1 MONTH OF
FREE
READING

at

www.ForgottenBooks.com

By purchasing this book you are eligible for one month membership to ForgottenBooks.com, giving you unlimited access to our entire collection of over 1,000,000 titles via our web site and mobile apps.

To claim your free month visit: www.forgottenbooks.com/free932797

ISBN 978-0-260-17892-3
PIBN 10932797

BOARD OF EDUCATION. VI. 15753
(C I. 33)

SPECIAL REPORTS

ON

EDUCATIONAL SUBJECTS.

VOLUME 4.

EDUCATIONAL SYSTEMS OF THE CHIEF COLONIES OF THE BRITISH EMPIRE.

(DOMINION OF CANADA: NEWFOUNDLAND: WEST INDIES).

Presented to both Houses of Parliament by Command of Her Majesty.

LONDON:
PRINTED FOR HIS MAJESTY'S STATIONERY OFFICE,
BY WYMAN AND SONS, LIMITED, FETTER LANE, LONDON, E.C.

And to be purchased, either directly or through any Bookseller, from
EYRE & SPOTTISWOODE, EAST HARDING STREET, FLEET STREET, E.C.; and
32, ABINGDON STREET, WESTMINSTER, S.W.; or
JOHN MENZIES & Co., ROSE STREET, EDINBURGH, and
90, WEST NILE STREET, GLASGOW; or
HODGES, FIGGIS & Co,. LIMITED, 104, GRAFTON STREET, DUBLIN.

1901.

[Cd. 416.] *Price 4s. 8d.*

SALE OF GOVERNMENT PUBLICATIONS.

The undermentioned Firms have been appointed sole Agents for the sale of Government Publications, including Parliamentary Reports and Papers, Acts of Parliament, Record Office Publications, &c., &c., and all such works can be purchased from them either directly or through retail booksellers, who are entitled to a discount of 25 per cent. from the selling prices :—

IN ENGLAND :—
> For all publications *excepting* Ordnance and Geological Maps, the Hydrographical Works of the Admiralty, and Patent Office Publications :—Messrs. EYRE AND SPOTTISWOODE, East Harding Street, E.C.
> For Geological Maps :—Mr. E. STANFORD, Cockspur Street, S.W.
> For Hydrographical Works of the Admiralty :—Mr. J. D. POTTER, 31, Poultry, E.C.
> Patent Office Publications are sold at the Patent Office.

> For all Publications *excepting* the Hydrographical Works of the Admiralty and Patent Office Publications :—

IN SCOTLAND :—Messrs. JOHN MENZIES & Co., Rose Street, Edinburgh, and 90, West Nile Street, Glasgow.

IN IRELAND :—Messrs. HODGES, FIGGIS, & Co., LIMITED, 104, Grafton Street, Dublin.

ORDNANCE SURVEY MAPS OF GREAT BRITAIN AND IRELAND :—There are Agents for the sale of these Maps in most of the chief towns. Copies can also be ordered at many Head Post Offices, and through any Bookseller, or from the Director-General Ordnance Survey, Southampton ; or, in the case of Ireland, from the Officer in Charge Ordnance Survey, Dublin.

The following is a list of some of the more important Parliamentary and Official Publications recently issued :—

Parliamentary :

Statutes—

Public General, Session 1899, Sess. 2, and 1900, Sess. 1 and 2. With Index, Tables, &c. Cloth. Price 3*s.*

Second Revised Edition. A.D. 1235-1713 to A.D. 1872-1883. XVI. Vols. Price 7*s.* 6*d.* each.

Revised Editions. Tables showing subsequent Repeals, effected by Acts of Session 62 & 63 Vict. 1899. Price 6*d.*

Statutes in Force. Index to. 16th Edition. To end of 63 & 64 Vict. 2 Vols. Price 10*s.* 6*d.*

The Statutory Rules and Orders revised. Statutory Rules and Orders, other than those of a Local, Personal, or Temporary Character, issued prior to 1890, and now in force. Vols. I. to VIII. Price 10*s.* each.

Statutory Rules and Orders other than those of a Local, Personal, or Temporary Character. With a list of the more important Statutory Orders of a Local Character, arranged in classes ; and an Index. Roy. 8vo. Boards. Issued in the years 1890, 1891, 1892, 1893, 1894, 1895, 1896, 1897, 1898, and 1899. Price 10*s.* each.

Statutory Rules and Orders in force on 31st December 1899. Index to. Price 10*s.*

Statutory Rules and Orders, 1901. Registered under the Rules Publication Act, 1893. In course of issue.

Acts of Parliament, Local and Private, Session 1901. In course of issue.

[Cd. 418.] EDUCATIONAL SUBJECTS. Special Report. Vol. VI. Preparatory Schools for Boys ; their place in English Secondary Education. Price 2*s.* 3½*d.*

[Cd. 419.] TECHNICAL AND COMMERCIAL EDUCATION in East Prussia, Poland, Galicia, Silesia, and Bohemia, by James Baker, F.R.G.S. Price 6*d.*

[Cd. 423.] INDIA AND THE COLONIES.—Regulations in force with regard to Commercial Travellers. Reports respecting. Price 4½*d.*

[Cd. 448.] IRISH INLAND FISHERIES COMMISSION. Report of, on Conditions and Laws. Price 2½*d.*

[Cd. 450.]   Do.   do.   do.   Part I. Evidence and Index. Price 4*s.* 1*d.*

[Cd. 453.] SOUTH AFRICAN HOSPITALS. Report of Royal Commission as to the Treatment of the Sick and Wounded during the Campaign. Price 8*d.*

[Cd. 454.] SOUTH AFRICAN HOSPITALS. Evidence and Index.   Price 5*s.* 2*d.*

[Cd. 455.]   Do.   do.   Appendix.   Price 3*s.*

[Cd. 459.] ARSENICAL POISONING ATTRIBUTED TO BEER. Report on the Recent Epidemic. Price 2½*d.*

[Cd. 134 and 134¹ to 134¹².] MINES. Reports of H.M. Inspectors for 1899, with Summaries of the Statistical portion under the provisions of the Coal Mines Regulation Act, 1887 ; Metalliferous Mines Regulation Acts, 1872-1875 ; Slate Mines (Gunpowder) Act, 1882, Districts Nos. 1 to 13. Complete. Price 7*s.* 7*d.*

MINES in the United Kingdom and the Isle of Man. List of, for 1899.   Price 3*s.* 1*d.*

QUARRIES.   Ditto.   ditto.   ditto. 1899.   Price 3*s.* 9*d.*

MINES ABANDONED. List of the Plans of. Corrected to 31st December 1899.   Price 1*s.*

ACCIDENTS AT DOCKS, WHARVES, AND QUAYS. Report upon.   Price 6*d.*

BOARD OF EDUCATION.

SPECIAL REPORTS

ON

EDUCATIONAL SUBJECTS.

VOLUME 4.

EDUCATIONAL SYSTEMS OF THE CHIEF COLONIES OF THE BRITISH EMPIRE.

(DOMINION OF CANADA: NEWFOUNDLAND: WEST INDIES).

Presented to both Houses of Parliament by Command of Her Majesty.

LONDON:
PRINTED FOR HIS MAJESTY'S STATIONERY OFFICE,
BY WYMAN AND SONS, LIMITED, FETTER LANE, LONDON, E.C.

And to be purchased, either directly or through any Bookseller, from
EYRE & SPOTTISWOODE, EAST HARDING STREET, FLEET STREET, E.C.; and
32, ABINGDON STREET, WESTMINSTER, S.W.; or
JOHN MENZIES & Co., ROSE STREET, EDINBURGH, and
90, WEST NILE STREET, GLASGOW; or
HODGES, FIGGIS & Co., LIMITED, 104, GRAFTON STREET, DUBLIN.

1901.

[Cd. 416.] *Price 4s. 8d.*

The Board of Education

[Introductory Letter to Volumes 4 and 5 of the Series.]

To Sir G. W. KEKEWICH, K.C.B.,

Secretary of the Board of Education

SIR,

I HAVE the honour to present to you the accompanying volumes of Special Reports, descriptive of the Educational Systems of the chief Colonies of the British Empire.

In 1897, after the celebration of the completion of the sixtieth year of Her Majesty's reign, it was decided that steps should be taken to prepare a series of reports on Colonial Education. The Secretary of State for the Colonies, when approached on the subject by the Lords of the Committee of Council on Education, approved the plan and forwarded, with a covering letter, to the Education Departments of Ontario, Quebec, Nova Scotia, New Brunswick, Manitoba, North-West Territories, British Columbia, Prince Edward Island, Newfoundland, New South Wales, Victoria, South Australia, Queensland, Tasmania, Western Australia, New Zealand, Jamaica, British Guiana, Cape Colony Natal, Malta and Ceylon,* a letter in which their Lordships requested the favour of the co-operation of the Colonial Authorities in the preparation of the projected reports.

With a view to facilitating a comparative survey of the systems of education now in force in different parts of the Empire, it was suggested that each report should give a short history of the growth of the present system, and refer, if possible, to the following subjects :—

(1) The central and local administration of education: the number of children and students at school or college; regulations for school attendance, and the methods by which they are enforced.

(2) Finance; the cost of education to the State and the amount of such cost borne respectively by the central authority, by the local authority, by the parents of scholars, or by voluntary subscribers, as the case might be; and the amount of school fees, if any are charged.

(3) How far private schools of different grades and types exist outside the State system of education.

(4) The arrangements made for the inspection of schools and the method of appointing the inspectorial staff.

(5) The provision made for the teaching of singing, drawing, cookery, and domestic economy; for manual training and practical instruction, and for drill and physical exercises.

---

* The selection of the above mentioned Colonies was made on the advice of the Colonial Office. It is hoped that a later volume will contain accounts of the educational systems of Mauritius, the Straits Settlements, Hong Kong, the Gold Coast, Lagos, and Sierra Leone. Students of education desiring information about education in India will find a valuable summary in Mr. J. S. Cotton's *Progress of Education in India*, 1892 3 to 1896-7; *Third Quinquennial Review.* (Cd. 9190, 5/5½.) 1898.

4296. Wt. 25796 3000—3/01. Wy. & S.   A 2

(6) The regulations for religious instruction.

(7) The method of appointing teachers in the elementary schools, the scale of their payment, the arrangements made for their professional training; how far there prevails a system of pupil teachers or apprentice-teachers; the proportions, respectively, of men and women teachers, and the arrangements made for pensions for teachers in elementary schools.

(8) How far, if at all, free meals are provided for needy scholars in elementary schools, and, if so, at whose cost.

(9) The arrangements for continuation schools or classes, where such exist.

(10) The provision of higher (including University) and secondary education, and how far such are subsidised by the State, and how far under its inspection and control.

(11) The arrangements for technical, commercial, and agricultural instruction.

(12) Reformatory and industrial schools.

(13) Schools for the blind, for the deaf and dumb, and for mentally defective children.

It was also suggested that each report should embody (preferably in the form of an Appendix) such part of the elementary school Code as dealt (1) with the course of studies, and (2) with regulations for the building and equipment of schools.

To the invitation thus given there was a cordial response, and in the course of the following year reports were received from sixteen out of the twenty-two Colonies approached.

In the remaining cases, however, long delay supervened and circumstances at length made it necessary to prepare a certain number of the reports from official materials supplied by the Colonial Authorities and supplemented by other documents available for the purpose.

In the meantime, however, considerable changes had been taking place in the educational systems of several of the colonies from which reports had been received in the course of 1898. Many of these changes were of an important character and of general interest to students of education all over the world. In several cases, also, important reports on education had been issued by the Governments concerned.

The whole series of reports, therefore, has been revised and greatly enlarged, and the statistics, as far as possible, have been brought up to date. Notices of material changes in the courses of study or in methods of educational administration, together with abstracts of recently issued official papers on colonial education, have been embodied in the reports, and some additional articles have been prepared on recent developments in agricultural education and manual training. It is hoped that in their present form the volumes may prove useful to those interested in studying and comparing the educational systems of the chief British Colonies.

As the work has proceeded, those engaged in the preparation of the reports have been increasingly impressed by the varied interest of the subject and by its growing importance. The most striking features of the reports, taken as a whole, may be summarised as follows:—

(i.) During the last two or three years there has been an evident growth of interest in educational questions in nearly every part of the Empire. Within the last twelve months there have been remarkable and significant changes in the educational systems of some of the Colonies.

(ii.) The chief characteristic of education throughout the British Colonies is the freedom with which it has been allowed to adjust itself to the different needs experienced by different parts of the Empire. There has been no centralised control over educational policy, though literary and other traditions have naturally had a strong influence on the scope and methods of instruction. The educational systems described in these volumes are marked by the utmost variety of legislative enactment.

(iii.) But, at the same time, it is impossible not to be struck by indications of an increasing sense of the importance of united effort in such branches of education as bear on the economic welfare or collective interests of the Empire as a whole. This shows itself in an evidently growing desire to compare notes on educational matters and to benefit by the educational experience of other parts of the Empire where similar difficulties have been encountered.

(iv.) There are many signs of uneasiness as to the possible dangers which may result from a tendency to bookishness in elementary education, and from a divorce between school studies and the practical interests of daily life.

(v.) As a corrective of what is hurtful in such a tendency, and in order to secure what is in itself a valuable and generally attractive element in education, there is a vigorous movement in favour of the introduction of various kinds of manual training and of simple forms of technical education into primary schools.

(vi.) There are indications of difficulty in regard to the aim, scope and subject-matter of the education of native races, and some signs of disappointment at the ethical and social results of purely literary forms of primary instruction.

(vii.) Speaking generally, there is comparative weakness in the provision of higher education, and especially of that type of secondary education which in this country is given at the great public schools. As a rule, secondary education has hitherto been left in the main to denominational and private effort.

I desire to take this opportunity of acknowledging the courtesy of the various Colonial Authorities in furnishing reports for publication in this volume, and for their assistance in many

other ways. I am indebted to the Agents General in London for New South Wales, Victoria, South Australia, Queensland, Tasmania, Western Australia and New Zealand for much help and valuable information. My special thanks are also due to Mr. J. G. Colmer, C.M.G., Secretary to the Office of the High Commissioner of Canada; to Mr. Just, Librarian in the same Office; to Mr. W. T. R. Preston, Inspector of Emigration Agencies for Canada; to Mr. Spencer Brydges Todd, C.M.G., Secretary to the Department of the Agent General for the Cape of Good Hope in London; to Dr. ThosMuir, F.R.S., Superintendent General of Education at the Cape of Good Hope; to Mr. R. Russell, junr., Secretary to the for Agent General for Natal in London: to Dr. Morris, C.M.G., Imperial Commissioner of Agriculture for the West Indies; to Mr. E. B. Sargant, formerly of the Civil Service Commission; to Mr. C. P.Lucas, C.B., Mr. H. W. Just, C.M.G., and Mr. E. im Thurn, C.B., C.M.G., of the Colonial Office; and to my colleagues Mr. A. E. Twentyman, Mr. R. Balfour, Miss Beard, Miss Green and Miss Matheson.

I have the honour to be, Sir,

Your obedient servant,

MICHAEL E. SADLER,

Director of Special Inquiries and Reports.

December, 1900.

CONTENTS.§

[In the case of reports marked thus *, supplementary notes have been added, or more recent statistics inserted by the Special Inquiries Section of the Board of Education.]

PAGE

A. Dominion of Canada—

1. Ontario, The System of Education in - - - 1

Prepared from official documents supplied by the Education Department of Ontario.

2. Quebec, The System of Education in the Province of 145

Prepared from official documents by Mr. R. Balfour.

3. *Nova Scotia, The System of Education in - - 263

By Mr. A. H. MacKay, Superintendent of Education, Nova Scotia.

4. *New Brunswick, The System of Education in - 335

By Professor J. Brittain, Instructor in the Provincial Normal School, Fredericton, New Brunswick.

5. Manitoba, The System of Education in - - - 349

Prepared from official documents by Mr. A. E. Twentyman.

6. North-West Territories, The System of Education in the - - - - - - - - - 409

Prepared from official documents by Mr. R. Balfour.

7. British Columbia, The System of Education in - 467

Prepared from official documents by Mr. R. Balfour.

8. *Prince Edward Island, The System of Education in 515

By Mr. D. J. MacLeod, Chief Superintendent of Education, Prince Edward Island.

§ Volume 5, which is also devoted to reports on the Educational Systems of British Colonies, contains reports on education in Cape Colony, Natal, New South Wales, Victoria, Queensland, Tasmania, South Australia, Western Australia, New Zealand, Ceylon and Malta.

PAGE

9. **Memorandum on Agricultural Education in Canada** - - - - - - - - - 533

    By Dr. W. Saunders, Director of Dominion Experimental Farms.

10. **Note on the Macdonald Manual Training Fund for the development of manual and practical instruction in primary schools in Canada** - - 537

    By Mr. M. E. Sadler.

B. **Newfoundland—**

   *Newfoundland, The System of Education in - - 541

    I. By the Rev. Canon W. Pilot, D.D., D.C.L., Superintendent of Church of England Schools in Newfoundland.

    II. By the Rev. G. S. Milligan, M.A., LL.D., Superintendent of Methodist Schools in Newfoundland.

C. **West Indies—**

   1. **Jamaica, The System of Education in** - - - 575

    Part I. with Appendices.
        By the Hon. T. Capper, Superintending Inspector of Schools, Jamaica.

    Part II.
        Prepared from official documents by Mr. M. E. Sadler.

   2. **British Guiana, The System of Education in** - - 751

    By Mr. W. Blair, Chief Inspector of Schools, British Guiana.

   3. **The Teaching of Agriculture in Elementary and Higher Schools in the West Indies** - - - 797

    Compiled from official documents by Mr. M. E. Sadler.

SYNOPSIS OF CONTENTS.

A.—DOMINION OF CANADA.

PAGE

1. Ontario - - - - - - - - - - -

PART I.—GENERAL DESCRIPTION OF THE SYSTEM - - - - 5

   INTRODUCTION - - - - - - - - - -
      Central Administration - - - - - -
      Local Administration - - - - - -
      The School and the Churches - - - - -

   PRIMARY EDUCATION - - - - - - - - 7
      Kindergartens - - - - - - - - 7
      Administration - - - - - - - - 8
      Compulsory Education - - - - - - 8
      Subjects of Instruction - - - - - - 9
      Leaving Examinations - - - - - - 9
      Statistics - - - - - - - - 10
      Separate Schools - - - - - - - 10
      Training of Teachers - - - - - - - 12
      County Model Schools - - - - - - 14
      Normal Schools - - - - - - - 15
      Inspection - - - - - - - - 16
      Teachers' Institutes - - - - - - 18

   SECONDARY EDUCATION - - - - - - - 19
      High Schools and Collegiate Institutes - - - 19
      Trustees - - - - - - - - 20
      Finance - - - - - - - - 20
      Entrance Examination - - - - - - 21
      Statistics - - - - - - - - 22
      Departmental Examinations - - - - - 22
      The School of Pedagogy - - - - - 25
      Inspectors of High Schools - - - - - 26

   UNIVERSITY EDUCATION - - - - - - - 27

   TECHNICAL EDUCATION - - - - - - - 34

   SPECIAL SCHOOLS - - - - - - - 37

   INDUSTRIAL SCHOOLS - - - - - - - 38

PART II.—THE SYSTEM IN 1899 ; EXTRACTS FROM THE REPORT OF
THE MINISTER OF EDUCATION FOR THE YEAR 1899. - - 40

   PUBLIC SCHOOL TEACHERS AND THEIR CERTIFICATES - - 40
      Certificates, 1899 - - - - - - 40
      Remarks on the supply of qualified teachers - - 40
      Teachers in training at Normal Schools, 1877–1899 - 41
      Teachers' Institutes, 1877–1898 - - - - 41
      Temporary and extended Certificates, 1899 - - 42
      Specialists' Certificates - - - - - 42

PAGE

THE PUBLIC SCHOOL LEAVING EXAMINATIONS - - - 44

CONTINUATION CLASSES - - - - - - - - 46

THE COURSE OF STUDY IN PUBLIC AND HIGH SCHOOLS - - 47

Agriculture - - - - - - - - 47
Manual Training - - - - - - - 49
Temperance and Hygiene - - - - - - 50

SEPARATE SCHOOLS IN 1898 - - - - - - - 50

Roman Catholic - - - - - - - 50
Protestant - - - - - - - - - 50

HIGH SCHOOLS - - - - - - - - 51

Diffusion of High School Education - - - - 51
Tendencies of High School Education, 1867–1898 - - 51
Departmental Instructions for the High School Entrance
Examination, 1900 - - - - - - - 52
The question of Free High Schools - - - - 54

EMPIRE DAY IN PUBLIC AND HIGH SCHOOLS - - - 54

Circular of March, 1899 - - - - - - 54
Remarks from the Report for 1899 - - - - 55

UNIVERSITY EDUCATION - - - - - - - 56

From the Report of the Council of the University of
Toronto for 1898–9 - - - - - - 56
Numbers attending Pass and Honour Lectures - - 57
The Laboratories - - - - - - - 58
Numbers examined in the Faculties and Departments - 58
Students in the Faculty of Medicine - - - - 58
Subjects taught in the Faculty of Science - - 59
University College—(i.) Registered Students; (ii.) Pass
and Honours Lectures - - - - - - 59
Subjects taught by the Faculty of the School of Science - 60

ART TEACHING - - - - - - - - 61

Art Schools and Departmental Drawing Examinations - 61
Certificates in Primary Art Course, 1882–1899 - - 61
        ,,   Advanced Art Course, 1883–1899 - - 61
        ,,   Mechanical Drawing Course, 1883–1899 62
        ,,   Industrial Art Course, 1885–1899 - 62
        ,,   Extra Subjects, 1885–1889 - - - 63
Literary and Scientific Societies receiving grants - - 63
Progress of School Architecture and Decoration - - 63

PUBLIC LIBRARIES - - - - - - - - 66

Public Libraries not free - - - - - - 66
Evening Classes in Public Libraries, 1898–1899 - - 67
Certificates in Primary Drawing Course, 1899 - - 68
Certificates in Mechanical Drawing Course, 1899 - 68
Number of Public Libraries in Counties and Districts - 68
Progress of Public Libraries, 1883–1899 - - - 69
Free Libraries - - - - - - - - 69

REPORTS OF THE INDUSTRIAL SCHOOLS, 1899 - - - 70

Victoria Industrial School - - - - - 70
Alexandra Industrial School - - - - - 70

EXAMINATION REQUIREMENTS 1900, 1901, 1902 - - 70

Junior Leaving Standing, Part I. - - - - 70
    do.   do.   do.   Part II. - - - - 71

EXAMINATION REQUIREMENTS, 1900, 1901, 1902—*cont.*   PAGE

Senior Leaving Standing, Part I. - - - - - - 76
   do.   do.   do.   Part II. - - - - - - 78
Question Papers - - - - - - - - 82
Percentages - - - - - - - - - 82
Commercial Diploma - - - - - - - 83

PART III.—STATISTICAL TABLES FOR THE YEAR 1898 - - - 85

Table 1. PUBLIC SCHOOLS. Pupils in the different branches - 85
  „   2. PUBLIC SCHOOLS. School population and pupils in
        attendance - - - - - - 86
  „   3. PUBLIC SCHOOLS. Teachers, their salaries and
        qualifications - - - - - - 87
  „   4. PUBLIC SCHOOLS. Receipts and expenditure - - 88
  „   5. HIGH SCHOOLS - - - - - - - 89
        a. Receipts and expenditure - - - - 89
        b. Miscellaneous information - - - - 89
  „   6. COLLEGIATE INSTITUTES - - - - - 90
        a. Receipts and expenditure - - - - 90
        b. Miscellaneous information - - - - 90
  „   7. COLLEGIATE INSTITUTES. Pupils in the different
        branches of Instruction - - - - - 91
  „   8. KINDERGARTENS - - - - - - 92
  „   9. NIGHT SCHOOLS - - - - - - 92
  „ 10. GENERAL STATISTICAL ABSTRACT, 1867 to 1898 - 93
  „ 11. SUMMARY OF STATISTICS FOR 1898 - - - 94
        a. Elementary Schools - - - - - 94
        b. Secondary Schools - - - - - 95

APPENDICES - - - - - - - - - - 96

A. Regulations of the Education Department of the Province
   of Ontario (1896) - - - - - - - 96
B. Certain Regulations as amended in 1898 and 1899 - 125
C. Duties of Inspectors - - - - - - - 127
D. Examinations and Examiners - - - - - 130
E. Uniform Text Books - - - - - - - 134
F. Regulations for the School of Pedagogy - - - 138
G. University Regulations - - - - - - 140

2. Quebec   - - - - - - - - - 145

INTRODUCTORY - - - - - - - - - 149

CENTRAL ADMINISTRATION - - - - - - - 151

The Lieutenant-Governor - - - - - 151
The Department and the Council - - - - 151
The Superintendent - - - - - - - 151
The Committees of the Council - - - - 152
The Classification of Creeds - - - - - 152

The Council of Public Instruction and its Committees - 152

Composition of the Council - - - - - 152
Special Meetings - - - - - - - 153
Definition of Powers of the Council and Committees - 154
Special provisions for each Committee - - - 155
Text-books - - - - - - - - 155
Appointments - - - - - - - - 156
Inquiries and Appeals - - - - - - 156
Donations and Legacies - - - - - - 156
School Exhibitions - - - - - - - 156

CENTRAL ADMINISTRATION—*cont.*   **PAGE**
 The Superintendent of Public Instruction and his Staff - - 157
  Salary, *ex-officio* position and powers   -   -   -   - 157
  The Secretaries of the Department -   -   -   - 157
  Special duties of Superintendent   -   -   -   - 157
  Additional duties   -   -   -   -   -   - 158

LOCAL ADMINISTRATION   -   -   -   -   -   -   - 158

 School municipalities   -   -   -   -   -   - 158
 Their abolition or annexation -   -   -   -   - 159
 School districts   -   -   -   -   -   - 160
 Power of Lieutenant-Governor to alter areas -   -   - 160
 Division into school districts -   -   -   -   - 160
 Dissentient Schools   -   -   -   -   - 161
 Notices of dissent -   -   -   -   -   - 161
 Alternation of majority and minority   -   -   - 162
 Union of dissentient municipalities   -   -   - 163
 Dissentients in towns   -   -   -   -   - 163
 Grant by Commissioners to Trustees   -   -   - 163
 Extinction of trustee corporation -   -   -   - 164
 Children taught in next municipality   -   -   - 164
 Erection of new municipality   -   -   -   - 165
 Annual meeting : procedure -   -   -   -   - 165
 Penalty for neglect in office   -   -   -   - 167
 Persons qualified to vote and to hold office   -   - 167
 Vacancies   -   -   -   -   -   -   - 167
 Term of office -   -   -   -   -   -   - 168
 Contestations and appeals   -   -   -   - 168
 Meetings of school corporation   -   -   -   - 169
 Duties of Commissioners and Trustees   -   -   - 170
  School Property   -   -   -   -   - 171
  School-Houses -   -   -   -   -   - 172
  Special tax   -   -   -   -   -   - 172
  School taxes   -   -   -   -   -   - 172
  Exemptions   -   -   -   -   -   - 173
  Appeals   -   -   -   -   -   - 174
  School site   -   -   -   -   -   - 174
  Union for Model School or Academy   -   - 175
  Monthly fees -   -   -   -   -   - 175
  Schools for Girls   -   -   -   -   - 176
  Annual census of children-   -   -   - 176
  Special powers of trustees-   -   -   - 177
 The Secretary-Treasurer   -   -   -   - 178
 Security and Sureties   -   -   -   -   - 178
 His duties   -   -   -   -   -   - 178
 His assistant -   -   -   -   -   - 179
 Examination of Accounts   -   -   -   - 180
  By School Corporation   -   -   -   - 180
  By Auditors   -   -   -   -   - 180
  By Superintendent -   -   -   -   - 181
 Fabrique Schools   -   -   -   -   - 182
 Statistics of 1898–99   -   -   -   -   - 182

FINANCE : PROVINCIAL AND LOCAL   -   -   -   - 183

 Conditions of aid   -   -   -   -   - 183
  Exemption of municipality   -   -   - 183
 Distribution of Local School Fund -   -   -   - 184
 Refusal of share in Common School Fund   -   - 185
 Sum reserved for three special purposes -   -   - 185
 Applications of Local School Fund -   -   -   - 186
 Valuation of property   -   -   -   -   - 186

FINANCE: PROVINCIAL AND LOCAL—*cont.* PAGE

Imposition of school taxes - - - - - - - 187
Collection by seizure - - - - - - - - 188
New and special taxes - - - - - - - 189
Voluntary Contributions - - - - - - - 191
Collection from religious and other corporations - - 191
Capitalisation of debt - - - - - - - 192
Statistical Tables - - - - - - - - 192
 Table of amounts expended on education - - - - 192
 Statistics of the cost of education - - - - - 193

SCHOOL VISITORS AND SCHOOL INSPECTION - - - - 194

Visitors for the whole Province - - - - - 194
Visitors in their own districts only - - - - 194
School Inspection - - - - - - - 194
Duties of Inspectors - - - - - - - 195
Qualifications - - - - - - - - 195
Salaries : instructions : number - - - - - 195
Specimen of Inspector's return - - - - - 196
Dismissal of Inspector - - - - - - 197
Circular of 1897 about Pedagogical Lectures - - - 197

TEACHERS: TRAINING AND DIPLOMAS - - - - - 200

Normal Schools - - - - - - - 200
 Financial provision - - - - - - 200
 Superintendent's control - - - - - - 201
 Normal school diploma - - - - - - 201
 Normal schools for girls - - - - - - 202
Pedagogical lectures - - - - - - 202
Central Board of Examiners - - - - - 203
Quebec and Montreal Boards - - - - - 204
Other Boards of Examiners - - - - - 204
Duties of Boards of Examiners - - - - - 204
Validity and necessity of diplomas - - - - - 206
Summary of statistics of teachers, 1897-98 - - - 207
From the Report for 1895-96 - - - - - - 207

COMPARATIVE STATEMENT OF PROGRESS, 1867-1899 - - - 208

SUPERIOR EDUCATION - - - - - - - - 209

Finance - - - - - - - - - 209
Roman Catholic Laval University - - - - 210
Branch of Laval University at Montreal - - - - 213
Statistics of Protestant Universities - - - - 215
Statistics of Model Schools, Academies, etc. - - - 216
Regulations for Academies - - - - - 218
Special rules for Model Schools - - - - - 219
Royal Institution for the Advancement of Learning - - 220

INDUSTRIAL SCHOOLS - - - - - - - 221

Certificates : Building : Inspection - - - - - 221
Finance - - - - - - - - - 222
Withdrawal of Certificate - - - - - - 222
Detention of Children - - - - - - 223
Penalties - - - - - - - - 224
Management of certified Industrial Schools - - - 224

THE POLYTECHNIC SCHOOL - - - - - - - 225

	PAGE
MISCELLANEOUS - - - - - - - - -	227
Remarks on educational progress - - - - -	227
Plans of school houses - - - - - -	229
Teachers' salaries - - - - - - -	229
Teaching of drawing - - - - - -	229
Manual training for girls - - - - - -	230
School holidays - - - - - - -	231
School libraries - - - - - - -	231
APPENDICES - - - - - - - - - - -	
A. An account of the Protestant Schools of Montreal, 1900. By the Secretary-Superintendent - - - - -	232
B. Extracts from the Regulations of the Protestant School Commissioners for Montreal, 1900 - - - - -	236
C. Regulations of 1890 for the issue of debentures by the Roman Catholic and Protestant School Commissioners for Montreal - - - - - - - - -	250
D. Special Regulation of 1893 concerning tenure of Roman Catholic School Commissioners for Montreal - - -	253
E. Course of study in Roman Catholic Academies and Model Schools - - - - - - - - -	254-5
F. Course of study in Protestant Elementary Schools - -	256
G. From the Report of the Montreal Protestant School Commissioners 1897-1899 - - - - - - -	257

3. Nova Scotia - - - - - - - - - - - 263

	PAGE
INTRODUCTORY - - - - - - - - -	265
EARLY HISTORY - - - - - - - -	267
Education Act of 1811 - - - - - - -	267
Rise of Denominational Colleges and Universities - -	268
Private Schools - - - - - - - -	269
PRIMARY AND SECONDARY EDUCATION - - - - -	270
The Rise of the Free School Idea - - - - -	270
First Superintendents of Education - - - -	270
Free School System - - - - - - -	271
Council of Public Instruction - - - - -	274
Superintendent of Education - - - - -	274
District Commissioners of Schools - - - -	274
The Inspector - - - - - - - -	274
The School Section - - - - - - -	275
The Annual School Meeting - - - - - -	275
Finance - - - - - - - - -	275
County Academies - - - - - - -	276
Courses of Study and Text-Books - - - -	277
Manual Training - - - - - - -	281
Religion - - - - - - - - -	281
Public Grants for Denominational Schools - - -	282
Licensing and appointment of Teachers - - -	283
Salaries, Classification, etc. - - - - -	286
Attendance - - - - - - - -	288
High School Classes carry forward Primary Education -	288
TECHNICAL, COMMERCIAL AND AGRICULTURAL INSTRUCTION	289
PUBLIC REFORMATORIES, INDUSTRIAL OR PARENTAL SCHOOLS	292
Free Meals - - - - - - - -	292
SCHOOLS FOR THE BLIND AND THE DEAF AND DUMB - -	292
SUPPLEMENTARY NOTE - - - - - - - -	293

PAGE

APPENDICES - - - - - - - - - 294

    A. Regulation of the Council of Public Instruction referring
        to " Devotional Exercises " - - - - - 294
    B. The Public School Course of Study as prescribed in 1898 - 294
    C. The General Regulations of the Provincial High School
        Examinations, 1898 - - - - - - - 312
    D. Regulations of the Council of Public Instruction referring
        to County Academies - - - - - - 319
    E. Regulations of the Council of Public Instruction referring
        to " Common " School Buildings - - - - 322
    F. Regulations of the Council of Public Instruction on the
        Licensing of Teachers and their professional qualifications 326

4. New Brunswick - - - - - - - - - 335

PRIMARY EDUCATION : - - - - - - - 336

    Brief Historical Sketch - - - - - - 336
    " Boarding Around " System - - - - - 336
    Assessment System - - - - - - 337
    Common Schools Act, 1871 - - - - - 337
    Central Administration - - - - - - 337
    Local Administration - - - - - - 337
    Finance - - - - - - - - 338
    Salaries of Teachers - - - - - - 339
    School Attendance - - - - - - 339
    Course of Study - - - - - - 340
    Manual Training and Needlework - - - - 340
    Instruction in Religion and Morals - - - - 340
    Training of Teachers - - - - - - 340
    School Inspection - - - - - - 341
    Teachers' Institutes - - - - - - 341

SECONDARY EDUCATION - - - - - - - 341

UNIVERSITY EDUCATION - - - - - - 342

TECHNICAL AND AGRICULTURAL EDUCATION - - - 342

INDUSTRIAL SCHOOLS AND REFORMATORIES - - - 342

SCHOOLS FOR THE DEAF AND DUMB AND THE BLIND - - 342

GENERAL RESULTS - - - - - - - 342

SUPPLEMENTARY NOTES - - - - - - 344

    University Education - - - - - - 344
    Government Training Farm - - - - - 344
    Provincial Dairy School - - - - - 346

APPENDIX. EDUCATIONAL STATISTICS, 1889–1899 - - - 347

5. Manitoba - - - - - - - - - 349

INTRODUCTION - - - - - - - 351

    The Settlement Period - - - - - 352
    The Denominational Period, 1870–1890 - - - 353
    The Public Schools Act of 1890 and the Religious Controversy 356

PAGE

CENTRAL ADMINISTRATION - - - - - - - 365
    The Education Department - - - - - 365
    The Advisory Board - - - - - - 365
    Inspection - - - - - - - - 367

LOCAL ADMINISTRATION - - - - - - - 367
    Rural School Districts - - - - - 367
        Annual School Meeting - - - - 368
        School Trustees - - - - - - 368
    Public School Boards in cities, towns and villages - - 370

FINANCE - - - - - - - - - 371
    Annual Grants :—
        Legislative Grants - - - - - 371
        Municipal Grants - - - - - 371
    Loans - - - - - - - - 372

TEACHERS - - - - - - - - 373
    Teachers' Certificates and Training - - - - 373
    Salaries - - - - - - - - 375

ATTENDANCE - - - - - - - - 375

CURRICULUM - - - - - - - - 376
    Religious Instruction - - - - - - 377

INTERMEDIATE AND COLLEGIATE SCHOOLS - - - - 377

THE UNIVERSITY OF MANITOBA - - - - - 377

THE NEGLECTED CHILDREN ACT - - - - - 378

APPENDICES - - - - - - - - 380
    A.—Educational Statistics. 1871–1898 - - - 380
    B.—Programme of Studies for the Public Schools - - 388
    C.—Regulations regarding Religious Exercises - - 396
    D.—Regulations as to Teachers' Certificates - - - 399

6. North-west Territories - - - - - - 409

INTRODUCTORY - - - - - - - - 411

CENTRAL ADMINISTRATION - - - - - - 414
    Council of Public Instruction (Central Authority) - - 414
    Classification of Schools - - - - - - 415

LOCAL ADMINISTRATION - - - - - - 416
    School Districts - - - - - - 416
    Inaugural School Meeting - - - - - 417
    Separate Schools - - - - - - 418
    Annual School Meeting - - - - - 418
    Union of Public and Separate School Districts - - 420
    Disorganisation of School Districts - - - 420
    Trustees - - - - - - - 421
        Secretary of Board of Trustees - - - 423
        Treasurer of Board of Trustees - - - 424
        Treasurer's Return - - - - - 425

PAGE

STATISTICS - - - - - - - - - - - 426
   School Districts - - - - - - - - 426
   Schools - - - - - - - - - 426
   Pupils Enrolled - - - - - - - - 427
   Pupils in Attendance - - - - - - - 427
      Attendance - - - - - - - - 427
      Classification - - - - - - - - 427
      Comparative Statement of Attendance and Classification 428
   Summary of Statistics 1885-1899 - - - - - 429

ATTENDANCE LAWS AND TRUANCY - - - - - 429
   Length of time during which Schools are open - - 429
   Penalties - - - - - - - - - 429
   Reasonable excuses - - - - - - - 430
   Truancy and Truant Officer - - - - - 430
   School Hours - - - - - - - - 430
   Period for which Grants are payable - - - 431
   Remarks on Attendance in 1898 - - - - 431

COST OF EDUCATION - - - - - - - - 432
   Legislative Grants - - - - - - - 432
      Scale - - - - - - - - 432
      Dates of payment - - - - - - 433
      Allowance on account of disease - - - 433
   Local Taxation - - - - - - - 434
      Assessment - - - - - - - 434
      Protestants and Roman Catholics - - - 435
      Assessment roll - - - - - - 435
      Exemptions - - - - - - - 436
      Complaints - - - - - - - 438
      Court of Revision - - - - - - 438
      Appeal to Superintendent - - - - 438
      Return of Trustees : Rebate - - - - 439
      Incurring Debt by Debenture - - - - 439
   School Fees - - - - - - - - 440
   Treasurer's Return - - - - - - - 440
   Public Notice of Poll on issue of Debentures - - 442

INSPECTORS AND INSPECTION - - - - - - 443

RELIGIOUS INSTRUCTION - - - - - - - 444

TEACHERS - - - - - - - - - - 444
   Their duties - - - - - - - - 444
   Teachers' Institutes - - - - - - - 445
   Supply of Teachers, &c. - - - - - 446
   Foreign Certificates - - - - - - 447
   Normal School - - - - - - - 447
   Form of Agreement between Trustees and Teacher - 447
   Certificates - - - - - - - - 448
   Summary of Examinations - - - - - 448
   Qualifications for High School Certificate - - 449
   General Regulations for Non-professional Examinations - 449
   Certificates without Examination - - - 450
   Certificates and Teachers' Examinations (1898) - - 450

SPECIAL SCHOOLS - - - - - - - - 451
   Night Schools - - - - - - - - 451
   Kindergartens - - - - - - - - 451

PAGE

APPENDICES - - - - - - - - - - 452
  A. EXTRACTS FROM THE PROGRAMME OF STUDY - - - 452
    Drawing - - - - - - - - - - 452
    Stimulants and Narcotics (Alcohol, Tobacco) - - - 453
    Manners and Morals - - - - - - - 453
    Hygiene - - - - - - - - - - 454
    Music - - - - - - - - - - 454
    " Programme of Studies " - - - - - - 454
      Reading and Literature - - - - - - 454
      Orthoepy and Spelling - - - - - - 455
      Composition - - - - - - - - 455
      Grammar - - - - - - - - - 455
      History - - - - - - - - - 455
      Geography - - - - - - - - 456
      Arithmetic - - - - - - - - 457
      Nature Study and Agriculture - - - - - 457

  B. EXTRACTS FROM THE REPORT FOR 1898 - - - - 457
    Agriculture - - - - - - - - - 457
    Domestic Economy and Hygiene - - - - 458
    Equipment - - - - - - - - 459
    Buildings - - - - - - - - - 459

  C. EXTRACTS FROM PAPERS SET IN PROFESSIONAL EXAMINA-
    TION FOR TEACHERS, 1898 - - - - - - 461
      First-Class Certificates - - - - - - 461
      First and Second-Class Certificates (Drawing) - - 462
      Second-Class Certificates - - - - - - 462
      Third-Class Certificates - - - - - 464

7. British Columbia - - - - - - - - 467

INTRODUCTORY - - - - - - - - - 469

CENTRAL ADMINISTRATION - - - - - - - 472
    Council of Public Instruction - - - - 472
    Its Powers - - - - - - 472
    Special Provisions - - - - - - 473
    The Superintendent of Education - - - - 474

LOCAL ADMINISTRATION - - - - - - - 475
    Rural School Districts - - - - - - 475
      Annual School Meeting - - - - - 475
      Challenge of Voter - - - - - - 476
      Order of Business - - - - - - 477
      Special Meetings - - - - - - 477
      Report of Trustees - - - - - - 478
    City School Districts - - - - - - 479
      Qualification of Voters - - - - - 479
      Meetings of Trustees - - - - - 480
      Their Powers and Duties - - - - - 480
      Statement of Accounts - - - - - 482
      High Schools and Collegiate Institutes - - 482
      Annual Reports - - - - - - 483
      Per capita Grants - - - - - - 483
      Non-sectarian Principles - - - - - 483

PAGE

REGULATIONS AS TO COMPULSORY ATTENDANCE - - - - 484

Fines - - - - - - - - 484
Exemptions - - - - - - - 484
Reasonable Excuses - - - - - - - 484

TEACHERS - - - - - - - - - 485

Grades of Certificate - - - - - - 485
Temporary Certificate - - - - - - 485
Terms of Validity - - - - - - - 485
Exemption from Non-Professional Examination - - 486
Moral Character - - - - - - - 486
Form of Candidate's Notification - - - - 486
Annual Renewal - - - - - - - 486
Certificate Statistics for 1898 - - - - - 486
Rights conferred by Certificates - - - - 487
Statistics of Permanent Staff, 1897-8 - - - 487
Statistics of Permanent Staff, 1894-5 - - - 488
Average Salaries - - - - - - 488
Duties of Public School Teachers - - - - 489
Notices of Appointment, Dismissal, &c. - - - 490
Teacher's Appeal against Dismissal - - - - 490

TRAINING OF TEACHERS - - - - - - 490

From the Report for 1893-4 - - - - - 490
From the Report for 1896 - - - - - - 491
Necessity of a Normal School - - - - - 491

TRUANCY : PUNISHMENTS - - - - - - 492

Expulsion and Suspension - - - - - 492
Corporal Punishment - - - - - - 492
Moral Suasion - - - - - - - 493

LEGAL PENALTIES - - - - - - - 493

Voter's False Declaration - - - - - 493
Disturbance of School Meeting - - - - 493

SCHOOL PROPERTY - - - - - - - 493

Trustees' Responsibility - - - - - 493
Misuse of School Buildings - - - - - 493
Teacher's Responsibility - - - - - 494

INSPECTION - - - - - - - - 494

Inspector's Report - - - - - - 494
Need of a third Inspector (1896) - - - - 494

HIGH SCHOOLS - - - - - - - - 494

Nanaimo High School - - - - - 495
New Westminster High School - - - - 495
Vancouver High School - - - - - 496
Victoria High School - - - - - 496
Diploma of Standing - - - - - 496
Subjects for Entrance Examination - - - 497
Paper on Agriculture - - - - - 497
Conditions of Creation of High Schools - - 497
Teachers as Pupils in High Schools - - - 497
Percentage of Marks Required - - - - 497
Courses and Classes - - - - - 498
Promotion from Graded to High Schools - - 498
From the Report for 185-6 - - - - 498
" Board of Governors of Vancouver College - - 499

	PAGE
GRADED SCHOOLS	- 499
Size of Divisions	- 499
Optional Subjects	- 499
"Limit Table	- 499
Semi-annual Examination	- 499
Suggestions from Circular of 1895	- 500
COMMON SCHOOLS	- 500
Optional Subjects	- 500
The Lord's Prayer	- 500
GENERAL REMARKS. STATISTICS OF EDUCATIONAL PROGRESS	- 501
Statistics for 1897-9	- 501
Cost per pupil, 1888-98	- 502
Attendance, 1897-8	- 503
Attendance and Expenditure, 1890-9	- 503
Attendance, 1894-5	- 503
Progress in Attendance, 1894-7	- 504
Teachers' Aims	- 504
Classification of Schools	- 505
APPENDICES	- 506
A. Subjects of Examination for Certificates and conditions of obtaining them	- 506
B. Courses of Study	- 510
High Schools	- 510
Graded and Common Schools	- 511
Optional Subjects	- 513
Agriculture	- 513

8. Prince Edward Island - 515

Early History	- 517
Administration and Inspection	- 517
Progress under the Act of 1877	- 517
Statistics	- 518
Prince of Wales College	- 518
Appointment of Teachers	- 519
Salaries	- 519
Special Subjects.	- 519
Private Schools	- 519

APPENDIX :—
Regulations of the Board of Education	- 520

9. Memorandum on Agricultural Education in Canada - 533

Provincial Aids	- 533
Agricultural Schools	- 533
Other Organisations	- 534
Dominion Aids to Agriculture	- 534

10. Note on the Macdonald Manual Training Fund for the Development of Manual and Practical Instruction in Primary Schools in Canada - 537

B. NEWFOUNDLAND.

PAGE

Newfoundland - - - - - - - - - - - 541

PRIMARY EDUCATION - - - - - - - - - 542

Historical Sketch : - - - - - - - - - 542

Chaotic period. 1726–1823 - - - - - 542
Period of individual enterprise, 1823–1836 - - - 543
Legislative action, 1836–1896—Creation of Local Boards of Education—Two Central Boards - - - - 546

Present system - - - - - - - - - 547

Act of 1874 - - - - - - - - - 547
Attendance - - - - - - - - - 549
Finance - - - - - - - - - - 549
Private Schools - - - - - - - - - 550
Inspection - - - - - - - - - 550
Singing, Drawing and Drill - - - - - 551
Religious Instruction - - - - - - 551
Teachers—Salaries and Training - - - - 551

SECONDARY EDUCATION - - - - - - - 552

METHODIST SCHOOLS AS RELATED TO THE NEWFOUNDLAND SYSTEM OF EDUCATION - - - - - - - - 554

Early History - - - - - - - - - 554
Present System - - - - - - - - 556

Primary Education - - - - - - - 556
Administration - - - - - - - - 557
Attendance - - - - - - - - 557
Cost - - - - - - - - - - 557
Subjects taught - - - - - - - 557
Religious Instruction - - - - - - 557
Teachers - - - - - - - - 557
Training of Teachers - - - - - - 558
Higher Education - - - - - - - 558

SUPPLEMENTARY NOTES - - - - - - - - 560

Education Estimates, 1898–99 and 1899–1900 - - - 560
Denominational Apportionment of Government Grants for Education, 1899–1900 - - - - - - - 561
Apportionment of Grants for Inspection, 1899–1900 - - 561
Statistics of Roman Catholic Schools - - - - 562
From the Report of the Colonial and Continental Church Society for 1899–1900 - - - - - - - 563

APPENDICES - - - - - - - - - - 566

A. Return of Schools for the year 1896–1897 - - - 566
B. Voluntary Contributions and Fees - - - - 567
C. Programme of Studies for Elementary Schools - - 568
D. Teachers' Pension Fund - - - - - - 569
E. Some Provisions of the Education Act of July, 1899 - - 573

C.—WEST. INDIES.

	PAGE
1. Jamaica - - - - - - - -	- 575
PART I.	
HISTORICAL SKETCH - - - - - - -	- 577
THE SYSTEM (AS IT WAS BEFORE THE NEW CODE, 1900)	- 585
Local Managers - - - - - - -	- 585
Finance - - - - - - - -	- 586
Attendance - - - - - - -	- 588
Private and Secondary Schools - - -	- 589
Administration - - - - - - -	- 590
Inspection - - - - - - -	- 591
Subjects of Instruction - - - -	- 592
Agriculture - - - - - - -	- 594
Manual Training - - - - - -	- 595
Religious Instruction - - - - -	- 595
Teachers' Salaries - - - - -	- 596
Pupil Teachers - - - - - -	- 597
Training - - - - - - - -	- 598
Secondary Education - - - - -	- 599
Technical Instruction - - - - -	- 600
Reformatory and Industrial Schools - -	- 600
APPENDICES - - - - - - - -	- 601
A. Denominational Summary of Elementary Schools in 1864 and 1865 - - - - - -	- 601
B. Statistics of Elementary Education from 1868 to 1899	602
C. Attendance Curves - - - - *To face page*	602
D. Statistics of Age - - - - - -	- 603
E. Synopsis of the principal changes in the Elementary School System between 1867 and 1897 - -	- 604
F. Standards of Classification down to the New Code, 1900	607
G. Subjects for Examination of Pupil Teachers -	- 616
H. Requirements at Examination of Training Colleges	· 618
PART II.	
SUPPLEMENTARY NOTES ON EDUCATION IN JAMAICA, 1898–1900	624
REPORT OF THE COMMISSION ON EDUCATION IN JAMAICA, 1898 ` - - - - - - -	- 624
System of Education in Jamaica - - -	- 625
Amalgamation of Schools - - - -	- 626
School Age- - - - - - -	- 629
Compulsion to Attend School - - -	- 630
Irregularity and Unpunctuality - - -	- 632
Education of Children of East Indians - -	- 634
School Managers - - - - -	- 635
Inspectors and Inspection - - - -	- 635
Grants - - - - - - -	- 636
Teachers and their Training - - -	- 636
Classification of Schools - - - -	- 643
School Organisation - - - - -	- 645
Proposed Changes in the Curriculum of Elementary Schools - - - - - - -	- 646
Religious Teaching - - - - -	- 656
Manual and Agricultural Instruction. - -	- 657
Continuation Schools- - - - -	- 662
Secondary Schools - - - - -	- 662
Effect of Home Conditions on School Life. -	- 663

SUPPLEMENTARY NOTES ON EDUCATION IN JAMAICA, 1896–1900—
cont.

REPORT OF THE COMMISSION ON EDUCATION IN JAMAICA,
1898—cont.   PAGE

Scholarships - - - - - - - - - 663
Board of Education and Education Department   -   - 664
Commissioners' Finding as to the State of Education in
Jamaica - - - - - - - - - 664

EXTRACTS FROM THE EVIDENCE GIVEN BEFORE THE EDUCA-
TION COMMISSION - - - - - - - 665

Is it desirable that the system of education should in the
main be organised on denominational lines ? -   -   - 665
Does Education tend to make the rising generation disinclined for manual labour, especially in Agriculture ? - 669
Is it desirable or practicable to have more agricultural
teaching in elementary Schools ? - - - - 672
Should Elementary Education be made more practical and
less literary ? - - - - - - - 676
What have been the general effects on the population of
the system of education in Jamaica ? - - - - 678

EDUCATION IN JAMAICA IN 1898–9 - - - - 681

Educational Statistics 1897–9 - - - - - - 681
Memorandum on Educational Matters addressed by Board
of Education to the Legislative Council, April, 1897 - 681
Educational Finance, 1897–9 - - - - - 682
Monthly Average Attendance at Schools and Classification
of Scholars - - - - - - - - 684
Teachers - - - - - - - - 685
Manual Training, Kindergarten Class, and Teaching of
Elementary Science in its bearing on Agriculture   - 685
Training Colleges - - - - - - - 686
Scholarships and Secondary Education   -   -   - 687
Remarks of the Superintending Inspector on the Report
of the Education Commission - - - - - 688

SELECTION OF THE ARTICLES CONTAINED IN THE NEW CODE
OF REGULATIONS OF THE EDUCATION DEPARTMENT, IN
FORCE FROM MAY 10, 1900 - - - - - - 689

2. British Guiana - - - - - - - 751

PRIMARY EDUCATION - - - - - - - 753

Introductory - - - - - - - - 753
Early History - - - - - - - - 753
Mr. Canning's Resolutions - - - - - - 754
First Grants for Educational Purposes - - - - 754
Lady Mico's Legacy, etc. - - - - - - 755
Establishment of the Grammar School - - - - 755
Education Commission - - - - - - 756
Ordinance of 1855 - - - - - - - 756
School Commission of 1874 - - - - - 757
Ordinance of 1882 - - - - - - - 758
Reduction of State Grants to Education - - - - 760
The New Code of 1890 - - - - - - 761
Schools for Aboriginal Indians - - - - - 762
Statistics - - - - - - - - 762

SECONDARY EDUCATION - - - - - - - 763

Queen's College - - - - - - - 763
The Catholic Grammar School - - - - - 765
Ursuline Convent High Schools - - - - - 766
Wesleyan High Schools - - - - - - 766

REFORMATORIES - - - - - - - - 766

EDUCATIONAL ENDOWMENTS - - - - - - 768

PAGE

SUPPLEMENTARY NOTE - . . . . - 770

APPENDICES - . . . . - 771

A. Report of the Commissioners on Primary Education, 1897- 771
B. Code of Regulations for Grant-in-Aid Schools, 1900 - - 774
C. An Ordinance (1900) to amend the Elementary Education
    Ordinance, 1876 - . . . . . . - 793

3. The Teaching of Agriculture in Elementary and Higher Schools in the West Indies - . . . . . - 797

Recommendations of the West India Royal Commission - 799
  Extracts from Report : A system of Peasant Proprietors. 799
    Establishment of a Department of Economic Botany
      in the West Indies - . . . . . - 801
    Education :—Elementary, Agricultural and Industrial 802
  Extracts from Subsidiary Report : - . . . - 802
    Scheme for the Establishment of a Department of
      Economic Botany and for Agricultural Instruction
      in the West Indies - . . . . . - 802
    Administration ; Head Office - . . . 803
    Tobago Botanic Station - . . . . - 804
    Grenada Botanic Station - . . . . - 804
    St. Vincent Botanic Station and Industrial School - 805
    St. Lucia Botanic Station and Industrial School - 805
    Barbados Botanic Station and Experimental Cane
      Cultivation - . . . . . . - 806
    Dominica Botanic Station and Industrial School - 806
    Montserrat Botanic Station - . . . - 806
    Antigua Botanic Station and Sugar Cane Experiments 807
    St. Kitts-Nevis - . . . . . . - 807
    Summary : Botanic Stations and Industrial Schools - 807
    British Guiana - . . . . . . - 808
    Horticultural Shows - . . . . - 808
    Grants to Elementary Schools - . . . - 808
    Bulletins, Leaflets, etc. - . . . . - 808
    Grants to Colleges and Schools - . . . - 808
    Summary : Botanic Department - . . - 809
  Debate in the House of Commons Aug. 2, 1898 - . - 809
  Letter from the Secretary of State - . . - 810
  First Agricultural Conference : President's Address - 811
    The Sugar Industry - . . . . - 812
    Other Industries - . . . . . - 815
    Botanical Institutions - . . . . - 817
    Agricultural Instructors - . . . - 817
    Agricultural Exhibitions - . . . . - 818
    Bulletins, Handbooks and Leaflets - . - 819
    Agricultural Teaching in Primary Schools - . - 819
    Agricultural Schools - . . . . . - 820
    Teaching Scientific Agriculture in the Higher Schools
      and Colleges - . . . . . . - 820
    Fungoid and Insect Pests - . . . - 821
    New Steamship Services - . . . . - 821
  Second Agricultural Conference - . . . - 821
    Extracts from President's Address : Agricultural
      Education - . . . . . . - 821
    Teaching Agriculture in High Schools and Colleges :
      Discussion - . . . . . . - 824
    Teaching Agriculture in Elementary Schools : Dis-
      cussion - . . . . - 828
  Postscript on Agricultural Education in the West Indies in
    1900 - . . . . - 833

Volume I. of Special Reports (1896–7), contains the following Papers:—

1. Public Elementary Education in England and Wales, 1870–1895.
   By Messrs. M. E. Sadler and J. W. Edwards.
2. English Students in Foreign Training Colleges.
   By Miss L. Manley, Miss Williams, and Mr. H. L. Withers.
3. Brush Work in an Elementary School (with illustrations).
   By Mr. Seth Coward.
4. The A B C of Drawing: an inquiry into the principles underlying
   elementary instruction in Drawing (with illustrations).
   By Mr. Ebenezer Cooke.
5. Domestic Economy Teaching in England.
   By Mrs. Pillow.
6. Technical Education for Girls.
   By Miss A. J. Cooper.
7. The Secondary Day School attached to the Battersea Polytechnic, London
   —an experiment in the co-education of boys and girls.
   By Mr. Sidney H. Wells.
8. The History of the Irish System of Elementary Education.
   By Mr. M. E. Sadler.
9. The National System of Education in Ireland.
   By the late Right Hon. C. T. Redington, D.L.
10. Recent Legislation on Elementary Education in Belgium.
    By Messrs. M. E. Sadler and R. L. Morant.
11. The Housewifery Schools and Classes of Belgium.
    By Miss K. S. Block and Miss L. Brackenbury.
12. The French System of Higher Primary Schools.
    By Mr. R. L. Morant.
13. The Realschulen in Berlin and their bearing on Modern Secondary and
    Commercial Education.
    By Mr. M. E. Sadler.
14. The Ober-Realschulen of Prussia, with special reference to the Ober-
    Realschule at Charlottenburg.
    By Mr. M. E. Sadler.
15. The Prussian Elementary School Code.
    Translated by Mr. A. E. Twentyman.
16. The Continuation Schools in Saxony.
    By Mr. F. H. Dale.
17. The School Journey in Germany.
    By Miss C. I. Dodd.
18. The Teaching of the Mother Tongue in Germany.
    By Mr. F. H. Dale.
19. Holiday Courses in France and Germany for Instruction in Modern
    Languages.
    By Messrs. F. S. Marvin and R. L. Morant.
20. Recent Educational Progress in Denmark (with maps).
    By Mr. J. S. Thornton.
21. Education in Egypt.
    By Mr. P. A. Barnett.
22. The Education of Girls and Women in Spain.
    By Señor Don Fernando de Arteaga.
23. The National Bureau of Education of the United States.
    By Mr. R. L. Morant.
24. The History of the Manitoba School System and the Issues of the Recent
    Controversy.
    By Mr. R. L. Morant.
25. Arrangements for the admission of Women to the chief Universities in the
    British Empire and in Foreign Countries.
    By Mr. M. E. Sadler, with the help of Mr. J. W. Longsdon.
26. Appendix giving a list of the chief official papers bearing on Education in
    Great Britain and Ireland.
    Prepared by Mr. M. E. Sadler.

This volume (Cd. 8447) can be obtained, either directly or through any Bookseller, from
EYRE AND SPOTTISWOODE, EAST HARDING STREET, FLEET STREET, E.C.;
JOHN MENZIES & Co., ROSE STREET, EDINBURGH;
HODGES, FIGGIS, & Co., LIMITED, 104, GRAFTON STREET, DUBLIN.

Price 3s. 4d.; Post free 3s. 10d.

Volume 2 of Special Reports contains the following Papers:—

1. The Welsh Intermediate Education Act, 1889: Its Origin and Working.
   Contributed by the Charity Commissioners for England and Wales.
2. The London Polytechnic Institutes (with illustrations).
   By Mr. Sidney Webb.
3. The London School of Economics and Political Science.
   By Mr. W. A. S. Hewins.
4. The Curriculum of a Girls' School.
   By Mrs. Bryant, Miss Burstall and Miss Aitken.
5. Physical Education at the Sheffield High School for Girls.
   By Mrs. Woodhouse.
6. Games and Athletics in Secondary Schools for Girls (with illustrations).
   By Miss P. Lawrence.
7. The Organisation of Games out of School for the children attending Public
   Elementary Schools.
   By Mr. George Sharples.
8. Physical Education under the School Board for London (with illustrations).
   By Mr. Thomas Chesterton.
9. Physical Education for Girls and Infants under the London School Board
   (with illustrations).
   By the late Mrs. Ely Dallas.
10. Physical Training in Birmingham Board Schools (with illustrations).
    By Mr. Samuel Bott.
11. Physical Training under the Leeds School Board.
    By Mr. R. E. Thomas.
12. The School Gardens at the Boscombe British School (with illustrations).
    By Mr. T. G. Rooper.
13. The Connection between the Public Library and the Public Elementary
    School.
    By Mr. John J. Ogle.
14. The Educational Museum of the Teachers' Guild.
    By Mr. John L. Myres.
15. The Haslemere Educational Museum (with plans).
    By Dr. Jonathan Hutchinson, F.R.S.
16. School Plays in Latin and Greek.
    By Mr. J. ff. Baker-Penoyre.
17. The Study of Education.
    By Mr. J. J. Findlay.
18. The Training of Secondary Teachers and Educational Ideals.
    By Mr. F. J. R. Hendy.
19. The Heuristic Method of Teaching.
    By Dr. Henry Armstrong, F.R.S.
20. Statistics, &c., of Elementary Education in England and Wales,
    1833-1870.
    By Messrs. M. E. Sadler and J. W. Edwards.
21. List of Publications on Educational Subjects issued by the chief Local
    Educational Authorities in England and Wales.
    Prepared by Miss M. S. Beard.
22. Les Universités Françaises.
    By Monsieur Louis Liard.
23. The French Universities (a translation of No. 22).
    By Mr. J. W. Longsdon.
24. The Position of Teachers in the State Secondary Schools for Boys in
    France.
    By Mr. F. B. Kirkman.
25. The French Leaving Certificate—Certificat d'Études Primaires.
    By Sir Joshua Fitch.
26. The Teaching of Modern Languages in Belgium and Holland.
    By Miss J. D. Montgomery.
27. School Hygiene in Brussels.
    By Miss J. D. Montgomery.

This volume (Cd. 8943) can be obtained, either directly or through any Bookseller, from
EYRE AND SPOTTISWOODE, EAST HARDING STREET, FLEET STREET, E.C.
JOHN MENZIES & Co., ROSE STREET, EDINBURGH;
HODGES, FIGGIS, & Co., LIMITED, 104, GRAFTON STREET, DUBLIN.

Price 6s. 2d. ; Post free 6s. 3d.

Volume 3 of Special Reports contains the following papers :—

1. The National Organisation of Education in Switzerlan .
   By Mr. R. L. Morant.

2. Problems in Prussian Secondary Education for Boys, with special reference to similar questions in England.
   By Mr. M. E. Sadler.

3. " The Curricula and Programmes of Work for Higher Schools in Prussia."
   Translated by Mr. W. G. Lipscomb.

4. The Higher Schools of the Grand Duchy of Baden.
   By Mr. H. E. D. Hammond.

5. Strömungen auf dem Gebiet des Schul- und Bildungswesens in Deutschland.
   Von Professor Dr. W. Rein in Jena.

6. Tendencies in the Educational Systems of Germany. (Translation of No. 5.)
   By Mr. F. H. Dale.

7. The Teaching of Modern Languages in Frankfort a/M and district.
   By Mr. Fabian Ware.

8. The Teaching of Modern Languages in Germany.
   By Miss Mary Brebner.

9. The Teaching of Foreign Languages.
   By Professor Dr. Emil Hausknecht.

10. The Teacher of Modern Languages in Prussian Secondary Schools for Boys. His education and professional training.
    By Mr. Fabian Ware.

11. Higher Commercial Education in Antwerp, Leipzig, Paris and Havre.
    By Mr. M. E. Sadler.

12. The Present Position of Manual Instruction in Germany.
    By Dr. Otto W. Beyer. (Translated by Mr. A. E. Twentyman.)

13. The Secondary Schools of Sweden.
    By Dr. Otto Gallander.

14. Elementary Education in the Grand Duchy of Finland.
    By the Baron Dr. Yrjö-Koskinen.

This volume (Cd. 8988) can be obtained, either directly or through any Bookseller, from
EYRE AND SPOTTISWOODE, EAST HARDING STREET, FLEET STREET, E.C. ;
JOHN MENZIES & Co, ROSE STREET, EDINBURGH ;
HODGES, FIGGIS & Co., LIMITED, 104, GRAFTON STREET, DUBLIN.

Price 3s. 3d. ; Post free 3s. 9d.

Volume 5 of Special Reports (published simultaneously with Volume 4) contains the following papers :—

A. AFRICA—

1. Cape Colony, The History and Present State of Education in.
    Part I., Sections 1–74.
        By Mr. G. B. Muir, B.A., of the Department of Public Education,
        Cape Town.
    Part I., Sections 75 to end, Part II. and Part III.
        Prepared from official documents by Mr. M. E. Sadler.

2. Natal, The System of Education in.
        By Mr. R. Russell, Superintendent of Education, Natal.

B. COMMONWEALTH OF AUSTRALIA—

1. New South Wales, The System of Education in.
        Prepared from official documents supplied by the Department of
        Public Instruction for New South Wales.

2. Victoria, The System of Education in.
        By The Hon. A. J. Peacock, late Minister of Public Instruction,
        Victoria.

3. Queensland, The System of Education in.
        By Mr. J. G. Anderson, M.A., Under Secretary for Public
        Instruction, Queensland.

4. Tasmania, The System of Education in.
        Prepared from official documents by Mr. A. E. Twentyman.

5. South Australia, The System of Education in.
        By Mr. C. L. Whitham, Member of the Board of Inspectors of
        Schools, South Australia.

6. Western Australia, The System of Education in.
        By Mr. Cyril Jackson, Inspector General of Schools, Western
        Australia.

C. NEW ZEALAND—

New Zealand, The System of Education in.
        Prepared by Mr. M. E. Sadler, from official documents supplied
        by the Department of Education for New Zealand.

D. CEYLON—

Ceylon, The System of Education in.
        By Mr. J. B. Cull, late Director of Public Instruction, and Mr. A.
        Van Cuylenburg, Inspector of Schools, Ceylon.

E. MALTA—

Malta, The System of Education in.
        By Mr. N. Tagliaferro, Director of Education, Malta.

—————————————

This volume (Cd. 417) can be obtained, either directly or through any Bookseller, from
    EYRE AND SPOTTISWOODE, EAST HARDING STREET, FLEET STREET, E.C. ;
        JOHN MENZIES & Co., ROSE STREET, EDINBURGH ;
    HODGES, FIGGIS, & Co., LIMITED, 104, GRAFTON STREET, DUBLIN.

Price 4s. 0d. ; *Post free 4s. 6d.*

Volume 6 of Special Reports contains the following papers:—

1. Introduction.
    By Mr. C. C. Cotterill.

2. The Masters of a Preparatory School.
    By Mr. C. C. Cotterill.

3. Preparatory School Equipment.
    By Mr. Frank Ritchie.

4. The Time-table of Work in Preparatory Schools.
    By Mr. H. Frampton Stallard.

5. The Preparatory School Curriculum.
    By Mr. G. Gidley Robinson.

6. The Place of the Preparatory School for Boys in Secondary Education in England.
    By Mr. M. E. Sadler.

7. Entrance Scholarships at Public Schools, and their Influence on Preparatory Schools.
    By the Rev. the Honourable Canon E. Lyttelton.

8. Examinations for Entrance Scholarships at the Public Schools. Their Character and Effect on the Educational Work of Preparatory Schools
    By Mr. C. C. Lynam.

9. The Teaching of Latin and Greek in Preparatory Schools.
    By the Rev. C. Eccles Williams, D.D.

10. The Teaching of the Mother-Tongue in Preparatory Schools.
    By Mr. H. C. Tillard.

11. The Teaching of History in Preparatory Schools.
    By Mr. A. M. Curteis.

12. The Teaching of Geography in Preparatory Schools.
    By the Rev. F. R. Burrows.

13. The Teaching of Modern Languages in Preparatory Schools.
    By Messrs. E. P. Arnold and Fabian Ware.

14. The Teaching of Mathematics in Preparatory Schools.
    By the late Mr. C. G. Allum.

15. Natural Science in Preparatory schools.
    By Mr. Archer Vassall.

16. The Teaching of Drawing in Preparatory Schools.
    By Mr. James T. Watts.

17. Art Teaching in Preparatory Schools.
    By Mr. W. Egerton Hine.

18. The School Workshop.
    By Mr. E. D. Mansfield.

19. Music in Preparatory Schools.
    By the Rev. W. Earle, with an Appendix by Mr. W. W. Cheriton.

20. Singing in Preparatory Schools.
    By Mr. Leonard C. Venables.

21. Gardening, its Role in Preparatory School Life.
    By Mr. A. C. Bartholomew.

22. Health and Physical Training in Preparatory Schools.
    By the Rev. C. T. Wickham.

23. Games in Preparatory Schools.
    By Mr. A. J. C. Dowding.

24. The Employment of Leisure Hours in Boys' Boarding Schools.
    By Mr. Arthur Rowntree.

25. Preparatory School Libraries.
    By Mr. W. Douglas.

26. A Day in a Boy's Life at a Preparatory School.
    By Mr. P. S. Dealtry.

27. School Management in Preparatory Schools.
    By the Rev. J. H. Wilkinson, with an Appendix by Mr. A. J. C. Dowding.

28. Economics of Preparatory Schools.
    By the Rev. C. Black.

29. Preparation for the Preparatory School.
    By Mr. E. D. Mansfield.

30. Preparatory Boys' Schools under Lady Principals.
    By Mr. C. D. Olive.

31. The Preparatory Department at Public Schools.
    By Mr. A. T. Martin.

32. The Preparatory Department at a Public School.
    By Mr. T. H. Mason.

33. The Relations between Public and Preparatory Schools.
    By the Rev. Herbert Bull.

34. The Preparatory School Product.
    By the Rev. H. A. James, D.D.

35. The Preparatory School Product.
    By the Rev. the Honourable Canon E. Lyttelton.

36. The Preparatory School Product.
    By Dr. Hely Hutchinson Almond.

37. The Preparatory School Product.
    By Mr. Arthur C. Benson.

38. The Home Training of Children.
    By Mrs. Franklin.

39. The Possibility of Co-education in English Preparatory and other Secondary Schools.
    By Mr. J. H. Badley.

40. Notes on a Preparatory School for Girls.

41. Appendix.

This volume (Cd. 418) can be obtained, either directly or through any Bookseller, from
EYRE AND SPOTTISWOODE, EAST HARDING STREET, FLEET STREET, E.C. ;
JOHN MENZIES & Co., ROSE STREET, EDINBURGH ;
HODGES, FIGGIS & Co., LIMITED, 104, GRAFTON STREET, DUBLIN,

Price s. 3½d.; Post free, 2s. 7½d,

The following Reports from Volumes 2 and 3 of Special Reports on Educational Subjects have been issued as Reprints:—

1. Special Reports on Intermediate Education in Wales and the Organisation of Education in Switzerland.

   (Nos. 1 in Vols. 2 and 3 respectively.)   Price 1s. 1d. ; post free, 1s. 3½d.

2. Special Reports on Modern Language Teaching.

   (No. 26 in Vol. 2 and Nos. 7, 8, 9, 10 in Vol. 3.)   Price 6½d. ; post free, 8½d.

3. Special Reports on Secondary Education in Prussia.

   (Nos. 2 and 3 in Vol. 3.)   Price 1s. ; post free, 1s. 3½d.

4. Special Report on Secondary Schools in Baden.

   (No. 4 in Vol. 3.)   Price 5½d. ; post free, 7d.

5. Special Reports on Education in France.

   (Nos. 22, 23, 24, 25 in Vol. 2.)   Price 4d. ; post free, 5½d.

6. Special Report on the Heuristic Method of Teaching.

   (No. 19 in Vol. 2.)   Price 3d. ; post free, 4d.

7. Special Report on the Connection between the Public Library and the Public Elementary School.

   (No. 13 in Vol. 2.)   Price 2½d ; post free, 3½d.

These can be obtained, either directly or through any bookseller from
EYRE AND SPOTTISWOODE, EAST HARDING STREET, FLEET STREET, E.C. .
JOHN MENZIES & Co., ROSE STREET, EDINBURGH ;
HODGES FIGGIS & Co., LIMITED, 104, GRAFTON STREET, DUBLIN,

THE
SYSTEM OF EDUCATION
IN
ONTARIO.

PART I.

GENERAL DESCRIPTION OF THE SYSTEM.

INTRODUCTION - - - - - - - - .5

    Central Administration - - - - - - 5
    Local Administration - - - - - - - 6
    The School and the Churches - - - - - 7

I. PRIMARY EDUCATION - - - - - - - 7

    Kindergartens - - - - - - - - 7
    Administration - - - - - - - - 8
    Compulsory Education - - - - - - 8
    Subjects of Instruction - - - - - - 9
    Leaving Examinations - - - - - - 9
    Statistics - - - - - - - - 10
    Separate Schools - - - - - - - 10
    Training of Teachers - - - - - - 12
    County Model Schools - - - - - 14
    Normal Schools - - - - - - - 15
    Inspection - - - - - - - - 16
    Teachers' Institutes - - - - - - 18

II. SECONDARY EDUCATION.

    High Schools and Collegiate Institutes - - - 19
    Trustees - - - - - - - - 20
    Finance - - - - - - - - 20
    Entrance Examination - - - - - - 21
    Statistics - - - - - - - - 22
    Departmental Examinations - - - - 22
    The School of Pedagogy - - - - - 25
    Inspectors of High Schools - - - - - 26

III. UNIVERSITY EDUCATION - - - - - - 27

IV. TECHNICAL EDUCATION - - - - - 34

V. SPECIAL SCHOOLS - - - - - - - 37

VI. INDUSTRIAL SCHOOLS - - - - - - 83

PART II.

THE SYSTEM IN 1899 : EXTRACTS FROM THE REPORT OF THE MINISTER OF EDUCATION FOR THE YEAR 1899.

I. PUBLIC SCHOOL TEACHERS AND THEIR CERTIFICATES.

    a. Certificates, 1899 - - - - - - 40
    b. Remarks on the supply of qualified teachers - - 40

C

I. PUBLIC SCHOOL TEACHERS AND THEIR CERTIFICATES—*cont.*

 c. Teachers in training at Normal Schools, 1877-1899 - 41
 d. Teachers' Institutes, 1877-1898 - - - 41
 c. Temporary and extended Certificates, 1899 - - 42
 f. Specialists' Certificates. - - - - - 42

II. THE PUBLIC SCHOOL LEAVING EXAMINATIONS - - 44

III. CONTINUATION CLASSES - - - - - - 46

IV. THE COURSE OF STUDY IN PUBLIC AND HIGH SCHOOLS.

 a. Agriculture - - - - - 47
 b. Manual Training - - - - - 49
 c. Temperance and Hygiene - - - - - 50

V. SEPARATE SCHOOLS IN 1898.

 a. Roman Catholic - - - - - 50
 b. Protestant - - - - - 50

VI. HIGH SCHOOLS.

 a. Diffusion of High School Education - - 51
 b. Tendencies of High School Education, 1867-1898 - 51
 c. Departmental Instructions for the High School
  Entrance Examination, 1900 - - - 52
 d. The question of Free High Schools - - - 54

VII. EMPIRE DAY IN PUBLIC AND HIGH SCHOOLS.

 a. Circular of March, 1899 - - - - 54
 b. Remarks from the Report for 1899 - - - 55

VIII. UNIVERSITY EDUCATION.

 a. From the Report of the Council of the University of
  Toronto for 1898-9 - - - - - 56
 b. Numbers attending Pass and Honour Lectures - 57
 c. The Laboratories - - - - - 58
 d. Numbers examined in the Faculties and Departments 58
 e. Students in the Faculty of Medicine - - 58
 f. Subjects taught in the Faculty of Science - 59
 g. University College—(i) Registered Students ; (ii)
  Pass and Honours Lectures - - - 59
 h. Subjects taught by the Faculty of the School of
  Science - - - - - - - 60

IX. ART TEACHING.

 a. Art Schools and Departmental Drawing Examinations 61

  (i.) Certificates in Primary Art Course, 1882-1889 - 61
  (ii.)   "   Advanced Art Course, 1883-1899 61
  (iii.)   Mechanical Drawing Course 1883–
     1899 - - - - - 62
  (iv.)   Industrial Art Course, 1885-1899 62
  (v.)   "   Extra Subjects, 1885-1889 - - 63

 b. Literary and Scientific Societies receiving grants - 63
 c. Progress of School Architecture and Decoration - 63

X. PUBLIC LIBRARIES.

 a. Public Libraries not free. - - - - 66
 b. Evening Classes in Public Libraries, 1898-1899 - 67
 c. Certificates in Primary Drawing Course, 1899 - - 68

X. PUBLIC LIBRARIES—*cont.*

    d. Certificates in Mechanical Drawing Course, 1899 - 68
    e. Number of Public Libraries in Counties and Districts 68
    f. Progress of Public Libraries, 1883–1899 - - - 69
    g. Free Libraries - - - - - - - 69

XI. REPORTS OF THE INDUSTRIAL SCHOOLS, 1899.

    a. Victoria Industrial School - - - - - 70
    b. Alexandra Industrial School - - - - - 70

XII. EXAMINATION REQUIREMENTS, 1900, 1901, 1902 - - 70

    a. Junior Leaving Standing, Part I - - 70
    b. do. do. do. Part II. - - - - 71
    c. Senior Leaving Standing, Part I. - - - 76
    d. do. do. do. Part. II. - - - - 78
    e. Question Papers - - - - - - 82
    f. Percentages - - - - - - - 82
    g. Commercial Diploma - - - - - - 83

PART III.

STATISTICAL TABLES FOR THE YEAR 1898.

Table 1. PUBLIC SCHOOLS. Pupils in the different branches 85

   „ 2. PUBLIC SCHOOLS. School population and pupils in attendance - - - - - - - 86

   „ 3. PUBLIC SCHOOLS. Teachers, their salaries and qualifications - - - - - - 87

   „ 4. PUBLIC SCHOOLS. Receipts and expenditure - - 88

   „ 5. HIGH SCHOOLS.

      a. Receipts and expenditure - - - 89
      b. Miscellaneous information - - - - 89

   „ 6. COLLEGIATE INSTITUTES.

      a. Receipts and expenditure - - - 90
      b. Miscellaneous information - - - 90

   „ 7. COLLEGIATE INSTITUTES. Pupils in the different branches of Instruction - - - - 91

   „ 8. KINDERGARTENS - - - - - - 92

   „ 9. NIGHT SCHOOLS. - - - - - - 92

   „ 10. GENERAL STATISTICAL ABSTRACT, 1867 to 1898 - 93

   „ 11. SUMMARY OF STATISTICS FOR 1898.

      a. Elementary Schools - - - - 94
      b. Secondary Schools - - - - - 95

APPENDICES.

A. Regulations of the Education Department of the Province of Ontario (1896) - - - - - - - 96
B. Certain Regulations as amended in 1898 and 1899 - - 125
C. Duties of Inspectors - - - - - - - 127
D. Examinations and Examiners - - - - - 130
E. Uniform Text Books - - - - - - - 134
F. Regulations for the School of Pedagogy - - - - 138
G. University Regulations - - - - - - 140

THE SYSTEM OF EDUCATION IN ONTARIO.

[NOTE.—Part I. of this Report consists in the main of extracts from the official handbook to the educational system of the Province, written in 1893 by Mr. John Millar, now Deputy Minister of Education. This useful book is entitled "The Educational System of the Province of Ontario." A copy of it was specially furnished by the Education Department of Ontario for the purposes of this Report.

Appendices C, D, E, F, and G have all been taken from the same work ; and Appendix A is part of an official document also supplied by the Education Department.

Part II., which deals only with the state of education in the Province in 1899 (as well as Appendix B, which gives certain recent regulations), has been compiled from the admirably arranged "Report of the Minister of Education for the year 1899," also furnished by the Ontario Education Department.

Part III. consists of statistical tables for the school year 1898, selected from among those given in the Appendix to the Report for 1899.]

PART I.—GENERAL DESCRIPTION OF THE SYSTEM.

INTRODUCTION.

" From the earliest settlement of Ontario," writes Mr. Millar in his account of the Educational System of the Province, "schools were established as the wants of the inhabitants required." . . . " The Legislature soon recognised the needs of the country, and made grants of land and money in aid of elementary, secondary, and superior education. Statutes were passed from time to time for the purpose of opening schools to meet the demands of the people. The sparsely settled condition of the Province delayed for a while the organization of the system. It was not until 1844 that the elementary schools were put on a comprehensive basis. In that year the Rev. Egerton Ryerson, LL.D., was appointed Chief Superintendent of Education, and the report which he presented to the House of Assembly sketched in an able manner the main features of the system of which he was the distinguished founder, and of which he continued for thirty-three years to be the efficient administrator. In 1876 the office of chief superintendent was abolished, and the schools of the Province placed under the control of a member of the Government with the title of Minister of Education. In this way they have been since administered, and such improvements as have been considered necessary have been made from time to time by means of amendments to the school law and regulations of the Education Department." Central Administration.

N.B.—Recent reports of the Minister of Education and other documents relating to education in Ontario may be seen at the Board of Education Library, St. Stephen's House, Cannon Row, Whitehall, London, S.W.

This Department consists of the members of the Executive Government: and its head, as already stated, is the Minister of Education. Subject to the provisions of any statute in that behalf, and the regulations of the Department, there may be established the following schools :—(1) Kindergartens, (2) Public Schools, (3) Night Schools, (4) High Schools, and Collegiate Institutes, (5) Art Schools, (6) County Model Schools, (7) Normal Schools, (8) Schools of Pedagogy, (9) Teachers' Institutes (10) Mechanics' Institutes, (11) Industrial Schools.

"It is the duty of the Minister to direct all the educational forces in the country: first from his place as a member of the Legislative Assembly, and secondly through the officers of his department. From the discussions of educational questions in the provincial parliament his position as a member gives him the best facilities for recognising the working of the school law, and ascertaining the trend of public opinion. As the head of his department his constant official intercourse with trustees, inspectors and teachers, gives him the greatest opportunity for prescribing from time to time whatever amendments to the regulations may be considered wise in the interests of high and public schools. From the wide sweep of the legislation which he is expected to direct, and from his position as a member of the Government responsible to the people's representatives, he is able to advance such legislation as will guard the unity of the system and preserve its symmetry."

"Ontario may claim to have some features of her system that are largely her own. Among them may be mentioned: a division of state and municipal authority on a judicious basis; clear lines separating the function of the university from that of the high schools, and the function of the high schools from that of the public or elementary schools; a uniform course of study: all high and public schools in the hands of professionally trained teachers; no person eligible to the position of inspector who does not hold the highest grade of a teacher's certificate, and who has not had years of experience as a teacher; inspectors removable if inefficient, but not subject to removal by popular vote; the examinations of teachers under provincial instead of local control; the acceptance of a common matriculation examination for admission to the universities and to the learned professions; a uniform series of text books for the whole Province; the almost entire absence of party politics in the manner in which school boards, inspectors and teachers discharge their duties; the system national instead of sectarian, but affording under constitutional guarantees and limitations protection to Roman Catholic and Protestant separate schools and denominational universities."

Local Administration.

"The municipal system of Ontario affords a full measure of local self-government. The province is for the most part divided into counties, which are subdivided into minor municipalities, consisting of townships, and of incorporated villages, towns, and cities. These corporations are given certain powers, and have certain responsibilities with respect to education. Through their muni cipal councils counties are under obligation to make grants of money to high schools, and both counties and townships must contribute certain sums in aid of public schools. Each township is divided into school sections and each of these sections is provided with a public school. There is a board of trustees for each school section, incorporated village, town, and city. Much the greater part of what is expended for public schools is provided by the school section, village, town, or city. The ratepayers (men and women) elect the trustees, who, within the provisions of the provincial statutes or regulations of the Education Department, appoint the teachers and determine the amounts to be expended for buildings, equipments, and salaries. It thus follows that the system of education in Ontario is essentially democratic, and in those matters which affect the sentiments or touch the pockets of the people, each locality has almost entire control. It is not, however, considered wise to decentralise as regards the granting of certificates to teachers and inspectors, the authorising of text-books, the fixing of courses of study, and the prescribing of the duties of trustees, inspectors, and teachers. These are questions which, though still under the control of the people, are regulated by a responsible government."

"There is no established church in Ontario, or connection   The School between Church and State. The constitution gives the Province   and the control of its educational affairs, and the great majority of the people   Churches. believe that schools and colleges should be non-denominational. No religious body has any voice in the management of the high and public schools, or the university. . . . They are institutions of a Christian p ople. The doctrines of no church are taught, but the principles of Christianity form an essential feature of the daily exercises. . . The co-operation of the clergy of all denominations in educational gatherings is quite common, and recognition of religion is fully shown in the regulations which have been prescribed by the Education Department."

1. PRIMARY EDUCATION.

"By the Public Schools Act each Board of Trustees in cities, towns, and incorporated villages has power to establish kinder-   Kindergar- gartens for children between the ages of four and seven years.   tens. The system has been introduced into all the large cities and into many of the principal towns. Each of the provincial normal and model schools in Toronto and Ottawa has also a kindergarten, with two regular teachers on the staff, assisted by those taking the training course. In all these schools the principles of Froebel's system are followed, and the effect has been to create much interest in this method of training young children. A small fee is generally charged, and the cost has to some extent militated against their establishment. Experience has, however, shown that the expense need not be high. A genuine kindergartner can, with the aid of her assistants in training, superintend from fifty to one hundred children, provided she begin with no more than twenty, adding ten or twenty more as she gets an assistant ready to take charge of them. These pupil teachers are not paid, and may not become teachers, as it is held that all women should learn to interest and train young children according to the Froebelian methods. It is found indispensable to the success of a school of the kind that the mothers of the community should take a lively interest in the training thus given to their children. Where this is the case, and a good kindergartner employed, cheerfulness, intelligence, activity, and a fondness for the school work are aroused among the pupils. At the normal kindergartens many visitors, especially ladies, are present almost daily, and wherever these institutions are established the results are quite observable in the superiority of the public schools."

In 1898 the province had 116 kindergartens attended by 11,083 pupils. 240 teachers were employed.

Administration.

"Townships are divided by their municipal councils into sections, and each of these has its own school (a few have two schools) managed by a board of three trustees, who hold office for three years—one going out of office annually, when his successor is elected. A grant of money is paid by the Government to each school according to the average attendance of pupils, and the county council is obliged to make an equal appropriation. In addition the township council must give a grant of 100 dollars (150 dollars if two teachers are employed) to each school, and the ratepayers of the section are taxed to raise whatever further sum the trustees require to maintain the school. Since 1871 the schools have all been free."

"Cities, towns, and incorporated villages in Ontario also receive their share of the legislative grant for public schools and the balance necessary is raised by the municipal council at the request of the board of trustees. The public school board consists of six or more members, two elected from each ward, of whom one retires annually. If the board so decides, the elections may be held by ballot, and on the same day as the municipal elections. The graded system of classification, under the direction of the principal or inspector, is adopted, and promotions are usually made twice a year. As in rural schools, the public schools are all free, and free text books, under the Act of 1891, may also be provided by the trustees in cities, towns, and villages, or each pupil may be charged a small fee for their purchase. Night schools and kindergartens may also be established."

"Trustees have extensive duties. To them is largely entrusted the amount of money to be expended for school sites, buildings, equipment, and maintenance. They select the teachers and determine the number, grade, and description of schools to be established and maintained. In cities and towns the boards have erected a large number of very handsome school buildings furnished with the latest improvements as to heating and ventilation, maps and apparatus, and provided with furniture of the most modern character."

Compulsory Education.

"It is assumed that the parent as well as the State has duties to perform regarding education. The parent is not denied the right to have his children educated at a private school, a church school or college, or a denominational university, but, if he so, decides, he is not thereby relieved of his duty in the way of paying his share towards the support of the institutions sustained, or partly sustained, by the State. It is held to be the duty of the state to provide free elementary schools. . . . All persons are taxed to support education, because its general diffusion is for the public good. It is held that compulsory education is a necessary corollary of free education. If the state gives the boon of free schools to all, it has a right to see that the expected advantages are realized. On this principle the Truancy and Compulsory Education Act of 1891 was passed. . . . By this Act all children between the ages of eight and fourteen are obliged to attend school for the full term during which the school is open, and parents or guardians who fail to send their children are subject to penalties. The rights of conscience are sufficiently guarded. Penalties are not inflicted if the child is under efficient instruction at home, or unable to attend through sickness or other unavoidable cause, or is excused by a justice of the peace, or by the principal of the school, or if he has passed the high school entrance examination. Any person employing a child under fourteen years of age during school hours is liable to a penalty of twenty dollars. When the services of a child are deemed urgent, an absence from school for six weeks of the term may be granted. Provision is made for sending a child who is vicious or immoral to an industrial school. To nip truancy in the bud is regarded as the most effective means of preventing a recourse to the penalties of the Act. Truant officers must be appointed for every city, town, and incorporated village, and may be appointed for every school section. These officers are vested with police powers, and have authority to enter factories, workshops, stores and other places where children may be employed, and ascertain whether there is any violation of the Act. Regulations may be made by the local authorities for the better enforcement of the statute. The truant officers must report annually to the Education Department according to prescribed forms."

" The public school has usually five successive classes, but in the case of towns in which instruction is given in the lowest class of the high school without the imposition of any fee, it is not compulsory on the public school board to maintain a fifth class in the primary school.

" There is a fixed course of study for each of the five classes, of the ordinary public school, which will be found in detail in Appendix A (Regulations of the Educational Department, Schedule A). It includes the following subjects:—Reading, Writing, Arithmetic, Grammar, Geography, History, Drawing, Music, Physiology, and Temperance. *Subjects of Instruction.*

" Public School Leaving Examinations are held each year, at the same time as the High School Entrance Examinations, for those pupils who take up fifth form work. The main object of this regulation is to afford the pupils of rural schools who cannot conveniently attend a high school an incentive for higher work. Only those pupils are eligible for this examination who have *Leaving Examinations.*

passed the entrance examination, or who have made at least the total number of marks required, and are recommended by the principal of the public school. The examination papers are prepared by the Education Department, and the questions are based upon the following subjects:—Arithmetic and Mensuration (value 200), English Grammar and Rhetoric (150), English Poetical Literature (150), English Composition (100), History (100), Geography (100), Book-keeping and Penmanship (100) Drawing (50), Reading (50); there are besides two optional papers, each valued at 75, one of them being on Temperance and Hygiene and the other on Agriculture. The standard required is one-third of the marks in each subject and one-half of the total marks obtainable. To meet the cost of the examination a fee of one dollar is required of each candidate, and the papers are read by the Inspector and the Principal of the county model school. Any public school pupil who has passed the high school Entrance Examination may be a candidate, and a special grant is made by the Legislature for those schools that successfully prepare pupils for this examination. No grant is, however, paid to a school in a city, town or village where there is a high school, as it is not deemed desirable for such schools to take up this work. To prevent the junior classes from being neglected it is necessary that at least two teachers be employed, and as a guarantee of ability to undertake the course, the principal must hold at least a second-class certificate."

Population of Ontario (1891), 2,114,321; school population 591,300. Total number of registered pupils, 478,194 (under 5 1,387; between 5 and 12, 476,584; over 12,223). Average attendance, 273,451. Percentage of average attendance to total number attending school, 57.

Classification of pupils. In 1st Reader, Parts I. and II., 179,360 2nd Reader, 90,624; 3rd Reader, 97,693; 4th Reader, 89,670 5th Reader, 20,847

Number of pupils learning writing, 464,460; arithmetic 469,603; drawing, 447,813; geography, 343,759; history, 245,370; grammar and composition, 313,637; temperance and hygiene 219,776.

Total number of public school houses, 5,587, of which 2,374 were brick, 487 stone, 2,355 frame, and 371 log.

Number of teachers employed in the public schools, 8,465 (male 2,656, female 5,809). Of these 3,585 have attended a normal school; 476 hold provincial first-class certificates or first-class certificates of the old County Board; 3,414 hold one or other type of second-class certificate; 4,333 hold third-class or other certificate.

In the public schools the highest salary paid to a teacher was 1,500 dollars; the average salary of male teachers 396 dollars and of female teachers 293 dollars.

"The Roman Catholics of Ontario have certain educational privileges guaranteed to them by the Act of Confederation. All ratepayers, no matter what may be their religious belief, are, however, liable [to pay public school rates, unless, in the manner provided they become separate school supporters. The term 'separate schools' applies to Protestant and coloured persons as well as to Roman Catholics. As a matter of fact, the exception to the general public school system is confined chiefly to Roman Catholics, who desire to establish separate schools in localities where their supporters are sufficiently numerous for the purpose. It is provided that any number of heads of family, not less than five, being residents of the place and Roman Catholics, may unite and establish a separate school. Such ratepayers are required to give notice to the clerk of the municipality of their intention to become separate school supporters, and they are then exempted from the payment of rates towards the public school until they give a contrary notice to the same municipal officer. It is optional with a Roman Catholic whether he continues to be a public school supporter, but in cities and towns where separate schools have been established most Roman Catholics have become supporters of these schools. In a few of the rural districts, and especially in Eastern Ontario, where there is a considerable French element, a number of separate schools have been formed, but in most counties of the Province the large majority of the people are Protestant, and very few separate schools have been established.

"The separate schools are all under Government inspection and are generally conducted in accordance with the same regulations as the public schools. Like the latter, they are under the control of boards of trustees, who are elected by the separate school supporters. The teachers, except those who are members of certain religious orders, are required to comply with the same regulations in order to receive certificates. The course of study pursued by the pupils is nearly the same as that for the public schools, and the text books, except those for religious instruction, are in many instances the same. Separate school pupils pass the same entrance examinations as public school pupils for admission to the high schools, and both classes of schools share in the legislative grant in proportion to the attendance."

STATISTICS OF SEPARATE SCHOOLS.

(i.) ROMAN CATHOLIC.

–	Schools Open.	Total Receipts.	Total Expenditure.	Number of Teachers.	Number of Pupils.
1898	345	$389,185	$349,481	744	41,667

(ii.) PROTESTANT.

–	Schools Open.	Total Receipts.	Total Expenditure.	Number of Teachers.	Number of Pupils.
1898	8	$5,567	$4,895	12	505

" One of the most valued features of the system of education in Ontario is the extensive provision made for the training of teachers. Every position from the lowest in the Kindergarten to the highest in a collegiate institute must be filled by a trained teacher. No teacher of a high or public school receives a permanent certificate who does not possess qualifications of a three-fold nature —(1) scholarship, (2) a knowledge of pedagogical principles, and (3) success shown by actual experience.

" Among educationists it is now fully admitted that scholarship alone does not fit a person to undertake the duties of a teacher. Just as the lawyer, doctor or clegyman receives professional training at a school of law, medicine or theology, so it has come to be admitted that the teacher should acquire special training at a normal school or a school of pedagogy. It was formerly customary for the candidate for the teaching profession to obtain his special training at the same time that he acquired his literary and scientific attainments. Under this system, normal schools undertook non-professional as well as professional work, and chairs of education were established in universities whereby the undergraduate in arts might receive such instruction in the science of education as would enable him as a newly-fledged B.A. to take charge of a school. In Ontario there is a clear separation of the professional from the academic courses. It is assumed that the professional training of a teacher should be taken up *after*, and not in conjunction with, the acquisition of knowledge at a high school or university. . . .

" A person who desires to become a teacher must first pass the ordinary departmental or university examinations which will be hereafter described. In this respect his course is nearly similar to that of the student who wishes to take up any other profession. He takes up his English Literature, his Algebra, his Botany and his Latin in the same class in school or college with those who intend to become farmers, mechanics, or editors. The successful candidates at the same university examinations are admitted a few month afterwards without any further non-professional tests—some to a course in law, some to a medical school, some to a theological college, and others to an institution for the training of teachers. To train students how to teach is not, it is held, the province of university or high school, and the graduates of these institutions, no matter how high their scholarship, could not, on the strength of their diplomas, hold positions as teachers. It is contended that a professional school should not be expected to give instruction in the ordinary branches taught in school or college, and that its functions are better discharged, and discharged in shorter time, when its students, before being admitted, have finished their course at university or high school.

" Another feature which characterizes the system of training teachers in Ontario is the value attached to experience. It is assumed that a person may pass his university examination, and, after taking a course at a training school, fail when in charge of his own school. It is held that the course for teachers-in-training at an ordinary practice school, though valuable, must necessarily be surrounded by conditions more or less artificial; that there cannot be given training in many points of discipline, and that the lack of continuity in the teaching done by students stands in the way of an estimate being made of their ability to bring on pupils. It is further contended that there are other necessary qualifications for a teacher which can be acquired or tested only by actual experience; that a teacher must learn how to govern himself, to 'get on' with pupils, parents, and trustees, and to show that he is capable of exercising a large amount of 'common sense.' For such reasons it is provided that no permanent certificate is given to any high or public school teacher who has not in the opinion of his inspector proved himself successful. The lowest grade of certificate is valid only for three years, and the holder who fails to 'work up' for one of a higher grade or who, in spite of his scholarship or professional training, shows that he has mistaken his calling, is obliged to give way and allow his position to be held by another. It is moreover felt that in a large graded school, where important administrative ability is required, the principal should have first shown his efficiency in a subordinate position. On this ground the B.A. who has received his professional certificate after attending the School of Pedagogy must serve as an assistant for at least two years in a high school or collegiate institute before becoming eligible for a head master's certificate. In other words, a high school teacher must serve an apprenticeship for two years before he can get the highest grade of certificate, and the public school teacher has a similar period of probation before he can secure a first class certificate. There is, at the same time, every incentive held out to the energetic teacher to rise in the profession. Many of the best positions as teachers, and nearly all the positions as inspectors, are held by those who started at the lowest step of the stairs.

" In the establishment of training schools it is assumed that the different grades of schools—kindergartens, public schools and high schools—require teachers of different qualifications, whose professional attainments should be gained at institutions specially provided in each case for the purpose. With this view there have been established in Ontario the following training schools for teachers :—

"(1.) Kindergartens, including the local schools of this kind where the training is given for assistants' certificates, and the provincial kindergartens connected with the normal schools where the training is given for directors' certificates.

"(2.) County Model Schools, where all public school teachers receive their first professional training, and from which third class certificates, valid for three years, are awarded.

"(3.) Provincial Normal Schools, for the further training of public school teachers who desire to obtain second class certificates, which are valid for life.

"(4.) The School of Pedagogy, for the training of those who desire to obtain certificates as first class public school teachers, assistant high school teachers, and specialists in one or more of the six departments of Classics, Mathematics, English, Modern Languages Natural Science, and the Commercial Course. The School of Pedagogy also gives the professional training which, with the necessary scholarship and experience, enables its graduates to obtain subsequently certificates as public school inspectors or principals of high schools and collegiate institutes.

ul organ-
T. achers.

"A young woman who desires to become a regular teacher in a Kindergarten must take one year's training at some local school of the kind which has been established by a public school board. If she is intelligent, fond of young children, and ready to read such literature as bears on her work, an extensive preliminary course at a high school is not essential, but she will be all the better qualified by having first attended one for three or four years. After the year's training an examination must be passed, conducted by the Education Department; but the certificate gained only qualifies to teach as an assistant. The holder of such a certificate becomes, however, eligible to attend either of the normal Kindergartens at Toronto or Ottawa, and a year's additional course there is required in order to obtain a certificate as director. This certificate qualifies her to take charge of any Kindergarten established by a board of public school trustees."

nnty
del
iools.

"To begin teaching in any public school in Ontario it is necessary to obtain what is called a third-class certificate from a county board of examiners, and only those are eligible for the examination who have attended a session at a county model school. To be admitted to a course of training at one of these institutions it is necessary to have first passed the high school primary examination. The board of examiners consists of the public school inspector and two other persons appointed by the county council holding first-class certificates and actually engaged in teaching. They receive for their services 4 dollars per diem and travelling expenses. This board, subject to the regulations of the Education Department, sets apart at least one public school in each county for the training of third-class teachers. The course of study for the pupils is the same as in any other public school. There are 59 county model schools in Ontario, and the average number of students-in-training at each is about 30. A grant of 150 dollars by the Legislature and an additional 150 dollars by the county council are made to each of these institutions, mainly to assist the trustees to provide an efficient staff. The course of professional training extends over about four months—from September to December. The time of the teachers-in-training is taken up with (1) observation of the work done by the regular teachers, (2) practice lessons given to the classes or to sections of a class, and (3) criticisms, discussions of methods, and lectures by the principal on pedagogical principles. A third-class certificate is valid for only three years, and if the holder has by that time no higher non-professional attainments than a high school primary certificate, or if he has not been successful in teaching, he is not eligible to enter a normal school, and may be obliged to retire from the profession. This regulation is based on the principle that a life certificate should be given to no teacher until he is tried by the only true test— that of experience. The object is to prevent incompetent persons from holding positions, and by offering their services at low salaries, shutting out energetic teachers and injuring the schools.

"It was intended that as far as possible third-class teachers should be assistants, and the intention has been observed in cities and towns, but the supply of second-class teachers is not yet sufficient to confine third-class teachers to subordinate positions in rural districts, where there is often only one teacher in each school. It is, however, quite common for third-class teachers to have passed the junior leaving or even senior leaving examination before attending a county model school, and the good education thus gained by a three or four years' previous attendance at a high school or collegiate institute gives even to rural schools a class of young men and women earnest in their work."

"To have a permanent licence to teach in a public school it is necessary to obtain at least a second-class certificate. This certificate can be secured only by teachers who have attended the normal school and passed an examination at the close of the session. The examination, which is both written and practical, is conducted by inspectors appointed from time to time by the Minister of Education. In addition to these tests a favourable report from the principal of the normal school is also essential. *Normal Schools.*

"Two normal schools, with large model or practice schools as adjuncts, have been established, one in Toronto and the other in Ottawa. There are two sessions each year, and only those students are admitted who have passed the high school junior leaving examination, and who have, as reported by the inspector under whom they have served, taught successfully one year as third-class teachers. It is customary, however, for the students to have taught two or three years before being admitted to the normal school. With this experience in their own schools, after having had their preliminary professional training at a county model school and with the scholarship gained previously by three or four years' attendance at a high school or collegiate institute, the teachers-in-training of the normal schools occupy valuable vantage ground in the acquisition of pedagogical knowledge and professional skill. In order still further to confine their attention during the session to practical work and the discussion of principles and methods, a preliminary entrance examination must be passed on most of the books prescribed for the course.

"The work of the pupils of the model schools is in harmony with that of ordinary public schools and several of the early weeks of the session are partly employed by the normal school students in observing the teaching done by the regular teachers. Subsequently they are required to take charge of the model school classes under the immediate direction and criticism of these teachers and with the advantage of lectures from the masters of the normal schools on Psychology, the Science and History of Education, and the application of the general principles of Pedagogy to the methods of instruction peculiar to each branch of study. The important aim of the normal school course is not to train teachers to become imitators, but rather to encourage individuality and self-reliance, not to cause them to become mechanical, or the slaves of methods, but to lead them to understand the principles upon which all good teaching and school management are based. About 100 students attend each normal school every session."

Inspection.

"The system of Education in Ontario makes provision for a thorough inspection of all classes of schools. School inspection is needed (1) to enforce the general rules and regulations sanctioned by the school authorities, and (2) to see that the proper methods of instruction are employed and that the teaching is made effective. In order to secure proper supervision it is necessary that the inspector should be well qualified, and that he should be invested with sufficient authority to enforce the pre-scribed regulations. It is assumed that no person is qualified for this important position who is not possessed of a wide range of scholarship, and who has not had several years of experience as a teacher. Without the latter, there can be no guarantee of fitness to deal with the many details of school management, and without the former there would be a lack of that culture and broadness of view which scholarly attainments are presumed to give. The public school inspector requires a knowledge of the work of elementary schools. Experience gained only in a high school will not suffice. The following is the regulation regarding the qualifications of public school inspectors :—

Any person with five years' successful experience as a teacher, of which at least three years shall have been in a public school ; who holds either specialist's non-professional standing obtained on a University examination, or a Degree in Arts from any University in Ontario, with first-class graduation honours in one or more of the other recognized departments in such University ; and who has passed the examinations of the Ontario Normal College for a specialist's certificate, shall be entitled to a certificate as an inspector of public schools.

"It is not deemed expedient to have these officers elected by a popular vote. Other elements than those of fitness might then determine the appointment. The high qualifications required limit the number of candidates and shut out the ordinary ' office seeker' from the list of applicants. County inspectors are appointed by the county councils, and city inspectors by the public school boards. When a vacancy occurs, the position is generally filled by appointing some teacher with the prescribed qualifications, who, by ability and application, has gained a reputation in his profession.

"The removal of an inspector seldom occurs. It is provided that the county or city inspector cannot be dismissed except by a two-thirds vote of the council or board appointing him, unless for misconduct or inefficiency, in which case he may be dismissed by a majority vote, or by the Lieutenant-Governor in Council It is quite customary for inspectors to hold their positions for more than twenty years, and when they keep themselves abreast of the educational progress of the country they become more useful with increased experience. By his intercourse with the members of the municipal councils, trustee boards, and the teachers of his district, the position of an inspector is a most important one for exercising through his scholarship, professional attainments, and character a valuable influence upon the pupils of the public schools.

"The statute requires each municipal council of a county to appoint an inspector of public schools. If there are more than one hundred and twenty schools in the county the council must appoint two inspectors. The salary of county inspectors varies from about 900 to 1,600 dollars according to the number of schools. The minimum rate is 10 dollars for each teacher, and 5 dollars of this is paid by the Legislature. In cities, if there are more than three hundred teachers, two inspectors must be appointed. In some of the smaller cities and most of the towns the county inspector is also inspector of the city or town schools. It is usual in these places for the principal to perform many duties pertaining to the organization of the schools that would otherwise be discharged by the inspector.

"In the larger cities, where the inspector devotes all his time to the service of the board, the salary varies from about 1,200 to 3,000 dollars, the Legislature allowing, as in the case of county schools, 5 dollars for each teacher.

". . . In the system of education for Ontario there has been a judicious division of responsibilities among different authorities. What has largely added influence for good to the position of inspector is the fact that he is free from many of the duties assigned to such an officer in some other countries. He has nothing to do with the authorization of text books or the fixing of courses of study. He does not engage the teachers, but in rural schools it is quite customary for trustees, in selecting teachers, to seek his advice. In cities his recommendations are almost invariably sought by the committee of the board to whom the selection of teachers is assigned, and it rarely happens that the trustees ignore his opinion on a matter of this kind.

"The inspector is not required to undertake the responsibility of licensing teachers in Ontario. By entrusting this duty to a board of examiners he is saved from the 'pressure' that might otherwise be brought to bear on him to grant certificates. He has, however, as chairman of the board of examiners, a proper influence in preventing incompetent persons from entering the profession, and without his approval no teacher in his inspectorate can attend a normal school. It therefore follows that inspectors have power to block incompetent teachers from receiving permanent certificates.

"The inspector is also relieved from a more embarrassing responsibility—that of determining the academic qualifications of applicants for teachers' certificates. This duty is entrusted to a board of examiners, acting not under local, but under provincial authority. The aim has been to place the inspector in such a position as will enable him to give his best thoughts and efforts to the most important duties of school supervision and to have his tenure of office so secured that he need not fear being disturbed so long as he discharges his duties energetically, honestly, and judiciously.

Teachers'
Institutes.
"The Educational Association of Ontario has been in existence for more than thirty years, and meets during the Easter holidays for the reading and discussion of papers relating to various questions of educational interest. The meetings of this body have done much towards giving direction to the school legislation of the Province. The association may be regarded, in fact, as an 'Educational Parliament.' It receives a grant of 200 dollars a year from the Legislature, and its proceedings are published for the information of its members. Besides the sessions of the general association, very many valuable papers are read and discussed in sections of that body. In this way there have been organized sections for the kindergartners, public school teachers, high school teachers, training school teachers, inspectors, etc. There have also been formed associations for the advancement of classics, mathematics, modern languages, and science. The high and public school trustees have organized a provincial association which has, in like manner, contributed much to the discussion of educational questions. It is now a section of the general 'Educational Association.'

"Besides the provincial association, there is organized in each county or inspectoral district a 'teachers' institute' for the purpose of imparting instruction in methods of teaching, and for discussing educational matters, subject to the regulations of the Education Department. A grant of 25 dollars is paid by the Legislature to each institute, and the county or city gives a grant of an equal amount. Many of the associations have valuable libraries of professional works. The public school inspector takes a leading part in the work of these county associations, and he is generally aided by the more experienced public school teachers, and the teachers of the one or more high schools or collegiate institutes situated within his district. A director of teachers' institutes, appointed by the Education Department, frequently attends these meetings, and very often other prominent persons are invited to give addresses on educational topics. The main object, however, is to have discussed pedagogical principles and methods of teaching, and to enable teachers to 'compare notes' regarding their daily duties. Dr. Arnold, of Rugby, felt it to be necessary that his pupils should 'drink from a running stream rather than from a stagnant pool.' . . . In cities these associations often meet monthly under direction of the inspector. Sometimes he finds it desirable to have teachers of the same grade meet together. These institutes have also had the effect of creating greater interest in school work among the general public."

II. Secondary Education.

" With the approval of the Lieut.-Governor in Council high schools may be established by the council of any county, in any municipality containing not fewer than one thousand inhabitants. If two or more municipalities form a district, with an adjacent incorporated village, a high school may be established in such district if it contains at least three thousand inhabitants. Each district is, however, generally confined to one municipality. The municipal council of a city may establish as many high schools as it may deem expedient, subject to the approval of the Lieut.-Governor in Council. The following are the requirements of a high school, and the Government grant may be withheld if its efficiency or the requirements are not maintained:--

(1) No connection with a public school as regards premises.

(2) A site of at least half an acre in extent, well fenced, well drained, planted with shade trees, and suitably provided with walks in front and rear.

(3) A playground, and all other necessary provision for physical exercise.

(4) A well or other means of supplying pure drinking water.

(5) Water-closets for the sexes, separate and in separate yards, and properly screened from observation.

(6) A building large enough to provide ample accommodation for every pupil in attendance, with all necessary provision for light, heat, and ventilation, and two entrances with covered porches.

(7) Suitable separate cloak rooms for boys and girls, furniture, desks, black-boards, and maps, apparatus, and library of reference of the maximum value recognised for schools with two masters.

(8) A principal, and at least two assistants.

"Collegiate institutes are nearly the same as high schools as regards the regulations by which they are governed. They receive larger grants from the Legislature in view of the superior equipment required for their establishment and the necessity of employing teachers of higher attainments, and a greater number of them, than for high schools. The following is the provision of the statute under which a high school may become a collegiate institute:—

On the report of the Minister of Education, and subject to the regulations of the Education Department, any high school having (1) suitable school buildings, out-buildings, grounds and appliances for physical training : (2) a library, containing standard books of reference in the subjects of the high school curriculum ; (3) a laboratory, with the necessary chemicals and apparatus for teaching the elements of the sciences ; (4) a staff of at least five teachers, four being specialists, one in each of the following departments : Classics, Mathematics, Natural Science, Modern Languages, including English, and any one of the staff being a specialist in the Commercial Department ; (5) such other assistants as will secure thorough instruction in all the subjects on the curriculum of studies approved by the Education Department for collegiate institutes ; may be constituted a collegiate institute by order of the Lieutenant-Governor in Council,

" The regulations also provide :—

> (1) No high school shall be raised to the status of a collegiate institute without such a minimum equipment in the way of library, physical and chemical apparatus, gymnasium, maps and globes, as is the maximum recognised for high schools with three or more masters."

> (2) Any collegiate institute that fails to comply with the conditions prescribed herein for the status of a collegiate institute may, on the joint report of the high school inspectors, be reduced to the rank of a high school, and deprived of the special legislative grant, at the discretion of the Minister of Education."

Trustees.

" Each high school or collegiate institute is managed by a board of trustees, whose duties are similar to those of public schools. Each board consists of at least six trustees, and, except in the case of cities and towns separated from the county, three of these are appointed by the county council, and three by the council of the town or village where the high school is situated. If the district is composed of more than one municipality, then each of these municipalities is represented on the high school board. In towns separated from the county all the trustees are appointed by the town council. In cities the council also appoints all the trustees, and if two high schools are established, twelve trustees are appointed, and if more than two, the council appoints eighteen trustees. Each trustee so appointed holds office generally for three years. Two other trustees holding office for one year may be added, one by the public school board and the other by the separate school board of the city, town or incorporated village where the high school or collegiate institute is situated. High school trustees cannot be members of the municipal council."

Finance.

" The cost of each high school and collegiate institute is made up of the expenditure required for ' Permanent Improvements and ' Maintenance.' The former of these must be met entirely by the district or municipality, and consists mainly of the expenditure for school site, building, furniture, and equipment. The latter consists of the usual outlay for the salaries of teachers and other officers, repairs, fuel, stationery, and sundry expenses for ordinary school purposes, and is met from four sources, viz.: (1) Government grants ; (2) county grants ; (3) district or municipal grants ; and (4) fees of students.

"(1.) Government grants to the high schools and collegiate institute are mainly based on the efforts made by the locality. If the local expenditure is good, a correspondingly liberal grant may be expected from the Legislature, so far as the annual appropriation will allow. As a minimum each high school receives a fixed grant of 375 dollars, and each collegiate institute an additional grant of 275 dollars. On the condition and suitability of the premises a high school is entitled to a maximum grant of 150 dollars and a collegiate institute to one of 200 dollars. For equipment there is a maximum grant of 200 dollars and one of 600 dollars on the basis of salaries of the teachers. The remainder of the grant is distributed on the basis of average attendance The grants in full vary from about 500 dollars to 1,800 dollars on the basis thus outlined.

"(2.) The county council is required to make a grant to each high school or collegiate‑institute in the county equal to the grant made by the Legislature. This grant is intended to meet the cost of instruction for county pupils; that is, for those pupils of the county who do not reside in the municipality or district where the high school is situated. It sometimes happens that the equivalent of the Government grant would not be sufficient to meet the cost of maintenance for county pupils, and in that case the county is liable for whatever additional amount is necessary to meet its share of the cost of maintenance. The principle involved in this part of the statute is that the county should pay for the education of county pupils.

"(3.) After the county and legislative grants have been received whatever further sums, in addition to any fees which have been paid, may be required to meet the cost of maintenance, must be made up by the municipality or district where the high school is situated, on the requisition of the Trustee Board. Under the provisions of the Act the municipal grant raised for this purpose is, as a matter of fact, its proportionate share of the cost of maintenance. If, for instance, there are as many county as resident pupils, the county and district pay equal shares of the cost of maintenance after deducting the legislative grant. Should there be any dispute as regards these amounts the Act provides a ready settlement by arbitration.

"(4.) County councils may require a portion of the liability of the county to be paid by the county pupils in fees not exceeding one dollar per month, the fee being uniform for all high schools in the county. Resident pupils may also be required by the board to pay fees, thus lessening the amount to be raised by the municipality. It thus follows that the question of free high schools is left to be determined by each locality, and it has been found that this option is more satisfactory than making all high school free by Act of Parliament, or fixing a uniform fee for the Province. Non-resident pupils, that is those from other counties, must pay such fees as the board deems expedient, but such fees must not be greater than the cost of maintenance or less than those of county pupils. Of the 128 high schools and collegiate institutes 48 of them are free, and the fees in the others vary from 2.50 to 26 dollars per year."

"A uniform examination is held every year about the first of July for admission to high schools and collegiate institutes. Each high school has a board of examiners for the purpose, consisting of the principal of the high school, the public school inspector, and two qualified teachers who have no pupils at the examination, one being appointed by the public school board and the other by the separate school board of the city, town, or village where the high school is situated. The examiners are paid 1 dollar per pupil for their services, and the cost may be met by fees from the candidates or by the county and district for their respective shares. The examination papers are prepared by the high school inspectors and public and separate school

[margin note: Entrance Examination.]

inspectors appointed by the minister of education and sent in sealed envelopes to the presiding examiner, to be opened during the hours of the examination. Only those pupils who pass the examination and whose admission has been confirmed by the high school inspectors can be admitted to a high school or collegiate institute. The examination is based on the course of the fourth form of the public schools, and includes the following subjects and values:—Reading, 50 marks; drawing, 50; neatness, 35; writing, 50; orthography, 30; literature, 100; arithmetic, 100; grammar, 100; geography, 75; composition, 100; history, 75. Optional papers are set in temperance and hygiene and agriculture, each valued at 75. The standard required to pass is one-third in each subject and one-half of the aggregate number of marks. There is also provision for recommending in case of failure the following classes of candidates:—(*a*) Those who fail to reach the standard prescribed in some subject, but who make considerably more than the aggregate marks required, and (*b*) those who in the opinion of the examiners, on account of age or for some special reason, should be recommended. The reasons should be set forth in each case. The report of the board of examiners and the answer papers (to provide for any appeals) are sent to the Education Department. The regulations also provide for the provisional admission, during the interval between examinations, of pupils who were unable to be present at the regular examination, and who would suffer if not allowed to attend a high school. Certificates are granted to all pupils whose admission has been confirmed by the high school inspectors. About 20,000 candidates annually write at the entrance examination and about half that number pass."

Statistics, 1898.

Number of collegiate institutes, 37; high schools, 93; total, 130.

Number of pupils enrolled, 23,301; percentage of average attendance, 60.

Number of teachers, 571. Average salary for principals, $1,177; for assistants, $814. The salaries of specialists in collegiate institutes range from about $1,000 to $1,500. The cost per pupil is about $34.26.

Departmental Examinations.

"The origin and development of the system of examinations conducted by the Education Department may be readily understood by considering the general aims of written examinations.

"(1.) Examinations furnish valuable aid to both teachers and students regarding the manner in which the work of the school should be taken up. They tend to give direction to the teaching, and to prevent faulty methods of instruction and a consequent waste of time and energy. It is held that a proper system of examination does much to improve the discipline of school or college, and that wherever examinations are ignored the *morale* of the institution will be found weak and the education inferior. In Ontario the aim has been, by making physical training compulsory and by emphasizing the inculcation of high moral principles, to reduce to a minimum the possible evils of examinations, and to guard carefully their educational value while utilizing them for other purposes for which their application is indispensable.

"(2.) Examinations are serviceable as tests for the promotion of pupils. They are almost essential, but do not supply the only *data* for this purpose. In the schools of Ontario promotions are generally made by the principal, aided by the members of his staff. The principal and his assistants prepare their own questions, and hold examinations at the close of each term. The promotions are not, however, based entirely on " percentages " gained at the final examinations. The daily, weekly, or monthly class records are also taken into account, and to some extent the general estimate made by the teachers as to the pupil's industry and ability. Evidence of *power* and fitness to begin the work of a higher class is recognized as the main consideration in deciding upon the promotion of a pupil.

The pupils in either a high or public school may be promoted from time to time and reach the highest form, on the recommendation of the principal, who is responsible for the organization of his classes. No pupil is obliged to take any examinations other than those prescribed by the principal, and parents are left free to have their children write or not at the departmental or any other examinations. It is found, however, desirable and expedient in practice to modify this feature of school organization in view of the third object of examinations."

"(3.) Examinations are held for the purpose of granting certificates that have a qualifying or commercial value. These cannot be left to be awarded by the teachers or other local authorities of each school. To do so would furnish no guarantee of uniformity in standards, and without such uniformity the value of the certificates granted would be slight. The estimate of teachers may, however, receive consideration in special cases where a candidate, through sickness or other cause, clearly fails to do himself justice. Uniformity is secured by the system of departmental examinations adopted for the entire Province. It is also found convenient for teachers in high schools to utilize generally the departmental examinations for purposes of promotion, and the regulations regarding the mode by which these are conducted have, moreover, in view the direction given to the teaching, and their consequent educational effect upon all the pupils of the schools.

" In short, the aim of the system is to secure at the same time the three objects of examinations here mentioned, and to lessen, as far as possible, the evils that are said to be associated with tests of this kind. The method is practically a combination of the systems of admission to college by certificate and by examination.

" The plan adopted in Ontario has greatly reduced the number of examinations. For instance, the high school entrance examination is conveniently used by public school teachers as a test for promotion to the fifth form, and the high school primary and leaving examinations serve as promotion examinations to higher forms in the secondary schools,

" Some years ago in Ontario each of the four or five universities held its own matriculation examinations. The law society, the medical council and the divinity schools had their own entrance examinations. There were besides, examinations held for admission to normal schools and other training institutions for teachers. Dentistry, pharmacy and engineering each had its own tests for admission to a course of study for these professions. What made matters worse was that the courses prescribed were not based on a common curriculum, the examinations were held at different periods of the high school term, and pupils were under the expense, in most cases, of going from home in order to write at any one of these examinations.

" This condition of affairs, so annoying to high school teachers in the organization of their classes, has been entirely changed by having prescribed a uniform course of study for all the schools, by the adoption of a system of uniform examinations for the Province, and by the acceptance on the part of the different universities and the various learned bodies of the certificates awarded by the Education Department. The examinations are held at the same time and on the same papers in every high school and collegiate institute. The student who passes the examination may secure a certificate or certificates which will admit him as a matriculant to any university in the Province; to the school of practical science; to a course of study in law, medicine, dentistry, or pharmacy; to a course of theology in any divinity school, or to a county model school, or some other institution for the professional training of teachers.

" The examination papers are prepared by examiners qualified by experience as teachers in high schools or universities to set suitable papers To avoid narrowness in style the examiners are selected from a wide field, and are changed from time to time. The answer papers of candidates are read by university graduates actually engaged in teaching. As a matter of fact, the papers are valued by teachers who are familiar with the same work in their own schools, and whose pupils are candidates at the same examination. The regulations make such necessary provision as prevents any identification of the papers read by any of the associate examiners.

" An important feature of the examination system in Ontario is that a student's calling in life need not necessarily be determined by the course taken up in school. If he has no special object in view but to secure a good education, no better plan is open to him for this purpose than to strive to gain a high school leaving certificate. Should he afterwards decide to enter a university, or to take up a professional course, he is in the possession of the necessary passport, without being obliged to turn again to his books and prepare for an examination.

" The course of study for Form I. in high schools is prescribed with the object of requiring all students to receive at first a good business education. The object in view is to guarantee that the interests of the great body of students will not suffer by having undue attention given to subjects required for entering the professions. The examinations that may be held in the junior classes, or Form I., are left almost entirely to the teachers. Those students who, in addition to the requirements in other subjects, show proficiency in reading, drawing, and the commercial course, receive commercial certificates signed by the principal. A student who receives a high school commercial certificate has taken about the same course as a pupil from the elementary schools who has passed the public school leaving examination.

"Examinations are held annually in July, in the courses of study prescribed for Forms II., III. and IV. of high schools. Candidates who pass the examination for Forms I. and II. receive high school primary certificates; for Form III. high school junior leaving certificates, or university matriculation certificates; and for Form IV., senior leaving certificates, and perhaps university matriculation certificates with honours."

"The highest positions in the teaching profession are open only to the graduates of the School of Pedagogy. This institution is located in Toronto, and in it are trained the first class public school teachers, the assistants and principals of high schools and collegiate institutes, and the public school inspectors. Its importance may be seen from the additional fact that only first class teachers are eligible to be appointed principals of county model schools or members of county boards of examiners. The associate examiners for the departmental examinations must be university graduates actually engaged in teaching, and this provision practically leaves the work of reading the papers in the hands of persons who have passed through the School of Pedagogy. *The School of Pedagogy.*

"The graduates of the School of Pedagogy are in fact the teachers of the teachers of the public schools. As high school teachers they educate the students of the secondary schools, and as principals of model schools they give the professional training required at first of every public school teacher. At the departmental examinations they may be said to guard the avenues for admission to the universities and to the professions, and at county board examinations they are the judges of the qualifications of those who become third class teachers. In fact their influence as inspectors and teachers is so far-reaching as to extend, it may be said, to the entire half million children attending the schools of the Province.

"To be admitted to the School of Pedagogy it is necessary for a student to have at least a high school senior leaving certificate. A large number of its students are, however, B.A.'s of the various universities of the Province, many of them being graduates of high honour standing. Teachers who hold second class certificates from one of the normal schools, and have taught two years, are exempted from attendance, but must, like others, hold senior leaving certificates and pass the final examination. When they pass this examination they receive first class public school teachers' certificates, which also qualify them to teach as assistants in high schools. Third class teachers, who have taught three years and hold senior leaving certificates, by attending the

School of Pedagogy and passing the examination, are entitled likewise to first class public school teachers' certificates. The other certificates granted qualify only to teach in high schools or collegiate institutes, but first class certificates answer for both purposes.

"As in the case of the normal schools the course of study is almost entirely professional. Besides observation of the teaching done in the provincial model schools, including the kindergartens, an important part of the course consists of model lessons given by the lecturers and practice lessons by the students themselves who are formed into classes for the purpose. It is held that much valuable training can be given, and many requisites of a good teacher tested, before he is allowed to take charge of a class, even as an assistant. The ability to show the logical arrangement of a subject to be taught, to recognise the salient points to be brought out in a presentation lesson, to show, as a teacher, accuracy of language and grasp of the matter to be taken up before a class—these and kindred characteristics of a good teacher should, and may, be acquired before any chance is given to experiment on a class of high school pupils. Those who desire to become specialists in collegiate institutes must first pass the non-professional examinations required at the university. For them an additional course of training is provided in methods and a higher standard is exacted at the professional examination.

"When a teacher-in-training shows that he possesses good teaching ability he may complete the course in half a year, but in many instances a year's work is found necessary. He then passes the examination of the School of Pedagogy and enters upon the practical part of his training. The "Interim Certificate" which he receives qualifies him to teach for six months in any high school or collegiate institute. He is thrown, as any regular assistant, upon his own resources, and he receives the advice and support of an experienced principal, who, as a rule, if teaching ability is exhibited, desires to retain him as a permanent member of his staff. At the close of the half year those who have been thus serving their "apprenticeship" are required to pass a practical examination in teaching, conducted by the high school inspectors or other persons appointed by the Minister. If successful they receive permanent certificates, but if they have proved themselves failures in the work, they are no longer allowed to remain in the profession.

The holder of an assistant's certificate, if a graduate in arts of a British or Canadian university, who has taught successfully two years in a high school, is entitled to a principal's certificate, and if before or after this he qualifies by examination as a specialist, he has gained the highest certificate awarded by the Department.

"About 100 students attend the School of Pedagogy each session."

Inspectors f High hools. "The inspectors of high schools are appointed by the Government, and are selected from principals of collegiate institutes, who have attained the front rank in their profession. The important functions of the secondary schools and the regulations under which they are conducted render their inspection a matter which largely affects elementary as well as higher education. . . . It has been fully acknowledged by educationists that work of this kind to be properly performed must be assigned to experts practically engaged as teachers in high school or university. The high school inspectors, like the public school inspectors, are also largely relieved from the responsibility of licensing teachers. They have, however, and properly so, a voice like public school instructors, in preventing incompetent persons from entering the profession.

" The high school inspectors have thus been enabled to devote their energies to the proper work of supervision, and acting under regulations of the Education Department, their official visits have tended much to improve the character of the schools. Their reports to trustees have in a few years brought about great improvements in the accommodations, large additions to the libraries and apparatus, and superior appliances for physical training. More satisfactory still has been the advance made in the qualifications of the teaching staffs . . ."

III. UNIVERSITY EDUCATION.

History of the University of Toronto (from the University of Toronto Calendar for 1896–97).—The movement which ended in the establishment of the University of Toronto as the centre of the educational system of the Province of Ontario originated with General Simcoe, the First Governor of Upper Canada, who repeatedly expressed his conviction, both before his departure from England and also during his term of office (1792–1796), that the best interests alike of the Government and of the inhabitants demanded the establishment of a University in Upper Canada. It was not, however, during his administration that the project assumed a definite form.

In 1797 the Legislative Council and House of Assembly in a joint address to King George III. asked " that his Majesty would be graciously pleased to direct his Government in the Province to appropriate a certain portion of the waste lands of the Crown as a fund for the establishment and support of a respectable Grammar School, in each district thereof ; and also a College or University for the instruction of youth in the different branches of liberal knowledge." To this address a favourable answer was transmitted, and the acting Lieutenant-Governor, the Hon. Peter Russell, was directed to determine the manner and character of the appropriation. In accordance with this request the Executive Council of Upper Canada reported on the 1st December, 1798, that an appropriation of 500,000 acres would be sufficient for the support and maintenance of four Grammar Schools and a University. For the foundation of the latter nothing was done until 1827, when a Royal Charter was granted for the establishment at or near York, as Toronto was then called, of a college " with the style and privilege of a University." to be called " King's College," having for its endowment that

The
Provincial
University.

portion of the grant of " waste lands " originally provided for the University in the report above referred to. These lands were in 1828 exchanged for 225,944 acres of Crown Reserves. . . . . The opening of the College was delayed for fourteen years. In consequence of public representations on the sectarian character of the College, all religious tests were abolished by an amended charter which passed the two Houses of the Provincial Legislature and received the Royal Assent in 1837. In 1842 the affairs of the University had assumed such a condition as to render its organisation possible, and Faculties of Arts, Medicine, Law and Divinity were established. In that year the erection of the College Building was begun. In 1843 the first matriculation of students took place, and inaugural addresses and lectures were delivered on the 8th and 9th June of that year.

The agitation which resulted in the amended charter of 1837 had continued after the opening of the College in 1842, owing to efforts made to defeat the purpose of the amendment, and in 1849 an Act of the Legislature effected important modifications in the constitution of King's College whereby all instruction in Divinity was discontinued, and a larger measure of public control of the affairs of the University instituted, through the formation of a Senate, of which a number of the members were appointed by the Crown. The name was now changed from that of the University of King's College to that of " The University of Toronto."

Three years afterwards the University underwent a further transformation, by which the Act of 1853 abolished its Faculties of Medicine and Law, and divided its functions between the two newly organised corporations of the "University of Toronto" and "University College." To the Senate were assigned the duties of framing the curriculum, holding examinations and admitting to degrees in Arts, Law and Medicine, while to the President and Professors of University College, as a distinct and independent corporation with special powers, were assigned the teaching in Arts and the entire discipline and control of students. The models followed in the reorganisation of the Universities, it was claimed, were the University of London and University College, London, both of which had then been only recently established. For thirty-four years the University of Toronto and University College performed the functions respectively assigned to them by this Act . . . and for thirty-four years the constitution of the two corporations above mentioned remained unchanged. Other collegiate bodies, principally denominational schools of theology, entered into affiliation with the University, and, with regard to their especial requirements, the course of study in Oriental Languages was augmented; but the Faculty of University College continued to do the work of instruction for nearly all the students in Arts who presented themselves for examination. The candidates for examinations and degrees in Medicine were trained in medical schools in affiliation with the University, and in the Faculty of Law the examinations were based upon text-books prescribed by the Senate, without teaching.

In 1887 both the University of Toronto and University College were remodelled by the University Federation Act. The main object of renewed legislation was to secure a more uniform standard of higher education by the union of the various denominational universities of Ontario with the Provincial University. Since the proclamation of the Act, Victoria University at Cobourg, representing the Methodist body, has entered into federation with the University of Toronto. The governing body of this institution is now represented on the Senate of the University of Toronto, its graduates elect representatives to the same body, and by the removal of the faculty and students of Victoria University to Toronto, the Union of the two Universities has been effected. Under the Federation Act, the theological colleges also, formerly in affiliation with the University of Toronto, have become federated colleges, and enjoy increased representation on the Senate.

"The faculty of University College, by the Act of 1887, consists of professors and lecturers in Classical Languages and Literature (including lecturers in Ancient History), Oriental Languages, English, French, German, and Moral Philosophy. All other portions of the Arts course are assigned to the Faculty of the University of Toronto, of which the lectures are made equally available to the students of University College, and those of all federating universities and colleges.

. . . . A Faculty of Medicine in the University of Toronto was established immediately upon the passing of the Act in 1887, and teaching is imparted in all branches of medical science. All the advantages of the Faculty of Arts are available for the students in Medicine, and the laboratories of the scientific departments are utilised equally by students in both faculties.

In 1888 a stimulus was given to the study of scientific methods of farming by the affiliation of the Ontario Agricultural College, and the adoption of a curriculum of study for the degree of Bachelor of the Science of Agriculture. Similarly an examination for the degree of Doctor of Dental Surgery was instituted, as a consequence of the affiliation of the Royal College of Dental Surgeons of Ontario. The College of Pharmacy was subsequently admitted to affiliation, and with the extension of the same privileges to the Toronto College of Music, a curriculum of study was prepared for the degree of Bachelor of Music. The School of Practical Science was affiliated in 1889, and graduates of the School are specially eligible on certain conditions for the degrees of Bachelor of Applied Science and of various degrees in Engineering in the University. By a recent enactment of the Senate a curriculum was prescribed leading to the degree of Bachelor and Doctor of Pedagogy.

Thus,[*] "the highest institution of learning in Ontario controlled by provincial authority is the University of Toronto. It is the

---

[*] Millar : Educational System of the Province of Ontario.

copestone of the educational structure . . . It is cheerfully
sustained by Protestant and Roman Catholic, and it has a large
body of devoted graduates representing all the leading religious
denominations. . . . It is a conservative force guarding the
educational citadel from ill-advised innovations, and at the same
time an agent of progress and enlightenment . . ."

" The entire system of education in Ontario has been established
with the object of making good citizens. It is assumed that the
state is benefited by having its educational facilities brought as
nearly as possible within the reach of all. With all our public
schools free, and our high schools either free or available by the
payment of comparatively low fees, the University of Toronto
also opens its doors on easy terms to all students who pass
the matriculation examinations . . . Accepting the honest
convictions of those favourable as well as of those adverse to
denominational oversight in the training of youth, the University
Federation Act has presented a solution of a problem at one time
embarrassing to statesmen and dangerous to the progress of
higher education."

"For many years the University experienced repeated changes
in its local habitation as well as in the scope of its functions. The
stately pile which forms the centre of the cluster of collegiate
buildings devoted to the work of the University was partly
destroyed by fire some years ago, but it has since been recon-
structed with many internal improvements. Considerable extension
has been effected in the numbers, capacity, and adequate equipment
of the lecture rooms and laboratories. Much attention has also
been given to improvements in heating, lighting, and ventilation.

"The new school of biology, which harmonises in structure with
the University, is one of the handsomest and most substantial
buildings on the Continent devoted to that department of science.
Its corridors, lecture rooms, and laboratories are of a very spacious
character. The central portion is assigned to the University
Biological Museum. This contains, in addition to other collections,
an extensive and valuable series of preparations used for illustrating the lectures in animal and vegetable morphology and
embryology.

" To the south and east of the University stands the School of
Practical Science, a large four-storey building, where students have
extensive facilities for gaining proficiency in the different departments of applied science. The accommodation has in view
extensive courses in chemistry, mineralogy, assaying and
engineering.

" A new building for chemistry was provided in 1893 to the
west of the School of Practical Science. This building is in the
form of a quadrangle, with the lecture-rooms on one side and the
laboratories on the other. There is laboratory accommodation for
200 students, and the lecture-rooms hold about 350. . . .
Between the School of Biology and the University has recently
been completed the new library, on plans embracing the most
recent improvements derived from the experience of leading
universities in Germany and the United States. It contains a

fire-proof room to accommodate 120,000 volumes, a reading-room to accommodate 200 students, and seminary rooms for various departments of instruction.

"The large number of ladies who have of late years taken up the B.A. course gave rise to a project for the erection of a residence for women attending the University. A suitable site has been offered for the purpose by the University authorities and a number of the citizens of Toronto have taken considerable interest in the object."

"By legislative enactment the Provincial University consists of the University and University College, which have their respective functions. Various bodies are entrusted with the management of these institutions. **Organization.**

1. *The Crown.*—The supreme authority in all matters continues to be the Crown, from whom emanated the charter that erected the University. All appointments, therefore, rest with the Lieutenant-Governor, and all statutes of the Senate to be binding must receive his approval. All property is vested in the Crown and is managed and administered by an officer appointed by the Government.

2. *The Board of Trustees.*—This body is entrusted with general powers as to the management of the endowment, and consists of ten members, viz., the Chancellor, the Vice-Chancellor, the President of University College, five members elected by, but not necessarily members of, the Senate of the University, and two members elected by, but not necessarily members of, the Council of University College.

3. *The Senate.*—This body consists of (*a*) ex-officio members, (*b*) appointed members, and (*c*) elected members, making 61 in all. The function of the Senate is the general administration of the University. It has to do with the appointment of examiners, the prescribing of courses of study, the fixing of standards for examination, the granting of degrees, and may be said to give general direction as regards the policy to be pursued in University matters. The Chancellor is elected by the graduates and the Vice-Chancellor is chosen from actual members of the Senate at its first meeting after a triennial election.

4. *Convocation.*—Convocation consists of the whole body of graduates of the University in all its faculties. It elects the Chancellor, and, in divisions according to faculty, it elects members of the Senate as its representatives in arts, law, and medicine. The result of its discussions is not binding on the Senate, but may be communicated to that body for action to be taken thereon.

5. *The University Council.*—This body is composed of a president, who shall also be president of the University College, and the professors in the University. It has full authority and responsibility of discipline over all students in relation to professors and other teachers. It has also entire authority respecting the societies and associations of the students. All

officers and servants of the University are also subject to its
authority, and on its report the laboratory fees to be paid by
students are determined by the Lieutenant-Governor in Council.

6. *The Council of University College.*—Like the University
Council, this body has control over students of University College
and authority over its servants.   It consists of the president and
professors of the college, together with the dean of residence.   It
has larger duties and powers, however, than the University Council, being constituted a corporation."

**Faculties –
The Arts
Course.**

"The University possesses teaching faculties in law and
medicine as well as in arts.   It was felt that the advantages of a
well-equipped faculty for the course in arts might readily be
made available for the students of medicine and thus elevate the
standard of medical education.   A similar opportunity gave rise
to the establishment of a faculty of law.   To furnish instruction
for students in arts has always, however, been held to be the main
object of the Provincial University.   Its endowment has been
regarded as primarily intended for the advancement of higher
education, and its resources have been guarded in the interests of
of those taking the B.A. course.   The close relations which exist
between the University and the secondary schools of Ontario have
given to the former a national position . . .   This connection
is now felt by the University to be far more valuable than a large
addition to its endowment . . .   The curriculum has been
arranged with due regard for the aims of those who desire
simply a liberal education as well as of those intending to enter
some profession.   It has provided such a course of literature,
mathematics, science, and philosophy as serves the purposes of
all students who desire a high academic training, and, by its
provisions for affiliation and federation, facilities are secured in
the interests of the various religious denominations and of the
learned professions.

"The division of the arts course into what are termed university
and college subjects respectively, marks an important develop-
ment of university organization.   To the university professoriate
are assigned the departments of Mathematics, Physics, Chemistry,
Biology, Physiology, Mineralogy and Geology, History and
Ethnology, Italian, Spanish, Comparative Philology, Political
Economy, Constitutional History, Logic, and Mental Philosophy.
In University College are taken up Greek, Latin, Ancient History,
English, French, German, Oriental Languages, and Ethics.   This
arrangement has the advantage of relieving the colleges of the
expense necessary for providing the costly laboratories required in
the teaching of modern science, and at the same time affording
better facilities for closer intercourse between teacher and
students in departments where smaller classes are desirable.
The division thus made has also introduced a principle which
gives every facility for the union or federation of different colleges
with the Provincial University."

**University
Federation.**

"The main object of the University Federation Act of 1887 was
to secure a uniform standard of higher education by the union
of the various denominational universities of Ontario with the

Provincial University. It was contended that a high standard can best be maintained when there are uniform examinations for graduation as well as for matriculation; that modern requirements—especially in the departments of science—call for extensive equipments which can be better provided by a union of resources; that the mingling of students of various sects tends to cultivate broader Christian sentiments and more patriotic views of citizenship; and that members of churches need not be taxed to maintain half a dozen universities to do work already provided by the State.

"It was moreover felt that all the advantages claimed for denominational oversight might be retained in connection with the plan of university federation. A college federated with the University of Toronto carries on the same work as University College; and its students have the same privileges secured to them as the students of the latter institution by the establishment of the university professoriate. For instance, the undergraduates, who one hour of the day receive instruction in Latin or Moral Philosophy in different colleges meet together another hour of the day to receive lectures from university professors in Mathematics, Civil Polity, Chemistry or Biology. A university federating with the Provincial University ceases to exercise its degree-conferring powers except in Divinity. Its students take the same university examinations in the different years as the students of University College, and the degrees conferred give them the status of *alumni* of the Provincial University. The governing authorities of a federated college are represented on the Senate of the University of Toronto, and its graduates elect representatives to the same body. Under the Federation Act the theological colleges also, formerly in affiliation with the University of Toronto, have become federating colleges and enjoy increased representation on the Senate. The following institutions are now federated to or affiliated with the Provincial University:—

> Victoria University (Methodist).
> Knox College (Presbyterian).
> St. Michael's College (Roman Catholic).
> Wycliffe College (Episcopalian).
> Huron College (Episcopalian).
> The School of Practical Science.
> The Ontario Agricultural College
> Trinity Medical School.
> Royal College of Dental Surgeons.
> Ontario College of Pharmacy.
> Women's Medical College.
> Toronto College of Music."

There are, however, other corporations with the power of granting degrees which are not affiliated to the University of Toronto. These institutions are more or less closely connected with various religious denominational bodies—thus Trinity College, Toronto, is connected with the Episcopal Church;

Queen's College with the Presbyterian community. The McMaster University is supported by the Baptists, while the Roman Catholic University is the University of Ottawa.

"The University of Ottawa* has no regular endowment. It is conducted by members of a religious order, the Oblates of Mary Immaculate. Some fifty members of this religious order are engaged in educational work here without salary. They receive from the University in return for their services, board, clothing, a small allowance for vacation annually, and an assurance of ample assistance in sickness and old age."

IV. TECHNICAL EDUCATION.

The School of Practical Science.

"The School of Practical Science was founded by Act of the Legislative Assembly in 1877. An arrangement was entered into with the Council of University College, whereby the students of the school received instruction in those university subjects which were included in the work of the school. In 1889 the school was affiliated to the University of Toronto. In 1890 very large additions were made to the original building. The latter was set apart for the work in chemistry, mineralogy, and assaying, while the engineering and architectural departments were accommodated in the new building, a large portion of which is occupied by the engineering laboratory. This laboratory has been equipped with the most modern machinery and apparatus for carrying on original investigations in steam engineering, hydraulic and electrical engineering, strength of materials of construction, standards of length, etc. The cost in fees for a full course is 120 dollars.

"The department of chemistry is provided with laboratories for qualitative and quantitative analysis, toxicology, etc. In the department of mining engineering there are laboratories for assaying, blowpipe analysis, microscopic lithology, etc. For instruction in surveying and practical astronomy the school is supplied with a good collection of the ordinary field instruments— transit levels, etc.—and also with a ten-inch theodolite for astronomical and geodetic work.

"The departments of instructions are :—

1. Civil engineering, including sanitary engineering.
2. Mechanical and electrical engineering.
3. Mining engineering.
4. Architecture.
5. Analytical and applied chemistry.

"The instruction given in each of these departments is designed to give the students a thorough knowledge of the scientific principles underlying the practice in the several professions, and also to give him such a training as will make him immediately useful when he enters into active professional work."

---

* See Papers relating to University Education of Roman Catholics in certain Colonies. (Colonial Office Return, London, 1900, Cd. 115.)

"The institution known as the "Ontario Agricultural College and Experimental Farm" is situated about a mile to the south of the city of Guelph, in the centre of an extensive agricultural and noted stock-raising district, readily accessible by rail from all parts of the province. The farm consists of 550 acres, about 400 of which are cleared. It is composed of almost every variety of soil, and hence is well suited for the purpose for which it was selected.

Ontario Agricultural College.

"The instruction given at the institution is embraced under two heads, a course of study and a course of apprenticeship. The latter is intended for special students who come in for practical farming for the autumn, winter, and spring terms, during which they are employed in the station in each of the six departments of practical farm labour. The course of study is for two years, at the end of which time a diploma is granted. Holders of a diploma who have attained a certain standard in the theoretical and practical work of the first two years, may remain for a third. In 1888 the college was affiliated with the University of Toronto, and an examination for the degree of Bachelor of the Science of Agriculture was instituted, to which only students of the third year in the Ontario Agricultural College may be admitted."

"The design of the Government of Ontario has been to provide a general education for all classes, and such a training as will enable any student who so desires to take a professional course. With the exception of the fees required, the academic training is provided at the public expense, but it is not the policy of the Province to provide free for students a professional education. Perhaps the only exceptions to this principle are to be found in the case of the Agricultural College and the School of Practical Science. As the interests of the farmers are largely bound up with those of the Province generally, the subject of agriculture has due recognition in the public school curriculum, and liberal grants from the Legislature have been made to farmers' institutes. The expenditure annually made in behalf of the Agricultural College at Guelph is justified by the growing importance of a knowledge of scientific agriculture to the farming community, and by the high position gained by the institution among colleges with a similar object. Encouragement is also generously given in the public and high schools, as well as in the mechanics' institutes, to drawing as a preliminary training for various industrial pursuits, and the erection and equipment of the School of Practical Science has been demanded in view of the immense mineral resources of the Province, which are only now beginning to be fully valued.

Professional Schools.

"In the case of other professions, such as law, medicine, dentistry, etc., the intention has been to require those who take up those pursuits to gain, at their own expense, the knowledge or training necessary. These professions have, however, been placed by law on such a basis as to guarantee to the public that those who follow such callings shall be persons of good education and high professional acquirements. The statutes give largely to the members of each profession the power to make regula-

tions regarding the examinations to be passed by those desiring
to enter such profession.

" The Law Society, which has its permanent seat at Osgoode
Hall, Toronto, makes regulations for admission to the profession
of law.   In order to enter upon the course a student must pass
the matriculation examination for admission to the arts faculty
of a university, and must then take a five years' course and pass
the examinations, which cover an extensive field of professional
reading.   Many students previously take the B.A. or LL.B. degree
in a university, and thereby shorten the course to one of three
years.   There has been established by this society a law school,
which students must attend for a portion of the time.

"The College of Physicians and Surgeons for Ontario prescribes
the course of study and conducts the examination for all
students who enter the medical profession.   To begin the study
a student must pass the matriculation examination (with the
addition of science) as conducted by the Education Department.
As in the case of law, five years are necessary to complete the
course.   There are six medical colleges in the Province, including
the medical department of the Provincial University, but a
degree from any university or college will not relieve a candidate
from passing the examinations prescribed by the College of
Physicians and Surgeons of Ontario.

"The College of Dentistry, Toronto, which is affiliated with the
Provincial University, controls the entrance to that profession,
and the College of Pharmacy, also affiliated with the Toronto
University, prescribes the course of study and conducts the
examinations for those who desire to become druggists.

" Powers somewhat similar in character are held by surveyors
and civil engineers.   The Ontario Veterinary College, Toronto,
has acquired a more than provincial reputation by the thorough
training it gives to those who intend to practise the veterinary
art.   A number of commercial colleges have been established
in the principal cities of the Province, where good facilities are
offered to those desiring a business education.   The increased
attention now required to be given in the high schools and
collegiate institutes to the different departments of a business
education has no doubt enabled these institutions to give a
good commercial training without requiring students to be at
the expense of attending a commercial college.   The incorporation of the "Stenographic Reporters' Association " is expected, by
the powers and privileges conferred, to give valuable aid towards
the study and practice of a profession growing in value.   Music,
both vocal and instrumental, has attained a high position in
Ontario through the efficiency of the College of Music (affiliated
with Toronto University), the Conservatory of Music, and the
various ladies' colleges.   These latter institutions, as well as the
different art schools, have contributed much towards the
progress of the fine arts, and the character of the exhibits made
at the Art School Examinations of the Education Department
has for years been most commendable."

V. SPECIAL SCHOOLS.

Institute for the Deaf and Dumb.

"The Legislature of Ontario has made ample provision to meet the educational requirements of the deaf mutes of the Province. The institution for the deaf and dumb, situated at the city of Belleville, is open to all deaf mutes from seven to twenty-one years of age who are residents of Ontario, and who are not deficient in intellect and are free from contagious diseases.

"The object in founding and maintaining this institute is to afford educational advantages to those who are, on account of deafness, either partial or total, unable to receive instruction in public schools. The period of instruction is seven years, with a vacation of nearly three months during the summer of each year. Parents or guardians who are able to pay are charged the sum of 50 dollars a year for board. There are no charges for tuition, books or medical attendance. Clothing must be furnished by parents or friends.

"The course of instruction is both scholastic and industrial. In the former the work is analogous, so far as the capacity of the pupils will allow, to that of the elementary schools. The modes of instruction employed are the manual alphabet, signs, writing, and articulation or visible speech.

"In the industrial department, the trades of printing, carpentering, and shoe-making are taught to boys, and girls are instructed in general domestic work, tailoring, dressmaking, sewing, knitting, the use of the sewing machine, and such ornamental and fancy work as may be desirable.

"Since the institution was opened in 1870, no fewer than 908 children have received the benefits of the instruction given. Most of those who have attended have turned out well, and have become an intelligent, law-abiding class. . . . . In the organisation and management of the institute, advantage has been taken of the most improved methods of instruction recognised in America and in Europe for training the deaf and dumb."

Institution for the Blind.

"The institution for the education of the blind was established in the city of Brantford in 1872. Like the institution for the deaf and dumb, it is intended to be supplementary to the public school system of the Province. Youths between the ages of seven and twenty-one are admitted who are not disqualified by disease or mental capacity, but whose sight is so defective or impaired as to prevent them from receiving education by the ordinary methods. No charges are made for tuition in the case of pupils admitted from Ontario. . . . .

"Pupils are taught arithmetic, grammar, geography, reading, writing, and at a more advanced stage, English literature and history. Reading is taught by the use of embossed type traced by the fingers, and writing with the aid of a grooved card, which acts as a guide to the hand. The ordinary expedients in the case of blind pupils are employed to give information in geography and natural history. Where the ability of the pupils justifies, very valuable instruction is given in vocal and instrumental music. Many graduates of the institution have shown marked proficiency with the pianoforte, organ, or violin. . . . . A kindergarten class is now an important department of the institution. . . . . Considerable attention is given to industrial training. . . . . In a few sessions an intelligent youth may graduate as a competent workman and become able to earn a living for himself. Girls are instructed in sewing and knitting, including the use of sewing and knitting machines, and have in this way been trained to provide for themselves a comfortable living.

"Attention is paid to physical training by instruction in gymnastic and calisthenic exercises. The health of the pupils is carefully looked after, and satisfactory provision is made for religious instruction by devotional exercises morning and evening, and by attendance at the churches of their respective denominations every Sunday. The pupils have access to a good library of embossed books which are increased in numbers from year to year."

VI. INDUSTRIAL SCHOOLS.

"According to the provisions of 'The Industrial Schools Act' of Ontario, Boards of Trustees in any city or town may establish schools in which industrial training is provided, and in which children are lodged, clothed, and fed, as well as taught. A Board of Trustees may delegate these powers, rights, and privileges to a benevolent or philanthropic society, but in such a case the chairman and secretary of the board and the school inspector become members of the board of management.

"The trustees provide the teachers necessary for the industrial school, and the general superintendent of the school must, when practicable, be selected from the teachers so appointed. Any person may bring before the police magistrate, or before some other competent authority, any child apparently under the age of fourteen years who comes within the following descriptions:—

1. Who is found begging or receiving alms, or being in any street or public place for the purpose of begging or receiving alms;

2. Who is found wandering, and not having any home or settled place of abode or proper guardianship or not having any lawful occupation or business or visible means of subsistence;

3. Who is found destitute, either being an orphan or having a surviving parent who is undergoing penal servitude or imprisonment;

4. Whose parent, step-parent or guardian represents to the judge or magistrate that he is unable to control the child, and that he desires the child to be sent to an industrial school under this Act;

5. Who by reason of the neglect, drunkenness, or other vices of the parents, is suffered to be growing up without salutary parental control and education, or in circumstances exposing him to lead an idle and dissolute life;

6. Who has been found guilty of petty crime, and who, in the opinion of the judge or magistrate before whom he has been convicted, should be sent to an industrial school instead of a gaol or reformatory.

"The judge or magistrate, if satisfied on enquiry that it is expedient to deal with the child under the Act, may order him to be sent to a certified industrial school for a period not extending beyond the time when the child will attain the age of sixteen years. The trustee board or society may admit into its industrial school all children apparently under the age of fourteen years who are committed by judge or magistrate: and it has power to place such children at such employments and cause them to be instructed in such branches of useful knowledge as are suited to their years and capacity.

"The Act provides for having, as far as practicable, Roman Catholic children sent to Roman Catholic industrial schools, and other children to other industrial schools. A minister of the religious persuasion to which the child appears to belong may visit the child at the schools on such days and at such times as may be fixed by the regulations of the Education Department.

"The Minister of Education may at any time order any child to be discharged under certain conditions from an industrial school.

"The school corporation or society may make rules for the management and discipline of the industrial school, but such rules must be consistent with the Act, and must be approved by the Education Department before being enforced.

"In case a child sent to an industrial school has not resided in the city or town in which the said school is situated, or to which it is attached, for a period of one year, but has resided for that period in some other county, city, or town, the school board or society may recover from the corporation of such county, city, or town the expense of maintaining the child.

"An Industrial School was established a few years ago at Mimico, a short distance from Toronto. The total expenditure was about 100,000 dollars, which was partly raised by subscription and partly met by the Legislature and city corporation. The buildings consist of one large and three smaller "cottages," besides workshops, and a large new building will soon be ready for occupation. There is a farm of fifty acres attached, and by working upon this as well as in the workshops, the boys are trained to industrious habits. About 200 children are in attendance. The cost is about 2 dollars a week for each, and the Legislature make a grant of 3,500 dollars to the institution."

PART II.—*THE SYSTEM IN 1899; EXTRACTS FROM
THE REPORT OF THE MINISTER OF EDUCATION
FOR THE YEAR 1899.*

I.—PUBLIC SCHOOL TEACHERS AND THEIR CERTIFICATES.

a. *Number of Public School Teachers' Certificates, 1899.*

	Male.	Female.	Total.
Third Class, per County Model School Reports - - - - - -	432	726	1,158
Second Class- -			
From Ottawa Normal School -	56	160	216]
Toronto Normal School -	36	226	262
First Class—			
From Ontario Normal College ;	43	20	63

b. *Remarks on the Supply of Qualified Teachers.*

It is to be hoped that the establishment of a third Normal
School will be followed by the appointment of a larger number
of second-class teachers in our Public Schools than heretofore.
It is unfortunate that Boards of Trustees do not yet fully
realise the advantage of having in our schools teachers of high
qualifications. Too often there is a disposition in some places to
secure the so-called cheap teacher, regardless of the important
interests involved. Teachers of character and ability cannot be
expected to remain in the profession unless their services are
better remunerated. Young men and young women of energy
cannot be blamed should they withdraw from a profession in
which they find high scholarship and valuable experience are
not properly appreciated. It may be doubted if a higher
standard is exacted in other countries for teachers' certificates.
In Ontario the standard has been very much advanced from
what it was a dozen years ago. With the abolition of the
Primary examination, a student who desires to become a teacher
will ordinarily attend a High School three years, and with a
year's professional training subsequently exacted, it will be
readily conceded that the expense involved in entering the
profession is considerable.

c. Teachers in training at Various Classes of Normal Schools, 1877–1899.

(Taken from the Report for 1899.)

Year.	County Model Schools.			Normal College.			Normal and Model Schools, etc.					
	No. of schools.	No. of teachers-in-training.	No. that passed final examination.	No. of teachers.	No. of students.	Receipts from fees of Normal College.	No. of Normal School teachers.	No. of Normal School students.	No. of Model Kindergarten teachers.	No. of Model Schools and Kindergarten pupils.	Receipts from fees of Normal Schools, Model Schools, and Kindergarten pupils.	Expenditure, Normal and Model Schools.
						$ c.					$ c.	$ c.
1877	50	1,146	1,124	—	—	—	13	257	8	643	7,909 22	25,780 88
1882	46	882	837	—	—	—	16	260	15	799	13,783 50	44,888 02
1887	55	1,491	1,376	—	—	—	13	441	18	763	16,427 00	40,188 66
1892	59	1,283	1,225	10	96	1,630 00	12	428	22	842	19,016 00	45,724 12
1897	60	1,645	1,384	12	180	4,374 00	13	447	23	832	18,797 59	46,390 91
1898	60	1,288	1,166	12	176	2,600 00	10	458	24	858	20,587 41	46,949 63
1899	61	1,271	1,158	12	148	1,845 00	10	478	25	863	19,908 00	46,835 08

d. Teachers' Institutes, 1877–1898.

(Taken from the Report for 1899.)

Year.	Receipts.							Expenditure.	
	No. of Teachers' Institutes	No. of members.	Total No. of teachers in province.	Amount received from Government grants.	Amount received from municipal grants.	Amount received from members' fees.	Total amount received.	Amount paid for libraries.	Total amount paid.
				$ c.	$ c.	$ c.	$ c.	$ c.	$ c.
1877	42	1,181	6,468	1,412 50	100 00	299 75	2,769 44	—	1,137 68
1882	62	4,395	6,857	2,900 00	300 00	1,088 84	9,394 28	453 02	5,855 33
1887	66	6,781	7,594	1,800 00	1,879 45	730 66	10,405 95	1,234 08	4,975 50
1892	69	8,142	8,480	1,950 00	2,105 00	875 76	12,043 54	1,472 41	6,127 46
1897	73	7,627	9,128	2,425 00	2,017 45	901 15	12,446 20	1,479 88	6,598 84
1898	75	8,238	9,209	2,650 00	1,857 50	876 25	12,629 49	1,526 34	6,730 60

e. Temporary and Extended Certificates issued during 1899.

COUNTIES.	Temporary Certificates authorised by the Minister of Education during the Year.	Third Class Certificates extended by the Minister of Education during the Year.
Essex - - - -	10	6
Frontenac - - -	4	—
Kent - - - -	—	1
Lanark - - -	1	1
Leeds - - - -	—	1
Norfolk - - -	2	—
Ontario - - -	—	2
Oxford - - -	—	1
Peel - - - -	1	—
Prescott and Russell -	1	—
Prince Edward - -	- -	1
Renfrew - - -	3	4
Stormont - - -	- -	2
Welland - - -		1
District of Parry Sound and Nipissing - -	11	2
Eastern Ontario, R.C.S.S.	20	4
Western Ontario, R.C.S.S.	5	- -
Total, 1899 - -	58	26
Total, 1898 - -	47	22
Increase - - -	9	

The periods of service were: three years and under, 6; seven years and over, 20.

f. Specialists' Certificates.

Among the "Revised Regulations" adopted in 1896 appears the following:—Any person who obtains an Honour Degree in the department of English and History, Modern Languages and History, Classics, Mathematics, or Science as specified in the calendars of any University of Ontario, and accepted by the Education Department, is entitled to the *non-professional qualification of a specialist* in such department. A graduate who has not taken an Honour Degree in one of the above courses is entitled to the non-professional standing of a specialist on submitting to the Education Department a certificate from the Registrar of the University that he has passed, subsequent to graduation, the examinations prescribed for each year of the Honour course of the department for which he seeks to be recognised as a specialist, and which he has not already passed in his undergraduate's course; or any examination which is recommended by the University as equivalent thereto, and accepted as such by the Education Department.

Professional qualifications.—Every candidate for the professional examinations must hold the necessary non-professional standing before writing at the examinations at the Normal College for a specialist's certificate. The holder of an Assistant High School Teacher's Certificate who has the necessary non-professional standing is not required to attend the Normal College, but may write at the examination for specialist on the paper in "Methods" only. This paper may be taken at Hamilton or at any other place in the Province if the candidate makes arrangements with the Public School Inspector to preside. The department must be informed of such arrangements at least one month before the examination.

Commercial Specialists.

Any person who passes an examination in the subjects set forth in the course for Commercial Specialists (each subject to be valued at 100), and who is the holder of a High School Assistant's Certificate, obtained either before or after passing such examination, shall be entitled to a Commercial Specialist's Certificate.

The course for Commercial Specialists is as follows :—

Book-keeping.—Single and double entry book-keeping; wholesale and retail merchandising, commission business, manufacturing; warehousing, steamboating, exchange, joint stock companies, municipalities, societies and public institutions, statements and balance-sheets, partnership adjustments, liquidation and administration of estates, auditing, filing papers, and the use of special columns and the various other expedients in book-keeping to save time and labour and secure accuracy of work.

Penmanship.—Theory and practice of penmanship, Spencerian and vertical ; ledger headings : marking and engrossing.

Commercial Arithmetic.—Interest, discount, annuities certain, sinking funds, formation of interest and annuity tables, application of logarithms, stock and investments, partnership settlements, partial payments, equation of payments and exchange.

Banking.—Money and its substitutes : exchange ; incorporation and organisation ; banks ; business of banks, their relation to each other and to the business community ; the clearing house system ; legal requirements as to capital, shares, reserves, dividends, note issue ; insolvency and consequent liability.

Business Forms.—Invoices, accounts, statements, due bills, orders, receipts, wages, house receipts, deposit receipts, deposit slips, bank pass books, promissory notes, bills of exchange, bank drafts, cheques, bonds, debentures, coupons, instalment scripts, stock certificates, stock transfers, proxies, letters of credit, affidavits, balance sheets, pay sheets, time sheets and special forms of general book-keeping, books to suit special cases.

Law of Business.—Contracts, statute of limitations; negotiable paper and endorsements; sales of personal property; accounts, invoices, statements, etc.; chattel mortgages; real estate and mortgages; interest; agency; partnership; corporations; guarantee and suretyship; receipts and releases; insurances; master and servant; landlord and tenant; bailment; shipping and trans-

ation; host and guest; telegraphs; auctions; patents; copy-
ts; trade marks and industrial designs; affidavits and
arations; subjects and aliens; wills, and joint stock comes.

enography.—The principles of Stenography; writing from
ation at a speed of sixty words per minute, and accurate
scription into longhand at a speed of twelve words per
ute; the dictated matter to comprise business correspondence
egal documents.

rawing.—Object and Model Drawing; Perspective and
metrical Drawing.

he examination in Drawing will be on the papers used at the
School examinations in Primary and advanced Geometry
Perspective and in Model, Memory and Blackboard Drawing.
or the rest of the course the examinations will be held in
, and application with the fee of $5 should be sent to the
lic School Inspector not later than the 24th of May.

ooks of reference recommended by the examiners:—

The Canadian Accountant.   By Beatty and Johnson.
Expert Book-keeping.   By C. A. Fleming, Owen Sound.
The Theory of Finance.   By Geo. King.   C. & E. Layton,
   Farringdon St., London, E.C.
Money and the Mechanism of Exchange.   By W. S. Jevons.
   The Humboldt Publishing Co., New York.
Banking Act of 1890.   The Carswell Co., Adelaide St.,
   Toronto, Ont.
The Laws of Business.   By C. A. Fleming.
Expert Book-keeping.   By C. A. Fleming.
Complete Phonographic Instructor.   By Sir I. Pitman.

II.—The Public School Leaving Examinations.

ie Regulations in regard to this were amended in 1899 and
read as follows:—

ie Public School Leaving Examination is identical with the
mination prescribed for Part I. of Junior Leaving Standing
ie School Leaving Certificates are issued by the Public
ool Inspector to all pupils of Public Schools in his inspector-
who pass the examination of Part I. of Junior Leaving
ding.   The holders of Public School Leaving Certificates
d before 1899 will be entitled to certificates of having passed
examination of Part I. Junior Leaving Standing by passing
examinations in Arithmetic and Mensuration, Grammar and
ory, the prescribed percentage on the total of these subjects
g also exacted.

irt I., Junior Leaving Standing.—The subjects prescribed
Part I. of Junior Leaving Standing are the following:
ling, Drawing, Geography, Botany (or Agriculture), Writing
   Book-keeping and Commercial Transactions, English
mmar, English Literature, Arithmetic and Mensuration,
ish Composition and History.   The course in Agriculture

will include part of what is taken up in the authorised text book. For 1900 no examination will be held in Reading, English Literature, Drawing, Book-keeping, Botany (or Agriculture), but no name of a student who has not given due attention to these subjects is to be included in the confidential report of the Principal.

No grant to a High School will be paid until the Principal and Chairman of the School Board report that each obligatory subject of the course, whether prescribed for examination or not, has, in their judgment, received due attention on the part of the pupils while attending the school.

It is expected that throughout the course, until pupils have completed what is required for Part I. of Junior Leaving Standing, at least two half-hour lessons per week will be given regularly to Reading, and an equal time to English Literature. Regarding Drawing, Book-keeping, Botany or Agriculture, at least two half-hour lessons per week for each of these subjects are to be given regularly to pupils enrolled in Form I. of the High School or Form V. of the Public School; that is, practically, during the first year of the course in preparation for Part I. of Junior Leaving Standing.

Public School Leaving Examinations 1892 99
(from the Report for 1899).

Year.	No. of Candidates examined.	No. of Candidates passed.
1892	432	195
1893	539	268
1894	2,021	690
1895	2,630	1,395
1896	3,239	1,826
1897	4,578	2,242
1898	5,280	1,980
1899	4,368	2,825

Entrance Examinations, 1877-1899 (taken from the
Report for 1899).

Year.	No. of Candidates examined.	No. of Candidates passed.
1877	7,383	3,836
1882	9,607	4,371
1887	16,248	9,364
1892	16,409	8,427
1897	16,314	10,502
1898	16,861	9,611
1899	16,309	10,604

III.—CONTINUATION CLASSES.

An interesting development of the Public Schools in Ontario is the "Continuation Classes," an outgrowth of the elementary school that connects it more closely with the higher educational grades, High School, &c. The following is taken from the Report for 1899 :—

Continuation Classes.—Under the provisions of the Amendment of 1899 to the Public Schools Act, the course of study for Continuation Classes is extended to include the subjects prescribed for Form II. of the High School course. More advanced work of the High School may be taken up if requested by the Trustees and approved by the Public School Inspector. In Class (*a*) the Principal must give regular instruction to pupils of Form V. or to those doing higher work. In the other classes, the teachers must have such qualifications as are approved by the Public School Inspector.

There are now four grades of Continuation Classes, viz.:— (*a*) Schools in which the Principal holds a First Class Certificate and gives regular instruction only to pupils of Form V., or to those doing higher work. (*b*) Schools in which there are at least two teachers, and a class in regular attendance of at least ten pupils who have passed the High School Entrance examination. (*c*) Schools where there are at least five; and (*d*) in which there are at least three, who have passed the High School Entrance examination, and are in regular attendance.

No grant will be paid for Continuation Classes unless the Inspector reports that the obligatory subjects, whether prescribed for examination purposes or not, have received proper attention. The grant will be paid according to the nature and extent of the work done, and not on the results of examinations. In order that a school may obtain the grant, it will be necessary that the minimum number of pupils be enrolled during each month of the full academic year.

It should be understood that no pupil, unless he intends to become a teacher, is required to write at the examination for Part I. Junior Leaving Standing (Public Schools Leaving). No grant will be paid to a school on account of the success of pupils at the Public School Leaving examination, and a school entitled to rank in one of the grades for Continuation Classes, will receive its share of the appropriation for such classes, even if no pupils from the school should become candidates at any examination. The Legislative Grant for a Continuation Class will depend upon the number of the different grades in the Province, and cannot be determined until the County Inspectors make their reports for Continuation Classes to the Education Department. It should be recollected that the success of pupils at the High School Entrance examination in no way affects the question of whether or not a school is entitled to be placed in any of the grades for the academic year then ending.

IV.—THE COURSE OF STUDY IN PUBLIC AND HIGH SCHOOLS.

(*Remarks from the Report for 1899*).

a. Agriculture.—It is of the first importance that the training given in our High and Public Schools should be as practical as possible, and that the subjects taken up in the Public Schools and also in the lower Forms of the High Schools should have in view the pursuits that will necessarily be followed by the great majority of our citizens. The fact should not, however, be over-looked, that the value of the training given in our schools does not depend so much upon the knowledge gained as the habits which the pupils form. If, in all matters that pertain to character building, the work of the schools is of the proper kind, he subjects to be taken up are of secondary importance. If the influence of the teacher makes the pupil intelligent, industrious and law-abiding, the amount of Grammar, Arithmetic, Algebra, etc., acquired will not be a matter of prime importance. After all, only the beginning of an education can be gained at best in our schools, and if pupils go forth to the active duties of life with correct principles of conduct inculcated, it may be assumed they will become valuable members of society. . . . It is a fact, however, that only a small proportion of the pupils attending the Public Schools ever enter a High School, and that of those who attend our secondary schools only a fraction will ever be enrolled in our Universities. Under these circumstances, it must be admitted that the requirements of the masses of children must control in determining the courses of study to be taken up. No course of study for our Public Schools can be commended that overlooks the needs of the farming community. For many years Agriculture was an optional branch for the elementary schools. For the first time the subject is made compulsory for rural schools. Every pupil in the Fifth Form, and even in the Fourth Form of these Schools, is now required to give attention to Agriculture. Valuable results may be predicted if the subject is taken up carefully by our Public School teachers. It is well known that the study of Agriculture really embraces the study of certain departments of elementary Science, and that the knowledge to be gained is not valuable to agriculturists alone, but should be valuable to every young person in the Province. In this connection it is to be hoped that " Nature Study," as work of this kind is often called, will hereafter receive greater prominence in all our elementary schools. Some of our Public School Inspectors are giving special encouragement to studies of this kind, and the pupils in our rural schools are having their attention more frequently directed to the beauties of nature and the intellectual gain resulting from an examination of the elementary features of Botany, Geology, Zoology, Chemistry, etc.

The following circular was issued by the Education Department in 1899:—

Circular to Members of Municipal Councils and School Boards.

I wish to call your attention to the provisions of an Amend-ment to the Public Schools Act, passed at the last Session of the Legislative Assembly, and assented to the 1st of April, 1899. This Statute, entitled "An Act to improve the laws respecting Public Schools," gives important powers to Municipal Councils and Trustee Boards. The section of the Act reads as follows:—

"(1) The council of every municipality may, subject to the Regulations of the Education Department, employ one or more persons holding the degree of Bachelor of the Science of Agriculture or a certificate of qualification from the Ontario Agricultural College, to give instruction in Agriculture in the separate, public and high schools of the municipality, and the council shall have power to raise such sums of money as may be necessary to pay the salaries of such instructors, and all other expenses connected therewith. Such course of instruction shall include a knowledge of the chemistry of the soil, plant life, drainage, the cultivation of fruit, the beautifying of the farm, and generally all matters which would tend to enhance the value of the products of the farm, the dairy and the garden.

"(2) The trustees of any public, separate or high school or any number of boards of such trustees, may severally or jointly engage the services of any person qualified as in the preceding section for the purpose of giving similar instruction to the pupils of their respective schools, providing always that such course of instruction shall not supersede the instruction of the teacher in charge of the school, as required by the regulations of the Education Department.

"(3) As far as practicable, the course of lectures in agriculture by such temporary instructor shall occupy the last school period of each afternoon, and shall be open to all residents of the school section or municipality."

By the late amendments to the Regulations of the Education Department, the programme of study for Public Schools has been amended so as to make Agriculture a compulsory subject in all rural schools. This addition to the course of study will enable the pupils of all country districts to gain some valuable though elementary knowledge of what must necessarily concern a farming community. As may be expected, the information gained by means of the instruction given by the teachers and by the study of the authorised text-book, will necessarily be limited, in view of the age of the pupils. At the same time, their minds will be prepared to take a deeper interest than they otherwise would do in matters concerning the most important industry of the Province. The provisions of the section of the Amendment quoted will show that the local authorities are now vested with power to supplement largely the instruction gained in the Public Schools. It is well understood that a keener interest in agricultural matters has been fostered by means of Farmers' Institutes. I wish to urge upon all persons concerned the importance of taking advantage of the provisions of the late Amendment to the Statute, in order to continue in a more advanced form that instruction in Agriculture, the foundations for which are laid in all our rural schools.

b. Manual Training.—Manual Training is now an optional subject of the High School and Public School courses of study, and much attention has been given in Canada within the last year to this modern department of educational work. The progress of science, in this latter part of the nineteenth century, has revolutionised all our industries, and it is safe to predict that in the approaching century many changes may be expected regarding the relative values of different branches of study. The curriculum of fifty years ago will not do to-day, and unless the Province realises the important changes in the world's progress, it would be unreasonable to expect the laudable position, which our schools have held in the past, to be retained. In the United States, as well as in England and Germany, technical training has come to the front as an educational topic of discussion. In those countries, manual training has become a well recognised department of elementary and secondary education. It will not suffice to limit the benefits of technical education to those who are enrolled in universities or even in attendance at High Schools. A limitation of this character would be unreasonable, in view of the fact that such a very small percentage of persons ever attend the higher seats of learning. Technical education must, in its more elementary forms such as manual training, be taken up in the Public Schools, if we are to have well trained mechanics, farmers and merchants.

Education, to be effective, must not be one-sided. The intelligent use of the brain is no more needed than the intelligent exercise of the physical activities. Skilful hand-work is really mind work in a high degree. The hand should be made to become the servant of the mind. Instruction in elementary science, free-hand and geometrical drawing, modelling in clay, etc., may be made to incite a love for that self-activity which it is the duty of the teacher to cultivate. Instruction in manual training will cultivate the perceptive faculties; will create love for manual skill, dexterity, and taste for design; it will induce young persons to observe for themselves, to acquire knowledge at first hand, and to make them more self-reliant. The fact should not be overlooked that by far the larger number of men in every civilised community are workers, and therefore a skilled hand becomes as important as a well filled head. It is unfortunately true that in many departments of industry at the present day, there are too few skilled artisans to put into form the ideas of the designers. The unrest sometimes found among working classes arises from a lack of that skilful training which would enable them to make good use of their opportunities. To furnish that training which enables boys and girls to earn an honest living should be an important aim of every school. It is often said that the brightest boys come from the country. If the statement is analysed, it will be found that the main advantage which the country boy has over the one from the city is that he has had the advantage of manual training, which is too often entirely denied to the one from the city.

The advance of applied science, with the resulting subdivision of labour so marked at the present day, has rendered instruction in technical education essential, in view of the changed economic conditions. Years ago the mechanic was usually proficient in the various departments of his work. His training enabled him to make a complete article, and he did not confine his attention to few processes. The work of the shoemaker, the blacksmith, the carpenter, etc., is very different from what it was half a century ago. The country must adapt itself to the new requirements.

c. Temperance and Hygiene.—It is also worthy of notice that the number of pupils receiving instruction in Temperance and Hygiene has increased from 33,926, in 1882, to 219,776, in 1898. Having regard to the great importance of the knowledge of physiology and the injurious effects of alcoholic stimulants on the human system, provision was made by the statute in 1886 for placing this subject on the course of study for Public Schools. Instruction was also provided under departmental regulation for teachers-in-training at County Model Schools and Normal Schools, to be followed by an examination as an essential pre-requisite to their final recognition as duly qualified teachers. In 1893, this subject was made compulsory for entrance to High Schools and Collegiate Institutes, so that no pupil who pursues his studies as far as the Fifth Form can fail to be reasonably well acquainted with the conditions on which his health and physical vigour depend, as well as with the dangerous tendency of stimulants and narcotics to produce weakness and disease.

V.--SEPARATE SCHOOLS IN 1898.

a. Roman Catholic Separate Schools.

Year.	Schools—Expenditure—Teachers.				Number of pupils attending—Number of studies.							
	School open.	Total receipts.	Total expenditure.	Teachers.	Pupils.	Reading.	Writing.	Arithmetic.	Geography.	Grammar.	Drawing.	Temperance and hygiene.
1867	161	48,628	42,719	210	18,924	18,924	10,749	10,559	8,666	5,688	—	—
1872	171	68,810	61,817	254	21,406	21,406	13,699	12,189	8,011	7,908	—	—
1877	185	120,286	114,806	334	24,962	24,962	17,982	17,961	13,154	11,174	—	—
1882	190	166,729	154,840	390	26,148	26,148	21,052	21,524	13,900	11,695	7,548	2,033
1887	229	229,848	211,223	491	30,373	30,373	27,824	28,501	19,608	18,678	21,818	8,573
1892	312	326,084	289,888	662	37,466	37,466	35,565	35,936	26,290	22,755	32,682	11,056
1897	340	335,324	302,169	752	41,620	41,620	39,724	40,165	27,471	26,071	36,462	18,127
1898	345	369,185	349,451	744	41,667	41,667	41,473	41,396	29,578	24,188	37,345	17,964

b. Protestant Separate Schools.

The complete list of Protestant Separate Schools is as follows: No. 5 Bromley, No. 9 Cambridge, No. 1 Marlboro', No. 6 Plantagenet North, Puslinch, Rama, L'Orignal, Penetanguishene.

They were attended by 505 pupils. The whole amount expended for their maintenance was $4,895. One teacher held a First Class, five a Second Class, five a Third Class, and one a Temporary Certificate.

VI.—HIGH SCHOOLS.

a. *Diffusion of High School Education (from the Report for 1899).*

When the High School System of the Province was first inaugurated, its primary object was to prepare pupils for the learned professions, and especially for the University. While in that respect our High Schools amply fulfil their original purpose, in later years the course of education which they provide has been considered a desirable qualification for various other pursuits in life. Many young men in preparing for mercantile life or for agriculture take advantage of the High School, perhaps not so much because of the direct training which it gives for their intended calling as for the superior culture which it provides. In 1872, 486 High School pupils when they had finished their High School education entered mercantile life. In 1898 the number had increased to 1,491. Similarly (in 1872) 300 High School pupils left the High School for agricultural pursuits, and in 1898, 1,050 pupils pursued a similar course. In all, the High Schools gave to mercantile life and to agriculture in 1898, 2,541 pupils of well recognised educational standing, and to the Universities and learned professions the same year, 1,336. The whole number who left the High School for mercantile life since 1872 was 24,094, and for agriculture, 18,920.

b. *Tendencies of High School Education, 1867 to 1898.*

The following figures in regard to High School studies, together with some remarks suggested by them, are taken from the Report for 1899 :—

| Year. | Languages. | | | | Drawing. | Vocal Music. | Book-keeping and commercial transactions. | Left for mercantile life. | Left for agriculture. | Who joined learned profession. | Matriculated. | Number of schools charging fees. |
	Latin.	Greek.	French.	German.								
1867	5,171	802	2,164	—	676	—	1,288	—	—	—	56	57
1872	3,800	900	2,828	341	2,176	—	3,127	486	300	213	78	28
1877	4,955	871	3,001	442	2,755	-	8,621	555	328	564	145	35
1882	4,591	815	5,383	962	3,441	,	5,642	881	646	751	272	37
1887	5,409	997	6,180	1,350	14,295	1,955	14,064	1,141	882	791	305	58
1892	9,006	1,070	10,398	2,796	16,960	948	16,700	1,111	1,006	398	471	77
1897	16,873	1,421	13,761	5,109	12,252	160	11,647	1,368	1,153	409	652	97
1898	19,513	1,456	18,866	6,288	10,947	30	11,026	1,491	1,050	499	837	79

From a study of the classification of High Schools and Collegiate Institutes, two or three very striking changes in the tendency of higher education may be worthy of notice. For instance, in 1867, only 1,283 pupils, or 23 per cent. of the whole number, studied commercial subjects, such as book-keeping; in 1898 this subject was taken by 11,026 pupils, or 47 per cent. of the whole attendance. In 1867, 5,171 pupils, or 90 per cent. of the whole attendance, studied Latin; in 1898 the number of pupils in Latin was 19,313, about 83 per cent. of the number in attendance. In 1867, 15 per cent. studied Greek; in 1898, only six per cent. were engaged in studying this subject. In 1867, 38 per cent. of pupils studied French, and none studied German; in 1898 these numbers had increased to 60 per cent. and 27 per cent. respectively. There also has been a large increase in the number studying Drawing, the total in 1867 being 676, and in 1898, 10,947.

c. *Departmental Instructions for the High School Entrance Examination, 1900.*

(i.) No teacher who has pupils writing at the High School Entrance Examination is eligible as Examiner where such pupils are writing.

When the County Council recommends the holding of an examination at any place other than the High School, the presiding examiner shall be paid the sum of $3 per diem, and travelling expenses, for conducting such examination, and the examiners shall be allowed the sum of $1 per candidate for reading the examination papers. It shall be lawful for the County Treasurer to pay all the expenses of such examination on the certificate of the County Inspector.

(ii.) *Duties of Inspector.*—The Inspector shall notify the Department not later than the 3rd day of May in each year, of the number of persons desiring to be examined at any High School or other authorised place within his jurisdiction.

In any city or town forming a separate inspectoral division, the Inspector or Inspectors of such city or town shall preside at the examinations, and in conjunction with the Board of Examiners for such city or town, shall read the papers and report to the Department.

In counties in which more High Schools than one are situated, the Inspector for the county shall elect at which High School he will preside, and shall notify the Department of the choice he makes, and in each of the other High Schools the Principal of the High School shall preside.

In the case of examinations affiliated with a High School, the Inspector, within whose district such affiliated examinations are held, shall appoint presiding examiners, who shall be teachers in actual service, notice of which shall be sent to the Education Department; and such Inspector, together with the examiners of the High School with which the examination is affiliated, shall be the Board of Examiners in all such cases

Where, from the number of candidates, or any other cause, additional presiding examiners are required, the Inspector shall make such appointments as are necessary, preference being given to the other members of the Board of Examiners. The inspector shall not appoint as presiding examiner any teacher who has taken part in the instruction of any of the candidates in the room where he presides, or who is not in actual service.

Where more examinations than one are held in an inspectoral division, the papers will be sent by the Education Department to the Inspector, or the presiding examiner, as the case may be.

The parcel containing the examination papers shall not be opened till the morning of the examination day, nor shall any envelope containing the papers in any subject be opened until the time appointed in the time-table for the examination in such subject.

(iii.) *Duties of Presiding Examiners.*—To be in attendance at the place appointed for the examination at least fifteen minutes before the time fixed for the first subject, and to see that the candidates are supplied with the necessary stationery, and seated so far apart as to afford reasonable security against copying.

To open the envelope containing the papers in each subject in full view of the candidates, at the time prescribed, and to place one paper on each candidate's desk.

To exercise proper vigilance over the candidates to prevent copying and to allow no candidate to communicate with another, nor permit any person except a co-examiner to enter the room during examination.

To see that the candidates promptly cease writing at the proper time, fold and endorse their papers properly, and in every respect comply with the instructions given.

To submit the answers of the candidates to the examiners, according to the instructions from the Board.

(iv.) *Duties of Candidates.*—Every candidate should be in attendance at least fifteen minutes before the time at which the examination is to begin, and shall occupy the seat allotted by the presiding examiner. Any candidate desiring to move from his allotted place or to leave the room shall first obtain permission from the presiding examiner to do so. Any candidate leaving shall not return during the examination of the subject then in hand.

Every candidate shall write his answers on one side only of the paper, and shall number each answer. He shall arrange the sheets numerically, according to the questions, and fold them once crosswise, endorsing them with his name, the name of the subject, and the name of the place at which he is examined. No paper shall be returned to a candidate after being placed in the hands of the presiding examiner.

Any candidate who is found copying from another or allowing another to copy from him, or who brings into the examination room any book, note, or paper having any reference to the - subject on which he is writing, shall be required by the presiding

G

examiner to leave the room and his paper and the papers of all
the guilty parties shall be cancelled.

(v.) *Duties of Examiners.*—The papers of the different
candidates shall be so distributed that the same examiner
shall read and value the answers in the same subject throughout.

Marks are to be deducted for mis-spelt words and for want of
neatness as indicated on the question papers.

d. *The Question of Free High Schools (from the Report for 1899).*

The opinion that High School Education is mainly for the
benefit of the wealthy classes is held by very few of our citizens.
The influence of secondary schools in promoting the excellence
of elementary schools is seen in the increased ambition of pupils,
who as a result not only stay longer in the Public Schools, but
who do better work in consequence of the goal placed before
them. The energies of Public School teachers are quickened on
account of the demand made upon them by the High Schools.

. . . .

Free elementary schools have, since 1871, been guaranteed to
Ontario. The question of free High Schools is left to be determined by the authorities of each municipality. Discussions have
frequently arisen in many parts of the Province regarding the
principle of free secondary education. The fees of county pupils
attending High Schools cannot exceed $10 per annum. In
many counties, commendable liberality has been shown in having
county pupils admitted free or by the payment of a less amount
than the minimum fee. The rule observed regarding resident
pupils varies. In 51 High Schools and Collegiate Institutes, no
fees are charged resident pupils. In the other institutions fees
vary from $1 to $32 per annum. It would be a misfortune
should the doors of our High Schools and Collegiate Institutes
be closed to the children of parents in the humbler walks of
life. . . . . To confine the benefits of our High Schools to
the children of parents who are in a position to pay high fees
will necessarily restrict the number of well-trained mechanics,
merchants, and farmers.

VII.—EMPIRE DAY IN PUBLIC AND HIGH SCHOOLS.

a. *Circular of March, 1899.*

The following extracts from a circular issued to Inspectors are
taken from the Report of the Minister of Education for 1899.

In accordance with a resolution adopted by the Dominion
Education Association at Halifax, N.S., in August, 1898, the
Education Department of Ontario adopted the following minute
on March 1st, 1899 :—

"The School Day immediately preceding the 24th of May shall
be devoted specially to the study of the history of Canada in its
relation to the British Empire and to such other exercises as
might tend to increase the interest of the pupils in the history of

their own country and strengthen their attachment to the Empire to which they belong—such day to be known as ' Empire Day.' "

" ' Empire Day ' this year falls on Tuesday, the 23rd of May. It is not necessary to specify in detail how the day should be observed. The outline given below might be taken generally as a guide to teachers and trustees :—

" *The Forenoon.*—Part of the forenoon might be occupied with a familiar talk by the teacher on the British Empire, its extent and resources ; the relation of Canada to the Empire ; the unity of the Empire and its advantages ; the privileges which, as British subjects, we enjoy; the extent of Canada and its resources; readings from Canadian and British authors by the teacher ; interesting historical incidents in connection with our own country. The aim of the teacher in all his references to Canada and the Empire should be, to make Canadian patriotism intelligent, comprehensive and strong.

" *The Afternoon.*—The afternoon, commencing at 2.30 p.m., might be occupied with patriotic recitations, songs, readings by the pupils and speeches by trustees, clergymen, and such other persons as may be available.

" The trustees and public generally should be invited to be present at these exercises.

" During the day the British Flag or Canadian Ensign should be hoisted over the school building.

" Will you kindly inform the teachers of your Inspectoral District of the action of the Department and of the purposes of ' Empire Day ' as herein set forth."

b. *Remarks from the Report for 1899.*

On the 23rd of May last, the day before the commemoration of Her Majesty's birthday, the schools of this Province, as well as of the other Provinces of the Dominion, celebrated what will hereafter mark a step in the advancement of that unity of the Empire, to which so much attention has been given of late years. It may be expected that the celebration of Empire Day will in future be characterised by the same objects as marked the event in 1899. The day is not a holiday in the ordinary sense of the term, but it may be presumed that hereafter its annual recurrence will be devoted to exercises of a patriotic character, like those of last year. Inspectors in all parts of the Province, as well as Principals of schools, deserve no small credit for the excellent manner in which the event was inaugurated. In most of the schools, part of the forenoon was taken up by the teachers with references to the history of the British Empire, and the admirable heritage which we, as subjects of Her Majesty, enjoy. In the afternoon, trustees, members of Municipal Councils, members of Parliament, clergymen, and other prominent citizens, gave addresses to the children assembled in the schcols or in halls, to which the public was generally invited. . . . . It is satisfactory to know that in no instance does there appear to have

been any disposition to cultivate what is termed the "jingo
spirit" among the pupils attending our Public Schools. . . . .
The events which have lately been transpiring in another part of
the Empire have brought to the attention of all our citizens the
common interest felt by all who live under the British flag. There
need be little fear, I think, of any tendency on the part of the
people of this Province to become fond of war or anxious to depart
from those principles of government which had influence for so
many years in the preservation of peace. . . . .   In the addresses
given in many places attention was directed to those ideals of
liberty which have guided our statesmen, to the advance of
education, the growth of tolerance, the progress of self-government,
and the improvement in the moral atmosphere among Anglo-
Saxon communities. Attention was doubtless called, and properly
so, to the magnificent resources of our country, to the literature and
art left us by our British ancestry, and to the distinguished men
and women who have given their talents, their means, and even
their lives, for the promotion of Christian civilisation. The
opportunity appears to have been well employed for filling the
minds of the pupils with the highest kind of patriotism—a
patriotism inspired by a higher conception of civic duty, improved devotion to the public interests, willingness to offer
personal service in behalf of one another, and a disposition to
give assistance for the promotion of social improvement. . . . .
It is evident that exercises of this character cannot fail to impress
the children attending our schools with the great blessings possessed by those who have reaped the advantage of centuries of
progress towards the highest type of constitutional government.

VIII.—University Education.

*a. From the Annual Report of the Council of the University
of Toronto for the academical year 1898–99.*

For some years past the Departments of Psychology and
Physics have been in urgent need of increased accommodation
for lecture rooms and laboratories. Previously to the present
session it has been impossible to provide for these requirements.
Owing to the closing of the University College residence, however,
the Council has been enabled to make arrangements for the utilisa-
tion of a portion of the residence wing for this purpose. Several
vacant rooms have been fitted up at small expense, and thus
temporary facilities have been furnished for some of the more
pressing needs of these Departments, as well as for the work
of advanced students, both graduate and undergraduate, who are
prosecuting researches under the direction of the staff.
In consequence of the increased numbers of students in
several Departments, there is a growing need for two large
lecture-rooms, similar to those in the Chemical and Biological
Buildings. This want is especially felt in the departments of
History and Psychology. Hitherto these Departments have
been obliged to make use of the examination halls in the main
building, which are extremely unsuitable for lecture purposes.

The Council begs to direct the attention of your Honour to the increased necessity which exists for the re-organisation of the Department of Mineralogy and Geology and for its establishment on a basis commensurate with the importance of these subjects of study, and on a parallel with the provision which has been made for the teaching of the other sciences.

With the close of the academic session, Dr. Pike severed his connection with the University, after almost twenty years of service as Professor of Chemistry. Under his administration the Department of Chemistry has made remarkable progress; especially in the practical work of the laboratory and in the introduction and encouragement of the work of research. Under his direction also the present Chemical Building was erected, and its admirable arrangements are almost wholly owing to his skill and foresight.

b. The following tables exhibit the numbers attending the Pass and Honour Lectures in University subjects.

PASS.

Subjects.	Mathematics.	Physics.	Chemistry.	Biology.	Mineralogy and Geology.	Philosophy.	Logic.	Political Science.	History.
First year	132	37	–	85	–	–	–	–	–
Second year	–	6	9	–	35	138	128	–	80
Third year	–	7	–	–	–	–	–	40	37
Fourth year	30	–	–	–	–	32	–	65	31
Totals	162	50	9	85	35	170	128	105	148

In no case do the numbers given above include honour students. Instruction in Physics, Biology and Chemistry was given to 63 students of the first year in Medicine, and in Physics to 73 students of the first year and to 40 students of the second year in the School of Practical Science.

HONOUR.

Subjects.	Mathematics.	Physics.	Chemistry.	Biology.	Mineralogy and Geology.	Philosophy.	Political Science.	History.	Spanish.	Italian.	Phonetics.
First year	36	42	55	15	–	–	–	–	13	44	47
Second year	52	32	33	12	14	18	24	27	4	21	–
Third year	13	18	17	12	13	20	24	48	4	14	–
Fourth year	7	12	3	11	2	16	24	48	2	6	–
Totals	108	104	108	50	29	54	72	123	23	85	47

The second year lectures in Chemistry and the fourth year lectures in Biology were attended by 49 students of the second year in Medicine. Instruction in Mathematics was given to 73 students of the first year and to 40 students of the second year in the School of Practical Science.

c. *The Laboratories.*

The following table exhibits the numbers taking the practical work in the laboratories of the University :—

Laboratories.	Physical	Chemical	Mineralogical.	Biological	Psychological
Fourth year	12	3	2	11	16
Third year	18	17	13	12	15
Second year	13	33	14	12	–
First year	17	15	–	15	–
Totals	60	68	29	50	31

d. *Numbers examined in the Faculties and Departments.*

During the year thirteen hundred and thirty-four candidates were examined in the different Faculties and Departments, as follows :—

Faculty of Law - - - - - -	6
Faculty of Medicine - - - - -	190
Faculty of Arts - - - - - -	905
Department of Agriculture - - - -	11
Department of Pedagogy - - - -	6
Department of Dentistry - - - -	137
Department of Music - - - -	10
Department of Pharmacy - - - -	63
Department of Applied Science - - -	6
Total - - - - -	1,334

e. *Students in the Faculty of Medicine.*

The following table exhibits the number of the students registered as in attendance upon the lectures given by the staff of the Faculty of Medicine :—

Students of the fourth year - - -	55
Students of the third year - - - -	56
Students of the second year - - -	54
Students of the first year - - -	73
Occasional students - - - -	70
Total - - - - - -	308

f. Subjects taught in the Faculty of Science.

Subjects taught in the Faculty of Science of the University of Toronto :—

Subjects.	Number of Students.	
	2nd Term. Session 1898-9.	1st Term. Session 1899-00.
Algebra - - - - - - - Euclid - - - - - - - Plane trigonometry - - - - - Analytical geometry - - - - - Calculus - - - - - - - Astronomy - - - - - - -	108	139
Sound - - - - - - - Light, heat, electricity and magnetism - Hydrostatics - - - - - -	108	131

Practical instruction in Chemistry and Biology was given to 63 students of the first year, and to 49 students of the second year in Medicine, and in Physics to 85 students of the School of Practical Science. During the session eleven graduates in Arts were engaged in original research in the Psychological Laboratory and one in the Biological Laboratory

g. University College.

(i.) The numbers of registered students taking full or partial courses in University College were as follows :—

	Fourth Year.	Third Year.	Second Year.	First Year.	Post-graduate.	Total.
Matriculated students	129	108	102	102	–	441
Occasional students -	26	25	21	70	–	142
Extra-mural students	–	4	6	6	–	16
Graduated students -	5	2	2	1	3	13
Totals - - -	160	139	131	179	3	612

(ii.) The following tables exhibit the number of students attending the Pass and Honour Lectures in University College subjects :—

PASS.

	Greek.	Latin.	English.	French.	German.	Orientals.	Ethics.	Ancient History.
Fourth year - -	7	25	54	28	11	4	–	–
Third year - -	5	26	67	21	12	6	38	–
Second year - -	20	70	65	38	35	9	–	–
First year - -	24	113	105	64	47	28	–	105
Totals - - -	56	234	291	151	105	47	38	105

HONOUR.

	Greek.	Latin.	English.	French.	German.	Orientals.	Ethics.	Ancient History.
Fourth year - -	12	12	49	21	19	3	10	–
Third year - -	8	11	27	23	21	4	29	–
Second year - -	10	9	36	21	17	4	–	50
First year - -	18	27	77	53	48	–	–	27
Totals - - -	48	59	189	118	105	11	39	77

There were during the session 170 women students in attendance at University College.

h. Subjects taught by the Faculty of the School of Science.

SUBJECTS.	Number of Students.	
	2nd Term. Session 1898-9.	1st Term. Session 1899-00.
Organic and inorganic chemistry - - -⎫ Applied chemistry - - - - -⎬ Assaying - - - - - -⎭	149	181
Mineralogy and geology - - -⎫ Petrography - - - - -⎪ Metallurgy - - - - - -⎬ Mining and ore dressing - - -⎪ German - - - - - -⎭	83	145
Statics - - - - -⎫ Dynamics - - - - -⎪ Strength of materials - - -⎪ Theory of construction - - -⎪ Machine design - - - -⎬ Compound stress - - - -⎪ Hydraulics - - - - -⎪ Thermodynamics and theory of the steam ⎪ engine - - - - - -⎪ French - - - - - -⎭	147	185
Drawing - - - - -⎫ Architecture - - - - -⎪ Plumbing, heating and ventilation - -⎬ Mortars and cements - - - -⎪ Brick and stone masonry - - -⎭	146	177
Surveying - - - - -⎫ Geodesy and astronomy - - -⎪ Spherical trigonometry - - -⎬ Least squares - - - -⎪ Descriptive geometry - - -⎭	144	177
Electricity - - - - -⎫ Magnetism - - - - -⎪ Dynamo-electrical machinery - -⎬ Mechanics of machinery - - -⎪ Rigid dynamics - - - -⎭	99	110

IX.—ART TEACHING.

a. Art Schools and Departmental Drawing Examinations.

Tables showing the number of Certificates awarded since the commencement of this branch of the Education Department.

(i.) Certificates awarded in Primary Art Course from 1882 to 1899.

Year.	Freehand Drawing.	Geometry.	Perspective.	Model Drawing.	Blackboard Drawing.	Teachers' Certificates.	Total.
1882 · ·	28	21	17	12	28	—	106
1883 · ·	84	89	58	47	76	—	354
1884 · ·	153	174	139	138	86	66	736
1885 · ·	214	529	301	168	198	122	1,532
1886 · ·	634	672	149	662	414	77	2,608
1887 · ·	643	1,204	428	444	122	103	2,944
1888 · ·	805	882	520	403	236	133	2,979
1889 · ·	1,002	961	394	470	494	187	3,508
1890 · ·	1,000	1,009	290	811	313	130	3,553
1891 · ·	1,085	1,569	292	746	422	164	4,278
1892 · ·	1,361	1,419	569	1,120	720	338	5,527
1893 · ·	1,769	1,277	439	876	392	220	4,973
1894 · ·	1,383	719	548	550	562	153	3,915
1895 · ·	1,813	1,429	658	1,311	991	341	6,543
1896 · ·	1,195	569	361	1,110	1,121	265	4,621
1897 · ·	716	500	212	704	516	114	2,762
1898 · ·	854	311	173	1,224	604	149	3,315
1899 · ·	1,062	465	168	1,128	1,170	160	4,153
Total · ·	15,801	13,799	5,716	11,924	8,465	2,722	58,427

(ii.) Certificates awarded in Advanced Art Course from 1883 to 1899

Year.	Shading from flat.	Outline from round.	Shading from round.	Drawing from flowers.	Ornamental Design.	Industrial Design.	Teachers' Certificates.	Total.
1883 · ·	5	5	12	18	–	–	–	40
1884 · ·	16	5	12	12	–	–	–	45
1885 · ·	33	18	35	29	–	–	4	119
1886 · ·	35	24	19	48	–	–	3	129
1887 · ·	59	27	28	25	34	–	14	187
1888 · ·	22	17	39	44	20	–	9	151
1889 · ·	65	36	58	24	25	–	14	222
1890 · ·	62	30	76	43	22	–	15	248
1891 · ·	80	52	67	66	38	–	23	326
1892 · ·	24	32	53	72	37	–	13	231
1893 · ·	58	54	73	62	54	–	13	314
1894 · ·	31	44	58	79	68	–	24	304
1895 · ·	56	52	78	58	29	–	11	284
1896 · ·	60	74	103	113	–	29	17	396
1897 · ·	61	47	126	95	–	41	18	388
1898 · ·	67	73	169	187	–	44	18	558
1899 · ·	61	69	152	160	–	57	22	521
Total · ·	795	659	1,158	1,135	327	171	218	4,463

(iii.) Certificates awarded in Mechanical Drawing Course from 1883 to 1899.

Year.	Advanced Geometry.	Machine Drawing.	Building Construction.	Industrial Design.	Architectural Design.	Advanced Perspective.	Teachers' Certificates.	Total.
1883	2	3	1	2	–	3	–	11
1884	1	1	1	1	–	1	–	5
1885	12	32	4	25	–	12	4	89
1886	14	13	5	28	–	14	3	77
1887	6	5	12	18	–	6	2	49
1888	8	7	7	15	–	11	2	50
1889	13	23	11	20	–	12	3	82
1890	11	23	5	8	–	12	2	61
1891	3	31	8	31	–	28	2	103
1892	17	25	13	38	–	15	2	110
1893	14	33	10	47	–	35	10	149
1894	12	17	6	90	–	9	3	137
1895	5	22	9	31	–	12	3	82
1896	7	9	5	–	9	12	3	45
1897	16	13	4	–	6	15	–	54
1898	6	19	2	–	7	8	–	42
1899	25	20	5	–	7	18	–	75
Total	172	296	108	354	29	223	39	1,221

(iv.) Certificates Awarded in Industrial Art Course from 1885 to 1899.

Year.	Modelling in Clay.	Wood Carving.	Wood Engraving.	Lithography.	Painting on China.	Total.
1885	14	–	–	–	–	14
1886	11	7	–	–	–	18
1887	8	2	–	–	–	10
1888	10	3	1	1	9	24
1889	7	1	3	2	6	19
1890	7	4	–	1	6	18
1891	5	2	1	–	7	15
1892	2	1	–	1	3	7
1893	5	2	–	1	3	11
1894	4	2	–	2	10	18
1895	5	3	2	6	18	34
1896	3	2	–	3	30	38
1897	5	3	1	4	17	30
1898	7	5	–	1	17	30
1899	9	14	–	2	17	42
Total	102	51	8	24	143	328

(v.) Certificates awarded for Extra Subjects from
1885 to 1899.

Year.	Drawing from the antique.	Shading from casts.	Architectural designs.	Drawing from life.	Painting from life.	Painting oil colours.	Painting water colours.	Sepia.	Monochrome.	Pastel.	Sculpture in marble.	Photogravure.	Repoussé work.	Industrial design.	Pen and ink.	Machine drawing.	Engraving on copper.	Crayon portraits.	Total.
1885	–	–	–	–	–	9	7	–	–	–	–	–	–	–	–	–	–	–	16
1886	–	–	–	–	–	12	7	–	–	–	–	–	–	–	–	–	–	–	19
1887	–	–	–	7	–	32	9	–	–	–	–	2	–	–	–	–	–	–	50
1888	–	–	–	15	12	25	14	13	1	–	2	–	2	–	–	–	–	–	84
1889	–	–	–	12	8	16	21	3	2	–	–	–	–	–	–	–	–	–	62
1890	–	–	–	7	4	28	18	10	4	–	–	–	–	–	–	–	–	–	71
1891	–	–	–	4	5	29	26	3	6	–	–	–	–	–	–	–	–	–	73
1892	–	–	–	2	6	21	16	7	1	–	–	–	–	–	–	–	–	2	55
1893	11	–	2	5	9	35	21	7	4	–	–	–	–	–	–	–	–	–	94
1894	11	–	2	8	6	29	16	5	7	–	–	–	–	10	–	1	–	–	96
1895	26	–	6	14	4	39	24	10	1	–	–	–	–	17	–	5	1	–	147
1896	14	–	–	12	6	34	38	6	1	2	–	1	–	13	1	1	–	–	129
1897	19	11	1	17	6	38	42	7	3	3	–	3	–	22	3	4	–	–	179
1898	22	12	–	12	9	37	28	7	6	6	1	6	–	15	4	6	–	–	171
1899	19	14	–	17	2	10	22	8	1	4	–	3	–	31	13	5	–	–	149
Total	122	37	11	132	77	394	309	86	37	15	3	13	4	108	21	22	1	2	1,894

b. Literary and Scientific Societies receiving grants.

The following Institutions receive Legislative Grants: 1.
Hamilton Literary and Scientific Institution; 2. Kingston
School of Mining; 3. Ontario Historical Society; 4. Ottawa
French Canadian Institute; 5. Ottawa Literary and Scientific
Society; 6. Ottawa St. Patrick's Literary and Scientific Associa-
tion; 7. Ottawa Field Naturalist Club; 8. Toronto Canadian
Institute; 9. Toronto Astronomical and Physical Society.

All of these Institutions give popular lectures on literature or
science; some of them publish their transactions and others
have museums, all of which are greatly appreciated by the
public and assist in developing a taste for Literature, Science
and Art.

c. Progress of School Architecture and Decoration.

Extract from an inaugural address given by Dr. S. P. May,
Superintendent of Art Schools, to the officers and members of the
Dufferin Art School League, in December 1899.

A History of the Progress of School Architecture and the
Decoration of School Rooms in the City.

It is not generally known, and I presume that even some members of the Advisory Board for School Art Leagues are not aware, that fifty years ago the Education Department supplied architectural plans for the erection of school houses. The late Chief Superintendent of Education, the Rev. Dr. Ryerson, the founder of the public school system, whose memory we all revere, and whose name will be handed down to posterity as a great Canadian educationist, philanthropist and true Christian, was the first man in Canada to direct public attention to the importance of school architecture.

It was through his exertions that in 1850 Parliament voted the sum of £200 per annum for purchasing plans, engravings, etc., for the improvement of school architecture; these plans were published and distributed from time to time through the Upper Canada Journal of Education, and eventually school trustees made so many applications for specifications for erecting school buildings, that it became necessary for a book to be published on this subject.

In 1857 Dr. Hodgins, then Deputy Superintendent of Education, published under the authority of the Chief Superintendent, "The School House, its architecture, external and internal arrangements." This book was profusely illustrated with engravings of elevations and plans for school buildings, and was of great value in awakening an interest in school architecture, for, as some of us remember, at that time we had a large number of log school houses, and the trustees of rural schools seemed satisfied that so long as they could afford shelter for the school children, they need make no attempt to make the school attractive to the pupils; they considered learning to be a good thing, and approved of children attending school, but they did not care about external architectural beauty, nor the internal decoration of school rooms.

In 1859, two years after the publication of "The School House," the grant for school architecture was increased to $800.00 per annum.

In 1872 the Education Department offered prizes to Inspectors and Teachers for the best architectual designs and plans for rural school houses. Thirty persons competed, and seventeen awards were made to the value of $230.00; seven prizes were taken by school inspectors, and ten by school teachers.

In 1876 a new edition of "The School House," with illustrated papers on School Hygiene and Ventilation, was published by Dr. Hodgins. I consider that a proper attention to Light, Heat, and Ventilation is of more importance than external decorations in the construction of school buildings. If school rooms are not well ventilated and lighted, most injurious effects are produced on the mental development and physical health of children, which are often felt in after life. It is a well known hygienic fact that if a child breathes foul air, he is in a state of physical discomfort; consequently in his undiscriminating mind the feelings of pain and lassitude are associated with school, and cause a dislike for books and study.

The ill health of pupils and teachers, sometimes credited to overwork, is frequently due to draughts and foul air in the school room.

Another important thing is the arrangement of light in the school room. We frequently find windows on the right of the desks of the pupils, and sometimes on three or four sides of a room ; this, together with the white walls, and interminable blackboards surrounding the children, no doubt produces Myopia or nearsightedness ; and how frequent it is that we now see school children using spectacles; fifty years ago such a thing was unknown.

In the same year, 1876, the Education Department exhibited at the Centennial Exhibition models of school buildings for Collegiate Institutes, Public Schools in cities and towns, also for Schools in rural districts, made to a working scale with ground plans and references as to cost of erection, accommodation, etc. At the close of the exhibition these models, which were much sought after by foreign educationists, were divided between the representatives of Japan and the United States. We also exhibited large framed photographs of Collegiate Institutes, High Schools, and Public Schools erected in different parts of this Province.

I may mention that a similar collection of large photographs for the Paris Exposition of 1900 has been prepared under the authority of the Hon. Mr. Harcourt, Minister of Education.

In 1886, Dr. Hodgins, under the direction of the Hon. Adam Crooks, first Minister of Education, published "Hints and Suggestions on School Architecture and Hygiene," with plans and illustrations, and I may here state that the Education Department is now offering prizes for the best architectural plans for school houses.

In regard to the internal decoration of school houses I may say that from 1851 to 1878 the Educational Depository supplied schools at half cost price with historical and other prints and engravings, which were reproductions of the works of Raphael and other old masters, together with plain and coloured engravings by Landseer and other modern painters, also small busts of eminent and celebrated men of ancient and modern times.

The annual reports of the Chief Superintendent and the Ministers of Education show that after good school houses had been erected, internal decoration was not uncommon. I claim, therefore, that the Education Department of this Province took the lead of all other countries in encouraging the decoration of public school walls with pictures, engravings, plaster casts, etc.

It was not until 1880 that France commenced the æsthetic culture of the pupils of common schools. In that year a commission of thirty eminent men were appointed to report on the decoration of schools, and art for schools. This commission was charged with the duty of studying the means of introducing into the system of instruction the æsthetic education of the eye. Its labours extended over a year. In the report it is said : " The special task of this commission was to devise means and ways for improving æsthetic education through the eye, not by specific direct instruction set forth in programmes, but by the operation of the environments of the school, and the artistic character of its appliances. These environments and appliances were considered by the commission mainly under four heads: 1. The æsthetic character of the school building, including its artistic ornamentation, both exterior and interior; 2. The furnishing of objects of art for the observation and study of the pupils; 3. The rewards of merit; 4. Illustrating apparatus."

Soon after this a Committee was appointed in Manchester, England, with similar functions to those of the French Commission. This was followed by the organisation of an association with the same object in view, in London, England, with Mr. Ruskin as President.

In 1883, the Committee on Drawing of the Boston School Board called attention to what had been done in this direction in Manchester and London, and suggested the advisability of organising a similar association for their schools. In this connection it remarks: "We hold with the English Committee that a love for the beautiful is perhaps only second to religion as a protection against the grosser forms of self-indulgence, and that it can best be kindled at an age when the mind is specially susceptible to the influence of habitual surroundings."

About the same time our present Premier, the Hon. Dr. Ross, then Minister of Education, introduced mural decoration in the school buildings under Government control; the walls of the Toronto and Ottawa Normal Schools were either tinted or papered, and decorated with oil paintings, reproductions of the different ancient and modern Schools of Art, and life-size busts of distinguished men of ancient and modern times, thus surrounding the teachers in training with examples of art, and studies of the great and good. The result which followed and will follow we cannot calculate, for we know that in human culture the most potential forces impressed on our minds are produced by our environments; that although these forces are imperceptible and scarcely seem to have existence, they cause an unconscious tuition, an invisible intangible influence on our minds, to which no resistance can be made because its very existence is unnoticed and unknown.

X.—Public Libraries.

a. Public Libraries (not free).

The following extracts are taken from the annual reports for the year ending 30th April, 1899 :—

1. *Classification of Public Libraries Reporting 1898–99.*

Public Libraries, with libraries, reading rooms and evening classes - - - - -	2
Public Libraries, with libraries and reading rooms - - - - - - -	128
Public Libraries, with libraries only - -	117
Total - - - - - -	247

2. *Public Libraries—Receipts and Balances on hand.*

The total receipts of Public Libraries
was - - - - - - $75,875 36
Balances on hand - - - - 5,969 83

3. *Public Libraries—Expenditure.*

The total expenditure of 247 Public
Libraries was - - - - $69,905 53

4. *Public Libraries—Assets and Liabilities.*

Assets of 247 Public Libraries - - $358,395 72
Liabilities of 247 Public Libraries - 16,021 00

5. *Number of Members in Public Libraries.*

247 Public Libraries have 32,249 members.

6. *Number of Volumes in Public Libraries and Number of Volumes Issued.*

Number of volumes in 247 Libraries - 436,124
Number of Volumes issued in 247 Libraries - - - - - - - 734,642

7. *Reading Rooms in Public Libraries.*

128 Libraries reporting have reading rooms.
128 Libraries subscribed for 2,717 newspapers and periodicals.

8. *Evening Classes in Public Libraries.*

2 Libraries had 35 pupils in the drawing courses.

*b. Evening Classes in Public Libraries, 1898-9
(from the Report for 1899).*

Public Libraries.	Number of Students.	Primary Course.
Galt - -	9	Practical Geometry.
	20	Descriptive Geometry, Machine Drawing and Advanced Perspective.
Peterboro' - -	14	Machine Drawing.
	43	

c. Certificates awarded to Public Libraries in 1899.
Primary Drawing Course.

Public Libraries.	Number of Students for Examination.	Number of Proficiency Certificates.					
		Freehand.	Geometry.	Perspective.	Model.	Blackboard.	Total Proficiency Certificates.
Galt - - - -	3	1	–	–	1	–	2
	3	1	–	–	1	–	2

d. Certificates awarded to Public Libraries in 1899.
Mechanical Drawing Course.

Public Libraries.	Number of Students for Examination.	Number of Proficiency Certificates.					
		Advanced Geometry.	Machine Drawing.	Building Construction.	Architectural Design.	Advanced Perspective.	Total Proficiency Certificates.
Galt - - - -	11	–	2	–	–	–	2
Peterboro' - - -	13	–	5	–	–	–	5
	24	–	7	–	–	–	7

e. Abstract showing Number of Public Libraries in each County and District.

Name.	No.	Name.	No.	Name.	No.	Name.	No.	Name.	No.
Addington -	6	Frontenac -	3	Lambton -	12	Northumberl'd	9	Renfrew	9
Algoma -	11	Glengarry -	3	Lanark -	8	Ontario -	12	Russell	2
Brant -	6	Grenville -	9	Leeds	4	Oxford -	12	Stormont	1
Bruce -	22	Grey -	17	Lennox -	1	Parry Sound -	6	Simcoe	15
Carleton -	8	Haliburton -	1	Lincoln -	6	Peel -	13	Victoria	12
Dufferin	10	Haldimand -	10	Manitoulin Isl'd	2	Perth -	9	Waterloo	13
Dundas	7	Halton -	5	Middlesex	12	Peterborough	3	Welland	9
Durham -	4	Hastings -	4	Muskoka -	5	Prescott -	1	Wellington -	13
Elgin -	11	Huron -	15	Nipissing -	4	Prince Edward	2	Wentworth	6
Essex -	7	Kent -	13	Norfolk -	4	Rainy River -	3	York -	21

The following Abstract *f* shows the progress of Public Libraries at intervals of five years since 1883, when only 93 libraries reported having 13,672 members, who borrowed 251,890 books; there are now (for the year ending 30th April 1899) 364 libraries reporting with 121,397 members and readers who borrowed 2,547,131 volumes.

In addition there are 42 libraries which did not report, or were incorporated after the 1st of May, 1899.

Free Libraries are rapidly increasing and are greatly appreciated. In 1883 only one Free Library had been established, but now the Superintendent's report shows that there are 120 Free Libraries, and that several others have been established since the 30th of April, 1899.

f.—Abstract showing the Progress of Public Libraries from 1883 to 1899.

Year.	Institutes reporting.	Number of members.	Number of evening classes.	Number of pupils.	Number of reading rooms.	Number of newspapers and periodicals.	Number of volumes in libraries.	Number of volumes issued.	Total receipts.	Total assets.
									$ c.	$ c.
1883 -	93	13,672	28	1,758	59	1,540	154,093	251,920	59,716 00	225,190 00
1886 -	167	52,016	41	1,102	104	3,041	311,048	744,466	103,843 68	408,573 75
1896 -	255	84,068	41	1,117	156	4,745	510,326	1,415,867	160,554 96	685,412 17
1898 -	347	111,206	2	79	200	5,834	789,062	2,858,140	118,783 21	870 167 54
1899 -	364	121,397	2	35	200	5,889	862,047	2,547,131	193,421 90	985,975 81

g. Free Libraries.

The following extracts are taken from the annual Reports for the year ending 30th April, 1899 (for details see Table C).

1. *Free Libraries' Receipts and Balances on hand.*

The total receipts of 117 Free
Libraries was   -   -   -   - $117,545 84
Balances on hand -   -   -   -   8,407 05

2. *Free Libraries' Expenditure.*

The total expenditure of 117 Free
Libraries was   -   -   -   - $109,138 79

3. *Free Libraries' Assets and Liabilities.*

Assets of 117 Free Libraries   -   - $577,580 09
Liabilities   „   -   -   113,902 49

4. *Number of Readers in Free Libraries.*

117 Free Libraries report having had 89,148 readers.

5. *Number of Volumes in Free Libraries, and Number of Volumes Issued.*

Number of Volumes in 117 Free Libraries   425,923
Number of volumes issued -   -   - 1,812,489

6. *Reading Rooms in Free Libraries.*

72 Free Libraries subscribed for 3,112 newspapers
and periodicals.

H

XI.—Reports of the Industrial Schools, 1899.

a. Victoria Industrial School.

The total attendance for the year was 47,529 days.
The total number registered for the year was 186.
69 boys were in attendance during the entire year.
55 were sent out during the year, and 62 came in.
The attendance at present is 132 boys.
The boys are employed as follows:—

Farm	- - - - 27	Printing	- - - 15
Carpenter shop	- - 17	Engine-room	- - - 7
Tailor shop	- - - 19	Conservatories	- - 9
Shoe shop	- - - 17	Cottages	- - - 22
Laundry	- - - 8	Bake-room	- - - 3
Kitchen	- - - 8	Office	- - - - 2
Dining-room	- - - 15	School all day	- - - 11
Knitting-room	- - 6		

b. Alexandra Industrial School.

The total attendance for the year was 9,177 days.
The total number registered was 36.
10 were in attendance during the entire year.
13 were sent out during the year and 13 came in.
The attendance at present is 25 girls.
The girls are taught to knit and sew, and to work in the kitchen, the laundry, and to do general household work.

XII.—Examination Requirements, 1900, 1901, 1902.

The following are the Examination Requirements for the years 1900, 1901, and 1902:—

  a. Junior Leaving Standing - - Part I.
  b. „ „ „ - - Part II.
  c. Senior Leaving Standing - - Part I.
  d. „ „ „ - - Part II.

Note.—It is expected that throughout the course, until pupils have completed what is required for Part I. of Junior Leaving Standing, at least two half-hour lessons per week shall be given regularly to Reading, and an equal time to English Literature. Regarding Drawing, Book-keeping, Botany or Agriculture, at least two half-hour lessons per week for each of these subjects are to be given regularly to pupils enrolled in Form I. of the High School or Form V. of the Public School; that is practically during the first year of the course in preparation for Part I. of Junior Leaving Standing.

a. Junior Leaving Standing, Part I.
Geography.

The building up of the earth; its land surface; the ocean; comparison of continents as to physical features, natural products and inhabitants; relations of physical conditions to animals and vegetable products, and of natural products and geographical condition to the occupations of the people and national progress. Form, size and motions of the earth; lines drawn on the map, with reasons for their position; relation of the positions of the earth with respect to the sun, to light and temperature; the air; its movements; causes affecting climate. Natural and manufactured products of the countries of the world, with their exports and imports; transcontinental commercial highways and their relation to centres of population; internal commercial highways of Canada and the chief internal commercial highways of the United States; commercial relations of Great Britain and her colonies. Forms of Governments in the countries of the world and their relation to civilisation. One examination paper.

Arithmetic and Mensuration.

Proofs of elementary rules in Arithmetic; fractions (theory and proofs); commercial Arithmetic; mental Arithmetic, Mensuration of rectilinear figures. One examination paper. (The questions will call for accuracy and will have special reference to the requirements of ordinary life.)

English Grammar.

Etymology and Syntax, including the inflection, classification, and elementary analysis of words and the logical structure of the sentence and paragraph; exercises chiefly on passages from authors not prescribed. One examination paper. (The questions will call for such an elementary knowledge of the subject as will be of special value in the ordinary use of the language.)

English Composition.

For examination purposes an essay of about two pages of foolscap on one of the themes prescribed by the examiners will be required. The penmanship, spelling, punctuation, construction of sentences, the logical arrangement of the thought, the literary accuracy and aptness of the language, and the general plan or scope of the whole essay will be specially considered by the examiners. One examination paper.

History of Great Britain and Canada.

Great Britain and Canada from 1763 to 1885, with the outlines of the preceding periods of British History.

The Geography relating to the History prescribed. One examination paper.

b. Junior Leaving Standing, Part II.

Note.—The subjects prescribed for Part II. of Senior Leaving Standing are the following (Regulations 46 amended); English

Grammar and Rhetoric, English Composition, English Literature Ancient History, Arithmetic and Mensuration, Algebra, Geometry, Physics, and Latin, and one of the following groups:—(*a*) French and Greek; (*b*) German and Greek; (*c*) French, German, and Chemistry; (*d*) French, Physics, and Chemistry; (*e*) German, Physics, and Chemistry; (*f*) Botany, Physics, and Chemistry.

A candidate, who has already obtained a certificate of having passed Part I. of Form II., will not be required to take the papers in Arithmetic and Mensuration, English Grammar and Rhetoric, and the obligatory Physics.

English.

ENGLISH GRAMMAR AND RHETORIC: Etymology and Syntax, including the inflection, classification and elementary analysis of words, and the logical structure of the sentence; rhetorical structure of the sentence and paragraph; exercises chiefly on passages from authors not prescribed; the main facts in the development of the language. One examination paper.

COMPOSITION: An essay, to which special importance will be attached, on one of several themes set by the examiners. In order to pass in this subject, legible writing, correct spelling and punctuation, and proper construction of sentences are indispensable. The candidate should also give attention to the structure of the whole essay, the effective ordering of the thought, and the accurate employment of good English vocabulary.

About two pages of foolscap is suggested as the proper length for the essay; but quality, not quantity, will be mainly regarded. One examination paper.

LITERATURE: Such questions only shall be set as may serve to test the candidate's familiarity with, and intelligent and appreciative comprehension of the prescribed texts. The candidate will be expected to have memorised some of the finest passages. In addition to the questions on the prescribed selections, others shall be set on a "sight passage" to test the candidate's ability to interpret literature for himself. One examination paper.

1900.

LONGFELLOW: Evangeline. A Psalm of Life, Wreck of the Hesperus, "The Day is Done," The Old Clock on the Stairs, The Fire of Driftwood, Resignation, The Warden of the Cinque Ports, Excelsior, The Bridge, A Gleam of Sunshine.

WORDSWORTH: The Education of Nature ("Three years she grew"), "She was a phantom of delight," A Lesson ("There is a flower, the Lesser Celandine"), To the Skylark, The Green Linnet, To the Cuckoo, To the Daisy, and the following Sonnets; To a Distant Friend ("Why art thou silent"), England and Switzerland ("Two voices are there"), "Milton, thou shouldst be living at this hour," Westminster Bridge, The Inner Vision ("Most sweet it is, with unuplifted eyes"), "O Friend! I know not which way I must look," To Sleep, Within King's College Chapel.

1901.

TENNYSON: Elaine, Lady of Shalott, St. Agnes' Eve, Sir Galahad, Lotos-Eaters, Ulysses, Crossing the Bar, Early Spring, "You ask me why," "Of old sat Freedom," "Love thou thy land," the six interlude songs and "Tears, idle tears," in "The Princess."

1902.

SCOTT: Lay of the Last Minstrel.

Ancient History.

(1) General outlines of Greek History to the Battle of Chæronea, 338 B.C.

(2) General Outlines of Roman History to the Death of Augustus, authorised text-book, omitting:—

(1) Greek History—Chaps. II., III., VI., VII., XI., XII. XXIV., XXX., XXXI.

(2) Roman History—Chaps. II., III., IV., V., XXIX.

NOTE.—It is desirable, however, that the teacher make oral use of such portions of the omitted chapters as are necessary to make clear the historical connections between important events.

One examination paper.

Mathematics.

ARITHMETIC AND MENSURATION: Proofs of elementary rules in Arithmetic: fractions (theory and proofs); commercial Arithmetic; mental Arithmetic; Mensuration of right parallelopipeds, pyramids and prisms; the circle, sphere, cylinder and cone. One examination paper.

ALGEBRA: Elementary Rules; Highest Common Measure; Lowest Common Multiple; Fractions; Square Root; Simple Equations of one, two and three unknown quantities; Indices; Surds; Quadratics of one and two unknown quantities.

One examination paper.

GEOMETRY: Euclid, Books I., II., and III.; easy Deductions. One examination paper.

Elementary Experimental Science (Physics).

Use of metre rule; use of calipers and vernier for more accurate metric measurements (*e.g.*, diameters of wires, thickness of glass, plates, etc.); numerical calculations in the metric system.

Use of balance.

Specific gravity, by specific gravity bottle and hydrostatic balance, of liquids and of solids.

Boyle's law; barometer; diffusion of gases.

Use of Fahrenheit and Centigrade thermometers; determination of zero and boiling point; boiling point dependent on pressure.

Expansion of solids, liquids and gases; examples.
Specific heat; latent heat; easy numerical examples.
Transmutation ot matter; indestructibility of matter.
Solution, precipitation, crystallisation and evaporation.
One examination paper.

Latin.

Translation into Latin of English phrases and easy sentences
to illustrate Latin accidence and the common rules of Latin
syntax.

Translation into Latin of easy narrative English based upon
the first twenty-five chapters of the prescribed Cæsar.

Translation at sight (with the aid of vocabularies) from some
easy prose author.

Translation from prescribed texts, with grammatical and other
questions naturally arising from the extracts set for translation.

The following are the texts prescribed :—

1900 : VERGIL, Aeneid, Book II.; CÆSAR, Bellum Gallicum,
Book V.

1901 : VERGIL, Aeneid, Book II.; CÆSAR, Bellum Gallicum,
Books II., III.

1902 : CORNELIUS NEPOS, Lives of Themistocles, Aristides and
Hannibal; CÆSAR, Bellum Gallicum, Book IV. (omitting Chap.
17) and Book V., Chaps. 1-23 ; VERGIL, Aeneid, Book II. (1-505).

Two papers will be set : (1) Translation of English into Latin.
(2) Prescribed texts and translation at sight, with questions on
Grammar, etc.

N.B.—The Roman method of pronouncing Latin is recommended.

French.

The candidates knowledge of French will be tested by (1)
simple questions on grammar, (2) the translation of simple
passages from English into French, (3) translation at sight of
easy passages from modern French, and (4) examinations on the
following texts :—

1900 : ENAULT, le Chien du capitaine; FEUILLET, la Fée.

1901 : DE MAISTRE, Voyage autour de ma chambre ; LABICHE,
la Grammaire.

1900 : LAMENNAIS, Paroles d'un croyant, Chaps. VII. and
XVII ; PERRAULT, le Maître Chat ou le Chat Botté ; DUMAS, Un
nez gelé, and la Pipe de Jean Bart ; ALPHONSE DAUDET, la
Dernière Classe, and la Chèvre de M. Seguin ; LEGOUVÉ, la Patte
de Dindon; POUVILLON, Hortibus, LOTI, Chagrin d'un vieux
forçat ; MOLIÈRE, l'Avare, Acte III., sc. 5 (Est-ce à votre cocher.
.   .   . sous la mienne). VICTOR HUGO, Waterloo, Chap. IX. ;
ROUGET DE L'ISLE, la Marseillaise ; ARNAULT, la Feuille ;
CHATEAUBRIAND, l'Exilé; THÉOPHILE GAUTIER, la Chimère ;
VICTOR HUGO, Extase ; LAMARTINE, l'Automne ; DE MUSSET,
Tristesse ; SULLY PRUDHOMME, le Vase brisé ; LA FONTAINE, le
Chêne et le Roseau.

MADAME EMILE DE GIRARDIN, la Joie fait peur.

Two papers will be set: (1) prescribed texts and translation at sight; questions on Grammar; (2) the translation of English into French.

Greek.

Translation into English of passages from prescribed texts.

Translation at sight (with the aid of vocabularies) of easy Attic prose, to which special importance will be attached.

Grammatical questions on the passages from prescribed texts will be set, and such other questions as arise naturally from the context.

Translation from English into Greek of sentences and of easy narrative passages based upon the prescribed prose texts.

The following are the prescribed texts:

1900: Selections from XENOPHON, Anabasis I., in White's Beginner's Greek Book (pp. 304-428) with the exercises thereon; HOMER, Iliad I.

1901: Selections from XENOPHON, Anabasis I., in White's Beginner's Greek Book (pp. 304-428) with the exercises thereon; HOMER, Iliad I.

1902: Selections from XENOPHON, Anabasis I., in White's Beginner's Greek Book (pp. 304-428) with the exercises thereon; HOMER, Iliad VI.

Two papers will be set: (1) prescribed texts and translation at sight; questions on Grammar; (2) the translation of English into Greek.

German.

The candidate's knowledge of German will be tested by: (1) simple questions on grammar, (2) the translation of simple passages from English into German, (3) translation at sight of easy passages from modern German, and (4) an examination on the following texts:—

1900: HAUFF, das kalte Herz, Kalif Storch.

1901: LEANDER, Träumereien (selected by Van Daell).

1902: GRIMM, Rotkäppchen; ANDERSEN, Wie's der Alte Macht, Das neue Kleid, Venedig, Rothschild, Der Bär; ERTL, Himmelsschlüssel; FROMMEL, Das eiserne Kreuz; BAUMBACH, Nicotiana, Der Goldbaum; HEINE, Lorelei. Du bist wie eine Blume; UHLAND, Schäfer's Sonntagslied. Das Schloss am Meer; CHAMISSO, Das Schloss Boncourt; CLAUDIUS, Die Sterne, Der Riese Goliath; GOETHE, Mignon, Erlkönig, Der Sänger; SCHILLER, Der Jüngling am Bache.

LEANDER, Träumereien (selected by Van Daell), pp. 1-44.

Two papers will be set: (1) Prescribed texts and translation at sight; questions on Grammar; (2) translation of English into German.

Elementary, Experimental Science (Chemistry).

Properties of Hydrogen, Chlorine, Oxygen, Sulphur, Nitrogen, Carbon and their more important compounds. Nomenclature,

Laws of combination of the elements. The Atomic Theory and Molecular Theory.

One examination paper.

Botany.

The practical study of representatives of the flowering plants of the locality and representatives of the chief subdivisions of cryptogams, such as a fern, a lycopod, a horsetail, a liverwort, a moss, a lichen, a mushroom, and a chara. The drawing and description of parts of plants and classification. Comparison of different organs, morphology of root, stem, leaves, and hair, parts of the flower, reproduction of flowering plants, pollination, fertilisation and the nature of fruit and seeds. At the examination two plants to be selected by the presiding examiner will be submitted, one for classification and one for description. In classification, candidates will be allowed to use their floras (the authorised text-book in Botany).

One examination paper.

Physics (of Optional Group).

ELECTRICITY.—Voltaic cells, common kinds; chemical action in the cell; magnetic effects of the current; chemical effects of the current; voltameter; astatic and tangent galvanometers; simple notions of potential; Ohm's law, with units; best arrangement of cells; electric light, arc and incandescent; magnetism; inclination and declination of compass; current induction; induction coil; dynamo and motor; electric bell; telegraph; telephone; electro-plating. SOUND. — Caused by vibrations; illustration of vibrations, pendulums, rods, strings, membranes, plates, columns of air; propagated by waves; its velocity; determination of velocity; pitch; standard forks, acoustical C = 512, musical A = 870; intervals; harmonic scale; diatonic scale; equally tempered scale; vibration of air in open and closed tubes, with wave-lengths; resonators; nodes and loops; vibration of strings and wires; reflection of sound; manometric flames. LIGHT. — Rectilinear propagation; image through a pin-hole; beam; pencil; photometry; shadow and grease spot photometers; reflection and scattering of light; laws of reflection; images in plain mirrors; multiple images in inclined mirrors; concave and convex mirrors; drawing image's refraction; laws and index of refraction; total reflection; path through a prism; lenses; drawing image produced by a lens; simple microscope; dispersion and colour; spectrum; recomposition of white light.

c. Senior Leaving Standing, Part I.

Note.—In order to obtain Senior Leaving Standing, a candidate must pass the examination of Part I. of Junior Leaving Standing, and in addition the subjects herein prescribed for Parts I. and II. of Senior Leaving Standing, which may be taken at one examination or at different examinations.

Unsuccessful candidates at any previous Senior Leaving Examination will be allowed to write in 1900 for Senior Leaving Standing by selecting the same options in the course as they were allowed to take in 1899.

The subjects of Part I. of Senior Leaving Standing are the following:—English Composition, English Literature, Algebra, Geometry, Trigonometry, English and Ancient History.

English.

COMPOSITION: An essay, to which special importance will be attached, on one of several themes set by the examiner.
One examination paper.

LITERATURE: The candidate will be expected to have memorised some of the finest passages. Besides questions to est the candidate's familiarity with, and comprehension of, the following selections, questions may also be set to determine within reasonable limits his power of appreciating literary art.

RHETORIC: Reading of prose authors in connection with the study of rhetoric.
One examination paper.

1900.

LONGFELLOW: Evangeline, A Psalm of Life, Wreck of the Hesperus, "The day is done," The Old Clock on the Stairs, The fire of driftwood, Resignation, The Warden of the Cinque Ports, Excelsior, The Bridge, A Gleam of Sunshine.

SHAKESPEARE: Macbeth.

MILTON: L'Allegro, Il Penseroso, Lycidas, On the Morning of Christ's Nativity.

WORDSWORTH: (Palgrave's Golden Treasury of Songs and Lyrics) The Education of Nature ("Three years she grew"), "She was a Phantom of Delight," A Lesson ("There is a flower, the Lesser Celandine"), To the Skylark, The Green Linnet, To the Cuckoo, To the Daisy, and the following Sonnets: To a Distant Friend ("Why art thou silent"), England and Switzerland ("Two voices are there"), "Milton, thou shouldst be living till this hour," Westminster Bridge, The Inner Vision ("Most sweet it is with unuplifted eyes"), "O Friend! I know not which way I must look," To Sleep, Within King's College Chapel.

1901.

TENNYSON: Elaine, Lady of Shalott, St. Agnes' Eve, Sir Galahad, Lotos-Eaters, Ulysses, Crossing the Bar, Early Spring, "You ask me why," "Of old sat Freedom," "Love thou thy land," the six interlude songs and "Tears, idle tears," in "The Princess."

MILTON: Paradise Lost, Book VII.

SHAKESPEARE: Julius Cæsar.

1902.

SCOTT: Lay of the Last Minstrel.
MILTON: Paradise Lost, Book I.
SHAKESPEARE: The Merchant of Venice.

Mathematics.

ALGEBRA: Elementary Rules; Highest Common Measure; Lowest Common Multiple; Fractions; Square Root; Simple Equations of one, two, and three unknown quantities; Indices; Surds; Quadratics of one and two unknown quantities; Theory of Divisors, Ratio, Proportion, and Variation; Progressions; Notation; Permutations and Combinations; Binomial Theorem; Interest Forms; Annuities.
One examination paper.

GEOMETRY: Euclid, Books I., II., III., IV., and V.; Definitions of Book V.; Deductions.
One examination paper.

TRIGONOMETRY: Trigonometrical ratios with their relations to each other; Sines, etc., of the sum and difference of angles with deduced formulas; Use of Logarithms; Solution of Triangles; Expressions for the area of Triangles; Radii of circumscribed, inscribed, and escribed circles.
One examination paper.

History.

English History from the discovery of America to 1763.
General outlines of Greek History to the battle of Chæronea, 338 B.C. Special attention to be paid to the following: General characteristics of Greece and the Greeks; ancient institutions; constitution of Athens and Sparta; Persian wars; growth of the Athenian Empire; characteristics of the age of Pericles; Peloponnesian wars; rise of Thebes; Theban Supremacy; rise of Macedon; downfall of Greece.
General outlines of Roman History to the death of Augustus. Special attention to be given to the following: General characteristics of Italy and the Roman People; struggle of the Plebeians for political and social equality; conquest of Italy; Punic wars; how Rome governed and was governed; internal and external history of Rome from the downfall of Carthage to the death of Augustus.
The Geography relating to the History prescribed.
One examination paper.

d. Senior Leaving Standing, Part II.

Note.—The subjects of Part II. of Senior Leaving Standing are the following:—Physics, Latin, and one of the following groups: (a) French and Greek, (b) German and Greek, (c) French and German, (d) French and Chemistry, (e) German and Chemistry (f) Biology and Chemistry.

Physics.

MECHANICS: Measurement of velocity; uniformly accelerated rectilineal motion; metric units of force, work, energy and power; equilibrium of forces acting at a point; triangle, parallelogram, and polygon of forces; parallel forces; principle of moments; centre of gravity; laws of friction; numerical examples.

HYDROSTATICS: Fluid pressure at a point; pressure on a horizontal plane; pressure on an inclined plane; resultant vertical pressure, and resultant horizontal pressure, when fluid is under air pressure and when not; transmission of pressure; Bramah's press; equilibrium of liquids of unequal density in a bent tube; the barometer; air-pump; water-pump, common and force; siphon.

ELECTRICITY: Voltaic cells, common kinds; chemical action in the cell; magnetic effects of the current; chemical effects of the current; volta-meters; electro-plating; astatic and tangent galvanometers; simple notions of potential; Ohm's law; shunts; measurement of resistance; electric light, arc and incandescent; current induction; induction coil; dynamo and motor; the joule and watt; electric bell; telegraph; telephone; elements of terrestrial magnetism.

One examination paper.

Latin.

Translation into English of passages from prescribed texts.

Translation at sight of passages of average difficulty, similar in style to the authors read.

Grammatical questions on the passages from prescribed texts will be set, and such other questions as arise naturally from the context.

Translation into Latin of easy passages of English, similar in style to the authors read.

The following are the prescribed texts:—

1900: CAESAR, Bellum Gallicum, Bk. V.; VERGIL, Aeneid, Bk. II.; HORACE, Odes, III., IV.; LIVY XXI.

1901: CAESAR, Bellum Gallicum, Bks. II., III.; VERGIL, Aeneid, Bk. II.; HORACE, Odes, I., II.; LIVY XXI.

1902: CAESAR, Bellum Gallicum, Bk. IV., omitting Chap. 17, and Bk. V., Chaps. 1–23; VERGIL, Aeneid II., lines 1–505; HORACE, Odes I., II.; CICERO, Pro Lege Manilia, Pro Marcello, Philippic XIV.

Two examination papers.

French.

The prescription of work in grammar, the translation of English into French and sight translation is the same for Senior Leaving Standing as for Junior Leaving Standing, but the examination will be of a more advanced character.

The following are the prescribed texts:—

1900: ENAULT: le Chien du capitaine; FEUILLET, la Fée, le

Roman d'un jeune Homme pauvre; LABICHE, Voyage de M. Perrichon.

1901: DE MAISTRE, Voyage autour de ma chambre; LABICHE, la Grammaire; ERCKMANN-CHATRIAN, Madame Thérèse; LABICHE, le Poudre aux yeux

1902: LAMENNAIS, Paroles d'un croyant, Chaps. VII. and XVII.; PERRAULT, le Maître Chat ou le Chat Botté; DUMAS, Un nez gelé and la Pipe de Jean Bart; ALPHONSE DAUDET, la Dernière Classe and la Chèvre de M. Seguin; LEGOUVÉ, la Patte de Dindon; POUVILLON, Hortibus; LOTI, Chagrin d'un vieux forcat; MOLIÈRE, L'Avare, Acte III., sc. 5 (Est-ce à votre cocher . . . . . sous la mienne); VICTOR HUGO, Waterloo, Chap. IX.; ROUGET DE L'ISLE, la Marseillaise; ARNAULT, la Feuille; CHATEAUBRIAND, l'Exilé; THÉOPHILE GAUTIER, la Chimère; VICTOR HUGO, Extase; LAMARTINE, l'Automne; DE MUSSET, Tristesse; SULLY PRUDHOMME, le Vase brisé: LA FONTAINE, le Chêne et le Roseau.

MADAME EMILE DE GIRARDIN, la Joie fait peur.

MÉRIMÉE, Colomba.

Two examination papers.

· *Greek.*

Translation into English of passages from prescribed texts.

Translation at sight of passages of average difficulty, similar to the authors read.

Grammatical questions on the passages from prescribed texts will be set, and such other questions as arise naturally from the context.

Translation into Greek of ordinary narrative passages of English, similar to the authors read.

The following are the prescribed texts:—

1900: XENOPHON, Anabasis, I. (Chaps. I.–VIII.); HOMER, Iliad, I., Odyssey XV.; LYSIAS, Contra Eratosthenem, and Epitaphius.

1901: XENOPHON, Anabasis I. (Chaps. I.-VIII.); HOMER, Iliad I., Odyssey XV.; LUCIAN, Charon, Vera Historia II.

1892: XENOPHON, Anabasis I. (Chaps. I.-VIII.); HOMER, Iliad VI.; Odyssey XVII.: LUCIAN, Charon, Vera Historia II.

Two examination papers.

German.

The prescription of work in grammar, the translation of English into German and sight translation is the same for Senior Leaving Standing as for Junior Leaving Standing, but the examination will be of a more advanced character.

The following are the prescribed texts:—

1900: HAUFF, das kalte Herz, Kalif Storch; EICHENDORFF, Aus dem Leben eines Taugenichts; WILHELMI, Einer muss heiraten; BENEDIX, Eigensinn.

1901: LEANDER, Träumereien (selected by Van Daell);

BAUMBACH, der Schwiegersohn; GERSTÄCKER, Germelshausen; ELZ, Er ist nicht eifersüchtig; WICHERT, Post Festum.

1902: GRIMM, Rotkäppchen; ANDERSEN, Wie's der Alte Macht, Das neue Kleid, Venedig, Rothschild, Der Bär; ERTL, Himmelsschlüssel; FROMMEL, Das eiserne Kreuz; BAUMBACH, Nicotiana, Der Goldbaum; HEINE, Lorelei, Du bist wie eine Blume; UHLAND, Schäfer's Sonntagslied, Das Schloss am Meer; CHAMISSO, Das Schloss Boncourt; CLAUDIUS, Die Sterne, Der Riese Goliath; GOETHE, Mignon, Erlkönig, Der Sänger; SCHILLER, Der Jüngling am Bache.

LEANDER, Träumereien (selected by Van Daell), pp. 1-44.

EBNER-ESCHENBACH, Die Frieherren von Gemperlein; WILHELMI Einer muss heiraten.

BENEDIX, Eigensinn.

Two examination papers.

Chemistry.

Chemical Theory. The study of the following elements, with their most characteristic compounds, in illustration of Mendelejeff's Classification of the Elements: Hydrogen; Sodium, Potassium; Magnesium, Zinc; Calcium, Strontium, Barium; Boron, Aluminium; Carbon, Silicon, Tin, Lead; Nitrogen, Phosphorus, Arsenic, Antimony, Bismuth; Oxygen, Sulphur; Fluorine, Chlorine, Bromine, Iodine; Manganese, Iron. Elementary Qualitative Analysis.

A practical examination shall be held in connection with the subject, a pure salt will be sent out for qualitative analysis, and the candidate shall be allowed the use of an analytical table. One examination paper.

Biology.

1. *Elements of Zoology:* Thorough examination of the external form, the gills, and the viscera of some common fish. Study of the prepared skeleton of the same. Demonstration of the arrangement of the muscular and nervous systems and the sense-organs, as far as these can be studied without the aid of the microscope.

Comparison of the structure of the frog with that of the fish. The skeleton of the pectoral and pelvic girdles and of the appendages of the frog should be studied, and the chief facts in the development of its spawn till the adult form is attained should be observed.

Examination of the external form of a turtle and a snake.

Examination of the structure of a bird.

Study of the skeleton and also of the teeth of a cat or dog.

Study of the crayfish as a type of the Arthropods.

Comparison of the crayfish with an insect (grasshopper, cricket, or cockroach); also with a millipede and a spider.

Examination of an earthworm.

Study of a fresh-water mussel.

The principles of zoological nomenclature as illustrated by some of the common fresh-water fish, such as the sucker and the herring, bass and perch.

Study of an amœba, or paramœcium as a type of a unicellular animal.

The modifications of the form of the body in vertebrates in connection with different methods of locomotion. The natural habits of the various animals examined.

2. *Elements of Botany :* The examination will test whether the candidate has practically studied representatives of the flowering plants of the locality in which the preparatory school is situated, and representatives of the chief subdivisions of cryptogams, such as a fern, a lycopod, a horsetail, a liverwort, a moss, a lichen, a mushroom, and a chara.

An elementary knowledge of the microscopic structure of the bean and the maize. Attention will be given in the examination to drawing and description of parts of plants supplied, and to their classification. Comparison of different organs, morphology of root, stem, leaves and hair, parts of the flower, reproduction of flowering plants, pollination, fertilisation, and the nature of fruit and seeds.

A practical examination shall be held in connection with this subject. The material for examination will consist of two plants, a microscopic section and an animal.

Two examination papers.

e. Question Papers.

The papers in Part I. for Junior Leaving Standing will be different from those set for Matriculation. The Examiners will be expected, moreover, to set papers for the purposes of candidates who desire to become teachers, but it is not intended that the questions shall be more difficult than the Regulations have called for since 1896. The papers in Arithmetic and Mensuration and Grammar and Rhetoric, as hereinbefore mentioned, shall be submitted to candidates, when writing on Part II. of the Junior Leaving Course, in addition to the papers in these subjects taken by candidates when writing on Part I. For the optional groups, the examinations will be equal in difficulty, as near as may be, in order that candidates who begin the optional subjects at the same time during their High School course may have equal advantages in preparing for the examinations.

f. Percentages.

Each question paper will hereafter be valued at 100 (Regulation 43). Candidates for Junior and Senior Leaving Standing will be required to make 50 per cent. of the aggregate marks prescribed for each of the parts into which the examinations are divided, as well as $33\frac{1}{3}$ per cent. on each paper. Seventy-five per cent. of the aggregate will be required for Honours. If, after all the answer papers are read, any question paper should be found, by the Board of Examiners, easier or more difficult than intended, the minimum on the paper shall be correspondingly raised or lowered, and the total number of marks correspondingly raised or diminished. Each candidate who makes the required aggregate may be awarded a certificate, even though he should fail to obtain the minimum in a subject, provided he was regarded as fit to pass in that subject by the staff, as shown from the confidential report sent to the Department before the examinations.

g. Commercial Diploma.

The course for a Commercial Diploma will, as heretofore, consist of two parts (I. and II.). Part I. will be the same as Part I. of Junior Leaving. Part II. will embrace the Commercial subjects mentioned in Regulation 50, viz.:—Book-keeping and Writing; Commercial Transactions; Business forms and usages; Stenography (Theory); Stenography (Dictation). Book-keeping shall be taken up in six sets as follows :—

Set I. shall show transactions extending over a period of two months ; the transactions of the first month being done by Single Entry, and of the second by Double Entry, and showing the change from Single to Double Entry. Books to be used : Day Book (1st month), Journal Day Book (2nd month), Cash Book, Bill Book and Ledger.

Set II. The transactions shall be the same as for Set I., those of the first month being done by Double Entry, and of the second month by Single Entry, and showing the change from Double Entry to Single Entry. Books to be used : Four Column Journal with special columns for Mdse. Purchases and Sales (1st month), Day Book (2nd month), Cash Book, Bill Book and Ledger.

Set III. A Double Entry set with two partners. Books to be used : Journal Day Book with a special column for Mdse. Sales, Cash Book, Invoice Book, Bill Book, and Ledger, the first three as books of original entry.

Set IV. A Double Entry set; a continuation of Set III., the posting being done in the same ledger. A third partner shall be admitted and the transactions shall include shipments and consignments. Books to be used : Journal Day Book, Cash Book, Invoice Book, Sales Book, Bill Book, and Ledger, the first four as books of original entry.

Set V. A Double Entry set: a continuation of Set IV., the posting being done in a new ledger. A fourth partner shall be admitted, and the transactions shall include wholesale merchandising, shipment companies, and merchandise companies. Books to be used : The same as for Set IV.

Set VI. A set in Manufacturing. Books to be used : Journal . Day Book, with a special column for Mdse. Sales, Cash Book, Time Book, and Ledger.

The Cash Book shall be a book of original entry in all of the Double Entry sets, various special columns being used in the different sets. A monthly Trial Balance shall be used in connection with Sets III., IV., and V., and Statements of Resources and Liabilities, and of Losses and Gains for all of the sets. The transactions in the different sets shall be different from year to year. The sets may recur triennially, and shall consist of not less than twenty pages of foolscap.

The book-keeping sets of pupils who write at the examination for a Commercial Diploma shall be examined by the teacher and a report sent to to the Education Department.

Business Forms and Usages.—Negotiable paper; promissory notes; special notes; bills of exchange; acceptance; negotiation of bills, notes; cheques; collection of accounts; discharge and dishonour; special forms of due bills and orders; accounts, invoices and statements; interest; partnerships; receipts and releases; banking; and commercial correspondence.

Stenography.—At the examination in dictation in stenography, the candidate shall be required to have attained the rate of fifty words per minute. He shall also be required to transcribe his work into longhand at the rate of twelve words per minute. The dictated matter shall consist of business letters and legal documents.

Four examination papers, each valued at 100.

PART III.—STATISTICAL TABLES FOR THE YEAR 1898.

The following statistical tables are taken from the Report of the Minister of Education for 1899:—

TABLE 1.—PUBLIC SCHOOLS.

	Reading						Number of pupils in the different branches of instruction, 1898.															
	1st Reader Part I.	1st Reader Part II.	2nd Reader.	3rd Reader.	4th Reader.	5th Reader.	Writing.	Arithmetic.	Drawing.	Geography.	Music.	Grammar and Composition.	English History.	Canadian History.	Physiology and Temperance.	Drill and Calisthenics.	Book-keeping.	Algebra.	Geometry.	Botany.	Elementary Physics.	Agriculture.
1. Counties, etc.	69,248	46,728	57,880	61,598	57,031	14,879	294,762	298,066	228,063	210,084	120,149	191,842	81,013	110,657	123,096	128,798	15,994	13,758	13,418	1,925	2,305	1,204
2. Cities	14,455	9,000	18,098	15,380	13,096	2,999	67,253	67,965	67,062	58,787	60,727	54,391	13,119	21,453	47,225	65,531	5,026	2,841	2,841	3,139	779	—
3. Towns	14,802	9,435	11,809	12,405	11,056	1,301	60,972	61,296	59,503	45,880	39,172	43,836	14,438	23,013	31,501	37,849	2,109	1,386	1,308	122	432	40
4. Grand Total, 1898	98,565	65,163	82,707	89,300	81,753	19,179	422,987	425,207	410,468	314,181	220,048	289,499	108,566	155,123	201,812	231,973	23,129	17,985	17,567	4,486	3,416	1,244
5. Grand Total, 1897	100,075	65,482	83,423	90,942	81,823	19,412	425,301	431,704	411,982	314,718	208,078	290,716	107,570	154,498	197,216	241,482	23,668	17,984	17,166	5,161	4,100	2,189
6. Increase											11,970		996		4,596			1	401			
7. Decrease	1,510	319	716	1,582	70	233	2,814	3,497	1,514	537		1,217		1,370		9,509	589			675	684	945
8. Percentage	33	15	19	59	19	4	97	98	94	72	51	06	35	36	46	53	5	4	4	1	1	4

I

Part III.—Statistical Tables for the year 1896.—continued.

TABLE 2.—PUBLIC SCHOOLS.

School population.—Pupils attending the Public Schools, 1896.

	School population by trustees, between 5 and 21 years of age.	Pupils under 5 years of age.	Pupils between 5 and 21 years of age.	Pupils over 21 years of age.	Total number of pupils of all ages attending school.	Boys.	Girls.	Attending less than 20 days during the year.	20 to 50 days.	51 to 100 days.	101 to 150 days.	151 to 200 days.	201 days to the whole year.	No. of children 8 to 14 (inc.) who did not attend any school during the year.	No. of children 8 to 14 (inc.) who did not attend any school for 100 days during the year.	Average attendance of pupils.	Percentage of average to local attendance.
1 Counties, etc.	302,6xx	1,774	300,846	192	307,362	161,518	145,784	27,191	44,353	65,080	72,123	87,423	10,824	2,238	57,775	157,196	52
2 Cities	121,912	2	67,362	3	67,967	34,611	33,846	1,908	4,453	10,251	11,978	39,237	10	42	3,301	50,280	74
3 Towns	50,717	21	61,450	18	61,406	31,232	30,594	2,875	4,972	10,409	13,112	30,149	151	286	5,394	40,305	66
4 Grand total, 1896	1,091,950	1,307	436,227	208	436,727	227,361	209,366	31,864	53,778	86,370	97,212	156,809	10,985	2,565	67,070	247,750	57
5 Grand total, 1897	1,091,855	1,259	489,642	246	441,167	230,335	210,822	32,446	54,725	90,147	97,884	157,836	8,180	2,243	68,791	248,548	56
6 Increase	1,846	28	4,415	48	4,430	2,974	1,456	582	947	3,765	—	1,026	2,505	322	1,721	798	1
7 Decrease	—	31	—	5	—	—	—	7	12	21	32	37	2	—	—	—	—
8 Percentage	—	30	99.09	—	—	52	48	—	—	—	—	—	—	—	—	—	—

Part III.—Statistical Tables for the year 1898—continued.

TABLE 3.—PUBLIC SCHOOLS

Public School Teachers, 1898.

	Total number.			Average Salaries.			Attended a Normal School.	Certificates.							
	Public School teachers.	Male.	Female.	Highest Salary Paid.	Average Salary, male teacher.	Average Salary, female teacher.	Number of teachers who have attended a Normal School.	Total number of certificates.	Provincial 1st class.	Provincial 2nd class.	1st class old County Board.	2nd class old County Board.	3rd class.	Temporary certificates.	Other certificates.
				$	$	$									
1. Counties, etc.	6,082	2,322	3,760	900	346	250	1,751	6,082	163	1,763	17	13	4,080	46	—
2. Cities	1,372	150	1,222	1,500	888	448	1,106	1,372	171	948	14	7	61	—	171
3. Towns	1,011	184	827	1,150	695	291	729	1,011	98	949	13	4	192	5	—
4. Grand Total 1898	8,465	2,656	5,809	1,500	396	293	3,586	8,465	432	3,410	44	24	4,333	51	171
5. " 1897	8,376	2,090	5,086	1,500	391	294	3,470	8,376	387	3,396	53	32	4,345	56	216
6. Increase	89	—	125	—	5	—	106	89	96	74	—	—	—	4	47
7. Decrease	—	34	—	—	—	1	—	—	—	—	9	8	12	—	—
8. Percentage	—	31	69	—	—	—	43	—	4	41	4	1	52	2	8

Part III.—Statistical Tables for the year 1898—continued.

TABLE 4.—PUBLIC SCHOOLS.

RECEIPTS AND EXPENDITURE.

	Legislative Grants.	Municipal Grants and Assessments.	Clergy Reserve Fund, Balance and other Sources.	Total Receipts for all Public School Purposes.	Teachers' Salaries.	Sites and Building School Houses.	Maps, Apparatus, Prizes, and Libraries.	Rent and Repairs, Fuel and other Expenses.	Total Expenditure for all Public School Purposes.	Balances.
	$ c.	$ c.	$ c.	$ c.	$ c.	$ c.	$ c.	$ c.	$ c.	$ c.
1. Counties, etc.	245,266 73	1,389,762 01	931,573 42	3,066,604 91	1,723,387 24	183,770 12	40,276 35	416,300 74	2,363,734 45	702,880 76
2. Cities	53,191 00	958,250 82	158,022 46	1,169,473 28	646,534 11	204,738 28	12,671 10	295,175 17	1,129,118 66	40,354 62
3. Towns	43,011 00	457,359 91	94,511 38	594,182 27	377,238 63	37,918 57	4,752 33	130,476 25	550,380 78	43,801 49
4. Grand Total, 1898	340,470 73	3,305,381 74	1,184,407 24	4,830,250 76	2,747,159 98	426,421 97	57,690 78	811,952 16	4,043,233 89	787,025 87
5. Grand Total, 1897	339,863 30	3,138,943 99	1,176,025 72	4,652,831 01	2,717,261 09	350,456 70	54,798 27	790,986 42	3,912,601 48	739,359 53
6. Increase	607 43	168,437 75	8,383 52	177,423 75	29,898 89	75,965 27	2,901 51	20,966 74	129,732 41	47,666 34
7. Decrease	—	—	—	—	—	—	—	—	—	—
8. Percentage	7	63	25	—	63	11	1	30	—	—
Cost per Pupil.										
1. Counties, etc.	7 60									
2. Cities	16 61									
3. Towns	8 96									
4. Province	9 26									

Part III.—Statistical Tables for the year 1898—continued.

TABLE 5.—HIGH SCHOOLS, 1898.

a. RECEIPTS AND EXPENDITURE.

	Legislative grants.	Municipal grants (county).	Municipal grants (local).	Fees.	Balances and other sources.	Total receipts.	Teachers' salaries.	Building, rent and repairs.	Maps, apparatus, prizes and libraries.	Fuel, books and contingencies.	Total expenditure.	Balances.	Charges per year.
1. Total, 1898	$83,279 41	87,660 35	116,870 28	37,897 86	60,289 08	390,966 98	242,664 98	22,644 17	3,519 52	49,982 06	323,750 66	32,216 28	43 free. 51 fee. 38 free. 60 fee.
2. " 1897	$55,653 84	89,209 75	117,167 04	40,287 04	69,479 79	372,796 46	244,067 00	23,249 41	5,708 65	61,124 45	339,144 51	33,651 96	9 free. 9 fee.
3. Increase	$1,626 57												
4. Decrease		$1,549 40	296 76	2,389 18	9,220 76	11,829 53	1,412 07	5,605 24	2,184 13	1,182 39	10,898 88	1,436 70	
5. Percentage	17	24	32	10	17		78	7	1	10			

Cost per pupil, $25.56.

b. MISCELLANEOUS INFORMATION.

	Brick, stone or frame school house.	Size of playground.	Schools under United Board.	Value of library.	Value of scientific apparatus.	Value of charts, maps and globes.	Gymnasium.	Value of gymnasium and appliances.	Museum.	Estimated value of museum.	Schools using authorised Scripture reading.	Schools opened and closed with prayer.	Schools using Bible.	Religious instruction imparted.	Commencement exercises.	No. of pupils in Form I.	Form II.	Form III.	Form IV.	No. of pupils from municipalities composing the High School district.	From other municipalities within the county.	From other counties.	Who entered mercantile life.	Who became occupied with agriculture.	Who joined a learned profession.	Who became teachers.	Who left for other occupations.	Commercial.	Agricultural.	Mechanical.	Professional.
1. Total, 1898	B 8 F 30 9 82	198	1	28,076	35,526	5,718	7	5,076	16	680	87	91	29	22	80	4,498	3,889	2,810	523	6,610	4,241	839	601	654	257	762	1,008	2,620	6,268	2,853	964
2. " 1897	30 9 92	185	1	20,612	34,578	5,545	10	6,731	15	706	40	90	31	32	66	4,853	3,974	2,856	499	6,685	4,696	861	588	650	165	808	1,070	2,542	5,655	2,969	1,016
3. Increase	2	1		364	1,548	173		655	1	115	3	1			6				24	16	445		77	4	72		110	21	93	116	62
4. Decrease			42				3		1	18	40	99	2			385	85	46	5	57	36	31				308			292	24	9
5. Percentage	87 10 3						8		18						105	33	33	24	5										40		

Part III.—*Statistical Tables for the year 1898—continued.*

TABLE 6.—COLLEGIATE INSTITUTES, 1898.

a. RECEIPTS AND EXPENDITURE.

	Legislative grants.	Municipal grants (County).	Municipal grants (local).	Fees.	Balances and other sources.	Total receipts.	Teachers' salaries.	Building, rent and repairs.	Maps, apparatus, prizes and libraries.	Fuel, books and contingencies.	Total expenditure.	Balances.	Charges per year.
1. Total, 1898	$41,923 59	46,606 86	315,210 77	65,687 31	49,164 60	418,483 68	289,231 94	29,621 85	3,859 01	77,876 83	400,358 33	18,225 30	9 Free. 28 Fee.
2. " 1897	$44,597 16	43,518 83	301,519 03	70,572 35	34,488 24	394,800 61	288,700 78	18,377 83	3,870 82	65,618 81	370,881 89	17,868 72	10 Free. 27 Fee.
3. Increase	—	$2,078 08	13,691 74	—	14,681 36	23,708 02	462 21	11,264 32	—	11,761 72	23,436 44	396 58	1 Fee.
4. Decrease	$2,673 57	—	—	3,984 54	—	—	—	—	41 81	—	—	—	1 Free.
5. Percentage	10	11	51	16	12	—	72	7	1	20	—	—	—

Cost per pupil, $34.54.

b. MISCELLANEOUS INFORMATION.

	Brick, stone or frame school house.	Size of playground.	Schools under United Board.	Value of library.	Value of scientific apparatus.	Value of charts, maps, and globes.	Gymnasium.	Value of Gymnasium and appliances.	Museum.	Estimated value of museum.	Schools using authorized Scripture readings.	Schools opened and closed with prayer.	Schools using Bible.	Religious instruction imparted.	Commencement exercises.	No. of pupils in— Form I.	Form II.	Form III.	Form IV.	No. of pupils from municipalities composing the High School district.	From other municipalities within the county.	From other counties.	Who entered mercantile life.	Who became occupied with agriculture.	Who joined a learned profession.	Who became teachers.	Who left for other occupations.	Occupation of parents. Commercial.	Agricultural.	Mechanical.	Professional.
1. Total, 1898	B. S. 33 4	acres 96	15	29,686	36,170	5,168	34	55,856	19	2,452	23	26	12	1	30	4,899	3,212	2,490	1,010	8,270	2,862	470	825	896	295	674	992	3,814	3,361	3,013	1,488
2. " 1897	33 4	99½	16	28,406	35,736	5,080	34	55,578	15	1,663	22	26	11	1	31	5,253	3,288	2,507	1,180	8,452	3,062	494	770	488	244	995	1,065	4,195	3,283	3,353	1,494
3. Increase	—	—	—	1,280	434	118	—	217	4	769	1	—	1	—	—	—	76	17	130	71	—	—	46	87	19	312	78	312	115	—	61
4. Decrease	—	3½	1	—	—	—	—	—	—	—	—	—	—	—	1	854	—	21	—	—	282	25	115	—	—	—	—	—	—	280	18
5. Percentage	59 11	—	41	—	—	—	90	—	61	—	02	100	33	—	82	462	28	21	9	71	25	4	—	—	—	—	73	83	99	25	—

Part III.—*Statistical Tables for the year 1898—continued.*

TABLE 7.—COLLEGIATE INSTITUTES, 1898.

	Examinations, etc.												Number of pupils in the different branches of Instruction.												
	No. passed the Preliminary Examination for a Student in Surveying, 1898.	No. passed Matriculation Examination, Medical Council, 1898.	No. passed Matriculation Examination, Law Society, 1898.	No. 2nd Class Matriculation Honours.	No. 1st Class Matriculation Honours.	No. passed the Senior Matriculation Examination at any University.	No. passed the Junior Matriculation Examination at any University.	No. passed Departmental Matriculation Examination.	No. passed Senior Leaving Examination.	No. passed Junior Leaving Examination.	No. passed Primary Examination.	How many pupils obtained Commercial Diplomas in 1898.	Gymnastics.	Calisthenics.	Drill.	Vocal Music.	Drawing.	Stenography.	Book-keeping and Commercial Transactions.	Writing.	German.	French.	Greek.	Latin.	Zoology.
1. Total, 1898	7	43	8	175	125	9	180	340	166	450	469	39	5,735	6,610	6,863	30	5,528	1,715	5,652	4,284	3,081	7,332	835	9,395	229
2. " 1897	7	38	9	178	161	8	128	270	333	865	500	9	5,689	7,162	8,313	30	6,144	1,906	5,652	5,204	2,869	7,453	871	8,054	361
3. Increase		5				1	11	70				30	34					509			212			441	
4. Decrease			1	3	36				166	415	91			552	1,450		616	15		920		121	36		132
5. Percentage		3		12	1		12	3	12	4	4	1	49	57	59	1	47	15	48	36	26	63	7	80	2

TABLE ·8.—KINDERGARTENS, 1898.

Note.—The system of Kindergarten instruction, first introduced into Ontario in 1882, and subsequently made part of the School System of the Province, by the Public Schools Act of 1885, has met with encouraging success. A report of the pupils receiving instruction in this way was first made in 1892. The report showed that in the short space of ten years, 69 Kindergartens were established, with 160 teachers, attended by 6,375 children under six years of age.

No. of Kindergartens.	Number of Teachers.	No. of Pupils attending.	Average attendance.
116	240	11,083	4,573.

TABLE 9.—NIGHT SCHOOLS.   1898.

No. of Night Schools.	No. of Teachers.	No. of Pupils attending.*	Average attendance.
18	42	1,504	363

* This number does not include the attendance at the classes established by Mechanics' Institutes and Art Schools.

Part III.—Statistical Tables for the year 1898.—continued.

TABLE 10.

A General Statistical Abstract, exhibiting the comparative state and progress of Education in Ontario, as connected with Public, Separate and High Schools (including Collegiate Institutes); also Normal College and Normal and Model Schools. From the year 1867 to 1898, compiled from Returns in the Education Department.

No.	Subjects compared.	1867.	1872.	1877.	1882.	1887.	1892.	1897.	1898.
1	Population	—	1,620,851	—	1,926,922	—	2,114,321	—	—
2	School population between the ages of five and sixteen years, up to 1884 (and five to twenty-one subsequently)	447,726	495,768	494,804	483,817	611,912	595,538	590,055	591,900
3	High Schools (including Collegiate Institutes)	102	174	104	104	112	128	130	130
4	Normal College and Normal and Model Schools	3	3	4	5	6	6	7	7
5	Total Public Schools in operation	4,201	4,490	4,956	5,013	5,377	5,577	5,574	5,587
6	Total Roman Catholic Separate Schools	161	171	185	190	239	312	340	345
7	Grand total of all schools in operation	4,527	4,758	5,248	5,313	5,924	6,023	6,051	6,099
8	Total pupils attending High Schools (including Collegiate Institutes)	5,996	7,968	9,229	12,348	17,459	22,637	24,390	23,301
9	Total students and pupils attending Normal College, Normal and Model Schools	900	900	900	1,059	1,294	1,270	1,492	1,492
10	Total pupils attending Public Schools	382,719	433,254	465,908	445,364	462,539	448,304	441,187	436,727
11	Total pupils attending Roman Catholic Separate Schools	18,924	21,406	24,962	26,148	30,373	37,466	41,020	41,067
12	Grand total, students and pupils attending High, Public, Separate, Normal College and Normal and Model Schools	408,139	463,457	500,999	484,919	511,875	509,777	508,659	508,187
13	Total amount paid for the salaries of Public and Separate School Teachers	1,003,516	1,371,594	2,088,099	2,144,448	2,456,540	2,782,028	2,986,061	2,914,830
14	Total amount paid for the erection and repairs of Public and Separate School Houses, and for libraries and apparatus, books, fuel, stationery, etc.	379,672	835,770	1,085,390	882,596	1,293,566	1,301,290	1,529,909	1,477,895
15	Grand total paid for Public and Separate School Teachers' Salaries, the erection and repairs of the school houses, and for libraries, apparatus, etc.	1,473,188	2,207,364	3,073,489	3,026,974	3,742,16?	4,063,917	4,215,670	4,392,715
16	Total amount paid for High School (including Collegiate Institutes), Teachers' salaries	94,820	141,612	211,867	253,864	327,462	470,628	532,337	531,687
17	Total amount paid for erection and repair of High School (including Collegiate Institutes) houses, maps, apparatus, prizes, fuel, books, etc.	12,190	31,360	51,417	99,157	168,160	215,871	168,139	292,067
18	Amount paid for other educational purposes	532,825	449,890	250,968	262,307	250,832	353,367	346,220	342,916
19	Grand total, paid for educational purposes	1,929,023	2,830,226	3,587,491	3,633,002	4,518,549	5,004,003	5,278,466	5,470,476
20	Total Public and Separate School Teachers	4,890	5,476	6,464	6,657	7,594	8,480	9,128	9,309
21	Total male teachers	2,849	2,625	3,021	3,082	2,718	2,770	2,784	2,743
22	Total female teachers	2,041	2,850	3,448	3,714	4,878	5,710	6,344	6,466

* Colleges and Private Schools are included for 1867 and 1872.

TABLE 11.

SUMMARY OF STATISTICS FOR 1898.

a. ELEMENTARY SCHOOLS.[1]

Number of Public Schools - - - - -		5,587
Increase for the year - - -	13	
Number of Roman Catholic Separate Schools -		345
Increase for the year - - -	5	
Number of Protestant Separate Schools - -		8
Number of Kindergartens - - - - -		116
Number of teachers - - - - - -		240
Number of Night Schools - - - - -		18
Number of teachers - - - - - -		42
Amount expended for Public School Houses (sites and buildings) - - - - - -		$426,422
Amounts expended for Public School teachers' salaries) - - - - - - -		$2,747,159
Amount expended for all other purposes - -		$869,652
Total amount expended on Public Schools - -		$4,043,233
Increase - - - - -	$129,732	
Number of persons in the Province between the ages of 5 and 21 - - - - -		591,300
Increase for the year - - -	1,245	
Number of registered pupils of all ages in the Public Schools during the year - - -		436,727
Decrease for the year - - -	4,430	
Average attendance of pupils in the Public Schools during the year - - - - -		247,780
Decrease for the year - - -	768	
Number of pupils in Roman Catholic Separate Schools - - - - - - -		41,667
Increase for the year - - -	47	
Average attendance of pupils in Roman Catholic Separate Schools - - - -		25,671
Increase for the year - - -	675	
Number of pupils in Protestant Separate Schools		505
Decrease for the year - - -	38	
Average attendance of pupils in Protestant Separate Schools - - - - -		266
Decrease for the year - - -	55	

[1] The Curriculum of Elementary Schools embraces the following subjects: Reading, Writing, Arithmetic, Composition, Drawing, English Literature, Geography, Music, Grammar, History, Physiology and Temperance, Drill and Calisthenics, Book-keeping, Algebra, Geometry, Botany, Elementary Physics, Agriculture.

a. ELEMENTARY SCHOOLS—*cont.*

Number of pupils attending Kindergartens - Increase for the year - - - 390	11,083

Number of pupils attending Kindergartens -   **11,083**
   Increase for the year -   -   -   390

Average attendance of pupils at Kindergartens -   **4,573**
   Increase for the year -   -   -   211

Number of pupils attending Night Schools .   **1,504**
   Increase for the year -   -   -   98

Average attendance of pupils at Night Schools -   **363**
   Increase for the year -   -   -   46

Percentage of average attendance to total attendance in Public Schools -   -   -   -   **57**

Number of persons employed as teachers in the Public Schools during the year: Men, 2,656; women, 5,809 ; total - -   -   -   **8,465**
Decrease: men, 34 ;
   Increase: women, 123 ; increase -   -   89

Number of teachers who have attended a Normal School -   -   -   -   -   -   **3,585**
   Increase for the year -   -   -   106

Number of teachers who have attended a County Model School in 1899 -   -   -   -   **1,271**

Average annual salary of male teachers in Public Schools -   -   -   -   -   -   **$396**
   Increase for the year -   -   - $5

Average annual salary of female teachers in Public Schools -   -   -   -   -   -   **$293**
   Decrease for the year -   -   - $1

b. SECONDARY SCHOOLS.[1]

Number of High Schools (including 37 Collegiate Institutes) -   -   -   -   -   -   **130**

Number of teachers in High Schools -   -   -   **571**
   Decrease for the year -   -   -   8

Number of pupils in High Schools -   -   -   **23,301**
   Decrease for the year -   -   -   1,089

Amount expended for High School teachers' salaries -   -   -   -   -   -   **$531,887**

Amount expended for High School houses (sites and buildings) -   -   -   -   -   **$52,266**

Amount expended for all other High School purposes -   -   -   -   -   **$144,856**

Total amount expended on High Schools   **$729,009**

---

[1] The Curriculum of Secondary Schools includes all the subjects required for Matriculation at the University (see below, Appendix G).

APPENDIX A.

REGULATIONS OF THE EDUCATION DEPARTMENT OF THE PROVINCE OF ONTARIO.

(Approved by the Education Department, October 20th, 1896.)

PUBLIC SCHOOLS.

Sites and School Houses.

1. THE site of every public school shall admit of easy drainage and shall be accessible by the best highways in the section. Its area shall be not less than half an acre, and if the school population of the section exceeds seventy-five, the area shall be not less than one acre. The grounds shall be levelled and drained, enclosed by a neat and substantial fence and planted with shade trees. The school house shall be placed at least 30 feet from the public highway.

2. There shall be a well or other means of procuring water, so placed and guarded as to be secure against pollution from surface drainage, or in any other way. Every rural school shall be provided with a woodshed.

3. The closets for the sexes shall be under different roofs. They shall be separated by a high close-board fence, their entrances screened from observation, and locked after school hours. They shall be properly cleansed and disinfected when necessary, and approached by proper walks from the school house so as to be accessible with comfort at all seasons of the year.

4. Where the average attendance of any section for three years exceeds 50 pupils a school house with two rooms shall be provided. An additional room and teacher shall be required for each additional 50 pupils in average attendance. Every school house shall afford separate entrances with covered porches and suitable cloak rooms for boys and girls.

5. Every schoolroom shall contain a superficial area of at least 12 square feet, and a cubic content of at least 250 feet, for each pupil in average attendance. A uniform temperature throughout the room of at least 67 degrees shall be maintained, and provision made for a complete change of atmosphere three times every hour. The windows, both sashes, shall be adjusted by weights and pulleys and provided with suitable blinds. Light, where possible, shall be admitted from the left of the pupil.

Furniture and Equipment.

6. Every school house shall be seated with either double or single desks, single desks being preferred. The desks shall be fastened to the floor in rows facing the teacher's platform, with suitable aisles between the rows and with passages at least three feet wide between the outside rows and

the walls of the school room. Desks according to the following scale shall be considered as meeting all legal requirements :—

Age of Pupils.	Seats.			Desks.			
	Height.		Slope of Back.	Length.		Width.	Height next Pupil.
	Front.	Rear.		Double.	Single.		
Five to eight years - -	11 in.	10½ in.	2 in.	36 in.	18 in.	12 in.	22 in.
Eight to ten years - -	12 „	11½ „	2 „	36 „	18 „	12 „	23 „
Ten to thirteen years -	13 „	12½ „	2½ „	36 „	20 „	13 „	24 „
Thirteen to sixteen years -	14 „	14½ „	3 „	40 „	22 „	13 „	26 „

7. There shall be one blackboard, at least four feet wide, extending across the whole room in rear of the teacher's desk, with its lower edge not more than 2½ feet above the floor or platform ; and, when possible, there should be an additional blackboard on each side of the room. At the lower edge of each blackboard there should be a trough five inches wide for holding crayons and brushes.

Note.—The following directions for making a blackboard may be found useful :—

(a) Where a brick wall is built solid, and also in cases of frame buildings, the part to be used for a blackboard should be lined with boards, and the laths for holding the plaster nailed firmly on the boards.

(b) The plaster for the blackboard should be composed largely of plaster of Paris.

(c) Before and after having received the first coat of colour it should be thoroughly polished with fine sand paper.

(d) The colouring matter should be laid on with a wide flat varnish brush.

(e) The liquid colouring should be made as follows :—Dissolve gum shellac in alcohol, four ounces to the quart ; the alcohol should be ninety-five per cent. strong ; the dissolving process will require at least 12 hours. Fine emery flour, with enough chrome green or lamp black to give colour, should then be added until the mixture has the consistency of thin paint. It may then be applied, in long even strokes, up and down, the liquid being kept constantly stirred.

8. Every school shall have at least one globe not less than nine inches in diameter, properly mounted ; a map of Canada ; a map of Ontario ; a map of the world and of the continents ; one or more sets of tablet lessons of Part I. of the First Reader ; a standard dictionary ; a gazetteer ; a numeral frame ; a suitable supply of crayons and blackboard brushes ; an eight-day clock ; shelving for baskets ; hooks for caps and cloaks ; and two chairs in addition to the teacher's chair.

9. The Trustees shall appoint one of their number or some suitable person to keep the school house and premises and all fences, outhouses, walks, windows, desks, maps, blackboards and stoves in proper repair. They shall also provide for whitewashing walls and ceilings if finished in plaster (or for washing if finished in wood), every year during the summer holidays, and shall employ a caretaker whose duty it shall be to sweep the floors daily, and wash them at least quarterly and to make fires one hour before the opening of school, from the 1st of November to the 1st of May in each year.

10. No public school house or school grounds, unless otherwise provided for in the conveyance to the trustees, shall be used for any other than public school purposes without the consent of the trustees, and no advertisements shall be posted in any school room or distributed to the pupils unless approved in the same way.

11. The first Friday in May each year shall in rural school sections and in incorporated villages be devoted to the planting of shade trees, the making of flower beds, and otherwise beautifying and improving the school grounds. Songs and recitations designed to cultivate greater interest in trees and flowers and in the study of nature shall form part of the exercises of the day.

Duties of Pupils.

12. Every pupil registered in a public school shall attend punctually and regularly every day of the school year in which his name is so registered. He shall be neat and cleanly in his person and habits, diligent in his studies, kind and courteous to his fellow-pupils, obedient and respectful to his teacher, and shall submit to such discipline as would be exercised by a kind, firm and judicious parent.

13. Every pupil on returning to school after absence from any cause shall give orally or in writing to the teacher, a proper reason for his absence. A pupil may retire from school at any hour during the day at the request, either oral or written, of his parent or guardian. A pupil may be suspended who fails or neglects to provide himself with the text books or other supplies required in his course of study, or to pay the fees imposed for such purposes by the trustees.

14. Every pupil shall be responsible to the teacher for his conduct on the school premises or on the way to or from school, except when accompanied by his parents or guardians, or by some person appointed by them on their behalf. Any pupil who injures or destroys school property or furniture may be suspended until the property or furniture destroyed or injured is made good by the parent or guardian of such pupil.   -

School Terms and Organization.

15. Unless otherwise directed by the Trustees, the pupils attending every public school shall assemble for study at nine o'clock in the forenoon, and shall be dismissed not later than four o'clock in the afternoon. One hour at least shall be allowed for recreation at mid-day, and ten minutes during the forenoon and afternoon terms, but in no case shall the hours of study be less than five hours per day, including the recess in the forenoon and afternoon, provided always the Trustees may reduce the hours of study for pupils in the First and Second Forms.

16. Pupils not registered in a day school may attend a night school from the 1st of October until the 31st of March. The hours of study in the night school shall not exceed 2½ hours per session. Pupils shall not be admitted to a night school who are under 14 years of age or who attend school during the day. Night schools shall be subject to the same regulations as public schools with respect to the discipline of pupils, the duties and qualifications of teachers and the use of text books.

17. The course of study for public schools shall be taken up in five forms as hereinafter set forth, and pupils shall be classified by the teacher with respect to their attainments in all the subjects of the form to which they are assigned or from which they are to be promoted. Pupils who have passed the high school entrance examination and such other pupils as are considered qualified by the teacher and inspector shall be entitled in both rural and urban schools to receive instruction in the subjects of the Fifth Form, provided that, in a municipality having a high school if resident pupils of the First Form are not charged fees it will not be deemed obliga-

tory for the public school board to have a fifth class. The amount of time to be given to any class is to be determined by the teacher, who shall be guided in this matter by the inspector. Subjects of the course of study marked with an asterisk are optional.

18. An optional subject shall be taken only with the consent of the Trustees and the Inspector, and where the teacher is the holder of a first or second class certificate and has passed an examination in the option which he undertakes to teach. The Trustees of any rural school may, by resolution passed at a regular meeting of the board, require agriculture to be taught in the fourth and fifth forms of the school, and in such cases the inspector shall report to the Trustees at least annually, the extent of the course taken by the pupils and their standing. Not more than three periods of 30 minutes each shall be given per week to the study of all the optional subjects. In urban schools such instruction may be given in domestic economy as the Trustees deem exedient.

19. In school sections where the French or German language prevails, the Trustee may, in addition to the course of study prescribed for public schools, require instruction to be given in reading, grammar and composition to such pupils as are directed by their parents or guardians to study either of these languages, and in all such cases the authorised text books in French or German shall be used. But nothing herein contained shall be construed to mean that any of the text book prescribed for public schools shall be set aside because of the use of the authorised text books in French or German.

Continuation Classes.

20. In schools where instruction for the primary examinations has been given under former regulations similar to what may be given by the establishment of a continuation class in connection with any public school under the provisions of Section 8 of the Public Schools Act, 1896, the principal of the school shall be deemed qualified so long as he remains principal of such school. In the case of any subsequent appointment as principal, the qualifications shall be a first class certificate for schools in class (*a*) hereinafter mentioned.

21. Any grant made by the Legislature for public school leaving examinations and continuation classes shall be distributed by the Minister of Education among the schools of the three grades hereafter mentioned, viz. : —(*a*) Schools in which the principal holds a first class certificate (unless occupying the position in 1896), and gives regular instruction only to pupils who have passed the high school entrance examination (one or more of whom have also passed the public school leaving examination) and who are taking the full course required for primary standing. (*b*) Schools in which there are two or more teachers and a class in regular attendance of at least 10 pupils who have passed the high school entrance examination (one or more of whom have also passed the public school leaving examination) and who are taking the full work required for primary standing. (*c*) Schools in which there is a class in regular attendance of at least five pupils who have passed the high school entrance examination (one or more of whom have also passed the public school leaving examination) and who are taking the full course prescribed for primary standing. Any person holding a second class certificate shall be deemed qualified to conduct the classes in schools under divisions (*b*) and (*c*). Before a grant is paid to any school for a continuation class the inspector shall certify to its efficiency, and to the competence of the teachers employed to give the instruction required by the regulations of the Education Department. Any school receiving a grant under this regulation shall not receive any additional allowance on account of pupils who may pass the public school leaving examination. (Modified in 1899, *see* § III. of Part II., above.)

Public School Courses of Study.

22. Subject to any instructions issued by the Minister of Education from time to time, the limitations and examination requirements of each Form in the public school shall be as set forth in Schedule A—Public School Courses of Study. (*See below.*)

High School Entrance Examinations.

23. At every high school and collegiate institute and such other places as may be recommended by the county council, examinations to be known as high school entrance examinations, to be conducted on the subjects prescribed for the Fourth Form of public schools, shall be held annually. The county council may impose a fee not exceeding one dollar upon each county pupil writing at the entrance examination. Boards of trustees may impose similar fees upon resident and non-resident pupils writing for the entrance examination at high schools and collegiate institutes.

24. Any person intending to write at this examination shall notify the inspector in whose district he proposes to write on or before the 1st day of May. Where more examinations than one are held in the same inspectoral division, he shall notify the inspector of the place at which he desires to be examined. The answer papers of the candidates shall be read by the Board of Examiners constituted under Section 38 of the High Schools Act, 1896.

25. The answers of candidates at the entrance examination shall be appraised according to the following scale, viz.: In reading, spelling, drawing, writing, 50 each ; in physiology and temperance, composition, history, geography, 100 each ; in grammar and literature, 150 each ; in arithmetic, 200. Two marks shall be deducted for each misspelled word on the dictation paper, and one mark for every misspelled word in any other paper. Reasonable deductions may also be made for want of neatness.

26. Any candidate who obtains one-third of the marks in each subject and one-half of the aggregate marks shall be considered as having passed the examination. The examiners may also award pass standing to candidates who have not made a bad failure in any subject but who have made a high aggregate above the half required, or whose case on account of age or other circumstances demands special consideration. The decision of the Board of Examiners shall be final with regard to the admission or rejection of any candidate, but the inspector may submit to the board for re-consideration the complaint of any candidate or any other person with regard to the examination.

27. In the interval between the annual examinations, pupils may be admitted to a high school by the Minister of Education on the joint report of the principal of a high school and the public school inspector, showing the attainments of such pupil, his age, and the reasons for his non-attendance at the entrance examination prescribed by the Department. No pupil shall be admitted until his case is disposed of by the Minister. The names of such pupils shall be included in the report of the Board of Examiners at the next annual examination.

Public School Leaving Examinations.

28. Public school leaving examinations will be held annually at every high school and collegiate institute, and at such other places as may be recommended by the inspector. A person who wishes to write at the public school leaving examination must, before the 24th of May, give the necessary notice to the inspector on a form to be obtained from him. The answer papers will be examined at the Education Department immediately after the examination is held, and a report of the results will be forwarded to the inspector, or to the high school principal, if the examination was held at a high school centre. The Board of Trustees where such examination is held shall pay all the cost of the examination, but will receive from the inspector half the fees paid by candidates.

29. Candidates at the public school leaving examination shall take the following subjects, to be valued as herein mentioned, viz.: reading, 50 ; drawing, writing with book-keeping and commercial transactions, English composition, English literature, history, geography, algebra, geometry, botany each 100 ; English grammar and rhetoric, arithmetic and mensura-

tion, each 150. Any candidate who obtains one-third of the marks in each subject and one-half (67 per cent. for honours), of the aggregate marks shall be considered as having passed the public school leaving examination, provided, also, that a candidate who fails on one or more subjects may, if he makes considerably more than 50 per cent. on the total, be awarded a public school leaving certificate. The Board of Examiners for high school entrance examinations may admit to a high school candidates who have failed at a public school leaving examination, providing they have made one-quarter of the marks on each entrance examination subject.

HIGH SCHOOLS AND COLLEGIATE INSTITUTES.

Accommodation and Equipment.

. 30. The plans of every high school hereafter erected, and the plans and site of every high school hereafter established, shall be subject to the approval of the Minister of Education. In all high schools established since July, 1891, or to be hereafter established, there shall be a principal and at least two assistants. No new high school shall be entitled to receive any grant that does not provide at least the amount fixed by the instructions of the Minister of Education with regard to accommodation and the equipment required as the maximum in distributing the legislative grant to schools with two masters.

31. Any high school may be raised to the status of a collegiate institute when it is shown to the satisfaction of the Education Department that the trustees have provided : (*a*) adequate school buildings ; (*b*) equipment of the value and character required as the maximum in the case of high schools with three or more masters ; (*c*) four specialists, viz., one in classics, one in mathematics, one in science, one in modern languages including English (one of whom or some other member of the staff being also a commercial specialist), and (*d*) such other assistants as will secure thorough instruction in all the subjects of the high school course as far as senior matriculation into the University of Toronto. A collegiate institute may be reduced to the rank of a high school on the joint report of the high school inspectors, approved by the Education Department.

32. Every high school that complies with the regulations of the Education Department shall be entitled to the following grants : (*a*) a fixed grant of 375 dollars ; (*b*) in respect of school accommodation, a maximum of 100 dollars in the case of high schools with two masters and of 150 dollars in the case of high schools with three or more masters ; (*c*) in respect of equipment, ten per cent of the total approved expenditure but so as not to exceed 110 dollars in the case of high schools with two masters ; or 220 dollars in the case of high schools with three or more masters ; (*d*) in respect of salaries ten per cent. of the expenditure over 1,500 dollars but so as not to exceed 600 dollars in any case ; (*e*) such amount *pro rata* in respect of average attendance as may remain unexpended of the grant.

33. Every collegiate institute that complies with the regulations of the Education Department shall be entitled ; (*a*) to a fixed grant of 375 dollars ; (*b*) to a grant in respect of equipment of 275 dollars ; (*c*) to a grant in respect of school accommodation of 200 dollars ; (*d*) to ten per cent. of the expenditure on salaries over 1,500 dollars but so as not to exceed 600 dollars ; and (*e*) to a grant on the basis of average attendance out of any unexpended balance of the legislative grant.

34. In apportioning the legislative grant on equipment, the maximum recognized in the case of high schools with two masters shall be as follows : library, 300 dollars ; physical and chemical apparatus, 300 dollars ; maps and globes, 50 dollars, and models for drawing, 50 dollars ; gymnasium, not including equipment, 400 dollars. In the case of collegiate institutes and high schools with three masters the maximum recognized shall be : library,

600 dollars ; physical and chemical apparatus, 600 dollars ; maps and globes, 100 dollars, and models for drawing, 100 dollars ; gymnasium, not including equipment, 800 dollars.

35. When the value of the library has reached the maximum herein recognized, ten per cent. of the annual expenditure by the High School Board on supplemental reading in English Literature will be allowed. The catalogue of the equipment shall be kept by the principal of the school and shall be accessible to any officer of the Education Department. The instructions of the Minister of Education in the matter of grading shall be followed in appropriating the grant for buildings and premises. On the report of a high school inspector, such reductions may be made in the grants payable upon the salaries of the staff, and the character and equipment of the school buildings and their appendages as the Minister of Education may deem expedient.

High School Organization.

36. In every high school or collegiate institute the head teacher shall be called the principal, and the other teachers assistants. The authority of the principal of the high school shall be supreme as to all matters of discipline on the school premises, where the public and high school occupy the same building. The provisions of the Public Schools Act, 1896, Section 76, and the regulations of the Education Department with respect to the duties of pupils attending a public school shall apply to teachers and pupils of high schools.

37. The principal of a high school or collegiate institute shall hold a principal's certificate and the assistants shall hold high school assistants' certificates. Special teachers of music, drawing, drill, gymnastics and calisthenics, shall possess qualifications satisfactory to the Minister of Education. If, after due advertisement, a high school board is unable to obtain a qualified assistant, a temporary certificate may be granted by the Minister of Education for the current half year to a suitable person on the application of the board.

38. The principal shall determine the number of pupils to be assigned to each form and the order in which the subjects in each form shall be taken up by the pupils. The principal shall make such promotions from one form to another as he may deem expedient ; he shall also assign the subjects of the course of study among the assistants.

39. The course of study in high schools shall be taken in four forms. The subjects marked with an asterisk in Forms I. and II. are optional ; all the other subjects are obligatory. No subjects shall be taken in any form other than the subjects herein prescribed. All pupils shall take the obligatory subjects in Forms I. and II. and such other subjects in any of the forms as may be required for departmental or other examinations or as may be chosen by their parents or guardians and the principal of the school, provided that pupils taking the course for a commercial diploma shall be required to take only the subjects of such course. Typewriters may be furnished by the Board of Trustees for the use of the pupils. At the option of the Board of Trustees and the principal, the art school drawing course may be taken in Forms II. and III., and agricultural chemistry, physiology and temperance and vocal music may be taken in any form.

40. Reading shall be taught twice a week during the academic year to all the pupils in each of the sub-divisions of Forms I. and II. and to the pupils in the other forms in connection with the English Literature. Writing shall be taught during the first term at least twice a week in the lowest division of Form I., and provision shall be made for additional practice in school hours. Half-hour periods separate from the other subjects shall be allotted to reading and writing in the time table. Where the average number of pupils in a class exceeds twenty-five, the time devoted to reading and writing shall be proportionately extended. On the report of a high school inspector a

deduction from the legislative grant may, at the discretion of the Minister of Education, be made of 50 dollars in the case of the non-observance of any high school or collegiate institute of any part of this regulation.

41. In high schools and collegiate institutes having a gymnasium, drill, gymnastics and calisthenics shall be taught in half-hour periods and in organized classes not less than three times a week in each division of Forms I., II. and III., but shall be optional in Form IV. ; additional time shall be allowed for practice by pupils under efficient supervision. No pupil shall be exempted from the course prescribed, except upon a medical certificate or on account of evident physical disability. During the months of May, June, September, October, and November, the principal may substitute for drill, etc., not more than twice a week, such sports and games as he may approve of. In high schools having no gymnasium, drill and calisthenics shall be taught as the weather may permit ; and gymnastics may be omitted.

High School Course of Study.

42. The details of the courses of study and examination requirements in each form in high schools shall be as set forth in Schedule B—High School Courses of Study. (*See* below.)

High School Examinations.

43. An examination will be held annually by the Education Department, subject to the conditions hereinafter contained, on the high school course of study at each high school and collegiate institute and at such other centres as may be approved. Candidates intending to write should make application to the public school inspector before the 24th of May on a form to be obtained from him. One examination paper will be given in each subject except in the case of Biology of Form IV., in which there shall be two papers, and of Latin, Greek, French, and German for Forms III. and IV., in which there shall be two examination papers—one in Authors and Grammar and one in Composition. The papers shall be valued as follows :—

Form I.– Reading (oral examination), 50 ; Drawing, English Composition History, Geography, Algebra, Geometry, Botany, Writing with Book-keeping and Commercial Transactions, English Grammar and Rhetoric, Arithmetic and Mensuration, each 150.

Form II.—Part I.—English Grammar and Rhetoric, 200 ; Arithmetic and Mensuration, 200 ; History of Great Britain and Canada, 150 ; Physics, 100 ; Part II.—English Composition, 100 ; English Literature, 150 ; Algebra, 150 ; Geometry, 100. Optional Subjects.—Latin, Greek, French, German, each 150.

Form III.—English Composition, 100 ; English Literature, 150 ; Algebra, 150 ; Geometry, 125 ; Ancient History, Physics, Botany, Chemistry, Latin, Greek, French, German, each paper 75.

Form IV.—Part I.—English Composition, 100 ; English Literature, 150 ; Algebra, 150 ; Geometry, 125 ; Trigonometry, 125 ; English and Ancient History, 100. Part II.—Physics, 100 ; Chemistry and Biology, each 75 ; Latin, Greek, French, and German, each paper 75.

Commercial Course.—The examination for Commercial Diploma will be as hereinafter defined and as set forth in Schedule B.

High School Certificates.

44. Candidates at high school examinations will be awarded a certificate in the form, or in Part I. or II. of the form, as the case may be (where part of a form is prescribed as a separate division of their examination) in which they may have passed. The examination in any form, or in Part I. or II. of any form (where a form is divided for examination purposes)

may be taken in such order or at such intervals of one or more years as the candidate may desire.   Candidates who fail in any subject in a form, or in the part of a form prescribed for their examination, shall, if they present themselves again, take the whole examination in such form or part of a form.   No candidate shall be required to pass a second time in the form or part of a form for which he has received a certificate.

45. To obtain primary standing candidates shall take the public school leaving examination as defined for public schools (which shall be that for Form I.), and at the same time or in a different year, both parts of Form II. taken together.   To pass the public school leaving examination or the examination of Form II., candidates must obtain one-third of the marks assigned to each subject, and 50 (67 for honours) per cent. of the aggregate of marks, provided that in the case of the former a candidate who fails on one or more subjects may, if he makes considerably more than 50 per cent. on the total, be awarded a certificate.   They may also write on the optional subjects of Form II.   The marks obtained on the optional subjects shall be added to the aggregate marks, by way of bonus, provided the candidate receives one-third of the marks assigned to the subject.

46. To obtain junior leaving standing candidates shall take the public school leaving examination and Part I. of the Second Form examination, unless they have already passed these examinations, and the following subjects of the Third Form examination, viz. :—English Composition, English Literature, Ancient History, Algebra, Geometry, Latin and one of the following groups, viz. :   (a) French and Greek ; or (b) German and Greek ; or (c) French, German and Chemistry ; or (d) French, Physics, Botany, and Chemistry ; or (e) German, Physics, Botany and Chemistry. Candidates who obtain one-third of the marks assigned to the subjects in Part I. of the Second Form shall be given a certificate to that effect.   A separate certificate will also be given to candidates who pass on the same standard in the subjects of the Third Form, no percentage on the total being required for either of these certificates, but 67 per cent. giving honours in the latter case. (*See* above, Part II., § XII., *a* and *b*.)

47. To obtain senior leaving standing candidates shall take the public school leaving examination and Part I. of the Second Form examination, unless they have already passed these examinations; and in addition Part I. of the Fourth Form examination ; and of Part II., Form IV., Latin and Physics, with one of the following groups, viz. :—(a) Greek and French, or (b) Greek and German, or (c) French, Chemistry and Biology, or (d) German, Chemistry and Biology.   Certificates will be given candidates who pass one or both parts of Form IV. at this examination, the standard for passing being one-third on each paper.   No percentage will be required on the total, but 67 per cent. will secure honours when Parts I. and II. are taken together. Candidates for senior leaving standing who hold junior leaving standing are required to take only Part I. of the Fourth Form examination and the subjects of Part II. of the Fourth Form, hereinbefore mentioned. (*See* above, Part II., § XII., *c* and *d*.)

48. A candidate for junior or senior leaving standing who has passed Part I. of the Second Form examination, shall be awarded a certificate on application to the Education Department of having passed in Form II., notwithstanding his failure to obtain junior or senior leaving standing, providing such candidate has obtained one-third of the marks at this examination in the subjects of Part II. of the Second Form examination.

49. The standing of the second, third, and fourth years in Arts after a regular course in any University in the British dominions, will be accepted in lieu of the primary, junior leaving and senior leaving standing respectively.

50. The course for a commercial diploma may be taken in two parts. Both parts may be taken in different years or in the same year, at the option of the candidate.   Part I. shall consist of book-keeping and writing, 200 marks ; commercial transactions, business forms and usages, 200 marks ;

stenography (theory), 100 marks ; stenography (dictation), 100 marks. Part II. shall consist of the examination papers in Form II. in arithmetic and mensuration, history of Great Britain and Canada, English composition, English literature and algebra. The marks in these subjects shall be the same as in Form II. Candidates shall be required to make one-third of the marks in each subject in each part, and one-half of the aggregate of each part to obtain pass standing. Candidates who hold a certificate of having passed in Form II., or in any part of a higher form, shall be required to write only on Part I. of the Commercial Course.

SPECIALISTS' STANDING.

51. Any person who obtains an Honour degree in the department of English and History, Moderns and History, Classics, Mathematics, or Science as specified in the calendars of any University of Ontario and accepted by the Education Department, shall be entitled to the non-professional qualification of a Specialist in such department. A graduate who has not taken an Honour degree in one of the above courses shall be entitled to the non-professional standing of a Specialist on submitting to the Department of Education a certificate from the Registrar of the University that he has passed, subsequent to graduation, the examinations prescribed for each year of the Honour course of the Department for which he seeks to be recognised as a Specialist, and which he has not already passed in his undergraduate course; or any examination which is recommended by the University as equivalent thereto and accepted as such by the Education Department.

EXAMINATION AND OTHER FEES.

53. The fees authorised by the Education Department shall be as follows : Candidates for the Entrance Examination, if so ordered by the Board of Trustees or the County Council, 1 dollar ; Public School Leaving, 2 dollars ; Commercial diploma, each part, 2 dollars ; Second Form examination, Part I., 2 dollars ; the whole of Form II., 5 dollars : Third Form examination, 5 dollars ; Fourth Form examination, Parts I. and II., each 3 dollars ; taken together, 5 dollars ; for candidates for examination in one or more subjects only, for the purpose of completing a course for pass matriculation into any university or learned profession, 2 dollars ; Tuition County Model School, when so ordered by the Board of Trustees, 5 dollars ; kindergarten assistants, 3 dollars ; directors, 5 dollars ; examination Normal School, 2 dollars ; examination Normal College, 10 dollars, appeals of all kinds, 5 dollars. (Fee to be refunded if the appeal is sustained.)

KINDERGARTENS.

54. No person shall be appointed to take charge of a kindergarten in which assistant teachers or teachers-in-training are employed, who has not passed the examination prescribed for a director of kindergartens ; and no person shall be paid a salary or allowance for teaching under a director who has not passed the examination prescribed for directors or assistant teachers. No person shall be admitted to the course of training prescribed for assistants who is not seventeen years of age and who has not primary standing, or who has not spent at least three years in a high school. Any person who has taken the equivalent of such a course at some other educational institution may, on the recommendation of the inspector, be admitted to training with the consent of the Minister of Education. No person shall be admitted to the course prescribed for a director unless such a person has obtained an assistant's certificate.

55. Any person who attends a kindergarten for one year and passes the examinations prescribed by the Education Department shall be entitled to an assistant's certificate. The holder of an assistant's certificate, or the holder of a second-class provincial certificate shall, on attending a provincial kindergarten one year and on passing the prescribed examinations, be entitled to a director's certificate.

56. The examination for directors shall include psychology and the general principles of Froebel's system ; history of education ; theory and practice of the gifts and occupations ; Mutter and Kose-Lieder ; botany and natural history ; miscellaneous topics, including discipline and methods of morning talks, each 100 ; practical teaching, 500 ; bookwork, 400. There shall also be a sessional examination in music, drawing, and physical culture to be reported by the principal to the examiners at the final examination. The examination for assistants shall include the theory and practice of the gifts (two papers) ; theory and practice of the occupations (one paper) ; miscellaneous topics, including the general principles of Froebel's system and their application to songs and games, elementary science, morning talks and discipline (one paper), each paper, 100 ; bookwork, 400. Any director sending up candidates to the examination for assistants' certificates shall certify that the Pease-work and Modelling have been satisfactorily completed.

County and City Model Schools.

57. The Board of Examiners for every county shall, and the trustees of any city, with the approval of the Minister of Education, may set apart at least one public school for the professional training of third-class teachers. The principal of such school shall be the holder of a first-class certificate from the Education Department and shall have at least three years' experience as a public school teacher. In every model school there shall be at least three assistants on the staff who shall be the holders of first or second-class certificates. The County Board of Examiners shall distribute the teachers-in-training among the county model schools as may be deemed expedient.

58. The model school term shall begin on the second of September and shall close on the fifteenth day of December. During the term the principal of the public school to which the model school is attached shall be relieved of all public school duties except the management and supervision of the public school. The assistants shall give such instruction to the teachers-in-training as may be required by the principal or by the regulations of the Education Department. There shall be a room for the exclusive use of the teachers-in-training either in the public school buildings or elsewhere equally convenient.

59. Application for admission to a model school shall be made to the inspector not later than the twenty-fifth of August. Any person who has primary or a higher standing, or who is considered eligible by the Board of Examiners for a district certificate and who will be eighteen years of age before the close of the term may be admitted as a teacher-in-training. The teachers-in-training shall be subject to the discipline of the principal with an appeal in case of dispute to the Chairman of the County Board of Examiners. Boards of Trustees may impose a tuition fee, not exceeding 5 dollars, on each teacher-in-training.

60. The course of study in model schools shall consist of instruction in school management, to be valued for examination purposes at 100 ; instruction in the science of education, 100 ; instruction in the best methods of teaching all the subjects on the public school course of study, two papers, 100 each ; instruction in the school law and regulations so far as they relate to the duties of teachers and pupils, instruction in school hygiene, music and physical culture, 50 each ; and such practice in teaching as will cultivate correct methods of presenting subjects to a class and develop the

art of school government. The final examination of the Education Department will be limited to school management, the science of education, methods, school hygiene, and the school law and regulations.

61. The principal of the school shall submit to the Board of Examiners a report with respect to the standing of every teacher-in-training, having regard to his conduct during the session, his aptitude as a teacher, his powers of discipline and government in the school room and such other qualities as in the opinion of the principal are necessary to a successful teacher. The principal shall also report the standing of each teacher-in-training in the subjects of hygiene, music and physical culture as determined by at least one sessional examination. These reports shall be considered by the Board of Examiners at the final examination in estimating the standing of the candidates for a certificate in all cases of doubt.

62. During the last week of the session the county board of examiners shall require each teacher-in-training to teach in the presence of such members of the board as may be appointed for that purpose, two lessons of 20 minutes each, one of which shall be assigned by the presiding examiner one day before, and the other 40 minutes before it is to be taught. Each lesson shall be valued at 100, shall be appraised by different examiners and shall not be taught in the same form nor in the same subject. The Board of Examiners shall also submit the candidates to a practical test of their ability to place upon the blackboard with neatness and despatch any exercise for pupils they may deem expedient. The time allowance for such a test shall not exceed 10 minutes and the valuation 50.

63. Any teacher-in-training having primary standing who obtains 40 per cent. of the marks assigned to each subject (including practical teaching), and 60 per cent. of the aggregate shall be awarded a third class certificate valid for three years. At the request of the county board and with the permission of the Minister of Education, a certificate for a shorter period and valid only within the jurisdiction of the county board, to be known as a district certificate, may be awarded to teachers-in-training who obtain a lower percentage, or to such other persons whose non-professional standing would entitle them only to district certificates. The board may reject any candidate whose scholarship appears to be defective. The decision of the board with respect to the examination shall be final.

DISTRICT MODEL SCHOOLS.

64. The Minister of Education may set apart two public schools in each of the districts of Thunder Bay, Algoma, Parry Sound and Nipissing as Model Schools for candidates for district certificates. No school shall rank as a district model school unless the teaching staff consists of at least three teachers, viz. : a principal holding a first class certificate and at least one of his assistants holding a second-class certificate. Teachers-in-training at district schools shall take the course of study and the final examinations prescribed for public school leaving examinations. Candidates for teachers' certificates at the district model school examinations shall be at least 18 years of age, and shall take such a course of professional training in the subjects prescribed for county model schools as the Inspector of the district may direct.

65. In cities and counties where the French or German language prevails, the Board of Examiners, with the approval of the Education Department, may establish a model school for the training of teachers of French or German origin ; such school shall hold one term each year, viz. : from the 1st of September to the 1st of July. The course of study shall be the non-professional course required for a public school leaving certificate and the professional course required for a county model school. The examination in English shall be conducted on the papers prescribed for the public school leaving certificate. The examination in French or German shall be limited

to reading, grammar, and composition, and may be both oral and written. The papers in French and German shall be prepared by the Board of Examiners. The board may submit the teachers-in-training to such an examination on the professional course as it deems expedient.

PROVINCIAL NORMAL AND MODEL SCHOOLS.

66. There shall be two sessions of the normal school each year ; the first session shall open on the third Tuesday in January and the second session on the third Tuesday in August. The sessions shall close in June and December at such dates as may be determined by the Minister of Education. Any teacher who has at least junior leaving standing, and who has taught a public school successfully for one year, or who, after passing the county model school examination, has taught under the supervision of the inspector of a city having a city model school, six months thereafter may be admitted as a normal school student.

67. Before being registered, every student admitted to a normal school shall be examined, in writing or orally, by the normal school masters upon the books prescribed for the calendar year as the reading course for teachers. Any teacher may be refused registration whose examination does not show a thorough acquaintance with such reading course. The course of study after admission shall be limited and valued for examination purposes as follows :—Psychology and Science of Education, 200 ; History of Education and School Management, each 150 ; Methods of Teaching (four papers), each paper 100 ; Practice Teaching in the Model School, 400.

68. The principal of the normal school shall be responsible for the discipline and management of the teachers-in-training. He shall prescribe the duties of the staff subject to the approval of the Minister of Education ; he shall cause sessional examinations to be held in temperance, agriculture, reading, writing, drawing, music and physical culture, each valued at 50 marks, and shall keep a record of the same. The staff shall carry out the instructions of the principal with regard to discipline, management, methods of study and all matters affecting the efficiency of the normal school and the progress of the teachers-in-training.

69. Teachers-in-training shall attend regularly and punctually throughout the session and shall submit to such discipline and direction as may be prescribed by the principal. They shall lodge and board at such houses only as are approved by the principal. . Ladies and gentlemen shall not board at the same house and shall have no communication with one another except by permission of the principal or one of the masters.

70. Teachers-in-training shall take a written examination towards the end of each session, to be conducted by the staff, covering every subject on the course of study. The standing of candidates at this examination shall be added to the marks prescribed for the final examination. At the close of each session candidates shall submit to a written examination conducted by the Education Department. The examiners shall have power to reject any candidate who shows deficiency of scholarship.

71. An examination in practical teaching, to be conducted according to the instructions of the Minister of Education, shall be required of every teacher-in-training. This examination shall be valued at 200 marks. Any candidate who obtains 34 per cent. of the marks in each subject of the written examinations (the sessional and final written examination being taken jointly), and 34 per cent. of the marks in teaching (the report of the staff and the report of the special examiners being taken jointly), and 50 per cent. of the aggregate marks shall be entitled to pass standing. Candidates making 75 per cent. of the aggregate marks shall be awarded honours.

72. The terms of the Provincial Model School shall correspond with the public school terms in cities. The hours of study shall be from 9.30 a.m. to 12 a.m., and 1.30 p.m. to 3.30 p.m. The regulations of the Education

Department with regard to pupils and teachers in public schools shall apply to the teaching staff and to pupils of the model school, subject to any modifications that may be made by the Minister of Education from time to time.

73. The head master and head mistress of each model school and the director of the Provincial Kindergarten shall act under the direction of the principal of the normal school to which their respective departments are attached, and shall be responsible to him for the order, discipline and progress of the pupils, and for the accuracy and usefulness of the lessons conducted by the teachers-in-training. All members of the teaching staff shall report themselves for duty to the principal of the normal school not later than one day before the re-opening of the school after the Easter, Mid-Summer and Christmas vacations.

ONTARIO NORMAL COLLEGE.

74. The Ontario Normal College shall open each year on the 1st of October and close on the 31st of May. Any person who has senior leaving standing or who is a graduate in arts of any university in the British Dominions, and who will be eighteen years of age before the close of the college year, may be admitted as a teacher-in-training on application to the Minister of Education on or before the 15th of September.

75. The course of study shall consist of lectures on Psychology, the History of Educational Systems, the Science of Education, the best methods of teaching each subject on the high school course of study, School management; instruction in Reading, School Hygiene, Writing, Drawing, Stenography, Physical Culture; practice teaching; and such other subjects as may be prescribed by the Minister of Education. The marks allowed for examination purposes shall be as follows: Psychology and Science of Education, each 200; History of Education, School Management, Methods in English, in Mathematics, in Science, in Classics, and in French and German, each 150.

76. Teachers-in-training shall lodge in such houses only as are approved by the principal; ladies and gentlemen shall not board in the same house nor shall they mingle together in the class-rooms or in the halls of the Normal College. They shall attend regularly and punctually upon lectures and shall submit to the rules of the college with regard to discipline, or any other matter required by the principal, and shall undertake such practice teaching as may be prescribed by the Minister of Education.

77. The principal shall be responsible for the organization and management of the college and for the discipline of the teachers-in-training. He shall prescribe the duties of his staff, and shall from time to time be present at their instruction and at the practice teaching of the teachers-in-training. He shall report the sessional examinations to the Education Department on the forms prescribed by the Minister of Education, and shall make in addition such observations with respect to the conduct of each teacher-in-training and his aptitude as a teacher as he may deem expedient.

78. Each lecturer shall explain and illustrate the best method of dealing with each branch of his department as it should be taught in the different forms of a high or public school, and shall, as far as possible, explain and justify his methods on scientific principles, giving model lessons for classes in different stages of advancement. He shall keep a record of the practice teaching of each teacher-in-training, and shall report to the principal from time to time any breach of discipline or any irregularity on the part of the teachers-in-training or any other matter that comes to his notice which may affect the work of the college.

79. Teachers-in-training shall take two written examinations during the session, viz., one in December and the other in March, and such oral examinations as may be considered necessary for testing their knowledge of methods and their teaching ability. These examinations shall be conducted by the staff of the college ; the number of papers at the sessional examinations and the value of the marks in each subject shall be the same as are prescribed for the final written examination. No teacher-in-training shall be recommended to pass by the examiners who has made less that 34 per cent. of the marks at the sessional examinations (50 marks being the maximum for each) in reading, writing, drawing, or physical culture. Any candidate who obtains 34 per cent. of the marks in each subject of the examinations (the sessional and final written examinations being taken jointly) and 50 per cent. of the aggregate marks, shall be entitled to pass standing. Candidates making 75 per cent. of the aggregate marks shall be awarded honours.

80. At the end of May in each year the teachers-in-training shall submit to an examination conducted by the Education Department. Any candidate who obtains the required standing in Psychology, the Science of Education, the History of Education, School Management, Methods in Mathematics, Methods in English, Methods in Latin, Methods in Elementary Science (the primary course in Botany and Physics) and methods in one of the following groups, viz. : (*a*) Greek, or (*b*) French and German, or (*c*) Chemistry, Physics and Biology, shall be entitled to a normal college interim certificate. The holder of a specialist's non-professional certificate in any of the courses recognised by the Education Department, who passes the final examination (including methods in the subjects of his non-professional certificate) shall be entitled to a normal college interim specialist's certificate in the subjects of his non-professional specialist's course.

THE EDUCATIONAL COUNCIL.

81. The Educational Council, authorised by the Education Department Act, 1896, to conduct departmental examinations, shall hold its first meeting each year as may be fixed by the Minister of Education and shall organise by electing as chairman one of its members. Subsequent meetings of the Council shall be held from time to time as may be determined by the Council.

82. The Council shall appoint examiners of well known ability as teachers either in a university or high school, to prepare examination papers for the examinations of the pupils in the second, third and fourth forms of high schools and collegiate institutes, and such other examinations as may be transferred to the Council with the approval of the Education Department. The Council shall also appoint examiners of well known experience as inspectors or teachers (from lists to be submitted by the Minister of Education), to prepare examination papers at all other departmental examinations.

83. For the purpose of reading the answer papers of candidates at the examinations of Forms II., III. and IV., the Council shall appoint, as associate examiners, graduates of any of the universities in the British dominions or specialists according to the regulations of the Education Department actually engaged in teaching. For the purpose of reading the answer papers of candidates of other examinations the Council shall appoint as associate examiners, persons holding first class certificates (in the case of kindergarten examinations, teachers specially qualified) in actual service. The lists from which such selection is made shall be furnished by the Minister of Education and shall, in each case contain, if required by the Council, the names of at least twice the number of associate examiners to be appointed. The number of examiners appointed by the Council for each examination shall be subject to the instructions of the Minister of Education from time to time.

84. All communications or references requiring the attention of the Council shall be addressed to the Education Department. The Registrar of the Council shall submit for consideration all matters referred by the Minister of Education. The Council shall report promptly to the Minister of Education all matters that require any action by the Education Department or any of its officers. The Council shall appoint an executive committee. The Education Department shall appoint a chairman of the Board of Examiners who shall exercise such supervision over the examinations as the Council may order. Candidates may have their papers re-examined on placing an appeal to that effect in the hands of the Minister of Education within 20 days after the publication of the results of the examination.

TEACHERS' CERTIFICATES.

85. The Minister of Education may issue certificates, on the report of the Educational Council or the Education Department, as follows, viz., any person who attends a public kindergarten for one year and passes the pre-scribed examination shall be entitled to an assistant's certificate ; any person who has obtained an assistant's certificate and who has attended a provincial kindergarten one year and passes the prescribed examinations shall be entitled to a director's certificate. Any person who attends a normal school one term and who passes the prescribed examinations shall be entitled to a second class public school certificate. Any person who has passed the final examinations of the normal college shall be entitled to a normal college interim certificate.

86. A normal college interim certificate shall entitle the holder, if under 21 years of age, to teach in a public school only, and if over 21 years, to teach in public or high school. After two years' successful experience as teachers, the holders of such certificates shall, on the report of the inspector concerned, be entitled to a permanent certificate as a first class public school teacher or as a high school assistant, ordinary or specialist, according to the class of school in which the experience was acquired. Normal college interim certificates may be extended from year to year on the report of a public or high school inspector. Any graduate in Arts in any university in the British Dominions, who holds a high school assistant's certificate, and who, as shown by the report of the high school inspector, has taught successfully three years (two of which at least were spent in a high school), shall be entitled to a certificate as principal of a high school or collegiate institute.

87. A third class certificate shall be valid for the full period of three years from the date thereof ; and may on expiration be renewed by any Board of Examiners for any period not exceeding three years, on the following conditions, viz. :—(a) Where the applicant has re-passed the Form II. exami-nation or holds any other non-professional certificate of a higher grade ; (b) where the applicant attempted such examination and obtained a standing acceptable to the Board ; (c) where the applicant has re-passed the county model school examination. The certificate of any teacher who has not taught the full period of three years for which his certificate was granted may be extended by the county board for any time lost by sickness or any other cause. In all cases the report of the inspector with respect to the efficiency of the applicant as a teacher must be satisfactory. All renewals shall be issued with the authority of the Board, and shall be limited to the jurisdiction of the Board of Examiners granting the same.

88. In case it appears that a duly qualified teacher is not available, and that it is in the public interest that a teacher should be temporarily retained in any school, the Minister of Education may, on the report of the inspector, extend a third class certificate for one year, such certificate to be valid only under the Board of Trustees applying for the same. With the consent of the Minister of Education, a temporary certificate may be given by the inspector to any person of suitable character and attainments where a qualified teacher is not available.

PUBLIC SCHOOL INSPECTORS AND DUTIES OF INSPECTORS GENERALLY.

89. Any person with five years' successful experience as a teacher, of which at least three years shall have been in a public school; who holds either specialist's non-professional standing obtained on a university examination, or a degree in arts from any university in Ontario with first class graduation honours in one or more of the other recognised departments in such University; and who has passed the examinations of the Ontario Normal College for a specialist's certificate shall be entitled to a certificate as an inspector of public schools.

90. Every inspector, of any class of schools conducted under the Education Department, while officially visiting a school, shall have supreme authority in the school, and may direct teachers and pupils in regard to any or all of the exercises of the school-room. He shall, by personal examination or otherwise as he may be directed by the Minister of Education, ascertain the character of the teaching in the schools which he is authorised to visit, and shall make inquiry and examination in such manner as he may think proper, into the efficiency of the staff, the accommodation and equipment of the school, and all matters affecting the health and comfort of the pupils. He shall report to the Minister of Education any violation of the Schools Act or the regulations of the Education Department in reference to the class of schools for which he is inspector.

TEACHERS' INSTITUTES.

91. Every teachers' institute shall have one meeting each year on a Friday and Saturday to be named by the management committee. The county council may allow Thursday to be taken also if considered expedient. The institute shall hold two sittings per day of three hours each for at least two days, and one evening sitting. All questions and discussions foreign to the teachers' work shall be avoided. The officers of the institute shall be a president, vice-president and secretary-treasurer. There shall be a management committee of five persons, to be appointed by the members of the institute. The officers and the management committee shall be elected annually.

92. The inspector shall furnish the secretary of the institute with a list of teachers in his county or inspectoral division. Every public school teacher shall attend continuously all the sessions of the institute of his county or inspectoral division and shall answer to the calling of the roll at the opening and closing of each session. A report of the sessions attended by each teacher shall be sent by the secretary to the Board of Trustees employing such teacher.

TEACHERS' READING COURSE.

93. The Minister of Education may prescribe a course of reading for the teachers of public schools. The course shall extend over three years and certificates for reading more than three books in one year shall not be granted by the Inspector. For the purposes of the course the year shall correspond with the calendar year. A teacher may enter on the course by taking any of the books prescribed for the year. The list of books for each year will be announced by the Education Department.

94. Any teacher who desires a certificate of having taken the public school teachers' reading course shall make a synopsis of not less than ten or more than fifteen pages of each book read, and shall transmit the same to the inspector of his district on or before the 30th of June in each year. Such synopsis shall be accompanied by a fee of twenty-five cents and a declaration that the books prescribed for the year were read and that the synopsis submitted was prepared without assistance by the person signing the same.

95. The management committee of each teachers' institute shall appoint two persons, who with the inspector shall form a committee for determining whether the synopsis made by the teacher desiring a certificate indicates that the books have been read intelligently. The inspector shall issue a certificate for each book so read, on the form prescribed by the Minister of Education to every teacher whose synopsis has been found satisfactory. If a teacher is unable to read all the books prescribed for the year or if his synopsis of any book has been rejected, he may substitute the books of the next year for those omitted or rejected.

96. Any teacher who submits to the Education Department certificates showing that he has satisfactorily read nine of the books prescribed, shall be entitled to receive from the Minister of Education a diploma certifying to the completion of one full reading course covering three years. Additional diplomas shall be awarded to teachers who complete additional courses of three years.

Religious Instruction.

97. Every public and high school shall be opened with the Lord's Prayer, and closed with the reading of the Scriptures and the Lord's Prayer, or the prayer authorised by the Department of Education. When a teacher claims to have conscientious scruples in regard to opening or closing the school as herein prescribed, he shall notify the trustees to that effect in writing; and it shall be the duty of the trustees to make such provision in the premises as they may deem expedient.

98. The Scriptures shall be read daily and systematically, without comment or explanation ; the portions used may be taken from the book of selections adopted by the Department for that purpose, or from the Bible, as the trustees, by resolution, may direct. Trustees may also order the reading of the Bible or the authorized Scripture Selections by both pupils and teachers at the opening and closing of the school, and the repeating of the Ten Commandments at least once a week.

99. No pupil shall be required to take part in any religious exercise objected to by his parents or guardians, and in order to the observance of this regulation, the teacher, before commencing a religious exercise, is to allow a 'short interval to elapse, during which the children of Roman Catholics, and of others who have signified their objection, may retire. If in virtue of the right to be absent from the religious exercises, any pupil does not enter the school room till the close of the time allowed for religious instruction, such absence shall not be treated as an offence against the rules of the schoo .

100. The clergy of any denomination, or their authorized representatives, shall have the right to give religious instruction to the pupils of their own church, in each school house, at least once a week, after the hour of closing the school in the afternoon ; and if the clergy of more than one denomination apply to give religious instruction in the same school house, the Board of Trustees shall decide on what day of the week the school house shall be at the disposal of the clergymen of each denomination, at the time above stated. But it shall be lawful for the Board of Trustees to allow a clergyman of any denomination, or its authorized representative, to give religious instruction to the pupils of his own church providing it be not during the regular hours of the school. Emblems of a denominational character shall not be exhibited in a public school during regular school hours.

Grants to Weak Schools.

101. Where on the report of the inspector or on other satisfactory evidence it appears that any school section is so limited in area, or is so remote from market or railway accommodation, or has suffered from any exceptional cause as to clearly establish the inability of the ratepayers to

bear the ordinary burdens of taxation for school purposes, the Minister of Education may appropriate to such section out of the grant to poor schools such sum of money from year to year as he may deem expedient.

102. The inspector shall submit to the county council at the regular meeting thereof in January or June of each year, a list of schools in his inspectoral division where the assessment for school purposes is insufficient for the proper maintenance of the school, and shall indicate in each case any special reason why the statutory grants for school purposes should be supplemented by the county council.

103. All schools receiving special grants, either from township or county councils, shall receive from the Poor School Fund, voted by the Legislature, the equivalent of such special grant, provided the sum voted by the Legislature is sufficient. When the legislative grant is not sufficient to admit of paying the equivalent of the county or township grant, then such grant shall be made *pro rata*. Any portion of the Poor School Fund remaining after such payments are made may be distributed among other weak schools on the report of the inspector.

SUPERANNUATED TEACHERS.

104. Any subscriber to the fund for superannuated teachers who fails or neglects to pay the annual subscription of four dollars on or before the 31st of December in any year, shall be required to pay for such year the sum of five dollars. In the case of persons under sixty years of age who have been placed upon the superannuated list, proof of disability for professional service shall be furnished annually to the Department. Should it appear that any superannuated teacher under sixty years of age is capable of resuming his profession, the allowance shall in the meantime be withdrawn. No allowance shall be paid unless satisfactory evidence of good moral character is furnished to the Education Department annually, or when required.

TEXT BOOKS.

105. The copyright of every authorised text book shall, where possible, be vested in the Education Department. The publisher of an authorised text book shall submit to the Minister of Education a sample copy of every edition for approval, and no edition of any text book shall be considered as approved unless a certificate to that effect, in writing, has been issued by the Minister of Education.

106. Before any authorised text book is placed on the market, the publisher thereof shall execute such agreements and give such security for the publication of such book as may be required by the Minister of Education. Any authorised text book shall be subject at every stage of its manufacture to the inspection and approval of the Education Department as regards printing, binding and paper, and may be removed from the list of authorised text books in case the publisher fails to comply with the regulations of the Education Department

107. Every authorised text book shall bear the imprint of the publisher, and shall show upon the cover the authorised retail price. No part of an authorised text book shall be used for advertising purposes, and no change shall be made in the letterpress, binding or paper of any authorised text book without the consent of the Minister of Education. Books recommended as reference books shall not be used as text books by the pupils, and any teacher who permits such books, or any other book not authorised as a text book for the public schools, to be used as such, shall be liable to such penalties as are imposed by the School Act.

GENERAL DIRECTIONS TO TRUSTEES.

108. The notice calling an annual or special meeting should be signed by the secretary or by a majority of the trustees. Any ratepayer may call the meeting to order and nominate a chairman as soon as the hour appointed arrives. The business of all school meetings should be conducted according to the following rules of order :—

(1.) *Addressing Chairman.*—Every elector shall rise previously to speaking and address himself to the chairman.

(2.) *Order of speaking.*—When two or more electors arise at once, the chairman shall name the elector who shall speak first, when the other elector or electors shall next have the right to address the meeting in the order named by the chairman.

(3.) *Motion to be read.*—Any elector may require the question or motion under discussion to be read for his information at any time, but not so as to interrupt an elector who may be speaking.

(4.) *Speaking twice.*—No elector shall speak more than twice on the same question or amendment without leave of the meeting, except in explanation of something which may have been misunderstood, or until every one choosing to speak shall have spoken.

(5.) *Protest.*—No protest against an election, or other proceedings of the school meeting, shall be received by the chairman. All protests must be sent to the inspector within twenty days at least after the meeting.

(6) *Adjournment.*—A motion to adjourn a school meeting shall always be in order, provided that no second motion to the same effect shall be made until after some intermediate proceedings shall have been had.

(7.) *Motion to be in writing and seconded.*—A motion cannot be put from the chair, or debated, unless the same be seconded. If required by the chairman, all motions must be reduced to writing.

(8.) *Withdrawal of a motion.*—After a motion has been announced or read by the chairman, it shall be deemed to be in possession of the meeting ; but may be withdrawn at any time before decision, by the consent of the meeting.

(9.) *Kind of motions to be received.*—When a motion is under debate no other motion shall be received, unless to amend it, or to postpone it, or for adjournment.

(10.) *Order of putting motion.*—All questions shall be put in the reverse order in which they are moved. Amendments shall be put before the main motion ; the last amendment first, and so on.

(11.) *Reconsidering motion.*—A motion to reconsider a vote may be made by any elector at the same meeting ; but no vote of reconsideration shall be taken more than once on the same question at the same meeting.

(12.) *Minutes.*—At the close of every annual or special meeting the chairman should sign the minutes, and send forthwith to the inspector a copy of the same, signed by himself and the secretary.

(13.) *Legal Trustee.*—Every trustee declared elected by the chairman of the school meeting is a legal trustee until his election is set aside by proper authority.

(14.) *Use of Seal.*—The seal of the school corporation should not be affixed to letters or notices, but only to contracts, agreements, deeds, or other papers, which are designed to bind the trustees as a corporation for the payment of money, or the performance of any specified act, duty or thing.

INSTRUCTIONS AND REGULATIONS.

109. Instructions may be issued by the Minister of Education from time to time to inspectors or other officers in carrying out the provisions of these regulations.

110. All former regulations of the Education Department are repealed, subject to such provisions for the years 1896 and 1897 as are contained in the Circular of Instructions issued by the Minister of Education on the date of the adoption of these regulations.

SCHEDULE A.—PUBLIC SCHOOL COURSES OF STUDY.

Form I.

Reading.—The use of the Tablets and Parts I. and II. of the First Reader.

Spelling.—Spelling from dictation and orally.

Writing.—Writing from blackboard copies.

Geography.—Conversations respecting the earth; its divisions of land and water; its plants and animals; explanation of any reference to places in the reading lessons.

English Language.—Oral exercises in language, correction of mistakes in conversation.

Arithmetic.—Notation and numeration to 1,000; addition and subtraction; mental arithmetic.

Drawing.—The exercises in first Reader and blackboard exercises.

Music —Rote singing.

Form II.

Reading.—The Second Reader; easy questions on the literature of every lesson.

Spelling.—Oral spelling, and dictation on slates and paper; blackboard exercises.

Writing.—Copy books Nos. 1 and 2.

Geography.—Local geography and elementary definitions; map of the world; map geography of all places referred to in reading lessons.

English Language.—Oral and written exercises in language and composition; correction of mistakes in conversation.

Arithmetic.—Notation and numeration to 1,000,000; multiplication and division; mental arithmetic.

Physiology and Temperance.—Conversations on temperance, the use of alcoholic stimulants, and the laws of health.

Drawing.—Authorised Drawing Course, Nos. 1 and 2.

Music.—Rote singing, continued; easy notation.

Form III.

Reading.—The Third Reader; literature of every lesson.

Spelling.—Course in Form II. continued.

Writing.—Copy Books Nos. 3 and 4.

Geography.—Definitions; general geography of the Dominion of Canada; North and South America; Ontario more particularly; map drawing.

Grammar and Composition.—Classes of words and their inflections ; simple analysis ; descriptive and letter writing.

History.—Conversations on British and Canadian History ; local history.

Arithmetic.—Reduction ; compound rules : bills and accounts ; averages and aggregates ; sharing and measurements ; mental arithmetic.

Physiology and Temperance.—Conversations on temperance ; the physical effects of intoxicating liquors ; importance of exercise.

Drawing.—Authorised Drawing Course, Nos. 3 and 4.

Music.—Easy exercises in musical notation ; songs.

Form IV.

Reading.—The Fourth Reader ; the literature of every lesson.

Spelling.—Systematic orthography and orthoepy.

Writing.—Copy Books Nos. 5 and 6.

Geography.—Geography of Canada and the British Empire ; the continents ; map drawing.

Grammar and Composition.—Elements of formal grammar, analysis and composition. Descriptive, narrative and letter writing.

History.—Leading events in Canadian and British History, with special attention to Canadian History since 1841.

Arithmetic.—Measures, multiples, fractions, percentage, interest, mental arithmetic.

Physiology and Temperance.—Digestion, respiration, the circulation of the blood, and the nervous system. The effects of alcohol and narcotics.

Drawing.—Authorised Drawing Course Nos. 5 and 6.

Music.—Course in Form III., continued.

Form V.

Reading.—Practice in oral reading continued.

English Grammar and Rhetoric.—Etymology and Syntax, including the inflection, classification, and elementary analysis of words and the logical structure of the sentence ; rhetorical structure of the sentence and paragraph ; exercises chiefly on passages from authors not prescribed.

English Composition.—Essays on familiar subjects ; familiar letters.

English Poetical Literature.—Intelligent and appreciative comprehension of the prescribed texts ; memorisation of the finest passages ; supplementary reading from authors prescribed by the teacher ; oral reading of the texts. The examination in literature will consist of "sight work" as well as of questions on the prescribed texts.

History.—The History of Canada ; British History.

Geography.—The building up of the earth ; its land surface ; the ocean ; comparison of continents as to physical features, natural products and inhabitants ; relations of physical conditions to animal and vegetable products, and of national products and geographical condition to the occupations of the people and national progress. Form, size and motions of the earth ; lines drawn on the map, with reasons for their position; relation of the positions of the earth with respect to the sun, to light and temperature; the air; its movements; causes affecting climate. Natural and manufactured products of the countries of the world, with their exports and imports; trans-continental commercial highways and their relation to centres of population ; internal commercial highways of Canada and the chief internal commercial highways of the United States ; commercial relations of Great Britain and her colonies. Forms of governments in the countries of the world and their relation to civilisation.

Arithmetic and Mensuration.—Proofs of elementary rules in arithmetic; fractions (theory and proofs); commercial arithmetic; mental arithmetic; mensuration of rectilinear figures.

Algebra.—Elementary rules ; highest common measure ; lowest common multiple ; fractions begun.

Geometry.—Euclid, Book I., propositions 1-26 ; easy deductions.

Drawing.—Object and model drawing ; High School Drawing Course, Books Nos. 1 and 2.

Bookkeeping.—Bookkeeping by single and double entry ; commercial forms, such as drafts, notes and cheques ; general business transactions. The Bookkeeping shall be specially suitable for farmers and artisans, or for retail merchants and general traders.

*Botany.—The practical study of representatives of the following natural orders of flowering plants : Ranunculaceæ, Cruciferæ, Malvaceæ, Leguminosæ, Rosaceæ, Sapindaceæ, Umbelliferæ, Compositæ, Labiatæ, Capuliferæ, Araceæ, Liliaceæ, Iridaceæ, Coniferæ, and Gramineæ (types contained in text-book). Drawing and description of plants and their classification. Comparison of different organs, morphology of root, stem, leaves and hairs, parts of the flowers, germination, reproduction of flowering plants, pollination, fertilization, and the nature of fruits and seeds. In the examination a plant belonging to one of the above-mentioned orders to be selected by the presiding examiner shall be submitted to the candidates for description and classification.

*Agriculture.—The course in the authorized text book.

*Latin and Greek.—The Elementary Latin Book, Grammar Composition and sight reading. The Beginner's Greek Book begun.

*French and German.—Grammar, Composition and sight reading.

Schedule B. —High School Courses of Study.

Form I.

Reading.—Practice in Oral Reading.

English Grammar and Rhetoric.—Etymology and Syntax, including the inflection, classification, and elementary analysis of words and the logical structure of the sentence ; rhetorical structure of the sentence and paragraph ; exercises chiefly on passages from authors not prescribed.

English Composition.—Essays on familiar subjects ; familiar letters.

English Poetical Literature.—Intelligent and appreciative comprehension of the prescribed texts ; memorization of the finest passages ; Supplementary Reading from authors provided in the High School library or supplied by pupils under the authority of the High School Board ; oral reading of the texts. The examination will consist of " sight " work as well as of questions on the prescribed texts.

History.—The History of Canada ; British History.

Geography.—The building up of the earth ; its land surface ; the ocean ; comparison of continents as to physical features, natural products and inhabitants ; relations of physical conditions to animal and vegetable products, and of natural products and geographical condition to the occupations of the people and national progress. Form, size and motions of the earth ; lines drawn on the map, with reasons for their position ; relation of the positions of the earth with respect to the sun, to light and temperature ; the air ; its movements ; causes affecting climate. Natural and manufactured products of the countries of the world, with their exports and imports ; transcontinental commercial highways and their relation to centres of population ; internal commercial highways of Canada and the chief internal commercial highways of the United States ; commercial relations of Great Britain and her colonies. Forms of governments in the countries of the world and their relation to civilization.

Arithmetic and Mensuration.— Proofs of elementary rules in Arithmetic ; Fractions (theory and proofs) ; Commercial Arithmetic ; Mental Arithmetic ; Mensuration of rectilinear figures.

Algebra.—Elementary rules ; Highest Common Measure ; Lowest Common Multiple ; Fractions begun.

Geometry.—Euclid, Book I., propositions 1-26 ; easy deductions.

Drawing.—Object and Model Drawing, High School Drawing Course, Books 1 and 2 ; * Perspective Drawing, Book 3.

*Bookkeeping. — Bookkeeping by single and double entry ; commercial forms, such as drafts, notes and cheques ; general business transactions. The bookkeeping shall be specially suitable for farmers and artisans, or for retail merchants and general traders.

*Stenography.— The elements of Pitman's system.

*Latin and Greek.—The Elementary Latin Book, grammar, composition and sight-reading. The Beginner's Greek Book begun.

*French and German. —Grammar, composition, conversation, dictation and sight-reading.

*Botany.—The practical study of representatives of the following natural orders of flowering plants : —Ranunculaceæ, Cruciferæ, Malvaceæ, Leguminosæ, Rosaceæ, Sapindaceæ, Umbelliferæ, Compositæ, Labiatæ, Cupuliferæ, Araceæ, Liliaceæ, Iridaceæ, Coniferæ and Gramineæ (types contained in text-book). Drawing and description of plants and their classification. Comparison of different organs, morphology of root, stem, leaves and hairs, parts of the flowers, germination reproduction of flowering plants, pollination, fertilization, and the nature of fruits and seeds. At the examination in Botany a plant belonging to one of the prescribed orders, to be selected by the presiding examiner, will be submitted to the candidates for description and classification.

Form II.

Reading.—The course in Form I. continued.

English Grammar and Rhetoric.—The course in Form I. continued, with the main facts in the development of the language.

English Composition.—The course in Form I. continued. For examination purposes an essay of about three pages of foolscap on one of the themes prescribed by the examiners will be required. The penmanship, spelling, punctuation, construction of sentences, the logical arrangement of the thought, the literary accuracy and aptness of the language, and the general plan or scope of the whole essay will be especially considered by the examiners.

English Poetical Literature.—The course in Form I. continued, with the prescribed texts. At the examination every candidate will be tested as to his familiarity with, and intelligent comprehension of the prescribed texts, and as to his knowledge from memory of the finest passages in prose and poetry. His ability to interpret literature for himself and his knowledge of English Literature generally will be tested by questions on a "sight" passage not contained in the text prescribed.

History.—Great Britain and Canada from 1763 to 1871, with the outlines of the preceding periods of British History. The Geography relating to the History prescribed.

Arithmetic and Mensuration.—Course in Arithmetic Form I. reviewed and completed. Mensuration ; right parallelopipeds, pyramids and prisms ; the circle, sphere, cylinder and cone.

Algebra.—The course in Form I. reviewed and completed, with simple equations of one, two and three unknown quantities ; simple products.

Geometry.—Euclid, Book I. ; deductions.

*Latin and Greek.—The course in Latin in Form I. continued, with the prescribed author. The Beginner's Greek Book, to page 301 ; sight translation. In Latin and Greek Grammar the examination questions in this Form shall be based mainly on prose passages. The sentences for translation into Latin and Greek shall be the same in idiom and vocabulary as in the text books ; the sentences for translation into English shall consist of " sight " work and shall be of the same character as the sentences in the text books.

*French and German. —The course in Form I. continued, with the reader. In French and German Grammar the examination in Form II. shall be based mainly on prose passages ; the sentences for translation into French or German shall be the same in idiom and vocabulary as in the authorised text books ; the sentences for translation into English shall consist of " sight " work and shall be of the same character as the sentences in the authorised text books.

*Physics. —An experimental course defined as follows :— Metric system of weights and measures. Use of the balance. Phenomena of gravitation. Matter attracts matter. Laws of attraction. Cavendish experiment. Attraction independent of condition. Illustration of weight of gases, liquids and solids. Specific gravity. Meaning of the term " a form of matter." All matter may be subjected to transmutation. " Chemistry," application of measurement by weight (mass) to such transmutation leads to the theory of elements. Matter indestructible. Meaning of "Force." Various manifestations of force, with illustrations from the phenomena of electricity, magnetism and heat. Force measured in gravitation units ; consequent double meaning of the terms expressing units of weight as mass and units of weight as force. Meaning of "work." Measurement of working gravitation units. Meaning of " Energy." Effects of force continuously applied to matter. Laws of matter in motion. Velocity ; Acceleration. Statement of Newton's laws of motion. Definition of "Mass." Meaning, value and application of " g." Mass a measure of matter. Conservation of energy. Energy, like matter, indestructible and transmutable. Study of the states of matter. Properties and law of gases, liquids and solids. Laws of diffusion. Elementary laws of heat. Mechanical equivalent. Latent heat. Specific heat. Caloric.

*Bookkeeping. —Bookkeeping by single and double entry ; business forms, usages and correspondence. The Principal and the Board of Trustees may arrange any other course in Bookkeeping that in their opinion is better adapted to the interests of the pupils taking up the subject.

*Stenography. —Course in Form I. continued.

Form III.

English Composition. —Essay-writing.

English Poetical Literature. —Course in Form II. continued, with the prescribed texts.

History. —Outlines of Roman History to the death of Augustus, and of Greek History to the Battle of Chaeronea. The geography relating to the history prescribed.

Algebra. —Course in Form II. reviewed ; Square Root ; Indices ; Surds ; quadratics of one or two unknown quantities.

Geometry. —Euclid ; Books I., II., and III. Deductions.

Latin and Greek. —Course in Form II. continued ; with the prescribed texts. The examination in Latin and Greek shall consist of translation into English of passages from prescribed texts ; translation at sight (with the aid of vocabularies) of easy Attic prose and of passages from some easy Latin prose author ; translation from English into Greek and Latin of sentences and of easy narrative passages based on the prescribed prose texts and such grammatical and other questions as arise naturally from the prescribed texts. Practice in the translation of Greek and Latin beyond the prescribed texts shall be expected of candidates.

French and German. —Course in Form II. continued ; with the prescribed texts. In Form III. the examination in Grammar shall consist mainly of translations into French or German of short English sentences as a test of the candidate's knowledge of grammatical forms and structure and the translation of passages from English into French or German and "sight" translation. Practice in French and German beyond the prescribed texts shall be expected of candidates.

Chemistry.—An experimental course defined as follows :—Properties of Hydrogen, Chlorine, Oxygen, Sulphur, Nitrogen, Carbon and their more important compounds. Nomenclature. Laws of combination of the elements. The Atomic Theory and Molecular Theory.

Physics.—ELECTRICITY.—Voltaic cells, common kinds ; chemical action in the cell ; magnetic effects of the current ; chemical effects of the current ; voltameter ; astatic and tangent galvanometers ; simple notions of potential; Ohm's law, with units ; best arrangement of cells ; electric light, arc and incandescent ; magnetism ; inclination and declination of compass ; current induction ; induction coil ; dynamo and motor ; electric bell ; telegraph ; telephone ; electro-plating. SOUND. Caused by vibrations ; illustration of vibrations, pendulums, rods, strings, membranes, plates, columns of air ; propagated by waves ; its velocity : determination of velocity ; pitch ; standard forks, acoustical $C = 512$, musical, $A = 870$; intervals : harmonic scale : diatonic scale ; equally tempered scale ; vibration of air in open and closed tubes, with wave-lengths ; resonators ; nodes and loops ; vibration of strings and wires ; reflection of sound : manometric flames. LIGHT. - Rectilinear propagation ; image through a pinhole ; beam ; pencil ; photometry ; shadow and grease-spot photometers ; reflection and scattering of light : laws of reflection ; images in plain mirrors : multiple images in inclined mirrors ; concave and convex mirrors ; drawing images : refraction ; laws and index of refraction ; total reflexion : path through a prism ; lenses : drawing image produced by a lens : simple microscope ; dispersion and colour ; spectrum ; recomposition of white light.

Botany.—The practical study of representatives of the flowering plants of the locality and representatives of the chief sub-divisions of cryptogams, such as a fern, a lycopod, a horse-tail, a liverwort, a moss, a lichen, a mushroom and a chara. The drawing and description of parts of plants and classification. Comparison of different organs, morphology of root, stem, leaves and hair, parts of the flower, reproduction of flowering plants, pollination, fertilisation and the nature of fruit and seeds. At the examination two plants to be selected by the presiding examiner will be submitted, one for classification and one for description. In classification candidates will be allowed to use their floras (the authorised text-book in Botany).

Form IV.

English Composition.—Course in Form III. continued.

English Poetical Literature.—Course in Form III. continued, with the prescribed texts. The examination questions will test within reasonable limits the power of appreciating literary art.

History. - English History from the discovery of America to 1763. Ancient History, the course in Form III. reviewed. The geography relating to the History prescribed.

Algebra.—Course in Form III. reviewed. Theory of Divisors ; Ratio, Proportion and Variation ; Progressions ; Notation ; Permutations and Combinations ; Binomial Theorem ; Interest Forms ; Annuities.

Geometry.—Euclid. The course in Forms II. and III. reviewed ; Books IV. and VI. ; Definitions of Book V. ; Deductions.

Trigonometry.—Trigonometrical ratios, with their relations to each other ; Sines, etc., of the sum and difference of angles with deduced formulas ; Use of Logarithms ; Solution of Triangles ; Expressions for the area of triangles ; Radii of circumscribed, inscribed and escribed circles.

Latin and Greek.—Course in Form III. continued, with the prescribed texts. In Form IV. the examination in Latin and Greek shall be of an advanced character and shall include the translation into Latin and Greek of ordinary narrative passages of English. The Roman method of pronouncing Latin is recommended.

French and German.—Course in Form III. continued, with the prescribed texts. The course of study in Form IV. in grammar, composition, and sight translation shall be the same as in Form III., but the examination shall be of a more advanced character.

Physics.—An experimental course defined as follows :—MECHANICS.— Uniformly accelerated rectilineal motion, particularly under gravity; composition and resolution of forces ; triangle and parallelogram of forces ; friction ; polygon of forces ; with easy examples. HYDROSTATICS.—Fluid pressure at a point ; pressure on a horizontal plane ; pressure on an inclined plane ; resultant vertical pressure, and resultant horizontal pressure, when fluid is under air pressure and when not ; transmission of pressure ; Bramah's press ; equilibrium of liquids of unequal density in a bent tube ; the barometer ; air pump ; water pump, common and force ; syphon ELECTRICITY. Voltaic cells, common kinds ; chemical action in the cell ; magnetic effects of the current ; chemical effects of the current voltameter ; astatic and tangent galvanometers ; simple notions of potential ; Ohm's law, with units, best arrangement of cells ; electric light, arc and incandescent ; magnetism ; inclination and declination of compass ; current induction ; induction coil ; dynamo and motor ; electric bell ; telegraph ; telephone ; electro-plating. SOUND.—Caused by vibrations ; illustration of vibrations, pendulums, rods, strings, membranes, plates, columns of air ; propagated by waves ; its velocity ; determination of velocity ; pitch ; standard forks ; acoustical $C = 512$, musical $A = 870$; intervals ; harmonic scale ; diatonic scale ; equally tempered scale ; vibration of air in open and closed tubes, with wave lengths ; resonators ; nodes and loops ; vibration of strings and wires ; reflection of sound ; manometric flames. LIGHT.—Rectilinear propagation ; image through a pin-hole ; beam ; pencil ; photometry ; shadow, and grease-spot photometers ; reflection and scattering of light ; laws of reflection ; images in plain mirrors ; multiple images in inclined mirrors ; concave and convex mirrors ; drawing images ; refraction : laws and index of refraction ; total reflection ; path through a prism ; lenses ; drawing image produced by a lens ; simple microscope ; dispersion and colour : spectrum : recomposition of white light.

Chemistry.—Chemical theory. The practical study of the following elements, with their most characteristic compounds, in illustration of Mendelejeff's classification of the elements. Hydrogen ; Sodium ; Potassium ; Magnesium, Zinc ; Calcium ; Strontium ; Barium ; Boron, Aluminum ; Carbon, Silicon, Tin, Lead ; Nitrogen ; Phosphorus ; Arsenic ; Antimony ; Bismuth ; Oxygen, Sulphur ; Fluorine, Chlorine, Bromine, Iodine ; Manganese, Iron. Elementary Qualitative Analysis. At the examination in Practical Chemistry for Form IV. the material for determination shall be sent from the Education Department, and shall consist of one pure simple salt. In the qualitative analysis of this salt the candidates shall not be allowed the use of text-books, analytical tables, notes, or charts. Places shall be allotted to the candidates so that each one shall be at least ten feet away from any other candidate. Each candidate shall have exclusive use of one set of reagents, apparatus and lamp, while at work. If the number of candidates should exceed the accommodations of the laboratory, the candidates shall be examined in sections.

Biology.—ELEMENTS OF ZOOLOGY.—Thorough examination of the external form, the gills and the viscera of some common fish. Study of the prepared skeleton of the same. Demonstration of the arrangement of the muscular and nervous systems and the sense organs, as far as these can be studied without the aid of a microscope. Comparison of the structure of the frog with that of the fish. The skeleton of the pectoral and pelvic girdles, and of the appendages of the frog, and the observation of the chief facts in the development of its spawn, till the the adult form is attained. Examination of the external from of a turtle and a snake. Examination of the structure of a pigeon or a fowl. Study of the skeleton and also of the teeth and viscera of a cat or dog. Study of the crayfish as a type of the Arthropode

Comparison of the crayfish with an insect (grasshopper, cricket, or cockroach), also with a millipede and a spider. Examination of an earthworm and a leech. Study of a fresh-water mussel and a pond snail. The principles of zoological nomenclature as illustrated by some of the common fresh-water fish, such as the sucker and herring, bass and perch. Study of an amœba or paramœcium as a type of a unicellular animal. The modifications of the form of the body in vertebrates in connection with different methods of locomotion. ELEMENTS OF BOTANY.—The practical study of representatives of the flowering plants of the locality in which the school is situated, and representatives of the chief sub-divisions of cryptogams, such as a fern, a lycopod, a horsetail, a liverwort, a moss, a lichen, a mushroom, and a chara. An elementary knowledge of the microscopic structure of the bean and the maize. The drawing and description of parts of plants and classification. Comparison of different organs, morphology of root, stem, leaves, and hair, parts of the flower, reproduction of flowering plants, pollination, fertilisation, and the nature of fruit and seeds. The material for examination will consist of two plants, a microscopic section and an animal. The plant designated " A " is to be identified by means of the flora. Twenty minutes shall be allowed for this operation. The text-books shall then be taken from the candidates and the paper with the plant designated " B," the animal and the microscopic section distributed. Each candidate is to be allowed the use of a compound microscope during the second period. The material for this examination will be sent from the Education Department.

COMMERCIAL DIPLOMA COURSE.

The course shall consist of bookkeeping, business forms and usages and stenography. Bookkeeping shall be taken in six sets as follows : -

Set I. shall show transactions extending over a period of two months, the transactions of the first month being done by Single Entry, and of the second by Double Entry, and showing the change from Single to Double Entry. Books to be used : Day Book (first month), Journal Day Book (second month), Cash Book, Bill Book, and Ledger.

Set II. The transactions shall be the same as for Set I., those of the first month being done by double entry, and of the second month by Single Entry, and showing the change from Double Entry to Single Entry. Books to be used : Four Column Journal with special columns for Mdse. Purchases and Sales (first month), Day Book (second month), Cash Book, Bill Book and Ledger.

Set III. A Double Entry set with two partners. Books to be used : Journal Day Book with a special column for Mdse. Sales, Cash Book, Invoice Book, Bill Book, and Ledger, the first three as Books of original entry.

Set IV. A Double Entry set ; a continuation of Set III., the posting being done in the same Ledger. A third partner shall be admitted and the transactions shall include shipments and consignments. Books to be used : Journal Day Book, Cash Book, Invoice Book, Sales Book, Bill Book, and Ledger, the first four as books of original entry.

Set V. A Double Entry set ; a continuation of Set IV., the posting being done in a new ledger. A fourth partner shall be admitted, and the transactions shall include wholesale merchandising, shipment companies, and merchandise companies. Books to be used : The same as for Set IV.

Set VI. A set in Manufacturing. Books to be used : Journal Day Book, with a special column for Mdse. Sales, Cash Book, Time Book and Ledger.

The Cash Book shall be a book of original entry in all of the Double Entry Sets, various special columns being used in the different sets. A monthly Trial Balance shall be made in connection with Sets III., IV., and V., and Statements of Resources and Liabilities, and of Losses and Gains for all of the sets. The transactions in the different sets shall be different from year to year. The sets may recur triennially, and shall consist of not less than twenty pages of foolscap.

The bookkeeping sets of pupils who write at the examination for a commercial certificate shall be sent, prepaid, to the Education Department, with the examination papers and shall be certified by the teacher to be the work of the candidate.

Business Forms and Usages.—Negotiable paper; promissory notes; special notes; bills of exchange; acceptance; negotiation of bills, notes; cheques; collection of accounts, discharge and dishonour; special forms of due bills and orders; accounts, invoices and statements; interest; partnerships; receipts and releases; banking; and commercial correspondence.

Stenography.—At the examination in dictation in stenography, the candidate shall be required to have attained the rate of fifty words per minute. He shall also be required to transcribe his work into longhand at the rate of twelve words per minute. The dictated matter shall consist of business letters and legal documents.

Schedule C.—Course for Commercial Specialists.

Bookkeeping.—Single and Double entry bookkeeping; wholesale and retail merchandising, commission business, manufacturing, warehousing, steamboating, exchange, joint stock companies, municipalities, societies and public institutions; statements and balance sheets, partnership adjustments, liquidation and administration of estates, auditing filing papers, the use of special columns, and the various other expedients in bookkeeping to save time and labour, and secure accuracy of work.

Penmanship.—Theory and practice of penmanship, Spencerian and vertical; ledger headings; marking and engrossing.

Commercial Arithmetic.—Interest, discount, annuities certain, sinking funds, formation of interest and annuity tables, application of logarithms, stocks and investments, partnership settlements, partial payments, equation of payments, and exchange.

Banking.—Money and its substitutes; exchange; incorporation and organization of banks; business of banks, their relation to each other and to the business community; the clearing house system; legal requirements as to capital, shares, reserves, dividends, not issue; insolvency and consequent liability.

Business Forms.—Invoices, accounts, statements, due bills, orders, receipts, warehouse receipts, deposit receipts, deposit slips, bank pass books, promissory notes, bills of exchange, bank drafts, cheques, bonds, debentures, coupons, instalment scrips, stock certificates, stock transfers, proxies, letters of credit, affidavits, balance sheets, pay sheets, time sheets, and special forms of general bookkeeping, books to suit special cases.

Laws of Business.—Contracts; statute of limitations; negotiable paper and endorsements; sales of personal property; accounts, invoices, statements, etc.; chattel mortgages; real estate and mortgages; interest; agency; partnership; corporations; guarantee and suretyship; receipts and releases; insurance; master and servant; landlord and tenant; bailment; shipping and transportation; host and guest; telegraphs; auctions; patents; copyrights; trade marks and industrial designs; affidavits and declarations; subjects and aliens; wills, and joint stock companies.

Stenography.—The principles of Stenography; writing from dictation at a speed of sixty words per minute, and accurate transcription into longhand at a speed of twelve words per minute; the dictated matter to comprise business correspondence or legal documents.

Drawing.—Object and Model Drawing; Perspective and Geometrical Drawing.

APPENDIX B.—CERTAIN REGULATIONS AS AMENDED IN 1898 AND 1899.

For the academic year 1898-99 the following modifications were made in the Revised Regulations, which came into force in October, 1896 :—

Public School Leaving Examination.

This examination will be conducted in 1899 on the course of study prescribed in the regulations, except that physiology and temperance, will as in 1896, be substituted for botany. High school pupils are not eligible to write at this examination. The examination will be conducted by the Entrance Board of Examiners, under the provisions of Section 38 of the High Schools Act, and Sections 23-29 of the Regulations, subject to the usual instructions to examiners.

First Form Examination.

This examination, which is open to all pupils, will be conducted as heretofore, the course embracing reading, writing and bookkeeping, drawing, geography, and botany. First Form certificates will have the same qualifying value for teachers' certificates as public school leaving certificates.

Primary Examination.

No examination will be held in Part II. of Form II. (Regulation 43), and no certificates that give mere primary standing (Regulations 45, 48 and 49) will be issued after 1898. No change is made in the course to be taken up in Forms I. and II. of the high school or for continuation classes in public schools, by the abolition of the primary examination.

Junior Leaving Examination.

The amendment of Regulation 46 made for 1898 is continued. This will allow, at the Form III. examination for junior leaving standing, the following options :—(a) French and Greek ; (b) German and Greek ; (c) French, German, and Chemistry ; (d) French, Physics, and Chemistry ; (e) German, Physics, and Chemistry ; (f) Botany, Physics and Chemistry.
The obligatory subjects of Form III. for junior leaving are as already prescribed—viz., English Composition, English Literature, Ancient History, Algebra, Geometry, and Latin.
Unsuccessful candidates at the junior leaving examination will be allowed to write in 1899 for junior leaving standing, by selecting the same options in the course as were allowed in 1898.

Senior Leaving Examination.

The amendment of Regulation 47 made for 1898 is continued. This will allow, at the Form IV. examination for senior leaving standing, the following options :—(a) French and Greek ; (b) German and Greek ; (c) French and German ; (d) French and Chemistry ; (e) German and Chemistry ; (f) Biology and Chemistry.
The obligatory subjects of Form IV. for senior leaving are as already prescribed—viz., English Composition, English Literature, Algebra, Geometry Trigonometry, English and Ancient History, Physics and Latin.

Unsuccessful candidates at the senior leaving examination will be allowed to write in 1899 for senior leaving standing by selecting the same options in the course as were allowed in 1898.

Percentage, &c

Candidates for junior and senior leaving standing will be required to make 50 per cent. of the aggregate marks allowed in the subjects prescribed in each of the forms or parts of forms, as well as one-third in each paper; 67 per cent. of the aggregate of each form examination will be required for honours in that form. The examinations in chemistry, physics, and biology in Forms III. and IV. will be equal in difficulty, as near as may be, to the examination in the language or languages for which these subjects are taken as options; and so far as necessary, the maximum marks in each of these subjects will be adjusted for the purpose. There will be two papers in biology of Form IV.; one in botany and one in zoology, with practical work distributed between the two. The time limit for those subjects will be extended.

These modifications, it will be understood make no change in the course or the percentage required by the University for matriculation.

County Model Schools.

(1898.)—The abolition of the primary examination will not affect the rights of holders of primary standing obtained in 1898, or in a previous year, to attend county model schools. If a scarcity of teachers should arise in any county after next year, in consequence of the higher requirements, provision will be made to meet the special conditions of the locality. It should be understood that County Boards of Examiners are not allowed to award third-class certificates to candidates who do not make the higher percentage required by Regulation 63. A district certificate shall not be granted under this section of the Regulations unless there is scarcity of teachers, and until the consent of the Department has been first obtained. Renewals, granted under Regulation 87, are valid only in the county where issued.

Beginning with the examinations of the Model Schools in 1900, an additional paper in Methods will be submitted to test the ability of the students-in-training to teach drawing, writing, bookkeeping, and elementary science (botany or agriculture). There will also be an examination in reading.

Normal College.

All students entering the Normal College, irrespective of the academic course which they may have taken, must take the subjects prescribed (*see* Appendix A., Regulation 80), subject to the following conditions :—

(1.) Holders of senior leaving certificates, granted on departmental examinations, may omit Latin if they do not select Greek.

(2.) Unsuccessful candidates at previous examinations will be allowed to write at the final examination in May of any year without attendance at the Normal College, and may confine themselves to the same subjects as taken previously.

Teachers of ten years' successful experience, who hold normal school certificates, and who have the necessary academic standing, may write at the final examination in May without attendance at the Normal College.

Beginning with the examinations of the Model Schools in 1900, an additional paper in methods will be submitted to test the ability of the students-in-training to teach Drawing, Writing, Bookkeeping, and Elementary Science (Botany or Agriculture). There will also be an examination in Reading.

APPENDIX C.—DUTIES OF INSPECTORS.

THE DUTIES OF COUNTY INSPECTORS.

It is the duty of a County Inspector :

1. To visit every Public School within his jurisdiction once in each term, unless required to do so oftener (for the adjustment of disputes or other purposes) by the county council which appointed him, and to see that every school is conducted according to this Act and the regulations of the Department ;

2. To examine, at his visits of inspection, into the condition of the school as respects the progress of the pupils in learning ; the order and discipline observed ; the system of instruction pursued ; the mode of keeping the school registers ; the average attendance of pupils ; the character and condition of the building and premises ; and to give such advice to the teachers, pupils and officers of the school as he may consider proper ;

3. To deliver from time to time, public lectures in his district on some subject connected with public school education ;

4. To withhold his order for the amount apportioned from the legislative or municipal grant to any school section ; (*a*) When the school was kept open for less than six months in the year ; or (*b*) When the trustees fail to transmit the annual or semi-annual school returns properly filled up ; or (*c*) When the trustees fail to comply with the school Act, or the regulations of the Education Department ; or (*d*) When the teacher uses, or permits to be used, as a text book any book not authorised by the Education Department ; and in every case to report to the trustees and to the Education Department his reasons for so doing ;

5. To give when desired any information in his power to the Minister of Education respecting any Public School matter within his jurisdiction, to prepare and transmit to the Minister of Education, on or before the 1st day of March, an annual report in the form prescribed by the Education Department ;

7. To recommend to the county or township council such special aid as he may deem advisable to be given to new or weak school sections in the county ;

8. To appoint, in his discretion, the time and place for a special meeting ;

9. To give, at his discretion, any candidate, on due examination, a certificate of qualification to teach a school within his district until the next ensuing professional examination of teachers ;

10. To deliver over to his successor, on retiring from office, copies of his official correspondence, and all school papers in his custody, on the order of the county council or public school board appointing him.

The Act also provides :—

No Inspector of schools shall, during his tenure of office, engage in or hold any other employment, office or calling which would interfere with the full discharge of his duties as Inspector.

In addition to these provisions of the statute the following regulations are prescribed.

It is the duty of every County Inspector :—

(1) *To spend at least half a day each term in each school.* Where a school has several departments, the Inspector should devote half a day to each department. When, however, from the character of the work done, an Inspector thinks it would be in the interest of the school to extend his visit over the whole day, he should do so.

(2) *To satisfy himself as to the progress made by the pupils from time to time.* This cannot be done without many memoranda of the standing of each class. It will therefore be necessary for the Inspector to make

4296.

M 2

copious notes in regard to each recitation, showing the condition of each class and the proficiency attained in the several subjects of the curriculum. This part of the work should be thorough and searching ; and the conclusions arrived at should be based on the Inspector's own observation.

(3) *To examine into the methods of instruction pursued by the teacher.* To do this the Inspector should require the teacher of the school to teach several lessons in his presence. In this way the teacher's methods can be observed and hints given for improvement, should he evince any faults of method or of manner. Great attention should be paid to methods ; the proper and logical presentation of a subject is so important that success is impossible without it. He should see that the prescribed time for instruction in Temperance and Hygiene is observed.

(4) *To teach a few model lessons himself.* The proper methods of teaching subjects that are found to be neglected or badly taught by the teacher should be exemplified by the Inspector. Here all the qualities which go to form the model teacher should be exercised. His methods of questioning and of receiving answers, of arousing the enthusiasm of the class, of securing attention, of reaching by apt illustration the judgment of the pupils, should serve the teacher both as a model and as a stimulus.

(5) *To ascertain the nature of the discipline exercised by the teacher.* This no doubt will appear from the attention and diligence of the pupils, without special enquiry. The *manner* of the teacher will very soon indicate the nature of the discipline. It would be well, nevertheless, to ascertain whether corporal punishment is frequently resorted to, and if not, what are the punishments (if any) usually inflicted.

(6) *To examine the registers, maps, seats and all the internal and external equipment of the school-house.* He should see (*a*) that the register and class book are properly and neatly kept, and ascertain whether or not entries are made therein daily ; (*b*) that the maps are suitable and well preserved ; (*c*) that blackboards are in proper repair, and that crayons and brushes are fully supplied ; (*d*) that the furniture is generally adequate ; (*e*) that proper attention is paid to the heating and ventilation of the rooms ; (*f*) that the fences and out-houses are in proper repair ; (*g*) that the School Library is suitably cared for.

(7) *To report to Trustees in regard to such matters as require their attention.* This duty the Inspector should never neglect. The trustees of a school expect to be informed and directed as to many matters coming under the cognizance of the Inspector, who is, in a certain sense, their officer, and is appointed for the very purpose of aiding them in the discharge of their duties. His report, therefore, on the school should be full. Every necessary change coming within the scope of the duties of the trustees should be mentioned in detail ; and in no case should the school grant be withheld until they have had an opportunity of removing any defect to which their attention has been called.

(8) *To give such advice to teachers as may be deemed necessary.* This part of the Inspector's duty should be performed with tact and delicacy, and perfect frankness. Whatever defects in the teacher's manner, or in his discipline of the pupils, or methods of instruction, are discovered during the inspection of the school, should be plainly pointed out. Wherever the Inspector has reason to believe that there is any defect in the organization of the school, or in its classification, or in attention on the part of the pupils, it should be referred to, and the proper remedy suggested. This, of course, should be done privately—not in the presence of the pupils.

(9) *To see that no unauthorized text-books are used in the school.* No text-books should be placed in the hands of the pupils except those authorised for their use. Under the disguise of being books for "home study," many unauthorised text books are introduced into the school. This should be prevented by the Inspector in the exercise of his authority as an officer of the Education Department.

(10) *To withhold the school grant in certain cases.* Before the school grant is withheld : (*a*) An opportunity should be afforded the Board of Trustees

to remedy the wrong complained of. (*b*) A full statement of the case should be sent to the Department, and the consent of the Minister of Education obtained. As the grant can be withheld for any violation of the School Act or Departmental Regulations, the power thus conferred should be exercised judiciously, and only when other remedies fail.

(11) *To divide the school grants.* Care should be taken to see that the semi-annual returns of the Boards of Trustees are properly added up, and if any doubt exists as to their accuracy they should be compared with the school register. When the division of the grant is made, as required by law, it will be sufficient for the Inspector to send a statement to the Township Treasurer of the amount due each school section, and at the same time to notify the Secretary-Treasurer of each Board of Trustees of the amount due its section. The Board of Trustees can then give an order either to the teacher or to some other person to whom it desires to have the money paid, and on this order the Township Treasurer is authorised to pay the money.

(12) *To decide complaints made within twenty days in regard to the election of Trustees and other matters.* In discharging this duty the Inspector should remember that he is exercising judicial functions, and should accordingly proceed with due deliberation. He has a right to withhold his decision until such evidence is produced as he may deem necessary in regard to the question at issue.

(13) *To grant, on examination, temporary certificates.* These certificates should be granted only (*a*) when petitioned for by a Board of Trustees, and only for the school over which such Board has jurisdiction ; and (*b*) until the date of the next ensuing Departmental Examination ; and (*c*) when it appears that a teacher holding a regular certificate is not available. The consent of the Minister of Education is also necessary in every case.

(14) *To suspend a teacher's certificate.* This should be done only when the Inspector is fully satisfied that the teacher is incompetent or immoral, or has wilfully violated the School Law or the regulations of the Education Department. In the final investigation by which such suspension is to be confirmed or set aside, the fullest opportunity should be afforded the teacher to vindicate himself. Judicial fairness should in this instance also characterise the conduct of the Inspector.

(15) *To visit the County Model School at least twice in each term.* It is very desirable that the Inspector should be present at the opening of the Model School, and assist the Principal in its organisation. He should also visit the school during the term, and by his presence and counsel encourage the teachers-in-training in the pursuit of their studies. For two such visits he should be paid by the county council at the same rate as he is paid for Public School inspection.

(16) *To examine carefully in English* every pupil according to the course of studies prescribed for Public Schools ; but he shall be at liberty to use his own discretion as to what explanations he will give in any other language that appears to be better known by the pupil. The standard of efficiency recognised in Public Schools where the English language only is taught shall be the standard for French and German schools, reasonable allowance being made for pupils whose mother tongue is French or German. The Inspector shall report at once to the Education Department any school in which the regulations respecting the study and use of English are disregarded by the teacher or trustees.

DUTIES OF CITY AND TOWN INSPECTORS.

Inspectors in cities and towns shall perform similar duties as County Inspectors so far as practicable, and shall, in addition, perform such other duties as may be prescribed by the Board of Trustees. In cities with more Inspectors than one, each Inspector may be required to report separately to the Education Department.

DUTIES OF SEPARATE SCHOOL INSPECTORS.

Inspectors of separate schools shall perform the like duties as Inspectors of public schools, and shall, with regard to separate schools, have, so far as the same is practicable, like power and authority as public school Inspectors have with regard to public schools.

DUTIES OF MODEL SCHOOL INSPECTORS.

The Inspector of model schools shall visit each model school at least once in two years, and shall devote a full day to the examination of the teachers-in-training and the inspection of the departments used for model school purposes, and shall report annually to the Minister of Education one the standing of each model school and all other matters affecting the efficiency of the schools.

DUTIES OF HIGH SCHOOL INSPECTORS.

(1) Each high school Inspector shall visit the high schools and collegiate institutes in the section of the Province assigned to him at least once in each year, and shall spend not less than one day in each school having two or three masters, and such additional time in a school with four or over four masters as the interests of the school may require.

(2) At each visit he shall ascertain the character of the teaching in the different departments of study ; and shall make enquiry and examination, in such manner as he may think proper, into the efficiency of the staff, the accommodation and equipment of the school, and all matters affecting the health and comfort of the pupils. He shall also report any violation of the High Schools Act or the Regulations of the Education Department in reference to high schools, after making such enquiry as he may think proper.

(3) He shall report to the Minister of Education, within one week after his inspection, the result of his observations and enquiry in a form pre-scribed for that purpose.

POWERS OF INSPECTOR.

The Inspector, while officially visiting a school, has supreme authority in the school, and has the right to direct teachers and pupils in regard to any or all of the exercises of the schoolroom. He may either examine the classes himself or direct the teachers to do so. He is at liberty to give such advice to pupils or to the teacher as he may deem necessary. All his counsels, however, should be given in a spirit of kindness, and his authority should be exercised, not with a view to over-awe or intimidate, but to reform abuses, correct mistakes, and inspire confidence and respect. He should be courteous and considerate, and when reproof is necessary it should be tempered with gentleness and sympathy.

APPENDIX D.

EXAMINATIONS AND EXAMINERS.

(1) Examinations will be held annually at each high school and collegi-ate institute, and at such other places as the Minister of Education may designate, in the courses of study prescribed for each of the Forms I. and II., III. and IV. These examinations shall be known respectively as the High School Primary, the High School Junior and Senior Leaving Examina-tions, and the University Pass and Honour Matriculation Examinations.

(2) The Minister of Education may act in conjunction with the Senate of the University of Toronto in conducting these examinations by means of a Joint Board of the Education Department and University of Toronto, to be appointed as soon after the first day of October in each year as is practi-cable.

(3) The Joint Board shall elect a chairman from their number who shall retain his right to vote as a member of the Board. In case of any vacancy on the Board the appointing body may fill the same for the remainder of the term.

(4) The Board shall appoint examiners to prepare the examination papers for the Departmental and university matriculation examinations, but such examiners shall not exceed fifteen in number. The Board shall also appoint such associate examiners as may be necessary for the reading of the answer papers of the candidates at the said examinations.

(5) The examiners shall be selected from persons qualified by experience as teachers in either a university or a high school to set papers suitable for candidates at such examinations.

(6) The associate examiners shall be selected from a list of graduates of universities in the British Dominions actually engaged in teaching, such list to be furnished by the Minister of Education, and to contain the names of at least double the number of associate examiners required.

(7) No examiner or associate examiner shall be appointed who is objected to by three out of the four representatives either of the university or of the Department of Education.

DUTIES OF EXAMINERS.

The following shall be the duties of the examiners :—

(1) To elect at the first meeting a chairman from their number, who shall retain his right to vote as a member of the Board.

(2) To assign at the first meeting the subjects of examination to the different members, and to arrange for having the manuscript of the examination papers in the hands of the Minister of Education at such dates as he may fix.

(3) To revise and approve of all examination papers and to assign values to the questions. The examiners are jointly and severally responsible for the character of the questions in each of the papers.

(4) To arrange in alphabetical order the names of the examiners in each department at the head of each paper in that department, and to give, as far as possible, instructions to candidates in the same form at the head of each paper.

(5) To avoid, as far as possible, questions that consist of numerous parts with different values for each part.

(6) To use capital letters, A, B, etc., to denote the sections of the papers, and figures 1, 2, etc., consecutively throughout, to mark the individual questions. To space in printing and to mark with letters (a), (b), etc., the several sub-sections under each number.

(7) To place, as far as the nature of the paper allows, optional questions, if any, at the end of the paper.

(8) To take the general management of the work of the associate examiners, and to settle such questions connected therewith as may be referred to them by the chairmen of the sections.

(9) To assist the associate examiners in each section in reading the answer papers and to report to the Minister of Education and Joint Board the results of the examinations.

(10) To settle the results of the examinations in accordance with the standards and regulations of the Education Department and the Senate of the University respectively

(11) To decide and report upon all appeals in conjunction with such persons as may be appointed for that purpose.

DUTIES OF ASSOCIATE EXAMINERS.

(1) The associate examiners shall be classified into sections according to the subject of examination. An examiner shall be the chairman of each section, or, where an examiner is unable to act, such person as may be appointed for that purpose by the Joint Board.

(2) The chairman of a section shall have general oversight of the work done thereby, and shall spend so much of his time as may be necessary in revising the work of his colleagues, with a view to remove clerical errors and secure practical uniformity in valuing the answers.

(3) Before commencing the actual work of examination the associate examiners of each section shall spend a sufficient time in discussing the answers and reading answer papers jointly, to enable the members to arrive at a consensus of opinion as to the valuation of answers, especially of partial or imperfect answers.

(4) When a section finds that the values assigned to the questions on the examination papers are unsatisfactory, or when it is evident that the examiner has not followed the course of study prescribed by the Education Department or by the curriculum of the University of Toronto, it shall report through its chairman to the chairman of the Examiners or the person acting on his behalf.

(5) No associate examiner shall have in hand more than twenty papers at one time, nor shall he have more than one envelope opened upon his table at one time, except in cases of suspected copying, in which case he shall return each sheet to its proper envelope. The papers shall be returned in the numerical order in which they were received. In cases of suspected copying, the associate examiner shall note on the face of the envelope " Copying, see No. ———, question ———."

(6) One mark shall be deducted for each misspelt word and for each instance of bad English from the marks obtained in each subject. At the Primary and the Junior Leaving Examination in English Composition, an essay will be expected of about sixty lines in length, and at the Senior Leaving Examination of about ninety lines.

(7) At all the examinations in Arithmetic, either arithmetical or algebraic solutions shall be accepted.

(8) In reading the papers each associate examiner shall mark distinctly in the left-hand margin the value assigned by him to each answer or partial answer, shall sum up the total on each page at the foot of the margin, and shall place the result on the face of the envelope, indicating the deductions for misspelt words and incorrect English thereon, thus, *e.g.*, History 80—2 sp.—4 f.s. = 74, and initialing the envelope of each paper examined.

(9) The hours of work shall be from 9 o'clock a.m. to 12 noon, and from 2 o'clock p.m. to 5 p.m. Examiners shall begin and stop work promptly, and shall abstain from all unnecessary conversation during working hours. The work of the examination shall be strictly confidential.

(10) Associate examiners shall be paid the sum of 6 dollars per day, the payment being subject to the restriction that the whole amount paid for the examination shall not exceed the sum of 1.50 dollar per candidate.

(11) Associate examiners who do not reside in Toronto will be allowed their actual railway expenses to and from their usual residences in Ontario.

EXAMINATION PAPERS.

(1) At all the examinations, each paper on the Latin, Greek, French, and German authors shall contain, in addition to questions on passages from the prescribed texts, questions on passages from works not prescribed but similar in style and of equal difficulty ; and the meaning shall be given of

words not likely to have been met with by the candidates. The examinations in the "Sight-work" shall determine, not whether the candidate has read more than the prescribed texts, but whether he is familiar with the idioms and constructions met in the prescribed course.

(2) At the Primary and Junior and Senior Leaving Examinations in Poetical Literature, "Sight-work" shall also be given ; but at the Leaving examinations the examination papers shall consist of three sections, two being on the prescribed texts, and the third on an "unseen" passage ; of these, university candidates shall take the first and second, and departmental candidates the third, with one of the others prescribed by the examiners.

(3) In the subjects of Mathematics, English, and History and Geography the papers for pass matriculants either shall be distinct from those for the Junior Leaving Examination, or shall be supplemented by questions specially adapted to the latter class of candidates.

(4) At the Primary and Junior Leaving Examinations the value of the questions on Grammar, in the paper on Grammar and Rhetoric shall be two-thirds of the value of the whole, and at the Primary examination the value of the questions in Algebra in the paper on Algebra and Euclid shall also be two-thirds of the value of the whole. The questions in Mensuration are for the Junior Leaving Examination only.

(5) At the Senior Leaving and Honour Matriculation Examinations in Botany and Zoology, the specimens for description and identification shall be sent from the Education Department where required, and at the primary examination in Botany they shall be provided by the presiding examiner.

(6) The subjects, number, and values of the papers of the different examinations shall be as follows :—

1. *Primary Examination.*

	No. of papers.	Value of subject.
English Grammar and Rhetoric	One	200
English Composition (Essay)	„	100
English Poetical Literature	„	200
History and Geography	„	150
Arithmetic, Mensuration, and Commercial Transactions.	„	200
Algebra and Euclid	„	200
Physics	„	100
Botany	„	100
Latin	Two—one on Authors and one on Composition and Grammar.	200
French	„	„ 200
Grammar	„	„ 200

2. *Junior Leaving Examination.*

	No. of papers.	Value of subject.
English Grammar and Rhetoric	One	150
English Composition (Essay)	„	100
English Poetical Literature	„	200
History and Geography	„	150
Arithmetic and Mensuration	„	200
Algebra	„	150
Euclid	„	150
Chemistry	„	200
Physics	„	200
Latin	Two—one on Authors and one on Composition and Grammar.	200
French	„	„ 200
German	„	200
Greek		200

3. *Senior Leaving Examination.*

	No. of papers.	Value of subject.
English Grammar, Philology, Rhetoric, and Prosody.	One	200
English Composition (Essay)	..	100
English Poetical Literature	..	200
History and Geography	..	150
Algebra	..	150
Euclid	..	150
Trigonometry	,.	150
Chemistry		125
Physics	Four —400	125
Botany		75
Zoology		75
Latin	Two—one on Authors and one on Composition and Grammar.	200
Greek	,, ,,	200
French		200
German		200

APPENDIX E.—UNIFORM TEXT BOOKS.*

PROVINCIAL CONTROL.

An important characteristic of the system of education for Ontario is the adoption of a uniform series of text-books for the schools of the Province. The statutes for both High and Public Schools provide :—

No teacher shall use or permit to be used as text-books any books in a model or public school, except such as are authorised by the Education Department, and no portion of the legislative grant shall be paid by the inspector to any school in which unauthorised books are used.

Any authorised text-book in actual use in any public or model school may be changed by the teacher of such school for any other authorised text-book in the same subject on the written approval of the trustees and the inspector, provided always such change is made at the beginning of a school term, and at least six months after such approval has been given.

In case any teacher or other person shall negligently or wilfully substitute any unauthorised text-book in place of an authorised text-book in actual use upon the same subject in his school, he shall for each such offence, on conviction thereof before a Police Magistrate or Justice of the Peace, be liable to a penalty not exceeding 10 dollars, payable to the municipality for public school purposes, together with costs, as the Police Magistrate or Justice may think fit.

The regulations also provide :—

(1.) No book shall be authorised as a text-book in any public school until the copyright thereof has been vested in the Education Department.

(2.) Every text-book for public or high schools printed and published in Canada, shall be subject, at any stage of its manufacture, to the inspection and approval of the department in regard to printing, binding and paper ; in case of using any book not published in Canada, the English edition shall be preferred to any other.

(3.) A sample copy of every edition of every authorised book shall be deposited in the Education Department by the publisher, and no edition of any book shall be considered as approved without a certificate from the Minister of Education approving thereof.

* From Mr. J. Millar's *Educational System of the Province of Ontario*, pp. 83, ff.

(4.) Every authorised book shall bear the imprint of the publisher, and shall show upon the cover or title page the authorised retail price, and no part of the book shall be used for advertising purposes, without the written consent of the Department.

(5.) The Education Department may require the publisher of any text-book to make such alterations from time to time as may be deemed expedient ; but no alterations in contents, typography, binding, paper or any other material respect, shall, in any case, be made by the publisher, without the consent of the Education Department.

(6.) Every publisher of an authorised text-book shall, before placing any edition of such authorised book upon the market, execute such agreements and give such security for the due fulfilment of these regulations as may be required by the Education Department.

(7.) All authorised text-books may be published by any firm or publishers in Ontario, on the payment to the original publishers of such sum or sums of money as may be agreed upon between the publishers concerned, and the Minister of Education respectively.

(8.) The Minister of Education may, at his discretion, after making full inquiry into the cost of manufacture, reduce the retail price of any authorised text-book ; he may also remove such book from the list of authorised text-books, if the publisher fails to comply with the regulations of the Education Department, or if it be considered to be in the public interest so to do.

(9.) In case the Education Department shall at any time recommend any books as aids to the teacher for private reference or study, it is to be distinctly understood that such books are not to be used as text-books by the pupils, and any teacher who permits such books or any other book not authorised as a text-book for the public schools, to be used as such, shall be liable to such penalties as are imposed by the School Act.

The adoption of a uniform series of text-books for the Province has been attended with many advantages. Among them the following may be mentioned : —

1. The cost to pupils has been less than if the selection of text-books were left to each locality.

2. There are better facilities thereby afforded for securing a uniform course of study, and a uniform standard for departmental and university matriculation examinations.

3. The difficulties have been minimised that arise when pupils remove from one school to another.

4. It has, by limiting their responsibilities, tended to render teachers, Inspectors and other school officials more useful in the discharge of their duties.

5. Annoyance and confusion resulting from the frequent changes of text-books by school boards have been avoided.

6. Parents, teachers, Inspectors and trustees are protected from the incessant importunities of book agents and publishing firms.

7. It is a measure of economy to parents and pupils, as they are saved from the too frequent changes of text-books.

To the Education Department has been given the power to authorise text-books for the high and public schools, and for the various institutions for the training of teachers. In preparing and authorising text-books the following objects have been kept in view :—

(1.) To cover the course of study in each subject so far as possible by one text-book.

(2.) To control and regulate the price of each text-book, and thus protect the public as well as act fairly towards the publishers.

(3.) To reduce the price of text-books should it appear to the Department that the profits are excessive.

(4.) To keep up a required standard as regards the binding, typography and general workmanship of the books.

(5.) To encourage Canadian teachers of well-known ability to undertake the preparation of text-books.

(6.) To manufacture, as far as possible, all authorised text-books in the Province.

(7.) To prevent frequent changes by teachers and trustees.

(8.) To reduce the number of text-books. This has been especially kept in view as regards the public schools. In high schools where fewer pupils are affected a choice has been allowed in the case of some departments.

By the Public Schools Act of 1891 it has been provided that the public school board of any city, town or incorporated village may provide free text-books for the pupils. In accordance with the democratic principles of the school system it has been considered preferable to leave a matter of this kind to be decided by the ratepayers themselves for each locality. It is yet too soon to say how far this optional power may be taken advantage of by municipalities.

LIST OF TEXT BOOKS.

1. The text-books named in Schedules "A" and "B" shall be the authorised text-books for the public schools, for Forms I., II., and III. of collegiate institutes and high schools of the Province of Ontario.

2. The text-books in French or German mentioned in schedule "A" are authorised only for schools where the French or German language prevails, and where the trustees with the approval of the inspector require French or German to be taught in addition to English.

3. The books named in Schedule "B" shall be the authorised text-books in the corresponding subject in the course of study prescribed for the Fifth Form of public schools.

4. All text-books prescribed or required for senior matriculation or for the courses in Form IV. of high schools and collegiate institutes may be used in addition to those mentioned herein.

5. For religious instruction, either the Sacred Scriptures or the Scripture Readings adopted by the Education Department, shall be used by teachers and pupils as prescribed by the regulations of the Education Department

Public Schools--Form I. IV. (Schedule A.)

	$	c.
The Public School Readers.		
First Reader, Part I.	0	10
First Reader, Part II.	0	15
Second Reader	0	25
Third Reader	0	35
Fourth Reader	0	45
Public School Arithmetic	0	25
Public School Geography	0	75
Public School Grammar	0	25
Public School History of England and Canada (new edition)	0	30
Public School Drawing Course—each number (new series)	0	05
Public School Hygiene and Temperance	0	25
Public School Agriculture	0	40
Public School Writing Course—each number to July 1894 (after July, 1894, five cents)	0	06

French-English Readers. $ c.

	$	c.
First Reader, Part I.	0	10
First Reader, Part II.	0	15
Second Reader	0	25
Third Reader	0	35
Les Grandes Inventions Modernes	0	50
Robert's French Grammar	0	25

German-English Readers.

	$	c.
Ahn's First German Book	0	25
„ Second „	0	45
„ Third „	0	45
„ Fourth „	0	50
„ First German Reader	0	50
Klotz's German Grammar	0	60

Collegiate Institutes and High Schools. *(Schedule B.)*

English.

	$	c.
High School Reader	0	60
High School English Grammar	0	75
High School English Composition	0	50
High School Geography	1	00
High School History of England and Canada	0	65
Schmitz's History of Greece and Rome	0	75
Green's Short History of the English People	1	50

Mathematics.

	$	c.
High School Arithmetic	0	60
High School Algebra	0	75
McLellan's Elements of Algebra	0	75
High School Euclid, McKay (Books I., II., III., 50 cents)	0	75

Classics.

	$	c.
Henderson and Fletcher's First Latin Book	1	00
Carruthers and Robertson's Primary Latin Book	1	00
Harkness' Introductory Latin Book	0	50
Harkness' Revised Standard Latin Grammar	1	00
Leighton's First Steps in Latin	1	00
Bradley's Arnold's Latin Prose	1	50
Goodwin's Greek Grammar	1	25
Harkness' First Greek Book	0	90

Moderns.

	$	c.
High School French Grammar	0	75
High School French Reader	0	50
High School German Grammar	0	75
High School German Reader	0	50
Lessons in French, complete (Fasquelles-Sykes)	0	75

Science.

	$	c.
High School Physics	1	00
High School Botany	1	00
High School Chemistry	0	75

Book-keeping and Drawing.

	$	c.
High School Book-keeping	0	65
High School Drawing Course—five parts—each	0	15

Dictionaries Recommended.

1. *English*—Stormonth's English Dictionaries (smaller and larger).
   Skeat's Etymological Dictionary (cheap unabridged edition)
   The Concise Imperial Dictionary.

2. *Latin*—Anthon's smaller Latin Dictionary.
   Harper's (Lewis and Scott's) Latin Dictionary.

3. *Greek*—Liddell and Scott's larger and smaller Greek Dictionaries.

4. *French*—Cassell's French and English, and English and French
   Dictionaries.
   Spiers and Surenne's French and English, and English and
   French Dictionaries.

5. *German*—Blackley and Friedlander's German and English, and English
   and German Dictionaries.
   Flügel's German Dictionary.

6. *Antiquities and Mythology*—Anthon's and Smith's.

APPENDIX F.

REGULATIONS FOR THE SCHOOL OF PEDAGOGY.

The following regulations have been prescribed for the School of
Pedagogy :—

(1) Only such persons shall be admitted to the provincial School of
Pedagogy or its final written examination as shall have completed at least
the twenty-first year of their age on or before the close of the session, and
as hold at least a high school senior leaving certificate.

(2) Teachers-in-training on admission to the school, and other candidates
at the final written examination, shall each pay a fee of 10 dollars.

(3) The following certificate shall be awarded candidates who pass the
prescribed written and practical examinations in December and June (or
April and December) : after a session at the school of Pedagogy, specialists'
certificates, high school assistants' certificates, and first class certificates to
candidates who have had three years' experience in a public school, or who
hold a second class certificate, and without a session at the school of
Pedagogy, first class certificates to candidates who, holding a second class
certificate, have had two years' successful experience in a public school, and
specialists' certificates to candidates who hold high school assistants' or first
class certificates.

Duties of Staff.

(1) The principal shall be the chief instructor in the theoretical and critical
course, and shall be responsible for the organisation and management of the
school. He shall have charge of the teachers-in-training and determine the
hours for instruction, observation and practice teaching in the School of
Pedagogy. He shall prescribe the duties of the lecturers on methods and
shall from time to time be present at their instructions and those of the
special instructors, and at the practice teaching of the teachers-in-training. He
shall, with the assistance of the lecturers and special instructors, furnish
the Minister of Education with the prescribed statement of the standing of
each teacher-in-training at the close of the session.

(2) Each lecturer shall develop systematically the best method of dealing
with each branch of his department in the various stages of a pupil's
progress, and shall, as far as possible, explain and justify his methods on
scientific principles, giving model lessons for classes in different stages of

advancement. He shall also criticise the practice teaching of the teachers-in-training in the School of Pedagogy, and shall, by suitable records, provide the means of forming a just estimate of the standing of each teacher-in-training.

(3) No certificate or testimonial shall be given to any teacher-in-training or other candidate at the final examination by any of the examiners or members of the staff of the School of Pedagogy.

Duties of Teachers-in-training.

(1) Teachers-in-training shall lodge and board at such houses only as are approved by the principal. Ladies and gentlemen shall not board at the same house. Communication between the sexes is strictly prohibited, except by permission of the principal or one of the lecturers or masters.

(2) Teachers-in-training shall attend regularly and punctually throughout the session, and shall submit to such discipline and perform such duties as may be prescribed by the principal.

(3) The teachers-in-training shall make no presentation to any member of the staff of the School of Pedagogy.

Course of Study and Text Books.

(1) The course of study and training shall be as follows : Psychology, the history and criticism of educational systems, the science of education, lectures with practical illustrations on the best methods of teaching each subject on the programme of studies for high schools, lectures on school organisation and management, observation and practice in the School of Pedagogy ; instruction in reading, temperance and hygiene, writing, drawing, stenography, drill, gymnastics and calisthenics, and such other subjects as may be prescribed by the Minister of Education.

(2) (a) In addition to the text books prescribed for collegiate institutes and high schools, the following are authorised for the School of Pedagogy : Quick's Essays on Educational Reformers (International Educational Series, 1890 edition), McLellan's Applied Psychology, Spencer's Education, Landon's School Management, Fitch's Lectures on Teaching, Manuel of Hygiene, and Houghton's Physical Culture.

(b) The following are recommended for reference : Mahaffy's Old Greek Education, Compayré's History of Pedagogy, Gill's Systems of Education, Radestock's Habit in Education, Dewey's Psychology, Sully's Teachers' Handbook of Psychology (Appleton), Ladd's Outlines of Physiological Psychology.

Examinations.

(1) Teachers-in-training shall take the following examinations :—(a) At least one written examination conducted, during the session, by the staff of the school, on the work of the sessions ; (b) final written examination (in December or April), conducted by the staff of the school and such other examiners as the Minister may appoint, in the following subjects, obligatory on all candidates :—Psychology, science of education, history of education, school organisation and management, methods in mathematics, and methods in English. In addition to the foregoing subjects, candidates holding university qualifications shall take methods in Latin, and methods either in Greek or in French and German ; and other candidates, methods in science or classics, or modern languages ; candidates for a commercial specialist's certificate shall take also methods in the commercial subjects ; (c) and a final examination in December, in reading and drill, gymnastics and calisthenics for male teachers, and drill and calisthenics for female teachers, conducted by the staff of the school, unless otherwise ordered by the Minister of Education.

APPENDIX G

UNIVERSITY REGULATIONS.

Matriculation,

Matriculation examinations, formerly conducted by the different universities, are now entrusted to examiners selected by the joint board, which is appointed by the Minister of Education and the Senate of the University of Toronto. This examination is held in the beginning of July, and is called the Junior Matriculation Examination. Candidates may also enter by passing the Senior Matriculation Examination (first year) or at the examination of the second year. High school leaving certificates are accepted *pro tanto* for entering the University. The following provisions have been made by the Senate regarding the matriculation examinations :—

All candidates entering at the junior matriculation examination must take the pass subjects in Latin, Mathematics, English History and Geography, and in one of the following groups : (*a*) Greek ; (*b*) French and German ; (*c*) French, and either Physics or Chemistry ; (*d*) German, and either Physics or Chemistry.

Candidates intending to take, during their university course, any one of the following honour departments, viz. : Political Science, Mathematics and Physics, Chemistry and Mineralogy, Natural Sciences, are recommended to take French and German at matriculation, since these languages must be taken in connection with the above-named honour departments. For a similar reason candidates intending to take, during the university course, either the honour departments of Philosophy or that of Oriental Languages, are recommended to take Greek, French and German at junior matriculation.

Regulations Relating to the Pass Course.

The subjects to be taken by those pursuing the pass course, with the options permitted, are set forth in the following schedule :—

First Year — { Latin ; English ; History ; Mathematics ; either Greek, or French and German ; any one of the three sciences— Chemistry, Biology, Geology.

Second Year — { Latin ; English ; History ; Philosophy ; Physics ; either Greek, or French and German.

Third Year — { Latin ; English ; either Greek, or French and German ; any two of the three departments —History and Political Science, Philosophy, Physics.

Fourth Year — { Latin ; English ; either Greek, or French and German ; any two of the three departments—Political Science, Philosophy, Mathematics and Physics.

NOTE.—Hebrew may be substituted for French or German in each of the four years.

. Undergraduates in the pass course in the third and fourth years may, in lieu of one or more of the subjects prescribed for each of these years, take certain of the following subjects—namely, Biblical Greek, Biblical Literature, Apologetics, and Church History.

Regulations Relating to the Honour Course.

In this course there are eight honour departments—viz. : I. Classics ; II. Modern Languages ; III. Oriental Languages ; IV. Political Science ; V. Philosophy ; VI. Mathematics and Physics , VII. Chemistry and Mineralogy ; VIII. Natural Sciences.

Candidates pursuing Department II. will be allowed at and after the examination of 1893 to take either Teutonic or Romance Languages in their fourth year.

Candidates pursuing Department VI. are allowed to take either Mathematics or Physics in their fourth year.

Candidates pursuing Department VIII. are allowed to take either Division I. or Division II. in their fourth year.

An undergraduate is entitled to admission to the degree of Bachelor of Arts, if in each year of his course he passes the examination in the pass and honour subjects of one of these departments (except in the department of Political Science, for which the honour subjects only are required), and also the pass examinations in the subjects and at the respective times mentioned in the following schedule :—

Undergraduates to the honour departments of Philosophy and Oriental Languages may, in the third year, substitute Biblical Literature or Church History for History. Undergraduates in the honour department of Philosophy may also substitute Biblical Greek for the pass Classical Greek (Plato) to be taken in the third year, and Biblical Literature or Apologetics for the pass Economics for the fourth year. Undergraduates in the honour department of Oriental Languages may also substitute Biblical Greek for the pass Classical Greek of the third and fourth years. Undergraduates in the honour department of Political Science may substitute Church History for the pass English of the second year, and Biblical Greek for the pass French or German of the third year. Those exercising these options must present certificates of having attended lectures and passed examinations in the subjects so selected at an affiliated or confederated college or university other than University College. The minimum for passing at such examinations must not be less than the minimum required at the University examinations of third year. These examinations do not count for honours.

In the honour department of Philosophy two distinct examinations are held in the fourth year upon the two systems of philosophy taught in the confederating Arts Colleges.

A candidate for honours in any of these departments is required each year to take the pass papers set in the subjects of his department for that year, except in the department of Political Science, in which only the honour papers are required.

Candidates in the honour subjects of Physics, Chemistry, Biology, and Mineralogy and Geology, will be ranked in the class lists on practical work done in the laboratories of the respective departments during the session ; and no candidate will be allowed to proceed to examination in any of these honour subjects unless he presents to the registrar a certificate from the professor that he has attained honour standing in the practical work of that subject.

Fees.

The following fees are payable :—

	Dols.
For each examination after matriculation	5
For change of faculty	5
For admission *ad eundem statum*	6
For the Degree of B.A.	10
For the Degree of M.A.	20
For admission *ad eundem gradum* { B.A.	20
{ M.A.	20
For admission to a higher year on the certificate of the head of an affiliated college	5
For dispensation from attendance at lectures in an affiliated college	2
For certificates of honour (each)	1
Annual library fee	2

Matriculated undergraduates who are registered students of University College, or at any federating university or college, may attend lectures of university professors and lecturers in the Faculty of Arts without payment or fees, except those imposed for laboratory work ; but such students must enter their name with the Registrar of the University.

Laboratory fees vary from about two to twenty-five dollars, according to the number of sub-departments. The library fee is two dollars.

Term Work.

Candidates in pass subjects in the Faculty of Arts shall be arranged in the annual class lists in three grades, A, B and C; the minimum for A being seventy-five per cent. of the marks, and for B fifty per cent.; all under fifty per cent. who pass shall be placed in C.

Reports of attendance at pass lectures in the first and second years shall be made in all departments except those of Chemistry, Natural Science and Physics, and marks for such attendance shall be assigned in connection with the May examinations as follows.

	Marks.
For attendance at four-fifths and over - -	20
„ two-thirds and over - -	13
„ one-half and over - -	7

No students attending less than one-half the lectures shall receive any marks for attendance.

Reports on term pass work in the first and second years shall be made in all departments except those of Chemistry, Natural Science and Physics. In the department of English five essays at least shall be required during the session from each student; and the reports on term work in that department shall be based on the essays. In other departments the report on term work shall be based on those parts of the work which the professor or lecturer may deem most appropriate as tests of proficiency. The maximum number of marks to be assigned for term work in connection with the May Examination shall be thirty, and no candidate earning less than ten marks shall receive any marks for term work.

Matriculation Scholarships.

Through the liberality of several persons, including the Hon. Edward Blake, M.P., Chancellor of the University, who has given the sum of twenty thousand dollars as a fund for an endowment for junior matriculation scholarships, valuable inducements are offered to deserving students desiring to take a course in arts in the Provincial University. These scholarships vary in value from 25 to 190 dollars. A large number of scholarships, medals and prizes are also awarded in the different years of the course.

University College Fees.

Graduates in Arts, who have pursued the undergraduate course in University College, may attend lectures free; but this privilege does not exempt them from laboratory and other special fees.

For regular students in Arts, "a course of lectures" means a continuous course of instruction offered to matriculated students in Arts in any one year in any subject.

"A partial course of lectures" means any special course or any subdivision, complete in itself, of a course of lectures as above defined.

"A matriculated student in Arts" means a student who is matriculated in the University, and enrolled in University College, and whose name is entered with the Registrar of the University.

"An occasional student" includes every student not being a matriculated student under the above definition, in whose case the Lieutenant-Governor in Council is by law authorised to determine fees for courses of lectures on the report of the Council of University College.

Every matriculated student in Arts shall, on each year's enrolment in University College, pay an enrolment fee according to the following table, which fee shall include all instruction for which fees are by law chargeable, except laboratory supply charges and library fees :—

		Dols.
First Year	- Any course or department - - -	25
Second Year	- Any course or department - - -	25
Third Year	- Chemistry and Mineralogy - -	20
	Natural Sciences - - -	20
	Any other course or department -	25
Fourth Year	- Chemistry and Mineralogy or Physics	20
	Biology - - - - -	15
	Any other course or department -	25

The annual enrolment fee of a matriculated student in Arts, taking under the regulations more than one honour course, shall be 25 dollars only.

Statistics.

		Dols.
Value of land reservation for building -	-	478,000
„ Buildings - - - -	-	640,000
„ Library books, apparatus, etc.		120,000
„ Unoccupied land - -		1,000,000
„ Land leased - -		326,000
„ Investments - -		1,000,000
Annual income - - - -	-	118,000
Graduates in Arts (Toronto, 1,660 ; Victoria, 644) - -		2,304
„ Medicine (Toronto, 808; Victoria, 937, of whom 80 are graduates in both) - - - -		1,665
„ Law (Toronto, 245 ; Victoria, 98) -		343
„ Engineering - - - - -		5
„ Agriculture - - -		33
„ Dentistry - - -		85
„ Pharmacy - - - -		22

THE
SYSTEM OF EDUCATION
IN
THE PROVINCE OF QUEBEC.

INTRODUCTORY - - - - - - - - - 149

I.--CENTRAL ADMINISTRATION.

    The Lieutenant-Governor - - - - - 151
    The Department and the Council - - - - 151
    The Superintendent - - - - - - 151
    The Committees of the Council - - - - 152
    The Classification of Creeds - - - - - 152

    (a.) *The Council of Public Instruction and its Committees* - 152

    Composition of the Council - - - - 152
    Special Meetings - - - - - - - 153
    Definition of Powers of the Council and Committees - 154
    Special provisions for each Committee - - - 155
    Text-books - - - - - - - - 155
    Appointments - - - - - - - 156
    Inquiries and Appeals - - - - 156
    Donations and Legacies - - - - - 156
    School Exhibitions - - - - - - 156

    (b.) *The Superintendent of Public Instruction and his Staff* - 157

    Salary, *ex-officio* position and powers - - - 157
    The Secretaries of the Department - - - - 157
    Special duties of Superintendent - - - 157
    Additional duties - - - - - - 158

II.—Local Administration.

School municipalities - - - - - - - 158
Their abolition or annexation - - - - - - 159
School districts - - - - - - - - 160
Power of Lieutenant-Governor to alter areas - - - 160
Division into school districts - - - - - - 160
Dissentient Schools - - - - - - - - 161
Notices of dissent - - - - - - - - 161
Alternation of majority and minority - - - - 162
Union of dissentient municipalities - - - - 163
Dissentients in towns - - - - - - - 163
Grant by Commissioners to Trustees - - - - 163
Extinction of trustee corporation - - - - - 164
Children taught in next municipality - - - - 164
Erection of new municipality - - - - - - 165
Annual meeting : procedure. - - - - - - 165
Penalty for neglect in office - - - - - - 167
Persons qualified to vote and to hold office - - - 167
Vacancies - - - - - - - - - 167
Term of office - - - - - - - - - 168
Contestations and appeals - - - - - - 168
Meetings of school corporation - - - - - 169
Duties of Commissioners and Trustees - - - - 170
    School Property - - - - - - - 171
    School-Houses - - - - - - - 172
    Special tax - - - - - - - - 172
    School taxes - - - - - - - - 172
    Exemptions - - - - - - - - 173
    Appeals - - - - - - - - - 174
    School Site - - - - - - - - 174
    Union for Model School or Academy - - - 175
    Monthly Fees - - - - - - - - 175
    Schools for Girls - - - - - 176
    Annual census of children - - - - - 176
    Special powers of trustees - - - - - 177
The Secretary-Treasurer - - - - - - - 178
Security and sureties - - - - - - - 178
His duties - - - - - - - - - 178
His assistant - - - - - - - - - 179

Examination of accounts :
    (a.) By School Corporation - - - - - 180
    (b.) By Auditors - - - - - - 180
    (c.) By Superintendent - - - - - - 181
(li.) Fabrique schools - - - - - - - 182
Statistics of 1898–99 - - - - - - - 182

III.—Finance: Provincial and Local.

Conditions of aid - - - - - - - - 183
   Exemption of municipality - - - - - - 183
Distribution of Local School Fund - - - 184
Refusal of share in Common School Fund - - 185
Sum reserved for three special purposes - - - 185
Applications of Local School Fund - - - 186
Valuation of property - - - - - - 186
Imposition of school taxes - - - - - 187
Collection by seizure - - - - - - 188
New and special taxes - - - - - - 189
Voluntary contributions - - - - - - 191
Collection from religious and other corporations - - 191
Capitalisation of debt - - - - - - 192
Statistical Tables :
   Table of amounts expended on education - - 192
   Statistics of the cost of education - - - 193

V.—School Visitors and School Inspection - - - - 194

Visitors for the whole Province - - - - 194
Visitors in their own districts only - - - - 194
School Inspection - - - - - - 194
Duties of Inspectors - - - - - - 195
Qualifications - - - - - - - 195
Salaries : instructions : number - - - - 195
Specimen of Inspector's return - - - - 196
Dismissal of Inspector - - - - - - 197
Circular of 1897 about Pedagogical Lectures - - - 197

V.—Teachers: Training and Diplomas.

Normal Schools :
   Financial provision - - - - - - 200
   Superintendent's control - - - - - 201
   Normal school diploma - - - - - 201
   Normal schools for girls - - - - - 202
Pedagogical lectures - - - - - - 202
Central Board of Examiners - - - - - 203
Quebec and Montreal Boards - - - - - 204
Other Boards of Examiners - - - - - 204
Duties of Boards of Examiners - - - - 204
Validity and Necessity of diplomas - - - 206
Summary of statistics of teachers, 1897-8 - - 207
From the Report for 1895-6 - - - - - 207

VI.—Comparative Statement of Progress, 1867-1899 - - 208

VII.—SUPERIOR EDUCATION.

    (i.) Finance - - - - - - - - 209
    (ii.) Roman Catholic Laval University - - - 210
    (iii.) Branch of Laval University at Montreal - - 213
    (iv.) Statistics of Protestant Universities - - - 215
    (v.) Statistics of Model Schools, Academies, etc. - - 216
    (vi.) Regulations for Academies - - - - 218
    (vii.) Special rules for Model Schools - - - 219
    (viii.) Royal Institution for the Advancement of Learning 220

II.—INDUSTRIAL SCHOOLS.

    Certificates : Building : Inspection - - - 221
    Finance - - - - - - - - 222
    Withdrawal of Certificate - - - - 222
    Detention of Children - - - - 223
    Penalties - - - - - - - 224
    Management of certified Industrial Schools - - 224

IX.—THE POLYTECHNIC SCHOOL - - - - - - 225

—MISCELLANEOUS.

    (i.) Remarks on educational progress - - - 227
    (ii.) Plans of school houses - - - - 229
    (iii.) Teachers' salaries - - - - - 229
    (iv.) Teaching of drawing - - - - 229
    (v.) Manual training for girls - - - - 230
    (vi.) School holidays - - - - - 231
    (vii.) School libraries - - - - - 231

APPENDICES.

A. An account of the Protestant Schools of Montreal, 1900. By the Secretary-Superintendent - - - - - 232

B. Extracts from the Regulations of the Protestant School Commissioners for Montreal, 1900 - - - - 236

C. Regulations of 1890 for the issue of debentures by the Roman Catholic and Protestant School Commissioners for Montreal 250

D. Special Regulation of 1893 concerning tenure of Roman Catholic School Commissioners for Montreal - - - 253

E. Course of study in Roman Catholic Academies and Model Schools - - - - - - - - -254-5

F. Course of study in Protestant Elementary Schools - - 256

G. From the Report of the Montreal Protestant School Commissioners 1897-1899 - - - - - - - 257

THE SYSTEM OF EDUCATION IN THE PROVINCE OF QUEBEC.

[This account has been compiled mainly from the " Revised Statutes" of the Province. Use has also been made of the annual reports of the Superintendent of Public Instruction for recent years, which have been supplied to the Board of Education by the Quebec Department of Public Instruction.]

INTRODUCTORY.

Among the Provinces of the Dominion, Quebec shares with Nova Scotia the distinction of having two Chambers constituting its Parliament. The Upper Chamber is called the Legislative Council, and the Lower, the Legislative Assembly. The total area of the Province is 347,350 square miles, of which 344,050 square miles are " land area."

Quebec was, of course, one of the original Provinces of the Dominion. The original Act of 1791 divided Canada into two Provinces, Upper Canada, now Ontario, and Lower Canada, now Quebec. The present constitution of the Province was, in its main outlines, fixed by the " British North America Act " of 1867.

It is not without reason that the experience of the Dominion of Canada is cited as showing how completely a fusion may be effected by judicious legislation between two races of different language, creed, and ideals. We need not stop to estimate how far this wonderful fusion of the French and the British, the Roman Catholic and the Protestant, population has been the result of the educational legislation in particular. It is at least obvious that in the three provinces of the Dominion where " separate " or " dissentient " schools are provided for the religious minority in each educational unit of the country, a working arrangement has been devised which recognises in large measure the rights of conscience, at least so far as two broadly distinguished types of religious belief are concerned, while maintaining effective Government control and securing to every school, whether sectarian or not, its *national* character.

The Provinces which first succeeded in this were Ontario, Quebec, and the North-west Territories. But in the last case a distinction must be made; for in the Territories little short of half the financial support of the schools comes from the Government, and it is not until differences of creed involve, or threaten to involve, some disputable incidence of local taxation that the problem becomes really difficult. In Ontario and Quebec, on the other hand, the difficulty of preserving the rights of con-science to " religious minorities " while providing for the local support of all schools by taxation, could hardly have presented itself in a more striking form.   The educational systems of the two Provinces should be studied side by side by those who wish to ascertain how this problem of religious creeds as affecting education has been solved.   They make an effective contrast, inasmuch as the preponderance of Protestants in Ontario though smaller is not less decisive than the preponderance of Roman Catholics in Quebec, while in both Provinces the privileges of the vast majority are secured to the dissentient few.   The statistics of the census of 1891 show that in Ontario out of a total population of 2,114,320, 358,300 were Roman Catholic, and 1,599,226 Protestant; while in Quebec out of a population of 1,488,535, 175,680 were Protestant, and 1,291,709 Roman Catholic.*

The Regulations which follow in this Report scarcely need any introductory comment, since the *corpus* of school law is admirably clear.   On the other hand, the task of abstracting what follows may be justified on the ground that much unnecessary and uninteresting detail has thus been omitted, and that a clearer idea of the main features of the system will be gathered from a study of it than from reading through the Revised Statutes of the Province in their entirety.

It may be as well, however, to draw special attention to one or two points.   All persons elected to serve on the local authorities for schools, except Roman Catholic and Protestant clergymen, are obliged to accept office.   The relations and the differences between school commissioners and school trustees will be clearly enough explained in what follows, but it must be pointed out here that any powers given to, or any obligations imposed upon, school commissioners apply also to trustees of separate schools in reference to the schools and school districts under their control. Special attention may be called to the provision giving power to school commissioners (*i.e.*, the local authority for the schools of the religious majority in the educational unit of the system) to grant annually a certain sum to school trustees in their municipality (*i.e.*, the local authority for the schools of the religious minority in the same unit) in respect of those children whose parents pay taxes to the school commissioners though they send their children to the dissentient schools.

Equally noteworthy are the financial regulations restricting the levying of taxes on corporations or incorporated companies, including religious, charitable, or educational institutions.   The tax may be imposed on such institutions only by the School Corporation (whether of commissioners or of trustees) of the same religious faith as is held in the institution; and must, when collected, be applied to the exclusive benefit of that religious majority or religious minority, as the case may be.   It should also be noted that, while the Superintendent is *ex officio* a member of both the Protestant and the Roman Catholic

---

* The only difference of creed recognised in the educational law of either Province is that between Roman Catholic and Protestant.   The Protestant Churches included in the census are Church of England, Presbyterian, Methodist, and Baptist.   In Ontario the Methodist is the largest Protestant Communion, and in Quebec the Church of England.

Committees of the Council of Public Instruction, he is entitled
to vote only in the Committee to which he, by religion, belongs.
The punctual payment of the teachers' salaries every six months
figures among the conditions to be fulfilled before a Government
grant can be received; and the elasticity of the provisions is well
exemplified in the exemption from taxes of poor municipalities
which can be shown to have "done their best" to fulfil all the
necessary conditions.

Attention may also be drawn to the principle which lies at the
root of the financial administration of the schools—the "dollar
for dollar principle." The wide power given to the local
authorities in the application of Government grants is also
notable. The School Corporation can either distribute the
money to the schools under it in proportion to the number of
children of school age (seven to fourteen years) capable of
attending school in each district; or it may make a common
fund from which teachers' salaries and all other expenses of the
schools are paid. By this method, given a well-constituted
school corporation, an elasticity is introduced that may often
prevent that objectionable feature of educational systems familiar
to any student of them—the *facilis descensus Averni* of the
necessitous school whose grant from Government decreases
almost in proportion to its need of assistance.

The protection afforded to teachers by the Regulations will
be frequently noticed in what follows, more especially in regard
to their dismissal and the term of their tenure.

I.—CENTRAL ADMINISTRATION.

The titular and, in many respects, actual head of the educa- Lieutenant-
tional system is the Lieutenant-Governor or "the Lieutenant- Governor.
Governor in Council." He appoints the Superintendent and the
officers of the Department of Public Instruction.

It is necessary to note that the Department of Instruction is Department
distinct from the Council of Public Instruction. The Depart- and Council.
ment is in reality the staff of the Superintendent;* the
Council is the body responsible for all important changes in the
method of providing public education, and has, within the limits
set by statute and subject to the approval of the Lieutenant-
Governor in Council, full power to control the management of
all schools.

The Superintendent (with the Department under him) is Superin-
subordinate to the Council in all matters not expressly assigned tendent.
to him. Such at least is the practical outcome of the system,
though it is not actually stated in the Statutes. The Superintendent is required to enforce regulations made by the Council
and approved by the Lieutenant-Governor.

* In the school year 1897-8 the Department consisted of the Superinten-
dent, a French Secretary, an English Secretary, a Special Officer and
Assistant Secretary, Curator of Museum, Accountant, Assistant Accountant
and Clerk of Statistics, Clerk of Records, Librarian and Clerk of French
Correspondence, Clerk of Accounts, Clerk of English Correspondence
Assistant Book-keeper, four ordinary Clerks, and three Messengers.

Committees.

For all practical purposes each of the two Committees of the Council has the same statutory powers in regard to matters specially concerning education of its own religious faith as the Council which those two Committees together compose has in regard to all matters not specially concerning one or the other of them. These Committees are called the Roman Catholic and the Protestant Committees.

Classification of Creeds.

This is perhaps the most distinctive feature of the educational system; and the religious division, which thus begins with the central authority, will be met with in almost every detail of the local administration. The Public Schools of the Province are classified as Roman Catholic or as Protestant schools; and no Public School exists which is not identified with one or the other of these religious classes.

The phrase used in the Statutes is "religious faith," not religious denomination; but it is hardly necessary to remark that the division is in reality an arbitrary one. For the purposes of education, all those persons who are not members of the Roman Catholic Church are by statute declared to be Protestants; and every school must, by statute, have a religious character and religious instruction corresponding with one or the other of these divisions.

In view of the difficulties that have been experienced elsewhere in elementary education it would be instructive to know what compromise has been devised by the three or four main religious interests that together compose the Protestant Committee, and how far that compromise has been found to satisfy each of the parties to it. Under such a system much would evidently depend on the nature of the compromise devised in practice by the representatives of the various types of belief found in the Protestant Churches. Experience elsewhere shows that on many important questions there is not always identity of positive religious conviction among those who, in contradistinction to Roman Catholics, are called Protestant. The official documents do not show what is the nature of the compromise arrived at. No information is available on this point, and it is therefore useless to speculate on the nature of the religious instruction given in public schools under the central control of the Protestant Committee.

a. The Council of Public Instruction and its Committees.

Composition of the Council.

The Council of Public Instruction, then, is composed of Roman Catholic and Protestant members, and is divided into two Committees, the one consisting of the Roman Catholic and the other of the Protestant members. The Superintendent is a member of the Council, and, *ex officio*, the chairman of it : * but, while he is *ex officio* a member of each of the Committees, he is entitled to vote only in the Committee to which he, by religion,

---

. * In the case of the absence or sickness of the Superintendent, the Council appoints one of its members present to act as chairman of the meeting.

belongs. Thus, like every school corporation (local authority for public education in all grades), every teacher, and nearly all officials connected with education, the Superintendent must be a member of one or the other of the classes of religious faith into which the-Province is divided for educational purposes. The position of the Superintendent is, however, exceptional, inasmuch as he alone is directly concerned with both divisions of the system and is the only member of both Committees of the Central Authority.

The Roman Catholic members of the Council (*i.e.*, the members of the Roman Catholic Committee) are the following:—

(1.) The Bishops, ordinaires, or administrators of the Roman Catholic dioceses and apostolic vicariates, situated either in whole or in part in the Province: *ex-officio members*.

(2.) An equal number of Roman Catholic laymen appointed by the Lieutenant-Governor in Council: *appointed members*.

The constitution of the Protestant Committee is not so carefully defined by statute It consists of "a number of Protestant members, equal to the number of Roman Catholic members appointed by the Lieutenant-Governor in Council, who are appointed in the same manner." The Lieutenant-Governor directly appoints the whole of the Protestant Committee and exactly half of the Roman Catholic Committee.

There is thus no statutory definition of the degree in which one or other of the various types of Protestant belief shall be represented on the Protestant Committee.

Those members of the Council who are appointed as such hold office during pleasure. In the discharge of their duties they are subject to the lawful orders and directions of the Lieutenant-Governor in Council.*

The two secretaries of the Department of Public Instruction are joint secretaries of the Council. They enter its proceedings in a book kept for that purpose, procure maps, books, stationery, etc., as directed, and keep the accounts of the Council.† The expenses of the acts and proceedings of the Council are defrayed and accounted for by the Superintendent as part of the contingent expenses of the Department of Public Instruction.

The Superintendent may call a special meeting of the Council Special at any time with due notice. Each Committee holds its meetings Meetings. separately and may fix their number.

The secretary of each Committee keeps a record of its proceedings and conducts its correspondence. He deposits the record of proceedings, the correspondence, and all other documents among the archives of the Department of Public Instruction.

---

* It does not appear whether the *ex-officio* Roman Catholic members are responsible to the Lieutenant-Governor or not ; nor to whom they are responsible if not to him. Nothing is said of their resignation or removal.

† It is not provided that one of these two secretaries to the Department should be a Roman Catholic and the other a Protestant. They are secretaries to the whole council; each Committee has, besides, its own secretary

After notice, given at least eight days in advance, special meetings of either Committee may be convened by the chairman or by the Superintendent, and special meetings of either Committee must be so convened if two or more members of either Committee make written request for it. ·

The Lieutenant-Governor in Council or either of the Committees may require the Superintendent to call a special meeting of the Council of Public Instruction.

The chairman of the Council and of each Committee has, on all questions in which the votes are equal, a second and casting vote. The Council and each of its Committees may appoint sub-committees (or one or two delegates) for the consideration of any matters submitted to them. Sub-committees (or delegates) report their proceedings to the Council or to the Committee by which they were appointed.

Powers of Council and Committees. The powers of the Council and its Committees are defined by two clauses which it may be as well to give in full. (Quebec Revised Statutes, 1910 and 1911.)

(1.) " The matters and things which by law belong to the Council shall be referred to it, in so far as they shall specially affect the interests of both Roman Catholic and Protestant education, and in such manner and form as the whole shall from time to time be determined by the Lieutenant-Governor in Council on the report of the Superintendent of Public Instruction."

(2.) " Everything within the scope of the functions of the Council of Public Instruction, which specially concerns the schools and public instruction generally of Roman Catholics, shall be within the exclusive jurisdiction of the Roman Catholic Committee of the Council. In the same manner everything within the scope of such functions, which specially concerns the schools and public instruction generally of Protestants, shall be within the exclusive jurisdiction of the Protestant Committee."

Except in so far as these two clauses may be held to assign certain matters to one or other of the Committees, the powers of the Council as a whole are as follows :—

(1.) To fix the time of their meetings and the mode of proceeding.

(2.) To make regulations respecting normal schools.

(3.) To make, from time to time, regulations for the organisation, government, and discipline of public schools,* and for the classification of schools and teachers.

(4.) To select and cause to be published text-books, maps, and globes, to be used, to the exclusion of all others, in the elementary schools, model schools, and academies under the control of school commissioners or trustees (powers are reserved to the two Committees in respect of text-books, and a special

---

* This covers practically all the elementary, and much of the secondary, education of the Province. " Model Schools " and " Academies " are of course public schools.

Provision secures to the *curé* of a Roman Catholic church the exclusive right of selecting the books having reference to religion and morals for the use of pupils of his religion).

(5.) To acquire the copyright of books, maps, pieces of music, and other publications made under their direction.

(6.) To cause to be inserted by the Superintendent, in a book to be kept for that purpose, the names and grades and classes of all teachers who have received diplomas from the Boards of Examiners ; and also, the names of all teachers who, after going through the regular course of instruction in any normal school, have received diplomas from the Superintendent.

There is one special provision in regard to the constitution of each of the Committees :— Special provisions for each Committee.

(i.) The members of the Protestant Committee may associate with themselves five persons to assist them in their labours, who shall not form part of the Council of Public Instruction, but shall have, in the Protestant Committee, the same powers as the ordinary members of that Committee.

(ii.) Each Roman Catholic Bishop, Vicar Apostolic, or administrator of a Roman Catholic Diocese, may appoint a delegate to represent him at the meetings of the Roman Catholic Committee, if he is unable to be present through illness or absence from the Province. The delegate has at the meetings all the rights of the person appointing him.

This last regulation in regard to certain Roman Catholic members applies also to meetings of the whole Council, but there is no such provision for Protestant members in respect of the meetings either of the Council or of the Protestant Committee.

Special provisions in regard to the powers of the Committees over Boards of Examiners, to cancel teachers' diplomas, and to inquire into the conduct of School Inspectors, will be found below.

Each Committee prepares and revises from time to time Text-books. a list of text-books, maps, globes, models, and other articles for use in the schools. The list of authorised text-books is revised once in every four years, and the changes made in it are published by the Superintendent in the *Quebec Official Gazette.* A text-book excluded from the revised list cannot be withdrawn from use until a year after the publication of the revision.

The Superintendent retains the grant of any municipality which allows text-books, not entered on the authorised list, to be used in its schools.

All text-books entered on the list may become the property of the Roman Catholic or Protestant Committee of the Council of Public Instruction, in consideration of an indemnity to the proprietors to be fixed by the Lieutenant-Governor in Council. Any contestation as to the amount of indemnity must be referred to three arbitrators appointed, one by the Superintendent, another by the owner of the work, and the third by the two first arbitrators. The award of these arbitrators is final.

Every person has the right to print, publish, and sell the works entered on the list (*i.e.*, the property of either of the Committees) by paying every five years a sum of ten dollars (£2) for each work. The form, paper, type, and binding of such books are determined by the Superintendent. In case any abuse arises from a combination of booksellers to raise the price of text-books, the Roman Catholic or Protestant Committee may fix a maximum price for such works.

Appointments. School Inspectors, professors, directors and principals of normal schools, the secretaries and the members of boards of examiners, are appointed or removed by the Lieutenant-Governor in Council, on the recommendation of the Roman Catholic or Protestant Committee, according as such appointments or removals concern Roman Catholic or Protestant schools.

Inquiries and Appeals. The Roman Catholic or Protestant Committee may cause inquiries to be made into all questions concerning public instruction which come respectively under their control.

Whenever the persons interested in the decisions of the Superintendent have no recourse before the Courts, an appeal lies by summary petition (except, of course, when the law declares the decision of the Superintendent to be final) to the Council of Public Instruction or to one of its Committees. In cases where the decision of the Superintendent refers to a difficulty between Roman Catholics and Protestants, the appeal lies to the Council of Public Instruction. In cases of a difficulty between persons of the same religious faith, the appeal is within the jurisdiction of the Committee which represents that faith.

Donations and Legacies. Each of the Committees may receive by donation, legacy, or otherwise, by gratuitous title money or other property; and may dispose of the same, in its discretion, for the purposes of education. In respect of property so acquired, each Committee has all the powers of a corporation. Should any person make a legacy to the Council of Public Instruction without stating the Committee for which he designed it, the legacy belongs to the Committee of the faith to which, at the time of his death, the testator belonged. If the testator belonged neither to the Roman Catholic nor to the Protestant faith, the legacy is divided between the two Committees, in the proportion of the Roman Catholic and Protestant populations of the Province.

The sums of money granted to Roman Catholics, or Protestants, for educational purposes and not expended, remain at the credit and disposal of the Committee which had the control of them.

School Exhibitions. The Lieutenant-Governor in Council may, on the recommendation of the Council of Public Instruction, or on the report of the Superintendent, make and promulgate regulations for establishing and maintaining *school exhibitions*, and may appoint one or more commissioners for that purpose, whose duty it shall be to obey the instructions given by the Lieutenant-Governor in Council.

b. *The Superintendent of Public Instruction and his staff.*

The Superintendent is appointed by the Lieutenant-Governor in Council. He holds office during pleasure, and must give a security to the sum of $8,000. His salary is $4,000 per annum. Salary and ex-officio Position.

The Superintendent, in the exercise of his functions, is bound to comply with the directions of the Council of Public Instruction or with those of the Roman Catholic or Protestant Committee. He is *ex officio* president of the Council, member of each of the Committees (though entitled to vote only in the Committee of his own religious faith), visitor-general of all public schools, and member of the Council of Arts and Manufactures (who control the teaching of drawing). He compiles and publishes statistics and information respecting educational institutions, public libraries, and artistic, literary, and scientific societies, and, in general, respecting all subjects connected with literary and intellectual progress. Every year he draws up, in accordance with the directions of the Council or of its Committees, a detailed statement of the sums required for public education, and submits this statement to the Government. He has power to hold inquiries, to summon before him and administer oaths to witnesses or parties in all difficulties which may arise in reference to schools or school-houses. He may also delegate this power to hold inquiries to the secretaries of the Department or to school inspectors. When the investigation is held at the request of one or more ratepayers, the Superintendent may require the person who applies for it to deposit an amount sufficient to cover the expenses.

The Superintendent is the depository of all documents respecting matters under the control of the Department of Public Instruction, and may deliver copies or extracts thereof, in consideration of a remuneration fixed by the Lieutenant-Governor in Council.

The secretaries of the Department of Public Instruction who may be appointed for the administration of the educational laws are deputy-heads of the Department and act under the direction of the Superintendent. Secretaries.

In the absence of the Superintendent, they may suspend any employé of the Department who refuses or neglects to obey their orders. The Superintendent may delegate to one of the secretaries of the Department all the powers conferred on him by law, if he be absent from the Province.

It is the special duty of the Superintendent :— Special Duties of Superin- tendent.

1. To receive from the Provincial Treasurer, in addition to the amounts appropriated for superior education, all sums of money appropriated for public school purposes, and to distribute them among the School Commissioners and Trustees of the

municipalities in proportion to their population as ascertained by the last census;

2. To prepare and cause to be printed recommendations and advice on the management of schools for the School Commissioners and Trustees, and for the Secretary-Treasurers and teachers;

3. To keep correct books and distinct schedules of all the matters under his superintendence, so that information may be promptly obtained by the Government, the Legislature, or the school visitors;

4. To examine and control the accounts of all persons, cor porations, and associations accountable for any public moneys appropriated and distributed under the laws relating to schools, and to report whether they are *bond fide* applied for the purposes for which they were granted;

5. To lay annually before the Legislature a detailed report of the actual state of education during the period to which the report relates; and

6. To state in the yearly report to the Legislature what he has done with the amounts voted for education during the period covered by it.

Additional Duties of Superintendent.
The Lieutenant-Governor in Council may, if he sees fit, assign to the Superintendent certain other duties. He may require him to effect the establishment of art, literary, or scientific societies, and of libraries, museums, and picture galleries, whether these be established by such societies or by the Government, or by institutions receiving Government aid. The Superintendent may be required to encourage competitions and examinations, and the distribution of diplomas, medals, or other marks of distinction for artistic, literary, or scientific work, or to establish schools for adults and instruction for workmen and artisans. In fact, all which in general concerns the support and encouragement of arts, letters, and science, and the distribution of the funds voted for those purposes by the Legislature, may be entrusted to the Superintendent as one of his special duties, if the Lieutenant-Governor in Council so desires.

II.—LOCAL ADMINISTRATION.

School Municipalities.
The Local Authorities for Public Instruction in the Province are called "School Corporations"; and the local areas controlled by them for school purposes are called "School Municipalities."

In the constitution of the Local Authorities, as in all other respects, due regard is paid to the rights of what are called the *religious majority* and the *religious minority;* but for the purposes of Public Schools only the two main divisions of Christian communions, Roman Catholic and Protestant, are recognised.

The *Ratepayers* of any municipality or district are defined as the proprietors, lessees, occupants, inhabitants, or others, who, by reason of the taxable properties they own or occupy in a municipality or district, are liable for the payment of school taxes.

The term " school municipality" properly means "any territory erected into a municipality for the support of schools under the control of school commissioners or school trustees;" and the term "school corporation" means indifferently a corporation either of school commissioners or of school trustees, commissioners being responsible for the schools of the majority and trustees for the schools of the dissentient minority.

For school purposes, then, the Province is divided into "municipalities." To the English reader this term is apt to be misleading. It does not imply in any sense what we should understand by a municipal organisation. It is in reality more like the "school district" of the North-West Territories or British Columbia, though in Quebec that expression is appropriated to the smaller educational units which constitute a "school municipality." The word "municipality " does not imply the existence of a city nor necessarily even of a town within its limits. It is, in fact, merely an area bearing to the smaller areas ("school districts") a relation similar to that between a "city district" and a "city ward" elsewhere, or, more nearly still, to the relation between an *arrondissement* and the *communes* of which it consists in France.

Once this misconception is removed, the local administration of education in the Province may be understood without much difficulty.

If, on account of the "erection" of new municipalities, the municipality from which they are detached ceases to exist, or if a school municipality is abolished and its territory annexed to a neighbouring municipality by the annexation or uniting together of two or more municipal corporations, the Superintendent must inquire into the state of affairs of the old municipality either personally or by a school inspector or by any other person specially appointed by him for that purpose. This inquiry must be undertaken within the three months following the abolition and annexation, and must be directed towards ascertaining what are the resources of, and the outstanding claims against, the municipality within the limits of which the abolished muncipality was situated. At the inquiry the municipalities concerned are represented, and notice of time and place must be given to the commissioners or trustees, as the case may be. The report of the examination is made to the Superintendent, who, after hearing the representations of all parties concerned, gives a final decision from which there is no appeal.

It would be unnecessary to give in detail the regulations that determine the affairs of school municipalities during the *interim* period that must usually follow such a readjustment (see § § 1977–1980, Revised Statutes). The Superintendent in his award on the enquiry above described, may order that the new municipality shall have the right to levy upon the territory from which it has been detached, or upon the abolished municipality, a

Abolition and Annexation.

special tax in addition to the ordinary school tax during one or more years.

School Districts. It has already been pointed out that a school municipality consists of smaller units, the school districts. Here, again, a student of Canadian education may easily be misled. In the North-West Territories and in British Columbia the local educational authority is called a school district. In Quebec the authority that deals locally with education in a direct manner is the school corporation of commissioners or trustees elected for any school municipality.

In every municipality, village, town, and city of the Province, one or more public schools for the elementary instruction of youth must be held, under the *control of school commissioners*, or, in the event of *dissentient schools* being established, under the control of *school trustees*. The inhabitants of any city, town, or village municipality, are subject to the jurisdiction of the school commissioners or trustees elected for the municipality of which the city, town, or village forms part, and have the right of voting at the election of such school commissioners or trustees.

Power of Lieutenant-Governor to alter areas. By the original Act establishing school municipalities all existing municipalities were constituted as school municipalities. It was, however, reserved to the Lieutenant-Governor in Council to alter the limits of existing municipalities for school purposes, to subdivide them and to erect new ones. This power may not be exercised without due notice given in a prescribed manner that will ensure the utmost publicity; nor can alterations or subdivisions be made until the school corporations affected by them have been notified, and their representations on the subject carefully considered. The Lieutenant-Governor in Council may provide that the changes so made shall apply to the religious majority only, or to the religious minority only, as the case may require, of the school municipalities affected by such changes (Statute of 1890).

Division into School Districts. The school commissioners or trustees divide the school municipality into school districts. The limits assigned by them to each district must be entered in the register of their proceedings. They may also, in their discretion, alter the limits of districts already existing, and erect new ones to suit local circumstances. But no school district may exceed five miles in length or breadth. The school commissioners or trustees must provide that there be a school in each district, and, when it is expedient, they may unite two or more districts for the same school, and again separate them. Notice of such union or separation of districts must be given to the superintendent.

The school commissioners or trustees of any incorporated town or village, which has been erected into a separate school municipality, need not divide such school municipality into school districts. They may even annul such a division if it has already been made.

The point of this regulation would seem to lie in the fact

that it is often convenient to treat a town or village of any considerable proportions as an educational unit for administrative purposes.

No section of territory under the school municipality may be erected by commissioners or trustees into a school district, unless it contains at least twenty children over five and under sixteen years of age. It is, however, provided that *one* of the school districts under any school corporation (commissioners or trustees) may contain a smaller number of children of school-age.

It is now necessary to indicate the difference between the functions of school commissioners and school trustee (Article 1985).

Dissentient Schools— Notices of Dissent.

If, in any municipality, the regulations and arrangements made by the school commissioners for the management of any school, are not agreeable to any number whatever of the proprietors, occupants, tenants, or ratepayers, professing a religious faith different from that of the majority of the inhabitants of the municipality, these proprietors, occupants, tenants, and ratepayers may signify their dissent in writing to the chairman of the school commissioners. Three copies of this notice of dissent must be made and signed, one for the chairman of the commissioners, one to be kept, subsequently to the formation of the dissentient schools, in the archives of the trustees of that school, and one to be sent to the Superintendent of Public Instruction.

The notice to withdraw from the school Corporation is made in the following form :—

"Province of Quebec,
        Municipality of
To the Chairman of the School Commissioners of the Municipality of
                    , county of   .
    Sir,
    We, the undersigned, proprietors, occupants, tenants, and ratepayers of the Municipality of   , county of   ,
professing the (*Catholic or Protestant*) religion, have the honour, under Article 1985 of the Revised Statutes of the Province of Quebec, to notify you of our intention of withdrawing from the control of the school corporation of which you are the chairman.
    Given at   , this   day of   , 19 .*

---

    * Notice to withdraw from control of *future* commissioners.

Province of Quebec,
        Municipality of
To the Chairman of the School Trustees of the Municipality of
                    county of   .
    Sir,
    We, the undersigned, proprietors, tenants, occupants, and ratepayers of the Municipality of   , in the county of   ,
professing the   religion, have the honour to inform you, in virtue of Article 1887a of the Revised Statutes of the Province of Quebec, that we do not intend to be governed by the school commissioners who shall be elected in July next, and that we intend to elect three trustees to administer our schools.
    Given at   this   day   of   , 189 .

When a notice of dissent is served in accordance with this form, the *status quo* is maintained until the date of the annual elections, and at that date the dissentients elect three school trustees, in the usual manner (*for the method of election prescribed, see below*); during the eight days following their election or nomination, the trustees must give notice thereof to the chairman of the school commissioners.

Alternation of Majority and Minority. If, in any municipality, the ratepayers who belong to the religious denomination of the dissentients become the majority, they may signify in writing their intention of organising themselves in consequence.

Such notice must be made and signed in triplicate, and is served and deposited in the same manner as the notice of dissent.*

It is also, like the notice of dissent, served upon the chairman of the commissioners and upon the Superintendent of Public Instruction. In such case, the *status quo* is maintained up to the month of July following, and at that date an election is held in the usual way of five school commissioners, either for all the ratepayers, if the former majority, which has become the minority, has not declared itself dissentient, or for the majority alone, if the minority has declared itself dissentient.

When the former dissentients have declared their intention of electing five commissioners, the former majority, which has become the minority, may at once declare itself dissentient by giving notice, in the usual manner, to the Superintendent of Public Instruction and to the chairman of the trustees.

The notice of dissent must, in such case, in order to have effect the same year, be served on or before the 15th of June. In such case, in the month of July, the new dissentients elect their school trustees in the usual manner.

If the notice of dissent is not served before the 15th of June, the minority is governed by the school commissioners until it declares itself dissentient in the usual manner (Statute of 1893).

Dissentients are not liable for any taxes or school-rates which may be imposed by the school commissioners, except for the taxes of the then current year, or for taxes for the building of any school-house previously contracted for, or for the payment

---

* *Notice of declaration of majority.*

Province of Quebec,
  Municipality of

To the Chairman of the School Commissioners of the Municipality of   , county of   .
  Sir,

We, the undersigned, proprietors, tenants, occupants, and ratepayers of the Municipality of   , in the county of   , now under the control of the School Trustees of the said Municipality, have the honour to inform you, in virtue of Article 1987 of the Revised Statutes of the Province of Quebec, that we have become the majority, and that we therefore intend to organise ourselves and elect five School Commissioners, for the administration of our schools, in the month of July next.

Given at   , this   day of   , 189 .

of debts previously incurred. But such taxes must always be imposed w thin six months from the date of the receipt of the notice of dissent.

In the case of newly organised municipalities, if the declaration of dissent be served upon the chairman of the school commissioners within one month after the organisation of the school corporation, the dissentients are not liable for any taxes imposed by the school commissioners.

The dissentients in any municipality, who, as such, form a school municipality, may, with the approval of the superintendent, upon the demand of both parties, unite with a neighbouring school municipality of their religious faith, situated at a short distance from their own, either completely or only for the purpose of sending their children to school. If the union be only for this latter purpose, the school trustees of these dissentients continue to collect the school taxes in their territory, but are bound to remit the amount within a fixed time to the school municipality to which they are united. *Union of dissentient municipalities.*

Any such union of dissentient school municipalities of the same religious faith may be made for the number of years that the Superintendent may fix. With his approval it may also be cancelled after twelve months' public notice. In such cases of union the trustees of the dissentients are obliged to levy the same rate of taxes in their municipality as that imposed by the school corporation to which they are united.

Hitherto, the regulations have only touched the case in which the school municipality is of itself an entire district. There are further provisions in regard to townships or parishes divided into two or more municipalities with ordinary schools controlled by school commissioners. *Dissentients in towns.*

Any number whatever of the proprietors, occupants, and ratepayers of such a township or parish, who profess a religious faith different from that of the majority of the township or parish, may dissent and maintain one or more dissentient schools, situated anywhere in that township or parish, by giving notice in writing to the chairman of the school commissioners of their respective municipalities, and electing three trustees for school purposes. The trustees of these dissentients in a township or parish thus elected must either maintain under their immediate control, or subsidise, a school of their own religious faith situated in that township or parish.

If the members of the religious minority in any one of the school municipalities, into which the township or parish is divided, desire to send their children to the school maintained by the trustees, without themselves becoming dissentients, it is lawful for the school commissioners of that municipality to make an annual grant from the school funds of the municipality to the trustees, in aid of that dissentient school. *Grant by Commissioners to Trustees.*

For readers in Great Britain it may be instructive here to elaborate an imaginary equivalent to this regulation in terms of our own educational system. It is similar to a possible arrangement by which, should any number whatever of the ratepayers in a district upon which local rates are levied by a School Board desire to send their children to a voluntary school situated within that district, it would be lawful for the School Board of the district to make from the school funds raised by it from local rates, an annual grant in aid of the voluntary school, proportionate to the number of children attending that school, whose parents are liable to pay rates to the School Board.

Extinction of Trustee Corporation. To return to the actual conditions of Quebec. Whenever the trustees of dissentient schools in any municipality have been a year without schools, either in their own municipality or jointly with other trustees in an adjoining municipality, it is lawful for the Superintendent, after giving three consecutive public notices to that effect, to recommend to the Lieutenant-Governor in Council, that the corporation of trustees of dissentient schools in that municipality be declared extinct. The ratepayers who were, up to the time of such extinction, under the control of those trustees, then become liable for all taxes levied by the school commissioners; and the trustees are further required to pay over to the commissioners a sum equal to their share of all school taxes levied by the commissioners during all the time for which they, as trustees of dissentient schools not in operation, had neglected to keep their schools in operation.

One year after the dissolution or extinction of a corporation of trustees, any number of proprietors, tenants, and occupants, professing the religious faith of the minority in such municipality, may again elect trustees, and form a new corporation.

Children Taught in next municipality. Whenever there is no dissentient school in a municipality, it is open to any resident head of a family professing the religious faith of the minority in that municipality, and having children of school age, to declare, in writing, to the chairman of the school commissioners, that he intends to support a school in a neighbouring municipality. But this school must not be more than three miles distant from his residence. After this declaration, he pays his taxes to the commissioners or trustees, as the case may be, by whom the school, which he has chosen to support, and to which in virtue of that support he sends his child or children, is maintained. Special mention must be made in all school returns of children belonging to a neighbouring municipality, and these children are not taken into account in apportioning the school grants between the commissioners and trustees.

Children from other school districts, of the same faith as the dissentients for whom the school was established, may attend that school whenever the dissentients for whom it was established are not sufficiently numerous in any district to support a school alone.

(*a*) Any person belonging to the religious minority may at any time become a dissentient; and (*b*) any dissentient may, in like manner, declare his intention of ceasing to be a dissentient. The receipt by the chairman of the commissioners of the declaration made in the former case (*a*) is sufficient to place the persons making that declaration under the control, for school purposes, of the trustees; and, similarly, the receipt by the chairman of the trustees of the declaration made in the latter case (*b*) is sufficient to place the persons making that declaration under the control, for school purposes, of the commissioners.

It may here be repeated that the terms "religious majority' and "religious minority" mean the Roman Catholic or Protestant majority or minority, as the case may be. Erection of new municipality.

It is now time to describe the method by which a new school municipality is erected. As a general rule, the first step is an application made by residents in any district for the alteration subdivision, or erection of a municipality. The Lieutenant-Governor in Council then exercises his power, giving public notice, for which the applicants must pay. At the first meeting of the newly created municipality the election of a board of school commissioners (or school trustees) takes place. Such a meeting is called, at eight days' notice, either by the senior justice of the peace or by any other resident justice of the peace, or, in their default, by any three proprietors of real estate. At this first meeting the justice of the peace, or one of the other persons responsible for the calling of the meeting, presides; but after the election of the commissioners (or trustees) has once been made at the first meeting, the chairman of the commissioners or trustees, or a person appointed to that effect by a resolution of the commissioners or trustees, presides; this person may be one of those members of the school corporation who do not go out of office at that date. If such an appointment be not made, or if the person appointed be absent or unable to act, the secretary presides *de jure* at the election.

On the first Monday in July in each year there is held a general meeting of all the proprietors of real estate paying taxes or monthly fees in each school municipality, for the election of a board of school commissioners or trustees. As a general rule it is the secretary-treasurer of the board of school commissioners or school trustees who calls this annual general meeting. In his absence the chairman of the commissioners or trustees acts for him in this respect; and in any case due public notice must be given. Annual Meeting.

The *quorum* of any corporation is, unless otherwise provided, an absolute majority of all its members; and the majority of the members present at any meeting regularly held at which there is a quorum may validly exercise all the powers of the corporation.

At the annual election of the commissioners or trustees, the following is the procedure in cases where the choice is contested. Any five persons present and qualified to vote may demand a poll to be held in the following manner:— Procedure.

1. The presiding officer requests the electors present to propose those persons whom they wish to be chosen as school commissioners or trustees.

2. He is bound to receive and propose as candidates the names

of all persons submitted to him, whether verbally or in writing, by at least two of the electors present.

3. If, during the first hour after the opening of the meeting, as many candidates as there are school commissioners or trustees to be elected, or fewer candidates than the required number, have been proposed for election, the election is declared closed and the presiding officer proclaims the candidates proposed for election duly elected.

4. If more candidates have been nominated than there are vacancies to be filled, the presiding officer, upon a requisition by five electors present, proceeds without delay to hold a poll, and to register the votes of the electors ; but if among those nominated there be any to whom there is no opposition, he proclaims such candidates elected, and the poll is held for the other opposed candidates only.

5. If five electors do not demand a poll, the candidates are proclaimed as elected on a show of hands, provided always that twenty electors present may appeal from such a count and demand a poll.

6. Every elector may vote for as many candidates as there are school commissioners or trustees to be elected in the municipality.

7. Any person tendering his vote must take the following oath or affirmation, if so required by the presiding officer, or by any elector, or by any candidate, or by the representative of any candidate: " I swear (*or* I affirm) that I am qualified to vote at this election, that I am at least twenty-one years of age, that I have paid all school taxes due by me, and that I have not already voted at this election ; so help me God."
If the elector refuses to take this oath when required to do so, his vote is rejected.

8. Entry is made in the poll book against the names of those persons required to take the oath or affirmation, *i.e.,*" sworn," " refused to swear," " affirmed," " objected to," as the case may be.

9. In the case of an equal division of votes in favour of one or more of the candidates, the presiding officer is bound under a penalty of not less than $20 nor more than $50 to give a casting vote.

At these election-meetings the proprietors of real estate paying taxes or monthly fees, and thus qualified to vote, elect five school commissioners or three trustees, as the case may be, or the number of commissioners or trustees required to fill the vacancies caused by the retiring of such of the commissioners or trustees as go out of office. *All persons so elected,* except Roman Catholic and Protestant clergymen, *are bound to accept office.* The provision of 1892 may here be quoted:—" The default on the part of any person, lawfully required to perform any duties under these regulations, to accomplish any one of the duties incumbent upon him, does not have the effect of preventing the execution of any provision of these Regulations for Public Instruction."

Every person duly called upon to accept office or to perform any functions implied by office, who refuses or neglects to perform these, or who in any way wilfully contravenes the regulations, incurs thereby for each offence, whether of commission or omission, a penalty of not less than five nor more than ten dollars, according to the gravity of the offence, in the discretion of the court or authority having cognizance thereof. And any justice of the peace residing within the county, as well as the Circuit Court, has jurisdiction with regard to such offences, and may, after judgment, cause the penalty to be levied, under warrant, by seizure and sale. The amount of every penalty so levied is paid into the hands of the Secretary-Treasurer of the school corporation of the locality in which the offence has been committed, and forms part of the local school fund. All persons qualified to vote at the election of school commissioners or trustees have competence to prosecute for the recovery of such penalties. *Penalty for neglect in offices.*

No person may vote at any election of school commissioners or trustees in any school municipality, unless he has previously paid all contributions then payable by him for school purposes in his municipality. A contravention of this enactment carries a penalty not exceeding $10. *Persons qualified to vote and to hold office.*

Clergymen of all religious denominations ministering in the school municipality, although not qualified with respect to property, and all qualified voters resident in it, are, without any (further) property qualification, eligible as school commissioners or trustees. But non-residents with interest in the municipality, other than such clergymen, are not eligible.

Individuals of the *dissentient minority* cannot be elected or serve as *school commissioners*, or vote at their election; nor can individuals of the *majority*, where there is a dissentient minority, be elected or serve as school trustees, or vote at their election.

No school commissioner or trustee may be a teacher in any school in his municipality; nor may he be a contractor for any work contracted for by any school corporation of which he is a member.

A school commissioner or trustee may not be re-elected, except with his own consent, during the four years next after his going out of office.

The proceedings of any general meeting for the election of school commissioners or trustees must be reported, within eight days, to the Superintendent, together with a list of the persons elected. The chairman of such a meeting is in this respect responsible, and the penalty attached is $5. The persons elected must also be notified of their election within eight days.

If any vacancy in the school corporation is caused by the death, absence, or incapacity from sickness, infirmity, or otherwise, during three consecutive months, of any commissioner or trustee, another must be elected in his stead at a meeting of qualified *Vacancies.*

voters called for that purpose by the chairman or temporary chairman of the school corporation, at which the chairman himself or a substitute, being one of the commissioners or trustees, named by him must preside.

Whenever, on the occurrence of such a vacancy, the election of another person to the office has not taken place within one month of the occurrence of the vacancy, the Lieutenant-Governor in Council may, upon the recommendation of the Superintendent, fill such vacancy.

For the municipalities in which no election of school commissioners or trustees has taken place within the time prescribed, the Lieutenant-Governor in Council may, upon the recommendation of the Superintendent, appoint commissioners or trustees.

Commissioners and trustees going out of office are replaced by election at a general meeting, or, in default of an election, by appointment by the Lieutenant-Governor in Council.

Term of office. The office of school commissioner or trustee is held for three years, whether the appointment has been by election or by the Lieutenant-Governor in Council. After the first election or nomination of a board of commissioners or trustees, two in the case of commissioners, or one in the case of trustees, determined by lot, retire from office at the end of the first year, two (or one) of the remaining officers, determined by lot, at the end of the second year, and the remaining commissioner or trustee at the end of the third year. The chairman is equally liable with the other school officers to go out of office, if the lot should fall on him.

It will be seen from the foregoing regulation that it is provided that *school corporations* shall consist of (a) five commissioners or (b), in the case of dissentient schools, three trustees.

It only remains to add that the secretary-treasurer, or in his absence, or incapacity, the chairman or the senior member of the school corporation, is compelled to convene the annual general meeting for the election of school officers under a penalty of not less than $10 nor more than $50.

Contestations and appeals. It is hardly necessary here to give in any detail the regulations governing contestation of elections, appeals, &c. Contestations with regard to elections or to the functions and powers assumed by school officers or by any persons claiming to be such officers, may be brought, by a petition (*requête libellée*) setting forth the case, before the Superior Court in the district or before the nearest Circuit Court. Such petitions may be brought by any person having authority as visitor or otherwise over the schools of the municipality; and the contestations are tried in a summary manner. Any school officer whose election has been obtained by fraud or stratagem, or by the votes of persons not qualified to vote, or any person usurping the functions of school commissioner or trustee, or illegally holding such office, may be summarily prosecuted at the instance of any person interested, or of several collectively interested, before the Superior or Circuit Court in the district, for the purpose of declaring such election, or usurpation or retention of office illegal, and the seat vacant. Contestations may be made by one candidate or by five electors on the grounds of violence, corruption, fraud, or incapacity, or on the ground of non-observance of necessary formalities. The petitioners may, in their petition, indicate the persons who have a right to the office in question and state the facts necessary to establish that right. ("Whosoever was aware of the tenor or object of anything, which was or should have been required by notice, cannot take advantage of the default of such formality or of the insufficiency of such notice." Statute of 1892.) Notice is given to every school officer whose election is contested. Petitioners must give security for the costs. The Court by its judgment may confirm or annul the election or declare another person to have been duly elected. If the Court by its judgment annuls the election of the school officer or officers without stating who should fill such office, it must in the same judgment order a new election to replace the school officer whose election is thus annulled, name for that purpose a person to preside at the election, and fix the day and hour upon which a meeting of the electors is to be held. As in the case of ordinary elections, due public notice must be given.

Such are in outline the regulations governing contested elections.*

We come now to the powers of school corporations and their meetings.

The commissioners or trustees in each municipality form a corporation under the name of "*The School Commissioners (or Trustees) for the Municipality of . . . . in the County of . . . .*" They have "perpetual succession" and a common seal, if they think proper to have one; they have the same powers as any other body politic and corporate, may sue and be sued, &c. Meetings of School Corporation.

The school corporation meets to elect a chairman on the next Monday after its election. It also appoints a secretary-treasurer, who is entrusted with the care and custody of the archives, and remains in office during the pleasure of the

---

* (From the Statutes of 1892.)—Before presenting such petition to the Superintendent, the ratepayers interested shall, by petition signed by at least five of them, require the school commissioners or trustees to revise their decision or to perform the duty or duties which they have refused or neglected to perform.

During the thirty days next after the receipt of such petition, the school commissioners or trustees shall, by a notice through their secretary or a bailiff, notify their decision to one of the first two persons who signed such petition.

During the fifteen days following the notification of such decision, or, in the absence of such notification, during the fifteen days following the expiration of the time during which such notification might have been made, a petition in appeal may be presented to the Superintendent, who shall then exact, from the petitioners in appeal, security that the costs of the proceedings on such petition in appeal shall be paid, and designate the person or persons who shall support such costs, of which he fixes the amount.

No school corporation may, without the approval of the Lieutenant-Governor in Council, upon the recommendation of the Superintendent of Public Instruction, hypothecate, alienate, sell, or exchange the property belonging to it, or borrow money thereon for school purposes.

School-Houses.

(b) *School-Houses.*—School-houses are built in accordance with and upon plans approved or furnished by the Superintendent.

If it be necessary to purchase or enlarge the site of a school-house, to build, rebuild, enlarge, repair, or maintain one or more school-houses, and purchase, repair, or maintain the school furniture or apparatus, the school commissioners or trustees may at all times for this purpose tax either the particular district or the whole municipality according as one or the other plan has previously been adopted in that municipality.

If a house for a model school be in question, the district in which such a school is situated is first taxed for an amount equal to that which it would have cost the district to erect an elementary school-house. The additional sum required for the model school house is then levied on the whole municipality, the district also paying its share.

The Superintendent may authorise the school commissioners or trustees of any municipality which is not an incorporated town or village municipality, to build and maintain two or more school-houses in any district.

Special Tax

In cases where the municipality is not divided into school districts, the commissioners or trustees may exercise the powers in regard to school property described above, upon the recommendation of the Superintendent, and with the approval of the Roman Catholic or the Protestant Committee, as the case may be. They may for this purpose raise by special tax the necessary funds, provided the total amount expended does not exceed, in any one year, $3,000.

The above limitation applies also to taxes levied for the construction of a school-house for a superior school, academy, or model school. The limit is fixed at $1,600 in the case of a tax for an elementary school-house. In either case the corporation may be authorised by the Superintendent to exceed the limit.

Upon the recommendation of the Superintendent, and with the approval of the Roman Catholic or Protestant Committee of the Council of Public Instruction, as the case may be, school commissioners and trustees may devote to the aid and mainten-ance of superior schools, academies, and model schools under their control, a sum not to exceed in any one year $1,000, to be divided by them among such educational institutions, according to their several wants. The amount thus appropriated must be included in the general tax raised by them.

School Taxes.

(c.) *School Taxes.*—It is the duty of the commissioners or trustees to levy by taxation in their municipalities the taxes they deem necessary for the support of the schools under their control. *The sum arising from such taxes must not be less than the sum allowed to such municipality out of the common school fund of the Province.* (This last may be described as the " $ for $ principle," on the analogy of the " £ for £ principle," as understood in the administration of public education elsewhere.)

To enable the commissioners or trustees to receive from the Superintendent their share of the common school fund, they must furnish him with a declaration from their secretary-treasurer that he has actually received a sum equal to that share.

School taxes are imposed uniformly according to valuation, upon all taxable real property in the municipality. They are payable by the owner, occupant, or possessor of the property, and may, in default of payment, become without registration a special charge on such property.

The Superintendent may allow commissioners or trustees to levy upon real estate, situated outside the limits of a town or village, but forming part of the same municipality as such town or village, a tax of not less than one-half the tax levied upon real estate comprised within the limits of the town or village.

The secretary-treasurer of the school commissioners or trustees collects from the ratepayers in the municipality a sum sufficient to pay the salaries of the teachers at the expiration of each half year of their engagement; and his half-yearly report to the Department of Public Instruction must show that this has been done; otherwise the Government grant will not be paid.

Commissioners or trustees who refuse or neglect to pay any teacher his salary, or any part of the salary due to him, may be sued by the Superintendent on behalf of the teacher, the amount of the salary being regarded as a personal debt due to the Superintendent, and payable by him to the teacher, after deduction has been made of all costs incurred by the Superintendent in recovering the amount due to the teacher.

Exemptions from School Taxes.—(1) All property belonging to Her Majesty, or held in trust for the use of Her Majesty; (2) all buildings set apart for purposes of education, or of religious worship, parsonage houses, and all charitable institutions or hospitals incorporated according to law, and the land on which such buildings are erected; also all cemeteries; (3) every educational institution receiving no grant from the school corporation of the municipality in which it is situated, and the land on which it is erected, and its dependencies; (4) all property belonging to or used especially for exhibition purposes by agricultural and horticultural societies is exempt from municipal and school taxes, though subject nevertheless to *les travaux mitoyens.* (Statute of 1889. The *travaux mitoyens,* lit. boundary works, are the compulsory repairs to roads.)

The school commissioners or trustees may make such necessary alterations in the valuation roll and collection roll of the municipality as may become necessary by the concession or separation of a lot, or the erection of a building. All such alterations must be made and published in the manner prescribed for the making and publishing of the valuation and collection rolls.

The school commissioners or trustees may, under authority from the Superintendent, exempt from school contributions any resident ratepayer living more than five miles from the nearest school of his religious faith, provided he does not send his children to such school.

Appeals.

In every case of special tax in a school district, or of a general tax on the whole municipality as above detailed, for building, repairing, &c., school-houses, other than model schools, any of the persons so taxed may appeal to the Superintendent, who may set aside the tax or relieve from it the school districts, or any one of them, so appealing, or may confirm the tax, at his discretion.

When a site for a school-house is chosen by the commissioners or trustees, or when a change is made in the limits of a school district, or when a new school district is established in a municipality, or when the commissioners or trustees refuse or neglect to fulfil any of the functions assigned to them in these respects, the ratepayers interested may at all times appeal by summary petition to the Superintendent, but such appeal is not allowed unless with the approval in writing of three visitors other than the school commissioners or trustees. The decision made by the Superintendent on such appeals is final, but he may from time to time alter or modify any decision given by him on an appeal.

School Site.

School Site.—If, after having selected a site for a school-house, the commissioners or trustees cannot make terms with the proprietor respecting the amount offered as indemnity, or in case the proprietor refuses to deliver possession of the land required, the matter is settled by arbitration. The school corporation appoints an arbitrator, and the owner of the land another. A third arbitrator is appointed by the Judge of the Superior Court of the district at the instance of either of the parties to the arbitration. The arbitrators so appointed have all the powers necessary for the summoning, hearing, swearing, and examination of witnesses; and the award of a majority of them is final, and shall designate the party liable for the costs of the arbitration. This award gives power to the commissioners or trustees, upon deposit of the sum of compensation awarded to the persons entitled thereto, to take immediate possession of the land for which the compensation has been awarded.

When a school-district is divided by the creation of a new district or new municipality, the part on which the school-house is situated retains the property and refunds to the other an amount to be established *pro ratu* by the valuation of the real property which was taxed for its erection.

The same rule is followed when the religious minority declare themselves dissentient. Unless an understanding to the con-

trary be come to with the minority, the majority keeps the
school-house on payment of an amount determined as above.

Two or more school municipalities may unite by mutual
agreement in maintaining a model school or an academy, and in
erecting a building for it. In these cases the school is under the
control of the municipality in which it is situated, but the commissioners or trustees of the other municipalities have the right
to be present at all meetings of that municipality, to take part
in the discussions, and to vote on all questions respecting the
affairs of the academy or model school.

Any school corporation that desires to co-operate in this
manner in the erection of a model school or academy must pass
a resolution to that effect naming the amount to be levied. The
sum may be paid in one amount, but, if it be paid in instalments,
at least one instalment must be paid annually. A school
corporation that desires to participate in the maintenance of a
school of this kind passes a resolution naming the amount to
be levied annually for the purpose. The amount named is paid
over each year until it is decided by vote of the ratepayers to
discontinue the payment. The consent of a majority of the
voters must be obtained before the annual amount to be spent in
co-operation for an academy or model school can be fixed. For
this purpose a special meeting must be held.

The acceptance by the school corporation in which the school
is situated, of aid in the erection of a model school or academy
granted by any other municipality carries with it the right of
the children in the latter municipality to attend the school upon
the same conditions as the children of the municipality in which
the school is situated.

(d.) *Monthly Fees.*—Over and above the taxes levied, the school
commissioners and trustees fix the amount to be paid to the
secretary-treasurer in monthly fees for the eight school months
by the father, or mother, tutor, curator, or guardian of each child
of school age. These fees are for the use of the school district
in which they are collected.

*Such fees may not in any case exceed 40 cents (i.e., may not
reach the amount of two shillings), nor fall below 5 cents per
month (i.e., 2½d.).* They may be diminished in the discretion of
the commissioners or trustees according to the means of the
parents, the age of the children, and the course of instruction.
Higher monthly fees may be asked for in model schools and
academies, and for the whole time such schools are in active
operation, not for eight school months only.

The monthly school fees shall not be exacted except for each
child from seven to fourteen years of age capable of attending
school; but, upon payment of such monthly school fees, children
from five to seven years and from fourteen to sixteen years have
a right to attend the school of the district in which they reside,
and those from sixteen to eighteen years the model school of
their municipality.

School commissioners or trustees cannot exact monthly school fees from parents—

(1) If they be indigent persons; (2) for insane, deaf, or dumb children; (3) for children who are unable to attend school owing to serious and prolonged illness; (4) for children who are absent from the school municipality for the purpose of receiving their education, or for children in a college or other incorporated educational institution, or one receiving a special grant from the public funds other than schools under the control of the commissioners or trustees.

Any ratepayer in a district where there is no school open may send his children to the school of a neighbouring district situated within the limits of his municipality, by paying the monthly school fee exacted for the children of that district.

The monthly fees payable for children attending a model school, a separate girls' school, or a school kept by some religious community forming a school district, do not form part of the school fund. Such fees are payable directly to the teacher, and are for his or her use, unless a different agreement has been made between the corporation and the teacher.

School commissioners or trustees, in the half-yearly reports which they are bound to transmit to the Superintendent, must state the amount of monthly fees fixed for each district, and the amount actually collected. The Superintendent, with the approval of the Lieutenant-Governor in Council, may refuse the school grant for the year if the commissioners or trustees fail to fix the amount of monthly fees to be paid for the children in each district, or to cause the money to be collected.

The payment of the monthly school fees may be exacted in advance, except in municipalities in which the manner of collecting them is regulated by a special act or by a bye-law of the school corporation. (Statute of 1892.)

Schools for Girls.

(e.) *Schools for Girls.*—The school commissioners or trustees may establish in the municipality a girls' school distinct from that for boys, and such girls' school shall be considered as a school district.

If any religious community has already established an elementary school for girls in any municipality, the community may place its school from year to year or for a term agreed upon under the management of the commissioners or trustees. It is then entitled to all the advantages of ordinary public schools.

Annual Census of Children.

(f.) *Annual Census of Children.*—Commissioners or trustees must cause to be made every year by their secretary-treasurer a census of the children in each school municipality, distinguishing those who are from five to seven years of age, those from fourteen to sixteen, those from seven to fourteen, and those actually attending school. The secretary-treasurer must transmit this census to the Superintendent in his half-yearly report.

Every father, head of a family, tutor, curator, or guardian who refuses to give to the secretary-treasurer the information required for the census of children, or who makes a false declaration, incurs a penalty of not less than five nor more than twenty-five dollars.

Special Powers and Duties of School Trustees.—Some special regulations determining the powers and duties of school trustees as distinct from school commissioners must now be given. School trustees, it will be remembered, form the school corporation for dissentient schools, *i.e.*, the schools of a dissentient religious minority in a school municipality.

For the management of the schools under their control trustees have in general the same duties as commissioners They are a corporation for the purposes of their own dissentient schools, and are entitled to receive from the superintendent shares of the general school fund, bearing the same proportion to the whole sums allotted from time to time to the municipality as the number of children attending the dissentient school or schools bears to the entire number of children attending school in the municipality at the same time.

Trustees alone have the right of imposing and collecting the taxes upon the dissentient inhabitants.

Whenever the school trustees in two adjoining municipalities are unable to support a school in each municipality, they may unite to establish and maintain under their first management a school situated as near the limits of both municipalities as possible, so as to be accessible to both. In such cases the trustees jointly report their proceedings to the superintendent, who shall remit the share of the common school grant to the secretary-treasurer whose name first appears in the signatures to the report.

In cases of annexation of any territory to a school municipality, the costs incurred for such annexation are at the charge of the municipality to which such territory is annexed. (1892.)

The trustees are entitled to a copy of the collection roll in force, to a copy of the list of children capable of attending school. and to a copy of all other documents in the hands of the school commissioners connected with the management of dissentient schools. If there is no tax imposed, or the tax imposed does not appear to them a proper one, the trustees may, in the months of July and August, impose the taxes deemed necessary by them upon the dissentient inhabitants.

Trustees may constitute their own school-districts independently of the school-districts established by the school commissioners of the municipality; they have the same rights and duties and are subject to the same penalties as school commissioners in respect to the collection and application of moneys levied by them, the rendering and examination of their accounts, and all other matters.

The trustees may also receive the amount of the monthly fees payable for the children of dissentient parents, tutors, or curators, and may institute all suits or prosecutions, and do all other things necessary for the recovery of taxes and monthly fees.

Special powers of Trustees.

The Secretary-Treasurer.—Every school corporation has an officer called the secretary-treasurer, who is appointed by the school commissioners or trustees, as the case may be, and holds office during their pleasure.

Security and Sureties.—Before entering upon his duties the secretary-treasurer is required to give security to the school commissioners or trustees, either by instrument, or by a bond under private seal signed and acknowledged before a justice of the peace. The security is given by at least two solvent sureties to the satisfaction of the school corporation for the total amount of the moneys for which the secretary-treasurer may at any time during his tenure of office be responsible. Security must be given not only for moneys arising from contributions or donations paid into his hands for the support of schools, but also for the general school fund. The security can at any time be renewed at the requisition of the school corporation. The sureties of the secretary-treasurer may, by giving notice of their intention in writing to the secretary-treasurer himself and to the chairman of the school corporation by which he is employed, free themselves at any time from future liability under their bond at the expiration of thirty days after their service of notice. The secretary-treasurer must, within the thirty days following this service of notice, furnish other sureties in lieu of those who have withdrawn. In default of this he cannot discharge any of the functions of his office without becoming liable to a penalty of $20 for each infraction. The same penalty is operative in cases where, after the death, insolvency, or removal of one of the sureties, the secretary-treasurer has failed to supply the place of that surety within thirty days following the notice he is required in such cases to give to the chairman of his school corporation. This notice itself is compulsory under a penalty of $100.

Duties and powers of Secretary-Treasurer.—He is the keeper of all the books, registers, plans, maps, archives, and other documents and papers which are either the property of the school corporation or are produced, filed, and preserved in its office. He cannot divest himself of the custody of the archives, except with the permission of the school corporation or under the authority of a competent court.

He attends all meetings of the school corporation and draws up minutes of all its acts and proceedings in a book kept for that purpose. These minutes must be approved by the school corporation, signed by the person presiding at the meeting to which they refer, and countersigned by the secretary-treasurer.

Whenever a bye-law or resolution is amended or repealed, mention must be made of this in the margin of the minutes opposite such bye-law or resolution.

Copies and extracts from all books, registers, archives, documents, and papers preserved in the office of the school corporation which are certified by the secretary-treasurer are evidence of their contents.

The secretary-treasurer collects and has charge of all moneys due or payable to the school corporation. He pays out of the funds of the school corporation all sums of money due by it, whenever authorised to do so. The authorisation of the chairman is sufficient for sums up to $10.

No secretary-treasurer can, under a penalty of $20 for each infraction, (1) grant discharges to ratepayers or other persons indebted to the school corporation for school taxes or other debts, without having actually received in cash or in lawful value the amount mentioned in such discharges, nor (2) lend directly or indirectly to ratepayers or other persons moneys received in payment of school taxes, or belonging to the school corporation.

The secretary-treasurer is bound to keep, in the form prescribed, books of account, in which he enters fully each item of receipt and expenditure. He must keep in the archives all vouchers for his expenditure. He is further bound to keep a "repertory," in which particulars are entered of all reports, apportionments, valuations, collections, judgments, maps, plans, letters, notices, or, generally, of all papers that have been in his possession during his tenure of office.

On office days any interested person, or his attorney for him, may inspect and examine the secretary-treasurer's books of account and vouchers for expenditure, as also all registers and documents in his archives. The secretary-treasurer is bound to deliver, upon payment of his fees, to any person applying for them, copies or extracts from any book, roll, register, document, or other paper which forms part of the archives. Copies must be supplied gratuitously to the Lieutenant-Governor and to members or officers of the school corporation.

No teacher can be appointed secretary-treasurer.

The school commissioners or trustees may at any time remove the secretary-treasurer and appoint another in his place.

The remuneration of the secretary-treasurer must not exceed seven per cent. of the moneys received by him as such, for all the services consistent with the duties of his office, which the school commissioners or trustees may require of him. Nevertheless, the school corporation may, by resolution and with the authorisation of the superintendent, grant a supplementary sum to the secretary-treasurer for the use of his office, as well as for any other specified consideration.

The secretary-treasurer may, under his signature, from time to time appoint an assistant secretary-treasurer, who has the same rights, powers, privileges, and obligations as himself, except as regards security. His Assistant.

The assistant secretary-treasurer enters into office as soon as he has received written notice of his appointment. He may be removed or replaced at pleasure by the secretary-treasurer. In the exercise of his functions he acts under the responsibility of the secretary-treasurer, and under that of the sureties of that officer. In the event of a vacancy in the office of secretary-treasurer, his assistant continues to exercise the duties until the vacancy is filled.

Examination of accounts of Secretary-Treasurer.—(*a*) By the School Corporation.—He prepares and submits to the school commissioners or trustees in July of every year a detailed statement of the receipts and expenditure of the school municipality for the year ending 30th June of that year. As soon as the statement has been approved by the commissioners or trustees he prepares an abstract of the receipts and expenditure, assets and liabilities, for which abstract he must obtain the approval of the school corporation. This abstract must be read, posted up, or otherwise published at least eight days before the meeting of the ratepayers called by him for the election of school commissioners or trustees (see above). He must furnish a copy of the abstract to any ratepayer upon the payment of twenty cents.

(*b*) By Auditors.—The school corporation appoints one or two auditors to examine and audit the accounts kept by their secretary-treasurer, whether in or out of office. Such auditors are bound to report respecting all accounts of the corporation and all accounts relating to any subject falling within their jurisdiction, whenever the school corporation may require them to do so.

In the case of a special audit of the accounts of the secretary-treasurer, the chairman of the school commissioners or trustees gives written notice of this audit to the secretary-treasurer requiring him to attend, so as to give all the explanations that may be required of him. This notice is served personally or by bailiff. And if the secretary-treasurer refuses or neglects to attend, the auditor proceeds with his work none the less, and forwards his report to the corporation. They then adopt the report in whole or in part, and certify the amount due to the auditor for his services, and communicate the result of their meeting to the secretary-treasurer by serving upon him by bailiff a copy of the resolutions adopted respecting the report.

The secretary-treasurer must, within fifteen days, pay the amount which is found deficient in his accounts. He may, however, contest the auditor's report by giving notice, within fifteen days, to the school corporation. This notice is served upon the chairman by a bailiff. The corporation then forward the auditor's report, together with a copy of their proceedings, of the notice given to them by the secretary-treasurer, and of other documents connected with the matter, to the Superintendent.

The Superintendent then appoints a school inspector or any other person to examine and audit the accounts in presence of the parties or after they have been duly summoned. The inspector or person appointed reports to the Superintendent the procedure followed by him, and the Superintendent then gives his decision, which is final. Debts declared to be such in his decision must be paid without delay, and legal proceedings must be instituted to execute the decision in default of such payment. The decision of the Superintendent fixes the amount of the costs and expenses of the inspector or other person appointed for this purpose. (For an alternative action open to the Superintendent or the school corporation in such cases see below.)

(c.) By the Superintendent.—Where difficulties arise between the school corporation and its secretary - treasurer, in or out of office, or when a written application to the superintendent is made by at least five ratepayers, having for its object the revision of the accounts submitted by the secretary-treasurer, the Superintendent may cause those accounts or copies of them to be laid before him, and may render judgment in detail and upon the whole of them. His judgment has the force of an award of arbitrators between all the parties. The superintendent may, also, himself proceed to the place in question, or appoint a delegate in his stead. The examination must take place on the day and hour and at the place fixed in a notice duly served five days previously by a bailiff upon the corporation and its secretary-treasurer, who shall have a right to attend or to be represented at the examination.

The secretary-treasurer may in certain circumstances apply to the corporation by written notice served by bailiff upon the chairman for the appointment of an auditor to examine his accounts within eight days; in default of his appointment, or in the auditor's default, he may apply by petition to the Superintendent.

Whenever the Superintendent is assured that a secretary-treasurer's accounts have not been rendered, or, having been rendered, are informal, irregular, illegal, fraudulent, or erroneous, he may, in his own individual name, sue the secretary-treasurer before any court of competent jurisdiction, in an action to render accounts, or to secure the reformation, correction, or revision of the accounts so rendered. He may demand that all agreements entered into between the school commissioners or trustees and their secretary-treasurer, or any other person, with reference to such accounts or their rendering be set aside, annulled, or modified in whole or in part. But the Superintendent may not enter into any such suit without first making a demand by notice upon the school commissioners or trustees to institute such action themselves within the delay indicated in the notice. The notice must be signed by the Superintendent, and is served upon the school corporation by a bailiff of the Superior Court. After the delay indicated in the notice has expired, the Superintendent must institute action if the corporation has not done so. The Superintendent has, however, power in any case to intervene to watch proceedings, and advance them in such a suit, if it be brought by the school corporation. And the suits or interventions of the Superintendent are at the expense of the school commissioners or trustees. (This procedure may also be adopted by the Superintendent or by the school corporation in the case provided for above.)

The sureties of any secretary-treasurer may be made parties to any action brought against a secretary-treasurer by the Superintendent.

Lastly, if the school corporation neglect or refuse to institute proceedings, the Superintendent may in his own name sue any secretary-treasurer in or out of office for the recovery from him of any sum of money which belongs to the school corporation, whether that money arise from the Government grants, the collection of school taxes, monthly fees, or other school dues received by him during the term of his office.

There are certain special rules about *Fabrique* Schools. The *Fabrique* of a parish is the vestry-board or board of church-wardens. The *Fabrique* of any parish and the school commissioners or trustees in charge of it may by mutual agreement unite the *Fabrique* schools in operation with any of the public schools for one or more years. Any *Fabrique* contributing not less than $50 annually towards the support of any school under the management of school commissioners or trustees thereby acquires a right for the *curé* and churchwarden in office to be commissioners for the management of that school only, if they were not so before. But no *Fabrique* may unite its school to those managed by commissioners or trustees of another faith, except under an express and formal agreement between the *Fabrique* and the school corporation of different faith.

· This account of the Local Administration may be concluded by the following statistics taken from the Superintendent's Annual Report for 1898–99.

Roman Catholic and Protestant Schools, Boards of Commissioners and Trustees, Schoolhouses Owned and Leased, Materials of School buildings.

GENERAL STATISTICS.	Roman Catholics.	Protestants.	Total.
Municipalities under control of commissioners or trustees.	1,016	304	1,320
Schoolhouses belonging to commissioners or trustees.	—	—	5,126
Schoolhouses leased to commissioners or trustees.	..	—	406
Houses used for independent schools -	—	—	270
Total - - -	—	—	5,802
Wooden houses - - - - -	—	—	5,171
Brick houses - - - - -	—	—	373
Stone houses - - - - -	—	—	258
Total - - -	—	—	5,802

III.—FINANCE, PROVINCIAL AND LOCAL.

There is little especially remarkable in the financial arrangements of the Quebec educational system. Accordingly, it will be unnecessary to give the regulations in such detail as seemed desirable in the matter of local authorities.

Schools are maintained (*a*) by grants from the "Common School Fund" of the Province, (*b*) by local school taxes, whether usual or special.

To entitle any school to its share, whether of the general common school fund or of the local school fund (*i.e.*, to grants from the "Common School Fund" of the Province or to apportionment from the school fund of the local authority, whether it be a corporation of school commissioners or of school trustees) it is *requisite* and *sufficient* that the school in question should fulfil the following conditions:— *Conditions of aid.*

(1.) The school must be conducted under the management of school commissioners or school trustees in accordance with the regulations;

(2.) The school must have been in actual operation during at least eight months;

(3.) The school must have been attended by at least fifteen children, periods of epidemic or contagious diseases being excepted. (A special indulgence is allowed whenever the school corporation can be shown to have endeavoured in good faith to carry out the law, by which a share of the school fund, general or local, may be paid for each school where there are fifteen or more children of school age, although the school has not been attended by that number during the year.)

(4.) Reports must have been made to the School Corporation by the teacher, and also by at least two of the school commissioners or trustees.

(5.) A public examination must have been held in the school.

(6.) A Report, signed by the majority of the School Corporation and by its secretary-treasurer, must have been transmitted to the Superintendent every six months.

(7.) A sum equal to the grant made by the Legislature for the municipality must have been raised. A special exemption can, however, be made in the case of poor municipalities.

The Superintendent may, upon a representation to the fact that the School Commissioners or trustees have in good faith carried out the provisions of the law, and upon proof of this fact to his satisfaction, exempt the municipality from the whole or part of the tax that would otherwise have to be raised in order to entitle the municipality to its share from the Provincial common school fund. He may pay the amount of share in this case, although the amount of the tax actually levied falls short of the amount required, *i.e.*, although the amount locally raised *Exemption of municipality.*

be not as great as the amount of share from the Provincial grant.

(8.) Teachers with diplomas must have been employed in the school.

(9.) Teachers must have been paid every six months.

(10.) Only those books authorised by the Roman Catholic or the Protestant Committee of the Council of Public Instruction should have been used.

(11.) The Regulations of the Council of Public Instruction or of the Roman Catholic or Protestant Committee, and the instructions of the Superintendent, must have been observed.

The sum annually voted by the Legislature in aid of poor municipalities is distributed by the Superintendent according to a division made by him and approved by the Committee of the Council of Public Instruction of the religious faith to which such school municipalities belong.

Distribution f Local chool Fund.

The Fund and its distribution.—The sums constituting the Common School Fund of the Province may be paid by the Superintendent in two semi-annual payments, under two accountable warrants to the Provincial Treasurer to be issued by the Lieutenant-Governor.

The Superintendent deposits these sums in some bank, according as the Lieutenant-Governor in Council may direct; and apportions it according to law among the various municipalities. He pays to the school commissioners or trustees the shares belonging to the municipalities they represent by cheques drawn upon the bank and made payable to their order; and he must account according to law for all moneys. The shares must be paid to the school corporations by the Superintendent in two half-yearly payments. The school commissioners or trustees may direct the payment, out of the general (local) school fund in their hands, of such contingent expenses as are not specially provided for in the Regulations

Any sums of money which have not been specially appropriated by provision of the donors, vendors, or others, and all sums arising from the allowance for schools, from school taxes or from any source *other than monthly fees*, form the *school fund* in each municipality under the control of the commissioners or trustees. The *school fund* thus formed is divided, distributed, and employed by them;

(1.) either in proportion to the number of children from seven to fourteen years in each school district capable of attending school; or,

(2.) by making a common fund, out of which the commissioners or trustees pay the expenses occasioned by the payment of teachers' salaries, the maintenance of school houses, the purchase of books, school furniture, and other contingent expenses.

The school commissioners or trustees after having adopted one or the other of these two methods, cannot change it within two years unless by the authority of the Superintendent.

In all cases, the school corporation must deduct from this school fund a sum of eighty dollars for the support of a model school, if there be one in the municipality, in addition to the share which such model school is entitled to receive from the fund.

The girls' school, if there be one in the municipality, is counted as constituting in itself one school district, and the model school as another school district. The share of the moneys to be allotted to the girls' school and the model school is determined by the number of children of the age prescribed for attending school, residing in the school district in which such schools are established.

The Superintendent may refuse the school grant for any year to any municipality in which the commissioners or trustees have not rendered sufficient accounts, accompanied by vouchers, of the application of the school moneys for the years preceding, or for any one of them, whatever be the source whence those moneys were derived.

The Superintendent may refuse to pay the whole or any part *Refusal of* of the share of the Common School Fund, which would other- *share in* wise be payable to any school municipality,— *Common School Fund.*

(1) if his instructions or those of the Council of Public Instruction, or of either of its committees, have been disobeyed; or,

(2) if unqualified teachers have been employed by the commissioners or trustees; or,

(3) if a qualified teacher has been dismissed by the school commissioners or trustees before the end of his engagement, and for no valid or just cause. He may, further, pay out of the share of the municipality such indemnity as appears to him justly due to any teacher unjustly dismissed by the school corporation of that municipality.

Out of the permanent and additional legislative grant for *Sum reserved* school purposes in the Province, the following sums may, with *for three* the approval of the Lieutenant-Governor in Council, be set apart *purposes.* and expended yearly by the Superintendent, for the following purposes:—

(1.) A sum for special aid to public schools in poor school municipalities.

(2.) A sum to encourage the publication and circulation of a journal of public instruction.

(3.) A sum towards forming a fund for the support of superannuated or worn out public school teachers in the Province, under such regulations as may be from time to time adopted by the Superintendent or by the Council of Public Instruction, and approved by the Lieutenant-Governor in Council.

Applications of Local School Fund.
Any sum of money whatever arising from the general or local school fund which is not employed by the School Commissioners, Trustees, or Secretary-Treasurers during the year in which it is received must be deposited by them or placed out at interest, in order to create revenue for the School Corporation.

If in any school district there is no school in operation, the School Commissioners or Trustees deposit the money to which the district would be entitled at interest in some savings or other chartered bank, where, with the consent of the rate-payers of the district, they allow it to accumulate during a term not exceeding four years, to be thereafter used by them either in the purchase of ground or in building a school-house, or towards other educational purposes in the school district.

The Superintendent may authorise the School Corporation in any municipality to apply the share coming for any one year to any school district, the inhabitants of which have contributed nothing or too little during the same year to the common fund of that municipality, in such manner as the Superintendent may direct, for the advancement of education in the municipality, instead of depositing the share in a bank. The amounts already placed in any bank for any school district in like cases may be dealt with in the same manner.

It is not necessary to give in full detail the regulations governing—

  a. Valuation.

  b. The Imposition of Taxes.

  c. Their Collection by Seizure..

  d. New and Special Taxes.

  e. Voluntary Contributions.

  f. Collection of Taxes from Corporations, including Religious or Educational bodies, and

  g. Capitalisation of Debt.

Nevertheless, certain distinctive features of the school finance of the Province may with advantage be given in rough outline under each of these headings.

Valuation of property.
a. Wherever a *Valuation of Property* has already been made

by order of the municipal authorities, it serves as the basis of the taxes to be imposed for school purposes. A copy of any such valuation must be furnished to the school corporation, on demand, by the municipal council. But if there be no existing property valuation upon which school taxes can be based, the school commissioners or trustees may cause a property valuation to be made by three valuators appointed and authorized by them for that purpose. A new valuation roll is necessary in cases where, a school municipality having been so formed as to include parts of other municipalities, the valuation rolls in force in those municipalities are not uniform. A penalty of ten dollars is attached to neglect on the part of the commissioners or trustees, either to demand a copy of an existing valuation roll or, failing that, to cause one to be made. The commissioners or trustees may amend a valuation roll when they deem it expedient to do so, provided eight days' public notice is given of their intention. Refusal or neglect on the part of persons in possess on of an existing valuation applicable to the levying of school taxes to hand over a copy of such valuation to the school corporation on demand carries a penalty of twenty dollars. The persons authorised to make the property valuation upon which school taxes are to be based, have the right to enter at all times in and upon any property to inspect it, and to require from the proprietor or occupant any information calculated to aid in the making or completing of the valuation. Obstruction or refusal on the part of occupants to give relevant or necessary information is punished by a penalty of four dollars. When a valuation for school taxes has once been made, it can only be amended by the authority which ordered it to be made. No person can act as valuator for school purposes unless he is a proprietor of real or personal property in the municipality to the amount of 400 dollars.

b. School taxes are imposed between July 1 and September 1, Imposition of in each year, and must be paid at any time on demand. At school taxes. least thirty days' notice must be given before enforcing payment. School corporations and their secretary-treasurers may, in their discretion, receive the amount of taxes and monthly fees in produce, at prices to be fixed by them. Even though no complaint be made, the commissioners or trustees must examine and amend the collection roll and rectify errors made in transcribing valuations or names of persons taxed; or insert names of persons and descriptions of lands which have been omitted, and strike out those erroneously inserted. The rate-payers must be informed of the day, hour, and place of the meeting at which the roll is to be examined and amended. Any rate-payer may demand that the collection roll be amended in any of the particulars just mentioned, either by producing a complaint in writing before or upon the day fixed for its examination, or by stating his complaint verbally at the examination. The commissioners or trustees must consider all complaints made verbally or in writing and hear all interested persons present. Amendments to the collection roll must be entered upon it or upon a paper annexed to it with the initials of the secretary-treasurer, and a declaration testifying to their accuracy and determining their number must be annexed to the collection roll under the signatures of the chairman and the secretary-treasurer of the corporation.

'ollection by
cizure.

c. Collection by Seizure—Public notice of 30 days having been given that payment of school taxes will be enforced, and twenty days after that delay having passed, the collection of school taxes may be enforced by the corporation, either by suit or prosecution, or by a warrant of distress, or by adjudication and sale by the municipality of the property liable for school taxes. A special notice of demand for payment accompanied by a detailed statement of the sums due, must be served by the secretary-treasurer upon ratepayers before proceeding by warrant, distress, or adjudication and sale. Seizure and sale are made under a warrant signed by the chairman of the school corporation, and addressed to a bailiff, who executes it under his oath of office. But the chairman does not incur any personal responsibility in giving and signing such a warrant. He merely acts under the responsibility of the school corporation in whose interest the distress is made. The day and place of sale of the goods and chattels seized must be announced by the bailiff by public notice; and the notice must state the names and quality of the ratepayers whose goods and chattels are to be sold. In the absence of the ratepayer, or if he refuses to open cupboards, chests, &c., the bailiff may, by an order of the chairman of the school corporation or of any justice of the peace, cause the same to be opened in presence of two witnesses with all necessary force. Any ratepayer who has been required to pay as school taxes a larger sum than he owes, or who has already paid, as well as any person having a right of ownership or a privilege on the property seized, may oppose the seizure and sale. His opposition must be supported by an affidavit attesting the truth of the allegations it contains, allowed by a judge of the Superior Court or by a clerk of the Circuit Court of the county or district, or by a clerk of the magistrates' court in the district. One of these authorities must endorse the affidavit and annex to it an order to the bailiff to return the warrant of distress to the Court whence the writ issued. But permission to make an affidavit of opposition is not granted unless a deposit of five dollars be made in the office of the secretary-treasurer, or of a sum equal to that claimed by the warrant, if that sum be less than five dollars. The opposition is subsequently heard and decided according to the ordinary practice of the Court. The proceeds of any sale are distributed by the Court and are paid by the secretary-treasurer according to its order. When no opposition to the distribution of the proceeds of the sale of moveables is made, the bailiff pays over the proceeds of the sale, after deducting the costs of seizure and sale, to the secretary-treasurer; and he applies the proceeds towards the payment of the school taxes, for which the warrant of distress was issued. If there be any surplus, it is paid by the secretary-treasurer to the ratepayer whose goods and chattels were sold.

d. New and Special Taxes.—Whenever a general or special tax in any school municipality is annulled or set aside, the school commissioners or trustees must forthwith, in a summary manner, cause a new tax to be imposed. This new tax is imposed and takes effect for the whole time, past and future, for which the tax so annulled or set aside would have been in force had it been valid. The annulling of a tax does not, however, have the effect of invalidating any payments made under the authority of the tax so annulled, but such payments go towards the discharge of the new tax for the period for which they have been made. The tax so annulled is declared invalid for the future only, and not with regard to any judgments then already rendered to enforce payment.

It is lawful for the school commissioners and trustees in every school municipality, with the approval of the Lieutenant-Governor in Council, upon satisfactory proof that the money to be levied had been *bona fide* expended in the construction of model or elementary school-houses, to impose a special assessment for the payment of debts contracted by the commissioners or trustees for the construction of the school houses, over and above the amount allowed by law ; and the amount of any such special assessment may also include the cost incurred by municipalities in suits respecting the previous assessment. In cases where a special assessment has been so annulled, the ratepayers who have paid their share have not the right to be reimbursed the amount so paid by them : but, in any subsequent assessment levied for the same purpose, credit is given them for the amounts so paid by them upon the assessment annulled.

The Superintendent may cause *Special Taxes* to be levied in any municipality or district, for the payment of the debts incurred by the school commissioners or trustees within the limits of their powers, or which have been adjudged by a Court of Justice to be due by such municipality or district ; and, whenever such debts have been contracted by a municipality subsequently divided into several municipalities, or the limits of which have been subsequently altered, the Superintendent apportions the payment of such debts equitably among the several municipalities liable for them. If there be no funds available for the payment of the sum of money which the school corporation is condemned by judgment to pay, the commissioners or trustees must apply to the Superintendent for authorization to levy a special tax to pay the amount of the judgment. If the Superintendent authorizes such a special tax, a special collection roll must forthwith be prepared. The judgment creditor may obtain the issue of a writ of execution against the school corporation in default, (1) if the Superintendent does not furnish the authority for the special tax within fifteen days from the time when it is demanded from him ; (2) if the amount of the special tax which he has authorized has not been collected; (3) if the school commissioners or trustees have not proceeded to complete the collection roll within the fifteen days following the date of the authorisation by the Superintendent; (4) if the commissioners or trustees refuse or neglect in any manner to proceed with the completion of the collection roll, or to collect the tax, in whole or in part. Such a writ of execution is addressed and delivered to the sheriff of the district in which the school municipality in question is situated, and enjoins him—(1) to levy from the school corporation, with all possible dispatch, the amount of the debt with interest, and the costs of the judgment and of the execution; (2) in default of immediate payment by the school corporation, to seize and sell any moveable property held by it, and any real estate belonging to it, upon which the judgment creditor may have a privilege or hypothec, and of which the seizure and sale may be ordered by the judgment. And in the event of there being no real or personal property to be seized or sold (or if the property is insufficient to satisfy the judgment) an *alias* writ of execution may be issued against the school corporation in default, addressed to the sheriff, and enjoining him—(1) to levy from the school corporation the whole sum (or the sum remaining due, as the case may be) of the debt, with interest and costs including those of the judgment, by apportioning the sum required on all the rateable real property in the school municipality liable for the judgment, in proportion to its value; and (2) to collect the tax imposed by him, and to make a return to the Court of the amount levied and of his proceedings, so soon as the amount of the debt, interest, and costs has been collected, or from time to time as the Court may order. The sheriff may then procure from the secretary-treasurer the valuation roll in force, and, on his refusal to supply this, may take possession of it. If no valuation roll exists, he proceeds to make a valuation of the taxable property himself. The sheriff publishes the special collection roll made by him for this apportionment; and hears and decides all complaints made either in writing or verbally by the ratepayers; and he then makes such amendments to the special collection roll as he may deem right. The special tax is payable at the sheriff's office at the expiration of a delay of thirty days. Almost the same regulations in regard to collection, the special notice for uncollected taxes, opposition, &c., apply in this case as in the case of an ordinary school tax collected by a school corporation. The sheriff finally transmits a copy of his special collection roll, showing therein what amounts have been collected, to the school commissioners or trustees, after having levied the whole amount set forth in the *alias* writ of execution, with interest and costs. And if any surplus remain in his hands it belongs to the school corporation, and is paid over by him to it. All arrears in ordinary school taxes belong to the school corporation. If judgment is rendered for a debt due for the building of a school-house for which a portion only of the school municipality is liable, the judgment, the writ of execution, and the *alias* writ of execution must mention the fact. The tax in this case is imposed only upon the real property situated in that part of the municipality which is liable under the judgment.

e. Voluntary Contributions.—When, in any school municipality, the valuation of property has been duly made and the school tax based upon it has been imposed before September 1 in any year, for the then following school year, the persons so taxed, or any other of the inhabitants of such school municipality or school district, may pay as a voluntary contribution into the hands of the secretary-treasurer, the sum required, for the school-year then commenced, to equal the amount of public moneys granted to the municipality out of the school fund for that school year. The payment of such voluntary contribution must be attested on oath before a justice of the peace, by the secretary-treasurer, and by the chairman or other member of the school corporation. This attestation must be transmitted to the Superintendent before November 10. The secretary-treasurer is not empowered to receive the amount of such a voluntary contribution by portions or otherwise than in one and the same payment. He holds the amount in lieu of the fund which would have been raised by taxation for the school year so commenced, and the tax thereupon becomes inoperative for that year in the school municipality or district; but the monthly school fees, and any tax imposed for the erection of school-houses, is levied by the school municipality or district, when they have not been voluntarily paid.

f. Collection of Taxes from Corporations.—The school commissioners for a school municipality alone have power to levy taxes on the lands and real estate of corporations and incorporated companies. But they pay over annually to the *trustees* a portion of all the taxes levied by them on corporations or companies, in the same proportion as the Government grant for the same year is divided between them and the trustees. The portion of the taxes levied for the building of school-houses and for the payment of debts which is thus paid over to the trustees, must be set apart by them for the building or repairing of their own school-houses. No religious, charitable, or educational institutions or corporations can be taxed for school purposes on the property occupied by them for the objects for which they were instituted. But they may be taxed by the school commissioners or trustees of the religious majority or minority to which they belong on all property held by them for the purpose of deriving any income for themselves. Such a tax must be used by the school commissioners or trustees, as the case may be, to the exclusive benefit of the religious majority or minority to which they belong, or else in conformity with the declarations which they may make in this respect. When the religious body to which they belong is not obvious, and where no such declaration has been made, the properties must be dealt with for the purposes of school-taxes in the same manner as is prescribed for the properties of other corporations and of incorporated companies.

Any non-resident proprietor may declare in writing to the school commissioners and trustees his intention of dividing his taxes between the schools of the majority and those of the minority. In that case the school commissioners continue to levy and receive such taxes and pay over to the trustees such part or proportion of them as the proprietor may direct to be so paid over.

Capitalisation of debt.

g. Capitalisation.—Any school corporation in a city or town may, with the authorisation of the Lieutenant-Governor in Council, upon the report of the Superintendent of Public Instruction, capitalise the debts by it lawfully contracted or to be contracted, and stipulate for the payment thereof by annuities covering a period of not more than fifty years. Such annuities include the interest and the proportion of the capital which is to be paid yearly to extinguish the debt at the date agreed upon. The corporation may, with the authorisation of the Superintendent of Public Instruction, issue, for the payment of such annuities, debentures maturing every six months or every year until the loan is paid off. (Statute of 1893.)

Statistical Tables.

This section of the subject may be concluded and illustrated by two statistical tables. The second of these gives in some detail the sources and applications of school funds, whether provincial or municipal (*i.e.*, local) :—

(i.)   AMOUNTS EXPENDED ON PUBLIC INSTRUCTION IN 1889-90.

	$	cts.	$	cts.
Amounts voted by the Legislature :				
Ordinary and special grants - -	386,835	00		
Amounts voted in aid of literary and scientific institutions - - -	19,650	00	406,485	00
Amounts paid by the Ratepayers :				
Annual taxes - - - - -	815,313	00		
Special taxes - - - - -	87,495	00		
Monthly contributions - - -	244,972	00		
Amounts expended by institutions of superior education - - -	1,292,617	00	2,440,397	00
TOTAL* - - - - -			2,846,882	00

* At $5 to £1 the amounts are : Legislature, £81,297 ; Ratepayers, £488,079½.   Total, £569,376½.

(ii.) (Compiled from statistics in the Report of the Superintendent of Public Instruction for the Year 1896–97.)

GENERAL STATISTICS OF THE COST OF EDUCATION.

COUNTIES.	Value of Taxable Real Estate.	MUNICIPAL CONTRIBUTIONS.			GOVERNMENT CONTRIBUTIONS.			Contributions of Subsidised Schools.	TOTAL.	Number of School-houses.	Value of School-houses, Furniture, and School Appliances.
		Annual Taxes.	Special Taxes.	Monthly Contributions.	For Public Schools.	For Superior Education.	For Poor Municipalities.				
	$	$	$	$	$	$	$	$	$		$
Argenteuil	2,033,450	11,327	709	2,887	1,670.66	397.91	750.46	2,130	20,072.03	87	48,910
Beauharnois	5,259,276	13,303	1,200	2,547	1,790.34	1,295.39	—	20,130	42,265.73	57	291,190
Charlevoix	3,737,909	5,782	167	774	2,046.87	459.86	417.19	3,280	12,926.92	96	52,750
Deux-Montagnes	3,711,152	10,469	1,368	362	1,582.62	289.65	96.81	6,480	20,628.08	69	83,610
Gaspé	1,897,121	12,303	450	1,455	2,953.89	398.55	1,911.66	1,300	20,772.10	125	35,695
Hochelaga	38,029,293	103,882	8,833	15,552	7,402.17	1,287.92	—	54,342	191,286.39	75	1,004,739
Iberville	3,635,433	10,052	1,065	664	1,279.51	329.74	—	14,633	27,903.25	61	141,620
Joliette	4,891,666	10,890	271	396	2,460.81	956.26	69.53	23,154	40,197.60	90	291,090
Laprairie	3,821,213	8,607	156	361	963.16	272.72	—	2,535	10,894.88	32	38,900
Maskinongé	4,721,145	8,848	—	563	1,911.80	236.18	73.36	8,267	19,899.34	67	103,855
Missisquoi	5,319,683	16,135	448	1,470	2,012.67	1,307.80	509.96	17,340	39,223.43	110	136,800
Napierville	3,150,928	6,919	139	318	1,065.34	204.98	—	6,428	15,044.32	39	72,045
Ottawa	5,422,001	46,563	2,858	8,912	6,505.47	1,442.43	1,734.38	4,901	72,816.28	226	209,283
Pontiac	1,635,821	16,508	1,226	1,913	2,182.09	569.33	1,024.94	—	23,423.36	106	37,900
Quebec, County of	4,793,479	11,133	360	2,778	2,594.18	916.16	421.04	27,605	45,807.38	72	276,500
Richelieu	4,205,917	10,543	—	928	2,294.42	515.61	—	12,006	28,287.03	60	161,075
Saguenay	254,564	1,092	271	350	904.15	178.24	2,099.20	1,336	6,249.59	22	15,690
Témiscouata	3,386,908	13,257	1,064	1,828	2,778.30	556.49	502.19	8,722	28,677.98	137	126,755
Vaudreuil	3,881,754	9,736	1,203	873	1,217.18	1,110.51	30.90	23,706	37,876.59	52	148,650
Wolfe	2,100,494	9,655	1,010	931	1,671.31	175.00	193.05	2,863	16,488.36	91	36,107
Yamaska	4,434,476	11,226	824	717	2,370.24	382.32	—	9,237	24,756.56	94	118,335

R

IV.—School Visitors and School Inspection.

School Visitors.—Certain persons are *ex officio* " visitors " with power to visit any public school in any municipality whether in town or country. But no visitor is entitled to visit a school belonging to inhabitants not of his own religious faith.

Visitors for the whole Province.

a. The school visitors for the whole province are—

(1.) members of the Roman Catholic, or of the Protestant, Committees of the Council of Public Instruction,

(2.) Judges of the Supreme Court, of the Court of Queen's Bench, and of the Superior Court, who are resident in the Province of Quebec,

(3.) Members of the Federal Parliament, who are resident in the Province,

(4.) members of the Legislature of Quebec,

(5.) the Secretaries of the Department of Public Instruction.

(6.) The Superintendent of Public Instruction, as visitor-general of all public schools, may take cognizance of disputes arising between school commissioners or trustees and teachers, and give a final dicision.

Visitors in their own districts only.

b. School inspectors are *ex officio* visitors of academies and model schools under the control of school commissioners or trustees in their districts of inspection, and it is lawful for any inspector to visit the schools within any district of inspection other than that assigned to him on receipt of an order from the Superintendent. An Inspector who holds such an order may report on the schools he visits outside his own district.

c. The following are visitors only for the municipality in which they reside;

(1.) Roman Catholic Priests and Protestant Ministers;

(2.) Members of the Council of Arts and Manufactures;

(3.) The Mayor and Justices of the Peace;

(4.) The Colonels, Lieutenant-Colonels, Majors, and Senior Captains of the Militia.

Each visitor is entitled to examine the regulations and other documents relative to each school, and to obtain all other information concerning it. A visitor may be present at examinations held by any board of examiners and may interrogate the candidates who offer themselves for examination, and give his opinion upon them.

School Inspection.

The districts into which the Province is divided for the purpose of school inspection are identical with the judicial districts. And each Inspector is *ex officio* a justice of the peace of the district for which he is appointed.

The initiative in the appointment of School Inspectors comes from the Roman Catholic or from the Protestant Committee. They recommend the appointment of one or more Inspectors for a certain judicial district to the Lieutenant-Governor, who makes the appointment for such a period as he deems necessary.

The Inspector's duties are defined thus by statute :— **Duties of Inspectors.**

(1.) to examine the school-teachers, and the schools and school-houses under their control in each school municipality ;

(2.) to inspect the accounts of the secretary-treasurers, and the register of the school commissioners or school trustees of every such municipality ;

(3.) to ascertain whether the provisions of the laws and regulations respecting public instruction are there carried out and obeyed.

In the performance of his duties each Inspector must comply with the instructions given to him by the Superintendent, in accordance with the regulations of the Committee of the Council of Public Instruction of the religious faith which he himself professes.

Unless otherwise defined or limited by the instrument appointing him, each such inspector has all the powers and authority of the Superintendent with reference to his visits and examinations. And when an Inspector makes his visits the secretary-treasurer of the municipality and all teachers of a public school in it are bound to exhibit to him all the documents in their charge belonging to or in any way relating to their respective offices. Every refusal or neglect to do so, when requested by an Inspector, carries with it a penalty of eight dollars.

No person can be appointed School Inspector unless, **Qualifications.**

(1.) he has attained the age of twenty-five years ;

(2.) he has obtained a diploma for teaching in an academy, model school, or elementary school ;

(3.) he has taught in a school for a period of at least five years,

(4.) at least five years have elapsed since he discontinued teaching in a school,

(5.) he has been examined before the Roman Catholic or Protestant Committee, or before a sub-committee of examiners appointed by one or the other of those Committees, upon his fitness and ability to fulfil the duties of the office in accordance with the regulations which each Committee may make.

Each Inspector is paid such a sum as the Lieutenant-Governor **Salaries.** in Council deems adequate remuneration for the duties performed by him. But his salary can in no case exceed the rate of $1,200 (£240) per annum. In all cases in which an Inspector is appointed by the Superintendent to make any special inspection, inquiry, or investigation in any municipality, the travelling and other expenses of the Inspector are paid by the party designated by the Superintendent. The person who is to pay the expenses of inspection is determined by the Superintendent upon the report of the Inspector. These last regulations apply only to inspections or inquiries which do not take place at the time of the Inspector's ordinary visit to the schools of the municipality in question.

Instructions and Number. Instructions to School Inspectors are from time to time issued from the Department of Public Instruction These are written by the Superintendent, and deal with particular points of importance for the time being. There is no annual publication issued to Inspectors similar to the "Revised Instructions to H.M. Inspectors" issued in England and Wales.

In 1897–8 there were 42 Inspectors.

Inspector's Return. The following is a specimen taken at random from the Annual Report for 1897–8, of the returns made by Inspectors to the Superintendent. In two cases, it would seem, no visit was paid by an Inspector to the schools.

MASKINONGÉ COUNTY. Municipality.	Grade of Institution.	Whether under Control of Commissioners or not.	Value of immoveable Property.	Expenditure for the Year.	Teachers. Male RELIGIOUS or Nuns.	Male.	Female.
a. Maskinongé	Model School Mixed	Under control	1,500	375	—	1	1
b. Rivière du Loup	Academy Boys	Under control and independent	15,000	1,060	4 *Frères de l'Instruction Chrétienne*	—	—
c. Rivière du Loup	Model Conventual	Independent	19,300	3,538	10 *Soeurs de l'Assomption*	—	2
d. Dumontier	Model Mixed	Under control	1,200	225	—	—	2
e. St. Paulin	Model Conventual	Under control and independent	8,725	841	6 *Soeurs de l'Assomption*	—	—
f. Ste. Ursule	Model Conventual	Under control and independent	30,640	7,420	3 *Soeurs de la Providence*	—	1
g. Ste. Ursule	Model Boys	Under control	1,700	231	—	1	1

Municipality.	Value note based solely on examination of the Annual Report.	Total Pupils.	Grants out of the Superior Education Fund.	From the Inspection Bulletins.				
				State of School House.	State of Furniture.	Is the Teacher competent?	Is there Progress?	General Note on School.
a. Maskinongé	Very Good	75	35.08	Fair	Fair	Yes	Yes	Very Good
b. Rivière du Loup	Very Good	203	35.08	Very Good	Good	Yes	Yes	Very Good
c. Rivière du Loup	Very Good	244	35.08	—	—	—	—	—
d. Dumontier	Good	88	26.33	Good	Good	Yes	Yes	Very Good
e. St. Paulin	Very Good	93	43.84	—	—	—	—	—
f. Ste. Ursule	Very Good	119	35.08	Very Good	Good	Yes	Yes	Excellent
g. Ste. Ursule	Very Good	66	22.28	Fair	Fair	Yes	Yes	Fair

The Roman Catholic or the Protestant Committee may, upon Dismissal of complaint to that effect, cause an inquiry to be held into the Inspector. conduct of any Inspector of Schools accused of bad conduct, immorality, or intemperance, or serious neglect in the execution of his duties. After the inquiry, all the documents are forwarded to the Lieutenant-Governor in Council, " praying, if there be occasion, for the dismissal of such Inspector and the cancelling of his commission." If an Inspector is dismissed in this manner he cannot afterwards hold office. Inspectors are strictly prohibited from having any interest, direct or indirect, in the sale of books or school supplies in their inspection districts.

The following passage from a circular issued by the present Circular of Superintendent in October, 1897 (Annual Report for 1896–7), 1897. is of interest as being typical of the instructions given to Inspectors from headquarters. Other instructions issued in the same year and dealing with the special subject of the *Pedagogical lectures* to teachers then instituted will be found under that head in Section V.

" By an Order-in-Council dated the 6th inst., the Government has confirmed the decision taken by the Roman Catholic Committee of the Council of Public Instruction to replace your autumn inspection by a series of Pedagogical lectures which you will be called upon to give to the teachers of your inspection districts :

" 1. To respond to the desire of the Roman Catholic Committee, you will organise this course by calling together in the village or in some central spot in each parish, all the teachers who teach therein. These lectures, to the extent of four or five, should last two days.

" 2. You will notify the teachers at least eight or ten days beforehand of the day and hour that the lectures will be given in the respective parishes.

" 3. In the event of there being several school municipalities in the parish, the lectures shall be given for all the teachers in such parishes. The same may be done in the case of two or three school municipalities of adjoining parishes when there are not more than three or four teachers in one of such municipalities.

" 4. Teachers who have to travel to attend the lectures will receive compensation at the rate of seventy-five cents per diem. You will take notice of their presence at the lectures, and forward their names and addresses to the Department of Public Instruction.

" At the conclusion of your visit you will also send to me a report containing your remarks on the result of these conferences, both from a pedagogical point of view, and with regard to their effect on the minds of the School Boards.

" 5. Teachers may give their pupils a holiday during the two days which these lectures last.

"6. It is desirable that the parish priest and the school commissioners should attend the lectures to enhance their value and to increase their efficiency.

"7. With a view of establishing as much uniformity as possible in the instruction to be given to the teachers, I take the opportunity of sending to you, with the present circular, some lectures which have been carefully prepared, and which you may study so as to be able to make use of them by adding such remarks as you may deem advisable and the instruction you may consider yourself called upon to give.

"8. I have no doubt that you yourselves will attach importance to these lectures; that you will display zeal in delivering them. You know, as I do, that many of our male teachers, and above all that a great many of our female teachers, have not had the advantage of attending the Normal School, and have not received the necessary professional training. The instructions you will give them will therefore be of very great assistance to them, and will open up entirely new horizons to several of them.

"In addition to the subjects dealt with in the lectures I send you, strongly recommend the teachers not to make their pupils learn anything by heart that they have not clearly explained to them; to carefully prepare their lessons and all explanations they have to give on the following day, even to the smallest children, so as to be understood by them; to study thoroughly so as to develop their own knowledge and make their teaching more beneficial. They will highly appreciate all this advice. You may also advise them to sometimes go beyond the teaching of the class subjects to give the children judicious instruction respecting the duties they will afterwards be called upon to perform when they leave school.

"Tell them to thoroughly inculcate upon the minds of the children great respect for paternal, civil, and religious authority. Let them warn them against intemperance, the source of so many evils, and against the extravagance that impoverishes our country parts. Let them recommend them to avoid quarrels and law suits, and let them lay great stress in the presence of the children on the necessity of honesty in contracts. Let them also teach them good manners, and insist upon politeness and cleanliness. They can be made to highly prize in school the benefits conferred by agriculture, in order to make the children like that calling; and let them not neglect to instil into their minds great love of country—in a word, please impress upon the teachers the necessity of making their schools attractive, and study agreeable to their pupils by not only carefully preparing their teaching but by reciting anecdotes culled chiefly from the history of Canada.

"With regard to the moral education of the children, about which you will have to speak to the school teachers, I cannot do better than repeat to you the admirable circular that M. Guizot addressed to the teachers of France in 1833. The words of that distinguished man are more than ever applicable at the present time.

"'As regards moral education,' wrote M. Guizot, 'I rely chiefly upon you. In you, a desire to do well is indispensable You are not ignorant of the fact that this is beyond a doubt the most important and most difficult part of your mission. You are aware that in confiding a child to you, each family asks you to return to it an honest man, and the country a good citizen. You see that virtue does not always follow upon enlightenment, and the lessons imbibed in childhood might become opposed to it, if they addressed themselves merely to its intelligence. Let the teacher, therefore, not hesitate to assume the rights of the family by giving his first care to the inward culture of his pupil's soul. Just as he should avoid opening his school to sectarian and party spirit and bringing up the children in religious or political doctrines which lead them to revolt against the authority of home counsels, so should he rise above the passing quarrels which agitate society to endeavour unceasingly to propagate and strengthen those imperishable principles of morality and reason, without which universal order is imperilled, and to sow deeply in their young hearts those seeds of virtue and of honour which age and passions will never stifle.

"' Faith in Providence, the holiness of duty, submission to paternal authority, the respect due to law and authority and the rights of all: such are the sentiments which he should endeavour to foster. Never by his conversation or by his example should he run the risk of weakening in the minds of the children the veneration due to what is good. Never by words of hatred or revenge should he predispose them to those blind prejudices which create, as it were, hostile nations in the very bosom of the nation itself. The peace and concord which he maintains in his school, should, if possible, prepare calmness for future generations.'

" I am happy to inform you that the Government has been pleased to comply with the request of the Roman Catholic Commissioners of the Council of Public Instruction, and to send free of charge "l'Enseignement Primaire" to each of the primary schools under control of Roman Catholic Commissioners and Trustees.

" This decision has been taken with a view of assisting teachers in their arduous tasks, of keeping them informed with respect to the progress of education, and of further developing their pedagogical knowledge.

" This review, under the management of an active and zealous teacher, and edited by competent writers, will be of great assistance to teachers, by showing them the best methods of teaching, and by becoming the faithful interpreter of the national aspirations of the people; therefore, each school will receive 'l'Enseignement Primaire' free of charge, and it will be the property, not of the teacher, but of the school itself.

" I beg you to see that the numbers of this review are carefully preserved in each school, so that at the end of the year they may be bound together and form the numbers of a pedagogical library.

"Please instruct the secretary-treasurer of your school municipality to have this review bound every year, and to cause to be printed on the cover the name of the school municipality and the number of the district to which it belongs.

"The teachers must not appropriate the numbers of ' l'Enseignement Primaire' at the end of the year, but send them to the office of the secretary-treasurer in order that he may get them bound during the vacation. They must also obtain themselves from the post-office of their parish the numbers of the reviews that are addressed to their schools."

V.—TEACHERS: TRAINING AND DIPLOMAS.

Normal Schools.—The Regulations touching Normal Schools are, briefly, as follows :—

Financial Provision.

The Lieutenant-Governor in Council may adopt all needful measures for the establishment in the Province of one or more normal schools, containing one or more model schools, for the instruction and training of teachers of public schools in the science of education and the art of teaching. · He may select the location of such schools, and cause to be erected or procured and furnished the buildings requisite for the purpose. To provide for the purchase of such sites and for erecting the buildings he may order that the sum of $8,000 be yearly set aside out of the superior education income fund and appropriated to form a fund called "The Normal School Building Fund of the Province of Quebec." Any sum so set apart yearly may be invested and placed at interest as the Lieutenant-Governor in Council may direct, and the income and interest shall, like the principal, form part of the fund. The moneys realised by the sale of any site and buildings, acquired for normal school purposes and not deemed convenient for such purposes, is also added to the fund and is invested and dealt with in the same manner as the other sums. It is the Lieutenant-Governor in Council who directs such a sale to be made. Any excess of the normal school building fund not actually required for the purpose for which the fund was constituted may, in the discretion of the Lieutenant-Governor in Council, either revert to and form part of the superior education income fund of the Province, or be invested as part of it and to the benefit of that fund.

Besides the annual sum set apart out of the superior education income fund, there is also allowed yearly out of the common school fund for the Province a sum not exceeding $6,000, to defray the salaries of officers and other contingent expenses of normal schools; and a sum not exceeding $4,000 is allowed yearly out of the common school income fund, as an aid to facilitate the attendance of teachers in training at normal schools.

And in case these two sums are found insufficient, the

Lieutenant-Governor in Council may order that a certain sum be yearly appropriated out of the common school income fund for the support and maintenance of normal schools. The sum so set apart and appropriated yearly must not exceed in any one year the sum of $10,000.

Thus it will be seen that the support of the normal schools comes mainly from two sources—the superior education income fund and the common school fund. By this method the normal schools are recognised as a particular type of secondary schools having for their special object the training of teachers for elementary schools.

Regulations are made by the Council of Public Instruction or by its Roman Catholic and its Protestant Committee, with the approval of the Lieutenant-Governor in Council, for the management of normal schools, for prescribing the terms and conditions upon which students shall be received and instructed in them, the course of instruction to be followed, the mode and manner in which registers and books shall be kept and diplomas granted to students; and the form in which shall be made the reports which the principal of each normal school is required to make to the Superintendent.

Normal schools are under the control of the Superintendent, Superin-who makes from time to time such arrangements for their tendent's establishment and maintenance as the Lieutenant-Governor Contro¹. in Council may direct. The principal of each normal school reports to the Superintendent, giving such details as he may require. The professors, directors, and principals are appointed or removed by the Lieutenant-Governor in Council, on the recommendation of the Roman Catholic or Protestant Committee of the Council of Public Instruction, according as such appointments or removals concern Roman Catholic or Protestant normal schools. The principal of every normal school must, before admitting any pupil into his school, make him sign, in presence of two witnesses, a document or obligation by which he binds himself to pay his board and to pay such sum as may be required, according to the conditions which shall, from time to time, be fixed by the Lieutenant-Governor in Council. A father, tutor, or friend may sign such a document and bind himself personally for payment of the sum. The Attorney-General, in the name of the principal and upon his recommendation, may sue for the recovery of all sums due in a competent court of justice. The principal must account to the Superintendent for all sums collected under such documents.

On the presentation by any student to the Superintendent Diploma. of a certificate under the hand and seal of the principal of any normal school that the student has gone through a regular course of study therein, the Superintendent may grant a diploma of qualification to the student, which shall be valid, until revoked for some breach of good conduct or of good morals. By virtue of this diploma and while it remains valid, the holder is eligible to .be employed as teacher according to the grade of the diploma obtained by him, in any academy, model school, or elementary school under the control of school commissioners or trustees.

The following is taken from the yearly report made to the Superintendent by the Principal of the Jacques Cartier Normal School (Montreal), for 1897–8:—" By drawing up programmes causing examinations to be passed, the Government has raised the level of the knowledge which the teacher should possess. That was the starting point, it was necessary; but we must not stay there for ever. It is not sufficient that the teachers be educated, they must also have acquired as great an experience as possible of children and of the application of pedagogical principles. With the exception of those who have been trained in the Normal Schools and teaching communities, how many are there who have any idea of the necessity of a good method for properly teaching the elements of arithmetic or merely of reading? Or, if they have studied it, how many of them can take advantage of it ?"

The Superintendent remarks in this connection that "among other remedies which have been sanctioned by experience in the old world, a suggestion has been made that all persons who desire to teach should be compelled to pass some time on trial under a teacher of some years' standing"—alluding, one may suppose, to the pupil-teacher and "provisional-assistant-teacher" system of England and Wales (Articles 34 and 49 Elementary Day School Code, 1900). The Superintendent says "this trial might be of greater or less duration. Six months would suffice to effect a complete change in a great many schools, and in the end perhaps the value of well trained teachers would be understood."

Normal Schools for Girls.

From the Superintendent's Annual Report for 1897–8.— " The good result of the pedagogical lectures shows how deserving of the attention of the Legislature is the foundation of Normal Schools for girls. I have had the honour of pointing out on several occasions how necessary is the establishment of such schools, and I consider that this is the first step to be taken in the reforms to be effected. Moreover, I merely express the opinion of the Roman Catholic Committee of the Council of Public Instruction."

There are only two Normal Schools for girls in the Province, one at Montreal for Protestants and the other at Quebec for Roman Catholics. Successive annual Reports have pointed out to the Government that no very decided results can be expected from elementary schools until more such institutions for the training of women teachers have been founded. The need seems to be greater among the Roman Catholics, and several Normal Schools are in reality needed now to provide training adequate to the number of women teachers in Roman Catholic schools.

Pedagogical Lectures. — These were inaugurated in the autumn of 1897, and have supplied a long felt want. They have to a certain extent made up for the absence of professional training in a great many teachers. " Of course they cannot supply the special knowledge which those who propose to become teachers could acquire in a Normal School; nevertheless the good effects have shown themselves in the very first year. There has been an improvement in a great many of the persons in charge of schools; they have taught with more method."

The following were the regulations on this subject given out in 1897 :—

" 1st. That, in the future, the School Inspectors shall not be obliged to make more than one visit to the schools in their respective districts, and that such visit shall be at the end of the school year ;

" 2nd. That the autumn visits shall be replaced by pedagogical lectures, which the School Inspectors shall give to the teachers in the schools of their inspection districts ;

" 3rd. That these lectures shall be under the direction of the Superintendent of Public Instruction, and shall be given on the days and at the places fixed by the School Inspectors, who shall give notice of them to the teachers ;

" 4th. That the teachers who will be obliged to travel to attend these lectures shall receive an indemnity of seventy-five cents per day ; the lectures not to last more than two days ;

" 5th. That the teachers may give holidays to their pupils during the two days that the lectures shall last."

The Boards of Examiners for Teachers' Diplomas.—(i.) *Central Board ;* (ii.) *Boards for Quebec and Montreal ;* (iii.) *Boards for other cities, towns, or counties.*

(i.) The Lieutenant-Governor in Council may, upon the recommendation of the Roman Catholic or Protestant Committee of the Council of Public Instruction, constitute by proclamation a Central Board of Examiners for the examination of candidates for teachers' diplomas. The Central Board, when constituted, alone has the right of issuing diplomas valid for the schools under the control of the Committee upon whose recommendation the Board was constituted. This Central Board must consist of five members and a secretary, who are appointed by the Lieutenant-Governor in Council upon the recommendation of the Roman Catholic or Protestant Committee, as the case may be. Its duties when constituted are or would be,

a. To prepare the examination questions in the different subjects prescribed.

b. To submit the examination questions to the candidates at certain centres,

c. To examine the answers given by the candidates and, after due deliberation, to grant diplomas to the candidates deemed worthy.

The examinations conducted by the Central Board are held at such time and place and in such manner as may be prescribed from time to time by the regulations of the Committee upon whose recommendation the Central Board of Examiners was constituted. The fees payable by the candidates are used towards defraying the expenses of the Central Board.*

(ii.) The Boards of Examiners for the cities of Quebec and Montreal do not, like the Central Board, depend for their existence on the recommendation of another body, but are constituted by statute. They are composed of fourteen persons, one-half of whom are Roman Catholics and the other half Protestants. The Lieutenant-Governor appoints the members upon the recommendation of the Roman Catholic and Protestant Committees of the Council of Public Instruction. The Boards examine candidates for teachers' diplomas and deliver or refuse to each, as the case may require, a diploma after due examination. The Board is in each case divided into two divisions, Roman Catholic and Protestant, and separately performs the duties imposed upon it.

(iii.) Other Boards of Examiners besides those for Quebec and Montreal may be at any time and for any city, town, county, or counties, be established by proclamation of the Lieutenant-Governor in Council upon the recommendation of either Committee of the Council of Public Instruction. Every Board so constituted by proclamation is composed of not less than five nor more than ten members; and, as is the case with the Boards for Quebec and Montreal, these Boards may be organised in two divisions, Roman Catholic and Protestant, each of which separately performs the duties devolving on it, if the Lieutenant-Governor so orders upon the report of either Committee of the Council of Public Instruction.

Duties. It is the duty of every Board of Examiners, (1) to meet at

---

* *Central Board of Examiners.* —"A regulation orders the foundation of a central board of examiners, which alone, with the normal schools, shall have the right to grant certificates of capacity, allowing the holders thereof to teach in Roman Catholic Schools. By this means it is hoped that certificates will have more prestige and greater value in the eyes of the public. The local boards of examiners will be abolished.'—*From the Report for* 1896.

10 a.m. on the twentieth day after nomination to choose a president, vice-president, and secretary ; (2) to hold examinations in accordance with the regulations of the Roman Catholic or Protestant Committee, as the case may be ;' and after due examination to grant or refuse, as the case may require, diplomas to the candidates presenting themselves for examination: (3) to admit to examination no candidate who is not provided with a certificate of good moral character, signed by the *curé* or minister of his own religious faith, and by at least three school commissioners or school trustees or school visitors of the locality in which he has resided for the previous six months, and with a certificate of his age, which must be of the age fixed by the Roman Catholic Committee of the Council of Public Instruction for Roman Catholic candidates, and by the Protestant Committee for Protestant candidates; (4) to require all candidates for a model or elementary school diploma to pay to the secretary of the board of examiners the sum of two dollars, and for an academy diploma, the sum of three dollars (such sums are not returned to candidates who have failed to obtain the diploma, but these may present themselves a second time at the next examination without paying further fees); (5) to deliver to each candidate deemed worthy, a diploma as a teacher, signed by the president, or vice-president, and the secretary, sealed with the seal of the Board, bearing a date and distinctly indicating :

a. That the candidate has prov ded the requisite certificates of moral character and of age;

b. His age, residence, and religious belief;

c. The grade of the diploma granted ;

d. The language which the diploma authorises the candidate to teach ;

(6) to classify the candidates in these grades, namely, elementary, model school, and academy grades ; (7) to enter the names and surname of each candidate admitted, as well as the grade to which he belongs ; (8) to require, in the course of examination, proof of the following qualifications, namely :—

a. For teachers of elementary schools, such qualifications as will enable them to teach, with success, reading, writing, the elements of grammar, geography, and arithmetic as far as the rule of three ;

b. For teachers of model schools, in addition to the foregoing, such qualifications as will enable them to teach grammar, analysis, composition, geography, use of globes, arithmetic in all its branches, the elements of mensuration book-keeping, and linear drawing;

c. For teachers of academies (besides the qualifications required for the above-mentioned two grades of teachers) all the branches of a classical education.*

d. And for all grades of teachers such other qualifications as may be required by the regulations passed from time to time by either Committee of the Council of Public Instruction and approved by the Lieutenant-Governor in Council;

(9) to keep a correct list of candidates admitted to the right of teaching; (10) to give notice to the Superintendent of the admission of each candidate to the right of teaching, within fifteen days after such admission; (11) to keep or cause to be kept a register of their proceedings properly signed for each meeting and containing lists of candidates, candidates admitted, certificates of age and moral character, &c.; (12) to have a particular seal and to make use of the forms of diplomas furnished by the Superintendent. The Lieutenant-Governor in Council may from time to time modify the details of the duties above given upon the recommendation of either of the Committees of the Council or of the Superintendent.

Validity of Diplomas. The diplomas granted to teachers by a board of examiners are valid only for the grade of schools for which they were granted and within the limits which may from time to time be prescribed. The Roman Catholic or Protestant Committee may, from time to time, provide in such manner and under such conditions as may be deemed expedient, for requiring any teacher, holding any diploma granted by any board of examiners, to submit to examination *de novo*, by such board; and, in default of any such teacher doing so, or in the case of failure of the teacher from any cause to obtain a new diploma, the diploma previously granted becomes null and void. Such procedure can only be taken with the approval of the Lieutenant-Governor in Council.

All persons desiring to act as teachers under these regulations or under any special act for the encouragement of education must, unless provided with a diploma from one of the normal schools of the Province, undergo an examination before one of the boards of examiners in the Province and obtain a diploma.

---

* How far changes may have been introduced in this matter cannot be ascertained from documents available. It is, however, notable that, so long ago as 1874, the Superintendent in his Annual Report pointed out that the curriculum of academies was too extensive. "It would be doubtless much better to restrict the studies to a more limited field, with the certainty of thoroughly going over the ground."

School commissioners and trustees, and all persons entrusted with the management of schools, may employ as teachers only those who are provided with diplomas, on pain of losing their share of the grants made for the encouragement of education. Nevertheless, any priest, minister, and ecclesiastic, and every person who is a member either of a religious order instituted for educational purposes or of a religious community of women, is exempt from undergoing an examination before any board of examiners.

SUMMARY OF STATISTICS RESPECTING TEACHERS—1897-8.

Teachers in Elementary and Model Schools, and Academies.	Without Certificates.	With Certificates.	Certificates for			Certificates from		Average Salary of Teachers with Certificates.		Total number of Teachers.
			Elementary Schools.	Model Schools.	Academies.	Normal Schools.	Board of Examiners.	In Elementary Schools.	In Model Schools and Academies.	
								$	$	
Male Teachers in Roman Catholic Schools	32	241	62	133	46	105	136	220	492	273
Male Teachers in Protestant Schools	17	114	19	37	58	40	74	570	824	131
Female Teachers in Roman Catholic Schools	313	4,308	3,206	1,098	4	209	4,090	102	190	4,621
Female Teachers in Protestant Schools	41	1,222	763	419	40	371	851	133	301	1,263
Totals and average	403	5,885	4,050	1,687	148	725	5,160	123.60	310.20	6,288
Lay professors teaching in Universities, Normal Schools, and Special Schools										358
Grand Total of lay teachers										6,646
Members of the Clergy in Colleges and some other Schools										549
Religious—Brothers 866, Nuns 2,432										3,298
Grand Total of religious teachers										3,847
GRAND TOTAL of all Teachers, Lay and Religious										10,498

In 1899 there were 788 male lay: 5,944 female lay, teachers: 1,431 male religious: 2,612 nuns: total, 10,755.

From the Report for 1895–96:—"We are striving to lower the number of teachers without certificates in the Province. . . . . In 1893–94 the number of lay teachers without certificates was 1,080. In 1894–95 it was 899, and this year it is 686, making a decrease of 394."

VI.—Comparative Statement of the Educational Movement, 1867 to 1899.

Number of	1867-68.	1872-73.	1877-78.	1882-83.	1887-88.	1892-93.	1895-96.	1898-99.
Elementary Schools - -	3,355	3,630	4,096	4,404	4,640	4,963	5,178	5,147
Model Schools - - -	318	343	260	333	485	493	514	539
Academies - - - -	190	212	282	246	149	141	164	160
Roman Catholic and Protestant Colleges - -	36	37	40	31	23	23	21	22
Special Schools - - -	2	6	17	18	18	18	19	16
Normal Schools - - -	3	3	3	3	3	3	3	31
Universities - - - -	3	3	3	4	4	4	4	4
Totals - -	3,907	4,234	4,701	5,039	5,322	5,640	5,903	5,895
Pupils of Elementary Schools - - - -	156,820	155,916	167,031	170,858	181,402	187,979	201,587	201,292
Pupils of Model Schools -	22,700	28,588	20,429	26,378	} 70,417	79,223	91,997	105,975
„ Academies - -	26,010	34,488	38,852	38,278				
„ Colleges - -	6,189	7,113	7,874	6,879	3,918*	5,024	5,302	5,681
„ Special Schools -	278	741	1,866	1,262	1,905	1,561	1,935	1,832
„ Normal Schools	256	246	306	330	296	284	377	} 1,303
„ Schools attached to Normal Schools -	—	—	—	—	—	789	893	
Students of University -	584	758	731	1,240	1,193	1,109	1,528	2,360
Totals - -	212,837	225,850	227,089	245,225	259,131	275,969	303,619	318,443
Male Lay Teachers - -	608	696	626	497	494	677†	752	788
Male Teachers in Religious Orders - - - -	311	498	593	602	912	1,128	1,200	1,431
Female Lay Teachers -	2,969	3,507	3,931	4,448	4,962	5,394	5,763	5,944
Nuns - - - - - -	648	956	1,028	1,324	1,804	2,096	2,265	2,612
Totals - - -	4,536	5,657	6,178	6,871	8,172	9,997	9,980	10,775

* In this number that of the students of industrial colleges, which was comprised in the previous figures, is not included. From 1887 these colleges have been known as boys' academies.

† This number comprises the professors of universities, normal schools, Protestant colleges, and special schools, which were not included in the previous figures.

‡ Including "schools attached to normal schools."

VII.—Superior Education.

(i.) *Finance.* — The Superintendent annually apportions amongst the universities, colleges, seminaries, academies, high or superior schools, model schools, or educational institutions other than the ordinary elementary schools, the whole or such part of the grants for education (according to the recommendation of the Roman Catholic or Protestant Committee) as the Lieutenant-Governor in Council prescribes, and in such proportions as he may approve. The grants so apportioned are paid by the Provincial Treasurer, on the warrant of the Lieutenant-Governor, to the Superintendent, who pays them to the educational institutions entitled to them.

The total aid granted to universities, classical colleges, industrial colleges, academies, and model schools, is divided between the aggregate of the Roman Catholic and Protestant institutions respectively, in the relative proportion of the Roman Catholic and Protestant populations of the Province according to the last census the results of which are available at the time. Grants so made out of the income fund are for one year only and are not permanent. The Lieutenant-Governor in Council may attach to them any conditions which are deemed advantageous for the furtherance of superior education.

The sums paid over to the Provincial Treasurer, arising from the celebration of marriages by Protestant ministers, are annually paid over by him to the Superintendent to be apportioned under the authority of the Lieutenant-Governor in Council, and, in accordance with the recommendation of the Protestant Committee of the Council of Public Instruction, among the Protestant institutions of superior education, in addition to and in the same manner as the other grants to these institutions.

The interest arising from the investment of $60,000 realised by the settlement of the Jesuits' Estates under the Act of 1889, is annually apportioned by the Protestant Committee, with the approval of the Lieutenant-Governor in Council, among the Protestant institutions of Superior Education, in addition to, and in the same manner as, any sums by law granted for the purpose of Protestant Superior Education.

No grant can be made to any superior-educational institution not actually in operation, or to any institution owning real estate, whose liabilities exceed two-thirds of the value of its real estate, nor to any ordinary model school or educational institution which has not fulfilled the conditions prescribed.

Any educational institution desirous of obtaining a grant out of the income fund must make an application to that effect to the Superintendent, and he may not recommend any grant to any such educational institution, the application from which is not accompanied by a report, showing :

(1.) the composition of the governing body ;

(2.) the number and names of the directors, principals, professors, teachers, or lecturers ;

4226.   S

(3.) the number of pupils, distinguishing those under, and those above, sixteen years of age;

(4.) the general course of instruction and the books used;

(5.) the annual cost of maintaining the institution and the sources from which the means are derived;

(6.) the value of the real estate of the institution, if it owns any

(7.) a statement of its liabilities;

(8.) the number of pupils taught gratuitously, or taught and boarded gratuitously;

(9.) the number of books, globes, and maps possessed by the institution, and the value of any museum and philosophical apparatus belonging to it.

The financial arrangement for 'Superior Education' cannot be properly understood without quoting the Act of 1889 confiscating the estates of "the late Order of Jesuits":—

" The estates and property of the late Order of Jesuits, whether in possession or reversion, including all sums funded or invested, as forming part thereof, and the principal of all moneys which have arisen or shall arise from the sale or commutation of any part of the said estates or property, are hereby appropriated, and shall form a fund to . be called the 'Quebec Superior Education Fund,' under the control and management of the Governor in Council.

" Whenever it appears to the Governor in Council that this Income Fund can be increased by the sale and by the investment of the proceeds of the sale of any portion of the Jesuit Estates, or of any *rente foncière* or *rente constituée* then forming part of them, the Governor in Council may order such sale to be made, and may direct that the moneys realised by it be invested in provincial debentures or other securities, the annual interest or income whereof shall form part of this Income Fund.

" There shall be annually placed to the credit of this Income Fund the sum of twenty thousand dollars out of the Consolidated Revenue Fund of this Province, which sum shall form part of this Income Fund, and be appropriated accordingly; and if in any year this Income Fund falls short of the sum of eighty-eight thousand dollars, then such sum as may be necessary to make it equal to eighty-eight thousand dollars shall be taken from the Common School Fund and added to it for that year as part thereof."

(ii.) *The Roman Catholic Laval University.*—(*Extracts from* " *Papers relating to University Education of Roman Catholics in certain Colonies," issued by the Colonial Office,* 1900.)

(*Translated from the original French.*)

" The Laval University was founded in 1852 by the Seminary of Quebec at the request of the Bishops of " Lower Canada." The aim was to throw open to the French Catholic population an institute of higher education capable of equalling in importance those frequented by persons of other language and religion. The then Governor of Canada, Lord Elgin, and his ministers wrote: "We have no hesitation in acknowledging the justice and propriety of securing to the numerous and important body of Catholics in Canada the benefit of a University of which they have been until now deprived." A Royal Charter was granted by Her Majesty and signed on December 8, 1852.

"Pope Pius IX, satisfied with the test of nearly a quarter of a century which the Seminary had undergone, granted its canonical status to the University by the Bull '*Inter varias sollicitudines*,' in which he recognised the good accomplished by this institution during its twenty-four years of existence.

"In virtue of this Royal Charter the Superior and Directors of the Quebec Seminary formed a legal corporation enjoying the same rights and privileges as before, together with all the rights, powers, and privileges of a University, for the education and instruction of youth and of the students of the various Faculties.

"The corporation of the University is styled 'The Rector and members of the Laval University at Quebec, in the Dominion of Canada." It is a body politic and corporate enjoying all privileges, including a common seal, &c. The University has a Council, consisting of the Rector, the Directors of the Seminary of Quebec, and the three senior Professors of each of the four Faculties, Theology, Medicine, Law, and Arts. All the powers granted by Letters Patent are exercised by the Council, which has full authority for making statutes, rules, and regulations concerning the government of the University, the studies, lessons, and other exercises, the degrees in the four Faculties, and, generally, all matters connected with these and concerned with the advancement of the University. It can also revoke, renew, and change all these statutes, rules, and regulations. But in any case it can do or ordain nothing contrary or opposed to the Laws and Statutes of the United Kingdom, of the Dominion of Canada, or to the terms of reference of the Letters Patent. The Council has power to nominate the Professors of the Faculties of Law, Medicine, and Arts, and to revoke and annul its own nominations on just and sufficient cause. It has also the right to lay before the Visitor of the University the names of those who are, in its opinion, suitable for the position of Professor in the Faculty of Theology; but it is the Visitor who makes this appointment.

"The University may confer the degrees of Bachelor, Licentiate, and Doctor on any student in any of the Faculties, whether he be a student of the University or no. It has besides all the privileges enjoyed by the Universities of the United Kingdom.

"In virtue of the Bull '*Inter varias sollicitudines*' the University has, for its protector at Rome at the Holy See, His Eminence the Cardinal Prefect of the Propaganda. The higher supervision of the doctrine and discipline of the University, in other words the supervision of "faith and morals," is entrusted to a superior Council consisting of the Archbishops and Bishops of the Province of Quebec under the presidency of the Archbishop of Quebec, who is called the Apostolic Chancellor of the University.

" The instruction is given by titular Professors, whether ordinary or extraordinary, by attached Professors (" *professeurs agrégés,* " *i.e.* similar to the Fellows of a College at one of the old English Universities), and by Professors in charge of particular branches. The ordinary titular Professors alone are Professors within the meaning of the Charter; and they alone can be members of the University Council. A titular Professor in one Faculty cannot be nominated titular Professor in another Faculty, though he can be an attached professor or a professor in charge of a particular branch in another Faculty (*professeur agrégé* or *chargé de cours*).

" The courses are private in the Faculties of Theology, Law, and Medicine. Any priest may, however, be admitted to the courses in Theology, and the same privilege belongs to advocates and notaries (barristers and solicitors) in the courses in Law, and to physicians and surgeons in the courses in Medicine. In the Faculty of Arts there are public and private courses, but these are confined to pupils or students of the Faculty.

" The Council of each Faculty is required to frame the complete programme of the instruction in that Faculty, and to revise it from time to time. This programme, after revision by the University Council, becomes obligatory upon the Professors as well as upon the pupils. It cannot be modified except with the approval of the University Council, which is not usually given in any important matter until the proposed modification has been discussed in a general assembly of the Professors of the Faculty.

" At the end of each term all the pupils are examined in the different subjects taught to them during the term. The results are entered in the registers. Every candidate whose work does not attain at least the standard denoted by the mark " fairly good " (*assez bien*) has a mark set against his name which prevents his proceeding to a degree, until it be replaced, at some subsequent examination, by a mark of satisfactory standard.

" There are two classes of pupils, (1) enrolled pupils or pupils proper (*élèves inscrits ou élèves*), who have successfully passed the examination of matriculation in the Faculty of Arts, (2) student pupils who have not passed this matriculation. For the Faculties of Law and Medicine, the students who intend to practise as barristers, solicitors, or physicians in the Province of Quebec, must have been admitted as students by the executive of the Bar, the Chamber of Notaries, or the College of Physicians, as the case may be, before they can be received as student pupils (*élèves étudiants*).

" By a law passed in 1891, Bachelors of Science, of Letters, or of Arts need only have their diplomas identified in order to be admitted as students of Law or of Medicine without examination."

After some details in regard to the scientific apparatus, the museums of mineralogy, geology, and botany, the botanical garden, the entomological collection, the picture gallery, and the library, in all of which points the University is well equipped, the Return proceeds to the work done by the Seminary :—

" The University was founded and has been exclusively

maintained by the Quebec Seminary, which has never refused any sacrifice in the endeavour to secure an institution likely to be an honour to the country and to meet the needs of its young men. It is hardly an exaggeration to estimate the sacrifices made by the Seminary for this purpose at one million dollars. Every year, the Seminary is still obliged to add from ten to twelve thousand dollars to the income of the University in order to pay the deficit on the annual receipts; and interest on the capital thus used is not thought of, it being regarded as *dead capital.* But the Seminary would never have been able to expend so much on the University had it been obliged to pay the priests charged with the instruction. The priest asks no more the ten dollars per month which serve for his main-tenance. The Rector, who is at the same time Superior of the Seminary, is no better off in this respect than his colleagues.

"There are now (1900) about 250 pupils every year in the four Faculties of the University of Quebec. Pupils who take up the classical course in the seventeen colleges affiliated to the University, present themselves as candidates in the exam-inations for the degree of Bachelor of Letters at the end of their course. . . . .

(iii.) "Some years ago the Laval University established a branch in Montreal, which has now a large number of pupils and is very prosperous.

"The Faculties of this Branch of the University at Montreal are a reproduction of those at Quebec. . . . The Faculties properly so called are four in number, Theology, Law, Medicine, and Arts. The schools attached are two in number, the Poly-technic school and the school of comparative medicine and veterinary science. Two of the Faculties, Theology and Arts, are for various reasons not under the administration of the University. The Faculty of Theology is identical with the Great Seminary (*grand séminaire*) of Montreal, which belongs to the 'Society of the Seminary of St. Sulpice.' Under the supervision of the Catholic Archbishop of Montreal, the members of the Society of St. Sulpice have exclusive direction of the Seminary. . . . . The University has nothing to say to the administration of this establishment nor to the direction of the instruction given in it. Its function in this matter is confined to the granting of certificates and diplomas to pupils whose competence is certified to the University, after special examinations by the Directors of the Seminary. Again, the Faculty of Arts does not give regular instruction, since the higher teaching of Literature and the Sciences does not yet exist in the University system of the Province. The only scientific instruction provided for so far is that in Civil Engineering at the Polytechnic School. This school, attached to the Faculty of Arts, receives diplomas from the University.

"It follows that the only Faculties of the University in its Branch at Montreal that can be, strictly speaking, considered as University Faculties are those of Law and of Medicine. The instruction in these is given in the University buildings, and part of the expense involved by it is defrayed by the general administration. . . . The Government grants (except in the cases of the Polytechnic School, the grant to which is guaranteed by a statute of the Province, and of the 'general administration,' the grant to which was made in 1896 for a period of seven years) are revocable at the pleasure of the Legislature. In the same way the Bishops have only undertaken to pay their share of the annual subsidy for a certain number of years. . . . The pupils taught at the Montreal Branch of the University do not all come from the dioceses of the Province, although the greater number of them do. A certain number are members of the neighbouring ecclesiastical provinces of Quebec and Ottawa, and some even of the dioceses of Upper Canada, of British Columbia, or of the United States. This is especially the case with the pupils in the Faculty of Theology, who are recruited to a large extent from the dioceses of the United States. . . . The double centre of instruction, at Quebec and at Montreal, implies a peculiar variety of life and of function. Consequently, the activity of the University could not become that of an absolutely normal organism."

The Return proceeds with a comparison and contrast drawn between the Catholic Universities of Washington, Louvain (Belgium), Lille, and Quebec, pointing out that the relations existing in these cases between the University corporations and the Catholic Episcopate are established on foundations which, though the same in principle as those of the Laval University, yet entail in practice a preponderance of episcopal direction which does not obtain to the same degree in the Faculties at Montreal. Some statistics in regard to the Branch University at Montreal are appended :—

I.---Ordinary sources of income of the Branch University at Montreal :—

   (i.) Annual subsidy from the Episcopate -   -   **$8,000**

   (ii.) Government grant, distributed among—

1. General administration	-	-	-	$4,000
2. Faculty of Law	-	-	-	$2,000
3. Faculty of Medicine	-	-	-	$2,000
4. Polytechnic School	-	-	-	$10,000
5. Veterinary School	-	-	-	$2,000
				$20,000

   (iii.) Receipts from fees paid by pupils for enrolment in Faculties and for courses of study :—

     1. Faculty of Law (125 pupils; three years' enrolment, $5; annual course, $50) - $6,458

     2. Faculty of Medicine (180 pupils, annual course, $50) $14,760

     3. Polytechnic School (20 pupils; four years' enrolment, $5; annual course, $50) $1,025

     4. Veterinary School (10 pupils, annual enrolment, $2) - $20

                                  $22,263

Total Income -   - - - - $50,263

Annual deduction for sinking fund   . $6,500

Nett annual Income   - -   **$43,763**

II.—Average number of pupils at Montreal, in the Faculties and affiliated Schools, during the last three years (1896–99) :—

Faculty of Theology - - - - - - -	225
Faculty of Law - - - - - - -	125
Faculty of Medicine - - - - - -	180
Polytechnic School - - - - - -	20
Veterinary School - - - - - -	10
Total - -	560

III.—Catholic population of the four dioceses of the ecclesiastical province of Montreal :—

Montreal - - - - - - -	400,000
St. Hyacinthe - - - - - -	115,000
Sherbrooke - - - - - -	60,000
Valleyfield - - - - - -	57,800
	632,800

(iv.) *Statistics of Protestant Universities,* 1897–8.

(1.) McGill University, Montreal, 1897–8.

Number of Faculties - - - - -	––	5
Number of Professors :		
Faculty of Arts - - - - -	27	
,, Medicine - - - -	54	
,, Law - - - - -	8	
,, Sciences - - - - -	17	
,, Veterinary Medicine - - -	11	
Total - - -		117
Number of Students :		
Faculty of Arts ; boys, 252, girls, 121 - -	373	
,, Medicine ; boys, 427, girls, 2 - -	429	
,, Law ; boys, 47 - - - -	47	
,, Sciences ; boys, 225, girls, 6 - -	231	
,, Veterinary Medicine ; boys, 23 -	23	
Total - - -		1,103
Graduates of the University :		
Doctors of Civil Law - - - -	1	
,, Medicine - - - -	72	
,, Veterinary Medicine - - -	12	
Masters of Arts - - - - -	8	
,, Sciences - - - -	3	
Mechanical Engineers - - -	3	
Bachelors of Arts - - - - -	47	
,, Sciences - - - -	42	
,, Law - - - - - -	11	
Total - - -		199

(2.) UNIVERSITY AND COLLEGE OF LENNOXVILLE, 1897-8.

Number of Professors :

In the College -	-	-	-	-	-	-	9	
Faculty of Arts	-	-	-	-	-	-	6	
„ Medicine -	-	-	-	-	-	27		
, Divinity -	-	-	-	-	-	2		
			Total	-	-			44

Number of Students :

In the College -	-	-	-	-	-	-	99	
Faculty of Arts	-	-	-	-	-	-	53	
„ Medicine	-	-	-	-	-	102		
„ Divinity -	-	-	-	-	-	16		
			Total	-	-			270

Graduates of the University :

Bachelors of Arts	-	-	-	-	-	15		
Masters of Arts	-	-	-	-	. -	10		
Doctors in Law, *Honoris causa*	-	-	-	7				
„ Medicine	-	-	-	-	13			
„ Dental Art	-	-	-	-	3			
Licentiates in Divinity	-	-	-	-	3			
			Total	-	-			51

(v.) *Statistics of educational institutions, other than Universities, receiving grants for "Superior Education" in 1897-8.*

(1.) *Protestant—Model Schools and Academies.*

Number of Protestant Model Schools	53
Number of Protestant Academies	26
Number of Male Lay Teachers in these schools, with certificates 68, without certificates 10	78
Number of Female Lay Teachers in these schools, with certificates 215, without certificates 13	228
Members of Protestant Clergy teaching in these schools	7
Average salary of Male Lay Teachers with certificate ...	$824
Average salary of Female Lay Teachers with certificates	$301

(2.) *Roman Catholic—Model Schools and Academies.*

Number of Roman Catholic Model Schools	481
Number of Roman Catholic Academies	127
Number of Male Lay Teachers in these schools, with certificates 188, without certificates 20	208
Number of Female Lay Teachers in these schools, with certificates 353, without certificates 41	394
Number of Religious Teachers, male 836, female 2,372	3,208
Average salary of Male Lay Teachers with certificates ...	$492
Average salary of Female Lay Teachers with certificates	$120

(3.) *Roman Catholic and Protestant Model Schools.*

a. *Roman Catholic.*

Schools under control of School Commissioners or Trustees.						Independent Schools.						Boys', Girls', or Mixed Schools.						Total of Pupils.
Number of Schools.	Roman Catholic Pupils.		Protestant Pupils.		Average Attendance of Pupils.	Number of Schools.	Roman Catholic Pupils.		Protestant Pupils.		Average Attendance of Pupils.	Boys' Schools.		Girls' Schools.		Mixed Schools.		
	Boys.	Girls.	Boys.	Girls.			Boys.	Girls.	Boys.	Girls.		Number.	Pupils.	Number.	Pupils.	Number.	Pupils.	
340	23,225	24,185	197	69	42,956	141	3,058	9,667	5	47	11,213	130	23,319	173	25,348	178	16,786	65,458

b. *Protestant.*

Number of Model Schools.	Protestant Pupils.		Roman Catholic Pupils.		Average Attendance.	Total of Pupils.
	Boys.	Girls.	Boys.	Girls.		
53	2,148	1,975	164	92	3,349	4,379

(4.) *Roman Catholic and Protestant Academies.*

a. *Roman Catholic.*

Academies under control of School Commissioners or Trustees.					Independent Academies.						Total Number of Pupils.	Boys' Academies.		Girls' Academies.		Mixed Academies.	
Roman Catholic Pupils.		Protestant Pupils.		Average attendance.	Number of Academies.	Roman Catholic Pupils.		Protestant Pupils.		Average attendance.		Number.	Pupils.	Number.	Pupils.	Number.	Pupils.
Boys.	Girls.	Boys.	Girls.			Boys.	Girls.	Boys.	Girls.								
10,369	1,496	33	3	10,290	94	2,549	10,787	217	186	11,575	25,640	45	12,687	77	11,834	5	1,119

b. Protestant.

Number of Academies.	Protestant Pupils.		Roman Catholic Pupils.		Average Attendance.	Total of Pupils.
	Boys.	Girls.	Boys.	Girls.		
26	2,201	2,051	152	62	3,668	4,466

(5.) *Roman Catholic Classical Colleges.*

Number...	...	...	...	...	19
Pupils in Classical Course	...		...		3,660
Pupils in Commercial Course...				...	1,814
Total pupils	...	...	...	...	5,474
Average attendance	...	...		...	5,018
Religious Professors	...	...		...	481
Lay Professors ...	...	...		...	40
Total Professors		...	...	...	521

(vi.) *Academies.*—The following are the Statutes dealing with the conduct of Academies :—

It is competent to the corporations of school commissioners or trustees in any counties or parts of counties to combine for the purpose of establishing one or more academies therein. The mode of procedure in such cases is as follows :— *a.* Wherever it appears desirable to the Roman Catholic or Protestant school commissioners or trustees, or to a majority of them, that an academy or academies should be established, the several chairmen of those school corporations may, by virtue of a resolution passed by each school corporation, be appointed academy delegates on behalf of the corporations; and the delegate last named convenes the first meeting of delegates by a notice of eight days of time and place; *b.* at the first meeting of these academy delegates those present or a majority of them elect a chairman and a secretary. If, in the opinion of the majority, it is thought necessary or desirable to establish one or more academies in the county or counties, a petition to that effect, founded on a resolution of the delegates, is prepared and forwarded to the Roman Catholic or Protestant Committee, stating the facts of the case, and the petition is signed by the chairman and secretary of the meeting; *c.* at the next meeting of the Roman Catholic or Protestant Committee, or at a meeting specially called for that purpose, the petition is taken into consideration, and, if approved by the majority of them, the petition is delivered by the Roman Catholic or Protestant Committee to the Superintendent for transmission to the Lieutenant-Governor in Council. If the Lieutenant-Governor approves the petition he may, by proclamation in the Quebec Official Gazette, signify his approval and establish such academy or academies; *d.* after this proclamation the board of delegates meet once more and elect three of their members to act as the first trustees of the academy, and these three trustees remain in office until the first day of the following August, when a regular · annual meeting of the board of delegates is held. At this first meeting, as well as at the meeting to be held annually in August, the board of delegates appoints three of its number to act as trustees of the academy for the ensuing year. They also appoint an auditor or auditors of accounts. The academy trustees annually present to the board of delegates at the annual meeting a report of the educational work of the past year done in the academy, with a balance sheet and statement of income and expenditure duly audited by the auditors. The secretary of the board of delegates may be the secretary-treasurer of each board of academy trustees, or the academy trustees may appoint their own secretary-treasurer. The academy trustees, their secretary, and the auditors, conform *mutatis mutandis* to the provisions of the school laws in all respects, as also to the rules of the Roman Catholic or Protestant Committee, as the case may be.

To provide for the building and maintenance of such academies the Roman Catholic or Protestant school commissioners or trustees of the county, part of country, or counties wherein an academy is established, may levy a tax on the taxable real estate of the school municipality under their control, sufficient to provide a sum not exceeding $3,000 for the purchase of a site and the building of an academy, and not less than $300 *per annum* towards the payment of teachers and the incidental expenses of the academy. The school commissioners or trustees are jointly and severally responsible to the academy trustees for the payment of the sums mentioned, and must pay over the sums to the academy trustees by equal half-yearly payments in January and July of each year.

The academy trustees are entitled to charge monthly fees to the scholars for the maintenance of the academy, provided the fees do not exceed $1.50 per month, to be paid monthly in advance. No scholar two months in arrears for such fees can be permitted to attend the academy.

Each academy fulfilling the conditions here stated and conforming to the rules and regulations in regard to academies from time to time adopted by the Roman Catholic or Protestant Committee, is entitled to a share of the legislative grant for superior education in the discretion of that Committee of the Council of Public Instruction which is of its religious faith.

(vii.) *Model Schools.*—Certain special rules in regard to the financial support of Model Schools should be given here:—

1. Commissioners or trustees may charge fees higher than the 40 cents per month allowed for elementary schools to the children attending model schools; and such fees may in model

schools be exacted for the whole time they are in active operation;

2. these monthly fees do not form part of the school fund, but are payable directly to the teacher and are for his or her use, unless a different agreement has been made between the school corporation and the teacher;

3. in all cases, the school commissioners or trustees deduct from the school fund of the municipality a sum of $80 for the support of a model school, if there is one in the municipality, in addition to the share which the model school is entitled to receive from the fund;

4. the model school in any municipality is counted as in itself a school district, without prejudice to the above grant of $80; and the share of the moneys to be allotted to the model school is determined by the number of children of the age prescribed for attending school residing in the school district in which it is established;

5. the Superintendent may retain, out of the school grant to which any municipality is entitled, a sum of $80 to support a model school therein.

(viii.) This section of the subject may well be completed by a short account of the *Royal Institution for the Advancement of Learning.* The Governor may appoint such and so many persons as he sees fit to be trustees of the schools of royal foundation in the Province and of all other institutions for the purposes of education and the advancement of learning. The trustees thus appointed are a body politic and corporate, and their powers include the administration and improvement of all estates and property appropriated to the institutions over which they have control as trustees. They may be replaced by the Governor at any time. As a corporation they have full powers of purchase, possession, &c., in regard to all property of institutions of royal foundation. The Governor may appoint a president or principal of the corporation, but otherwise the senior member in order of appointment presides over the corporation. They may make by-laws, rules, and ordinances for the conduct and government of the corporation of free schools and other educational institutions of royal foundation, for the direction of the masters, professors, and students in them, and for the management and improvement of all estates and property belonging to these institutions. But their powers do not in any way, directly or indirectly, prejudice those of existing religious communities, schools, corporations, or private schools. The Governor may appoint "a fit and proper person" to be the school-master of each free school of royal foundation, and may from time to time remove him and appoint another in his stead. The Governor may, further, fix the salary to be allowed to each school-master. No master may teach in any free school of royal foundation without a commission for that purpose from the Governor.

The rents, profits, and other sums of money are received by the treasurer of the corporation and deposited or disposed of by him according to the directions of the Corporation. A detailed statement and account, affirmed by the treasurer before a magistrate, of the receipts and the expenditure must be annually presented to the Governor before February 1. The Corporation has power to invest money in buildings or other real estate required for the actual use of the McGill College or any department or branch of it, or for the use of any other royal foundation wholly or in part under its control. The Corporation may also take loans of money on the security of the properties under their control up to a specified limit.

This Royal Institution for the Advancement of Learning has always been intimately connected with the financial administration of the great Protestant University of the Province, the McGill College at Montreal. By an Act of 1863, provision may from time to time be made by any statute of McGill College and University for augmenting the number of trustees, members of the Royal Institution for the Advancement of Learning, and governors of the McGill College to not more than fifteen in number ; for regulating their selection and appointment; and for fixing and limiting their term of office.

It is further provided in the Act of 1863 that only the McGill University and "such institutions of education as from time to time may have been, or hereafter may be, affiliated to it in terms of its statutes," can be deemed to be schools and institutions of royal foundation under the control of the Royal Institution for the Advancement of Learning.

VIII.—INDUSTRIAL SCHOOLS.

Those who wish to study the system of industrial schools in Quebec in detail may consult the Revised Statutes, 3128 to 3173. Here only a brief summary of the main provisions in regard to them can be given.

In the first place, it is important to note the meaning in which the term Industrial School is used. It is confined to residential schools in which clothing, board, and lodging are free, and in which training definitely industrial is given: "a school in which industrial training is provided, and in which children are lodged, clothed, and fed, as well as taught, shall exclusively be deemed an Industrial School." (Revised Statutes, 3128.)

Granting of Certificates.—By the original Act constituting these schools it was provided that the managers of then existing industrial schools might apply for certification to the Lieutenant-Governor. On such application, the Lieutenant-Governor would direct the "inspector of industrial schools" to examine into the conditions of the school and its fitness for the reception of children, and report his impressions and conclusions. If the report of the inspector be satisfactory the Provincial Secretary may certify that the school is fit for the reception of children. A notice of the grant of each certificate thus constituting a school a "certified industrial school" must be published in the Quebec Official Gazette.

Building : Inspection.—No substantial addition or alteration may be made to or in the buildings of any certified industrial school without the approval of the Lieutenant-Governor. He it is who appoints the inspector for these schools from among the inspectors of prisons, hospitals, &c.; and he may also appoint someone to assist the inspector, and to work under his direction. Every certified industrial school must be from time to time, and at least once in every year, inspected by the inspector or by his assistant.

Finance.—Any municipal council may contribute sums of money on their own conditions towards the alteration, enlargement, or rebuilding of a certified school of this class, or towards the support of its inmates, its management, or the establishment and building of a new school. But this right of municipal councils to contribute is restricted by three conditions, viz., (1) that previous notice of its intention to take into consideration the giving of such a contribution be given not less than two months beforehand; (2) that the order for the contribution be made at a special meeting of the council; and (3) that when the contribution is for the alteration, rebuilding, establishment, or building of a school or projected school, or for the purchase of land, the approval of the Lieutenant-Governor be previously obtained.

The Provincial Treasurer may, from time to time, contribute, out of money provided by the Legislature for the purpose, such sums as the Lieutenant-Governor may see fit to recommend for the custody and maintenance of children detained in certified industrial schools, provided that such contributions do not exceed 50 cents per head per week for children detained on the application of their parents or tutors. Further, any municipal council may contract with the managers of a certified industrial school for the reception and maintenance of children ordered by justices to be sent there from the municipality the council represents. And the managers of any incorporated municipal institution may contribute towards the maintenance of children detained in a certified industrial school on their application.

Withdrawal and Resignation of Certificate.—If at any time the Lieutenant-Governor be dissatisfied with the condition of a certified industrial school, the Provincial Secretary may serve on the managers a notice declaring that their certificate is withdrawn. The managers, or the executors of a deceased manager, of such a school may, by previous notice of their intention given to the Provincial Secretary, resign their certificate. A notice of such resignation or withdrawal must be published. Whenever notice of the resignation or withdrawal of the certificate is given, no child can be received into the school for detention after the date of the notice of resignation, or the receipt of the notice that the certificate will be withdrawn. But the obligation of the managers to teach, train, clothe, lodge, and feed any children already detained in the school continues until the withdrawal or resignation of the certificate takes effect, or until the contribution made by the Legislature towards the custody and maintenance of the children detained is discontinued, whichever first happens. And when a school ceases to be a certified industrial school the children detained there are either discharged or transferred to some other certified industrial school by order of the Provincial Secretary.

Detention of Children.—*a.* Two ratepayers of any municipality may bring any child under the age of twelve years before two justices of the peace or a magistrate, provided (1) that he is fatherless or motherless and that his surviving parent is guilty of misconduct; or (2) that both parents are criminals condemned to the penitentiary. In any case it must be shown that the child is without any means of subsistence and has no relation legally liable for his support. If the justices of the peace or the magistrate are satisfied by the evidence given to this effect by the ratepayers, they may order the child to be sent to a certified industrial school.

b. The father or mother, tutor or relative, of a child under twelve years of age may obtain an order for the detention of a child in an industrial school for a time to be specified in the application for this made by them to two justices of the peace or to a magistrate. Such an application must represent on oath that the applicant is unable to control the child in question by reason of his bad and vicious habits; and, before an order for the detention of the child can be obtained, the justices of the peace or magistrate must be satisfied on inquiry that this course is necessary. No such order can be made out unless the parent, tutor, or relative-of the child deposits a sum sufficient to cover the cost of his maintenance in the industrial school for one month.

c. The mayor of any municipality may also, with the consent of his municipal council, by a similar application to two justices of the peace or to a magistrate, obtain from them, after the usual inquiry into the facts of the case, an order for the detention of a child under twelve years of age in a certified industrial school. It must in such cases be shown that the child requires to be protected and cared for owing to the continual sickness or extreme poverty or habitual drunkenness or other vicious habits of his parents. The municipality is in these cases liable for one-half of the cost of the child's maintenance in the certified industrial school. It is, however, lawful for the corporation to obtain the repayment of the money paid by them to the Government in respect of the child so detained by means of suit and distress upon the property of the child, or of those who were legally obliged to provide and care for him.

No order can be given for the detention of any child in a certified industrial school until he is seven years of age, nor can he be detained after he is twelve years of age, unless his parents oblige themselves to pay the cost of his board and maintenance, or unless the child be prevented from leaving by sickness or infirmity. It is the duty of the prison inspectors to see that no child remains after the age of twelve years.

No order for detention can be executed unless the papers on the case have been submitted to, and the order has been approved by, the Provincial Secretary. He has power, when approving such an order, to limit the period for which it shall remain in force.

The reception of a child by the managers of a certified industrial school is equivalent to an undertaking by them to teach, train, clothe, lodge, and feed him during the whole period for which he is liable to be detained in the school. The term of detention can in no case exceed three years; it is fixed by the justices or magistrates making the order, subject always to alteration of the term of detention by the Provincial Secretary. In determining on the certified industrial school to which the child is to be sent the justices or magistrate must endeavour to ascertain the religious persuasion of the child and to select a school conducted in accordance with it. The parents or guardians of any child detained in an industrial school may apply for and obtain his removal from one such school to another, if they can satisfy the authorities responsible for the order that the school to which the child has been sent is of a different religious persuasion from their own, and that there exists one of the same religion in the Province to which they would wish their child to be sent. Such a removal, however, is always dependent upon the willingness of the managers of the school designated by the parents or guardians to receive the child.

Penalties.—So much for the preliminary conditions and the steps by which a child is detained in an industrial school. When established at such a school he becomes liable to imprisonment for any term between fourteen days and three months if he wilfully neglects, or wilfully refuses to conform to, the rules of the school. The imprisonment is imposed by two justices or a magistrate on summary conviction. At the expiration of the term of imprisonment the child may be sent to a reformatory school (*see Revised Statutes* 2892–2910 *for the regulations in regard to reformatory schools*). But imprisonment can only be ordered in cases where the child is over ten years of age. Punishments are also attached to the offences of inducing a child to escape from an industrial school, concealing a child who has so escaped, or preventing his return. When a child over ten years of age escapes he is liable to imprisonment; otherwise he is brought back to the school to complete his term of detention.

Management of Certified Industrial Schools.—A minister of the religious persuasion specified in the order of detention may visit the child at the school for the purpose of giving him religious instruction on certain days at certain times. After the expiration of eighteen months of the period of detention fixed for any child, the managers may permit him to live with any trustworthy and respectable persons who may be willing to take charge of him. Such permission is given by a "licence," which must be renewed or terminated every three months, and can be revoked at any time by the managers. A child who escapes from the person with whom he is placed under a licence, or who refuses to return to the school on its expiration, is deemed to have escaped from school and may be punished accordingly. The managers may bind a child, with his own consent, apprentice to any trade, calling, or service, although his period of detention has not expired, provided always that when placed with some person under licence he conducted himself well. The managers of a school may make rules for the management and discipline of the school, but such rules cannot be enforced until they have been approved by the Lieutenant-Governor through the Provincial Secretary. There must be a printed copy of the approved rules of the school signed by the inspector of industrial schools. Managers may also hire out the children under their care either as apprentices or as domestic servants: but such an arrangement must bring no money either to the managers or to the child, and must guarantee to the master the gratuitous services of the child, and to the child board, lodging, and maintenance. Provided that the managers of the certified industrial school teach, train, clothe, and feed the child in the school as though he were actually lodging in the school itself, they may permit a child sent to their care to lodge at the dwelling of his father or of any trustworthy person. But managers are bound to report to the Lieutenant-Governor every instance in which they exercise their discretion in this manner.

Inasmuch as the regulations bearing on industrial schools are given among the statutes in regard to charitable and other associations, it may be concluded that industrial schools of this nature, whether certified or not, are generally supported and managed by private persons, whether for charitable purposes or not.

IX.—THE POLYTECHNIC SCHOOL.

The nature of the Polytechnic School of Montreal and the work undertaken by it may best be understood by consulting the original terms of its foundation. It is an important though an isolated development of the educational system of Quebec.

The Polytechnic School is incorporated under the title of "La Corporation de l'Ecole Polytechnique," and the corporation consists of the principal and director; two engineers, residing in Montreal, holding diplomas from the Polytechnic School, chosen outside of the corps of professors, who are elected by the other members of the corporation; two members of the Roman Catholic Committee of the Council of Public Instruction residing in Montreal, and chosen by that Committee of the Council; and the president of the Roman Catholic Board of School Commissioners for the City of Montreal. The corporation may, further, associate to itself other members to the number of four, who, being donors, have complied with the conditions and bye-laws made respecting benefactors of the institution. The principal and director of the Polytechnic School, as well as the other members of the corporation just mentioned, cease to be members of it on the day upon which they are replaced in their official capacities; the engineers are named for three years, and, in the case of death or absence from the Province, are replaced by the corporation for the balance of their term of office. The principal of the Polytechnic School is *de jure* the president of the corporation as well as of the executive committee, and has a casting vote.

The corporation has the right to acquire and hold, by donation, legacy, or purchase, moveable and immoveable property, and to perform all acts of ownership in connection with it. It has also power to sue and be sued, to borrow, to sign and negotiate promissory notes and bills of exchange, and to become a party under any title whatever; and it possesses, moreover, all the rights and powers belonging generally to corporations.

The corporation of the Polytechnic School has power to make regulations:

(1) To define the duties and functions of the professors and employees, and to fix their salaries;

(2.) for the administration of the school, the conduct of the students, and the fees payable by them;

(3.) to modify or extend the programme in force in the school;

(4.) for the management of its affairs or for any purpose whatever of the corporation.

Such regulations, however, cannot have effect until after they have been sanctioned by the Archbishop of Montreal, Apostolic Vice-Chancellor of Laval University, and by the University Council of the said University; and have been approved by the Lieutenant-Governor in Council.

The appointment of the principal and professors of the school must be confirmed by the Archbishop of Montreal, and, when confirmed, must be submitted to the University Council of Laval University; and the appointment only becomes final from the date of its acceptance by the Council.

The carrying out of the bye-laws adopted by the corporation is entrusted to an executive committee, composed of three members, *viz.*:—1, The principal of the Polytechnic School; 2, the director of studies of the school; 3, one of the members of the Catholic Committee of the Council of Public Instruction, named by the committee.

The executive committee reports to the corporation and to the

Lieutenant-Governor in Council every year, or oftener if required to do so.

A council of improvement may be established which is composed of the professors of the Polytechnic School, and of three pupils, holding diplomas from the school, selected by the corporation.

This council gives advice as to the modifications that it may be advisable to make in the curriculum of studies and on all matters upon which the management of the school may consult it.

Considering the services rendered by the school, and the necessity that there should be such an institution in the country, the school receives, out of the fund for superior education, an annual grant of ten thousand dollars.

A report is made each year to the Superintendent of Public Instruction, containing:—1, The course of study followed in the school and the modifications or extensions of the programme; 2, the number and classification of the students; 3, the condition of the collections, instruments, laboratory, and library; 4, a statement of the receipts and expenditure of the school.

The diploma of civil engineer is granted to the students capable of conducting and executing all works of art and of construction upon the surface of the soil ; the diploma of mining engineer is granted to the students capable of conducting and executing all works of discovering, extracting, and working ores and minerals, and their reduction to useful metals ; the diploma of mechanical engineer is granted to the students capable of designing, combining, and constructing engines and machines used in manufactures ; the diploma of industrial engineer is granted to the students capable of applying the principles of physics and of chemistry to productions and manufactures.

X.—MISCELLANEOUS.—(*From Annual Reports of recent years.*)

(i.) *Remarks on Attendance and Educational Progress from the Report for* 1895–6.

(ii.) *Plans of School Houses.*

(iii.) *Teachers' Salaries.*

(iv.) *The Teaching of Drawing.*

(v.) *Manual Training for Girls.*

(vi.) *School Holidays.*

(vii.) *School Libraries.*

i.) *Remarks from the Annual Report for* 1895–6 :—

"The number of school municipalities increases gradually as the wild lands are settled, and the number of children attending school last year amounted to 303,619.

"The inspectors' reports show that the average attendance is higher. In some country districts the percentage is 78, 79, and even over 80.

"Throughout the Province the average attendance at elementary schools was 71 per cent. for Roman Catholic pupils and 74 per cent. for Protestant pupils. In the model schools and academies the average attendance was 83 for Roman Catholics and 79 for Protestants.

"The general average attendance for the Province was 76 per cent.

"A general comparative table drawn up respecting education in this Province from 1867 to 1896 shows that the total number of educational establishments which, at Confederation, was 3,907, is now 5,903; and that the number of pupils at school has increased by 90,782, the difference between 212,837 in 1867 and 393,619 in 1896.

"According to the statistics obtained, the number of children between five and sixteen years in 1895-6 was 328,420. Of this number, the proportion of those attending school was 88·30 and the proportion of those not attending school was 11·70.

"Still, the figure 88·30 is below the real proportion, for in the towns and in some villages, where there are a great many independent schools, the majority of the latter do not send in reports to the Department of Public Instruction, as they are not compelled by law to do so; and, consequently, the number of pupils attending them is not included in the proportion just mentioned.

"It is unfortunate that the census of children old enough to attend school is incomplete.

"For some time past a great deal more attention seems to have been paid to certain facts connected with education. Have the elements which have brought these facts about, or which may explain them, been taken into consideration? To do so it would be advisable to study the composition of Canadian families, the progress of colonisation, as well as the history of education in the Province of Quebec at various periods of our civil history—under the French Government, under the English Government before the constitution of 1791, and afterwards up to 1842, and from the Union to the present day.

"Without doubt it does not suffice to explain the facts; we must know how to profit by the lessons they give us. From about fifty years ago, that is to say from 1849, the date of the regular organisation of our school system, we have progressed; our progress cannot be said to be slow when we consider that the generation which was fifteen years old at the time has not yet disappeared. It would not be fair to compare a country in embryo, which requires a number of material and intellectual instruments, with the countries of the Old World where revolving cycles have accumulated all kinds of resources. The comparison, however, would not be all to our disadvantage. Since 1849 we have had in succession the formation of school municipalities, the organisation of the inspectorate, the founding of normal schools and the journals of education, the establishment of boards of examiners, and the regulations respecting diplomas for teaching. This is what has been done, and it cannot be denied that it is a great deal, even in comparison with what remains to be done. We can claim ameliorations and improvements of the existing system, rather than the creation of a new organisation. But to safely effect these improvements we must not hesitate to seek and study them."

(ii). *Plans of School Houses.*

A series of plans for country school houses has been drawn up by the architects of the Department of Public Works. These have been lithographed and distributed, free of charge, to school boards applying for them.

Several school municipalities have written to the Department for the plans they needed. They can readily be followed by country workmen, for they are simple and easy to understand. They also have the advantage of being in accordance with the rules of hygiene and the regulations of the Council of Public Instruction.

Hitherto the school houses have not been built on any specified plan, and the Superintendent frequently had much difficulty in getting the school boards to adopt the dimensions required by law.

(iii.) *Teachers Salaries.*

"The small salaries paid to the teachers have just been mentioned, but Mr. Brault's district, comprising the counties of Jacques Cartier, Vaudreuil, and Soulanges, may be cited as a pattern for the others. Mr. Brault's report shows that the average salary paid to certificated male lay teachers was $343.00, and to certificated female lay teachers was $144.00. In the parish of St. Polycarpe especially from 1879 to 1896, the average of the salaries has increased by 80 per cent. It is very desirable that this example be followed, and, as the Inspector very properly says, the school commissioners of that section of the Province appreciate the services rendered to society by those whose mission it is to educate young people.

"The Roman Catholic Committee, with the approval of the executive, fixed the minimum salary to be paid to school masters and school mistresses at $100 : and every municipality that does not comply with this regulation will forfeit its school grant. Let us hope that better days are coming for the female teachers, who received too small a stipend for the services that they rendered."

(iv.) *The Teaching of Drawing.*

"One of the suggestions made in the consolidation of the school laws arranged by the Roman Catholic and Protestant Committees is to make the teaching of drawing compulsory in primary schools, and to leave its control to the Department of Public Instruction, to which it was not given by law.

"Heretofore the teaching of this branch has been confined, in most instances, to having lithographs or prints copied, or dotted models filled in, thereby paralysing all spirit or initiative in the pupil, and completely doing away with the educational value of drawing.

"This branch of education has been the least appreciated and most neglected, and there are few female teachers who are capable of teaching drawing to children. But to reach the pupil, and to teach him to draw, it is necessary in the first place to properly train the teaching staff and make them familiar with the most improved methods now followed in Belgium, in France, and elsewhere.

"Correspondence that has been undertaken with several teaching communities of nuns, where young girls undergo a special training to prepare them for obtaining certificates of capacity, shows that these houses are endeavouring to reform their method of teaching drawing; and in order to complete the instruction of their own teachers in that branch, they have even secured the services of special professors.

"If we wish to teach drawing in our elementary schools as it should be taught, it is necessary that programmes be drawn up by competent men so as to give the teaching of that branch a well defined bearing; consequently the means of attaining the desired end cannot be adopted too soon."

It is laid down by statute that drawing shall, as far as possible, be taught in all schools, and that the Council of Arts and Manufactures shall make regulations for the establishment of a system of teaching drawing in all its branches. This Council determines the manner and method to be followed in teaching drawing, approves the text-books, drawing-books, and plans to be used for that purpose in each school. They are responsible for causing the system prescribed by them to be followed in all schools under the control of commissioners or trustees, and are urged to make it, as far as possible, uniform.

The regulations on drawing made by the Council of Arts and Manufactures are submitted to the approval of the Roman Catholic or Protestant Committee, as the case may be; and, when they have been approved, are published by the Superintendent.

(v.) *Manual Training for Girls.*—"The education of women is certainly one of the most serious questions of the day. The well-being of families requires that girls should, during the course of their education, receive practical instruction and learn how to manage a household. The subject of manual training in the normal and public schools is now being agitated; for, in Canada, where large fortunes are the exception, and where every mother is called upon to attend to household duties, it is necessary for domestic happiness that a girl should learn at school what she will require to know properly to fulfil her future duties as mistress of a house.

"This question is not a new one, however, in the Province of Quebec, for manual training has always been taught in Roman Catholic educational institutions for girls and in orphan asylums under the direction of communities of nuns, as well as in several Protestant institutions; and, of all the provinces of the Dominion, that of Quebec possesses an organisation which, without being perfect, is the most complete in this respect. Reference to the statistics of the Department on the matter shows that in the Roman Catholic institutions of superior education under the control of religious communities, that is to say, in girls' model schools and academies to the number of 193, out of 37,377 children attending them 13,107 learn domestic economy, 16,772 learn knitting, and 12,704 learn sewing and embroidery."

(vi.) *School Holidays.*—Saturday is a holiday in every school under the control of commissioners or trustees, unless a regulation to the contrary be adopted by a school corporation and approved by the Superintendent. Such a regulation can, however, be repealed by the Superintendent at any time or by the school corporation after notice to the Superintendent.

The Roman Catholic and the Protestant Committee may, with the approval of the Lieutenant-Governor, fix the other holidays in the schools respectively under their control.

(vii.) *School Libraries.*—A sum not exceeding $2,000 may be annually, or for a certain number of years, appropriated from the Superior Education Fund by order of the Lieutenant-Governor in Council, to assist the establishment of city, town, village, parish, or township libraries in school municipalities in which suitable contributions have been made by the school corporation for that purpose. The assistance is given in money or in books, on the conditions deemed requisite by the Lieutenant-Governor in Council.

Municipalities and school corporations may appropriate such a portion of their revenues as they may deem expedient for the purpose of libraries, and they may, with the authority of the Superintendent, issue debentures or bonds with the view of creating a fund for that purpose.

Libraries so formed or maintained are under the management, inspection, and regulations which the Roman Catholic or Protestant Committee may from time to time prescribe. The regulations are published by the Superintendent in the Quebec Official Gazette.

[Reports of the Superintendent of Public Instruction for recent years, embodying the returns of Inspectors and other documents relating to education in Quebec, may be consulted at the Board of Education Library, St. Stephen's House, Cannon Row, Whitehall, London, S.W.]

APPENDIX A.

PROTESTANT SCHOOLS.

MONTREAL.

[The following general account of the Protestant Schools was kindly written for this Report in October, 1900, by Mr. E. W. Arthy, Secretary-Superintendent of the Protestant Board of School Commissioners.]

SCHOOL GOVERNMENT.

The Protestant Board of School Commissioners for the city of Montreal was appointed under an Act of the Provincial Legislature, 9 Vic., cap. 27 (1846). It is composed of six members, viz. :—

Three Commissioners appointed by the Provincial Government and three appointed by the City Council.

School Commissioners hold office for three years, two of the six retiring annually in rotation. Retiring Commissioners are eligible for reappointment.

SCHOOLS.

I.—PUBLIC SCHOOLS.

Ann Street School, founded in 1850, rebuilt in 1872, capacity 600, enrolment this year 427.

Panet Street School, founded 1852, rebuilt 1860, enlarged 1870, abandoned and replaced by Lansdowne School 1892.

Lansdowne School, founded 1892, capacity 800, enrolment this year 719.

British and Canadian School, founded 1822, transferred to Board 1866, remodelled 1873, superseded by Dufferin School 1894.

Dufferin School, founded 1894, capacity 700, enrolment this year 638.

Royal Arthur School, founded 1870, remodelled 1888, capacity 600, enrolment this year, 466.

Sherbrooke Street School, founded 1874, superseded by Aberdeen School 1895.

Aberdeen School, capacity 900, enrolment this year 835.

Riverside School, founded 1876, remodelled 1894, capacity 700, enrolment this year 671.

Berthelet Street School, founded 1886, capacity 700, enrolment this year 534.

Hochelaga School, transferred to Board 1884, rebuilt 1890, capacity 200, enrolment this year 99.

Mount Royal School, transferred to Board 1886, rebuilt 1889, enlarged 1894 and again 1899, capacity 900, enrolment this year 841.

Lorne School (St. Gabriel), transferred to Board 1887, rebuilt 1891, capacity 750, enrolment this year 614.

Britannia School, founded 1875, rebuilt 1887, capacity 150, enrolment this year 71.

Victoria School, founded 1888, capacity 700, enrolment this year 564.

II.—SENIOR SCHOOL.

Founded in 1877 to give an advanced education in English ; present building erected 1883, capacity 300, enrolment this year 267.

III.—SUBSIDISED SCHOOLS.

McGill Model School (subsidised), enrolment 422.

Baron de Hirsch Free Day School (subsidised), enrolment 363.

IV.—HIGH SCHOOLS.

The High School of Montreal (boys), was founded in 1843 by a Board of Directors, incorporated in 1845, substituted in 1846 by order in council in the privileges and duties of the Royal Grammar School (which was founded in 1816), united with McGill College in 1853, and placed under the direction of the Protestant Board of School Commissioners in 1870 ; rebuilt in 1877, burned in 1890, present building opened 1892, enrolment this year 650.

The High School for Girls, founded 1875, building erected 1877, burned 1890, present buildings erected 1892, enrolment this year 477.

The Board has, accordingly, under its control fifteen schools in active operation, with capacity for 9,200 pupils, and an enrolment so far this year of 7,873, not including the 785 pupils in the two subsidised schools.

COURSE OF STUDY.

I.—PUBLIC SCHOOLS.

The elementary course of study, as laid down for the Public Schools, apart from the Kindergarten, extends over six years, and includes reading, writing, spelling, grammar in its practical aspects, including language lessons, geography, Canadian history, observation lessons, physiology, arithmetic, including the elements of bookkeeping, singing by Tonic Sol-fa methods, drawing and form study, cooking, and calisthenics.

Morals are included not only by example and right discipline, but by precept also, through instruction in the Holy Scriptures, in the elements of morality, and in so much of the principles of the Canadian constitution and law as may cause intelligent children to comprehend their relations to the State and to act the part of good citizens. French, being a colloquial language of the city and province, is so taught throughout the full course.

II.—SENIOR SCHOOL.

The course of study in the Senior School is a direct continuation of the course in the Public Schools. Into it are drafted year by year scholars who, having successfully completed the elementary course, desire to continue their education. Its curriculum is consequently advanced, and requires for its completion three years, comprising mathematics, botany, English literature, advanced drawing, including industrial designing, book-keeping, stenography, and typewriting. This school differs from the High Schools chiefly in the exclusion of the classics, and in the nominal fees charged.

III.—HIGH SCHOOLS.

The High Schools for girls and boys provide a complete education in all branches, elementary and advanced. In this respect they differ from most schools of the same name both in Canada and the United States.

The course of instruction includes the Latin, Greek, French, and English languages ; geography and history ; arithmetic, algebra, geometry, mensuration, plane trigonometry, physics, chemistry, and botany ; drawing and manual training ; writing, shorthand, and commercial work ; gymnastics and military drill. Biblical instruction is required only from Protestants. An examination of the course of study will show that while Latin and Greek have the prominence which belongs to them in higher education, provision is made for thorough training in English, French, German, and mathematics. French, being a colloquial language of the country, receives special attention.

The course covers a period of ten years, apart from the Kindergarten, as follows :—

(a) A preliminary course of six years. This includes a half-day class for transition work, into which pupils are received at seven years of age, the second, third and fourth year classes, and the first and second forms, leaving (b) four years for the regular work of the High School.

The work of the preliminary course is uniform for all pupils. In addition to the usual elementary subjects, special attention is given in this course to instruction in form study, drawing, manual training, nature study, French and to moral and physical training. By a careful selection of teachers who have by training and experience special qualifications for this work, by limiting the number of pupils in each class, and by careful supervision of the work of the various classes, provision has been made for a thorough preliminary training which will enable the pupils to enter with advantage upon the more advanced work of the higher forms.

HIGH SCHOOL COURSE.

During the first two years of the High School work one course is prescribed for all pupils, except that pupils are allowed to substitute extra English for Latin. During these two years, special attention is given to the elementary subjects, and to Literature, French, Latin, drawing, and vocal music. Every pupil is strongly recommended to take at least this two years' course in Latin in order that he or she may be qualified to carry on the English work with advantage.

During the last few years of the course the following subjects will receive systematic and thorough treatment : English language and literature, general history, Latin, Greek, French, German, mathematics, science, drawing, and music. These subjects will be arranged in optional courses so that students may prepare for the A.A. Examinations and for the entrance to the University, or may secure that preparation for life which comes from a thorough and systematic educational course. The subjects of history, drawing, vocal music, and calisthenics are given the special attention which they are entitled to receive in a high school for girls.

Admission to all classes is by examination in accordance with the limit-tables. Candidates for admission must satisfy the Rector, by such examination as he may institute, that they are prepared to take up with advantage the course which they desire to follow. The selection of optional courses is subject to the approval of the Rector.

In addition to the courses of study already outlined, provision will be made for special courses to meet the requirements of special students.

FINANCIAL.

CITY SCHOOL TAX.

The operations of the Board since its institution have extended over a period of more than fifty years. From 1847 to 1869 its revenue was derived from two sources, an allowance from the City Council and a grant from the Provincial Government, the City Council being bound to pay an amount equal to three times the Government grant. The annual receipts from these sources scarcely averaged $1,500. In 1869 a system of taxation for school purposes was established, the rate being fixed at one-twentieth of one per cent. on the assessed value of all rateable property and the amount thus raised being divided between the Roman Catholic and Protestant Boards of School Commissioners according to the religious persuasion of the taxpayers. This rate and basis of division gave the Protestants an income of about $17,000. In 1871 the rate was increased to one mill (one-tenth of a cent), in 1872 to two mills, and in 1892 to two and a-half mills on the dollar. This last rate of the City School Tax yielded last year to Protestants the sum of $155,484.76 for school purposes.

DEBENTURES.

The School Boards of Montreal have no power to levy a special tax for the purchase of sites and construction of school-houses, but they are authorised by the Legislature to issue debentures up to $500,000 for that purpose, redeemable in 20, 30, and 40 years. The Protestant Board has now issued debentures up to the full amount, the interest and sinking fund for which, amounting to $30,897.39 a year, form a first charge upon the school tax.

FEES.

PUBLIC SCHOOLS.

In respect of fees, the Board has always been of opinion that education for which a small or moderate fee is charged, is more appreciated by the community than that which is entirely free. In order to enforce this principle, but at the same time to place education within the reach of all, fees in the public schools are fixed at fifty cents per month per pupil, but all children from the same family after the second are admitted free. Inability to pay this moderate sum, never exceeding one dollar a month, does not exclude children from school privileges. Applications for free admission on plea of indigence, when recommended by reliable persons, are never refused. At the present time, for one or other of the above reasons, 1,535 pupils in the public schools pay no fees.

SENIOR SCHOOL.

In the Senior School, the fee charged is one dollar a month in the two lower grades, and two dollars in the more advanced.

HIGH SCHOOLS.

The Board has laid it down as a guiding principle that every Protestant child in the city attending its schools has an equitable and legal claim to an expenditure on his education of an equal share of the amount provided by taxation for the maintenance of schools. On this consideration, the fees charged in the High Schools for boys and girls were fixed at such rates that, after making an allowance *per capita* from the city school-tax equal to that expended *per capita* on pupils in the public schools, the additional cost of education could be defrayed from the higher fees. At the present time these fees vary from $5.00 to $15.00 per quarter, according to class, but where more than three children from a family are in attendance at the same time, only the three most advanced are charged fees.

SCHOLARSHIPS.

In order to enable the sons and daughters of the poorer classes to avail themselves of the higher and more costly education given in the High Schools, free scholarships have been instituted. These scholarships are of two kinds, namely :—

(*a*) Government scholarships, which are not competitive. These are thirty in number, and are awarded by the Provincial Government on the recommendation of the School Board. The fees of those who hold them are defrayed by an annual Government grant of $1,185.

(*b*) Commissioners' scholarships, which are competitive. Forty such scholarships are awarded annually by the School Board, twenty to girls and twenty to boys. They are tenable for four years, and under certain provisions, all pupils in the Sixth year classes of the public schools are entitled to compete for them.

Thus in the city of Montreal there is no Protestant child of promise who may not obtain, free and with honour to himself, an education equal in all respects to that given to the sons and daughters of the wealthier classes.

APPENDIX B.

PROTESTANT BOARD OF SCHOOL COMMISSIONERS FOR THE CITY OF MONTREAL.—EXTRACTS FROM REGULATIONS FOR CITY SCHOOLS, 1900.*

CITY SCHOOLS UNDER THE CONTROL OF THE PROTESTANT BOARD OF SCHOOL COMMISSIONERS.

These are the High School of Montreal, the High School for Girls, the Senior School, and the Public Schools. These schools are subject to the school laws of the Province of Quebec, except as modified by special legislation.

SCHOOL OFFICERS.

School Officers are a Secretary-Superintendent, a Treasurer, a Rector of the High Schools, Principals of the Senior and Public Schools, Directors of special subjects, Class teachers, Supernumerary teachers, Special teachers, and Caretakers.

The High Schools are, by resolution of the Board, under the immediate management of a High School Committee, composed of the School Commissioners, the Secretary-Superintendent and the Rector. This Committee has full control of all matters concerning the organisation and management of the High Schools, unless otherwise provided for under these regulations.

In the discharge of his duties as head of the two High Schools, the Rector is directly responsible to the High School Committee, from which he receives his instructions and to which he must report at least quarterly.

All action of the High School Committee is subject to the approval of the Board.

THE SECRETARY-SUPERINTENDENT.

To the Secretary-Superintendent is committed the task of securing the proper grading and harmonious working of the schools as parts of a general system. He must visit each school monthly, except in December, May and June, for the purpose of advising with teachers in regard to any matters en which they wish to consult him, of examining any class in any portion of its work ; of seeing that school records are properly kept ; and generally of inquiring into school work, discipline, and condition of property and making suggestions for their improvement. He must furnish a monthly report to the Board, act as its secretary, and see that its decisions are carried out.

THE TREASURER.

The Treasurer shall be responsible for all receipts and expenditures, collect all fees and other moneys due to the Board, deposit all moneys received in the bank, so that the debit side of the bankbook shall correspond month by month with the sum of receipts in the statement of accounts, pay all amounts authorised by the Board, by cheque, signed by the Chairman, or in his absence by the Senior Commissioners in the city, and himself, paying small amounts from the proceeds of a collective cheque given him by the Board each month, so that the total of the credit side of the bank-

---

* A copy of the Regulations was kindly furnished by the Secretary-Superintendent of the Board.

book may correspond month by month with the total expenditure of the month ; keep the accounts of the Board by double entry, prepare a monthly statement of accounts and submit it to audit by the Secretary-Superintendent and auditor in time for the Board meeting of the succeeding month. He shall act as recording secretary at meetings of the Board and High School Committee, and perform such additional clerical and other work as may be required of him.

PRINCIPALS.*

Every school is under the immediate control of a Principal, whose duty it is to exercise close supervision over the course of instruction and methods of presentation employed in it ; to maintain with justice, kindness, and discretion efficient discipline ; to secure the cheerful and faithful co-operation of teachers ; to enforce upon caretakers due attention to their duties ; and to observe, and cause to be observed by pupils and subordinates in office, the regulations of the Board. In order to do this he shall from time to time read to the assembled school such regulations as pupils ought to know.

In the Public and Senior Schools, it shall be the duty of the Principal to report to the Secretary-Superintendent any case of inattention to duty on the part of a subordinate, unless by previous remonstrance he shall have secured immediate reformation. Should the Secretary-Superintendent fail to secure amendment, he shall report to the Board.

In similar cases in the High Schools, the Rector shall report the matter to the High School Committee.

The Principal must carefully keep the register of progress of pupils and report to the Board the names of all pupils withdrawn from the school and the reasons for their withdrawal. He shall also keep the register of attendance of teachers. He must prepare his monthly report for the Board, and send it to the Secretary-Superintendent not later than the first day of the month following, with the written explanations of absence required by the provisions in regard to the attendance of teachers. He must take an inventory of moveables in his school, and send a copy of it to the Treasurer's office. This inventory must be compared from time to time with the moveables actually in the school, and must be renewed during the month of June of each year. He must take supervision of the school buildings and property, and report from time to time upon their condition in sanitary and other respects.

The home work assigned to pupils must be carefully supervised by the Principal, so that it may not exceed in amount the provisions of the limit tables, or burden parents with what is properly the work of teachers.

SPECIAL DIRECTORS.

Special Directors have supervision under the Secretary-Superintendent of the methods of teaching the subjects assigned to them. For this purpose they shall have, when visiting classes, the same power of inspection and direction as the Superintendent. Their visits shall be made as far as possible in conformity with pre-arranged time tables ; and in other cases they shall notify Principals beforehand of intended visits, in order that the routine of the classes may suffer as little disturbance as possible. They shall report from time to time to the Secretary-Superintendent and annually in writing to the Board. They shall attend all meetings to which they are summoned by the Board or Secretary-Superintendent.

No special directors are employed in the High Schools.

CLASS AND SUPERNUMERARY TEACHERS.

Class and supernumerary teachers are primarily responsible to the Principal for the discharge of the duties assigned to them under these regulations

---

* In the following Regulations where the word *Principal* occurs, it must be held to include the Rector of the High Schools, except where special provision is made to the contrary.

and by the time table of the school, and for the progress and good order of
each scholar in their respective classes. They are therefore entitled to all
reasonable liberty in the class methods to be employed. In cases of
difference of opinion, however, the instructions of the Principal are to be
followed. They are expected to attend monthly meetings of the staff, to
bear cheerfully their share of all extra duties, and to co-operate heartily with
others for the success of the school.

Each teacher must carefully keep and make up monthly the register of
attendance of his class, must notify the Principal of any infringement of
the regulations respecting fees or attendance, and must not enter a new
name without receiving from him a register number, nor drop a name
without his concurrence.

SPECIAL TEACHERS.

Such teachers as are employed in the High and Senior Schools part of the
time only, are designated Special teachers. They bear all the responsibilities
and exercise all the powers of class teachers while in charge of any class, but
they are not required to keep a class register, nor to perform any duties out
of the hours of their attendance, except that they may be required, at the
request of the Principal, to give one hour a week after school hours to weak
or delinquent pupils, and to attend the monthly meetings of the staff. They
must be provided by Principals with a list of the names of the pupils in
each of their classes.

The Board, however, reserves to itself the right of requiring from special
teachers, when employed full time, all the duties of class teachers, in some
one, but not more than one, of the schools in which they are employed.

ENGAGEMENTS.

No teacher is held to be engaged by the Board until the authorised form
of engagement has been signed. All class and supernumerary teachers shall
serve four months on trial before being permanently engaged.

Unless it be expressly stipulated in the engagement, no teacher is
employed to teach any particular class in any particular school, as the
Board reserves to itself the right to re-arrange the teaching staff of the
various schools when and how it may deem best ; and the Secretary-
Superintendent is authorised annually to re-arrange the teaching staff of
the Public schools and at his discretion to give teachers charge of boys and
girls alternately.

The Board will not hereafter employ teachers who have not sufficient
acquaintance with French, especially with its pronunciation, to enable
them to teach creditably so much of that language as may be demanded
by the limit tables of their classes. All female teachers when not disqualified are expected to take their own classes in Tonic Sol-fa. Teachers
not qualified to do this must suffer the reduction of salary provided for in
the 7th paragraph of the regulations as to salaries.

Teachers may be required to attend any lectures or discussions that may
be instituted by the Secretary-Superintendent for the improvement of
methods of teaching.

SALARIES.

Salaries in the High Schools and Senior School are considered and
determined individually by the Board ; but male teachers engaged at less
that $1,000 per annum, and female teachers engaged at less than $440 in
classes up to and including the third year of the preliminary Course, or
$500 in the Fourth or Fifth years, will receive, if employed full time,
regular annual increase up to these amounts.

In the Public Schools, male Principals of schools containing classes of all
grades receive from the time of engagement, $1,000 per annum with increase
up to $1,500 as determined by the Board. Second masters receive $600 per
annum. Salaries of female Principals are determined individually by the
Board.

Female teachers of Kindergarten, Preparatory, and other classes up to
and including the Third Year, and Supernumerary Teachers, receive $275

per annum on engagement, and, provided they prove themselves punctual, faithful, and efficient, the Board will, on the recommendation of the Superintendent, raise their salaries annually in the month of September, so that they will receive $300 in the second, $320 in the third, $340 in the fourth, $365 in the fifth, and $385 in the sixth year of service.

Female teachers of Fourth, Fifth, and Sixth Year classes will receive $330 during their first year of service, and, on the conditions of advance above stated, will receive $350 in the second, $375 in the third, $400 in the fourth, $420 in the fifth, and $440 in the sixth year of service.

Assistants in the Kindergarten, being teachers in training, receive no salary, but qualified teachers when acting as assistants will receive $125 per annum.

Teachers engaged temporarily to supply the place of absentees receive one dollar per day of actual teaching.

Teachers not qualified to take their own classes in Tonic Sol-fa shall be engaged at a rate of salary $10.00 per annum below the above scale.

The above scale, however, does not prevent the Board from engaging skilful and experienced teachers at higher than the minimum or maximum rates, nor from augmenting their salaries year by year, as it may determine, nor for diminishing or withholding any or all augmentations in case of financial necessity.

Applications for special increase of salary are considered only at the regular meeting of the Board in June, and teachers who desire to urge their claims in this or any other relation otherwise than in writing, must apply in writing to the secretary to be heard before the full Board, but must not interview individual Commissioners.

Teachers are forbidden to transfer their salaries except by special permission of the Chairman.

Limit Tables, Time Tables and Rules.

The work proper to each year of the course is defined in the limit tables published annually in the school prospectuses.

The time table of each school shall be drawn up by the Principal in consultation with the other teachers, conforming as nearly as practicable to the limit tables of the Board. In the case of the Public and Senior Schools it must, when drawn up, be submitted to the Superintendent, discussed and approved by him at a meeting of teachers ; if, after hearing the opinion of teachers, it be satisfactory to him he shall sign it. No time table shall be binding without his signature, and, except to meet a temporary emergency, no time table, so approved, shall be altered or departed from without his approval signified in writing. A similar course must be followed in respect to any rules which it may be thought desirable to enact in any school.

In the case of the High Schools the time tables when drawn up must be submitted and approved at a meeting of the High School Committee.

School Districts.

Pupils are required to attend the school provided for the district in which they reside. No exception to this rule can be allowed except on the written order of the Board or Secretary-Superintendent.

No school districts are assigned to the High School of Montreal, the High School for Girls, or the Senior School.

Who may be admitted to Schools.

Children of Protestant parents, resident in Montreal, and of others, resident or non-resident, who pay into the Protestant Panel school tax upon real estate owned by them in the city,* of school age,† of sound mind, in possession of their senses, properly vaccinated, free from infection, and not under suspension from another school, are admissible to any school

---

* Jews and Roman Catholics may be admitted to schools where there is room, at the same rate of fee as Protestants, but subject in other respects to the conditions imposed on non-residents of the City.

† School age is defined by law to be between five and sixteen years.

in which there is suitable accommodation, provided that no child residing in one school district shall be admitted to the school of another district without a written order from the Secretary-Superintendent, addressed to the Principal of the school to which admission is sought, which order may be revoked at the close of any school month if the seat is required for a resident of the district.

Reception of Pupils.

Pupils who have not previously attended school are admitted in the months of September, October, February, and March, and Principals are authorised at other times to refuse admission to those who cannot enter with advantage any one of the established classes.

It shall be the duty of the Principal before admitting a pupil :—

1st. To ascertain his residence so that he may not be unwittingly admitted if residing out of the city or in some other school district.

2nd. To enquire as to his religious faith, whether Protestant, Jew, or Roman Catholic.

3rd. To secure and preserve the authorised statements as to his vaccination, and the absence of any infectious disease in the household from which he comes, signed by a parent or guardian.

4th. To enquire if he has previously attended any school under the control of the Board ; and, if so, to ascertain and record what school, and the standing and register number of the pupil in it.

When children apply for admission to any school where there is no room for their reception, the Principal must carefully examine the applicants, and send to the Secretary-Superintendent forthwith a statement of their names in full, ages, addresses, religious faith, and attainments, so far as may be necessary to determine the grade of class to which they shall be admitted. It shall then be the duty of the Secretary-Superintendent to endeavour to find suitable vacancies in other accessible schools.

Should the parent be unwilling to send the child to a school outside his district, he may enter his name upon the application list kept by the Principal, whose duty it shall be to notify such applicants, in order of the date of their applications, of vacancies as they occur.

All transfers given by the Board or Secretary-Superintendent shall be good only for the remainder of the school year then current, unless a statement to the contrary is given in writing at the time ; and it shall be the duty of Principals, on 1st September following, to refer pupils thus admitted to the school situated in the district in which they reside.

Transfers made on account of discipline shall be subject to reconsideration annually, and the Secretary-Superintendent shall then determine on the course to be pursued in each such case. In the absence of any order to the contrary, these transfers shall be considered permanent

Conditions of Continuance in School.

The continuance of a pupil in school is conditional upon the due payment of fees, upon his being furnished with prescribed text-books, his attention to studies, punctuality, respectful obedience to teachers, pleasant intercourse with school-fellows, personal cleanliness, freedom from infection, avoidance of injury to school premises and furniture, and abstinence from immorality in speech and action.

No pupil may bring to school or have in his possession fire-arms or any explosives.

Fees.

In public schools the fee is 25c. per month for each pupil in the half-day classes, and 50c. in other classes ; but no more than two children of the same family shall be charged school fees. In the Senior School the fee is $1.00 in the lower, and $2.00 in the two upper grades, per pupil per month. Attendance in the Senior School does not count towards remission of fees in the Public Schools.

The Treasurer will visit the schools on the eighth school day of each month, for the purpose of receiving the fees for that month. Principals are required to pay into the hands of the Treasurer, at his office, all balances of fees collected after the eighth school day as soon as any balance amounts to five dollars, and to pay in like manner the final balance of the month's fees not later than 11 a.m. on the last Saturday of the month.

In the High Schools fees are payable quarterly, and vary in the different grades.

In the Kindergarten and Transition Classes the fee is $5.00 per term.
In the First and Second Preparatory Classes the fee is $6.25 per term.
In the Third Preparatory Class the fee is $7.50 per term.
In the First Form the fee is $8.75 per term.
In the Second Form the fee is $10.00 per term.
In the Third Form the fee is $11.25 per term.
In the Fourth Form the fee is $12.50 per term.
In the Fifth Form the fee is $13.75 per term.
In the Sixth Form the fee is $15.00 per term.

When four or more children belonging to one family are in attendance at the same time in either of the High Schools, only the three most advanced will be charged fees.

All fees are payable in advance, monthly fees on the first school day of each month ; quarterly fees on the first day of each term, namely, 1st September, 16th November, 1st February, 16th April. Any teacher permitting a pupil to remain in school more than five days without payment of the monthly fee or eight days without payment of the quarterly fee, becomes responsible to the Board for it. Teachers in the High Schools will be relieved from this responsibility upon reporting to the Treasurer, in writing, the fact of nonpayment.

No application for remission of fees in the High Schools will be entertained where the pupil has not been absent for more than one-half the term. Pupils entering after the Christmas holidays will be charged proportionate fees for the month of January.

EXEMPTIONS.

In the Public Schools, children of persons in the employment of the Board are exempt from the payment of fees. In the Senior and High Schools a discount of 50 per cent. will be allowed them, except that children of teachers employed in the High and Senior Schools pay no fees while attending the schools to which parents are attached.

Exemptions from fees on the plea of poverty may be made by the Principal of any Public School, with the knowledge and consent of any member of the Board, or of the Secretary-Superintendent, given in writing.

TEXT-BOOKS.

Every pupil is required to procure all such text-books and other school requisites as are enumerated in the limit table of the class to which he or she belongs, and none other.

In cases of deserving indigence, the Secretary-Superintendent may provide and lend, with due precautions for their proper preservation, text-books and other school requisites, preserving a record of each case.

SCHOOL HOURS.

The school hours for each class in all the schools are defined in the limit tables, and are binding alike on teachers and pupils.

The opening or closing of the play-grounds and school buildings shall be determined by the Principal of the school, subject to the approval of the Secretary-Superintendent, or in the case of the High Schools, the High School Committee, and pupils shall not have admission to them at any other times. Arrangements must be so made as that teachers shall be in attendance—one in the building and one in each of the play-grounds—during intervals of school work, and at such other times as they are open by order of the Principal.

Each class-room shall be assigned by the Principal to the particular charge of a teacher, whose duty it shall be to inquire promptly into the cause of all damage, when any such occurs, and to report the same to the Principal. Damage due to rough or improper conduct must be repaired at the expense of the pupils in fault. A teacher failing to make prompt inquiry and report becomes responsible for damage done. Teachers left in supervision of a building will in like manner be held responsible for damage outside the class-rooms.

School doors shall be closed at ten minutes past the time of opening of each session, after which no children shall be admitted to any class without the permission of the Principal, except when, in cold or wet weather, the health of the children would be endangered by their being compelled to return home.

If any pupil in the Senior or any Public School is late or absent at more than ten sessions of the school during the month, without satisfactory explanation by a parent or guardian, or leaves the school premises during any school session without permission of the teacher in charge, the Principal may, at his discretion, declare the seat forfeited, and must notify the parents to that effect. He must then send a statement of the case to the Secretary-Superintendent, who is empowered to readmit the pupil upon the application of his parents or guardians.

School Studies.

The limit table for each class states the time to be devoted to each subject and the progress which the class is expected to make in one half year or year. The Board does not minutely direct the manner of giving instruction, preferring that teachers, aided by the advice of the Superintendent and of the Principal should exercise their talents and skill with as little interference as possible. It, however, reminds teachers that class-work is not mere recitation, but is also, and to a great extent, study under the eye and with the aid of the teacher ; and forbids the giving of any home work to junior classes that has not been carefully explained beforehand.

Every statement made to the class by a teacher must be so made as to arrest the attention, and to convey a distinct and correct conception to the understanding. The memory must be trained to remember facts accurately, and to recall expressions of sufficient importance, whether for their concise truth or for their beauty, with verbal exactness and with promptitude. So much only as can be thoroughly done should be attempted.

Teachers must carefully prepare the day's work beforehand. Exercises must be written on the blackboard, and all appliances placed in readiness before the opening of each session. The general work of preparation and the correction of exercises should occupy at least an hour daily.

Fuller directions respecting certain work may be found in the Memoranda and Instructions issued for the use of teachers.

Discipline.

Discipline in the schools is founded on instruction in duty, and is maintained by appeals to reason and right moral feeling, aided by rewards to the diligent and obedient, the reproof and punishment of those neglect-fully and wilfully wrong, and the expulsion of the incorrigible.

It is expected that no pupil will be punished for a fault committed in ignorance, nor for a fault not distinctly brought home to him. Teachers are therefore required to be careful that the children understand their duties. Care must be taken that school regulations be not too minute, nor school duties unnecessarily multiplied or onerous.

Habits of diligence and good conduct must be fostered by reward. One of the best rewards is private or public commendation from a judicious teacher. Prizes are provided for the diligent and successful.

If rewards, admonition, and reproof fail to secure good conduct and diligence on the part of any child, punishment must be resorted to.

In resorting to punishment teachers must take care to ascertain that the punishment is merited, and to select that form which is best suited to the offence. To secure this end, the Board recommends that teachers, while taking note of misconduct during a lesson, shall not punish until its close.

PUNISHMENTS

Permitted methods of punishment are : ·

(a) Setting a pupil to stand on the floor. This punishment must not be prolonged beyond the continuance of one lesson.

(b) Keeping him after school in the afternoon.

This must in no case be for longer than one hour a day.

(c) Reporting him to the Principal of the school.

No pupil should be sent to report himself verbally, but reports must be made by the teacher in person or in writing.

Pupils should be reported by teachers to the Principal only in cases of a grave character.

When a pupil is reported, the Principal must, before inflicting punishment for the offence, see that he has received a correct report.

(d) Deprivation of credit marks. This punishment must not be used capriciously.

(e) Corporal punishment, except in the case of girls.

Corporal punishment must be applied only on the palms of the hands and with the strap supplied by the Board, after the boy has been made aware that such punishment is about to be inflicted. If a boy refuse to submit he must be sent to the Principal.

All other methods of corporal punishment, such as shaking, pulling the ear, slapping with the hand, striking with the pointer or without warning, are strictly forbidden.

The giving of one or more strokes for the same offence to the same pupil at the same time constitutes a case of corporal punishment.

If the same pupil be whipped more than once during any month, each whipping must be recorded as a separate case of corporal punishment.

If more than one pupil be whipped for the same offence at the same time each whipping must be recorded specifically as a case of corporal punishment.

The strap shall be kept in the Principal's room, sent for as required, and immediately returned.

The pupil to be punished shall not be sent for the strap.

A book provided by the Board for the purpose must be kept for recording cases of punishment in each school. This book shall be kept in the Principal's office, and sent with the strap when a whipping is to be inflicted. All punishments must be recorded in it at the time in accordance with the form there prescribed It shall be the duty of the Principal of the school to countersign each record after the book has been returned, and to include in his monthly return to the Board a statement of the number of corporal punishments administered in each class.

Corporal punishment shall not be inflicted upon any pupil who refuses to submit to it. The insubordinate pupil shall be sent home by the Principal, either at once or at the close of the session, with a written statement of his offence and of the penalty to be inflicted, of the fact of the pupil's refusal to submit and of his consequent exclusion from the school, until he is willing to submit.

No record of "*sending home*" shall be entered in the Principal's punishment book.

In cases where the offence of the pupil has been peculiarly grave, or his conduct in refusing punishment has been insolent or impertinent (and only in such cases), the Principal instead of sending the pupil home may resort at once to suspension under clause (*f*).

(*f*) Suspension.

When the ordinary discipline fails to secure becoming conduct in a pupil, the Principal may suspend him from the school for a period not exceeding five school days, sending by the delinquent a written statement addressed to one of his parents or guardians, informing him of the length of time for which the pupil is suspended, and the reasons of suspension.

If the suspension be for refusal to do some definite act that may rightfully be demanded, it may be extended until the offender return and do that which he had refused to do ; but a statement, as provided for in the foregoing paragraph, must be sent to a parent or guardian.

If a suspended pupil remain away from school more than five school days from the date of suspension, a report of the case must be sent to the Secretary-Superintendent, who shall then take measures to prevent his admission to any other school.

All cases of corporal punishment by the Principal, as such, and of suspension, must be fully and permanently recorded in a book provided for that purpose, and open to the inspection of any member of the Board and of the Secretary-Superintendent. Punishment inflicted by the Principal, when taking temporarily the place of a teacher, will be noted in the corporal punishment book of the school only.

EXPULSION.

When it becomes obvious that the conduct of a pupil is such as to endanger the authority of competent teachers, or the morals of his companions, and the modes of discipline detailed above fail to secure amendment, the case must be reported to the Secretary-Superintendent, who shall appoint a time to meet the pupil, his parents or guardians, and the teacher concerned, at the school, and· shall send to each party a notification specifying the time, place, and the object of the meeting. If neither the pupil nor his parents or guardians attend, he shall be considered withdrawn, and forbidden admission into any school.   If he or they attend, the matter shall be carefully investigated, all parties having a dispassionate hearing, and, according to the merits of the case, the Secretary-Superintendent may warn the delinquent and his parents or guardians, by note if the latter be absent, of the danger of expulsion, may suspend him for a time not exceeding a month, may remove him to another school, or may submit the matter to the Board, with which alone remains the power to suspend indefinitely, or to expel.   If the Secretary-Superintendent remove the delinquent to another school, he must make provision for his reception there

EXAMINATIONS.

Public oral examinations will be held from time to time by appointment of the Commissioners.

Written examinations shall be held annually or oftener, as the Board may direct.   At their close, and in accordance with their results, prizes shall be awarded, promotions made, and classes re-arranged.

A scheme, giving the day on which each examination shall be held, will be sent to the Principals by the Board sufficiently early to afford time for preparation and arrangement.

For all such examinations the Board will furnish the questions, and will determine the manner in which the marks assigned to the subjects shall be given.

The scale of values assigned to the subjects is given on the Examination Sheets provided under the regulation for the reporting of results.

The questions shall be distributed to the schools in sealed parcels, each bearing on the outside the name of the examination paper contained within, and the number of copies.   No parcel shall be opened until the hour at which the examination is to be held.

As far as possible all pupils taking the same examination paper must be examined simultaneously in the school, but when the accommodation is insufficient for this, especial care must be taken that the children first examined shall have no communication with those still to be examined. No two children taking the same examination paper shall sit at the same desk.

The children about to be examined being assembled, the teacher must furnish each with pen, ink, blotting paper, a known and sufficient quantity of blank paper, which must all be returned untorn, and, after silence is enforced, one examination paper only.

Each child must write his name, age last birthday, name of the school, and rank in the school in appropriate places. Then, having marked the time, and giving no explanation of the questions, the teacher must direct the children to begin work, must see that no use is made of any slate, book, pencil, other paper than that furnished, or of any extraneous aid, and must arrest all work at the end of the assigned time, and collect the answers. Any pupil detected in contravening this regulation shall forfeit all marks assigned to the paper upon which he is engaged.

In giving out dictation, the teacher should read once before writing begins and before the time is marked, and should then read at his discretion, while the pupils write, giving the punctuation unless otherwise directed, and, if he chooses, the meaning of detached words.

All answers shall be read, valued, and signed in accordance, first with any instructions that may be issued by the Board ; secondly, with instructions issued by the Principal. The precise method of distributing the marks assigned for each question and paper shall be determined by the Principal in consultation with the teachers interested before the answers of the pupils are marked. All doubtful points arising during the process of marking shall be referred to the Principal, whose decision must be followed ; and in schools where two or more classes taught by different teachers take the same examination paper the answers shall be valued by the teachers concerned in consultation with one another. All answers must be filed in an orderly manner in the school, must be preserved for one year, and shall be open to the inspection and subject to the call of the Board or Superintendent.

PROMOTIONS.

In cases where the desirability of promoting a pupil is doubtful, because such a pupil in the written examinations has acquitted himself either better or worse than could have been expected, it shall be in the power of the Secretary-Superintendent to take into consideration in determining the pupil's fitness for promotion, the results of all tests recorded during the year, and the teacher's impressions, as well as marks gained in the examination.

When a pupil has satisfactorily completed a course of any school or class, he shall be removed to a higher. No deviations from this rule will be permitted, unless expressly sanctioned by the Secretary-Superintendent.

In the High Schools promotions shall be made by the Rector under the regulations in consultation with the teachers in charge of their respective classes, subject to the approval of the High School Committee.

PRIZES.

Prizes for general proficiency are provided in all classes of the Public and Senior Schools, except Kindergarten, Preparatory, and First Year grades. All pupils are eligible for these prizes.

A pupil, transferred from one school to another during the course of the year, must, in order to be eligible for a prize, establish his school record for the year by the production of the monthly reports received in the former school.

To be entitled to a prize, a pupil in the Public Schools, must have obtained : —

(a) Eighty per cent. of the total marks obtainable in all examination papers set by the Board or by Principals in grades not examined by the Board ;

(b) A similar percentage of the total marks attainable for lessons during the year where some scheme of marking school-work, approved by the Secretary-Superintendent, has been consistently maintained throughout the year ; and

(c) Ninety per cent of the maximum marks in conduct and punctuality, also awarded on some approved scheme.

In the Senior School to be entitled to a prize the pupil is required to obtain seventy-five per cent. only of the marks attainable in examinations and lessons.

A First General Proficiency prize will be given in each class to that boy and that girl, whose aggregate marks—not less than the minimum above stated—are the highest.

All pupils who have not remained in the grade of their classes more than twelve school months in the Public and Senior Schools, or more than five terms in the High Schools, and who have not been entered in the punishment book of the Principal during the six months preceding, may compete for First General Proficiency prizes.

In the High Schools medals are the only prizes awarded by the Board.

COMMISSIONERS' SCHOLARSHIPS.

The Board will award, annually, a number of Commissioners' Scholarships, not more than forty (40) in all.

In awarding scholarships to the candidates entitled to compete, the following principles will be observed :-

(a) Two scholarships will be awarded in each Public School, and in the McGill Model Schools one to the first boy and the other to the first girl.

(b) The remaining scholarships will be divided between boys and girls of the Public Schools in proportion to the number of boys and girls of Sixth Year Grade who enter upon the final examinations.

(c) The scholarships assigned to boys will be distributed among the various schools as nearly as possible in the ratio which the number of boys of Sixth Year Grade in each school bears to the total number of boys as determined by principle (b).

(d) Principle (c) will be applied to girls.

(e) Where the girls of a school are entitled to a certain number of scholarships with a fraction over, and the boys are entitled to another certain number with a fraction over, and the two fractions nearly equivalent, when added together, are sufficient to entitle the school to an additional scholarship, such a scholarship may be won either by a boy or by a girl.

(f) The scholarships thus assigned to each school will be awarded in order of merit, except that candidates qualifying under the second of the two conditions of qualification mentioned below, must obtain 5 per cent. more marks on their aggregate than candidates qualifying under the first condition, in order to take precedence.

All candidates must be pupils in the Sixth Year of the Public Schools who are entitled to compete for first General Proficiency prizes, who are not less than twelve nor more than sixteen years of age on the first of June of the year in which they are candidates, who have spent the two years previous in the Public Schools, and have not doubled the Fifth Year Grade except on account of age or illness, and who have fulfilled one or other of the following conditions :—

1st That they take seventy-five per cent. of the total marks attainable in examinations and in the subject of English, and not less than two-thirds of such marks in each and every other subject.

2nd That they obtain eighty per cent. of the total marks as above with seventy-five per cent. in English, and do not fall below the above-mentioned standard of two-thirds in more than two subjects ; and in case the failure be in French or Arithmetic, pass a supplemental examination on the first of September next ensuing.

The Commissioners' Scholarships are tenable either in the High Schools for a classical course, or in the Senior School for a non-classical course, but can be retained only from year to year, and for their retention the holders of them must give satisfactory evidence of continued good conduct and application.

A scholarship is forfeited if the holder thereof, except in case of illness, fails to gain promotion to the next higher grade at the end of any year.

The Rector of the High Schools and the Principal of the Senior School, on receiving Commissioners' Scholars, are authorised to demand from parents some reasonable assurance that their children will complete the school course, and they shall report annually to the Board at its September meeting, upon the progress of those enjoying this benefit.

GOVERNMENT SCHOLARSHIPS.

Thirty free tuitions in the High School of Montreal are awarded by the Lieutenant-Governor-in-Council upon the recommendation of the Board. These scholarships are not competitive, and candidates in order to be eligible for appointment, must give satisfactory proof of good character and of their being qualified to enter at least the Third Form. These scholarships are tenable from year to year, and their tenure is conditional upon good conduct and satisfactory progress. Nominations are made annually at the September meeting of the Board, and it shall be the duty of the Rector of the High School to report in writing to that meeting upon the conduct and progress of pupils enjoying this benefit, as well as upon the qualifications of new applicants. Applications must be sent in writing to the Secretary of the Board not later than the first week in September.

REPORTS TO PARENTS.

Monthly reports of attendance, and reports of the results of written examinations, shall be sent to the parents or guardians of all pupils. In addition to these, reports of progress and standing shall be sent to parents at least three times a year. All forms of report shall be approved by the Board.

MEETINGS OF TEACHERS.

At least one meeting of teachers shall be held in the Senior and each Public School during the year, at the call of the Secretary-Superintendent, at such time out of school hours as may appear to him convenient for the teachers. At it, one of the Commissioners, the Secretary-Superintendent, or the Principal of the school, shall preside, and all teachers are expected to attend. All matters affecting the interest of the school may be discussed, and all proposed Regulations and Time Tables shall be submitted previous to receiving the sanction of the Superintendent.

CONFERENCES OF TEACHERS.

Conferences of teachers shall be held in the High School at half-past three o'clock in the afternoon, from time to time as occasion arises. Such conferences shall be called (a) by the Board, (b) by the Secretary-Superintendent, (c) at the request of six teachers given in writing to the Secretary-Superintendent. A week's notice of meeting shall be given, except in cases of emergency, and a statement of the special business to be brought forward shall be embodied in the notice of meeting. All teachers are expected to attend.

HOLIDAYS.

Holidays shall be as follows :—

1st. Every Saturday.

2nd. Good Friday and Easter Monday.

3rd. The Queen's birthday.

4th. Such days as may be proclaimed by Authority.*

5th. The Superintendent is directed to make such arrangements as may be necessary to allow any teacher two days annually to visit other schools under the control of the Board, or to attend the Convention of Protestant Teachers of the Province of Quebec.

6th. Monthly half-holidays for punctual attendance are allowed in schools in which the attendance does not fall short of 90 per cent. of the perfect attendance.

---

* These holidays cannot be given by the Principals of Schools without receipt of special authorisation from the Board.

The schools will close for about ten days at Christmas and two months in the summer, as may be determined each year by the Board.

Any other holidays may be given by the Board or by its Chairman only.

SUPPLIES AND REPAIRS.

All school supplies and small repairs, when sanctioned by the Treasurer, will be provided by him upon the receipt of a requisition from the Principal, so that no expenses on behalf of the schools shall be incurred by Principals or Caretakers, without his written order. It will then be the duty of each Principal to consider beforehand what supplies are needed monthly, and to send his requisition in sufficient time to allow of its being met. The Principal must give the Treasurer a receipt for all goods delivered.

FIRE-DRILL.

Fire-drills must be conducted at least once a month, sometimes during the forenoon, and sometimes during the afternoon session, but not at regular or prearranged periods.

There shall be a special signal placed in some accessible part of the building, which must be used for fire-drill only. Every member of the school staff, as well as the caretaker, must know how to give the fire-signal.

Teachers must dismiss pupils immediately on hearing the signal and always in the same way. Pupils must not stay to put on clothing.

Pupils must walk in quick step, keeping in time, but not crowding, teachers being in advance of their classes.

Teachers or reliable older pupils, should be stationed on staircase landings, at the foot of stairways, at exits, and other important positions, to assist, and should be especially trained to take these positions with promptness.

Pupils in drilling should be confined occasionally to one staircase, and one means of exit ; and should be trained to halt instantaneously at word of command, and to obey promptly all directions.

Note.—The treasurer of the City of Montreal annually pays to the Protestant Committee of the Council of Public Instruction, out of the moneys payable to the Protestant Board of School Commissioners for the City of Montreal, the sum of two thousand dollars for the education of children, resident in the City of Montreal, and attending the McGill Model Schools.

Protestant Schools in Montreal.—The following report as to the course in manual training in the institutions under the control of the Protestant Schools of Montreal, was recently made by the superintendent of them, and is taken from the Report for 1897.

"*a.* Kindergartens.—Kindergarten departments have now been established in all the High and Public Schools with the exception of two small schools situated on the outskirts of the city. The Kindergarten occupations are the basis of all manual training. The Kindergarten begins the training of the hands in exactness, deftness, and neatness, educating them to do the will of the brain which stands behind them. The course deals with solids, by means of clay, sand, and cardboard work ; surfaces, through paper-folding, paper-cutting, and painting with brush ; lines, by means of weaving, sewing, and drawing ; and points, by means of bead-stringing, perforating, etc.

"*b.* Transition Work. — It has been felt for some time that some special provision is necessary in order to make a natural connection between the Kindergarten or the Home and the regular school work. The difficulty is now met by what is called Transition Work during the first year of school. This work forms a prominent feature of first year classes, more especially in the High Schools, and is under the direction of specialists trained and experienced in this work. The children are taught Reading,

Writing, and Arithmetic, in connection with Manual Work and Form Study. Beginnings are made in Literature and Science, History and Geography, by means of stories, poems, and observation lessons, with the aid of the sand and clay modelling. Correlation of studies is the aim, that interest may be stimulated and the connection between the Kindergarten and Preparatory Classes made as close and natural as possible.

"*c.* Form Study and Drawing. — The manual work begun in the Kindergarten is systematically carried on in the junior classes of all schools under the head of Form Study and Drawing. This includes paper-folding and paper-cutting, sticklaying, clay modelling, and colour work. The results of the work in this direction have been very satisfactory.

"The work is strictly educational, it deals with the mind ; the hand and eye are trained to express thought through the study of concrete objects. It aims to cultivate the imagination, to develop the sense of beauty, to lead to the expression of artistic ideas, to teach in true historic order what the course of the world's great art has been, and the function of beauty in education and in life.

"The course followed is the Prang course, and will be found fully explained in the three following books published by the Prang Co., viz., 'The Use of Models,' 'Suggestions for Instruction in Colour,' and the 'Primary Course in Art Education, Parts I. and II.'

"*d.* Sloyd. — Educational Sloyd now forms a regular part of the course of the Boys' High School. The system of educational handwork in wood is generally recognised as an important instrument in the development of the mental, moral, and physical powers of children. The advantages to be derived from it are numerous. It inspires respect for rough, honest, bodily labour ; it cultivates manual dexterity, self-reliance, industry, perseverance, and patience ; it trains to habits of order, exactness, cleanliness, neatness ; and it develops the physical powers. A Sloyd room has accordingly been fitted up with thirty-six adjustable work-benches, each bench being provided with the necessary tools for an elementary course of woodwork. The course, which extends over a period of three years, beginning with the first form, consists of a series of models in wood so arranged as to involve a well-graded series of exercises in the use of common tools. Eight classes, including over two hundred boys, are drafted in turn into the Sloyd room, where they are required to take up the regular course in Sloyd. Three steps are involved in the study of each model. First, the model is carefully examined by each boy ; second, a working plan of the model, drawn to scale, is prepared by each boy ; and third, the model is reproduced in wood from the working plan. From the beginning the pupil is taught to make and interpret working drawings, and to reproduce from them the indicated forms."

The following note has been kindly supplied by the present Superintendent of Protestant Schools in Montreal :—

e. Cooking.—Three cooking centres in convenient schools have been established. Classes from the ten large public schools are now drafted into one or other of these centres, each school contributing a class of not more than 28 girls. Instruction in cooking is given during the regular school hours, each class spending half a day in the work, and no fee is charged. The method of instruction provides for a demonstration lesson to a full class during the first hour, and for practice lessons in two sections during the remainder of the time. The services of a competent instructress have been secured in the person of a graduate of the School of Cookery and Domestic Economy, Manchester, England.

APPENDIX C.

REGULATIONS OF 1890 EMPOWERING THE ROMAN CATHOLIC
AND PROTESTANT BOARDS OF SCHOOL COMMISSIONERS
IN MONTREAL TO ISSUE DEBENTURES.

Whereas the Board of Roman Catholic School Commissioners of the City
of Montreal, and the Board of Protestant School Commissioners of the
City of Montreal have, by their petition, established that it is expedient to
consolidate, explain, and give a permanent character to, the various statutes
which have been, from time to time, enacted, granting the said Boards
power to issue debentures for the purpose of enabling the said boards to
erect suitable school-houses in the City of Montreal, under their respective
control ; and whereas some of the debentures issued under the authority
of the said statutes have become paid up and extinguished, by means of
the sinking fund provided for the regular redemption of the said debentures ; and whereas the growing wants and necessities of primary education
in the said City of Montreal, as well as the facilities offered for obtaining
loans on debentures, render it expedient that the said school boards should
be invested with the permanent power of raising money by debentures to a
limited amount for the construction of school-houses when necessary,
without being obliged to obtain new legislative authority, upon each and
every issue of such debentures.

Therefore, Her Majesty, by and with the advice and consent of the
Legislature of Quebec, enacts as follows :

1. The Board of Roman Catholic School Commissioners of the City of
Montreal, and the Board of Protestant School Commissioners of the City of
Montreal, are hereby, severally and separately, authorised to issue debentures or bonds for the purpose of raising money to build schools, under
the control of the said Boards, and acquire land for school sites, as well as
to pay off any mortgages upon their immoveable property to the extent of
five hundred thousand dollars for each Board.

2. The said debentures or bonds shall be issued in sums of one hundred,
five hundred, or one thousand dollars each ; no issue shall be of less than
twenty-five thousand dollars in bonds of equal denomination ; the said
issue to be redeemable, as herein provided, in fifteen, twenty, twenty-five,
thirty, thirty-five, or forty years, and the said debentures or bonds shall
bear interest at a rate not exceeding five per cent. per annum, payable
annually or semi-annually.

3. The payment of the interest and capital of the said debentures or
bonds shall be provided out of the income of the said Boards, derived from
the school tax in the City of Montreal :

(*a*) Whenever the Board shall have decided upon an issue of debentures
or bonds, the said Board will give a notice in writing to the treasurer of
the City of Montreal specifying the date and the amount of issue decided
upon, the denomination of the bonds, the rate of interest, and the date of
the redemption of the said debentures or bonds.

(*b*) The bonds or debentures issued conformably to the said notice and
signed by the president or chairman and treasurer of the Board, shall be
presented to the treasurer of the City of Montreal, whose duty it shall be to

sign the said bonds, provided they do not exceed the issue authorised by the present act.

(c) Such signature, by the treasurer of the City of Montreal, shall be an acknowledgment that the said bonds or debentures have been served upon him, and that the payment of interest and capital of the said bonds shall be provided for by the said treasurer out of the school tax, which the said treasurer is bound to pay yearly for the said Boards after collection of the same by the Corporation of the City of Montreal according to law, and the said signature of the said treasurer shall be sufficient proof to third parties, that the said bonds or debentures have been issued conformably to the present act, and are not in excess of the power to issue, authorised by the present act.

(d) It shall be the duty of the Treasurer of the City of Montreal, out of the yearly proceeds of the school tax in the City of Montreal, to retain in his hands a sufficient sum to pay all the interest which shall become due and payable, in each and every year, upon the said bonds or debentures, and, furthermore, to retain, in addition, a sufficient sum to form a sinking fund to provide for the repayment of the capital of the said debentures or bonds at their maturity; and the bearers of the said bonds or debentures shall have the right to claim from the Corporation of the City of Montreal payment at maturity of the said bonds or debentures in capital and interest.

(e) Upon the amounts thus retained in his hands, the said treasurer shall allow the Board entitled to the same the rate of interest which the particular issue of the bonds may bear, which interest shall be capitalised yearly whilst the said bonds or debentures shall remain outstanding and unpaid; and the said treasurer shall, out of the amount so by him retained, pay the interest upon the said bonds or debentures, as the same become due, and out of the amount retained by him for a sinking fund and the interest accrued upon the said sinking fund, he shall redeem the said bonds as the same become due; and he shall render an account to the said Board, and shall pay over to them any amounts remaining in his hands to their credit upon any separate issue of bonds, or shall be entitled to claim from them any deficit, should such deficit exist.

(f) The Corporation of the City of Montreal and the said Board may mutually agree upon some different system as to the creation and maintenance of a sinking fund for the redemption of the said debentures or bonds as well as the investment of the same; but, in the absence of such special agreement, the foregoing dispositions shall apply, and, under any circumstances, the signature of the Treasurer of the City of Montreal, acknowledging as aforesaid, the service upon him of the said bonds or debentures, will be sufficient proof, in favour of the bearers of the said bonds or debentures, that the issue of the same has been duly authorised, according to law, and that their redemption shall be provided out of the said sinking fund.

4. Nothing in this act shall be construed as giving the said Board power to issue and keep outstanding more than the said sum of five hundred thousand dollars of bonds or debentures; and, in consequence, the debentures issued under the authority of the statutes 32 Victoria chapter 16, 33 Victoria chapter 25, 34 Victoria chapter 12, 36 Victoria chapter 33, 39 Victoria chapter 16, 42–43 Victoria chapter 14, by either of the said Boards, and still unredeemed, are to be taken into account when the said Boards exercise the said powers hereby conferred to issue debentures or bonds to the extent of the said sum of five hundred thousand dollars; nor shall this act be interpreted as authorizing either board to issue five hundred thousand dollars of debentures in addition to those already issued and still unredeemed at the time of the coming into force of this act; but only as conferring upon the said boards the power to issue, from time to time, as the necessity for which the said issues are authorised occur, and to keep

outstanding the said sum of five hundred thousand dollars in bonds or debentures in the manner aforesaid, inclusive of those bonds which have been, from time to time, issued under the above-mentioned statutes, and which shall still be unredeemed at the time of the coming into force of this act.

Nevertheless, the debentures issued by the Board of Protestant School Commissioners of the City of Montreal, to the amount of fifty five thousand dollars and signed by the Treasurer of the City of Montreal, bearing date the first day of January, eighteen hundred and ninety, redeemable in *twenty** years, are hereby declared legal, valid, and binding, as though the said debentures had been issued under the authority and provisions of the present act.

---

* Amended by an Act passed the same day, 30th December, 1890, and " thirty " substituted.

APPENDIX D

SPECIAL REGULATION OF 1893 IN REGARD TO THE TENURE OF OFFICE IN THE ROMAN CATHOLIC BOARD OF SCHOOL COMMISSIONERS, MONTREAL.

1. All the Commissioners of the Roman Catholic Board of School Commissioners of the City of Montreal shall go out of office on the first day of July next.

2. Before the said day, the Lieutenant Governor in Council, upon the recommendation of the Superintendent of Public Instruction, shall appoint three commissioners, chosen as much as possible from among the members of the universities of Montreal, the Archbishop of Montreal shall appoint three selected from the members of the clergy, and the Corporation of the city of Montreal shall also appoint three selected from the Roman Catholic aldermen of the said city, to form part of the said Board.

3. If the Archbishop of the diocese of Montreal, or the corporation of the City of Montreal, or both, shall have neglected to notify the Superintendent of Public Instruction, in writing, of the appointments which they are obliged to make, the said appointments shall be made by the Lieutenant Governor in Council in the manner above provided ; and the commissioners so appointed, shall be deemed to have been named by the authority which failed to appoint them.

In case the appointments or some of the appointments to be made by the Lieutenant Governor in Council have not been made they shall be made by him within the shortest possible delay thereafter, and the commissioners so appointed shall enter into office immediately after their appointment.

4. The commissioners shall remain in office during three years, except that, after their nomination, one of the commissioners in each of the above categories, designated by lot, shall go out of office at the end of the first year, another of each category at the end of the second year, and the three others at the end of the third year.

5. Any vacancy in the said Board, by death or absence from the Province, shall be filled according to the manner in which the appointment of the commissioner to be replaced was made, and the person filling such vacancy shall remain in office only during the time his predecessor would have continued in office.

APPENDIX E.

ROMAN CATHOLIC SCHOOLS: COURSE OF STUDY FOR MODEL SCHOOLS AND ACADEMY.

SUBJECTS.	MODEL SCHOOLS.		ACADEMY.	
	FIFTH YEAR.	SIXTH YEAR.	SEVENTH YEAR.	EIGHTH YEAR.
Moral and Religious Instruction	Catechism. Latin reading.	Catechism. Latin reading.	Catechism	Catechism.
French	Expressive reading Oral résumé of lesson read. Memorizing (Committing to memory) and reciting interesting and simple selections from the best prose and poetry. Grammar Review of elements, syntax. Parsing. General principles of logical analysis. Letter Writing—Familiar letters, business letters, recits, descriptions, narrations.	Expressive Reading Oral résumé of lessons read. Reciting selections from the best prose and poetry. Grammar—Review, syntax. Parsing and logical analysis. First principles of literature. Letters, narrations, descriptions.	Expressive Reading Elocution, declamation. Grammar - Complete analysis. Literature - Qualities of style. Figures Letters, narrations, descriptions.	Expressive Reading -- Elocution, declamation. Grammar complete—Logical analysis. Literature - Qualities of style. Figures. Literary Analysis—Letter, narrations, descriptions.
English. (For schools in which as much attention is given to English as to French.)	Expressive Reading—Spelling and meaning of words of the reading lesson, dictation, Translation. Writing of stories read or related by teacher. Letter Writing—Letters, narrations.	Expressive Reading Dictation, translation. Writing of stories read or related by teacher Grammar and analysis. Letter Writing—Letters, narrations, descriptions.	Reading and recitation of selections from best prose and verse. Dictation, translation. Grammar - Analysis. Literature - Letters, narrations, descriptions.	Expressive Reading -- Dictation, translation. Grammar—Analysis. Literature — Letter, narrations, descriptions.
Writing	Copy writing Exercise copy-books.	Copy writing Exercise copy-books.	Copy writing Exercise copy-books.	Copy writing. Exercise copy-books.

Mathematics	Review common fractions, decimal fractions, and compound rules. The unitary method, elementary percentage, simple interest, miscellaneous problems, mental arithmetic. Elementary mensuration. Book-keeping—Double entry.	Review work of the preceding year. Percentage and its application: commission, discount, insurance, interest, profit and loss, etc. Miscellaneous problems. Mensuration—Mensuration of surfaces. Book-keeping—Double entry.	Percentage, general review. Square root, cube root. Practical exercises—Mental arithmetic. Review of mensuration of surfaces. Algebra—General definitions; algebraic addition, subtraction, multiplication, and division. Equations of the first degree. Book-keeping—Double entry. Commercial correspondence.	General review. Miscellaneous exercises. Mental arithmetic. Mensuration of surfaces and solids; Algebra to equations of second degree inclusive. Book-keeping—Double entry. Commercial correspondence.
Geography	Europe and Asia. Map Drawing.	Review of preceding year—Africa, Oceania.—Review Canada. Map drawing.	General review. Use of globes. Map drawing.	General review. Terrestrial Globe. Oral lessons on elements of cosmography. Map drawing.
History	Canadian History—French Rule. Sacred History—General review.	Canadian History—English Rule. Sacred History—General review.	History of the Church to the Crusades. Canadian History, review. French History, principal events.	History of the Church, from the Crusades to the present time. History, principal events. United States History.
Drawing	Drawing	Drawing	Drawing	Drawing.
Useful knowledge	Object lessons and written résumé—Subjects: commerce, industry, navigation, hygiene, &c. Canadian Civics. Agriculture—Oral lessons.		Agriculture—A regular course of oral lessons on agriculture. Elements of philosophy, of physics, of geology, and of botany. Political Economy (for boys). Canadian Civics. The agricultural, forest mining, and industrial products of Canada. Its internal and foreign trade. Domestic Economy (for girls).	

APPENDIX F.

PROTESTANT SCHOOLS: ELEMENTARY COURSE OF STUDY.

SUBJECTS.	GRADE I.	GRADE II.	GRADE III.	GRADE IV.
Scripture Knowledge	The first half hour of each day to be devoted to the Opening-Exercises—Scripture Reading, Singing, and Prayer, Instruction in Scripture and Morals, including readings and lessons upon Godliness, Truthfulness, Honour, Respect for Others, Good Manners, Temperance, Health, Kindness to Animals, &c.			
English	The meaning of words with the subject matter of the reading lesson. Special attention to be given to pleasantness and brightness of tones, fluency, clearness and correctness of pronunciation, and to writing and spelling in all written work.			
	Copying words and sentences, oral and written reproduction, Memoriter work. Special attention to pen-holding and hand movements.	Copying words and sentences, Dictation, oral and written, Reproduction, Sentence Composition, Memoriter work.	Copying, Dictation, Word Building, Special Study of Simple Selections, from best prose and poetry, with Memoriter work, Sentence Drill, the parts of Speech.	Dictation, Special Study of Selections, including Definitions, Derivations, Analysis and Synthesis of Sentences, Parsing, Letter Writing, Accounts, Descriptive Composition, and Recitation of selected passages.
Arithmetic	Mental Arithmetic, Addition and Subtraction, with objects, and with numbers of two figures. Reading and writing numbers to 100.	Mental Arithmetic, Four Simple Rules to Short Division inclusive. Multiplication Table. Avoirdupois Weight, Long and Liquid Measures.	Mental Arithmetic, Long Division, Simple Examples in Fractions and in Compound Numbers in ordinary use, and review.	Mental Arithmetic, Simple Examples in Fractions, Decimals, Percentage, Interest, Mensuration; and Review.
Geography and History	Elementary terms. Divisions of land and water. Map of the school neighbourhood.	Outline of the Map of Canada.	Map of Western Hemisphere, Map Drawing, Outline of Canadian History, French Rule.	Map of Eastern Hemisphere, Map Drawing, Outline of Canadian History, including points of contact with British History.
Object Lessons or Useful Knowledge.	Form Study and Drawing, Colour, Size, Weight, Motion, First Notions of Agriculture. (Special attention to the Plants, Animals, Forest Trees. and Minerals of the Province, and their uses.)			
French (Optional)	Names of objects in conversation.	Names of objects and phrases.	Easy sentences with simple forms of familiar verbs.	Reading, easy exercises in translation, regular verbs.
Text-Books necessary for each Grade.	Reading Book, Table-card, Slate, Slate-Pencil.	Reading Book, Table-Card, Slate, Slate-Pencil, Copy-Book, Ink.	Reading Book, Slate, Pencils, Copy-Book, Blank Book, Pen, Ink, Arithmetic, Geography, Canadian History, Drawing Book, No. 1.	Reading Book, Slate, Pencils, Spelling Book, Copy Book, Blank Book, Pen, Ink, Arithmetic, Grammar, Geography, Canadian History, Drawing Book, No. 2.

N. B.—Music and Physical Exercises are required to form part of the School Course

APPENDIX G.

FROM THE REPORT OF THE PROTESTANT BOARD OF SCHOOL COMMISSIONERS FOR MONTREAL FROM SEPTEMBER, 1897, TO SEPTEMBER, 1899.[*]

ATTENDANCE.

The Board has under its direct control fifteen schools with an actual daily attendance of 8,206 pupils, as may be seen from the following returns. It also subsidises two other schools, the McGill Model Schools, and the Baron de Hirsch Day School.

ATTENDANCE FOR OCTOBER, 1899.

Name of School.	No. of Pupils.
High School of Montreal	669
High School for Girls	520
Senior School	258
Aberdeen School	849
Ann Street School	481
Berthelet Street School	599
Britannia School	71
Dufferin School	584
Hochelaga School	95
Lansdowne School	746
Lorne School	682
Mount Royal School	867
Riverside School	679
Royal Arthur School	509
Victoria School	597
	8,206
McGill Model School, boys and girls	485
Baron de Hirsch School	358
	9,049

This attendance shows an increase of 63 pupils only as compared with the same returns last year. A further analysis, however, shows that the number of Roman Catholics has decreased by 75, and the number of non-residents by 76. It follows, therefore, that the number of Protestant and Jewish pupils residing within the City limits has increased by 214, which a final analysis sub-divides into 124 Protestants and 90 Jews. The total enrolment for October is made up as follows :

Protestants residing within the city limits			-	7,638
Jews „ „ „ „			-	1,107
Roman Catholics -	-	-	-	214
Non-resident Protestants and Jews	-	-	90
				9,049

It has been a noticeable fact for some years back that the school population has been growing rapidly in the outskirts of the city, and in the

---

[*] This Report was kindly supplied by Mr. E. W. Arthy, Secretary. Superintendent to the Protestant Board.

X

suburban municipalities, but has been stationary, or even decreasing in the central districts of the city. This year, for example, there has been a very considerable increase, amounting to 185 pupils in Mount Royal and Aberdeen Schools, while there has been an actual falling off in the attendance of Ann Street, Berthelet Street, and Dufferin Schools.

School Accommodation.

Since the date of the last report (November, 1897) an extension of six rooms to the Mount Royal School has been erected to meet the urgent needs of that growing district. The expenditure for the purpose, amounting to some $14,000.00, has increased the floating debt of the Board by about $8,000. The building was completed in the spring of the present year, and on the re-assembling of classes in September every classroom was occupied. The present schoolrooms of the Senior School are much needed to furnish accommodation for an extension of the High School. Last year a committee of the Board spent much time in the consideration of ways and means, but was unable either to find a desirable site or to advise the Commissioners, in view of their financial position, to undertake the large capital expenditure necessary for the erection of a suitable building.

The difficulty of adjusting school attendance to school accommodation is likely to be an increasing one. At the present time, two class rooms only, one in Victoria and one in Royal Arthur School, are not in regular daily use. On the other hand, there are eleven half-day classes which meet in the afternoon, because there are no class rooms vacant for their reception in the forenoon. This arrangement is open to obvious objections on the ground of both health and convenience. Apart from this double use of certain rooms, there are not a few other classes which have grown beyond the normal capacity of their rooms, and yet cannot be divided for lack of space.

Course of Study.

The course of study in the Public Schools has been divided into half-yearly instead of yearly sections. This change has been introduced to meet the requirements of a system of classification which provides for the grading of pupils by intervening steps of six months instead of twelve months. Apart from the general improvement gained by more exact classification throughout the school, two particular advantages have resulted from the change. First, when a pupil for any reason fails to gain promotion he loses, not a full year, but a half-year only. Second, the facilities for placing new pupils with advantage are increased. In the Public Schools the names of the grades, as Preparatory, Primary, Intermediate, and Senior, have been abandoned, since these names carried no meaning to those unfamiliar with the system. The simpler method of naming the grade by the year which it occupies in the school course has been substituted. The course is now divided into six grades known as First to Sixth Years. Preliminary to this, two classes are provided, a Kindergarten class, and a Preparatory class for the benefit of very young children who are unable to enter upon the regular First year work. These classes are alternative, not successive, stages in the course.

The Commissioners, being of opinion that upon the whole the best interests of education will be served by eliminating the principle of competition and emulation among pupils, are moving in the direction of limiting and eventually abolishing the present system of prize-giving. With this end in view all prizes, with the exception of medals, have been given up in the High Schools. In the Senior and Public Schools non-competitive prizes for General Proficiency are still maintained, but to secure these, pupils must have reached the required standard, not only in the marks allowed for lessons, but also in those for good conduct and punctuality.

Latin has been introduced as an optional subject into the course of the Senior School. This step has been found necessary in order to enable the graduates of the school to enter with advantage the classes of the McGill

Normal School. Provision has also been made in the High School for the preparation of pupils of the Sixth Form for the special examinations required for admission to the study of Law, Medicine and Dentistry.

SPECIAL SUBJECTS.

A third centre for instruction in cookery was opened in October, 1898, in the Royal Arthur School, and is attended by classes from that school and from Victoria School. In this way provision has now been made for the instruction in this subject of classes selected from all the Public Schools.

The Prang system of instruction in form and colour which had been in use for several years in the first three grades of the Public Schools, was adopted in 1899 in the remaining grades. Miss Phillips, an expert in this system, visited the city last spring, and besides giving lectures and demonstrations to the teachers, rendered valuable assistance in drawing up the new course of study. For the help of teachers in this and other work normal classes in observation work, form, and colour have been instituted. These classes are under the direct instruction of Mrs. Simister, who is being assisted by many others.

FINANCIAL.

The financial and statistical statements for the year ending June 30, 1899, accompany this report, together with a comparative statement of income and expenditure for 1897-8 and 1898-9. The diminution in the amount yielded by the City School tax, the principal item of the Board's revenue, was totally unexpected, and was due chiefly to a marked decrease in the valuation of property belonging to Protestant owners. As there was at the same time a considerable increase in the disbursements for the year, and as the whole expenditure of the Board, whether on income or on capital account, must be met from its ordinary annual income, a deficit amounting to $7,820.90 was created and added to the existing floating debt That debt, after deducting the value of all assets available towards its liquidation, amounted in the 30th June, 1899, to $8,429.33, for which provision can only be made by savings from the income of future years. The Board has already sold off all the available portion of the Aberdeen School property, as well as its property on Fullum Street, and has also taken into account in this calculation the value of the lot on the corner of Marlborough and St. Catherine Streets, still remaining unsold.

The arrangement with the Jewish ratepayers under which they have agreed to pay their school taxes into the Protestant Panel has been modified so that in future the subsidy to the Baron de Hirsch Day School will be a *per capita* allowance of $8.00, but will not exceed the gross amount of $2,000 per annum. The Board has now in its own schools 749 Jewish pupils, and it also supports the Baron de Hirsch Free Day School, on which there are 358 more, or 1,107 in all. The school tax paid by Jewish proprietors into the Protestant Panel amounted in 1898 to $4,519, a sum very far below the cost of educating the Jewish children resident in the city. On the basis of the expenditure for that year, $19.32 per pupil (see Table II., page 21), the Board has disbursed over and above the school taxes paid by Jewish proprietors a sum of $10,951.68 out of the Protestant school tax for the education of Jewish children.

(1.) Statistics of Attendance in the High, Senior, and Public Schools for the Year 1898–99.

NAME OF SCHOOL.	No. of school days.	Average Monthly Enrolment.	Average daily Attendance.	Percentage of daily Attendance.	Average No. of times late.
High School of Montreal · · ·	192	625	595	95·2	1·2
High School for Girls · · ·	192	465	435	93·5	1·3
Senior School · · · · ·	190	241	229	95·	2·
Public Schools · · · · ·	190	6,252	5,742	91·9	2·3
Total, 1898-99 · · ·	—	7,583	7,001	—	—
Total, 1897-98 · · ·	—	7,293	6,710	—	—
McGill Model Schools 1898-99	—	451	—	—	—
Baron de Hirsch Day School · ·	—	332	—	—	—
Total including subsidised schools, 1898-99 · · · · ·	—	8,366	—	—	—

(2.) Statement of Attendance and Average Cost.

This Statement includes all expenditure made upon Income Account, as shown by the Statement of Receipts and Disbursements.

NAME OF SCHOOL.	Average Monthly Enrolment.	Net cost of Mainten- ance.	Proportion of undistri- buted Expenses.	Total.	Cost per pupil.
Aberdeen · · · · ·	774	$8,278.62	$7,050.00	$15,328.62	$19.80
Ann Street · · · · ·	449	6,406.29	1,535.00	7,941.29	17.68
Berthelet Street · · · ·	612	7,364.94	2,312.00	9,676.94	15.81
Britannia · · · · ·	71	1,415.17	473.00	1,888.17	21.12
Dufferin · · · · ·	548	7,386.39	4,371.00	11,757.39	21.45
Girls' High · · · ·	465	2,786.06	8,323.00	11,109.06	23.89
High · · · · ·	625	8,717.08	8,323.00	17,040.08	27.84
Hochelaga · · · ·	121	2,104.29	1,313.00	3,417.29	28.24
Lansdowne · · · ·	712	8,168.77	3,441.00	11,609.77	16.31
Lorne · · · · ·	649	7,036.29	2,916.00	9,952.29	15.33
Mount Royal · · · ·	668	7,746.76	2,732.00	10,478.76	15.69
Riverside · · · ·	651	7,871.78	3,141.00	11,012.78	16.92
Royal Arthur · · · ·	432	5,795.68	2,508.00	8,303.68	19.43
Senior · · · · ·	241	5,414.81	2,014.00	7,428.81	30.82
Victoria · · · · ·	565	6,760.64	2,836.00	9,596.64	16.99
	7,583	$93,253.57	$53,288.00	$146,541.57	$19.32

(3.) COMPARATIVE STATEMENT OF INCOME AND EXPENDITURE.

Total ordinary expenditure · · · · · · · ·	$224,732.35
,, ,, Income · · · · · · · ·	216,911.45
Deficit · · · · · · ·	$7,820.90

INCOME.

—	1897-8.	1896-9.	Increase.	Decrease.
City school tax · · · · ·	$154,302 01	$151,529 94	—	$2,772 07
Neutral tax, Hochelaga, etc. · ·	947.13	484.91	—	462.22
Government grants · · · ·	6,831.36	6,831.36	—	—
High School fees · · · · ·	17,646.05	19,749.88	2,103.83	—
Girls' High School fees · · ·	12,027.64	13,452.63	1,424.99	—
Public, Senior, and Night Schools ·	23,408.81	24,210.48	801.67	—
Interest received · · · · ·	764.84	652.25	—	112.59
Total ordinary income · ·	$215,927.84	$216,911.45	$983.61	—

EXPENDITURE.

—	1897-8.	1896-9.	Increase.	Decrease.
General charges of maintenance ·	$161,704.93	$167,691.92	$5,986.99	—
Subsidies · · · · · ·	6,856.83	5,955.36	—	901 47
Interest · · · · · ·	29,715 37	28,948.75	—	766.62
Sinking fund · · · · ·	8,244.09	8,197.43	—	46.66
	$206,521 22	$210,793 46	—	
Land, buildings, and furniture · ·	5,359.62	13,988.89	8,579.27	—
Total ordinary expenditure ·	$211,880.84	$224,732.35	$12,851.51	—

NOTE.—The detailed information about the Montreal Protestant Schools given in Appendices A., B., and G., was obtained in response to an application made to the Protestant Board of School Commissioners. A similar application was made by the same mail to the Roman Catholic Board of School Commissioners for Montreal, but no answer had been received at the time of going to Press.

THE
SYSTEM OF EDUCATION
IN
NOVA SCOTIA.

INTRODUCTORY - - - - - -   265

I. EARLY HISTORY.

Education Act of 1811 - - - - - - -   267
Rise of Denominational Colleges and Universities   - 268
Private Schools - - - - - - -   269

II. PRIMARY AND SECONDARY EDUCATION.

The Rise of the Free School Idea - - - - - 270
First Superintendents of Education - - - - 270
Free School System - - - - - - - 271
Council of Public Instruction - - - - - 274
Superintendent of Education - - - - - - 274
District Commissioners of Schools - - - - 274
The Inspector - - - - - - - - 274
The School Section - - - - - - - 275
The Annual School Meeting - - - - - 275
Finance - - - - - - - - - 275
County Academies - - - - - - - 276
Courses of Study and Text Books - - - - 277
Manual Training - - - - - - - 281
Religion - - - - - - - - - 281
Public Grants for Denominational Schools - - 282
Licensing and Appointment of Teachers - - 283
Salaries, Classification, etc. - - - - - 286
Attendance - - - - - - - - 288
High School Classes carry forward Primary Education - 288

III. TECHNICAL, COMMERCIAL AND AGRICULTURAL INSTRUC
TION - - - - - - - - - 289

IV. PUBLIC REFORMATORIES, INDUSTRIAL OR PARENTAL
SCHOOLS - - - - - - - - 292
Free Meals - - - - - - - - 292

V. SCHOOLS FOR THE BLIND AND THE DEAF AND DUMB - 292

SUPPLEMENTARY NOTE - - - - - - - 293

APPENDICES.

A. Regulation of the Council of Public Instruction re-
ferring to "Devotional Exercises" - - - - 294
B. The Public School Course of Study as prescribed in 1898 294
C. The General Regulations of the Provincial High School
Examinations, 1898 - - - - - - 312
D. Regulations of the Council of Public Instruction
referring to County Academies - - - 319
E. Regulations of the Council of Public Instruction
referring to "Common" School Buildings- - 322
F. Regulations of the Council of Public Instruction on
the Licensing of Teachers and their professional
qualifications - - - - - - 326

THE SYSTEM OF EDUCATION IN NOVA SCOTIA.*

INTRODUCTORY.

The area of the province of Nova Scotia is given at 20,550 square miles.   According to the census of 1891 it had a population of 450,523.   Of these 160,073 were scheduled as wage earners engaged in one of the following different classes of occupations :

Agriculture	53,340
Mining and Fishing	29,893
Manufactures and Mechanical work	26,541
Domestic and Personal service or trades	23,463
Trade and Transportation	18,117
The learned Professions	6,100
Living on Incomes	2,619

These figures, aggregating more than one third of the total population, give an approximate idea of the different future employments of those who are being educated for wage earners of the general classes specified.   The mothers and younger children form nearly two thirds of the population, the former requiring, for reasons which need not be stated here, an education as full, as general, and as practical as the wage earners.

Their religious classification in 1891 was as follows :—

Roman Catholics	122,452
Presbyterians	108,952
Baptists	72,731
Church of England	64,410
Methodists	54,195
Free-Will Baptists	10,377
Lutherans	5,882
Congregationalists	3,112
Disciples	1,728
Salvation Army	1,377
Others	5,307

* The statistics in this Report, which was prepared in 1898, have been corrected, where possible, from official documents since received.

The outline statistics of all the educational institutions of the province, public and private, for the year ended July, 1897, may be stated as follows :—

PUBLIC SCHOOLS.	
School sections maintaining school during the year - -	1,743
Valuation of property subject to assessment in the same	80,738,448 *dols.*
Valuation of the average school section - - - -	46,322 „
Regularly licensed teachers in Elementary and Secondary Schools - - - - - - - - -	2,485
Pupils enrolled in the Elementary and Secondary Schools	101,150
Pupils daily present on an average during the whole year - - - - - - - - -	53,817
Pupils in Deaf and Dumb Institution from the province-	85
Pupils in the School for the Blind from the province -	60
Students in the Provincial Normal School - - -	152
Students in the Provincial School of Agriculture - -	70
Students in the Provincial Mining Schools - - -	52
Students in the Nova Scotia School of Horticulture -	50
Annual cost of education per pupil in daily attendance -	15.06 *dols.*
Total cost of public education for the year - - -	810,676 „
Revenue from local assessment in the 1,743 school sections	448,263 „
Revenue from County assessment (paid to trustees of section) - - - - - - - - -	119,602 „
Revenue from Provincial Grants (182,500 *dols.* for teachers' Elementary Schools) - - - -	242,811 „

PRIVATE SCHOOLS.	
Enrolled in attendance at five Ladies' Colleges, Seminaries, or Convents, two Business Colleges, three secondary schools, and thirteen elementary schools and kindergartens - - - - - -	1,973
Enrolled in the Universities not affiliated with the public school system (secondary or high school system) - -	548

I. EARLY HISTORY.

The Society ·for the Propagation of the Gospel in Foreign Parts, at the request of the Lords of Trade and Plantations by letter dated, Whitehall, England, April 6th, 1749, resolved to send six clergymen and six schoolmasters to the settlement at Chebucto (Halifax) as soon as it should be formed. Two of these came out with the 2,576 settlers under Edward Cornwallis, the convoy of whose fleet of transports arrived in the present harbour of Halifax on the 21st of June, 1749. Schools were then mainly supported by fees; but towards the end of the century more particularly, the provincial Government began to aid many by small grants. The provincial Legislature, which dates from the year 1758, established a seminary at Windsor in 1788. Next year a grammar school was established at Halifax, the capital; and an Act incorporating King's College at Windsor was passed. In 1790 £500 for the site of the college and an annual grant of £400 were voted by the Legislature. These institutions were under the control of the Church of England. In 1802 King's College was granted a Royal Charter from England with £1,000 a year, which was not withdrawn entirely until 1834. But one of its statutes contained the following clause: "No member of the university shall frequent the Romish Mass "or the meeting-houses of Presbyterians, Baptists, or Methodists, "or the Conventicles or places of worship of any other dissenters "from the Church of England, or where Divine Service shall not "be performed according to the liturgy of the Church of England." As a consequence, a movement commenced as early as 1805 at Pictou, in the north of the province, under the leadership of the Rev. Dr. Thomas McCulloch, in favour of the creation of an institution of the higher education free from religious tests. This movement was aided at Pictou by the Education Act Education of 1811, which established "grammar schools" in each of Act of 1811. the ten most important districts of the province, each with an allowance of £100 for the head master, and £50 for an assistant when the pupils numbered over thirty. This Act remained in force until 1825. But in Pictou more was demanded, and in 1816 the Pictou Academy was incorporated after the plan of one of the Scottish universities. Opening shortly after, this institution prepared students for graduation at the University of Glasgow, Scotland; but still neither the power of conferring degrees nor the encouragement of a permanent grant was given it, although four-fifths of the population of the province, and on some occasions the House of Assembly, unanimously pressed its claims upon the Government. After a few annual grants of £400 about the middle of the twenties, the Governor's Council of nine by a majority of one vetoed from year to year any further grants proposed by the House of Assembly, until the institution accepted the position of a secondary school. It was under these circumstances that the representatives of the people began that agitation for an Executive Council, having the confidence of the popular branch of the Legislature, which resulted in 1848 in the concession of the principle of responsible government.   After a vain though nearly successful struggle for more than a decade, the one brilliant fight for an undenominational university was fought and lost.   The later attempts have little dramatic interest.   In the meantime elementary education was progressing.   In 1814 a large school on the Lancastrian plan was started in Halifax, and three years later another on the Madras system, both of which were in receipt of public grants.

The Rise of Denominational Colleges and Universities.   In 1820 the corner stone of Dalhousie College was laid in Halifax by the Governor, Earl Dalhousie.   Its initial endowment of £9,750 was from the proceeds of the Custom duties collected at Castine, a town which was captured from the United States in the war of 1814.   It was to be a provincial university such as the Pictou Academy was then striving to develop into in the north.   Not, however, until the collapse of all the expectations of the latter institution in 1838 was this college opened.   For seven years it functioned with a staff of Presbyterian professors, starting out with such an appearance of exclusiveness (which might have resulted from the defeat of the more generous aspirations of the promoters of the Pictou Academy and the success of the King's College idea), as to alienate the Baptists and give rise in its turn to the establishment of Acadia College at Wolfville, in the same year, 1838.   Dalhousie College paid the penalty of its mistake and was closed in 1845 until it was reorganised by the Legislature in 1863 as an undenominational and provincial university.   In recent years its students have numbered more than those of all the other universities combined.

The " Presbyterian College " is a purely theological institution which originated in 1820 in affiliation with the Pictou Academy, and after migration in succession to West River, Truro, and the City of Halifax, settled down at Pine Hill, in the suburbs of Halifax, in 1878.

In 1854 the Roman Catholic College, St. Francis Xavier, was established at Antigonish.   (*See also Supplementary Note.*)

In 1860 the Roman Catholic College, St. Mary's, was started in the City of Halifax.

In 1862 the Methodists established the University of Mount Allison in the province of New Brunswick, near the border of Nova Scotia, and like the Nova Scotian colleges proper, it received a similar grant from the provincial treasury for its services to the Methodist denomination.

In 1876 the University of Halifax, on the model of that of London, was incorporated by the Legislature with the hope of eventually contracenting the power of the conferring of degrees in one provincial institution.   For Dalhousie, though undenominational in its constitution, Board of Governors, and professoriate, was of necessity patronised by the majority of Presbyterian students, who had only a Theological College of their own, in preference to the denominational colleges ; and it was therefore naturally represented from the denominational point of view as the Presbyterian University. But the colleges with a few exceptions refused to surrender their degree granting powers even for the promise of the continuation of the college grants. A new provincial administration determined to exercise economy accepted this refusal as an occasion to terminate the system of public aid to the universities. The last of such grants was paid in the year 1881, the aggregate for the last year being $15,800.

With this stroke the University of Halifax, depending solely on the legislative grants, and St. Mary's College collapsed.

But in 1890 another degree conferring college was added to the list. The Eudist Fathers from France founded the college of Sainte Anne at Church Point in the midst of the largest French settlement in the province. (*See also Supplementary Note.*)

These universities with a few secondary, special, and elemen- Private tary schools, including ladies' colleges, seminaries, convents, busi- Schools. ness colleges, primary schools and kindergartens, which enrolled in 1897 only 1,973 pupils with an estimated average attendance of 1,297, are the only educational institutions not under the direct control of the Education Department. Among the universities the two Roman Catholic colleges are affiliated to the public school system, functioning under the law as County Academies for their respective counties, for which they receive their share of the Academic grant.

To conclude this subdivision of our historic sketch, a summary of the statistics of all these private educational institutions (which are the only ones which are to-day independent of provincial aid and control), is given in the following two tables :—

A.—The Universities, with 548 students.

B.—Secondary, elementary, and special private schools, with 1,973 pupils.

A.—THE UNIVERSITIES OF NOVA SCOTIA, YEAR ENDED 1897.

| NAME. | Opened. | Location. | Affiliation. | Professors. | Lecturers. | Students. | | | | | Total Students. | Total Graduates. |
						Arts.	Science.	Medicine.	Law.	Theology.		
Dalhousie . .	1863	Halifax .	Undenom.	11	20	194	25	62	67	—	348	72
Acadia . . .	1838	Wolfville ·	Baptist	8	2	124	—	—	7	—	124	46b
Pine Hill . .	1820	Halifax ·	Presbyterian	4	1	—	—	—	—	47	47	6
King's . . .	1790	Windsor ·	Ch. of Eng.	6	4	19	7	—	—	14	29	21b
St. Fr. Xavier ·	1854	Antigonish	R. Cath. (Eng)	—	—	—	··	·	·	—	a	10
Sainte Anne ·	1890	Church Pt.	R.C. (French)	—	—	—	—	·	·	—	a	—
				29	27	337	32	62	74	61	548	155

a. Academic students enrolled among those of the public schools.

b. In the second line seven students are counted twice, and in the fourth line eleven are counted twice—once in the Arts and again in Law or Theology.

B.—PRIVATE, SPECIAL, SECONDARY, AND ELEMENTARY SCHOOLS OF NOVA SCOTIA,
YEAR ENDED 1897.

NAME.	Location.	Teachers	Annual roll.	Average Attendance.
Halifax Ladies' College and Conservatory of Music	Halifax	23	362	200
Mount St. Vincent Academy	Rockingham.	15	93	90
Church School for Girls	Windsor	12	80	80
Acadia Seminary	Wolfville....	10	86	70
Academy of the Sacred Heart	Halifax	26	105	100
Whiston and Fraser's Commercial College	Halifax	8	361	87
Seventeen other Academies, Elementary Schools, and Kindergartens	....	50	1,086	670
Totals.....................	....	144	1,973	1,297

II. PRIMARY AND SECONDARY EDUCATION.

The Rise of the Free School Idea.
In 1825 the Legislature had a breezy discussion of the question of a public school system; but the principle of free schools supported by compulsory assessment, which was advocated on this occasion with much eloquence, was rejected by a vote of 24 to 12, so great was the fear of legislation which would confer the power of local taxation.

In 1832 the province was divided into districts averaging the size of half a county, each under a board of School Commissioners appointed by the Governor-in-Council. These boards were entrusted with the power of organising school sections approximating four miles in length and breadth where possible, and of otherwise stimulating and directing the formation and maintenance of schools in the district under their charge. The funds for each school were obtained mainly from local subscriptions which were supplemented by the grant from the provincial treasury. In 1841 the Legislature was opened by a speech of Lord Falkland, the Governor, in which he advocated the adoption of the principle of assessment; but the House of Assembly was still afraid, and contented itself with the further amendment of the Act of 1832. Provision was also made at length in nearly all the schools for the education of free scholars, but they were a small minority.

The First Superintendents of Education.
In 1850 a provincial superintendent of education was appointed in the person of the late Sir John William Dawson, of McGill University. Under his short term of three years there was a rapid advance in the education of the Legislature and the country with respect to the advantage of improved buildings and methods, the establishment of a Provincial Normal School, and the adoption of the system of local assessment. In 1855 the Normal School was opened under the principalship of the second superintendent, Rev. Dr. Forrester. Under his advocacy from the platform and the Press the time came in 1864 for the establishment of the free school system.

The present Sir Charles Tupper, who was leader of the Free School Government in 1864, was able to introduce the bill with the System. ultimate concurrence of the leader of the opposition, the late Sir Adams G. Archibald; and without any serious resistance it was eventually passed. But in every school section throughout the land there were several families whose education was practically completed under the old conditions, who were now without consideration taxed heavily for the education of their neighbours who in many cases never aided them in the support of their schools. By these and others who were often well off, yet without any children to send to school, the Act was considered outrageously unjust beyond experience or tradition. But as the intelligent representatives of both political parties were committed to a principle which had been glorified for thirty years as the unapproachable ideal, it never became a party question directly. The same parliament accepted confederation with the other provinces of the Dominion of Canada in 1867. So it fortunately happened for the school question that the vials of popular wrath were poured out on the supporters of that administration, ostensibly because the question of confederation was not first presented to the electorate before being acted upon by the legislature. For the next few years the province had therefore to pose as extremely anti-confederate; but no voice was ever raised in Parliament against the principle of assessment and of free schools.

Although during these years a generous interest in education had been increasing fast, the census of 1861 showed that out of a population of some 300,000 over the age of five years there were 81,000 who could not read. It was estimated that in 1863, while some 37,000 were enrolled as attending school for some portion of the year, there were more who were receiving no educational training whatever — 50,000 according to some estimates.

The two tables following show the growth of educational effort for a series of years before and after this event. It should be observed that the numbers of teachers and pupils in the first table are inflated as compared with those of the second which gives the mean of the respective numbers for each half of the year, while the former gives the total numbers of different teachers and pupils for any and every portion of each year. It will also be observed in the first table, that during those years the average attendance was not considered of sufficient importance to record in the reports made to the legislature, from which these statistics are taken.

Before the Free School System.

YEAR.	Number of Teachers.	Number of pupils enrolled.	Local Funds $4—£1.	Provincial Grants, $4—£1.	Total Cost of Schools.	Annual Cost per pupil "enrolled."	Superintendents.
			$	$	$	$	
1820	....	....	....	....	34,720	....	
1824	217	5,514	....	....	....	....	
1828	....	6,639	....	....	....	....	
1829	....	12,000	....	....	....	....	
1831	375	12,941	48,792	....	....	....	
1832	423	11 771	31,367	7,338	38,705	3 29	
1833	457	13,161	57,602	16,628	74,230	5 64	
1834	444	12,573	37,468	17,865	55,333	4 40	
1835	530	15,292	49,813	27,323	77,136	5 04	
1836	550	16,000	60,000	18,000	78,000	4 88	(*)
1841	643	20,910	....	....	....	....	
1842	854	92,383	83,973	36,122	120,095	4 09	
1843	939	29,723	92,972	34,396	126,668	4 26	
1844	985	30,979	88,190	36,255	124,445	4 02	
1846	1.001	33,960	79,828	37,712	117,540	3 46	
1847	1,041	34,729	93,172	43,394	136,566	3 93	
1850	896	25,398	100,556	42,368	142,924	5 64	Dawson.
1851	878	29,579	93,611	42,675	136,286	4 61	
1852	967	32,762	107,407	47,982	155,389	4 74	
1854	907	31,010	103,608	46,642	150,250	4 85	M. & R.
1856	....	31,307	104,047	42,355	146,402	68	Forrester.
1857	1,002	34,356	128,222	53,519	181,741	5 29	
1858	1,127	33,742	129,672	53,319	182,991	5 42	
1859	1,061	35,581	135,041	46,891	181,932	5 11	
1860	1,059	35,203	121,873	45,742	167,615	4 75	
1861	1,043	33,652	129,775	46,833	176,608	5 25	
1862	1,092	36,087	129 999	47,888	177,887	4 93	
1863	1,072	37,483	130,664	45,472	176,136	4 70	
1864	1,112	35,405	115,226	47,930	163,156	4 01	Rand.

* Up to the year 1836 these statistics include only the elementary schools. After this date the secondary schools are also included, *i.e.*, the grammar and high schools or academies,

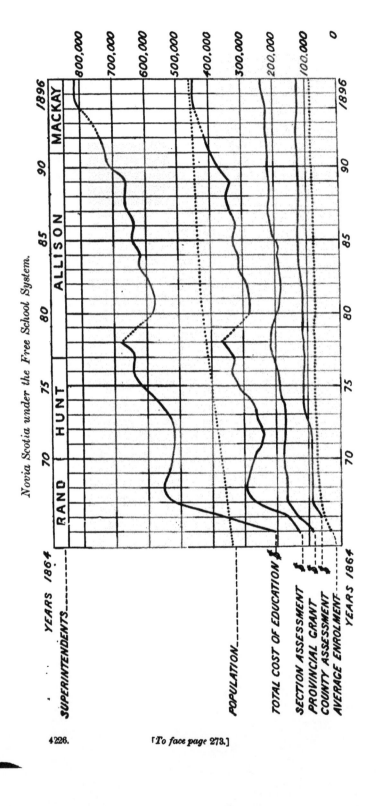

Novia Scotia under the Free School System.

Under the Free School System.

Years.	Av. No. of Teachers W. and S. Terms.	Average enrolment of Winter and Summer Terms.	Average Daily Attendance Winter and Summer Terms.	Av. p.c. of enrolment in Daily Attendance.	School Section Assessments.	County Assessment.	Provincial Grants.	Total Cost of Public Education.	Annual cost per pupil in Daily Attendance.	Superintendent.
					$		$	$	$	
1865	916	39,461	23,572	60.0	124,673	—	87,085	211,758	8.98	Rand
1866	1059	50,574	29,239	57.8	176,252	55,462	136,821	368,533	12.60	
1867	1360	65,396	36,943	56.1	252,913	91,477	162,000	516,390	13.98	
1868	1390	68,612	39,731	58.2	298,659	91,968	164,750	555,367	13.98	
1869	1515	74,139	43,078	58.1	286,754	91,760	167,387	545,901	12.67	
1870	1565	75,279	42,177	56.0	266,160	91,762	174,602	532,524	12.62	Hunt
1871	1620	75,995	43,612	57.4	247,209	91,762	176,174	515,145	11.81	
1872	1592	73,638	40,806	55.4	245,759	95,461	171,395	512,615	12.56	
1873	1624	74,297	41,392	55.3	265,274	105,029	165,562	535,865	12.94	
1874	1658	76,277	44,143	55.0	287,349	107,301	175,013	569,668	12.90	
1875	1775	79,123	44,229	55.3	320,130	107,396	185,565	613,091	13.86	
1876	1810	79,813	45,373	56.3	338,338	106,781	194,605	640,224	14.11	
1877	1888	83,364	46,690	56.3	324,550	106,833	204,266	635,649	13.61	Allison
1878	1964	82,346	48,951	59.0	368,282	106,920	208,115	683,317	13 96	
1879	1985	82,996	45,857	55.4	—	107,181	205,575	—	—	
1880	1809	76,393	42,580	55.7	281,561	107,181	196,217	584,959	13.74	(a)
1881	1881	78,323	43,461	55.1	286,086	106,695	185,519	578,300	13.36	
1882	1922	79,042	43,746	35.3	290,564	106,949	184,627	582,140	13.31	
1883	1961	80,477	45,650	56.7	316,477	120,340	186,088	622,905	13.65	
1884	2014	83,153	47,280	57.5	314,172	120,345	191,124	625,641	13.23	
1885	2054	84,025	48,398	57.8	334,044	120,328	199,188	653,560	13.50	
1886	2111	85,714	51,142	59.6	321,954	120,377	209,834	652,165	12.75	
1887	2143	85,474	50,655	58.5	337,216	119,047	216,085	672,348	13.43	
1888	2153	84,534	48,707	57.6	346,314	118,485	211,196	675,995	13.88	
1889	2182	84,429	50,033	59.2	341,716	118,281	212,922	672,919	13.45	
1890	2214	85,482	49,620	58.0	377,529	118,349	213,434	709,312	14.29	
1891	2229	83,548	49,347	59.0	393,077	118,301	213,906	725,284	14.60	Mackay
1892	2268	85,077	50,975	59.8	410,017	120,127	216,430	746,574	14.65	
1893	2319	85,733	49,391	57.6	413,449	80,623	166,040	669,112	13.55	(b)
1894	2351	87,595	49,806	56.9	454,200	120,507	220,436	795,144	15.96	
1895	2399	89,126	51,528	57.8	453,144	119,900	238,760	811,804	15.75	
1896	2438	90,270	53,023	58.7	450,972	120,018	242,345	813,335	15.34	
1897	2485	90,918	53,317	59.2	448,263	119,602	242,811	810,676	15.06	
1898	2510	91,615	55,715	60.8	473,106	119,869	245,837	838,810	15.06	

(a) The grants to the universities (denominational colleges, &c.) which amounted to $15,800 annually were discontinued from the year 1881.

(b) In 1893 the school year was changed so as to close in the middle of the summer vacation—the end of July instead of the end of October. This transition school year therefore consisted of only nine months or three-fourths of a calendar year. Instead of the averages for the previous winter and summer terms, after this date the averages are those of the four quarters of the school year.

The Council of Public Instruction. The Council of Public Instruction consists of the members of the executive council of the Provincial Government, five of whom constitute a quorum. This body determines the regulations for the expenditure of the funds appropriated for educational purposes, the classification of teachers, and for the administration of all matters generally which fall within the scope of the educational statutes. It prescribes the school books and the courses of study for the schools of all grades. It directs the normal school, appoints the provincial examiners of the high school students, inspectors, district school commissioners, and has power to make provision for any exigency not inconsistent with the statutes.

The Superintendent of Education. The Superintendent of Education is appointed by the Governor in Council, and is also the Secretary of the Council of Public Instruction. His duties are generally the same as those of a Minister of Education, with the exception that he has not to find a constituency for election; and is answerable directly to the Government instead of to the House of Assembly. The Education Department in Nova Scotia has hitherto had the good fortune of being considered non-partizan, although the Council is exclusively made up of the members of the Provincial Cabinet and its secretary the superintendent.

The District Commissioners of Schools. The District Commissioners of Schools are continuations of the boards which were in 1832 invested with the power of directing and stimulating education in the days of voluntary subscriptions for the support of schools, when local efforts of specified degrees were rewarded by certain provincial grants There were recently thirty-three such boards presiding over as many divisions of the province, but their functions are now mainly confined to the rectification of the bounds of the school sections, and the determination of those which, owing to their geographical and other conditions, should be placed on the list of those receiving special aid one-third more of both the county and provincial grants than the normal ratio.

The Inspector The inspector, who is appointed by the Council of Public Instruction, on the recommendation of the Superintendent of Education, is the secretary of each of these boards within his inspectorate, but this duty is merely an incidental part of his work. The province is subdivided into ten inspectorates, which gives on an average over two hundred schools to each inspector. This office is one of the most important in the whole system, for the inspector directly inspects each school within his district, makes up the pay list from the returns from each of the schools, pays the provincial and county grants to the teachers and trustees, when the same is authorised to be paid from the Education Department. to which a summary of all returns, etc., are promptly sent as the basis of the division of the funds; withholds approval from returns of schools in which the law has not been observed until there is the required reform, etc. The inspectors are the direct agents of the Education Office, reporting monthly on all the schools visited by them, and coming into authoritative contact with teachers and trustees in every section of the province.

The school section is the unit corporation for school purposes, and geographically includes a territory about four miles in extent, with the school near the centre. There is an injurious tendency in many sections to reduce the geographical limits of the section for the purpose of having all the children near the school, while neither the wealth nor the population of the section will allow a good teacher to be employed. The experience of the educational authorities proves that under ordinary circumstances it is better to be two miles distant from a good school than to be only one mile from a poor school. The section is governed by a board of three trustees, one of whom retires each year at the annual meeting of the section, when his successor is elected. In towns having a municipal government the board of trustees is known as the school commissioners, three of whom are appointed by the municipal council and two by the provincial government, one member each retiring annually. In the City of Halifax there is a board of twelve school commissioners, six appointed by the city council and six by the provincial government, the two senior of each group retiring after serving three years. Cities or towns, no matter how much their extent may exceed the normal four miles, form but one school section. The great mass of school sections are rural, with a simple board of three trustees; the number of sections in 1898 was 1,874.

The School Section.

The annual school meeting is the most important educational event in the rural school section. Except in certain specified sections it is fixed by law to be held on the last Monday of June, just before the close of the schools for the year, and seven or eight weeks or more before the opening of the schools in the new school year. It is the annual parliament of the section, where the taxpayers assemble to discuss the educational administration, elect the new trustee, and vote the amount of supply to be levied upon the section for the support of the school for the following year. The sum of the valuations of the property within school sections having schools was in 1897 $80,738,448, and in 1898, $81,726,341. The value of the school property itself was in these years $1,484,635 and $1,502,711 respectively. The total amount voted at the annual meetings of 1898 to be assessed on the section property was $473,104, $77,935 of which was for building and repairs, and $368,567 to supplement the funds from the other two sources for the salaries of teachers. One of these sources is the county fund, which is raised under the statute by the collection, with the rates of each county, of an additional sum equal to thirty cents per head for each inhabitant within the county at the last decennial census. This fund is distributed annually to the board of trustees of each section which conducts an approved public school as follows: first, a small grant of $25 for each teacher employed for the year in the section, then the balance and greater portion is divided to each section in the municipality in proportion to the grand total days' attendance made by the pupils in each school according to the returns sent

The Annual School Meeting.

Finance.

The County Fund.

in at the end of the year.   This stimulates the trustees to secure as large an attendance of pupils as possible, in order to increase their revenue from this source.

The provincial grant is the third source of revenue for the support of the school ; but it is paid directly to the teacher, and is dependent on the class of licence held, as well as on the number of days taught.   Originally a Class D, or Third Class, teacher received a grant of $60 per annum, Class C, or Second Class, teacher $90, Class B, or First Class, $120, as well as Class A, or County Academy, teachers who were not engaged in a county academy.   But in 1888, in order to prevent an excessive growth of the grant from the provincial treasury, the sum total was definitely fixed at $167,500, and in 1895 at $182,500, to be paid in joint proportion to the days taught and the scale above given. The scale was extended to allow $180 for Class A teachers as subordinates, and $220 as principals of schools, with high school departments of prescribed magnitude.   For 1897 the total amount of county grant to the school sections was practically the $120,000 authorised, and the total amount of the provincial grant to teachers, 2,485 in number, was practically the $182,500 authorised by the statute.*   This sum does not include the grants to the county academies, which in 1897 amounted to nearly $16,000.   The county academy is that high school

within the county which receives a special grant on account of its agreement to admit free any students from the county who are able to pass the county academy entrance examination. This examination is conducted by the staff of the institution under general regulations upon question papers prepared by the Education Department on the first eight years' work of the public schools, generally known as the " common " school grades. The county academies are of four orders, determined merely by the extent of their equipment, and receive annually the respective grants of $500, $1,000, $1,500, and $1,720 in lieu of the provincial grant to its teachers.   These grants are an induce- ment to the shire town of each county to make its high school of superior merit, as compared with the other high schools which may be within the county, and which may capture the grant if the shire town fails to provide the required accommodation.   As a matter of fact, there are many high schools in some of the eighteen counties of the province which are superior to the county academies in the poorer counties.   The course of study for these institutions is that of the Grades IX., X., XI., and, if desirable and possible, XII.   The number of high school students enrolled in the academies during 1898 was 1,733.   Those enrolled in the other high schools, or high school departments, doing exactly the same kind of work, without participation in the academic grant, but in the enjoyment of the less liberal pro- vincial grants to teachers according to the general system, were 3,738.   Not being subject to the special testing of the county academies, these numbers include a greater proportion of pupils

---

* The Provincial grant to teachers, 1897–8, was $182,592.

who are not so fully up to the standards. In many of the "common" schools a few of the pupils are doing a portion of the high school work, as are also some special students in the high schools proper. These numbered during the same year 1,652.

From 1864 to 1880 the only suggestion of a course of study for the common (elementary) schools was the list of books prescribed, and for the high (secondary) schools the syllabus of the teachers' examination, of which there were four grades, known as D, C, B, and A, one advancing above the other by about an average year's work, except the latter, which meant about two years' additional work, and fitted a candidate for a county academy headmaster's diploma. *Courses of Study.*

From 1880 to 1885 the Education Department, assisted by the Provincial Educational Association, developed a course of study for the common schools first, then for the high schools. In 1893 the high school course was made the basis of a system of high school examinations, which are now held at forty different stations throughout the province in the first week of July, the closing week of the school year. Provincial certificates of grades D, C, B, and A are given to all candidates with the value of each subject or paper as marked by the provincial examiner of that subject, those not reaching the prescribed standard for a "pass" receiving a "decapitated" certificate bearing simply the full details of the examination record. Foreign languages are optional in this course. In the twelfth grade of the public schools, which is the fourth grade of the high schools, or grade A, there is a bifurcation into a classical side and a scientific side, with a nucleus of subjects in common, leading respectively to the certificates of A (classical) and A (scientific). The secondary schools are in this manner federated into a species of provincial university of secondary rank. The certificates of scholarship of the various grades are accepted as the scholarship qualifications of the different classes of teachers, and also in lieu of the entrance examinations into the various universities and technical colleges, thus doing away with the former necessity of having different classes in the same school if students in it were preparing for different colleges. In this manner the articulation of all private as well as public institutions of the higher education with the public school system is perfectly accomplished. Even when the unsuccessful candidate has not "passed," his certificate, if bearing marks high enough on the various subjects required by the entrance standard of any given institution will exempt him from examination upon those subjects. As the examination is conducted in the most impersonal manner by provincial examiners whose scholarship is universally acknowledged, and as the course of study and the examination papers themselves, as well as the results, are published in the official Journal of the Education Department, the standards can be most easily understood by all educational officers who accept them at their value.

Conspectus
of the Public
School
Course of
Study up to
Grade XI.

A SUGGESTIVE PERCENTAGE OF TIME FOR CLASS-ROOM TEACHING IN EACH
SUBJECT, ON THE SUPPOSITION THAT THERE IS ONE TEACHER FOR EACH
GRADE. WHEN ONE TEACHER HAS THE WORK OF MORE THAN ONE
GRADE, THE TIME TO EACH SUBJECT IN THE CLASS-ROOM MUST BE
LESSENED.

SUBJECTS.	PERCENTAGE OF TIME IN EACH GRADE.									EXAMINATION VALUES FOR PROVINCIAL CERTIFICATES.		
	I	II	III	IV	V	VI	VII	VIII	High School.	IX	X	XI
English - -	40	40	40	40	40	40	35	30	20 {	Lang. 100 Gram. 100	Lang. 100 Gram. 100	Lit. 100 Gram. 100
Mathematics - -	20	20	20	20	20	20	25	30	20 {	Arith. 100 Alg. 100 Geom. 100	Arith. 100 Alg. 100 Geom. 100	P. Mat. 100 Alg. 100 Geom. 100
Science and Manual } Art	20	20	20	20	20	20	20	20	20 {	Dr. &c 100 Botany 100	Dr. &c. 100 Chem. 100	Physiol.100 Physics 100
Geography & History —	—	—		5	10	10	10	10	10	G. & H. 100	G. & H. 100	G. & H 100
Music,Calisthenics, Moral and Patri- } otic Duties	20	20	20	15	10	10	10	10	5			
Optional. { Languages, Latin and Greek -					-	-	-		25	Latin 100 {	Latin 100 Greek 100	Latin 200 Greek 200
Or, French and German - -					-	-	-		25	Frnch 100 }	Frnch. 100 Germ. 100	Frnch. 100 Germ. 100

The average of the actual number of *minutes* of the *teachers'*
time in the 2,346 school rooms of the province of *all* grades,
absorbed in teaching the several subjects named *each day* on an
average during the year ended 1897, was as follows, correct to
the nearest minute :—

English (Spelling, 32 ; Reading, 66 ; Grammar, Composition, etc., 22)	120
Mathematics (Arithmetic, 60 ; Book-keeping, 5) - - - -	65
Science and Art (Nature Lessons, 7 ; Writing, 20 ; Drawing, 12) -	39
Geography and History (Geography, 20 ; History, 17) - - -	37
General (Calisthenics and Drill, 4 ; Music, 6 ; Hygiene and Temperance, 9 ; Moral and Patriotic Duties, 4) - - -	23
Total minutes, on average, each day - - -	284

In the high schools no time is given to some of these
elementary subjects, and in many rural schools high school
subjects absorb a portion of the teacher's time. All this time is
abstracted from the average which would be found by taking the
common school grades alone. And again, the great majority of
the schools are yet very far from having an ideal teacher who
can distribute his time in the most effective manner. It is
simply the facts which are given here, and they should be
supplemented by the following measure of the time absorbed in
certain numbers of the 2,346 school rooms above discussed, in
teaching the following high school subjects. The number of

school rooms and the average number of minutes spent per day correct to the nearest integer, are given here:—

In 200 schools practical mathematics absorb on an average 14 minutes daily; in 1,135 schools, Algebra, 15 minutes; in 909 schools, Geometry, 13 minutes: in 849 schools, Botany, etc., 7 minutes; in 172 schools, Physiology, 8 minutes; in 618 schools, Physics, 7 minutes: in 344 schools, Chemistry, 12 minutes: in 100 schools, Latin, 21 minutes; in 24 schools, Greek, 16 minutes; in 82 schools, French, 18 minutes: in 8 schools, German, 18 minutes: in 77 schools, Manual Training, 7 minutes.

While the time here has been reduced to a *daily* standard, it will not of course be assumed that each subject is taught every day. Most subjects are taught alternately but three or two days in the week, and some on one day only: while such a subject as Book-keeping may be taken up for a month or two only during the year. The reduction has been made to the daily average for the purpose of comparison. There are 18 county academies and perhaps as many more high schools. It will be seen, therefore, that there are quite a number of mixed common and high schools in the country, i.e., schools with a few pupils doing more or less high school work under the eye of the teacher of the miscellaneous school.

The numbers of pupils returned as studying in each grade during the years 1897 and 1898 are as follows:—

	1897.	1898.
Grade I. (and Kindergartens)	19,116	18,929
Grade II.	13,232	13,128
Grade III.	12,541	12,532
Grade IV.	13,007	13,275
Grade V.	11,136	11,007
Grade VI.	9,193	9,015
Grade VII.	9,305	9,344
Grade VIII.	7,064	6,850
Total in common school grades	94,594	94,080
Grade IX.		4,202	4,530
Grade X.		1,692	1,885
Grade XI.		590	608
Grade XII.		72	100
Total in high school grade	6,556	7,123
Total in public schools	101,150	101,203

The detailed course of study for fully graded schools, together with contracted forms for village and rural schools and a specimen time table for a miscellaneous school with one teacher, are given in Appendix B. The general principles governing them are indicated in the following comments introducing them:—

1. The public school course of study may be considered under its sub-divisions of the common and high school courses. They furnish a basis for the classification of pupils by the teachers, and

Public School Course of Study. Comments.

for the examination of schools by the inspectors, while they also secure a definite co-ordination of all the work attempted in the public schools of all grades, thus fostering the harmonious inter-action of all the educational forces of the province.

2. These courses are to be followed in all schools, particu-larly with reference to (1) the order of succession of the subjects, and (2) the simultaneity of their study. The fulness of detail with which they can be carrried out in each school must depend upon local conditions, such as the size of the school, the number of grades assigned to the teacher, etc. As suggestive to teachers with little experience, contracted forms of the detailed common school course for miscellaneous and partially graded schools are appended.

3. The public school course of study is the result of the obser-vation and experience of representative leading teachers of the province, under the suggestion of the experiments of other countries, and the criticism of our own teachers in provincial conventions assembled for many years in succession. A system developed in such a manner must necessarily in some points be a compromise, and presumably therefore at least a little behind what we might expect from the few most advanced teachers. But it is also very likely to be a better guide than the practice of a majority without any mutual consultation for improvement. The successive progression of studies is intended to be adapted to the order of development of the powers of the child's mind, while their simultaneous progression is designed to prevent monotony and one-sidedness, and to produce a harmonious and healthy development of the physical, mental, and moral powers of the pupil. The apparent multiplicity of the subjects is due to their sub-division for the purpose of emphasizing leading features of the main subjects which might otherwise be overlooked by inexperienced teachers. The courses have been demonstrated to be adapted to the average pupil under a teacher of average skill. The teacher is, however, cautioned to take special care that pupils prematurely promoted or in feeble health should not run any risk of "over pressure" in attempting to follow the average class work.

Changes in these courses of study must always be expected from year to year, but to a very small extent it is hoped, except in the prescription of certain texts in the high school course. These will be published from time to time in the organ of the Department, the JOURNAL OF EDUCATION, published in April and October of each year.

Text Books.   In performing the duty of selecting and prescribing text books for the public schools, the Council of Public Instruc-tion has availed itself as fully as possible of the knowledge and experience of those who are engaged in the practical work of education. The sole aim of recent modifications has been to secure, at reasonable cost, a series of texts *adapted for use in schools.* Change in authorized books is *in itself* a very unde-sirable thing.

The prescribing of new books is one of such importance to the country that the most extraordinary care has to be taken to make sure that the ultimate advantages of a change will more than compensate the people for the temporary loss or annoyance always involved in making a change. But change there must be. It is the essential condition of all growth; and we ought under such circumstances to be always prepared for it.

Inspectors and teachers are reminded—

1. That the course of study for common schools encourages an economical expenditure for text-books by providing a system of oral instruction for junior classes. Too many teachers try to satisfy themselves in respect to their more youthful pupils by placing in their hands text-books not needed in any case, and worse than useless when unaccompanied by proper oral exposition. A text-book should not be required for a child until he is prepared to use it intelligently.

2. That the regulation which makes it illegal and improper for a teacher to introduce unauthorised texts, by no means hinders him from giving his pupils the benefit of other treatises to whose explanations he may attach importance. The progressive teacher will always have such aids within reach, and will so use them as to impart variety and interest to his instructions.

The subjects named on the course of study are either " impera- *Optional* tive " or " optional." The optional need not be provided for by *Subjects.* the Boards of Trustees if they so determine, and if provision is made for them the pupil is not compelled to take the subject. The imperative subjects must be provided for in every school according to its grade, and as a rule all pupils are required to take them in their regular course.

In the high schools, for instance, all foreign languages are optional. But all the more clever students are encouraged to take one or two if not more of these, the points made enhancing their standing in the obtaining of " pass " certificates.

In the common schools " manual training " is optional, as it *Manual* also is in the high school. Needle-work for the girls is very *Training.* common in the more progressive portions of the country. And in the city of Halifax a course in cookery is provided for the girls of grades VII. and VIII. A course in woodwork is also provided for the boys of grade VIII. and the high schools in Halifax. In a few of the other towns beginnings have been made in the same direction, iron work being provided for in a private school at Wolfville in addition to woodwork. Boards of trustees are encouraged to develop such extensions in connection with the public schools in the larger towns more especially ; and all teachers are required to take a course in woodwork in the Provincial Normal School. Practical work in chemistry and physics are insisted upon in all schools, and students are stimulated to make as much of their own apparatus as may be possible in any given locality.

Although religion is not even mentioned as an optional sub- *Religion.* ject, it will have been noticed that instruction in moral and patriotic duties is imperative in every school either in regular

order or in connection with history and incidents in the daily
school life, and anniversary days. It is also the duty of the
teacher "to inculcate by precept and example respect for
religion and Christian morality." But Regulation I. of
the Council of Public Instruction (see Appendix A.), acknow-
ledges the existence of old customs in connection with many
of the schools with which it does not mean to interfere
beyond the protection of persons who object in writing to
"devotional exercises," from being compelled to take part in
them or be present at them. In other words, the regulation
allows "devotional exercises" to be conducted in any school
so long as no "parent or guardian" objects thereto "in writing."
If the objection be made, the exercises may be held within
regular school hours if so modified as to give no offence to anyone.
But if no such modification can be made, the exercise may be
held immediately before the opening of the secular work of the
school or after its close. The trustees are assumed to understand the local conditions of their section, and have, therefore,
very large powers for regulating such exercises where people
desire to have them in the public school, but limited first by the
provision that no one shall be compelled to be present at devotional exercises formally objected to, and second by the condition that they shall not encroach excessively on the regular and
imperative work of the school.

The trustees of public schools may rent the schoolrooms of
denominational schools, appoint teachers nominated by the
owners of such rooms, provided that the teachers hold provincial
licences to teach, and otherwise control the school in strict
accordance with the law. Such schools having the regularly
licensed teachers, the regularly prescribed school books, the
public school register to keep, the same form of return to make
out and attest, the same inspectors as the other schools, are in
every respect public schools, and are therefore as eligible for the
public grants as if the buildings were erected by the board of
trustees itself. When it does not interfere with the proper
grading, the Council of Public Instruction permits trustees in
some cases to provide separate rooms for boys and girls,
although coeducation is not only the rule in rural sections but
in the academies and the other high schools.

In the City of Halifax the Roman Catholic members of the
Board of School Commissioners are accustomed to nominate
teachers to the schools belonging originally to the ecclesiastical
corporation, although the appointments are always made by the
full Board.

Public Grants for Denominational Schools. In a few of the towns a small proportion of the children were
withdrawn from the public schools to form convent schools. In
most of these at date, the parties responsible for this schism
acted with so much tact as eventually to see elected to the town
councils and school boards in their localities those who affiliated
the "separate schools" as above indicated to the public schools
of the section. The fact that such schools thus win recognition
from the local educational authorities in whose section they

originate, is a very high premium on their peaceful evolution.
For the trustees are as free to change their policy when they
consider it advantageous to the section, as they were formerly to
make their policy. The fact that a school also performs other
functions useful to all or a portion of a community does not
disqualify it under these circumstances from participation in the
public grants, if it is in every respect a public school under the
control of the legal trustees of the section. This explains why the
two Roman Catholic Colleges of the Province, St. Francis Xavier
(English) and Sainte Anne (French), and most of the convents
are affiliated with the public school system. In fact, no
corresponding institutions of any other of the religious denominations are thus affiliated, although the law leaves it as open to
the one as to the other.

Although the Roman Catholic denomination is thus the
only one to develop affiliation of this kind with the public
schools, it must be remembered that the law makes no
concession in favour of one denomination more than another.
For any other body, philosophic coterie or business corporation has the same privilege of impressing and con-
vincing the local school authorities. Neither the statutes nor
the regulations, nor the statistical forms contain a single reference
to any religious sect or feature, excepting that injunction of the
statutes requiring the teacher to inculcate by precept and example
a respect for religion and Christian morality. The moral and
patriotic training, with practical and objective methods in developing good character in the school children, combined with
such dogmatic instruction as may be given under the direction
of the clergy and others specially qualified in connection with the
several church organisations, appear to produce at least as good
results as the formal teaching of religion in the schools of many
other countries.

A provincial syllabus for third, second, first, and county Licensing
academy headmaster's classes of licence was one of the features and Appoint-
of the Act of 1864. At first the examinations were held by the Teachers.
different boards of examiners appointed by the various boards of
district school commissioners, then in 1867 by one provincial
board. In 1893 this examination was changed into the provincial
high school examination, a certificate of which is the basis of the
scholarship of the candidate for licence. To this qualification
he must add that of professional qualification, which may be of
the normal order or minimum order. The first is graduation
from the normal school of the rank corresponding to the grade of
scholarship, which, with evidence of the prescribed age and
character, will entitle the candidate to receive the class of licence
corresponding to the grade of his high school certificate. The
minimum professional qualification examination is the continuation of the old professional papers of the original "teachers'
examination" on "teaching" and "school management," to which
have been added "hygiene and temperance." This M.P.Q (minimum professional qualification) examination does not require
attendance at the normal school, and everything else being

equal qualifies for a licence one degree lower than the corresponding grade of scholarship. Graduation from the normal school will enable a candidate to advance one degree beyond the licence held on entering if his work is approved. The advancing of his general scholarship by attendance at a high school for a year might enable him to make the same advance without attending the normal school, while it would be also advancing him towards some of the other professions for which, in this province, that of teaching is still too often a stepping stone. But the present law takes away to some extent the actual discrimination against the normal school up to the year 1893. Since that date the number of normal school trained teachers employed in the schools out of the 2,500 of all combined has risen from 400 to 800. In 1898 there were 30 per cent. of trained teachers to 70 per cent. of untrained, examination-selected teachers. But the Council of Public Instruction, the Government, cannot yet venture to make normal school training compulsory on all, for the teaching profession has for so long been recognised as the general avenue into the learned professions. The regulations under which the licences are granted are given in Appendix F.

These are determined by the boards of trustees or commissioners of each school section, who advertise for and engage their own teachers. Such teachers must hold a licence of some class, and the provincial grant payable to each different class is known to the trustees, who as a rule find it to their advantage to obtain a teacher of as high a class as possible, not only on account of the more advanced scholarship alone, but on account of the larger grant paid to him. Without a licence the teacher would be simply a private teacher, and the school a private

Few Private Elementary Schools.

school unrecognised by the Education Department. Of such elementary schools there are now scarcely one dozen in the whole province, and such as are to be found are small and exist for some special reason.

The Sex of Teachers.

Sixty years ago, on the 22nd of March, 1838, the Report of the Committee on Education of the House of Assembly was presented to the Parliament. It expresses itself strongly in favour of a uniform provincial system of education, and of compulsory assessment. The following two paragraphs are quoted to throw a light on the state of public education and sentiment at that time.

"With these views the Committee decided to state the difficulties which pressed upon them frankly to the House, leaving it to a majority to decide either for or against assessment for the ensuing year. If they decided in favour, then, taking our population at 180,000, and assuming that the children of a school-going age, either between five and twelve, or seven and fourteen, amount to 26,000, we would require 886 teachers to educate the whole. To sustain these would require a very large sum, and deducting the amount now paid from the provincial fund, and all that is voluntarily contributed for the support of common schools, the amount to be raised would be so considerable that public opinion should be fully prepared for its imposition before such a law was passed."

"Should it be determined to continue the present law, the Committee recommend that an addition of £100 be added to the

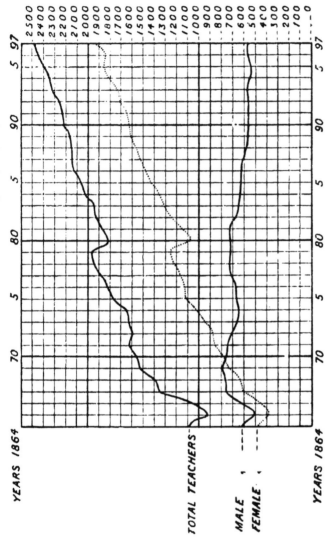

Public School Teachers, Nova Scotia, 1864 to 1897.

YEARS 1864

TOTAL TEACHERS

MALE

FEMALE

YEARS 1864

amount now granted under it ; that a new and a more equitable distribution of the whole sum be made, and that such improvements be carried out in the details as will make it more efficient. Among these the Committee recommend the introduction of itinerating schoolmasters in scattered settlements : *and the admission of female teachers, who are often the most valuable that can be obtained, to some participation in the benefits of the law."*

The following table will show at a glance the rapid increase of female teachers from the year 1864 to 1898 :—

Year.	Male.	Female.	Total.
1864	615	478	1,093
1865	520	397	917
1866	618	442	1,060
1867	761	599	1,360
1868	763	627	1,390
1869	798	717	1,515
1870	767	798	1,565
1871	754	866	1,620
1872	704	889	1,593
1873	665	959	1,624
1874	647	1,010	1,657
1875	672	1,103	1,775
1876	687	1,124	1,811
1877	717	1,171	1,888
1878	740	1,214	1,954
1879	735	1,251	1,986
1880	720	1,089	1,809
1881	724	1,157	1,881
1882	677	1,256	1,933
1883	656	1,305	1,961
1884	635	1,379	2,014
1885	631	1,424	2,055
1886	627	1,484	2,111
1887	605	1,539	2,144
1888	586	1,568	2,154
1889	577	1,605	2,182
1890	580	1,635	2,215
1891	574	1,656	2,230
1892	565	1,703	2,268
1893	582	1,737	2,319
1894	541	1,810	2,351
1895	540	1,859	2,399
1896	582	1,856	2,438
1897	576	1,909	2,485
1898	614	1,896	

The amount of salary is determined by each board of school
trustees. The provincial regulations merely fix the grant payable to each class of teachers. In the City of Halifax Class B
female teachers generally start with $300 a year, and Class C
with $250, the salary rising annually in case of success by the
amount of $30 until $450 is attained. The principal's salary
may go up to $500 as a rule, and higher in the case of a
specially valuable teacher. Class C male teachers start at $700
and if principals at $800, which may gradually rise to $1,000.
The following table shows the maximum salaries given in the
province, the average salaries in the most progressive county, the
average salaries in the least wealthy county, and the average of
the eighteen county averages which may be called the provincial
average :—

SALARIES, 1897.

—	A (M.)	A (F.)	B (M)	B (F.)	C (M.)	C (F.)	D (M.)	D (F.)
	$	$	$	$	$	$	$	$
Maximum salaries	1,000	800	900	750	830	600	350	300
Highest county average	1,194	800	816	392	322	272	232	180
Lowest county average	617	442	259	254	194	174	133	123
Provincial average	836	651	401	303	284	228	184	162

Average Salaries, 1898 -   -   - A (male), $841.03
           „   „   -   - A (female), 552.86
                              -     - B (male),   400.09
                              -     - B (female), 291.20
                              -     - C (male),   286.77
                              -     - C (female), 225.76
                              -     - D (male),   178.98
                              -     - D (female), 164·21

Class A (male), 53, 58; Class A (female), 8, 12; Class B (male),
141, 150; Class B (female), 225, 250: Class C (male), 186, 194;
Class C (female), 838, 795: Class D (male), 196, 212: Class D
(female), 838, 839. Totals, 2,485, 2,510.

From these figures it can be readily inferred that the teaching
profession in Nova Scotia is still largely in the hands of those who
are making it a stepping-stone to some other profession, for the
average salaries are not at all comparable with those of the
ordinary life professions. The lower class teachers may be
looked upon, however, as to a certain extent qualifying for
higher classes and the better schools. But, as the following table
shows, the higher class teachers and the best positions are not
at all so numerous as the others.

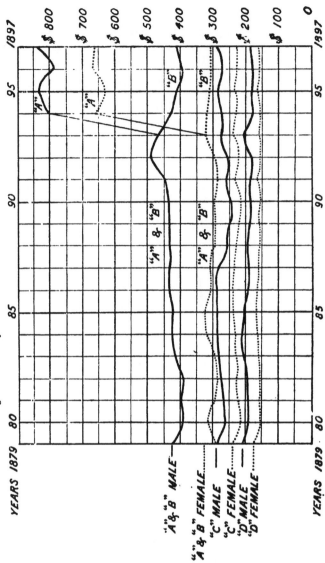

Average Salaries of Public School Teachers, Nova Scotia.

YEARS 1879   80   85   90   95   1897

$ 800
$ 700
$ 600
$ 500
$ 400
$ 300
$ 200
$ 100
O

"A"
"A"
"B"
"B"
"A" & "B"
"A" & "B"

"A" & "B" MALE
"A" & "B" FEMALE
"C" MALE
"C" FEMALE
"D" MALE
"D" FEMALE

The following table shows that the provincial averages oi salaries for each class for the last nineteen years have not fluctuated in any extraordinary manner.

PROVINCIAL AVERAGES OF SALARIES, NOVA SCOTIA, FROM 1879 TO 1898.

YEAR.	A. and B. (M.)	A. and B. (F.)	C. (M.)	C. (F.)	D. (M.)	D. (F.)
	Dols.	Dols.	Dols.	Dols.	Dols.	Dols.
1879	425	293	290	232	204	174
1880	393	.319	262	218	194	157
1881	397	294	207	224	193	160
1882	389	289	272	226	198	159
1883	409	298	279	231	206	165
1884	423	311	287	236	212	169
1885	422	312	287	237	205	170
1886	439	304	288	237	199	170
1887	438	305	274	231	183	162
1888	438	298	254	228	190	161
1889	438	297	250	223	182	161
1890	440	299	249	221	182	158
1891	449	286	261	233	186	164
1892	489	296	255	224	180	158
*1893	348	240	205	178	152	122

	A. (M.)	B. (M.)	A. (F.)	B. (F.)			
	Dols.	Dols.	Dols.	Dols.			
1894	602	438	653	319	276	228	181	157
1895	838	419	534	310	288	232	182	163
1896	789	398	622	302	275	227	182	161
1897	836	406	651	303	284	228	184	162
1898	841	409	553	291	287	226	179	164

* Three-quarter year.

The salaries of the higher classes tend to rise, those of the lower classes to fall. This indicates the gradual increase of those making teaching a life profession, and a lower appreciation of the merits of those having the lowest qualifications, although these qualifications have been advanced all round by at least the equivalent of one year more of study since the nomenclature of the classes was adopted.

There is no general system of apprenticeship, except in the city schools to a very limited extent. In the Normal School there are practice lessons in the Model Schools under the criticism of fellow students and one of the Faculty.

No system of pensions for teachers has yet been devised to be satisfactory at the same time to the majority of the teachers and the Legislature. In fact, no plan has had sufficient backing to bring it before the Legislature.

Attendance.   Over 98 per cent. of all elementary and secondary education of the province is conducted under the Public School Laws, perhaps 99 per cent., as a large portion of those enrolled in private schools are studying special subjects, such as commercial or art branches. The 101,203 enrolled during the year 1897–8 made an average daily attendance for the full year of only 57,771. The number between the ages of five and fifteen who were reported as not having attended school at all during the year 1896–7 was 6,102.

Small Proportion of Education Private.

Compulsory Attendance.   A general compulsory attendance law is in existence requiring every school section in the province to vote yea or nay on the adoption of the law at every annual meeting, until it is once adopted, when it remains permanently in force. The trustees are then able to notify this fact to all parents and guardians whose children between the ages of seven and twelve are not likely to make the required minimum attendance of 120 days in the year. At the end of the year a fine of two dollars can be imposed on the parent or guardian for each child absent the whole year, and *pro ratu* in the case of each who has not made an attendance of 120 days. Exemptions are allowed if education is being given otherwise or elsewhere, and for other special reasons. But, although many sections have adopted the law, the trustees are very averse to the execution of it. The fact is, that after several years' experience of the law it is found to be practically inoperative in rural sections. A modification of the general law called the " Town's Compulsory Attendance Act " is being administered with good effect at times in the city of Halifax and a few of the towns, the thoroughness of the administration depending on the administrators for the time being.

High School Classes carry forward Primary Education.   The public school course of study is very definitely organised, having eight (annual) grades in the " common " school (where possible, with a preliminary year of Kindergarten for pupils under five years of age) and four grades in the " high " school, making altogether a twelve year course, free to all who are able and willing to take advantage of the same.   In the high school grades ancient and modern languages are optional subjects to the student : while drawing, book-keeping, geography, and the elements of the natural sciences are imperative up to the end of the eleventh year. The completion of the work of each year of the high school course in a satisfactory manner as demonstrated by the annual terminal provincial examinations is recognised by the award of a certificate containing on its margin the percentage marks given by the board of provincial examiners on each subject : thus, even should the certificate be not a " pass " from one grade to another, it may still serve the purpose of exempting the holder from the passing of the examination upon particular subjects in the matriculation of students into the various colleges, etc. In other words, the high school system is a sort of provincial university, under which all the high schools and academies are federated. All this has already been pointed out in more detail.

Every "common" school in the country as well as in the towns is allowed to carry on high school classes to any extent compatible with the interests of the community in the judgment of the trustees. All such classes are as free as those of the most elementary department. Trustees can also open "Evening Schools" under the same conditions as day schools, each two and a half hours session counting as half a day of "day school" in the drawing of public grants.

There is therefore no necessity for any special arrangements for "Continuation Schools," for where there is population sufficient the whole range of elementary and secondary grades is open free to those who have the scholarship qualifications to enter the grade desired.

III. Technical, Commercial, and Agricultural Instruction.

For some time there has been a growing impression that the courses of study were tending to stimulate the youth of the country more propor iona ely to the literary and learned professions, in which onlyt some 6,000 out of 160,000 are employed, than towards the industrial occupations in which the masses are engaged. As the sentiments-determining the occupations of the future citizens are generally called into existence during the period of common school life, it was deemed advisable to so modify the old literary courses from the kindergarten up to the high school as to develop *pari passu* industrial and patriotic sentiments and the sense of the dignity and pleasure of intelligent and skilled labour. This is now attempted to be done by "nature study," etc., the accurate observation and correlation of all the common phenomena, natural and artificial, in each locality, leading up to the character and functions of our national institutions and the glorious inheritance of our best traditions.

I.—In the Regular Public Schools.

Since 1893 the Provincial Normal School (annual cost $9,175) admits as candidates for the professional qualification of teachers only such as have already passed the required standard of scholarship at the provincial high school examinations. Pedagogy, the practice and theory of education, etc., as in normal schools generally, are important subjects in this institution, in addition to the general polishing of work already more or less completed in the high school, and "practice" teaching in the Model schools, special stress is now laid upon the further development of the practice and teaching of modelling in clay, freehand and mathematical drawing, woodwork and the use of tools generally, practical demonstrations in physics, chemistry, botany, geology, entomology and general biology, in agriculture, horticulture, dairying, etc. Manual subjects, such as cookery, can be introduced into any school at the option of the boards of trustees of the school section. The Provincial Normal School at Truro is affiliated to the provincial School of Agriculture about a mile distant, and all candidates for a diploma are required to take one or more subjects according to the class in which they have entered, so that they may be prepared to give successful object lessons adapted to the industries of the school sections in which they may some time be engaged. The teacher is expected to be able to develop in pupils, from the lowest grade upwards, the habit of accurate observation and the study of all common phenomena and objects, with the action and inter-action of law natural, social, and civil, so far as exemplified in the local environment. This habit, it is hoped, may make the work of the common schools more valuable as a general foundation for all professional and even literary careers, as well as for the varied and increasingly complex industrial conditions of our times. While an interest and an intelligent pleasure may in many cases be thus created in occupations otherwise uninviting or repellent, the scientific principles conditioning their most successful exploitation are simultaneously revealed. These object lessons of the common school are carried on in a more specialized form in the several grades of the high school.

II.—In the Special Public Schools. Manual Training.

Affiliated to the public school system or otherwise aided by public grants are the following institutions of secondary rank which do work in general technical education.

1. The Manual Training Department of the Provincial Normal School at Truro was established as at present in 1893. The attendance in 1898 was 152 There is also a manual training department in woodwork, opened in Halifax in 1891, free to selected classes from the highest grade of the common schools and the lower grades of the high schools. In Wolfville, established shortly after this Halifax school, there is the best equipped school of the kind in the province, including in its course ironwork as well as woodwork. It can be utilised by the public schools of the town and by Acadia College in its vicinity, but it receives no provincial or civic grant, and is supported by fees in addition to the original private foundation bequeathed to the trustees.

School of Agriculture.

2. The Provincial School of Agriculture at Truro, established in 1885, has now two instructors, in addition to the manager of the farm. The attendance in 1897 was 70 for full and special courses, besides the 152 students taking the normal school special courses. The school has conveniences for the practical study, free, of all branches of agriculture, horticulture, and dairying. The school building proper is fitted up with qualitative and quantitative chemical laboratories, a dissecting room biological laboratory and apparatus, with a general and technical library.

Under the annual inspection of the principal of the school there are eight local agricultural schools in the charge of graduates who also conduct, in affiliation with the agricultural work, the ordinary public school of the section.

Horticulture.

3. The Provincial School of Horticulture at Wolfville, was established in 1893, by the Fruit-Growers' Association, with the aid of an annual grant of $2,000 from the Provincial Government. The enrolment in 1898 was sixty-one.

4. The Mining Schools were established within the last four Mining or five years. They are carried on under the direction of the Schools. Inspector of Mines. By the Mines Regulation Act, all managers, underground managers, and overmen are required to hold certificates of competency gained by examination. These examinations are conducted in writing by a Board representing equally the mining profession, the employers, and the employees. Instructors are appointed at the principal mining centres, and are charged with the preparation of candidates for the examination. The courses extend over the winter months, and the instructors are paid according to results. The candidates for certificates as managers have no special instructors, they being usually men already holding underground managers' certificates, and having at their disposal one or more instructors capable of imparting the additional information distinguishing managers from the lower grades. A large number of men have successfully passed these examinations, and now fill the positions of trust about our coal mines. In 1897 forty certificates were issued to managers, underground managers, and overmen. A similar system of examination and instruction is pursued in the case of men employed about machinery used for raising and lowering persons in mines. There are three classes of these certificates, and altogether there were twelve granted during 1897.

5. The Victoria School of Art and Design was established in School of Art Halifax in the year 1887, in commemoration of the fiftieth anni- and Design. versary of the accession of Her Majesty Queen Victoria. It is subsidized annually by grants from the Province and the City. There is a staff of four instructors, and the attendance of students for 1897 was classified as follows:—Freehand and Object Drawing, 31; Painting and Life class, 23; Senior Mechanics, 10; Junior Mechanics, 23; Architecture, 12; Children's class, 6; Deaf and Dumb, 22. Total, 127. It must be remembered in noting the number of students in this institution that many of the subjects taught here are also taught in their elementary stages in the public schools and in the ladies' colleges and convents. As more progress is made the character of this institution will further improve, confining its attention to the higher art and design education—which it already successfully affects.

6. A school of cookery has been opened in the City of Cookery. Halifax as part of the public school system. The members of the local branch of the Women's National Council very materially assisted in creating a sentiment in favour of the fuller development of the principles underlying the domestic sciences in the public schools. The School of Cookery was opened by them under the approval of the Education Department before the City Board of School Commissioners was ready to make it an integral part of their school system. It is now wholly supported and managed by the Board, and is open free as an alternative course in manual training for pupils of Grade VIII.

There are three ladies' colleges and two conventual colleges III.—In the which give attention to the development of art and some of the Private practical applications of science to the domestic and technical Secondary Schools.

z 2

arts. There are two small navigation schools, but the mathematical principles of navigation are imperative on all public school candidates for the Grade XI. " pass." There are at least two institutions which give special attention to commercial subjects, but in the Grades IX. and X. of the public schools the principles of book-keeping by single and double entry respectively are imperative. The Business College at Truro reported 87 different students during 1897, and the Commercial College at Halifax as many as 361. Much of the work of these institutions is more or less elementary, so that their statistics should not be taken to mean so much pure secondary education. They will be found summed up in Table B. at the end of Section I. of this report.

IV.—In the Universities. As can be inferred from Table A. (Section I. of this report) the University of Dalhousie provides for a very considerable range of technical instruction. The other colleges incidentally or directly include in their curricula subjects of technical value. It must be remembered here that Nova Scotia is not dependent on its own institutions for the various technical avocations followed in the province; and the large number of those who go abroad for such instruction contributes very materially to the deliberate development of the institutions at home.

IV. PUBLIC REFORMATORIES, INDUSTRIAL OR PARENTAL SCHOOLS.

Reformatories and Industrial Schools. Public reformatories, industrial or parental schools are required in order to complete a compulsory system satisfactorily. In the city of Halifax there are two quasi-public industrial schools, to which truants from the city are being sentenced, but the schools are for the city itself rather than for the province. While there has been a movement made in the direction of agitating for the erection of provincial parental schools for truants and incorrigibles, it has not yet acquired force enough to move the Government.

Free Meals. Except in the city of Halifax, there appears to be no occasion for the providing of needy scholars with free meals. The few cases occurring in the city have been attended to by charitable persons, aided by some members of the Board of School Commissioners. With the increase of population and " bad times," it may become necessary to make arrangements for the systematic aid of the needy in this matter.

V. SCHOOLS FOR THE BLIND AND THE DEAF AND DUMB.

Schools for the Blind and Deaf and Dumb. The blind and the deaf and dumb are educated at the public expense in two very well-equipped and well-officered institutions in Halifax. The Halifax School for the Blind furnishes accommodations also for the blind of the Atlantic provinces of Canada and Newfoundland; the Deaf and Dumb Institution for the same, except the province of New Brunswick, which has a small institution of its own. In the former there were in 1898 eighty-eight blind from the province of Nova Scotia, for whose education the Government grants were $4,500, in addition to the endowment of the school. In the latter for the same time eighty-nine deaf and dumb from the province, for whom the provincial grant was $5,737, in addition to proceeds of the endowments.

A. H. MacKay,

April, 1898. *Superintendent of Education.*

NOTE.—Recent Reports of the Superintendent of Education on the Public Schools of Nova Scotia and other documents relating to Education in Nova Scotia can be seen at the Board of Education Library, St. Stephen's House, Cannon Row, Whitehall, London, S.W.

SUPPLEMENTARY NOTE.

The following information is taken from " Papers relating to University Education of Roman Catholics in certain Colonies." (Colonial Office Return, 1900. Cd. 115.)

There are in Nova Scotia at the present time two Catholic Universities, called respectively St. Francis Xavier's in the County of Antigonish, and St. Anne's in the County of Digby.

The revenue derived from the endowments, fees, etc., of the University of St. Francis Xavier's College is in the vicinity of $12,000. The number of students attending the session in the summer of 1898 was 101; the Catholic population, according to the census of 1891, in the whole Province of Nova Scotia was 122,452. . . The Bishop of Antigonish is Chairman (*ex officio*) of the Board of Governors.

St. Anne's University was founded in 1890. On 30th April, 1892, in virtue of an Act passed by the Provincial Parliament of Nova Scotia, the College was incorporated and chartered " as a University with all and every the usual privileges of such an institution"; and the Directors of said Corporation then or hereafter appointed were entrusted with the power and privilege of conferring the degrees of Bachelor, Master, and Doctor in the several Arts and Faculties, and of making such bye-laws and regulations as they may deem necessary to govern the granting of such degrees, and determining the scholastic requirements therefor.

The University of St. Anne receives an annual grant from the Local Government of $1,600, as the institution acts in the capacity of a County Academy. The University was destroyed by fire in 1898, but a new building, larger and more commodious, is now almost completed.* The number of students attending, previous to its destruction by fire, was 107, and, as before mentioned, the total Catholic population, according to the last census taken, was 122,452. The Archbishop of Halifax is (*ex officio*) Chairman of the Board of Governors.

---

* Since the above was published the building has been completed.

APPENDIX A.

REGULATION OF THE COUNCIL OF PUBLIC INSTRUCTION REFERRING TO DEVOTIONAL EXERCISES.

TRUSTEES.

A relation being established between the trustees and the teacher, it becomes the duty of the former, on behalf of the people, to see that the scholars are making sure progress ; that there is life in the school, both intellectual and moral—in short, that the great ends sought by the education of the young are being realised in the section over which they preside. All may not be able to form a nice judgment upon its intellectual aspect, but none can fail to estimate correctly its social and moral tone. While the law does not sanction the teaching in our public schools of the peculiar views which characterise the different denominations of Christians, it does instruct the teacher "to inculcate by precept and example a respect for religion and the principles of Christian morality." To the trustees the people must look to see their desires in this respect, so far as is consonant with the spirit of the law, carried into effect by *the teacher*.

REG. I. *Whereas*, It has been represented to the Council that trustees of public schools have, in certain cases, required pupils, on pain of forfeiting school privileges, to be present during devotional exercises not approved of by their parents ; *And whereas*, Such proceeding is contrary to the principles of the school law, the following regulation is made for the direction of trustees, the better to ensure carrying out of the spirit of the law in this behalf :—

Ordered, That in case where the parents or guardians of children in actual attendance on any public school or department signify in writing to the trustees their conscientious objection to any portion of such devotional exercises as may be conducted therein under the sanction of the trustees, such devotional exercises shall either be so modified as not to offend the religious feelings of those so objecting, or shall be held immediately before the time fixed for opening, or after the time fixed for the close of the daily work of the school ; and no children, whose parents or guardians signify conscientious objections thereto, shall be required to be present during such devotional exercises.

APPENDIX B.

THE PUBLIC SCHOOL COURSE OF STUDY AS PRESCRIBED IN 1898.

COMMENTS.

1. The public school course of study may be considered under its subdivisions of the common and high school courses. They furnish a basis for the classification of pupils by the teachers and for the examination of schools by the inspectors, while they also secure a definite co-ordination of all the work attempted in the public schools of all grades, thus fostering the harmonious interaction of all the educational forces of the Province.

2 These courses are to be followed in all schools, particularly with reference to (1) the order of succession of the subjects, and (2) the simultaneity of their study. The fulness of detail with which they can be carried out in each school must depend upon local conditions, such as the size of the school, the number of grades assigned to the teacher, etc. As suggestive to

teachers with little experience, contracted forms of the detailed common school course for miscellaneous and partially graded schools are appended.

3. The public school course of study is the result of the observation and experience of representative leading teachers of the province, under the suggestion of the experiments of other countries, and the criticism of our our teachers in provincial conventions assembled for many years in succession. A system developed in such a manner must necessarily in some points be a compromise, and presumably therefore at least a little behind what we might expect from the few most advanced teachers. But it is also very likely to be a better guide than the practice of a majority without any mutual consultation for improvement. The successive progression of studies is intended to be adapted to the order of development of the powers of the child's mind, while their simultaneous progression is designed to prevent monotony and onesidedness, and to produce a harmonious and healthy development of the physical, mental, and moral powers of the pupil. The apparent multiplicity of the subjects is due to their subdivision for the purpose of emphasizing leading features of the main subjects which might otherwise be overlooked by inexperienced teachers. The courses have been demonstrated to be adapted to the average pupil under a teacher of average skill. The teacher is, however, cautioned to take special care that pupils prematurely promoted or in feeble health should not run any risk of "over-pressure" in attempting to follow the average class-work.

Changes in these courses of study must always be expected from year to year, but to a very small extent it is hoped, except in the prescription of certain texts in the high school course. These will be published from time to time in the organ of the Department, the JOURNAL OF EDUCATION, published in April and October in each year.

GENERAL DIRECTIONS.

(FOR ALL PUBLIC SCHOOLS.)

(The paragraph numbers below refer to corresponding columns in the statistical tables of the Register.)

65. *Calisthenics and Military Drill.*—As often as found convenient ; but "physical exercises" should be given once in the middle of every session over one hour in length, and in the lower grades more frequently than in the higher. Correct position, etc., in sitting, standing, and walking, polite behaviour, and good manners generally, are most important, and should in every school be made habitual to each pupil. The more useful words of command and corresponding movements of "military drill" should be thoroughly known in all schools.

66. *Vocal Music.*—All pupils (excepting of course those known to be organically defective as regards music) should be able to pass an examination in vocal music before promotion to a higher grade. For the present the following minimum is prescribed for each grade. At least one simple song with its tonic sol-fa notation for Grade I· An additional melody and its notation for each succeeding Grade, with a correspondingly increased general knowledge of music. Vocal music may be combined with some forms of "physical exercise," as marching and light movements. Recommended, "National and Vacation Songs" for Common and High Schools. Teachers musically defective may comply with the law by having these lessons given by any one qualified.

67. *Hygiene and Temperance.*—Orally in all grades, and as incidents or occasions may suggest. Text books for pupils' use as follows : Grades V. and VI., Health Reader No. 1 ; Grades VII. and VIII., Health Reader No. 2.

68. *Moral and Patriotic Duties.*—As enjoined by the School Law and when found most convenient and effective. Some lessons in reader, in history, in biography, etc., as well as public anniversary days may be utilised incidentally.

69. *Lessons on Nature.*—The noting, examination, and study of the common and more important natural objects and laws of nature, as they are exemplified within the range of the school section or of the pupils' observations. Under this head pupils should not be required to memorise notes or facts which they have not at least to some extent actually observed or verified for themselves. Brittain's "Nature Lessons," and Payne's "Nature Study" (U.S.A.), or Garlick and Dexter's "Object Lessons for Standards I., II., and III." (England), are useful guides to the teacher for portions of the work prescribed in some of the grades. There should be a short "Nature Lesson" given every day, as often as possible on the daily collections and observations of the pupils themselves instead of those of the teacher—the lesson always to be based on the objects or observations. These guide books are to be used only to show the teacher how to give such lessons ; and they are entirely prohibited as text books for either pupil or teacher, for under no circumstances should " notes " from the books be given to pupils. All such studies must be from the objects. Observations under this head form some of the best subjects for English Composition Exercises in all the grades.

70. *Spelling and Dictation.*—It should be strictly insisted upon that, from the very commencement in the first grade, the pupil should spell every word read in the lessons, and common words of similar difficulty used in his conversation. Writing words in the lower grades. Transcription and dictation in the higher grades should be utilised more and more as facility in writing increases.

71. *Reading and Elocution.*—Pupils must be enabled to clearly understand the portion to be read, then to read it with proper expression. 2. Faults of enunciation, pronunciation, etc., of tone, of posture, and manner, etc., must be carefully noted and corrected. 3. Choice passages should be memorised occasionally for recitation with the proper expression. Ten lines per year at least for Grade I., twenty lines at least for Grade II., and a similar increase for each succeeding grade is prescribed. In the High School Grades the memorising and effective recitation of choice extracts in every language studied, is also imperative on each pupil. Reading should be taught at first, partly at least, by word building from the phonic elements, occasional drills of this kind being continued in all the grades to obtain clear enunciation.

72. *English.*—In all grades practice should constantly be given in expressing the substance of stories, lessons, or observations orally in correct language, and in the higher grades in writing also. Discussion of subject matter of lesson. Attention to the use of capitals, punctuation marks, paragraphing, etc., should be introduced gradually and regularly, so that at the end of the common school course, language in correct form can be fluently used in description or business letters, orally and in writing. The practical rather than the theoretical knowledge of English is what is specially required in the common school, and a large portion of the school time should be given to it. Pupils should be continually exercised in finding synonyms or substituting "their own made meanings" for difficult words in their reading lessons, instead of merely memorising definitions often given at head of lesson.

73. *Writing.*—Styles most easy to read should be cultivated. Simple vertical writing is generally preferable to the sloping styles. No exercise in writing should be accepted by the teacher from the pupil unless its form shows evidence of care. Should begin in the first grade with letters formed from the simple elements properly classified, and should be taught in the order of difficulty.

77. *Drawing.*—Thompson's "Manual Training, No. 1," is recommended to the teacher as covering to some extent the *Drawings and Lessons* on *Nature* as they may be taught to pupils of the first five grades, and No. 2, the next five grades ; or McFaul's "Public School Drawing Manual" (Canada Pub. Co., Toronto), as covering generally the work of the Common and High Schools. Drawing of objects studied under the head of Nature Lessons to be constantly practised, and carried on even in the High School.

78. *Arithmetic.*—It is of the highest importance to secure the habit of obtaining accurate answers at the first attempt. Every slip in mental or written arithmetical work is not only unnecessary, but is a positive education in a habit which will tend to render useless the most strenuous efforts afterwards to become accurate or even to make satisfactory progress in mathematics. Accuracy is of supreme importance from the first. Rapidity should follow as the secondary consideration. Appropriate exercises in Mental Arithmetic should be given in every grade, and proficiency in it should be required in all promotions.

75 and 76. *Geography and History.* The verbal memorising of these lessons at home by the pupil is for the most part injurious to the character of the memory, and useless as practical knowledge. For, in spite of all cautions and instructions to the contrary, most pupils, when left to themselves, mentally associate the facts memorised with the wording, the paragraph and the page of a book, instead of with the proper locus in the map, or with the proper system of related facts. These lessons should therefore be prepared under the careful and philosophic direction of the teacher in the schoolroom, at least until the pupils are trained how to study aright. The home work would then be only the review and perfecting of the lessons by the pupils in the proper manner by reference to the several items in the text. Local or current events, historical, economic, or scientific, should be skilfully used to interpret the remote in time and place.

90. *Manual Training*—(Optional). This may often be introduced as an alternative or recreation, and without therefore. materially increasing the real labour of the pupil. Clay modelling, wood-work, needle-work, cookery, &c., as most appropriate or expedient, may be introduced with the consent of the Trustees and Education Department. Teachers should at all times encourage the pupils in the production of any specimens of home-made handiwork or apparatus, in scientific experiments at home, and in the formation of collections of plants, minerals, and other natural productions of their own part of the country.

CONSPECTUS OF PUBLIC SCHOOL COURSE OF STUDY TO GRADE XI.

With a suggestive percentage of Time for Class-room teaching in each subject, on the supposition that there is one Teacher for each Grade. When one Teacher has the work of more than one Grade, the time to each subject in the Class-room must be lessened.

SUBJECTS.	PERCENTAGE OF TIME IN EACH GRADE.									EXAMINATION VALUES FOR PROVINCIAL CERTIFICATES.		
	I.	II.	III.	IV.	V.	VI.	VII.	VIII.	High School.	IX.	X.	XI.
English	40	40	40	40	40	40	35	30	20	Lang. 100 Gram. 100	Lang. 100 Gram. 100	Lit. 100 Gram. 100
Mathematics	20	20	20		20	20	20	25	30	20	Arith. 100 Alg. 100 Geom. 100	Arith. 100 Alg. 100 Geom. 100	P. Mat 100 Alg. 100 Geom. 100
Science and Manual Art	20	20	20		20	20	20	20	20	20	Dr.&c. 100 Bot'ny 100	Dr.&c. 100 Chem. 100	Phys'l 100 Physics 100
Geography and History	—	—	—	5	10	10	10	10	10	G.& H. 100	G.& H. 100	G.& H. 100
Music, Calisthenics Moral and Patriotic Duties	20	20	20	10	10	10	10	10	5			
Optional { Languages, Latin and Greek	.	.	.	.	.	.	.	.	25	L'tin 100 {	Latin 100 Greek 100	Latin 200 Greek 200
Or, French and German	.	.	.	.	.	.	.	.	25	Fnch 100 {	Fr'nch 100 Germ. 100	Fr'nch 100 Germ. 100

SPECIAL DIRECTIONS FOR COMMON SCHOOLS.

GRADE I.

Reading.—Primer with Wall Cards or Blackboard work.

Language.—Story-telling by pupil. Writing easy vertical letters, words and sentences.

Writing and Drawing.—Writing on slate, paper, or blackboard. Drawing of easy, interesting figures, as in *Manual Training*, to end of Section II.

Arithmetic.—All fundamental arithmetical operations with numbers, the result of which do not exceed 20, to be done with concrete or abstract numbers, accurately and rapidly. See General Directions, 78.

Lessons on Nature.—Power of accurate observation developed by exercising each of the senses on simple or appropriate subjects. Estimation of direction, distance, magnitude, weight, &c., begun. Common colours, simple regular solids, surfaces and lines. Simple observations on a few common minerals, stones, plants, and animals.

Music, &c.—As under General Directions, 65, 66, 67 and 68.

GRADE II.

Reading.—Reader No. 1.

Language.—As in Grade I., but more advanced. See General Directions, 70, 71, 72.

Writing and Drawing.—As in Grade I., but more advanced. Angles, triangles, squares, rectangles, plans of platform and of schoolroom, or as in *Manual Training*, No. 1, to end of Section IV., with *Public School Drawing Course*, No. 1.

Arithmetic.—Numbers up to 100 on the same plan as in Grade I.

Lessons on Nature.—As in Grade I., but more extended. See General Directions, 69.

Music, etc.—As under General Directions, 65, 66, 67, and 68.

GRADE III.

Reading.—Reader No. 2. See General Directions, 71.

Language.—As in II., but more advanced. Subject and predicate. Nouns and verbs.

Writing and Drawing.—Vertical letters on slate and in copy books. Freehand outlines on slate, blackboard, etc. Common geometrical lines and figures, with their names. Map of school grounds and surroundings. As in *Manual Training*, No. 1, to end of Section VI., with *Public School Drawing Course*, No. 2.

Arithmetic.—As in Common School Arithmetic, Part I., first half. See General Directions, 78.

Lessons on Nature.—Geography of neighbourhood, use of local or county maps. Estimation of distances, measures, weights, etc., continued. Colour. Study extended to, say, three or four each of common metals, stones, earths, flowers, shrubs, trees, insects, birds, and mammals. See General Directions, 69.

Music, etc.—As under General Directions, 65, 66, 67, and 68.

GRADE IV.

Reading.—Reader No. 3. See General Directions, 70 and 71.

Language.—Oral statements of matter of lessons, observations, etc. Written sentences, with punctuation, etc. Modifiers of subject and predicate, of noun and verb.

Writing and Drawing.—Copy Book. Drawing as in *Manual Training*, No. 1, to end of Section VIII., with *Public School Drawing Course*, No. 3, and drawing from objects.

Geography.—Oral lessons on Physiography, as on pages 85 to 99, Introductory Geography, with the general geography of the Province begun on the school map. See General Directions, 75 and 76.

Arithmetic.—As in Common School Arithmetic, Part I., completed. See General Directions, 78.

Lessons on Nature.—As in Grade III., but extended so as to include four or five objects of each kind, as in General Directions.

Music, etc.—As under General Directions, 65, 66, 67, and 68.

GRADE V.

Reading.—Reader No. 4, Part I. See General Directions.

Language.—As in Grade IV. and General Directions. All parts of speech and of sentences with inflections of noun, adjective, and pronoun orally. Composition practice on " nature lessons," etc., increasing.

Writing and Drawing.—Copy Book. Drawing as in *Manual Training,* No. 1, with *Public School Drawing Course,* No. 4, etc.

Geography and History.—Ideas of latitude and longitude, physiography, etc., developed. Oral geography of Nova Scotia on map in fuller detail. General geography of the Provinces of Canada and the Continent, as on the Hemisphere maps. Oral lessons on leading incidents of Nova Scotia history.

Arithmetic.—As in Common School Arithmetic, Part II., first half.

Lessons on Nature.—From mineral and rock to soil, as shown in neighbourhood, and extended to, say, five or six each of the common plants, trees, insects, other invertebrates, fish, reptiles, birds, mammals, and natural phenomena, such as ventilation, evaporation, freezing, closely examined. Health Reader, No. I., begun.

Music, etc.—As under General Directions.

GRADE VI.

Reading.—Reader No. 4, completed. See General Directions.

Language.—As in Grade V., extended. Formal composition (simple essays) twice each month. Paradigm of regular verb. Simple parsing and analysis begun. More important rules of Syntax applied. Short descriptive sketches of observations, etc., and letters. All from oral instruction.

Writing and Drawing.—Copy Book. Drawing as in *Manual Training,* No. 2, to end of Section II., with *Public School Drawing Course,* No. 5, etc. Increasing practice in representing common objects in outline.

Geography.—Introductory Geography text to end of Canada. Thorough drill in outlines of Hemispheres, with map drawing.

History.—British American History : text, chapters 3, 5, 10, 11, 13 (in part) and 14.

Arithmetic.—As in Common School Arithmetic, Part II., completed.

Lessons on Nature.—As in Grade V., but extended, say to at least six or seven objects of each class specified. Distribution and values of all natural products of the Province. Health Reader No. 1, completed.

Music, etc.—As under General Directions.

GRADE VII.

Reading.—Reader No. 5 begun. Character of metre and figures of speech begun to be observed. See General Directions.

Language.—Leading principles of Etymology with paradigms as in a prescribed text. Exercises, parsing, and analysis of simple sentences, with application of rules of Syntax.

Written abstracts of oral or reading lessons. Simple description of " nature " observations, etc., narrative and business forms. Punctuation and paragraphing.

Writing and Drawing.—Copy Book. Drawing as in *Manual Training* No. 2 to end of Section IV., with *Public School Drawing Course,* No. 6, etc. Plotting of lines, triangles, rectangles, etc., according to scale. Simple object drawing extended.

Geography.—Introductory Geography to end of Europe, with thorough map drill, and map drawing. See General Directions.

History.—British American History completed. See General Directions.

Arithmetic.—As in Common School Arithmetic, Part III., first half.

Lessons on Nature.—As in Grade IV., and with the study of specimens illustrating the stones, minerals, etc. ; each class, sub-class, and division of plants ; and each class of animals, found in the locality. All common and easily observed physical phenomena. The Introductory Science Primer, and Health Reader No. 2 begun. See General Directions.

Music, etc. --As under General Directions.

GRADE VIII.

Reading.—Reader No. 5 completed. Elements of prosody and plain figures of speech, as illustrated in reading, to be observed and studied. See General Directions 71.

Spelling.—Prescribed Speller in addition to General Directions.

Language.— Parsing, including important rules of Syntax, as in prescribed text. Analysis of simple and easy complex sentences. Correction of false Syntax.

Composition Exercises as in Grade VII. extended. Pupils at this stage should be able to express themselves fluently and with fair accuracy in writing, for all ordinary business purposes. See General Directions.

Writing and Drawing.—Copy Book. Model and object drawing. *Manual Training,* No 2 to end of Section V., with review of *Public School Drawing Course,* Nos. 5 and 6, etc. Construction of angles and simple mathematical figures to scale, and their measurement. T. C. Allen's Card Scale recommended. See General Directions.

Geography.—Introductory Geography completed and reviewed, with latest corrections and map drill and map drawing. See General Directions.

History.—As in "Brief History of England," with review of British American History. See General Directions.

Arithmetic.—Common School Arithmetic completed. See General Directions.

Algebra.—Fundamental rules, with special drill on the evaluation of algebraic expressions.

Book-keeping.—A simple set.

Lessons on Nature.—As in Grade VII., extended to bear on Health, Agriculture, Horticulture, and any local industry of the School Section. Local "Nature Observations." Oral lessons from Science Primers - specially the Chemistry Primer. Health Reader No. 2 completed. See General Directions.

Music, etc.--As under General Directions.

CONDENSED COMMON SCHOOL COURSES.

[The following condensations of the Common School Course of Study are given here merely as suggestions for the benefit of untrained teachers who may require such aid. In connection with the special directions given hereunder, the teacher should study thoroughly the meaning of the general directions given first under the various subjects numbered from 65 to 90 These general combined with the following special directions, form the prescribed Courses of Study.

FOR A COMMON SCHOOL WITH FOUR TEACHERS.

PRIMARY.

Reading. —Primer and Reader No. 1, with wall cards or blackboard work.

Language.—Story-telling by pupil. Easy vertical letters, words and sentences.

Writing and Drawing.—Writing on slate, paper, or blackboard. Drawing of easy interesting figures, plans of platform and schoolroom, etc., or, as in *Manual Training,* No. I. to the end of Section IV., with Drawing Book No. 1.

Arithmetic.—All fundamental arithmetical operations with numbers, the results of which do not exceed 100, to be done with concrete and abstract numbers, accurately and rapidly.

Lessons on Nature, &c.—Power of accurate observation developed by exercising each of the senses on simple and appropriate objects. Estimation of direction, distance, magnitude, weight, etc., begun. Common colours, simple, regular, solids, surfaces, and lines. Simple observations on a few common minerals, stones, plants, and animals. Simple songs. Hygiene and Temperance.

ADVANCED PRIMARY.

Reading.—Readers Nos. 2 and 3 with spelling.

Language.—Oral statements of matter of lessons, observations, etc. Written sentences with punctuation, etc. Subject, predicate, noun, verb, and their modifiers.

Writing and Drawing.—On slate and blackboard. Common geometrical lines and figures with their names, map of school-ground. Copy books. Drawing as in *Manual Training*, No. 1, to the end of Section VIII., and Drawing Books Nos. 2 and 3, with outline drawings of common objects.

Arithmetic.—As in Common School Arithmetic, Part I.

Lessons on Nature, &c.—Geography of neighbourhood and the use of map of province with easy geographical terms, explanation of the change of seasons, etc. Estimation of distance, measure, weight, etc., continued. Colour. Study of four or five each of the common metals, stones, earths, flowers, shrubs, trees, insects, birds, and mammals. Simple songs. Hygiene and Temperance.

INTERMEDIATE.

Reading.—Reader No. 4 with spelling. Health Reader No. 1.

Language.—Formal compositions (simple essays twice a month), short descriptions of "Nature lesson" observations, etc., and letters as well as oral abstracts. Simple parsing and analysis begun, with the application of the more important rules of syntax, exercises selected from reading lessons. (No text-book of grammar in the hands of pupils.)

Writing and Drawing.—Copy Books. Drawing as in *Manual Training*, No. 1, complete, and drawing books Nos. 4 and 5. Model and object drawing.

Arithmetic.—As in Common School Arithmetic, Part II.

Geography.—Introductory Geography to end of Canada. Thorough drill in outlines of Hemisphere maps.

History.—Nova Scotia, to 1756, as in prescribed British American History.

Lessons on Nature.—From minerals and rock to soil, as shown in neighbourhood, and say six or seven each of the common plants, trees, insects, other invertebrates, fish, reptiles, birds, mammals, and natural phenomena, such as ventilation, evaporation, freezing, closely examined. Distribution and values of the natural products of the Province. Music, at least half-a-dozen songs (tonic sol-fa notation).

PREPARATORY.

Reading.—Reader No. 5. Health Reader No. 2. Elements of prosody and plain figures of speech as illustrated in readings to be observed and studied.

Spelling.—Readers and prescribed Spelling Book, etc.

Language.—Leading principles of Etymology and Syntax as in prescribed "Grammar." Parsing. Analysis of simple and easy complex sentences. Correction of false syntax. Written abstracts of oral and reading lessons.

Si ple description of "Nature lesson" observations, etc., narrative and business forms. Punctuation and paragraphing.

Writing and Drawing.—Copy Books. Drawing as in *Manual Training*, No. 2, to end of Section V., with Drawing Book No. 6, Model and Object drawing with simple drawing from nature. Construction of angles and simple geometrical figures to scale and their measurement. The use of scales on T. C. Allen's Card Scale.

Geography.—Introductory text-book with latest corrections and thorough map drill.

History.—"British American," completed, with "Brief History of England."

Arithmetic and Algebra.—Common School Arithmetic. Fundamental rules of Algebra, and evaluation of algebraic expressions.

Book-keeping.—A simple set.

Music.—At least eight songs and the tonic sol-fa notation.

Lessons on Nature.—The study by examination of the minerals, stones, earths, etc.; of specimens of each class, sub-class, and division of plants; and of each class of animals, as found in the locality, with particular reference to the bearing of the knowledge on any useful industry, as agriculture, horticulture, etc. All common and easily observed physical phenomena. Oral lessons with experiments on subject matter of Introductory Science Primer.

FOR A COMMON SCHOOL WITH THREE TEACHERS.

LOWER.

Reading.—Primer and Readers, Nos. 1 and 2, with spelling.

Language.—Story-telling by pupil. Printing or writing simple words and thoughts.

Writing and Drawing.—Vertical letters, etc., on slate, paper, or blackboard and copy book. Drawing from objects, and of easy interesting figures, plans of school grounds, or as in *Manual Training* No. 1, to end of Section VI., with Drawing Books, Nos. 1 and 2.

Arithmetic.—As in Common School Arithmetic, Part I., first half.

Lessons on Nature.—Power of accurate observation developed by exercising each of the senses on simple and appropriate objects, geography of neighbourhood and local map. Estimation of direction, magnitude, distance, weight, measure, etc., begun. Colours. Objective study of at least a few of each class of the natural history objects in the locality.

Music.—At least three simple songs (tonic sol-fa notation).

MIDDLE.

Reading.—Readers Nos. 3 and 4, with spelling. Health Reader, No. 1.

Language.—Oral statement of matter of reading lessons and oral lessons. Simple description of "nature lesson' observations, etc., narrative and letter writing. Parts of speech and sentences with the easier inflections and rules of syntax. Parsing and analysis of simple passages in reading lessons begun.

Writing and Drawing.—Copy books. Drawing as in *Manual Training* No. 1, complete, with Drawing Books, Nos. 3, 4, and 5, and outline drawing from objects.

Arithmetic.—As in Common School Arithmetic, Parts I. and II.

Geography and History.—Drill on the Hemisphere maps and Introductory text-book to end of Canada. Oral lessons on the leading incidents of the history of Nova Scotia.

Music.—Five or six songs (tonic sol-fa notation).

Lessons on Nature.—Estimation of weights, measures, distances, etc., in connection with reduction exercises. Six or seven each of every class of natural history objects (mineral, vegetable, and animal), in the neighbourhood, examined and classified. Common physical phenomena observed and studied.

HIGHER.

Reading.—Reader No. 5 and Health Reader No. 2, with spelling and prescribed spelling book, elements of prosody and plain figures of speech in passages read observed.

Language.—Leading principles of Etymology and Syntax as in prescribed "Grammar," Parsing, analysis of simple and easy complex sentences, correction of false syntax, oral and written abstracts of interesting lessons. Essays, including narrative, description of "nature lesson" observation, etc., and general letter writing with special attention to punctuation, paragraphing, and form generally.

Writing and Drawing.—Copy books. Drawing as in *Manual Training* No. 2, to end of Section V. with Drawing Book No. 6, Model and Object drawing with simple drawing from nature. The construction and measurement of angles and mathematical figures. The use of scales on Allen's Card Scale.

Geography.—Introductory Geography, complete with latest corrections, and general map drill on the Hemisphere maps.

History.—As in " British American," and the " Brief History of England."

Arithmetic and Algebra.—Common School Arithmetic, and evaluation of algebraic expressions and four fundamental rules.

Book-keeping.—One simple set with commercial forms.

Music.—At least eight songs and the tonic sol-fa notation.

Lessons on Nature.—The study objectively of a number of the typical natural history objects of the locality, their distribution, value, and bearing on native industries in the Province. The observation and explanation of common physical phenomena, oral lessons and experiments as in the Introductory Science Primer.

FOR A COMMON SCHOOL WITH TWO TEACHERS.

JUNIOR (at least two divisions).

Reading.—Primer and Readers Nos. 1, 2, and 3, with spelling, and oral abstracts of interesting lessons ; nouns, verbs, subjects, predicates, etc., in lessons of higher classes ; writing sentences, and description of "nature" observations.

Writing and Drawing.—Letters, words, geometrical figures, etc., on slate, paper, and blackboard. Copying from cards. Copy books and drawing as in *Manual Training* No. 1, to the end of Section VIII., with Drawing Books Nos. 1, 2, 3, and drawing from common objects.

Arithmetic.—As in Common School Arithmetic, Part I.

Music.—Four or five songs with tonic sol-fa notation.

Lessons on Nature.—Practice in the estimation, by guessing and testing, of weights, measures, distances, etc., referred to in reduction tables. Study of regular solids, surfaces, lines, and colours. Observation of simple physical phenomena. Examination and classification of representative specimens of minerals, stones, etc., plants and animals, to be found in the locality. Training the eyes to see everything around and the mind to understand explanations and relations.

SENIOR (at least two divisions).

Reading.—Readers Nos. 4 and 5. Health Readers Nos. 1 and 2. Spelling and definition. Oral abstracts of lessons. Elementary grammar and analysis drill on sentences in reading lessons. Observations of figures of speech and the character of metre in poetical passages read in the advanced division.

Language.—Leading principles of Etymology. Syntax, etc., as in Grades VII. and VIII. Written and oral abstracts, narratives and description of ."nature lesson" observations, etc., with attention to punctuation, paragraphing, and form.

Writing and Drawing.—Copy books. Drawing in *Manual Training* No. 1, complete, and No. 2 to end of Section V., with Drawing Books

Nos. 5 and 6, Model and Object drawing ; and lessons on mathematical construction of figures in advanced division.

Geography.—Text book (introductory) in advanced division. For all, thorough drill in the general geography of the Hemisphere maps.

History.—" British American " text book and " Brief History of England " in advanced division.

Arithmetic.—Common School Arithmetic, Parts II. and III., with evaluation and fundamental rules of Algebra for advanced division.

Book-keeping.—Simple set for advanced division.

Music.—At least eight songs and the tonic sol-fa notation.

Lessons on Nature.—One daily to all pupils on one or other subject such as : Estimation of weights, measures, distances, etc., properties of bodies, common physical phenomena, local representative specimens or species of the mineral, vegetable, and animal world in the locality, the natural resources of the Province, and the bearing of these on our industrial development, etc., etc. ; experiments, etc., as in the Introductory Science Primer.

FOR A COMMON SCHOOL WITH ONE TEACHER.

(UNGRADED, "MISCELLANEOUS," OR "RURAL" SCHOOL.)

[As a general rule there should be at least four classes or divisions in such a school ; (a) those in Reader No. 5, (b) Reader No. 4, (c) Reader No. 3, and (d) Reader Nos. 2 and 1 and Primer. The pupils in such a school must be drilled to move without the loss of an instant of time, if the teacher is to be successful. There cannot be the leisure of a graded school in it.]

Reading.—(d) Four lessons a day, very short, with spelling, grammar and composition questions on them ; (c) three short lessons in like manner ; (b) two short lessons, one from Health Reader No. 1, with full range of questions on them ; (a) one lesson (Health Reader No. 2 on alternate days), with questions covering spelling, definitions, grammar, analysis, prosody and composition, more or less partially.

Writing and Drawing.—(d) On slate or paper from a blackboard or cards during specified times of the day ; (c) same, more advanced ; (b) copy books and drawing books, once each day ; (a) the same once each day.

Language.—Text book only in (a) and once a day or every other day, with written compositions in (a) and (b) as indicated in the other courses. Class instruction or essay criticism once or twice a week.

Geography.—Oral lessons once or twice a week to (d) and (c) and (b). Text book twice a week (b) and (a).

History.—Oral lessons once or twice a week to (c) and (b). Text book twice a week for (a).

Arithmetic.—Each class to receive attention twice a day as a class from the teacher ; (d) a very few minutes at a time ; (a) more time, which might vary with the difficulty of the points to be reasoned out. This will form the main subject for "seat work," while the teacher is engaged with other classes.

Music.—At least twice a day for a few minutes. Exercises short and often are more useful for many purposes than exercises long and seldom.

Lessons on Nature.—Once every day so as to select during the year the most important points specified in the uncontracted course.

Two specimen time tables are given below.

SUGGESTIVE TIME TABLES.

(DESIGNED TO AID INEXPERIENCED TEACHERS AND TRUSTEES.)

There are two specimens given here for a rural school in which it is assumed there is only common school work to be done—the work of the first eight " Provincial Grades."

Every teacher should have a *time table,* giving all these details posted up in the school room, so that pupils can be guided by it even at their "desk" work. Inspectors are required to insist on this in every school.

Time Table A.

[For a "rural" or "miscellaneous" common school (of eight Grades grouped in four classes, (a), (b), (c) and (d), as directed on the previous page, with about 44 pupils 2 in 8th, 3 in 7th, 4 in 6th, 5 in 5th, 6 in 4th, 7 in 3rd, 8 in 2nd, and 9 in 1st grade.].

Time when Begun.	Duration (Minutes).	RECITATIONS TO TEACHER. Monday. Wednesday. Friday.	Tuesday. Thursday.	SILENT WORK AT DESKS OF THE FOUR CLASSES. (a)	(b)	(c)	(d)
9 (a) 9.15 9.30 9.45 10.00 10.15 10.20	15 15 15 15 15 15 5 30	Opening, Song, and Roll-call. (d) Reading, Spelling, etc. (c) " " (b) " " (a) " " Song and Calisthenics. (a), (b), (c), and (d), Arithmetic, etc.		Arith. Arith. Spelling.	Arith. Spelling. Spelling.	Spelling. Spelling. Drawing. Drawing.	Spelling. Drawing. Arith.
10.50	10	RECESS.					
11.00 11.15 11.30 11.35	15 15 5 25	(a) Gram. and Anal. | (a) Language. (d) Reading, Spelling, etc. Mental Arithmetic. Writing. | Drawing		Arith.	Arith. Arith.	Arith. Arith.	Arith.
12.00	60	NOON INTERMISSION.					
1.00 1.05 1.20 1.35 1.50 2.05 2.10	5 15 15 15 15 5 20	Song and Roll-call. Geog. etc. (oral) | Hist. etc. (oral). (a+) Geog. | (a+) Hist. (c) Language. | (d) Language. (b) " | (a) Tues. } Health | (b) Thurs. } Reader. Song and Calisthenics. Arith., Alg., B.K., or Math. Drawing.		MapDraw. Language Arith.	Arith. Language.	Arith. Language. Spelling.	Arith. Language Spelling.
2.30	10	RECESS.					
2.40 2.55 3.05 3.20 3.35 3.50	15 10 15 15 15 10	" Nature " and Science lesson from objects. } Writing or Drawing notes on lesson. (d) Reading, Spelling, etc. | (a), (b), (c), and (d), Recitations (Elocutionary), on (c) " " | Fridays. (b) " " | Announcements, etc., and song.		Math. Math. Math.	Math. Spelling. Spelling.	Arith. Spelling.	Spelling. Arith.

Notes on Time Table A.

* Desk work, Mathematics, when teacher is not engaged with the class.

† Desk work, description in writing (and drawing when necessary) of natural objects or observations, when the teacher does not require the attention of the class to the "lesson" for the day. Some lessons may be adapted to all classes, others to the senior or junior. When an elementary lesson is given to classes (c) and (d), the classes (a) and (b) should be working on a written description of a plant, an insect, or other phenomena observed, or experiments in physics, etc, with drawings. And *vice versa.*

‡ *Class* (d) may be necessarily made of *two* or *three*, and if not more sub-classes, each of which must be rapidly taken in turn. Some in their letters, some in the primer, etc., but all must receive attention in these subjects three or four times a day, for they can do but a very little at a time.

Reading should combine, when there is time, spelling, definition of words, grammatical peculiarities, etc., and the meaning of the literature and useful ideas in it should always be made clear to the pupil. See General Directions, 70 and 71.

Language.—See General Directions, 72. The "desk" work should require every day, if possible, the expression of the pupil's thoughts about something on which he can have clear ideas. To read a short story, or choice description once, to the class; giving all, say, exactly five or ten minutes to write rapidly their remembrance of it substantially, is a good exercise; especially if the errors are corrected before the class or otherwise shortly after. Or to give them an object or a picture to "write up" rapidly in a limited time. This will develop facility of composition. Some grammar and analysis, of course, will be necessary to enable the pupils to understand the reasons why some methods of expression are better than others.

Mathematics.—Several subjects need be taken up only for a month or two, such as the elementary rules of algebra, accounts, the use of the mathematical scales, as in Allen's Card Scale, and the compass in mathematical drawing. Some of these might be taken instead of arithmetic, say, in the afternoon, or on alternate days.

High School Work.—Where work of this kind has to be done, those studying the high school subjects might aid the teacher with some of the classes so as to obtain time for the high school studies, which otherwise might cut down the time given each class too much.

Lessons on Nature.—In many of these lessons the whole school may profitably engage. In nearly all the whole senior or whole junior division of the whole school can take part. A skilful teacher can thus give profitable object lessons to several grades of scholars at once; at one time giving a Grade V. lesson, at another time a Grade VI. or Grade VII. or Grade VIII. lesson, which will also contain enough for the observation and interest of Grade I., Grade II., Grade III., and Grade IV. pupils. An object lesson given to the highest class can thus to a certain extent be made a good object lesson for all the lower classes. The older pupils will see more and think more. It must be remembered that the memorising of notes or facts merely stated to pupils is strictly forbidden under this head. Such memorising is pure cram, injurious instead of being useful. The teacher may not have time to take up in *class* every object indicated in the Nature Lessons of the Course. In such cases the pupils should be given, say, two or three objects nearly related to the typical specimen examined in school with direction to search for them and examine them at home as illustrated in specimen class lesson. Without much expenditure of time the teacher can note that this work has been honestly attempted to be done by each pupil. The lessons must be direct from nature itself, but under the guidance of the teacher who can save time in bringing the pupils to the point desired from his own more mature experience. They are intended to train the observing and inductive faculties, to show the true way of discovering something of the nature of the world which immediately surrounds us, and which is and will continue to be reacting upon us in one manner or another. This knowledge is so much power over nature from which we have to win our material existence. It is also the basis of any useful philosophy.

More stress has been laid on the natural history of each section than on elementary physics and chemistry. Not because physical phenomena are less important, but because the elements of these sciences are the same all the world over, and there is no end to the cheap and well illustrated guides to practical work in them which will suit a section in Nova Scotia as well as one in England or in the United States. But there are no such simple guides to the biology of each section, and many of its other scientific characters. The teacher must become a student and master them; for they are of the most special importance in developing the habits of accurate observations from childhood, which is the soundest basis for any career ranging from that of the poet and professional man to the tiller and lord of the soil, the tradesman, the manufacturer and the inventor; and, in developing in connection with history and civics an intelligent attachment even to the soil of our country.

Time Table B.

		RECITATION		DESK WORK							
TIME											
Exercise begins.	Length in Mts.	M., W., F.	Tu., Th.	I.	II.	III.	IV.	V.	VI.	VII.	VIII.
9–9.10	10	Opening.	Opening.								
9.10–9.25	15	I. and II. Read.	I. and II. Read.			Copy Reading Lesson.	Copy Reading Lesson.	Arithmetic.	Arithmetic.	Arith.	Arith.
9.25–9.40	15	III. and IV. Read.	III. and IV. Read.	Copy Reading Lesson.	Copy Reading Lesson.	Tables in Arithmetic.	Tables in Arithmetic.				
9.40–9.55	15	V. and VI. Read.	V. and VI. Read.							Spelling.	Spelling.
9.55–10	5	Song.	Song.								
10.00–10.40	40	Arith. and Algebra.	Arith. and Algebra.								
10.40–10.50	10	Recess.	Recess.								
10.50–11.05	15	VII. and VIII. Gram.	VII. and VIII. Comp.	English Exercise.	English Exercise.	English Exercise.	English Exercise.	Eng. Exercise.	Eng. Exercise.	English Exercise.	English Exercise.
11.05–11.20	15	V. and VI. Lang.	V. and VI. Gram.			English Exercise.	English Exercise.	English Exercise.	English Exercise.	English Exercise.	English Exercise.
11.20–11.30	10	III. and IV. Lang.	III. and IV. Lang.			Spell. Exercise.	Spel. Exercise.				
11.30–11.40	10	I. and II. Lang.	I. and II. Lang.								
11.40–12	20	Writing.	Drawing.								
12.00											
1.00–1.05		Song.	Song.								
1.05–1.15	10	I. and II. Read.	I. and II. Read.								
1.15–1.35	20	VII. and VIII. Georg.	VII. and VIII. Hist.	Copy lesson.	Copy lesson.	Arithmetic.	Arithmetic.	Arithmetic.	Arithmetic.	Arith.	Algebra.
1.35–1.50	15	V. and VI. Georg.	V. and VI. Hist.	Number Tables.	Number Tables.	Copy lesson.	Copy lesson.	Spelling.	Spelling.	English.	English.
1.50–2.05	15	III. and IV. Read.	III. & IV. Geog. & Hist.								
2.05–2.15		Song and Calisthenics.	Song and Calisthenics.								
2.15–2.35	20	Arith. and Algebra.	Arith. and Algebra.								
2.35–2.45	10	Recess.	Recess.								
2.45–2.55		I. and II. Read.	I. and II. Read.	Copy lesson.	Copy lesson.						
2.55–3.15	20	VII. & VIII. Health K. and Science.	VII. & VIII. Health K. and Science.	English.	English.	Review of Science (written.)	Review of Science (written.)	English Exercise.	English Exercise.	Spelling.	Spelling.
3.15–3.30	15	V. and VI. Health K. and Science.	V. and VI. Health K. and Science.	English.	English.						
3.30–3.40	10	III. and IV. Science.	III. and IV. Science.	Drawing.	Drawing.	Drawing.	Drawing.	Review of Science.	Review of Science.	Review of Science.	Review of Science.
3.40–3.55	15	VII. and VIII. Read.	VII. and VIII. Read.								
3.55–4	5	Closing.	Closing.								

Notes and Suggestions on Time Table B. for Miscellaneous School.

In grouping grades it may be found better to group differently ; as II., III., IV., and V., etc.   In that case I. would be taken alone ; also VIII. Or VII. and VIII. may work well together, while VI. would be taken alone.

It would never be practicable to combine Grades I. and II. in reading, in such a way as to have both classes read the same lesson.   A period may be set apart, as in the table, for the two classes.   Then Grade I. is taken first, Grade II. meanwhile is set to study the lesson, or to copy it.   At the close of lesson for Grade I., this grade is sent to copy lesson just read, while Grade II. reads.   The proportion of time given to each grade (I. and II.) will vary on different days according to circumstances, such as slim attendance of one grade and full attendance of the other.

Deal similarly with other combinations as III. and IV.   If they cannot read the same lesson profitably, take the lower grade first, then the other. In some cases the bad readers of the advanced grade should get additional practice by reading with the lower grade as well as with their own.   Also clever pupils in the lower grade may be allowed to read both lessons, and in this way become prepared for transfer to the higher grade in advance of their class.

All classes are taken together in arithmetic.   That is, the time is not divided up among the classes, as shown in the time table.   The teacher takes the different classes in such order and for such length of time as circumstances suggest.

Somewhat similar is the plan in English.   While one class is reciting or receiving instruction, others have some kind of work as desk-work.   The teacher may sometimes stop the desk-work of one or more classes temporarily and invite the attention of these classes to some point under discussion.

Spelling is to be combined with every lesson to some extent, especially with the reading lessons and the language lessons.   Also at desk-work pupils are set to copy from books, from the blackboard, to write names of objects, plurals of nouns, words exemplifying rules of spelling, etc.

High School Curriculum.

Special Directions, Year Ending July, 1899.

The subjects, number and value of the papers for the different High School examinations, and the general scope of examination questions, are indicated in the prescribed curriculum which follows.   Examination questions may demand description by drawing as well as by writing in all grades.   In any subject, also, a question may be put on work indicated under the head of General Directions, Course of Study for Public Schools.

GRADE IX.

1. *English Language.*—100 : [a] The Sir Roger De Coverley Papers (35), and Evangeline (T. C. Allen and Co.), with critical study, word analysis, prosody and recitations ; [b] English Composition as in Dalgleish's Introductory, or an equivalent in the hands of the teacher only, with essays, abstracts, and general correspondence, so as to develop the power of fluent and correct expression in writing.

2. *English Grammar.*—100 : Text Book [excepting " notes " and " appendix "] with easy exercises in parsing and analysis.

3. *Latin.*—100 : As in Collar and Daniell, to end of Chapter LIII., or any equivalent grammar with very easy translation and composition exercises. [To secure uniformity in pronunciation the Roman (or Phonetic) pronunciation of Latin is recommended to be used in all grades.]

4. *French.*—100 : As in Fasnacht's Progressive Course, First Year, with Progressive Reader, First Year, Sections 1 to 15 (MacMillan and Co.).

5. *History and Geography.* : [a] Text Book of British History up to the House of Tudor, and oral lessons on "How Canada is Governed." [b] Geography of North America and Europe as in Text Book.

6. *Science.*—100 : [a = 30] Physics as in Balfour Stewart's Primer [b = 70] Botany as in Gray's How Plants Grow, substituting for the details of "Flora," Part II., common or prescribed native plants ; or Spotton's. Drawing of parts of plants.

7. *Drawing and Book-keeping.* 100 : [a = 20] Construction of geometrical figures and solution of mensuration and trigonometrical problems by mathematical instruments, and T. C. Allen's Card Scale. [b = 30] High School Drawing Course No. 1, with model and object drawing and Manual Training No. 2 completed. [c = 50] Commercial forms and writing, with Single Entry Book-keeping Problems.

8. *Arithmetic.*--100 : As in Hamblin Smith to end of Section 21 (with a practical, knowledge of the metric system, which will be required in all grades).

9. *Algebra.*—100 : As in Hall and Knight's Elementary Algebra to end of Chapter XVI.

10. *Geometry.*—100 : Euclid I., with very easy exercises, as in Hall and Stevens to page 86.

Note.—Latin and French are optional ; all others imperative. The minimum aggregate for a "pass" is 400, with no subject below 25.

GRADE X.

1. *English Language.*—100 : [a] Same subjects as in previous grade, but more advanced scholarship required. [Composition as in Dalgleish's Advanced, or an equivalent in the hands of the teacher only, with special attention to the development of readiness and accuracy in written narrative, description, exposition, and general correspondence.]

2. *English Grammar.*—100 : Text Book (excepting "appendix") completed with exercises in parsing and analysis.

3. *Latin.*—100 : As in Collar and Daniel, complete, and "Cæsar's Invasion of Britain," by Welch and Duffield (MacMillan and Co., London).

4. *Greek.*—100 : As in Frost's Greek Primer (Allyn and Bacon, Boston), to end of Part III., or Initia Græca, Part I.

5. *French.*—100 : As in Fasnacht's Progressive Course, second year, with Progressive Reader, first year, selections 16 to 62.

6. *German.*—100 : As in Fasnacht's First Year (MacMillan and Co.).

7. *History and Geography.*—100 : [a] Text Book of British History from the House of Tudor to the present time. [b] Text Book of Geography, excepting North America and Europe.

8. *Science.*—100 : [a = 70] Chemistry as in Williams, but with 25 per cent. of optional questions at examination. [b = 30] Mineralogy as in Crosby's Common Rocks, or Agricultural Chemistry as in Tanner.

9. *Drawing and Book-keeping.*—100 : [a] Mathematical drawing as in previous grade, but more advanced ; Faunce's Mechanical Drawing recommended to teachers for "proper use of instruments" and problems. High School Drawing Course, No. 2, and model and object drawing, with simple drawing from Nature. [b] Book-keeping : Double Entry forms and problems.

10. *Arithmetic.*—100 : Text Book complete without appendix.

11. *Algebra.*—100 : As in Hall and Knight's Elementary to end of Chapter XXVII.

12. *Geometry.*—100 : Euclid I., II., and III. to Prop. 20, as in Hall and Stevens.

Note.—Latin, Greek, French, and German optional ; all others imperative. The minimum for a pass, 400, with no subject below 25.

GRADE XI.

1. *English Literature.*—100 : Authors prescribed from year to year, with critical study. [a = 80] Milton's L'Allegro, Il Pensoroso, Comus and Lycidas. Macaulay's Essay on Milton. [b = 20] A general acquaintan e with the prescribed literature of the previous grade, as above.

2. *English Grammar.*—100 : History of English Language and Text Book, completed, with difficult exercises. [b] History of English Literature, as in Meiklejohn.

3. *Latin.*—100 : Grammar and easy composition partly based on Prose author read.

4. *Latin.*—100 : [a] Cæsar's De Bell. Gall., Books II. and III., and [b] Virgil's Æneid, Book III. ; with grammatical and critical questions.

5. *Greek.*—100 : Grammar and easy composition based partly on author read and Frost's Primer completed.

6. *Greek.*—Xenophon's Anabasis, Book II., with grammatical and critical questions.

7. *French.*—100 : As in Fasnacht's Progressive Course, Third Year, with Souvestre's Un Philosophe Sous les Toits (MacMillan and Co.)

8. *German.*—100 : As in Fasnacht's Second Year (MacMillan and Co.).

9. *History and Geography.*—100 : General History and Geography as in Swinton.

10. *Physiology.*—100 : As in prescribed text, "Martin's Human Body and the Effects of Narcotics."

11. *Physics.*—100 : As in Gage's Introduction to Physical Science.

12. *Practical Mathematics.*—100 : As in Eaton.

13. *Algebra and Arithmetic.*—100 : As in Hall and Knight's Elementary Algebra.

14. *Geometry.*—100 : Euclid I. to IV. with exercises, the more important definitions and algebraic demonstrations of Euclid V., and Euclid VI. (text) to Prop. 19, as in Hall and Stevens.

Note.—Latin, Greek, French, and German optional ; all others imperative. The minimum aggregate for a pass, 400, with no subject below 25. The examination on this syllabus may also be known as the Junior Leaving Examination of the High School.

GRADE XII.

The examination on this syllabus may be known as the Senior Leaving Examination of the High School. This portion of the course of study may be profitably undertaken on the lines best adapted to the staff of instructors or the demands of students in the larger High Schools or County Academies. There is in this grade a bifurcation of the course into a classical side and a scientific side, with minor options leading to the certificates of " A " (classical) and " A " (scientific) respectively.

(A.) IMPERATIVE FOR BOTH SIDES.

1. *English Language.*—100 : As in Lounsbury's English Language, with prescribed authors. Chaucer's Canterbury Tables : The Prologue in detail (as in Skeat's Shilling Edition) ; with a general knowledge of the following Tales : 1, Knight's ; 2, Monk's ; 3, Clerk's ; 4, Squire's ; 5, Man of Law's ; 6, Pardoner's (any edition of the Canterbury Tales).

2. *English Literature.*—100 : Stopford Brooke's Primer (latest edition), with prescribed authors. Carlyle's Essay on Burns ; Macaulay's Essay on Milton ; Shakespeare's The Merchant of Venice.

3. *British History.*—100 : As in Green's Short History of the English People, and Clement's History of Canada.

4. *Psychology.*—100 : As in James's Text Book of Psychology (MacMillan and Co., London), or Maher's (Stoneyhurst Series).

5. *Sanitary Science.*—100 : As in the Ontario Manual of Hygiene.

(B.) IMPERATIVE FOR CLASSICAL SIDE.

1 *Latin Composition.*—100 : Grammar as in Bennett, and Composition as in Bradley's Arnold, or equivalents. Latin translation at sight.

2. *Tacitus.*—100 : Agricola and Germania.

3. *Cicero.*—100 : Pro Milone.*

4. *Virgil.*—100 : Æneid, Books V. and VI.

5. *Horace.*—100 : Odes. Books II. and IV.*
6. *Roman History and Geography.*—100 : As in Liddell's.
7. *Greek Composition.*—100 : Grammar as in Goodwin and composition as in Fletcher and Nicholson, or equivalents. Greek translation at sight.
8. *Xenophon.*—100 : Hellenica Books I. and II. (Clarendon Press).
9. *Plato.*—100 : The Apology and Crito.*
10. *Sophocles.*—100 : Ajax.
11. *Grecian History and Geography.*—100 : As in Smith's.

(C.) IMPERATIVE FOR SCIENTIFIC SIDE.

1. *Physics.*—100 : As in Gage's Principles of Physics.
2. *Chemistry.*—100 : As in Storer and Lindsay's Elementary.
3. *Botany.*—100 : As in The Essentials of Botany by Bessey (Henry Holt and Co., New York, latest edition) with a practical knowledge of representative species of the Nova Scotia flora.
4. *Zoology.*—100 : As in Dawson's Hand Book, with dissection of Nova Scotian species as in Colton's Practical Zoology.
5. *Geology.*—100 : As in Sir William Dawson's Hand Book of Canadian Geology (excepting the details relating to other Provinces from page 167 to 235).
6. *Astronomy.*—100 : As in Young's Elements of Astronomy.
7. *Navigation.*—100 : As in Norie's Epitome.
8. *Trigonometry.*—100 : Locke's Elementary Trigonometry.
9. *Algebra.*—100 : As in Hall and Knight's Higher Algebra, omitting " * " paragraphs and chapters xxvii. to xxxi.
10. *Geometry.*—100 : Euclid, particularly VI. & XI., as in Hall and Stevens, with exercises " Loci and their Equations," as in Chapter I. Wentworth's Elements of Analytic Geometry.

(D.) OPTIONAL FOR EITHER SIDE.

1. *French Grammar and Composition.*—100.
2. *French Authors.* — 100 : Voltaire's Charles XII., and Corneille's Horace.
3. *German Grammar and Composition.*—100 : As in Joynes-Meissner or equivalent.
4. *German Authors.*—100 : Wildenbruch's Kinderthränen (Freund and Jeckell, Berlin) ; Schiller's Der Neffe als Onkel, and Fritz auf Ferien by Babette von Bülow.

To pass Grade A (scientific) a minimum aggregate of 1000 must be made on twenty papers, including all in groups (A) and (C) and any other five papers.

To pass Grade A (classical) a minimum aggregate of 1000 must be made on twenty papers, including all in groups (A) and (B) and any other four papers.

No paper should fall below 25 (see Reg. 10 under Appendix C below).

For Grade A (classical and scientific), all the subjects in group (D) must have been taken as well as those in (A), (B), and (C). No paper to fall below 50.

GRADE "A" BY PARTIAL EXAMINATIONS.

A candidate at the Provincial Examination who makes an aggregate of 600 on any ten papers of the "A" syllabus, and an aggregate of 500 on a different set of ten papers of the syllabus at a subsequent examination, or who makes an aggregate of 1000 on twenty papers of the syllabus, or who has already taken an A (cl), an A (sc), or an "A" License, may thereafter present himself for examination on any of the subjects on which he may not have made at least 50 per cent. at a previous examination ; and so long as the Council of Public Instruction deems the character of the examination

---

* *For* 1900, *Cicero.*—Against Catiline, I. to IV.
  ,,   *Horace.*—Satires, Books I., omitting the 2nd and 8th Satires, and Book II.
  ,,   *Thucydides.*—Book VII.

on the subjects not materially changed, all the valuation marks 50 per cent. or above made on each subject at the said and following examinations may be incorporated into a single certificate, provided at least 50 per cent. be made on each of the (twenty) subjects required for the Grades A (cl), or A (sc), or on each of the (thirty) subjects in the full course for A (cl and sc).

UNIVERSITY MATRICULATION.

The leading universities and colleges of the Provinces have agreed to accept the Grade B or Junior leaving High School certificate in lieu of their Matriculation examination, when the certificate indicates a pass on each subject required by the particular matriculation standard concerned. For example, a university may fix 50 or 60 per cent. more or less in Latin, Greek, or any other subject, as its standard. Again, a candidate may fail to take a "pass" High School Certificate through a low mark in a subject not required for matriculation, yet make sufficient high marks, as shown by his "examination record," on the subjects required to admit him to the university. This constitutes a practical affiliation of the Public High Schools with the Universities, which will save division of energy in many high schools, while it will place each of the Universities in the same relation to the public schools.

APPENDIX C.

THE GENERAL REGULATIONS OF THE PROVINCIAL HIGH SCHOOL EXAMINATIONS, 1898.

PROVINCIAL EXAMINATION OF HIGH SCHOOL STUDENTS.

REG. 1. "High School Students" will be held to mean all pupils who passed the regular County Academy Entrance Examination, or who are certified by a Public School teacher as having completed one or more years of the High School Course of Study.

REG. 2. A terminal examination by the Provincial Board of Examiners shall be held at the end of each school year on subjects of the first, second, third and fourth years of the High School Curriculum, to be known as Grades IX, X, XI and XII respectively of the Public Schools, or Grades D C, B and A respectively, of the High Schools.

REG. 3. The examination sessions shall commence each day at nine o'clock, A.M., for Grade A on the first Monday of July, at the following stations *only*:—Sydney, Antigonish, Pictou, Amherst, Truro, Halifax, Kentville, and Yarmouth; for Grades B C and D on the following Wednesday, and for "minimum professional qualification" of Public School Teachers on Saturday following; and shall be conducted, according to instructions, under a Deputy Examiner appointed by the Superintendent of Education, at each of the following stations, viz.:—1, Amherst; 2, Annapolis; 3, Antigonish; 4, Arichat; 5, Baddeck; 6, Barrington; 7, Berwick; 8, Bridgetown; 9, Bridgewater; 10, Canso; 11, Cheticamp; 12, Church Point; 13, Digby; 14, Guysboro; 15, Halifax; 16, Kentville; 17, Liverpool; 18, Lockeport; 19, Lunenburg; 20, Maitland; 21, Margaree Forks; 22, Middleton; 23, New Glasgow; 24, North Sydney; 25, Oxford; 26, Parrsboro; 27, Pictou; 28, Port Hawkesbury; 29, Port Hood; 30, River John; 31, Sheet Harbor; 32, Shelburne; 33, Sherbrooke; 34, Stellarton; 35, Springhill; 36, Sydney; 37, Tatamagouche; 38, Truro; 39, Windsor; 40, Wolfville; 41, Yarmouth.

REG. 4. (a) Applications for admission to the Provincial High School Examination must be made on the prescribed form to the Inspector within whose district the examination station to be attended is situated, not later than the 24th day of May.

(b) Candidates applying for the Grade D examination, or for the same grade written for unsuccessfully at a previous examination, or for the next grade above the one already successfully passed by them, shall be admitted free. But a candidate who has not passed Grade D must have his application for C accompanied by a fee of one dollar ; if he has passed neither D nor C the application for B must be accompanied by two dollars ; and if he has passed neither D, C, nor B, the application for A must be accompanied by three dollars. Generally, one dollar must accompany the application for each grade before the one applied for, which the candidate has not regularly passed.

(c) For the Teachers' Minimum Professional Qualification Examination a fee of two dollars is required, but it should not be forwarded with the application, it having been found more convenient to pay the same to the Deputy-Examiner on the Saturday when the candidate presents himself for examination, the Deputy-Examiner transmitting the same to the Superintendent with his report.

(d) The prescribed form of application, which can be freely obtained from the Education Department through the Inspectors, shall contain a certificate which must be signed by a licensed teacher having at least the grade of scholarship applied for by the candidate, whose legal name must be carefully and fully written out. If the application is defective on account of the omission of the proper fee, or on account of the omission or incorrect statement of any fact called for in the prescribed form, the application is null and void, and even should the Deputy-Examiner admit the candidate provisionally to the examination, his papers will be intercepted at the Education Office.

(e) When a candidate presents himself for examination and his name is not found on the official list as having made regular application in due time, the Deputy-Examiner may admit him to the examination provisionally on his written statement that application was regularly made in due time and on the payment of one dollar, which are to be transmitted with the Deputy's report to the Superintendent ; and if such candidate's statement is proven to be correct, the error being due to causes beyond his control, the dollar shall be returned and his papers shall be forwarded to the Provincial Examiners.

(f) Prescribed form of Application. (See below.)

REG. 5. Each Inspector shall forward, *not later than June 1st*, to the Superintendent of Education, a list of the applications received for each grade of examination at each station within his district, on a form to be supplied from the Education Office, transmitting therewith all moneys, having duly classified and checked the same in the form aforesaid.

REG. 6. The Deputy Examiner, when authorised by the Superintendent of Education, shall have power to employ an assistant or assistants, who shall receive two dollars per day for the time so employed.

REG. 7. The Superintendent of Education shall have prepared and printed suitable examination questions for each grade at each examination, in accordance with the prescribed course of study, and shall also forward to each Deputy Examiner a sufficient supply of the printed questions, together with copies of such rules and instructions as may be necessary for the due conduct of the examination.

REG. 8. The maximum value of each paper shall be 100 ; and the numbered questions composing it shall be constructed with the intention of making each equal in value though not necessarily of equal difficulty, Thus, when 5 questions constitute one paper, the value of each when answered accurately with reasonable fulness and in good form will be 20.

PRESCRIBED FORM OF APPLICATION FOR PROVINCIAL HIGH SCHOOL EXAMINATION.

At ....Station, ...May, 189....

To..............

I......................................a duly licensed teacher of Class ....do hereby certify that the candidates whose names are given below from No. 1 to No......... inclusive, will, to the best of my knowledge, have completed, before the date of next examination, the full imperative Course of Study up to and including the Grade for which they respectively apply ; that they are good "*readers and writers* ; and in case of those who have not "passed" the previous Grade or Grades, that they have specially proved their proficiency (equivalent to a 50% "pass") in each of the subjects of the said course of study not virtually covered in the Grade applied for, such as the "science" of Grade B, the "Science, and Book-keeping and Drawing" of Grade C, and the imperatives of Grade B. I also forward herewith on behalf of these candidates................................ dollars, being the amount of fees required under sub-section (*b*) of Regulation 4, "Provincial Examination of High School Students" as specified in the list below.

Candidates intending to take the M. P. Q. Examination (fee $2.00) payable to the Deputy-Examiner at Examination) are indicated by the letters M. P. Q. in the column headed "remarks" below.

Signed..

.........................*Inspector of Schools :*

.............................*Principal of* ....*School* ....*Co.*

No.	NAMES OF CANDIDATES (in full). [This forms part of the permanent and official record of the Education Department. The names must therefore be written herein distinctly, correctly and without contraction.]	Age 1st August next.		Post Office Address of each Candidate.	Grade applied for.	PROVINCIAL GRADE NOW HELD.					Fee under Reg. 4 (*b*).	REMARKS.
		Yrs.	Mos.			Grade.	No.	Station.	Year.			

*If a candidate has a physical defect preventing good reading or writing, application may be made if qualified by and accompanied with a particular and authentic description of the case for the consideration of the Education Department.

no matter whether it should be easier or more difficult than its fellow questions.

REG. 9. Each examiner shall mark distinctly by coloured pencil or ink at the left-hand margin of each question on the candidate's paper its value on the foregoing assumption ; and shall sum up the total, placing it on the back of the sheet ; and underneath, the number of misspelled or obscurely-written words, which number is to be deducted from the total for the true value of the paper. Thus, should the sum of the marks of a paper be 54, and the misspelled or obscurely-written words be 6, the marks on the back would stand as follows, *e.g.*, English Grammar [54-6]=48.

REG. 10. To make a "pass" in the grade of examination applied for, the candidate must make *at least the minimum* aggregate of the grade and at least a *minimum* of 25 on each imperative subject or paper of the grade ; but this minimum of 25 may be lowered one unit for every 50 the candidate's aggregate may be above the "minimum aggregate" in the case of Grade A, and for every 25 in the cases of Grades B, C, and D. A mark below 25 on any optional subject will not be counted in the aggregate.

REG. 11. Candidates failing to make a pass in the grade applied for may be ranked as making a pass in the next grade below, provided 75 per cent. of the *minima* be made ; and as making a pass on the grade second below, provided 50 per cent. of the *minima* be made.

REG. 12. Each candidate shall receive from the Superintendent of Education a certificate containing the marks given in each subject by the examiners, and the High School Grade which the candidate may have successfully "passed." If the candidate has not "passed," the certificate will *not* bear the head title "HIGH SCHOOL CERTIFICATE" with the arms of the Education Department.

REG. 13. Candidates for High School Certificates will be expected to pass the various grades in order. Candidates will not be admitted to the examinations of the higher grades without evidence of their proficiency in the subjects of the preceding grades.

REG. 14. The subjects, number, and values of the papers for the different examinations, and the general scope of examination questions, are indicated by the prescribed High School curriculum. Examination may demand description by drawing as well as by writing in all grades.

PROVINCIAL EXAMINATION RULES.

COMMENT.

No envelopes shall be used to enclose papers. One hour is the maximum time allowed for writing each. One sheet of foolscap will therefore hold all that will be necessary to be written on any paper, if it is properly put down.

1. Candidates shall present themselves at the examination room punctually half an hour before the time set for the first paper of the grade for which they are to write, at which time the deputy examiner shall assign each a seat, and a number which shall represent the candidate's name, and must therefore be neither forgotten nor changed. The candidates who *present* themselves shall be numbered from 1 onwards in consecutive order (without a hiatus for absent applicants, who cannot be admitted after the numbering) beginning with the A's, then coming to the B's, C's, and D's in order.

2. Candidates shall be seated before the instant at which the examination is fixed to begin. No candidate late by the fraction of a minute has the right to claim admission to the examination room, and any candidate leaving the room during the progress of any examination must first send

his or her paper to the deputy examiner, and not return until the beginning of the next, paper.

3. Candidates shall provide themselves with (for their own exclusive use) pens, pencils, mathematical instruments, rulers, ink, blotting-paper, and a supply of good heavy foolscap paper of the size thirteen inches by eight.

4. Each candidate's paper must consist of one sheet of such foolscap, which may be written on both sides, and must contain no separate sheets or portions of sheets unless inseparably attached so as to form one paper. Neat writing, and clear, concise answers are much more likely to secure high values from examiners than extent of space covered or a multiplicity of words.

5. Each such paper must be *exactly* folded, 1st by doubling, bottom to top of page, pressing the fold (paper now 6½ by 8 inches) ; 2nd by doubling again in the same direction, pressing the fold flat so as to give the size of 3¼ by 8 inches.

6. Finally the paper must be exactly endorsed as follows : A neat line should be drawn across the end of the folded paper ½ inch from its upper margin. Within this space, 3¼ inches by ½ inch, there must be written in very distinct characters, 1st, the letter indicating the grade, 2nd, the candidate's number, and 3rd, a vacant parenthesis of at least one inch, within which the deputy examiner shall afterwards place the private symbol indicating the station. Immediately underneath this space and close to it should be neatly written the title or subject of the paper.

For example, candidate No. 18 writing for B (Grade XI.) on Algebra should endorse his paper as shown below :—

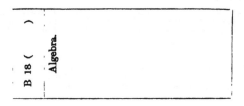

7. The subject title, grade and candidate's No. may be written within over the commencement of the paper also ; but any sign or writing meant to indicate the candidate's name, station, or personality may cause the rejection of the paper before it is even sent to the examiners.

8. Any attempt to give or receive information, even should it be unsuccessful, the presence of books or notes on the person of a candidate, or within his reach during examination, will constitute a violation of the examination rules, and will justify the deputy examiner in rejecting the candidate's papers, and dismissing him from further attendance. No dishonest person is entitled to a provincial certificate or teacher's licence. And where dishonesty at examination is proven, provincial certificates already obtained and licences based on them will be cancelled.

9. It is not necessary for candidates to copy papers on account of erasures or corrections made upon them. Neat corrections or cancelling of errors will allow a paper to stand as high in the estimation of the examiner as if half the time were lost in copying it. Answers or results without the written work necessary to find them will be assumed to be only guesses, and will be valued accordingly.

10. Candidates are forbidden to ask questions of the deputy examiner with respect to typographical or other errors which may sometimes occur in examination questions. The examiner of the paper alone will be the judge of the candidate's ability as indicated by his treatment of the error. No candidate will suffer for a blunder not his own.

11. Candidates desiring to speak with the deputy examiner will hold up the hand. Communication between *candidates* at examination, even to the extent of passing a ruler or making signs, is a violation of the rules. Any such necessary communication can be held through the deputy examiner only.

12. Candidates should remember that the deputy examiner cannot overlook a suspected violation of the rules of examination without violation of his oath of office. No consideration of personal friendship or pity can therefore be expected to shield the guilty or negligent.

13. All candidates will be required to fill in and sign the following certificate at the conclusion of the examination, to be sent in with the *last* paper :

CERTIFICATE.

Examination Station ....Date......July, 189 .

Candidate's No. (   ).

This is to certify that I have not omitted in my course of study any of the imperative subjects in the prescribed High School Curriculum up to Grade......, for which I have now been writing, and that I already hold a Provincial Certificate of Grade......*

I also do truly and solemnly affirm that in the present examination I have not used, or had in the Examination Room, any book, printed paper, portfolio, manuscript, or notes of any kind, bearing on any subject of examination ; that I have neither given aid to, nor sought nor received aid from any fellow-candidate ; that I have not wilfully violated any of the rules, but have performed my work honestly and in good faith.

Name in full   }
(*without contraction in any of its parts*).} ....

P.O. to which memo. or certificate is to be sent.............................

---

* A Teacher's Licence is a Prov. Certificate of the same grade as its class If no licence or certificate is held, the blank is to be filled in with a dash.

TIME TABLE.

PROVINCIAL EXAMINATION, BEGINNING FIRST MONDAY IN JULY, 1896.

TIME.	GRADE A.	COUNTY ACADEMY ENTRANCE.			
MONDAY. A.M. 9.00 to 10.10 10.10 ,, 11.10 11.15 ,, 12.15	Roman History. Chemisty. Xenophon.	English.			
P.M. 2.00 to 3.00 3.10 ,, 4.10 4.15 ,, 5.15	Greek History. Botany. Homer.	Mathematics.			
TUESDAY. A.M. 9.00 to 10.00 10.10 ,, 11.10 11.15 ,, 12 15	Cicero. Zoology. Navigation.	Drawing, etc. Geography and History.			
P.M. 2.00 to 3.00 3.10 ,, 4.10 4.15 ,, 5.15	Plato. Sanitary Science. Astronomy.	Useful Knowledge.			
A.M. 8.30 to 9.00	Seating of Grade B, C and D.				
WEDNESDAY. A.M. 9.00 to 10.00 10.10 ,, 11.10 11.15 ,, 12.15	Algebra. Latin Composition French Authors.	Algebra. Latin Compos'n.	Algebra. Latin.	Algegra. Latin. ....
P.M. 2.00 to 3.00 3.10 ,, 4.10 4.15 ,, 5.15	English Language. French Compos'n. Geology.	Eng. Language. French. Greek Authors.	Eng. Language. French.	Eng. Language. French. ....
THURSDAY. A.M. 9.00 to 10.00 10.10 ,, 11.10 11.15 ,, 12.15	Geometry. Greek Composition Tacitus.	Geometry. Latin Authors.	Geometry. Greek.	Geometry. ....
P.M. 2.00 to 3.00 3.10 ,, 4.10 4.15 ,, 5.15	Physics. German Compos'n. Virgil.	Physics. German. Greek Compos'n.	Science. German.	Science. ....
FRIDAY. A.M. 9.00 to 10.00 10.10 ,, 11.10 11.15 ,, 12.15	Trigonometry. Psychology. Horace.	Prac. Math. Physiology.	Arithmetic. Drawing & B.K.	Arithmetic. Draw'g & B.K.
P.M. 2.00 to 3.00 3.10 ,, 4.10 4.15 ,, 5.15	British History. English Literature. German Authors.	Geog. and Hist. English Gram.	Geog. and Hist. English Gram.	Geog. and Hist. English Gram. ....
SATURDAY. A.M. 9.00 to 10.00 10.10 ,, 11.10 11.15 ,, 12.15	M. P. Q. EXAMINATION. Hygiene and Temperance. School Law and Management. Theory and Practice of Teaching.				

APPENDIX D.

REGULATIONS OF THE COUNCIL OF PUBLIC INSTRUCTION REFERRING TO COUNTY ACADEMIES.

[1.] A County Academy is the high school in a county which under the statute is entitled to draw a special grant, called the academic grant, when the following regulations are satisfactorily observed.

Reg. 1. The board of trustees or commissioners of a school section in which a county academy is situated, in order to draw the academic grant authorized by the statute, shall make satisfactory provision for the instruction of all common school pupils within the section, as well as for all qualified high school students within the county, who may present themselves for admission.

Reg. 2. The buildings, grounds, outhouses, class rooms, laboratories or subsidiary rooms, warming and ventilation, books of reference, maps, charts, models, collections of specimens for illustration and object study, apparatus, etc., shall be of that degree of excellence compatible with the general progress in educational effort in the province, with the grade of grant competed for, and with effective instruction in the course of study prescribed, according to the judgment of the Council of Public Instruction on the report of the Superintendent of Education, under section 3, subsection 10 of the statute.

Reg. 3. The duly qualified teachers referred to in the statute shall hold a provincial academic license of class A (cl), or A (sc), except in the case of a teacher recognized as duly qualified at the inception of the system under the Act of 1885.

Reg. 4. The properly certified yearly average of high school students referred to in the statute shall be the average attendance of regular students who shall have demonstrated their being of full high school grade at the provincial high school examination, or at the annual examination of the academy by the Superintendent of Education.

Reg. 5. Regular pupils or students are those who have regularly entered the county academy under the regulations, and are pursuing the prescribed course of study. Other pupils or students, who may be known as *special* students, may be admitted, provided they can be accommodated without encroaching on the rights of the regular students. They are not, however, legally entitled to admission, except at the option of the trustees or commissioners of the academy ; nor are they counted as qualifying the academy to any extent for the academic grant under the law. In other respects their names, attendance, etc., are recorded in the register and entered into the annual returns as are those of the regular students.

Reg. 6. Students in other respects entitled to admission may be admitted without examination on presentation of provincial or other certificates (such as 300 on grade D, 200 on grade C), recognised by the Superintendent of Education as satisfactory proof of full high school grade.

Reg. 7. The ordinary mode of admission shall be by the county academy entrance examination, held on the Monday and Tuesday of the provincial examination week in July, on the common school course of study, the questions being prepared by the Education Department, arranged in five papers such as, (1) English, (2) mathematics, (3) drawing, writing, and simple accounts, (4) geography and history, and (5) useful knowledge.

Reg. 8. These question papers shall be sent to each principal immediately before the date of examination, under seal, which is not to be broken until the moment of examination specified on each envelope, and the results of the examination must be reported to the Education Office within one week from its close, on the form and with the certification prescribed.

Reg. 9. The examination shall be conducted by the principal and such persons as may be associated with him for the purpose by the board of trustees or commissioners, in strict accordance with the directions issued from the Education Office. All answer papers, with the examiners' values endorsed on the margin of each question, shall be preserved for *two* years, ready for examination or re-examination by the Superintendent of Education. The rules and proceedings of the provincial examination shall be followed in these examinations so far as they are applicable.

Reg. 10. A supplementary entrance examination for such applicants as can show good reason for not having presented themselves at the regular examination in July may be held at the opening of the academy after the summer vacation. The questions for this examination (should one be found necessary) shall be prepared by the principal (or faculty), and must be transmitted with the regular detailed report to the Superintendent of Education immediately after the examination ; and in every other respect shall be subject to the same conditions as the regular examination. No candidate failing at the July examination should be re-examined at a supplementary, unless he shall have made the prescribed aggregate, and shall also present a certificate of at least four weeks' study, in the interim, on the subjects in which he failed.

No supplementary entrance examination shall be held later during the year, except on the express permission of the Superintendent of Education, after good cause has been shown, when the examination shall be subject to the conditions already stated, except that the questions shall be so advanced as to cover, in addition to the common school work, that portion of the high school course already taken up at the date of examination.

[2.] *Comment.* As supplementary examinations under the foregoing regulation are specially open to the suspicion of an attempt on the part of candidates to gain an easy entrance, and on the part of the academy an unfair hold on public funds, principals would do well to discountenance them, except under urgent and justifying circumstances. In order that the public may observe what the facts are in connection with each institution, the following regulation is made :

Reg. 11. Each candidate passing the academy entrance examination shall be returned on the form prescribed, in the order of merit, numbered in consecutive order, so that each can be quoted by his *number, year, and county.* Those passing at any supplementary examinations shall receive the next consecutive numbers in order under the date of the initial entrance examination. Each such successful candidate shall be entitled to a certificate supplied by the Education Department, and signed by the principal who conducted the examination, and the said certificate shall also contain the candidate's name (in full) with number, year, and county, as above mentioned ; and these items shall be regularly published in the JOURNAL OF EDUCATION, as the list of the successful candidates at each academy.

Reg. 12. Each county academy shall be examined annually, when possible, by the Superintendent of Education in conjunction with the inspector of schools for the district. The examination shall be conducted orally or in writing, at the discretion of the examiners, and in its scope shall have regard to the time of the school year at which it may be held. The names of students in the lower classes on the register shall be carefully compared with the entrance examination lists, and the answer papers shall be inspected. Students on the register who are not present at such examination (unless they have already a high school certificate), or who fail to satisfy the examiners, shall not be held to be properly certified high school students under the statute, and their attendance shall therefore be deducted from that given in the "return," in order to determine the grade of academic grant to which the institution is entitled.

Reg. 13. Students may be admitted to the higher classes in any academy or standing shown by provincial certificates of scholarship, or by examination, at the discretion of the principal (or faculty) of each academy. The grading of any institution should for economy and efficiency be adjusted to its local conditions—*i.e.*, to the number of the students and of the staff of instructors, etc.

But in all academies and high schools, students who hold a provincial grade D shall be entitled to be enrolled in the register as *in* grade X with an asterisk or star thus, X*; those who hold grade C as *in* grade XI*; and those who hold grade B as *in* grade XII*. The star will thus indicate provincial classification, as its absence will denote merely local classification as permitted above. An error in the use of this star will be *prima facie* a falsification of the register.

Reg. 14. It shall be the duty of the trustees or commissioners of each county academy to supply for the teachers' use all text-books which by the prescribed course of study are made the basis of oral lessons and lectures. They must also provide the philosophical and chemical apparatus essential for the experiments and demonstrations required by the course as a regular part of the teaching. A selection of physiological and zoological diagrams, models and specimens, is deemed necessary. The teachers should encourage pupils to collect cabinets illustrating the geology, varied mineral resources, botany, zoology, etc., of Nova Scotia; and the museum and general equipment of the institution are required to be superior to those of the same grade of high schools not drawing academic grants.

Reg. 15. When the equipment of a county academy as generally indicated above and in regulation 2 is not decidedly superior to that of a high school in a section of nearly similar means in any part of the province, or when the trustees fail to make satisfactory provision for the effective teaching of any subject in the prescribed course of study, or for the health or comfort of the students, or of the common school pupils within the section, it shall be the duty of the superintendent to report the same to the Council. If, in case the Council notifies the trustees or commissioners of the defect reported, and within reasonable time the defects are not remedied, then the academy shall forfeit its claim to public grants until such time as the improvements required are made.

Reg. 16. The county academy entrance examination papers may be sent by the Superintendent of Education to the principals of high schools making application for them, under exactly the same conditions and obligations as to the principals of academies with respect to the conducting, reporting and certifying of the examination. But the successful candidates shall not be entitled to "academic certificates," although they shall be entitled to enrolment in the register as high school students.

Reg. 17. The schools entitled to employ a class A teacher under section 37 of the statute shall comprise at least two departments, each in charge of a separate teacher, shall be regularly graded according to prescribed course of study, and shall maintain in the principal's department a certified average of at least ten pupils regularly pursuing the studies of the prescribed high school course.

A class A teacher being a subordinate teacher, in order to draw the provincial grant under the said section 37 of the statute, must be certified by the inspector as being employed in doing regular high school work with a daily average attendance of at least twenty high school pupils.

It is also provided that in all cases the inspector of schools shall certify that the equipment and management of these schools are such as to warrant the payment of the special grant.

Any class A teacher proposing to claim the provincial grants under this regulation shall within three weeks of the opening of the school notify the inspector of the district in writing of his intention to qualify for such claim, and endorse his claim on his "return."

APPENDIX E.

REGULATIONS OF THE COUNCIL OF PUBLIC INSTRUCTION REFERRING TO "COMMON" SCHOOL BUILDINGS.

SCHOOL ACCOMMODATION.

The school house with its grounds is a very true index of the general public spirit and intelligence of the school section. Being the common centre of habitation for a large portion of the day of that part of every family naturally drawing forth the deepest emotions of affection and interest, the character of the school house and its environment must substantially reflect the sentiment of the community. Here we should expect to see the accumulation of efforts constantly made from year to year, embellishing grounds at first selected for their convenience, salubrity and beauty of position, and adding to the useful apparatus and general equipment of the school room, originally constructed with a view to healthy, physical, intellectual and moral development. When the people have reason to be proud of their school house, it may bear on its front the name of the school and the year of its erection. The following directions are intended more particularly for rural schools, as in the towns the custom has already been established by trustees and school commissioners of examining the most modern improvements before proceeding to build :

[1.] *School Sites.* In selecting the site for a school house, the trustees should see that the following conditions are fulfilled as far as possible, and that the sanction of the inspector is secured in writing before any contract whatever is entered upon. (*a*) The situation should be the most accessible to the majority of the people of the section. (*b*) It should be from 50 to 150 feet from any public highway, and should be far removed from railroads, mills, factories, taverns, noisy surroundings, stagnant pools, swamps, or noxious effluvia from any source. (*c*) It should have a dry, airy position, with a gentle slope and southern exposure if possible, and command as attractive a prospect as natural facilities will permit.

[2.] *School Grounds.* (*a*) In rural sections the ground should contain, when convenient, *one* acre, never less than *half* an acre ; in thickly peopled localities, or villages, a *half* an acre or more, but never less than *one-third* ; and in towns never less than *one-quarter*, if possible. (*b*) The form should be, perhaps, more than twice as long as broad, in order to furnish proper separate playgrounds for the boys and girls. (*c*) It should be properly levelled, drained when necessary, neatly fenced around, ornamented with desirable shade trees, which should neither interfere with the play grounds nor the light of the school room. (*d*) Clean water, free from the suspicion of taint from surface drainage or other impurities, should be within easy reach of the school house.

[3.] *School Houses.* (*a*) For a rural section not likely to have more than 30 pupils for twenty years to come, the school house should have the following *inside* measurements : Width 23 feet, length 31 feet (hall 6 feet teacher's platform 5 feet, clear space 4 feet, seats and desks 13 feet, clear space 3 feet), and 11 to 12 feet high.

(*b*) For a section with 42 pupils : Width 24 feet, length 36 feet (hall 6 feet, platform 5 feet, space 4 feet, seats and desks 18 feet, space 3 feet) and height 12 to 13 feet.

(*c*) For a section with 54 pupils : Width 25 feet, length 41 feet (hall 6 feet, platform 5 feet, space 4 feet, seats and desks, 23 feet, space 3 feet), and height 13 to 14 feet.

(*d*) For a section with a greater number of pupils, there should be, as required by the statute a separate class room, large enough to be converted into a primary department of a graded school should the attendance increase.

(*e*) When a building is situated with its length north and south, the entrance doors can be at the south end, the teacher's platform next the entrance hall, the stove at the north end, so that on cold, windy days the heated air may drift through the whole room ; the light coming principally from the east will obviate the glare of the midday sun, and the maps can be hung on the north wall to secure their proper orientation in the minds of the pupils (a very important matter), the west wall being used temporarily for maps when the convenience of teaching requires it.

(*f*) School houses with several departments should be so planned as to admit of extension without interfering with the principles of proper lighting of the rooms, etc., as elsewhere directed, and should not be more than two stories in height, exclusive of the basement, which should be airy and well lighted for a play room, and of the attic which might be utilised as a general assembly room.

[4.] *Lighting, Ventilation and Warming.* (*a*) The windows should be principally on the left of the pupils. There may be two behind them, but none in front of them or on the right. The front and right can be utilised for an unbroken blackboard, which should reach to within two and a half feet of the floor, and have a width of five feet, the upper portion being useful for the more permanent illustrations.

(*b*) The lower window sill should be at least *four* feet from the floor, and the top of the window as near the ceiling as possible. The left wall above the four foot line should be about one-half glass.

(*c*) The upper part of each window should be a transom, hinged below, or the upper sash should be hung on pulleys, as well as the lower for ventilation purposes.

(*d*) The size of a school room is determined by the greatest number of pupils it is intended to hold, 200 cubic feet of air being required for each. When the room is full of pupils this air should be entirely changed at least two or three times every hour. In some of the more expensively ventilated school buildings in the province, the air is warmed and changed every ten minutes.

(*e*) In rural sections where economy has to be carefully considered, a *large* stove surrounded by a sheet metal jacket closely fitted to the floor and around the door, separated from the rest of the stove by an air space, and rising up over three feet and nearly to the top of the stove, makes an excellent ventilating and warming furnace. Underneath the stove and shut off from the schoolroom by the jacket should be a large opening for the admission of pure, fresh air through a large tin pipe or air-tight wooden funnel running underneath the floor and through the foundation, then turning up and terminating at least six or eight feet above the ground on the side of the house, the entrance to the funnel being lateral and covered with a grating to prevent the throwing of anything into it. The stove should be two or three times larger than one necessary to warm the room without such an air draught. The stove, when practicable being at the north end of the room and opposite the teacher's desk, should have its pipe traverse the room at least 9 or 10 feet above the floor into the flue. The average temperature, 6 inches from the floor, should be 65° Fahrenheit (over 18° Centigrade). In a cold day the air cannot be kept pure without fresh incoming air, and this cannot be warmed without a very large expenditure of heat, necessitating a large stove and plenty of fuel. In such schools where in-going and out-going currents of air cannot be maintained as in the more expensive ventilating systems, the windows should be thrown open at every recess, and when physical exercise is being taken. The evil effects of impure air are so insidious and unobservable that even cautious teachers are apt to allow very serious injury to be inflicted on the general health of the school without being aware of it.

[5.] *Seating.* (*a*) The best arrangement for seating is that of single desks and seats adjustable to the sizes of the pupils. Next come single desks and seats of assorted sizes. But where economy is desirable, double desks and seats of no more than five assorted sizes serve very well, especially when, as in some patent forms, each seat moves automatically as the pupil sits or stands, so as to give the fullest freedom in standing.

(*b*) The seats should be arranged in three rows facing a wall (the south end when practicable) in which there are no windows, the light falling principally from the left and above. There should be a space of 4 feet between the front row and the teacher's platform, with at least 3 feet between the seats and the walls. The aisles should not be less than 2½ feet. In the schoolroom [3.] (*a*), about 13 feet will be occupied by five ranks of desks and seats, three in each rank, each rank on an average requiring about 2½ feet. In [3.] (*b*), about 18 feet in depth will be occupied by seven ranks, three in a rank. And in [3] (*c*), about 23 feet in depth will be occupied by nine ranks of double desks and seats, three in each rank.

(*c*) Dimensions of the five sizes of double desks and seats :—

Size.	Age of Pupil.	Height of Seat.	Desks.			Space between Desks and Seats.
			Height of side next Pupil.	Length.	Width.	
No. 1	5—7	11½ in.	21 in.	36 in.	12 in.	Edge of desk almost
„ 2	7—9	12½ „	22½ „	39 „	13 „	directly above edge
„ 3	9—11	13½ „	24 „	42 „	14 „	of seat.
„ 4	11—14	15 „	26 „	45 „	15 „	
„ 5	14—16	16 „	27 „	48 „	16 „	

(*d*) For the average rural school the following might be a good arrangement and distribution of the seats and desks : Front half of row on pupils' right (next the blackboard side), No. 1 seats ; back half, No. 2 seats ; central row, No. 4 seats ; front half of row on pupils' left (next the light side), No. 4 seats ; back half, No. 5 seats. The older pupils using the text books with smaller print would by this arrangement have the best light. Another plan is to have the seats arranged in ranks according to size, the smallest being in front, the largest farthest back.

[6.] *Outhouses.* (*a*) It is required that separate and comfortable outhouses be provided, and kept in good sanitary condition, for the use of pupils of different sexes.

(*b*) A high and perfectly tight board fence should extend from the rear of the school house to near the rear of the grounds, on each side of which should be placed one of the houses. Their approaches should be protected by a suitable screen or hedge.

(*c*) Each should be supplied with a well-cemented vault, so placed as to be easily cleaned, and a quantity of dry loamy earth or ground gypsum for daily use as absorbents, and care should be taken to exclude the rain or surface water from the vault.

(*d*) The night soil should be removed as early as possible in the spring, at the beginning of the summer holidays, and before the frost of winter sets in ; and the houses should be regularly washed every week, and during warm weather or the appearance of an epidemic should be frequently disinfected with the chloride of lime, sulphate of iron, or other convenient disinfectant.

(e) The doors should be provided with good locks, the plaster should be finished rough, and the paint should be heavily sanded so as to offer no temptation to the use of the pencil, and all offensive odours should be kept repressed by the use of absorbents or disinfectants.

(f) The foregoing are the minimum requirements for rural sections. In villages and towns, more expensive and thorough systems compatible with the facilities of the locality are demanded.

[7.] *School Equipment.* (a) Every school must have the prescribed registers carefully preserved, and should have such books of reference as may be recommended by the Council of Public Instruction, including a dictionary. In addition there should be maps of the Province, Dominion and the hemispheres, a terrestrial globe, wall cards, colour charts, music chart (modulator), ball frame, clock, hand bell, thermometer, blocks of geometrical solids, the common and the metric standards of weights and measures, and a box of coloured crayons for special black board illustrations.

(b) Every school should have a black board, five feet wide and two and a half feet from the floor, around the room, especially to the front and right of the pupils when the lighting is as previously recommended. At the lower edge there should be a concave shelf two or three inches wide for holding the chalk and brushes. *Brushes* can be made very cheaply as follows : Take a piece of light wood, not over six inches in length, two in breadth and one in thickness, trim it, making a groove along the two edges for the fingers. To the face glue a piece of half inch saddle cloth for the erasing surface, and it is complete. A number of these should be in each school room to facilitate class work on the black board. *Black boards* should be plastered down on laths nailed to a *solid* backing of boards, and should be composed largely of plaster of Paris, the surface being made very hard and smooth before applying the first coat of colour. Liquid slating, sold in cans, is very convenient for this latter purpose. Chrome green in liquid slating, containing fine emery flour, gives a green shade, which is considered by some more agreeable than dead black.

(c) In addition to the above requirements, advanced rural schools should be provided with maps of the continents, collections of the natural history of the locality, and some apparatus for the practical teaching of all the subjects of the prescribed course of study required to be taught in the school.

(d) In graded common schools the lower departments should be furnished in addition to (a) and (b) with a more extensive assortment of objects and pictures for object lessons, common and metric weights and measures, with a pair of small scales, and collections of local natural history objects.

(e) In graded common schools the higher departments should show a similar but more advanced adaptation to the work of their grades of the prescribed course of study leading up to that of the high school.

(f) In mixed or partial high school departments as far as possible, but especially in pure high school departments, in addition to the principal requirements of common schools, there should be full sets of ancient and physical maps, historical charts, physiological diagrams both vegetable and animal, celestial globe, gazetteer, classical dictionary, adequate apparatus and facilities for the practical study of chemistry, mineralogy, physics, surveying and navigation, botany, zoology and geology, so far as the high school course of study is pursued : and to aid the practical study of the latter subjects, a museum containing scientifically classified specimens of all the local species of each natural history department should be started and kept growing until it becomes as complete as possible.

APPENDIX F.

REGULATIONS OF THE COUNCIL OF PUBLIC INSTRUCTION ON THE LICENSING OF TEACHERS AND THEIR PROFESSIONAL QUALIFICATIONS.

COMMENT.

No person can, under any circumstances, be a teacher in a public school entitled to draw public money on his or her account without a License from the Council of Public Instruction. Before obtaining such a license a candidate must obtain, first, a certificate of the prescribed GRADE of scholarship at the Provincial High School Examination ; second, the prescribed certificate of professional RANK as a teacher either from the Provincial M. P. Q. Examination or the Provincial Normal School, and third, the prescribed certificate of age and character from a minister of religion or two Justices of the Peace. The value of a License is distinguished by the term CLASS, of scholarship by the term GRADE, of professional skill by the term RANK. The following collocation of the terms used will help to explain their significance and relation :—

Generally,

——	(1) Scholarship.	(2) Normal Prof. Skill.	(3) Age & Character
Class A (cl & sc) requires	Grade A (cl and sc)......	Academic Rank	20 years, &c.
Class A (cl) "	Grade A (cl)	Academic Rank	20 years, &c.
Class (A sc) "	Grade A (sc)	Academic Rank	20 years, &c.
Class B	Grade B	First Rank.........	18 years, &c
Class C	Grade C	Second Rank........	17 years, &c.
Class D "	Grade D	Third Rank	16 years, &c.

No certificate, combination of certificates, nor any other qualification except the possession of a lawfully procured License, gives a person authority to teach under the law in a public school. The Regulations governing the issuance of Licenses are as follows :

Reg. 1. The permanent Licenses of Public School Teachers shall be under the SEAL of the Council of Public Instruction, signed by the Secretary of the Council, shall be valid for the whole Province during the good behaviour of the holder, and shall be granted on the fulfilment of the three conditions more fully specified in the succeeding Regulations, namely : the presentation of the prescribed proof of (1) age and character, (2) scholarship, and (3) professional skill.

[After the year 1898 no License except that of Class D (provisional) shall be granted to any candidate without graduation of the required Rank from the Provincial Normal School, who has not made at least thirty-three per cent. on each imperative subject of the High School Course of Study up to and including the Grade corresponding to the Class applied for.

Thirty-three per cent. or more, on the subjects of a higher Grade will be taken as the equivalent of the "teachers' pass" on the same subject in any lower Grade. The following subjects are not repeated in the Grade next above : "Science" of Grade D, "Chemistry," "Drawing and Bookkeeping" of Grade C. They are represented in and will be covered by the "teachers' pass" of thirty-three per cent. on the corresponding subjects of Grade A, except "Drawing and Book-keeping."]

Reg. 2. There shall be four Classes of such Licenses, which may be designated as follows :

Class A (cl and sc), A (cl) or A (sc)—Academic (classical and scientific) Academic (classical) or Academic (scientific).

Class B—First Class.

Class C—Second Class.

Class D—Third Class.

Reg. 3. The certificate of professional qualification or skill shall be (a) the normal, academic, first, second, or third RANK classification by the Normal School, or (b) the minimum (which shall rank one degree lower than the normal), and shall be the first, second, or third rank pass on the following papers written on the Saturday of the Provincial Examination week : of School Law and Management, value 100 ; (2) Theory and Practice (1) Teaching, value 100 ; and (3) Hygiene and Temperance, value 100. First rank pass : an aggregate of 200 with no paper below 40. Second rank pass 150 with no paper below 30. Third rank pass : 100 with no paper below 20.

Reg. 4. The Provincial Normal School at Truro is recognised as the appropriate source of certificates of professional qualification for public school teachers ; but the certificates of other Normal or teachers' training schools whose curricula may be satisfactorily shown to the Council to be at least the equivalent of those of the Provincial Norman School, may be accepted when qualified by the addition of the two following conditions : (a) a pass certificate of the Provincial "minimum" professional qualification examination of the corresponding rank, and (b) a certificate of a Public School Inspector, before whom or under whose supervision the candidate has demonstrated his or her qualifications for the Class of License sought by the test of actual teaching for a sufficient period.

Reg. 5. The prescribed certificate of age and character is given in the following blank form of application for License, which will be supplied to candidates by the Education Department, through the Inspectors or the Principal of the Normal School :

FORM OF APPLICATION FOR A TEACHER'S LICENSE.

To........................

Inspector of Schools, District No. ...., Nova Scotia.

I hereby beg leave through you to make application to the Council of Public Instruction for a Teacher's License of Class............, and herewith I present evidence of compliance with the conditions prescribed, namely :

I. The prescribed certificate of age and character hereto attached which I affirm to be true.

II. My High School certificate of grade..............obtained at......... .... Examination Station as No...... ......, in the year 189... (Further information below.)

III. My certificate of professional qualification of .... Rank, No. ...... obtained at ....in the month of..................... 189....

(Name in full)...

(Post Office Address).......................

(County):...........................

CERTIFICATE OF AGE AND CHARACTER.

I, the undersigned, after due inquiry and a sufficient knowledge of the character of the above-named candidate for a Teacher's License, do hereby certify :—

That I believe the said candidate.. (name in full), was born on the.......................day of ...., in the year.. ; and

That I believe the moral character of the said candidate is good, and such as to justify the Council of Public Instruction in assuming that the said candidate will be disposed as a teacher "to inculcate by precept and example a respect for religion and the principles of Christian morality, and the highest regard for truth, justice, love of country, loyalty, humanity, benevolence, sobriety, industry, frugality, chastity, temperance, and all other virtues."

....(Name and title).
....(Church or Parish).
....(P. O. Address).

When the certificate given above is signed by "two Justices of the Peace," instead of a "Minister of Religion," the word "I" should be changed by the pen into "we," and after the signature on the second line the words "Church or Parish" may be cancelled by a stroke of the pen.

The correct quotation of the High School certificate in the application form given above, II., will be considered as equivalent to its presentation.

The correct quotation of the Provincial M. P. Q. Certificate or the Provincial Normal School Diploma in the application form above, III., will be considered as equivalent to its presentation.

Any certificate from Normal Schools, etc., which are not regularly recorded in the Education Office, must accompany this application as evidence of the correctness of the quotation.

———

FURTHER INFORMATION FROM APPLICANT.

1. Class of license already held.................., No. ...., year ....

2. University Degrees, Scholarship, Professional training, experience, or any other information candidate may wish to state, if any :

....
....

3. Provincial High School Examinations taken in addition to that specified in II. above : ·
On Grade A syllabus at Examination Station.............,No......., year.........
 „ B „ „ ...., „ ...., „ ....
 C „ ...., „ ...., „ ....
 D „ ...., „ ...., „ ....

———

GENERAL OR SPECIAL ENDORSATION OR REMARKS BY INSPECTOR (OR PRINCIPAL OF NORMAL SCHOOL).

....
....
....
...., Inspector.
Place and date...

Reg. 6. For an Academic or Class A License the three conditions are :—
(1.) A certificate signed by a Minister of Religion or two Justices of the Peace, as in the preceding form, to the effect that the candidate is of the full age of twenty years, and capable of fulfilling the duties specially mentioned in the statute. (2.) A pass certificate of the Grade A High School examination. (3.) A certificate of Academic first rank professional qualification from a Normal School [for which may be substituted a Provincial Grade A (cl & sc), with a first rank M. P. Q. (with no paper below 50), and at least one year's successful service as a *first* class teacher in a superior school, evidenced by the high testimonials of the Inspector and others having cognizance of the same, to the satisfaction of the Superintendent of Education.]

Reg. 7. For a First Class or B License the three conditions are :—(1.) A certificate of the full age of eighteen years and moral character as in the foregoing Regulation. (2.) A pass certificate of the Grade B High School examination. (3.) A certificate of first rank professional qualification from a Normal School, or a pass certificate of the Grade A High School examination with the first rank minimum professional qualification.

Reg 8. For a Second Class or C License the three conditions are :—(1.) A certificate of the full age of seventeen years and moral character as in the foregoing Regulation. (2.) A pass certificate of the Grade C High School examination. (3.) A certificate of second rank professional qualification from a Normal School or a pass certificate of the Grade B High School examination with the second rank minimum professional qualification.

Reg. 9. For a Third Class or D License the three conditions are :—(1.) A certificate of the full age of sixteen years and moral character as in the foregoing Regulation. (2.) A pass certificate of the Grade D High School examination. (3.) A certificate of third rank professional qualification from a Normal School or a pass certificate of the Grade C High School examination with the third rank minimum professional qualification.

TEMPORARY LICENSE.

Reg. 10. A Third Class (provisional) or D (prov.) License, valid only for one year, shall be granted on the regular application when the following conditions are fulfilled :—(1) A certificate of age and moral character as in the foregoing Regulation. (2) A pass certificate of the Grade D as in the foregoing Regulation. (3) The third rank minimum professional qualification. Such a License can be renewed for another year on condition that the candidate has demonstrated an advance in his qualifications by his record at a subsequent Provincial Examination.

SYLLABUS OF M. P. Q. EXAMINATION.

Reg. 11. The questions set in the minimum professional qualification examination paper shall be within the limits indicated by the books recommended by the Council of Public Instruction, and shall be as follows :—

School Law and School Management.—(a) To be familiar with the Acts relating to Public Schools in Nova Scotia and Regulations of the Council of Public Instruction as appearing in the *Journal of Education* from time to time, particularly those portions bearing on the relations and duties of teachers and on the organisation and operation of all grades of Public Schools.

(b) To understand thoroughly the principles of school organisation, the principles and methods of classification, the proper correlation and sequence of studies, the true aim and right modes of discipline, and the proper condition for securing the moral and physical well-being of pupils.

(c) To be familiar with the history of leading Educational Reformers and their systems.

Theory and Practice of Teaching. (*a*) To have an understanding of the fundamental laws of the human mind in their relation to the science and art of education generally, including the principles and practice of vocal music.

(*b*) To practically apply the principles thus derived to the teaching of particular subjects, especially those embraced in the Common and High School courses of study.

Hygiene and Temperance. (*a*) Hygiene as in recommended or prescribed books with special reference to school room, school premises, and the health of pupils. (*b*) Temperance as in recommended or prescribed books with special reference to requirements of the school law.

PROVINCIAL NORMAL SCHOOL.

INTRODUCTORY.

The object of the Provincial Normal School is the professional training of teachers for service in the public schools of Nova Scotia. While attendance is not compulsory, yet the importance and value of professional training are such as to justify the Council of Public Instruction in ranking all licences to be hereafter awarded one grade below that indicated by the scholarship certificate in the case of candidates not possessing such training.

The Institution is centrally located in the town of Truro, and, in order to make it equally accessible from all points of the province, students duly qualified for admission, whose homes are not less than ten miles from Truro, are allowed travelling expenses at the rate of five cents per mile going and returning.

The Provincial School of Agriculture, about a mile distant, is affiliated with the Normal School for the purpose of securing to Normal School Students practical instruction in microscopy, chemistry, and biology etc.

COURSE OF STUDY.

When entering on a course of study, students will be required to present a Provincial License or the Provincial High School Certificate corresponding to the rank of Diploma for which they are to compete.

The work of the normal school is chiefly of a professional character, including the study of Educational principles and Model School practice. Students are required to review the various subjects of the course of study from a professional standpoint, for the purpose of discovering their historic development in the mind of the child, noting their correlation, their educational values as means of mental discipline, and the mode of treatment or presentation required in order to secure to the learner both knowledge and power.

It will at the same time be the constant aim of the Institution to round out and enrich the scholarship of its students, endeavouring to inspire them with higher ideals and stimulate them to effort for higher attainment in knowledge. To this end it will require of them some advanced work, especially in the critical study of literature, and in laboratory work in natural science.

The course, modified in adaptation to the different classes, includes the following :

1. Psychology, General Principles of Pedagogy.
2. History of Education, application of the principles of method to the various subjects of the School Course.
3. Drawing and Calisthenics.
4. Vocal Music.
5. Natural History and Science.
6. Manual Training.
7. Observation and Practice in the Model School.

PSYCHOLOGY AND GENERAL PRINCIPLES OF PEDAGOGY.

While text-books will form a general guide in these subjects, the utmost freedom will be exercised in dealing with the matter they present. Topics will be examined in such a way as to elicit thought. It will be the aim to secure this end by introspection, by studying child-nature, and by comparing the views of different authors. Leading topics to be considered are :—

Perception, Reproduction, Conception, Apperception, Attention, Interest, Association, Thinking, Expression of Ideas, the Feelings, the Will, Character. The systematic study of the child's mental character and growth will be encouraged.

It will be the endeavour to show that right methods of teaching and sound maxims of school management are based on Psychological principles.

The scope and character of education, educational agencies, function of the school, correlation of studies, and educational values of different studies will be considered.

TEXT-BOOKS :—Halleck's Psychology, Lindner's Psychology, James' Psychology, Calkin's Notes on Education, Compayré's Pedagogy, De Garmo's Essentials of Method, and McMurry's General Method.

HISTORY OF EDUCATION.

This course consists of lectures, recitations on the history of education, and essays on educational topics. The students will be directed in studying the growth and relations of educational systems, with special attention to the trend of education at the present time.

TEXT-BOOKS :—
A Class.—*Compayré's History of Education.*
B Class.—*Quick's Educational Reformers.*
C Class.—*Hall's Outline History of Education.*

GEOGRAPHY, HISTORY, CIVICS, AND LANGUAGE.

This course consists of lectures and text-book work.

It will be the design in this work to base method on psychological principles.

Some attention will be given to the historical development of subjects, relative values, and concentration of studies.

A written outline of the lessons taught by the student based on these principles will afford a practical application of this work.

MATHEMATICS AND PHYSICS.

The following is an incomplete outline of the scope of the work in this department.

A review of the subjects of the various classes, special attention being given to the rationale of processes.

Development of the idea of number—the decimal system of notation examined and compared with other systems.

Units of weight, measure, time, etc.—their origin—comparison of systems and formulæ deduced therefrom, with methods of development—excellence of the metric system illustrated.

Division of subjects into topics and sub-topics, related groups of topics compared—logical articulation traced out.

When to use the Analytic method of presentation—when the Synthetic—why? Progress from the concrete to the abstract—from the Simple to the Complex.

Practical utility of Mathematical studies to go hand in hand with intellectual discipline. The framing and solving of problems arising out of the affairs of every day life.

A short course in mathematical drawing, including both lines and orthographic projection. (Text-book mathematical drawing by Linus Faunce, seventh edition.)

Object teaching in mathematical studies—when and how to use it.

The assignment, preparation, and recitation of lessons—what to aim at and what to avoid.

Examinations—their frequency and character. Preparation of examination questions.

Motives to be appealed to in pupils, and how to awaken them. Natural aptitudes of pupils to be turned to best account.

The management of classes studying the same branches in different grades of a miscellaneous school.

Sense-perceptions—their training and relation to studies in Physics.

Order and accuracy in conducting observations and experiments in Physics of paramount importance. The use of diagrams and drawings to illustrate thought and to develop faculty of imagination.

The use and adjustment of angular instruments. Practical work in field, including Surveying and Levelling.

Tabulation of results of experiments, with deductions therefrom.

The aim throughout will be to give prominence to such methods as are best calculated to stimulate inquiry and arouse mental energy.

NATURAL SCIENCE AT SCHOOL OF AGRICULTURE.

The course for Normal School students in the natural sciences at the School of Agriculture will embrace the following sciences :—Chemistry, Botany, General Biology, Entomology, Anatomy, and Physiology (human).

The course will be arranged so that each pupil will be able to review or continue the sciences he may have previously studied, and also receive an introduction to the study of the sciences of the next higher grade.

It will comprise laboratory or field work, accompanied with Reviews, Recitations, and Essays.

Options, subject to the approval of the Faculty, from the sciences named above, will be allowed students of the advanced classes.

Students taking laboratory work will be required to deposit with the Principal of the School of Agriculture at the commencement of the term a small sum of money to cover breakage of apparatus and cost of chemicals. Any balance of deposit will be returned at the close of term.

DRAWING.

Form study and modelling in Clay, Freehand Drawing, Model and Object Drawing, Shaded Drawing from the Round, Colour, Principles and Practice of Decorative Design, History of Art, Geometrical Drawing, Perspective, Preparation of Working Drawings to scale, and Methods in Teaching Drawing.

SINGING, READING, AND VOCAL CULTURE.

Singing.—This course consists of a study of the *Tonic Sol-fa* system of sight singing, and its application to the needs of all public schools ; also a comparison of the Tonic Sol-Fa and staff notation.

Reading and Vocal Culture.- The aim in this department is to cultivate a clear and natural mode of expression. Attention is given to correct breathing, proper placing of the voice, distinct and definite enunciation, correct emphasis and inflection, literary analysis, and intelligent interpretation of an author. Books used :—Vol. I. Evolution of Expression, with its application to the Readers used in the public schools.

DEPARTMENT OF MANUAL TRAINING AND SCIENCE.

This department is well equipped for practical work in its various subjects. The Manual Training room is fitted with model work benches, complete sets of wood-working tools, and drawing boards. The main purpose of the shop work is not so much the making of useful things as the training of mind, eye, and hand. The students do all their work in wood from their own drawings, so that the hand is trained to execute the purposes of the mind, and the object made is an expression of the mental image.

In Chemistry, while a text-book is taken as a general guide, the "laboratory method" of experimentation and original work by the student is demanded. Accuracy in observation, skill in manipulation, and general neatness are cultivated. Careful and complete notes of all work done are required.

In Mineralogy each student studies a set of typical specimens of native minerals, and applies the more simple tests for their various properties. Descriptions based on the results of the student's observation, together with such aditional information as to the formation, occurrence, etc., as can be obtained by supplementary reading, are recorded in note-books, which thus form elementary local text-books.

In all the work throughout the department special stress is laid on the pedagogics of the subject. The student is guided along the course which he is expected to follow as a teacher, and in his teaching in the Model School he is trained in the practical application of this method. In the subjects discussed regard is had to the course of study with the view of making the students familiar with its requirements.

The text-books used are Crosby's Common Minerals and Rocks, Clapp's Observation Lessons on Minerals, Williams's Introduction to Chemistry, and J. D. Dana's Manual of Mineralogy.

MODEL SCHOOL.

The Model School includes two departments, comprising the eight grades of the Common Schools. Students under training visit the Model School for observation and practice. Throughout the term they are required to teach classes under the supervision of the different members of the Faculty and the Model School teachers. Thus with the aid of criticism and suggestion, they are trained in the practical application of pedagogical principles inculcated in the lecture-room.

KINDERGARTEN.

A well equipped Kindergarten under the management of a special committee, is provided with accommodation in the Normal School Building, and has such general affiliation with the Institution that the Normal School Students have opportunity of observing the application of the principles and methods of Froebel's system of child training ; and the students under training as Kintergarteners are admitted to the classes in psychology and history of education in the Normal School.

TEXT BOOKS.

Halleck's Psychology, Lindner's Pyschology, James' Pyschology, Calkin's Notes on Education, Compayré's History of Education, Compayré's Pedagogy, Quick's Educational Reformers, Hall's Outline History of Education, McMurray's General Method, De Garmo's Essentials of Method.

The library is well supplied with the leading pedagogical works which the students are required to use for reference.

In the exemplication of method and in Model School practice the authorised text books for the Public Schools of the province will be used in the various subjects which they represent.

THE LIBRARY.

The Library contains about 1,500 volumes, selected chiefly for their fitness to aid students and teachers in the special work of the Institution. It comprises the most important pedagogical works in the English language, including educational books, reviews, and magazines. In addition to many other valuable works that have been added during the year, special mention may be made of the Century Dictionary, in six volumes.

EXPENSES.

1. Board can be obtained at prices varying from $2.25 to $3.00 per week.
2. Travelling expenses will be paid to students at the rate of 5 cents per mile to and from the Institution, at the end of the session, provided the distance is not less than ten miles.

THE ALUMNI ASSOCIATION.

All former students of Normal School, teachers of three years' experience, and all school officials are eligible to membership.

THE

SYSTEM OF EDUCATION

IN

NEW BRUNSWICK, CANADA.*

I. PRIMARY EDUCATION :
Brief Historical Sketch - - - - - - 336
"Boarding Around" System - - - - - 336
Assessment System - - - - - - - 337
Common Schools Act, 1871 - - - - - 337
Central Administration - - - - - - 337
Local Administration - - - - - 337
Finance - - - - - - - - 338
Salaries of Teachers - - - - - - 339
School Attendance - - - - - - 339
Course of Study - - - - - - - 340
Manual Training and Needlework - - - 340
Instruction in Religion and Morals - 340
Training of Teachers - - - - - - 340
School Inspection - - - - - - 341
Teachers' Institutes - - - - - - 341

II. SECONDARY EDUCATION - - - - - - 341

III. UNIVERSITY EDUCATION - - - - - 342

IV. TECHNICAL AND AGRICULTURAL EDUCATION - - 342

V. INDUSTRIAL SCHOOLS AND REFORMATORIES - - - 342

VI. SCHOOLS FOR THE DEAF AND DUMB AND THE BLIND - 342

VII. GENERAL RESULTS - - - - 342

SUPPLEMENTARY NOTES.
(i) University Education - - - 344
(ii) Government Training Farm - - - - 344
(iii) Provincial Dairy School - - - - - 346

APPENDIX. EDUCATIONAL STATISTICS, 1889–1899 - - - 347

* Since the receipt of this Report, which was prepared in 1898, the statistics have been amended in accordance with the latest available tables.

THE SYSTEM OF EDUCATION IN NEW BRUNSWICK, CANADA.

I. PRIMARY EDUCATION.

Brief Historical Sketch.

When in 1874 New Brunswick became a separate province, it had no large towns, and the rural districts were very sparsely settled. The homes of the pioneers were connected by rough forest roads or foot-paths. The settlers had to work hard for long hours. Their means were small and often their stock of learning slender. Under such conditions general illiteracy must soon have prevailed had not the Government come to the aid of the people. At first the legislative grants were small, nothing further being contemplated than the instruction of the young in reading and writing and perhaps the elements of arithmetic.

Still, parents who had enjoyed good educational advantages in their youth found their children growing up around them with no school within reach. In such cases the father and mother, in intervals stolen from the laborious duties of life on a new farm, usually found time to teach their children how to read and write, but seldom to raise them to their own standard of intelligence and culture. And many, the children of negligent or ignorant parents, were allowed to grow up quite illiterate.

The Legislature, however, gradually became more generous in its grants, until the annual allowance to teachers holding the several classes of licence had reached the following figures :—

	Male Teachers.	Female Teachers.
1st class - - - - -	$150.00	$110.00
2nd class - - - -	120.00	90.00
3rd class - - - -	90.00	70.00

The class of licence held depended upon the scholarly attainments of the candidate.

"Boarding Around" system

Very often, in the rural districts, the teacher received but little remuneration, save board and lodging, in addition to this provincial grant. In the more populous localities the practice of "boarding around" prevailed. The teacher in search of employment, having first obtained the permission of the school committee, set out to canvass the district for subscriptions. Each father or guardian was expected to subscribe so many "scholars" at so much per term or quarter, and in addition, to board and lodge the teacher for a term proportionate to the number of "scholars" subscribed. The custom of "boarding around" sometimes subjected the teacher to very trying experiences—at the best the accommodations and management of some of his temporary homes would be far from ideal; and, after all, having completed his term of service, he had to make another round or more among his constituents to collect the small cash subscriptions.

In the towns and villages also, payment was made by voluntary subscriptions, but the teacher as a rule "boarded himself."

This system, both in town and country, placed the financial burden mainly on the parents of large families and on the few public-spirited residents who were willing to contribute in proportion to their means. It is true that the Government on more than one occasion endeavoured to introduce the principle of general assessment, even offering a premium to any county, municipality, parish, or district which would support its schools in that way; but the assessment system made no headway against the opposition of that numerous and influential class whose sense of private ownership exceeds their public spirit. *Assessment system.*

In the early days of the Province, the rectors and missionaries of the Church of England were required to examine the public schools, and were accustomed to conduct religious exercises on the occasion of their visits; but, as the population increased the non-episcopal Protestant denominations and the Roman Catholics grew in numbers and influence. Persons, too, of any religious faith were allowed to qualify as teachers. In consequence the prestige of the English Church declined, and most of the schools receiving the Government grant became practically non-denominational.

In 1869-70 a great educational wave passed over the Province, which resulted in the passage of the present law, the "Common Schools Act, 1871." This act made local assessment for the support of schools compulsory, and provided for the free tuition of all children of school age. *The Common Schools Act.*

The central administrative power is invested in the Board of Education, which consists of the Governor, the members of the Executive Council, the Chancellor of the Provincial University, and the Chief Superintendent of Education. The Chief Superintendent is the secretary and chief executive officer of the Board. His position is understood to be non-political, professional fitness and executive ability being the sole qualifications. There have been three appointments under the present Act: Theodore H. Rand, D.C.L., who had successfully inaugurated the free schools system in Nova Scotia, was Chief Superintendent in New Brunswick from 1871 to 1883. He was succeeded by William Crocket, A.M., who had conducted the Provincial Normal School for over 12 years. In 1891 J.R. Inch, LL.D., President of Mount Allison University, was appointed to the position. *Central Administration.*

For the local administration of the Common Schools Act, the Province is divided into school districts. Each of the cities and incorporated towns is constituted one district, and the parishes of the 16 counties are divided into districts, none of which should contain less than 50 children of school age unless the district is at least four square miles in extent. *Local Administration.*

Every school district has a board of school trustees. In cities and incorporated towns, the members of the school board are appointed for a term of three years, part by the Governor in Council and part by the City or Town Council. Two members of the board must be women. Any trustee may be reappointed at the end of each term of three years. In the villages and rural districts, the school board consists of three trustees, elected by the ratepayers of the district at the annual school meeting. One trustee retires each year, but may be re-elected. The school meeting also determines, by vote, the amount which shall be assessed upon the district for the support of schools. Should the school meeting fail to provide the necessary means, the Board of Education may authorise the trustees to levy and collect a sufficient sum.

There is no school meeting in cities and incorporated towns. In them, the school board determines the amount to be assessed (subject to a maximum limitation fixed by law).

The trustees have the general management and oversight of the schools of the district. They select the teachers, engage them for a definite period, and, if they deem it best, may re-engage them. They may dismiss any teacher for immorality or gross neglect of duty. They may suspend or expel from the school any pupil addicted to vicious practices or who is persistently disobedient to the teacher.

Finance. The funds for the support of schools are drawn from three sources, the Provincial Grant, the County School Fund, and the District Assessment.

Each teacher is paid from the Provincial Treasury a fixed amount per school year. This allowance depends partly on the class of licence held by the teacher, and partly on the grade of school in which he is employed and his position therein. The allowances given to teachers in the ordinary schools during recent years have been approximately as follows:—

Male Teachers.			Female Teachers.		
1st Class	-	-	$ 135.00	1st Class	-	-	$ 100.00
2nd „	-	-	108.00	2nd „	-	-	81.00
3rd „	-	-	81.00	3rd „	-	-	63.00

The allowance to teachers in poor districts is increased one-third. The Province also makes grants to poor districts for the erection of school buildings.

The Provincial expenditure for the school service during the year 1897, not including grants to school libraries and for the education of the deaf-mutes and the blind, amounted to $161,446. The total Provincial income for the same year was $745,202.59. It will be seen, therefore, that the Province expends a large proportion of its income in support of education. The Provincial expenditure on education during the year 1898 was $163,022, and the total Provincial income $1,254,348.

The County School Fund is provided for by an annual assessment upon the county sufficient to yield a sum equal to thirty cents per head of the population. It is distributed among the school districts of the county, in part according to the number of teachers employed and in part in proportion to the average attendance at school. This money must be applied by the trustees in payment of the salaries of teachers. Besides this, the counties contribute towards the education of deaf-mutes and the blind. The money for school purposes raised by county assessment during the year 1896–7, amounted to $94,421, and in 1899 to $90,857.

The local assessment in every district is applied in support of the schools of the district, in payment of teachers' salaries, partly in defraying the cost of school buildings, furniture, apparatus, repairs, fuel, and other necessary expenses.

The amount assessed upon the districts of the Province, for salaries, etc., during 1898 approximated to $340,000.00. The assessment is levied partly as a poll-tax of one dollar on each adult male resident and the balance upon property and income.

No tuition fees are charged for pupils whose parents or guardians reside in the district. In general parents provide their children with text-books; but in the case of persons in indigent circumstances, the trustees are empowered to supply the necessary text-books at the expense of the district.

The public schools are provided for quite independently of subscriptions or endowments; yet school boards may legally receive benefactions in aid of popular education. This form of generosity has not, however, been largely indulged in by our philanthropists.

The average annual salaries from all sources, of the various classes of teachers, as shown by the returns for 1898, were :— Salaries of Teachers.

Grammar school teachers (principals) -	-	$939.47
Superior school teachers (principals) -	-	608.55
First class male teachers - -	-	463.99
Second „ „ „ -	-	278.40
Third „ „ „ -	-	224.25
First class female teachers	-	309.03
Second „ „ „ -	-	229.75
Third „ „ „ -	-	187.65

In the first Term of 1898, 1,864 teachers were employed in the public schools, of whom 402 were males, and 1,462 females.

There is no provision made for pensioning teachers.

The school laws of New Brunswick do not compel parents to send their children to school. When a pupil has been enrolled, however, he is expected to attend school regularly, and in case of absence or tardiness to present an excuse to the teacher from his parent or guardian. School Attendance.

The number of children enrolled in the public schools during the first term of 1898 was 63,333, which is about 20 per cent. of the total population. The average attendance for the Province is about 55 per cent. of the number enrolled. In the cities and towns the average is much higher than this, but lower in the country districts. The average cost per pupil per year is about 8.00 dollars.

Course of Study

The course of study for the common schools includes reading and spelling, writing, arithmetic, grammar, geography, British and Canadian history, health lessons, lessons on nature, drawing, singing, and in the higher grades algebra, geometry, and Latin. Physical exercises are conducted by the teachers.

Manual Training and Needlework.

In 1900 a manual training school for boys and a manual training class for teachers were opened in Fredericton, all expenses (except the provision of a room) being defrayed out of the Macdonald Manual Training Fund. In some schools the girls are taught needlework. There are no cooking departments connected with the schools.

Instruction in Religion and Morals.

The school law explicitly declares that all schools conducted under its provisions are to be non-sectarian. No dogmatic religious teaching is allowed by the law or regulations. Practical Christianity, however, is encouraged. Every teacher is expected to maintain a deportment becoming an educator of the young. Any teacher guilty of immorality may be discharged by the trustees; and, if the charge be established, his licence will be cancelled by the Board of Education. The teacher is directed to strive diligently to inculcate the principles and encourage the practice of Christian morality, and to give instruction, as occasion may offer, concerning those virtues and habits which contribute to the happiness, effectiveness, and social fitness of the individual.

In addition, the teacher has the privilege of opening and closing the school by reading a portion of the Scripture (either from the common or Douay version), and repeating the Lord's Prayer. These religious exercises are purely voluntary, however, and no pupil can be required to be present at them contrary to the will of his parent or guardian. No religious Catechism may be used in the schools.

The law was vigorously opposed at first by the Roman Catholics on account of its undenominational character. Some concessions have since been made in the administration of the law, which have had the effect of rendering the system less distasteful to them. In most of the towns, the Roman Catholic children are grouped together in the same schools under teachers of their own faith. While subject, during the regular school time, to the regulations of the Board of Education as to religious teaching and the use of the prescribed text-books, this arrangement renders it possible for the teachers to instruct the pupils in the dogmas of their religion before or after the prescribed school hours.

In the villages generally, and in country places, the children of all faiths attend the district school, which is often taught by a Roman Catholic teacher. The clergy of all denominations are encouraged to visit the schools.

Training of Teachers.

Every teacher in the public schools must obtain some professional training at a recognised training or normal school before receiving a permanent licence. By far the greater number attend the Provincial Normal School, where all except third class candidates and college graduates are required to attend for at least one year. The aim of this school is to acquaint the candidates with the best methods of teaching and school management, to instruct them in the principles and working details of the school system, and at the same time supply deficiencies in and supplement their general scholarship.

The attendance at the normal school for the year 1897-8 was 281. The candidates in attendance are all, or nearly all, natives of New Brunswick and come from all parts of the province. Their religious creeds are as various as those of the mass of the people, yet the utmost harmony prevails among them.

All candidates for Provincial licence to teach are required to pass the Government Examinations based upon the prescribed syllabus for the various classes of licence.

For the purpose of inspectoral visitation and supervision the Province is divided into six inspectoral districts. One inspector is appointed to each district by the Board of Education. The inspectors are usually teachers of experience, and must be holders of grammar school licences. *School Inspection.*

The regulations of the Board of Education provide for a system of annual gatherings for professional instruction and culture, called institutes: one for each county to continue for two days, and a general educational institute for the Province, whose sessions extend over a period of three days. These institutes are generally well attended and have done much to keep up the professional spirit and interest of the teachers. *Teachers' Institutes.*

II. SECONDARY EDUCATION.

There are three ranks of schools in the State system: ordinary common schools, superior schools, and grammar or high schools. *Secondary Education.*

The superior schools are advanced common schools. The law permits one to every 6,000 inhabitants. The Provincial Grant to the principal, who must hold a "Superior School" licence, is $250 per year. The superior school is free to qualified pupils from any district in the parish in which it is located.

The grammar schools are, or are intended to be, secondary schools proper. Each county is entitled to one. During the last few years a marked improvement has taken place in the equipment and efficiency of the grammar schools and other high schools. The Provincial Grant to the teachers has been increased, and several fine High School buildings have been erected. The Province contributes $350 per year toward the salary of every teacher in a Grammar School who holds a "Grammar School" licence. The Grammar Schools are free to qualified pupils from any part of the county. The High Schools in some of the towns are quite equal to the Grammar Schools in staff and equipment.

The High School course is an extension upward of the common school course. Greek and French are added. Health lessons become physiology, and nature lessons develop into physical science and botany.

Private and
Denomina-
tionalSchools
and Colleges.

Nearly all the elementary schools in the Province belong to the State system. A Madras school at St. John and another at Fredericton are controlled by the Church of England. The two commercial schools, one in each of the before-mentioned cities, are both conducted as private enterprises.

There are some denominational academies and boarding schools, but their attendance is small compared with that of the public Grammar, and High Schools.

There are also two well-attended denominational colleges— Mount Allison College, at Sackville, under the control of the Methodists, and the Roman Catholic College, St. Joseph's, at Memramcook. The greater part of those who attend the denominational secondary schools and colleges received their early education in the Provincial common schools.

III. UNIVERSITY EDUCATION.

University
Education.

There is a Provincial university at Fredericton. It has a considerable endowment, and receives, besides, a grant of about $9,000 from the Provincial Treasury. A moderate tuition fee is paid by the students.

IV. TECHNICAL AND AGRICULTURAL EDUCATION.

Technical
and Agricul-
tural Educa-
tion.

Under this head mention should be made of the Government Training Farm, and of the Provincial Dairy School, particulars of which are given in Supplementary Notes to this Report It may also be observed that the courses in nature study and physical science in the primary schools are, when taught in an earnest and practical way, a good preparation for technical work.

V. INDUSTRIAL SCHOOLS AND REFORMATORIES.

Industrial
Schools and
Reforma-
tories.

There is a reformatory near St. John, supported by Government, and two industrial schools in that city, one Roman Catholic and the other Protestant, supported by the gifts of the charitable.

VI. SCHOOLS FOR THE DEAF AND DUMB AND THE BLIND.

Schools for
the Deaf and
Dumb and
the Blind.

There is a school for the deaf and dumb at Fredericton. The Government has assisted in providing suitable buildings, and allows $60 per year from the County School Fund toward the support of each deaf and dumb mute person boarded and educated at the institute. This school also receives a special grant of $500 per annum from the Province.

There is no institution in the Province for the education of the blind, but the school for the blind at Halifax, in the adjoining province of Nova Scotia, is entitled to receive $75 per year from the Provincial Treasury, and an equal amount from the County School Fund, for each pupil from New Brunswick.

VII. GENERAL RESULTS.

General
results.

When we take a general view of the history of public education in New Brunswick, several tendencies may be observed arising in the earlier or later past, and taking their course toward the present. Some of these are here enumerated.

Methods of teaching have received increased attention, especially in the direction of making the school work easier and more pleasant for the pupil.

The curriculum of the Common and High Schools, at first very simple and exclusive, has become more complex and comprehensive. Methods of school discipline have been greatly softened. Corporal punishment is now little used.

The number of women teachers relatively to the number of men has steadily risen. At present over three-fourths of the teachers are women. For the first term of 1898, the class and sex of the teachers were as follows:—

Male Teachers.		Female Teachers.	
Grammar School -	20		
1st class - -	153	1st class - - -	274
2nd „ - - -	118	2nd „ - - -	786
3rd „ - - -	108	3rd „ - - -	377
Assistants - -	3	Assistants - -	25
Total - -	402	Total - -	1,462

There has been a great improvement in public school buildings, especially in the cities and towns.

The qualification of teachers, both in regard to scholarship and professional training, has been advanced, and the tendency is still in this direction.

The annual increase in the number of schools, and the consequent increase in expenditure, has caused a movement towards the union of rural school districts with the object of establishing one central graded school in place of several separate ungraded schools. This will involve the making provision for the transportation to the school at public expense of children living at a distance. If this plan prove successful it will have a tendency to increase the efficiency of the schools and at the same time decrease the expenditure of maintaining them.

The principle of assessment upon the property of the country for the support of public schools has been almost universally accepted. In some districts there is still occasionally manifested a passive resistance which tends to retard the machinery of the law, but any attempt to repeal any of the essential features of the Free School Act would be defeated by an overwhelming majority of votes. There is still a difference of opinion in regard to the proper limits of the Free School Act. Some maintain that a merely elementary education is all that the country should provide free of expense to the pupils; others would not only include secondary and collegiate schools in the free school class, but would provide at the public expense text-books for all pupils. There is but little doubt that a larger proportion of the cost of the schools will soon have to be borne by local taxation for the purpose of relieving to some extent the demand upon the Provincial revenues, nearly one-third of which is now expended for educational purposes.

J. BRITTAIN,

Instructor in the Provincial
Normal School.

SUPPLEMENTARY NOTES.

(i).

The following are extracts from *Papers relating to University Education of Roman Catholics in certain Colonies.* (*Colonial Office Return, 1900. Cd. 115.*)

" In the Province of New Brunswick no State provision is made for the University education of any particular denomination or class. The Provincial University is open to Roman Catholics, as to all other citizens, upon equal terms."

" There are in the Province, besides the Provincial University, two colleges with University powers under charter from the Provincial Legislature; one of these is under the control of the Roman Catholic Church and the other of the Methodist Conference."

" These denominational institutions are maintained wholly by fees and private endowments, and receive no grants whatever from the Public Treasury."

(ii).

GOVERNMENT TRAINING FARM.

The following letter appeared in the *Times* for November 22, 1900:—

"Sir,—I wish to call attention through the columns of *The Times* to a late move on the part of the Government of New Brunswick, Canada, which must impress one as a most practical plan in the direction of providing a young Englishman, Irishman, or Scotchman with an efficient training in agriculture that will fit him thoroughly for farming intelligently and with profit in the delightful colony mentioned.

"Heretofore, in the case of a boy who has but a small amount of capital at his disposal, not sufficient to enable him to begin life as a gentleman farmer in this country, but ample to make him at once practically independent in a province like New Brunswick, the various types of training at his disposal, whether in Great Britain or the colony itself, have had their distinct disadvantages, which space will not allow me to enumerate, not the least of which has been the expense, and, in some cases, the inefficiency. It was the careful consideration of these and other such facts that led the Government of New Brunswick--the largest of the maritime provinces, that portion of Canada which bears the distinction of lying nearer Great Britain than any other important food-producing area of the Empire, and of which the resources, climate, and agricultural conditions are unexcelled in the world—to encourage the establishment of a training farm that would offer to boys and young men, especially of the class that come from the great English public schools, a thorough practical three years' training in agriculture without the payment of any fees whatever.

"This training farm has already been established and is in active operation. The gentleman in charge of it is an Englishman, Mr. A. W. Pratt, a graduate of Cambridge and of the Royal Agricultural College at Cirencester, the late headmaster of Tamworth. It is felt that, being a thorough agriculturist and an efficient teacher, and knowing the English schoolboy as he does, he is well fitted to make the plan most efficient in operation.

"The farm is designed to carry on all its work in the most practical manner, and to be throughout on a paying basis and thoroughly self-supporting : presenting all the conditions of a farm, as such, in practical operation. The boys will themselves do practically everything that is to be done, getting direct experience of stock raising, dairying, crop raising, marketing, and so forth. The farm is inspected from time to time by members of the Department of Agriculture of the New Brunswick Government, who see that only the most approved methods obtain. Though no fees for instruction are charged it is necessary to charge a small fee, from £30 to £40 for the first year only, when the boy is practically of no service. This fee is asked simply to cover the cost of board and that of breakage of farm machinery, which usually suffers somewhat severely in the hands of the novice.

"The situation and the farm itself have been carefully chosen. It lies in the beautiful Kennebecasis Valley at the village of Penobsquis, near Sussex, in Southern New Brunswick, only about 50 miles by rail from St. John, the chief winter port of Canada, from which several lines of steamers run direct to Great Britain. The farm, comprising in all some 900 acres, includes both upland and rich, deep-soiled "intervale" land, and through its very centre run the Kennebecasis River and the main line of the Intercolonial Railway between Moncton and St. John, with many trains in both directions constantly. Penobsquis Station is on the farm itself.

"At the end of the period of training the director will personally assist each boy in his selection of a situation. In the meantime, what capital he has may be invested and accumulating, instead of a large percentage of it being paid out for instruction.

"Application to the Hon. C. A. Duff Miller, the Agent-General for New Brunswick, 17, Leather-Market, London, S.E., will elicit an illustrated prospectus and any further details of this training farm, and also full information with regard to the unexcelled portion of Canada where it is established. I have just returned from Canada and must say that everything is progressing most favourably, the English boys already on the farm being delighted with the country and prospects. The plan is one which seems to solve thoroughly the problem of how best to introduce a young Englishman, Scotchman, or Irishman to agricultural life in that beautiful and fertile country over seas, which offers so many advantages to both young and old, and the further development of which is always a step in the building of the Empire."

I am, yours sincerely,

W. ALBERT HICKMAN,
New Brunswick Government Commissioner.

(iii).

PROVINCIAL DAIRY SCHOOL (SUSSEX, N.B.).

(See *Report on Agriculture for the Province of New Brunswick, 1899.*   Fredericton, N.B.).

The work in
the winter,
1898–99.

The Dairy School which was first opened at Sussex during the winter of 1893–94, has been kept in operation every winter since that time.   The increasing interest and the large increase in the number of students from year to year has brought about many much-needed changes.   Work in the new building with its new and up-to-date machinery was of the most satisfactory nature. No better evidence of this can be had than the fact that dairymen attended, not only from New Brunswick, but also from the Provinces of P. E. Island and Nova Scotia.

The instruction given is of the most practical nature; theory is in no case advanced unless the same can be put in practical use.

The time for opening the school was changed in 1899 to a later date, and both the cheese and butter making courses will be carried on at the same time.

Since the first opening of the school, the session usually opened early in February and continued until about the middle of March. The milk at this season of the year had to be handled in a different manner than it does in the summer season. Consequently the students get training in the cheese-making department that they cannot put into practical use when they return to their factories and obtain the best results. However, some makers, who perhaps have not had very much experience at the work, follow the teaching at the school and get results that are not what are desired by the Inspector or the buyer; therefore by opening the school on the 12th March and continuing it until the 12th April, it is hoped in a measure to overcome this difficulty.

APPENDIX.

The following statistical tables have been taken from the Statistical Year Book of Canada for 1899 :—

TABLE I.—PUBLIC SCHOOLS.

Term ended	Number of Schools.	Teachers & Assistants.	Number of Pupils.	Boys.	Girls.	Average Attendance.	Proportion of Population at School.
June 30, 1889 -	1,505	1,597	59,819	31,847	27,972	33,785	1 in 5·84
Dec. 31, 1889 -	1,565	1,657	56,384	28,847	27,538	34,822	1 ,, 5·70
June 30, 1890 -	1,517	1,617	58,570	31,053	27,517	32,542	1 ,, 5·49
Dec. 31, 1890 -	1,557	1,641	55,622	27,964	27,658	33,512	1 ,, 5·78
June 30, 1891 -	1,536	1,632	59,568	31,196	28,372	34,394	1 ,, 5·39
Dec. 31, 1891 -	1,604	1,674	56,217	28,459	27,758	35,203	1 ,, 5·71
June 30, 1892 -	1,585	1,669	60,786	31,967	28,819	35,220	1 ,, 5·28
Dec. 31, 1892 -	1,633	1,710	57,547	29,092	28,455	37,373	1 ,, 5·58
June 30, 1893 -	1,614	1,693	60,154	31,576	28,578	35,940	1 ,, 5·34
Dec. 31, 1893 -	1,644	1,725	57,195	28,818	28,377	35,381	1 ,, 5·62
June 30, 1894 -	1,653	1,749	61,280	32,149	29,131	37,260	1 ,, 5·29
Dec. 31, 1894 -	1,685	1,761	57,282	28,894	28,388	36,295	1 ,, 5·60
June 30, 1895 -	1,695	1,790	62,518	32,659	29,859	38,447	1 ,, 5·13
Dec. 31, 1895 -	1,724	1,799	57,889	29,155	28,734	37,876	1 ,, 5·54
June 30, 1896 -	1,720	1,829	61,918	32,315	29,603	37,176	1 ,, 5·18
Dec. 31, 1896 -	1,722	1,782	57,200	28,660	28,540	37,085	1 ,, 5·61
June 30, 1897 -	1,737	1,829	61,908	32,297	29,611	37,154	1 ,, 5·18
Dec. 31, 1897 -	1,749	1,820	58,174	29,180	28,994	38,999	1 ,, 5·52
June 30, 1898 -	1,778	1,864	63,333	32,315	30,353	38,874	1 ,, 5·07
Dec. 31, 1898 -	1,797	1,882	59,457	28,660	29,695	38,978	1 ,, 5·40
June 30, 1899 -	1,806	1,912	63,536	32,297	30,564	37,771	1 ,, 5·05

TABLE II.—GRAMMAR SCHOOLS.

Term ending.	Teachers and Assistants.	Number of Pupils.	Average Attendance.
June 30, 1889 -	62	700	485
,, 1890 -	55	577	392
,, 1891 -	64	665	456
,, 1892 -	66	683	488
,, 1893 -	68	697	500
,, 1894 -	68	749	578
,, 1895 -	68	750	577
,, 1896 -	71	690	523
,, 1897 -	82	732	569
,, 1898 -	27	791	—
,, 1899 -	34	980	—

TABLE III.—NORMAL SCHOOLS.

Year.	Males.	Females.	Total.
1889 - - -	45	179	224
1890 - - -	49	190	239
1891 - - -	36	207	243
1892 - - -	38	231	269
1893 - - -	47	217	264
1894 - - -	59	255	314
1895 - - -	54	215	269
1896 - - -	65	175	240
1897 - - -	66	196	257
1898 - - -	54	227	281
1899 - - -	61	255	316

TABLE IV.—RECEIPTS AND EXPENDITURE.

(Not including amounts spent on school buildings.)

| Year. | Receipts. | | | | Expenditure. |
	Government Grant.	Municipal Aid.	District Assessment.	Total.	
	$				
1889 -	153,641	94,508	174,499	422,648	404,146
1890 -	157,062	94,505	183,636	435,203	416,551
1891 -	157,603	94,505	186,083	438,191	419,547
1892 -	163,058	94,467	174,866	432,391	410,717
1893 -	170,581	94,430	181,177	446,188	421,384
1894 -	* 171,561	92,281	183,166	447,088	427,215
1895 -	180,269	92,140	187,161	459,570	436,618
1896 -	182,018	91,528	211,115	484,661	461,733
1897 -	198,483	90,909	† 208,027	497,419	473,994
1898 -	188,104	90,807	† 230,000	508,911	483,829
1899 -	193,730	90,857	† 318,373	602,960	577,219

* For 10 months.   † Approximate.

THE
SYSTEM OF EDUCATION
IN THE
PROVINCE OF MANITOBA.

INTRODUCTION - - - - - - - - 351
   The Settlement Period - - - - - 352
   The Denominational Period, 1870--1890 - - 353
   The Public Schools Act of 1890 and the Religious
      Controversy - - - - - - - 356

I.—CENTRAL ADMINISTRATION - - - - - 365
   The Education Department - - - - 365
   The Advisory Board - - - - - 365
   Inspection - - - - - - - 367

II. —LOCAL ADMINISTRATION - - - - - - 367
   Rural School Districts - - - - - 367
      Annual School Meeting - - - - 368
      School Trustees - - - - - 368
   Public School Boards in cities, towns and villages - 370

III.—FINANCE - - - - - - - 371
   Annual Grants : -
      Legislative Grants - - - - 371
      Municipal Grants - - - - - 371
   Loans - - - - - - - - 372

IV. —TEACHERS - - - - - - - 373
   Teachers' Certificates and Training - - - 373
   Salaries - - - - - - - 375

V.—ATTENDANCE - - - - - - - 375

VI.—CURRICULUM - - - - - - - 376
   Religious Instruction - - - - 377

VII.—INTERMEDIATE AND COLLEGIATE SCHOOLS - 377

VIII.—THE UNIVERSITY OF MANITOBA - - - 377

IX.—THE NEGLECTED CHILDREN ACT - - - 378

APPENDICES.
A.—Educational Statistics. 1871-1898. - - 380
B —Programme of Studies for the Public Schools - 388
C.—Regulations regarding Religious Exercises - 396
D.—Regulations as to Teachers' Certificates - 399

THE SYSTEM OF EDUCATION IN THE PROVINCE OF MANITOBA.

[Compiled from recent reports of the Department of Education for the Province of Manitoba and other documents relating to education in Manitoba, which can be seen at the Board of Education Library, St. Stephen's House, Cannon Row, Whitehall, London, S.W.]

INTRODUCTION.

For the last thirty years Manitoba has enjoyed the status of a self-governing province and the privileges of membership in the Canadian Federation. Originally "an agricultural settlement peopled by emigrants from Scotland and Ireland under Lord Selkirk,* this district passed, in 1821, into the hands of the Hudson Bay Company. Unincorporated, however, with their other territories, it retained its separate existence till the rights of the Company were purchased by the Government for the purpose of creating the new federal province. Up to this date the little colony, known as the Red River Settlement, had been administered by a Governor appointed by the Company and assisted by a Council selected from men of local importance.

The population has been slowly increased by immigration not only from the United Kingdom but also from the neighbouring provinces of Ontario and Quebec. In 1869 this stood at some 12,000, and it has been estimated that of this number about 1,000 were whites, 5,000 Scotch and Irish half-breeds, and about 6,000 French half-breeds (métis). From the date of the Union (1870) immigration has continued to swell these numbers but at a quickened rate, so that in 1891 the enumerated population was 154,442, and it is calculated that it now nearly attains to 200,000. It is a very heterogeneous population both in race and religious belief, including as it does English, French, Germans, Icelanders, Hungarians and Finns; and the difficulties due to this admixture of races are largely responsible for the bitter struggles that have disturbed the peace of the new province for the last ten years. These struggles have centred round the problem of the schools, and considered in this light the history of educational effort in Manitoba falls naturally into three periods :—

(*a*) The period of unorganised effort in the settlement.
(*b*) The denominational period—1871–1890.
(*c*) The unsectarian system of the Act of 1890.

* *Cf.* Mr. R. L. Morant's report on "The Manitoba School System" in the first volume of "Special Reports on Educational Subjects," from which much valuable information has been derived.

(a) *The Settlement Period.*

During the period of the Company's administration it was no part of their policy to make any provision of financial aid towards establishing schools a permanent charge upon their revenues, though occasionally assistance was granted towards maintaining poor schools already in existence. The work of education was undertaken by the various religious communities within the territory. "Each Church had by its side a school under the control of the missionary. There was no system of taxation in vogue; the school was sustained by private subscriptions or by grants from the missionary societies." The results of these early missionary efforts were by no means inconsiderable ; education is said to have been in a much better condition than the isolated and scattered state of the population would have led one to expect, and in 1857 there were 17 schools in operation; but in view of the subsequent controversy it is well to remember that it is admitted on both sides that at the time when the Union was effected these schools were neither supported by grants from public funds nor controlled in any way by public officials.

At this date the Catholic and Protestant parties were almost equal in numbers and each supported their own schools, and though the proposed inclusion of this territory in the Dominion was met in some quarters with the violence of open rebellion, and in others with serious apprehensions of a possible curtailment of privileges hitherto freely enjoyed, it does not appear that there was any special anxiety with regard to the schools as then established. The notable Section 22 of the Manitoba Act is the result of the struggles in other provinces rather than due to any anticipation of immediate difficulties under the new conditions, though no doubt, as has been suggested, the idea of a possible shifting of the relative strength of religious parties helped to recommend its adoption.

As in the subsequent development of events much weight was attached to the interpretation of this section and of the similar one in British North America Act (1867), it may be well to quote the full text of the article in the Manitoba Act.

Section 22. The Legislature makes laws in relation to education subject and according to the following provisions :—

(1.) Nothing in any such laws shall prejudicially affect any right or privilege with regard to denominational schools which any class of persons have by law or practice in the province at the Union.

(2.) An appeal shall lie to the Governor-General in Council from any act or decision of the legislature of the province or of any provincial authority affecting any right or privilege of the Protestant or Roman Catholic minority of the Queen's subjects in relation to education.

(3.) In case any such provincial law as from time to time seems to the Governor-General in Council requisite for the due execution of the provisions of this section is not made, or in case any decision of the Governor-General in Council on any appeal under this section is not duly executed by the proper provincial authority in that behalf, then and in every such case and as far only as the circumstances of each case require, "the Parliament of Canada may make remedial laws for the due execution of the provisions of this section and of any decision of the Governor-General in Council under this section."

(b.) *The Denominational Period*, 1870–1890.

Such were the conditions under which the new province opened its educational legislation with the Manitoba Schools Act. This measure was passed in 1871 and established a State system of strict denominational schools.

The following is a summary[*] of the main provisions of this measure and of the principal amendments:—

1. The whole education of the province was placed under a central board of education, appointed by the Lieutenant-Governor in Council.

2. This board was composed of two sections, one Protestant, the other Catholic, equal in number. One-third of each section retired every year, and the Governor appointed their successors.

3. To this board was handed over the grant made for education every year by the provincial legislature to be divided equally between the two sections.

4. Each section of the board had exclusive and independent control over its own schools,[†] made its own regulations, and appointed and supervised its own inspectors, conducted the licensing and examination of its own body of teachers, and selected its own books for school use, especially on religious subjects.

5. For the actual management of schools, the whole province was divided up into school districts, in each of which the inhabitants elected a board of trustees, with duties similar to those of our school managers; a certain number of the trustees retired every year, and others were elected. These school districts were 24 in number, corresponding to the electoral divisions.

6. As the population was then more or less definitely segregated in certain areas corresponding with their differences of religious beliefs, it was arranged that 12 of these school districts, "comprising mainly a Catholic population,"[‡] should be Catholic, under the Catholic section of the central board, and 12 in the same way Protestant.

7. Each board of trustees had authority, in his own district, to make all arrangements for providing and managing schools,

---

[*] This summary is taken from Mr. Morant's Report on "The Manitoba School System."

[†] Their only *joint* function was to make regulations for registering and reporting the daily attendance of scholars.

[‡] Sessional Papers, 33a, p. 7.

appointing teachers, building, repairing, and furnishing school premises, and controlling the general working and expenditure.

8. To meet expenses not covered by the fees and the central grant, the inhabitants of each school district, assembled at an annual meeting, decided in what manner funds should be raised. One of the modes prescribed was an assessment and rate upon the property of the school district, the amount to be fixed by the Board of Trustees, but collected from the people and paid over to the trustees by the municipal authorities.*

9. In the event of assessment there was no provision for exemption except in the case of the father of a child actually attending a public school—a Protestant in a Catholic school district or a Catholic in a Protestant—who was exempt from contributing to a school not of his own faith in the event of his sending the child to the school of the nearest district of the other section, and contributing to it an amount equal to what he would have paid if he had belonged to that district.

10. But there could not be more than one school in any one given district, except by the special sanction of that section of the central authority to which the district originally belonged.

*   *   *   *   *

Various modifications were introduced in subsequent years, which are worth noticing in detail, as showing the persistent and increasing effort towards a more thorough application of the denominational system. As the Protestant population was increasing far more rapidly than the Catholic, this tendency appeared to redound chiefly to the benefit of the Protestants. Thus :—

11. By the Act of 1873 the legislative grant was no longer to be equally divided between the Catholic and Protestant sections,† but proportionally to the total average attendance at all the schools under each section respectively during the preceding year.

12. This was again altered in 1875, and the grant was made proportional to the total number of children of school age,‡ whether Protestant or Catholic, residing in all the school districts of each section respectively.

13. In the same year a change was also made in the composition of the Central Board which, to correspond with the great increase of Protestant relatively to Catholic immigration, was now fixed at the ratio of 12 Protestants to 9 Catholics.§

14. It was further enacted in 1876 that the establishment or existence of a school district belonging to one section of the Board should not prevent the establishment *in that same place* of a school district of the other section.‖

15. Protestant and Catholic districts could, in fact, either co-

---

* Canadian Economics, p. 302.   § *Cf.* 2 above.
† *Cf.* 3 above.   ‖ *Cf.* 9 and 10 above.
‡ 6-16 in towns ; 5-16 in rural districts.

exist or overlap; thus making it much easier. than before for a man to send his child to school under his own section of the board and so of his own faith.

16. This was the more necessary because school attendance was in this same year made compulsory in towns on all children, from 7 to 12 years old.

17. And the trustees were now empowered of their own authority to levy a rate on *all* the inhabitants of a district for school expenses.*

18. But the incidence of this rate was restricted in the following year by the Act of 1877, which expressly enacted that in no case shall a Protestant ratepayer be obliged to pay towards a Catholic school, nor a Catholic ratepayer towards a Protestant one.†

* * * * *

Further modifications were introduced from 1881 to 1884, but always in the direction of facilitating denominational privileges, not only as between Catholics and Protestants, but even as between different sects of the Protestants, who gradually formed distinct school districts of their own, under the one Protestant section of the Central Board.

19. In 1881 it was provided that a school could be opened, or a school district called into existence, *anywhere*, if there were ten children of school age residing within three miles of the proposed school site: it being only necessary for five resident heads of families to petition the municipal council under which they resided, to form a district; and in case of difficulty, an appeal lay to that section of the Central Board under whose jurisdiction the said five residents would belong.

20. In 1884 largely increased powers were given to the trustees for issuing debentures and borrowing money for building and improving their schools.

21. Denominational normal colleges, assisted by the rates and by provincial grants, were authorised to be established by *each* section of the Board independently, in connection with the denominational colleges of Winnipeg, and St. Boniface respectively

22. In 1886 the law stood that in municipalities including different school districts, rates were to be fixed by the district to which the majority of the residents belonged; but the municipality were to hand over to the district of the minority, a share of the total, proportionate to the number of children in attendance in the minority's schools.‡

---

* *Cf.* 8 above.
† *Vide* memorandum prepared by the Catholic Superintendent of Education, for the Colonial Exhibition, 1886. Mr. McCarthy, representing the Manitoba Government, stated before the Privy Council in Ottawa, March 5, 1895 :—" A man who was neither a Protestant nor a Catholic was exempt from taxation." But Principal Grant, who made an exhaustive inquiry into the Manitoba school question, says that this statement is quite inaccurate ; and that there was not any arrangement to that effect.
‡ *Vide* Catholic Superintendent's Report, 1886

23. It was also laid down that no educational buildings or institutions were to be rated or taxed for school purposes.

24. And that when two or more persons were sharing the interests of any taxable property, the taxes of each of them should be handed over independently to whichever school district (*i.e.*, Catholic or Protestant) each belonged, in respect of his own faith, without reference to the locality of the property.

* * * * *

Of the results of this system Mr. Somerset, Superintendent of Education for the Protestant section of the Board, wrote officially in 1886 :—" The history of the educational system of this province since its establishment in 1871 to the present time, affords very satisfactory evidence of the fulfilment of those conditions of usefulness and adaptation to the wants of the people, and justifies us in regarding its operation in the past with satisfaction. It is gratifying to all lovers of good citizenship as well as of educational progress to note that from the organisation of this system in 1871, at which period the Protestant schools numbered 16, and the Catholic 17, up to the present time,* there has been an almost entire absence of the friction and disagreement that have marked the progress of education in some of the sister provinces."

While Mr. Macoun, the Dominion Government explorer of the North-West, wrote in 1883† :—" Perhaps the most satisfactory chapter in the history of Manitoba is its peaceful and harmonious educational development. In every other province of the Dominion long and angry wars have been waged over the common schools. Well may the province that has no history in this respect be called happy." And this was written at a time when there were many varieties of religious beliefs in the province, the respective churches being represented in the following proportions :—Episcopalians 14, Presbyterians 14, Roman Catholics 13, Methodists 2, Lutherans and Mennonites 7, Baptists and Congregationalists 2 ; or, following the two divisions of the Board of Education, Catholics 13, non-Catholics 46.

And Dr. Morrison writes. "Throughout all these years, from 1871–1888, no complaint was ever made with the working of the separate school system. The people, Protestant and Catholic alike, were perfectly contented with the school system as it then existed."

(c) *The Public Schools Act of* 1890, *and the Religious Controversy.*

But the same feeling of satisfaction does not seem to have been shared by the provincial statesmen. Their aims were directed towards the creation of a " homogeneous Canadian people," and to the realisation of such aspirations these separate schools for Catholic, Episcopalian, Presbyterian, and Mennonite,

---

* *i.e.*, 1886, at which date Protestant Schools (according to another report) were 426 in number and Catholics 53.
† Manitoba and the Great North-West, p. 533.

for English, French, Hungarian, Icelander, and Finn offered the greatest hindrance, perpetuating the barrier raised by the diversity of language, and fostering by this variety the separatist point of view on matters concerning the general welfare of the whole community. Considerations of economy and efficiency also had their weight, and the Executive Council were fully alive to the enormous waste necessarily occasioned by a system of numerous small schools.

So convinced was the provincial administration of the necessity of finding some remedy that the Cabinet resolved in 1889 entirely to reverse the policy that had been pursued up till then. In view of the resulting agitation the question might be raised whether the historical position of the French Catholics throughout the Dominion did not entitle them to a differentiation of treatment from that dealt out to the immigrants from the Continental countries of Europe, but the measure introduced to the Provincial Legislature in 1890 applied the principle of undenominational education with strict logical consistency to all schools. That the Ministers had rightly interpreted the wishes of the province is proved by the large majority with which the Bill was carried—25 to 11—in a House which only contains 40 members, and by the fact that the new Parliament, elected mainly on this issue in 1893, rejected a proposal for the repeal of the new law by a still greater majority of 34 to 4.

As this Statute is still the valid law of the province, its provisions will be given in greater detail later on; here it is sufficient to state (in explanation of the intense agitation that followed its adoption) that it absolutely rejected the principle of denominationalism in education and recognised only one kind of school; the instruction was to be non-sectarian, and the local taxes raised towards the support of these schools to be collected from all ratepayers without any regard to their religious convictions.

This Act met with the most determined opposition from the Catholic party. It was held that under Section 22 (i.) of the Manitoba Act the entire measure was *ultra vires*. A test case was brought before the Courts, which after passing the primary instances in Canada with varying results, was finally decided by the Judicial Committee of the Privy Council in February, 1893. The judgment of the court was that since no *public* or state-recognised schools had existed before or at the union, this Act could not be held to have contravened "any denominational school rights or privileges existing by law or practice at the Union," and it was therefore not *ultra vires* but valid.

Before this decision had been published, the Catholics put forth another plea, viz. that under Section 22 (ii.) of the same Act they were entitled to appeal to the Governor-General in Council. This question in its turn occupied the attention of the law courts and passed through the various stages of judicial procedure, till the Judicial Committee of the Privy Council gave their decision in favour of the validity of the appeal. As the effect of this judgment has at various times been misrepresented and even held to uphold the claim of the Catholics to their separate schools, it is advisable to give the Court's own statement of its ruling :—

"With the policy of these Acts their Lordships are not concerned, nor with the reasons which led to their enactment. It may be that as the population of the province became in proportion more largely Protestant, it was found increasingly difficult, especially in sparsely populated districts, to work the system inaugurated in 1871, even with the modification introduced in later years. But whether this is so or not is immaterial.

"The sole question to be determined is whether a right or privilege which the Roman Catholic minority previously enjoyed has been affected by the legislation of 1890. Their Lordships are unable to see how this question can receive any but an affirmative answer. Contrast the position of the Roman Catholics prior and subsequent to the Acts from which they appeal.

"Before these passed into law there existed denominational schools, of which the control and management were in the hands of Roman Catholics, who could select the books to be used and determine the character of the religious teaching. These schools received their proportionate share of the money contributed for school purposes out of the general taxation of the province, and the money raised for these purposes by local assessment was, so far as it fell upon Catholics, applied only towards the support of Catholic schools. What is the position of the Roman Catholic minority under the Acts of 1890? Schools of their own denomination, conducted according to their views, will receive no aid from the State. They must depend entirely for their support upon the contributions of the Roman Catholic community, while the taxes out of which State aid is granted to the schools provided for by the Statute fall alike on Catholics and Protestants. Moreover, while the Catholic inhabitants remain liable to local assessment for school purposes, the proceeds of that assessment are no longer destined to any extent for the support of Catholic schools, but afford the means of maintaining schools which they regard as no more suitable for the education of Catholic children than if they were distinctively Protestant in their character.

"In view of this comparison, it does not seem possible to say that the rights and privileges of the Roman Catholic minority in relation to education, which existed prior to 1890, have not been affected. . . .

"It is certainly not essential that the Statutes repealed by the Act of 1890 should be re-enacted, or that the precise provisions of these Statutes should again be made law. The system of education embodied in the Acts of 1890 no doubt commends itself to and adequately supplies the wants of the great majority of the inhabitants of the province. All legitimate grounds of complaint would be removed, if that system were supplemented by provisions which would remove the grievance upon which the appeal is founded and were modified so far as might be necessary to give effect to these provisions."

In accordance with this judgment an Imperial Order was issued on February 2, 1895, and the case was heard before the Privy Council for Canada, the hearing lasting from February 27th to March 7th. Mr. Ewart presented the case for the Catholics and Mr. McCarthy defended the policy of the Provincial Government. At the end of the hearing the Council found that by the Acts of 1890 "the rights and privileges of the Roman Catholic minority of the said province, in relation to education, prior to 1st day of May, 1890, have been affected by depriving the Roman Catholic minority of the following rights and privileges which, previous to and until the 1st day of May, 1890, such minority had, viz. :—

"(a.) The right to build, maintain, equip, manage, conduct, and support Roman Catholic Schools in the manner provided for by the said statutes, which were repealed by the two Acts of 1890.

"(b.) The right to share proportionately in any grant made out of public funds for the purposes of education.

"(c.) The right of exception of such Roman Catholics as contribute to Roman Catholic Schools from all payment or contribution to the support of any other schools."

The Remedial Order embodying this finding intimates that it was the Governor-General's decision that the Manitoban Legislature must modify the Acts of 1890 accordingly. The provincial Ministers refused to comply, and the Remedial Bill which was consequently introduced into the Dominion Parliament roused a very bitter feeling in Manitoba. It is stated that the Conservative party at that time in power did not push the Bill with any vigour, and that the Bill was "talked out" by the Opposition. It now appears to be generally admitted that the Bill was a mistake. Mr. Blake, the "greatest authority on constitutional law in the Dominion," and at one time counsel for the Catholic minority of Manitoba, says :—" I think no thinking man who knows Canada and the Provinces can doubt there would be the greatest practical difficulty in enforcing on an unwilling Province many provisions of the Remedial Bill, and that in the attempt the interests of the Roman Catholic minority in Manitoba and six other provinces would be but too likely to suffer."

On April 24, 1896, the Canadian Parliament was dissolved, and one of the chief issues placed before the electors was the settlement of the Manitoban School Question. The Conservative policy of coercion received the active support of the Catholic clergy; yet even in Quebec from 50 out of the 65 seats members were returned to support Mr. (now Sir Wilfrid) Laurier, a Liberal, but also a French Catholic, who had pledged himself to settle in six months in a manner satisfactory to both parties this matter that had been troubling the country for the last six years. The results of the election placed Mr. Laurier in a position to redeem his promise.

But prior to the dissolution an effort had been made by the Dominion Government to arrive at some compromise acceptable to both Catholic and Protestant. It had appointed a small Commission of three or four members (Sir Donald Smith, now Lord Strathcona, being one of them) to proceed to Winnipeg and there meet the representatives of the Manitoban Government. But nothing came of the Commission. Subsequently, however, an arrangement was arrived at between Sir Wilfrid Laurier and the Provisional Government of Manitoba, on the following basis:—In towns and villages where there were resident twenty-five Roman Catholic children of school age, and in cities where there were fifty such children, the Board of Trustees should arrange that such children should have a school house or a school room for their own use, where they should be taught by a Roman Catholic teacher. Other points had reference to Catholic text-books, Catholic representation on the Advisory Board, Catholic representation on the Board of Examiners, and a Catholic Normal School. All these concessions were to be made under statutory enactments. The representatives of the provincial Government objected that the effect of such legislation would be to establish a system of State-supported separate schools for the Roman Catholic people, and to compel their support by the school taxes and legislative grants. "Not only so, but the whole school organisation—text-book regulations, constitution of Advisory Board, Boards of Examiners, and Normal School—would be modified to bring it into accord with the separation principle to an extent not usual even in places where regularly constituted separate school systems obtain."

It was found impossible to arrive at any satisfactory settlement, but the discussion was probably not without influence on the course of events when the negotiations were resumed by the new Dominion Government. The proposals put forward by Mr. Laurier, less favourable to the Catholics than those of Sir Donald Smith's Commission, were as follows.—

(1.) Legislation shall be introduced and passed at the regular session of the Legislature of Manitoba embodying the provisions hereinafter set forth in amendment to the "Public Schools Act," for the purpose of settling the educational questions that have been in dispute in that province.

(2.) Religious teaching to be conducted as herein-after provided: (1) If authorised by a resolution passed by a majority of the school trustees; or (2) if a petition be presented to the Board of School Trustees asking for religious teaching, and signed by the parents or guardians of at least ten children attending the school in the case of a rural district, or by the parents or guardians of at leasty twenty-five children attending the school in a city, town, or village.

(3.) Such religious teaching to take place between the hours of 3.30 and 4 o'clock in the afternoon, and to be conducted by any Christian clergyman whose charge includes any portion of the school district, or by any person duly authorised by such clergyman, or by a teacher when so authorised.

(4.) Where so specified in such resolution of the trustees, or where so required by the petition of the parents or guardians.

religious teaching during the prescribed per od may take place only on specified days of the week instead ofi on every teaching day.

(5.) In any school in towns and cities where the average attendance of Roman Catholic children is 40 or upwards, and in villages and rural districts where the average attendance of such children is 25 or upwards, the trustees shall, if required by the petition of the parents or guardians of such number of Roman Catholic children respectively, employ at least one duly certificated Roman Catholic teacher in such school. In any school in towns and cities where the average attendance of non-Roman Catholic children is 40 or upwards, and in villages and rural districts where the average attendance of such children is 25 or upwards, the trustees shall, if required by the petition of the parents or guardians of such children, employ at least one duly certificated non-Roman Catholic teacher.

(6.) Where religious teaching is required to be carried on in any school in pursuance of the foregoing provisions and there are Roman Catholic children and non-Roman Catholic children attending such school, and the school-room accommodation does not permit of the pupils being placed in separate rooms for the purpose of religious teaching, provisions shall be made by the regulations of the Department of Education (which regulation the Board of School Trustees shall observe) whereby the time allotted for religious teaching shall be divided in such a way that the religious teaching of the Roman Catholic children may be carried on during the prescribed period on one half of the teaching days in each month, and the religions teaching of the non-Roman Catholic children may be carried on during the prescribed period on one half of the teaching days in each month.

(7.) The Department of Education shall have the power to make regulations, not inconsistent with the principles of this Act, for the carrying into effect the provisions of this Act.

(8.) No separation of the pupils by religious denominations shall take place during the secular school work.

(9.) Where the schoolroom accommodation at the disposal of the trustees permits, instead of allotting different days of the week to the different denominations for the purpose of religious teaching, the pupils may be separated when the hour for religious teaching arrives, and placed in separate rooms.

(10.) Where ten of the pupils in any schools speak the French language (or any language other than English) as their native language, the teaching of such pupils shall be conducted in French (or such other language) and English upon the bilingual system.

(11.) No pupils to be permitted to be present at any religious teaching unless the parents or guardians of such pupils desire it. In case the parents or guardians do not desire the attendance of the pupils at such religious teaching, then the pupils shall be dismissed before the exercises, or shall remain in another room.

This compromise was objected to by the Catholic hierarchy, though not by large numbers of the representative Catholic laity. The latter made a representation of their views to the Pope. Subsequently M. Mery de Val sailed, as Papal Ablegate, for Canada at the end of March, 1897.

The result of this mission is best stated in the words of the Pope contained in an encyclical letter to the Archbishops, Bishops, and other ordinaries in the Federated States of Canada:—

"Very many expect a pronouncement from us upon the question, and look to us to point out what course they should pursue. We determined not to come to any conclusion upon the matter until our Delegate Apostolic had examined it upon the spot. Charged to make a careful survey of the situation, and to report upon it to us, he has with fidelity and ability fulfilled the task we imposed upon him.

"The question at issue is assuredly one of the highest and most serious importance. The decisions arrived at seven years ago on the school question by the Parliament of the Province of Manitoba must be remembered. The Act of Union of the Confederation has secured to Catholics the right to be educated in the public schools according to their consciences; and yet this right the Parliament of Manitoba abolished by a contrary law. This is a noxious law. For our children cannot go for instruction to schools which either ignore or of set purpose combat the Catholic religion, or in which its teachings are despised and its fundamental principles repudiated. Wherever the Church has allowed this to be done, it has only been with pain and through necessity, and at the same time surrounding her children with many safeguards which, nevertheless, it has been too often recognised have been inefficient to cope successfully with the danger attending it. Similarly, it is necessary to avoid at all costs, as most dangerous, those schools in which all beliefs are welcomed and treated as equal, as if, in what regards God and divine things, it makes no difference whether one believes rightly or wrongly, and takes up with truth or error. You know well that every school of this kind has been condemned by the Church, because nothing can be more harmful or better calculated to ruin the integrity of the faith and to turn aside the tender minds of the young from the way of truth.

"There is another point upon which those will agree with us who differ from us upon everything else, it is not by means of a purely scientific education and with vague and superficial notions of morality that Catholic children will leave at school such as the country desires and expects. Other serious and important teaching must be given to them if they are to turn out good Christians and upright and honest citizens; it is necessary that they should be formed on those principles which, deeply engraven on their consciences, they ought to follow and obey, because they naturally spring from their faith and religion. Without religion there can be no moral education deserving of the name, nor of any good, for the very nature and force of all duty comes from those special duties which bind man to God, who commands, forbids, and determines what is good and evil. And so, to be desirous that minds should be imbued with good, and at the same time to leave them without religion, is as senseless as to invite people to virtue after having taken away the foundations on which it rests. For the Catholic there is only one true religion, the Catholic Religion; and therefore, when it is a question of the teaching of morality or religion, he can neither accept nor recognise any which is not drawn from Catholic doctrine.

"Justice and reason then demand that the school shall supply our scholars not only with a scientific system of instruction, but also a body of moral teaching which, as we have said, is in harmony with the principles of their religion, without which, far from being of use, education can be nothing but harmful. From this comes the necessity of having Catholic masters and reading-books and text-books approved by the Bishops, of being free to regulate the school in a manner which shall be in full accord with the profession of the Catholic faith as well as with all the duties which flow from it. Furthermore it is the inherent right of a father's position to see in what institutions his children shall be educated, and what masters shall teach them moral precepts. When, therefore, Catholics demand, as it is their duty to demand and work, that the teaching given by schoolmasters shall be in harmony with the religion of their children, they are contending justly. And nothing could be more unjust than to compel them to choose an alternative, or to allow their children to grow up in ignorance or to throw them amid an environment which constitutes a manifest danger for the supreme interests of their souls. These principles of judgment and action, which are based upon truth and justice, and which form the safeguards of public as well as private interests, it is unlawful to call in question or in any way abandon. And so, when the new legislation came to strike Catholic Education in the province of Manitoba, it was your duty publicly to protest against injustice and the blow that had been dealt; and the way in which you fulfilled this duty has furnished a striking proof of your individual vigilance and of your true episcopal zeal.

.   .   .   .

"We are not ignorant that something has been done to amend the law. The men who are at the head of the Federal Government and of the Government of the Province have already taken certain measures to diminish the grievances of which the Catholics of Manitoba rightly persist in complaining. We have no doubt that these measures have been inspired by a love of fair dealing and by good intention. But we cannot conceal the truth. The law made to remedy the evil is defective, imperfect, insufficient. Catholics demand, and have a right to demand, much more. Besides, the arrangements may fail of their effect, owing to the variations in the local circumstances; enough has not yet been done in Manitoba for the Catholic education of our children. The claims of justice demand that this question should be considered from every point of view, that those unchangeable and sacred principles which we have enunciated above should be protected and secured. This is what must be aimed at, and this the end which must be pursued with zeal and prudence. But there must not be discord; there must be union of mind and harmony of action. As the object does not impose a line of conduct determinate and exclusive, but on the contrary, admits of several, as is usual in such matters, it follows that there may be on the line to be followed a certain number of opinions equally good and acceptable. Let none lose sight of the value of moderation, gentleness, and brotherly love. Let none forget the respect due to his neighbour, but let all, weighing the circumstances, determine what is best to be done and act together after having taken counsel with you.

"As to what regards particularly the Catholics of Manitoba, we have confidence that, God helping, they will one day obtain full satisfaction. This confidence is founded, above all, on the goodness of their cause; next, on the justice and wisdom of those who govern; and, lastly, on the goodwill of all upright Canadians. In the meantime, till they succeed in their claims, let them not refuse partial satisfaction. This is why, wherever the law or administration or the good dispositions of the people offer some means of lessening the evil and of warding off some of the dangers, it is absolutely necessary and expedient and advantageous that they should make use of them and derive all the benefit possible from them. Wherever, on the contrary, there is no other remedy, we exhort and conjure them to use a generous liberality. They can do nothing better for themselves or more calculated to redound to the welfare of their country than to contribute, as far as their means will allow, towards the maintenance of their own schools.

"There is still another point which calls for your united attention. Under your authority and with the help of those who direct your schools, a complete course of study ought to be carefully devised. Special care should be taken that those who are employed as teachers should be abundantly provided with all the qualities, natural and acquired, which are requisite for their profession. It is only right that Catholic schools, both in their educational methods and in the standard of their teaching, should be able to compete with the best."

This message did not remain without effect; it was dated 18th December, 1897. It was read in the Canadian churches on the third Sunday in the New Year. In February the *Times* correspondent reported that Archbishop Langevin, who at time of its first publication was the chief opponent to the Laurier-Greenway compromise, had agreed with the Canadian Premier to forego any insistence on legislative changes, provided that the Acts were administered in a liberal spirit, guided by the concessions granted. The Archbishop asked that Catholic teachers should be employed in Catholic school districts, that in Winnipeg the 500 Catholic children should attend the National schools and be taught by teachers of their faith, and, further, that in the French rural schools, instead of the bilingual text-books, only French books should be used in the earlier years of the pupil's school life. It was stated as probable that if these terms were accepted by the Manitoban Government the Archbishop would join the Advisory Board. This has not yet taken place, but it is noteworthy that the Board for 1898 contains a representative from St. Boniface. Further testimony as to the working of this conciliatory spirit is given by a special correspondent of the *Tablet* writing from Winnipeg on October 22, 1898. He concludes his article with these words: "The seed sown by Leo XIII. is already beginning to bear fruit in Canada, and a new spirit of charity and forbearance and hopefulness is abroad in the land. For my part, I have little doubt that before long Manitoba will range itself in line with the rest of the Dominion, and that whatever the letter of law, wherever there are enough Catholic children to warrant a separate school, there a separate Catholic school will be found."

I.—CENTRAL ADMINISTRATION.

The Education Department Act which immediately precedes the Public Schools Act in the Statute Book of the province of Manitoba, was passed in the year 1890. Under this Act the Executive Council, which at the present time consists of five members, or a committee thereof appointed by the Lieutenant-Governor in Council, was constituted the Education Department. The Education Department.

The following are the chief functions assigned to this office:—

(1) To appoint Inspectors of High and Public Schools, teachers in Provincial, Model and Normal Schools, and Directors of Teachers' Institutes.

(2) To fix the salaries of all Inspectors, Examiners, Normal and Model School Teachers and other officials of the Department.

(3) To provide for Provincial, Model and Normal Schools, and Intermediate and Collegiate Departments or schools.

(4) To arrange for the examination of teachers and for the issue of teachers' certificates.

(5) To prescribe the length of vacation and the number of teaching days in the year.

Side by side with the Education Department is the *Advisory Board* endowed with statutory powers under the same Act. This Board consists of seven members, four of whom are appointed by the Department of Education for a term of two years, two are elected annually by the Public and High School teachers actually engaged in teaching in the Province, and the seventh member is appointed by the University Council.* The Advisory Board.

---

* The following was the constitution of the Board at the time of the publication of the last Report:—Representing Manitoba University Council —The Most Reverend Robert Machray, M.A., LL.D. Elected by the Teachers of the Province—J. D. Hunt, B.A., Daniel McIntyre. Appointed by the Department of Education—Rev. George Boyle; E. W. Montgomery, B.A., M.D.; S. A. D. Bertrand; Professor R. R. Cochrane; G. D. Wilson, B.A. It will be observed that the last category contains five names instead of four as required by the Act.

The duties of the Board have reference mainly to the internal organisation of the school, they have power—

(1.) To make regulations for the dimensions, equipment, style, plan, furnishing, decoration, and ventilation of school houses, and for the arrangement and requisites of school premises.

[Such regulations have apparently not yet been issued. In the Inspectors' reports for the year 1898 there is frequent mention of the great improvement in the character of the buildings used for school purposes. But this is not everywhere the case. The Inspector for the North Western Division says:—

"It would be a very great advantage to all concerned if the Advisory Board would make regulations for the dimensions, equipment, style, plan, decoration, and ventilation of school houses, and for the arrangement and requisites of school premises. Not only are there many new school districts organised every year, but there are also many old districts in which the school buildings have outlived their usefulness and are being replaced by new ones. Where this is the case efforts are put forth, and usually with fair success, to secure a building suitable in plan, style, and dimensions for the needs of the district. But there are cases where the trustees are not alive to the importance of the matter, and the interests of the schools are neglected. There ought to be regulations strictly governing the erection of new buildings. A satisfactory solution of this problem might be reached, if experts on school buildings were invited to submit for approval sets of plans showing proper construction, heating, ventilation, lighting, and cost of school houses of one-room and two-room buildings, with and without basement. A moderate sum of money as a prize for the best design would be well invested."

Another inspector re-inforces this opinion:—

"As the country advances the necessity for increased attention to the element of hygiene in connection with the architecture of the school becomes more and more pressing. A small pamphlet containing a plan and specification for a rural school and other suggestions, if placed in the hands of school boards, would have a beneficial effect. Such plans and suggestions should represent the best ideas of provincial architects and be endorsed by the staff of Inspectors."]

(2.) To examine and authorise text-books and book of reference for the use of pupils and school libraries.

(3.) To determine the qualifications of Teachers and Inspectors for High and Public Schools.

(4.) To determine the standard to be obtained by pupils for admission to High Schools.

(5.) To decide or make suggestion concerning such matters

as may, from time to time, be referred to them by the Department of Education.

(6.) To appoint Examiners for the purpose of preparing examination papers for teachers' certificates and for examination of pupils seeking to enter High Schools, which Examiners shall report to the Department of Education.

(7.) To prescribe the forms of religious exercises to be used in schools.

(8.) To make regulations for the classification, organisation, discipline, and Government of Normal, Model, High, and Public Schools

(9.) To determine to whom teacher's certificates shall be granted, and to cancel certificates at any time granted, with power to recognise certificates granted outside the province, instead of an examination.

(10.) To decide upon all disputes and complaints laid before them, the settlement of which is not otherwise provided for by law.

The Central Authority exercises its power of control through its inspectors. No person is eligible for this office who does not hold a legal certificate of qualification, granted according to the Regulations of Education Department and the Advisory Board. No teacher in a public or high school, nor a school trustee, can be made an inspector, so long as he continues to hold such office. *Inspection.*

Besides the usual duties of school inspection, the inspector acts as arbitrator in disputes between school trustees and rate-payers in respect of school sites, or between school districts in matters of adjustment of boundaries, or between auditors of school accounts, where objection is taken to certain items of expenditure; and in unorganised districts he assumes the functions of a court of revision for the correction of the assessment roll. The inspector is also empowered to suspend any teacher who wilfully neglects or refuses to carry out the agreement made with a board of trustees. All cases of suspension must be immediately notified to the Education Department.

Besides the inspector, school visitors have the right to visit the school, to examine the progress of the pupils, and to give advice to the teacher and pupils. All clergymen, members of Advisory Board, judges, members of the Legislature, and members of the municipal councils, are school visitors in the district in which they reside; the clergymen must have a pastoral charge.

II.—LOCAL ADMINISTRATION.

The local authorities are divided into two classes, (*a*) the Trustees in rural districts, (*b*) Public School Boards in cities, towns, and villages.

(*a.*) *Rural School Districts.*

The council of each rural municipality may by bye-law form portions of the municipality when no schools have been established into school districts, provided— *Formation of Rural School Districts.*

(a) That no school district shall be so formed unless there

shall be at least ten children of school age living within the same:

(b) That no school district shall include more territory than twenty square miles, exclusive of public roads.

In unorganised territory the inspector of the district can form a portion or the whole of such territory into a school district, provided that it does not exceed, in length or breadth, five miles in a straight line, and that it is formed only on the petition of five property owners in the territory. Every rural municipal council, moreover, has the power to unite two or more districts in the same municipality into one, if at a public meeting called for that purpose by the trustees or the inspector in each district a majority of the ratepayers present at each meeting request the same to be united. The council can also alter the boundaries of a school district, or divide an existing district into two or more districts and unite portions of an existing district with another district, provided that all persons affected by the new arrangement have been duly notified. In case of dissatisfaction, a majority of the trustees or any five ratepayers may appeal to a Judge of the County Courts, who has the power to settle the dispute, which settlement remains in force for three years. If the school district happens to be situated in the district of more judges than one, the Department of Education directs to which judge the appeal shall be made. It is provided that where the decision of the judge does not affirm that of the council, and an application for reconsideration, signed by a majority of the ratepayers affected by the decision, or signed by a majority of the trustees of the district affected, is delivered to the judge within three months from the date of the decision, the judge may reconsider the matter and, if he think fit vary his decision.

Annual school meeting. A meeting of the ratepayers in each rural school district is held on the first Monday in December in each year, unless that day happen to be a public holiday. After the election of one of their number to be chairman of the meeting the business of the day is conducted in the following order:—

> (i.) The Annual Report of the Trustees is received and discussed.
> (ii.) The Annual Report of the Auditor is presented.
> (iii.) Election of an Auditor for the following year.
> (iv.) Miscellaneous business.
> (v.) Election of Trustee or Trustees to fill vacancy or vacancies.

All assessed ratepayers of the full age of twenty-one years are entitled to vote at such meeting.

School Trustees. For each rural district there are three trustees, one of whom retires each year. The necessary qualifications for the position of trustees are that the person should be an actual resident ratepayer within the school district, rated on the last revised assessment roll of the municipality or one of the municipalities in which the school district is situate, and of the full age of twenty-one, and able to read and write.

If the ratepayers of any school district for two years neglect or refuse to elect Trustees, the Council of the Municipality has the power to nominate Trustees, who shall act as if they had been elected by the ratepayers.

Any complaints as to proceedings at elections are heard by the Inspector, if made within thirty days after the election. Under these circumstances the Inspector has power to administer oaths, summon witnesses, enforce their attendance, and compel them to produce documents and to give evidence on oath.

The newly-elected Trustee, after he has accepted office, has to make the following declaration in writing:—

"I, A. B., do solemnly declare that I will truly, faithfully, and to the best of my ability and judgment discharge the duties of the office of School Trustee for the school district of   ."

(1.) To make arrangements for the annual school meeting and for any other special meeting as may be required for the purpose (a) of electing a Trustee or Auditor; (β) of selecting a new school site; (γ) of dealing with any other lawful school matter as the Trustees may think proper. (All meetings can only be held after six days' notice posted in three or more public places of the district.)

(2.) To provide adequate accommodation and a legally qualified teacher or teachers, according to the regulations prescribed by law, for two thirds of the actual resident children, between the ages of five and sixteen years.

(3.) To apply to the municipal council, at or before its first meeting after the thirty-first of July, for the levying and collecting by rate of all sums for the support of their schools authorised by the Public Schools Act, and also for the purchase of sites and erection of school buildings, either by one yearly rate or by the issue of debentures.

(4.) To arrange for the payment of teachers' salaries at least quarterly.

(5.) To see that the fabric of the school is kept in proper repair.

(6.) To exempt, either wholly or partially, indigent persons from payment of school rates.

(7.) To visit, from time to time, every school under their charge, and see that it is conducted according to law and the authorised regulations, and to provide school registers and a visitors' book.

(8.) To see that no unauthorised books are used in the school, and that the pupils are duly supplied with a uniform series of authorised text-books sanctioned by the Advisory Board.

(9.) To prepare for the annual meeting a report containing a summary of their proceedings during the year, and a full and detailed account of the receipt and expenditure of all school moneys.

(10.) To collect at their discretion, from non-resident pupils, and from pupils whose parents or guardians reside on land in

Duties of Trustees.

4226.   2 E the school district exempt from taxation, a sum not exceeding fifty cents per month for each pupil attending school, and pupils may be excluded from school for non-payment of fees.

(b) *Public School Boards in Cities, Towns, and Villages.*

In every village or town not divided into wards there are three elected school trustees holding office under similar conditions as the trustees in rural districts. In all larger villages and towns, and in cities which are so divided, two trustees are elected for each ward, one of whom retires each year.

The nomination and election of public school trustees are held at the same time and place and by the same returning officers as the municipal nominations and election of aldermen and councillors, and the provisions of the "Municipal Act," respecting the qualification of voters, the time for opening and closing the polls, etc., apply to the election of public school trustees.

The Act assigns the following duties to board of school trustees:—

(1) The appointment of a secretary and treasurer or secretary-treasurer, and one or more collectors, if required, of such school fees or rate bills as the Board may have authority to charge.

(2) The provision of adequate accommodation for all the children between the ages of 6 and 16 resident in the municipality.

(3) The determination of the number, kind, grade, and description of schools (such as male, female, infant, ward, or central schools) to be established and maintained, of the teachers to be employed, of the terms on which they are to be employed, the amount of their remuneration, and the duties they are to perform.

(4) The preparation of an estimate of expenditure to be laid before the Municipal Council.

(5) The collection at their discretion from the parents or guardians of children attending any public school under their charge a sum not exceeding 20 cents per month per pupil to defray the cost of text-books, stationery and other contingencies, and to see that all the pupils in the schools are duly provided with the uniform system of authorised text-books, and the collection at their discretion from non-resident pupils, and from pupils whose parents reside on land exempt from taxation, of a fee not exceeding a dollar a month for each pupil, and for a collegiate department an additional two dollars per month.

(6) The constitution at their discretion of one or more of the public schools of the city to be a model school for the preliminary training of public school teachers.

(7) The publication in one or more public newspapers or otherwise, and the transmission to the Department of Education of a report signed by the Chairman and containing all the information required by the regulation of the Department.

Furthermore, such Boards are empowered, if it is considered expedient, to provide a course of kindergarten instruction for children between the ages of three and six, to appoint a superintendent (so far Winnipeg is the only community which has availed itself of this right). They may also, with the consent of the Department, establish night schools for pupils over 14 years of age, unable to attend during ordinary school hours.

III.—FINANCE.

(a.) *Annual Grants.* (b.) *Loans.*

(a) *Annual Grants.*—The two main sources from which funds are derived for maintaining public schools are (*i.*) the Legislative Grants, and (*ii.*) the Municipal Taxes.

(*i.*) *Legislative Grants.*

Out of the sums placed at the disposal of the Education Department by the Legislature, a sum of sixty-five dollars is paid semi-annually for each teacher* employed in each school district, if the school has been in operation for the full term of the preceding period, otherwise a sum proportionate to the length of time for which the school was opened. No school, however, except in the case of a new school, is entitled to receive a larger amount than one half of the sum required by the trustees for the current expenses of the school ; and, moreover, the grant may suffer a reduction should the average attendance fall below 40 per cent. of the numbers on the roll.

To entitle the school to any share in the grant its trustees must have made the returns to theDepartment required by law, and the school must be conducted in accordance with the regulations of the Education Department and of the Advisory Board. Unless this last condition be fulfilled the school is not considered to be a public school, nor permitted to receive municipal grants.

The Legislative Grant during the year 1898, as recorded in the published report of the Department, amounted to $175,857 (£35,174), *i.e.*, about 25 per cent. of the total amount derived from public funds (*i.e.*, legislative and municipal grants), but only some 16 per cent. of the full sum available for the support of the public schools; it should also be mentioned that the sum entered for the year 1898 does not represent the amount actually expended, since some of the school grants remained unpaid at the time of the making up of the figures.

(*ii.*) *Municipal Grants.*

It is the duty of the local authority to provide such sums of money as are requisite for maintaining the efficiency of the school beyond the amounts received from the central authority. These local grants contain two elements, (*a*) a fixed rate per teacher employed, (*b*) a variable rate dependent on the amount of current expenditure.

---

* On the wisdom of the policy of giving the same amount of grant in aid of the salary of the oldest and most experienced teacher and the merest beginner, see the remarks of the Principal of the Provincial Normal Schoo quoted below, Section IV, of this report,

Under (a) the School Trustees are entitled to receive from the municipal authorities a sum of twenty dollars per teacher for each month the school has been kept opened. Every school that has been open for 102 teaching days is held to have been open for six months, and 204 teaching days constitute a full teaching year of twelve months. It is the duty of the Trustees to lay before the Municipal Council at its first meeting after July 31 in any year the number of months the school has been kept open and the number of months they intend to keep the school open, together with the number of teachers employed. If the trustees fail to make this return they cannot claim any sum beyond that which the Municipal Council may, at its discretion, fix for them.

Beyond this fixed grant the school law enacts that the council of every rural municipality, and the municipal council of every city, town, or village, shall levy and collect such sums as may be required by the public school trustees for school purposes. All unexpected balances are to stand to the credit of the school fund, and all moneys collected by the Municipality but unpaid to the School Trustees constitute a debt due from the Municipality to the Trustees.

The area of taxation for school purposes is the widest possible. Article 124 of the Revised Statute of Manitoba, c. 127, says :—

"The taxable property in a municipality for school purposes shall include all property liable to municipal taxation, and also all property which has heretofore been or may hereafter be exempted by the Municipal Council from municipal taxation but not from school taxation. No Municipal Council shall have the right to exempt any property whatsoever from school taxation."

Moreover, as the schools are public schools, no one is released from the obligation to contribute to their support by reason of the fact that he does not avail himself of the advantages which they offer. In view of the circumstances prevailing at the time of the passing of this measure, it is expressly laid down in the Act that any person residing in one school district and sending his children to the school of a neighbouring one, is, nevertheless, liable for the payment of rates assessed on his property for the support of the school in which he resides.

(b) Loans.

For certain purposes (such as the purchase of school sites, the erection and furnishing of school houses, or their purchase, the purchase or erection of a teacher's residence) the trustees may, under certain restrictions, borrow the necessary funds.

In the first instance the loans must be authorised at a meeting of the ratepayers called for this special purpose, and after, at least, two weeks' notice. No loan of more than 700 dollars nor one which would make the outstanding liabilities of the school community exceed that amount, can be authorised by a resolution of the ratepayers. If it is desired to raise a larger loan, a special bye-law must be passed in accordance with the terms of the Municipal Act; and it is the duty of the Municipal Council to submit any such bye-law to a vote when so requested by the School Trustees. In the case of rural school districts the persons entitled to vote on such bye-laws are all owners of real property within the district, whose names are on the last revised list of municipal electors. A majority of three-fifths of those voting is necessary for the adoption of the bye-law.

No loan under 2,000 dollars can be made for any term over 10 years, and the longest term in any case permissible is 20 years. The principal of the loan must be made repayable in annual instalments, and all boards having debentures not complying with this regulation have been obliged to establish a sinking fund. All loans must be sanctioned by the Education Department, and for this purpose the minutes of the meeting at which the loan was authorised must be forwarded to the central office; and the sanction of the Department is given, the debentures are issued, signed and sealed by the Provincial secretary. If in the opinion of the Department the interests of the holders of previous debentures are likely to prejudiced by this new issue, assent may be withheld.

The debenture indebtedness of the School Authorities has risen from $413,478 in 1889, to $841,103 in 1898.

IV.—TEACHERS.

All teachers in the public schools must be holders of certificates granted by the Advisory Board of Education. There are three classes of certificates, first, second, and third; the first class includes certificates of two grades, the other two classes have but one. Teachers' Certificates and Training.

The examinations, on the results of which these certificates are awarded, consist of two parts, (a) the non-professional examination, (b) the professional examination. No student can enter for a professional examination without having attended at least one session either at the Provincial Normal School at Winnipeg, or at one of the local Normal Schools situated in each of the inspectoral districts. The full syllabus for these examinations will be found in Appendix D.

The minimum requirement demanded from persons wishing to serve in a public school is the possession of the third class professional certificate. No one is allowed to enter for any class of professional examination unless he holds the non-professional certificate of corresponding rank or some recognised proof of equivalent attainment. Up till a very recent date there existed a system which enabled temporary " permits " to be issued to persons of but scant attainments and with no professional training. This procedure was on numerous occasions very adversely criticised by the inspectors; and it has now been abolished, or rather replaced by the third-class certificates, which are only valid for a period of three years, and cannot now be renewed, as was hitherto the case. It has been found possible to carry out this reform, because the supply is in some cases above the demand. but the tendency still exists for the better qualified teachers to be crowded out of the profession. In this connection the principal of the Provincial Normal School makes the following remarks in the course of his report for 1898 :—

" The number of persons licensed to teach during the year has had its effect on the standing of those engaged in the profession. There is no special inducement to school trustees to secure teachers of the higher grades, except it be that better work may be expected in the school, and this does not seem to some a matter of such vital importance as obtaining a teacher at a small salary. This works in favour of the lower grade teachers who are willing and able to serve for a smaller remuneration. Care must be taken that our schools do not suffer by the employment of too many teachers of this type. Judging by the number of better teachers who are drifting out of the work, it would seem that the pressure from below is beginning to be felt. It may be that our schools would be benefited by the adoption of the principle of graded legislative grants—a principle that has operated so successfully in some other places. This makes it as easy for any school district to support a teacher of the higher grade as one of the lower, and it tends to keep in the schools those who have the ripest scholarship, most complete training and longest experience."

Other defects on which the inspectors comment are :—

(i.) The shortness of the session at the Normal Schools, which only extends to ten weeks.

(ii.) The low minimum age limit, which it is generally agreed should be raised to 18 for women and 20 for men.

(iii.) The inadequacy of a purely written test for admission to a profession in which clear and correct oral expression is a matter of the first importance.

Another difficulty which greatly hampered the work of the Provincial Normal School—viz., that of being obliged to train together in the same classes students who had never taught and others who had had such experience—has been remedied by the regulation compelling all candidates for the first or second class professional examination to hold the third-class certificate, and to have taught successfully for one year after having obtained the non-professional certificate of a rank corresponding to that grade of teacher's licence which they are soliciting. This restriction has conduced to work of a much more satisfactory character; though even now the classes at the Provincial Normal School are too crowded and of too limited duration to enable each student to receive that individual attention from the staff and to obtain that sufficient opportunity for practical work which are most essential features in a really efficient system of training.

Besides the regular opportunities for training offered by the Normal School, there exists in each inspectoral division a Teachers' Institute or Association, which deals with matters directly concerning the inner-life of-the schools ; and the inspectors' reports contain most frequent allusions to the deep interest displayed by the teachers in this work and to the large numbers attending these meetings.

Principal McIntyre says : "These Institutes are useful in many ways. They assist in making clear to the teachers the aims and methods of education ; they settle many of the practical difficulties of the schoolroom ; they arouse a fresh enthusiasm for the work of teaching. They bring the Normal School into closer touch with the schools of the country, and thus prevent the training of teachers from becoming too theoretical. They also bring the schools and the people into more friendly relation, as at all gatherings many of the parents of the district attend, and frequently take part in the proceedings."

The teacher is engaged under a written agreement between him and the trustees of the school district in which he intends to serve. Changes from school to school and from district to district are very frequent; the number of teachers who have a recorded service of five years in the same school is small.

No system of graduated salaries exists; the actual amount Salaries. received by the teacher is settled in private agreement between him and the local trustees who are his employers. But it is felt that the trustees are not always the best judges of the interests of the school in this matter.

In 1894 Mr. E. E. Best writes : "The teachers in charge held all grades of certificates and represented all stages of proficiency, from the very highest standard of moral and professional excellence, down to those who had neither training, experience, nor aptitude ; the law of uniformity in the teacher's vocation applies only in the case of salaries. Even here, however, there are faint signs of reformation. Formerly the skilful and cultivated teacher was remunerated on the same basis as the novice, the ubiquitous tramp and adventurer. In some quarters the trustees are beginning to discriminate between the work of an artist and that of an artisan, and it is to be hoped that the near future may witness the grading of teachers' salaries and the proper compensation of those who are our real teachers."

The same hopefulness does not possess Mr. T. M. Maguire, who says in his report for the following year (1895) : "It is to be regretted that trustees do not make more distinction in the matter of salary between third and second class teachers. The neophyte who has just passed his examination, or the inexperienced teacher looking for his first school, can usually do as well in the matter of salary as the trained and experienced teacher."

The highest salary paid in 1898 was $1,800: the average salary for the province was $344, in towns and cities $563, in rural schools $397. The highest salary paid in rural schools was $700.

V.—ATTENDANCE.

There is no clause in the Act of 1890 which makes attendance compulsory. The Trustees in rural districts are bound by law to provide school accommodation for two-thirds of the actual resident children between the ages of five and sixteen ; the town authorities for all children between six and sixteen. Any child between these limits of age has a right to free instruction, but persons up to the age of twenty-one may attend school.

The absence of any compulsory regulations makes attendance irregular, but there are few advocates for their introduction. Mr. Rose, an Inspector, writes:—" Attendance should be in a measure at least compulsory. If the education of the child is a subject of such vast importance that every citizen may with justice be required to contribute towards the maintenance of the public school, then the State should have some adequate means of controlling the expenditure of their money. It is probable that if the payment of the various grants were made in some measure proportionate to the attendance, some slight improvement would follow. I visited one school in which there had not been a single pupil for six weeks. The teacher, who was in the habit of visiting the school each morning, was in receipt of a salary of $40 per month." Other inspectors are more disposed to rely rather upon a larger measure of zeal on the part of the teachers and upon the greater interest of parents in the work of education. The necessities of home requirements, it is admitted, account largely for this irregularity, but it is also in no small degree due to the carelessness and indifference of parents and guardians.

VI.—CURRICULUM.

The full programme of studies for the public school is given in Appendix B. Reading, Writing, and Arithmetic, together with " Observation Lessons," are the main subjects in the three lowest grades. The study of Geography is begun in Grade III., and of History in Grade V. With reference to the teaching of this last branch the Superintendent of the Winnipeg Schools, writes:— " All classes above five study British and Canadian History. This study is carried on with a view to leading our boys to appreciate their birthright as British subjects and citizens of Canada, to acquaint them with the duties and privileges of the citizenship, and to familiarise them, in an elementary way, with the nature of the problems, which the past presented, thus laying the foundations for intelligent participation in public matters when in mature years the exercise of that citizenship shall fall to them."

Elementary Science replaces the Observation lessons in the Fifth grade, Physiology is added in the Sixth, and Grammar in the Seventh ; Agriculture is also taught in certain schools.

The object of " Programme of Studies " is formulated by the Superintendent of the Winnipeg schools as follows :—" No attempt is made to have each pupil master the prescribed allotment of each subject specified in the course. The programme of studies is used as a guide to the teacher to indicate the material to be employed for the mental and moral development of the pupils. The primary aim is development ; the communication of knowledge is the secondary aim, although the most certain means of reaching the latter object is the faithful pursuit of the former. In determining when pupils are to be promoted, the question asked is not whether all the assigned subjects have been mastered to some specified degree expressed in percentage, but whether the educational progress of the pupils will be best served by advancement to another grade or by retention for a longer time in that in which he has been working."

The religious instruction may be given in school hours, but the Regulations of the Advisory Board with regard to religious exercises in the public schools permit the reading, without note or comment, of certain selected passages from the authorised English version or the Douay version of the Bible, and the use of a prescribed form of prayer.* Religious Instruction.

VII.—INTERMEDIATE AND COLLEGIATE SCHOOLS.

(a.) *Intermediate Schools.*—Intermediate schools are always combined with ordinary public schools, and it is usually only a small proportion of the pupils that are doing intermediate work. This consists in a more advanced study of the branches of the public school curriculum rather than in the introduction of new subjects. These schools are largely used by intending teachers as places of preparation for the non-professional examination for third class certificates.

(b.) *Collegiate Schools.*—The secondary schools proper of the province are the so-called Collegiate Schools. There are three such schools in Manitoba, situated at Winnipeg, Brandon, and Portage la Prairie. The Advisory Board has authority to regulate the standard of admission to these schools, but it is usual to admit boys after a special examination, a practice frequently criticised as tending to lower the standard of attainment. The number of pupils in attendance at each of these schools in 1898 was 525, 210, 126 respectively. These institutions prepare their pupils for the first class certificates and for the entrance examination of the University of Manitoba. In 1896 a commercial course was started at the Winnipeg Institute, where instruction is given in the following branches: English, Mathematics, History and Geography, Book-keeping, Agriculture, Shorthand. The number of pupils attending this course in 1898 was 43.

VIII.—THE UNIVERSITY OF MANITOBA.

The University of Manitoba was incorporated by an Act of the Manitoban Legislature in 1877. It was constituted on the model of the old London University, as a purely examining body. But certain teaching institutions are affiliated to the University, and have the right to nominate seven representatives to the University Council. The Colleges† thus affiliated at the

---

* The full text of these Regulations will be found in Appendix C.
† *Cf.* Papers relating to University Education of Roman Catholics in Certain Colonies (Colonial Office Return, Cd. 115, 1900, p. 10.)

present time are the St. Boniface College (Roman Catholic), St. John's College (Episcopalian), Manitoba College (Presbyterian), Wesley College (Methodist), and the Manitoba Medical College. The University has an endowment of 150,000 acres of land, and enjoys an income of $5,500. The number of students is about 135. In the University there are three faculties—Arts, Medicine, and Law, though the Statutes permit, under certain conditions, the establishment of a Faculty of Theology. No such faculty has yet been created. Students may matriculate after passing the Preliminary examination or the Medical Entrance examination. At the end of his first year of study the student may enter for the Previous examination, and subsequently after at least two years' further study he may present himself for the Senior B.A. examination, either in the General B.A. Course or in some special course of study. These special courses are five in number: (i.) Classics, (ii.) Mathematics, (iii.) Modern Languages, (iv.) Natural Science, (v.) Mental and Moral Science. The schedule of the subject matter dealt with in these examinations will be found in the Calendar of the University.

Scholarships are awarded on the results of most of the University examinations, except the final examinations for degrees. Before payment is made a certificate of satisfactory attendance must be returned by the Head of the College to which the student is attached. Catholics and Protestants are both represented on the Board of Studies and on the various examination Committees, and in Mental and Moral Science papers are set both in Latin and English, and in the Preliminary and Previous French and English versions of the questions set are distributed. In 1898 there were admitted to graduation 40 Bachelors of Arts, 11 Masters of Arts, 20 Doctors of Medicine, 11 Masters of Surgery, and 3 Bachelors of Laws; of these graduates 9 were women, who are admitted to the examinations on the same terms as men.

IX.—The Neglected Children Act.

The following are the chief provisions of an Act passed in 1898 for the better protection of neglected and dependent children:—

The Lieutenant-Governor may appoint an officer, to be known as the Superintendent of Neglected Children. The duties of this officer are (1) to encourage and assist in the organisation and establishment in various parts of the province of societies for the protection of children from neglect or cruelty. He shall exercise, by virtue of his office, the powers conferred on such societies of placing such children in properly selected foster homes. He is to visit all temporary homes and shelters where children are placed, to provide for the visitation of children in foster homes, and to see that a record of all committals is kept by the societies and of all children boarded out.

Children are liable to be apprehended—

(1) If they are found begging in any street or place of public resort.

(2) If they are found wandering about at a late hour or sleeping at night in barns, outhouses, or in the open air.

(3) If they are found dwelling with a thief, drunkard, or vagrant, or from such causes are allowed to grow up without salutary parental control.

(4) If found guilty of petty crimes and likely to develop criminal tendencies if not removed from their surroundings.

The Judge before whom the child is brought may make an order for its delivery to the custody of a society, and may order the municipality to which the child belongs to contribute a reasonable sum, not less than one dollar weekly, towards the expense of supporting the child. The society is empowered to place the child in a foster home, but must always retain the right to terminate the contract if the welfare of the child demand it. The Lieutenant-Governor may discharge any child from the custody of the society.

APPENDIX A.

EDUCATIONAL STATISTICS, 1871-1898.

1.—SCHOOL POPULATION.

Year.	School Population.	Pupils Registered. Under 5.	Pupils Registered. 5-21.	Pupils Registered Over 21.	Total No. of Pupils Registered.
1871 · ·	- ·	—		· ·	817
1881 · ·	7,000		—	· ·	4,919
1882 · ·	9,641	—	· ·	— ·	6,972
1883 · ·	12,346		10,484	—	10,831
1884 · ·	14,129	·	·	— ·	11,708
1885 · ·	15,850	—	11,046	744	13,074
1886 · ·	16,834		14,246	1,000	15,926
1887 · ·	17,600	· · ·	14,484	—	16,940
1888 · ·	18,850	—	14,996	· ·	18,000
1889 · ·	21,471	57	17,275	1,027	18,358
1890 · ·	25,077	65	21,972	1,219	23,256
1891 · ·	28,678	58	22,488	1,325	23,871
1892 · ·	29,564	130	23,022	94	23,243
1893 · ·	34,417	80	28,393	233	28,706
1894 · ·	36,459	74	32,403	203	32,680
1895 · ·	44,932	87	35,062	222	35,371
1896 · ·	50,093	85	37,701	201	37,987
1897 · ·	51,178	84	39,569	188	39,841
1898 · ·	57,431	88	43,825	157	44,070

2.—ATTENDANCE.

Year.	Pupils who attended less than 100 days.	Between 100 and 150 days.	Between 151 days and the whole year.	Average Attendance.	No. of School Days in year.
1883 · ·	—	· ·	· ·	5,064	—
1884 · ·	—	—	· ·	6,520	—
1885 · ·	—	—	· · ·	7,847	—
1886 · ·	—	—	· ·	8,611	203
1887 · ·	9,878	4,410	3,607	9,715	228
1888 ·	7,302	—	—	9,856	198
1889 · ·	11,807	5,770	4,033	11,242	212
1890 · ·	12,461	5,256	3,860	11,627	213
1891 · ·	13,990	7,321	5,424	12,433	215
1892 · ·	12,306	5,762	5,766	12,976	218
1893 · ·	15,958	7,983	6,180	14,180	215
1894 · ·	16,845	7,486	8,707	16,260	218
1895 · ·	16,768	8,643	9,913	19,516	212
1896 · ·	18,439	9,654	9,894	20,247	216
1897 · ·	18,725	10,082	10,835	21,500	216
1898 · ·	20,557	10,036	13,477	24,958	217

3.—TEACHERS EMPLOYED AND STANDING.

Year.	No. of Teachers.	Male.	Female.	Collegiate.	1st Class.	2nd Class.	3rd Class.	Interim Certificates.
1883	246	123	123	9	37	77	88	35
1884	359	170	189	—	47	118	138	56
1885	476	231	245	6	47	148	200	75
1886	525	242	283	7	44	148	236	89
1887	581	285	296	7	55	149	255	115
1888	675	267	408	8	62	190	298	117
1889	668	320	348	9	71	207	258	123
1890	840	451	389	5	68	279	369	100
1891	866	412	454	6	88	318	414	40
1892	902	390	512	9	86	392	341	74
1893	997	435	562	10	94	448	392	53
1894	1,047	500	547	15	126	467	383	56
1895	1,093	570	523	18	121	525	395	34
1896	1,143	585	558	20	140	539	401	43
1897	1,197	601	596	23	219	625	319	11
1898	1,301	654	647	25	224	658	379	4

4.—EXAMINATION OF TEACHERS.

Year.	1st Class.		2nd Class.		3rd Class.		Certificates Granted on standing obtained elsewhere.				Total Number receiving Certificates.
	No. Examined.	No. Passed.	No. Examined.	No. Passed.	No. Examined.	No. Passed.	1st Class.	2nd Class.	3rd Class.	Interim.	
1886	–	14	–	80	265	201	4	10	..	81	398
1887	23	10	61	19	265	92	18	12	–	186	337
1888	15	6	72	29	264	181	14	32	–	159	421
1889	17	7	81	28	268	150	21	74	–	137	417
1890	14	10	128	31	419	201	15	110	16	124	610
1891	15	9	152	78	393	263	24	112	60	40	687
1892	19	8	193	86	328	122	30	140	90	74	777
1893	22	12	137	50	433	131	65	122	41	53	723
1894	28	19	225	67	616	181	49	106	19	56	816
1895	22	14	235	90	499	118	41	106	23	34	886
1896	42	29	246	164	294	135	58	141	24	43	1,017
1897	44	23	235	97	305	165	76	174	24	11	1,133
1898	32	18	216	90	276	189	41	67	5	4	1,209

5.—NORMAL SCHOOL.

Year.	Teachers.		Students at Long Sessions.	Students at Short Sessions.	Number of Long Sessions.	Number of Short Sessions.
	Provincial Normal.	Local Normal.				
1883 . . .	1	—	16	—	2	—
1884 . . .	1	—	35	89	2	5
1885 . . .	1	—	31	93	1	4
1886 . . .	1	—	38	83	1	3
1887 . . .	1	—	31	99	1	1
1888 . . .	2	—	42	108	1	2
1889 . . .	2	—	35	122	1	3
1890 . . .	2	—	28	59	1	2
1891 . . .	2	5	67	122	1	5
1892 . . .	3	12	60	153	1	6
1893 . . .	3	9	63	85	1	4
1894 . . .	4	8	75	124	1	5
1895 . . .	4	9	189	149	2	5
1896 . . .	4	9	136	102	2	5
1897 . . .	4	9	143	101	2	4
1898 . . .	6	9	184	204	2	5

6.—RECEIPTS AND EXPENDITURES.

Year.	Receipts.			Expenditures.					
	Legislative Grant.	Municipal Taxes.	Total.	Teachers' Salaries.	Building, Furnishing and School Sites.	Fuel.	Repairs, Cleaning and care of School Houses.	Salaries of Sec.-Treasurers.	Total.
	$ c.	$	$	$	$	$	$	$	$
1883	20,596 81	—	—	—	97,068	—	—	—	363,775
1884	37,301 50	149,494	328,847	129,376	67,281	—	—	—	302,273
1885	40,916 01	195,640	338,996	150,759	50,393	—	—	—	320,899
1886	47,277 01	246,597	380,623	168,042	47,785	—	—	—	352,849
1887	54,478 75	226,813	357,267	181,042	38,734	—	—	—	420,055
1888	76,336 36	—	—	198,882	42,577	....	—	—	—
1889	96,111 38	282,204	436,721	206,813	70,464	—	—	—	413,478
1890	99,257 62	225,089	426,705	200,929	61,036	11,634	9,857	7,671	388,981
1891	95,306 71	312,396	502,640	251,719	198,403	19,944	10,446	9,521	457,231
1892	105,575 33	262,297	500,227	291,329	199,637	44,332	17,916	6,709	636,592
1893	108,071 55	329,562	760,583	317,119	134,590	24,108	12,356	6,293	744,178
1894	117,347 67	354,963	875,156	359,076	132,932	20,567	33,478	4,749	774,865
1895	129,099 13	481,828	892,056	378,656	118,519	18,166	32,084	12,070	797,542
1896	136,582 03	472,039	857,153	441,185	96,863	25,074	32,670	17,699	810,912
1897	143,561 41	525,482	825,774	445,204	57,370	26,648	34,265	11,928	805,417
1898	175,874 23	522,035	1,098,796	465,371	163,281	26,850	38,572	13,159	1,011,368

NOTE.—In the above Table the Legislative grant and total receipts are incomplete for the year 1898, as some of the grants to Schools have not yet been paid,

7.—SCHOOLS, SCHOOL HOUSES AND APPARATUS.

Year.	Number of School Districts Organized.	Number of Schools in Operation.	Number of School Houses.	Frame.	Brick.	Stone.	Log.	Schools using Maps.	Number of Maps.	Number of Globes.	Number of Trees planted during Year.
1871	16	–	–	–	–	–	–	–	–	–	–
1881	128	–	–	–	–	–	–	–	–	–	–
1882	182	–	–	–	–	–	–	–	–	–	–
1883	272	256	–	–	–	–	–	–	–	–	–
1884	359	326	–	–	–	–	–	–	–	–	–
1885	468	390	–	–	–	–	–	–	–	–	–
1886	549	465	–	–	–	–	–	–	–	–	–
1887	575	506	–	–	–	–	–	–	–	–	–
1888	639	547	–	–	–	–	–	–	–	–	–
1889	700	592	543	432	19	6	84	487	1,594	–	–
1890	719	712	554	450	21	6	77	509	1,796	293	–
1891	774	746	629	532	15	6	76	567	1,849	346	–
1892	821	789	653	563	23	7	58	586	1,905	364	1,224
1893	874	860	669	568	27	10	64	611	2,273	462	2,475
1894	916	884	744	627	37	11	69	704	2,113	541	2,223
1895	956	982	761	636	38	16	71	759	2,445	557	5,595
1896	985	1,032	854	703	39	16	96	804	2,625	596	3,231
1897	1,018	1,068	860	730	39	16	75	809	3,056	614	5,249
1898	1,042	1,250	924	763	49	18	94	852	3,256	659	2,996

8.—TEACHERS' SALARIES.

Year.	Highest Salary Paid.	Average Salary for the Province.	Average Salary in Cities and Towns.	Highest Salary in Rural Schools.	Average Salary in Rural Schools.	Number of Teachers Attending Normal Five Months or more.	Number Attending less than Five Months.	Untrained Teachers.
	$	$ c.	$ c.	$	$ c.			
1883	—	522 00	670 00	– –	456 50	—	—	—
1884	—	—	699 00		433 50	—	—	—
1885	—	—	554 00	· ·	425 10	—	—	—
1886	1,500	459 00	· ·		—	—	—	—
1887	1,500	—	· ·	800	—	143	210	288
1888	1,500	· ·	· ·	850	—	194	258	223
1889	1,500	483 20	602 16	900	463 70	185	302	178
1890	1,500	488 13	741 30	800	453 46	189	289	180
1891	1,600	474 05	661 23	900	426 60	269	431	166
1892	1,600	490 15	700 52	900	461 00	343	366	192
1893	1,800	479 36	642 68	800	456 24	419	356	222
1894	1,800	480 00	631 90	720	410 00	452	290	147
1895	1,800	427 89	604 94	720	368 67	487	390	216
1896	1,800	434 73	604 94	750	411 85	654	341	148
1897	1,800	495 21	533 56	750	484 48	709	352	136
1898	1,800	433 80	562 96	700	397 21	795	409	97

9.—ASSETS AND LIABILITIES.

Year.	Assets.			Liabilities.		
	Taxes due from Municipal Councils.	Value of School Houses, Sites and Furniture.	Total	Amount due Teachers.	Debenture Indebtedness.	Total.
	$	$	$	$	$	$
1883	--	411,596	.--	--	295,785	—
1884	--	334,824	—	--	372,980	—
1885	...	—	..	---	448,426	—
1886	--	581,442	.-	---	459,791	—
1887	--	434,072	--	--	420,055	—
1888	--	—	--	--	—	—
1889	--	615,319	—	--	413,478	—
1890	253,847	647,355	904,682	91,319	454,546	551,208
1891	249,561	668,272	928,442	84,201	449,489	679,449
1892	232,028	796,413	1,232,675	70,921	537,676	674,687
1893	401,262	852,335	1,263,447	91,773	555,856	761,577
1894	312,665	975,112	1,468,282	96,070	655,723	939,881
1895	289,687	1,128,518	1,560,700	100,226	741,134	972,912
1896	407,976	1,164,569	1,677,037	92,065	750,351	1,015,546
1897	350,344	1,226,423	1,754,875	83,228	740,444	1,018,568
1898	418,598	1,394,906	2,057,453	84,892	841,103	1,309,876

10.—EXPENDITURE OF LEGISLATIVE GRANT.

Year.	Payment to Schools.	Inspection of Schools.	Examination of Teachers.	Normal School.	Office.	Total.
	$ c.	$ c.	$ c.	$ c.	$ c.	$ c.
1883	20,596 81	1,361 00	1,059 71	1,090 00	5,133 18	29,242 70
1884	37,301 50	3,609 50	732 44	3,100 65	6,683 32	51,500 30
1885	40,916 01	3,914 40	1,174 85	3,145 71	6,463 86	55,794 85
1886	47,277 01	4,360 30	1,377 22	3,417 48	6,599 23	62,980 94
1887	54,478 75	5,442 04	1,676 12	4,910 35	8,160 92	74,668 18
1888	76,336 36	7,092 35	1,587 68	5,263 94	8,010 43	97,051 96
1889	96,111 38	7,439 40	1,583 13	6,595 52	8,279 92	118,809 05
1890	99,257 62	7,715 65	1,762 46	5,542 86	3,833 43	118,292 97
1891	95,306 71	7,838 78	1,814 74	5,184 30	3,692 53	113,837 16
1892	105,575 33	8,351 64	2,081 43	5,913 30	4,020 70	127,036 93
1893	108,071 55	8,626 80	2,803 46	8,802 92	3,706 22	136,968 49
1894	117,347 67	9,531 85	3,815 07	5,369 98	4,040 58	140,562 68
1895	129,099 13	9,878 67	2,993 03	5,440 10	4,003 41	152,386 54
1896	136,582 03	9,806 75	1,707 12	5,628 09	3,989 78	171,546 81
1897	143,561 41	10,496 85	2,138 02	5,988 92	3,955 53	166,903 48
1898	175,874 23	10,966 50	2,255 90	8,202 46	3,926 42	201,557 81

NOTE—In the above table the payments to schools and the total amount of expenditure are incomplete for the year 1898, as some of the grants to schools have not yet been paid.

11.—LEGISLATIVE GRANT FOR 1898.

EXPENDITURE.

PAYMENTS FOR OFFICE:

	$ c.	$ c.
Salaries	3,071 00	
Printing and Stationery	445 54	
Postage and Telegraph	312 73	
Incidentals	12 15	
Typewriter	90 00	
		3,926 42

PAYMENTS FOR INSPECTION OF SCHOOLS:

Salaries	10,925 00	
Printing and Stationery	11 60	
Incidentals	29 90	
		10,966 50

PAYMENTS FOR NORMAL SCHOOL:

Salaries	4,860 88	
Printing and Stationery	148 83	
Travelling Expenses	85 00	
Library	174 20	
Furniture and Repairs	174 30	
Incidentals, Rent of Piano, Caretaking, Light, etc.	141 75	
Examinations	473 70	
Rent	2,143 80	
		8,202 46

PAYMENTS FOR EXAMINATION OF TEACHERS:

Examiners' Fees	1,798 50	
Printing and Stationery	457 40	
		2,255 90

PAYMENTS FOR ADVISORY BOARD:

Members' Travelling Expenses		282 80

PAYMENTS FOR TEACHERS' INSTITUTES:

Travelling Expenses		49 50

PAYMENTS TO COLLEGIATE INSTITUTES:

Grants	7,794 51	
Expenses of Inspection	227 25	
		8,021 76
Grants to Intermediate Schools		9,100 00
Ordinary Grants to Schools		158,752 47
		201,557 81
Grant to Manitoba University		3,500 00
Grant to Manitoba University (Special)		750 00
Grant to Manitoba University (Building Fund revote)		60 00
		$205,867 81

4226.

2 F

12.—SCHOOLS.

Year.	School Districts.			Expenditure to Schools.		
	Organized.	In Operation.	No. of Departments.	Maximum Grant to each School per Year.	Total Grant to Schools.	Total Expenditure.
				$ c.	$ c.	$ c.
1885 · ·	468	343	390	100 00	40,916 01	55,794 85
1886 · ·	549	422	465	100 00	47,227 01	62,980 94
1887 · ·	575	464	506	100 00	54,478 75	74,668 18
1888 · ·	639	495	547	150 00	80,641 00	93,546 00
1889 · ·	700	574	592	150 00	96,111 38	118,809 05
1890 · ·	719	627	712	150 00	99,257 62	118,192 97
1891 · ·	774	612	746	150 00	95,306 71	113,837 16
1892 · ·	821	660	789	150 00	105,575 33	127,036 39
1893 · ·	874	713	860	130 00	108,071 55	136,968 49
1894 · ·	916	751	884	130 00	117,347 67	140,562 68
1895 · ·	956	786	982	130 00	129,099 13	152,386 54
1896 · ·	985	833	1032	130 00	136,582 03	171,546 81
1897 · ·	1018	843	1068	130 00	143,561 41	166,903 48
1898 · ·	1042	928	1250	130 00	175,874 23	201,557 81

NOTE.—In the above table the payments to schools and the total amount of expenditure are incomplete for the year 1898, as some of the grants to schools have not yet been paid.

13.—RELIGIOUS EXERCISES, ETC.

Year.	School Districts in operation.	Schools closed with Religious Exercises.	Schools closed with Prayer.	Bible used.	Schools giving Temperance Instruction.	Schools teaching Ten Commandments.	Schools giving Moral Instruction.
1893 · ·	713	451	407	339	398	343	550
1894 · ·	751	594	545	533	494	272	645
1895 · ·	786	433	396	295	674	205	629
1896 · ·	833	361	327	236	637	196	708
1897 · ·	843	333	368	282	633	237	746
1898 · ·	928	325	362	255	569	258	814

14.—CLASSIFICATION OF PUPILS.

Year	Reading	Spelling	Composition	Grammar	Arithmetic	Book-keeping	Writing	Geography	History, English	History, Canadian	Physiology	Literature	Algebra	Physics	Botany	Euclid	Music	Agriculture	Temperance	Drawing
1886	16,205	14,474	13,140	10,393	15,258	2,779	15,851	11,217	5,638	–	2,263	–	–	–	–	–	–	–	–	–
1889	20,489	19,014	17,854	10,522	20,349	2,649	20,389	15,774	6,922	–	13,007	–	–	–	–	–	–	–	–	–
1890	20,898	20,080	18,785	11,625	21,376	3,616	21,621	15,717	7,842	–	15,259	–	–	–	–	–	–	–	–	–
1891	23,871	21,080	21,291	9,844	23,454	7,417	23,317	18,027	8,359	–	14,368	6,182	652	276	–	–	–	–	–	–
1892	24,625	23,957	23,685	14,376	24,625	6,576	23,896	19,376	6,957	–	8,623	5,891	872	973	–	–	–	–	–	–
1893	28,706	25,275	16,569	16,569	25,269	4,720	26,643	17,876	7,510	7,623	4,317	7,021	2,961	2,928	1,648	1,368	10,096	–	–	–
1894	31,667	29,415	22,575	22,575	32,053	4,119	31,415	21,325	8,202	7,707	9,357	7,107	3,303	2,016	2,484	2,637	19,032	647	3,961	14,677
1895	34,592	29,145	24,948	13,226	34,592	5,393	31,552	25,203	10,256	10,238	11,878	9,766	5,012	–	6,871	4,788	21,445	6,974	15,130	17,751
1896	38,005	34,942	27,975	15,228	35,490	4,460	35,485	24,849	10,468	11,300	12,094	9,954	4,370	–	14,106	4,186	23,503	13,132	19,094	23,611
1897	39,702	37,066	32,508	12,169	39,040	3,696	39,702	26,849	11,331	12,602	14,283	12,204	4,477	–	16,505	4,292	29,216	12,674	19,397	28,734
1898	42,306	38,773	33,148	12,480	42,518	3,876	42,071	28,288	11,863	12,986	14,429	12,896	4,560	–	16,193	4,439	33,106	11,599	22,055	32,230

APPENDIX B.

PROGRAMME OF STUDIES FOR THE PUBLIC SCHOOLS.

The work to be done in the Public Schools is divided into nine Grades, as follows:—

GRADE I.

Reading.—First Reader, Part I.

Composition.—Ready and correct use of Simple Sentences in familiar conversation growing out of reading and observation lessons.

Writing.—In exercise books with lead pencil.

Arithmetic.—Numbers 1 to 20, their combinations and separations.
Use and meaning of one-half, one-third, one-fourth, &c., to one-twentieth (no figures).
Relation of halves, fourths, eighths; thirds, sixths, twelfths; thirds, ninths (no figures)
Simple problems and practical measurements introducing gallons in peck, pecks in bushel, months in year, inches in foot, pound, current coins up to 20.
Addition in columns, no total to exceed 20.

Observation Lessons :—

1. Plant Life.—Study of the plant as a whole. Name of parts—root, stem, leaf. Experiment to determine the use of each part to the plant. Observation of the uses that animals and insects make of the plant.

    Leaves.—(*a.*) Recognizing and naming a few common leaves.
        (*b.*) Drawing and describing each leaf as studied. Noting size, shape, colour, margin, veining. Colouring of some drawings.
        (*c.*) Memorizing appropriate poems and reproducing stories told.
    Flowers.—(*a*), (*b*), (*c.*) Same as under leaves. Observing the parts in each and distinguishing between them.
    Seeds.—(*a*), (*b*), (*c.*) Same as under leaves. Planting many seeds of some one kind, a few of several kinds; some in the light, some in the dark, some in dry earth, some in moist earth, some in cotton. Observing results.

2. Animal Life.—Insects—grasshopper, butterfly and allied insects.
Birds—Habits of the more familiar birds.

NOTE.—A calendar may be made to show changes in climate; the migration of birds; appearance of flowers; ripening of seeds, etc.

Spelling.—Copying words.

Music.—Singing of rote-songs. Drill on the scale and intervals as found in Exercises 1, 2, 3, 4 on second page, first series of Charts, Normal Music Course. (These four exercises are also printed on four cards, one on each card.)

Drawing.—Study of first year models as outlined in Primary Manual, Part I. (sphere, cube, cylinder right-angled triangular prism, square prism and hemisphere)

GRADE II.

Reading.—First Reader, Part II.
Phonic Analysis.
Exercises in Articulation and Pronunciation.
Reading at sight from books used in Grade I.
Reading stories and poetical selections from blackboard.
Appropriate selections of poetry memorized and recited.

Composition.—The substance of the reading lesson, and of short stories told or read to pupils, to be reproduced by them orally.
Oral expression in complete sentences of simple thoughts suggested by reading, observation lessons and personal experience.

Writing.—Copy Book No. 1, with lead pencil.

Arithmetic—Numbers 1 to 20, their combinations and separations.
Use and meaning of one-half, one-third, one-fourth, etc., to one-twentieth (no figures).
Relation of halves, fourths, eighths ; thirds, sixths, twelfths ; thirds, ninths (no figures).
Simple problems and practical measurements introducing gallons in peck, pecks in bushel, months in year, inches in foot, pound, current coins up to 20, etc.
Addition in columns, no total to exceed 20.

Observation Lessons.—Simple study of familiar plants and animals, as in Grade I.

Spelling.—From Readers only—such words from each lesson as pupils can learn while mastering the reading matter.

Music.—Singing of rote-songs. Review. Drill in Interval. Easy exercises from the Chart in each of the nine keys.

Drawing.—Study of second year models as outlined in Primary Manual, Part II. (ovoid ellipsoid, cone, pyramid, equilateral, triangular prism and vase form).

GRADE III.

Reading.—Second Reader.
Phonic Analysis.
Exercises in Articulation and Pronunciation.
Appropriate selections of poetry memorized and recited.

Composition.—Brief oral expression in complete sentences of thoughts suggested by pictures, observation lessons, etc.
Narrative of occurrences within pupil's experience.
Written exercises on the foregoing after oral work has been carefully done.
Oral and written reproduction of the substance of the reading lesson.

Writing.—Copy-books 2 and 3.
Careful attention to penmanship in all written exercises.

Arithmetic.—Numbers 1 to 100.
Their combinations and separations (oral and written).
Use and meaning of one twenty-first, one twenty-second, etc., to one one-hundredth (no figures).
Addition, Subtraction, Division and Partition of Fractions dealt with in Grade II.
Roman Numerals, I to C.
Simple problems, introducing seconds in minute, minutes in hour, hours in day ; pounds in bushel ; sheets in quire, quires in ream, &c.

Observation Lessons :—
1. Plant Life.—Continuation of the work of Grades I and II.
Study of growth, circulation of sap, &c.
Roots.—Fibrous and fleshy ; comparing, describing, naming.
Stems.—Erect, climbing, running ; manner of growth.
Leaves.—Parts, comparisons.
Flowers.—Parts, arrangement.
Fruit.—Fleshy and dry ; comparisons.
II. Animal Life.—Insects—Ants, Bees.
Birds—Continuation of work of Grades I and II.

Spelling.—From Reader.
Words to be arranged as far as possible in groups according to similarity
in form and sound.
Dictation.
Careful attention to spelling of all words used in written exercises.

Music. · Completion of work found in the first series of charts and
singing of easy exercises in all keys from Part I., First Reader, Normal
Music Course.

Drawing.—Prang's Drawing Book No. I., as outlined in Teachers
Manual Part I., also blank book for application of the work done in
Book I.

Geography.—Development of geographical notions by reference to
geographical features of neighbourhood.
Elementary lessons on direction, distance, extent.

GRADE IV.

Reading.—Third Reader.
Continuation of exercises of previous Grades.
Exercises to secure projection of tone and distinct articulation.
Memorizing of Poetical Selections.

Composition. — Exercises based on Observation Lessons, Reading
Lessons, Historical Tales, Geography, personal experience.   Special
attention to :
(1) Language as an expression of thought.
(2) Order of thought.
(3) Correction of common errors in speech.
Letter writing.

Writing.—Copy-books 4 and 5.
Careful attention to penmanship in all written exercises.

Arithmetic.—Numeration and Notation.
Simple Rules.
Addition, Subtraction, Division and Partition of Fractions already
known (figures).
Introduction of terms Numerator, Denominator, &c.
Roman Notation.
Graded Problems, introducing remaining Reduction Tables.
Simple Problems, introducing the use of dollars and cents.
Daily practice in Simple Rules to secure accuracy and rapidity.

Observation Lessons.—Grade III. continued.

Spelling.—From Reader.
Exercises as in Grade III.

Music.—Completion of the work found in part I., First Reader, and
reading all Music in parts II. and III. (First Reader.)

Drawing.—Prang's Drawing Book No. II., as outlined in Teacher's Manual, Part I., also blank book for application of work done in Book II.

Geography :—

(a) Review of work of Grade III.

Lessons to lead to simple conception of the earth as a great ball, with surface of land and water, surrounded by the air, lighted by the sun, and having two motions.

(b) Lessons on Natural Features, first from observation, afterwards by means of moulding board, pictures and blackboard illustrations.

(c) Preparation for and introduction of maps. (Review of lessons in position, distance, direction with representations drawn to scale.) Study of map of vicinity drawn on blackboard. Maps of natural features drawn from moulded forms. Practice in reading conventional map symbols on outline maps.

(d) General study from globe and maps. The hemisphere, continents, oceans and large islands, their relative positions and size. The continents, their position, climate, form, outline, surroundings, principal mountains, rivers, lakes, the most important countries, productions, people, interesting facts and associations.

GRADE V.

Reading.—Fourth Reader.
Continuation of exercises of previous Grades in pronunciation, &c.
Memorizing of Poetical Selections.

Composition.—The work of Grade IV. continued, with exercises based on the History of this Grade.

Writing.—Copy Books 6 and 7. Careful attention to penmanship in all written exercises.

Arithmetic.—Notation and Numeration.
Formal Reduction.
Easy Vulgar Fractions.
Denominate Fractions.
Daily practice to secure accuracy and rapidity in simple rules.
Graded Problems.
Reading and writing Decimals.

Elementary Science.—

1. Plant Life—Relation of plant to soil, light, heat and moisture. Comparisons. Continued study of growth.
Trace the changes in vegetables and selected trees, keeping a record of such changes.
Roots—Primary and secondary ; annuals, biennials and perennials.
Stems—Compare underground stems and stems above ground ; compare endogens and exogens.
Buds—Situation and kinds ; arrangement.
Leaves—Peculiar forms ; arrangement.
Flowers—Position and arrangement ; analysis and description of common flowers ; this should lead up to that orderly description which is necessary in classification.
Fruit—Kinds ; how formed ; how distributed, &c.

2. Animal Life—Continuation of work of previous Grades.

Spelling.—From Reader. Exercises as in Grades III. and IV.

Music.—Review of the most difficult songs and exercises in Part II., First Reader, giving special attention to two-part songs and exercises, so that each pupil may be able to sing either a soprano or an alto part. Commencement of work laid down in the second series of charts, and Second Reader, Part II.

Drawing.—Prang's Drawing Books Nos. III. and IV. as outlined in Teachers' Manual, Part II.

Geography.—Simple study of the important countries in each continent. The position of the country in the continent; its natural features, climate, productions; its people, their occupations, manners, customs; noted localities, cities, &c. Manitoba and Canada to be studied first. Moulding boards and map-drawing to be aids in the study.

History.—Tales and Biography.

A.

Leonidas and Ancient Greece.
Hannibal and the two great nations of his time.
Alfred the Great— or Early England
Charlemagne or Medieval Europe.
Peter the Hermit and the Crusades.
Joan of Arc or the English in France.
Wolsey—his great ambition.
The Armada, or England on the Seas.
John Eliot and the rights of the people.
Wm. Pitt— England's Colonies.
Wilberforce—The Slave Trade.
Stephenson—The story of invention.
Havelock—The Indian Empire.

B.

Columbus—Discovery of America.
Magellan—Circumnavigation of the Globe
Cartier—Early Canadian Discovery.
Champlain—and early settlement.
Cortez—The story of Mexico.
De Soto and the Mississippi.
La Salle and Western Exploration.
Madeleine de Vercheres and Daulac, or Indian Warfare.
D'Iberville and the Hudson's Bay Co.
Wolfe and Montcalm—The great struggle.
Captain Cook and Vancouver—Our Pacific Coast.
Lord Selkirk and the Red River Settlement.
Laura Secord and Canadian Loyalty.

Physiology.—Child's Health Primer (Pathfinder No. 1).

GRADE VI.

Reading.—Evangeline. Riverside Lit., Series No. 1 (Houghton, Mifflin & Co.).
Biographical Stories, Hawthorne, Riverside Lit., Series No. 10 (Houghton, Mifflin & Co.).
Sharp Eyes and other papers Riverside Lit., Series No. 36 (Houghton Mifflin & Co.).

Composition.—Same as Grade V., with exercises based on the History of this Grade.

Writing.—Copy Book No. 8. Careful attention to penmanship in all written exercises.

Arithmetic.—Factors, Measures and Multiples.
Vulgar Fractions.
Easy application of Decimals.
Easy application of Square and Cubic Measures.
Daily practice to secure accuracy and rapidity in simple rules.
Easy application of Percentage.
Graded Problems.

Elementary Science.—As outlined in Course of Agriculture Series I.

Spelling.—From Reading matter. Careful attention to spelling of all words used in written exercises.

Music.—Completion of work found in Second Series of Charts, and Part II. of Second Reader.

Drawing.—Prang's Drawing Books Nos. V. and VI. as outlined in Teachers' Manual, Part III.

Geography :--

(*a*) The earth as a globe. Simple illustrations and statements with reference to form, size, meridians, parallels, with their use ; motions and their effects, as day and night, seasons ; zones with their characteristics, as winds and ocean currents ; climate as affecting the life of man.

(*b*) Physical features and conditions of North America, South America and Europe studied and compared --position on the globe, position relative to other grand divisions, size, form, surface, drainage, animal and vegetable life, resources, causes determining growth of cities ; inhabitants, their occupations and social condition ; important localities, cities and towns.

(*c*) Observation to accompany the study of Geography—apparent movements of the sun, moon and stars, and varying time of their rising and setting ; difference in heat of the sun's rays at different hours of the day ; change in the direction of the sun's rays coming through a school room window at the same hour during the year ; varying length of noon-day shadows ; changes of the weather, wind and seasons.

History.—English History, Creighton, Chap. 1 to 9.
Canadian History, to taking of Quebec.

Physiology.—Physiology for Young People (New Pathfinder No. 2, Chap. 1 to 9).

GRADE VII.

Reading.—Story of Iliad.—Church. English Classic Series No. 59.
Story of Æneid.—Church. English Classic Series No. 58.
Birds and Bees.—Riverside Literature Series No. 28.
Christmas Carol (condensed).—English Classic Series No. 32.
The Children's Treasury of English Song, Part I., Palgrave. (McMillan & Co.)

Composition.—Oral and written exercises as in previous Grades.
Making of abstracts ; expansion of narrative sentences into paragraphs ; topical analysis ; proportion in the paragraph.

Writing.—Careful attention to penmanship in all written exercises.

Arithmetic.—Decimals.
Percentage without time.
Easy problems in Interest.
Application of Square and Cubic Measures.
Problems.

Elementary Science.—As outlined in Course of Agriculture Series II., pages 1-124.

Spelling.—As in Grade VI.

Music.—Third Reader, Normal Music Course.

Drawing.—Prang's Drawing Books Nos. VII. and VIII. as outlined in Manual.

Geography.—Physical and Political Geography of the countries in Europe and North America.
General review of the physical features of the grand divisions ; position of the countries in the grand divisions : surroundings, surface, climate : animal and vegetable life ; resources ; inhabitants, their occupations and social condition ; important localities, cities and towns.

History.—English History.   Creighton, Chap. 10 to 19.
Canadian.   From taking of Quebec to Confederation.

Physiology.—Physiology for Young People (New Pathfinder No. 2. Chap. 10 to 17).

Grammar.—Inductive study of the sentence, with results put in clear and concise language.

1.—Examination and comparison of easy sentences leading to classification into Declarative, Interrogative, &c.

2.—Division of compound sentences into independent propositions.

3.—Division of easy sentences into subject and predicate.

4.—Division of : (a) Complete subject into bare subject and modifiers : (b) Complete predicate into bare predicate and modifiers.

5.—Comparison of word groups leading to the distinction between :
   (a) Phrases and clauses.
   (b) Principal clauses and subordinate clauses.

6.—Examination and comparison of words, phrases and dependent clauses with regard to their use in the sentence.

7.—Analysis of compound sentences ; easy complex sentences and continuous prose.

GRADE VIII.

Reading.—Cricket on the Hearth.   English Classic Series, No. 86.
Lays of Ancient Rome.   English Classic Series, Nos. 76, 77.
Irving's Legend of Sleepy Hollow, English Classic Series, No. 41.
The Children's Treasury of English Song, Part II., Palgrave.   (McMillan & Co.)

Composition.—Continuation of exercises of previous Grades.
Direct instruction in choice of words, arrangement of words in sentences, structure of paragraphs, narration, description, common figures of speech.

Writing.—Careful attention to penmanship in all written exercises.

Arithmetic.—Percentage, Insurance, Commission and Brokerage, Profit and Loss, Duties, Interest and Discount, Measurement of surfaces of Rectangular solids and of Cylinders, Square Root with easy applications.

Elementary Science.—As outlined in Prairie Agriculture Series II.

Spelling.—As in Grade VII.

Music.—Third Reader.

Drawing.—Prang's Drawing Books Nos. IX. and X., as outlined in Manual.

Geography.—Physical Geography.
General review of the continents with special reference to British possessions.
Topics as in Grade VII.

History.—English History. Creighton reviewed.
Canadian. From Confederation to present time.

Algebra.—Simple rules ; simple equations ; problems ; easy exercises in factoring.

Geometry.—Euclid, Book I., Propositions I.-XXVI.

Grammar.—Exercises similar to those in Grade VII., but on more difficult sentences, and on continuous prose.

1.—Clasification of words into parts of speech, following the order suggested by the work of Grade VII.

2.—Distinguishing between
   (*a*) The different naming words.
   (*b*) The different modifying words.
   (*c*) The different connecting words.

3.—Parts of speech accurately defined.

4.—Inflection.

5.—Analysis and parsing.

GRADE IX. (Optional).

In cities and towns Boards of School Trustees may establish a new Grade, to be known as Grade IX.

The programme of studies for this Grade is now under the consideration of the Advisory Board.

APPENDIX C.

REGULATIONS REGARDING RELIGIOUS EXERCISES.

REGULATIONS

OF THE

ADVISORY BOARD

REGARDING

RELIGIOUS EXERCISES IN THE PUBLIC SCHOOLS.

Adopted May 21st, 1890.

The Religious Exercises in the Public Schools shall be :—
(*a*) The Reading, without note or comment, of the following selections from the authorised English Version of the Bible or the Douay Version of the Bible.
(*b*) The use of the following forms of prayer.

SCRIPTURE READINGS.

PART I.—HISTORICAL.

1. The Creation	Gen. i,	1-19
2. The Creation continued	Gen. i,	20-31
3. The Fall of Man	Gen. iii,	
4. The Deluge	Gen. viii,	1-22
5. The Covenant with Noah	Gen. ix,	1-17
6. The Trial of Abraham	Gen. xxii,	1-18
7. Isaac Blesses Jacob	Gen xxvii,	1-29
8. Esau's Blessing	Gen. xxvii,	30-45
9. Jacob's Vision	Gen. xxviii,	10-22
10. Jacob's Return to Bethel	Gen. xxxv,	1-15
11. Joseph and his brethren	Gen. xxxvii,	1-22
12. Joseph Sold into Egypt	Gen. xxxvii,	23-36
13. Pharaoh's Dreams	Gen. xli,	1-24
14. Joseph's Interpretations	Gen. xli,	25-43
15. Jacob's Sons' Visit	Gen. xlii,	1-20
16. Jacob's Sons' Return from Egypt	Gen. xlii,	21-38
17. The Second Visit to Egypt	Gen. xliii,	1-14
18. Joseph and his Brethren	Gen. xliii,	15-34
19. Joseph and his Brethren—continued	Gen. xliv,	1-13
20. Joseph and his Brethren—continued	Gen. xliv,	14-34
21. Joseph Discovers himself to his Brethren	Gen. xlv,	
22. Jacob and his Household go into Egypt	Gen. xlvi, 1-6,	28-34
23. Jacob's Interview with Pharaoh	Gen. xlvii,	1-12
24. Death of Jacob	Gen. xlviii,	1-21
25. Burial of Jacob	Gen. l,	1-26
26. Moses at the Burning Bush	Exod. iii,	1-20
27. Grievous Oppression of the Hebrews	Exod. v,	
28. The Passover	Exod. xii,	1-20
29. The Israelites Escape Through the Red Sea	Exod. xiv,	10-31
30. The Song of Deliverance	Exod. xv,	1-22
31. Giving of Manna	Exod. xvi,	2-35
32. The Water from the Rock	Exod. xvii,	
33. The Ten Commandments	Exod. xx,	1-17
34. The Covenant with Israel	Exod. xxiv,	
35. The Tabernacle	Exod. xl,	17-36
36. Spies sent into Canaan	Num. xiii,	17-33
37. The People Rebel at the Report of the Spies	Num. xiv,	1-30
38. The Song of Moses	Deut. xxxii,	1-14

39. The Death of Moses .... Deut. xxxiv,
40. Joshua Succeeds Moses...—................................... Josh. i,   1-17
41. The Covenant with Joshua................................ Josh. xxiv,   1-28
42. The Call of Samuel... I Saml. iii,
43. The Israelites Desire a King .... I Saml. viii,   1-20
44. Samuel Anoints Saul .... I Saml. ix, 21-27, xi,   1-11
45. Samuel Anoints David....................................... I Saml. xvi,
46. David and Goliath... I Saml. xvii,   1-27
47. David Overcomes Goliath .... I Saml. xvii, 28-54
48. David and Jonathan .... I Saml. xviii,   1-16
49. David Instructed as to the Building of the Temple
                                                        I Chron. xvii,   1-17
50. David's Advice to Solomon.......................... I Chron. xxviii,   1-20
51. David's Preparation for Building the Temple...... I Chron. xxix,   1-19
52. Solomon's Wise Choice...................... ....I Kings iii,   1-15
53. Preparations for Building the Temple .... I Kings v,
54. Solomon's Prayer at the Dedication of the Temple...II Chron. vi,   1 21
55. Solomon's Prayer—continued .... II Chron. vi,   22-42
56. Elijah .... I Kings xvii,
57. Elijah and the Prophets of Baal........................ I Kings xviii,   1-21
58. Discomfiture of the Prophets of Baal .... I Kings xviii,   22-46
59. Elijah in the Wilderness .... I Kings xix,   1-13
60. Elijah and Elisha .... ·........................ II Kings ii,   1-15
61. Naaman the Leper ....II Kings v,   1-19
62. The Fall of Israel................................II Kings xvii,   6-24
63. Public Worship of God Restored .... II Chron xxix,   20-36
64. Deliverance under Hezekiah ....II Kings xix,   1-19
65. Deliverance nnder Hezekiah—continued.............II Kings xix,   20-36
66. Rejoicing of the Israelites at the Restoration of Divine Worship
                                                        II Chron. xxx,
67. Jerusalem Taken by Nebuchadnezzar .... II Chron. xxxvi,   5-21
68. The Golden Image.. Dan. iii,   1-18
69. The Fiery Furnace... Dan. iii,   19-30
70. Daniel in the Lion's Den.. Dan. vi,
71. The Temple Rebuilt .... Ezra i, 1-6 & iii,

PART 2.—THE GOSPELS.

1. Christ the Word ....John i,   1-18
2. The Birth of Christ Announced................................ Luke ii,   8-20
3. The Visit of the Magi.. Matth. ii,   1-12
4. The Song of Simeon .... Luke ii,   25-40
5. Jesus in the Temple .... Luke ii,   41-52
6. The Baptism of Jesus Christ .... Matth. iii,   1-17
7 The Temptation of Our Lord ....Luke iv,   1-15
8. Testimony of John the Baptist .... John i,   19-34
9. The First Disciples .... John i,   35-51
10. Jesus at Nazareth ....Luke iv,   16-32
11. At Capernaum .... Matth. iv,   13-25
12. Sermon on the Mount .... Matth. v,   1-12
13. Sermon on the Mount—continued................. Matth. v, 13-20,   33-37
14. Sermon on the Mount—continued.............. Matth. v,   38-48
15. Sermon on the Mount—continued.......................... Matth. vi,   1-18
16. Sermon on the Mount—continued.................. Matth. vi,   19-34
17. Sermon on the Mount- continued...................... .... Matth. vii,   1-14
18. Sermon on the Mount—continued.....................Matth. vii,   15-29
19. The Miraculous Draught of Fishes .... Luke v,   1-15
20. The Healing of the Paralytic .... Luke v,   16-26
21. The Twelve Apostles Sent Forth .... Matth. ix, 36-38, x,   1-11
22. The Centurion's Servant—The Widow's Son .... Luke vii,   1-17
23. The Declaration Concerning John....................... Matth. xi,   2-19
24. The Feast in Simeon's House...................................Luke vii,   36-50
25. Privileges and Responsibility .... Matth. xi,   20-31
26. The Sabbath .... Luke vi.   1-11
27. Parable of the Sower ....Mark iv,   1-20

28. Parable of the Tares, etc.. Matth. xiii, 24-35
29. Parable of the Tares Explained, with other Parables
                Matth. xiii, 36-52
30. Children Brought to Jesus—Conditions of Discipleship...Mark x, 13-30
31. Tribute to Cæsar—The Widow's Offering
          Matth. xxii, 15-22, Mark xii, 41-44
32. Christ Confessed .... Matth. xvi, 13-28
33. Christ Feeding Five Thousand ....Mark vi, 30-41
34. Christ Walking on the Sea .... Matth. xiv, 22-33
35. The Transfiguration .... Matth. xvii, 1-13
36. The Great Supper .... Luke xiv, 7-24
37. The Lost Sheep and Lost Piece of Silver ....Luke xv, 1-10
38. The Two Sons ....Luke xv, 11-32
39. The Pharisee and the Publican ....Luke xviii, 9-17
40. Blind Bartimeus-Zaccheus the Publican ...Luke xviii, 35-43, xix, 1-10
41. The Good Samaritan................................... Luke x, 25-37
42. The Good Shepherd .... John x, 1-18
43 Christ One with the Father................................ John x, 22-42
44. Humility .... John xiii, 1-17
45. The Death of Lazarus .... John xi, 30-48
46. The Triumphal Entry into Jerusalem
        Mark xi, 1-11, Matth. xxi, 9-16
47. Parable of the Ten Virgins .... Matth. xxv, 1-13
48. Parable of the Talents.................................... Matth. xxv, 14-30
49. The Judgment .... Matth. xxv, 31-46
50. Christ Comforts the Disciples .... John xiv, 1-14
51. The Holy Spirit Promised .... John xiv, 15-31
52. Christ the True Vine ....John xv, 1-17
53. Last Sayings of Jesus ....John xvi, 1-15, 26-33
54. The Prayer of Christ .... John xvii, 1-26
55. The Box of Precious Ointment .... Matth. xxvi, 1-13
56. The Last Supper .... Matth. xxvi, 17-29
57. The Agony in the Garden—Betrayal of Jesus ..... Matth. xxvi, 30-56
58. Christ before Caiaphas and Peter's Denial .... Matth. xxvi, 57-75
59. Christ before Pilate ....Matth. xxvii, 1-25
60. The Crucifixion ....Matth. xxvii, 26-43
61. The Crucifixion—continued...............................Luke xxiii, 39-56
62. The Resurrection .... Mark xvi, 1-7, John xx, 3-18
63. The Journey to Emmaus ....Luke xxiv, 13-35
64. Jesus Appears to His Disciples—the Doubt of Thomas
              John xx, 19-29
65. Jesus Appears again to His Disciples....................... John xxi, 1-23
66. The Ascension .... Matth. xxviii.

FORM OF PRAYER.

Most merciful God, we yield Thee our humble and hearty thanks for Thy fatherly care and preservation of us this day, and for the progress which Thou hast enabled us to make in useful learning ; we pray thee to imprint upon our minds whatever good instructions we have received, and to bless them to the advancement of our temporal and eternal welfare ; and pardon, we implore Thee, all that Thou hast seen amiss in our thoughts, words, and actions. May Thy good Providence still guide and keep us during the approaching interval of rest and relaxation, so that we may be prepared to enter on the duties of the morrow with renewed vigour both of body and mind ; and preserve us we beseech Thee, now and forever, both outwardly in our bodies and inwardly in our souls, for the sake of Jesus Christ, Thy Son, our Lord. Amen.

Our Father, who art in Heaven, hallowed be Thy name. Thy kingdom come. Thy will be done on earth, as it is in Heaven ; give us this day our daily bread ; and forgive us our trespasses, as we forgive them that trespass against us ; and lead us not into temptation, but deliver us from evil. Amen.

The Grace of our Lord Jesus Christ, and the love of God, and the Fellowship of the Holy Ghost, be with us all evermore. Amen.

APPENDIX D.

REGULATIONS OF THE ADVISORY BOARD AS TO TEACHERS' CERTIFICATES.

Revised August 31st, 1899.

The following regulations have been adopted by the Advisory Board in regard to the examination of teachers and granting of certificates :--

TEACHERS' CERTIFICATES.

1. The certificates hereafter granted by the Advisory Board of Education for the public schools of the Province of Manitoba shall rank as first, second, or third class. Those of the first class shall be sub-divided into grades A and B ; those of the second and third classes shall be each of one grade. The first and second shall be valid during the pleasure of the Board : the third class certificates shall be valid for three years.

2. There shall be two parts in the examination for granting certificates —one for testing the literary acquirements of the candidates, to be known as the non-professional examination ; the other for testing their knowledge of the theory and practice of education, to be known as the professional examination.

NON-PROFESSIONAL EXAMINATION.

THIRD CLASS.

1. *Reading and Orthoepy.*—Oral reading with proper pronunciation and expression. [Value 100 ; minimum required 60.]

Writing and Spelling.—On all papers.

2. *English Grammar.*—Etymology and Syntax. Exercises.

Text Book.—Tweed's Grammar for Common Schools—Lee and Shepard. Supplementary—West's Grammar.

3. *Composition and Rhetoric.*—Familiar and business letters ; themes based upon prescribed prose literature ; principles of rhetoric as outlined in prescribed text book.

Text Book.—Welsh's English Composition.
1900. Composition from Models (new edition), pages 1-184.

4. *Poetical Literature.*—Intelligent comprehension of and familiarity with the prescribed poems ; memorising the finest portions ; oral reading of prescribed poems.

1900. The following selections from Tennyson : Recollections of the Arabian Nights, the Lady of Shalott, Œnone, The Lotos-Eaters, "You ask me why, tho' ill at ease," "Of old sat Freedom on the Heights," "Love thou thy land with love far brought," The Epic, Morte d'Arthur, Ulysses, St. Agnes' Eve, Sir Galahad, "As thro' the land at eve we went," "Sweet and low, sweet and low," "The splendour falls on castle walls," "Tears, idle tears, I know not what they mean," "Thy voice is heard thro' rolling drums," "Home they brought her warrior dead," "Ask me no more ; the moon may draw the sea," Lancelot and Elaine, To Virgil, Early Spring, Freedom, Crossing the Bar.

5. *History.*—The leading events of Canadian and English History.

Text Book—Arabella B. Buckley's History of England; Clement's History of Canada.

6. *Geography.*—The general geography of the world; geography of Canada and the British Empire more particularly.

Text Book—The High School Geography.

7. *Arithmetic.*—

Text Book—Hamblin Smith's Arithmetic to the end of Chapter XXVI. Supplementary for schools requiring additional exercises :— Thompson, Ballard & McKay's High School Arithmetic.

8. *Algebra.*—Fundamental laws of algebra; elementary rules; simple equations of one, two, and three unknown quantities; factoring; problems.

Text Book.—C. Smith's Elementary Algebra, Chapters I. to X. inclusive. Supplementary for schools requiring additional exercises :—Robertson & Birchard's High School Algebra.

9. *Euclid.*—Book I. with exercises.

Euclid's definitions will be required, and no axioms or postulates except Euclid's may be assumed unless in the case of the 12th axiom.

The actual proof of propositions as given in Euclid will not be required, but no proof of any proposition occurring in Euclid will be admitted in which use is made of any proposition which, in Euclid's order, occurs subsequently. The enunciations will be set according to Euclid. Abbreviations for words may be used, but not the algebraical symbols + and − , or indices.

(The definitions, axioms, postulates, enunciations as required will be found in Todhunter's Euclid.)

Note.—The First Book of Hall and Stevens' Euclid and the first ten chapters of Stringham's revision of C. Smith's Algebra, are bound together and contain all that is required for this examination in the subjects of Algebra and Euclid.

10. *Botany.*—Elements of Structural Botany.

The course in third-class Botany shall be entirely practical and descriptive, and shall cover the following :

The flower, its parts, their functions and relations as observed in the actual study of specimens of the following orders :—Ranunculaceæ, Cruciferæ, Leguminosæ, Rosaceæ, Onagraceæ, Saxifragaceæ, Sapindaceæ and Liliaceæ.

The classification of members of these orders to their species (Spotton's Botany being the limit).

The leaf in vernation, venation, phyllotaxis, surface, margin, outline, base, apex and function.

The study of flower arrangement and opening.

The simple study of fruits and their classification—as apocarpous and syncarpous, dehiscent and indehiscent.

The simple study of the root and stem, with drawings of cross section and branch systems.

Pollination, fertilisation, and the development of the seed from the ovule. The study of hairs, tendrils, runners and such modification of parts.

Germination, illustrating the growth of the seed and conditions. Plant food, assimilation, respiration and transpiration. Simple drawings of all the parts.

Plants shall be submitted at the examination.

Text Books—Spotton's High School Botany (Manitoba edition), and Manitoba Course of Agriculture, Series 1.

Book of reference for Teachers.—Bergen's Elements of Botany (Ginn & Co.).

11. *Agriculture.—*
Text Book—Manitoba Course of Agriculture, Series 2.

12. *Physiology.—*
Text Book—Physiology for young people (New Pathfinder, No. 2)

13. *Book-keeping.—*
Text Book.—High School Book-keeping, chapters 1 to 6 inclusive, chapters 8 to 10 inclusive, precis-writing, indexing.

14. *Drawing.—*Prang's Elementary Course, Books 8 and 9. Teachers' Manual, Part IV

Sketches from nature—more stress on rapid sketching, noticing the masses of form and colour, trees, flowers, bits of landscape ; guidance as to the use of copying.

Study of appearances—some lessons on Theory, drawing from the rectangular object below the eye, above the eye ; observing convergence, finding vanishing points, etc. Books, chairs, tables, simple school room objects thoughtfully drawn, brightly rendered (freehand work throughout).

Foreshortening, proportion, convergence as principles to be observed in good drawing ; stress on simplicity and grace, on character in the rendering of a sketch ; free sketching for criticism and comparison ; thoughtful selections for the books.

First steps in instrumental drawing ; use of a few geometrical problems (*See* 1 to 9), ability to read the working drawings illustrated in Book 8, to make a simple pattern accurately, to show from a single object two or three views figured.

Special features of the senior work—as the lessons under design, studies in light and shade, and colour, etc., to be met or adopted according to local conditions, (read notes on covers of pupils' drawing books.)

15. *Music.—*Normal Music Course Third Reader. Chromatic Scale, Minor Scales. Third Time Chart. Modulation. Exercises in vowels. Humming exercises. Breathing exercises.

Candidates will not be allowed to write for a second third-class certificate.

SECOND CLASS.

ENGLISH.

1. *Reading and Orthoepy.—*Oral reading, with proper pronunciation and expression. [Value 100, minimum required 60.]

2. *Writing and Spelling.—*On all papers.

3. *Grammar.—*(One paper.) West's English Grammar.

4. *Rhetoric and Composition.—*(One paper.)
(*a*) The reading of the selections contained in Alexander and Libby's Composition from Models, pages 249 to 457, in connection with the investigation of rhetorical principles, along the lines laid down in Genung's "Outlines of Rhetoric."

(*b*) The writing of an essay on one of a number of subjects to be assigned by the examiner. The essay should not exceed two foolscap pages in length.

Text Books—Composition from Models, Alexander and Libby ; Outlines of Rhetoric, Genung (Ginn & Co.)

5. *Poetical. Literature.—*(One paper.)
1900. Coleridge—The Ancient Mariner, Youth and Age.
Longfellow—Evangeline, A Psalm of Life, The Wreck of the Hesperus, "The Day is Done," The Old Clock on the Stairs, The Fire of Driftwood, Resignation, The Warden of the Cinque Ports, Excelsior, The Bridge, A Gleam of Sunshine.
Wordsworth—(Palgrave's Golden Treasury of Songs and Lyrics), The Education of Nature, ("Three Years She Grew,") "She was a Phantom of

Delight," A Lesson, ("There is a Flower, the Lesser Celandine"), To the
Skylark, The Green Linnet, To the Cuckoo, To the Daisy; and the follow-
ing sonnets: To a Distant Friend, "Why Art Thou Silent?" England and
Switzerland, "Two Voices are There," "Milton! Thou Should be Living
at this Hour," Westminster Bridge, The Inner Vision, "Most Sweet it is,
With Uplifted Eyes," "O Friend! I know not which way I must look,"
To Sleep, Within King's College Chapel.

HISTORY AND GEOGRAPHY.

1. (*a.*) *English History* from the Revolution of 1688 to the peace of 1815
Green's History.

   (*b.*) *Roman History* (Creighton's Rome—Primer).
   (*c.*) *Greek History* (Fyffe's Greece—Primer)

2. (*a.*) *Canadian History.*—Clement's History of Canada.
   (*b.*) *Geography.*—Outlines of physical and mathematical geography;
commercial and physical geography of Europe and America.
Text Book.—The High School Geography.

MATHEMATICS

1. *Arithmetic.*
Text Book.—Hamblin Smith's Arithmetic
Supplementary for schools requiring additional exercises.—Thompson,
Ballard & McKay's High School Arithmetic.

2. *Algebra.*—Elementary rules; easy factoring; highest common measure;
lowest common multiple; square root; fractions; simple equations of one,
two, and three unknown quantities; indices; surds; easy quadratic
equations of one and two unknown quantities.
Text Book.—C. Smith's Elementary Algebra.
Supplementary for schools requiring additional exercises.—Robertson &
Birchard's High School Algebra.

3. *Euclid.*—Bb. I., II., III.
Euclid's definitions will be required, and no axioms or postulates except
Euclid's may be assumed, unless in the case of the 12th axiom.
The actual proof of propositions, as given in Euclid, will not be required,
but no proof of any proposition occurring in Euclid will be admitted, in
which use is made of any proposition which, in Euclid's order, occurs
subsequently. The enunciations will be set according to Euclid. Abbreviations for words may be used, but not the algebraical symbols + and −,
or indices.
(The definitions, axioms, postulates, enunciations as required will be
found in Todhunter's Euclid.)

4. *Book-keeping.*—High School Book-keeping, chapters 1 to 6 inclusive,
chapters 8 to 10 inclusive, precis writing, indexing.

SCIENCE.

1. *Botany.*—Elements of structural botany.
Plants will be submitted to the candidates for examination and
identification.
Texts Books—Spotton's High School Botany (Manitoba edition) and the
Manitoba Course of Agriculture, Series 1.

2. *Physics.*—The elements of physics.
Text Book—Gage's Introduction to Physical Science, (*See* page 7).

3. *Agriculture* ⎫
4. *Music* ⎬ Same as for Third Class Certificate.
5. *Drawing* ⎭

(Candidates who have passed the examination in Book-keeping, Agriculture, Music, and Drawing, for third class certificates, will be exempt from
examination in these subjects for second class.)

FIRST CLASS.

ENGLISH.

1. *Writing and Spelling.*—On all papers.

2. *Rhetoric and Composition.*—(Two papers.)
(*a*) The reading of selected prose authors in connection with the investigation of rhetorical principles along the lines laid down in Genung's Outlines of Rhetoric.
(*b*) The writing of an essay on one of a number of subjects based on the selections prescribed for rhetorical study.

Texts for 1900 · The following selections from Representative Essays : Conversations—De Quincey ; Compensation—Emerson ; On a certain Con descension in Foreigners—Lowell ; Kin Beyond the Sea—Gladstone. Outlines of Rhetoric, Genung.

3. *History of the English Language and Literature.*—(One paper.)
History of English Language—Lounsbury, Part 1 ; English Literature—Stopford Brooke.

4. *Literature.*—(Two papers.)
(*a*) Shakespeare—Macbeth, The Tempest.
(*b*) Chaucer—The Prologue to the Canterbury Tales (Clarendon Press, Text).
Milton—Paradise Lost, Book I.

MATHEMATICS.

1. *Algebra.*—The Algebra prescribed for the second class examination, together with cube root, quadratic equations, ratio, proportion, variations, and the progressions.—(C. Smith's Elementary Algebra, inclusive of the whole of Chapter 28.)

2. *Euclid.*—Definitions and books I., II., III., IV., definitions of book V., book VI., propositions 1, 2, 3, A, 4, 33.
Euclid's definitions will be required, and no axioms and postulates except Euclid's may be assumed unless in the case of the 12th axiom.
The actual proof of propositions as given in Euclid will not be required, but no proof of any proposition occurring in Euclid will be admitted, in which use is made of any proposition, which in Euclid's order occurs subsequently. The enunciations will be set according to Euclid. Abbreviations for words may be used, but not the algebraical symbols + and −, or indices.
(The definitions, axioms, postulates, enunciations as required will be found in Todhunter's Euclid.)

3. *Trigonometry.*—Up to and including the solution of plane triangles.—Hamblin Smith's.

SCIENCE

1. *Geography.*—The Eclectic Physical Geography. — American Book Company.

2. *Chemistry.*—Elements of Inorganic Chemistry. — Remsen's Briefer Course.

NOTE.—A practical as well as theoretical knowledge of the subject is required.

3. *Physiology.*—Huxley's Elementary Lessons.

HISTORY.

English.—Green's Short History of the English People, Chapters iii., vii., ix.

Canadian.—Bourinot's How **Canada** is Governed.

Holders of Second Class Certificates, actually employed in teaching, who have had five years' successful experience, may be permitted to take the first class examination in two parts.

Part 1.—Mathematics and History.

Part 2.—English and Science.

Candidates must write on Book-keeping, Botany, Agriculture, Music, and Drawing if they have not passed in these subjects before.

MARKS REQUIRED TO PASS.

Candidates must obtain at least 50 per cent. of the aggregate marks, and 34 per cent. on each subject, except in the case of oral reading, where 60 per cent. is required.

SCIENCE TEACHING IN THE PUBLIC SCHOOLS OF MANITOBA.

COLLEGIATE AND INTERMEDIATE SCHOOLS.

1. *Chemistry.*—At the examination for first class teachers it is the intention to make the examination practical. Forty per cent. of the paper will be on practical work.

Practical examinations in this subject will be held in the Laboratories of Winnipeg, Brandon, and Portage la Prairie Collegiate Institutes.

2. *Physics.*—The examination for second class teachers shall be an experimental course, defined as follows :

Chapter I. Meaning of " Matter," " Energy," " Motion," " Rest," and Force." Three states of matter ; Constitution of matter. Volume, mass, density. Various manifestations of Force. Measurement of force in gravitation units. Molar and molecular forces. Properties of matter. Equilibrium of forces. Gravitation. Meaning of weight. Distinction between hypothesis, theory and law.

Chapter II. Properties and laws of gases, liquids and solids. Buoyancy. Archimedes' principle. Determination of the specific gravity of bodies. The barometer. Air pump. Common and force pumps. Syphon. Boyle's tube. Brahma Press. The hydrostatic paradox.

Chapter III. The meaning of Momentum, Acceleration, Velocity. Effects of force continuously applied to matter. Meaning of equal masses. Statement of Newton's Laws of Motion. The application of these laws. Centre of Gravity. Determination of centre of gravity. Equilibrium of bodies. Curvilinear motion. The pendulum. Graphic representation of force and motion. Composition and resolution of forces.

Chapter IV. Meaning of Work. Measurement of work in gravitation units. A practical acquaintance with the C. G. S. system of units. The law of machines. The pulley, wheel and axle. Levers. Use of the balance. Inclined plane.

Chapter V. Theory of heat. Sources of heat. Temperature. Effect of heat. Elementary laws of heat. Latent heat. Specific heat. The calorie. Thermometry. Use of Fahrenheit and Centigrade. Heat convertible into potential energy, and *vice versa*. Mechanical equivalent. Steam engine. Coservation and correlation of energy.

Chapter VI. The voltaic cell. Study of common kinds of cells. Polarisation of plates. Direction of current. Some effects produced by an electric current. Potential and electro-motor force. Ohm's law. Methods of combining cells. Laws of currents. The galvanometer. Laws of resistance of a conductor. Magnets and magnetism. Electric light, arc and incandescent. Telegraph. Telephone. Static electricity.

Chapter VII. Sound caused by vibrations. Method of propagation. Velocity, Reflection, Interference, Intensity, Pitch, Quality, Resonators, Vibrations of strings and wires. Nodes and loops. Noise and music.

Chapter VIII. Nature of Light. Rectilinear propagation. Images through a pinhole. Beam, Pencil, Ray. Photometry. Laws of reflection and refraction. Images in plane, concave and convex mirrors. Drawing of images. Lenses. Drawing images produced by a lens. Prism. Dispersion and colour. Spectrum. Recomposition of white light.

Text—Introduction to Physical Science—Gage. Fifty per cent. of the paper will be practical.

The following physical apparatus is required for the second class course :— Balance, Metric System of Weights, two Dynamometers, ½lb. Glass tubing, sizes ¼″ to ¼″, Spirit Lamp, Barometer Tube, Boyle's Tube, Air Pump and Receiver, two Flasks, Glass Models of Common and Force Pumps, Glass Models of Hydrostatic Press, Glass Models for showing that liquids transmit pressure equally in all directions, Syphon, Archimedes' Principle, Specific Gravity Bottle, Apparatus for illustrating Hydrostatic Paradox, Hydrometer, Set of Pulleys (4), Wheel and Axle, Ball and Ring to illustrate expansion under heat, Compound Bar, Fahrenheit Thermometer, Centigrade Thermometer, Pith Ball Pendulum, Stick Sealing Wax and Glass Rod for illustrating positive and negative electricity, large Bar Magnet, Horseshoe Magnet, Bi-chromate of Potash Cell (bottle form), four feet Copper Wire for Conductor, one Measuring Stick (metrical), Electric Machine, Electrophone, Leyden Jar and Discharger, Galvanometer, Electroscope, Magnetic Needle, Tuning Fork, two Triangular Prisms, one Plane Prism, Set of Lenses (6), Apparatus for studying Reflection of Light, Concave and Convex Mirrors (combination).

3. *Botany.*—At the examination for second and third class teachers fifty per cent. of the paper will be practical.

Attention is called to the fact that the new Manitoba edition of Spotton's Botany is now the authorized ;text book for Manitoba. The first part of this book substitutes Manitoba plants for a number of those in the old edition not found in this Province. The second part of the Manitoba edition, called "Wild Plants of Canada," is now perfectly adapted for practical work in Manitoba, having a full list of Manitoba wild flowers, as well as a list of the scientific names and orders of garden and hot-house plants.

The examination will be conducted on the Manitoba edition.

The attention of inspectors and teachers is called to the requirements of the Department as to submitting botanical note-books for inspection, and also as to the formation of a Herbarium in every Collegiate and Intermediate school.

Agriculture.—At the examination for second and third class teachers forty per cent. of the paper will be practical.

The attention of teachers is called to the necessity of familiarizing the candidates with the forty prescribed experiments before other experiments are undertaken.

Inasmuch as the teaching of agriculture in the public schools generally is necessarily confined to the chemical and physical apparatus provided by the Department, teachers preparing candidates for the examination are reminded of the importance of having the candidates instructed in the use of the apparatus provided by the Department, on which the examination will be conducted.

Candidates for entrance to the Collegiate Schools, in addition to the other work in agriculture, will be examined in the prescribed experiments.

PERSONS ELIGIBLE WITHOUT EXAMINATION.

1. The following persons shall be eligible for certificates :—

Holders of First or Second class professional or non-professional certificates, obtained on examination in the North-West Territories since January, 1894, to receive certificates of equal standing in this Province.

2. The following persons shall be eligible for non-professional certificates :—

(*a*) Undergraduates of the University of Manitoba, who have passed the Preliminary Examination (1892 and thereafter) to receive second class certificates on passing in book-keeping, agriculture, botany, music, and drawing, as prescribed for second class certificates ; those who have passed the previous Examination (1893 and thereafter), and have reached 50 per cent. of the aggregate marks, and 34 per cent. on each subject, and who present a certificate to that effect, to receive a certificate of first class, Grade B, on passing in book-keeping, agriculture, botany, music, and drawing, as prescribed for second class certificates.

(*b*) Graduates of the University of Manitoba, who have first or second class standing in Honour Courses, or in the General Course, to receive a certificate of first class, Grade A, on passing in book-keeping, agriculture, botany, music, and drawing, as prescribed for second class certificates.

(*c*) Graduates of any other University in Her Majesty's Dominions, on the presentation of satisfactory documents, to receive certificates of such class as the Advisory Board may deem them entitled to.

NORMAL SCHOOL COURSE.

1. Before being allowed to take professional training, all teachers shall have at least the corresponding non-professional standing.

2. Only those who have had third class professional training and at least one year's successful experience in teaching, shall be allowed to take the first or second class professional course.

THIRD CLASS.

The Science of Education.

Nature and aim of education, teaching, instruction. Outline of useful portions of mental science ; application of the principles derived therefrom to teaching and government.
Text—White's Pedagogy. Unconscious tuition—Huntingdon. Quick's Educational Reformers. Lectures.

The Art of Education.

(1) Methods of teaching each subject on the programme of studies. School Organization. School Management. Duties of teachers and pupils as set forth in the Public School Law and Regulations. Physical culture.

(2) Practice in teaching.
Texts—Public Schools Act ; Blaikie's Sound Bodies for our Boys and Girls. High School Cadet Drill Manual. Lectures.

SECOND CLASS.

The Science of Education.

The nature and aim of education, teaching and instruction. Psychology and ethics as the scientific basis of the art of education : their application to the development of the intellectual and moral powers.
Texts—White's Pedagogy. Sully's Psychology. Lectures.

The Art of Education.

(1) Outlines of general method ; its application to the teaching of each subject on the public school course of studies ; school organization ; school management ; physical culture ; practical training in music and drawing.

(2) Practice in teaching.

Texts.—White's Pedagogy. Public Schools Act. Lectures.

The History of Education.

Systems and theories of education ; eminent educators.
Texts.—Quick's Educational Reformers (Appleton's Edition, 1890).
Lectures.

FIRST CLASS.

The Science of Education.

Nature, form, and limit of education ; development and training of man , educational values ; psychological and logical sequences of subjects ; general method.

Texts.—Rozenkranz' Philosophy of Education ; Sully's Handbook of Psychology ; Jevon's Elements of Logic (Hill), selected portions ; Correlation Report and Report of Committee of Ten. Lectures.

The Art of Education.

(Application of principles derived from method and sequence to the teaching of each subject in the course of study ; school organization ; school management ; physical culture ; practical training in music and drawing.)

(2) Practice in teaching.
Texts--Public Schools Act. Regulations of the Department of Education and of the Advisory Board, so far as printed. Lectures.

The History of Education.

Systems and theories of education.
Text—Rosenkranz' Philosophy of Education, Part III. Lectures.
Quick's Educational Reformers (Appleton's Edition, 1890) ; Spencer's Essay on Education ; History of Educational Sloyd. Lectures.

COLLEGIATE OR HIGH SCHOOL.

The same as for First-class Certificate.

MARKS REQUIRED TO PASS WRITTEN EXAMINATION.

Candidates must obtain at least 34 per cent. on each subject, and 50 per cent. on all subjects.

GENERAL RULES.

NON-PROFESSIONAL CERTIFICATES.

1. All non-professional certificates shall issue on August 10th of each year, or, should that be a legal holiday, on the following day.

2. No non-professional certificate shall issue until the applicant therefor shall have filed with the Department of Education a certificate of moral character, signed by a clergyman or other responsible person.

3. No non-professional certificate shall be a license to teach in a public school in Manitoba.

PROFESSIONAL CERTIFICATES.

Professional certificates shall be issued to persons who have fulfilled the following requirements :—

THIRD CLASS.

1. To have at least a non-professional third class certificate.

2. To have attended at least a full session at a normal school, after obtaining such non-professional certificate, and to have passed the professional examination.

3. To have received a satisfactory report on conduct and practical teaching from the Principal of the Normal School.

4. Those third class teachers who have attended the Normal School for third class teachers in this province for a period not less than nine weeks, and whose non-professional third class certificates have expired, may on the recommendation of a Public School Inspector, have their professional training allowed them on any further non-professional certificates of higher grade obtained by them in the province.

5. No professional third class certificate shall be valid as a license to teach for a longer period than three years.

SECOND CLASS.

1. To have a non-professional second class certificate.

2. To have attended at least one full session after obtaining such non-professional certificate, to have passed the professional examination, and to have received a satisfactory report on conduct and practical teaching from the Principal of the Provincial Normal School.

3. To have taught successfully in this province for one year, after having obtained a non-professional second class certificate.

FIRST CLASS.

1. To have a non-professional first class certificate, or a degree in arts entitling the holder to a non-professional first class certificate.

2. To have attended at least one full session, either for first or second class candidates, at the Provincial Normal School, to have passed the professional examination for a first class certificate, and to have received a satisfactory report on conduct and practical teaching from the principal of the Provincial Normal School.

3. To have taught successfully in this province for one year, after having obtained a non-professional first class certificate.

COLLEGIATE OR HIGH SCHOOL CERTIFICATE.

(Principals of Collegiate or High Schools must hold this certificate.)

1. To have the degree of Bachelor of Arts from some university in Her Majesty's Dominions.

2. To have a professional first class certificate.

COLLEGIATE OR HIGH SCHOOL ASSISTANT'S CERTIFICATE.

1. To have standing equivalent to that of the previous examination in the University of Manitoba.

2. To have a professional first class certificate.

SPECIALIST'S CERTIFICATE.

1. Candidates on presenting to the Advisory Board sufficient evidence of being able to read French or German and to speak either of these languages fluently and correctly, may receive a temporary certificate, entitling them to teach in a Collegiate or High School as specialists in such language. Such certificates may be made permanent after a year on evidence of successful teaching.

2. Specialists in drawing, music, elocution, and calisthenics, may secure certificates on such conditions and for such periods as the Advisory Board may from time to time determine.

THE

SYSTEM OF EDUCATION

IN

THE NORTH-WEST TERRITORIES OF THE

DOMINION OF CANADA.

INTRODUCTORY - - - - - - - - 411

I. CENTRAL ADMINISTRATION.
    a. Council of Public Instruction (Central Authority) 414
    b. Classification of Schools - - - - 415

II. LOCAL ADMINISTRATION.
    a. School Districts - - - - - - 416
    b. Inaugural School Meeting - - - - 417
    c. Separate Schools - - - - - 418
    d. Annual School Meeting - - - - 418
    e. Union of Public and Separate School Districts - 420
    f. Disorganisation of School Districts - - 420
    g. Trustees - - - - - - 421
        Secretary of Board of Trustees - - 423
        Treasurer of Board of Trustees - - 424
        Treasurer's Return - - - - 425

III. STATISTICS.
    a. School Districts - - - - - 426
    b. Schools - - - - - - - 426
    c. Pupils Enrolled - - - - - 427
    d. Pupils in Attendance - - - - 427
        (1.) Attendance - - - - 427
        (2.) Classification - - - - 427
        (3.) Comparative Statement of Attendance
            and Classification - - - - 428
    e. Summary of Statistics 1885–1899 - - - 429

IV. ATTENDANCE LAWS AND TRUANCY.
    a. Length of time during which Schools are open - 429
    b. Penalties - - - - - - 429
    c. Reasonable excuses - - - - 430
    d. Truancy and Truant Officer - - - 430
    e. School Hours - - - - - 430
    f. Period for which Grants are payable - - 431
    g. Remarks on Attendance in 1898 - - - 431

V. COST OF EDUCATION.
    a. Legislative Grants - - - - 432
        (i.) Scale - - - - - 432
        (ii.) Dates of payment - - - 433
        (iii.) Allowance on account of disease - - 433

    b. Local Taxation - - - - - - - 434
        (i.)   Assessment - - - - - - 434
        (ii.) Protestants and Roman Catholics - 435
        (iii.) Assessment Roll - - - - - 435
        (iv.) Exemptions - - - - - 436
        (v.) Complaints - - - - - 438
        (vi.) Court of Revision - - - - 438
        (vii.) Appeal to Superintendent - - 438
        (viii.) Return of Trustees : Rebate - - 439
        (ix.) Incurring Debt by Debenture - - 439
    c. School Fees - - - - - - - 440
    d. Treasurer's Return - - - - - 440
    e. Public Notice of Poll on issue of Debentures - 442

VI. INSPECTORS AND INSPECTION - - - - 443
VII. RELIGIOUS INSTRUCTION - - - - - 444
VIII. TEACHERS.
    a. Their duties - - - - - - - 444
    b. Teachers' Institutes - - - - - 445
    c. Supply of Teachers, &c. - - - - 446
    d. Foreign Certificates - - - - - 447
    e. Normal School - - - - - - 447
    f. Form of Agreement between Trustees and Teacher 447
    g. Certificates - - - - - - - 448
    h. Summary of Examinations - - - - 448
    i. Qualifications for High School Certificate - - 449
    j. General Regulations for Non-professional Exami-
        nations - - - - - - - 449
    k. Certificates without Examination - - - 450
    l. Certificates and Teachers' Examinations (1898) - 450

IX. SPECIAL SCHOOLS.
    a. Night Schools - - - - - - 451
    b. Kindergartens - - - - - - 451

APPENDICES.

A. EXTRACTS FROM THE PROGRAMME OF STUDY - - - 452
    (i.)   Drawing - - - - - - - 452
    (ii.) Stimulants and Narcotics (Alcohol, Tobacco) - 453
    (iii.) Manners and Morals - - - - 453
    (iv.) Hygiene - - - - - - - 454
    (v.) Music - - - - - - - 454
    (vi.) " Programme of Studies " - - - 454
        (*a.*) Reading and Literature - - - 454
        (*b.*) Orthoepy and Spelling - - - 455
        (*c.*) Composition - - - - 455
        (*d.*) Grammar - - - - - 455
        (*e.*) History - - - - - 455
        (*f.*) Geography - - - - - 456
        (*g.*) Arithmetic - - - - - 457
        (*h.*) Nature Study and Agriculture - - 457

B. EXTRACTS FROM THE REPORT FOR 1898.
    (i.)   Agriculture - - - - - - 457
    (ii.) Domestic Economy and Hygiene - - - 458
    (iii.) Equipment - - - - - - 459
    (iv.) Buildings - - - - - - - 459

C. EXTRACTS FROM PAPERS SET IN PROFESSIONAL EXAMINATION
   FOR TEACHERS, 1898.
    (i.)   First-Class Certificates - - - - 461
    (ii.) First- and Second-Class Certificates (Drawing) 462
    (iii.) Second-Class Certificates - - - - 462
    (iv.) Third-Class Certificates - - - - 464

THE SYSTEM OF EDUCATION IN THE NORTH-WEST TERRITORIES OF THE DOMINION.

Compiled from Documents supplied by the Council of Public Instruction.

INTRODUCTORY.

In 1882 the Dominion Government formed, out of the vast Territory from the boundary of the United States to the most northerly point in the continent, and from the western shores of Hudson's Bay to the Rockies, four provisional districts. The educational system of the Territories deals with three of these four Territories—namely, Assiniboia, 89,535 square miles ; Saskatchewan, 107,092 square miles ; and Alberta, 106,100 square miles. This makes a total area of 302,727 square miles.

The population of such parts of this area as were then settled was, in 1891, 66,799, and, in 1894, 86,851. But of these 86,000, over 13,000 were Indians.

In 1898 there were nearly 16,754 pupils on the registers of the schools.

While the people are chiefly of British origin, other nationalities are represented in sufficient numbers to increase the school difficulties. The occupations are farming, cattle ranching, lumber, and mining, and in consequence the population is widely scattered. The following pages will show with what vigour and enthusiasm the Council of Public Instruction in the Territories has addressed itself to its difficult task.

The decade 1886 to 1896 witnessed a remarkable growth in the schools. The number rose from 76 to 336, an increase of 381 per cent., and the enrolment from 2,553 to 12,796, an increase of 400 per cent.

In 1899 there were 453 schools, and 18,801 pupils on the rolls.

In 1896 the number of teachers was 433, and, in 1898, 483 (232 men and 251 women). In 1899 the number of teachers had risen to 543.

Efforts were early made to provide professional training for teachers. By a regulation of 1893 it is declared that, to make it possible for remote districts to keep their schools open, " provisional certificates are issued to persons who present such evidence of scholarship that there is a reasonable probability of their being able to pass the next teachers' examination." But these certificates may not be issued until the trustees declare that they advertised for a properly qualified teacher, but have not succeeded in obtaining one. The provisional certificate is valid for that school only, and terminates. at the opening of the next examination for teachers.

Schools are maintained (1) by legislative grants and (2) by local taxation. In 1896, the last year for which accurate figures can be obtained for such a comparison, the *legislative grants* reach the figure of $126,218, while *local taxation* yielded $148,430. Thus in 1896 the legislative grants met 46 per cent. of the total expenditure, which was in that year $274,648. In 1897 the legislative grants amounted to $121,457, and in 1898 to $133,642.

Some idea of the purposes for which the money is expended may be given by this from the report for 1898.

"In school districts the principal expenditure, other than the districts' proportion of their teachers' salaries, and maintenance and equipment of buildings, has been the payment of debenture indebtedness, insurance, fuel, and caretaking, salaries of secretaries and collectors and the treasurers' commissions. The salaries of the district officials vary considerably, and it might be well if some uniform scale were to be laid down."

In noticing any omissions in the educational system of the Territories, it must be remembered that the area to be administered is immense, the difficulty of communication very great, the population very sparse, and the winter extremely rigorous. In all these respects the difficulties of providing educational facilities press with unusual weight upon the educational authority. It is only to be expected, therefore, that that authority should be compelled to confine its activity mainly to the bettering of the elementary education.

But, though there are no separate secondary schools, the sixth, seventh, and eighth standards (the enrolment of which was in 1896, 126, 39, and 5, and, in 1898, 221, 153, and 28 respectively) are termed "High School" standards, and have an entirely separate programme, based upon the matriculation examinations of the Universities of Toronto and Manitoba.

A comparison between the statistics of the years 1895 and 1898 in regard to teachers and their certificates (see below) shows that the proportion of women to men teachers has slightly increased—viz., 1896, 222 women to 211 men; 1898, 251 women to 232 men. On the other hand, the number of men, is very much larger than the number of women, holders of first-class certificates (1896, 62 men, 34 women; 1898, 74 men, 42 women). The preponderance of women over men teachers is accounted for by the holders of second-class certificates (1896, 98 men, 109 women; 1898, 118 men, 153 women).

There is a Normal School at Regina, the capital of the Territories, where sessions are held during the last four months of the year (see below).

Agriculture has been a compulsory subject of the curriculum for eight years, and has been on the whole very successfully taught. Some remarks made on this subject will be found below. Instruction is also given in domestic economy.

As will be seen from the following remarks (taken from the Report of the Council of Public Instruction 'for the year 1898) one of the principal educational difficulties of the country is the difference of nationality in the population :—

"The increase in the number of schools, pupils, higher grade teachers, the larger attendance in the higher standards and the improvements in buildings and grounds, are evidences of continued and improved educational progress commensurate in most respects with our growth and increase in population.

"One of our most serious and pressing educational problems arises from the settlement among us of so many foreign nationalities on the block or 'colony' system. There are colonies of Swedes, Finns, Bohemians, Hungarians, Jews, Austrians, Germans, Russians, Icelanders, Mennonites, Gallicians, and Doukhobors.

"In addition to the foreign colonies there are also exclusively French-speaking districts in Saskatchewan that, for a variety of reasons, have not been able to keep their schools in operation. In the interests of the children as well as of the country at large every means should be taken to encourage the opening and maintenance of schools among these non-English speaking communities.

"It would be criminal to shut our eyes to the fact that this rapid increase of a foreign and relatively ignorant population is at once a challenge and invitation to our institutions. These 'colonies' will add to our numbers, to our wealth in grain and cattle, to our material progress, but it will not be reasonable to expect them for many years to add much to that other wealth which is a nation's truest wealth—educated men with refined tastes, sound moral perceptions, a keen sense of civic responsibility and duty, and an adequate conception of the purposes of life. It is this latter wealth which determines the ranking of nations in the scale of civilisation. It is a sordid ideal that makes what a man has of greater value than what he is. It is not the quantity but the quality of its manhood that determines the status of a nation.

"To assimilate these different races, to secure the co-operation of these alien forces, are problems demanding for their solution patience, tact, and tolerant but firm legislation. Modes of life, customs, political forms, thoughts, and ideals differing from ours have made these peoples what they are, and have dowered them with an inaptitude for our political forms and a disregard of our social customs that tend to keep them apart from us. The older people will not give up the forms to which they have been accustomed, and the younger people cannot soon acquire ours, except perhaps where, at the edge of the 'colony,' they come into frequent contact with us. The block or colony system retards assimilation. Mr. Greenway, the Premier of Manitoba, speaking of the Mennonite colony there, said: 'Many of these, though they have been here for twenty-five years, do not know English and are not assimilated.'

"Only through our schools getting an early hold of the children of these settlers can we hope to train them to live according to our social system, and to understand and appreciate the institutions of the country which they have adopted.

"A common school and a common tongue are essential if we are to have a homogeneous citizenship. Strange as it may seem to some, it is nevertheless a fact that the most effective work in the schools of such 'colonies' has been done by Canadian teachers practically unacquainted with the language of the 'colony.' The advantage of a knowledge of the language is more evident in the teacher's influence with the parents than in his work in the schoolroom. But it is difficult to get Canadians to live in these recently formed colonies. The difference in modes of life and the lack of congenial society and comfortable boarding-houses deter most of them."

The following remark is taken from the Report for 1898 :—

"In two instances where the trustees declined to carry out the instructions of the department they were superseded by a commissioner until the required action was carried out. In a few instances where all the settlers were unable to speak English, commissioners have been appointed to conduct the affairs of the district."

I.—Central Administration.

a. Council of Public Instruction (Central Authority).

The members of the Executive Council of the Territories and four persons, two of whom shall be Protestants and two Roman Catholics, appointed by the Lieutenant Governor in Council, shall constitute a Council of Public Instruction, and one of the Executive Council, to be nominated by the Lieutenant Governor in Council, shall be chairman of the Council of Public Instruction. The appointed members shall have no vote, and shall receive such remuneration as the Lieutenant Governor in Council shall provide. The duties of the appointed members are purely advisory.

The Executive Council or any sub-committee thereof appointed for that purpose shall constitute a quorum of the Council of Public Instruction, but no general regulations respecting :

(*a*) The management and discipline of schools ;
(*b*) The examination, grading, and licensing of teachers ;
(*c*) The selection of books ;
(*d*) The inspection of schools ;
(*e*) Normal training :

shall be adopted or amended except at a general meeting of the Council of Public Instruction duly convened for that purpose.

It shall be the duty of the Council of Public Instruction—

i. To make regulations for the government and discipline of

schools and institutes and for the training and certification of teachers;

2. To prescribe programmes of study and text-books;

3. To define by "standards" the studies to be pursued in all schools, such standards to be numbered from I. upwards; standards above Standard V. to be further denominated "High School Standards";

4. To provide for the examination of persons, other than teachers, who may desire to enter professions or who may wish certificates of having completed courses of study in any school;

5. To prepare suitable forms and give such instructions as may be necessary for making all reports and conducting all proceedings;

6. To determine all cases of appeals, disputes, and complaints arising from decisions of trustees or inspectors, and to make such orders thereon as may be required;

7. To make any provision that may be necessary to meet exigencies occurring under the operation of these regulations.

The Council of Public Instruction shall report annually to the Lieutenant Governor in Council upon all schools and institutes with such statements and suggestions for promoting education generally as they may deem useful and expedient.

The Council of Public Instruction shall have power to suspend for cause the certificate of any teacher, and also to cancel the same.

The chairman of the Council of Public Instruction may empower any person to call any school meeting required to be held, when the person or persons invested with the power to do so neglect or refuse to act.

The chairman of the Council of Public Instruction may appoint a commissioner to examine into and report upon the condition of any one or more schools, and such commissioner shall have the power of a school inspector for the purpose. He may at any time appoint a commissioner to inspect the financial condition of any school district.

The chairman of the Council of Public Instruction may appoint a commissioner to conduct the affairs of any school district.

The Lieutenant Governor in Council may from time to time determine what officers or persons it is necessary to employ for any of the purposes above mentioned, assign their names of office, prescribe their duties and salaries, and make the necessary appointments.

b. Classification of Schools.

There may be established subject to the regulations of the Council of Public Instruction the following classes of schools, namely:

1. Public schools, for pupils over five years of age in which

instruction shall be given in the elements of an English and commercial education;

2. Separate schools, for pupils over five years of age in which instruction shall be given in the elements of an English and commercial education;

3. Kindergarten schools, for pupils between four and six years of age in which instruction shall be given according to kinder-garten methods;

4. Night schools, for pupils over fourteen years of age who are unable to attend during the usual school hours;

5. Normal schools, for the training of candidates for first, second, and third class teachers' certificates;

6. Teachers' institutes, for the reading of papers and the general discussion of educational topics.

NOTE.—*All schools shall be taught in the English language, but it shall be permissible for the trustees of any school to cause a primary course to be taught in the French language.*

NOTE.—*The title " High School " may be used to designate that department of any school which has a daily average attendance of thirty pupils in High School Standards, and in which not less than two teachers of that department are employed. For the qualifications required for assistant-masters and headmasters in High Schools see below.*

II. LOCAL ADMINISTRATION.

a. School Districts.

A school district must comprise an area of not more than twenty-five square miles nor more than five miles in breadth or length, and shall contain not less than four resident ratepayers and twelve children between the ages of five and sixteen inclusive; provided always that any person not living within a school district may apply to the trustees of any organised school district to have his or her property . . . assessed in any such school district to secure the advantages of education for his or her children; and in such case the trustees shall receive such application and place such property on the assessment roll of such district; provided always that in special cases the Chairman of the Council of Public Instruction may permit the boundaries of any school district to exceed five miles in breadth or length, such permission being only given in cases where all the resident ratepayers affected by such permission have agreed in writing to the same.

Any three ratepayers resident in any area as above defined may form themselves into a committee to procure its erection into a school district, and may petition the Chairman of the Council of Public Instruction for such erection.

Such a petition must specify—

1. The proposed name, limits, location, and approximate area of the proposed school districts.

2. The total population and the number of adults and children between the ages of five years and sixteen

years, inclusive, and the number of children below the
age of five years resident within the proposed district;

3. The total number of ratepayers in the district and the
number of Protestant and Roman Catholic ratepayers
respectively; and such petition shall be accompanied
by a sketch, plan, or map of the proposed district showing its boundaries, principal legal subdivisions, physical
features, and general location; and (except in the case
of town school districts) the quarter sections or river
lots, if the land is surveyed, on which the children of
school age reside.

The petition must be accompanied by a solemn declaration of
a member of the committee that the members thereof are *bonâ
fide* resident ratepayers of the proposed school district, and that
the statements made in the petition are correct.

b. Inaugral School Meeting.

On receiving the approval of the chairman of the Council of
Public Instruction to the limits of any proposed district, a notice
calling a meeting of the ratepayers shall be posted up by the
petitioners.

At the *School Meeting* thus convened the resident ratepayers present shall organise the meeting by appointing a chairman (who shall be a resident ratepayer), and a secretary.

Only resident ratepayers shall be entitled to vote at or take
any part in a first school meeting.

Every resident ratepayer shall have as many votes as there are
trustees to be elected, but shall in no case vote more than once
for one candidate at the same election.

Upon a petition signed by at least four-fifths of such resident
ratepayers of any school district as are the parents or guardians
of children between the ages of five years and sixteen years
inclusive, the Lieutenant Governor in Council may empower the
trustees of such district to enter into an agreement with the
trustees of any other school district for the education of their
children for a term of not less than three years.

Provided that in all cases where such an agreement is in force
grants shall be paid in respect of children attending the school
maintained in another school district than the one in which
they reside, as though the parents or guardians of such children
were resident ratepayers of the school district in which their
children are being taught:

Provided further that the school districts acting under such
an agreement shall have full power and authority to make the
necessary levy and assessment for the purpose of carrying out
the terms of the agreement and for providing for the conveyance
of the children to and from school.

Provided that the Lieutenant Governor in Council may
terminate any such agreement upon such terms as to him may
seem fit.

(From the Report of the Council of Public Instruction for the year 1898).

"It has been found necessary in several instances to alter the

4226.   H boundaries of existing districts in order to take in land newly settled by persons desiring the means of educating their children. A few school sites have been changed to meet the requirements of increased population. Twenty-two new districts were proclaimed during the year and several others had petitioned for erection but had not completed the prescribed proceedings at the close of the year. Seven districts that had not been in operation for a considerable time (in some instances had not opened at all) engaged teachers and started their schools."

c. Separate Schools.

The minority of the ratepayers in any organised public school district, whether Protestant or Roman Catholic, may establish a separate school therein and in such case the ratepayers establishing such Protestant or Roman Catholic separate schools shall be liable only to assessments of such rates as they impose upon themselves in respect thereof.

The petition for the erection of a separate school district shall be signed by three resident ratepayers of the religious faith indicated in the name of the proposed district. The petition shall set forth—

(a) The religious faith of the petitioners;

(b) The proposed name (stating whether Protestant or Roman Catholic) of the district;

(c) Its proposed limits, definite location, and approximate area;

(d) The total number of ratepayers and of children between the ages of five years and sixteen years inclusive, of the religious faith (Protestant or Roman Catholic) of the petitioners, residing within the limits of the proposed district;

(e) The total assessed value of their real and personal property according to the last revised assessment roll of the district;

and such petition shall be accompanied by a solemn declaration of one of the petitioners verifying the facts set forth in their petition.

The persons qualified to vote for or against a petition for the erection of a separate school district shall be the ratepayers resident therein being of the same religious faith (Protestant or Roman Catholic) as the petitioners.

After the establishment of a separate school district under the above provisions such separate school district shall possess and exercise all rights, powers, privileges, and be subject to the same liabilities and method of government as are provided in respect of public school districts. And any person who is legally assessed or assessable for a public school district shall not be liable to assessment for any separate school established therein.

d. Annual School Meeting.

At the annual meeting of the ratepayers of every school district (except town school districts), which is called by the trustees, the board of trustees submit and read to the meeting—

1. A statement of the teacher, signed by him, giving the following particulars :—

    (a) The number of days on which school was kept open during each term succeeding the last annual meeting;

    (b) The total number of children attending school during that period, specifying the number of males and females respectively;

    (c) The average daily attendance during each term;

    (d) The branches of education taught in the school and the number of children studying each;

    (e) The number of dismissals of scholars for misbehaviour or other causes;

2. The report of the inspector on the occasion of his last inspection of the school.

3. A statement showing—

    (a) The names of the trustees;

    (b) The vacancies created in the board during the year, if any, giving the reasons therefor, with an account of the elections held to fill such vacancies and the results thereof;

    (c) The engagements entered into during the year by the board as well as an account of those entailed upon them by their predecessors;

    (d) The amount of assessable property in the district according to the last finally revised assessment roll;

    (e) Rate of school tax per dollar;

    (f) Rate of tax per dollar to pay off debenture indebtedness;

    (g) The appeals against assessment made to a judge of the Supreme Court and the result of such appeals;

    (h) The times of holding meetings of the board of trustees during the year and the resolutions adopted at such meetings.

    (i) Particulars of the real and personal property held in the district:

4. The treasurer's statement showing—

    (a) The amount of money received by the district from all sources during the year, with particulars;

    (b) The amounts accruing to the school district funds of the past year on account of Government grants;

    (c) The amount of money due to the district from all sources, with particulars;

    (d) The amount of money paid out by the district during the year, with the particulars of payment;

    (e) The amounts, if any, due by the district, to whom due and the terms and times of payment;

5. The auditor's report.

6. Such further statement in relation to the affairs of the district as may be deemed advisable.

(No person shall be entitled to vote at any school meeting or for the election of a trustee or trustees, or to be nominated as trustee in any school district, who has not paid all taxes in arrear due by him to such district.)

e. Union of Public and Separate School Districts.

If in any area there exist a public school district and a separate school district, and it is resolved by the ratepayers of each of such school districts, at a public meeting of all the ratepayers called for the purpose of considering the question, that it is expedient that such districts should be disorganised for the purpose of the union of the same, and the erection of the area into a public school district, the chairman of the Council of Public Instruction may order the disorganisation of such existing districts, and order the erection of their area into a public school district with such name as he may decide upon; and thereafter the said chairman may make such orders, provisions, and appointments as to him shall appear proper for the completion of such disorganisation and the erection of the public school district, and as to all matters incident thereto and necessary for the establishment and operation of the same as a public school district, and for the adjustment, arrangement, and winding up of all the affairs of such disorganised districts, and for the settlement of their liabilities and disposition of their assets.

Provided that, unless the liabilities of such disorganised districts are not otherwise liquidated, the same shall be assumed by and imposed upon such newly-created district, and any debentures issued by the disorganised districts or either of them shall have the same force and effect upon the newly-established district and the property and rates thereof as they had upon the district by which they were respectively issued and its property and rates; and the trustees of such newly-organised district may authorise and direct the levy and collection of such rate or rates as may from time to time be necessary for the discharging of any liability or debenture indebtedness of a disorganised district assumed by or imposed upon such new district.

f. Disorganisation of School Districts.

The Lieutenant Governor in Council may by order declare that on and after a day therein to be named any school district shall be disorganised, and thereupon the same shall cease to have or enjoy any of the rights, powers, and privileges vested in such corporations; and upon any such disorganisation of a school district the chairman of the Council of Public Instruction may appoint one or more persons as commissioners to adjust and settle the assets and liabilities of such district: and the commissioners so appointed shall have full power and authority to sell and dispose of and convert into money all the assets and property of such district and apply the same so far as the same will extend.

(*Report for* 1898.)—" Ten school districts which, by reason of the settlers having removed to other parts of the Territories, had failed for years to be in operation, have been disorganised. The assets have, as far as possible, been realised and paid over to the creditors of the various districts. A liberal offer was made to those holding unpaid coupons against any of these districts for the relinquishment of their debenture claims but it was not generally accepted."

g. Trustees.

In school districts other than town school districts there shall be three trustees, each of whom, after the first election, shall hold office for three years and until his successor shall have been appointed.

The trustees elected at a *first* school meeting shall hold office as follows :—

1. The candidate receiving the highest number of votes (or the first one nominated if no vote has been taken, *i.e.*, in cases where the number of nominations does not exceed the number of trustees to be elected) shall be elected to serve until and including the thirty-first day of December of the second year following the election;

2. The candidate receiving the second highest number of votes (or second in order of nomination if no vote has been taken) shall be elected to serve until and including the thirty-first day of December of the year following the election;

3. The candidate receiving the third highest number of votes (or the third in order of nomination if no vote has been taken) shall be elected to serve until and including the thirty-first day of December following the election.

The persons qualified to be elected trustees shall be actual resident ratepayers within the district, able to read and write. No trustee shall hold the office of teacher within the district in which he is a trustee.

It shall be the duty of the board of trustees of every school district to—

1. Elect a chairman within ten days after the annual school meeting in each year;

2. Select and acquire a school site, which shall be in the centre of the district or as near thereto as the situation of the road-allowances and the securing of a dry, healthy, and suitable location will permit. In the event of it not being found convenient to have the school house located exactly in the centre of the school district the trustees may locate it elsewhere within the district upon receiving the consent of the chairman of the Council of Public Instruction to such location ;

Provided that in town school districts the trustees may select such site as in their judgment is desirable, subject to ratification by the ratepayers in the case of debentures being issued.

3. Engage a qualified teacher or teachers on such terms as the board may deem expedient, the contract for which shall be in writing, and a certified copy of such contract shall be at once forwarded to the Department of Public Instruction.

4. Forthwith report to the Department of Public Instruction

the appointment, resignation, or dismissal of a teacher or teachers in their district, and in the case of dismissal the reason for such dismissal;

5. To take possession and to have the custody and safe keeping of all school property which has been acquired or given for all school purposes to their district;

6. Do whatever they may judge expedient with regard to building, repairing, renting, warming, furnishing, and keeping in order the school houses in their district, their furniture and appendages, and the school lands and inclosures held by them, and for procuring apparatus and school books for their school;

7. Make such assessments on real and personal property of the district and levy such taxes as may be necessary to defray all lawful expenses and liabilities of the school district for the year or that part thereof for which such taxes are required to be levied;

8. Suspend or expel any pupil whose habitual conduct or condition is found to be injurious to the other pupils;

9. Keep a record of their proceedings signed for each sitting by the chairman and secretary, and see that true accounts both of the school and district are kept, and the affairs of the district generally are conducted in due order and with due regard to efficiency and economy; the accounts shall at all reasonable hours be open to the inspection of the ratepayers of the school district;

10. Select and provide for all such reference books for the use of pupils, maps, globes, and other apparatus as may be prescribed by the Council of Public Instruction;

11. Provide free of cost out of the funds of the district books and slates for the use of those children attending school whose parents cannot afford to procure the necessary books and slates for them;

12. Provide, when deemed expedient, a suitable library for the school;

13. See that all the reports required by the regulations are duly submitted without delay;

14. Call special meetings for any purpose whatever when required to do so by the Council of Public Instruction, or, in town school districts, by ten resident ratepayers, or, in other school districts, by a majority of the resident ratepayers;

15. See that the law with reference to compulsory education and truancy is carried out;

16. Provide wholesome and pure water for the use of children during school hours;

17. Provide separate buildings for privies for boys and girls respectively. The buildings shall be erected in the rear of the schoolhouse, at least ten feet apart, their entrances facing in opposite directions, or otherwise effectually screened from each other.

The trustees of any school district may by resolution enter into a contract to have a school house built at a cost not to exceed $500, payment for which may extend over a period of not more than five years at a rate of interest not to exceed eight per cent. per annum.

The Board of Trustees of any school district may authorise the chairman and treasurer thereof to borrow from any person or bank or corporation such sum of money as may be required to meet the expenditure of the school district until such time as the taxes levied thereon can be collected, or, in the case of school districts situated within a municipality or partly within a municipality, until such time as the municipal council can pay the school taxes to the trustees ; such authorisation shall be by bye-law of the Board of Trustees.

Any person eligible and elected to the office of school trustee who refuses to serve as such shall forfeit the sum of $20, and his neglect or refusal, if resident at the time within the district, to take declaration of office before the first regular meeting of the trustees shall be construed as such refusal, after which another person shall be elected to fill the place; but no school trustee shall be re-elected, except by his own consent, during the two years next after his going out of office.

Any person chosen as trustee may resign with the consent, expressed in writing, of his colleagues in office, but such resignation shall only take effect upon the election of his successor.

The Board of Trustees at the first meeting in each year appoints a secretary, among whose duties it shall be to answer all communications on school matters in such a manner as he may be directed by the Board, to examine the records and register of the school kept by the teacher and see that they are correct, to forward to the Department of Public Instruction the requisite reports, and give any further information that may be required by the Department or the Board of Trustees, to keep and produce on demand of an inspector, the minute books, papers, accounts, assessment rolls, and other documents committed to his charge. Secretary of Board of Trustees.

The minute book and other books of secretaries of all school boards shall be inspected annually, and, if irregularities are found, the inspector shall report the same to the Department of Public Instruction and shall make such recommendation to the trustees as he may deem necessary.

One of the trustees or a teacher may be secretary of the Board, but a teacher shall not be appointed treasurer.

The secretary of every Board of Trustees shall within one month of the date of the opening of the school notify the Department of Public Instruction of the opening of such school and the qualification of the teacher or teachers employed and the amount of the salary or salaries paid.

The secretary of every Board of Trustees shall forward to the Department of Public Instruction on the fifteenth day of April in each year (or as soon thereafter as the school shall open) a report giving the following information, namely :

(*a*) Name of teacher ;

> (*b*) Class of certificate held by each teacher and the date
>   thereof;
> (*c*) Salary paid each teacher per month;
> (*d*) Number of children attending school (per register);
> (*e*) If school open for the whole year or for only certain
>   months during summer, naming the months during
>   which it is intended to keep school open.

Treasurer of Board of Trustees.

By resolution of the Board one of its members may, with his consent, be appointed treasurer of the district for the whole or part of the term for which he was elected trustee. During his service as treasurer he receives remuneration, but the treasurer may be a responsible person appointed by the Board for the purpose, but not belonging to the Board.

It shall be the duty of the treasurer to collect, receive, and account for, all school moneys, whether derived from the Government or otherwise, for the purpose of education within the district of which he is treasurer; and to distribute such moneys in the manner directed by the Board of Trustees, and to keep a record of the same in a book provided for the purpose by the Board of Trustees: and he shall give and take receipts for all moneys so received and paid out by him, and shall produce, when called for by the trustees, auditor, or other competent authority, all books, papers, and moneys belonging to the corporation, and shall hand over the same to the trustees or any person named by them upon his ceasing to hold office.

The treasurer of every school district shall at the end of each term furnish to the Department of Public Instruction a solemn declaration giving the information required for the purpose of computing the grants payable to each school in such school district. In any term during which any school in such school district has not been kept open, the treasurer shall furnish a copy of the return with a notification to that effect written upon its face. See below.

The treasurer of every school district shall furnish to the Department of Public Instruction at the end of each year a statement showing the cash receipts and expenditure, amounts due to and by the district, particulars of the assessment, assets of district, cost of land and buildings, together with the auditor's report.*

The account books of treasurers of all school boards shall be inspected annually, and the inspector shall have power to call for all vouchers, receipts, auditor's reports, statements of accounts, and assessment rolls. Any irregularities shall be reported to the trustees and the Department of Public Instruction.

Any trustee, officer, or employee of a school district neglecting or refusing to discharge any duty assigned to him shall for each offence be liable to a fine not exceeding $50; and any trustee who, after ceasing to hold office, detains any money, book, paper, or thing belonging to the school district, shall thereby incur a penalty not exceeding $100 for each day of such wrongful detention. Any returning officer of any school district or proposed school district who shall knowingly and wilfully prejudice the result of any voting by preventing votes from being taken,

---

* See below, Section V., *d*.

taking unlawful votes, altering returns, or by any other means, shall be liable to a fine not less than $100. Should the trustees of any school district wilfully contract liabilities in the name of the district greater than are allowed to be contracted, such sum or sums may be recovered from them as a debt in a court of competent jurisdiction.

The prescribed form for the treasurer's return gives the best summary of the functions he exercises in a school district.

Treasurer's return.

TREASURER'S RETURN FOR TERM ENDING   1

I,   treasurer of   School District No.
of the North-West Territories do solemnly declare as follows :—

1. That the name of the teacher in the
   department of the above school district is   -   -   -

2. That the class of certificate granted by the Council of
   Public Instruction, N.W.T.,   he holds is -   -   -

3. That the salary paid to h   per   is -

4. That the amount of salary earned by h   during the
   term was -   -   -   -   -   -   -   -

5. That the amount of salary due h   at the end of the
   term was -

6. That the names of previous teachers (if any) in the said
   department to whom salary is still due and the amounts
   so due, are   -   -   -   -   -   -   -

7. That I have examined the school register and find :

   (a) That the department was opened for the current
       year on   -   -   -   -   -   -   -

   (b) That the department was open for the term on   -

   (c) That the department was closed during the term
       from   -   -   -   -   -   -   -
       until -   -   -   -   -   -   -

   (d) That the number of legally authorised teaching
       days the school was thus closed was   -   -

   (e) That the reason for so closing the school was   -
           (*Medical certificate if any attached hereto.*)

   (f) That the department was closed for the term on   -

   (g) That the number of legally authorised teaching
       days during the term on which the department was
       open was   -   -   -   -   -   -   -

   (h) That the annexed abstract from the school register
       as prepared by the teacher of this department and
       showing the number of pupils with their names,
       ages, sexes, and school standing, the pupils who
       have removed from the district or have died during
       the year, the pupils who have been absent all term
       with the reason therefor, the pupils who have been
       in attendance during the term with their aggregate
       and average attendances, is correct in every essen-
       tial and particular to the best of my knowledge
       and belief.

And I make this solemn declaration conscientiously believing it to be true and knowing that it is of the same force and effect as if made under oath and by virtue of "The Canada Evidence Act, 1893."

Declared before me at
this   *C.D.*
of   19   } day   Treasurer.
                                   P.O. address :

III.—STATISTICS.

The following is a summary of the statistics in regard to the number of school districts and schools, pupils enrolled, attendance, etc., for the year ending on December 31, 1898.

a. School Districts.

—	Erected.	In Operation.
Assiniboia.		
Public school districts	277	244
Protestant separate school districts	2	2
Roman Catholic public school districts	11	9
Roman Catholic separate school districts	4	1
	—294	—256
Alberta.		
Public school districts	143	114
Protestant separate school districts	0	0
Roman Catholic public school districts	15	10
Roman Catholic separate school districts	5	5
	—163	—129
Saskatchewan.		
Public school districts	45	32
Protestant separate school districts	1	1
Roman Catholic public school districts	18	7
Roman Catholic separate school districts	2	1
	— 66	— 41
	523	426
Unorganised school districts participating in grants	—	3
		429

b. Schools.

(1) Number of school districts in operation - - - - * 426
      (Increase for the year 1898, 32)
(2) Number of new school districts proclaimed - - - 22

          Total - - - - - - - 448*

---

* At the close of 1899, 453 schools were in actual operation.

c. *Pupils Enrolled.*

1. Number of pupils enrolled - · · · · ·	—	16,754*
Increase for the year · · · · ·	2,178	—

* The number of pupils enrolled in 1899 was 18,801, an increase of 2,047.

d. *Pupils in Attendance.*

d. (1) *Attendance.*	Increase.	Total.
Total number of pupils attending school during the year - · · · -	2,178	16,754
,, of boys - · · · -	1,228	8,694
,, of girls - · · · -	950	8,060
,, who attended school less than 20 days during the year - ·	—18	1,797
,, who attended between 20 and 50 days, inclusive - · ·	44	3,015 ·
,, who attended between 51 and 100 days, inclusive - · ·	813	4,928
,, who attended between 101 and 150 days, inclusive - · ·	411	3,622
,, who attended between 151 and 200 days, inclusive - · ·	678	2,775
,, who attended between 201 and the whole year - · · ·	230	617
,, of school age who did not attend at all - · · · ·	69	190
Total aggregate attendance of first term · -	—	806,879
,, ,, during the second term	—	730,492
,, ,, for the year -	—	1,537,371
Daily average attendance during the year · -	—	8,826·64*

d. (2) *Classification.*	Increase.	Total.
Total number in Standard I., Part 1 · · -	661	4,710
,, ,, I., Part 2 · · -	338	2,924
,, ,, II. · · · -	351	3,193
,, ,, III. · · · -	219	3,105
,, ,, IV. · · · -	416	1,782
,, ,, V. · · · -	124	638
,, ,, VI. "High School Stand."	23	221
,, ,, VII. Do. ·	45	153
,, ,, VIII. Do. ·	1	28
Total number in all Standards - · · -	2,178	16,754

* In 1899 the daily average attendance was 9,415.

d. (3) *Comparative Statement respecting Attendance and Classification.*

—	Public.	Roman Catholic Public Schools.	Roman Catholic Separate Schools.	Total.
Number of pupils on register -	14 970†	1,045†	739†	16,754†
„ of boys - - - -	7,812	566	316	8,694
„ of girls - - - -	7,158	479	423	8,060
„ who attended less than 20 days - - -	1,602	115	80	1,797
„ who attended between 21 and 50 days - -	2,726	190	99	[3,015
„ who attended between 51 and 100 days - -	4,415	293	220	4,928
„ who attended between 101 and 150 days -	3,307	181	134	3,622
„ who attended between 151 and 200 days -	2,461	171	143	2,775
„ who attended between 201 and the whole year	459	95	64	617
„ who did not attend any school during the year	146	37	7	190
Aggregate attendance during first term - - -	730,716	47,680	28,483	806,879
„ attendance during second term - -	653,679	42,644	34,168	730,492
„ attendance for the whole year - -	1,384,395	90,324	62,651	1,547,271
Daily average attendance during the year - - - -	7,925·43	549·42	351·79	8,826·64
Total number in First Standard, Part I. -	3,950	469	291	4,710
„ First Standard, Part II. -	2,553	247	124	2,924
„ Second Standard	2,876	197	120	3,193
„ Third Standard -	2,893	91	121	3,105
„ Fourth Standard	1,684	38	60	1,782
„ Fifth Standard -	614	2	22	638
„ *Sixth Standard -	219	1	1	221
„ *Seventh Standard	153	0	0	153
„ *Eighth Standard	28	0	0	28
Total number in all Standards -	14,970	1,045	739	16,754

* Total number in High School Standards (vi., vii., viii.) = *Public,* 400 ; *Roman Catholic Public,* 1 ; *Roman Catholic Separate,* 1 ; *total,* 402.

† The corresponding figures for 1899 are 16,825 pupils in Public Schools, 1,092 n Roman Catholic Public Schools, 884 in Roman Catholic Separate Schools. Total, 18,801.

(6.) *Summary of the Educational Statistics of the North-West Territories since 1885, when the management of the schools was vested in a Board of Education.*

Year.	Schools in Operation.	Pupils Enrolled.	Teachers Employed.	Expenditure by the Legislative Assembly.
				$
1886	76	2,553	84	8,908
1887	111	3,144	125	36,897
1888	131	3,453	150	44,547
1889	164	4,574	183	56,984
1890	195	5,398	224	85,002
1891	213	5,652	248	129,042
1892	249	6,170	295	121,056
1893	262	8,214	307	106,578
1894	300	10,721	353	113,999
1895	341	11,972	401	112,182
1896	366	12,790	433	120,218
1897	394	14,570	457	121,457
1898	426	16,754	483	133,642
1899	453	18,801	543	142,455

IV.—ATTENDANCE LAWS AND TRUANCY.

a. In every school district where there are at least fifteen children between the ages of seven and fourteen resident within a radius of one mile and a half from the school house it shall be compulsory for the trustees of such district to keep the school open during the whole year. *[Length of time during which Schools are open.]*

In every school district where there are at least ten children between the ages of seven years and fourteen years it shall be compulsory for the trustees of such school district to have their school in operation at least six months in every year.

b. Every parent, guardian, or other person resident in a school district having charge of any child or children between the ages of seven years and twelve years inclusive shall be required to send such child or children to school for a period of at least sixteen weeks in each year, at least eight weeks of which time shall be consecutive ; and every parent, guardian, or other person who does not provide that every such child under his or her care shall attend school or be otherwise educated shall be subject to the penalties provided by law. *[Penalties.]*

It shall be the duty of the trustees of every school district, or any person authorised by them, after being notified that any parent, guardian, or other person having control of any child or children neglects or violates the provisions of the preceding section, to make complaint of such neglect or violation to a justice of the peace ; and the person complained against shall, on summary conviction, be liable to a fine not exceeding one dollar for the first offence and double that penalty for each subsequent offence.

Reasonable excuses.

c. It shall be the duty of the justice of the peace to ascertain as far as may be the circumstances of any party complained of for not sending his or her child or children to school or otherwise educating him or them, and he shall accept any of the following as a reasonable excuse :—

1. That the child is under instruction in some other satisfactory manner ;

2. That the child has been prevented from attending school by sickness or any unavoidable cause ;

3. That there is no school open which the child can attend within a distance not exceeding two and one-half miles, measured according to the nearest passable road from the residence of such child ;

4. That such child has reached a standard of education of the same or of a greater degree than that to be attained in the school of the school district within which such child resides ;

5. That such parent or guardian was not able by reason of poverty to clothe such child properly, or that such child's bodily or mental condition has been such as to prevent his or her attendance at school or application to study for the period required.

Truancy and Truant Officer.

d. The trustees of each school may appoint a truant officer who shall be vested with police powers; and the trustees shall have authority to make regulations for the direction of such officer in the enforcement of these provisions as they may deem expedient, provided such regulations have been approved by the Chairman of the Council of Public Instruction.

If the parent, guardian, or other person having the legal charge of any child shall neglect or refuse to cause such child to attend some school within five days after being notified, the truant officer shall make or cause to be made a complaint against such person before any justice of the peace having jurisdiction in the school district ; and such person shall be liable on conviction to a fine not exceeding $1 and costs for the first offence, and double that penalty for each subsequent offence.

NOTE.—The above provisions do not apply in country school districts to children residing more than one mile from the school-house.

School Hours.

e. School shall be held between nine o'clock and twelve o'clock in the forenoon and half-past one and four in the afternoon of every day, standard time, not including Saturdays, Sundays, or statutory holidays; but the school trustees may alter or shorten the school hours upon receiving the permission of the chairman of the Council of Public Instruction.

A recess of fifteen minutes in the forenoon and in the afternoon shall be allowed.

The school year shall begin on January 1 and end on December 31, and shall be divided into two terms, ending on June 30 and December 31.

In all schools open during the whole year there shall be seven weeks' holiday, of which not less than two nor more than six shall be given in summer, and not less than one nor more than five in winter, to be apportioned at the discretion of the various boards of school trustees. The summer holidays shall fall between July 2 and August 31, and the winter holidays shall commence on December 24 in all schools.

The trustees of any school district in which the school is open during the whole year may allow two weeks' additional holidays.

f. The total number of school days in each year for which grants may become payable is 210, and most yearly schools are open for that period. The summer or short term schools are open for periods ranging from six to nine months.

g. (*From the Report for* 1898.)—" The average length of the school year 1898 for all schools was 159 days ; according to the latest report of the United States Commissioner of Education it was 140 days for the entire United States. The average attendance was 52 per cent. of the enrolment ; in Manitoba and Ontario it was 56 per cent. Far too many pupils fail to take proper advantage of the schools provided for them. Rather less than 36 per cent. of the pupils were under instruction for over 100 days in the year 1898.

" It is worth considering whether the present fixed grant should not be reduced and the variable grant on attendance increased to such an extent as to induce trustees, ratepayers, and teachers, from the monetary if no higher reason, to make much greater efforts than many of them now do to secure an improved attendance. The energy that can be put forth in this respect is shown when the attendance in small schools comes near the minimum for which grants are payable. The activity displayed then, if kept up during the year, would produce a great gain in attendance and a consequent improvement in the usefulness of the school through the amount and character of the instruction thus rendered possible.

" When the Assembly provides a large fixed grant and a liberal variable grant, and the people a local tax to supply schools it would seem wise to take a further step and see that such advantage was taken of this provision as would accomplish the end in view. The power that creates the necessary institution and furnishes the needed funds should wield the required coercive authority. If, when the schools are opened and their cost provided for, many of the children attend but half time, there is not only a waste of money and teaching power, but there is a loss of intelligence that will count against the welfare of the individual and the civic and industrial future of the nation.

" It may be doubted whether this relation of intelligence to earning power is sufficiently appreciated and whether it is realised that education is one of the best forms of national investment.

" To increase the average length of our school year and the average attendance of our pupils, and therefore their average intelligence, is to increase the industrial and political power of the

next generation. The discovery of some influence potent enough
to bring about this increase is a present need,

"The small number of children in attendance at many of the
schools and the consequent increased cost of their education
continues to engage attention.   There are schools within a few
miles of Regina, Qu'Appelle, Indian Head, Wolseley, and such
towns, with an average attendance of less than ten children and
a school year of only seven months.   If these children were conveyed to the town schools, they would have a full year's schooling,
and the cost, including their daily transportation, would not be
greater than it now is.   Their attendance would be more regular
and, generally, they would have the benefit of better buildings,
better classification, and better teaching.   The consolidation of
weak schools in outlying districts might follow later where
physical conditions were favourable.   There would always remain
certain areas in which this would not be feasible."

V.—Cost of Education.

Schools are maintained by *Legislative grants*, by *local taxation*,
and *by school fees.*

a. Legislative Grants.

The *Legislative grants* are fixed by Ordinance, and the
following are the provisions governing them :—

(i.) There shall be paid from and out of any moneys appropriated by the Legislative Assembly for schools (night schools,
normal schools, and teachers' institutes excepted) an amount
to be calculated as follows:—

(1) To each school having an average attendance of at least
six pupils for the days during which it has been open in
any term, a sum of $1.40 for each day the school
is open : Provided that the total number of days in each
year for which grants may become payable shall not
exceed 210 ;

(2) For every pupil in average daily attendance an additional amount of $1.50 (six shillings) per school year
of 210 days :

(3) To each school where a teacher is employed who holds a
first-class professional certificate the sum of 20 cents
for each day (not exceeding 210) in the year such
teacher is actually engaged in teaching; and to each
school where a teacher holding a second-class certificate
is so employed, the sum of 10 cents for each day (not
exceeding 210) in the year such teacher is actually
engaged in teaching ;

(4) To each school attaining a minimum grading upon the
reports of its inspection, as prescribed by the Council of
Public Instruction, on its efficiency in respect to buildings, equipment, government, and progress, a sum not
exceeding 15 cents nor less than 5 cents may be paid according to such grading, for each day (not exceeding 210)
on which the school has been kept open during the year

(5) To any High School complying with the regulations of the Council of Public Instruction, a special grant of seventy-five dollars (about £17) per term;

Provided, that in case the sum of the grants to be paid in any term under (*a*), (*b*) and (*c*) of this section shall exceed 70 per cent. of the salary actually earned by the teacher during that term, the amount of the grant under these subsections shall be reduced to the amount of the said 70 per cent. of salary paid;

(ii.) Provided further, that payment may be made in respect of the amounts earned under (*a*), (*b*), and (*c*) of this section at the end of the terms closing on the thirtieth day of June and the thirty-first day of December, on receipt of the return prescribed by the Council of Public Instruction; but the grant earned by any school under clause (*d*) shall be paid only with the last payment of the year;

Provided further, that in schools that are only open during a portion of the year payment may be made in respect of the amounts earned under clauses (*a*), (*b*), and (*c*) as soon as the school closes for the year, on receipt of the return prescribed by the Council of Public Instruction;

Provided further, that in schools where more than one teacher is employed, each department shall rank as a school under the provisions of clauses (*a*) and (*d*) of this section, when the average attendance of the whole school shall equal at least twenty pupils to each teacher employed; but no board of trustees shall engage an assistant teacher (expecting Government aid on that account) without having given the Department of Public Instruction at least three months' notice of their intention to do so and having received its approval;

Provided that the amounts shown in the treasurer's return to be due to any teacher or teachers shall be paid direct to such teacher or teachers, and proportionately to the extent of the grant.

Any school that has been closed on account of the absence of the teacher in attending a teachers' institute shall be entitled to all grants as if the school had been actually in operation during such period. For the purpose of computing the grant for such period the average attendance for the week preceding the closing of the school shall be taken as the actual attendance during the period the school remains closed from this cause.

Upon special recommendation of the Council of Public Instruction payment of a special grant may be made to any school, whether organised or not, out of the general revenue fund of the Territories.

Whatever additional sums may be necessary for the conduct of the school are raised by local taxation.

The daily average attendance shall be computed by dividing the aggregate attendance of the pupils for a term by the total number of days in such term in which the school was kept open.

(iii.) If a school has been closed by the written order of a duly qualified medical practitioner on account of the prevalence of the

[margin note: Dates of Payment.]

[margin note: Allowance on account of disease.]

within the district of any disease, the Lieutenant-Governor in Council may, upon the recommendation of the chairman of the Council of Public Instruction, pay grants in respect of such days as the school has been closed, but in no case shall such grants be paid for more than thirty days in the calendar year.

If, on account of the prevalence of any disease in the district, the average daily attendance falls below the number requisite to earn the grants, the Lieutenant-Governor in Council may, upon the recommendation of the chairman of the Council of Public Instruction, pay the grants on the basis of the actual attendance for such term.

New districts shall only become entitled to Government aid on the first day of the school term following the Order in Council for their erection.

Any school the officers of which shall allow such school to be taught or conducted in violation of the regulations of the Council of Public Instruction shall be liable to forfeit all rights to participate in any of the grants to aid the schools of the Territories, and upon satisfactory evidence of such violation such grants may be withheld.

b. Local Taxation.

Assessment.   (i.) Where a school district is situated within a municipality the trustees may, as soon as may be after the final revision of the assessment roll of the municipality, make a demand on the council of such municipality for the sum required for school purposes for the then current year ; but such sums shall not exceed an amount equal to twelve mills on the dollar (1¼ cents per dollar) according to the last revised assessment roll, on the property liable to assessment in such school district for ordinary school purposes, with such additional amount as may be necessary to meet any debenture indebtedness that may have been incurred and may be coming due.

The trustees of any school district the whole or any portion of which is situated within a municipality, may demand of the council of the municipality that the amount for which the school district (or the part thereof situated within the municipality) is liable for school purposes shall be imposed and collected by the municipality ; and the lands and property of persons liable for such amounts shall be assessed, and the same shall be collected, as other rates by the municipality.

If the amount collected falls short of the sum required, the council may direct the deficiency to be made up from any fund belonging to the municipality except sinking funds.

If there be no unappropriated funds the deficiency may be deducted from the sums estimated as required or from any one or more of them but not from the estimates supplied by the school trustees.

Should the amount collected exceed the estimates, the sum in excess shall be paid over to the treasurer of the school board.

In cases where the amount collected has been on account of some special purpose and is not required for such purpose, it shall form part of the general fund of the municipality.

(ii.) In cases where separate school districts have been esta- Protestants blished, when property owned by a Protestant is occupied by a and Roman Catholics. Roman Catholic and *vice versâ*, the tenant in such cases shall only be assessed for the amount of property he owns whether real or personal, but the school taxes shall in all cases (whether or not the same has been or is stipulated to the contrary in any deed, contract, or lease) be paid in the school district to which such owner is a ratepayer.

In cases where separate school districts have been established, whenever property is held by two or more persons as joint tenants or tenants in common, the holders of such property being Protestants and Roman Catholics, they shall be deemed and held accountable to the board of trustees for an amount of taxes in proportion to their interest in the premises; and such taxes shall be paid to the school district of which they are ratepayers.

A company may by notice to the secretary treasurer of any municipality wherein a separate school district is either wholly or in part situated, and to the secretary of the board of trustees of any school district in which a separate school has been established, require any part of the real property of which such company is either the owner and occupant or the tenant, and any part of the personal property (if any) of such company, liable to assessment, to be assessed for the purposes of said separate school; and the proper assessor shall thereupon enter said company as a separate school supporter in the assessment roll in respect of the property specially designated.

Provided always that the share or portion of the property of any company assessed in any municipality or in any school district for separate school purposes under the above provisions shall bear the same ratio and proportion to the whole property of the company assessable within the municipality or school district as the amount or proportion of the shares or stock of the company (so far as the same are held and possessed by persons who are Protestants or Roman Catholics as the case may be) bears to the whole amount of such paid or partly paid-up shares or stock of the company.

If a school district be situated partly within two or more municipal corporations, then the Board of Trustees may make a demand upon each of such corporations for that proportion of the amount of money required by such district which may justly be demanded by such district according to the amount of property included within the limits of the district and situated within the limits of such municipality; or the trustees may themselves or by means of an assessor levy an assessment.

(iii.) The trustees of any school district or an assessor whom Assessment they may appoint, as soon as may be in each year, shall prepare Roll. an *assessment roll* for the school district or for that part of the district which is not within the limits of any municipality. in which shall be set down, according to the best information to be had, a list of all the property taxable for their school in the district, with the names of the occupants and owners if such can be procured ; and such list shall contain the following information—

1. Name of occupant or person in possession (if there be no occupant a statement to that effect):

(a) Religion of occupant (whether Roman Catholic or Protestant) ;

(b) Sex ;

(c) Age ;

(d) Occupation ;

(e) Place of residence.

2. Name of owner if it can be ascertained (if owner's name be unknown such particulars concerning ownership as may be known):

(a) Religion of owner (whether Roman Catholic or Protestant) ;

(b) Sex ;

(c) Age ;

(d) Occupation ;

(e) Place of residence and post office address.

3. Description of real property in occupation of each person:

(a) Part and number of section, township, range, and meridian, or number and description of lot in special survey, or number of lot or house or other particulars of each parcel ;

(b) Improvements in cultivated lands (giving area) and buildings on each parcel ;

(c) Area in acres or the number of feet frontage of each parcel ;

(d) Value of each parcel ;

(e) Total value of real property.

4. Description of taxable personal property:

(a) Taxable personal property other than income, with particulars ;

(b) Value of such personal property ;

(c) Taxable income ;

(d) Total value of personal property, including taxable income.

5. Total value of taxable, real, and personal property ;

Exemptions.   (iv.) All real and personal property situated within the limits of any school district, or income derived by any person resident within the limits of such district, and live stock which is within the limits of a school district for a portion of the twelve months prior to the assessment shall be liable to taxation subject to the following provisions and exemptions—

1. All property held by Her Majesty or for the public use of the Government of the Territories or specially exempted by the Parliament of Canada;

2. All property held by or in trust for the use of any tribe of Indians or the property of the Indian Department;

3. Where any property is occupied by any person otherwise than in an official capacity the occupant shall be assessed in respect thereof, but the property itself shall not be liable;

4. The buildings and grounds, to the extent of two acres, of all public and separate schools and the personal property belonging to the same, being used for school purposes, and under the management of the Council of Public Instruction of the Territories;

5. A building used for church purposes and not used for any other purpose for hire or reward, and the lot or lots whereon it stands not exceeding one-half acre, except such part as may have any other building thereon;

6. Gaols and court houses and the necessary land attached thereto;

7. Any land in use as a public cemetery not exceeding twenty-five acres;

8. The books of every public library;

9. The income of a farmer derived from his farm and the income of merchants, mechanics, and other persons derived from capital liable to taxation.

The annual income of any person derived from his personal earnings provided the same does not exceed $600.

10. Grain, household effects of every kind, books, and wearing apparel;

11. The increase in the value of the land by reason of the annual cultivation thereof, together with the growing crops, or by reason of the cultivation of trees;

12. All works constructed, operated, and used in connection with irrigation ditches as well as the ditches themselves operated under and subject to the provisions of *The North-West Irrigation Act, 1898*;

Provided that live stock which has been assessed against the owner thereof in the school district in which he resides shall not be liable to assessment in any other school district.

A person occupying property or deriving income not liable to taxation may compel the assessor, on written demand, to assess him for such property or income in order that he may hereby be qualified for voting or holding office.

Real and personal property shall be estimated at their actual cash value as would be appraised in payment of a just debt from a solvent debtor.

Taxes may be recovered either from owner or occupant as a debt due to the school district; in which case the production of the collector's roll or a copy of so much thereof as relates to the taxes payable by such person, certified as a true copy by the secretary of the school district, shall be *prima facie* evidence of the debt.

Complaints.

(v.) If any ratepayer within the school district thinks that any person has been assessed too high or too low or has been wrongly inserted in or omitted from the assessment roll or that the property of any person has been misdescribed or omitted from the roll or that the assessment has not been performed in accordance with the above provisions and requirements, the secretary of the board of trustees shall, on his request in writing, give notice by post or otherwise to such person and the assessor, of the time when the matter will be tried by the court; and the matter shall be decided in the same manner as complaints by a person assessed.

The secretary of the board of trustees shall post up in some convenient place within the school district a list of all complaints made by persons on their own behalf against the asssessor's return and of all complaints on account of assessment or want of assessment of other persons, stating the names both of the complainant and of the party complained against with a concise statement of the matter complained of, together with an announcement of the time when the court will be held to hear the complaints; and no alteration shall be made in the roll unless under a complaint formally made according to the above provisions.

Court of Revision.

(vi.) If at any time before the day fixed for the sitting of the court of revision it shall be discovered that the property or income of any taxable person or part thereof has been omitted from the roll, the secretary shall notify such taxable person, if known, by registered letter, that at the sitting of the court of revision, to be held at least fifteen days after such notice, an application will be made to the said court to assess such taxable property for such sum as may be deemed right; and that such taxable person is required to attend such court to show cause why the said taxable property should not be assessed, and as to the amount the same should be assessed for.

The board of trustees of any school district shall sit as a court of revision not more than thirty days from the filing of the roll, and shall hear all complaints notice of which shall have been given.

The roll as finally passed by the court and certified by the secretary as passed shall (except in so far as the same may be further amended on appeal to a judge of the Supreme Court) be valid and bind all parties concerned.

Appeal to Superintendent.

(vii.) If a person be dissatisfied with the procedure of the court of revision he may appeal therefrom to a judge of the Supreme Court. In all cases of such appeals the person appealing shall in person or by his agent serve upon the secretary of the school district, within eight days after the decision of the court of revision, a written notice of his intention to appeal to a judge of the Supreme Court.

And in all such proceedings the judge shall possess all the powers for compelling the attendance and for the examination on oath of all parties whether claiming or objecting, or objected to, and all other persons whatsoever, and for the production of books, papers, rolls, and documents, and for the enforcement of such orders, decisions, and judgments as belong to or might be exercised by him in the Supreme Court.

(viii.) The Board of Trustees shall cause to be made out a collector's roll for the district on which shall be set down the name of every person assessed, the assessed value of his real property, and the amount with which such person is chargeable according to the rate of taxation computed in respect of sums ordered to be levied by the Board of Trustees, with any other particulars that may be necessary; and such roll shall be placed in the hands of the treasurer or collector duly appointed by the trustees for collection. Return of Trustees: Rebate.

The Board of School Trustees may by resolution allow a rebate not to exceed 10 per cent. upon all taxes paid within thirty days after the same have become payable.

(ix.) Should it appear desirable to the Board of Trustees of any school district that a sum of money should be borrowed upon security of the district for the purchase of a school site, or for the erection, purchase, or improvement of a school building or buildings, or for furnishing the same, or for the purchase of suitable play grounds for the children attending the school or schools of the district, they shall pass a bye-law to that effect; and, before proceeding to borrow such sum of money, shall receive the sanction of a majority of the votes of the ratepayers of the school district voting thereon. Incurring Debt by Debenture.

Upon receipt of the return of the voting and upon being satisfied that the necessary conditions have been complied with, the Lieutenant-Governor in Council shall in writing empower the trustees to borrow the sum or sums of money mentioned in the bye-law and shall publish the same in the official gazette of the Territories; and the assent of the Lieutenant-Governor in Council (published as aforesaid) to any such loan, shall be conclusive evidence that all the necessary formalities have been complied with and that such loan is one which the school district may lawfully make.

All money thus borrowed shall be borrowed by debenture.

The total face value of the debentures issued shall not be for a greater sum than one-tenth of the total assessed value of the real property within the district, according to the last finally revised assessment roll of the district.

Debentures shall not run for a longer term than twenty years, if the school buildings are of brick, concrete, or stone; and shall not run for a longer period than ten years, if the buildings be of frame or log.

Debentures shall not carry interest at a greater rate than eight
er cent. per annum.

The trustees of any school district, having received notice from
1e Lieutenant-Governor in Council authorising them to contract
loan, shall issue debentures therefor to secure the amount of
1e principal and interest of such loan upon the terms specified;
nd the said debentures and the coupons thereof shall be suffi-
ient, when signed by two of the trustees of the school district, to
ind such school district and to create a charge or lien against
ll school property or rates in the school district for which such
an is made.

All debentures shall on redemption be marked "cancelled"
d signed by the secretary of the board of trustees across the
ce thereof.

All debentures before being issued shall be sent for registration
the department of public instruction and such department
ill keep a book in which shall appear:

1. The name and number of each school district issuing
bentures;

2. The amount of debenture indebtedness incurred by such
strict from time to time;

3. The purposes for which the indebtedness was incurred, with
rticulars of the amount for each specific purpose;

4. The date of redemption of each debenture.

Two sections of land (1,280 acres) in each township are reserved
d held in trust by the Dominion Government as school lands
r aiding and promoting education. This means an endowment
about eleven million acres.

c. School Fees.

Except for pupils in High School departments, no fees shall be
arged by the trustees of any school district on account of the
tendance at the school thereof of any children whose parents
lawful guardians are ratepayers of such school district; but a
te not exceeding five cents per day per family payable monthly
advance may be charged for any children whose parents or
wful guardians are not ratepayers to such school district.

In High School departments the trustees may charge pupils,
iose parents or lawful guardians are resident ratepayers, a fee
t to exceed nine dollars for the first term and six dollars for
e second term.

In High School departments the trustees may charge pupils,
iose parents or lawful guardians are not resident ratepayers, a
not to exceed thirteen dollars in the first term and eight
llars in the second term.

d. Treasurer's Return.

The foregoing analysis of the financial administration of
ucation in the Territories may best be summarised by giving
full the prescribed form for the return made at the end of each

term by a treasurer of a board of trustees of any school district (public or separate) to the department of Public Instruction :—

School District No.

The following statement of cash received and expended by me on account of the above school district for the year ended December 31st, 1   , together with the other information furnished by me is correct and true in every particular.

RECEIPTS.			EXPENDITURE.	
Government grant for first term ended · · ·			For teachers' salaries ·	
Government grant for second term ended ·			On account of debenture indebtedness · ·	
Taxes collected during the year · · · ·			For rent of buildings ·	
Received for fees from pupils · · ·			„ school apparatus ·	
Proceeds of sale of debentures · · ·			„ library · · ·	
....			„ caretaker and fuel ·	
....			On school buildings ·	
....			....	
			....	
			....	
			....	

AMOUNT DUE TO AND BY THE DISTRICT.

Arrears of taxes due to district · · · ·			Balance due on teachers' salaries · ·	
Fees from pupils · ·			Balance due on outstanding accounts ·	
... .			Balance due on buildings and land · ·	
....			....	

PARTICULARS OF ASSESSMENT.			ASSETS OF DISTRICT.	
Amount of assessable property from last revised assessment roll ·			Estimated value of real estate · ·	
Rate of school tax per dollar · · · ·			Estimated value of school buildings · ·	
Rate of school tax per dollar to pay debenture indebtedness · · ·			Estimated value of furniture · · · ·	

AUDITOR'S REPORT.			COST OF LAND AND BUILDINGS.	
I hereby certify that I have compared the above statement with the books kept by the district and find the same correct. Auditor.			Amount paid for school site „ „ „ buildings „ „ „ furniture, &c. · · · ·	

(Signed) .... Treasurer.

e. *Public Notice of Poll on Issue of Debentures.*

The form prescribed for the *public notice of a poll on the issue of debentures* gives some idea of the share of the voters in the financial affairs of their school district :—

By the trustees of the (*give full corporate name of school district*).

Whereas it is deemed expedient by the trustees of the (*give full name of the school district*) that the sum of   dollars should be borrowed on the security of the said school district by the issue of debentures repayable to the bearer in equal consecutive annual instalments from the issue thereof with interest at the rate of   per cent. per annum for the following purposes, namely :

Therefore notice is hereby given by the trustees of the said district that a poll will be opened by the undersigned chairman of the said trustees at the   on   the day of   , 1   , at the hour of ten o'clock a.m., and will continue open until four o'clock p.m. of the same day, when the votes of those duly qualified to vote thereon will be taken for or against raising the said sum of   dollars by way of a loan on the security of the said school district as hereinbefore set forth.

The qualification of voters is expressed in the following oath or affirmation, which persons desiring to vote must take if required : " I, *A. B.*, do solemnly swear that I am a *bona fide* ratepayer of the (*name of school district*); that I am of the full age of twenty-one years ; that I am not an unenfranchised Indian ; that I have paid all taxes due by me to the said school district ; that I have not voted before at this election, and have not received any reward either directly or indirectly, nor have I any hope of receiving any reward for voting at this time and place."

Of which all persons interested are hereby notified and are required to govern themselves accordingly.

Chairman.

}Trustees.

Dated at

this   day of   19.

VI.—INSPECTORS AND INSPECTION.

Inspection. (*From the Report for* 1898.).—" The increase in the number of schools and pupils and the distances to be travelled made it impossible for the inspectors to visit all schools twice during the year.

" Through joint inspections and periodical conferences an attempt has been made to arrive at methods that secure substantial uniformity of judgment and practice.   An inspection implies observation and examination, with a view to determining how far the school meets the needs of the pupils and the requirements of the State.

" The inspector observes the children entering and leaving the school-room, coming to and retiring from class, and notes promptness of movements, economy of time, simplicity of class tactics, and positions of desks.   He observes the teacher's tone of voice, manner, watchfulness, decision, courtesy, consideration for the weaker and slower children, sympathy, and power to inspire.   He observes whether the children are punctual, polite, cheerful, interested, orderly, and systematic.   He observes the neatness, cleanliness, and orderly arrangement of the school room, its furniture and decoration, and the provisions made for heating, lighting, and ventilation, and notes the conditions of the school grounds.   He observes the teacher's conduct of a lesson, definiteness of aim, selection of facts, clearness of presentation, character of drill ; and notes the habits of work of the pupils in seats during this period.   He examines the time-table to learn what subjects are taught and how the children are employed ; he expects to find an analysis of it showing the amount of time devoted to class work in each subject.   He examines the children in several subjects to discover what knowledge they possess, what power to master new work they have acquired, and what ability they have to give correct expression to their thoughts.   He does not test all work at each visit, it being assumed that if a subject is well taught in one class it will probably be well taught in the remaining classes.   He examines the registers to see that they are kept correctly and to learn something of the pupils' regularity of attendance and length of time in their several standards.   He examines the pupils' text books to see that they are clean and free from markings.

" At the close of his inspection he has a brief conference with the teacher at which he praises excellent work, approves good work, and suggests remedies for inefficient work.   He encourages the teacher to continue to be a student and recommends books and journals that will add to his general culture and professional knowledge.   He leaves the teacher with a feeling that an inspector, while a skilled critic, is a sympathetic friend who helps and inspires, yet respects individuality and independence.

" He makes written reports of his inspection to the trustees and the Council of Public Instruction, in which he expresses brief judgments upon the general character of the school, makes particular comments upon any special excellences or defects, and suggests needed improvements. Where opportunity permits he has personal conferences with the trustees.

" He examines treasurers' books, aids in the settlement of district disputes, encourages the formation of new districts, meets with his teachers once a year in convention, and assists in the preparation of examination papers and the training of third class teachers.

" It is a pleasure to state that teachers and trustees are showing an increasing appreciation of the work of our inspectors and that there is in so many instances, an easily discernible relation between their frank reports and marked improvements in the quality of the teaching and the condition of the school houses and grounds."

VII.—Religious Instruction.

No religious instruction shall be permitted in any school in the Territories from the opening of such school until one half hour previous to the closing of such school in the afternoon, after which time any such instruction permitted or desired by the trustees may be given.

It shall, however, be permissible for the trustees of any school district to direct that the school be opened by the recitation of the Lord's prayer.

Any child attending any school shall have the privilege of leaving the schoolroom at the time at which religious instruction is commenced, as provided for in the preceding section, or of remaining without taking part in any religious instruction that may be given, if the parents or guardians so desire.

No teacher, trustee, or inspector shall in any way attempt to deprive such child of any advantage that it might derive from the ordinary education given in such school ; and any such action on the part of any trustee, inspector, or teacher shall be held to be a disqualification for and voidance of the office held by him or her.

VIII.—Teachers.

a. Their Duties.

It shall be the duty of every teacher—

1. To teach diligently and faithfully all the subjects required to be taught in the school according to the terms of his engagement with the trustees and according to the provisions of the Council of Public Instruction ;

2. To maintain proper order and discipline ;

3. To hold during each year public examinations of his school, of which he shall give due notice to the trustees, and through the pupils to their parents or guardians ;

4. To make at the end of each school term, or at such other time as may be approved by the inspector and subject to revision

by him, such promotions from one class to another as he may deem expedient ;

5. To give strict attention to the proper heating, ventilation, and cleanliness of the school house, and report to the trustees any necessity for cleaning and ventilating the school building and outhouses in connection with the same, and report to the school inspector any neglect on the part of the trustees in this respect ;

6. To report to the secretary of the trustees any necessary repairs to the school buildings or furniture and any required supply of fuel and drinking water ;

7. To keep in the prescribed form the school registers and to give access to them to trustees, inspectors, and any other person authorised thereto by the Chairman of the Council of Public Instruction ;

8. To assist the board of trustees in making the required returns to the department of Public Instruction ; and to furnish to the department, the inspector of schools, or the board of trustees, any information which it may be in his power to give respecting anything connected with the operations of his school or in any wise affecting its interests or character ;

9. To deliver up any school registers, school house key, or other school house property in his possession on the written order of the board of trustees ;

10. The teacher of a school may be secretary of the trustees but not treasurer.

A teacher whose agreement with a board of trustees has expired or who is dismissed by them shall be entitled to receive forthwith all moneys due to him for his services as teacher while employed by the said board. If such payment be not made by the trustees or tendered to the said teacher by them, he shall be entitled to recover from the said trustees the full amount of his salary due and unpaid, with interest, until payment is made by a suit in a court of competent jurisdiction.

Within ten months after the issue of the Order in Council erecting a newly-organised school district, the trustees shall engage a qualified person as school teacher for such period, not being more than one year, and at such salary as may be agreed upon.

In every school in which more teachers than one are employed the head teacher shall be called the principal and the other teachers assistants.

The principal shall prescribe, with the concurrence of the Board of Trustees, the duties of the assistants, and shall be responsible for the organisation and discipline of the whole school.

b. *Teachers' Institutes.*

Any number of teachers may organise themselves into a teachers' institute for the purpose of receiving instruction in the methods of teaching and for discussing educational matters subject to the regulations of the Council of Public Instruction.

brief judgments upon the general character ⌐   ᵍh the co-
particular comments upon any special ⌐   ..achers these
and suggests needed improvements. Wᵇ   ᵤf aims. They
he has personal conferences with the ⱼ   ᵢng the isolated

" He examines treasurers' books   .essional thought
district disputes, encourages the fᵣ   ᵢ. They are the
with his teachers once a year iᵣ   of work and giving
preparation of examination pᵉ   fhrough the evening
teachers.   veloping a right educa-

" It is a pleasure to staᵗ   ..d encouraging the school
an increasing appreciatⁱ
there is in so manʸ   ⱼ *of Teachers, etc.*
between their franᵗ
quality of the teaᶜ   ..eachers in well-settled districts is
grounds."   ..tlying districts there is difficulty in
  ..achers to accept pioneer conditions; into
  very few teachers have gone. The difficulty
  ...hers is increased when some trustees require

No reᶫ   ..in addition to the legal qualifications, to speak
Territ   ...modern language and be a member of a certain
prevⁱ   We are not yet wholly free from appeals of
whⁱ   and relatives to grant provisional certificates to
tr   ...ons persons without the required scholarship or
The rights of the children, quite ignored by these
..ple, are considered of paramount importance by the Council;
and provisional certificates are refused till it is made manifest
that qualified teachers cannot be obtained. The rule is: ' Provisional certificates are issued to persons who present such
evidence of scholarship that there is a reasonable probability of
their being able to pass the next teachers' examination.' These
certificates are not issued till the trustees declare that they have
advertised for a qualified teacher and have used all reasonable
effort to secure one but without success. Then upon application
of the trustees—not of the would-be teacher—a provisional
certificate is issued, valid for that school only, and terminating
at the opening of the next examination for teachers.

" In the engagement of teachers, willingness to accept a small
salary is too frequently a more potent influence than good
character, graceful manners, broad scholarship, and professional
skill. So long as this continues these schools will fail to secure
and retain the best class of teachers. Progress in the education
of the people to a juster recognition of the essential qualities of
a good teacher is slow. Permanency of tenure is the rule in
village and town schools, the exception in rural schools. Progress
is much retarded by frequent changes of teachers.

" Mental and moral tests of qualification are required of all
teachers. There should be a physical test as well. Tuberculosis
is known to be a contagious disease; yet persons infected with it
come here seeking relief in our climate and secure employment
in our schools. Candidates for certificates should be free from
any disease or infirmity which would unfit them for the work of
teaching.

d. Foreign Certificates.

 ...nditions specified in the regulations persons holding
...tificates, other than third class, issued in any of
...he British Islands may receive certificates here
... further examination or training. Each year
...rs are admitted under this regulation, and
...aw attention to certain difficulties arising
...ors as a rule are not lacking in general
...ility, but they do not understand our
...u of our school laws, fail to appreciate our
..., to a surprising extent, to read and interpret
...programme of studies. As a result, too much of
...ot year's work is misdirected if not wasted, and the
...pectors, with the limited time at their disposal for each school,
can do but little to remedy these defects. The inspectors are
unanimous in recommending that before receiving authority to
teach, these persons should be required to take such a course of
training as would make them familiar with our conditions and
laws, and put them in touch with our aims and methods. A
number of our best teachers have urged the necessity for such a
course."

e. Normal School.

The only Normal School in the Territories is at Regina,
the capital. The preparation for the first and second class
professional certificates is given during the last four months
of every year. Sessions for third-class candidates are conducted
at convenient local centres by the inspectors under the supervision of the superintendent, who delivers a course of lectures at
each.

In 1896, of the 433 teachers in employment, 96, of which 34
were women, held first-class certificates; 207, of whom 109 were
women, second-class certificates; and 130, of whom 79 were
women, held third-class certificates

f. Form of Agreement between Trustees and Teacher.

We, the undersigned, trustees of (*here insert name of school
district or separate school district in full*) have chosen
           who holds a   class certificate of quali-
fication to be a teacher in the said district; and we do hereby
contract with and employ such teacher at the rate of
           per annum (*or as the case may be*) from and after
the date hereof, and we do further bind and oblige ourselves and
our successors in office faithfully to collect and pay the said
teacher during the continuance of this agreement the sum or
sums for which we hereby become bound.

And the said teacher hereby contracts with the said trustees
and their successors in office, and binds himself to teach in and
conduct the school or schools of the said district (*or separate
school, as the case may be*) according to the provisions of *The
School Ordinance* and the regulations of the Council of Public
Instruction in force under its authority.

This agreement shall continue in force
from the date hereof unless the certificate of the said teacher
should in the meantime be revoked, and shall not include any
teaching on Saturdays or on other lawful holidays or vacations
decided on, *e.g.*,   all
such holidays and vacations being at the absolute disposal of the
teacher without any deduction from his salary whatever.

Witness ⎫   *A. B.* ⎫   Corporate
         ⎬   *C. D.* ⎱ Trustees.   seal.
         ⎭   *E. F.* ⎰
                             G. H., Teacher.
Dated this   day of   A.D. 19   .

g. Certificates.

The teachers' certificates granted by the Council of Public
Instruction shall be denominated third class, second class, first
class, and High School certificates.   These may be obtained by
fulfilling the following conditions :—

(*a*) Furnishing a certificate of moral character of recent date.
(*b*) Passing the prescribed non-professional examination.
(*c*) Passing the prescribed professional examination.
(*d*) Receiving a satisfactory report from an inspector after
having taught one year in the Territories on an interim
certificate.

Certificates of the third class shall be valid for three years.
All other certificates shall be valid during the pleasure of the
Council.

These certificates are competed for, not in one examination
in which the order of achievement would correspond to the grade
of the certificate given, but in four separate examinations corresponding to the four grades of certificate.   Each of these four
examinations consists of two parts, (*a*) non-professional, (*b*) professional.

For the non-professional examinations for first, second, and
third class, and High School certificates, candidates must obtain at
least 34 per cent. on each subject, and 50 per cent. on the total
number of marks.

If any subject is divided for the purpose of examination, candidates must obtain at least 34 per cent. on each subdivision.

*h. The following is a rough summary of the professional exami-
nation for the lowest and highest certificates, i.e., third-class
and first-class certificates :—*

THIRD CLASS.

1. *The Science of Education.*—The nature and aim of education, teaching, and instruction ; outline of helpful portions of
mental science ; application of the principles derived therefrom
to teaching and government.

2. *The Art of Education.*—Methods of teaching each subject
on the programme of studies for schools ; school organisation ;
school management ; school hygiene ; duties of teachers and
pupils.   Practice in teaching.

Text-book.—Gerlich's "New Manual of Method," "Manual of
Hygiene" (Ontario series).

1. *The Science of Education.*—Nature, form, and limits of education; development and training of man ; education values; psychological and logical sequence of subjects ; general method.

2. *The Art of Education.*—Application of principles derived from the science of education to the teaching of each subject on the programme of studies; school organisation; school management; school law; practice in teaching.

3. *The History of Education.*—Systems and theories of education ; eminent educators.

Text-books. — Rosenkranz's "Philosophy of Education"; Sully's "Handbook of Psychology"; De Garmos' "Essentials of Method"; Landon's "Teaching and Class Management"; White's "School Management"; Laurie's "Lectures on Linguistic Method"; Herbert Spencer's "Education"; "Report of the Committee of Ten."

i. Qualifications for High School Certificate.

The qualifications necessary for a High School certificate enabling a teacher to become the head-master of a High School are as follows :—

1. To have the degree of Bachelor of Arts from some University in Her Majesty's dominions, and

2. To have a professional certificate of the first class.

Persons holding a professional certificate of the first class, or a High School assistant's certificate obtained after a course at an approved school of pedagogy, may teach in a High School, but not as head-master.

NOTE.—A certificate from a school of pedagogy is not valid as a licence to supervise or teach in other than High Schools.

j. General Regulations for Non-Professional Examinations.

1. The examination of candidates for teachers' non-professional certificates shall commence on the first Monday of July in each year at such places as the Council of Public Instruction may announce.

2. No male teacher under eighteen years of age, nor female under sixteen, shall be allowed to write at these examinations.

3. Males under eighteen years of age and females under sixteen, who desire to test their scholarship may, upon payment of a fee of $5.00, write with the candidates for teachers' non-professional certificates. A statement of the marks awarded will be given them, but this statement will not be accepted as the equivalent of a certificate, even when the age limit has been attained.

4. Each candidate shall notify the Secretary of the Council of Public Instruction, not later than June 1st, of the class of certificate for which he is an applicant and the place at which he desires to write. Each such notice shall be accompanied by a fee of three dollars.

5. A non-professional certificate shall not be valid as a licence to teach.

6. During the sessions of the Normal School only those holding non-professional certificates are admitted.

Candidates who have previously taken the training prescribed for second class are permitted to write on the final examinations for first class without attendance during the session.

Persons whose teaching has been favourably reported on by an inspector, but whose third class professional certificates have expired, may, with the permission of the Council, renew these by passing the prescribed non-professional examination for third class and an additional examination based on White's "Pedagogy" and Landon's "Teaching and Class Management."

k. Certificates without Examination.

1. A person who holds a certificate, other than third class, issued since 1st January, 1886, in any province of the Dominion or in the British Islands, and who presents (a) a statement from the Department of Education in his province that his certificate is still valid, (b) a certificate of moral character of recent date, (c) a certificate from his last inspector of having taught successfully, may receive a certificate of such class as the Council of Public Instruction may deem him entitled to.

2. Graduates in any university in Her Majesty's Dominions may, on the presentation of proofs of scholarship, character, and age, receive non-professional certificates of the first class.

3. Persons holding certificates of educational value from institutions other than those mentioned may receive such certificates as the Council of Public Instruction may deem them entitled to.

The Academic Certificate.—Preparation for this certificate is given to teachers in the High School standards (Standards VI., VII., and VIII.). The examination comprises the following subjects: Spelling and writing, the English language, rhetoric and composition, poetical literature, history, geography, arithmetic, algebra, geometry, trigonometry, chemistry, botany, and physics.

l. Certificates and Teachers' Examinations in 1898.

(i.) TEACHERS AND CERTIFICATES.		
1. Number of teachers employed		483
Increase for the year	26	
2. Number of men employed		232
3. Number of women employed		251
4. Number of first-class teachers: men 74, women 42. Total		116
Increase for the year: men 1; women 9. Total	10	—
5. Number of second-class teachers: men 118; women 153. Total		271
Increase for the year: men 3; women, 23. Total	26	—
6. Number of third-class teachers (including provisional licences): men 40; women 56. Total		96
Decrease for the year: men 7; women, 3 Total	10	

(ii.) EXAMINATION OF TEACHERS. (Non-professional.)

First Class.

Number examined	12
Number passed	8

Second Class.

Number examined	58
Number passed	32
Given standing on first-class examination	1

Third Class.

Number examined	101
Number passed	47
Given standing on second-class examination	15

Number of Certificates granted during 1898 :—

First Class.—Male 16, Female 1. Total	17
Second Class.—Male 22, Female 26. Total	48
Third Class.—Male 11, Female 32. Total	43
Interim Certificates, to those qualified from other Provinces	136
Provisional Certificates, including temporary licences to substitutes for teachers who were ill, or who were attending Normal School	24
Total	268

(iii.) NORMAL SCHOOL.

Number attending First Class Session	23
„ Second Class Session	35
Third Class Session	28
Total	86

IX.—SPECIAL SCHOOLS.

a. Night Schools.

Trustees of any school district may engage a qualified teacher and make necessary arrangements at the expense of the school district for the maintenance of a night school, *provided* that, if the school is kept open for one month, a fee may be charged of not more than $2 a month for each month or portion of a month that the pupil is in attendance.

b. Kindergartens.

Kindergarten classes may be established in any school in the Territories for the teaching and training of children between the ages of four and six years according to kindergarten methods, and in such schools a fee may be charged, not exceeding $1 a month for each pupil, to cover the cost of maintaining such department.

Recent Reports of the Council of Public Instruction and other official documents relating to education in the North-West Territories can be seen at the Board of Education Library, St. Stephen's House, Cannon Row, Whitehall, London, S.W.

APPENDIX A.

EXTRACTS FROM THE "PROGRAMME OF STUDIES."

The following recommendations and rules were made in the "Programme of Studies" issued in 1895, and still in force.

(i.) DRAWING.

Drawing is to be taught as an added means of expression. Pupils are to draw in blank books after observing the type solids and objects. (From the Report for 1898):— "Drawing can be taught to all pupils who can learn to write, and it is of use to all. It trains the powers of observation, for the child must observe carefully to represent truly. It gives an added means of expression—clearer perhaps than either speaking or writing. It makes the hand skilful and enables every artisan to construct and read working drawings, and so aids him in his life work. It arouses and makes active the creative ability of the child, and it leads him to see and appreciate the beauty in what surrounds him, and strengthens his desire therefor. Our course is necessarily an elementary one, and prominence is given to objective and industrial drawing. In the study of pictures we have made a beginning."*

Standard I.

Teach the following forms as wholes from type solids and objects :
> *Sphere* and similar forms, natural and artificial, *e.g.*, ball, marble, apple, tomato, cherry, lemon, etc.
> *Cylinder* and smaller forms, natural and artificial, *e.g.*, pencil, bottle, spool, pint measure, cup, rope, ladder, mallet, etc.
> *Cube* and similar forms, natural and artificial, *e.g.*, box, chest, basket, inkstand, lumps of sugar, etc.

Teach their parts—surfaces, faces, edges, and corners, and the relation of these parts ; compare them.
Illustrative sketching in connection with Nature Study.

Standards II. and III.

The work of Standard I. and the following :
> The type solids bisected and studied as new wholes.
> *Hemisphere* and similar forms, natural and artificial, *e.g.*, half an apple, dish, bowl, cap, oil can, etc.
> *Half Cylinder* and similar forms, natural and artificial, *e.g.*, bandbox, coin, etc.
> *Half Cube*, square prism, right angled triangular prism, and similar forms, natural and artificial, *e.g.*, box, trunk, car, roof of a house, etc.

Teach their parts—surfaces, faces, edges, and corners, and the relation of the parts. Compare them.
Teach geometric figures—triangle, square, and rectangle from the solid, Draw objects based on these figures, *e.g.*, pennant, envelope, door, cross, flag, etc.
Illustrative sketching in connection with Nature Study.

Standards IV. and V.

The work of previous standards and forms derived from the type solids by variation.
> *Spheroid*, ellipsoid, ovoid, and similar forms natural and artificial, *e.g.*, lemon, cucumber, watermelon, egg, hops, pear, strawberry, vase, etc.

---

* See below, *note.*

Cone, circular frustrum, and similar forms, natural and artificial, *e.g.,* carrot, volcano, mountain peak, hour glass, wine glass, etc.

Pyramid, square frustrum and similar forms, natural and artificial, *e.g.,* cupolas, pyramids of Egypt, basket, etc.

Draw, from the solids, the geometric figures, circle, ellipse, and oval ; and learn the terms circumference, diameter, radius, arc, centre, focus, axis. Draw objects based on these figures, *e.g.,* target, circular window, hand mirror, eye glasses, horse shoe, padlock, fan, spoon, etc.

Illustrative sketching in connection with other studies.

(ii.) STIMULANTS AND NARCOTICS, WITH SPECIAL REFERENCE TO THE USE OF ALCOHOL AND TOBACCO.

The great purpose is to build up in the mind a theory of self-control and a willingness to abstain from acts that may grow into dangerous habits. The moral and social effects should be made prominent and abstinence be inculcated from higher ends than such as concern only the body. Technicalities and persistent dwelling upon details of disease should be avoided. Special delicacy of treatment is needed in those unfortunate cases in which children find themselves between the safe teaching of the school and the counter practices and influences of the home. Refrain from assertions of what is uncertain or sincerely doubted by high authority, or likely to be repudiated by the pupil when he is mature enough to judge for himself, since the admitted and unquestioned facts about the more dangerous stimulants and narcotics, the alcoholic drinks in particular, furnish invincible reasons why people in general should do without them, and young people above all others.

Teach what a stimulant is, what a narcotic is, what each may cause effects of alcohol on the digestive, circulatory, muscular, and nervous system.

Teach that tobacco contains a poisonous substance called nicotine, that it frequently injures the throat, lungs, heart, and other organs in adults, that it is far more harmful to young and growing persons than to adults, that it is particularly objectionable in the form of a cigarette, that children should avoid it in all its forms, and that the more sparingly grown people use it the better, as a rule, they are off.

(iii.) MANNERS AND MORALS.

It is the duty of the teacher to see that the pupil practices those external forms of conduct which express a true sense of the proprieties of life, and that politeness which denotes a genuine respect for the wants and wishes of others. It is his duty to turn the attention of the pupils to the moral quality of their acts and to lead them into a clear understanding and constant practice of every virtue. His own influence and example ; the narration of suitable tales to awaken right feeling ; the memorising of gems embodying noble sentiments, and maxims and proverbs containing rules of duty ; direct instruction, etc., are means to be employed.

Topics : Cleanliness and neatness, politeness, gentleness, kindness to others, kindness to animals, love, truthfulness, fidelity in duty, obedience, nobility, respect and reverence, gratitude and thankfulness, forgiveness, confession, honesty, honour, courage, humility, self-respect, self-control, prudence, good name, good manners, temperance, health, evil habits, bad language, evil speaking, industry, economy.

From the Report for the year 1898 : — "In 'Manners and Morals' our inspectors are informed too frequently that 'incidental instruction is given as occasion demands.' Observation of the behaviour of the children, and examination of what they know about the topics named in the Programme of Studies reveal the effects of this incidental work and emphasise the value, here as elsewhere, of systematic and definite instruction. 'Manners' is a fine art based on imitation, and on a genuine respect for the rights and duties of others. A knowledge of these rights and duties does not come by instinct. It has to be taught. The relations of a pupil to his fellows and to society are not known intuitively. This necessary knowledge must be taught, if moral action is to have a rational basis. Inspectors report that there are schools where the external forms of conduct are satisfactory, yet the pupils are not honest in their work, given to falsehood rather than confession in cases of clear wrong-doing, and do not appreciate the necessity for respecting and protecting the reputation of others.

"More attention is given to this subject each year, yet progress is slower than it need be. Our teachers are drawn not only from our own schools, but from every province in the Dominion. As a consequence some give this subject due attention, others are content with incidental instruction, too many ignore it, except when a case of discipline forces them to deal with some phase of it. If, as Matthew Arnold has said, 'Conduct is three-fourths of life,' and if school is a preparation for life, surely the subject has a right to a prominent place in the teacher's thought and a definite position in his school work. Those who have made little or no preparation for the systematic presentation of this subject will find White's 'School Management' a very suggestive book."

(iv.) Hygiene.

Topics : Lessons on cleanliness, proper clothing, pure air, good water, exercise, rest, avoidance of draughts, wholesome food, temperate habits, bathing, accidents, poison, disinfectants, digestion, circulation, respiration, care of the eye and ear.

(v.) Music.

Standard I.

Singing of rote songs clearly and sweetly. Drill on the scale and intervals. Exercises in time given with the time names and the metronome.

Standard II.

Easy exercises in each of the keys D, A, E, A♭, E♭, B♭, and F. Continued exercises in time, undivided pulsations.

Standard III.

Reading music (alto part). Time work on elementary rhythms, completed and divided pulsations commenced.

Standard V.

Completion of above.

From the Report for 1898.—"In music there is a marked improvement in the quality of the selections used for rote songs. The number of schools giving systematic teaching in singing is greater than at any previous period, but there are many schools where the teachers do not know how to give instruction in this subject. . . .

"The chief hindrances to progress lie in a number of teachers now in the schools who have had no training in these phases of art study, and in the continued admission of teachers from provinces where this work is not done."*

(vi.) Programme of Studies.

The programme now in force was issued in 1895. It is based on a minimum requirement for each standard. It is prescribed by the Council of Public Instruction as a guide in classifying pupils. It may be modified to meet the needs of special schools, but not without the written consent of an inspector, who shall forthwith report to the Council. The work in each standard includes a review of the essentials in previous standards.

It shall be the duty of each teacher to make a time table, based on this programme, and to present it to the inspector at each visit for his approval and signature.

The following descriptions of the aims in view and the methods in use in the various subjects give some idea of the character of the programme of 1895 :—

(a.) *Reading and Literature.*

Silent reading is used to obtain ideas and thoughts through printed or written words --to comprehend the subject matter as a whole and to grasp

---

These remarks are applied to drawing as well as to music (see above).

the significance of the parts, as well as to discover and appreciate beauties of thought and expression.

Oral reading is used to express these ideas and thoughts so as to be heard, understood, and felt. It involves systematic training in the principal elements of expression—quality of voice, pitch, force, time, stress, inflection, emphasis, pause.

Supplementary reading is used to furnish additional reading matter ; to provide reading collateral to the studies in nature, geography, history, literature, etc. ; to cultivate a taste for good literature. Its use is optional.

Sight reading in silence is used to give power to glean thought quickly and intelligently from the printed page. It is followed by logical statement, in the pupil's own words, of what he has gleaned.

Selections of poetry and prose inculcating reverence, love of country, love of nature, and admiration of moral courage are to be committed to memory and recited.

(b.) *Orthœpy and Spelling.*

Much attention should be given to accurate pronunciation. Pupils of the third, fourth, and fifth Standards should have constant practice in finding the pronunciation and meaning of words from the dictionary.

Special drills should be given on such words as are in their nature difficult to spell, and such as have been frequently misspelled in compositions. Pupils should not be drilled on the spelling of words which they may seldom or never have occasion to use.

(c.) *Composition.*

(i.) Compositions should consist, almost entirely, of expressions of thoughts evolved in the teaching of such studies as Geography, History, Agriculture, Literature, etc. (ii.) Through progressive exercises both critical and constructive the pupils should be led to discover and apply the leading principles of expression. Only the most important errors should be corrected in any one composition.

(d.) *Grammar.*

Grammar shows the structure of language. By revealing the rules of sentence-building it helps the pupil in using correctly the forms of speech which the necessities of expression require.

Through the logical forms of subject, predicate, and modifier, it reveals the essential nature of thought, and is an aid to the more thorough understanding of reading lessons.

The teaching of formal grammar should be brought into close connection with the work in reading and composition. Routine parsing and minute analysis should be avoided.

(e.) *History.*

Training of the moral judgment, and preparation for intelligent citizenship, are important aims in teaching history. History should be associated with geography and literature - historical poems, etc.

(i.) The *Canadian History* for Standards II. and III. is thus outlined :—

Standard II.—Lives of distinguished men described, *e.g.*, Columbus, the Cabots, Jacques Cartier, Champlain, Bishop Laval, Frontenac, La Salle, Montcalm, Wolfe, Sir Guy Carleton, Lyon Mackenzie, Papineau, Joseph Howe, Alexander Mackenzie, Sir John Macdonald, etc. Discussion of the chief excellences and defects in their characters to teach moral discrimination, and ultimately to derive principles of conduct. Reading and reciting of patriotic poems.

Standard III.—Outline study of leading features, *e.g.* Discovery ; exploration ; struggle between the French and English Colonists ; Treaty of Paris ; Quebec Act ; Constitutional Act ; War of 1812 ; Rebellion of 1837 ; Union Act ; Clergy Reserves ; Land Tenures — Feudal, Freehold, Leasehold, Seignorial ; Reciprocity Treaty ; British North America Act, etc.

(ii.) *English History for Standard IV.*—Outline study of each people or period to exhibit its chief characteristics, *e.g.*: Saxons — a farmer people; brought with them the germs of our political institutions—a limited monarchy, parliament, courts of justice, personal holdings of land; gave us the body of our English tongue; became Christian from choice. The presentation of this outline is to be oral. Supplementary reading in history should be encouraged.

English History for Standard V.—The text book studied as a review and expansion of the topics discussed in previous standards. Grouping of the essential facts in each period under topics indicating phases of progress, *e.g.* Political, industrial, intellectual, æsthetic, religious—to show the growth of the nation.

(iii.) *Canadian History for Standard V.*—An intelligent comprehension of the prescribed text; comparison of constitutional struggles in Canada with corresponding ones in England; outline study of how we are governed —parliamentary, judicial, municipal, and school systems; our civic duties —voting, office-holding, tax-paying, support of law, etc.

(f) *Geography.*

Standard I.—Direction.—Position of the sun in the morning at noon, in the evening; cardinal points of the compass; position of important places and objects by pointing with the hand and naming the direction.

Water.—Observation of forms of water such as clouds, fog, mist, rain, dew, frost, snow, and ice, as they occur, to find the more obvious qualities and uses of each.

Winds.—Recognition of calm, breeze, gale.

Standard II.—Direction.—Semi-cardinal points of the compass; observation of the direction of winds bringing heat, cold, rain, snow, moisture, dryness.

Land.—Hills, mountains—direction and nature of their slopes; plain, valley, prairie; cape, peninsula, isthmus, island; relation of these bodies to one another; their uses. (Teacher's reference: "How to study Geography," pp. 145-159.)

Water.—Fuller study of clouds, fog; mist, rain, dew; snow, ice, hail; as to uses and effects of each. Effects of sun and wind on these.

Spring, brook, river—source, banks, branches, mouth—lake; bay, sea, strait; relation of these bodies to one another; their uses.

Winds. — Calm, breeze, gale, storm, hurricane; effects on land and sea, on plants, animals, people, vessels.

Maps.—Construction of maps of school room, school grounds, neighbourhood; map representation of geographical objects studied.

The World as a Whole.—Outline study of its form, rotation, axis, poles, equator, hemispheres; hot, temperate, and cold parts.

Continents.—Their relative positions and sizes; characteristic animals and plants in each; occupations, habits, dress, and modes of life of the eading peoples in each.

Oceans.- Their relative positions and sizes; some characteristics of each.

Standard IV.—Dominion of Canada studied as a review (with additions) of a section of the continent of North America. Same topic as for continent study. (Teacher's reference: "The Geography of the British Colonies," by Dawson and Sutherland.)

South America.—Outline study, comparing its structure, drainage, coastline, climate, and productive regions with those of North America. Political divisions—mainly Brazil, the Argentine Republic and Chili. (Teacher's reference: "How to study Geography," pp. 218-224. The "Geographical Reader."

Eurasia. (Europe and Asia).—General structure of Eurasia compared with that of North America and that of South America. (Teacher's reference: "How to study Geography," pp. 224-263.)

Europe. Under the same topics as North America. Comparisons.

Asia. Only a very general study of climate, natural productions, productive regions, trade routes, cities. Political divisions—mainly India, Japan, and China. Comparisons.

(g.) *Arithmetic.*

Every new thought process in this subject should be developed objectively. Principles and rules should be arrived at inductively. Accuracy and rapidity in the simple fundamental processes are important.

(h.) *Nature Study and Agriculture.*

(Teacher's reference books: Newell's "From Seed to Leaf," Goodale's "Concerning a Few Common Plants," Grant Allen's "The Story of the Plants.")

To interest pupils in Nature, to train them in habits of careful observation and clear expression, and to lead them to acquire useful knowledge are important aims in teaching this subject.

The pupil must study the plant, the animal, and the soil rather than book descriptions of them. He may consult books after he has made his observations. The study of plant life should be emphasised in spring, though not restricted to that season.

This study should be connected with language, drawing, and geography.

Standard IV.—Plants.—Their food—its sources, how taken up, how assimilated; their reproduction, propagation; dissemination of seeds.

Weeds.—Bindweed or wild buckwheat, tumble-weed, hedge mustard, stink-weed, Russian thistle; methods of destroying.

Soils.—Preparation of, for seed.

Animals.—Feeding, care and management of horses, cattle, sheep, and swine.

Insects.—Growth, classification, remedies.

Standard V.—Tillage.—Drainage, fertilisers, subsoiling.

Crops.—Their growth, management, rotation; diseases, remedies; soiling crops.

Animals.—Principles of feeding; dairying.

APPENDIX B.

EXTRACTS FROM THE REPORT FOR 1898.

(i.) AGRICULTURE.

The instruction in agriculture given in the schools does not teach the pupil the art of growing different grains, but it does teach him how a grain of wheat or barley or a pea germinates, gets needful air and warmth, obtains nourishment from the soil, and how tillage is related to deep-feeding or shallow-feeding grains. It does attempt to teach pupils the principles upon which sound agricultural practice is based, and it is accomplishing its task year by year with increasing success.

The reports of inspectors confirm the statements of our best teachers that where this subject has received its due share of attention its right to a prominent place on our curriculum is undoubted, whether judged by its disciplinary effect or its practical value. That it has been taught badly by some teachers and neglected by others during the six years it has been a compulsory subject on our curriculum is admitted, but there are few subjects that have not suffered similarly. The teaching of it has been opposed by some who think of agriculture only as an art, tolerated by others who consider it a concession to an important element of our population that may not be ignored with safety, and warmly supported by many who see in it not only a useful subject of study, but also a means of increasing an intelligent sympathetic interest in agricultural problems and adding value and dignity to farm life.

In the examination of Public School leaving candidates and candidates for teachers' non-professional and professional certificates agriculture continues to be a compulsory subject. The course in the elementary schools deals in outline with soils—their formation, composition, classification, and preparation for seeding; with drainage, sub-soiling, and fertilising. It deals with plants --their food supply and modes of propagation; weeds-their causes and remedies : trees - their cultivation for shade, ornament, and protection. It deals with animals - the feeding, care, and management of horses, cattle, sheep, and swine. In the High School standards this course is reviewed and expanded, and the principles re-studied with the aid afforded by the pupil's knowledge of physics, which helps to explain "the influences of light and heat, and the movements of fluids in soil, plant, and animal, and the forces concerned in every machine and appliance" : of chemistry, which throws light upon life processes of plants and animals and the fertilisation of soils; of botany, which is systematised plant-knowledge ; of physical geography, which shows how soil conditions the growth and habitat of plant and animal.

In the Normal School the course is again reviewed from the standpoint of method and the student's knowledge widened by the reading of reports of experimental stations, bulletins, and monographs. It is recognised that in the elementary classes the pupils can know practically nothing in a scientific way of physics, chemistry, and botany, and that accordingly principles must be illustrated in a non-technical way with the materials available in the environment of the ordinary rural school. The Normal School trains intending teachers to do this.

The school districts of Lacombe and St. Albert have large gardens in which the children assist in the preparation of the soil and the planting and care of flowers, vegetables, root crops, and trees ; keep observations of their growth, and in a simple way combine the study of principles with practice. The effectiveness of the instruction is greatly aided by its concreteness.

Many teachers illustrate their lessons by references to farming operations in progress at the time in the neighbourhood, and require pupils to report the results of their observations of these ; but the work would be more systematic and effective if school grounds were fenced and small plots in them set apart for purposes of demonstration

(ii.) DOMESTIC ECONOMY AND HYGIENE.

The importance of keeping the school curriculum in touch with the practical interests of life is, in theory at least, admitted by all. The general arguments that can be advanced in support of the teaching of the principles of agriculture to boys can to a still greater degree be applied to the teaching of the principles of domestic economy and hygiene to girls. When school life ends there is a home life to be lived ; and no woman can afford to be ignorant of the general principles that underlie the sanitation of the home, the selection and preparation of foods, the laws of health, and the treatment of common accidents and ailments. The State which compels instruction to be given in reading, writing, and the elementary studies on account of their effect on the intelligence of the individual and on the civic and industrial welfare of its people, should take the next logical step and make compulsory a knowledge of the principles of sanitation and housewifery on which, to so great an extent, the health and happiness of its citizens depend. The economic value of such instruction is evident.

The girl, in after life, will have occasion to use this knowledge hundreds of times for the once she will have to use her knowledge of much of the geography, history, arithmetic, and algebra she has learned. It can be presented in such a way as to lead her to observe carefully, infer cautiously, judge accurately, and so benefit intellectually by the discipline afforded. It will increase her practical power. It will, through a knowledge of underlying principles, tend to convert what is too often in the home an unintelligent drudgery into an interesting and even attractive service. It will dignify housecraft and add to the health, comfort, and happiness of the family.

There is no institution in the State other than the school that can undertake this work. A series of lessons may be given that will illuminate and systematise the knowledge that the girls may have acquired in a practical way at home, and that will lead them to continue reading and reflecting after their school course ends. There are inexpensive text books containing much of this information. In the Normal Schools, where teachers can be prepared to present this subject as intelligently as any other, there can be given, in addition, the results of experiments on human foods and the rational feeding of man as recorded in the bulletins of experimental stations.

The practice of domestic economy cannot be taught now in our schools, but its principles can. We cannot, for example, bring the kitchen range into the school yet, but we can make clear to girls the food va'.ie and digestibility of the potato, and how this food value may be wasted when the potato is boiled in certain ways. From similar examples we can deduce a principle in cooking that will give intelligent direction to practice in the home.

(iii.) EQUIPMENT.

Progress in equipment is slow but steady. Better desks and an increasing number of single desks, better and larger blackboards, more globes and maps, more reference and reading books are reported. Some trustees have been more liberal than wise in their expenditure for equipment. In one part of the Territories a shrewd agent disposed of a number of quite expensive but rather useless geography charts which the Council had refused to authorise. Half this money expended on suitable reference books in geography would have been of much greater service. In rural districts, to the minimum requirements of a dictionary, a numeral frame or its equivalent, a set of weights and measures, a globe, and maps of the world and the Dominion of Canada, a number of schools have added sets of supplementary readers in literature, history, geography, and nature study, and have begun to form school libraries.

Some departmental aid and direction should be given to the establishment of libraries in every district. It is unnecessary to urge the stimulating effect of these on pupils and parents. They supply the best reading for the largest number at the smallest cost. Through their books on literature, history, science, and art they aid the teacher in his daily task, and continue his work after his pupils have ceased to attend school. Progress, so far, is due mainly to the teachers who secure funds for the maintenance and extension of libraries through entertainments and subscriptions. In comparatively few schools have trustees voted money for this purpose.

(iv.) BUILDINGS.

In the erection of new buildings greater care is given to sanitary conditions than formerly. Letters come to the Department asking for plans showing the best devices for heating, lighting, and ventilation. If there were prepared several plans of buildings suitable for rural and smaller urban schools where the services of a school architect are not easily obtained, trustees would use them to the manifest advantage of health, education, and architecture.

Inquiries are frequently made as to the methods of improving the inadequate ventilation of rural school buildings erected years ago. As these buildings are generally heated by stoves, a plan is recommended by which the foul air is drawn off at the floor by a flue at each side of the room at the back of the seats. These two flues are carried up along the wall to the height of the stove pipe, and then taken horizontally across to a half-drum partitioned at the end which rests upon the stove pipe for six to twelve feet of its length. From this drum the air is conducted up through the ceiling and roof by a vertical flue.

The total capacity of these flues should be not less than 2½ square inches for each pupil. They are provided with slides at the floor, to be closed in the evening, so that, by opening the side-slides in the jacket, exclusively internal circulation is secured.

Another slide at the ceiling, pulled down to open and pulled up to close by a couple of light chains, opens to cool the room when it becomes too warm, and is left open in the hot weather in summer.

("The plan described is applicable to new or old buildings, is economical in its use, and has been installed with slight modifications to suit special circumstances in a number of schools at a cost varying from 25dols. to 45dols. The stove commonly used here in schools is a heavy oblong box, but the description is modified to suit other forms.—A tight-fitting 24-gauge galvanised iron jacket is constructed over the rear half of the stove. The fresh air is brought in by a pipe of 144 to 200 square inches, in cross section (or through a duct made by 'under-flooring' two of the joists) under the floor from openings, covered with heavy screens in the outside wall, to an opening under the stove (jacketed part). If the duct is carried through from side to side of the building, it should be partitioned in the middle under the stove so that the air shall come into the room instead of blowing directly through the duct.—The slide under the stove is closed when the schoolroom is not occupied, and at such times two slides in the sides of the casing are opened so that the air of the room circulates through the casing.—The jacket being on the rear half of the stove (which should be placed as near the door as possible) serves as a screen from excessive radiation for those seated near the stove. The other half of the stove being uncovered affords considerable radiant heat, which is a valuable means of quickly warming children coming in cold in the morning. The stoves are commonly from 36 to 50 inches long.")

In some of our "colonies" certain influences have been brought to bear upon the people to induce them to erect churches, and use them or parts of them for school purposes. Recently it has become evident that there is a growing determination on the part of a number of these people to erect school buildings first and use them for church services until they are able to erect churches.

In outlying districts there are still some log buildings open to the rafters, "chinked" with clay, and banked with manure, which is not always removed in the early spring. Dirty within and cheerless without, their effect upon the children is bad. Too frequently it is negligence, not poverty, that is the cause; and the inspector finds ample scope for missionary work in his visits to the trustees. There are still some villages and towns where the janitor thinks he has done his duty when he scrubs the floor and dusts the walls once in three to six months. There are trustees who deem it a sufficient reply to an inspector's complaint of lack of cleanliness at his spring visit to assure the department that their "schools were cleaned thoroughly last midsummer!" But there are also schools, and an increasing number of them, where cleanliness reigns; and flowers in the windows and pictures on the walls give a happy home-like look to the rooms where the child spends so many of his formative hours.

APPENDIX C.

EXTRACTS FROM PAPERS SET IN THE PROFESSIONAL EXAMINATION FOR TEACHERS IN 1898.

NOTE.—*It should be remembered that candidates for any certificate of whatever grade must obtain 34 per cent. on each subject and 50 per cent. on the total number of marks.*

(i.) CANDIDATES FOR TEACHERS' FIRST-CLASS CERTIFICATE, 1898.

(a.) *The Philosophy of Education.*

1. Explain the following views of education and show how the acceptance of either will affect the teacher's work ; (a) The soul is a self-active power appropriating from its surroundings what is useful for its development. (b) The soul is the resultant of the manifold forces of its environment.

2. Give arguments for and against making the curriculum from the utilitarian standpoint ; from the disciplinary standpoint ; from the standpoint of the civilisation into which the child is born.

3. From the standpoints of nutrition, training, and discipline compare mathematics, natural science, and literature.

4. Describe the work of the school in preparing pupils for citizenship.

5. Discuss the duty of the school towards the moral and æsthetic life of its pupils.

p Describe, after Rosenkranz, the relation of the state and the church to the school.

7. Describe the dialectic method : show its relation to the principle of self-activity and make clear the educational value of this principle.

8. Compare oral instruction with instruction through books.

9. Write a note on habit in its relations to education.

(b.) *Organisation, Management, and Law.*

1. Give reasons for or against a double basis of classification.

2. State the conditions under which you would promote a pupil who had not covered the prescribed work of his class.

3. What do you consider the work of the principal of a school in the classification, promotion, attendance, and government of pupils ?

4. State and criticise the doctrine of the discipline of consequences.

5. How does the obedience yielded by a child in school differ from the obedience of an adult to the obligations imposed by a " sense of duty," and how can the one be developed into the other ?

6. Compare the good and evil effects of competitions for prizes or scholarships, with regard to their influence upon health, temper, and the true ends of education.

7. Discuss the use and abuse of home work.

8. State the teacher's legal duties with regard to contagious diseases, public examinations, and returns to the Council of Public Instruction.

(c.) *History of Education.*

1. Show how the Roman national ideals conditioned their educational ideals.

2. Describe chivalric education, showing its relation to humanistic education.

3. Write a note on Rousseau, describing his influence and criticising his educational theories.

4. Describe the chief characteristics of the methods of Froebel, and show how they affect the schools of to-day.

(d.) *Elementary Science.*

1. Discuss the aims and methods of Nature Study.
2. "Nature Study will not succeed unless it is co-ordinated with other studies." Explain.
3. Make a lesson plan on the duck—its adaptation to its mode of life Make illustrative drawing to accompany the lesson.
4. Make a lesson plan to show whether a cucumber is a botanical fruit.
5. Compare the germination of a bean and a grain of corn. From the manner of growth infer soils suitable for each.
6. From the standpoint of "exhaustion of soils" compare cereals with forage crops.
7. How would you lead a class to see the value of under-draining and summer-fallowing in "restoration of soils"?
8. Discuss the value of laboratory work in the study of plants and animals.

(ii.) Paper set to Candidates for First and Second Class Certificates.

Form Study and Drawing.

1. Outline a course of study for the first term in a rural school, stating what differences you would make between senior and junior work.
2. Make a shaded drawing of any three type solids pleasantly grouped.
3. Illustrate simply : −

   (*a*) "A peninsula is a body of land almost surrounded by water."

   (*b*) "On either side the river lie
   Long fields of barley and of rye,
   That clothe the wold and meet the sky ;
   And thro' the field the road runs by
         To many-tower'd Camelot ;'

   (*c*) The germination of a Bean.

4. Give a lesson plan for the presentation of the new type, cylinder, to a class that has already had sphere and cube.
5. A group suggesting lemonade would be :—Lemon, loaf-sugar, glass spoon. Sketch in outline the type forms on which these objects are based.
6. The square prism is placed with the long edges horizontal :—Draw front, top, and right end views.
7. Draw a group of objects--two or three—suggesting to a boy an afternoon's sport.

(iii.) Candidates for Second-Class Certificates.

(a.) *Psychology.*

1. Distinguish between voluntary and involuntary attention. Describe the conditions under which the powers of fixing and concentrating the attention of scholars may best be strengthened.
2. Give a brief account of the mental process by which we see and recognise a familiar object, say, our hat among other hats in a rack, bringing out more particularly the parts played by discrimination and assimilation.
3. Show how a habit of close observation of the distinctive characteristics of objects may best be cultivated in children.
4. Give a full analysis of the process of learning by heart a stanza of poetry.
5. Take any fact, not directly presentable to the senses, such as a historical event, and explain fully the process which the child's mind goes through in grasping the fact.
6. Explain the steps by which a concept is formed. How far does the choice of examples by a teacher assist the pupils in forming distinct and accurate concepts?
7. Distinguish between inductive and deductive reasoning ; and illustrate the place of each in school work.
8. Indicate ways in which the teacher may stimulate feeling judiciously.
9. How may the training of the will be both directly and indirectly developed at school? Give examples.

(.) *History of Education.*

1. Describe Athenian Education under the following heads : Its general aim, persons educated, subjects taught, proposed effects of musical training, of gymnastic training, points worthy of imitation in methods of teaching.

2. Describe Ascham's methods of teaching ; and show how they may be applied in the teaching of any English poem.

3. Describe Rousseau's ideal scheme of education. Criticise it. Account for its influence.

4. Write a note on Froebel describing the principles he advocated and outlining his modes of teaching in accordance therewith.

(*c*.) *Algebra and Geometry.*

1. State somewhat fully the different aims to be accomplished in teaching Algebra to pupils in Standard V.

2. (*a*) Illustrate to these pupils the uses of the symbols *plus* and *minus*.

(*b*) Illustrate a method of leading pupils to discover the Commutative Law for multiplication.

5. Show inductively and then deductively, how you will lead a pupil to see that if two triangles have their bases and box angles equal each to each, the triangles will coincide.

6. Show how you will lead a pupil to the solution of : " In a given time find a point such that lines drawn from it to two other points on the same side of the given line shall make equal angles with it."

(*d*.) *Arithmetic and Mensuration.*

1. " The educational value of arithmetic is thus indicated both as concerns its psychological side and its objective practical uses in correlating man with the world of nature."—Explain.

2. Write a series of questions to test the child's knowledge of the number *twelve.*

3. Make and explain diagrams to illustrate $\frac{1}{2}(\frac{1}{3}-\frac{1}{4})=\frac{1}{24}$.

4. Show how you would teach the solution of the following problem to a class unable to solve it : "A labourer in one week dug 5 rods more than half the length of a ditch, and the next week he dug the remaining 20 rods ; how long was the ditch ?"

5. Assuming that a class is prepared to begin the subject of commission, teach the first lesson, stating definitely the nature of the problems and explanations you would give.

6. Illustrate a method of discovering the surface area of a cylinder. Note specially the parts where you would expect a class to have difficulties. Find the area of a cylinder whose diameter is 7 inches and height 15 inches.

7. Illustrate a method of discovering the volume of a pyramid.

8. At $2.64 per cubic foot, find the cost of digging a ditch $\frac{1}{4}$ mile long, 23 feet wide at the top, 5 feet wide at the bottom, and 12 feet deep, the sides sloping equally. Write what you consider a proper solution of this.

(*e*.) *Geography and History.*

1. State the respective uses of the ordinary map, relief map, and globe in teaching geography to pupils in Standard III.

2. Outline a lesson on the formation and uses of rivers, to pupils in Standard III.

3. Outline a lesson on the industries of the North-West Territories, the rainfall of British Columbia, or the noted trade routes of Canada, to pupils in Standard IV.

4. From the continent of North America illustrate how geography and history may be taught so as to mutually assist each other.

5. Describe somewhat fully the educational values of history.

6. Write notes of lessons on any two of the following : Feudal System, Great Charter, Spanish Armada, Wellington, Corn Laws, Laval, Reciprocity Treaty (1854). State the purposes of each lesson.

(iv.) CANDIDATES FOR THIRD CLASS CERTIFICATES.

(a) *Organisation, Management, and Law.*

1. Describe practical methods of lighting and ventilating school buildings.

2 What considerations determine the classification of a new pupil?

3. State the uses of a time-table, and the principles that should govern its construction.

4. If you found your class getting listless and sleepy, what causes would you suppose to be at work, and what would be your remedies?

5. How should (a) want of punctuality, (b) copying, and (c) impudence be treated?

6. Outline a lesson for pupils in Standard II. on truth-telling.

7. Give your opinion as to the value of rewards and punishments; and state the principle on which they ought to be administered.

8. State the duties of teachers (as defined by the School Ordinance) with reference to promotions, official returns, contagious diseases, and religious instruction.

(b) *Reading, Spelling, and Writing.*

1. State the advantages and disadvantages of teaching elementary reading by the word (Look-and-Say) method.

2. State the uses and limits of simultaneous reading and pattern-reading in the first three Standards.

3. What is meant by distinct articulation in reading: Name any words which present special difficulty to learners; and mention any form of exercise that is most useful in correcting faulty articulation.

.   .   .   .   .

6. State the uses of word-building. With any two of the following words illustrate a method of teaching word-building: Forbidden, peaceful, baker, foretell.

7. Write in vertical style six capital letters so as to show the proper forms and proportions of their parts.

8. Describe the best way of conducting a class lesson in writing.

(c) *Grammar and Composition.*

1. State somewhat fully the value of grammar as a subject of instruction below the High School.

2. Give notes of a lesson on any one of the following? Relative pronoun, indirect object, adverbial clause, "the verb agrees with its subject in number." Show which of the values referred to in the first question your lesson illustrates.

3. Show how you would lead a pupil in Standard V. to analyse :—

> You asked me why, tho' ill at ease,
> Within this region I subsist,
> Whose spirits falter in the mist,
> And languish for the purple seas.

What use to the pupil should such an exercise be?

4. Show how you will prepare pupils in Standard II. to write a composition on Wolfe, the uses of clouds, the pumpkin, the Eskimo, or the hen.

5. After pupils have reproduced in writing an historical tale, outline a method of revising the exercise.

6. Show how you will prepare pupils to correct the error of sentence-tructure in "This great and good man died on September 17th, leaving behind him the memory of many noble actions and a numerous family, of whom three were sons."

(d) *Elementary Science.*

1. Make a lesson plan for Standard IV. pupils on the dissemination of seeds. Show how the lesson illustrates the leading aims in nature study.

2. Outline a lesson plan on the hawk—the adaptation of its structure to its mode of life. Make illustrative drawings to accompany the lesson.

3. Give notes of a lesson on the composition of soils, or on the drainage of soils, to pupils in Standard III.

4. How will you lead pupils to account for the difference in modes of cultivating soils for beets and for oats ?

5. Give notes of a lesson on how to disinfect a room in which a patient has had measles, or on how to recover a person apparently drowned.

6. Give notes of a lesson to boys on smoking cigarettes.

7. Mention precautions that a teacher should take to preserve the eyesight of his pupils.

(e.) *Geography and History.*

1. What are the respective uses of the ordinary map, relief map, and globe in teaching geography ?

2. Outline a lesson plan for any two of the following : Cape, uses of mountains, formation of rivers, climate as affected by prevailing winds and rainfall.

3. Make notes for a lesson on any one of the following : The mining districts in the North-West Territories, the exports of British Columbia, the commercial centres of the Dominion with their trade routes, the drainage of Asia, the products of the Argentine Republic.

4. Give two illustrations of how the geography of a country has affected its history.

5. Make a lesson plan for teaching the life of Champlain, Lyon McKenzie, Sir John Macdonald, Cardinal Wolsey, or Nelson. Show that your plan illustrates one or more of the aims you have in view in teaching history.

6. Write notes of a lesson on any one of the following : Magna Charta, Quebec Act, Canadian Rebellion of 1837, Reciprocity Treaty, 1854. State the purposes of the lesson.

THE
SYSTEM OF EDUCATION
IN
THE PROVINCE OF BRITISH COLUMBIA.

INTRODUCTORY - - - - - - - - - 469

I.—CENTRAL ADMINISTRATION.

    (i.) Council of Public Instruction - - - - 472
    (ii.) Its Powers - - - - - - - - 472
    (iii.) Special Provisions - - - - - - 473
    (iv.) The Superintendent of Education - - - - 474

II.—LOCAL ADMINISTRATION - - - - - - 475

    (a.) Rural School Districts - - - - - - 475

        (i.) Annual School Meeting - - - - 475
        (ii.) Challenge of Voter - - - - - 476
        (iii.) Order of Business - - - - - 477
        (iv.) Special Meetings - - - - - 477
        (v.) Report of Trustees - - - - - 478

    (b.) City School Districts - - - - - 479

        (i.) Qualification of Voters - - - - 479
        (ii.) Meetings of Trustees - - - - 480
        (iii.) Their Powers and Duties - - - 480
        (iv.) Statement of Accounts - - - - 482
        (v.) High Schools and Collegiate Institutes - - 482
        (vi.) Annual Reports - - - - - 483
        (vii.) *Per capita* Grants - - - - 483
        (viii.) Non-sectarian Principles - - - 483

III.—REGULATIONS AS TO COMPULSORY ATTENDANCE.

    (i.) Fines - - - - - - - - 484
    (ii.) Exemptions - - - - - - - 484
    (iii.) Reasonable Excuses - - - - - 484

IV.—TEACHERS.

    (i.) Grades of Certificate - - - - - 485
    (ii.) Temporary Certificate - - - - - 485
    (iii.) Terms of Validity - - - - - - 485
    (iv.) Exemption from Non-Professional Examination - 486
    (v.) Moral Character - - - - - - 486
    (vi.) Form of Candidate's Notification - - - 486
    (vii.) Annual Renewal - - - - - - 486
    (viii.) Certificate Statistics for 1898 - - - 486
    (ix.) Rights conferred by Certificates - - - 487
    (x.) Statistics of Permanent Staff, 1897–8 - - 487
    (xi.) Statistics of Permanent Staff, 1894–5 - - 488
    (xii.) Average Salaries - - - - - 488
    (xiii.) Duties of Public School Teachers - - - 489
    (xiv.) Notices of Appointment, Dismissal, &c. - - 490
    (xv.) Teacher's Appeal against Dismissal - - 490

V.—TRAINING OF TEACHERS

    (i.) From the Report for 1893–4 - - - - 490
    (ii.) From the Report for 1896 - - - - 491
    (iii.) Necessity of a Normal School - - - 491

VI. —TRUANCY : PUNISHMENTS.

    (i.) Expulsion and Suspension - - - - - 492
    (ii.) Corporal Punishment - - - - - - 492
    (iii.) Moral Suasion - - - - - - 493

VII.—LEGAL PENALTIES.

    (i.) Voter's False Declaration - - - - 493
    (ii.) Disturbance of School Meeting - - - - 493

VIII.—SCHOOL PROPERTY.

    (i.) Trustees' Responsibility - - - - 493
    (ii.) Misuse of School Buildings - - - - 493
    (iii.) Teacher's Responsibility - - - - 494

IX —INSPECTION.

    (i.) Inspector's Report - - - - - 494
    (ii.) Need of a third Inspector (1896) - - - - 494

X. -HIGH SCHOOLS.

    (i.) Nanaimo High School - - - - - 495
    (ii.) New Westminster High School - - - 495
    (iii.) Vancouver High School - - - - 496
    (iv.) Victoria High School - - - - 496
    (v.) Diploma of Standing - - - - 496
    (vi.) Subjects for Entrance Examination - - 497
    (vii) Paper on Agriculture - - - - 497
    (viii.) Conditions of Creation of High Schools - 497
    (ix.) Teachers as Pupils in High Schools - - 497
    (x.) Percentage of Marks Required - - 497
    (xi.) Courses and Classes - - - - 498
    (xii.) Promotion from Graded to High School - 498
    (xiii.) From the Report for 1895–6 - - - 498
    (xiv.) "Board of Governors of Vancouver College" - 499

XI. —GRADED SCHOOLS.

    (i.) Size of Divisions - - - - - 499
    (ii.) Optional Subjects - - - - - 499
    (iii.) "Limit Table" - - - - - 499
    (iv.) Semi-annual Examination - - - - 499
    (v.) Suggestions from Circular of 1895 - - 500

XII.—COMMON SCHOOLS.

    (i.) Optional Subjects - - - - - 500
    (ii.) The Lord's Prayer - - - - - 500

XIII.— GENERAL REMARKS. STATISTICS OF EDUCATIONAL PROGRESS.

    (i.) Statistics for 1897–9 - - - - 501
    (ii.) Cost per pupil, 1888- 98 - - - - 502
    (iii.) Attendance, 1897–8 - - - - 503
    (iv.) Attendance and Expenditure, 1890–9 - - 503
    (v.) Attendance, 1894–5 - - - - 503
    (vi.) Progress in Attendance, 1894–7 - - 504
    (vii.) Teachers' Aims - - - - 504
    (viii.) Classification of Schools - - - 505

APPENDICES.

A. Subjects of Examination for Certificates, and con-
    ditions of Obtaining them - - - - 506
B. Courses of Study :
    (i.) High Schools - - - - - 510
    (ii.) Graded and Common Schools - - 511
    (iii.) Optional Subjects - - - - 513
    (iv.) Agriculture - - - - - 513

THE SYSTEM OF EDUCATION IN THE PROVINCE OF BRITISH COLUMBIA.

Compiled from the " Manual of School Law," the Superintendent's Annual " Public Schools Reports" from 1893 to 1898, and official statistics for 1899.

INTRODUCTORY.

THE portion of the Province of British Columbia that was earliest connected directly with the Crown was Vancouver Island, which was "discovered" in 1762, and leased to the Hudson Bay Company in 1843. It became a Crown Colony in 1849. British Columbia, that is to say the territory between the Rocky Mountains and the Pacific Coast, bounded on the north by the 60th parallel, and on the south by what was until recently the United States territory of Washington and is now Washington State, was constituted a Crown Colony some ten years later than Vancouver Island, in 1858. A large immigration into this territory had then just taken place, owing to the recent discovery of gold. In 1866 the Crown Colonies of British Columbia and Vancouver Island were united, and in July 1871 British Columbia entered the Canadian Confederation. The Province is now represented in the Dominion Parliament by three members in the Senate and six members in the House of Commons.

The Provincial Government is administered by a Lieutenant-Governor, appointed by the Governor-General of the Dominion, and holding office during his pleasure, though not removable within five years of appointment. There is also a Legislative Assembly for the Province, consisting of thirty-three members. The Assembly is elected for four years by what is practically a manhood suffrage.

The average breadth of the country on the mainland from the Rocky Mountains to the Pacific Coast is about 450 miles and the length of coast-line is 550 miles. The total area of the Province, including Vancouver and Queen Charlotte Islands, is about 383,000 square miles. The population in 1891 was estimated at 98,173, but it has probably increased of late years at a higher rate than it did previous to 1891. The population was estimated at 36,240 in 1871, and at 49,450 in 1881. It may, therefore, be conjectured that the population is by this time (1900) about 140,000. Of these it may be reckoned that quite 25,000 are Indians and about 7,000 Chinese, thus leaving the European population at rather over 100,000.

There is naturally much diversity of climate within the Province, a factor that should be taken into account in any estimate of the educational conditions prevailing within its borders. Only in the North-East is there any considerable tract of land on the eastern slope of the Rockies, so that, speaking generally, the climate of the coast-line west of the Cascade Range is that of what is known as the Pacific Slope, common to the States of Oregon and Washington in the Union, although it is naturally milder there than in British Columbia. The trade of the Province has developed rapidly. The coal-mining industry centres in Nanaimo, a city of about 10,000 inhabitants, in Vancouver Island. There is also, of course, a great wealth of gold, and within the last five years in the Kootenay District, the South-Eastern corner of the Province very rich deposits have been found. The lumber trade is very large.

The educational system of British Columbia dates from 1872, the year after its incorporation in the Canadian Confederation. The main provisions of this Act remain in force to this day, although many amendments of detail have been made from time to time. Education, by the Act of 1872, took the character known as the free common-school type. The main outlines of the system will be sketched below. In the meantime some kind of summary and estimate may be attempted.

Perhaps the most distinctive part of the system is the distinction, a very important and real distinction, between the Local Authorities of Cities and Rural Districts. This distinction will not be found in the system of the North-West Territories described in this volume. It is due, one may suppose, to the great importance from the earliest times of the Province of the cities of Vancouver and Victoria. These, together with New Westminster, near Victoria, and Nanaimo, near Vancouver, are the only cities that have the distinctive organisation of the " City School District."

As will be seen below, the control exercised by the voters over the management of the common schools of any School District is intimate if indirect. Their approval or disapproval of the general conduct of the affairs of the school or schools in their District is expressed once a year at the Annual School Meeting, when a new Trustee is elected to serve on the Board of Trustees. This is equally true of the City and of the Rural School Districts.

Schools are maintained chiefly by legislative grants. In the four City School Districts the legislative grant, a *per capita* grant of $10 based on the average daily attendance of pupils, is supplemented by an apportionment from the Treasury of the Municipal Corporation. The Board of Trustees of any School District have power to raise money by Debenture.

Teachers are paid directly by the Government on a uniform scale proportionate to the grade or class of certificate obtained and the length of service as teacher. The statistics in regard to teachers on the permanent staff for 1897–8 show a considerable preponderance of women over men in City School Districts, and a narrow majority in Rural School Districts.

The Province is especially rich in its High Schools, of which there are four ; and local experts feel that the principal defect of its educational system is its lack of a Normal School, and indeed of any attempt at the professional training of teachers, if we except the voluntary effort of teachers that takes the form of the Teachers' Institutes. Full details in regard to the High Schools will be given below, and some remarks in regard to the need of a Normal School will be quoted from successive Annual Reports.

There is no University in the Province, but this defect (which, one may suppose, has only recently been felt) will probably be remedied before long. In the meanwhile a most interesting experiment has been made, by which any High School may become a "Collegiate Institute" and enter into an affiliation with some Canadian University. This has already been done in the case of the High School at Vancouver, now the "Vancouver College." It depends upon the Board of Trustees of any School District in which a High School is situated, whether or no they shall constitute themselves as (for the purpose of management of the High School) a "Collegiate Institute Board."

Certain Crown lands are set apart in a large number of the School Districts as School Reserves. These have been conveyed to the corporations of certain cities in trust for school purposes.

British Columbia contrasts favourably with its neighbour, the North-West Territories, in the matter of High Schools, there being only a device in the Territories by which the sixth, seventh, and eighth standards of common schools are called "High School Standards," and have a special curriculum taught by specially qualified teachers. But the North-West Territories have a Normal School at Regina, and it is in this respect that British Columbia is behindhand.

Since 1897 candidates for teachers' certificates of all grades, and applicants for admission to High Schools, have been required to take an examination in agriculture. Among other optional or "specific" subjects, "Temperance," as distinct from Hygiene and Physiology, can be made a compulsory part of the school curriculum by any Board of Trustees that so chooses. Physiology, Hygiene, and Agriculture are compulsory subjects in all graded and common schools, but there seems to be no special provision for the teaching of domestic economy ; nor do manual or "hand and eye" training, drill, and physical exercises play, as yet, an important *rôle* in the common school education.

It will be observed that in what follows no mention is made of any existing Normal School or of a University or of Technical and Industrial Schools, all of which would be generally regarded as necessary and desirable features of a public system of education. A perusal of the official documents shows that these important questions have already begun to engage the anxious attention of the educational authorities of the Province.

The report for the school year 1895–6 contains certain comparisons between the then state of educational progress and the conditions of the year 1872, when the "Public School Act" first came into force.

During these twenty-five years the number of schools had increased to nine times, and the number of enrolment to nearly fourteen times the corresponding figures for 1872 :—

1872.	25 schools	-	1,028 pupils enrolled.
1882.	50 „	-	2,653 „ „
1892.	154 „	-	10,773 „ „
1896.	233 „	over 14,000 „ „

[In 1899 there were 280 schools and 17,648 pupils enrolled.]

During nearly twenty-five years, from April 11, 1872, to December, 1896, the total expenditure from the Provincial Treasury for " education proper " was $2,146,114; the expenditure by the Lands and Works Department for construction of school-houses, furniture, repairs, etc., was $402,479, making the total outlay for all purposes of education $2,548,593. It is obvious that the Public School system at once took root in the Province, supplied existing needs from the first, raised the standard of educational requirement, and, generally, kept pace with the growth and development of the Province, whether in population, wealth, or importance.

I.—CENTRAL ADMINISTRATION.

Council of Public Instruction.   *Central Authority.*—(i.) The members of the Executive Council of the Province of British Columbia constitute, by the law of 1891, a " *Council of Public Instruction.*"

It is, however, the Lieutenant-Governor in Council who appoints the Superintendent of Education for the Province. It is not stated in the " Manual of School Law " for what period the Superintendent, thus appointed, holds office, from which it may perhaps be concluded that he holds office at the pleasure of the Lieutenant-Governor, as modified by the relations existing between the Council of Public Instruction (*i.e.*, the Executive Council) and the Superintendent, who is their Secretary.

Its Powers.   (ii.) The powers of the Council of Public Instruction may be summarised as follows :—

(1) To create school districts (see below), in addition to those already existing, and to define the boundaries thereof, and from time to time to alter the boundaries of existing school districts.

(2) To set apart in each school district such a quantity of the waste lands of the Crown as, in their opinion, may be necessary for school purposes in that district.

(3) To grant, on the application of the school trustees of any school district, such sum of money as may be required to pay the salary of the teacher in that district; and in rural school districts to defray the cost of erecting a school-house, or providing a house or room in which the public school of the district may be held, as also the cost of all furniture and apparatus necessary for the use of any such school, and the current expenses connected with it.

(4) To grant such sum as shall be thought proper in aid of the establishment of a school in any part of the Province, not being a school district. (For restrictions see below).

(5) To appoint two or more Examiners, who, together with the Superintendent of Education, shall constitute a Board of Examiners, and shall examine teachers and grant certificates of qualification.

(6) To appoint one or more Inspectors to visit the public schools, and to require such Inspectors to enquire and report to the Superintendent of Education the result of their enquiries, into the progress and attendance of pupils, the discipline and management of the school, the system of education pursued, the mode of keeping the school registers, the condition of the buildings and premises, and such other matters as they may deem advisable in the furtherance of the interests of the schools.

(7) To make rules and regulations for the conduct of the public schools, to prescribe the duties of teachers, and to determine their classification.

(8) To determine the subjects and percentages of marks in the subjects required for all classes and grades of certificates of teachers, as well as to make and prescribe rules for the governance of candidates for certificates of qualification as teachers (*i.e.* without examination).

(9) To select and prescribe a uniform series of text-books to be used in the public schools of the Province, as well as the courses and standards of instruction and study for schools.

(10) To suspend or cancel for cause the certificate of qualification of any teacher.

(11) To establish a High School in any district where it may be expedient to do so. In such schools the higher branches of instruction are to be taught; and every such High School shall be under the control of the Local Board of Trustees of the district. It is provided, however, that no High School shall be established in any school district in which there are less than twenty persons duly qualified and available to be admitted as High School pupils.

(12) To determine all cases of appeal arising from decisions of trustees.

(13) To make any other necessary provisions that are not inconsistent with the powers above detailed.

(14) To establish a Normal School, with model departments, and to make regulations for its conduct and management.

(iii.) Of these fourteen defined powers, three are subject to the Special approval and sanction of the Lieutenant-Governor in Council, Provisions. viz., (3), (4), and (10). Grants for teachers' salaries in any school district, and for the erection and proper maintenance of schoolhouses in rural school districts, grants in aid of the establishment of new schools outside school districts, and the cancellation of teachers' certificates are thus made subject to the approval of the Lieutenant-Governor.   Besides these restrictions there are other more detailed provisions.

A special proviso is made restricting the power of the Council of Public Instruction to create new school districts.   No district can be formed in which there are not at least fifteen children of school age, *i.e.*, between six and sixteen years of age.   (See above.)

Similarly the Council's power to grant sums in aid of the establishment of a school outside existing school districts is restricted to localities in which there are not less than seven nor more than fourteen children of school age.   And such grants in aid can only be given upon the application of a majority of the parents resident in that part of the Province.   (See above.)

Superintendent of Education.

(iv.) The duties of the *Superintendent of Education* are as follows :—

(1) To take charge of and safely keep all apparatus that may be procured for school purposes, and to furnish, at his discretion, on the application of the trustees of any district, such apparatus as may be required for the schools in such district.

(2) To establish a separate school for girls in any district where he may deem it expedient to do so ; and the school, when so established, may be presided over by a female teacher or teachers, but otherwise shall be subject to the same obligations and regulations as ordinary public schools.

(3) To examine and enquire into, from time to time, the progress of the pupils in learning, the order and discipline observed, the system of instruction pursued, the mode of keeping the school registers, the average attendance of pupils, the character and condition of the buildings and premises, and to give such directions as he may judge proper.

(4) To do all in his power to persuade and animate parents, guardians, trustees, and teachers to improve the character and efficiency of the public schools, and to secure the sound education of the young generally.

(5) To have, subject to the Council of Public Instruction, the supervision and direction of the inspectors and schools.

(6) To enforce the regulations and decisions of the Council.

(7) To organise Teachers' Institutes under the Council's regulations.

(8) To grant temporary certificates of qualification, countersigned by the Provincial Secretary, which temporary certificates shall be valid only till the next examination of teachers.

(9) To make annually, for the information of the Legislature, a report of the actual state of the public schools throughout the Province, showing the number of pupils taught in each school district, the branches taught, the average attendance, the amount expended by each school, the number of official visits made to each school, the salaries of teachers, the number, standing, and

sex of qualified teachers, together with any other information that he may possess respecting the educational state and wants and advantages of each school and school district in the Province, and such statements and suggestions for improving the school laws or the public schools or for promoting education generally as he may deem useful.

(10) To be responsible for all moneys paid through him on behalf of the public schools.

(11) To prepare suitable forms and give such instructions as he may judge necessary for the making of reports, &c.

(12) To investigate complaints made to him in regard to the mode of conducting any election of trustees and to report to the Council upon such complaint.

(13) To close schools when the average attendance falls below ten children.

(14) To cause copies of the Council's regulations to be published and furnished free of charge to trustees and teachers.

II.—LOCAL ADMINISTRATION.

(*a*) *Rural School Districts.* (*b*) *City School Districts.*

The School Districts of the Province are divided by the "Public School Act" into City Districts and Rural Districts, the former including the schools established within the municipal boundaries of each of the four cities of Victoria, Vancouver, New Westminster, and Nanaimo, the latter embracing all other Public Schools maintained. In each of the City Districts there are one High School, two or more Graded Schools, and one or more Ward Schools, while in the Rural Districts there are only Graded Schools and Common Schools.

The cost of education in a City District is met by the City Council, the Provincial Government paying a *per capita* grant of ten dollars per head per annum, based on the average actual daily attendance of the pupils. In addition to this grant, each municipal corporation receives the amount collected from its Provincial Revenue Tax.[1]

(*a*) *Rural School Districts.*—(i.) For each of these there must be three Trustees. An annual meeting for the election of School Trustees is held in all Rural School Districts, when the voters present elect one of their number to preside over the meeting, and to use, if necessary, a casting vote. Votes are recorded by poll, *Annual School Meeting.*

---

[1] The amount of *per capita* grant paid to each of the four cities in the school year 1894-5 was as follows :—

Victoria -	-	-	-	-	-	-	$17,390.80
Vancouver	-	-	-	-	-	-	15,895.25
New Westminster -	-	-	-	-	-	5,989.20
Nanaimo	-	-	-	-	-	-	6,129.55

Total	**$45,404.80**

and the names of all voters present are recorded. Trustees elected by this method at the *first annual school meeting* in any district hold office as follows :—

(1) The person receiving the largest number of votes continues in office until two years have passed since the next, or second, annual school meeting ; (2) the person receiving the next largest number of votes continues in office until one year has elapsed after the next, or second, annual school meeting; and (3) the person receiving the smallest number of votes of the three elected Trustees holds office until the next annual school meeting. In no case can any person resign his office as Trustee until his successor has been appointed.

Immediately after the formation of any *new School District*, the Superintendent of Education prepares notices in writing, describing the district, and appoints a time and place for the election of Trustees as above described. A correct copy of the proceedings of the first, and of every annual, and every special school district meeting must be sent to the Superintendent of Education, signed by the Chairman and Secretary of the meeting, and countersigned by the Secretary of the Board of Trustees.

Trustees serve without emolument or reward, and must not be interested, directly or indirectly, in any contract authorised by the Board of Trustees. But this regulation does not, of course, apply to the Secretary of the Board of Trustees, who is always one of their number, and whose salary is fixed by his colleagues previous to his selection.

One trustee is elected to office at each ensuing annual school meeting, in place of any trustee whose term of office is about to expire; and the same individual, if willing, may be re-elected ; but no school trustee can be re-elected, except by his own consent, during the four years next after his going out of office.

Any householder or freeholder resident in any school district for a period of six months previous to the election, provided he be twenty-one years of age, or the wife of such a householder or freeholder, is entitled to vote at any school meeting of the district as well as for the election of trustees. Chinese and Indians have no votes.

Challenge of Voter. (ii.) Any legal voter may challenge as unqualified to vote any person who offers to vote at an annual or other school meeting. The chairman of the meeting shall then require the person so challenged to make the following declaration :—

" I do declare and affirm that I am a resident householder (*or* freeholder, *as the case may be*) in this school district, and that I have been continuously a resident householder in this district for the last six months."

Or, in the case of a wife, a corresponding declaration in regard to the length of residence and household of her husband.

Every person who makes such a declaration shall be permitted to vote on all questions proposed at the school meeting; but, if any person refuse to make the declaration, his or her vote shall not be accepted.

No trustee may hold the office of teacher within the district of which he is a trustee ; and no clergyman of any denomination is eligible for the position of Superintendent of Education, inspector, trustee, or teacher. Any trustee who, during his trusteeship, is convicted of any criminal offence, or who becomes insane, or ceases to be an actual resident within the school district of which he is a trustee, shall, *ipso facto*, forfeit and vacate his seat, and the remaining trustee or trustees shall declare his seat vacant, and forthwith call a special meeting for the election of his successor (1894).

In rural school districts the notice calling an annual or special meeting may be signed by the Secretary to the Board by the direction of the trustees, or by a majority of the trustees themselves.

(iii.) The following is the order of business at all annual meetings of school districts :— Order of business.

(1). Calling the meeting to order.

(2). Election of chairman and secretary.

(3). Reading trustees' annual report, including statement of receipts and expenditure.

(4). Receiving and deciding upon trustees' report.

(5). Election of trustee to fill the vacancy at the end of the past year.

(6). Election of trustee to fill any other vacancy

(7). Any other business of which due notice has been given.

The voters present determine whether the poll shall be open or by ballot.

All protests against an election or other proceedings of a school meeting must be sent to the Superintendent of Education.

A motion to reconsider a vote may be made by any voter, but no vote of reconsideration may be taken more than once at the same meeting.

At the close of the proceedings of every school meeting, the chairman and the secretary should sign the Minutes, as entered by the Secretary in the Minute-book ; and the Secretary of the Board of Trustees must forthwith transmit to the Superintendent of Education a correct copy thereof, signed by himself.

(Rural School Districts). In every school district, any person being a householder in the school district, and being a British subject of the full age of twenty-one years, and otherwise qualified to vote at an election of trustees in the said school district, shall be eligible to be elected and to serve as a school trustee (1896). Any trustee elected to fill an occasional vacancy shall hold office only for the unexpired term of the person in whose place he is elected.

(iv.) Trustees may, after due notice, call a special school meeting for any special purpose they may think proper. But in cases where, from want of proper notice or other cause, any annual school meeting or special school meeting is not held at the Special Meetings.

proper time, any five voters in the district may call a meeting at ten days' notice within twenty days of the time at which such a meeting should properly have been held. The meeting thus called possesses all the powers and performs all the duties of the meeting in place of which it is called.

Any person chosen as trustee may resign, by giving written notice of his intention to his colleagues.

Every Board of Trustees appoints one of its number to be Secretary and Treasurer to the Corporation which it constitutes. These officers must give the security required by a majority of the trustees, for the correct and safe keeping of the papers and moneys of the Corporation. Their salary is paid by the Board, and is agreed upon before their selection for office. They are required to keep a correct record of their proceedings in a book procured for the purpose. They also receive and must account for all school moneys which come into their hands, and for disbursing the same as directed by a majority of the trustees.

The Board of Trustees meets once in every three months.

The trustees take possession and have the safe custody of all public school property which has been acquired or given for public school purposes in their district. They have power to acquire, and hold as a corporation by any title any land, moveable property, or income for school purposes, and to apply these according to the terms upon which they were acquired or received. With the approval of the Council of Public Instruction they may do whatever they judge expedient with regard to the building, repairing, renting, warming, furnishing, and maintaining the district school-houses, and the appendages belonging to the schoolhouses, as well as the school lands and enclosures held by them. They are required to visit each school under their charge at least three times a year, and to see that it is conducted according to the regulations. They must see that the pupils in their schools are duly provided with the authorised text-books, and use no unauthorised text-books.

Report of Trustees.

(v.) Every year at the annual meeting of the Rural School District the trustees, must read their annual school report for the year just terminated. The report must include, among other things, a full and detailed account of the receipt and expenditure of all school moneys received and expended on behalf of the district for any purpose during the past year.

The trustees must prepare and transmit annually to the Superintendent of Education before July 15, a report signed by a majority of their number. The report shall specify :

(1.) The whole time during which the school or schools in their district were kept by a qualified teacher during the year just ended (June 30);

(2) The amount of money raised for the school district, and the manner in which it has been expended ;

(3) The whole number of children residing in the school district : (*a*) who are under the age of six years; (*b*) who are between six and sixteen years old; and also the number of

children taught in the schools of the district, with a separate return for each school, and distinguishing the sexes, and the average attendance of pupils during the year

(4) The branches of education taught in the school, the number of pupils in each branch, the number of visits made by each trustee, the number of public school examinations, visits, and lectures, and such other information as may be required :

(5) The uses to which the school buildings and lands have been applied during the year, and the damage arising or the revenue derived from them.

The trustees select the site on which a school-house in a rural district is to be erected by the trustees. They shall then immediately call a special school meeting of the voters to approve the selection made. But (1) if a majority of the voters present do not ratify their selection of a site, this majority shall at the same meeting decide upon a suitable site, and this decision shall finally decide the matter, subject always to the approval of the Council of Public Instruction. (2) In case the voters of a school district neglect or refuse to select a site which meets with the approval of the Council of Public Instruction, the Superintendent of Education, or any person appointed by him, shall visit the school district and, after careful inspection, shall select a site: and such selection, subject to the approval of the Council of Public Instruction, shall finally decide the matter (1896).

(*b.*) *City School Districts.*—For each of the school districts of the City of Victoria, the City of Vancouver, the City of New Westminster, and the City of Nanaimo, there are seven trustees constituting the Board of Trustees for each city respectively. Every such Board, in cities as in rural districts, is a " body corporate."

(i.) The Board for each city school district is elected by voters Qualification duly qualified to vote for a mayor (see " Municipal Act " of the of Voters Province of British Columbia, § 36); and when preparing the annual voters' list in cities where the " Municipal Elections Act " does not govern the election of mayor, a list of the names of those entitled to vote for school trustees, but not included in the city annual voters' list as entitled to vote for mayor, shall be added thereto (1897).

No person liable to pay the Revenue Tax shall be permitted to vote until he has paid the tax for the current year.

At the first election each voter shall be entitled to six votes for members of the Board of Trustees, and at each subsequent election to as many votes as there are trustees to be elected No person may give more than one vote for any one candidate. The nomination and election of the Board of Trustees shall be held at the same time, and by the same Returning Officer, and shall be conducted in the same manner as the municipal nomination and election for mayor would be conducted ; and all the regulations and their amendments (respecting the times for opening and closing the poll, the mode of voting, corrupt or improper practices, vacancies, and declarations of challenged voters) shall hold good also for the election of the Board of School Trustees.

At the first election, the three candidates receiving the highest number of votes shall be declared elected to serve for two years, and the three candidates receiving the next highest number of votes shall serve for one year. At each subsequent annual election three trustees shall be elected to serve for two years. But any election to fill a vacancy may be held concurrently with the annual election. All trustees remain in office and exercise all the powers of trustees until their successors have been elected. The election to fill a vacancy is conducted in the same manner and is subject to the same provisions as an annual election; the Public School Board names a returning officer to act at such an election, and six days' notice of the nominations must be given.

Any person, being a British subject of the full age of twenty-one years, who is a resident householder or a resident freeholder in a school district, and who is otherwise qualified to vote at an election of School trustees in the said school district, and the wife of such householder or freeholder, shall be eligible to be elected and to serve as school trustee; provided always, that the wife of an acting school trustee shall not be eligible for election (1896).

Meetings of Trustees. (ii.) The Board of Trustees meets at least once in each month, and four members constitute a quorum (contrast similar regulation in regard to rural school districts).

The Board of Trustees at its first meeting after the annual election appoints one of its number to be Chairman of the Board, and the member so appointed presides at all meetings of the Board. He has a casting vote in case of an equality of votes between the other members of the Board upon any question, but shall not otherwise vote as a member of the Board.

Each Board of Trustees appoints its own Secretary and fixes his salary. The Secretary must keep a record of the proceedings of the Board, and perform such other duties as the Board may prescribe in relation to its corporate affairs. This record, as well as all books, accounts, vouchers, and papers of the Board are at all times subject to the inspection of the Council of Public Instruction, and any Committee of the City Council appointed by resolution for that purpose.

The salaries of the teachers employed in the public schools of the cities of Victoria, Vancouver, New Westminster, and Nanaimo shall be fixed and paid at the discretion of the school trustees of the said cities; and such salaries and all other expenses for the purchase or lease of school sites, erection, enlargement, or rent of school buildings, for furniture and repairs, and all other incidental expenses incurred by the Board of Trustees, shall be borne and paid by the Municipal Corporations of the said cities.

Their Powers and Duties. (iii.) The Board of Trustees is required to provide school accommodation and tuition, free of charge and sufficient for all children in the district between six and sixteen years of age, inclusive, and for this purpose shall organise and establish such and so many schools as it shall deem requisite, with powers to alter or discontinue the same, to purchase or lease lands or buildings for school purposes, to erect, enlarge, alter, repair, and improve school buildings and their appurtenances, to furnish school-houses and procure maps and apparatus, and to provide text-books for indigent pupils, fuel, and light. They shall also defray the contingent expenses of the several schools and of the Board of Trustees, and shall have the custody of the school property of the district. They may insure school buildings and furniture, must determine the sites of school-houses, and appoint the number of teachers for whose salaries provision has been made in the estimates, appoint, dismiss, and fix the salaries, wages, or remuneration of such other officers or employés as may, from time to time, be deemed necessary by the Board to secure the efficient management of the schools. They must report annually to the City Council upon the expenditure of the moneys received by the Board, and furnish annually, on or before July 15 of each year, to the Superintendent of Education, a full report of their proceedings, together with returns of all schools in accordance with the forms supplied by him.

The Board of Trustees must, further, prepare and lay before the City Council a detailed estimate of the sums required by the Board for the current year's ordinary expenses of maintaining the schools as they exist at the time of the making of the estimate. These sums are paid over, from time to time, as required by the City Treasurer to the several persons or cor-porations for whose use such moneys are payable. The Board shall further prepare the like detailed estimate of the sums required to meet any special or extraordinary expenses legally incurrible by the Board, and this last-mentioned estimate shall be subject to the consideration, alteration, and final approval of the Council. If the City Council finally rejects any such sum or sums, it shall be the duty of the Council, not more than thirty days after the receipt by the mayor of the written request of the Secretary of the Board in that behalf, to submit for the assent of the electors, a by-law authorising the proposed expenditure, and, if necessary, the raising of the moneys required to defray the same upon the credit of the municipality. In the event of such a by-law receiving the assent of the electors, the City Treasurer shall pay out of the proceeds of the debentures so issued all expenses connected with the issue of the loan, and the balance shall be paid out in the manner hereinbefore provided.

The City Treasurer shall, upon the receipt of any moneys from time to time paid into his hands on account of the rates and taxes, set apart and keep in a separate account so much and such proportion of the moneys as will cover the amount ordered to be levied and assessed for school purposes. The money so set apart shall be paid over to the Board by the City Treasurer, who shall exhibit to the Board the state of the account whenever so requested. The money so set apart shall not be applied to any other purpose whatsoever by the City Treasurer. It shall not be lawful for the Board of School Trustees to incur any liability beyond the amount shown to be at their disposal by this account.

No property acquired by a Board of Trustees, whether in city or country, shall be subject to taxation or be liable to be taken in execution; but in case of any judgment being recorded against the Board of Trustees, they shall forthwith notify the City Council in the City School Districts of the amount thereof, and the City Council shall levy the same.

The City Council annually appoints an Auditor to audit the accounts of the Board of Trustees, and the expense of this audit is paid out of the contingent expenses of the Board.

Statement of Accounts. (iv.) The Board of Trustees in every City School District shall cause to be published annually in January, in at least three issues of some newspaper circulating in the district, a detailed and audited statement of all receipts and expenditures for the year ending the 1st December. This statement must be signed by the Chairman and Secretary of the Board, and countersigned by the Auditor appointed in that behalf by the City Council.

High Schools and Collegiate Institutes. (v.) The Board of Trustees of any City School District may, by resolution, declare that it is desirable that tuition fees should be paid in respect of pupils attending at any High School situate within its limits, so as to make such High School more or less self-supporting. It shall then be the duty of the Board to settle the amount to be paid by parents and guardians for each pupil attending the High School, and to fix the time of payment, and, when necessary, to sue for and recover such amounts, in the name of the City Treasurer, who shall receive and apply the same to school purposes. But in settling such amount the Board shall make provision by which pupils, whose parents or guardians find it beyond their means to pay the tuition fees imposed by the Board, may have the advantages of the High School, either altogether without fee, or at some smaller fee within the means of the parent or guardian in each case.

The Board of Trustees of each School District wherein a High School or Collegiate Institute is situated shall, for the purposes of the control and of the management of the affairs of such High School or Collegiate Institute, be a body corporate and politic, under the name of "the Collegiate Institute Board" (1894).

It shall be lawful for any Collegiate Institute Board to enter into affiliation with any one or more of the following Canadian Universities, viz.:—The University of Toronto; the University of Queen's College, Kingston; the University of McGill College, Montreal; the University of New Brunswick; Fredericton or Dalhousie University, Halifax; which may by its charter and regulations be authorised to admit such Board into affiliation, and for the purpose of carrying out any agreement for affiliation there is hereby conferred upon each Collegiate Institute Board all necessary powers and authorities (1894).

" Whereas it is in the interest of advanced education to enable the High Schools of the Province to become affiliated with one or other of the Canadian or foreign universities: and whereas the charters and constitutions of certain of the said universities only

to be admitted into affiliation schools managed by an
porated Board of Governors: Therefore be it enacted as
ws, etc." An Act then follows empowering the Lieutenant-
rnor to grant, by Letters Patent charters of incorporation to
of the Boards of School Trustees of the cities of Victoria,
couver, New Westminster, or Nanaimo, who shall petition
for constituting the Board, and their duly elected successors,
dy corporate and politic under the name and style of 'The
of Governors of the . . . . . . College.'" The Letters
t is to specify the powers, rights, and immunities of the
hus constituted (1896). (See below, Section x. (xiv.).)
on failure of the Corporations of the cities of Victoria,
uver, New Westminster, or Nanaimo, or of the school
s in these cities to comply with and carry out the
ions, the lands formerly set apart as school reserves or
d by the Crown for school purposes, and conveyed in
the Corporations of those cities in trust for school
and as school sites, revert to the Crown.

he reports from school districts required by the Educa- Annual
e are:— Reports.

port of Annual School Meetings.

stees' Annual Report.

nal Report of Teachers, certified by the Secretary of
e Board of Trustees.

orts must be received at the Education Office before
the incidental expenses of schools in rural school
be certified.

cial regulation controls the grants to be given by Per capita
to cities. A *per capita* grant of ten dollars per grants.
num, based on the average actual daily attendance
School pupils, may be paid quarterly by the
nance, out of the Consolidated Revenue Fund of
to the Municipal Corporations of the cities of
uver, New Westminster, and Nanaimo; provided
schools are conducted in accordance with the
the Council of Public Instruction. And the
daily attendance must be calculated upon the
e half-year preceding the payment.

ic schools must be conducted on strictly secular Non-secta-
principles. The highest morality is to be in- rian
religious dogma or creed may be taught. The principles.
be used in opening or closing the school.

and school lands in rural districts are under
Lands and Works Department; but no public
y be alienated without the consent of the
ool District in which the reserve is situated.

Governor in Council may convey from time
l lands within a municipality, or portions
ration of the municipality in trust for school

purposes and the conducting of Public Schools in accordance with the regulations. But this power is subject to further trusts, conditions, and restrictions that may from time to time be determined by Order in Council.

The officer in charge of the treasury for the time being is required to set apart out of the general revenue of the Province, in each year, the sum that is voted by the Legislative Assembly for public school purposes and this sum is called the "Public School Fund."

III.—Regulations as to Compulsory Attendance.

Fines. (i.) Every child from the age of seven to twelve, inclusive, must attend some school, or be otherwise educated for six months in every year; and any parent or guardian who does not provide that every such child under his care attends some school or is otherwise educated, is subject to certain penalties. The fine imposed must not exceed five dollars for the first wilful offence, nor ten dollars for each subsequent offence. All such fines and penalties may be sued for, recovered, and enforced, with costs, before any Police Magistrate, Stipendiary Magistrate, or Justice of the Peace having jurisdiction within the district in which the fine or penalty has been, or is alleged to have been, incurred. And if the fine or penalty and costs be not at once paid, it can be enforced, levied, and collected, with costs of distress and sale of goods and chattels of the offender, under the warrant of the convicting Justice. The Justice must then pay over to the Treasurer of the Board of Trustees of the district the sum so recovered. In default of such distress, the Justice shall, by his warrant, cause the offender to be imprisoned for any time not exceeding thirty days, unless the fine and costs, and the reasonable expenses of collecting them, be paid before the expiration of the term of imprisonment. Before the penalty can be inflicted the trustees of the public school or the Superintendent of Education, or any person authorised by them or by him, must have received notice that the parents or guardians of the child continue to neglect or violate the compulsory regulations. They are then required to communicate this notification, and to make complaint upon it, to a Magistrate or Justice of the Peace. Such a Magistrate or Justice must investigate and decide in a summary manner upon any such complaint made by the Trustees or by the Superintendent.

Exemptions. (ii.) There are, however, certain *exemptions* from these compulsory regulations. It is the duty of the Police Magistrate or Justice of the Peace to ascertain, as far as may be, the circumstances of any person complained of for not sending his child or children to school or otherwise educating him or her or them.

Reasonable excuses. (iii.) Any of the following may be accepted as *reasonable excuses :—*

(*a.*) That the child is under instruction in some other satisfactory manner ;

(*b.*) That the child has been prevented from attending school by sickness, or by any other unavoidable cause ;

(*c.*) That there is no public school open which the child can attend, within a distance not exceeding three miles, measured according to the nearest passable road from the residence of the child in question ;

(*d.*) That the child has reached a standard of education of the same, or of a greater, degree than that to be attained in the public school.

IV.—Teachers.

(i.) No person can be appointed or retained as a teacher in any public school unless he or she holds a First, Second, or Third Class Certificate or a Temporary Certificate of Qualification. Such temporary certificates are granted according to the following regulations :— *Grades of Certificate.*

(ii.) The Trustees, upon satisfying the Superintendent of Education of their inability to secure a person properly qualified (*i.e.,* holding a First, Second, or Third Class Certificate), and, at the same time, suitable for their school, may appoint as a temporary teacher the holder of a temporary certificate, which shall be valid until the next public examination of teachers has been held, but no longer. And no person to whom a temporary certificate has been issued, and who has neglected or failed to obtain at the next public examination a first, second, or third class certificate, is entitled to receive a second temporary certificate. But the holder of an expired first, second, or third class certificate may obtain a second temporary certificate upon satisfying the Superintendent of Education that he or she was prevented by illness or other satisfactory cause from attending at the public examination. *Temporary Certificate.*

(iii.) The terms during which certificates of the various grades hold good are as follows :— *Terms of Validity.*

(1.) Third Class, Grade B, valid for one year ;

(2.) Third Class, Grade A, valid for two years ;

(3.) Second Class, Grade B, valid for three years ;

(4.) Second Class, Grade A, valid for five years ;

(5.) First Class, Grade B, valid for life, or during good behaviour ;

(6.) First Class, Grade A, valid for life, or during good behaviour.

Every certificate of qualification obtained at any examination must be signed by the Superintendent of Education, and by at least one Examiner; and it must be countersigned by the Provincial Secretary.

(iv.) Graduates in Arts, of recognised British or Canadian Universities, who have proceeded regularly to their degrees, shall be exempt from examination, except in professional subjects. They may be required by oral examination to further satisfy the Examiners as to their knowledge of the Art of Teaching, School Discipline and Management, and the School Law of the Province.

(v.) No certificate can be given to any person as a teacher who does not furnish satisfactory proof of good moral character, and satisfy the Board of Examiners that he or she is a fit and proper person to be granted a certificate.

The Legislature considers the moral fitness of the candidate to be of paramount importance. The Examiners must, therefore, be satisfied that the applicant is a fit and proper person for the position of teacher before they can deem him eligible to be admitted to the examination, or to be granted a certificate. Every person sending in notification of his intention to be a candidate at the Teachers' Examination must forward credentials of character satisfactory to the Board of Examiners. These testimonials should be of late date and should bear the signatures of those in responsible positions, such as clergymen, magistrates, or trustees.

(vi.) "*Form of notification of intention to be a candidate at Teachers' Examination.* Sir,—Being of the full age required by the regulations, I hereby give notice of intention to write in.........at the forthcoming Teachers' Examination for.........Class, Grade ....Certificate.

The optional subjects selected by me are.....................

Enclosed please find certificate of moral character, which I trust will prove satisfactory to the Board of Examiners. I am, yours truly,.............. ....(Name in full)."

(vii.) All holders of certificates who have taught in Public Schools of the Province for a period of fifteen years are entitled to have their certificates renewed annually without examination while they continue actively engaged in the service.

(viii.) In the examination for teachers' certificates in 1898, 286 candidates presented themselves, 115 in Victoria, 135 in Vancouver, and 36 in Kamloops. Out of the 286, 223 were successful, as follows:—

First Class, Grade A	9
" " " B	20
Second Class, Grade A	40
" " " B	78
Third Class, Grade A	21
" " " B	55

223

53 failed to obtain a certificate of any kind, and 10 withdrew from the examination.

In addition to these, 3 certificates were issued for length of service.

(ix.) A temporary certificate valid until the next examination of teachers, entitles the holder to teach temporarily in any school.

A Third Class, Grade B, certificate entitles the holder to teach in any common school, or to be assistant in any graded school for one year

A Third Class, Grade A, certificate entitles the holder to teach in any common school, or to be assistant in any graded school for two years.

A Second Class, Grade B, certificate entitles the holder to teach in any position in a graded school or in a common school for three years; and a Grade A certificate of the Second Class confers the same right for five years.

A First Class, Grade B, certificate entitles the holder to teach in any position in a graded school or in a common school or to act as an assistant in a high school during his life or good behaviour.

A First Class, Grade A, certificate entitles the holder to teach in any position in any public school for life or during good behaviour.

Rights conferred by Certificate.

(x.) Certificates of Teachers on Permanent Staff for the year :— *Statistics of Permanent Staff, 1897-8.*

1897-8.	CITY DISTRICTS.			RURAL DISTRICTS.		
CLASS AND GRADE.	Males.	Females.	Total.	Males	Females	Total.
First Class, Grade A - -	16	7	23	17	1	18
First Class, Grade B - -	18	18	36	30	10	40
Second Class, Grade A -	5	35	40	33	33	66
Second Class, Grade B -	3	23	26	32	67	99
Third Class, Grade A - -	-	4	4	..	8	8
Third Class, Grade B - -	-	4	4	7	14	21
Length of Service* - -	-	1	1	1	1	2
Temporary - - -	1	2	3	1	1	2
	43	94	137	121	135	256

* i.e. Certificates given on length of service without examination.

In 1897-8 there were in city districts 137 teachers, with an average monthly salary of $60·83, and in rural districts 256 teachers, with an average monthly salary of $53·74.

'tatistics of
'ermanent
taff, 1894-5.
(xi.) For the sake of comparison the corresponding figures for the school year 1894-95 are here added:—

GRADE.	Males.	Females.	Total.	Highest Salary Per Month.	Lowest Salary Per Month.	
				Dollars.	Dollars.	
First Class Grade A.	19	1	20	135	70	Teachers on Permanent Staff in City Districts.
„ „ „ B.	15	6	21	100	50	
Second „ „ A.	5	30	35	100	50	
„ „ „ B.	4	26	30	75	40	
Third „ „ A.	–	5	5	65	40	
„ „ „ B.	–	1	1	50	50	
Length of Service ·	..	2	2	65	55	
Temporary · ·	–	1	1	60	60	
	43	72	115	[Average monthly salary = $66.62].		
First Class Grade A.	12	1	13	60	50	Teachers on Permanent Staff in Rural Districts.
„ „ „ B.	23	2	25	100	50	
Second „ „ A.	26	25	51	80	50	
„ „ „ B.	23	42	65	70	50	
Third „ „ A.	6	12	18	60	50	
„ „ „ B.	3	5	8	60	50	
Length of Service ·	1	1	2	70	50	
Temporary · ·	–	1	1	50	50	
	94	89	183	[Average monthly salary $3·55·46].		
TOTALS · · ·	137	161	298	[Average monthly salary = $61.]		

'erage
laries.
(xii.) Putting the figures of the salaries approximately into terms of English money we find that in 1894-95 the average *monthly* salary was in *City Districts*, £13 17s. 6d., in *Rural Districts*, £11 11s. 0d. and in *the Province*, generally, £12 14s. 2d.; in other words, the average *annual* salaries of the teachers were in 1894-95, in *City Districts*, £166 10s., in *Rural Districts*, £138 12s., and in *the Province* generally £152 10s.

The corresponding figures in English money for the year 1897-98 were, approximately, as follows:—

	£	s.	d.
Average monthly salary in City Districts -	12	13	4
„ „ „ Rural Districts -	11	4	–
„ „ „ The Provinces -	11	18	8
Average salary per annum in City Districts	152	–	–
„ „ „ Rural Districts	134	8	–
„ „ The Province -	143	4	–

Salaries of public school teachers in rural districts are paid from the Provincial Treasury, but no public school teacher in rural districts is entitled to draw more than one salary for any month or portion of a month.

In case a school is summarily closed for any cause, the teacher shall not be paid salary for a longer period than one month from the date of such closing (1896).

(xiii.) The *duties of a Public School Teacher* are thus defined in the School Manual.

Duties of Public School Teachers.

(1.) To teach diligently and faithfully all the branches required to be taught in the school, according to the regulations.

(2.) To keep the daily, weekly, and monthly registers of the school.

(3.) To maintain proper order and discipline in his school, according to the authorised regulations; and to send to the parent or guardian of each pupil a monthly report of the progress, attendance, and punctuality of such pupil.

(4.) To keep a visitors' book (which the Trustees shall provide) and enter therein the visits made to his school, and, if deemed advisable, to present such book to any visitor, and request him to make therein any remarks suggested by his visit.

(5.) To give access to Inspectors and Trustees, at all times when desired by them, to the registers and visitors' book appertaining to the school, and, upon leaving the school, to deliver up the same to the order of the Trustees.

(6.) To hold at the end of each half year, public examinations of his school, of which he shall give due notice to the Trustees of the school, and, through his pupils, to their parents or guardians.

(7.) To furnish to the Superintendent of Education, monthly or when desired, any information which it may be in his power to give respecting anything connected with the operation of his school, or in any way affecting its interests or character.

(8.) To verify by affidavit before any Justice of the Peace, the correctness of such returns as the Superintendent of Education may, from time to time, require to be so verified.

(9.) To give at least thirty days' notice to the Trustees of his or her intention of resigning.

(xiv.) The Trustees of any School District must forthwith report to the Superintendent of Education the appointment, resignation, or dismissal of any teacher or teachers in their district, and in case of dismissal must state the reasons for such dismissal.

The Trustees shall, from time to time, select, from amongst those persons properly qualified, and appoint the teacher or teachers in their school district; and may remove and dismiss such teacher or teachers upon giving at least thirty days' notice of such intention of removal or dismissal, and of their reasons for so doing.

Upon notification from the Council of Public Instruction of the inefficiency or misconduct of any teacher, the trustees must give such teacher thirty days' notice of dismissal.

But, when a teacher has been suspended by the trustees for gross misconduct, he has no right to thirty days' notice, nor to salary in lieu of notice.

(xv.) A teacher suspended or dismissed by the Trustees on a charge of gross misconduct may appeal to the Council of Public Instruction, which has power to take evidence, and to confirm or reverse upon evidence the decision of the Trustees. When a decision is reversed, the teacher shall not be reinstated in the same school without the consent of the Trustees.

Trustees cannot give authority to teachers to violate the regulations in any particular.

Trustees cannot appoint or retain as teacher a person who does not hold a certificate from the Education Department of the Province.

V.—The Training of Teachers.

(i.) The following is taken from the Report for 1893-4.— " Our schools have increased in number and importance to such an extent as to require an expansion of the system. The experience of past years has shown that teachers before assuming active duties should be required to have a good general knowledge of the work that they undertake. In order that this be accomplished, it is necessary that a Normal School be established for the training of those who are about to engage in the instruction of youth. In every professional pursuit special training is a requirement, and particularly should this be the case with those who have to deal with child-mind. Only those who have at least some knowledge of psychology and proper methods of school management should be granted certificates in public schools.

" To place a school in charge of a teacher who possesses no other recommendation than a certificate is not, as a rule, doing justice to the pupils who have to attend the school.

" Experience has proved that it is a wise economy for any country to give to her teachers thorough instruction as to methods and general knowledge of school management. This can only be done by the establishment of a Normal School. Such an institution under two teachers, as a commencement, would be of invaluable benefit to the schools of the Province thereby every school under the charge of a trained teacher would receive direct benefit for every outlay made in this direction."

(ii.) The following remarks are quoted from the Public Schools Report for 1896 :— From the Report for 1896.

"We again beg to recommend that immediate steps be taken towards the establishment of a Normal School in this Province. It is of paramount importance that the young and inexperienced aspirants for the position of teachers should have some special preparation for their work. The success of the school is wholly dependent on the capability and fitness of the teacher, and the vital interests of children should not be intrusted to one who is ignorant of the first principles of the art of teaching. . . . If in other pursuits special training is necessary to success, certainly teachers require preparation for *their* work. . . . A Normal School affords to teachers the opportunity of properly preparing themselves for the achievement of the best results. While it is true that every teacher who has attended a Normal School may not prove to be a successful instructor, yet we believe that he will accomplish much more from the training he received in such an institution. It is also true that some of our best teachers have never attended a Normal School, but their success must be attributed either to natural aptitude or to many years of experience, or to both combined. . . . When it is taken into consideration that the Government is now paying about \$140,000 a year for salaries of teachers alone, the extra cost of maintaining a Normal School, say \$5,000 a year, is very small in comparison with the many benefits to our school system, which the establishment of such an institution would afford. British Columbia is the only Province in the Dominion which does not support one or more Normal Schools."

(iii.) The Inspector for the District of Nelson in 1898 records his conviction of the "absolute necessity" for a Normal School. Necessity for a Normal School. The majority of the teachers employed in the district are educated in the schools of British Columbia. Their knowledge is unquestionably adequate, he says, but they are deficient in ability to instruct and to use modern methods of teaching. He observes that the practical training of teachers is too often acquired at their pupils' expense, and that poor results are in consequence attained. A similar complaint is made by the Inspector for the Vancouver district. Many of the teachers know little of the art of teaching, and until the Province has a Normal School and a Model School, it is certain that the work of many of the young teachers will continue to be experimental. He recommends that the salary of inexperienced teachers should begin at a lower figure, and should increase regularly as the teacher proves his efficiency. One observation of the Inspector for Vancouver is remarkable and important. He suggests that the lack of interest taken in the schools by the people may be because "education is too cheap; what one gets for nothing is apt to be lightly prized." In view of this he would like to see the grant for "incidental expenses ' cut off, except in exceptional cases. In some country schools the work of the upper classes is to a certain extent hampered by the preparation of pupils for teachers' certificates. This would be obviated by the establishment of a Normal School, or by an arrangement for such instruction of intending teachers among the classes of the High Schools.

The necessity for the establishment of a Normal School in the Province is commented on in Inspector Wilson's Report for 1894-5 (Public School Report, p. 213). It is to this deficiency that he attributes the noticeable inferiority of the methods of primary instruction in the Province, as compared with the other Provinces of Nova Scotia and New Brunswick. The work of the advanced grades showed no such inferiority. But suitable professional training was, in his opinion, a real need.

VI.—TRUANCY: PUNISHMENTS.

Expulsion
and
Suspension.

The record of the rural schools in regard to the severest punishments—suspension and expulsion—is a better one than that of the city districts. That *truancy* is more prevalent in city districts than in rural districts is the natural consequence of the difference in home-training and modes of life in a considerable number of the children.

A pupil can only be *expelled* when his example is very injurious and there is no apparent prospect of reformation. For gross misconduct, or a violent and wilful opposition to authority, a pupil may be *suspended* from attendance at a school for a specified period, not to exceed one week. It is enjoined by the Department upon the teacher not to suspend or expel a pupil until all other means have failed to bring the child to obedience and good conduct.

Corporal
punishment.

(ii.) The teacher of a public school derives his authority for the use of the rod in *corporal punishment* from the regulations, of which the following is a portion :—" Every teacher shall practice such discipline as may be exercised by a kind, firm, and judicious parent in his family, avoiding corporal punishment, except when it shall appear to him to be imperatively necessary." While, therefore, the teacher is given authority to use the rod, he is admonished to avoid corporal punishment except when it is absolutely necessary. Too frequent or too severe use of the rod is indicative of the teacher's incompetency as a proper trainer of those entrusted to his care. One remedy for the abuse of this power is vested in the Board of Trustees of every school district; they may dismiss any teacher at thirty days' notice provided they state the cause of dismissal. It rests, therefore, with the trustees whether they will retain or dismiss the teacher who abuses his authority by the excessive use of corporal punishment. This is the only way, other than by counsel, in which trustees are authorised to interfere with the teacher in regard to the use or abuse of the rod.—(From the Report for 1894-5).—In some schools " the rod would appear to be the chief means employed to obtain discipline. It is proper to state, however, that more than half of the cases of corporal punishment reported are credited to less than twenty schools; one graded school reporting 108 cases, and one common school 91 cases.

(iii.) "It is to be feared that the use of the power of moral suasion **Moral** in obtaining good government in the schools is neglected, in **suasion.** great part, by a few of the teachers. Physical force is certainly not the only nor the best means at the command of the teacher for securing good discipline. The teacher who uses moral suasion effectively in the government of his school will accomplish the *best* results, not only in the moral training of the pupils but in their intellectual advancement."

VII.—LEGAL PENALTIES.

(i.) Any person wilfully making a false declaration of his right **Voter's false** to vote shall, on a summary conviction before any justice of the **declaration.** peace, be sentenced therefor to imprisonment for any period not exceeding three months, or to a fine not greater than one hundred dollars.

(ii.) Any person who wilfully disturbs, interrupts, or disquiets **Disturbance** the proceedings of any school meeting authorised to be held, or **of school** any school established and conducted according to the regula- **meeting.** tions, or who interrupts or disquiets any public school by rude or indecent behaviour, or by making a noise, either within the place where the school is held, or so near to it that he disturbs the order or exercises of the school, shall for each offence, on conviction before a justice of the peace, on the oath of one credible witness, forfeit and pay for public school purposes to the school district within which the offence was committed, a sum not exceeding twenty dollars, together with the costs of the conviction.

For the prescribed method of recovering these penalties, see the regulation already given above, Section III. (i.)

VIII.—SCHOOL PROPERTY.

(i.) In rural school districts the trustees are responsible for the **Trustees' re-** good repair of the school-house. They should see that the **sponsibility.** windows are properly fitted with glass; that at the proper season the stove and pipe, or fireplace, are in good condition, and that suitable wood or coal is provided; that the desks and seats are in good repair; that the outhouses are properly provided with doors; that the blackboards are kept painted, the water supply abundant, and that everything necessary for the comfort of the pupils and the success of the school is provided.

(ii.) No public school-house, or school plot, nor any building, **Misuse of** furniture, or other thing belonging to it, should be used or **school** occupied for any other purpose than for the use or accommoda- **buildings.** tion of the public school of the district, without the express permission of the trustees as a corporation: and then only after

school hours, and on condition that all damage be made goo
and cleaning and sweeping properly done.

Teacher's re-
sponsibility. (iii.) The teacher has charge of the school-house on behalf of
the trustees. He has no authority to use it otherwise than as
directed by them, nor to use it at any other time than during
school hours without their sanction. At the request of the
trustees he must at once deliver up to them the keys of the
school-house.

IX.—INSPECTION.

Inspector's
report. (i.) The supervision of the schools is the duty of the Superintendent of Education, and he is assisted in this work by
two Inspectors. When a school is visited by an inspector,
he is required to make a written report to the Department
immediately on his return to the Education Office, on the
internal work of the school-room, methods employed, and
on the condition of the school-grounds and the buildings:
in short, to report on all matters connected with the proper
working and the welfare of the school. The Department,
through the reports on inspections made, as well as through
information furnished by trustees and teacher, is kept fully
informed as to the condition of each school.

Need of a
third
Inspector. (ii) The Superintendent of Education wrote as follows, in his
Report for 1896 :—

"A school system, to be effective, must have vigilant supervision. Owing to the large extent of territory to be traversed
by representatives of the Department, and the yearly increasing
number of schools, it has not been possible to make as frequent
visitations as are desirable, or even to reach all the schools in
any one year.
"The first Inspector of Schools was appointed in 1887, to
assist the Superintendent in his work. At that time there were
92 schools in operation, under the charge of 118 teachers. In
1892, the number of schools having increased to 149, and the
number of teachers employed to 228, a second Inspector was
appointed. In view of the fact that in 1896 there were 233
schools under a staff of 368 teachers, the necessity of the
appointment of a third Inspector of Schools should be
considered."

X.—HIGH SCHOOLS.

There are four public High Schools in the Province, viz.,
the Nanaimo, New Westminster, Vancouver, and Victoria High
Schools. The salaries of the head-teachers vary from $135 to
$108 a month. In all these schools, co-education takes place
and the honours of the examinations, as well as of other school
activities, seem to be about equally divided between the boys and
the girls.

(i.) Taking first the Nanaimo High School, we find that in 1898 the enrolment of pupils reached 77, and the average actual daily attendance 40·68. In numbers the two sexes have recently been equal, though in 1898 the girls had the preponderance. The figures are as follows :— Nanaimo High School.

Nanaimo High School.

Year.	Boys enrolled.	Girls enrolled.	Total enrolment.	Average daily Attendance.
1892–3 - - -	14	25	39	23·37
1893–4 - - -	19	29	48	34·50
1894–5 - - -	36	34	70	41·56
1895 6 - - -	29	29	58	32·02
1896–7 - - -	27	26	53	33·74
1897·8 - - -	32	45	77	40·68

The average *monthly* attendance was 50.

(ii.) New Westminster High School has besides its principal an assistant master or mistress. Its average *monthly* attendance in 1898 was 47. New Westminster High School.

The following are the figures of enrolment, etc., since 1892 :—

New Westminster High School.

Year.	Boys enrolled.	Girls enrolled.	Total enrolment.	Average daily attendance.
1893 4 - - -	49	34	83	44·63
1894–5 - - -	48	37	85	51·01
1895–6 - - -	48	39	87	56·61
1896–7 - - -	55	39	94	50·36
1897·8 - - -	33	39	72	36·76

The official report contains no explanation of the sudden fall in the number of boys, as well as in the average daily attendance in the school year, 1898.

(iii.) The Vancouver High School has besides the principal, four
assistant masters at $100 a month. Its average *monthly* atten-
dance in 1898 was 107 out of an enrolment of 156.

Vancouver High School.

Year.	Boys enrolled.	Girls enrolled.	Total enrolment.	Average daily attendance.
1893-4 · · ·	52	92	144	92·77
1894-5 · · ·	58	101	159	108·44
1895-6 · · ·	55	79	134	87·74
1896 7 · · ·	55	98	153	88·73
1897-8 · · ·	55	101	156	94·35

(iv.) The Victoria High School has a principal at $110 a
month, two assistants at $90 a month each, and one assistant at
$75 a month. Its average monthly attendance in 1898 was
117 out of an enrolment of 154.

Victoria High School.

Year.	Boys enrolled.	Girls enrolled.	Total enrolment.	Average daily attendance.
1893 4 · · ·	78	81	159	121·00
1894-5 · · ·	96	105	201	130·28
1895-6 · · ·	80	101	181	111·50
1896-7 · · ·	74	87	161	106·85
1897-8 · · ·	58	96	154	104·65

(v.) By a regulation of the Council of Public Instruction, pupils
who have attended a High School for not less than two years
can obtain a Diploma or Certificate of Standing by undergoing
the annual Departmental Examination, provided they obtain at
least 30 per cent. of the marks in each subject. This Diploma
is granted only when the pupil is leaving school, and may be
considered equivalent to a Certificate of "Graduation." Seven
such certificates were granted to girls in 1898, and four to boys.

(vi.) The following are the subjects of examination for admission to a High School :—

1. *Spelling.*—To be able to spell correctly the ordinary words in the Fifth Reader and Spelling Book.

2. *Reading.*—To read correctly and intelligently any passage in the Fifth Reader.

3. *Writing.*—To write neatly and legibly.

4. *Arithmetic.*—To have a good general knowledge of numeration, notation, the four simple and compound rules, reduction, vulgar and decimal fractions, proportion, simple interest and percentage, compound interest, and discount.

5. *Mental Arithmetic.*—To be able to solve, mentally, any ordinary problems.

6. *Grammar.*—To know the principal grammatical forms and definitions, and to be able to analyse and parse any ordinary sentence.

7. *Geography.*—To have a good knowledge of the earth's planetary relations, of the general principles of physical geography, and of the outlines of the maps of Europe, Asia, Africa, America, Oceanica, and of the British Empire, and more particularly of that of the Dominion of Canada.

8. *English History.*—To know the different periods and outlines of English History.

9. *Canadian History.*—To have a knowledge of the outlines of Canadian History.

10. *Composition.*—To be able to write a letter correctly as to form and punctuation, and to write a brief composition on any simple subject.

11. *Anatomy, Physiology, and Hygiene.*—To have a general knowledge of the subject.

(vii.) Applicants for admission to a High School have been required since 1897 to pass an examination in Agriculture.

(viii.) An entrance examination upon these lines must be passed by all those who wish to enter a High School ; and, as has been seen, there must be at least twenty persons duly qualified in such subjects in any School district, before the Council may establish a High School in that district.

(ix.) On the other hand, there are certain exemptions. Teachers in the Public School, for example, who have already obtained teachers' certificates in the Province may be admitted to High Schools as pupils without an entrance examination.

(x.) The examination is on paper when deemed necessary, but candidates may in any case be subjected to an additional *viva voce* examination. The examination for entrance to a High School is held in each rural school when visited by the Superintendent or by an Inspector. Candidates must obtain at least 30 per cent. of the maximum marks in each subject ; and at least 60 per cent. of the aggregate maximum of all subjects. Pupils who have not been in attendance at a High School for two years, shall not be readmitted without examination.

(xi.) On entering the High School a pupil may for the first six months receive instruction in the English course only, but after that period he must take at least five of the additional subjects included either in the Commercial Course or in the Classical Course. The High School pupils are arranged in classes according to their proficiency; and each pupil is advanced from one class to another without regard to the length of time he may have spent in his class or division and solely with reference to his attainments as judged in the half-yearly official examination. Pupils from rural districts are admitted as candidates in the half-yearly examinations for entrance at the High Schools of Nanaimo, New Westminster, Vancouver, and Victoria.

(xii.) It should be noted that members of a Public School in a district that contains a High School cannot be received as pupils in the Graded School of the district after they have, on passing a satisfactory examination, been declared eligible for promotion from the Public School to a High School. The object of this is to prevent a development in the upper classes of Graded Schools that would inevitably mean overlapping and would seriously interfere with efficiency.

High Schools have three courses of study,—English, Commercial, and Classical.

(xiii.) The following is taken from the Report for 1895-6.— "The many benefits conferred by the four *High Schools* are fully proved by the work accomplished since the establishment of each, and by the high esteem in which each is held. These schools not only afford to all children who pass the standard required for admission the opportunity of obtaining a knowledge of the advanced subjects of study essential to a higher education, but they elevate the character of the lower grades and perfect and diffuse (*sic*) all the most valuable points of our school system. The scholarship demanded for entrance to a High School is certainly equal to, if not higher than, that required in the other Provinces. The necessity of this arises from the fact that these schools form the apex of the system of British Columbia, while in the other provinces, in addition to High Schools, there are Collegiate Institutes, Normal Schools, Colleges, and Universities. The High Schools of the Province have therefore to afford to the children, as far as possible, all the benefits accruing from these other higher institutions of learning—the University excepted."

"Taking into consideration the large number of subjects of study required to be taught in a High School, it must be apparent that the more complete the staff of teachers, the greater is the assurance of the best results; yet it may be proper in this connection to state that, as a rule, each teacher should have twenty-five or more pupils under his charge."

The advisability of granting diplomas to pupils on finishing one of the prescribed High School courses of study was under consideration in 1896.

(xiv.) *From the Report for* 1896.—"Under an amendment Board of made to the Public School Act, 1891, providing for the incor- Governors of poration of Boards of School Trustees of city districts the College. Lieutenant-Governor in Council has been pleased, by Letters Patent, to incorporate the Board of School Trustees of the City of Vancouver as a body corporate and politic, under the name and style of the 'Board of Governors of the Vancouver College.'"

The object of this change of names of trustees and High School is to enable the High School of Vancouver City to affiliate with a Canadian University.

Since 1894 only holders of "First Class, Grade A, certificates" have been allowed to teach, even as assistants, in High Schools.

XI.—Graded Schools.

"The success of a *Graded School* depends on the ability of its staff of teachers, its *grading* and general management. Experience has shown it to be impracticable to grade all schools on a common standard, hence each principal is required to frame a Limit Table deemed to be the most suitable for his school.

(i.) "The first division of a Graded School should certainly have Size of the best number of pupils, but in no division should there be less divisions than from thirty to forty; and not more than sixty in any division.

"In schools that have been in operation for three or more years, it is but reasonable to expect that an approximate equality of work can be assigned to each teacher. When some teachers have to perform almost double the work of others in the same school, it is evident either that there is a defect in the Limit Table, or that one or more of the teachers on the staff are incompetent.

"The teachers of these schools are, generally speaking, thorough in their work, and not slow to utilise all the good features of new methods advanced by the best authorities of the day; and hence the work accomplished in the Graded Schools is, on the whole, of a most satisfactory character." (Report of 1895–96.)

(ii.) In case one of the *optional subjects* of Drawing, Calisthenics, Optional or Temperance is begun in the fourth or fifth division, it should subjects. be taught in each of the succeeding higher grades, in order that the pupils may obtain such knowledge of the subject as will prove of future value.

It should be noted that in the school year 1894–5 the Council of Public Instruction, wishing to secure greater uniformity in the management of Graded Schools, issued the following new regulations :—

(iii.) The Principal shall prepare the Limit Table (*i.e., a table of* Limit table. *standards on which the grading is based*) for each division of his school, and must forward a copy of it to the Education Department for approval.

(iv.) Semi-annual written examinations for making promotions Semi-annual shall be held in the different divisions of each Graded School. Examination.

The Principal shall prepare the questions for these examinations, and shall fix the time of holding the same, but the promotion lists must be read on the date on which each public examination of the school is held.

As it is not deemed proper to place too great reliance upon a single written examination the Principal shall consult the assistant teacher of each division, in preparing the promotion list. The assistant's recommendation, based upon record kept as to progress and standing of pupils claimed to be worthy of promotion, shall be accorded proper consideration.

A copy of all questions set for each promotion examination, together with a statement of the results of the examination of each division must forthwith be forwarded to the Education Department. The list of children in the returns should contain the names of all pupils who received instruction in each division during the whole year, the names of those who were promoted at the examination being specially marked.

Suggestions from circular of 1895. (v.) *From a Circular dated December* 17, 1895—" By a public examination of a school is meant the examining orally of classes in at least four or more of the subjects of study taught in the school-room. If the teacher desires to vary the exercises of the day with recitations, singing, calisthenics, or other work in which instruction has been given, there cannot be any valid objection raised unless the time occupied by these last subjects directly interferes with the time which should be devoted to the *viva voce* examination.

" The public examination day should be regarded as affording the teacher the opportunity of showing to the trustees, parents, and other visitors, not only the advancement made by the pupils in the different subjects of study, but of presenting to them the methods used to secure this progress. If the teacher desires, he may call upon visitors to assist him in examining classes, but to do so must be regarded as a voluntary act on his part."

XII.—COMMON SCHOOLS.

The course of study prescribed for *Common Schools* embraces Reading, Writing, Arithmetic, Composition, Geography, Grammar, Canadian History, English History, Physiology, Hygiene, and Agriculture. All of these subjects must be taught in each school, provided the pupils are far enough advanced to receive instruction in them.

Optional subjects. (i.) In addition to these branches the following optional subjects may be taught :—Book-keeping, Mensuration, Algebra, Geometry, Drawing, Temperance, Music, Needlework, and Calisthenics. The trustees may require that " Temperance " should become part of the compulsory course (1896).

The prescribed subjects alone are deemed to be amply sufficient to afford to all pupils the opportunity of obtaining a good Common School education; but among the optional subjects are several branches of knowledge which would undoubtedly the better prepare them for entering upon the ordinary vocations of life.

The Lord s Prayer. (ii.) In a school in which more than one teacher is employed, if the Lord's Prayer is used in the opening or the closing of any of the divisions, it should be used in *all* the divisions of the school. " It is a pleasure to be able to report that this devotional exercise is used by more than two-thirds of the teachers in the opening or the closing of their schools."

XIII.—General Remarks and Statistics of Educational Progress.

(i.) *From the Report for* 1897–1898.—" The record of the past year shows marked improvement in the condition and management of the schools.   Their efficiency may be inferred from the high percentage of average daily attendance, from the very liberal amount expended for their maintenance, and from the lively interest shown by the people generally in their welfare.

Statistics for 1897-9.

" The main instrumentalities that have produced, and continue to produce, marked results for good in our public schools are better judgment displayed in the selection of teachers, the careful and constant supervision by the inspectors, the practical and beneficial work of the various teachers' institutes, and the increased interest and vigilance of trustees and parents.

" The whole number of pupils enrolled was 17,648, an increase of 1,850 over that of the previous year, and the average actual daily attendance was 11,055·65, an increase of 1,056·04 for the same period.   The total number of teachers and monitors employed was 422, an increase of 38 over that for the previous year.

" There were 261 *[280] schools in operation during the year, as follows :—

4	[4] High Schools.	228 [244]	Common Schools.
25 [28]	Graded Schools.	4 [4]	Ward Schools.

" In city districts the percentage of average daily attendance was 69·47, in rural districts 57·31, and for the whole Province 62·64.

" The expenditure from the provincial treasury for education proper during the year was as follows :—

Teachers' salaries	- - - -	$180,437.58	[$198,464
Per Capital Grants to City Districts	-	52,922.64	56,692
Education Office	- - - -	14,396.15	13 497
	Total - -	$247,756.37	$268,653]

(*i.e.*, about £50,000.)

" The expenditure by the Lands and Works Department for the construction of school-houses, furniture, repairs, and improvements to school property was as follows :—

School-houses in Rural Districts	-	$34,438.23	
Furniture, repairs, &c.	- - -	8,060.66	
	Total - -	$42,498.89	[$67,363]

" The total cost to the Provincial Government during the fiscal year 1897–8, for all purposes of education was as follows :—

Education proper	- - - -	$247,756.37	[$268,653
Lands and Works Departments	-	42,498.89	67,363
	Total - -	$290,255.26	$336,016]

(*i.e.* about £60,500.)

---

* The figures enclosed in brackets are those for 1899.

(ii.) The following table shows the cost of each pupil on enrolment, and on average daily attendance during the past ten years :—

Year.	Cost of each Pupil on enrolment.	Cost of each Pupil on averge daily attendance
1888–9 - - - -	$15.92	$29.39
1889 -90 -	15.29	28.37
1890–1 - - - -	14.78	26.66
1891–2 - - - -	14.91	25.79
1892–3 - - - -	16.57	26.79
1893–4 - - - -	13.40	21.71
1894–5 - - - -	14.02	22.95
1895–6 - - - -	14.17	22.14
1896–7 - - - -	13.97	22.08
1897–8 - - - -	14.03	22.40

In 1897–8 there were 57 "*assisted schools*" maintained during the year, and fifteen other schools began to receive "*assistance*" during the year, making a total of 72 assisted schools.

Schoolhouses were erected, or additions were made to school buildings, in eighteen instances.[1]

[1] It is desirable to give here some data for estimating the educational progress of the Province. Accordingly we give below the corresponding figures for 1894–5 :—

———	1894–5	1897–8
Number of Pupils enrolled - - -	13,482	17,648
Average actual daily attendance -	8,610·31	11,055·65
Total number of Teachers and Monitors	319	422
Number of Schools in operation - -	202	261
Number of High Schools in operation	4	4 (*stationary*)
Number of Graded Schools - -	20	25
Number of Common or Rural Schools	172	228
Number of Ward Schools - - -	6	4 (*decrease*)
Percentage of attendance in City Districts	69·93	69·47 (*slight decrease*)
Percentage of attendance in Rural Districts	57·66	57·31 (*slight decrease*)
Percentage of attendance in the Province	63·86	62·64 (*slight decrease*)
Expenditure on Education Proper -	$189,037.25	$247,756.35
Teachers' Salaries - - - -	$169,447.85	$180,437.55
Education Office - - -	$11,887.80	$14,396.15
Per capita Grant to City Districts -	$45,404.80	$52,922.64
Expenditure Lands and Works Department (*All on Rural Districts except $5,000*)	$18,963.35	$42,498.89 (*Rural Districts*) only)
Total Cost to Provincial Government -	$208,000.00	$290,255.00
School Houses erected or Additions made	11	18

(iii.) ATTENDANCE 1897–8.

Number of Pupils enrolled during the year - 17,648
 Increase for the year -   -   - 1,850

Number of Boys enrolled -   -   -   -   - 8,983
 Increase for the year -   -   - 878

Number of Girls enrolled -   -   -   - 8,665
 Increase for the year -   -   - 972

Average actual daily attendance   -   -   - 10,055·65
 Increase for the year -   -   - 1,056·04

Number of Pupils enrolled in High Schools   - 459
 Decrease for the year -   -   - 2

Average actual daily attendance in High Schools 276·44

Average actual daily attendance in Graded and Ward Schools   -   -   -   -   - 6,704·20

Average actual daily attendance in Rural Schools 4,075·01

Number of School Districts at the close of the year 213
 Increase for the year   -   - 14

(iv.) The gradual growth of the schools and the cost of main- taining them is fully shown by this record of attendance and expenditure :—

	Number of School Districts.	Aggregate Enrolment.	Average Daily Attendance.	Percentage of Attendance.	Expenditure.
1890–91 - -	141	9,260	5,134·91	55·45	$136,901.75
1891–2 - -	154	10,773	6,227·10	57·80	160,627.80
1892–3 - -	169	11,496	7,111·40	61·85	190,558.30
1893–4 - -	178	12,613	7,785·50	61·72	169,050.20
1894–5 - -	183	13,482	8,610·31	63·86	189,037.25
1895–6 - -	193	14,460	9,254·25	64·00	204,930.30
1896–7 - -	199	15,798	9,999·61	63·29	220,810.35
1897–8 - -	213	17,648	11,055·65	62·64	247,756.35
1898–9 - -	—	19,185	12,302·00	64.13	268,653·00

(v.) The progress made in recent years may be judged by a comparison of the figures for 1897–8 with those for 1894–5.

ATTENDANCE, 1894–5.

Number of Pupils enrolled during the year - 13,482
 Increase for the year -   -   - 869

Number of Boys enrolled -   -   -   - 6,848
 Increase for the year -   -   - 464

Number of Girls enrolled - - - - - 6,634
    Increase for the year - - - 405

Average actual daily attendance - - - 8,610·31
    Increase for the year - - - 824·81

Number of Pupils enrolled in High Schools - 515
    Increase for the year - - - 81

Average actual daily attendance in High Schools 331·29

Average actual daily attendance in Graded and
    Ward Schools - - - - - - 5,396·30

Average actual daily attendance in Rural Schools 2,882·72

Number of school districts at the close of the
    year - - - - - - - 183

Increase for the year - - - - - 5

Thus for the four years from 1893 to 1897 we can tabulate the following figures :—

INCREASE FROM 1893 TO 1897 (INCLUSIVE).

Enrolment - - - - - - - 5,035
Boys' enrolment - - - - - - 2,599
Girls' enrolment - - - - - - 2,436
Average actual daily attendance - - - - 2,270·15
Enrolment in High Schools - - - 54·
Number of School Districts - - - 35·

Progress in attendance, 1894-7. (vi.) Between the years 1894 and 1897 the progress in attendance was most marked in the Graded and Ward Schools, and a considerable decrease is noticeable in the attendance at High Schools.

PROGRESS 1894 TO 189".

Average actual daily attendance in High Schools
                             Decrease - - 54·85
Average actual daily attendance in Graded and Ward
    Schools   Increase - - 1,307·90
Average actual daily attendance in Rural Schools
                             Increase - - 1,192·29

Teachers' aims. (vii.) The Inspector for the Victoria district in 1898 observes in his report that there has been a general improvement in the character of the primary instruction given, that there is developing, more and more every year, a disposition among teachers to keep themselves prepared for their work; and that, although the greater part of the teachers do their work with the educational aim implied in the phrase " knowledge is power," the higher aim expressed in " *character* is power," becomes more and more prevalent. In this district there were in 1898 several Teachers' Institutes. They do much to stimulate teachers and to help in improving the schools. At the close of each Institute a public meeting is held, to which parents and others interested in education are usually invited.

(viii.) Some sort of classification of the "Ward Schools" and Classification "Graded Schools" in 1897–98 may be made thus:— of schools.

Cities.	Number of Grades.		Percentage of Regular Attendance.	
Nanaimo - - -	Central - - -	10	68·06	
	North Ward - -	1	79·01	75·16
	South Ward - -	1	78·40	
New Westminster - -	Boys' - - -	6	62·22	
	Girls' - - -	7	63·30	
	Sapputon - -	3	65·36	63·50
	Westside - -	2	63·13	
Vancouver - - -	Central - - -	10	65·11	
	East - - -	14	70·89	
	West - - -	13	73·67	69·91
	Mount Pleasant -	10	68·35	
	Fairview - -	4	72·13	
Victoria - - - -	Boys' - - -	8	69·91	
	Girls' - - -	8	73·39	
	North Ward - -	11	76·23	
	South Park - -	9	74·37	72·34
	West - - -	6	67·65	
	Springbridge - -	2	72·47	

	No. of Grades.	Percentage of regular Attendance.
Chilliwhack - - - -	3	69·79
Kamloops - - - -	4	58·04
Kaslo - - - - -	3	70·08
Mission - - - -	2	57·82
Nelson - - - -	4	59·79
Northfield - - - -	3	48·87
Rossland - - - -	7	57·02
Trail - - - -	3	51·50
Union Mines - - - -	4	62·27
Vernon - - - -	4	49·95
Wellington - - - -	8	62·55

Thus we find that in the Graded Schools of the large cities the percentage of regular attendance was, in 1898, 70·23; and in other Graded Schools, 58·88.

APPENDIX A.

SUBJECTS OF EXAMINATION FOR CERTIFICATES; AND CONDITIONS OF OBTAINING THEM.

(a) SUBJECTS OF EXAMINATION.

THIRD CLASS CERTIFICATES.

1. *Reading.*—To read intelligently and expressively.

2. *Writing.*—To write legibly and neatly, and to understand the principles of writing as given in any standard text-book.

3. *Spelling.*—To have a good knowledge of orthography and orthoepy.

4. *Written Arithmetic.*—To be thoroughly familiar with the subject.

5. *Mental Arithmetic.*—To show readiness and accuracy in solving problems.

6. *Geography.*—To have a good knowledge of the subject.

7. *English Grammar.*—To have a thorough knowledge of the subject, and to be able to analyse and parse any sentence.

8. *Canadian History.*—To have a good knowledge of the subject.

9. *English History.*—To have a good knowledge of the subject.

10. *Anatomy, Physiology, and Hygiene.*—To have a good general knowledge of the subject.

11. *Composition.*—To be familiar with the forms of correspondence, and to be able to write a composition on any simple subject, correct as to spelling, punctuation, and expression.

12. *Education.*—To have a thorough knowledge of the approved methods of teaching the various subjects prescribed for Common Schools: to be well acquainted with formation of time tables, classification of pupils, and modes of discipline, to be familiar with the School Act, and Rules and Regulations prescribed for the government of the Public Schools.

SECOND CLASS, GRADE B, CERTIFICATES.

1 to 12, as for Third Class Certificates.

13. *Mensuration.*—To know the application of the rules for the measurement of surfaces.

14. *Book-keeping.*—To understand the keeping of accounts by single entry.

15. *Music (Theory), Drawing (Linear), Botany.*—To have a fair knowledge of *one* of these subjects.

Second Class, Grade A, Certificates.

1 to 15, as for Second Class, Grade B, Certificates.

16. *Algebra.*—To know the application of the rules preceding and including simple equations.

17. *Geometry.*—Book I.

18. *Zoology, Astronomy, Rhetoric.* —To have a fair knowledge of *one* of these subjects.

First Class, Grade B, Certificates.

1 to 18, as for Second Class, Grade A, Certificates.

13. *Mensuration.*—To know the application of the rules for the measurement of volumes.

14. *Book-keeping.*—To understand the keeping of accounts by double entry.

16. *Algebra.*—To know the subject.

17. *Geometry.*—Books II., III., and IV., with problems.

19. *Natural Philosophy.*—To know the subject, and to be able to work problems in *Statics, Dynamics,* and *Hydrostatics.*

20. *English Literature.*—To have a good general knowledge of the subject.

21. *General History, Chemistry, Geology.*—To have a good knowledge of *one* of these subjects.

First-Class, Grade A, Certificates.

1. to 21., as for First-Class, Grade B, Certificates.

17. *Geometry.*—Books V. (Definitions) and VI.

22. *Practical Mathematics.*—To be familiar with *Plane Trigonometry,* including *Land Surveying* and *Navigation.*

23. *Ancient History.*—To have a general knowledge of the subject to the Fall of Rome.

24. *Latin.*—To have a good knowledge of Prose Composition ; to be able to translate and parse the following :—

    Cæsar, De Bello Gallico, Books I. and II.

    Virgil, Æneid, Books I. and II.

    Horace, Odes, Books I. & III.

25. *Greek and French :—*

> *Greek.*—To have a good knowledge of Prose Composition, and to be able to translate and parse the following :—
>
> > Xenophon, Anabasis, Books I. and II.
> > Homer, Iliad, Books I. and II.

> *French.*—To have a good knowledge of Prose Composition, and to be able to translate and parse the following :—
>
> > La Fontaine, Fables, Livres I. et II.
> > Voltaire, Histoire de Charles XII., Livres I. et II.
> > Corneille, Le Cid.

Note.—Since 1897 Candidates for Teachers' Certificates have been required to take a paper set on Agriculture.

(b.) Conditions of Obtaining Certificates.

Certificates of qualification shall be granted according to the following regulations :—

For a Temporary Certificate.—A candidate for a Temporary Certificate must give satisfactory information as to his character and scholastic qualifications, and must forward an application from a Board of School Trustees desiring his services as teacher. The Board of Trustees must satisfy the Superintendent of Education of their inability to secure a person properly qualified, suitable as a teacher for their school.

For a Third Class, Grade B, Certificate, a candidate must obtain 30 per cent. of the marks attached to each of the subjects of examination for that class and grade, and 40 per cent. of the total number of marks attached to the subjects of examination for that class and grade.

For a Third Class, Grade A, Certificate, a candidate must obtain 40 per cent. of the marks attached to each of the subjects of examination for that class and grade, and 50 per cent. of the total number of marks attached to the subjects of examination for that class and grade.

For a Second Class, Grade B, Certificate, a candidate must obtain 40 per cent. of the marks attached to each of the subjects of examination for Third Class Certificates, and not less than 30 per cent. of the marks attached to each of the subjects of examination peculiar to that class and grade, and 50 per cent. of the total number of marks attached to the subjects of examination for that class and grade.

For a Second Class, Grade A, Certificate, a candidate must obtain 40 per cent. of the marks attached to each of the subjects of examination for Second Class, Grade B, Certificates, and not less than 40 per cent of the marks attached to each of the subjects of examination peculiar to that class and grade, and 60 per cent. of the total number of marks attached to the subjects of examination for that class and grade.

For a First Class, Grade B, Certificate, a candidate must obtain 40 per cent. of the marks attached to each of the subjects of examination for Second Class, Grade A, Certificates, and not less than 40 per cent. in each of the subjects of examination peculiar to that class and grade, and 60 per cent. of the total number of marks attached to the subjects of examination for that class and grade.

For a First Class, Grade A, Certificate, a candidate must obtain 40 per cent. of the marks attached to each of the subjects of examination for First Class, Grade B, Certificates, and not less than 40 per cent. in each of the subjects of examination peculiar to that class and grade, and 60 per cent. of the total number of marks attached to the subjects of examination for that class and grade ; or he must be a graduate in arts of some recognised British or Canadian University, who has proceeded regularly to his degree, and *must satisfy the examiners as to his knowledge in the art of teaching, school discipline and management, and the School Law of the Province,* and may be further required to undergo an oral examination on these subjects.

Whenever it shall be deemed necessary to raise the standard of examination, at least twelve months' notice of such intention shall be given.

Since 1896, the age of male candidates for Teachers' Certificates has been fixed as over twenty years of age, and the age of female candidates as over eighteen.

Since 1894, holders of First Class, Grade B, Certificates, have not been entitled to act as assistants in High Schools.

A candidate who fails to obtain the certificate written for shall not be awarded marks for answers to the papers set in subjects peculiar to that class and grade.

A candidate at the Teachers' Examination may claim to have his papers re-read on the following conditions :—

1. The appeal or claim must be in the hands of the Minister of Education within twenty days after the publication of the results of the examination in the " British Columbia Gazette."

2. The ground of the appeal must be specifically stated.

3. The examiners shall dispose of all appeals with as little delay as possible, and no appeal shall subsequently be entertained on any ground whatever.

4. A deposit of $5 must be made with the department, which deposit shall be returned to the candidate if his appeal or claim is sustained.

APPENDIX B.

— — ——

COURSES OF STUDY.

(i.) HIGH SCHOOLS.

English Course.—All subjects ·prescribed for Graded and Common Schools.

Commercial Course.—Book-keeping—Single and Double Entry—including Banking, Commercial Correspondence, Commercial Law, &c., together with all subjects prescribed for the English Course, and other subjects in which candidates for First Class, Grade B, Certificates are examined.

Classical Course.—Latin, Greek, French, together with all subjects in which candidates for First Class, Grade A, Certificates are examined.

The following are the details of the regular High School Course of Study :—

1. *English Language :*—

(*a*) Reading—Sixth Reader ; the principles of orthoepy and elocution, spelling and syllables, derivation of words, rendering of poetry into prose, and generally the formation of a good English style.

(*b*) Composition.—The structure of sentences and paragraphs, correction of errors, familiar and business letters, themes on familiar subjects.

(*c*) Grammar.—Prescribed text-book completed, analysis and parsing of passages from authors not prescribed.

(*d*) English Literature.—Prescribed text-book.

2. *Geography.*—Mathematical, physical, and political. Uses of Terrestrial globe.

3. *History.*—The leading events of

(*a*) Canadian History,

(*b*) British History,

(*c*) Roman History,

(*d*) Grecian History,

(*e*) Ancient History.

4. *Physiology.*—Prescribed text-book on Anatomy, Physiology, and Hygiene completed.

5. *Book-keeping and Writing :*—

   (*a.*) Single Entry Book-keeping.

   (*b.*) Double Entry Book-keeping.

   (*c.*) Commercial Forms, etc.

   (*d.*) Writing, according to prescribed text-book.

6. *Mathematics :—*

   (*a.*) Arithmetic.—Prescribed text-book completed.

   (*b.*) Mensuration.—Lengths of lines, areas of surfaces, and volumes of solids.

   (*c.*) Algebra.—All rules prior to equations ; simple equations, quadratics, surds, proportion, progressions, permutations and combinations, binomial theorem, evolution and properties of numbers.

   (*d.*) Geometry.—Books I., II., III., IV., VI., and definitions of Book V. ; deductions.

   (*e.*) Trigonometry.—Plane Trigonometry.

   (*f.*) Natural Physiology.—Prescribed Text-book ; also prescribed text-books on Statics, Hydrostatics, and Dynamics.

7. *Ancient Languages :—*

   (*a.*) Latin.—Grammar, prose composition, and the prescribed texts.

   (*b.*) Greek.—Grammar, prose composition, and the prescribed texts.

8. *Modern Language.*—French.—Grammar, prose composition, and prescribed texts.

9. Any of the following optional subjects may be taught :—

Music (Theory).	*Zoology*	*Geology,*
Drawing (Linear).	*Astronomy,*	*Chemistry,*
Botany,	*Rhetoric,*	*General History.*

(ii.) GRADED AND COMMON SCHOOLS.

The course of study prescribed for Graded and Common Schools embraces the following subjects :—

1. *Reading.*—From Primier to Fifth Reader, inclusive. Special attention should be given to correct pronunciation, distinct articulation, and proper expression.

Declamation of selections from prose and poetry committed to memory tends to awaken a taste for good language, as well as aids in the development of a natural and easy delivery.

2. *Writing.*—The systems of penmanship authorized are Gage's copy-books, and Payson, Dunton, and Scribner's series. If the teacher prefer, he can use plain copy-books, setting the headlines.

Particular attention should be given to the proper manner of holding the pen, and correct position at the desk.

3. *Spelling.*—Gage's Speler is the authorised text-book. It should be used by all pupils in the Third, Fourth, and Fifth Readers.

Instruction should be both oral and written.

Dictation should commence with the ability of the child to write legibly, and should continue through the entire course.

4. *Written Arithmetic.*—Principles and methods should be thoroughly explained,

After *accuracy* in work, *quickness in calculation* is most desirable. To attain this, frequent practice in the simple rules is essential.

Practical examples—those that the pupil is liable to meet in every-day life—should be given frequently.

5. *Mental Arithmetic.*—Instruction should be begun with questions in the simple rules, and should expand according to advancement.

In teaching this branch, the chief object aimed at should be to impress firmly on the mind the facts and processes of arithmetic.

6. *Geography.*—Thorough knowledge of the *terms* used and explanations given in the introductory chapter of the text-book is essential.

The wall maps should be used freely. A globe should be used in teaching the shape of the earth, its motions, the seasons, &c.

Map drawing, or the sketching of maps from memory, will be found to be of great value in impressing upon the mind physical geography.

7. *English Grammar.*—Every pupil in the Third Reader should commence this branch, although oral instruction of an elementary character may be given to advantage at an earlier period.

A good knowledge of the parts of speech and their inflections, together with the rules of syntax, is of primary importance.

Construction of sentences and correction of errors should receive early attention.

The teaching of analysis should proceed slowly and carefully—the simple sentence being thoroughly understood before the complex or the compound sentence is attempted.

Parsing should be regarded by the teacher as a test of thorough knowledge of the accidence and rules of grammar.

8. *English History.*—Pupils in the Fourth Reader should be required to begin this subject. Prescribed lessons should be read in class.

The points of the lesson which are required to be memorized should be written on the blackboard.

Pupils should be taught the relative importance of events ; for example, that the story of Becket's parentage is not of equal historical value with the signing of Magna Charta, or the passing of the Habeas Corpus Act.

Oral reviews should be more frequent than written examinations on the subject. Geographical references should be pointed out on the map :— "Geography and chronology are the two eyes of history."

9. *Canadian History.*—Outlines of method given for English History are applicable to this subject.

10. *Composition and Letter Writing.*—The slate may be used in teaching this subject, but special care should be taken that its use does not lead the pupil into the habit of scribbling.

Reproduction as an occasional exercise may be used profitably, but the bringing out of originality is of the most permanent value.

Instruction should be given as to the proper method of opening, closing, folding, and addressing a letter.

A good knowledge of the forms used in general correspondence should be given.

11. *Anatomy, Physiology, and Hygiene.*—Oral primary instruction in these allied subjects may be given to the whole school, but pupils in the Fourth and Fifth Readers should be required to use the text-book.

The teaching of Physiology and Hygiene affords the teacher the opportunity of imparting practical instruction on many points of vital consequence to the pupil.

In giving instruction in Hygiene, the branch subject of Temperance, with reference to the evil effects of stimulants and narcotics on the human system, should not be overlooked.

(iii.) OPTIONAL SUBJECTS.

In addition to the above, the following subjects may be taught :—*Bookkeeping, Mensuration, Geometry, Drawing, Algebra, Music, Needlework, Calisthenics.*

The teaching of optional subjects, such as music, needlework, algebra, geometry, &c., is necessarily left to the discretion of the teacher, for the reason that every teacher may not be qualified to give instruction in these branches

By a regulation made in 1896 by the Council of Public Instruction it is provided that the Board of Trustees of any school district may require that *Temperance*, as a separate subject from anatomy, physiology, and hygiene, be taught in their school or schools, provided the authorized text-book on the subject is used.

(iv.) AGRICULTURE.

In 1896 the subject of agriculture was added to the course of study prescribed for Graded and Common Schools. Instruction in this branch must be given at least twice a week to all pupils in the Fourth and Fifth Divisions.

THE

SYSTEM OF EDUCATION

IN

PRINCE EDWARD ISLAND.

Early History - - - - - - - - - 517
Administration and Inspection - - - - - - 517
Progress under the Act of 1877 - - - - - 517
Statistics - - - - - - - - - 518
Prince of Wales College - - - - - - 518
Appointment of Teachers - - - - - - 519
Salaries - - - - - - - - - - 519
Special Subjects - - - - - - - - 519
Private Schools - - - - - - - 519

APPENDIX.

Regulations of the Board of Education - - - - 520

THE SYSTEM OF EDUCATION

IN

PRINCE EDWARD ISLAND.*

Up to the year 1852 the schools of this province were mainly Early upported by voluntary subscriptions and such local efforts as History. could be secured by mutual co-operation. In 1852 the Free Education Act was passed, under which the salaries of teachers were paid almost entirely from the provincial treasury. The stimulus thus given to education resulted in the establishment of the Provincial Normal School in 1856, and of the Prince of Wales College in 1860. From 1860 until 1877 very little was effected in the way of legislation for the improvement of the schools, although the administration was very effective during that period. In 1877 the Public Schools Act was passed, which provided for the establishment of a department of education, and introduced into our public school system many of the most approved principles and most modern methods of other countries.

The administration of the educational interests of the Administra- province is vested in a Board composed of the Members of tion and the Executive Council, the Chief Superintendent of Education, Inspection. the Principal of the College and Normal School, and two inspectors. Each district has a local Board of Trustees elected annually by the ratepayers.

The number of pupils enrolled in the Public Schools of the province in 1898 was 21,852. The average daily attendance was 13,377, or 61·58 per cent. of the pupils enrolled. There is a compulsory clause in the School Act, but it has never been enforced, consequently the attendance of pupils is entirely voluntary. The work of inspection is carried out by two inspectors of schools appointed by the Government.

In 1879 the College and Normal School were amalgamated, and Progress ladies were admitted for the first time into the former institu- under the tion. Many improvements in the administration of the educa- Act of 1877. tional affairs of the island for the advancement and encourage- ment of the teachers, and for the grading of the different schools, have been introduced since 1879, and are now beginning to be in effective operation.

---

* Since the receipt of this Report, which was prepared in December, 1897, the statistics have been amended in accordance with the latest available tables. The Appendix has also been added.

The effects of the different changes and legislative enactments will best be represented by giving the statistics for each decade since 1841 :—

—	*Schools.	Pupils.	Population of Province.
1841	121	4,356	47,034
1851	135	5,366	66,457

1852.—Free Education Act passed.
1856.—Normal School established.
1860.—Prince of Wales College opened.

—	*Schools.	Pupils.	Population of Province.
1861	302	12,102	81,000
1871	381	15,795	94,021

1877. Public Schools Act passed.
1879. College opened to ladies.
1879. College and Normal School amalgamated.

—	*Schools.	Pupils.	Population of Province.
1881	486	21,601	108,981

It will be observed from the statistics here given that during the period previous to the introduction of the Free Education Act not more than one in twelve of the population attended school. From the period between the passing of the Free Education Act, 1852, and the enactment of the Public Schools Laws of 1877 the attendance was one in six of the population. Under the Public Schools Act of 1877 and its amendments the attendance was one in five.

—	*Schools.	Pupils.	Population.
1891	531	22,330	109,078
1890	582	21 550	?

The Prince of Wales College, which includes the Normal School, is situated in Charlottetown, and its staff consists of a

---

* In this statement school departments are counted as separate schools.

principal and four professors. Attached to it as an adjunct to the Normal Department is the Model School with two teachers.

Teachers are appointed by a majority of the Board of Trustees of each school district. These teachers are trained in the Prince of Wales College and Normal School. Candidates for positions as teachers are required to spend a portion of their time in the Model School, but there are no apprentice teachers. The number of male and female teachers employed in 1898 was as follows:— Appointment of Teachers.

—	Class I.	Class II.	Class III.	Total.
Male Teachers · · ·	71	181	68	320
Female Teachers · ·	30	143	88	261

There are no pensions paid to teachers.

The salaries of the teachers are paid from the Provincial Treasury, but may be supplemented by local assessment, in which case the Treasury pays a further equal amount up to twenty-five dollars. As an inducement to teachers to continue in the profession a small bonus is paid them after a service of five years. The salaries paid by the Government vary according to grade: First-class male teachers received in 1898 $401 per annum; first-class female teachers, $335; second-class male teachers, $234; second-class female teachers, $188; third-class male teachers, $185; third-class female teachers, $141. The supplements (which are voluntary), paid by local assessment and an equal amount up to $25 paid by the Government, are not included in the foregoing salaries. Salaries.

Singing is taught in nearly all the schools, but no cooking and domestic economy. Manual training schools have been started, in 1900, in Charlottetown and Summerside. The cost is defrayed by the Macdonald Manual Training Fund. Special Subjects.

No provision is made for free meals; nor is there any system of continuation schools in existence.

In addition to these public sources of education, there are some few private institutions, mostly denominational in character —viz., in connection with the Roman Catholic Church, Saint Dunstan's College in the vicinity of Charlottetown, two Convent Schools within the city, and several others located in various parts of the island, in all of which both boarders and day scholars are received, and St. Peter's School in connection with the English church of that name, giving opportunities of tuition to children whose parents are willing to pay for the same. Private Schools.

D. J. MacLeod,

Chief Superintendent of Education.

Charlottetown, P.E.I.

APPENDIX.

REGULATIONS OF THE BOARD OF EDUCATION.

School Site and Outside Premises.

1. The school lot should be chosen with regard to healthiness of site; it should be dry and airy, as retired as possible, properly levelled, planted with shade trees, and enclosed by a substantial fence. It should be not less than half an acre in extent. If the school population of the district exceeds seventy-five the area should be one acre.

2. Every country school should be provided with a wood shed and two water closets, under different roofs. It is recommended that they be kept under lock and key.

3. Proper care should be taken to secure cleanliness and to prevent unpleasant and unhealthy odours.

Schoolhouse.

4. The schoolhouse should be placed at least thirty feet from the public highway, and provided with a cloak-room or entry.

5. Where the school population of the section exceeds one hundred, the schoolhouse should contain two rooms; where it exceeds one hundred and fifty, three rooms—an additional room being required for each additional fifty pupils.

6. An assistant teacher cannot be appointed in any school without the written approval of the Chief Superintendent of Education. A teacher engaged without such sanction must be paid entirely by the Trustees who employed him.

7. A first-class school must have at least two rooms and two teachers, in order to enable the Principal to carry out the work efficiently in the higher branches of study without detriment to the younger children; but it must be clearly understood, that no school can be ranked as a first-class school, unless the elementary instruction is of such a high character as to warrant the granting of this privilege.

8. At least 150 cubic feet of air should be allowed for each scholar, and a schoolroom to seat forty should, therefore, be about 25 feet by 20, and 12 feet high. If this size be larger than the district can afford, smaller dimensions may be allowed, on the written approval of the Inspector.

9. Ample provision must be made for ventilation. There should be a complete change of atmosphere in the room three times every hour. A uniform temperature of at least sixty-seven degrees should be maintained throughout the whole school day.

School Furniture and Apparatus.

10. A sufficient number of seats and desks should be provided for the accommodation of all the pupils usually in attendance at the school. There should be at least two chairs in addition to the teacher's chair.

11. Seats and desks should be so arranged, that the pupils may face the teacher. They should be single, if possible, but at any rate limited to two pupils, provided with suitable backs, graduated so that the feet of all the pupils may rest on the floor. The seats and desks must be fastened to the floor in paralle rows with aisles between.

12. A space of four or five feet should intervene between the front desk and the teacher's platform, and passages, at least three feet wide, should be left between the outside rows and the side and rear walls of the room.

13. The following dimensions for chairs and desks are recommended :—

| AGE OF PUPILS. | CHAIRS OR SEATS. | | | DESKS. | | | |
| | Height. | | Slope of Back. | Length. | | Width. | Height next Pupil. |
	Front.	Rear.		Double.	Single.		
Five to eight years	12 in.	11½ in.	2 in.	36 in.	18 in.	12 in.	22 in.
Eight to ten years	13 „	12½ „	2 „	36 „	18 „	12 „	23 „
Ten to thirteen years	14 „	13½ „	2½ „	36 „	20 „	13 „	24 „
Thirteen to sixteen years	16 „	15½ „	3 „	40 „	22 „	13 „	26 „

14. There should be one blackboard at least four feet wide, extending across the whole room in rear of the teacher's desk, with its lower edge not more than two and a half feet above the floor or platform, and, when possible, there should be an additional blackboard on each side of the room. At the lower edge of each blackboard there should be a shelf or trough five inches wide for holding crayons and brushes.

The following directions for making a blackboard may be found useful :—

(*a*) If the walls are brick the plaster should be laid upon the brick and not upon the laths as elsewhere ; if frame, the part to be used for a blackboard should be lined with boards, and the laths for holding the plaster nailed firmly on the boards.

(*b*) The plaster for the blackboard should be composed largely of plaster of Paris.

(*c*) Before and after having received the first coat of colour, it should be thoroughly polished with fine sandpaper.

(*d*) The colouring matter should be laid on with a wide, flat varnish brush.

(*e*) The liquid colouring should be laid as follows :—Dissolve gum shellac in alcohol, four ounces to the quart ; the alcohol should be 95 per cent. strong ; the dissolving process will require at least twelve hours. Fine emery flour with enough chrome green or lampblack to give colour, should then be added until the mixture has the consistency of thin paint. It may then be applied, in long even strokes, up and down, the liquid being kept constantly stirred.

15. A well equipped Primary Department should contain a ball frame, reading cards, and any such simple illustration of colour, measures, form, number and natural history, as may be within the means of the district to purchase. Advanced Departments should have in addition a set of modern maps, a dictionary, and a terrestrial globe.

16. All schools ought to be furnished with a clock, thermometer, a globe not less than nine inches in diameter, properly mounted, a map of the Maritime Provinces, maps of Dominion of Canada, maps of the world and of the different continents, and a suitable supply of crayons and blackboard brushes.

COURSE OF STUDIES.

17. The course of studies prescribed by the Board of Education shall be followed by the teacher as far as the circumstances of his school will permit. Any modifications deemed necessary should be made only with the concurrence of the inspector and the Trustees. In French schools the English Readers shall be used in addition to any prescribed text books in the French language.

DUTIES OF TEACHERS.

18. In every public school in which more teachers than one are employed, the head teacher should be called the Principal, and the other teachers Assistants.

19. The Principal shall prescribe (with the concurrence of the Trustees) the duties of the Assistants, and shall be responsible for the organisation, classification, and discipline of the whole school.

20. Every Public School Teacher has power and is required to manage his school in accordance with the School Law, and the regulations of the Board of Education.

21. The teacher (with the consent of the Trustees) may suspend pupils for persistent truancy, violent opposition to authority, habitual and determined neglect of duty, improper language, destruction of school property, or any conduct likely to injure the school. If any of these are persisted in, after one or more suspensions, the Trustees and teacher must expel the pupil.

22. In addition to the duties prescribed by the School Act, it shall be the duty of every teacher in a Public School :—

(1) To see that the schoolhouse is ready for the reception of pupils at least fifteen minutes before the time prescribed for opening the school in the morning, and five minutes before the time for opening in the afternoon.

(2) To classify his pupils strictly according to the programme of studies prescribed by the Education Department, and to make no departure from such classification, without the consent of the Board of Trustees and the Inspector.

(3) To prepare a time-table to be posted in some conspicuous part of the room for the guidance of himself and his pupils, which time-table should be submitted to the Inspector for his approval, on his first visit to the school, after the same is adopted or changed.

(4) To prevent the use by the pupils of unauthorised text-books.

(5) To make at the end of each school term, or at such other time as may be approved by the Inspector, and subject to revision by him, such promotions from one class to another as he may deem expedient.

(6) To practise such discipline in his school as would be exercised by a kind, firm, and judicious parent ; to reprove his pupils with tenderness and becoming deliberation, and to aim at governing them through their affections and reason rather than by force ; to encourage his pupils to cultivate kindly feelings towards one another, respect for one another's rights, politeness in and out of school, habits of honesty and truthfulness, and obedience to all persons in authority over them ; and to discountenance quarrelling, cruelty to animals, and the use of profane and other improper language.

(7) To give strict attention to the proper ventilation and cleanliness of the schoolhouse ; to make and enforce such rules as will ensure the keeping of the school grounds and outbuildings in a neat and cleanly condition.

(8) To see that the school grounds, sheds, and water-closets are kept in proper order ; that no damage is done to the furniture, fences, outbuildings, or other school property ; to give notice in writing to the Trustees of any necessary repairs or supplies.

(9) To make up all returns to the Inspector or the Education Department, as far as the information required can be supplied from the school register ; and to furnish such other information affecting the interests of his school as may from time to time be required by the Department or the Inspector.

(10) To attend regularly the Teachers' Institutes held in his county, and to contribute from his experience and observation to their general usefulness.

23. The teacher is required to keep the school open on every legally authorised teaching day throughout the term.

24. Teachers are to be punctual and constant in their own attendance, and to require the same from the pupils. Cases of absence and lateness are to be satisfactorily accounted for.

25. To be successful they must command the respect and goodwill of their pupils, and should strive diligently that the practice of all Christian virtues may prevail among those who are under their charge. Though they are precluded from sectarian teaching, it is their duty to inculcate those principles of morality which are revered in common by all good men. Teachers, however, must neither interfere nor permit interference with the religious tenets of the pupils.

26. When a register has been completed it must be handed to the Secretary of Trustees intact, and shall remain among the school papers for at least one year after. Any infringement of this regulation shall be reported to the Superintendent of Education by the Inspector, and will necessitate a deduction from the teacher's salary, unless satisfactory explanation be made.

27. The following are the duties of pupils in Public Schools :—

(1) Every pupil whose name is entered on the register of a Public School shall attend punctually and regularly every day of the school term in which his name is so entered ; he shall be neat and cleanly in his person and habits, and diligent, truthful, honest, kind, courteous, respectful, and obedient, and shall conform to all the rules of the school.

(2) Any pupil not present at the time prescribed for opening the school may be required to furnish forthwith a written excuse from his parent or guardian, or may be denied admittance to the school for the day or half day, at the discretion of the Principal.

(3) Any pupil absenting himself from school, except on account of sickness, shall forfeit his standing in his class, or shall be liable to such other punishment as the teacher may lawfully inflict.

(4) No pupil shall be allowed to leave school before the hour appointed for closing, except in case of sickness, or at the request, either oral or written, of the parent or guardian.

(5) Any pupil guilty of any of the following offences, viz. :—[a] persistent truancy ; [b] violent opposition to authority ; [c] the repetition of any offence after being warned ; [d] habitual and wilful neglect of duty ; [e] the use of profane or improper language ; [f] cutting, marring, destroying or defacing any part of the school property ; [g] writing any obscene words on the fences, water-closets, or any part of the school premises ; [h] general bad conduct, injurious to the moral tone of the school, may be suspended by the teacher for one month, or until such suspension is removed on assurance of better conduct, or by order of the Board of Trustees.

(6) Whenever a teacher suspends a pupil for any of the causes herein named he shall at once-notify his parents or guardians and the Board of Trustees, stating the reasons for such suspension.

(7) The parent or guardian of any pupil suspended may appeal to the Board of Trustees against the action of the teacher, and the decision of the Trustees shall be final.

(8) Any pupil who shall be adjudged so refractory by the Board of Trustees and by the Teacher, that his presence in the school is injurious to the other pupils, may be expelled ; and no such pupil shall be re-admitted to any school without the written consent of the Public School Inspector.

(9) No pupil who is affected with or exposed to any contagious disease shall be permitted to attend school until he produces the certificate of a medical man that there are no sanitary objections to his re-admission.

(10) Pupils shall be responsible to the teacher for their conduct on the school premises, or in going to or returning from school, except when accompanied by their parents or guardians, or by some person appointed by them or on their behalf.

(11) No pupil shall be allowed to remain in school unless he is furnished with the books and other requisites to be used by him in school, but it shall be lawful for the Board of Trustees to supply him with such books and other requisites.

(12) Any school property or furniture injured or destroyed by a pupil shall be made good forthwith by the parent or guardian under penalty of the suspension of the delinquent.

(13) Every pupil entitled thereto shall, on application, when he leaves or removes from the school, receive a certificate of good conduct and standing.

HOLIDAYS.

28. No teacher shall make up lost time by teaching on a holiday, or during vacations, and any attendance during such time shall be disallowed.

29. The year shall consist of two terms, one ending on June 30th, the other on December 31st. The vacations will be three weeks in May and three weeks in October, as well as the first week in July or the last week in December.

30. In Charlottetown and Summerside the Trustees may make their own arrangements for vacation and school sessions, subject to the approval of the Board of Education.

31. Trustees can, if required to do so by a majority at the annual meeting, substitute a midsummer vacation of six weeks, for the present spring and autumn vacations.

32. Every Saturday, every statutory holiday, and every day proclaimed a holiday by the Provincial or Dominion authorities, shall be a holiday in the Public Schools.

SCHOOL HOURS.

33. From the May vacation to the October vacation, the school session shall be from nine to four o'clock, with one hour's intermission at noon : and from the October vacation to the May vacation the session shall be from ten to three o'clock, with one half hour's intermission. There shall also be two recesses of ten minutes each, when the schoolroom must be aired.

34. The Trustees may, by resolution, prescribe as school hours from half-past nine to three o'clock, with an hour's intermission, for the period from the October to the May vacation, instead of the time specified in Section 33.

Note.—In schools having midsummer vacations, the hours should be changed on the 15th May and October.

35. In Summerside and Charlottetown the school hours may, if so decided by the Trustees, be from nine in the forenoon to two o'clock in the afternoon, with two intermissions of ten minutes each.

PAYMENT OF TEACHERS' SALARIES.

36. The salaries of Teachers shall be paid quarterly on the eighth day of October, January, April and July in each year, or rateably, according to the number of legally authorised days the teachers shall have satisfactorily taught for any portions of such quarters. All School Returns must be lodged in the Education Office at least four days before payment will be made. A teacher engaging at any other time than the beginning of the school year, can only engage for the remaining portion of the year.

37. The Inspectors' Reports as to the ranking of teachers in accordance with Section IX., must be lodged at the Education Office by the last day of each term.

38. The Inspectors' Reports ranking teachers entitled to a bonus under Section XII. of the Public Schools Act must be forwarded to the Education Office on or before the 15th of July in each year.

39. The bonus is payable on or before the 20th day of August in each year.

40. Partial orders, *i.e.*, orders given by teachers for part of the sum due them, will not be received at the Education Office.

41. No salaries can be paid from the Treasury to teachers until they have obtained a license under the Public Schools Act, 1877, and until all the necessary returns from the School District have been sent to the Office.

DUTIES OF TRUSTEES.

42. It is the duty of the School Trustees to keep the schoolhouse in suitable condition for use by the teachers and pupils.

43. The Trustees must pay the teacher any amount deducted from his statutory allowance, owing to loss of time occasioned by the neglect or refusal of the Trustees to comply with Regulation No. 42.

44. The Trustees must present, for inspection, all Books and records kept by them as a Board of Trustees, when required to do so by the Inspector of Schools.

NORMAL DEPARTMENT OF PRINCE OF WALES COLLEGE.

45. The entrance examinations to the Normal School Classes shall be held under the direction of the Chief Superintendent of Education, and in such places as may be deemed necessary, not to exceed five at any one examination.

46. The Chief Superintendent shall appoint, when necessary, one or more deputies to preside at the examinations.

47. Four Examiners shall be appointed under Section 3rd of the Public Schools Act.

48. The annual entrance examination to the Normal School shall be held on the first Tuesday in July ; and a semi-annual examination, if necessary, on the 3rd Tuesday in December.

49. The Chief Superintendent shall prepare and have printed suitable questions for each class in accordance with the prescribed syllabus of examination. The examination papers shall be securely sealed, and the seal on each pac age broken only in the presence of the candidates when required for actual use in the examination.

50. Each deputy, who presides at any of the stations at which examinations are held, shall immediately thereafter forward the papers returned by the candidates to the Chief Superintendent, with a statement that the examination was conducted in good faith, and that no infringements of the law or regulations of the Board were known to him.

51. Where, from the number of Candidates or any other cause, additional presiding Examiners are required, the Chief Superintendent shall make such appointments as are necessary ; but no person shall be eligible to be appointed presiding Examiner who has any pupils writing for admission at the station where he is presiding.

52. Application for admission to the examination must be forwarded to the Education Office not later than two weeks previous to the date of the examination. Before taking the examination, each candidate must pay a fee of fifty cents, to defray expenses of examination. The examiner will receive the same, and remit it to Chief Superintendent of Education.

53. Each letter of application shall give the name of the school to which the applicant belongs, his post office address, his age, and the station at which he intends to present himself for examination.

54. The following are the subjects upon which candidates for admission to the Normal School shall be examined :—

JUNIOR ENTRANCE EXAMINATION.

ENGLISH—Fifth or Sixth Reader—Parsing, Analysis, Orthography, Composition, Reading and Literature.

HISTORY—General Outlines of British and Canadian History.

GEOGRAPHY—Geography of the Dominion. Outlines of General Geography.

ARITHMETIC—Smaller Arithmetic throughout, Advanced Arithmetic to the end of Decimal fractions.

SENIOR ENTRANCE EXAMINATION.

ENGLISH,
ARITHMETIC,
GEOGRAPHY,
HISTORY,
} as prescribed by junior entrance examination.

GEOMETRY—Euclid, Book I.

ALGEBRA—Colenso's (Twenty Exercises, or equivalent).

LATIN—Beginner's Latin Book, or its equivalent.

54½. Each candidate to be entitled to attend the Normal School Department must obtain 50 per cent. of the attainable marks in English ; 50 per cent. in Arithmetic ; 35 per cent. in History and 50 per cent. in Geography : and not less than 50 per cent. of the total number of marks.

COLLEGIATE DEPARTMENT, PRINCE OF WALES COLLEGE.

55. The annual entrance examination to the College shall be conducted by the Principal and his Assistant Professors in July of each year.

56. The College and Normal School shall open on the Monday following the third Tuesday in August, and shall continue in session until the Friday next previous to the 25th December.

57. The second term shall open eleven week days (other than Saturdays) after the closing of the preceding session, as in Section 56, and shall close on the last Friday in May.

58. No candidate shall be admitted to the College who has not previously passed an examination in the following subjects :—

ENGLISH,
ARITHMETIC,
GEOGRAPHY,
HISTORY,
} as prescribed for junior entrance examination.

GEOMETRY—Book 1.

ALGEBRA—Colenso's Twenty Exercises, or equivalent.

LATIN—Beginner's Latin Book, or its equivalent.

59. Each candidate must make at least 50 per cent. of the marks attainable in these subjects, and at the close of the examination a report giving the number of marks made by the candidates in each subject shall be sent to the Education Office by the Principal of the College.

60. The Principal may, if he thinks proper, hold a semi-annual examination for entrance to the College at the beginning of the second session, a report of which must be made as in Section 59, but no other examination for entrance shall be held except as provided for in Section 55.

61. The Tuition Fee for students attending the Prince of Wales College and Normal School shall be as follows, viz. :—

For students residing in the Town or Royalty of Charlottetown the sum of fourteen dollars each, annually ; for students residing in any other portion of the Province, the sum of seven dollars each, annually—in all cases payable half-yearly in advance.　42 Vic. Chap. 3, Sec. 8.

TEACHERS' LICENSES.

No person shall be entitled to receive a license to teach under this Act unless [1] *if a male, he is eighteen years of age, or, if a female, she is sixteen years of age ; and* [2] *unless he or she is of temperate habits and good moral character : and* [3] *has attended the Provincial Training School at least one term.* —[40 Vic. Chap. 1, Sec. 85.]

62. Before the close of each semi-annual session of the Normal School an examination shall be held, under the direction of the Chief Superintendent of Education, in the following subjects, viz. :—

Third Class.

I. READING—A portion of the Sixth Royal Reader, or equivalent.

II. ORTHOGRAPHY—From Reader as above. Penmanship.

III. ARITHMETIC—General Arithmetic—methods of working to be judged.

IV. ENGLISH—Currie's Grammar. Literature. Reader.

V. GEOGRAPHY—Canada and the Continents. Map Drawing.

VI. HISTORY—A period of British History.

VII. SCHOOL MANAGEMENT—Theory and Art of Teaching, including principles and methods of instruction.

VIII. ORGANISATION—School organisation and government. School Laws of P. E. Island. Regulations of Board of Education.

IX. TEACHING—Marks for Teaching will be given by the Principal of the Prince of Wales College and Normal School and the Training Master. The marks will be based upon actual practice in the Normal School.

AGRICULTURE—First Principles.

63. Each candidate in Training for Third Class shall be required to take this examination before receiving a license to teach.

64. All who make an average of 80 per cent. of the marks assigned to the subjects in Section 59, and not less than 75 in teaching, shall be entitled to First Class Rank for professional work ; an average of between 70 and 80, with at least 60 in teaching, will entitle candidates to Second Class Rank ; and candidates receiving an average of 60 per cent., and not less than 50 in teaching, will be entitled to Third Class Rank. For a less average than that for Third Class Rank no candidate can obtain a Third Class Provincial License.

65. The following are the subjects on which candidates for Second Class License will be examined :—

Second Class.

I. ENGLISH—Selections in Prose and Poetry from English authors.

II. HISTORY—A period of British History.

III. GEOGRAPHY—Canada and any one of the continents.

IV. ARITHMETIC—Advanced Arithmetic.

V. ALGEBRA—To the end of simple equations of one or more unknown quantities.

VI. GEOMETRY —Euclid, Books I., II., III. Exercises.

VII. PHYSICS.

VIII. LATIN GRAMMAR—Cæsar's Gallic War, one or two Books ; Arnold's Prose Composition (30 Exercises).

IX. FRENCH—Selections from French authors. Grammar. Composition.

X. SCHOOL MANAGEMENT—Swett's Methods of Teaching.

XI. MUSIC.

XII. TEACHING—Practice in Model Schools.

Note—Book-keeping will be accepted as an equivalent for French.

66. Candidates for First or Second Class License must, in order to be successful, obtain at least 50 per cent. of the attainable marks in English, 50 per cent. in Arithmetic, 35 per cent. in each of the other subjects, and not less than 60 per cent. of the total number of marks.

67. Candidates for First Class License cannot receive a higher License than Second Class unless they have at least one year's experience in teaching.

68. The following are the subjects for the examination of candidates for First Class License :—

First Class.

I. English—A Play of Shakespeare. Some other English Classic. Literature. Mason's Grammar [Advanced].

II. English Literature—Brooke's throughout. The Literature of one period more minutely. English Composition.

III. History—Ancient History of the East, Grecian or Roman History.

IV. Physical Geography—Lawson's Text-Book of Physical Geography.

V. Arithmetic—Advanced Arithmetic.

VI. Geometry—Euclid, Books I.-IV. Exercises.

VII. Chemistry—Remsen's Elements of Chemistry.

VIII. Latin—Grammar. Selections from two authors. Arnold's Prose Composition to Exercise 61.

IX. Algebra—To the end of quadratics.

X. Greek—Bryce's First Greek Reader, Part I. Xenophon's *Anabasis*, one or two Books.

XI. French—Grammar. Fasquell's Introductory French Course.

XII. Trigonometry — Plane Trigonometry. Practical Mathematics. Solution of Triangles. Heights and distances.

XIII. Teaching—Practice in Model Schools.

Note.—Drawing will be accepted as an equivalent for Greek.

Academic Class.

69. The examination for Academic License will be open to all First Class Teachers of two years' experience, who have obtained first rank in professional work, or who hold a First Class Diploma.

Latin—Arnold's Prose Composition, Part I. Horace, Odes, Book I. Livy, Book XXI., Chaps. 1-37.

Greek—Arnold's Prose Composition. Homer, Iliad, Book I. Herodotus, Book I., Chaps. 1-42.

French—Molière, *Le Bourgeois Gentilhomme* ; Racine, *Iphigenie.*

Mathematics—Algebra, Colenso's Students' Algebra [throughout].

Geometry—Euclid [with exercises]. Solid Geometry. Conic Sections.

Trigonometry—Plane and Spherical Trigonometry, with practical examples from Chambers' Mathematics.

English and English Literature—The History and Literature of the Nineteenth Century. An acquaintance with the principal works of the period required.

School Management—Swett's Methods of Teaching ; Page's Theory and Practice of Teaching.

Of the four parts of this course, viz., Latin, Greek, and French ; Mathematics ; English ; and Professional Work, three must be taken by each candidate, the choice of selection being limited to the first two.

70. The examination of all candidates for Teachers' Licenses shall be held under the direction of the Chief Superintendent of Education. The papers shall be valued by Examiners appointed by the Board of Education.

71. There shall be one examination in each year for candidates for First and Second Class Licenses, beginning on Monday following the last Friday in May.

72. The results shall be announced about the first day of July.

Assistant Teachers.

73. In Graded Schools of two departments female teachers of the Third Class should be employed as assistants.

74. The Chief Superintendent shall have power to issue local licenses valid for the school year in which they are issued to persons of fair education, who shall receive the amount of twenty dollars per quarter.

75. A local license shall only be valid in the district for which it is issued, and cannot be renewed unless upon the report of the Inspector that the work done by such assistant is efficient, and satisfactory to the Trustees of the school, and then only for one additional year.

DAILY AVERAGE ATTENDANCE OF PUPILS.

76. In every school the average attendance of pupils must be, *at least*, 50 per cent. of the children of school age in the district. In districts employing more than one teacher, the average attendance must be as follows :—

2 teachers 80 pupils or under, an average attendance of 40.
2   ,,   80 pupils or over,   ,,   ,,   ,,   ,, 50 per cent
3   ,,   140 pupils or under, ,,   ,,   ,, 70.
3   ,,   140 pupils or over,   ,,   ,,   ,,   ,, 50 per cent.
4   ,,   200 pupils or under, ,,   ,,   ,,   ,, 100.
4   ,,   200 pupils or over,   ,,   ,,   ,,   ,, 50 per cent
5   ,,   250 pupils or under, ,,   ,,   ,,   ,, 125.
5   ,,   250 pupils or over,   ,,   ,,   ,,   ,, 50 per cent.

and so on for every additional fifty pupils.

77. When a larger attendance than 50 per cent. of the number in the district is required by the Public Schools Act or the Regulations of the Board of Education, the attendance of non-resident pupils, as well as of pupils under or over the specified school ages may be counted ; but in every case the average attendance of resident pupils of school age must be 50 per cent. or over, and made so to appear on the Trustees' Returns.

78. When the total average attendance in schools of two or more departments is less than 50 per cent. of the number of pupils in the district, a deduction from the salaries of all the teachers in the school shall be made as in Section 15 of the Public Schools Act, 1877.

79. When the total average attendance is 50 per cent. or upwards, and yet less than the average required by Regulation No. 76, a deduction shall be made from the Provincial allowance of the teachers similar to that provided for in Section 5 of the 48th Vic., chap. 2, the required average being the basis of payment instead of twenty, as in the section referred to.

ARBOUR DAY.

80. Some day in May should be set apart by the Trustees of every school throughout the Island for the purpose of planting shade trees, making flower beds, and otherwise improving and beautifying the school grounds. Arbour Day, when observed in this way, will be considered as a Holiday.

81. The Chief Superintendent of Education shall have power to appoint an Arbour Day for the whole Province, or for a portion thereof. When a day is so appointed, the school authorities shall observe it instead of a day appointed as in Regulation No. 80.

School Property.

82. No schoolhouse, or any building or ground, or furniture pertaining thereto, shall be used or occupied for any other than Public School Purposes without the express permission of the Trustees acting in their corporate capacity.

Temporary Third Class Licenses.

83. When the Board of Trustees of any school district report that they cannot obtain a suitable teacher, the Chief Superintendent may, if he deems it necessary in the interest of the school service, issue a temporary Third Class License to any suitable person of fair qualification to teach the school in such district. Such license shall be valid for the school year in which it is issued, and shall entitle the holder to a salary from the Provincial Treasury at the rate of $80 per annum.

Teachers' Institute.

84. On giving notice to the Trustees and pupils, teachers shall be entitled to be absent from their schools, for the purpose of attending Teachers' Associations, or the Provincial Education Institute, two legally authorised teaching days in each school year. The time so taken must be exclusively devoted to the work of the Association or Institute.

Inspection.

85. The Inspectors shall report monthly to the Chief Superintendent, upon forms furnished by the Education Department, the result of their observation and enquiry. They shall also make a general annual report to the Chief Superintendent on or about the 31st day of December.

86. In addition to the duties assigned to Inspectors by law and by existing regulations, it shall be their duty, and they are hereby required:—

(a) To report on applications for new school districts, or for a change of school boundaries.

(b) To examine the records of the Boards of School Trustees, when deemed necessary, and to see that they are properly kept and entered into a Minute Book.

(c) To examine the Register, and enter therein the date of their visit.

(d) To note the condition of the schoolhouse and premises, and to see that the school is in all respects conducted and maintained in conformity with the Law and the Regulations of the Board of Education.

87. When the Trustees of any school refuse or neglect to provide sufficient school accommodation, or to conduct the school in conformity with the Law and the Regulations and orders of the Board of Education, the Chief Superintendent shall have the power to withhold all Government allowances from the teacher.

88. The Inspector, while officially visiting a school, has supreme authority in the school, and has the right to direct teachers and pupils in regard to any or all of the exercises of the schoolroom. He may either examine the classes himself or direct the teacher to do so. He is at liberty to give such advice to pupils or to the teacher as he may deem necessary.

Miscellaneous.

89. All teachers remaining unemployed for more than two consecutive years must again qualify by passing a satisfactory examination, according

to law, before entering into an agreement to teach in the Public Schools, unless such teachers have been attending an institution of learning.

90. Academic Licenses do not lapse under Section 89 of the Regulations of the Board of Education.

91. Licenses of the First Class, if obtained upon making an average of over 75 per cent. of the marks attainable at any examination held subsequently to the 1st of January, 1881, do not lapse under Section 89.

SCHOOL LIBRARIES.

92. No book hostile to the Christian religion, or of an immoral or sectarian tendency, shall be permitted in a School Library.

93. The School Library shall be held by the Trustees in trust as a part of the school property. They shall appoint a Librarian, and make such rules and regulations for the preservation and circulation of the books as they may deem necessary.

94. After July, 1896, all Candidates for Matriculation into the Prince of Wales College and Normal School shall be required to take the Junior and Senior Examinations.

MEMORANDUM
ON
AGRICULTURAL EDUCATION
IN CANADA.

By Wm. Saunders, LL.D., Director of Dominion
Experimental Farms.*

PROVINCIAL AIDS - - - - - - - - - 533

   Agricultural Schools - - - - - - - - 533
   Other Organisations - - - - - - - - 534
DOMINION AIDS TO AGRICULTURE - - - - - - 534

Information relating to agriculture in Canada is given to
the farming community by both the Provincial and Dominion
Governments.

PROVINCIAL AIDS.

1. *Agricultural Schools.*—Some of the Provinces maintain
agricultural schools for the practical education of young men
in farming. The Ontario College of Agriculture at Guelph,
Ontario, is the best of these institutions in Canada. It is well
equipped and well managed and has been in operation for
about twenty-five years. There a large number of the sons
of Canadian farmers receive practical training in their calling.
An experimental farm is also carried on in connection with
this institution. The full course of study covers a period of
three years. The fees for tuition are nominal, and the cost of
living is reduced to a very small figure owing to the practice of
crediting students with the value of the labour performed by
them on the farm.

In the Province of Quebec there are several smaller agricultural
schools in different parts of the Province, the most important
of which is located at Compton, Quebec, in connection with
an experimental farm.

---

* For the use of this memorandum, the Editor of these volumes is
indebted to the High Commissioner for the Dominion of Canada.

Reference should also be made to an interesting paper on *Agricultural
Education in Greater Britain* read by Mr. R. Hedger Wallace to the
Society of Arts (London), on February 27, 1900, and printed in the
Society's *Journal* for March 9, 1900.

A school of Agriculture has been in operation at Truro, Nova Scotia, associated with an experimental station, for ten or twelve years past, and in the same Province a school of Horticulture has been in operation for the past three or four years, at Wolfville, Nova Scotia. Tuition is free in both schools. In New Brunswick a Government Training farm has been opened at Penobsquis, near Sussex. Tuition is free.

2. *Other Organisations.*—Other agencies which also render valuable help in this connection are Dairy Schools, Travelling Dairies, Farmers' Institutes, Livestock and Dairy Associations, Fruit Growers' Associations (associated, in Ontario, with a number of Fruit Experiment Stations), Poultry Associations, and Agricultural and Horticultural Societies. These are all maintained or assisted by the several Provinces by annual grants, and there are many of such organisations in every Province. The members connected with these associations, &c., meet from time to time to discuss matters relating to the branches of agriculture they represent, and the more important papers read at such meetings are published by the Provincial Governments and distributed, free of charge, to farmers who desire to receive them.

Dominion Aids to Agriculture.

The progress of agriculture in Canada has been greatly stimulated by the organisation and maintenance of experimental farms by the Dominion Government. Five of these farms have been established in different parts of the Dominion. This work was begun in 1887, the institutes being so located as to render efficient help to the farmers in the more thickly settled districts, and at the same time to cover the most varied climatic and other conditions which influence agriculture in this country. The Central Experimental Farm is situated at Ottawa, near the boundary line between Ontario and Quebec, where it serves as an aid to agriculture in these two important Provinces. A site for one of the four branch experimental farms was chosen at Nappan, Nova Scotia, near the boundary between that Province and New Brunswick, where it serves the purposes of the three Maritime Provinces. A second branch farm has been established at Brandon, in the central portion of Manitoba; a third at Indian Head, a town in Assiniboia, one of the North-west Territories; and a fourth at Agassiz, in the coast climate of British Columbia.

At all these farms experiments are conducted to gain information as to the best methods of preparing the land for crop and of maintaining its fertility, the most useful and profitable crops to grow, and how the various crops grown can be disposed of to the greatest advantage. To this end experiments are conducted in the feeding of cattle, sheep, and swine for flesh, the feeding of cows for the production of milk, butter, and cheese, and of poultry both for flesh and eggs. Experiments are also conducted to test the merits of new or untried varieties of cereals and other field crops, of grasses, forage plants, fruits, vegetables, plants, and trees: and samples, particularly of the most promising cereals, are distributed freely among farmers for trial, so that such as promise to be most profitable may be rapidly brought into general cultivation. New varieties of cereals and fruits are also produced by cross fertilising and selection.

At the Central Experimental Farm there is a scientific staff engaged in solving such problems as may arise in connection with the chemistry of agriculture, the diseases to which cultivated plants and trees are subject, the ravages of insect pests, and the spread of noxious weeds. Experiments are also conducted in the planting of trees for timber and shelter, and in the testing of ornamental trees, shrubs, and plants.

An annual report is published containing particulars of the work done at each farm, and this report is sent free of charge to every farmer in the Dominion who asks for it. The annual edition now required to meet the demand is 60,000. Occasional bulletins on special subjects of immediate importance are also issued from time to time as required. A large correspondence is conducted with farmers in all parts of the Dominion, who are encouraged to ask advice and information from the experimental farms, in reference to all questions affecting their calling. Farmers are also invited to visit the various farms and inspect the work in progress. The officers attend many of the more important gatherings of farmers in different parts of Canada, at which opportunities are afforded of giving fuller information regarding the work conducted and the results achieved from year to year.

No pupils are received at any of these Federal Government agricultural stations for training in experimental work.

NOTE ON THE MACDONALD MANUAL TRAINING FUND FOR THE DEVELOPMENT OF MANUAL AND PRACTICAL INSTRUCTION IN PRIMARY SCHOOLS IN CANADA.

One of the most remarkable features of the educational movement which is stirring the world at the present time is the growing sense of the importance of Manual and Practical Instruction, especially in primary schools. There is a widespread feeling that it is a mistake to confine education too closely to the study of books. The training of hand and eye in early childhood is alike of educational and of practical benefit. It cultivates the faculty of observation; it strengthens and enlarges the powers of exact expression; it corrects a tendency to one-sided intellectual development; it makes school life more interesting; it discloses aptitudes and interests which school teaching in the past has too often stunted or ignored; it provides a basis for later technical education, and it checks the growth of a foolish contempt for manual labour. All over the world different forms of manual and practical training are receiving increased recognition as indispensable elements in liberal education. "Unfortunately," to quote the Report of the Committee of Council on Education for England and Wales, 1897-8, "a mechanical form of bookish instruction is the cheapest kind of teaching. It calls for the least thought on the part of the teacher, and it requires the smallest outlay of funds or trouble on the necessary apparatus. Consequently it tends to prevail in inferior schools, staffed by inferior teachers. Of all kinds of education it is the least fruitful of permanent good."

Throughout the British Empire the feeling in favour of manual and practical instruction has been strengthened and guided by the valuable report of the Commission on Manual and Practical Instruction in Primary Schools under the Board of National Education in Ireland. This report, published in 1898,* together with the volumes of evidence and appendices,† has evidently made a deep impression on the minds of teachers and educational authorities in many different parts of the Empire. Traces of its influence and quotations from its recommendations crop up in educational memoranda published in almost all the colonies. The Commissioners based their recommendations in

---

* Cd. 8923, 7½d.

† First Report, with Evidence, Cd. 8383, 10½d.; second volume of Evidence, 1897, Cd. 8532, 2s. 3d.; third volume of Evidence, 1897, Cd. 8619, 1s. 4d.; fourth volume of Evidence, 1898, Cd. 8924, 3s. 7d. Appendix containing Evidence, 1899, Cd. 9512, 5s. 7d.; Appendices (various documents and reports), 1898, Cd. 8925, 4s. 10½d.

favour of introducing manual and practical instruction into the curricula of primary schools on educational reasons, on grounds of practical experience, and for reasons of practical utility. They held it to be important "that children should be taught, not merely to take in knowledge from books, but to observe with intelligence the material world around them; that they should be trained in habits of correct reasoning on the facts observed: and that they should, even at school, acquire some skill in the use of hand and eye to execute the conceptions of the brain." Such training the Commissioners regarded as "valuable to all, but especially valuable to those whose lives are to be mainly devoted to industrial arts and occupations." And, in the course of their inquiries, they had found that the introduction of manual training had contributed greatly to stimulate the intelligence of the pupils, to increase their interest in school life, and to make school life generally brighter and more attractive. "The development of Manual and Practical Education," wrote the Commissioners in their closing paragraphs, "will not disturb what is good in the present system, but only supply what is lacking. It will quicken the intelligence of the children, brighten the tone of school life, and make school work generally more interesting and attractive. . . . . The children will be taught not by means of books only, but also by the more simple and effective agency of things; they will be trained in the skilful use of all their faculties; and they will be better prepared for their work in life, which, for the great bulk of them, must consist mainly of manual occupations."

In a pamphlet on Manual Training in Public Schools,* Mr. James W. Robertson, Commissioner of Agriculture and Dairying for the Dominion of Canada, strongly emphasises the importance of manual training as a corrective to what he calls "the spirit of bare scholasticism," and announces an offer made by Sir William C. Macdonald, of Montreal, "to pay for the equipment required for educational manual training in one place in every province of the Dominion; and also to meet the expenses of qualified teachers, and of maintenance for three years in all those places." † Sir William offered to equip and maintain for three years in Ottawa as many centres as might be required to give all the boys (about 1,000) between the ages of 9 and 14 in the public schools an opportunity to receive this training. "It is hoped," writes Mr. Robertson, "that after a year or two an equally valuable course of practical instruction suited for girls of the same age may somehow be provided; and doubtless 'nature studies' will be given a proper place in rural schools. Sir William has authorised me to make a similar offer to the school authorities of Brockville, Ont.; of Charlottetown and

---

* Ottawa, E. J. Reynolds, Sparks Street, 1899.

† Sir William C. Macdonald, who is a native of Prince Edward Island, but has for over 40 years been resident in Montreal, is distinguished by his zeal for the advancement of education in Canada, and for his munificent gifts, exceeding two-and-a-half million dollars, to McGill University, Montreal.

Summerside, P.E.I.; of some place in the Province of Quebec; of Truro, N.S.; of Fredericton, N.B.; of Winnipeg, Man.; of Calgary, N.W.T.; and of some place in British Columbia.

"To begin the work on right educational lines, thoroughly trained and experienced teachers of high attainment will be brought at first from Scotland, England, or the United States.

" Next summer it is proposed to pay the expenses of several teachers from Canada to Great Britain and Sweden to take the course of training there, to see for themselves the educational systems and methods of those countries, and to meet teachers and other educational reformers in them. When these Canadian teachers return, they will be as lights set on hill-tops. The fire of their inspiration, information, and enthusiasm will spread."

In a later article, published in the present year,* Professor Robertson gives further particulars of the progress of this important scheme. "Under the Macdonald Manual Training Fund I was able to arrange for the opening of a manual training school at Fredericton, N.B., in April of the current year. The school authorities provided a room. All the other expenses were borne by the Macdonald Manual Training Fund. A Saturday forenoon class for teachers was also provided. It was taken advantage of and highly appreciated by them.

" A manual training school was also opened in April at Brockville, Ont. The School Board arranged for a commodious room, and, as in Fredericton, the expenses were met from the Macdonald Manual Training Fund.

" A summer course for teachers has been provided during the holidays at Brockville. Ont., and Fredericton, N.B.

" To introduce this improvement into the school system of the various provinces of Canada, with the best possible results, it has been necessary to engage teachers who have been specially trained and who have had experience elsewhere. At this date seven teachers who have come to Canada from Great Britain are engaged in giving manual training or in preparing for the opening of the schools early in September. Two instructors have been engaged in the United States. Seven others are expected to arrive from England before the end of September. These will complete the number of teachers of experience who are required in the various schools where manual training is being established. Several assistant teachers will be engaged in Canada, who will have an opportunity to become thoroughly proficient as full instructors.

" So far as the places are arranged for at present, they are Ottawa, Ont.; Brockville, Ont.; Waterloo, Que.; Knowlton, Que.; Fredericton, N.B.; Truro, N.S.; Charlottetown, P.E.I.; and Summerside, P.E.I. I intend to make similar arrangements with the school authorities at Winnipeg, Man.; Calgary, N.W.T., and Victoria, B.C., to have manual training in connection with their public schools before the end of October of the current year.

---

* *Manual Training in the Public Schools* in the *Farming World* (Toronto), September 4, 1900.

" All boys of suitable age attending the public schools in those places may have the benefit of the course of instruction free and practically without expense to the School Boards. As soon as practicable an equal opportunity will be provided for the boys in the public schools at Regina, N.W.T., and for the teachers in training there. The teachers in training in the Normal School at Montreal will be afforded the same privilege as those in the other provinces.

" Altogether provision will be made for about 5,000 boys and 600 teachers attending the normal schools to receive manual training during each of three years.

" In choosing the place to receive the offer of these manual training schools, consideration has been given to the desirability of selecting centres from which the movement could spread most rapidly throughout each province, and most quickly and effectively benefit its school system and its children.

" Manual training develops in children habits of industry, and leads them thoughtfully to adjust their acts to desired ends. That of itself is of great educational value. It brings about the mental habit of appreciating good work for its own sake, and is quite different from that sort of education which consists in informing the pupils about the facts within a definite area of knowledge in order that they may be able to pass examinations on the subjects included within it. The so-called dull boys, who are not quick at book studies, have in many cases been found to show great aptness in the manual training part of education. It prevents them from being discouraged with school life, and from feeling any sense of inferiority to the quick children. It gives them self-reliance, hopefulness and courage, all of which react on their mental and physical faculties. It also is a soothing and strengthening corrective to the quick and excitable children who become over-anxious about examinations on book studies."

To these excellent remarks it may perhaps be added that really educational forms of manual and practical instruction involve small classes, and therefore tend to increase the cost (as undoubtedly they do the value) of education. Furthermore it is not easy to bring the best use of manual and practical instruction into harmony with the (often mischievous) requirements of written examination tests, according to the results of which scholarships are sometimes too exclusively given. Nor should it be forgotten that manual and practical instruction, given in a wrong way, may become as dangerously mechanical a part of education as any of the bookish methods so justly reprobated by educational critics.

October, 1900.   M. E. Sadler.

THE

SYSTEM OF EDUCATION

IN

NEWFOUNDLAND.

I. (a) PRIMARY EDUCATION :

Historical Sketch - - - - - - - - 542
    Chaotic period, 1726-1823 - - - - - 542
    Period of individual enterprise, 1823-1836. - - 543
    Legislative action, 1836-1898—Creation of Local
      Boards of Education—Two Central Boards - - 546
Present system - - - - - - - - 547
    Act of 1874 - - - - - - - 547
    Attendance - - - - - - - 549
    Finance - - - - - - - - 549
    Private Schools - - - - - - 550
    Inspection - - - - - - - 550
    Singing, Drawing and Drill - - - - 551
    Religious Instruction - - - - 551
    Teachers—Salaries and Training - - - 551
(b) SECONDARY EDUCATION - - - - - - 552

II. METHODIST SCHOOLS AS RELATED TO THE NEWFOUNDLAND
    SYSTEM OF EDUCATION :

Early History - - - - - - - 554
Present System :
    (a) Primary Education - - - - - - 556
    Administration - - - - - - 557
    Attendance - - - - - - 557
    Cost. - - - - - - - 557
    Subjects Taught - - - - - 557
    Religious Instruction - - - - 557
    Teachers - - - - - - 557
    Training of Teachers - - - - 558
    (b) Higher Education - - - - - 558

III. SUPPLEMENTARY NOTES.

    (a) Estimated Expenditure of Legislature upon Public
      Education 1898-9, and 1899-1900 - - - 560
    (b) Denominational Apportionment of Government
      Grants for Education, 1899-1900 - - - 561
    (c) Apportionment of Grants for Inspection 1899-1900 561
    (d) Statistics of Roman Catholic Schools - - 562
    (e) From the Report of the Colonial and Continental
      Church Society for 1899-1900 - - - - 563

APPENDICES.

A. Return of Schools for the year 1896-7 - - - 566
B. Voluntary Contributions and Fees - - - 567
C. Programme of Studies for Elementary Schools - 568
D. Teachers' Pension Fund - - - - - - 569
E. Some Provisions of the Education Act of July, 1899 573

THE SYSTEM OF EDUCATION IN NEWFOUNDLAND.

I. (*a*.) PRIMARY EDUCATION.

Historical sketch.

Newfoundland stands first in point of time of all the colonial possessions of Great Britain. From the date of its discovery by Cabot (1497) down to 1813 it was regarded merely as a fishing ground, and not as a colony or place of settlement. Desultory attempts were made by Guy (1609), Calvert (1618), Whitbourne (1624), and others, at permanent residence, but colonisation was not merely discouraged but actually prohibited. Trade, settlement, and family life were alike discountenanced.

In 1776 an attempt was made to recall from the island all shopkeepers who were not fishermen. In 1783 Governor Elliott asked the British Ministry to prohibit the residence of women on the island, and even so late as 1811, dwelling-houses could not be built without special licence. Land grants were made first in 1813. Notwithstanding these prohibitions the island began to be peopled by arrivals from England, Scotland and Ireland, and at the commencement of the present century contained a population of 25,000 people, who were for the most part scattered among innumerable harbors along more than a thousand miles of sea coast, inaccessible except by water.

There is no lack of material for showing the depravity and barbarous condition of the people in these early days, but little to record the efforts made to improve the morals and intelligence of these settlers by the Government of England. It was left to private individual enterprise or some charitable institution to commence the work.

Chaotic Period, 1726-1823.

The pioneer of education in Newfoundland was the venerable Society for the Propagation of the Gospel in Foreign Parts. The material for this part of the sketch on education is very meagre, and is found scattered throughout their printed reports from 1726 to 1823, covering a period of nearly one hundred years. In 1726 this Society had established a school ("for all the poor people") in Bonavista, under their Missionary, the Rev. Mr. Jones, and kept it annually supplied with books, &c. In 1744 they established their first school in St. John's, under Rev. Mr. Peasely, and continued it under his successor, the Rev. Edward Langman, M.A. In 1766 the first school was established in Harbor Grace, under a Mr William Lampen, at a salary of £15 per annum. In 1777 the Society appointed John Thomas schoolmaster at Scilly Cove. In 1788 the Rev. Mr. Price opened a school in St. John's in his parsonage, and paid the salary of an assistant. In 1790 a school was opened in Burin by Rev. Mr. Evans, and Mr. Saunders was appointed teacher at a salary of £15 per annum. In 1798 Mr. Price's school, established in St. John's, was placed under Mr Lionel Chancey, assisted by his wife, on a salary of £20 per annum. In 1810 the first school was opened in Bay Roberts, under Mr Williams, and in 1811 the first school was opened in Brigus, under Mr. Plumleigh. Other schools were established by this Society in various parts of the island, as at Twillingate, Exploits, Trinity, Bare Need, Bonaventure, Greenspond, and several other settlements, and though they may have been few as compared with the great need everywhere apparent, yet so far as the work of those established extended, they were priceless in days when the ignorance of the common fisherman was described as "barbarous." Of these early teachers, what they were doubtless produced results of no less worth than what they did. With their civilizing habits and christian character, the indirect influence for good of their daily life in uplifting the people cannot be reckoned of less value than what was accomplished by direct instruction in school and in church, where the masters, as "Readers" under S.P.G. regulations, on Sundays conducted the service for morning and evening prayers and read a sermon.

Governors of the colony, Waldegrave, Gambier, Pole and Gower, were not slow in recognising their power and influence, and often testified to the good effects produced, as well in the degree of knowledge imparted as in their civilizing and christianizing power generally. The Rev. Mr. Anspach (S.P.G.), of Harbor Grace, from 1802 to 1812, says: "I attribute the improvement of parents and children to the advantage of these schools; they have been productive of much good." The first Archdeacon of Newfoundland, Coster, says: "It is surprising to see so much effected with so little means; in them (the schools) many are the children which have learnt to read and to pray, who but for the teachers of these schools would have known nothing."

The effects of the labours of John Thomas, schoolmaster at Scilly Cove, were reported to be visible, not only at that "barbarous and lawless" settlement, but for many miles around.

Such is the brief account of the first schools in Newfoundland, and though we have little means of comparing efficiency in those days with what we require in these, yet the system and the men were quite equal to what could be expected under the circumstances.

In addition to paying the stipends of these teachers, the Society supplied all schools with necessary material, established a lending library in each, and presented each child, when able to read, with a Bible and book of Common Prayer.

The annual cost of these schools to the Society for the Propagation of the Gospel was £325. The fees required were a quintal of fish for each child in attendance, and the hours were in summer, from 6 in the morning till 6 in the evening.

The educational work of this society in Newfoundland was discontinued shortly after the establishment of the Newfoundland School Society, 1823.

The year 1823 marks the introduction of a system of education into Newfoundland which was unknown before, and which has largely moulded all subsequent operations and influenced all subsequent legislation. The sixteen schools of the Society for the Propagation of the Gospel were of contracted operations, and lacked the advantages of a system of education. The growing feeling for something better and wider in its scope and efficiency took shape first in the mind of Mr. Samuel Codner, a successful merchant from Devonshire, and for a considerable period a

Period of individual enterprise, 1823-1836.

resident in St. John's. His signal deliverance from shipwreck while on a voyage to England was the occasion of a resolution to establish schools of a superior class, which should embrace the whole population of the island, then numbering 75,000 people. With this single purpose in view, and with a zeal that up to the time of his death knew no abatement, he interviewed and interested in his scheme the leading business men of England concerned in the Newfoundland trade, an undertaking which involved journeys into Scotland and throughout the greater part of England. His efforts were crowned with success, and a "Society for educating the poor of Newfoundland" was established in London, June 30th, 1823. The following resolutions proclaim the spirit which pervaded the first promoters of this Society :—

1. "That the colony of Newfoundland is the oldest and one of the most important possessions of the British Crown, and has always proved a considerable source of wealth, and the main cause of our national prosperity.

2. "That the obligations of the Mother Country to its ancient colony of Newfoundland, as well on account of the national wealth derived from its fisheries, as of the maritime strength afforded by its trade, demand of us both in policy and gratitude the most ample returns of both social and religious blessings to the settlers there which we can extend to them as fellow subjects and fellow men."

In its first Report the Society says : —"The elements of social and moral institutions are in a great measure wanting (in Newfoundland), and it is by encouraging education among the lower classes and affording them scriptural instruction that your Society hopes, under the blessing of Almighty God, to supply in some degree this lamentable deficiency. It is by giving the descendants of our own countrymen in Newfoundland wholesome moral institutions, and especially schools, that we shall best discharge the claims of kindred and of philanthropy, and most effectually teach them to understand and rightly appreciate their connection with, and interest in the moral as well as national greatness of their Mother Country. They will soon be able to value the blessings which we trust this Society has in store for them; for in proportion as the poor are made intelligent they will become industrious, and if moral and religious principles are wisely and diligently inculcated on the minds of the rising generation we may confidently expect to find what is the never-failing result—that they will grow up a happy and useful people; and your Committee beg leave explicitly to state it as their opinion that any other mode of relief than that of schools for the poorer classes of Newfoundland must fall short of producing these desirable effects."

Her Majesty's Government in England aided the design by grants of land for school purposes, free passages from England on board the ships of war to its teachers, and pecuniary assistance towards the erection of schools and payment of the salaries of masters.

The first Agents of this Society, Mr. and Mrs. Jeynes and Mr.

Fleet arrived in Newfoundland in August, 1824, and on September 20th a school was opened to which the "poor of all denominations" were invited to send their children, the Society wisely accommodating its means to the character of the soil it had undertaken to cultivate. These teachers had received their training at the National Society's Training School, Baldwin's Gardens, London. The system was monitorial, after the model of Dr. Bell, of Madras fame. The improvements made under this scheme were so rapid, and the popularity of the school was so great, that it created a desire for education in the outharbors, from whence several applications to establish schools were forwarded to the Committee in London. Schools were multiplied rapidly, settlements vieing with one another to erect schools at their own charges, in order to be first supplied with teachers.

The liberality of the merchants helped on the work, so that in 1842 the Society had sixty schools in operation and an attendance in them of about 3,500 scholars. One unique feature connected with the operation of these schools was the opening of what were called branch schools. A trained teacher from London was stationed at one of the most populous settlements, whose duty was not only to attend to his own school, but also to open up, under local agents whom he had previously instructed, schools in the small neighbouring settlements. Thus at St. John's, under the principal teacher in the central school, branch schools were opened at Quidi Vidi, Torbay, South Side, St. John's, and Petty Harbor; and in like manner the principal teacher at Trinity had under his care also the branch schools at Cuckolds Cove, Salmon Cove, Ship Cove and Bonaventure. He made periodical visits to inspect the schools and advise the teacher, and thus the system and the instruction were brought into one harmonious whole.

In 1836, when the Newfoundland Legislature made its first vote for educational purposes, the Society, now known as the Colonial and Continental Church Society, had extended its operations to the neighbouring continent, and left some of the work it had begun to be taken up by boards of education, then for the first time called into existence.

No estimate can be placed upon the good work which this Society has done for Newfoundland, the cradle of its birth. Their schools, although conducted as Church schools, were open to all, no attempt being made to proselytize, and every care taken to regard the religious principles of the people. Their early teachers were not only trained, but were picked men, of sterling worth and exemplary lives, who exercised an uplifting influence never before experienced in this country, where at the time the elements of social and moral institutions were in a great measure wanting.

The Colonial and Continental Church Society still carries on its beneficent work in this country on a contracted scale. During the seventy-five years of its existence it is estimated that the amount of money it has expended on schools in Newfoundland reaches a quarter of a million dollars. The operations of the Society now stretch all around the globe, and its work for good in Newfoundland is only limited by its means.   To-day it is doing admirable work in our midst in training, under an experienced educationist from Battersea, many students who will become the future teachers of the country.   To-day the Society maintains in this Island under twenty-four teachers, twenty-one schools, which have an attendance of 2,069.

Legislative action, 1836–1898.   In 1832 a representative Government was granted to Newfoundland, and in 1836 the Assembly passed its first Educational Act, based upon a report made by Messrs. Carson, Martin, Keough and Hoyles.   In this report, after speaking of the importance of education to the subject, and its advantage to the State, they add—" Your Committee consider that the voluntary system works advantageously, and therefore they would recommend that assistance be given by the Legislature, by immediate grants of money to be placed at the disposal of the several societies and individuals who direct and govern, for the gratuitous education of the poorer classes, schools of such importance as to claim the attention of the Legislature."   They further recommend that in those parts of the Island where education has hitherto been promoted, the seeds already sown shall be fostered by the Legislature, and according as the means of the country will permit, and the growing intelligence of the people require, it is their anxious desire "that Grammar schools be instituted and schools even of a higher order to succeed them."

Creation of Local Boards of Education.   The Island was divided into nine educational districts, each respectively co-terminous with the electoral districts into which the Colony was then divided, and boards of education were then appointed, each consisting of twelve persons, to administer the appropriations.   Out of the grant of £2,100, six hundred pounds were paid in equal proportions to the Newfoundland School Society and to the Roman Catholics, towards the support of schools then established.   The Act was purely undenominational in its character, embracing the education of all classes.

Two central Boards of Education.   It appears that in two of the most important districts of the island no action was taken, as they were without school houses in which to carry on the work, and the money voted, £525, was ordered to be expended in the erection of school houses.   In 1838 the Act was amended providing that ministers of religion may visit schools but not be permitted to impart any religious instruction or in any way to interfere with their proceedings.   The books prescribed for use were the "Irish National School Series" to the exclusion of all of a distinctly denominational character.   The Bible as a text-book was used in all schools.   This latter provision created much dissatisfaction among the Roman Catholics, and an agitation was set on foot for a division of the grant.   In 1843 an Act was passed by the assembly recognising the principle contended for by the Roman Catholics, and a grant of £5,100 was divided equally between Roman Catholics and Protestants.   The country was divided into eighteen Roman Catholic and eighteen Protestant districts, and boards of education were appointed in each to expend their respective allocations. Fees for the first time were made compulsory, and provision was made for the appointment of an inspector at a salary of £300 sterling per annum. This Act continued to govern all educational operations until 1851, when an Act was passed by the Legislature increasing the grant to £7,500, and creating a central board of education for each of the two religious sections, for the administration of £2,400 only. In the following year (1852) the principle of centralisation was further carried into effect by the establishment of two central boards of education, one for Roman Catholics and one for Protestants, for the administration of the whole of their respective grants. Local boards were appointed to act under the control of the central boards, and to carry into effect their regulations. This arrangement met with determined opposition, and in the following year (1853) an Act was passed repealing this Act and re-establishing the former method of administration by local boards. The country was mapped out into twenty-three districts, and an additional sum of £380 was granted for the establishment of commercial schools in nine of the principal settlements. By this Act, the course of instruction in schools was to consist of reading, writing, arithmetic, and English grammar, and where required, geography, history, and navigation. Also such industrial instruction was to be given as might be deemed necessary by the boards of education. £200 was provided for instruction of Protestant masters in training, which sum was deducted from the Protestant grant : before division among the districts. The Act was continued from year to year until 1858, save that in 1857 the grant to fifteen commercial schools was raised to £755

The year 1858 marks a further step in advance in education. The grant was increased to £10,525 and divided among Protestants and Roman Catholics according to their respective numbers. £750 were allocated for the training of teachers, £400 for the inspection of schools, and £1,000 for commercial schools.

The selection of teachers for training was given to boards of education in rotation. This Act, with some slight alterations made in 1866, 1867, and 1870, continued to govern all educational proceedings until 1874, when the grant was further divided among all the religious denominations of the Colony.

The existing system of education in Newfoundland is purely denominational and is the development of all former systems. It was inaugurated by the Legislature in 1874 and came into practical operation in the following year. *Present system.*

This Act provides for a sum of money for Protestant educational purposes equal in proportion, according to population, to the sum of money appropriated to Roman Catholics for educational purposes, and, further, that this sum shall be apportioned among the various Protestant denominations according to population. For this purpose a census of the Colony was taken in 1874. Three inspectors, one each for Church of England, Roman Catholic, and Methodist, were appointed for the inspection of schools of their respective denominations. The inspection of six schools of other denominations is undertaken by the Church of England and Methodist superintendents in alternate years. *Act of 1874.*

In the first year of their work the inspectors of Church of England and Methodist schools presented a joint report on the condition of education throughout the country. In this they pointed to the difficulty of finding competent persons to take charge of schools, and recommended certain regulations as well for the appointment, supervision and training of teachers as for the examination of teachers then employed. They directed attention to the dingy, cheerless buildings erected without regard to ventilation, and devoid of almost everything to render school work pleasant. The Legislature voted 40,000 dollars for school-houses, which were to be erected under rules and regulations prescribing the capacity and construction of school-houses required, ventilation, outhouses, site and grounds. They described the great diversity of books in the hands of scholars of similar attainments preventing all proper classification, and needlessly retarding the progress of the school, and recommended the adoption of a series of "Royal Readers" by Messrs. Nelson of London.

They outlined a programme of studies for common schools and issued time tables and rules for the management of schools. These recommendations were embodied in an Act which passed the Legislature in 1876, and all subsequent educational operations have been in the direction of improvement on those lines. Pupil teachers are no longer appointed by rotation from the various boards, but are now admitted in training after a competitive examination. A board of examiners was appointed for each denomination to examine all candidates for pupil teacherships, to prescribe their course of study, and to look after their proper education, and after the period of training was ended to grant certificates of qualification, according to merit, of first, second or third grade.

The Governor in Council is the ultimate source of all jurisdiction over the entire education of the Colony. Under an Act passed in 1898 the Colonial Secretary is charged more particularly with the oversight of this department. There is no Minister of Education, and no educational department proper. The superintendents before referred to have, under this limitation, the general oversight and direction of all educational proceedings. The local administration is by boards of education. The country is mapped out into districts respectively coincident with the several ecclesiastical jurisdictions of the clergy of the various denominations, and boards of education are appointed for each by the Governor in Council, consisting of five or seven members of the respective denominations, one of whom is always the resident clergyman.* These boards are required to organise annually for the purpose of electing officers, and to make bye-laws and regulations for the establishment and management of schools within their respective districts, and for the appropriation of the respective sums of money granted to their districts.

They are required to furnish annually audited accounts of income and expenditure, and returns of all schools under their

See Appendix E, 3, for provisions of Education Act, 1899.

management, to the proper superintendent. The table in Appendix A gives details of all schools in the colony, with their attendance, &c.

There were on 30th June, 1897, 628 schools and colleges in Attendance. operation, with an attendance of 34,408. The cost per pupil to Government was 4.32 dollars, or 17*s.* 3*d.* sterling, and the proportion of the entire population attending school for the year was 17 per cent. or one in every 5·8.

There is no law governing school attendance. The necessity and importance of a compulsory enactment have often been brought before the Legislature, but up to the present it is urged that there are insuperable difficulties in the way of making it law, owing to the scattered nature of the population and the want of means of communication.

There is no system of school tax whatever. The Government Grant is the only reliable source of the income of the boards.

The total amount of the annual Legislative Grant for elemen- Finance. tary and secondary schools for the whole Island of Newfoundland, and the Labrador is 154,089.19 dollars. Taking the population of the last Census, 1891, at 200,653, this gives a per capita amount of 76 cents for the entire population for all educational purposes :—

	Dollars.
Grant for Elementary Schools - - -	102,351.19
„ to Augment teachers' salaries, according to grade - - -	25,297.87
„ for Training teachers - - -	5,610.84
„ „ Inspection, office and incid. -	6,060.00
„ „ Colleges - - - - -	9,565.29
„ „ Council of Higher Education -	4,000.00
„ „ Pensions to retired teachers -	700.00
„ to pension scheme, about - -	500.00
	154,085.19

The per capita grant for elementary education is 69 cents; for the Colleges and Council of Higher Education, 6¾ cents per caput of the entire population.

The Educational Grant is divided among the religious denominations of the Colony according to population, as follows :—

	Dollars.
Roman Catholics - - - - -	54,085.04
Church of England - - - -	51,732.99
Methodist - - - - - -	39,468.73
Presbyterian - - - - -	1,073.54
Congregationalists - - - -	579.39
Reformed Episcopal - - - -	360.81
Salvation Army - - - - -	1,466.15
	148,766.65

Appendix B gives the amount of voluntary contributions and school fees for the year ended 30th June, 1897.

From this table it will be seen that the amount, contributed by the people towards the support of schools during the year, was 37,190.85 dollars, and is 24½ per cent. of the entire Government Grant for Education.

Private Schools. Outside of the State system there are not more than half a dozen private schools of any kind. They are chiefly in St. John's.

Inspection. By the Education Act, 1895, the Governor in Council may nominate and appoint three superintendents. One a member of the Church of England, for the superintendence and inspection of Church of England Schools. One a member of the Roman Catholic Church, for the superintendence and inspection of Roman Catholic Schools. One a member of the Methodist Church, for the superintendence and inspection of Methodist Schools. The schools of all other Protestant denominations, with the exception of the Presbyterian and Congregationalist, are placed under the Church of England and Methodist superintendents in alternate years. The law requires that each of these shall be sworn before a Justice of the Peace well and faithfully to discharge the duties of his office. Under the limitations before referred to :—

1. The Superintendent has a general supervision and direction of all schools and training schools of his denomination: and,

2. Is required to enforce the provisions of the Act, and the regulations and decisions of the Governor in Council in reference to the same.

3. To forward to Boards of Education all necessary forms of returns provided in the Act.

4. To prescribe the duties of an assistant with which each superintendent is provided.

5. To visit annually, with the aid of the assistant, each school, training school, and college of his denomination to examine the state and condition thereof as respects the qualifications of teachers, the system of instruction pursued, the order and discipline observed, the mode of keeping school registers, suitability and condition of school buildings and premises, and to give such advice as he may judge proper to teachers and boards.

6. To prepare annually a report of all schools, training institutions and colleges of his denomination, with full details of income and expenditure, and other school statistics. This report is laid before the Legislature in printed form within a month after its next opening.

The salary of each superintendent is 1,620 dollars, or £333 6s. 8d. sterling, which amount covers all travelling expenses, stationery and rent of office. The sum of £82 6s. 1d. is provided for the assistant, supplemented from other sources to £123 9s. 1d.   All the clerical work connected with his schools and all payments of his department are (under the Governor in Council) managed by the proper superintendent. In addition he is, by virtue of his office, Chairman of the Board of Examiners appointed to grant certificates of qualification to teachers, and, further, he has the oversight of all pupil teachers sent forward for training.

Singing and drawing are taught in a few schools as a part of the ordinary school work. In the Central Training School of the Church of England, a Bachelor of Music gives special instruction in singing to the teachers in training. In the colleges these subjects are taught by competent masters. No provision is made for lessons in cooking and domestic economy, nor for manual training. Drill forms a part of the discipline in the majority of schools. Singing, Drawing, and Drill.

Each denomination gives instruction in those distinctive matters of faith and duty which each recognises as the groundwork of its system, but no teacher is allowed to impart to any child attending his school any religious instruction which may be objected to by the parent or guardian of such child. With this limitation the Education Act takes no cognizance of religious instruction. Religious instruction.

Teachers are appointed by Boards of Education assisted by the proper superintendent, and must possess a certificate of qualification from the Board of Examiners empowered for this purpose. There are three Grades, I., II., and III. To these there is a direct money value attached, *e.g.*, teachers of first grade receive 75 dollars per annum, of second grade 55 dollars per annum, and of third grade 32 dollars per annum. The syllabus for grading these teachers is given in Schedule E of the Education Act, 1895. The following is a scale of their payments:— Teachers' salaries and Training.

CHURCH OF ENGLAND.

	Teachers of First Grade.		Teachers of Second Grade.		Teachers of Third Grade.	
	Male.	Female.	Male.	Female.	Male.	Female.
Average Salary -	$ 434.96	$ 308.26	$ 274.09	$ 191.81	$ 198.87	$ 152.76
Highest Salary -	727.52	417.75	468.73	308.00	345.37	195.82
Lowest Salary -	335.00	225.00	180.14	152.00	102.11	129.30

ROMAN CATHOLIC.

	Male.	Female.	Male.	Female.	Male.	Female.
Average Salary -	264.00	218.00	202.00	156.00	166.00	125.00
Highest Salary -	435.00	250.00	270.00	216.00	248.00	163.00
Lowest Salary -	175.00	185.00	135.00	110.00	89.00	91.00

METHODIST.

	$	$	$	$	$	$
Average Salary	391.95	265.13	281.75	219.98	247.57	187.90
Highest Salary	631.25	331.41	367.25	283.33	328.00	256.50
Lowest Salary	243.90	210.00	194.90	164.74	205.50	116.00

There is no training college in the country in the proper professional sense of that term, and no one denomination has the means at present to create and support one. In the absence of such, intending teachers and pupil teachers attend the various colleges, which are supposed to afford facilities for the illustration and practice of the most improved method of teaching. After going through a course of education these pupil teachers have to undergo examinations, are graded according to their merit, and on passing receive certificates without which they are not eligible to be appointed to take charge of schools. Each male pupil teacher in training is allowed by Government 100 dollars per annum, and each female teacher 80 dollars per annum towards board, lodging, education, &c. Each of the leading denominations has attached to its college a residence or home for these pupil teachers, and the charge for their maintenance is a trifle over the Government grant. All pupil teachers are indentured to their proper superintendents under a bond of 400 dollars. The period of training is limited to three years.

Of the total teachers (759) the females are 63 per cent., and the males 37 per cent., but omitting the ladies of the convent schools (Roman Catholic), the females are 56·7 and males 43·3 per cent. of the whole staff.

A scheme for pensions in the elementary schools was established by Act of Legislature in 1892. The scheme is printed in Appendix D.

No free meals are provided in any schools, nor is there at present any arrangement made for continuation schools.

I. (b.) SECONDARY EDUCATION.

Four colleges subsidized by the Legislature to the extent of $9,565.29, are established in St. John's. The course of study is similar to that pursued in grammar schools in England. Pupils are prepared for the examinations of the London University, for which St John's has been appointed a centre.

An Act to encourage higher education was passed by the Legislature in 1893. This Act provides for the appointment of an examining body styled the "Council of Higher Education," which is empowered to institute a system of uniform competitive examinations for the pupils of the different schools throughout the colony, and to induce students to present themselves at these examinations by offering in connection therewith diplomas, prizes, and scholarships. The examinations are conducted in a manner similar to that obtaining at the examinations for the London

University, and are divided into a junior and senior grade. Superintending committees and centres for holding the examinations are appointed by the council in any place upon applicants complying with certain forms and conditions. These examinations have had a most healthy stimulus in the larger centres of population, and have tended to give increased method and continuity to the course of instruction pursued in schools. In order to secure the uniform grading of teachers of all denominations, all candidates for pupil teacherships, and for the office of teacher are required to pass the examinations of the council before presenting themselves for examination before the Board of Examiners for certificates of qualification.

The denominational system is working well. It is consonant with the convictions and sentiments of the people generally. To give proof of these convictions, each denomination has expended large sums of money in the erection of school buildings, and particularly in the capital, St. John's, the centre of all movements affecting the welfare of the colony. The Church of England has spent during the last four years on schools and training schools 60,000 dollars. The Methodists have spent more. The Roman Catholics have equalled if not exceeded either, and the splendid colleges which are the result are not only conspicuous ornaments to the city, but as educational establishments would do credit to places otherwise more favourably situated. In addition the annual average expenditure by all denominations for school purposes is $37,190.85, or 24 per cent. of the entire Government grant for elementary and secondary schools.

The Christian Brothers and the convent schools of the Roman Catholic Church are prominent voluntary factors, and the work gratuitously done by these agencies is valued at 10,000 dollars per annum.

WILLIAM PILOT, D.D., D.C.L., &c.,
Superintendent of Church of England
Schools in Newfoundland.

St. John's, Newfoundland,
22 March, 1898.

II. Methodist Schools as Related to the Newfoundland System of Education.

Early History.

In presenting a summary of facts and events relating to the establishment, development and progress of Methodist schools, it may be convenient, perhaps necessary, to revert briefly to the condition of education in the Colony prior to 1836, when action was first taken by the Legislature to encourage public schools. This will enable us more readily to trace the origin and history of a movement within the denomination at an early date, which showed a hearty approval and high appreciation of educational efforts; but which from force of circumstances remained for a long time but a feeble factor in regard to direct educational work. From their introduction into Newfoundland the Wesleyan Methodist missionaries, here as everywhere else, attached due importance to the right training of youth. They bewailed the prevailing ignorance and unblushing immorality of the fishing population, that had settled or grown up in settlemerts around the principal bays. In Blackhead, for example, as late as 1820, there never had been a day school. Hence, October 20th, 1819, the missionary appealed to the Missionary Committee to establish a Mission Day School at that station. Similar appeals were made for other missions. Not much, however, could be accomplished for a time, except by way of Sunday Schools, in which in 1824, twelve hundred pupils had been gathered, many of whom therein learned to read their Bibles and Hymn Books. Soon after, as the result of earnest appeals, the parent Wesleyan Missionary Society made a small annual grant whereby in 1825 three Wesleyan Day Schools were put in operation. Besides, as in 1823, the Newfoundland School Society (now the C.C.C. Society) had been organized to provide for the education of the poor in Newfoundland, some of the missionaries gave it countenance and help, and for three successive years, 1824–1826, obtained free from the parent society a donation of £20 per year.

From this time efforts of Wesleyans were continued in some places directly and in others indirectly, till 1836, when an Act to encourage education was passed by the Legislature, providing £300 for the Newfoundland School Society, £300 for certain Roman Catholic schools, and £1,500 for elementary schools, under the direction of education boards, of which the senior or superior clergyman, resident, was made a member. This Act was amended in 1838, providing that ministers of religion should be visitors of schools, without power to give religious instruction therein, and further, that £150 should be granted to purchase books, which should not on any pretence contain or include the doctrines or tenets of any particular Church or religious society. This Act also provided that money granted in 1836 for Conception and Trinity Bays but not expended, might be used for the erection or procuring of school-houses. Of the total population (75,094,) Wesleyan Methodists numbered only 10,636 in the census of 1838. Hence with privileges secured by the above Acts and 9 Wesleyan day schools in 1840, they had ample opportunity for maintaining an interest in education.

In 1843 an Act was passed granting £5,100, and providing that of the Protestant share £500 should be appropriated for the use of the Newfoundland School Society, and £250 for the use of Wesleyan Methodist schools in the following districts :—Carbonear, Harbor Grace, Brigus, Trinity Bay (North), Trinity Bay (South), Burin, and St. John's.

Wesleyans were also specially interested in Acts passed the same year, to establish and maintain a grammar school at Carbonear, and another at Harbor Grace, for each of which £400 were appropriated per year, besides large amounts at different times towards procuring suitable school-houses. In accordance with certain local efforts, Wesleyans, like other denominations, obtained from the Legislature in 1844–45, for the erection of school-houses, £206 for St. John's, £100 for Cupids, £75 for Harbor Grace, and £75 for Carbonear.

In 1844, £3,000 were appropriated by the Legislature to establish an academy, under a joint directorate, in St. John's. This proved unsatisfactory, and an amending Act was passed in 1850, providing for three academies, namely, one for the Church of England, one for the Roman Catholics, and one for the general Protestants. On the last a board was appointed of five, of whom two only were Methodists, for its population of 14,239.

In 1851 Wesleyans formed the Newfoundland Wesleyan School Society, whose object was to promote the efficiency of Methodist schools, and under its auspices, in 1852, the Wesleyan Normal Day School was opened in St. John's, under two superior teachers from the Glasgow Normal School. This institution succeeded well until failure of health compelled the head master, after three years, to leave the Colony, which was deeply regretted on general educational grounds, but particularly because the Legislature had appropriated in 1853, among other things, a grant of £200 for training Protestant masters in the Newfoundland School Society School or in the Wesleyan Training School, and sundries amounting to £7,880, as the total grant for that year. This Act enjoined that no teacher in the public schools be allowed to impart any religious instruction which may be objected to by parents or guardians. In 1856, £8,080 were granted for ordinary education, and £200 for school-houses, and in the following year a further grant of £375 was made for commercial and other schools.

In 1858 an Act was passed for £10,525 for the maintenance of education, from which, besides the ordinary vote of £250 for Wesleyan schools, £20 for Burin and £20 for Cupids, a special appropriation of £100 from the Protestant share was made for

Wesleyan schools. It was further enacted, that there be two Inspectors of schools, one for the Roman Catholics, and one for the Protestants, at a salary each of £200 a year; and that £750 be granted for training Pupil Teachers, each to receive an allowance of £25 towards his expenses. In 1858 also another Act was passed providing for the Wesleyan Academy, with £200 as its share of the academic grant per year, also for the division of £600 between Wesleyans and the representatives of the General Protestant Academy, voted in Supply Act, 1857, but unexpended. This Act, passed by the Legislature in response to numerous signed petitions, gave much satisfaction, as it placed under the direction of a Methodist Board a classical and mathematical school which, while affording facilities for a good commercial education, should also serve as a training school for teachers for other Wesleyan schools. A suitable building was erected and furnished, and a principal was obtained to commence academic work January 9th, 1860. He was aided from time to time by active and well qualified assistants. Judged by reports to the District Committee, the Wesleyan Academy afforded, from date of opening till 1875, opportunity to hundreds of students to get a thorough and fair education, and to not a few expecting to teach some useful preparation. During that time also Wesleyan schools whose number and attendance varied considerably, according to circumstances, were the means of instructing in useful knowledge from about 300 to 500 pupils a year, or a total of many thousands. This it must be remembered was effected in distinct localities, while education grants were divided between Roman Catholics and Protestants, and while the Methodists, who would have preferred the joint system throughout the Colony, received from Protestant Boards help to run Wesleyan schools in certain settlements. Thus far, however, Methodists claimed an interest in common with other Protestants in Board Schools generally, and wherever found were ready in all districts to co-operate for promotion of education.

PRESENT EDUCATIONAL SYSTEM.
(a) *Primary Education.*

This was fully introduced by Education Acts 1874 and 1876. which rendered it completely denominational, and provided for separate denominational schools, which however should be public schools and restricted in their operation by a Conscience Clause. Both Roman Catholics and Episcopalians had declared in favour of subdivision, and Methodists somewhat reluctantly complied with their arrangement, as justice was done to all religious bodies by giving to all alike Education Grants per capita. By the 1874 Act 40,000 dollars were provided for school houses and school property, and arrangements made for sub-division of property on an equitable basis, which was in due course accomplished without difficulty. By the 1876 Act $88,251.92 were provided for all purposes, which amount has been increased from time to time according to increase of population, &c., till now it has reached a total of $149,585.19 per year, besides $4,000 for purposes of the Council of Higher Education.

These grants provide $90,251.65 for general purposes, $4,000 to aid poor districts, $5,297.57 to encourage on certain conditions, involving hearty co-operation, the maintenance of superior schools, $9,565.29 to sustain colleges, $25,297.87 for the encouragement of teachers and supplementing salaries, according to character and certificate of grade, and $4,860 for the salaries, travelling and other expenses of three superintendents.

The chief and central authority is vested in H.M. Government. Administra-
The Governor in Council has power to appoint in each educa- tion.
tional district, as defined in the Act, a board of five or seven members of the respective denominations, on which the senior or superior clergyman, resident or officiating in the district, shall be one, to manage and expend all moneys, &c. Such boards in St. John's and in districts in which are superior schools, may consist of nine members; vacancies occurring by death, resignation, or absence from the Colony for twelve months may be filled by the Governor in Council. The annual meeting of every board shall be held on the first Wednesday in July, or as soon as practicable thereafter, when a chairman and other officers shall be elected, accounts submitted and audited, and other business transacted which may be necessary, and correct returns transmitted to the superintendent according to form of schedules prescribed. For public schools there are 152 education boards, of which Methodists have 61. Similar boards are appointed in like manner for the four colleges, but nomination of members is with the respective denominations.

There were 591 schools in 1896, 33,742 pupils, or an attendance Attendance.
of 16·81 per cent. of total population. In 1897, in Methodist public schools, there were 4,695 boys and 4,118 girls, total 8,813. In Methodist colleges there were 260 pupils, 137 males and 123 females. Attendance as yet is voluntary, but as the result of a growing interest in education it is steadily increasing.

In 1896 the cost of each pupil to Government was $3.64 on Cost.
an average for all denominations. In 1897 Methodist boards returned fees $5,374.98 and voluntary contributions towards current expenses $614.66. Methodist College Board returned fees $4,700.73.

In public schools, classes are conducted in six standards, in Subjects
reading, writing, arithmetic, geography, grammar and composi- taught.
tion, history, book-keeping, mensuration, geometry, navigation, algebra, drawing, needlework and vocal music. Singing and drawing are taught in many Methodist schools and domestic economy in a few of them.

Methodist schools are opened by singing a hymn, reading the Religious
Scriptures, and prayer daily. This constitutes usually the amount instruction.
of religious instruction, which, however, in no case contradicts the Conscience Clause.

Teachers are appointed by Education Boards, must be engaged Teachers.
according to prescribed form, and must have three months'

notice in writing, in case of dismissal, but may be dismissed summarily for immorality. They must hold certificates of qualification from Boards of Examiners, of third, second, or first or associate grade, and faithfully discharge duties distinctly defined in Education Act.

Training of teachers.

Pupil teachers are regularly indentured to the Superintendents of Education, for one, two, or three years, and must attend certain recognised institutions. The Methodist College, with its primary and model school, serves as training and practising school for regular or special pupil teachers. Of total grants before mentioned, $5,610.84 are appropriated for training teachers, of which the Methodist share is $1,489.76 per year. The maximum amount annually paid towards the board, lodging, and training of any male pupil teacher, per Act, is $100, and of females the maximum is $80. By special arrangement with the college executive, and the payment of $400 annually, provided under the Education Act, reduced rates of cost are made applicable to Methodist pupil teachers in the College Home, under the guardianship of the reverend chaplain and guardian. Selection, oversight, and gradation of pupil teachers is conducted by Board of Examiners for the denomination, and upon the completion of term of training such persons are required, under a penalty of $400, to serve as teacher in a public school for three years, or, if their course of training has extended over two years, one and a-half times as long as the term of training.

Certificated teachers may be admitted to a second course of training for a period not exceeding twelve months, provided they serve as teachers in a public school for at least eighteen months, under a penalty of $200 in case of breach of said contract. During 1897 there were twenty-five regular pupil teachers and four specials admitted for training to prepare them for teaching in Methodist public schools.

Sex of teachers.

In 1897 sixty-one teachers in Methodist schools were males, and one hundred and nineteen females, and of pupil teachers in college, fourteen were males and fifteen were females.

(b) *Higher Education.*

In the Colleges provision is made for teaching advanced classes, in ordinary commercial subjects, in Latin, Greek, French, German, Algebra, Geometry, Mensuration and Land Surveying, Chemistry, Magnetism and Electricity, Freehand and Geometrical Drawing, Trigonometry and Navigation, Shorthand, Music, and School Management. These Colleges are all under Government inspection, and reports of their condition and progress, and a detailed account of income and expenditure, must be transmitted to their respective Superintendents to be laid before the Legislature, in accordance with prescribed forms.

The Methodist College has for its principal a B.A., F.S.S. (London), who has five well-qualified assistants in the Upper School, besides two highly accomplished Professors—one of Music and one of Drawing and Painting. It has also in the model school four other certificated teachers from kindergarten upwards.

The Methodist College has a new and valuable property which has cost about $80,000, apart from buildings consumed by fire in 1892, which cost about $40,000, and by the hearty contributions of its friends liabilities amounting to nearly $50,000 are being, by voluntary efforts, regularly and steadily reduced. Current income for 1897, comprising grants and fees, was $8,477.61, and expenditure for salaries and current expenses was $7,697.83. Besides 260 reported as above in Upper School, there were 200 pupils in Model School, or a total of 460 under instruction during the past year.

This body represents the denominations and secures the combined thought and action of twenty-three members, appointed by H.M. Government, including three Superintendents of Education and the four Principals of Colleges, *ex-officio*. Its chief object is to promote education by holding examinations by a competent and independent Board of Examiners outside the Colony, and to awaken honourable competition in the schools of Newfoundland, by awarding diplomas, prizes and scholarships to successful candidates. In my judgment, despite certain drawbacks in the way of its success, the Council of Higher Education has had a healthful influence upon public education. It gives diplomas for Junior, Senior, and Associate Grades. In June last pupils in Methodist College won 56 Junior, 40 Senior, and 5 Associate, and in twenty-seven Methodist Public Schools, 92 Junior, 28 Senior, and one Associate, making a total of 222 diplomas.

(margin note: Council of Higher Education)

GEORGE S. MILLIGAN, M.A., LL.D.,
Supt. of Methodist Schools.

St. John's,
    March 22nd, 1898.

Copies of the Education Act of 1895 and of the Amending Acts of 1896 and 1899 may be seen at the Board of Education Library, St. Stephen's House, Cannon Row, Whitehall, London, S.W.

III. SUPPLEMENTARY NOTES.

(a) EDUCATION ESTIMATES, 1898–99 AND 1899–1900.

The following tables, summarised from the Journal of the Legislative Council of Newfoundland for 1899, show the Education Estimates for the years 1898–99, and 1899–1900.

A. *Expenditure for which votes of the Legislature are required.*	Estimate. 1898-9.	Estimate. 1899-1900.
Contingencies	$1,500.00	$1,500.00
Gould's School	120.00	120.00
Council of Higher Education	4,000.00	4,000.00
	$5,620.00	$5,620.00
B. *Expenditure authorised by Statute.*		
Scholarships	$600.00	$600.00
Pensions	700.00	700.00
Grants to Boards	89,551.65	98,551.65
Destitute Places	5,526.39	5,526.39
Higher Education	5,297.87	5,297.87
Pupil Teachers	5,610.84	5,610.84
Encouragement of Teachers	5,297.87	5,297.87
Supplemental Vote	20,000.00	20,000.00
Colleges	9,565.29	9,565.29
Inspection (a) Salaries	6,060.00	7,020.00
(b) Additional	1,975.28	1,379.07
	$152,685.19	$150,548.98
SUMMARY.		
A. To be voted	$2,620.00	$5,620.00
B. Authorized by Statute	$152,685.00	$150,548.00
	$155,305.19	$156,168.98

(*b.*) DENOMINATIONAL APPORTIONMENT OF GOVERNMENT
GRANTS FOR EDUCATION, 1899–1900.

The Grants to Boards, Grant for Destitute Places, Grant
for Higher Education, Grant for Pupil Teachers, Grant for
Encouragement of Teachers, Supplementary Vote, and Grant for
Colleges, the aggregates of which are given under *B* above,
were all divided among various denominations.

The apportionment prepared for the year 1899–1900 was as
follows :—

	Grants to Boards.	Destitute Places.	Higher Education.	Pupil Teachers.	Encouragement of Teachers.	Supplementary Vote.	Colleges.
	$	$	$	$	$	$	$
Roman Catholic	32,589.39	2,002.21	1,919.41	2,032.80	1,919.41	7,245.98	3,465.49
Church of England	31,083.15	1,923.08	1,843.56	1,952.46	1,843.56	6,959.61	3,328.53
Methodist	23,716.91	1,467.34	1,406.66	1,489.76	1,406.66	5,310.29	2,539.72
Presbyterian	645.05	39.91	38.26	40.52	38.26	144.43	69.06
Congregational	348.13	21.54	20.65	21.87	20.65	77.95	37.28
Reformed Episcopal	216.80	13.41	12.86	13.62	12.86	48.51	23.22
Salvation Army	931.30	57.62	55.24	58.50	55.24	208.52	99.73
Other Denominations	20.92	1.28	1.23	1.31	1.23	4.68	2.24

(*c.*) APPORTIONMENT OF GRANTS FOR INSPECTION, 1899–1900.

The Government Grants for Inspection were thus apportioned
in the Estimates for 1899–1900.

(i.) Salaries. $

Roman Catholic Superintendent   -   -   1,500.00
Roman Catholic Superintendent, Harbor
    Grace   -   -   -   -   -   -   1,000·00
Church of England Superintendent   -   1,620.00
Church of England Assistant   -   -   700.00
Methodist Superintendent   -   -   -   1,500.00
Methodist Assistant   -   -   -   -   700.00

(ii.) Additional. $

Roman Catholic   -   -   -   -   -   504.04
Church of England   -   -   -   -   569.14
Methodists   -   -   -   -   -   111.39
Presbyterian   -   -   -   -   -   58.03
Congregational   -   -   -   -   31.32
Reformed Episcopal   -   -   -   -   19.52
Salvation Army   -   -   83.77
Other Denominations   -   -   -   1.88

(d.) Statistics of Roman Catholic Schools.

The following statistics in regard to the Roman Catholic
Schools of Newfoundland are taken from the " American Catholic
Directory " for 1900. The figures given follow the ecclesiastical
division of the country into the two dioceses, Harbor Grace and
St. John's, and the Vicariate-Apostolic of St. George's. At the
end will be found the totals for the whole province but it has
not been possible to test the accuracy of these from other sources
than that first mentioned.

(i.) *Diocese of Harbour Grace.*
Catholic Population   -   -   -   -   29,000
Convents (Sisters of the Presentation, 3 ;
Sisters of Mercy, 2)   -   -   -   -   5
Catholic Schools   -   -   -   -   -   90

There is also a Roman Catholic Academy in this diocese.

(ii.) *Diocese of St. John's :*
Catholic Population   -   -   -   -   **45,000**
Convents (Sisters of the Presentation, 9 ;
Sisters of Mercy, 5 ; 10 Brothers of
Christian Schools)   -   -   -   -   15

There are in each parish Roman Catholic schools under the
care of the parochial clergy, and supported by Government
Grants. There are about 30 parishes outside St. John's city.

Besides the parochial schools there are also :—St. Patrick's
Schools, kept by the Christian Brothers; Holy Cross Schools,
kept by the Christian Brothers; St. Bride's Academy for young
ladies, kept by the Sisters of Mercy; St. Bonaventure's College,
under a Board of Directors; St. Michael's Orphanage for Girls,
kept by the Sisters of Mercy; Boys Orphanage and Industrial
School, kept by the Christian Brothers.

(iii.) *Vicariate-Apostolic of St. George's ;*
Catholic Population   -   -   -   -   7,000
Convents (Sisters of the Presentation and
Sisters of Mercy)   -   -   -   -   2
Parochial Schools -   -   -   -   -   24
Children attending Parochial Schools,
about   -   -   -   -   -   -   650

(iv.) *Approximate Totals for Roman Catholic Schools in
Newfoundland :*
Catholic Population   -   -   -   -   81,000
Catholic Schools (parochial)   -   -   -   146
Catholic Academy -   -   -   -   -   1
Schools kept by Christian Brothers (in-
cluding one Industrial School)   -   -   3
Schools kept by Sisters of Mercy   -   -   2
Catholic College   -   -   -   -   -   1

No estimate of the numbers of children attending Catholic Schools can here be attempted. On the ratio of children to schools which obtains in the Vicariate-Apostolic of St. George's, the number for the whole country would be a little short of 4,000 in the parochial schools alone.

(d.) FROM THE REPORT OF THE COLONIAL AND CONTINENTAL CHURCH SOCIETY FROM 1899--1900.

By kind permission of the Colonial and Continental Church Society the following extracts from their Report for the year 1899–1900 are here reprinted. The work of this Society, originally founded in Newfoundland and called for some years the Newfoundland School Society, has been already referred to in the report by Dr. Pilot, I. (a), above.

The work of the Central Training Schools, St. John's, is of special importance, inasmuch as at present not only all the teachers of Church of England Schools but also a large number of teachers in other schools receive their preparation for the work of teaching there.

The following passage is taken from the general summary of the Society's work in its Annual Report for 1899 to 1900.

"By the training of teachers from the out-harbours the Society exercises a wide and far-reaching influence upon the whole country, for upon the Christian character and qualifications of its teachers must depend in large measure the moral qualities and knowledge of those who in the future will have the destiny of their country in their keeping.

"The offertories in the St. John's churches on one Sunday during the past year, amounting to £18 12s., were set apart for educational purposes, and sent home to the Society. This would appear to be the first time the Society's work had been thus publicly recognised.

"The Society's schools in the island are attended by about 2,000 children. under the care of more than twenty teachers. They are conducted with great efficiency, and were never more useful than at present."

The following is taken from a more detailed report of the Colonial and Continental Church Society's work in the Diocese of Newfoundland, and contains certain remarks made by Dr. Pilot. "Sharing in the wider interest now taken in education throughout the colony, the schools of the Society have improved in numbers and in efficiency.

"During the year twenty-five schools have been kept in continuous operation under twenty-five teachers, with a total enrolment of 2,136, and an average daily attendance of 1,112 scholars.

"These schools have been reported upon by the Rev. Canon Pilot, Government Superintendent of Church of England Schools, a copy of which is appended ; and in a letter to Mr. Marriott, the

Secretary, he had added some further particulars. He says:
' I forward to you a copy of my official report to his Excellency the
Governor. From this you will gather my impressions of the
Society's schools as ascertained at their examination. In a
general way I may say that these schools are doing an excellent
work. As a whole they are superior to any equal number of
Board Schools.

"'Of those in St. John's I can add nothing to your own
knowledge, save to say that I do not know what we should do
without them. . . . . In the examinations of the Council of
Higher Education last year, the Central Training School again
headed the list of all Church of England schools that sent up
candidates, and its pupils gained 50 per cent. more honours than
did any of our schools in the colony outside of the colleges.
Candidates from sixteen other Church of England schools were
presented for these examinations, of which schools all the
teachers, save one, had received their training in the Central
Schools. Considering that the scope of these examinations is
widening year after year, this is a most creditable record, and
if there were nothing else to say, it should satisfy the Society and
its friends that their efforts on behalf of the poor of Newfoundland have not gone for nothing, and that their present work
justifies the continuance of their help and support.

" But it is not in sharpening wits, imparting information and
cultivating faculties, that the chief work of this Society lies.
These modes may make children sharp and keen in matters
appertaining to this life. There is another and a nobler side
to this Society's work. These schools of theirs are first and
foremost schools for religious instruction. The education given
in them embraces the whole man, his body, mind and spirit,
and only so far as these receive appropriate attention and
culture, can education be said to be either successful or
profitable. This then is the aim and object of these schools
—a religious and secular education. Children are taught
that they are sinful, yet capable of being good—that they
are liable to temptation, and yet may find help to resist it
—that this life is but a trial period and a time of preparation
for that redemption of body, soul, and spirit, purchased by
a Saviour's Death and Passion. After over a quarter of a
century's experience in the examination of schools, I give
it as a confirmed opinion that where religious instruction is
best attended to, there also is there more and more conscientious
work performed in secular instruction.

"In work with pupils in training, the Central Schools have
had a year of marked success. Thirty-eight pupil-teachers
have been in attendance, twelve males and twenty-six females.
Twelve of these are with us to-day. The others have passed
the Government examinations for certificates, and are now
employed in schools in all parts of the colony.'"

The Report of the Corresponding Committee of the Colonial
and Continental Church Society in Newfoundland concludes

with the following words :—" To the Government for the usual grants in aid, to the subscribers for their increased interest and increased subscriptions, and to the Parent Society without whose help much ignorance must of necessity exist in this colony, the thanks of this Committee are most cordially tendered."

During the year ending April 1, 1900, the Society expended in grants and by salaries of missionaries £740, upon its work in Newfoundland. It is, however, impossible to ascertain what proportion of this sum was devoted to purposes purely educational.

APPENDIX A.

RETURN of SCHOOLS in NEWFOUNDLAND for year ended 30th June 1897.

Denomination.	Population.	Total Government Grant.	Character of School.	Number of Schools.	Teachers. Male.	Teachers. Female.	Total Teachers.	Whole Number attending for Year.	Cost of each Pupil to Government.	Percentage of Attendance compared with Total Number on Register.	Percentage of Denominational Population attending School.
Church of England	69,823	*Dollars.* 52,259.14	Public (Board) Schools	197	109	85	194	9,511			
			Colleges	2	5	3	8	238			
			Colonial and Continental Church Society Schools	21	17	3	20	2,069			
				220	131	91	222	11,818	*Dollars.* 4.42 or 18s. 2d.	51	16·9 or 1 in 5·9.
Roman Catholics	72,696	54,085.04	Public (Board) Schools	190	60	140	200	8,983			
			Colleges	1	6	—	6	166			
			Academies	8	4	4	8	243			
			Convent Schools	21	—	116	116	2,584			
			Christian Brothers School	2	11	—	11	902			
				217	81	260	341	13,180	4.10 or 17s. nearly.	55·5	18 or 1 in 5·56.
Methodist	53,276	40,395.14	Public (Board) Schools	185	61	119	180	8,890			
			Colleges	1	5	9	14	290			
				196	66	128	194	9,150	4.42 or 18s. 2d.	55	17·1 or 1 in 5·8.
Others	4,888	2,027.06	Public (Board) Schools	5	2	3	5	230			
			Presbyterian College	1	1	—	1	130			
				6	3	3	6	360	5.63 or 1l. 3s. 2d.		7·4 or 1 in 13·4.
				639	281	482	763	34,508	4.51 or 17s. 3d.		17·1 or 1 in 5·4.

APPENDIX B.

VOLUNTARY CONTRIBUTIONS, FEES, &c., towards EDUCATION in NEWFOUNDLAND.

Denomination.	Voluntary Contributions in Money.	Voluntary Contributions in Kind.	Fees.	Total.	Percentage of Contributions compared with Government Grant.	Government Grant per head.	Voluntary Contributions per head.
	Dollars.	*Dollars.*	*Dollars.*	*Dollars.*		*Cents.*	*Cents.*
Church of England	4,904.00	2,100.00	7,981.48	14,985.48	29	75 or 3s. 1d.	22
Roman Catholics	2,000.00	1,500.00	4,965.00	8,465.00	15·6	74 or 3s. 0¼d.	12 nearly
Methodist	614.66	1,000.00	10,575.71	12,190.37	30	78 nearly or 3s. 1¼d.	22
Other	950.00	—	600.00	1,550.00	76	42 nearly or 1s. 9½d.	31
	8,468.66	4,600.00	24,122.19	37,190.85	24	76½ or 3s. 2d.	18

APPENDIX C.

PROGRAMME of STUDIES for ELEMENTARY SCHOOLS, NEWFOUNDLAND.

Grade of School	Standards	Reading and Spelling	Writing	Arithmetic	Grammar	Composition	Geography	History	Remarks
Third Grade	I.	To read in mono-syllables.	To print letters or figures on slate.	Simple exercises in Arithmetic, Ball Frames, &c.	—	—			It will be seen by reference to this Schedule that in Third Grade, scholars are required to pass in Standards I., II.; and in Second Grade I., II., III., and IV.; and in First Grade they are required to pass in all Standards. The subjects presented in this Schedule are regarded as essentials: schools in which Singing, Drawing, Drill, Book-keeping, Geometry, Algebra, Navigation, other Languages, or other higher branches are taught, will receive honourable mention. Two-thirds of those in attendance will be required to pass in each standard, in order to qualify for any grade.
	II.	To read a paragraph from an elementary book.	To transcribe a sentence correctly.	Simple addition and Subtraction, and Multiplication Tables to six times 12.	—	—			
Second Grade	III	To read with intelligence a short paragraph from a more advanced class book.	To write on slate from Dictation correctly in copy-books, elements of simple letters.	To work an exercise in any of the compound Rules.			Elementary, and particularly a map of Newfoundland.		
	IV.	To read with accuracy a passage in poetry or prose.	Copy-books to show improvement.	Practice, Bills of Parcels and Simple Proportion.	To point out Nouns, Verbs and Adjectives in a sentence.	Easy composition.	Outlines of Western Hemisphere, particularly British North America.	Introductory.	
First Grade	V.	To read with fluency and expression a passage in poetry or prose.	Same as above	Simple Interest, Vulgar and Decimal Fractions.	Parsing and analysis of simple sentences.	To write from memory the substance of a story read out twice.	Outlines of Eastern Hemisphere, particularly the British Isles.	History of Newfoundland.	
	VI.	To read and recite with taste and expression.	Same as above	Compound Interest, Compound Proportion, and Discount.	Parsing and analysis advanced.	Original	The world, with map drawing.	British History.	

APPENDIX D.

TEACHERS' PENSION FUND.

59. For the purpose of providing for the retirement of all teachers of public schools upon their reaching the age of sixty years, there shall be established a fund, to be known as "The Teachers' Pension Fund," in the manner hereinafter specified, that is to say,—

(1.) From the appropriation made under section 11 of this Act to each teacher who has received a certificate of grade from any Board of Examiners appointed under this Act, the Governor in Council shall deduct, every six months, one half of the annual premium required to be paid by such teacher, according to age, as fixed in the six per cent. columns in Schedules J and K of this Act, which sums so deducted shall be deposited in the Savings Bank of this Colony to the credit of the said fund.

(2.) Upon the amount accumulated to the credit of the fund at the beginning of each calendar year there shall be allowed by the Government interest for the ensuing twelve months, at the rate of three per cent. in addition to the interest paid by the Savings Bank, which amount of interest so allowed by the Government shall be deposited to the credit of the said fund in the Savings Bank.

(3.) In consideration of the regular payment of the annual premiums provided for in sub-section 1, each male teacher shall, upon reaching the age of sixty years, be entitled to receive a pension of one hundred dollars per annum, during the remainder of his life, and each female teacher, during the remainder of her life, a pension of eighty dollars.

(4.) The Government of the Colony shall be trustees and managers of this fund, which shall be deposited in the Savings Bank, and the pensions shall be paid quarterly during the lifetime of the respective pensioneers, at the office of the said Bank, upon the order of the Colonial Secretary. An annual report of the condition of the fund shall be laid before the Legislature within one month after the opening of the next succeeding session.

(5.) In the case of the death of any contributor to this fund, before he shall have entered upon his pension, the whole sum he has contributed, with compound interest at six per cent., shall be returned to his legal representatives, provided he has not forfeited his claim under sub-sections 9 and 13.

(6.) Any contributor to this fund who shall cease to follow the occupation of a teacher shall be permitted, provided he has made twenty annual payments to the fund, to secure to himself the pension by paying thenceforth, until he arrive at the age of sixty years, the annual premium fixed for his age at entrance as stated in the three per cent. columns contained in Schedules J and K of this Act.

(7.) After the provisions relating to this fund shall have come into operation, any contributor thereto who shall cease to follow the occupation of a teacher, after five full years' service as such, and payment of five annual premiums, shall be permitted to withdraw from the fund all his contributions, with compound interest at three per cent.

(8.) Should any contributor to this fund, who has taught a public
school for a period of five full years, after this scheme has come
into operation, cease to follow the occupation of a teacher for
not more than two years, he shall, if he again become a teacher
of a public school, within the said period of two years, and have
not withdrawn his deposits, as provided for in sub-section 7,
resume his connection with this fund by paying his arrears of
contributions, with compound interest at six per cent.

(9.) Should any contributor to this fund, who has taught a public
school for a period of less than five full years, cease to follow
the occupation of a teacher, he shall forfeit all claim upon this
fund, and if he again become a teacher, shall resume his connection with the fund by paying the annual premium based
upon his age at re entrance : provided that, where such teacher
has retired, owing to failure of health, he shall, if he again
become a teacher, within two years from the date of his retirement, resume his connection with the fund on his former footing
without such forfeit, by payment of his arrears with compound
interest at six per cent. ; provided further, that any teacher
employed on or before the first day of July, 1892, may, upon
ceasing to follow the occupation of a teacher, withdraw all his
contributions to the fund, with compound interest at three per
cent. ; provided he has taught a public school five full years at
the time of his retirement.

(10.) No teacher beyond the age of forty years shall be permitted to
become a contributor to this fund ; provided this shall not
apply to teachers over forty years, employed on or before the
first July, 1892, such teachers shall have the option of becoming
contributors to this fund within a period of two years therefrom,
by signifying their desire in writing to the managers of the fund.

(11.) All premiums required in connection with this fund shall be made
in half-yearly instalments on the 30th day of June and 31st day
of December in each year. Teachers, on first being employed,
if they have taught for less than six months at either of the
above dates, shall pay proportionate parts thereof.

(12.) For the purposes of this fund, the age of every teacher contributing thereto shall be taken to be his age on his birthday
nearest to the date of his employment as a teacher.

(13.) Any teacher whose certificate has been cancelled for drunkenness,
or other immoral conduct, shall forfeit all claim upon this fund.

60. No payments shall be made from this fund except in accordance with
the provisions of the next preceding section.

61. After the lapse of twenty years from the first day of July, 1892, any
funds which shall be found to have accumulated over and above the amount
necessary to secure the payment of all claims provided for in section 59,
shall be applied either in diminution of the future annual premiums of the
contributors, or in augmentation of their pensions, as the trustees and
managers of this fund shall determine.

62. The provisions of section 59 shall not apply to teachers who are
members of any religious Order, unless they so desire.

SCHEDULE J.

Annual Premiums required to be paid by each Male Teacher, according to age, as provided for in Sub-section 1 of Section 64 of this Act, in order to secure·to himself, upon his reaching the age of Sixty years, a pension of 100 dollars per annum during the remainder of his life, expectation of life at that age being taken at 12·5 years, and premiums being calculated on the scale of three and six per cent. compound interest.

AGE.	Number of Payments.	Annual Premiums on the Scale of Three per Cent. Compound Interest.	Annual Premiums on the Scale of Six per Cent. Compound Interest.	AGE.
		Dollars.	Dollars.	
16	44	11.56	4.29	16
17	43	12.04	4.57	17
18	42	12.68	4.87	18
19	41	13.09	5.19	19
20	40	13.66	5.54	20
21	39	14.25	5.91	21
22	38	14.90	6.31	22
23	37	15.28	6 73	23
24	36	15.56	7.19	24
25	35	17.03	7.69	25
26	34	17.84	8.22	26
27	33	18.52	8.80	27
28	32	19.61	9.43	28
29	31	20.60	10.10	29
30	30	21.65	10.84	30
31	29	22.78	11.63	31
32	28	23.97	12.50	32
33	27	25.30	13.43	33
34	26	26.72	14.47	34
35	25	28.25	15.60	35
36	24	29.92	16.85	36
37	23	31.74	18.21	37
38	22	33.73	19.72	38
39	21	25.92	21.40	39
40	20	38.33	23.31	40
41	19	41.08	25.41	41
42	18	44.00	27.75	42
43	17	47.79	30.39	43
44	16	51.10	33.39	44
45	15	55.38	36.82	45
46	14	60.28	40.77	46
47	13	65.95	45.37	47
48	12	72.58	50.77	48
49	11	80.42	57.23	49
50	10	89.93	64.92	50

SCHEDULE K.

Annual Premiums required to be paid by each Female Teacher, according to age, as provided for in Sub-section 1 of Section 64 of this Act in order to secure to herself, upon her reaching the age of Sixty years a pension of 80 dollars per annum during the remainder of her life, expectation of life at that age being taken at 13·5 years, and premiums being calculated on the scale of three and six per cent. compound interest.

AGE.	Number of Payments.	Annual Premiums on the Scale of Three per Cent. Compound Interest.	Annual Premiums on the Scale of Six per Cent. Compound Interest.	AGE.
		Dollars.	Dollars.	
16	44	9.85	3.61	16
17	43	10.26	3.84	17
18	42	10.69	4.10	18
19	41	11.13	4.37	19
20	40	11.63	4.66	20
21	39	12.14	4.98	21
22	38	12.68	5.31	22
23	37	13.25	5.67	23
24	36	13.86	6.06	24
25	35	14.50	6.48	25
26	34	15.18	6.93	26
27	33	15.92	7.41	27
28	32	16.70	7.94	28
29	31	17.54	8.51	29
30	30	18.43	9.13	30
31	29	19.39	9.80	31
32	28	20.42	10.73	32
33	27	21.54	11.32	33
34	26	22.74	12.19	34
35	25	24.05	13.14	35
36	24	25.47	14.19	36
37	23	27.02	15.34	37
38	22	28.71	16.61	38
39	21	30.57	18.02	39
40	20	32.63	19.64	40
41	19	34.90	21.40	41
42	18	37.45	23.37	42
43	17	40.29	25.59	43
44	16	43.49	28.12	44
45	15	47.14	31.02	45
46	14	51.30	34.34	46
47	13	56.13	38.21	47
48	12	61.79	42.76	48
49	11	68.45	48.15	49
50	10	76.51	54.68	50

APPENDIX E.

SOME PROVISIONS OF THE EDUCATION ACT OF JULY, 1899.

1. The Governor in Council may nominate or appoint an Assistant both to the Superintendent of Church of England Schools and to the Superintendent of Methodist Schools. Such assistants are called Assistant-Superintendents, and act under the directions of the Superintendents.

2. *Salaries.*—

	$
Superintendent of Church of England Schools -	1,620
Assistant do. - - - - - - -	700
Superintendent of Roman Catholic Schools, except Diocese for Harbor Grace - - -	1,500
Superintendent of Roman Catholic Schools, Diocese of Harbor Grace - - - -	1,000
Superintendent of Methodist Schools - -	1,500
Assistant do. - - - - - - -	700

3. In districts where superior schools are or may be established, Boards of Education, whether Church of England, Roman Catholic, or Methodist Boards, may consist of nine or more members. They may consist of nine members in St. John's districts. One layman shall retire annually, but shall be eligible for reappointment at the end of the next, second, or other succeeding year. The members of existing Boards retire in order of seniority of appointment.

4. No Superintendent or Assistant-Superintendent shall engage directly or indirectly in any commercial undertaking or business.

THE
SYSTEM OF EDUCATION ·
IN
JAMAICA.

PART I.

I. HISTORICAL SKETCH - - - - - - - - 577

II. THE SYSTEM (AS IT WAS BEFORE THE NEW CODE, 1900).
 Local Managers - - - - - - - - - 585
 Finance - - - .- - - - - - 586
 Attendance - - - - - - - - - 588
 Private and Secondary Schools - - - - - 589
 Administration - - - - - - - - 590
 Inspection - - - - - - - - 591
 Subjects of Instruction - - - - - - 592
 Agriculture - - - - - - - 594
 Manual Training - - - - - - - 595
 Religious Instruction - - - - - - 595
 Teachers' Salaries - - - - - - 596
 Pupil Teachers - - - - - - - 597
 Training - - - - - - - - 598
 Secondary Education - - - - - - 599
 Technical Instruction - - - - - - 600
 Reformatory and Industrial Schools - - - - 600

APPENDICES.

A. Denominational Summary of Elementary Schools in 1864
 and 1865 - - - - - - - - - 601
B. Statistics of Elementary Education from 1868 to 1899 - - 602
C. Attendance Curves - - - - - To face page 602
D. Statistics of Age - - - - - - - - 603
E. Synopsis of the principal changes in the Elementary School
 System between 1867 and 1897 - - - - - 604
F. Standards of Classification down to the New Code, 1900 - 607
G. Subjects for Examination of Pupil Teachers - - - 616
H. Requirements at Examination of Training Colleges - - 618

PART II.

SUPPLEMENTARY NOTES ON EDUCATION IN JAMAICA,
1898-1900.

I. REPORT OF THE COMMISSION ON EDUCATION IN JAMAICA,
 1898 - - - - - - - - - - 624
 System of Education in Jamaica - - - - 625
 Amalgamation of Schools - - - - - 626
 School Age - - - - - - - - 629
 Compulsion to Attend School - - - - - 630

Irregularity and Unpunctuality - - - - - - 632
Education of Children of East Indians - - - - 634
School Managers - - - - - - - 635
Inspectors and Inspection - - - - - - 635
Grants - - - - - - - - 636
Teachers and their Training - - - - - 636
Classification of Schools - - - - - - 643
School Organisation - - - - - - - 645
Proposed changes in the Curriculum of Elementary Schools 646
Religious Teaching - - - - - - - 656
Manual and Agricultural Instruction - - - - 657
Continuation Schools - - - - - - 662
Secondary Schools - - - - - - - 662
Effect of Home Conditions on School Life - - - 663
Scholarships - - - - - - - - 663
Board of Education and Education Department - - 664
Commissioners' Finding as to the State of Education in
Jamaica - - - - - - - - - 664

II. EXTRACTS FROM THE EVIDENCE GIVEN BEFORE THE EDUCA-
TION COMMISSION - - - - - - - 665

Is it desirable that the system of education should in
the main be organised on denominational lines ? - - 665

Does Education tend to make the rising generation disinclined for manual labour, especially in Agriculture ? - 669

Is it desirable or practicable to have more agricultural
teaching in elementary schools ? - - - - 672

Should Elementary Education be made more practical and
less literary ? - - - - - - - 676

What have been the general effects on the population of
the system of education in Jamaica ? - - - - 678

III. EDUCATION IN JAMAICA IN 1898-9.

Educational Statistics 1897-9 - - - - - 681

Memorandum on Educational Matters addressed by Board
of Education to the Legislative Council, April, 1897 - 681

Educational Finance, 1897-9 - - - - - 682

Monthly Average Attendance at Schools and Classification
of Scholars - - - - - - - - 684

Teachers - - - - - - - - - 685

Manual Training, Kindergarten Class, and Teaching of
Elementary Science in its bearing on Agriculture - 685

Training Colleges - - - - - - - 686

Scholarships and Secondary Education - - 687

Remarks of the Superintending Inspector on the Report
of the Education Commission - - - - 688

IV. SELECTION OF THE ARTICLES CONTAINED IN THE NEW CODE
OF REGULATIONS OF THE EDUCATION DEPARTMENT, IN
FORCE FROM MAY 10, 1900 - - 689

THE SYSTEM OF EDUCATION IN JAMAICA.*

I. HISTORICAL SKETCH.

1. Elementary education cannot be said to have existed in Jamaica prior to Emancipation in 1834. Slavery in this Island, as in all other countries, debarred the people not only from education, but also from all the means calculated to advance their moral and intellectual improvement. It was popularly held and stoutly maintained in the public papers that knowledge would entirely unfit the negroes for the labour to which they were subjected. *Emancipation in 1834.*

2. The advantages of education were therefore only available for the children of free people and certain privileged classes. For these provision was made by bequests, at various periods, of money, lands, and slaves, in various parts of the Island, which were the original endowments of the existing schools known as Wolmer's, Manning's, Rusea's, Munro and Dickenson's, etc., so called after the names of the testators. Unfortunately, however, the funds were in many cases misappropriated, and in nearly all mismanaged. It would not be too much to say that the bulk of the money left for educational purposes was squandered or stolen. Had not the necessities of the government of the day led them to appropriate all the money belonging to these educational trusts that could be recovered, for which they undertook to pay, and have since paid a high rate of interest, there might have been no endowed school now in existence that was founded before Emancipation. Even up to 1870, and in some cases later still, the income derived from the Government was to a large extent wasted on giving in the endowed schools elementary education of a character little if at all higher than that given at a comparatively insignificant cost in the ordinary elementary schools, to the children of persons much better able to educate them than the parents of the vast majority of fee-paying children in the latter. Gardner, in his " History of Jamaica," says : " The influence of the endowed schools, with the single exception of Wolmer's " (which gave mainly elementary teaching) " was small in the extreme. Upwards of £3,000 per annum was spent to about as little purpose as it is possible to conceive." I shall return to the later history of these trusts further on. *Misuse of early bequests.*

3. Two or three elementary day schools for children of free parents appear to have existed in the Island previous to 1820. Between 1820 and 1834 seven schools were opened for children of free parents only, all by the Church of England ; whilst forty were opened for the children of slaves, viz., nine by the Church of England, twelve by the Moravians, six by the Presbyterians, four by the Baptists, and nine by proprietors of *Particulars of the first schools.*

---

* Part I. of this Report, with its Appendices, was prepared by the Hon. T. Capper in 1898. Part II. brings the account of the Educational System of Jamaica down to the publication of the New Code in May, 1900. It will be seen that the years 1898–1900 have been important in the educational history of the Island.

estates. In 1835 and 1836 about £50,000 was given by the British Government for the erection of school houses, and in 1837 when Mr. Latrobe made at their request an exhaustive report (from which my figures are taken) upon the condition of the schools in the colony, especially those which had received building grants, there were 12,580 children on the books of the 183 elementary day schools then in operation, the average attendance being 9,789, or 77·7 per cent. (it is now about 60 per cent.), whilst there are 139 Sunday schools with 20,870 scholars on the books, and 95 evening schools with 5,304 scholars. Besides these schools there were 124 private schools, as to which little information was available. Of the 12,580 children in the day schools of the Island 2,531, or 20 per cent., were to be found in Kingston. The proportion is now about 5 per cent. Besides the 2,531 in the regular day schools in Kingston, it was estimated that there were 2,245 in private schools, 1,000 "supposed to receive instruction from day-scholars and from itinerant teachers," and 150 in evening schools, making nearly 6,000 under instruction, of whom, however, a considerable number must have been adults. Of the 1,182 in Kingston Sunday schools a large proportion doubtless also attended day schools. A large number of the teachers in the Island had been brought from England; out of 153 schoolmasters and 104 schoolmistresses mentioned by Mr. Latrobe only 41 of the former and 61 of the latter were coloured. The following were the salaries paid by the Church Missionary Society, and it is probable that those given by other bodies were about the same :—

Coloured males, from	£42 to £84.	
„ females „	£18 to £48.	
Europeans, unmarried	£120.	
„ married	£144 and upwards.	

In 1837 and in each succeeding year up to 1842 the sum of £30,000 was given by the British Parliament to Jamaica for education. In 1842 this amount was reduced by £6,000, and £5,000 was taken off the grant every succeeding year till 1846, when it ceased. "About 80 schools were aided by the grants for building, more than half being connected with the Established Church, and to these by far the largest proportion of succeeding grants was given."[*] Whilst these large grants were given by Parliament, the public enthusiasm on behalf of the freed slaves found expression also in large subscriptions for educational purposes to the various religious bodies, so that no lack of funds for the inauguration of school work was experienced.

Lady Mico's Charity.

4. The commencement of the operations of the Mico Charity in 1836 must not be passed over without special notice. More than 100 years before, Lady Mico had left £1,000 for the redemption of Christian captives in Algeria. In 1836 this application of the revenue derived from the trust, the capitalised value of which was now over £100,000, having become

---

[*] Gardner's History of Jamaica.

impossible, an order in Chancery was obtained allowing it to be employed in the education of the emancipated negroes. Schools were at once established in Mauritius and in Jamaica and other West Indian Islands, and about 20 schoolmasters were sent out to the latter. In the country parts of Jamaica several schools were established, besides the training institution and schools in Kingston. Gradually the plan of operations was changed, the elementary schools were given up, and the portion of the resources of the Charity devoted to Jamaica was concentrated on the training institution, without which, for many years after the cessation of the Imperial grant, no efficient elementary education of any kind would have been possible, and to which Jamaica owes a debt which it is impossible to over-estimate.

5. Whilst all these efforts were being made to provide elemen- Reaction. tary instruction for the people, the people themselves displayed the greatest enthusiasm in availing themselves of it. The numerous schools opened in all parts of the Island were rapidly filled to repletion with the most eager and docile of pupils. This enthusiasm was justly regarded as most encouraging and hopeful, and it is to be much regretted that in spite of the zeal displayed by the ministers of the various denominations and others, and of the importation of English masters and mistresses, the schools established were for the most part of a very inferior description. The teaching was almost entirely by rote, "sound without sense." This so-called education naturally did little to fit its recipients for the most ordinary duties of life, and still less for the advancement in social position which many had anticipated and hoped for as its result; reaction, as might have been expected, set in, gradually producing utter indifference towards education in the minds alike of the labouring population and of the more intelligent classes. Education, or what was called such, having failed to show them how to cultivate the soil better, to make more money, to improve their circumstances, or to advance themselves in life, was considered a failure. Fortunately, a few good schools here and there served to show that when properly managed in the hands of competent teachers, education was a real power, and capable of conferring benefits of the highest value upon its recipients by stimulating and arousing the intelligence without which success in any pursuit is impossible.

6. The result of this reaction was that elementary education Mr. Savage's became almost entirely neglected. The Government gave in Report in all about £3,000 annually to the schools, but there was no 1864. regular system of inspection, and the great majority were practically worthless as educational agencies. That any schools at all remained in existence at this time was due to the efforts of the religious bodies, which from local resources and subscriptions received from England, managed to keep some hundreds of schools alive, some at least of which were fairly efficient. That these were the exception, however, was shown by the report of Mr. Savage, who found on his appointment in 1864 that of 289 schools examined by him and arranged in four classes, only 25

might be regarded as efficient, whilst in 154, or more than one-half, he stated that there was no regular system, nor any moral training whatever, and that no attempt was made to teach the pupils to think, or to explain or elucidate the meaning of any of the lessons. In Appendix "A" I give the results of this examination, and also figures showing that of the total cost of schools at that time one-half was met by denominational funds, one-fourth by school fees, and one-fourth by Government, mainly in support of schools in connection with the Church of England.

7. A revival of popular interest had already taken place in 1863, when a measure was adopted by the Colonial Legislature to establish a system of "competitive examination" of schoolmasters, with the view of securing a more competent class of men as teachers of the elementary schools. A board of public examiners with the Bishop at its head, was duly appointed by the Government to carry out this project. One examination only was held by this Board, at which thirteen candidates presented themselves, of whom four were said to have passed. The list of subjects included Greek and Roman History and Optics, and the standard aimed at was far too high. In 1864 Mr. Savage was first appointed to examine into and report upon the state of elementary education in the colony, with the results referred to in the previous paragraph. He was requested to give his views on the subject generally, and on the form of a scheme of supervision and inspection of schools suited to the condition of the country, and ultimately in 1867 the regulations were adopted, upon which, with various alterations and modifications from time to time, our whole educational system in Jamaica has been founded. Sir John Peter Grant had just assumed the Government, and he, personally, with the assistance of Mr. Savage, settled the details of the new plan. It proved a great success, and gave, Mr. Savage says, "universal satisfaction." The schools were "rigidly examined in reading, dictation, arithmetic, Scripture knowledge, grammar, geography, singing, organisation and discipline. The tests were thorough and the examination impartial." The collection of school fees was made imperative, as one of the conditions of receiving aid. From 1867, when the system was introduced, until 1880, there was a steady and almost unbroken advance in the number of schools under inspection, in the average attendance, and in the efficiency of the teaching given. (*See* Appendix B.)

Regulations of 1867.

8. Under the regulations promulgated in 1867 elementary schools that met the Government requirements received (1) a management grant of £20, £15 or £10, and (2) a capitation grant of 6s., 5s. or 4s. per unit of average attendance, according to the class of the school. They also received 3s. for every girl in average attendance at a sewing class. In addition to these grants it was provided that "schools in which the pupils devoted not less than three hours of every school day to manual labour upon a regular system, should be considered industrial schools," and should receive a further allowance of one-half the amount of the management grant or £10, £7 10s., or £5 according

to the class of the school. Industrial schools were also exempted from the obligation to charge fees. In March 1870, Mr. Savage reported that "the number of industrial schools had not increased as much as could be desired," owing to the objection of parents to send their children to school to learn what they could teach them themselves, and to the difficulty experienced in selecting the best and most remunerative industries, and in disposing of the products. The special grants to industrial schools were therefore increased by giving an addition of half the capitation grant, besides half the management grant, making a total special allowance to these schools of, in some cases, over £22 a year. Under this stimulus the total amount of the special grants to industrial schools rose , from £90 in 1871 to £586 in 1874. In 1875, however, Mr. (now Bishop) Douet, who was acting for Mr. Savage, reported that it had been found necessary to reduce these grants, and stated that "when any work had been attempted the teacher had failed to give satisfaction, owing to his want of knowledge." The total amount of these grants declined again from £586 in 1874 to £308 in 1877, when Mr. Savage reported, "After all that has been said and written on the subject of industrial schools, the problem still remains unsolved, as far as Jamaica is concerned. All the inspectors concur in stating that the feeble attempts hitherto made by some of the schools to combine manual labour with school instruction have been most unsatisfactory, and in view of the intentions of the Government, nearly all have been entire failures." The regulations providing for special grants to industrial schools were therefore rescinded, and the grants ceased. Regulations for providing aid to schools in which "skilled manual labour and improved systems of cultivation on really useful and successful methods" are combined with school instruction, have been nominally in force ever since 1878, but in consequence of the great expense it would have been necessary to incur to earn a comparatively very small grant, these regulations remained a dead letter.

It has seemed to me worth while to give somewhat fully the details of the failure of this determined and persevering attempt, extending over a period of ten years, to secure the combination in the elementary schools of mental and intellectual training with actual labour, agricultural or industrial, an attempt made by men who at first fully believed in its practicability, but were slowly and reluctantly convinced by experience that they had been mistaken.

9. In 1877 a small Commission, consisting of the Chief Justice, the Attorney-General, one of the leading physicians of the Island, and a minister of religion of very wide and varied experience, was appointed to enquire into the condition of the juvenile population. The Commission of necessity dealt with the education question, and in its report, made in 1879, recommended, *inter alia*, the introduction of compulsion, at first in the towns, and afterwards, by degrees, in the rural districts where sufficient accommodation existed. The Commission was of opinion that "The existing system including management, Government grants in aid, Government

Commission of 1877.

inspection and fees, had worked well, and would serve, with necessary additions and modifications, as the basis of a compulsory system."

School Commission Law, 1879.

10. In 1879 the Schools Commission Law was passed, giving the Governor power to nominate a Commission to deal with the various endowed schools in the Island. The Commission was entrusted with the direct control of one of the best endowed schools, the Jamaica Free School, and was empowered in the case of other endowed schools, if it considered the trust funds were being improperly applied, to remove existing bodies of trustees and replace them by others, to prepare and put in force new schemes for the management of the schools, and as a last resort to take over the funds of any endowment and apply them, with due reservation of the rights of existing beneficiaries or classes of beneficiaries, to the purpose of the Jamaica Free School, re-named by the law the Jamaica High School. This last extreme step has never been taken, but the Commission appointed, under the chairmanship at first of the Chief Justice, Sir J. Lucie Smith, and subsequently of the Bishop of Jamaica, now Archbishop of the West Indies, at once took in hand the remodelling of the constitution of the Jamaica High School, removing it to the neighbourhood of Kingston, where, with its offshoot, University College, it is now doing excellent work ; and then proceeded to deal in succession with the various endowed schools mentioned in Paragraph 2 of this sketch, which are now, under their new scheme of management, giving general satisfaction.

Progress since 1883.

11. In the year 1880, Jamaica had the experience—fortunately a rare one—of a severe cyclone, which amongst other serious results to the colony threw back the progress of education several years at least. The falling-off in average attendance at the inspections in 1881 amounted to nearly 20 per cent., and the efficiency of the schools was also found to be seriously affected, mainly in consequence of the greatly increased irregularity of attendance. It took three years for the attendance and six for the efficiency of the schools to reach again the high-water mark of 1880. Appendix B will, however, show that the advance from 1886 to 1894 was phenomenally rapid, the attendance increasing by 88·5 per cent. and the number of first-class schools by 142·9 per cent. The greater part of the increase in attendance took place in 1893 and 1894, the two years immediately following the abolition of fees in 1892. Since 1894 there has been a falling-off of 10 per cent. in average attendance, though the efficiency of the schools has been fairly well maintained. The consequent reduction in the average size of the schools has, under the provisions of the new Code, explained below, caused an increase in the cost per unit of average attendance. In Appendix C. is given a graphic representation of the fluctuation in the average attendance in Jamaica and its several parishes from August, 1892, to March, 1897. It will be seen that in Kingston alone there has been a continuous and rapid advance. The natural reaction from the enthusiasm for education coincident with the abolition of fees, and special circumstances such as droughts, have affected the attendance in

the country generally, but with returning prosperity there can be no doubt that the number of children in the schools will again largely increase.

12. Between 1880 and 1885 Pupil Teachers' Examinations at local centres were established, in place of the former individual examinations at the time the schools were inspected: a regular system of aid to voluntary denominational training colleges, and of increased aid to the Mico Charity, was introduced; an annual examination of all the students in training colleges, at which teachers also might be examined for certificates, was established, bringing the training colleges for the first time into direct relations with the Education Department; and the pupil teachers' examinations were thrown open to voluntary candidates on payment of a nominal fee. *Pupil-Teachers' Examinations.*

13. In 1885 a Commission was appointed, under the chairmanship of the Colonial Secretary, and including also seven representatives of the principal religious bodies, two heads of Government departments, and three prominent laymen interested in education, to enquire into the whole system of elementary education in the colony. After holding 34 meetings, and taking oral and written evidence from persons believed to be interested in education and able to afford valuable information on the points submitted to them, it reported in 1886 in favour of (1) Grants for teachers' residences; (2) Superannuation allowances to teachers; (3) Compulsory attendance; (4) Abolition of fees; (5) The imposition of special taxation for educational purposes; (6) The establishment of a central board of education, and (7) of local boards. In an *ad interim* report presented in September, 1885, the Commission had strongly recommended a still further increase in the grants to training colleges, with a view to doubling the number of students under training as soon as possible, and steps to that end were immediately taken. There are now 191 students under training, as against 78 in 1885. The Commission expressed the opinion that the existing system of inspection and examination was a sufficient test of the working of the schools, and had proved effective in promoting the interests of education. *Elementary Education Commission, 1885.*

14. No action was taken on this report until 1892, when two laws were passed by the Legislative Council giving effect to some of its recommendations. The first of these provided for the creation of a central board, to be presided over by the head of the Education Department, whose functions should be mainly advisory, but without whose recommendations no new schools should receive aid, nor any change be made in the Code of Regulations. Provision was also made for the imposition of an education tax, for the payment of a grant in lieu of fees to all schools where fees were not charged, for the enactment by the governor, in his discretion, on the recommendation of the Board, of compulsory attendance at elementary schools in such towns or districts as he might designate, for the establishment of small scholarships to assist needy scholars from the elementary schools *Educational Legislation in 1892.*

to obtain higher education in secondary schools, and for the enforcement of a conscience clause similar to that which is in use in England. The Code then in force was to remain so until altered on the recommendation of the Board.

The Secondary Education Law provided for the establishment of secondary schools in any important centres declared by the Governor in Privy Council, on the recommendation of the Board, to be without adequate provision for secondary education, and for the granting of scholarships to scholars in such schools to enable the more promising of them to continue their education at high schools or colleges. A central board was at once nominated by the Governor, and it proceeded to revise the Education Code and to perform the other duties laid upon it by the law. The first Revised Code came into force on August 10, 1893, and a second, the existing Code, in March, 1895. The chief object aimed at in the first revision of the Code, disregarding minor points of detail was to secure that however small a school might be, so long as it was really necessary, the teacher should earn enough to maintain himself respectably. The amount earned by the smallest schools was raised by the new Code from 50 to 100 per cent. Of course such a system could only be maintained if no small school were allowed that was not absolutely necessary. Provision was also made by the Revised Code for building grants for teachers' houses, as recommended by the Commission of 1885. At the meetings of the Board held regularly every quarter in accordance with the law, applications for 223 new schools have been considered, of which 148 were declared necessary by the Board, but the net increase in the number of schools on the annual grant list has been only 12, owing mainly to the voluntary closing of schools found not to be needed.

The establishment of a school under the Secondary Education Law, at Montego Bay, was in 1895 recommended by the Board of Education and sanctioned by the Governor in Privy Council. It was opened in September, 1896, and it is now in operation with 14 pupils.

15. An interesting sidelight is thrown on the educational progress in the twenty years from 1871 to 1891 and in the twelve years from 1884 to 1896 by the Census and Marriage Statistics given at the foot of Appendix B. It will be seen that the number that could read and write in every hundred of the population in 1891 was twice as large as in 1871, and the percentage attending school was also twice as large. The actual numbers had increased by about 150 per cent. The proportion of persons signing the marriage register with a written signature increased between 1884 and 1896 by nearly 30 per cent. These facts indicate much more than the mere capacity to sign names; they prove a general advance in the intelligence of the population.

The Education Commission, 1897-8. 16. In the legislative session of 1897 a resolution was carried in favour of the appointment of another Education Commission, which was nominated by the Governor later in the year. The chairman is a Judge of the Supreme Court, and of the other five members two are elected members of the

Legislative Council and three are representatives of some of the religious bodies which have been associated with so much of the educational work in the past. It may be anticipated that the result of their enquiries and deliberations will be the recommendation of measures which will gradually cause the children to attend school in greater numbers and with more regularity, which as quickly as may be will bring suitable hand and eye training and the inculcation of elementary agricultural principles into their due and important places in the curriculum, and which will greatly improve our system generally.* The children are thus in a fair way to have these subjects brought more clearly to their notice, and they will be shown, in the best ways that can be devised, how they may help to develop useful industrial pursuits and to foster the agricultural interests of the Island.

II. THE SYSTEM (AS IT WAS BEFORE THE NEW CODE, 1900).

1. Elementary education in Jamaica is conducted entirely by Local local managers, the vast majority being ministers of the various Managers. religious bodies. Though the Board of Education through the Code, and the Education Department in administering the Code, have done their best to secure the nomination of at least two co-managers for each school, it is still, and must inevitably be for some time to come, the rare exception for any school to have more than one local manager. The educated and influential people in the country are almost universally too busy or too indifferent to take any but a purely nominal part, and that only in a very few instances, in the management of schools. As a consequence, when any pressure is brought to bear on the responsible manager of a school to nominate colleagues, the only persons he can find to present are, though possibly unexceptionable as to moral character, and very likely not lacking in shrewdness and common sense, educationally altogether unfit for the position. The name of a person has been sent up for approval as a manager of a public elementary school whose *mark* is affixed to his declaration of willingness to serve. Thus in the case of nearly every elementary school in the Island there is one person and one only, in whose hands the whole management of the school rests. The grants made by Government were originally what they are still called, grants in aid, that is, they supplemented other sources of income mainly derived from the central funds of the various religious bodies, but for some time now the salaries of practically all teachers, and the cost of most of the school appliances have been met entirely from the Government grant. The managers own the buildings (even though in many cases a considerable proportion of the cost of erection and of repairs, sometimes as much as one-half, has been supplied by the Government), and they appoint and dismiss the teachers without appeal.

* For Summary of the Report of the Commission, and Extracts from the Evidence, *see* Supplementary Notes to this Report.

Except in the case of some half-dozen schools, there is no local authority which has anything at all to do with elementary education, and even in these the powers of management are practically exercised by the manager.

Finance.

2. The total amount expended on education by the State (all provided from the general revenue of the Island) out of which all the salaries of the teachers, very nearly all the cost of appliances, and an appreciable proportion of the cost of erection and repair of school buildings are met, is distributed as follows (the figures are for 1896):—

	£
Direct Grants to Elementary Schools and Teachers -	50,893
Building Grants - - . - - - - -	1,320
Cost of Central Office - - - - - -	3,237
Salaries and Travelling Allowances of 8 Inspectors -	2,600
Cost of Government Training College for Women— 30 Students - - - - - - - - -	1,800
Subventions to Training Colleges not under Government Management - - - - - - - -	5,155
Expenses of Board of Education - - - -	221
Grant to Jamaica High School - - - - -	1,300
Scholarships to pupils from all classes of schools -	925
Cost of Government Secondary School, Montego Bay -	189
Total - -	67,640

3. Direct Government grants, which amount at present to about £52,000, or an average of about £56 to each school, are paid solely on results, subject to conditions laid down in the code of regulations. These results are estimated, and the conditions enforced, by the Education Department alone, between which and the managers there is no intervening authority. The mode of estimating results and of calculating grants, and the various conditions imposed, are laid down in the Code of Regulations. This Code, until the passing of the Education Laws in 1892, had been drawn up and from time to time amended by the Education Department and derived its validity from the authority of the Government.

The Elementary Education Law of 1892 provided for the nomination by the Governor of a Board of Education, of which the superintending Inspector of Schools is *ex officio* Chairman, and whose functions are mainly consultative and advisory. Changes in the Code, however, can only be made on the initiative of the Board, subject to approval by the Governor in Privy Council and to possible disallowance within twelve months by the Legislature. There is a special provision in the law that no school shall receive aid from Government until the Board has declared it necessary, and the law further charges the Board with the duty of "considering the advisability of closing superfluous schools, of amalgamating or reorganising existing schools and opening new schools where needed, for the management of which latter it shall make such arrangements as it shall think fit."

4. For about twenty years previous to 1897, £1,500 was annually voted by the Legislature to be expended in grants for the erection or repair of school buildings. At the session of the Legislative Council held in 1897, however, in consequence of a serious falling-off in the revenue, this amount was reduced to £500, or a little more than 10s. for each school on the Annual Grant List. For many years the grants were made as free gifts in aid of local efforts which were expected to provide at least half of the total amount spent, and practically no conditions were insisted upon. The present regulations which have remained substantially unaltered since 1887, require the signing of a guarantee that the work to be aided shall be completed in two years, that the site shall be central and suitable, and that the building erected or repaired shall be such as is approved by the Education Department, and shall be made available for the purposes of a public elementary school for twelve years, after which the Government retains no lien of any kind upon it. No grant can be made unless at least one-half of the total amount to be expended be raised locally; and unless the work is undertaken by a responsible central body of trustees, such, for instance, as the Diocesan Financial Board of the Church of England, the grants are paid in small instalments as the work progresses.

5. School fees were abolished by the Law of 1892, which substituted a compulsory tax on houses, realising about 50 per cent. more than had previously been voluntarily paid by the parents of a small proportion of the children. There are practically no voluntary subscribers to school funds, but the greater part of the cost of the erection and repair of the school buildings used for school purposes (whether (*a*) churches or chapels used as schools; (*b*) school-houses used occasionally or habitually as churches or chapels : (*c*) dwellings of teachers who are also catechists or lay preachers : (*d*) buildings used only as schools, or (*e*) dwellings for teachers who do not perform any work of a catechetical character), forming an appreciable part of the total cost of elementary education, is still either borne by the central funds of the different churches, or collected locally by ministers of religion from members of their congregations and others.

The fact that many teachers are also catechists or lay preachers undoubtedly tends to attract a higher class of men into the teaching profession, both from the addition they thus obtain to their salaries and from the hope of promotion to the ministry of the different churches, which is in many cases recruited from the best of the teachers, whilst the religious bodies of course benefit greatly by having a living income secured to their catechists independently of anything they may get from Church funds. The drawbacks to a system under which teachers are often practically compelled to be catechists or lay preachers are obvious, and need not be dwelt upon. In the absence of returns or published information, it is impossible to give a full return of the financial help that has been given to education by the religious bodies, but I have ascertained that about £8,000 was spent on buildings and stipends of catechists during 1896, as follows :—

	Church of England.	Baptists.	Wesleyans.	Moravians.	Presbyterians.	Congregationalists.	United Methodists.	Roman Catholics.	Christian Church (American Union).
		£	£	£	£	£	£	£	£
School Buildings proper, including Teachers' homes.	No information available. "Several thousands."	–	561	306	1,146	94	180	765	0
School Chapels			258	0	0	78	–	0	0
Stipends to Teachers, as such.		64	400	120	161	–		90	} 60
Stipends to Teachers, as Organists, Catechists, &c.		0	612	80	0	58	170	0	
School Appliances					7				
	–	64	1,831	506	1,314	230	350	855	60

Total, exclusive of Church of England, £5,210.

With reference to the third and fourth items in the above list, I may quote from a letter from one of my informants. "A grant is made to each of our schools, used in some instances to supplement salary, in others to pay house rent, in others to provide appliances, in others to aid in building teachers' cottages, but the majority of our teachers do some catechetical work, and when the allowance is made to them it is regarded as a consideration for that service, though theoretically such service is free and voluntary."

Attendance. 6. The estimated population of Jamaica on the 31st March, 1897, was 694,865. The number of children on the registers of the 932 public elementary schools in the year 1896–7 was 98,559, or 14·2 per cent. of the population, and the number in average attendance 58,411, or 8·4 per cent. of the population. The percentage of children on the registers in average attendance is 59·61 per cent. It has fluctuated in the past thirty years between 54 and 66, and corresponds pretty closely with the percentage in the other West India Islands. The irregularity of attendance which these figures show, seriously affects the efficiency of the schools, and it is certain that nothing short of compulsory attendance will completely cure it.

7. The Elementary Education Law of 1892 gave power to the Governor to make, on the recommendation of the Board of Education, regulations for the compulsory attendance at school in any specified towns or districts of all children between the ages of seven and thirteen. For various reasons these powers have not yet been exercised in any town or district, though recom-

mendations to that effect have been made by the Board of Education. That the time has come when the principle having been conceded, as it was by the Law of 1892, compulsion might be put in force in selected districts, seems to be indicated by the fact that the average attendance of pupils at the elementary schools in Jamaica is now, as stated above, 8·47 per cent. of the population, whilst in England, at the commencement of compulsion in 1871, it was 6·31; in 1876, when the obligation was made universal, though the means of enforcing it were not, it was 8·06; and in 1881, when it was both made universal and universally enforced, it was 10·99. Other circumstances, however, have to be taken into consideration, such as the supply of competent teachers, and the quality of the education given in the schools; the probable financial results of the establishment of compulsion—a far more serious question for a colony like Jamaica, with two-thirds of its children illegitimate, and especially so just now, than in a country like England—and the available accommodation. With regard to the last-named point, it may be observed that many schools are held in churches or chapels, to the use of which for school purposes the Government has no claim, and that while in such cases there would be apparently an excess of school accommodation reckoned by floor space, and the aggregate of the available school places might therefore appear to be equal to anything likely to be required for some years, yet owing to the irregularity of the distribution, and the unsuitableness of a good deal of the space nominally available for school purposes, there would be a great local deficiency of school places in many districts. Cubic space is of comparatively small importance in a tropical climate, where doors and windows are kept constantly wide open.

8. As stated in the preceding paragraph the limits of age laid down for compulsory attendance at school, if and when the regulations for such attendance are put into force, are seven and thirteen. At present the limits of age between which children are allowed to attend public elementary schools are five and fourteen, except when special provision is made for the education of infants, in which case three is the lower limit, and in certain other exceptional cases. It will be seen by the Tables in Appendix D that 83 per cent. of the children are between the ages of six and twelve inclusive, 8 per cent. are thirteen years of age, 6 per cent. are five, 3 per cent. (admitted for the most part under temporary exceptional regulations) are fourteen, and only about 1 per cent. are under five and over fourteen. That three-fifths of the children are below the second standard is a fact that is much to be regretted; but it is not without a parallel in colonies which have a longer educational history than Jamaica, and in which much larger sums proportionately have been spent on elementary schools. In the absence of compulsory regulations, moreover, it cannot be considered · altogether surprising.

9. Private elementary schools are practically non-existent except in Kingston, where there are a few, of which little is practically known, except that they are for the most part select

Private and Secondary Schools.

and inefficient.   Private secondary schools are to be found in
Kingston and in the large towns, but as they are not in any way
assisted by the Government, information about them is difficult
to obtain.   That the education given in them is improving seems
to be shown by the increasing number that send up scholars
who pass the Cambridge Local Examinations.   Of the endowed
schools of the Island, of which a good deal has already been
said in the Historical Sketch, one, the Jamaica High School, is
largely assisted from Government funds, and would take a high
place amongst institutions of the same class anywhere; two
boarding schools for boys and girls respectively, supported out
of one endowment and situated in one of the healthiest and
coolest districts in Jamaica, are thoroughly efficient and well
conducted; and five day schools in various towns of the Island
supply satisfactorily the higher educational needs of those
towns.   There are two successful residential high schools, one
for boys and one for girls, well-managed and maintained by the
Wesleyan Methodist Society, without any aid from endowments
or public funds.   One day school of about the same standing as
the five endowed- day schools have been founded under the
Secondary Education Law of 1892.   It is unendowed, sustained
by Government grant and fees alone, and managed by the
Board of Education.   There are at least two good unassisted
private high schools for boys in Kingston, and several girls'
schools of varying degrees of efficiency, mainly for day scholars.
University College, founded in 1888 and attached to the Jamaica
High School, is the only educational institution of collegiate
standing in the Island.   It is largely supported by Government
and has accommodation for twelve students.   Four of its students
have taken the London University B.A. degree and one the M.A.
without leaving the Island; but many high school and college
students, with the assistance of Government scholarships, complete their course and take their degrees in England.

10. I may here refer to the system of Government scholarships,
whereby in Jamaica promising boys and girls, even the poorest,
may be assisted throughout their whole school career, and if they
prove their fitness for higher education, a university career also.
Scholarships tenable at secondary schools are awarded annually
under Law 31 of 1892, on the results of the first year pupil
teachers' examination, to pupils from the elementary schools.
Scholarships of gradually increasing value are awarded upon the
results of the Cambridge Local Examination to scholars at the
secondary schools, culminating in the Jamaica scholarship of
200*l.* a year for three years tenable at any English university.
Thus it may be said that no boy or girl of conspicuous ability
need spend anything on tuition, or in the higher part of an
educational course even for maintenance, from the first rudiments
up to the instruction necessary to gain a university degree.*

Administra-
tion.
11. The administrative staff of the Education Department
consists of a superintending inspector, an examiner, and five
clerks on the permanent establishment, besides one or two

---

* For the revised arrangements, by which the number of scholarships
has been greatly reduced, *see* Supplementary Notes to this Report.

additional clerks employed as required. The Superintending Inspector of Schools is also a member of the Legislative Council, Inspector of Industrial Schools, Chairman of the Board of Education, and of three other Boards, Vice-Chairman of the Board of Directors of the Mico Training College, a member of the (Endowed) Schools Commission, of the Board of Management of the Government Training College for Women, and of two other Boards. Besides carrying on a large correspondence with managers and others, the Central Office administers the whole of the Education Vote, including the payment of the annual grants to schools in advance in monthly instalments, tabulates the results of the annual examinations of teachers, pupil teachers and voluntary candidates, prepares the statistical tables for the departmental reports, keeps the register of teachers, prepares and issues the educational bulletin (*see* below, Paragraph 13), and exercises a general control over the inspection of schools and the working of the whole system.

12. A staff of eight inspectors is employed to examine the schools Inspection. and determine the grant earned. Six of these are graduates of English universities. The qualifications of those now appointed are substantially the same as those of English inspectors, whilst the commencing salary is slightly more than a third, and the maximum salary rather less than a fourth of that of an English inspector. Each has about 120 schools on his list, some of them twenty or thirty miles from the nearest public lodging house of any kind, and many only accessible on horseback. Besides the work of inspection and examination of elementary schools, which can practically only be carried on for nine months in the year, the inspectors have many special enquiries to undertake, involving often long special journeys, and they are also, for about three months, continuously employed in presiding over examinations, and in setting and marking examination papers. At the examination of pupil teachers and volunteer candidates in November, 1897, there were 1,752 candidates, and the number is rapidly increasing, whilst 185 students at training colleges and seventeen teachers were examined in the following month, the examination lasting for six days. The inspectors have also to conduct investigations into charges against teachers of serious professional misconduct or grave moral delinquency.

In Jamaica, appointments of inspectors, like those of other civil servants in the Island, are made by the Governor, subject to confirmation by the Secretary of State for the Colonies. Of the eight Inspectors at present on the staff two belong to Jamaica families, four had been domiciled here for several years previous to their appointment, one had just taken up his residence here when appointed, and one was transferred by the Secretary of State from another appointment in the British West Indies.

13. A bulletin is issued by the Department, as occasion arises, for the purposes of giving information to managers and teachers on subjects of general interest and importance, such as the interpretation placed by the Department on particular Articles of the Code, the reports of the proceedings of the Board of

Education, and notes (written by the Inspectors) on the pupil teachers and training college examinations. Changes in the register of teachers are also included. The numbers issued between December, 1896, and December, 1897, contain the names of 33 teachers struck off the register for serious professional misconduct or in consequence of charges of immorality either admitted or found to be true after a full enquiry. A correct estimate of the state of education cannot be made without this brief reference to a deplorable fact, nor should it be overlooked that changes of teachers are very frequent and that, for this reason alone, the efficiency of many schools is often seriously impaired.

Subjects of Instruction.   14. The subjects in which schools are examined, and for which marks or grants are given, are the following :—

	Marks.
Chief Subjects :	
Reading and Recitation - - - - -	15 ⎫
Writing (including Dictation and Composition) -	15 ⎬ 45
Arithmetic (on slate and paper, and mental) -	15 ⎭
Obligatory Subject :	
Elementary Science, having Special reference to the Principles of Agriculture and Handicrafts.	6
Secondary Subjects :	
Scripture (including the Teaching of Morals) - -	6 ⎫
Organization and Discipline - - - -	6 ⎪
Geography and History - - - - -	6 ⎬ 33
English - - - - - - - -	5 ⎪
Elementary Geometrical Drawing - - - -	5 ⎪
Singing - - - - - - - -	5 ⎭
Special Subjects :	
Higher Drawing.	
Needlework.	
The Practical Teaching of Agriculture, Horticulture, and Handicrafts.	
IN INFANT SCHOOLS.	
Chief Subjects :	
Reading and Recitation (including English) - -	15 ⎫
Writing (including Dictation and Composition) -	15 ⎬ 45
Arithmetic (on slate and paper, and mental) - -	15 ⎭
Secondary Subjects :	
Organization and Discipline - - - - -	15 ⎫
Scripture (including the Teaching of Morals) - -	6 ⎪
Singing - - - - - - -	6 ⎬ 39
Geography and History - - - - -	6 ⎪
Elementary Facts of Plant Life, General Knowledge, and Elementary Geometrical Drawing.	6 ⎭

The above tables must be considered as provisional only, as a thorough revision of the Code is in contemplation.

Standards of classification in these subjects are supplied to all the schools, and all the schools on the annual grant list are required to be classified according to these standards.

The marks given at inspection are according to the following

scale, viz.:—Little, one-sixth of the maximum number of marks
attainable; moderate, one-third; fair, one-half; good, two-thirds;
very good, five-sixths; and excellent, the total maximum
number of marks attainable. This latter mark is only given
when the school as a whole has attained to the highest degree of
proficiency that could be expected under the best teaching.
Marks intermediate between these are also given. Individual
examination for passes has never been a part of the Jamaica
school system. A school is marked on its general results, not
on individual passes. This is of course a much more elastic
system than that in which each individual is examined and
marked separately, and gives more freedom to the Inspector; but
it also calls for much more care in the marking. In this
feature of our system we to a great extent anticipated the
English Code; whilst in another, the substitution of special
visits for a regular inspection, we are tentatively and in a few
instances following it.

15. The schools are ranked in three classes according to the
number of marks that may be awarded to them at the annual
inspections, when the results achieved during the year are measured
by the scale mentioned above, thus:—A first class must obtain 56
marks, and 10 marks in each of the chief subjects, or two-thirds of
the total obtainable; a second class, 42 marks and 7 marks in each
of the chief subjects; a third class, 30 marks and 5 marks in each
of the chief subjects. Grants are made by the Government, based
on the number of marks obtained by each school, and to some
extent also on the average attendance. In schools with an
average attendance of 80 or over, a grant is given of one pound
per mark for the principal teacher with possible additions for the
teaching of Drawing, Agriculture and Handicrafts, and for training pupil teachers, and 4s. to 6s. per unit for any excess in the
average attendance above 80. In addition to this, grants are made
depending on the average attendance, for the payment of such
assistant teachers as the school may require, and a grant, fixed for
the present at 6d. per unit of average attendance, is made for
school appliances. A registered teacher engaged as an assistant
in a school with over 150 in average attendance, gets £25 a year
and 4s. per mark, or about £40 in the case of a good first class school.
In every school with 60 or more in total average attendance and
a separate infant department, an additional woman teacher, who
gives her whole time to the ordinary work of the school, besides
teaching the sewing, earns for the school a grant of £12 a year
and 2s. per mark per annum, or in general about £17 or £18,
besides the sewing grant of 3s. per unit of average attendance at
the sewing class. Schools with less than 80 in average attendance
earn for their principal teacher grants which can in no case be less
than 15s. a mark, and which rise gradually from that amount for
an average of 20 by an addition of 1d. per mark for every unit of
average attendance above 20 to the full 20s. per mark when the
average is 80.

16. Though the secondary subjects of the list in Paragraph 13
are not strictly compulsory, yet they are practically always taught,

although teachers have been informed by the Department that they may often get better marks and grants by omitting one or more of them. Prominence is given to elementary geometrical drawing because of the utter incapacity of the Jamaica population at present, not excepting carpenters and masons, to recognise a right angle, a square, etc. The present very low requirements will be raised as soon as this can be done with any prospect of better results.

17. Singing is taught in every school and is an essential part of the curriculum. For drawing of a little higher character than the compulsory minimum which does not go beyond the square, hexagon, and equilateral triangle and the use of compasses, a grant of 1s. or 2s. is made for every scholar efficiently taught. Very few schools have as yet applied for or received this special grant.

Cookery has not yet been taught at all.

Domestic Economy is included under Elementary Science, and embraces elementary Hygiene and Dietetics. A regular system of physical drill is strongly recommended in the Code, and in a few instances successfully carried out.

18. A fixed grant of 3s. per unit of average attendance is given for sewing. The grant is large compared with the amount that other subjects gain for the school, yet considering that the majority of schools have less than thirty girls learning sewing it is difficult to see how it could be lowered. The teaching of this subject is perhaps less satisfactory than that of any other. The smaller schools have sometimes to be satisfied with a sewing mistress who can neither read nor write. To encourage good work a bonus of £1, £2 or £3 is given in all cases of specially good results, but this is earned by few schools. Schools with an average attendance of over sixty may, however, employ an additional woman teacher, who is employed in the general instruction of the scholars and in teaching needlework, and who is better educated and more intelligent than the average sewing mistress.

Agriculture.

19. Allusion has been made to the fact that special grants are given for agricultural teaching. This subject has occupied the attention of the Board of Education from its first appointment, and arrangements have been now made in considerable detail for its encouragement. Two classes of schools receive grants of this kind. The first class, A, receives grants of from £1 to £3 for each school for work which should in strictness form and will probably form at no distant date part of the regular curriculum, and be compulsory. It consists of the careful illustration by experiments of the theoretical teaching included in the regular syllabus, by means of a very small plot of land, or earth in flower pots, boxes or barrels. The schools in class B, which receive grants of from £5 to £10, are required to have at least a quarter of an acre of land under cultivation, and the practical instruction, which must be of an educative character, and must occupy four hours per week, is not allowed to encroach on the regular school hours. One of the regulations is that no credit will be given in this class "for ordinary cultivation on the unscientific methods too usually practised in the Island, but only for cultivation on

improved and scientific methods," which may form an object lesson to the neighbourhood, especially when economic plants are grown which are not generally known in the district. Several grants have been awarded to schools in both classes. The requirements of class A are on the same lines as the system now laid down for the rural primary schools in France; those of class B have some of the drawbacks that have made similar schemes inoperative in former years, both in Jamaica and elsewhere. This practical work, which is for obvious reasons viewed more favourably perhaps by the teachers than by the scholars and their parents, may, if it does no more, widen the views of the peasant population as to the dignity of daily work of body as well as of mind, and after a while it may give place to the more strictly educational training for children previously spoken of.

20. For some years past the Board of Education and the Department have been endeavouring to take some effectual steps *Manual Training.* towards introducing manual training into the schools. The great difficulty in the way has been the necessity of bringing out teachers from England or the United States. The Government have secured a suitable site in Kingston for a large day school, with separate departments for infants, boys, and girls respectively, now called the "Board School," and it is intended to make the training of hand and eye the main features in all branches. The Board has succeeded, after many disappointments, in securing an experienced English teacher, who has been through a thorough training in manual work; the practical instruction in the Board School, open to qualified scholars from any elementary school in Kingston, was commenced in January, 1898. It is proposed to give students in the training colleges, and teachers, the opportunity of sharing in the benefits of this instruction, and of familiarising themselves with the methods employed, with a view to the gradual spread of hand and eye training in the schools generally. The Board has also secured a trained Kindergarten mistress for the infant school, and it is intended that cookery shall be taught in the girls' school. When this school is successfully at work in all its branches, endeavour will be made to extend its methods to other schools.

21. Religious instruction has been included in the Code on precisely the same footing as other subjects, ever since the *Religious Instruction.* commencement of the present system in 1867. For twenty-five years, what was required to be taught in the schools was laid down in the regulations as "the leading facts of the Old and New Testament, especially the history and teaching of the Lord Jesus Christ, and the essential truths of the Gospel, familiarly known." No religious or sectarian difficulties have ever arisen in Jamaica schools. There is a conscience clause, but I have never heard of its being invoked. The Department has never been officially notified that any distinctive sectarian teaching was given in the schools, nor have I ever heard of any child being withdrawn from any such teaching. Teaching of a denominational character may be given in some

schools at specified hours, in accordance with the Conscience Clause, but it is never brought under the notice of the Department.

The present requirements under the head of religious instruction are very much the same as for the twenty-five years referred to, with the addition of prescribed passages of the Bible to be learnt by heart, and lessons to be given on morals.

22. Throughout Jamaica, and, I believe, throughout the British West Indies generally, no elementary school in the country is held regularly for more than four days in a week. Repeated endeavours have been made to introduce Friday school, but, except in the towns, altogether without success. Friday school in the towns is now compulsory for half the day at least, but the attendance is generally far below that for the other four days. The opinion is held by some that the freedom from school-work on Fridays and Saturdays gives the children of the peasantry their only opportunity of keeping up their familiarity with the practical manual work by which they will have to live; but those parents who do give their children of school age such work to do, do so in the early mornings of school days, and there can be little doubt that very many, if not the majority of school children, are simply idle for the greater part of Friday and Saturday. In consequence of this custom of making Fridays and Saturdays whole holidays, the possible number of school sessions in the year (morning and afternoon) is of course consider-ably reduced. The minimum required by the Code to entitle a school to full annual grant is 336, or 42 school weeks of eight sessions each, in the country, and 360, or 40 school weeks of nine sessions each, in the towns.

Teachers' Salaries.

23. The teachers are appointed by the local managers without reference to the Department, and nearly always on the condition that they receive the whole of the grant (except such part of it as is otherwise specially appropriated by the Code). The engage-ment is frequently verbal, in spite of the strong recommendation of the Code and the Department that it should invariably be in writing, and the exception in the parenthesis is seldom made explicitly. In consequence, disputes between managers and teachers are not uncommon. Under the present Code the portion of the grant available for the remuneration of the principal teacher varies from £22 10s. in the smallest and poorest schools up to £120 in the largest and best. In the largest school of all the portion of the grant which goes to the principal teacher must be much larger, but this is altogether an exceptional case. Assistant teachers get from £35 to £40, and additional women teachers from £16 to £20, besides the sewing grant, which may be from £5 to £12. Training college students who have completed three years at a training college, and successful teachers who pass the third year training college examination, receive certificates which entitle them to personal payments of £5, £10 or £15 for every year during the whole of which they have been teaching in a public elementary school according to the class of the school. These payments are in

addition to the amounts already mentioned. Since the passage of the Law of 1892 registration has been compulsory, and no unregistered teacher can now be employed except temporarily. Teachers who were at work when the Code was revised in 1893 are admitted to the register on easy terms, but no new teacher can now be registered without passing an examination which is held annually. Of the teachers on the register at present, 815 are men and 125 women. In addition to these there are about 100 additional women teachers who are not required to be on the register. 394 teachers have passed the certificate examination, of whom 241 have already taught for the prescribed probationary period and received their certificate.

24. Every school whose teacher, besides being registered, Pupil Teachers. has done successful work or can show other proof of efficiency, may have one or more pupil teachers not exceeding in all (1) one for every for₊y scholars in average attendance, or (2) two for a principal teacher and one for each registered assistant.

There is no entrance examination for pupil teachers before engagement, but they must be certified to possess good health and character and aptitude to teach, to be at least 13 years of age, and to have reached the fifth standard in reading, writing, and arithmetic at least six months before engagement. The usual term of engagement is for four years, and at the end of each year, if a pupil teacher has passed the examination corresponding to that year, he or she receives a payment of £4 for the first year, £5 for the second, and £6 each for the third and fourth.

The teacher of the school receives for the training of the pupil teacher during the year, if the corresponding examination is passed, the sum of £3 for the first, and £1 10s. for every additional pupil teacher.

Though pupil teachers at the close of their engagement are free to choose their employment, the training colleges are, as might be expected, largely recruited from their number. The number of pupil teachers examined in November, 1897, was 590, of whom 330 passed, according to the following table :—

Year.	1	2	3	4	Total.
Presented - - - -	212	194	110	74	590
Passed - - - -	93	97	74	66	330
Per cent. passed - - -	43·9	50	67·3	89·2	56

The term of engagement until October 1893 was for three years only.

25. About twelve years ago persons other than pupil teachers, for the most part the more advanced scholars from the elementary schools, were for the first time admitted to the pupil teachers' examinations, then recently instituted at local centres, for a nominal fee of 2s. 6d. The number of candidates availing them-

selves of these facilities has grown enormously, until in November, 1897, no fewer than 1,162 presented themselves.

The following gives the result of their examination :—

Year.	1	2	3	4	Total.
Presented - - - -	560	176	153	273	1,162
Passed - - - -	114	55	41	98	308
Per cent. passed - - -	20	31·2	27	36	26·5

The fourth year examination has been made the entrance examination for training colleges, and the registration examination for teachers, and upon its results are awarded training college exhibitions. Scholarships tenable at secondary schools under the Education Law, and trade scholarships, given to boys willing to be properly apprenticed to a trade, are awarded on the first and third year examination respectively. With reference to the last mentioned, it may be of interest to state that without some such inducement the apprenticeship law would be practically a dead letter in the colony, and the apprenticeship system non-existent. The word "apprenticeship" has associations for the older inhabitants which strongly prejudice them against it, and the semi-servitude which it suggests to them is abhorrent to the mind of men whose immediate ancestors were slaves.

Training. 26. There are six training colleges containing 132 men and 61 women students. Only one of these, the Shortwood Training College for Women, with 30 students, is exclusively managed and supported by the Government.* The largest training college for men—that maintained by the trustees of the Lady Mico Charity in London, with the assistance of a yearly payment by the Government of £2,250 — contains 80 students. The other colleges are denominational, two being for men and two for women students. The denominational colleges receive a maintenance grant of £25 from Government for each student admitted under the regulations and a further grant of £10 for each who passes the annual examination. The course in all the colleges is one of three years. The curriculum includes Reading and Elocution, English Grammar, English Orthography and Composition, Arithmetic, Geography, History, Scripture, Elementary Science, Music (both vocal and instrumental, and theory), School Management, Algebra (except in women's colleges), Euclid and Drawing. Women's colleges take Needlework in place of Algebra. Specially promising students are allowed to take up Latin, French and Higher Mathematics, and grants are given for passes in those subjects. All the training college students are examined in the same week, just before Christmas, and only those who pass all their annual examinations receive certificates entitling them to the annual payments of special grants as explained in Paragraph 22.

* For the recent change in the status of the Shortwood College, *see* Supplementary Notes to this Report.

Teachers are not appointed or paid (directly) by the Government; there is no system of pensions, and none has ever been given.

27. No free meals are supplied to needy scholars in any of the elementary schools. Scarcity of food is a most unusual thing in Jamaica, except in great droughts and in isolated localities. In such cases private individuals have been known for a few days or weeks to supply cornmeal or flour to one or two schools. Very often it is when there is a superabundance of unsaleable food that the peasantry find times the hardest. Want of money and want of clothing are at times keenly felt; and inability to procure decent clothes, whilst causing little or no suffering such as is experienced in colder climates, seriously affects the attendance at the schools. In a drought such as Jamaica experienced in the spring of 1897 over a considerable part of the country the children are largely occupied in fetching water from any distance up to six or seven miles, and the falling-off in the attendance at the schools is very marked.

28. There are no continuation schools or classes. Work Continuation begins for the labouring class about six o'clock in the morning Schools. and ends about five o'clock in the afternoon, and the great majority of the people go to bed very early. A system of evening continuation schools would mean little less than a revolution in the social habits of the people, and would be very difficult to introduce, except to a limited extent in towns.

29. As secondary and higher education is mainly under Secondary private management, it has been to a considerable extent dealt Education. with in paragraph 9. A Secondary Education Law was passed in 1892 (at the same time as the Primary Education Law) providing for the gradual establishment in all important centres where efficient endowed or private secondary schools did not exist, of secondary day schools supported by the Government and managed by the Board of Education. One such school has been established in Montego Bay, the second town in the Island, and is doing well.

The endowed schools of the Island were, as has already been said, brought by a Law passed in 1879 under the control, direct or indirect, of the Schools Commission. The only school under the Commission's direct control and management is the Jamaica High School, with accommodation for over 50 boys, with which is associated University College. These institutions receive £1,000 a year from endowments and £1,300 a year from the Government. There are 23 foundation scholars in the school, who pay no fees, besides six scholars sent from lower endowed schools, and the receipts from paying scholars have amounted to as much as £1,600 per annum. No school in the British Empire takes a higher position than this (for its size) in the Cambridge Local Examinations.

The other endowed schools in the Island receive no aid from Government, except in the form of a high rate of interest on moneys held for them by the Government. They are managed in detail for the most part by local Boards of management, but are subject to the supervision of the Commission, as explained in section 10 of the Historical Sketch. Examinations of all these schools are annually held under conditions approved of by the Commission.

Technical Instruction. 30. Nothing has yet been attempted in the way of technical instruction, and nearly all the commercial education that is given is given in the schools referred to in Paragraph 9. All elementary schools are expected to teach ordinary business forms, and a little more is taught in some of the larger elementary schools in the towns, but it is not included in the Code schedules As stated above, we are only at the very beginning of the introduction into the schools of manual, or more strictly, hand and eye training, and what little has been and is being done in the way of agricultural training is mainly of a tentative character. What is being aimed at is the inculcation by practical illustration and experiment of sound agricultural principles.

Reformatory and Industrial Schools. 31. There is one large combined reformatory and industrial school for boys, one reformatory for girls, one industrial school for boys and one for girls, all maintained entirely by Government. Besides these there are large industrial schools for boys and girls in Kingston under the management of the Roman Catholics, and a small industrial school for girls in connection with the Church of England, a fixed sum per head being paid to these institutions for the maintenance of each child therein by the authorities of the parish from which the child comes. The elementary schools in connection with these institutions are inspected and reported on by the Education Department, and the general management is reported on by the Superintending Inspector of Schools as Inspector of Industrial Schools. There is also an industrial school in Spanish Town, altogether unsupported by Government. The number of children in these schools is 408 : 293 boys and 115 girls, and the total cost to the Government is £6,948.

Schools for the Blind, etc. 32. There are no schools for the blind, for the deaf and dumb, nor for other defective children. Enquiries have been made with reference to the number of blind children, but it is found that they are so few and so scattered that arrangements for giving them special instruction would be difficult and expensive.

T. CAPPER,
Superintending Inspector of Schools.

Recent Reports of the Education Department and of the Board of Education, the Report of the Commission appointed to enquire into the System of Education in Jamaica, 1898, and other documents relating to Education in Jamaica, can be seen at the Board of Education Library, St. Stephen's House, Cannon Row, Whitehall, London, S.W.

APPENDIX A.

DENOMINATIONAL SUMMARY of ELEMENTARY SCHOOLS in Jamaica in 1864 and 1865, exclusive of Endowed and Private Schools.

Religious Denominations.	Schools.	Average attendance.	Receiving Government Aid. Annual Income.						Average salary of teachers.*	Class of Schools.				Not receiving Government aid.		Totals of all the Schools connected with each Denomination.	
			Per School.	From Government.	From the Society.	From Vestries.	School fees.	Total.		1.	2.	3.	4.	Schools.	Average attendances.	Schools.	Average attendances.
			£	£	£	£	£	£	£								
Established Church	180	5,100	11	1,406	962	981	671	3,980	28	1	4	27	94	36	1,888	162	6,988
Moravians	54	2,688	5	270	863	—	584	1,727	24	1	1	38	17	1	50	53	2,058
Wesleyans	38	1,854	6	211	1,216	—	896	1,823	55	1	6	19	7	3	78	36	1,332
Presbyterians	17	679	8	248	214	—	235	697	44	—	5	7	3	29	1,417	44	2,096
Baptists	16	550	5	84	182	—	202	468	27	—	—	6	9	74	2,798	89	3,348
London Missionary (Congregationalists)	4	143	19	58	44	—	60	142	38	—	—	4	—	11	634	15	777
United Meth'odists	9	282	7	72	138	—	82	292	33	—	1	6	3	—	—	9	282
Wesleyan Association	5	167	7	35	65	—	81	181	36	—	—	—	5	—	—	5	167
Roman Catholic	3	74	15	46	51	—	—	97	27	—	1	1	2	—	—	3	74
Hebrew	2	36	—	45	—	—	—	45	—	1	—	—	—	—	—	1	36
Undenominational	19	701	11	235	†1,500	—	415	2,140	72	4	1	4	11	47	890	66	1,661
American Mission	7	181	14	98	143	—	38	280	41	1	—	3	3	—	—	7	181
TOTALS	255	11,956	—	2,779	5,338	981	3,716	11,712	38	8	17	110	154	201	7,645	490	18,850

* These averages chiefly represented the money stipends of the teachers, and various allowances that were in many cases given in addition. The Moravians' average, which appears the smallest, is really by no means so, when other things are taken into account—residence, pension, privileges, &c.
† Miss.

APPENDIX B.

STATISTICS showing the progress of Elementary Education in Jamaica from 1868 to 1899.

Years ending	Number of Schools on Annual Grant List.	Number of Scholars on books.	Number of Scholars Average Attendance.	1st Class Schools.	2nd Class Schools.	Grants to Schools, excluding Building Grants.	Building Grants.	Fees.	Grant per School aided.	Grant per Scholar in average attendance.
						£	£	£	£ s.	s.
30 September :										
1868	286	19,764	12,216	1	6	2,978	–	–	10 8	4
1869	262	20,439	11,680	3	20	4,161	–	3,106	15 19	7
1870	329	25,961	14,609	4	35	5,857	1,250	3,785	17 16	8
1871	408	33,343	19,644	6	68	8,960	1,200	5,215	20 5	8
1872	438	38,006	22,435	7	94	9,897	1,500	5,873	22 12	8
1873	456	37,496	22,044	11	125	10,961	1,400	5,812	24 2	10
1874	500	43,135	25,160	17	145	12,807	1,586	6,087	25 12	10
1875	526	41,023	24,586	31	144	12,974	1,484	5,911	24 13	10
1876	569	46,654	27,270	45	157	14,756	1,500	6,610	25 19	10
1877	583	50,832	29,185	51	161	15,707	1,573	6,680	27 0	10
1878	617	51,488	29,679	54	176	16,304	1,500	6,775	26 9	11
1879	646	52,243	28,661	64	202	16,977	1,500	6,123	26 6	11
1880	681	56,382	32,871	70	238	18,992	1,500	6,763	27 18	
1881	687	48,960	26,649	52	195	16,024	1,520	5,380	23 7	
1882	677	53,386	29,894	47	164	16,724	1,500	4,783	24 14	
1883	688	56,312	32,203	47	212	17,754	1,500	6,478	26 12	
1884	701	57,557	33,294	60	216	17,661	1,500	7,148	25 3	
1885	728	62,106	36,079	65	251	20,170	1,410	7,908	27 14	
1886	723	61,571	34,825	70	254	20,150	1,500	6,928	27 18	
1887	725	62,424	35,613	91	235	20,078	1,500	6,738	27 16	
1888	771	71,643	41,920	100	280	23,383	1,500	7,904	30 5	
1889	826	75,613	43,563	104	288	26,398	1,305	8,050	31 19	
31 March :										
1891	836	80,199	44,410	115	319	*42,597	*1,943	*10,903	33 19	
1892	872	84,119	46,161	130	329	29,005	1,443	8,842	33 5	
1893	912	92,135	52,983	143	389	†‡43,560	1,680	6,649	†147 15 †	
1894	957	97,456	64,695	169	367	‡56,435	1,455	45	‡50 0	
1895	962	104,149	62,589	160	345	52,828	1,490	–	54 18	
1896	932	100,352	59,617	154	355	50,203	1,495	–	53 17	
1897	932	98,550	58,411	166	347	50,893	1,320	–	54 12	
1898	913	98,205	57,983	160	389	53,554	510	–	56 13	
1899	896	97,091	57,508	176	397	51,561	–	–	57 8	

* 18 months.
† Including part of first grant in lieu of fees of 4s. per unit of average attendance.
‡ Including also special grant for compensation where fees had exceeded 4s. per unit of age attendance.

CENSUS RETURNS.

—	Population.	Could Read.	Per Cent.	Could Read and Write.	Per Cent.	Attending School.
1871	506,154	452,472	30·1	71,074	14·0	40,610
1881	580,804	231,068	39·8	115,418	20·0	67,402
1891	639,491	292,288	45·7	177,795	27·8	99,769
Percentage of advance in the 20 years.	26·3	81·2	52	150·3	97·6	145·7

REGISTRAR-GENERAL'S MARRIAGE RETURNS.—The percentage of brides and bridng the Marriage Register with a mark has decreased from 59·2 in 1883–4, the first year we have reliable statistics on this point, to 47·8 in 1895–6, a decrease of 20 per cent. 1 ber of these, therefore, who affix a proper signature increased during the same period to 52·2, or by 27 per cent.

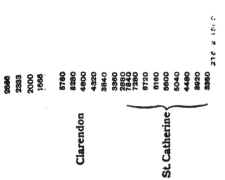

2666
2333
2000
1666

5760
5280
4800
4320
3840
3360
2880
7840
7280
6720
6160
5600
5040
4480
3920
3360

Clarendon

St. Catherine

8

APPENDIX D.

STATISTICS of Age.

TABLE I.

Standard	A.	B.	1	2	3	4	5	6	7
Average Age of the Scholars	7	8¾	10	10	10¾	11	12	12¾	13½

TABLE II.

Reading and Writing Standard	A.	B.	1	2	3	4	5	6	7
Per cent	33·11	15·04	14·31	11·37	9·86	7·78	5·49	3·03	·0009

TABLE III.

Years of age	3	4	5	6	7	8	9	10	11	12	13	14	15
Per cent	·14	·53	6·02	9·95	11·96	12·05	12·58	12·43	11·80	10·47	8·02	2·97	·48

TABLE IV.

Standard.	3	4	5	6	7	8	9	10	11	12	13	14	Sp. Reg. Art. 20. 14	Sp. Reg. Art. 20. 15	7th Std. Schools. 15	
A	131	505	5,558	7,931	6,791	4,656	2,917	1,828	1,000	537	192	23	3	1	-	32,073
B.	1	15	204	1,170	2,648	3,019	2,629	2,018	1,432	840	471	100	20	6	1	14,574
1.	-	-	64	413	1,439	2,380	2,753	2,526	2,015	1,288	762	171	32	13	-	13,856
2.	-	-	7	104	512	1,326	1,9u7	2,194	2 023	1,555	1,070	288	55	22	-	11,013
3.	-	-	-	23	161	617	1,204	1,829	2,084	1,907	1,310	306	70	33	4	9,550
4.	-	-	-	2	43	212	588	1,139	1,649	1,937	1,435	362	112	48	-	7,5:7
5.	-	-	-	-	5	31	171	423	952	1,409	1,510	466	206	133	7	5,313
6.	-	-	-	-	-	6	22	90	276	661	1,011	401	280	173	3	2,923
7.	-	-	-	-	-	-	-	2	5	15	14	28	8	1	15	58
Total	132	520	5,833	9,643	11,599	12,247	12,191	12,049	11,436	10,149	7,775	2,097	786	430	35	96,922

APPENDIX E.

1867.—Introduction of the system. All schools aided (except industrial) were required to charge fees. Schools were awarded marks on examination up to a maximum of 84. Those with two-thirds of the possible maximum or over called first class, one-half to two-thirds second, and one-third to one-half third. This proportion required for each of the principal subjects, reading, writing, and arithmetic, as well as in the aggregate. Age limits, four to seventeen.

Grants :—

First class schools received 20*l.* and 6*s.* per unit of average.
Second   „   15*l.* and 5*s.*   „
Third   „   10*l.* and 4*s.*   „

Sewing 3*s.* per unit of average at sewing class. Industrial schools, in which three school hours a day were devoted to manual labour on a regular system, £10, £7 10*s.*, or £5.

1870.—Building grants given for new schools.
Government Training College opened and Mico College subsidised.

1873.—Industrial schools required to give only two school hours to manual labour. Grants to these schools as above, and in addition 3*s.*, 2*s.* 6*d.* or 2*s.* per unit of average.

1875.—Grants to industrial schools reduced.
Grants to 1st class schools made 8*s.* per mark instead of the sum of £20.
     „   2nd   „   7*s.*   „   „   £15.
     „   3rd   6*s.*   „   „   £10.

1877.—Grants given to pupil teachers of £4, £5 and £6 for the first, second and third year of service respectively, subject to their passing an examination by means of printed cards at the time the schools they were employed in were inspected.
Grants to schoolmasters for instructing them out of school hours, £3 for one, £4 10*s.* for two, and £1 10*s.* for each additional pupil teacher.

1878.—Grants to industrial schools discontinued.

1879.—Grant of £15 given for each resident student in a voluntary training college on his passing an annual examination.

1881.—Teachers convicted of any offence against morality not permitted to take employment in Government aided schools. (Restoration possible after one year at least.)
Only 144 days out of the 180 school days in the year required to be taken for calculating average attendance. (As many as 36 days, when attendance was exceptionally low owing to severe weather or other causes, could thus be omitted.)
Advances on account of the annual grants expected to be earned at next inspection made quarterly.

1882.—Pupil teachers first examined in centres at a fixed date with papers that had not been used before. Fifty-nine examined.

First Government examination of training colleges in December with freshly set papers. Twenty-six candidates.

Grant of £7 given for each non-resident student at a voluntary training college on his passing the annual examination.

Teachers admitted to third year training college examination.

Certificates granted on the passing of the third year examination, to teachers at once, and to training college students after two years' successful work as teachers, with an accompanying payment of £10 in each case.

Grants made to holders of certificates of £15, £10 or £5 according to the class of schools examined under them during the year.

1887.—An additional grant of £20 per annum paid monthly for each resident student under training at a voluntary training college.

An additional grant of 10s. to each school on annual grant list for keeping clock in proper order, and for appliances.

Voluntary candidates first admitted to pupil teachers' examinations on payment of a nominal fee of 2s. 6d.

1892.—Passing of Elementary and Secondary Education Laws and appointment of Board of Education. Age limits made five to fourteen, infant schools and departments, three to ten. Governor given power to introduce compulsion locally or generally by proclamation. Advances to schools paid monthly instead of quarterly. Abolition of fees, substitution of grant of 4s. per unit of average to be paid out of a special tax on houses. New schools not to be aided before being declared necessary by the Board of Education. Small scholarships given to best scholars from elementary schools tenable at secondary schools. Provision made for establishment of secondary schools under general control of Board of Education in places which were without adequate provision for secondary education. Scholarships of £10 to £60 a year given on results of Cambridge Local and London Matriculation Examinations.

1893.—First Revised Code came into force. The main provisions as to grants were as follows :—

Schools under 80 in average attendance for every mark 15s. and 1d. per unit of average over 20. The whole of this grant to be paid to the principal teacher in the absence of a special agreement to the contrary.

Schools of 80 in average attendance and over, £1 per mark, and 4s. to 6s. per unit of average attendance over 80, for additional remuneration to the principal teacher.

Appliances grant, 6d. per unit of average attendance.
Schools over 150, 25l., and 4s. per mark for assisted teacher.

Schools over 60 and with infant department -   -
Schools over 80 and not entitled to pupil teacher -
Schools over 100 and entitled to only one pupil   £15 for additional
  teacher - - - - - - - -   woman teacher.
Schools over 120 and entitled to two pupil teachers
  or more - - - - - - - -

Drawing—1s. or 2s. per scholar satisfactorily taught.

Agriculture—Grants not exceeding £10, according to circumstances and value of work done.

The principal changes not affecting grants were (1) the increase of the marks given for the principal subjects of Reading, Writing, and Arithmetic, from 12 to 18 each, or from 36 to 54 in the aggregate ; and the reduction of them for the secondary subjects from 48 to 30 : (2) the addition of elementary geometrical drawing to the curriculum of the schools ; (3) the requirement that as far as practicable every school should have three managers ; (4) the opening of a register of teachers, admission to which, except in the case of successful teachers of some standing, was to be regulated by examination ; (5) the provision for the regular investigation, with the assistance when possible of disinterested managers, of charges of immorality and misconduct not otherwise established to the satisfaction of the Department ; (6) the extension of the pupil teachers' course by one year ; (7) provision for the admission of teachers for one year to training colleges ; and (8) the introduction of regulations as to minimum school staff and floor space.

1895.—Second Revised Code approved and brought into force. The changes were of slight importance. The marks for the principal subjects were reduced to 45, and those for the secondary subjects raised to 39.

Detailed regulations were made as to the grants for agricultural teaching, which ranged from £1 to £10.

It was provided that where handicrafts were properly taught a grant not exceeding £10 might be given. The appropriation of the grant of 4s. to 6s. per unit of average over 80, to the further remuneration of the principal teacher was discontinued, and it was allowed to be used for the general purposes of the school.

First publication of the educational bulletin for the information of managers and teachers.

[1900.—A number of important Articles in the New Code which came into force on May 10, 1900, will be found in the Supplementary Notes at the end of this Report.]

APPENDIX F.*

STANDARDS OF CLASSIFICATION DOWN TO THE NEW CODE, 1900.

SCHEDULE A.

STANDARDS OF CLASSIFICATION.

All schools on the Annual Grant List will be examined according to these Standards. The maximum marks attainable will only be given at inspection when the whole of the subjects mentioned in the syllabus are taken, and when the school as a whole has attained to the highest degree of proficiency that would be possible under any teaching. Every lower degree of efficiency will receive a proportionately smaller number of marks, which may be fractional.

Children in higher standards (chief subjects) or divisions (secondary subjects) may be examined in any of the subjects for lower standards or divisions as well as in their own.

1. CHIEF SUBJECTS.

[All scholars are required to be placed in the same classes in reading and writing ; and the marks for arithmetic will be lower in proportion as this is not the case in that subject also. The inspector must be satisfied that the *principles* of arithmetic are properly taught in the school.]

---

* Appendix F, with Appendices G and H, are necessary to an understanding of the educational system described in Mr. Capper's foregoing report and reviewed by the Jamaica Education Commission, 1898, in the report summarised below.

The Courses of Study and Standards of Classification laid down by the New Code of May, 1900, will be found at the end of Part II. of this Report.

APPENDIX F.—Schedule A.—Chief Subjects—*continued.*

Subjects.	Standard I.			Standard II.
	A. Children under Seven (the majority from Four to Six).	**B.** Children under Ten (the majority from Five to Seven)		Standard II.
Reading ·	To read simultaneously, and separately from blackboard, simple sentences containing words of elementary sounds. To analyse (vocally) such words into their component sounds, recognising and naming the letters that represent them. To build up (vocally) these components into new words.	As before, but including words up to the standard of Infant Readers.	To read familiar words, phrases and simple sentences from blackboard, chart, &c. To read a short passage from a First Standard Reader.	To read a short passage from a Second Standard Reader.
Recitation · ·	To recite simultaneously and separately a simple school song or hymn.	To recite three verses as before.	To recite four verses as before.	To recite 20 lines of simple verse as before.
Writing and **Orthography.**	To form letters (print and script) with sticks and rings, and draw them on the slate from blackboard or from dictation.	As before, also words and short easy sentences, from the Infant Reader.	To copy on slate in manuscript characters two lines of print, commencing with a capital letter.	A passage of not more than four lines from an elementary reading book, slowly read once and then dictated word by word. Copy books (half text or medium hand) to be shown.
Composition · ·	To answer direct questions in the form of simple sentences.	To tell simple facts about objects in pictures exhibited, in complete sentences. To turn these into negative and interrogative sentences.	Answering questions orally in whole sentences	Answering on the slate questions about familiar scenes and objects in whole sentences.
Arithmetic ·	To tell at sight the number of objects in a group up to six without counting. To add and subtract up to 10. To represent these processes by figures and symbols.	To add and subtract up to 100. To count by twos, threes, and fours up to 100. Multiplication table up to five times five. To tell at sight the number of objects in a group up to 10 without counting.	Notation and numeration of numbers not exceeding 1,000. Simple addition and subtraction of numbers of not more than three figures. (In addition not more than five lines to be given.) The multiplication table to six times 12.	Notation and numeration of numbers not exceeding 100,000. The four simple rules. Multiplication and division to be by numbers not greater than 12. The multiplication table up to 12 × 12 and pence table to 12s.

Mental Arithmetic.—Short exercises in mental arithmetic may be given in the examination of all Standard quantities and should be preparatory to the work of the next.

* Reading with intelligence will be required in all the Standards, and increased fluency and expression in successive years. Two sets of reading books must be provided in all Standards, one of which in Standards above the Second should relate if possible to Jamaica. The Inspector may examine from any of the books in use in the Standard, and from Standard III. and upwards from any book or passage suitable for the purpose which he may select. The intelligence of the reading will be tested partly by questions on the meaning of what is read.

† Intelligence and expression with due attention to articulation, inflection and emphasis will be required in the recitation of all Standards.

‡ The writing and arithmetic of Standards I., II., III. may be on slates or paper, at the discretion of the Managers; in Standards IV. and upwards it should be on paper. Either the vertical or sloping system will be accepted.

APPENDIX F.—SCHEDULE A.—CHIEF SUBJECTS—*continued.*

Standard III.	Standard IV.	Standard V.	Standard VI.	Standard VII
To read a passage from a Third Standard reader.	To read a passage from a Fourth Standard reader.	To read a passage from some standard author, or from a Fifth Standard reader.	To read a passage from one of Shakespeare's historical plays, or from some other standard author.	To read a passage from Shakespeare or Milton, or from some other standard author.
To recite 30 lines of poetry and to know their meaning.	To recite 40 lines of poetry, and to know their meaning.	To recite 50 lines of poetry and to explain the words and allusions.	To recite 60 lines from some standard poet, and to explain the words and allusions.	To recite 60 lines from Shakespeare or Milton or some other standard author, and to explain the words and allusions.
Six lines from one of the reading books of the standard, slowly read once and then dictated. Copy books (capitals and figures, large and small hand) to be shown.	Eight lines of poetry or prose, slowly read once, and then dictated. Copy books to be shown.	Dictation. Copy books to be shown.	Dictation. Copy books and exercise books to be shown.	Dictation. Note books and exercise books to be shown.
Writing on slate simple sentences containing specified nouns, verbs, adjectives and adverbs.	Exercise in the transposition of words in simple poetry into the order of prose. Very simple friendly letters and receipts for money.	Writing from memory the substance of a short story read out twice. Paraphrase of simple poetical passages. Writing friendly letters. The simplest business forms.	A short theme or letter on an easy subject. Business correspondence. Paraphrasing. Letter writing.	Précis or abridgment of document or statement showing its most important contents. Exercises in the right use of commercial terms.
The former rules, with long division. Addition and subtraction of money. Roman numbers to MM. Time by a clock or watch.	Compound rules (money) and reduction of common weights and measures. ‡ §	Compound rules, weights and measures. Practice, bills of parcels, and simple proportion. The unitary method. Addition and subtraction of proper fractions, with denominators not exceeding 12.	Fractions, vulgar and decimal; compound proportion and simple interest.	Averages, percentages, and stocks.

These should not involve large numbers, should from the first deal with concrete as well as abstract higher Standard.

‡ The scholars of the Fourth Standard and upwards should be required to add columns of pounds, shillings, and pence within a specified time in order to show readiness and accuracy.

§ The tables to be learned include those weights and measures only which are in ordinary use viz.:—

Length.—The mile, furlong, chain, rod or pole, yard, foot, and inch.

Weight.—The ton, hundredweight, quarter, stone, pound, ounce, and drachm.

Capacity.—Quarter, bushel, peck, gallon, quart, and pint.

Area.—The square mile, acre, rood, square pole or perch, the yard, foot, and inch.

Time.—Year, month, week, day, hour, minute, and second.

APPENDIX F.—SCHEDULE A.—SECONDARY SUBJECTS.

N.B.—The scholars in any school may be arranged in more or fewer divisions than are suggested below, according to the size of the school, so long as the whole ground is covered; but any arrangement of this kind must be approved by the Inspector of Schools at his annual visit.

	SCRIPTURE (including the Teaching of Morals).	GEOGRAPHY AND HISTORY.
I. A. (As in Chief Subjects.)	To answer intelligently questions on thirty lessons given during the year in the subject according to a scheme approved of by the Inspector at the previous annual examination.	Points of the compass. Land and water on the map. Some knowledge of the locality round the school.
I. B. (As in Chief Subjects.)	As above.	Important geographical definitions, illustrated by reference to the map. Simple facts relating to the Geography of Jamaica. Stories of great men.

	SCRIPTURE KNOWLEDGE. / MORALS.	GEOGRAPHY AND HISTORY
LOWER DIVISION.	**SCRIPTURE KNOWLEDGE.** To learn by heart (i.) Lord's Prayer, Psalm xxiii., Prov. xii. 17, 18, 19, 22. (ii.) Ten Commandments, Matt. v. 1-12, xxii. 35-40. Leading facts in Life of our Lord, simple stories from lives of Abraham, Moses, David. **MORALS.** Instruction and training throughout the year in reverence for God, truthfulness, honesty, purity, gentleness, obedience to parents, to teachers, to persons in authority, politeness, kindness towards playmates and animals.	A plan of the school and playground. The four cardinal points. Meaning and use of a map. The size and shape of the world. Geographical terms simply explained and illustrated by reference to maps. Physical Geography of hills and rivers. Stories of great men and great events.
MIDDLE DIVISION.	To learn by heart (iii.) Deut. xxviii. 1-14, (iv.) St. John xiv. 15-31. Fuller facts of our Lord's life; some of chief parables; history of Creation and Flood; chief facts in lives of Jacob, Joseph, Joshua, Solomon, Ahab, Hezekiah, Nehemiah. Reverence, love of country, respect for authority, obedience to law, honour, industry, temperance, purity, politeness, good behaviour at home, in school, in places of worship, in company, avoiding evil-speaking and profanity.	Physical, political, and commercial Geography of Jamaica and the British Isles, with special knowledge of the district in which the school is situated. Map of Europe and North America. Simple stories relating to English and Jamaican History.
UPPER DIVISION	To learn by heart (v.) Proverbs xiv. 25, xvi. 24, xix. 22; xx. 1, xxiii. 31, 32, xxvi. 28, and xxviii. 13; Ephesians, vi. 1-9; (vi.) 1 Cor. xii. 31, and xiii. Our Lord's life and teaching; teaching of Law of Moses as to duties of parents and children, duty to poor, fatherless, and widows; main facts of Old Testament history; main facts in lives of the Apostles. Reverence, self-respect, patriotism, courage, self-control, self-denial, confession of wrong, forgiveness, duties of the citizen, fidelity to official trust.	Physical, political, and commercial Geography of the United States and British Empire, and general outlines of the Geography of the World. Interchange of productions. Circumstances which determine climate. Latitude and longitude. Day and night. The seasons. Broad outlines of English and Jamaican History. Biographies of six leading persons in English or Jamaican History, such as Alfred, Henry V., Columbus, Queen Elizabeth, Cromwell, Robert Nelson, Wellington, &c. Principal events in life of Queen Victoria.
	MEANS—Stated lessons provided for in the time-table, as well as in incidental teaching; stories, brief biographies, illustrative examples, verses, proverbs, maxims of the wise, literary gems fitted to cultivate the qualities named above, and to mould character and direct action.	

APPENDIX F.—Schedule A.—Secondary Subjects—*continued.*

ELEMENTARY SCIENCE.

I. (A. & B.).—To answer intelligently questions on 30 lessons given during the year in the subject according to a scheme approved of by the Inspector at the previous annual examination.

	ALTERNATIVE. ONE ONLY REQUIRED.			COMPULSORY.
—	Physics and Mechanics. (In Town Schools).	Agriculture. (In Country Schools).	Domestic Economy (in Girls' Schools or for the girls in mixed Schools when practicable).	Natural History. Physiology and Hygiene.
LOWER DIVISION.	The three states of matter. Ordinary tools and machines (*e.g.*, a clock, a pair of scales, level, carpenter's tools, &c.) Building a house.	Usefulness of the various domestic animals, and how they repay kindness and care. Tools, and how they need keeping in order. Work at different periods of the year. The common objects of cultivation in Jamaica.	Ordinary articles of food, clothing, and washing. Neatness and cleanliness in house and person ; purity of air. The dwelling ; neatness, cleanliness, and ventilation.	The build and chief organs of the human body. Need of exercise, clearliness, temperance in all things. A few main laws of health. A course of simple lessons (to be approved by the Inspector) on the lion, tiger, camel, elephant, leopard or other animals.
UPPER DIVISION.	Common properties of matter. Barometer, thermometer. Practical measurement, measures of length, time, velocity and space. Matter in motion, weight, inertia, momentum.	Need of plants (air, soil, water). Need of cultivation, and what makes it more or less effective. Regulation of plant food ; manure ; folly of burning the plant food supplied by nature.	Food and beverages: their properties and nutritive value. Purity of water. Rules of health, common ailments, treatment of the sick. Management of the house.	Mechanism of motion. Alimentation, circulation, respiration. Properties of nerve. Simple lessons of hygiene. Outlines of the classification of the animal kingdom.

ORGANIZATION AND DISCIPLINE.

The Inspector in awarding marks under this head will have special regard to the moral training and conduct of the children, to the neatness and order of the school premises and furniture, and to the proper classification of the scholars, both for teaching and examination.

To meet the requirements respecting discipline, the managers and teachers will be expected to satisfy the Inspector that all reasonable care is taken ; in the ordinary management of the school, to bring up the children in the habits of punctuality, of good manners and language, of cleanliness and tidiness, and also to impress upon the children the importance of cheerful obedience to duty, of consideration and respect for others, and of honour and truthfulness in word and act.

The ordinary discipline of the School must be prompt and exact, and yet maintained without harshness and without noisy demonstration of authority.

In particular, the honesty of the scholars under examination, and the degree of interest they show in their work, will be taken into account ; and high marks will not be given unless the Inspector is satisfied that the school is a place for the formation of right habits, as well as a place of instruction.

The Inspector will also take into account the condition of the School Records, and the faithfulness with which the requirements of the Department with regard to them have been met. The marking of this subject will largely depend upon the results of any special visits the Inspector may have been able to pay during the year.

A regulation system of physical drill will be found most useful in securing punctuality and obedience.

APPENDIX F.—SCHEDULE A.—SECONDARY SUBJECTS—*continued.*

ENGLISH.

Standard I.—Pointing out the subject in an easy sentence.
　　Pointing out nouns.

Standard II.—Pointing out the subject and predicate in an easy sentence.
　　Pointing out nouns and verbs.

Standard III.—Modification of subject and predicate by single words. Formation of illustrative sentences.
　　Pointing out parts of speech and making sentences containing them.

Standard IV.—Modification of subject, predicate and object by words and phrases. Simple analysis. Formation of illustrative sentence. Easy parsing.

Inflection of the noun and pronoun. Elementary word-building.

Standard V.—Modification of subject, predicate and object by words, phrases and sentences. Word-building, a little more advanced.

Standard VI.—Parsing and analysis of complex sentences. Word - building. Knowledge of English prefixes. Correction of sentences containing common faults in speech.

Standard VII—Parsing. Making sentences illustrating the right use of given words and phrases. Knowledge of English terminations. Correction of common errors in the use of words and in the formation of sentences.

SINGING.

More than half marks will in no case be given unless some success is attained in teaching by note in accordance with the Schedule.

For Schools using the Staff Notation.	*For Schools using the Tonic Solfa Method and Notation.*

I. (*A. & B.*)—To sing by ear simple songs and hymns and without action. To mark the varieties of simple time with hands and feet. To sing the scale of C Major from the staff and name the notes.

DIVISION I.

Note Test.—1. To sing as pointed out by the examiner, the notes (of the key chord of C *in an easy order*, using the Sol-fa syllables *Do Mi Sol; Do*).

Song Test.—2. To sing sweetly any one of at least three easy school-songs or action songs previously prepared.

The compass of these songs should not exceed the limit of an octave, say from C to C or D to D, in the treble staves, and the words should be such as children can understand.

DIVISION II.

Note Test.—1. To sing slowly as pointed out by the examiner and using the Sol-fa syllables, the ascending and descending notes of the scale of C (*Do*) the notes of the key-chord of C (*Do Mi Sol Do*), in any order, and also small groups of consecutive notes of the scale of C as written by the examiner.

Time Test.—To sing on one sound to the syllable "*laa,*" an exercise in $\frac{2}{2}$ or $\frac{4}{4}$ time, which shall include minims or crotchets.

Ear Test.—3. To repeat (*i.e.,* imitate not name) a simple phrase of not more than four notes, using the syllable "*laa,*" after hearing the examiner or teacher sing (or play) it twice through.

Song Test.—4. To sing in unison, in good time and tune, and sweetly, any one of at least five school songs set to words previously prepared.

DIVISION I.

1. To sing from the examiner's pointing on the modulator the tones of a *Do*A chord in any easy order, using the Sol-fa syllables.

2. To sing sweetly any one of at least three easy school songs or action songs previously prepared.

The compass of the music should not if possible exceed the limit of an octave, and the words should be such as children can understand.

DIVISION II.

Note Test.—1. To Sol-fa slowly from the examiner's pointing on the modulator, in any key—the key tone and chord being given, the tones of the *Do* chord in any order, and the other tones of the scale in stepwise succession.

Time Test.—2. To sing on one tone to the syllable "laa," an exercise including one pulse and two pulse tones, in two pulse or four pulse measure.

Ear Test.—3. To imitate a simple phrase of not more than four notes using the syllable "laa," after hearing the examiner or teacher sing or play it twice through.

Song Test.—4. To sing in unison in good time and tune, and sweetly, any one of at least five school songs (set to words) previously arranged.

APPENDIX F.—SCHEDULE A.—SECONDARY SUBJECTS—*continued.*

SINGING—*continued.*

More than half marks will in no case be given unless some success is attained in teaching by note in accordance with the Schedule.

For Schools using the Staff Notation.	For Schools using the Tonic Solfa Method and Notation.
DIVISION III.	**DIVISION III.**
Note Test.—1. To sing slowly as pointed out by the examiner, using the Sol-fa syllables, a series of notes in the key of C, containing an F sharp contradicted by an F natural, and a B flat contradicted by a B natural. The F sharp should be approached by the note G and return to G, and the B flat should be approached by C and followed by A.	*Note Test* (Modulator).—(*a*) To Sol-fa from the examiner's pointing on the modulator, or from dictation, in any key, simple passages in the major diatonic scale, including fe and ta in step-wise progression, used thus, s fe s—d ta l.
	Note Test (*written or printed*) (*b*). To Sol-fa at sight a written or printed exercise, including the notes of the Doh cord in any order, and any other notes of the major diatonic scale in step-wise succession. The exercise not to contain any difficulties of time.
Time Test.—2. To sing on one sound to the syllable "laa" an exercise in $\frac{4}{4}$ or $\frac{3}{4}$ time containing semibreves, minims, crotchets, and quavers, with dotted minims; and rests on non-accented portions of the bar.	*Time Test.*—2. To sing on one sound to the syllable "laa" an exercise in three-pulse or four-pulse measure, containing one-pulse notes, half pulse notes and whole-pulse rests on the non-accented pulses of the measure.
Ear Test.—To repeat and afterwards name any three consecutive notes of the scale of C, which the examiner or teacher may twice sing to the syllable laa (or play) each time, first giving the chord or the scale of C.	*Ear Test.*—3. To imitate to "laa," and afterward name any three consecutive tones of the scale, which the examiner or teacher may twice sing to laa (or play), each time first giving the doh cord or the scale.
Song Test.—To sing in unison or parts, in good time and with due expression, any one of at least five school songs or rounds (set to words) previously prepared.	*Song Test.*—4. To sing in unison or parts, in good time and tune, and with due expression, any one of at least five school songs or rounds (set to words) previously prepared.

ELEMENTARY GEOMETRICAL DRAWING.

STANDARD I.—Draw on slate, with and without ruler, from illustration on blackboard, or from dictation, straight lines, vertical, horizontal, oblique; angles, right, acute, obtuse, one side of each angle being horizontal; letters formed of horizontal, vertical, and oblique lines.	STANDARD IV.—Draw on slate, with and without ruler, rhombus; concentric squares, sides four inches, two inches, one inch, on diagonals or diameters.
STANDARD II.—Mark off on vertical, horizontal, and oblique lines, one, two, three and four inches; divide lines by points into two, four, and eight equal parts; draw two familiar objects, without perspective effect, represented by straight lines.	STANDARD V.—Draw on slate parallel lines, vertical, horizontal, oblique, with half-inch spaces between them. Draw a regular octagon.
STANDARD III.—Draw on slate, with and without ruler, equilateral and isosceles triangles. Draw with and without ruler a square, side three inches, divided by diameters.	STANDARD VI.—Draw a regular hexagon. Two or more symmetrical arrangements of straight lines in the square, hexagon and equilateral triangle. Use of compasses.
	STANDARD VII.—As in previous Standards, but with greater accuracy.

APPENDIX F.

Schedule A.—Special Subjects.

NEEDLEWORK.	DRAWING.
I. (A. & B.) Needle Drill. Thimble drill. Knitting pin drill. To hem three inches one colour, to show specimens of Kindergarten work in some of the following gifts, 1, 8, 10, 11, 12, 14, 17, 19 and 20, and to do one such exercise before the Inspector ; or to go through the routine of some household pursuit	

Lower Division.
 	
  1. Hemming, seaming, felling. Any garment or other useful article showing these stitches.
  2. Knitting, 2 needles, plain and purled, *e.g.* a strip, or comforter or cuffs.	

Middle Division.
 	
  1. The work of the previous group, stitching, pleating, and sewing on strings. Garments showing these stitches.
  2. Herring bone stitch. The stitch only on canvas or flannel. Darning, simple, on canvas.
  3. Knitting, 4 needles, plain and purled, *e.g.*, cuffs.
	Middle Division.
	Standards.
	
	III.—Freehand drawing of regular rectilineal forms such as are contained in the first part of No. 3 of the Whitehall Series of Drawing Books.
	IV.—Freehand drawing from the flat or curved figures, such as are contained in the second part of No. 3 of the Whitehall Series of Drawing Books.

Upper Division.
 	
  1. The work of previous groups, gathering, setting-in, button hole, sewing on button. Any garment shewing these stitches.
  2. Darning stocking web material (thin places and holes).
  3. Patching in calico, print and flannel.
  4. Knitting, 4 needles, a sock or stocking.
  5. Cutting out two simple garments.
	Upper Section.
	
	V.—Freehand drawing from the simple curved figures in No. 4 of the Whitehall Series of Drawing Books, and from simple rectangular models.
	VI.—Freehand drawing from simple circular models such as spheres, cylinders and cones.
	VII.—Drawing any common objects. Drawing to scale geometrical figures with instruments.

NOTES.
 	
  1. Garments must be shown in each Division, but not necessarily those specified in this Schedule, which are mentioned merely as examples. They must be presented in the same condition as when completed by the scholars.
  2. At least half as many garments or useful articles should be shown as there are children on the books in the Lower Division. Each garment or useful article must be entirely made by its own Division. In the Middle and Upper Divisions each girl must (if she has attended school six months or upwards) present a garment made by herself.
  3. The Girls in the Upper Division should, as a rule, cut out the garments made by the children in the two Lower Divisions.
	NOTE.
	
	  In order to interest the children it will be advisable to teach them to draw as early as possible from actual objects, such as the doors and windows, furniture and apparatus of the school room.

APPENDIX F.

SCHEDULE A.—SPECIAL SUBJECTS—*continued.*

PRACTICAL TEACHING IN AGRICULTURE AND HORTICULTURE.

All Schools which claim a grant under Article 112 of the Code must present in Elementary Science at the annual inspection a course of 40 object lessons from Nature.

The Schools to which grants may be made under this Article will be of two kinds.

Class A.—Schools in which the elements of Scientific Agriculture are satisfactorily taught and illustrated by practical experiments on a small scale carried out by the teacher and observed by the children.

Class B.—Schools in which the elements of Scientific Agriculture are intelligently taught and illustrated by practical work in the field done by the children and directed by the Teacher.

CLASS A.—REQUIREMENTS.

The careful illustration by experiments of the Agricultural teaching required under the Elementary Science Schedule (A) of the Code.

A very small plot of land, or some earth in flower pots, boxes or barrels will be sufficient to conduct the illustrations required in this Class.

CLASS B.—REQUIREMENTS.

1. The principles explained in Tanner's Alphabet of Agriculture and further steps, comprising 40 lessons, must be intelligently taught in the school.

2. A plot of land of at least a quarter of acre in extent must be provided.

3. This plot must be surrounded by a good and sufficient fence and the possession of it legally defined.

4. The kind of plants to be cultivated and the exact number and kind of tools required must be decided by the Department on the report of qualified persons.

5. As a rule the following tools will be required for each dozen children.

    3 Light machettes.
    2 Rakes.
    2 Garden spades ; small size.
    2 Demerara forks, three or four prongs.
    3 Hoes, small size only, for friable soils (loam or marls).

6. Credit will be given for the cultivation of economic plants not generally grown in the district, when the size and character of the plot renders this advisable.

7. The time to be given to practical work in the field must be as a rule four hours per week. This work, for which a separate grant is given, must not occupy any part of the school hours.

8. Boys above ten must attend the practical teaching in the field, and boys under ten may be permitted to do so.

9. The agricultural teaching and the lighter practical work shall be open to girls.

10. A manure heap of road scrapings and other refuse should be formed in some suitable place.

11. Everything grown should if possible be sold, and after the payment of necessary expenses, one-third of the net proceeds must go to the teacher, and the other two-thirds must be equitably divided amongst the scholars who had taken part in the cultivation.

12. No credit will be given to any School in Class B for ordinary cultivation conducted on the unscientific methods too usually practised in the island ; but only for cultivation conducted on improved scientific methods.

PRACTICAL TEACHING IN HANDICRAFTS.

The requirements in this Subject have not yet been settled.

APPENDIX G.*

SCHEDULE D.—SUBJECTS FOR EXAMINATION OF PUPIL TEACHERS.

	Reading and Recitation.†	Dictation.	Arithmetic.‡	Grammar.
First Year.	To read with fluency, ease, and just expression, and to recite 60 lines from some standard poet.	A passage of moderate difficulty to be correctly written on paper from dictation in a fair, legible hand. To write a short letter.	To be fairly proficient in the practical application of all the Compound Rules, *i.e.*, of money, and the weights and measures in general use.	The parts of speech with their relations in a sentence. Simple analysis.
Second Year.	To read as above, and to recite 60 lines from some standard poet, with knowledge of meanings and allusions.	As above ; also the substance of a passage read by the Examiner to be written down from memory. Good penmanship required.	Elementary Vulgar Fractions. Practice. Tradesmen's and household accounts.	Analysis and parsing of simple sentences.
Third Year.	To read as above, and to recite as above 70 lines from some standard poet.	As above ; also business forms such as bills and receipts. The requirement of good penmanship will this year be more rigidly enforced.	Simple Interest. Simple Proportion. Vulgar Fractions. Unitary Method. Decimals.	Analysis and parsing of complex sentences.
Fourth Year.	To read as above, and to recite 80 lines of Shakespeare with clearness and force, and knowledge of allusions.	As above ; also a short essay on a given subject.	Compound proportion. Percentages. Averages.	Paraphrasing. Fuller knowledge of Grammar.
Text Books Recommended.				

* For the requirements of the New Code of May, 1900, see Part II. of this Report.
† To be prepared for the annual inspection of the school.
‡ The figures in the Arithmetic work must be well formed, and the examples worked out methodically and as good models for children to imitate.

APPENDIX G.

SCHEDULE D.—SUBJECTS FOR EXAMINATION OF PUPIL TEACHERS.

Geography.	History (including Scripture History).	Science.	Teaching.
Physical geography of mountains and rivers. Jamaica and the British Isles. Map of Jamaica.	Leading facts of Bible History. Chief events in History of Jamaica.	Colour, form, principal divisions of the animal and vegetable kingdom.	To teach a class in reading or writing to the satisfaction of the Inspector. How to question.
Rains and springs, Europe and North and Central America. Map of England and Wales.	As above. Life of Christ in greater detail. Outlines of British History from Julius Cæsar to Magna Charta.	Stones and soils. Elementary facts in physics.	As above, with increased skill in instruction and discipline. To answer simple questions on how to teach reading, and how to secure attention.
British possessions. Outline map of Caribbean Sea, Gulf of Mexico, West Indies. Latitude and longitude. Zones.	As above. Jewish History to end of Judges in greater detail. Outlines of British History to the Restoration of Charles II.	Elementary facts in animal and vegetable Physiology.	As above, also to conduct a class in arithmetic to the satisfaction of the Inspector. To answer simple questions on how to teach arithmetic.
Asia, Africa, South America, map of British India.	As above. Acts of the Apostles in greater detail. Outlines of British History to the Battle of Waterloo.	First principles of agriculture.	As above, also to give a lesson to pupils of the pupil teacher's own sex in any secondary subject taught. To prepare notes of a lesson.
Hughes's Elementary Class Book, 1s. 6d. Simms's Geography of Jamaica.	Nelson's History of England for the Young, and Fyfe and Sinclair's History of Jamaica.	First Year of Scientific Knowledge(Paul Bert). J. B. Lippincott & Co., 60c.; and Relfe Bros., London, 2s. 6d. First Principles of Agriculture, Tanner, Macmillan, 1s.	The Art of Questioning. How to Secure Attention, J. G. Fitch, M.A.

Defects in these particulars will be more severely visited with loss of marks in the Second and Third Years.

APPENDIX H.

SCHEDULE N.*—REQUIREMENTS AT EXAMINATION OF TRAINING
COLLEGES.

PRIMARY SUJECTS.

N.B.—Candidates in the Second and Third Year are liable to be examined in any of

	Reading and Elocution.	English Grammar.
First Year.	To read with fluency, ease, and expression from approved Reading Books, with full understanding and ability to explain clearly to a class. Vol. III. of "Great Authors," published by T. Nelson & Sons. To repeat 80 lines of poetry from any of the poets mentioned in Vols. II. and III. of "Great Authors," † with correct expression and knowledge of the meaning.	Analysis of simple and compound sentences. To parse fully sentences of ordinary difficulty. Chief rules of syntax. Elementary History of English Language and Literature.
Second Year	To read as above, from approved Reading Books, a Text Book in History, an educational periodical, or a newspaper. Vol. II. of "Great Authors." To repeat as above, 120 lines of poetry from Wordsworth, Tennyson, Cowper, Longfellow, or Goldsmith, or any of the poets mentioned in Vol. II. of "Great Authors."	Analysis and complete parsing of complex sentences. Correction of erroneously - constructed sentences.
Third Year.	To read as above, passages of moderate difficulty from the best authors, and from newspapers. Humorous passages from Standard Authors to be read intelligently. Vol. I. of "Great Authors." To repeat as above 120 lines of poetry from Milton or Shakespeare and 50 lines of prose from the Essays of Bacon or Macaulay.‖	Structure and derivation of words. Roots, prefixes, and Affixes. Word-building.
Books Recommended.	"Great Authors," 3 vols., T. Nelson & Sons -	Salmon's English Grammar. Morris's Primer of English Grammar. Daniel's History, Grammar, and Derivation of the English Language. Campbell's History of English Language and Literature.

* For the curriculum for Training Colleges as laid down by the New Code of May, 1900, see Part II. of this report.
† Or from some other book or author, upon approval by the Department.
‖ Or from some other standard essayist approved by the Department.
‡ In all years the teaching of physical geography should be, as far as possible, exemplified and illustrated by the natural features of Jamaica.

APPENDIX H.

Schedule N.—Requirements at Examination of Training Colleges.

Primary Subjects.

the Subjects in previous Standards.   Subjects in *Italics* not required in Female College.

English Orthography and Composition.	Arithmetic.	Geography.
To write from dictation passages (prose and poetry) of moderate difficulty. To write from memory the substance of a passage of simple prose read with ordinary quickness. Bills, receipts, business letters. Use of marks of punctuation, capitals, diacritical marks and italics. Copies set in large text and small hand. Rules for the formation of letters (rules for either upright or sloping style will be accepted).	Weights and measures, reduction, practice, vulgar fractions. Practical examples in the use of linear, square, and cubic measure. (Carpeting rooms, plastering walls, fencing, contents of tanks, &c.) The reasons of the processes in addition, subtraction, multiplication, and division explained as to a class. Mental arithmetic.	Meaning and uses of maps—exemplified by map drawing of school premises and district round school. ‡ Physical geography, formation of land by the action of water, ice, volcanoes, and other natural agencies. Mountains, rivers, and river-valleys. In 1895 and every third year thereafter, geography as above of Asia, Africa, America, South of the United States ; and maps as above of Asia (especially China and Japan), Africa and America. (The whole college takes the same subjects. For subjects in other years, *see* note ‡.)
To write a short descriptive piece on a specified subject. To correct errors in orthography and composition. Notes of first lessons in connected composition (letter writing, &c.)	Proportion, unitary methods, decimals, simple and compound interest, true and bankers' discount. The reason of the processes in adding, subtracting, multiplying, and dividing vulgar fractions explained as to a class.	Physical geography. Climate currents of the air and ocean, rain dew, &c. Physical, political, and commercial geography, and maps as above.
To paraphrase a passage of moderate difficulty. Essay writing ; different kinds. General laws of style.	Percentages, profit, and loss, stocks, square and cube roots, scales of notation. The reasons of the processes in multiplying and dividing decimals explained as to a class.	Physical and mathematical geography. The earth as a planet, its size and motions, with the phenomena dependent upon them, the seasons, day and night, latitude and longitude. Physical, political, and commercial geography, and maps as above.
Salmon's English Composition. Longmans. Nichol's Primer of English Composition. (Macmillan, 1s.).	Sonnenschein's Arithmetic. Pendlebury's Arithmetic. Deighton Bell & Co.	Hughes's Class Books of Geography and of Physical Geography, Geikie's Primers of Physical Geography and Geology, Geikie's "On the Teaching of Geography," Macmillan, Simm's History and Geography of Jamaica, Fyfe and Sinclair's ditto. Physiography, Elementary Course (Chambers 2s).

‡ In 1896 and every third year thereafter physical, political, and commercial geography of the British Empire, and maps (including natural features and chief political divisions) of Jamaica, the British Isles, Canada, Australia, and South Africa, roughly drawn from memory.
In 1897 and every third year thereafter geography as above of Europe and the United States ; and maps as above of any European country, of the United States as a whole, and of any well defined group of States (New England States, Southern States, &c.)

APPENDIX H.—Schedule N.—*continued.*

Secondary Subjects.

N.B.—Candidates in the Second and Third Year are liable to be examined in any of the

	History.	Scripture.	Science. (Strictly Elementary.)	
First Year.	Principal facts in History of Jamaica up to Emancipation. Broad outlines of History of England to the end of the 17th Century.	In 1896 and every third year thereafter the subjects will be—Genesis, Exodus, I.-XX., Matthew, for the whole College. For subjects in other years see note. †	Botany.—Characters of the root, stem, leaves, and parts of the flower, illustrated by specimens of common flowering plants. Chemistry.—Elementary and compound matter. Illustrations of combination and decomposition in such bodies as hydrochloric acid, water, oxide of mercury, and rust of iron. Preparation and properties of the common gases, such as oxygen, hydrogen, nitrogen, and chlorine. The chemical character and constituents of air and water, and the nature of the impurities sometimes found in both. Effects of plants and animals on air. The properties of carbon and its chief inorganic compounds. Differences between metallic and non-metallic bodies. Combination by weight and volume. The use of symbols and chemical formulæ. Physics.—Chief forces of nature. Gravity. Properties of solids, liquids, gases. Domestic Economy.‡—Food; its composition and nutritive value. Clothing and washing.	
Second Year.	History of England from the Conquest to the Restoration of Charles II. Broad outlines of European History up to 1660 A.D.	As above	Botany.—Structure of wood, bark and pith. Cells and vessels. Food of plants, and manner in which a plant grows. Function of the root and different parts of the flower. The comparison of a fern and a moss with a flowering plant. The formation of different kinds of fruits. The structure of a bean and of a grain of corn. The phenomena of germination. *Agriculture.—The principles regulating the more or less perfect supply of plant food; manures as supplemental sources of plant food. The principles regulating the growth of crops and the variations in their yield and quality.* Physics.—Moving bodies. Vibrating bodies. Sound. Domestic Economy.‡—Food; its functions, preparation, and culinary treatment. The dwelling; warming, cleaning, and ventilation. Rules for health; the management of a sick room.	
Third Year.	History of Jamaica to the present time. History of England from the Restoration to present time. Broad outlines of European History to the present time.	As above	Animal Physiology.—The build of the human body. Names and positions of the internal organs. The properties of muscle. The mechanism of principal movements of the limbs, and of the body as a whole. The organs and functions of alimentation, circulation, and respiration. The general arrangement of the nervous system. The properties of nerve. Reflex action. Sensation, organs and functions of touch, taste, smell, hearing and sight. Physics.—Heat. Light. Electricity. Hygiene.	
Books Recommended.	Fyfe and Sinclair's History of Jamaica, Edith Thompson's History of England, Gardiner's Student's History of England, Green's Short History of the English People, Sanderson's Outlines of World's History.	Cambridge Bible for Schools. Maclear's Old Testament. 1s. (Macmillan).	Bland's Botany, Bemrose, 1s. Furneaux' Chemistry, Longmans. London's Hygiene, Chambers. Balfour Stewart's Physics Primer, Macmillan, 1s. Text Book of Tropical Agriculture, Jamaica, 2s. Tanner's First Principles of Agriculture, Macmillan, 1s. Fream's Elements of Agriculture.	Sight Singing and Theory of Music, National Society, 1s. 8d., Curwen's How to Read Music, Tonic Sol-fa Association, 1s.

† In 1896 and every year thereafter Judges I. and II., Samuel, and Luke. In 1897 and every third year thereafter the subject will be Kings I. and II., Acts, Outlines of History of Israel from the Captivity to the Christian Era.
‡ Only in colleges for women.

APPENDIX H.—Schedule N.—*continued.*

Secondary Subjects.

Subjects in previous Standards. Subjects in Italics not required in Colleges for Women.

Music.	School Management.	*Algebra.*	Euclid.	Drawing.*
Singing from modulator, value of notes, simple time, major scales, intervals.	Characteristics of children; simple analysis of the mental powers; order of their development; leading principles of teaching cultivation of the senses. How to question; how to secure attention; how to teach the elementary subjects. Keeping of school registers.	*To least common multiple. Simple equations, and simple problems involving the same.*	Definitions. Postulates. Axioms. Book I., 1-5, and easy riders. *Book I., 6-26, and easy riders.*	French and drawing (First Grade) on paper and blackboard.
Elements of theory of music, compound time, minor scales, modulation, transposition, Sol-fa notation; reading an easy passage in any key or mode from the treble staff at sight.	Cultivation of the memory. On the use of words. How to teach grammar, geography, history. Notes of lessons. A lesson in reading, dictation, or arithmetic, or an object lesson, is required to be given in the presence of the examiner. Knowledge of Code.	*Fractions, simultaneous simple equations, and problems involving the same.*	Book I., 1-26, and easy riders. *Book I., 27-48, and easy riders.*	Practical Geometry. Rawle, latest edition (15th) pp. 1-52. (Method and principles of construction of every figure must be fully explained.)
Common dominant and subdominant chords, fundamental discords, inversions; class teaching from modulator; to play simple tunes on the piano or harmonium; ear tests.	Discipline; school furniture and apparatus and their uses; educational reformers; time table and method of organising an elementary school. Lessons as above, or in grammar, composition, Scripture, or morals.	*Problems leading to simple equations, involution, quadratics, and simple problems involving the same.*	Book I., and easy riders. *Book II., and easy riders.*	Model drawing and rudiments of perspective. Proficiency in drawing on the blackboard to illustrate practice lessons.
Teacher's Manual of the Science and Art of Teaching, National Society. Salmon's Object Lessons, Longmans. Rick's Object Lessons. Emerson White's Pedagogy. Fitch's Art of Questioning Fitch's Art of Securing Attention. Teacher's Manual of Instruction, Education Department, State of New York. Primer of Pedagogy, Professor Putman.	Hall and Knight's Algebra.	Hall and Steven's Euclid.	Rawle's Class-book. Practical Geometry (National Society). Freehand Drawing (First Grade). Kensington Drawing to Scale 1d. Whitehall Drawing Course, G. Gill and Son.

* The pass requirement in drawing will be leniently enforced.

APPENDIX H.—*continued.* SCHEDULE P.

NEEDLEWORK FOR TRAINING COLLEGES FOR WOMEN.

Standard.	Needlework.	Darning and Mending.	Knitting.	Class-work.
First Year.	1. *To show an unlined canvas sampler*, with the following stitches worked to the thread. Sewing, running, hemming, gathering, stitching, herring-bone, chain stitch, whip-stitch, button-hole stitch. 2. *To show on separate pieces of material* (2 in. by 5 in.). (a) Hemming in two colours, joining a fresh thread. (b) A sew and fell seam, with a string sewn on. (c) A piece of flannel herring-bone. (d) A wrist band stitched, with button and button hole, and a piece of calico, gathered, stroked, and set in. (e) A piece of twilled long cloth with binders and gussets. (f) A set of tucks on longcloth, with a whipped frill. 3. *To make up:*— (1) An infant's print frock. (2) A print or diaper pinafore. (3) A plain shift or chemise.	1. A sample of knitted stocking web material, showing a straight twill and bird's eye darn. 2. A cross cut darned in linen. 3. A hedge-tear darned in cloth or flannel.	1. To show squares (3 by 5 in.) of : (a) Knitting. (b) Alternate knitting and purling. (c) Ribbing ; the specimens to be made with chain edge and cast on and off by the maker. 2. A pair of infant's socks on two needles, or pair of ribbed cotton garters.	To draw to scale cut out and fix : (1) An infant's frock. (2) A pinafore. (3) A plain shift or chemise.
Second Year.	1. A linen stitch sampler showing the stitches of the first year, and adding marking in large and small letters. 2. A pair of child's first knicker-bockers gathered into bands. 3. A flannel gored skirt, or woman's white slip-body. 4. A gored and tucked longcloth skirt.	1. A linen or calico patch set in. 2. A print patch matching the pattern. 3. A flannel or cloth patch.	1. Specimens of : (a) Intaking. (b) Heels. (c) Ankle - gussets. 2. A woollen vest on two needles, or knitted cotton wash - cloth on four needles.	To draw to scale, cut out and fix : (1) A pair of child's first knickerbockers. (2) A flannel gored skirt. (3) A longcloth gored skirt.
Third Year.	1. A linen sampler, showing braiding, feather-stitch, cable stitch, and knotting. 2. A woman's yoked nightdress. 3. A man's shirt with gussets.	1. A stocking web sampler, showing :— (a) Swiss darning. (b) Grafting. (c) Stocking-web stitch. 2. Taking up ladders in stockings.	1. A pair of women's stockings. 2. A pair of child's socks.	1. Thimble, needle, and folding drill to an infant class. 2. To teach the sampler stitches to a school class on the demonstration frame. 3. To cut out and fix :— (1) A shirt. (2) A nightdress.

Materials Required.		Books Recommended.
White cheese cloth for canvas samplers. Red cotton for working cotton samplers. Marking linen for linen samplers. Stocking web material for darning samplers. Red knitting cotton for knitting specimens. Blue and red marking cotton for specimens of stitches.	Messrs. Venables & Co., Whitechapel, London, E.C.	Demonstration frame and cord — National Society, London. Infant-threaders for needle drill—Venables & Co. Sectional paper for cutting out to scale—National Society. Chequered black-board for cutting out to scale.

Self - teaching Needlework Manuals — (E. Jones). Hughes, Ludgate Hill. Plain cutting out—Griffiths & Farran. Diagrams for above — Griffiths & Farran.

APPENDIX H.—*continued.* SCHEDULE Q.

REQUIREMENTS IN EXTRA SUBJECTS AT TRAINING COLLEGES.

—	Latin.	French.	Mathematics.
Second year	Nouns, adjectives, pronouns, regular verbs. Principia, to p. 65. Gradatim, Nos. 1–46.	Nouns, adjectives, pronouns, regular verbs. French Course, year I. 1st French Reader, 1–140.	*Algebra.*—Indices, Surds, Ratio, Proportion, Variation, Arithmetical and Geometrical Progression, Logarithms. *Euclid.*—To Book III. 29. *Mechanics.* — Kinematics, Measurement of Force. (Magnus, 1892 edition pp. 1–126.)
Third year	Irregular verbs, prepositions, conjunctions, with elementary syntax. Principia to end Gradatim, Nos. 41–80.	Irregular verbs. French Course, year II. Introduction and Exs. 1–80. 1st French Reader, No. 141–200.	*Euclid.*—To Book IV. *Trigonometry.*—The relation between the circumference and diameter of a circle. Measurement of angles. The trigonometrical ratios (Lock, stereotyped edition, 1898, pp. 1–86.) *Mechanics.*—Laws of motion. Energy. Machines Centre of gravity (Magnus, 1892 edition, pp. 127–226, and 317–358.)
Books recommended.	Smith's Principia Heatley's Gradatim.	Macmillan's French Course. Caron's 1st French Reader.	Hall and Knight's Algebra. Hall and Steven's Euclid. Magnus's Elementary Lessons in Mechanics. Lock's Elementary Trigonometry.

SUPPLEMENTARY NOTES ON EDUCATION IN JAMAICA, 1898–1900.

Since the above report was written by the Hon. T. Capper, the Education Commission, referred to in paragraph I. 16 above, has issued its report. As the matters inquired into and discussed by the Commissioners are of great importance and general educational interest, it has seemed best to append, in the form of Supplementary Notes to the foregoing report, a summary of the chief recommendations of the Commissioners, together with a few illustrative extracts from the accompanying volume of evidence. The following notes also contain extracts from the Annual Report of the Education Department and of the Board of Education of Jamaica for the years 1898 and 1899, the latter having been issued in the present year 1900. The reader will thus be enabled to follow the development of education in Jamaica down to a recent date. It should be borne in mind that the elementary schools referred to are almost exclusively attended by coloured children.

I.—Summary of the Report of the Commission appointed to enquire into the System of Education in Jamaica, 1898.

The Commission appointed in December, 1897, consisted of His Honour C. F. Lumb, LL.D., one of the Judges of the Supreme Court of Jamaica; the Most Rev. Dr. Nuttall, Archbishop of the West Indies; the Right Rev. Dr. Gordon, Bishop of Thyatira and Vicar Apostolic of Jamaica; the Hon. D. S. Gideon, member of the Legislative Council; the Hon. James Johnston, M.D., member of the Legislative Council, and the Rev. Dr. William Gillies. The letter of the Governor appointing the Commission stated, as the reason for its appointment, the fact that "representations have been made by members of the Legislature and other persons from time to time that the present system of education in the colony has not produced satisfactory results; that the curriculum adopted by the Board of Education is not suitable to the needs of the population; that the cost of education is too high in proportion to the financial resources of the Colony; and that it is expedient that full and authentic information should be obtained as to the system of education pursued in Elementary, Secondary, and Industrial Schools and Reformatories, and the training of teachers thereof." The Commissioners were charged "to make full and diligent inquiry into the system of education adopted in the Colony, and its cost; to report whether the education at present given is calculated to inculcate a sense of duty and responsibility and to impart useful knowledge; and to suggest such changes in the educational system as might appear to them calculated to secure efficiency and economy." By a later instrument (Feb. 2, 1898) the Commissioners were empowered, if they should judge the same to be desirable, to take evidence privately in the course of the inquiry, such evidence to be regarded by the Commissioners as confidential and the persons giving it to be so informed beforehand. The Commissioners' report is dated November 26, 1898, and was signed by all six Commissioners, but each of them appended a "supplementary statement," recording dissent on certain points. The following is an abridged summary of the chief recommendations of the report, which is stated, in the Superintending Inspector's report for 1898–9, to have been long out of print and not procurable.

(1) *System of Education in Jamaica.*

The Commissioners write:—" The existing system of Elementary Education in Jamaica may be briefly described as a Denominational System, with respect to the establishment and management of schools, under which scholars pay no fees, and almost the whole of the annual expense of the schools and a very small part of the cost of school buildings are contributed by the Government from general revenue. It must not be forgotten that hitherto representatives of the various religious denominations have been almost the only persons who have practically interested themselves in the education of the young from its moral and intellectual standpoint. Although the results produced may not be as satisfactory as could be desired, yet to them and to their efforts is due the undoubted educational advance that has been made, and it would be unjust and ungrateful to overlook this important result and to withhold from them a due recognition of their work in the past.

" Many witnesses have suggested that the present system should be supplanted by a National or entirely secular system, with the establishment of numerous School Boards," . . . . . but, the Commissioners added, " we cannot recommend the adoption of such a complete revolution in our education system."

" It was proposed, and the Board of Education on the 27th October, 1896, and in January, 1897, carried resolutions to the effect that, with certain exceptions, no more new Denominational Schools receiving Government aid should be established. By a majority we recommend this.

" Apart from any theory, we have arrived at the conclusion that a dual system of Voluntary and of Government schools in Jamaica will best utilise all the educational forces of the island at least cost to the public revenue. At present there is only one Board School in Kingston, and that of a special kind; and there are two or three public elementary schools elsewhere under joint management; but all the rest (numbering over nine hundred) are Denominational or Voluntary schools. This fact largely explains why we recommend that after our report comes into force no new voluntary schools should be established. This arrangement is necessary to give anything like a fair opportunity of developing Government schools and testing that method of meeting difficulties which have arisen. But another fact should be mentioned which has an important bearing on the case. There appears to be scarcely a district of the Island (if there be even one) in which voluntary schools have not been planted; and in many districts the total of such schools is in excess of the needs of the population. There is hardly (if at all) a district where one religious denomination could now be authorised to establish a new school without other denominations feeling aggrieved—for there is hardly a place left where a particular denomination, on the ground of the people of the district belonging solely or chiefly to such denomination, can claim the right of establishing a fresh denominational school.

" Moreover, such is the pressure of financial difficulty in regard to the establishment and maintenance of schools, arising partly from the unwillingness or inability of the people to give much free labour or financial assistance, and partly from the withdrawal of British voluntary contributions and subsidies, that most, if not all, of the religious bodies, even those which are greatly in favour of the denominational system of education, appear to have come to the conclusion that the best they can do is to endeavour to conserve and sustain the most necessary and the most efficient of their existing schools. So that arranging to maintain on the Government list efficient and necessary voluntary schools, to amalgamate small and inefficient schools and to make all new schools Government schools, as we have suggested, seems the best and in fact the only solution of the various difficulties of the case.

" As there will henceforth be two classes of public elementary schools, it is necessary to give each class a name.

" (1) The schools which have been established by various religious denominations largely at their own cost, and which will still be managed by them, and need their special care and assistance, we recommend should be called Voluntary Schools. This is the name which on the whole seems to be generally preferred, and it has the advantage of being the term used in English Law or Code for somewhat similar schools.

" (2) We recommend that the other schools should be called Government Schools."

(2) *Amalgamation of Schools.*

It will be convenient to take next the recommendations of the Commissioners with regard to the amalgamation of schools, though the section under this heading comes somewhat later in the original report.

The Commissioners remark: " One of the weakest parts of the present system is the multiplicity of schools, resulting in (1) increased expenditure, as small schools are relatively more expensive than large schools ; (2) small salaries of head teachers; (3) inferiority of teachers, as small schools mean small salaries; (4) weakening of discipline and teacher's influence ; (5) waste of teachers' and inspectors' time. A judicious system of amalgamation would (1) promote combination of weak and inefficient schools, greater efficiency, better organisation and discipline; (2) increase salaries of many teachers and induce a better class to enter the profession, and (3) allow of the employment of more trained women teachers, and of teachers fresh from college as assistants, and of boys and girls being in different departments."

"The effect of amalgamation on the teachers will be that (1) the incompetent will be dismissed; (2) the inferior can be employed as assistants; (3) it will give the teachers more responsibility; (4) it will prevent any injustice that may now exist of a teacher's form of religion being a factor considered in his appointment."

The Commissioners point out that the amalgamation of schools would not necessarily mean in all cases the building of a new school, and urge that "amalgamation and closing of schools should take place at as early a date as possible." "We are aware," they proceed, "that this is a most difficult and delicate matter to deal with, and we do not consider that we are the proper persons to deal with it in detail. We are also of opinion that the settlement of this matter should not be left to the Board of Education or to the Education Department, but that it should be dealt with by an outside independent committee of three gentlemen specially appointed for the purpose. We therefore recommend that three entirely disinterested gentlemen be specially appointed by the Governor to be a committee to deal with this matter in the following manner: (1) A special Inspector should be appointed by the Governor to report upon all the proposed cases of amalgamation or closing of schools referred to him by the Education Department. (2) Such reports, together with the opinions thereon of the Superintending Inspector, and all objections, if any, of persons interested, should be referred from time to time to this committee, whose decision (subject to the general principles set out below) shall be final, unless revoked by the Governor. The following should be the general principles which should guide the Committee in dealing with the proposed amalgamation:—

"(1) The aim should be to establish one good school in the place of several small ones, especially in towns or populous centres.

"(2) Due regard should be paid to the population, educational needs, and facilities for scholars getting to school.

"(3) Due regard should be paid to the fact that Voluntary schools (where of sufficient size and not too numerous for the need of a district) cost the State less than Government schools. Nor should it be forgotten that the establishment of many Voluntary schools in Jamaica is the outcome of past effort, and represents deep local interest, the loss of which would be injurious to the State and to the cause of education. On the other hand, we consider there is now a considerable number of small voluntary schools which may well be amalgamated.

"(4) In the case of a large and efficient school and a small or inefficient school, the latter is to be amalgamated with the former, and the amalgamated school is to remain a voluntary school of the denomination of the former, and the manager (and his successors) of the former shall be the corresponding manager of the amalgamated school, with the right, under the Code, of appointment of teachers, and the manager (and his successors) of the small school shall be co-manager.

"(5) In towns where there is not more than sufficient school accommodation no school should be compulsorily amalgamated which is efficient according to the Code, and which is sufficiently large to prevent the waste of public money.

"(6) The provisions in the next preceding sub-section shall also apply to schools in country districts, with the further condition that amalgamation shall not leave an appreciable number of children resident more than two and a half miles from a school.

"(7) . . . On determining on the renting of buildings as Government schools, preference should be given to such buildings as are detached, as are not used as places of worship, and as are suitable."

"In the case of Roman Catholic Schools," continued the Commissioners, " we, by a majority, recommend as follows :—

"(1) Existing Roman Catholic Schools should be exempted from any proposed arrangement of amalgamation with other voluntary schools on condition that such exemption causes no more expense to the Government than if the scholars in such schools were in attendance at such amalgamated schools.

"(2) Before the new permanent arrangements suggested in this report come into force the Roman Catholic authorities should be allowed to start and have placed on the Government list (subject to all the other usual requirements) other schools not now recognised, where these are needed by Roman Catholic communities—say, to the number of not exceeding six in the country and one in Kingston—provided that such schools come within the provisions of the new Code as regards numbers for exceptional schools in the country, and that the number in average attendance in the one proposed in Kingston should be not less than 80 ; and provided that the education of the children shall not cost more to the Government than if they were being educated in a Government school.

"(3) Roman Catholics shall erect and maintain at their own expense such school buildings as may be required under the last preceding sub-section.

"(4) Non-Roman Catholic children shall not be compulsorily required to attend any Roman Catholic school."

The chairman, Justice Lumb, dissented from the recommendation that, with certain exceptions, no more Denominational schools receiving Government aid should be established. He wrote : " I believe in a dual system of Denominational and Undenominational or Government Schools, by which a meritorious educational rivalry is fostered and the conscientious objections of all are respected. Hitherto the system has been Denominational, and to allow none but Government schools would be going from one extreme to the other. I also think that the privilege of establishing schools should be granted to all denominations alike, and therefore I do not approve of the form of the recommendation above [*sc.*, as to exemption of Roman Catholic Schools], although I have no objection whatever to Roman Catholics having the privileges therein." The Bishop of Thyatira recorded his "dissent from the sweeping statements that ' after our report comes into force no new Voluntary Schools shall be established.' My reason is that as Voluntary Schools have been admittedly necessary and useful in the past, and are recommended as useful and necessary for the present, so they may be found to be useful and necessary in future." Mr. Gideon similarly dissented, recording his opinion that "the proposed scheme of amalgamating existing schools may have the effect of those of one denomination swallowing up those of others in certain districts," and stating that he could " see no reason why the special privileges recommended for Roman Catholic schools " (with which he agreed) "should not be conceded to all denominations, especially as it is provided that such privileges shall not cause more expense to the Government."

(3) *School Age.*

Under this head the Commissioners remark as follows : " At present the school age is from five to fourteen years, except in infant schools, which scholars may enter at three years, and except in Seventh Standard schools, in which they may remain till they are sixteen. We recommend that the school age in elementary schools should be from six to twelve years of age. This term of years will (1) give free education for six years to every child ; (2) be sufficient, if attendance be compulsory, and if the new curriculum we shall recommend later be adopted ; (3) aid amalgamation, as children of such ages can walk greater distances than infants ; (4) probably increase punctuality and regularity, the want of which is greatest among the younger children ; (5) cause a greater number of children to pass through the schools ; (6) prevent girls over twelve being taught by men.

" Twelve years of age will be high enough because (1) the children by that time will have mastered the curriculum ; and (2) that age will admit of two years for manual and practical agricultural instruction.

" In Seventh Standard schools some scholars may now remain till they are sixteen years of age. We recommend that Seventh Standard schools should be abolished.

" The majority of us recommend that provision be made in the Law and the Code for infant schools for children between the ages of four and six to be be taught on Kindergarten methods ; that such schools be for the present limited to the towns ; but if increased public funds should become available they be extended to other centres of considerable population ; but that in every case such schools be only retained or placed upon the Government

list if and when the Governor as the final authority is satisfied
that they are needed and can be efficiently conducted according
to the regulations as to the number of children and the intelligent
use of Kindergarten methods.   The number of infants to entitle
a school to be on the Government list should be not less than
fifty . . ."

" With respect to scholars who intend to become Pupil
Teachers, we recommend that they should be allowed to continue
as scholars until they become thirteen years of age, in order that
they should not lose any of the education they have acquired by
their school life being interrupted for a year."

(4) *Compulsion to attend School.*

On this subject the Commissioners stated that diversity
of opinion existed among themselves as amongst those who had
given evidence on the question.   " Taking everything into
consideration," they state, " we, by a majority, recommend that
compulsion should be enforced under the following conditions :—

"(1) Compulsion should first take effect from the 1st January,
1900, and should apply in that year to the age of six years, and
each succeeding year one year should be added up to the age of
twelve.

"(2) It should be for 240 attendances in each school year.

"(3) The fine for non-attendance should never exceed 5s., with
an alternative imprisonment for not more than seven days.

"(4) Any of the following reasons should be a reasonable excuse
or exemption, namely :—

"(a) That the child is under efficient instruction in some
other manner ;

"(b) That the child has been prevented from attending school
by sickness or any unavoidable cause ;

"(c) That there is no public elementary school open which
the child can attend within such distance, not exceeding two and a half miles measured according to the
nearest road from the residence of such child, as
may be prescribed in the regulations ; and the magistrate should be allowed in his discretion to reprimand
for the first offence.

" The arrangements for carrying out compulsion should be as
follows :—

"(1) There should be one Attendance Officer in every suitably
defined area, which should embrace many school districts. In
the country we suggest that he should be a rural headman or
policeman, and in towns a member of the constabulary, the
former to be paid not more than 1s. 6d. a day when so-employed.

"(2) Managers and teachers should in the first instance aid
in preparing and keeping lists of children of the schoolable age
to whom compulsion applies.

"In the event of failure to get the children on the list, the attendance officer should be responsible, and should call on parents and guardians to give in the names and ages of the children.

"(3) The managers and co-managers will be able to give valuable aid in the matter of attendance. The managers, with, if possible, the corresponding manager present, should meet monthly at the school. The locally resident managers and the teacher should report the result of their efforts to get the children to school. Parents considered culpably negligent in not sending their children to school should be warned to attend such meeting. Excuses should be granted by the managers for valid reasons, such as sickness in the house, want of clothes, need for children's services during pimento, orange, or other crop time. Those without sufficient excuse should be warned that, if the children's proper attendance does not commence before the next monthly meeting of the managers, they will be placed on the list of defaulters.

"(4) A list of defaulters (that is, those considered by the managers without sufficient excuse) to be kept at the school, and a certified copy of this supplied by the teacher monthly to the attendance officer.

"(5) The attendance officer should then summon before the magistrate the parents or guardians of the children on the list, and the magistrate would deal with them subject to the conditions already laid down.

"(6) In towns some of the preceding arrangements may require modification.

"(7) In carrying out these arrangements, voluntary aid should be largely relied upon, and paid services availed of as little as possible, so as to keep down expense."

"That there are difficulties in the way of carrying out compulsion" write the Commissioners, "we are well aware, but we cannot see that (to the extent we recommend that compulsion should be attempted) the difficulties are greater in Jamaica than in any other countries where compulsion is carried out with manifest advantage. With the voluntary co-operation, which we suggest should be sought, the expense of the machinery of compulsion will be comparatively small. If there be additional cost to the country, it will chiefly result from the eventual bringing into the schools of a greater proportion of the population. But no intelligent citizen who believes in the value of a proper education will object to this; for, in the event of compulsion having this result, it will be the means of preventing a great waste of public money arising from irregularity of attendance, and will make the school effective for the education of a greater proportion of the population. . . . . Why should we tax the community to support schools, and then permit children to pass school age without using them? We believe that, if our suggestions are adopted, the difficulties will be minimised both as to cost and method. And compulsion will become practicable and efficient by being carried out simultaneously under the operation of a general law, but beginning with the younger children.

" We are of opinion that this arrangement will not rapidly force up the attendance, but will gradually increase it. Nowhere has compulsion brought into the schools all the schoolable children; but judiciously applied it does tend gradually to increase the percentage of attendance. As we recommend that compulsion should come into operation in and after January, 1900, for children between the ages of six and seven, and in and after January, 1901, for those between six and eight, and so on up to twelve, we think that for the first three years beginning with the year 1900, the gradual enforcement of the compulsory arrangements will do little if anything more than counterbalance the withdrawals from school on account of reduction of school years, whereby those from twelve to fourteen and those in country places younger than six will be removed from school. Compulsory attendance thus carried out will not necessitate any immediate outlay in building. . . .

" We believe that the fact of the law requiring the attendance of children at school will have great weight with our people generally, and will in itself tend to greatly improve the attendance. Some considerable time should elapse after compulsion comes into operation before other means besides moral influence are resorted to; and full allowance should be made for all reasonable excuses; so that there will be no real hardship created.

" Some of the direct advantages which may be expected to result from compulsory attendance are the following :—

" Full value will be more reliably obtained for outlay of public funds on education.

" The greater regularity of attendance will tend to prevent wastefulness of teaching power.

" While in the first years compulsion will only be applied to the younger children, this will help to keep up the attendance of the older ones on the list, because their parents in many cases will require them to travel with the younger children to take care of them.

" If a right education is good for the people as a whole, no recommendations would be wise which did not provide for gradually bringing all the children under the influence of such good and practical education.

" . . . The proposed arrangements for itinerant teachers in sparsely populated districts [see below] will be futile without compulsory attendance.

" In fact a large part of our proposals for securing efficiency combined with economy can only be expected to be successful if strengthened by compulsion."

(5) *Irregularity and Unpunctuality.*

Under this head (which is closely connected with iii. and iv. above) the Commissioners write :—" All of the witnesses who are in any way connected, practically, with education, complain of the great want of regularity and punctuality, especially in the younger children. As irregularity and unpunctuality are such great drawbacks to efficiency and to the maintenance of school discipline, they require serious consideration. It should not be overlooked that in England, where there are both compulsion and comparative irregularity of attendance, there are complaints about efficiency, caused, as some believe, by attempts to teach too many subjects.

" Irregularity of attendance may be owing to the economic conditions of Jamaica, which can only be removed gradually, and to parents keeping children at home for trivial reasons. Unpunctuality may be in part owing to the teachers themselves by not assembling or dismissing the school at the fixed hours, or by not calling the rolls at the proper time, or by permitting unpunctuality without dealing with it, or by not keeping their clocks in order."

The Commissioners point out that "greater regularity of attendance will be probably secured by compulsory attendance, by raising the minimum school age, and by the growth of public opinion. . . . Inspectors' surprise visits will also keep the teachers on the alert to be punctual. . . . With the same object in view, we recommend that the morning work should be commenced with drill and singing, which are the most pleasing and attractive part of school work to children, and that scholars should not be admitted after ten a.m. in the morning session and two p.m. in the afternoon session, and that the Head Teacher should enter the times of opening and dismissing school each day in his Log Book. . . . As an inducement to scholars to become regular and punctual we recommend that medals and certificates be given annually for punctuality and regularity and proficiency, the distribution to be publicly made by prominent persons. This will not entail an expenditure of more than a very few pounds each year, and we hope that it will be attended by results similar to those obtained in places where such a system is in operation."

The following dissentient notes, signed by individual Commissioners, touch on topics referred to under the headings iii., iv., and v. above. The Chairman writes : " I cannot agree to any of the recommendations for compulsion. First, its adoption will increase the cost of education. It will either increase the numbers in attendance or not; if the former, then the cost will increase ; if the latter, there is no necessity for it. Second : When the finances will allow, it might be fixed tentatively in one or two towns, and, if successful, be applied to other towns. Third : In the country its enforcement would be difficult or dangerous. The written opinions of seven medical men of the highest repute and resident in different parts of Jamaica were laid before us, and it would appear that it would be physically injurious for young children to walk four or five miles a day and have five hours' school work, for at least 120 days in the year. To avoid this would require a multiplicity of schools." The

Chairman expresses a preference for a thorough trial of various means of persuasion, such as the offer of medals for regularity of attendance, changes in the time table, improvements in the teaching, the offer of leaving certificates of good character, &c., rather than a resort to compulsion. "My experience of compulsion has forcibly impressed on me the advisability of keeping the policeman and gaol far apart from elementary education." Justice Lumb also called attention to unfavourable reports of the school attendance in London. He added that he should have "preferred the school age to be from seven to thirteen," but that he deferred to the majority in this respect. He further expressed the opinion that " being sent to school when very young does not hasten a scholar's mental development," and that " believing the educational result to be very meagre, he could not concur in the recommendation for admission from four to six in towns." His reasons for dissenting from the recommendation to recognise, under the new conditions, in towns, a number of infant schools, are worded as follows: "(*a*) It will increase expense, as it will increase the number of scholars, of departments, and of teachers, and will require Kindergarten methods; (*b*) it will require specially trained teachers; (*c*) infant schools are so expensive; (*d*) I think six years are sufficient for the taxpayers to pay for; (*e*) by confining it to towns, an injustice will be done to children in country districts. . . . Nor can I agree in the recommendation for the adoption of kindergarten methods. . . . Whether it has all the merits that its supporters claim for it or not, I do not consider, but its great expense must be taken into account. It will require specially trained teachers and expensive apparatus and equipment involving not only initial cost but also that of replacement."

The Archbishop of Jamaica and Dr. Gillies signed a memorandum suggesting certain modifications in the Commissioners' recommendations in regard to school age, and the dates and modes of giving effect to proposed changes introducing compulsory attendance.

Mr. Gideon recorded his opinion in the following terms: " I do not consider the country is yet in a condition to render compulsion practicable or desirable; and I am of opinion that compulsory education even on the lines indicated will be costly. If, however, it is intended to give effect to the recommendation of the Commission to reduce the school age, then, to counterbalance the disadvantage resulting therefrom, I should withdraw my objection. I cannot concur with the recommendation that the school age should be from six to twelve instead of five to fourteen."

(6) *Education of Children of East Indians.*

The Commissioners found that, except in a few cases, there was no evidence of any special effort having been made for the education of the children of East Indians. " It also appears," they write, "that there are many difficulties in obtaining their attendance in the ordinary elementary schools, one of which is the racial jealousy of the parent for the protection of his female child. . . . . Considering that there are now about 15,000 East Indians in the island, of whom not more than 2,000 are indentured, and that except as to these 2,000 they are under the same regulations as others as to taxation, &c., we are of opinion that some effort should be made to give them the advantages of education, and we therefore recommend that special schools should be established in centres, where necessary under the following conditions:—

" (1) That such schools be Government schools;
" (2) That the minimum attendance should be 30;
" (3) That the teaching should be given in the English language;
" (4) That the teacher should be able to speak English and Hindi;
" (5) That West Indian children should not be refused admission when no other school is accessible to them."

(7) *School Managers.*

The Commission found " the present system unsatisfactory, because—
" (1) There is difficulty in obtaining co-managers;
" (2) There is a great absence of laymen as co-managers;
" (3) There is an insufficiency of proper supervision, as some managers have as many as nine or ten schools."
They recommended that, in regard to Voluntary schools, there should, if possible, be three managers for each school, and that it should be made clear that women are eligible for appointment as co-managers, and that their co-operation is sought. In regard to Government schools, the Commissioners advised that the Governor should appoint a board of six managers for each school, women being eligible for appointment, but that " no teacher or any person who derives any profit or emolument from any Government school should be a manager." " In England," the Commissioners write, " professional men, merchants, shopkeepers and others engaged in earning their living, give their services free, as such managers, and we hope a similar public spirit will be displayed in Jamaica, and that there may be no difficulty in the future in obtaining the services of ladies and gentlemen for such positions."

(8) *Inspectors and Inspection.*

" It would appear," state the Commissioners, " that during recent years only persons possessing University Degrees have been appointed Inspectors. We are of opinion that the services of University graduates are very desirable, but we recommend that the possession of such degrees should not be an indispensable qualification for such appointments. . . ."
" The Commission is strongly of opinion that great good will probably result from a system of surprise visits by Inspectors, by

which teachers will be kept on the alert and during which an Inspector can point out bad habits, make suggestions for improvement, give model lessons, and help and direct teachers."

" We therefore recommend that—

"(1) Each school should be examined once in two years;

"(2) Surprise visits be made varying in number inversely as the efficiency of a school, and be not less than once in each non-examination year.

"(3) Great attention should be paid to the examination of discipline and organisation. . . .

"(5) Teachers should give lessons in the presence of the Inspector.

"It may be reasonably expected that each Inspector should spend not less than 180 days in a year in actual examination and visiting schools on the following basis—say 200 schools to each Inspector, 100 days for the examination of 100 schools in each year; 80 days for surprise visits, and this at the rate of two surprise visits a day will allow of 100 surprise visits to the second 100 schools, and extra visits to any schools that he considers may require it."

" We do not consider the annual conference of Inspectors referred to in the Colonial Secretary's letter of 21st February, 1898, will be necessary if our recommendations be adopted."

(9) *Grants.*

"Grants on examination will be abolished if the salaries of teachers are fixed. For the same reason the attendance grant will cease. We recommend that Voluntary schools now in existence should be eligible for the same amount of building grant as is now provided for in the Code. . . . As it is so necessary for the efficiency of a school that its materials and appliances should be sufficient and up to date, we regret that the financial position will not admit of a recommendation of an immediate increase of the capitation grant of 6d. a head, but we hope this can and will be remedied before long. Whatever the amount may be, we recommend that (1) Inspectors should have the power to order the providing of the necessary apparatus; (2) which should be within the amount of the grant and be a fixed charge upon it. . . ."

" We recommend that special grants should cease for Drawing, Agriculture and Horticulture,* Handicrafts,* and special grants for schools over 80."

(10) *Teachers and their Training.*

The Commissioners record their opinion (paragraph 158), that "the teachers, as a body, are probably the weakest and most unsatisfactory part of the present system, though the evidence shows an improvement in those who have been trained in recent years. Students are however trained in too much that is unnecessary and unfitting, and too little in what is useful and practical, at the expenditure of much public money, producing, in many cases

---

* For new proposals in regard to these subjects, see Section xv. below.

teachers who are imbued with false ideas of their duties and occupation. As some explanation for this state of affairs, it is but right to remember that neither the present curriculum in Schools nor in the Training Colleges will allow of the adoption of a different and useful training. Therefore we consider it to be all the more necessary for us to endeavour to remedy this by the changes which we are about to recommend."

(a) *Training of Teachers.*

The Commissioners wish "to emphasise their opinion that the training of women teachers should be combined with subjects of a practical nature," and suggest that this would be attained if the women students were to "take part and receive instruction in the cookery, laundry, and domestic arrangements" at the Training Colleges.

A majority of the Commissioners recommend that the period of training for teachers (men and women) should be reduced from three to two years. "This will reduce the cost of each student, will provide more trained teachers, and will be long enough for the reduced curriculum we propose." Dr. Gillies dissents from this view, on the ground that a two years course of training is not sufficient to secure true efficiency. In any case, he would give a third year's training to students showing special ability.

The following is a summary of the changes in the curriculum of the Training Colleges proposed by the Commissioners (except Dr. Gillies, who dissents "in the interests of efficiency with economy, and the welfare of the schools ") :—

Reading School Management Drill · Agricultural Instruction Domestic Economy	To be extended.
Composition History Geography Grammar Drawing	To be curtailed.
Elocution Science Latin French Algebra Euclid Mechanics Trigonometry Instrumental Music	To be struck out.
Object Lessons Laundry Work Cooking Manual Instruction	To be introduced.

With regard to these suggested changes, which are in the direction of giving a more " practical " trend to the studies of teachers in training, the Commissioners make the following remarks:—" We are of opinion that the present curriculum (*i.e.* in the Training Colleges) contains too much of the higher subjects and too little of the primary and practical subjects, and that too many text books are indicated.

" *Reading:* Great attention should be paid to reading aloud and to a conversational discussion and explanation of the lesson.

" *Composition:* Should comprise letter-writing and short essays in plain and simple language.

" *Arithmetic:* There should be great attention paid to Mental Arithmetic and to Weights and Measures.

" *History:* Should be confined to English and Jamaica History, and to that of the United States of America.

" *Geography:* Too extensive, especially as to physical and mathematical Geography.

" *Grammar:* The history of the English language and literature might with advantage be omitted.

" *Music:* Should be confined entirely to singing by note. The teaching of instrumental music might be available out of working hours for those who will pay for it.

" *School Management:* This subject requires the greatest attention, and 50 additional hours in each year at least should be given to it. Work in the practising school should be done for one week continuously, and this would . produce better results. . . .

" *Drill:* Should be compulsory for men and women.

" *Object Lessons:* These should be introduced, and great attention paid to them. . . .

" *Drawing:* Freehand and elementary geometrical for men and women. Freehand drawing will often be necessary to teachers to illustrate lessons.

" *Scripture and Good Manners:* These subjects may remain as in the present Code.

" *Domestic Economy for Women:* Should be taught both theoretically and practically.

" *Sewing for Women:* Should be absolutely confined to plain sewing, cutting out, repair of garments, and knitting of useful articles.

---

* Dr. Gillies dissents from this recommendation, believing that the omission would inflict a great loss on students who are to be teachers of English. He would rather give the subject a larger place.

"*Laundry-work and Cooking for Women:* [To be taught by taking part and receiving instruction in the cookery, laundry work and domestic arrangements of the training colleges. 'This will reduce the large staff of servants, and will be of great benefit to the students and to others when they leave the College, for it must not be forgotten that female teachers, by their example to others, may be of incalculable good or evil.']

"*Manual Instruction for Men:* It should be compulsory on each male student to receive two years' instruction at the Board School on the Sloyd system.

"We do not approve of the suggestion made to us that each student should be taught a trade, as the difficulties and cost of doing so are too great.

"*Agricultural Instruction:* This should be a compulsory subject, and should be given on fixed days in each week.

"The following subjects should be omitted:

"*Elocution : as reading aloud is sufficient.

"†Science: What is necessary can be given in object lessons and agricultural instruction.

"†Euclid †Algebra	} at present compulsory	} as we consider these
Latin French Mathematics	} at present optional	subjects entirely unnecessary."

(b) The Teaching Staff in the Schools.

The following points in connection with the teaching staff are dealt with, *inter alia,* by the Commissioners in their report:—

Pupil Teachers.—"It has been suggested to us that the pupil teacher system should be abolished, and that more assistants should be employed. We cannot approve of this, as pupil teachers are a valuable aid to education, and provide candidates for our training colleges, and the proposed change would involve greater expense. We are of opinion: (i.) That the present restriction as to age—not less than 13 or more than 17—should remain; (ii.) that there should be no check upon pupil teachers choosing another vocation at the end of their four years' training; and (iii.) that any pupil teacher failing in two

---

* The Archbishop of the West Indies and Dr. Gillies demur to this omission on the ground that the exercise improves the vocabulary and creates a taste for good literature.

† Dr. Gillies writes that "to exclude Science, Euclid, and Algebra from the Training Colleges would, keeping in view the other subjects as outlined, result in a Training College course greatly inferior to any known to me in any part of the world."

successive examinations should not be retained on the paid staff of any school."

Women Teachers.—"As there are so few qualified women teachers employed, and as we think it is desirable that much school teaching should be done by women, we recommend that a greater number of women should be employed (i.) as head-teachers and assistants, and as far as possible where only two teachers are employed they should be of the same sex; (ii.) to teach in girls', boys', mixed or infant schools; but that (iii.) care should be taken not to produce a supply greater than the demand."

Monitors.—"There should be no restriction upon the employment of unpaid monitors approved by the Department."

Veto of Education Department on Appointment of Teachers.—"We consider that the appointment of teachers should be subject to the approval of the Education Department, and that its veto should only be exercised on any one of the following grounds:—(1) Failure to meet any of the requirements of the Code; (2) Lack of qualification for the particular post; (3) Frequent or capricious changing of schools."

(c) Teachers' Salaries.

Under this head the Commissioners report as follows:—"In considering the amount of teachers' salaries it must not be forgotten (1) that they will have received five years' free education as pupil teachers; (2) and maintenance and training in the college free; (3) that school work (*a*) in town is 4½ days a week, (*b*) in the country is 4 days a week; (4) that they have opportunity of supplementing their incomes from some other occupation on Fridays and Saturdays; (5) that they have several weeks of holiday in each year.

"We are of opinion that salaries should be fixed."

The advantages of fixed salaries are summed up as follows:—"If salaries are paid, (1) persons of superior qualifications will be induced to enter the profession: (2) better attendance will be promoted, as small attendance will mean smaller salary; . . . (4) there will be a check upon teachers capriciously changing schools; (5) teachers will not have to wait until the inspection to know what their salaries will be. The system will also save much work in the Department in calculating grants-in-aid or attendance grants, and will abolish the present complicated system of advances in respect of grants-in-aid."

The Commissioners recommend the following scale of salaries for Head Teachers, Assistants, Additional Women Teachers (*i.e.*, women over 18 years of age, whose character and attainments satisfy the Department, and who should be qualified to teach sewing), Itinerant Teachers (*i.e.*, Teachers who would divide their time in each week between two schools situated in sparsely populated districts), and Pupil Teachers.

Head Teachers.

Numbers in attendance at the School.	Salaries.	
	Male.	Female.
	£	£
From 50 to 80 - - - - -	50	36
„ 81 to 140 - - - - - -	60	40
„ 141 to 200 - - - - - -	80	54
„ 201 to 300 - - - - - -	100	66
„ 301 to 400 - - - - - -	120	80

Schools below 50 in attendance in thinly populated districts to be considered as exceptional schools, and the Head Teacher to receive a salary of £35 a year.

In order to offer a further inducement to Head Teachers and to recognise marked excellence in teaching, each Head Teacher distinguished for the excellence of the work done by his school in the Government examination should receive an extra payment (in the discretion of the Department) of from £5 to £10 per annum. [The Archbishop of the West Indies and Dr. Gillies think that the salaries recommended above for large schools are not high enough, especially for large towns.]

Assistants.—Males - - - - £35 to £45.
Females - - - - £25 to £30.
Additional Women Teachers - - £18.

Itinerant Teachers.—Same as Head Teachers for the same number of scholars in the two schools, with an additional £10 a year for travelling.

Pupil Teachers at present are paid for—1st year £4.
2nd year £5.
3rd year £6.
4th year £6.

" Suggestions have been made to us (1) that they should have increased payments; (2) that they should receive no payment; (3) that they should be paid for part only of their time.

" Considering (*a*) that the supply is greater than the demand, (*b*) that they will have received an additional five years' free education, (*c*) that they are free to choose any other walk in life after this additional free education, (*d*) that they will be trained free, and (*e*) that their work in their first and second years is of such small value, we recommend that they should receive no payment for the first and second years, and that they should be paid for the third year a sum of £5, and for the fourth year £6. We are of opinion that the result of this arrangement will be that (i.) there will be a sufficient inducement for earnest

4226.

2 Y

workers who intend to follow the profession, and (ii.) the over-supply will be checked."

The Commissioners recommend that the total amount of salaries due in respect of each school should be paid by draft or order by the Department to the managers of the school, at the end of each month, for payment by the managers to the teachers; that the managers should pay all such salaries within ten days from the receipt of such draft or order; that the teachers should give a receipt on a paysheet drawn up according to a form presented in detail; and that the receipted paysheet should be returned by the managers to the Department within fourteen days of the receipt of the remittance.

(d) *Teachers' Pensions.*

The Commissioners write with reference to this subject: "We are strongly of opinion that the time has arrived for the establishment of a pension system for Head Teachers and Assistants. We suggest the following as an outline of such a scheme, subject to its more careful elaboration by an actuary or other expert.

"(1) Male Head Teacher to contribute   30/- a year.
    Female „   „   „   „   20/-   „
    Assistants   „   „   15/-

"(2) Pensions to be payable at 60 years of age.

"(3) At 60 years of age a teacher should be entitled to (a) a return of all his or her contributions, and (b) a pension from the Government of 7s. 6d. per annum for every year of complete service.

"(4) If a teacher breaks down after fifteen years of service, he or she should have his or her contributions returned and a proportionate pension.

"(5) In case a teacher dies before earning a pension, the total amount contributed should be paid to his or her personal representatives.

"(6) Contributions to the pension fund should be optional with teachers.

"(7) All teachers, like civil servants, to be subject to conditions set out in section 79 of the Colonial Office Rules and Regulations.

"(8) In case a teacher is removed from the register for misconduct, such teacher shall forfeit and lose every claim under this section and shall forfeit all contributions made.

"We consider that this generous system, which contains some of the most valuable provisions of a Widows' and Orphans' Fund, ought to be an important inducement for a desirable class of persons to enter and remain in the profession."

The Commissioners considered that residences should not be provided for any teacher at the expense of the Government, but the Archbishop of the West Indies and Dr. Gillies held that, when funds become available, the State should aid in providing teachers' houses.

(e) *Itinerant Teachers.*

In order to meet the difficulties of supplying the educational wants of sparsely populated districts, the Commissioners recommend the trial of a system of itinerant teachers. They propose that each itinerant teacher should divide his time in each week between two schools situated in a thinly populated district and not more than five miles apart. They contend that "two consecutive days' instruction in each week in the reduced curriculum proposed below ought to produce educational results of considerable value." The following advantages are claimed for the proposed system :—

"(i.) It can be adopted where distances, roads, rivers, &c., make amalgamation of schools impossible.

"(ii.) It will avoid causing children to walk too great distances.

"(iii.) It will allow of teachers giving more attention to individual scholars.

"(iv.) It will admit of the teacher having better emoluments than if he had only one such school.

"(v.) It will attract good teachers and prevent the employment of inferior teachers.

"(vi.) It will reduce the number of teachers required.

"(vii.) It will consequently reduce the cost of education."

(11) *Classification of Schools.*

The Commissioners state that a suggestion had been made to them that there should be two classes of Public Elementary Schools :

(1) Central schools in which the curriculum should follow the more extended lines of the existing code.

(2) Feeders or smaller schools in which "a reduced curriculum should be taught."

But they express themselves as unable to adopt this suggestion as "amongst many other objections, it would make the system costly and complicated."

The Commissioners report : "There are now about 900 public elementary schools in the island. We believe this number to be too many, and in many places the schools to be too near for educational wants. This multiplicity is due in many instances to denominational rivalry, and may have been encouraged by the low average attendance of 30 as now required by the Code. This is to be deplored, as it unnecessarily increases the cost of education, the number of teachers, and the work of the Inspectors and of the Department; it also creates small inefficient schools, lowers the salaries of the teachers, and wastes public money."

The Commissioners recommend that the following conditions should be complied with before the establishment of any new public elementary school:—

(i.) The application should be published in the Jamaica Gazette.

(ii.) The application should be decided by the Governor.

(iii.) Regard should be paid to the sufficiency of accommodation already existing in the locality and to the facilities for travelling, and to the avoidance of waste of public money.

In all schools now existing and hereafter to be established, the minimum average attendance to be (i.) in towns 80, (ii.) in country districts 50; (iii.) in districts sparsely populated and difficult of access 30 (such schools to be styled "exceptional schools"); the transition from the old to the new regulation to be so arranged as to permit readjustment to the new conditions.

"The Governor should have power to withdraw assistance from a school, although the required attendance is complied with, for any or all of the following :—

"(i.) Failure to comply with provisions of the Law or Code.

"(ii.) The dilapidated, unhealthy, or unfit condition of the school buildings.

"(iii.) When an inspector has thrice successively reported within 18 months that the educational standard is unsatisfactory, and the manager, having been so notified by the Department, neglects to dismiss the head or other teacher, or to take the necessary steps to raise the educational standard.

"(iv.) When any manager or any teacher with the manager's knowledge interferes or attempts to interfere with the religion of any scholar.

"(v.) Or when for any other declared reason the school is not conducted to the satisfaction of the Department."

The Commissioners make the following proposals as to the classes of schools and mixed education of boys and girls: "Schools may be boys', girls', or mixed schools or infant schools. We see no real danger in, or sound objection to, boys and girls under twelve years of age being educated in the same class, especially if the boys are placed together and the girls are so placed. And when the numbers in attendance warrant it, they may be kept apart in separate rooms, or by dividing rooms by screens in the same building. . ."

The Commissioners recommend that in Government (as distinguished from Voluntary) schools, "no applicant should be refused admission into any school on account of the religious persuasion, race, or language of such applicant or of either of his parents or guardians."

In his Notes appended to the report the Chairman observes on the subject of the schools:—" My experience in such matters has proved to me that the only safe way of arriving at a sound and reliable decision is to inspect schools and examine the scholars. Accordingly I have examined over fifty schools in various parts of the island, occupying a considerable time and involving no little labour. The result has been disappointing.

" *As to Teachers—*

" (*a*) In many cases school discipline, cleanliness, and tidiness were wholly or in part neglected.

" (*b*) Too often a lack of ability to impart knowledge intelligently.

" *As to Scholars—*

" (*a*) Imperfect grounding in primary subjects—*e. g.* Reading and Arithmetic.

" (*b*) Too much appealing to their memory and too little to their intelligence.

" (*c*) Very little, or imperfect, knowledge of the geography of Jamaica.

" (*d*) In Recitation and Science the results were lamentably poor."

(12) *School Organisation.*

The Commissioners recommend, *inter alia,* that (i.) the length and dates of holidays should be fixed by the Board of Education, which should also have power to close schools during any part of crop time.

(ii.) Two breaks, of about ten minutes each, in the morning and one in the afternoon, should be compulsory.

(iii.) Morning school should begin with drill and singing. " This change will probably have a beneficial effect, as children enter into this work with much zest, and in order not to miss it would probably be punctual."

(iv.) " Children should be in one class for all subjects."

(v.) " Greater attention should be paid to (*a*) the organisation of, (*b*) the discipline in, and (*c*) the cleanliness of the school."

(vi.) " There should be more individual attention in the teaching, and there should be less of general questioning and of children answering together."

(vii.) " Government should provide certificates of character and proficiency, to be given by managers to deserving scholars leaving school. These would be guides to employers. This may improve (*a*) regularity, (*b*) punctuality, (*c*) good manners, and (*d*) efficiency."

(viii.) Under the present financial circumstances of the colony the units of teaching power, as given in the Code, continue to be recognised, viz.:—

Head Teacher - - - -	*80 children.
Assistant Teacher - -	80 „
Additional Woman Teacher	30 „
Pupil Teacher - - -	30 ..

with provision that—

(*a*) In a school with an average attendance between 60 and 80 one pupil teacher may be employed, if the Department thinks it desirable.

(*b*) When the average attendance exceeds one-half of the difference between the above numbers, it shall be considered as equal to the higher number.

(13) *Proposed Changes in the Curriculum of Elementary Schools.*

On this subject, and on xiv. and xv. below, the Commissioners' recommendations are as follows:—

The Code makes arrangements for two classifications of subjects of instruction, calling them standards when applied to the chief subjects, and divisions when applied to the secondary subjects. We find that in the chief subjects there are nine standards (including the sub-division of the first standard), and that the secondary subjects are thus divided:—

Science - - - -	2 divisions
History - - -	
Geography - - -	
Grammar - - -	3 divisions each.
Scripture - - -	
Singing - - -	
Geometrical Drawing -	

The same scholar may be in different standards and divisions, thereby creating such a complication as is pointed out by Mr. Williams, Inspector of Schools. We are of opinion that there are too many standards and divisions and that their multiplicity adds to the complexity of the Code and to the work of Inspectors and teachers, and tends to militate against efficiency, as so little time can be given to each subject.

We *recommend* that there should only be six classes (and no standards or divisions), and that each scholar should be in one class for all subjects.

In our opinion the curriculum should only include obligatory subjects. We find that only three-fifths and one-tenth of

---

* The Archbishop of the West Indies and Dr. Gillies think that in large schools the head teacher, having heavier duties of superintendence, should count for fewer units of average attendance.

the scholars now reach the second and third standards respectively, and that there are only 88 scholars in the seventh standard in the whole island. These figures appear to us to be extremely disappointing, and the causes of and remedies 'or them should be pointed out.

Judging from personal observation and from every source of information, we are of opinion that the curriculum has led to superficial teaching, and that too much has been attempted for the capacity of many of the teachers and scholars. It also appears from the evidence that some teachers neglect the chief subjects to obtain marks in the secondary subjects, in the belief that if their attention be confined to the former, with whatever result, their grant will be cut down, and some witnesses attribute the backward condition of our schools largely to this.

Recognising that the economic conditions of Jamaica are not such as to call for a curriculum that is suitable for Europe or the United States of America it appears to us that our aim should be—

to give a thorough foundation in primary Education,
to train the eye and hand,
to form accurate ideas of shape, distance, and time,
to give fundamental manual and agricultural instruction,

and so help scholars to earn their living and to discharge their duties as citizens.

We think that Reading requires great improvement, and that greater attention and more time should be devoted to it. It would probably be improved and made more interesting, and at the same time a love of reading might be created:

(1.) By a conversational discussion and explanation of each lesson, in which attention should be paid to grammar, punctuation, and vocabulary.

(2.) By the use of Reading Books more appropriate to Jamaica scholars, and comprising in their subjects broad outlines of the history and geography of Jamaica. Selected newspapers and "Penny Selections" from standard authors might also be used.

Although Writing seems to be well taught generally, yet more attention should be paid to letter-writing in simple language, to business forms, and to dictation.

We are of opinion that too much is attempted in Arithmetic, and the proposal at the meeting of the Jamaica Union of Teachers on 30th November, 1897, illustrates this.

We *recommend* that it should be confined to Simple and Compound Rules, Reduction, Practice, Bills of Parcels, Simple Proportion, Simple Interest, and Fractions with denominators not exceeding 20;

And that great attention should be paid to Mental Arithmetic, Tables of Weights and Measures, and to questions arising in ordinary life.

Geography should be taught in the reading lesson and should comprise the ordinary definitions, the geography of Jamaica, and outlines of the geography of the British Empire and the United States of America, illustrated by reference to maps.

History should be taught in the reading lesson and to the upper classes only, and should be confined to Jamaica and to two brief chapters, one on English History and one on the History of the United States of America.

Grammar and Word Building should only be taught in the Reading lesson and in the grammatical explanations at the end of the lessons in the improved Reading Books.

Scripture, Morals and Good Manners should be taught as at present, with a distribution over all of the classes.

The teaching of Sewing now costs £4,200 a year, and it is found to a large extent to be very unsatisfactory, and not to justify such an expenditure, owing to the want of competent teachers. We *recommend* that it should be confined to plain sewing, cutting out, repairs of garments and knitting of useful articles; that it should at once cease to be taught in any school where there is not a Registered Woman Teacher and that all women teachers should teach it without addition to their ordinary salaries.

Physical Drill should form part of the curriculum for boys and girls.

The singing of approved songs and hymns should be taught by note. If children learn to sing by note this will help them to brighten and cheer their homes in after life.

The drawing and sub-division of lines and ordinary plane figures should be taught to boys and girls so as to obtain accuracy and to give eye and hand training; and a detailed syllabus should be drawn up.

Object lessons to boys and girls should be introduced suitable to Jamaica, which should refer to common objects and animals, and to theoretical elements of agriculture according to a detailed syllabus, and also lessons on thrift.

Domestic Economy and Household Duties should be taught to girls in the three upper classes.

[Manual and Agricultural Instruction is dealt with in detail in Section xv. below.]

It appears to be almost universally agreed that Kindergarten methods of teaching are very valuable in the case of young children; that they greatly assist in training the faculties of observation and the dexterity of hand and eye, which specially need to be developed in our Jamaica children. And this form of teaching also increases the power intelligently to take in the more advanced teaching in the juvenile school, and particularly helps to lay a good foundation for the manual training which we propose should be given in the last two years of school life.

We therefore desire to see these principles of teaching in use in all infant schools which may hereafter be maintained at public expense, and as far as possible in the teaching of the children between six and eight years of age in the ordinary elementary schools. In the present state of the finances we cannot recommend grants of public money for Kindergarten apparatus, and this will no doubt prevent the rapid introduction on any large scale of Kindergarten teaching. But simple and inexpensive apparatus will suffice for the introduction and practical use of Kindergarten methods in a modified degree, which is all that can be expected in schools generally for a long time to come: and the cost of such apparatus we hope may in many instances be borne by managers and friends of the school. A great difficulty in Jamaica hitherto in this matter has been the absence of qualified teachers, but this difficulty will gradually be removed if, as we recommend, and as is now partially the case, teachers in and near to Kingston and students obtain a course of instruction in the Kindergarten section of the Board School, Kingston.

We do not consider it feasible to introduce Cooking and Laundry work into schools, because of the expense of apparatus, materials, and of specially trained teachers, and for other obvious reasons.

We also *recommend* that fewer text-books should be in use and fewer changes made in them, thereby reducing the cost to parents; that one Reading Book, including the instruction in History and Geography, be specially composed and be sold at a price not exceeding 6*d.*, if possible; and that the Tropical Readers now in use be continued, and also that the curriculum should be fixed and obligatory for all schools, and so avoid the invidious work now thrown upon Inspectors by Article 28A of the Code.

By reducing the curriculum, greater efficiency will be obtained, the cost of education will be reduced, greater attention can be paid to individual and backward scholars, and there will be less work for the Inspectors.

By the above suggested changes in the curriculum:

Reading   -   -
Writing   -   -
Dictation   -   - } will be extended.
Agriculture -   -
Drill   -   -

$$
\left.\begin{array}{ll}
\text{Arithmetic} & \text{-} \\
\text{History} & \text{-} \\
\text{Geography} & \text{-} \\
\text{Grammar} & \text{-} \\
\text{Composition} & \text{-} \\
\text{Sewing} & \text{-} \\
\text{Drawing} & \text{-}
\end{array}\right\} \text{will be reduced.}
$$

$$
\left.\begin{array}{l}
\text{Object Lessons} \\
\text{Manual Instruction}
\end{array}\right\} \text{will be introduced.}
$$

and some subjects will be entirely eliminated.

We suggest the following as the Curriculum in Elementary Schools :*—

CLASS I.

Reading—

Alphabet.
Read and spell monosyllables.
To read a short passage from a "Primer" or "Infant Reading Sheet."

Scripture—

(1) To learn by heart the Lord's Prayer; Psalm xxiii.: Prov. xii. 17, 18, 19, 22. (2) Some leading facts in the Life of our Lord: Simple stories from the life of Abraham.

Morals and Good Manners—

Instruction and training in reverence for God, in truthfulness, honesty, gentleness, obedience to parents and teachers.

Writing—

To form on slates from copies, letters, small and capital. Text hand.

Arithmetic—

Write on slates numbers 1 to 99.
To add and subtract numbers 1 to 9.
Mental operations in simple addition and subtraction (concrete examples).
Days of week, months and year.

Drawing—

On the Froebel system.
Vertical and horizontal lines and combinations of these to form simple figures or patterns.

---

* Dr. Gillies dissents in the following terms : "Apart from the question of allowing optional subjects under proper conditions, I cannot approve of the curriculum here outlined."

Object Lessons—

Common objects (*e.g.,* clock, money, cutlass, hoe, &c.).
Food and Clothing (*e.g.,* bread, milk, cotton, wool, &c.).
Familiar animals (*e.g.,* horse, cow, dog, &c.).
Good manners and Thrift.

CLASS II.

Reading—

Read, speak fluently and spell monosyllables.
To read a short passage from an " Infant Reader."
Discussion of reading lesson.

Scripture—

(1) To learn by heart the Ten Commandments: Matt. v.
1-12 ; xxii. 35-40.
(2) Further leading facts in the Life of our Lord;
Simple stories from the lives of Moses and David.

Morals and Good Manners—

Obedience to persons in authority, purity, politeness,
kindness towards playmates and animals.

Writing—

Small and capital letters.
To transcribe accurately a short passage from the reading
book in text hand.

Arithmetic—

Notation, 1 to 999.
Simple addition and subtraction.
Mental arithmetic bearing on the above (using concrete
examples).
Names and number of days of week, month and year.

Drawing—On the Froebel System.

Vertical, horizontal and diagonal lines, and combinations
of these to form simple figures or patterns.

Object Lessons—

Common objects, as 1st year.

CLASS III.

Reading—

Fluent and intelligent reading of Elementary Book, and
Spelling from same.
Regard to grammar and pronunciation.
Discussion and explanation. Conversation thereon.
Exercises in articulation and pronunciation.

Scripture—

(1) To learn by heart Deut. xxviii. 1-14. (2) Fuller facts
of our Lord's Life ; History of Creation and Flood ;
Chief facts in lives of Jacob and Joseph.

Morals and Good Manners—

Reverence, respect for authority, good behaviour at home, in school, in places of Worship, in company.

Writing—

On slates from memory and dictation.
In books from copies.
Words from one to three syllables.

Domestic Economy—

To girls.

Drawing—

Freehand and with the ruler of lines, angles, parallels and simple right lined forms.

Arithmetic—

Notation: The four simple rules of Arithmetic: Multiplication Table to 12 times 12: Troy and Avoirdupois Weights: Money Table: Roman Numerals I. to C.: Time by the clock: Use and meaning of $\frac{1}{2}$, $\frac{1}{4}$, $\frac{1}{3}$ to $\frac{1}{10}$.
Relation of halves, fourths, eighths; thirds, sixths, twelfths; thirds, ninths.
Mental Arithmetic.

Object Lessons—

As in 1st year.

*Sewing—*Girls.

Drill—

Singing—

Class IV.

Reading—

Fluent and intelligent reading of Advanced Reading book and Spelling therefrom.
Reading books to include History of Jamaica, Geographical Definitions, Geography of Jamaica, with reference to maps.
Conversational discussion, explanation of lesson.

Scripture—

(1) To learn by heart Prov. xiv. 25; xvi. 24; St. John xiv. 15-21. (2) Some of the chief parables of our Lord: Chief facts in the lives of Joshua, Solomon, Ahab, Hezekiah, Nehemiah.

Morals and Good Manners—

Love of country, obedience to law, honour, industry, temperance, purity, politeness, avoiding evil-speaking and profanity.

Writing—

In copy books text and half text; and from dictation from Reading Book.

Arithmetic—

Compound Rules and Reduction.
Tables of Length.
   Capacity.
   Area.
   Time.
Mental Arithmetic.

Domestic Economy and Household Duties—Girls.

Drawing—

Draw on slates, with or without a ruler, straight lines, horizontal, vertical or oblique, and their combination to form simple geometrical figures: angles, acute, right and obtuse.
To mark off on straight lines 1–4 inches.
To divide straight lines into 2, 4 and 8 equal parts.

Object Lessons —

Common minerals, plants and animals.
The simpler manufacturing and agricultural processes with especial reference to Jamaica.

Sewing—Girls.

Drill—

Singing—

CLASS V.

Reading—

To read with fluency piece of prose or poetry or newspaper and spell words from same.
Reading book also to teach Geography of United States of America and British Empire.
Conversational discussion and explanation of lesson.

Scripture—

(1) To learn by heart Prov. xix. 22; xxi. 1; xxiii. 31, 32; xxvi. 28; xxviii. 13. (2) Our Lord's life and teaching; teaching of law of Moses as to duties of parents and children, duty to poor, fatherless and widows.

Morals and Good Manners—

Reverence, self-respect, patriotism, courage, self-control, self-denial.

Writing—

> In copy book half-text and small hand: and from Dictation.
> Letter and ordinary business forms.
> From memory substance of short story.

Drawing—

> Ordinary plane geometrical figures, free hand and with ruler and compass.

Arithmetic—

> Practice, Bills of Parcels, Simple Proportion.

Domestic Economy and House Duties— }
Sewing—   } Girls.

Object Lessons—

> Similar to Class 4.

Manual Instruction—

> To Boys in Kingston (at present) and to such Girls as desire it.

Agricultural Instruction—

> In all country schools and in schools in towns where practicable.

Drill—

Singing—

CLASS VI.

Reading—

> To read with fluency piece of prose or poetry or newspaper and spell words from same.
> Reading book also to teach Geography of United States of America and British Empire and History of England and of the United States of America.
> Conversational discussion and explanation of lesson.

Scripture—

> (1.) To learn by heart Ephesians vi. 1–8; 1 Cor. xii. 31 and xiii. (2.) Main facts of Old Testament history; revision of the facts of Gospel History, main facts in lives of the Apostles.

Morals and Good Manners—

> Confession of wrong, forgiveness, duties of the citizen, fidelity to official trust.

Writing—

In copy book half-text and small hand : and from dictation.
Letter and ordinary business forms.
Short theme on easy subject.

Drawing—

Simple scales and drawing to scale.
Drawing to scale to be limited to the following subjects :
    1. To draw and take dimensions from a scale of feet
      and inches.
    2. To draw a plan or other figure on squared paper
      from a sketch having dimensions marked on it.
    3. To enlarge or reduce plain figures to scale.

Arithmetic—

Simple Interest, and Vulgar Fractions with denominators
not exceeding 20.
Easy application of square measure.
Examples in all Standards.
Mental Arithmetic.

Domestic Economy and Household Duties—⎫
                              ⎬ Girls.
Sewing—⎭

Object Lessons—

Similar to 3rd Class.

Manual Instruction—

To Boys in Kingston (at present) and to such Girls as
desire it.

Agricultural Instruction—

In all country schools and in schools in towns where
practicable.

Drill—

Singing—

General Instructions to Teachers—

In Reading and Spelling each scholar should be heard by
the whole class.
In Arithmetic the object should be to explain the reason
for every operation : and to teach methods of proving
results, and so exercise reasoning powers and not make
mere calculating machines.
Short examples should be given.
The black-board should be used.
In Dictation.   Prevent copying.
                Do not give long passages.
                Read slowly, loudly and distinctly.
Always use simple language.
Speak loudly so as to be heard by each scholar.
Correct errors in grammar and pronunciation.

(14.) *Religious Teaching.*

In Voluntary Schools religious teaching should be given and be the same as in the present Code, with the conscience clause.

In Government Schools the religious teaching should be the same as in the present code with a conscience clause. We believe that this simple arrangement will meet all requirements in the case of most Government Schools. But in order to meet some cases which may arise, we *recommend* that when religious bodies have only a few adherents in a locality, and it is difficult for the ministers to make satisfactory regular arrangements for supplementing the teaching of the school, such ministers shall on their occasional visits to a school be permitted (if they so desire), at any time convenient to them, after proper notification, to withdraw the scholars of their denomination, from the general work of the school, to a class room or a neighbouring house or other meeting place for the purpose of giving them religious instruction—provided, however, that the entire withdrawal of the scholars from the school for denominational religious teaching, shall not, during any month, exceed the number of hours specified for religious teaching for the whole school.

As far as we can forecast the future circumstances of Jamaica the foregoing arrangements are likely to meet the requirements of public opinion and of the various religious denominations. But if there should arise a more acute division of opinion on the question of religious teaching, then we further *recommend* the following regulations :—

(i.) In every Government school a portion of each day, not more than one hour, shall be set apart, when the scholars of any one religious denomination may be instructed by the clergyman of such denomination or other person appointed by him in writing, or by a teacher, when so authorised, and any class room may be set apart for such religious instruction, but in all cases the scholars receiving such religious instruction shall be separated from the other scholars :

Provided, that if two or more clergymen of different denominations desire to give such instruction at any school, the scholars of each such different denomination shall be so instructed in separate rooms or on different days :

Provided also that the religious instruction to be so given shall in every case be the religious instruction authorised by the denomination to which the clergyman or other religious instructor may belong :

Provided further that in case of non-attendance of any such clergyman or religious instructor during any portion of the period so set apart for religious instruction, such period shall be devoted to the ordinary secular instruction in such school :

Provided further that no scholar shall be allowed or permitted to receive any religious instruction if either of the parents or the guardian of such scholar objects to such religious instruction being given:

Provided lastly that no separation of scholars by religious denominations shall take place during the secular school work.

(ii.) In any Government school where the average attendance of scholars of one denomination will admit of it, there shall be employed at least one duly certificated teacher of such denomination in such school.

(iii.) Where there are scholars attending a Government school which does not permit of the scholars being placed in separate rooms for the purpose of religious instruction, the Department shall, where denominational teaching is called for by any Religious Body, make regulations whereby the time allotted for religious instruction shall be divided in such a manner that the religious instruction of such scholar shall be carried on during such period as may be prescribed.

(iv.) Where the school-room accommodation permits, instead of allotting different days of the month to different denominations for the purpose of religious instruction, the scholars may be separated when the hour for religious instruction arrives, and placed in separate rooms.

With reference to the improvement or otherwise in the morals and good manners of scholars who have passed through the Elementary Schools, the evidence is so conflicting that we are not in a position to arrive at a definite conclusion. But we hope that the changes we recommend will produce better results.

(15) *Manual and Agricultural Instruction.*

In our opinion the efforts in this instruction should be such as are suitable to the children and to the wants and resources of the island. Its objects should be to train the mind, hand and eye, and to teach that labour is honourable. And in order that it should not be irksome to the children we think it should form part of the ordinary curriculum and should be given during school hours.

We do not contemplate that by Manual Instruction specific and various trades should be taught; it will be sufficient, as in many other countries, that boys should be taught the Sloyd system, as adopted in England and America, which prepares for all handicrafts.

A school has recently been established by the Board of Education in Hanover Street, Kingston. It is called the Board School. The principal objects aimed at have been to give the usual elementary education on improved methods, and to prepare the scholars for receiving the manual training which is intended to be the principal feature of the school; and the Head Master has been selected for the purpose of giving this manual instruction. The time during which the manual training has been given has been too short to allow of a just estimate of the result;

but there seems every reason to expect that it will be satisfactory.
At present there are sixty Scholars and seventy Students and
Teachers taking weekly lessons, and as the school has become
affiliated with "The City and Guilds of London Institute," their
work will be subject to examination.

We think that this school should be continued, but that in
justification of the special expenditure incurred steps should at
once be taken for hastening the carrying out of the intention of
making the school principally a Manual Training School for the
benefit of Kingston scholars generally, and of the whole Island.

We *recommend* that the following changes be made:—

(1) That the name of the school, which leads to mis-
understanding, be changed to—The Manual Training School.

(2) That the boys' elementary department be closed when
the use of the buildings is required for manual training
purposes. This will save the cost of that department.

(3) That from and after the 1st January, 1899, boys be
selected from all the schools in Kingston and brought in
from time to time in batches for manual instruction. And
that steps be taken for giving preliminary instruction to
boys whose preparation for receiving manual instruction
is defective.

(4) At present no new building will be necessary, and
the number of boys who are taught at one time can be
increased to about 100. It is also proposed that only boys
in the last two years of their school course should receive
this instruction and for two consecutive hours each week.
This will provide for 800 boys receiving this instruction for
two hours every week for two years. The boys from the
various schools will assemble at the Board School in batches
of about 100 at fixed times on fixed days. This scheme
will eventually require one or two assistants, at about £80 a
year each, a mechanic to look after lumber and tools, and
about £100 for tools.

This Manual Instruction should be available to girls whose
parents or guardians desire them to have it.

We do not consider it necessary to recommend any change
in the Girls' Department of this school.

There is a department of the school for Kindergarten
teaching, the objects in view being (a) to teach a number of
Infants on this method and (b) to instruct Teachers, in and about
Kingston, and Students in Kindergarten methods. A competent
Kindergarten Teacher is at the head of this department at a
salary of £150 per annum, and the number of scholars having
steadily increased, an Assistant has been employed who is paid
at the rate of £25 per annum. As there are no other means of
introducing Kindergarten methods of teaching into schools
generally, or infant schools, except by teachers taught at this

school, we *recommend* that the school be continued, but under the following modified arrangements :—

(1) That the amount spent on the staff which may be reckoned as for the teaching of the Infants be kept within the arrangements of the Code.

(2) That the greater portion of the Head Teacher's time be devoted to the teaching of teachers and students; and that, as regards students, if it be found desirable, the Head Teacher should attend Shortwood College at fixed times once or twice a week for the purpose of giving instruction in Kindergarten methods.

As in other Government Schools we *recommend* that this school should be managed by a Committee of Managers to be appointed by the Governor.

In England boys' manual work is examined by an Inspector from the Science and Art Department : this being impossible here, we *recommend* that this work should be done by any person having practical knowledge of the subject.

We *recommend* that Agricultural Instruction should be given to boys and to girls.

The objects should be to give sound theoretical and practical teaching :

To help them to earn their living :
To teach them that there is scope for trained intelligence in agriculture :
And to create a taste for agriculture.

It should be practical and not laborious : and should have special reference to the products of the district in which the school is situated.

We find that various attempts, to a more or less limited extent, have been made to give agricultural instruction in Jamaica from 1874 onwards. Temporary success has been achieved in a few cases, but nearly all have resulted in failure owing to

The teacher not having been trained in this subject :
Or want of funds : or both.

Another cause of failure is the misconception in the popular mind that this instruction means

Cutlass and hoe work in the field :
Or a scholar tilling the ground for the teacher's benefit :
and this misconception may have arisen, to some extent, from the wording of Schedule A of the Code, where it speaks of the "elements of Scientific Agriculture . . . illustrated by practical work in the field."

We consider that the agricultural instruction we *recommend* should be given in country schools and in such town schools as may be considered advisable, but only in schools where the teacher has been trained in this subject, and should be confined to ordinary school hours, for one hour a day or for four hours a week at least.

Theoretical teaching should be by object lessons and demonstrations in the simple principles of plant life.

Practical teaching—

(1) Should be in a small piece of land adjoining or near the school:

(2) Or, if this is not possible, in boxes and pots;

(3) Should not be field work:

and the teacher should—

(*a*) Set the example and work with his own hands:

(*b*) Make the children familiar with the use of implements: and

(*c*) Explain the reason for every operation.

The above principles, combined with the system of elementary instruction in Agriculture in Rural Schools in France, will in our opinion produce a system adapted to the requirements of this island.

Although the conditions at the Boys' Reformatory and at the Hope Industrial School are more favourable for the teaching of this subject than at an elementary school, yet the success achieved in those institutions and in the elementary school at Mt. Fletcher, leads us to believe that a great and useful result will be ultimately gained, if instruction in this subject is made almost universal, as we recommend.

We also *recommend* that provision be made for resident or non-resident paying boys at Hope Agricultural Industrial School. This we consider an important suggestion, by which the best scientific instruction in agriculture can be given to boys of all classes in the island. In this connection we may refer to the remarks of the Director of Public Gardens and Plantations in his Annual Report for 1895-96.

Various suggestions have been made as to the manner in which agricultural instruction should be given, amongst others:

(1) By the establishment of Farm Schools:

(2) By the establishment of an Agricultural School in each Parish:

(3) By the establishment of one or more Agricultural Colleges.

We consider that each of these schemes would entail too much expense for the Colony at the present time, or for the scholars, or for both, though some of them may be capable of being carried out in the future. In view of the present state of the finances we cannot recommend any immediate expenditure in this direction beyond what is involved in the re-arrangements which we propose for agricultural teaching at the Hope Agricultural Industrial School. But with a view to action as soon as funds will allow, we *recommend* that the following provisions for Continuation Agricultural Schools, to be called Farm Schools, be inserted in the Law—

    (1) One Farm School may, on funds being voted for the purpose, be established in each Parish of the Island.

    (2) The management of each such School so established shall be in accordance with the provisions of a scheme made by the Governor in Privy Council after receiving the advice of the Board of Education and after two months publication of it in the Gazette.

We further *recommend* that as soon as the Governor considers that the finances will warrant it steps should be taken for the establishment of one such school as an experiment.

The opinion seems to be held that the present system of education tends to encourage a distaste for manual labour in favour of clerkships and such occupations and to create an exodus from country into town. This complaint is not confined to Jamaica, but is made in England and other countries, and it is probable that this result is to be looked for in some stages of education or of the social life of a people, although a wide observation of the facts shows that there must also be other causes than education. We cannot say that it has been shown to us or that we are of the opinion that matters are worse in this respect in Jamaica than in many other places. But any such general distaste for manual and agricultural labour must be felt to be an evil, and we believe that, to whatever extent it may at present exist in Jamaica, the carrying out of our recommendations will tend to check it. When a thoroughly sound, simple, and practical education, such as we are endeavouring to establish, becomes universal, it may be expected that, owing to the increased intelligence thereby gained, agriculture and handicrafts will be estimated at their true value by a steadily increasing number of persons.

We fully adopt and endorse as our view the following remarks: "Schools should confine themselves to preparing children for an intelligent apprenticeship in the calling that will yield them a livelihood and to cultivate in them a taste for their future profession. A teacher should never forget that the best way to make a workman love his work is to make him understand it. The end to be attained by elementary instruction in agriculture is to give the greatest number of children in rural districts the knowledge indispensable for reading a book on modern agriculture, or attending an agricultural meeting with profit, to inspire them with a love of country life and the desire not to change it for the city or manufactures, and to inculcate the truth that the agricultural profession, the most independent of all, is more remunerative than many others for industrious, intelligent and well instructed followers."

(16) *Continuation Schools.*

A majority of the Commissioners "recognise the fact that further educational facilities will be required, after the age of 12 years has been reached, for some who may be intended for special callings, artisan work and the like." To meet this want the Commissioners recommend that Government Continuation Schools should be established in certain places, when funds will allow, with the approval of the Governor in each case and on certain other stringent conditions.

The cost of maintaining such a school would be partly met by a payment from the Government of £30 towards the salary of the Head Teacher, and of half the amount of the salary of any other teacher required. The other part of the salary of the teachers, and other working expenses of the school to be provided from fees to be paid by each scholar at the rate of sixpence a week. The subjects taught to be of a character between the elementary and the secondary schools, and to include manual and agricultural instruction. Pupils to be allowed to attend such schools between the ages of 12 and 15. Scholarships from the elementary schools should be tenable at Continuation Schools, as well as at Secondary Schools, and "thus capable but poor children from the elementary schools would have a chance of benefiting by the continuation schools."

(17) *Secondary Schools.*

The Commissioners recommend that "Manual or Agricultural Instruction might form part of the curriculum in every secondary school."

On the subject of the relation of the State to secondary and higher education and to private secondary schools, the Commissioners remark as follows: "A majority of us consider that the State has a duty to care for and assist Secondary and Higher Education. This is recognised in all British countries and is now being increasingly recognised in Great Britain itself, where large private endowments and much available private effort were, until recently, considered sufficient to meet the ordinary wants of the country in these respects. In the Colonies generally, and especially in those situated like Jamaica, experience shows that there cannot be efficient, continuous, and sufficient provision for Secondary and Higher Education without some assistance from the State, endowments being limited as to amount and locality. And failure to make adequate provision for placing such education within the reach of those who need it for their own benefit and the service of the State, is unfair to them and injurious to the State. It is not meant that the State should meet the entire cost, as is the case in Elementary Education ; but should place it within reach of those who need it, and who either by private resources can meet the remainder of the cost or by exceptional ability can secure available scholarships or other personal financial assistance to meet the cost.

" Therefore, although in the present state of the finances of the colony nothing further can be done immediately in the matter, we recommend that provision be made by law, on points not already provided, for giving hereafter, as soon as public funds are available, the following further assistance to Secondary and Higher Education.

" (1) Establish Secondary Public Schools like that at Montego Bay (it that should prove a success), where such are wanted, under the provisions of the present Law.

" (2) Assist Private Secondary Schools for boys and girls by a limited payment for those within specified ages who annually pass a specified examination."

(18) *Effect of Home Conditions on School Life.*

Referring to the effect of the House Tax the Commissioners remark :—" Witnesses state that the House Tax is a bar to the progress of education ; that it is one cause of overcrowding and immorality ; that the poor are dissatisfied with it, and that it is a check upon the improvement of their houses, because if they build a second room, so as to allow of the separation of the sexes, or of parents from their children, their tax will be increased.

" The Commission is strongly of opinion that much of what is now gained in the school is lost in the home, and that it is quite hopeless to expect any system of education to be a complete success until the homes are better and illegitimacy less. . Having called attention to this subject, we do not consider that it comes within the scope of our Commission to deal with it, but we hope that some scheme of readjustment of this tax will soon be adopted, which will facilitate and allow of the improvement of the houses of the people."

(19) *Scholarships.*

The Commissioners report as follows (a note signed by two of the Commissioners being given below):—" While we recognise the enormous good produced by these Scholarships, yet the financial position compels us reluctantly to recommend that (1) subject to the rights of the present holders, all be suspended for the present with the following exception, viz., that the Jamaica Scholarship should be given once in three years, (2) all be re-established when the finances will allow, with the following extensions and alterations :—

"(a) Girls to have equal advantages with boys in all Scholarships.

"(b) The Jamaica Scholarship may also be tenable from now at some recognised Engineering, Agricultural, cr Veterinary College.

"(c) That the 28 Scholarships at £5 each in Art. 124 of the Code be increased to £10 each."

On this subject the Archbishop of the West Indies and Dr. Gillies append the following note:—"Being deeply convinced that one of the greatest wants of Jamaica at the present time is scientific knowledge practically applied to the cultivation of the soil, the preparation of products for market, and the management of stock; and that, if this be not secured, the pressure of our agricultural and financial difficulties cannot be removed: we urge that, instead of suspending any of the larger scholarships, they be maintained in the re-arranged form recommended, so as to be available at the present time *chiefly* for those Jamaica young men who would use them for gaining scientific and practical knowledge at Agricultural, Veterinary, and Engineering Colleges. The agricultural teaching in elementary and other schools, as recommended in the report, will gradually benefit the people generally; but this development needs to be supplemented by increasing the knowledge and practice of scientific methods among those who will employ or direct labour."

(20) *Board of Education and Education Department.*

Under these heads the Commissioners make a number of recommendations, some of them very detailed in character. With regard to the Board of Education, they advise that, in the main, its duties should be advisory only, and that it should have no power of voting or expending public money; that a member of the Legislative Council should be a member; that women should be eligible for membership; that it should be representative of all parts of the island; that, if possible, there should be more lay members than hitherto; that the superintending inspector should not be a member but that his advice should be at all times available to the Board; and that the Chairman of the Board should be the Governor, or other person appointed by him. The Commissioners propose that the Board of Education should act as a Court of Appeal to hear appeals from the decision of the Education Department in regard to complaints made against teachers or by teachers against school managers.

Under the heading "Education Department," the Commissioners express the opinion that "considerable reductions can be made in the work, expenses, and office staff of the Department."

(21) *Commissioners' finding as to the state of Education in Jamaica.*

The Commissioners conclude by remarking that in their opinion, formed after "full and diligent inquiry," "the education at present given is not sufficiently calculated to inculcate a sense of duty and responsibility, and to impart useful knowledge."

II.—Extracts from the Evidence given before the Jamaica Education Commission, 1898.

In addition to their report, the Commissioners issued a volume containing the evidence tendered to them in the course of their public sittings in different parts of the Island. They invited the assistance and testimony of "Ministers of Religion, Newspaper Editors, School Managers, Teachers in Public and Private Schools, Members of Public Boards, Government Officials, Planters, Peasant Proprietors, Employers of Labour, and Artisans, and representatives of every class and phase of opinion interested in education." The result of this general invitation is embodied in a large volume containing much valuable evidence which touches, from many points of view, on several educational problems now attracting attention in different parts of the world. This volume of evidence is of special value, as there have been few, if any, public inquiries into the working of an educational system, in the course of which so much interesting testimony has been given on the general question by witnesses of such varied experience and from so many standpoints. The following extracts from the evidence illustrate the complexity of the questions at issue, and show what different judgments may be formed, on the working of an educational system, by practical men of business as well as by persons more closely connected with the details of school work. The extracts are arranged below under headings for convenient reference, but it will be understood that they cover only a very small part of the topics dealt with by the witnesses. They have been selected with a view to showing the different types of opinion represented in the evidence published by the Commissioners, and to indicating the number of different factors which have to be taken into account in estimating the results or influence of an educational system. The figures in brackets refer to the numbers of the answers as printed in the report of the evidence.

(1) *Is it desirable that the system of education should in the main be organised on denominational lines?*

The Rev. C. E. Randall (Minister of the Church of the Disciples) said: "The present system, which is almost entirely denominational, should be superseded as rapidly as possible by one that is undenominational. I am of this opinion because I believe that denominational interests have frequently been sought rather than those of education. Schools have been unnecessarily multiplied, and expense thereby caused." (558.)

The Rev. Jonathan Reinke (a Moravian Minister), speaking of the present system of education generally, did not feel that it was one which, as a citizen, he would adopt, because he was not in favour of denominational control; but at the same time he felt that, although a national system would be a great improvement, it could not be considered in the present financial condition of the island. Although he was not in favour of the present system, still he thought that in the present condition of the colony it could not be changed with advantage: they could not change it, and therefore a change was not desirable. His ideas on the subject were that the Government could better look after its own work than by sharing it with denominations or churches, and if the Government did that, the educational result would be a great deal better than it was at present. At present the schools had two aims before them—the denominational aim and the educational aim, while the Government under the national system would only have one aim, and that was the advancement of education in these schools. He believed in Bible teaching, but not in the way in which it was taught at present. Now, the teachers were biassed by their own views. They might not directly teach dogmas, but they explained the Scriptures according to their individual views. He had been present at inspections, and there was always a doctrinal tendency in the answers of the children, and that was evidently the result of the teaching." Asked by the Archbishop which school he thought to be carried on in the interests of the denomination, Mr. Reinke answered, " My own."

The Archbishop.—I am sorry to hear that.

Mr. Reinke.—And I believe that every school is carried on in the interests of the denomination. That is my view. I am sorry to say it, but I believe that every denominational manager carries on his school for the benefit of the denomination.

The Archbishop.—It is so contrary to my experience——

Mr. Reinke.—I do not mean to say that any denominational crusade is carried on; but children naturally attach themselves to the place of worship with which the school is connected. (794, 797, 831–833.)

Mr. R. Craig (Justice of the Peace for the Parish of Clarendon) stated that "there was a terrible waste of money by the multiplicity of schools, which was due to denominational rivalry." (878A.)

The Rev. H. B. Wolcott (Presbyterian Minister of Richmond. St. Mary) said: " The sooner the country adopts what the people call a National system in place of the denominational system, the better it will be for all concerned. It is either the business of the Church or of the State to manage elementary education. I do not think the union of the two, as at present arranged, is conducive to the highest or best results. It leads to denominational jealousies, and to a great many difficulties that might be avoided. . . . . I am not acquainted with England. My experience is in America." (2502, 2503.)

Mr. R. C. Guy (Editor of the *Jamaica Post*) said: " I am an opponent of the existing denominational system, because it is both expensive and ineffective." (2640.)

The Synod of the Presbyterian Church of Jamaica forwarded to the Commission a number of resolutions (adopted in 1896), numbers 3 and 4 of which were as follows:

> "That, while appreciating the countenance and aid the Government of this country now gives to education, and thankfully recognising the progress the country has in consequence made, the Synod is strongly of opinion that the existing State-aided denominational system should be regarded as only a temporary arrangement, to be continued only so long as the Government may be unwilling to undertake the task of establishing a more adequate system."
>
> "That in the opinion of the Synod the educational condition and needs of the country call for a radical change in the relations of the Government to this question, and point to the introduction of a National system as the only satisfactory solution." (Appendix, p. 20.)

On the other hand, the Rev. Father Lynch, speaking of the general system of education in the Colony, said that "it had always struck him that its defects had been exaggerated: that pupils had clamoured without knowing that the same defects might be found in a different system. . . . He believed that the present Board and Department of Education had quite ability and authority enough to bring about needed reforms. The present defects were a good deal the result of depression in the island rather than defects in the system proper." (654.)

The Rt. Rev. C. F. Douet, Assistant Bishop of Jamaica, said: "The term commonly used in describing the system of education pursued in Jamaica is the Denominational system. I should like to drop the term ' Denominational ' and to use the term that is used in the Code, ' Public Elementary Education aided by the Government.' I say that advisedly, because I travel about the country a good deal, and I meet a good many intelligent and educated people of the country, and they have a very strong objection to the word denominational. It puts some of them quite into a feverish state, because they connect it with what they call denominational wrangling. I think that our present system is the best under existing circumstances, and the best for the condition of things in Jamaica. The people as a rule have confidence in the ministers of religion, and they are satisfied to leave the teaching of their children in their hands. There ought to be more elasticity and more co-operation among the managers of schools, and therefore I should not object myself to having Boards of Managers made up of the managers of schools of different denominations. I do not see that we should gain anything by enlarging those Boards and taking in, either by election or any other process, other people, because we find very great difficulty in this country in getting anyone to take any interest in education." (1041.)

Mr. C. P. Bovell, J.P., said: "One of the greatest mistakes is

that the schools are not more particularly denominational than
they are. A teacher of one belief should teach in a school
of that belief. A teacher cannot be expected to teach a code
of religion which is not in accordance with his belief. . . .
Unless religion is taught according to a man's own belief, he
cannot carry that force into the teaching which he would
otherwise do." (1385–6.)

The Rev. J. N. Somerville (Rector of Holy Trinity, Green
Island) expressed himself as being "in favour of the present
system because of the influence that managers have on the
parents to get them to send their children to school. With
a few exceptions those people who are outside of the influence of
the Church are careless about the education of their children."
"I mean by the Church the whole Christian Church, not a
denomination. It is the only system which will keep up the
attendance at school." (1435.)

Mr. J. R. Williams, M.A. Oxford (Inspector of Schools),
"considered the existing association between religion and
morality, as represented in the ministers who manage the
schools, and elementary education, invaluable, and likely to be
necessary in the best interests of the people for an indefinite
time. At present its value varied considerably with the personal influence of the manager, and with the attention he gave to
the school, but it was always something, and disconnection
would be a moral loss to the schools, which such advantages as
removal of denominational friction, increased supervision, and
improved organisation would by no means compensate." (1464.)

Mr. Wellesley Bourke (solicitor, and formerly Member of the
Legislative Council), quoted a petition which had been extensively signed by the members of the Roman Catholic community. In this petition the following paragraphs occur:—

"Catholics regard the education of their children as a duty
and right divinely transmitted to them—and for the State to
deprive the parent of that right they regard as tyranny and
State despotism. To Catholics education means a complete
work, covering the growth of mind and heart, demanding instruction in matters secular and matters religious; the development of man's bodily, mental and moral faculties, which in the
child must be strengthened and developed that they may be
used for the end for which God gave them. Therefore it is that
Catholics cannot and will not suffer their children to be forced
into schools where either their moral development will be left to
chance, or where it will be directed by teachers whose Protestant
training has been one long course of fabulous misrepresentations
and perversions of Catholic doctrine and practices. Catholics
are not thereby inimical to State schools as such, but only to the
manner in which State schools are generally conducted, a
manner perilous to the Catholic faith.

" . . . . It is but a vain delusion for any person, or any
honestly intentioned body of persons, to pretend that education
can, under existing circumstances, be given in any part of the
world, freed from religious or irreligious training or bias, where

the youth have to be trained and taught by persons professing or not professing religious belief; and Catholics will not allow themselves to be blinded by such a delusion. While Catholics do not pretend to believe that all religions are equally good, still they are ready to admit that the teaching of any form of the Christian religion is better for the good of society and of the State than that no religion at all should be taught in the schools of this island—and to that end, for the good of society, they advocate the continuance of denominational elementary schools in this island." (2634.)

The Jamaica Union of Teachers passed, in 1898, a resolution that the present system of elementary education in Jamaica "should remain as at present, with such modifications as may be considered necessary." (Appendix, No. 17.)

(2) *Does education tend to make the rising generation disinclined for manual labour, especially in agriculture?*

Inspector McCrea (in charge of the Constabulary Division of Clarendon) said that "education tended to detract from the dignity of labour. The youth of the country were looking forward to positions in shops, and, if they did not obtain them, they went to swell the idle class." (889.)

Mr. Jas. W. Mitchell (Custos of Clarendon) said that "the system of education had unfitted the people for their station in life. He agreed with the complaint that the people turned from agriculture and wanted to be clerks." (926.)

Mr. George Nash (storekeeper, of Mandeville) said that "there was a distaste among the younger men for hard work, there was a distaste for labour. All aspired to clerkships and none to wield a hoe. It was not the school system which was entirely at fault. It was the result of the desire of the children to emulate their betters, and it caused them to aspire too much. . . . Some of the distaste probably arose from the fact that the present education gave no knowledge whatever of practical training. That might answer for some of it, but not for all." (959–961, 962.)

The Hon. J. P. Clark (Custos of the Parish of Manchester) said that "very often the education seemed to take them out of their sphere of life and created a contempt for agricultural labour, although the young fellows who had refused work were, he knew, hard pressed for a living. Their fathers and mothers would labour in the fields, but they would never dream of it. He was not condemning education, of course, but the question was whether it was carried too far or not." (1027.)

Mr. Arthur Levy (Advocate) gave his evidence "not as a specialist on education but as a citizen, and his statements were suggested by things which had struck him. . . . Education ought to improve the agricultural prospects of the country, but it had not done so. Its principal product was a hybrid, a man whose education did not make him intellectually useful, but at the same time a man who was too good for agricultural labour. . . . There is a hybrid class which is neither an educated class nor a labouring class, but one which produces a vagabond. It makes him above labouring." (1030, 1037.)

Mr. T. S. Tomlinson (shopkeeper and member of the Westmoreland Parochial Board) said: "Too much of the State's money is spent on book-learning. I would have all the subjects taught which are now in the Code, but I would teach the children less of each. In the time thus saved I would give them some practical training. . . . ." He noticed an indisposition to agricultural work on the part of children who had been through the elementary schools. "Their object is to become something higher by means of education, and they consequently ignore the very source of the country's income. Parents can scarcely command their children to the ground. If the children are made to know, while they are at school, that they have to work, it would help at once to check and curb this indisposition to agricultural labour." (1402.)

Mr. Besley (shoemaker, of Lucea) said: "When the children have a certain amount of education they do not care about going to a trade. They just go idling unless they can get into shops as clerks. Very few wish to be shoemakers. I have only had one for some time now." (1449.)

Mr. Rattigan (collector of taxes for Hanover) said: "The present system of education is far from satisfactory to the public, who observe that an ignorance and false pride is the outcome of elementary education only, when the young man from school seeks employment in offices, stores, etc., and is positively ashamed of honest and honourable manual labour of any description, and the young woman prefers a rocking chair and a piano, and is also ashamed to cook or to be seen in a laundry." (1484.)

Mr. Calder (Resident Magistrate for Trelawny) said that he thought the present system of education had been an entire failure. "One has only to visit a school to see that the children are taught by rote like parrots. The people are being taught to think that they are better than their fathers, that it is a disgrace to handle a pickaxe and hoe. They want to be clerks, teachers, or in the Government service. The girls are taught to think it a disgrace to do what their mothers did before them." (1742.)

The Rev. P. J. Hall (Rector of Brown's Town), asked by the Archbishop whether he thought that education was lifting the children above their station, replied: "We find that there are many who will not go and work in the field. Agriculture is certainly not their domain after they have passed the fifth standard. It seems to me that we spend a great deal of the £70,000 devoted to education to spoil our labour market." (1815.)

Mr. R. L. Young (planter, of Tobolski) said, in answer to a question whether "the people are more or less willing to labour now than they were before education was so extensive," "I think they are rather against agriculture. They think it is bemeaning, and they scoff at work in the field. The country man is looked upon as a bumpkin when he comes to town. The town youth

looks upon agriculture as little less than disgraceful to him."
(1885.)

Mr. C. N. Dias (druggist and storekeeper, of Morant Bay), said :
"With regard to the results of the present system, I find when a
boy leaves school, he thinks himself an educated man who
ought not to follow agricultural pursuits . . . The parents of
such a boy have always made their living by agriculture, but he
thinks it *infra dig.*, if he has been to school, to go into the field
to work." (2377–8.)

A rather different view was taken by Mr. T. C. Garrett
(Superintendent of the Public Works Department), who said
that during the whole 28 years which he had spent in Jamaica
he had never had any difficulty in getting labour. "He had
had trouble as to the quality and quantity, but not as to the
getting of men. The younger generation, which was rather
more educated, did not care to work. It was not exactly that
those who had no education were the real labourers, but there
were many of those who left school with a good education who
looked rather for pen-and-ink work. He believed, however, that
when such youths found that they could not get any but
manual labour, they would return to it. He would not by any
means stop education because of this preference for more
intellectual labour. He did not think much could be done to
encourage a love for manual labour by training the hand and
eye in the schools. They would have to go back to home
influence. He did not think that it was the system of education
which was altogether at fault." (975–6.)

The Rev. H. L. Webster (Baptist Minister, of Montego Bay)
said : "Education has not, even under the present system, turned
away the minds of the people from industrial and agricultural
occupation. It is the want of education that has done it." (1630.)

Mr. L. C. Shirley, J.P. (proprietor and planter, of Duncans,
and Chairman of the Parochial Board of Trelawny), said that
he did not find any unwillingness to labour which he could
attribute to education. (1813.)

The Rev. G. House (Baptist Minister, of St. Ann's Bay) said
that he did not believe the people were as unwilling to labour
as had been said. "The Jamaica labourers are not the lazy,
worthless set they are put down to be, if they are treated and
paid well. If they are paid sufficiently, you would not [find
a better class of labour anywhere." (1988.)

Special interest will be found to attach to the evidence of the
following witnesses, who also referred to the above questions,
but from a somewhat different standpoint.

Mr. C. A. Cover (Headmaster of Rusea School) said: " The
effect of education on industrial and agricultural occupations
has certainly been in some cases to lead to a contempt of these
employments. I think it is due to the fact that the people
were tied down to agriculture in former times, and naturally
there is a revulsion. The people should therefore be taught
to see that there is scope in agriculture for their highest intelligence. I do not think the number of idlers has increased

as an outcome of education. In some cases it is due to the folly of the parents, who have kept their children at home as gentlemen—so called—and so for a time, at any rate, they become idlers. I think, however, they have been eventually forced into an occupation of some kind. The idea of the parents, which is in one respect laudable enough, is to better the condition of their children; but the error is made of thinking that they cannot be bettered by returning to agricultural employment.' (1504.)

Mr. A. N. Dixon, J.P. (retired land surveyor and planter, of Lime Hall), said that the younger generation were generally more unwilling to accept agricultural work. But he added: "I do not attribute that to education at all, but rather to a general upward movement all through the world. As time goes by, there is a general levelling up. It will rectify itself in time." (2076.)

Mr. R. M. Cocking (clerk to the Parochial Board of St. Mary), asked by the Archbishop whether " within the last ten years he had seen a change for the better or worse in the willingness of the young folks to work," said : " I think the people have a great deal of ambition, which naturally arises from their being educated. That ambition is keeping them from their agricultural work, and they are looking more towards becoming teachers, parsons, or clerks. The general feeling is against (agricultural) work, and education is responsible for it, although I am not against education for one moment. Education has created an ambition to go higher." (2081.)

(3) *Is it desirable or practicable to have more Agricultural Teaching in Elementary Schools?*

The Rev. Wm. Griffith (in charge of the United Methodist Free Church in Kingston) said that " he believed that there was a misconception in the popular mind as to what was meant by agricultural training in the elementary schools. The parents believed that it meant going into a field with cutlass and hoe. That would be a dirty piece of business. The children would tear and spoil their clothes and be unfitted for study. But he could not understand why the elder children should not be taught the practice and theory of horticulture and agriculture without dirtying themselves at all. The real difficulty was the lack of competent teachers. Horticulture could be taught in the backyard of a school by plants in boxes, and agriculture might be adequately taught in a plot of land about a quarter of an acre in extent. The children would be very much interested in the work, and the criticism of the parents would be disarmed." (761.)

Mr. H. M. Farquharson, J.P. (storekeeper and proprietor at Black River), considered that " the present system of education should be at once considerably modified. The education now being given to the people does not teach them to be useful members of society. The capabilities of the ordinary negro, at present, for education are very limited, and the attempt to cram him with a smattering of abstruse subjects, which can be of no possible use to him in after life, only imbues him with a mistaken idea of his own importance and effectually prevents his success. . . . The education most likely to be beneficent to this country would be agricultural and industrial . . . In a central spot an agricultural and industrial college should be started. Import, for preference from the Southern States of America, where the conditions of climate more nearly resemble ours, men thoroughly qualified to instruct pupils in agriculture. This college would primarily be a training place for teachers, for those who had passed through it could teach others. . . . The negro people are imitative, and if they see that a new method is to their benefit they will follow it." . . . "The most worthless people in our district are those with a little education. They are too idle to work. They loaf about the place and steal whenever they get an opportunity. I have a great deal of acquaintance with the people, and I think at present anything beyond the three R's is superfluous. They are capable of taking in that amount of education, but they have not yet reached the stage when they can take more. Of course there are exceptions. The people are now in the position we were in about the Norman Conquest. We were practically savages then. If there had been a nation in those days as enlightened as ourselves, and they had endeavoured to teach us as our people are taught, it would have been a failure. . . . A little geography, history, and so on is all right, but the future of the country lies more in the hands of the people than in their heads. . . By teaching a man geography and history you do not teach him to hold a hoe and till the land. . . The labourer's hand is what is to support him, and his head having too much in it makes him not a labourer and unfits him for work." (1224, 1230, 1246–9.)

Mr. W. J. F. Walker (schoolmaster of Holy Trinity School, Montego Bay) said: "Agricultural teaching for the children was a very important matter, and more attention should be given to it. . . . Jamaica is an agricultural country, and if it is to improve to any extent, it must be through agriculture." (1561–2.)

Mr. J. Arnold Jones (assistant-manager of the Boston Fruit Company) said: "Taking education from my own experience, I have perhaps a dozen applications each week from young men for employment. . . . The almost invariable question I put to them is, 'What can you do?' and the invariable answer is that they can do anything. I tell them that that will not do, and I ask for something that they can do, and it turns out that they cannot do anything. These people do not want any higher education. They want an education which will enable them to do something practical, so that if they are going to saw a board in two, they would be able to saw it within three inches of a mark laid out for them." (2260.)

The Director of the Public Gardens at Kingston, in a letter to the Commission, enclosed extracts from his annual report 1895–6. In the course of that report the following paragraphs occur.

" If the education of the present day has to some extent failed, it has done so in so far as it has depended solely on books and mere oral instruction. Such exclusive dependence is not wise even for literary culture, but should be combined with the training of the hand, eye, and the whole body, in order to turn out men and women fit for their work in the world.

" It is a question whether it matters very much what this practical training consists of, so long as it is based on sound theoretical principles. But if it can be made the foundation of the child's life-work afterwards, he starts with this double advantage over children who have learnt from books.

" In our island the practical training should be almost universally one in agriculture.

" If so, it is even more important that the teachers of elementary schools should have a thorough training in this respect than those who are going to be actually engaged in agricultural work; for the latter get their training somehow and after a fashion, whereas the others, who have to teach, cannot find the time, even if they had the inclination." (Appendix, No. 21.)

On the other hand, Mr. J. R. Williams, M.A. (Inspector of Schools), remarked that " one of the effects of our efforts at agricultural teaching hitherto has been to bring agricultural teaching into contempt. . . . We have created a prejudice against agricultural training in schools by allowing it to be attempted by incompetent men." Mr. Williams made a number of interesting suggestions for the development of agricultural education, and strongly urged that " higher agricultural training with the cultivation of a plot of land and practical demonstrations in the use of tools, different processes in cultivation, the making of manures, such processes as grafting, etc., etc., should only be undertaken by really competent men who have had special education in the work at the training colleges, and hold certificates of proficiency, or who really qualify themselves by courses of practical training at such a place as the Botanical Gardens." He also recommended " a small special grant for a well kept school garden, either of vegetables or flowers, or both, rather for its æsthetic value—for the cultivation of taste—than because of any direct commercial value; but anything that might lead to the encouragement of cottage gardens might eventually produce results of some importance." In all country schools he would have compulsory instruction in the principles of cultivation, nature and improvement of soils, growth of plants, etc. (1464.)

The Rev. P. Williams (Baptist Minister, of Chester Castle) thought it " impracticable to teach (practical) agriculture in ordinary elementary schools. . . . . . It would so upset them as to bring confusion." He quite approved of theoretical instruction in agriculture being given in the schools. " It is the practical agriculture which I say cannot be taught in our ordinary schools."

Hon. Dr. Johnston.—You mean you would favour such instruction as the manner of attending to the coffee plant, the kind of product to put into the soil for the first time . . . . . the general principles which govern cultivation. Then there is the question of allowing air to reach the soil by forking, the lack of which hinders very materially the growth of plants?

Rev. Mr. Williams.—The more of that kind of instruction the better.

Hon. Dr. Johnston.—But you don't see your way to children dirtying their clothes by working in a field and getting into trouble when they get home?

Rev. Mr. Williams.—That is not the most serious part of it They dirty their clothes as it is.

Hon. Dr. Johnston.—What is the serious part of it, then?

Rev. Mr. Williams.—Parents do not consider that schoolmasters can teach agriculture better than they can themselves. They have objected to it in the past . . . . . when attempts were made to establish industrial schools, as they were called. Teachers in a few instances got the children to work a ground for them, and the parents objected. They said they sent their children to learn something, and not to work grounds for the teacher." (1546–7.)

Mr. Hawthorne (Teacher at Adelphi School, Martie) said that he did a little cultivation of his own, but the boys did not help. " I did try to teach them gardening and get them to take an interest in it, but I lost about six children by trying to get them to do the work, and by calling upon them to keep the school yard clean. I came down on one or two of the boys for refusing to clear up the yard, and the parents took offence and took the children away. . . . They say that they send their children to school to learn lessons and not to work. . . . The complaint about taking them into the field is that they get their clothes dirty." (1717.)

Mr. A. N. Dixon, J.P. (retired surveyor and planter, of Lime Hall), regarded " agricultural teaching in the elementary schools as impracticable." " In the first place," he said, " the teachers themselves have never been taught the subject practically, and it is not therefore to be expected that they could teach it. I think it would have the effect of taking away from their efforts to teach the literary part of education properly. Parents, too, would have the right to object to the teaching of agriculture in the schools if their children were not thoroughly grounded in other subjects." Mr. Dixon thought it would be quite possible for the teacher to teach some of the principles of agriculture out of a text book, but " taking up land and taking a class to cultivate it would draw away the time of the teacher from things of greater importance. At the same time such things would draw out a child's intelligence in a certain direction." (2071–2.)

Mr. Elias Stuart (agriculturist, and member of the Parochial Board of St. Thomas) would not have the schools teach agriculture. " You would embarrass the teacher a good deal. How can a teacher who has not been trained as an agriculturist teach agriculture?" But he thought it would be a wise provision if, when a boy left school, he could go into an agricultural class

and be taught there, and he would have special schools founded
for the teaching of agriculture. (2317.)

(4) *Should Elementary Education be made more practical and less literary?*

Mr. A. G. Nash, B.Sc. Edin. and F.R.S.E. (civil engineer
Mandeville), " would have a portion of the Education Grant
devoted to the encouragement of industrial tastes. With it he
would import a number of skilled tradesmen and let them
go from place to place in the country imparting this technical
knowledge. . . . The old class of tradesmen in Jamaica
had died out, and the younger generations were not up to
their standard. It would be an advantage for boys to be taught
the rudiments of a trade at school. A man could attend for a
few hours at the school and teach the children, and such
instruction would be attended with great advantage to the
colony. He thought that a great deal of the money applied
to education at the present time was misapplied. It should
have a more practical turn entirely." (1089.)

Mr. Stanley Delapenha (solicitor, of Black River) "would
teach the children reading, writing and arithmetic, but anything
beyond that makes them worse." He would teach them the
rudiments of trade and agriculture in school, and thought that
in Black River good tradesmen could be got to undertake the
tuition." (1334.)

Mr. G. D. Robertson (deputy clerk of the courts, Brown's
Town) held that " while people are being educated, there does
not seem to be much consideration as to what we are to do with
them after they are educated. . . . Jamaica being an agricultural and industrial community, he recommended that parallel
with the elementary education should run the teaching of agriculture, the industries and trades." (1904.)

Mr. Jacobs (storekeeper, of Bath) " believed that the present
system of education was a very good one, but not in the right
groove. Unless the Government should see their way to
improve the homes of the peasants, all the money was a waste.
. . . Children at school should be taught domestic pursuits. If
in after years they wanted to go to a higher branch of education,
there should be opportunities for them to do so. It should
be instilled into the minds of the boys that they must do
something to earn their living, and it should be compulsory for
them to learn a trade. As it was, they all wanted to be parsons
and lawyers. Girls are badly in need of useful training."
(2282.)

The Synod of the Presbyterian Church of Jamaica, in 1896,
adopted a resolution recognising " the great importance of providing practical instruction in agriculture and the handicrafts,"
but declaring itself " satisfied that to attempt to introduce it into
the elementary schools would be to court failure. The Synod
would welcome any scheme whereby Trade and Farm Scho
might be established at convenient centres for boys who have

completed the curriculum of the elementary schools." In 1897 the Synod further expressed itself as "fully alive to the importance of providing practical teaching in agriculture and handicrafts." (Appendix, No. 18.)

The Rev. Robert Johnson, M.A. (Theological Tutor to the Presbyterian Church), informed the Commission that "with regard to industrial and agricultural education, his impression was that not much could be done in that direction with school children beyond what the Code provided for. . . He supposed that it would be quite possible to introduce manual training, but whether it would be desirable to introduce the actual teaching of trades he was not prepared to say. If they had in certain centres a school where trades and agriculture were taught, and one that could be reached by the boys residing in the neighbourhood without the necessity of paying board and lodging, it would be taken advantage of and would accomplish good results. To such a school children might go after they were 14 years of age. . . Boys who were prepared to receive this instruction would be big, and there was no reason why they should not go many miles each day to a central school." (987.)

The Rev. C. Melville (Rector of St. John's, Black River) said that he was "cognisant many years ago of the efforts made to establish industries in connection with elementary schools. The attempt was soon abandoned. He could say nothing about the efforts which had more recently been made, but he had little belief in their usefulness or permanent success." (1282.)

Mr. John Besley (shoemaker, of Lucea) was asked by the Chairman : "Supposing attempts were made to introduce the teaching of trades into the schools and shoemaking were chosen, would you see any difficulty in a practical shoemaker going in for two or three hours on one day in the week and teaching in the school how to make shoes ? "

Mr. Besley.—I do not think that would be advisable. There would not be enough time to impart a trade to them.

The Chairman.—How much time would be necessary to familiarise them with the use of the tools ?

Mr. Besley.—For that perhaps one day in the week would suffice.

The Chairman.—Don't you think that would be useful for those who wanted to be shoemakers in after life ?

Mr. Besley.—Yes.

The Chairman.—And would it not get over the foolish idea of not wanting to work at a trade ?

Mr. Besley.—Yes. But if a lot of boys were to learn shoemaking I do not see where they would get sufficient work, unless they were protected against the importation of boots. (1453.)

Mr. J. R. Williams, M.A. (Inspector of Schools), said : "If the object be to teach boys in attendance at elementary schools a trade, the result must be disastrous, but we certainly should do what we can to cultivate hand and eye (1) by such manual training as Sloyd work and, in junior classes, Kindergarten work, or whatever else is useful for the purpose in cases where (*and only in cases where*) we can secure competent teaching of a really educative character, and (2) by developing drawing, geometrical or freehand, and especially model drawing, as a school subject. . . . .

" Another way of encouraging industrial training by teachers of elementary schools seems to me very feasible, very important, and likely to cost very little. . . . I would have every training college student learn a trade—if possible of his own selection— to be learnt thoroughly in a workmanlike manner, with as much instruction in the principles of the art as is possible. If contempt for manual labour exists among the teachers, as some people say, nothing is more likely to cure it than thorough competence in one particular branch; an equipment in the tools of their trades would be a suitable bonus for these men leaving college; the means of supplementing their income by work in the trade in the spare time at their disposal would be an adjunct which no industrious man would despise. The object lesson of a teacher working with his hands would be useful to the surrounding population: we should, I have no doubt, see these men finding apprentices amongst their scholars or their former scholars, and their influence might mean a considerable increase in the productive skill of the country." (1464.)

(5) *What have been the general effects on the population of the system of education in Jamaica ?* *

On this subject, and with regard to the results of the system of education on morals and good manners, there was great variety in the opinions expressed by the witnesses. Some commented unfavourably on the results. Mr. C. G. Aitken (Acting Registrar-General), for example, said : " It seems to me that we are educating the lower classes out of their sphere and unfitting them for thorough good work in the sphere in which they are. If boys and girls were well taught to read, write, and do sums, it would be far better for them and for the community, than having them take these higher subjects in the schools, which are not and cannot be thoroughly taught. I get many letters from school-masters who are registrars of births and deaths, and I find the greatest difficulty in finding out what they mean. I infer from that that they cannot teach their scholars. If you take the average schoolboy and let him read from a book in which he has not been coached, he cannot explain to you at the end what he has been reading about. He has only a vague idea. I do not think you can get men to teach thoroughly and properly for the present salaries." (2472.) And Mr. C. P. Lazarus (Mechanical Engineer) said : " I know no country where the boys have such liberty and insolence. . . . I would not say that it is the result of education, because it would be foolish. It is due to imperfect education. Our people do not seem to know their position. Every little fellow thinks he is as good as anyone else because he

---

* It should be borne in mind that the elementary schools referred to are almost exclusively attended by coloured children.

can read and write." (2554.) On the other hand, the Rev. W. Simms, M.A. (Principal of University College and Headmaster of the Jamaica High School), "did not think that the public expression of dissatisfaction with the system as a whole was at all an intelligent dissatisfaction. The public had expected the impossible. The defects in the system were being eradicated by degrees, and the results now obtained were very much better than those of twenty years ago." (338.) The Rt. Rev. Dr. Douet, Assistant Bishop of Jamaica, thought that "the complaints that education is having very bad effects on the industrial occupations of the people were very much exaggerated." "As one witness has stated," Dr. Douet continued, "many people of the labouring class do not encourage their children to work in their grounds. They prefer them to sit in the house and to read their lessons. I know a good many people who are bringing up their children with what they call an education, and they think it derogatory to them to send them to the soil. They look upon them as ladies and gentlemen, and they call them ' Massa ' and ' Missy.' It is perfectly true that they spoil their children utterly. We are passing through a transition state. When the people begin to get out of their ignorant state and into a higher state of civilisation, they do not want to work on the soil. I think, therefore, we must make allowances for our people on that point. They think they can better themselves by being clerks and by using their fingers in the way of penmanship. We must not always put it down to education. People say, ' Look at your schools. You are driving the people away from the soil.' That is one cry all through the country. I say there are other reasons for it besides education." (1043.)

Mr. Frantz Guiselin (storekeeper, Falmouth) could "testify to the great improvement in the education of the country during some twenty years. . . . During the last thirty years there has been a stiffening of the people, and there is not that servile politeness there used to be." (1801–3.) Mr. W. H. Plant (head-master of the Titchfield School, Port Antonio, Member of the Board of Education) said : " It would appear at first sight that manners have deteriorated, but I do not believe it is so Many people consider the bowing and scraping of the people as good manners, but it is a mistake. I think those who have passed through the schools compare favourably with the previous generation . . . . There is a spirit of independence, but that is not peculiar to Jamaica, and it will cure itself in time." (2161.) Mr. Johns (headmaster of the Mandeville Boys' Middle Grade School) said that " the children who pass through the schools are undoubtedly superior in manners and morals to those whose attendance has been such that they cannot be said to have come under the influence of the schools at all." (951.) The Hon. W. Ewen (Custos of the Parish of Westmoreland) said : " I now see a marked difference in the manners of the more youthful population. There is much more civility and propriety, and I conclude that greater attention is paid to this matter than in years gone by. This matter was neglected up to a comparatively recent period." (1349A.) Dr. R. S. Turton (District Medical Officer, St. Ann's) said: " I think there is distinct improvement in the morals and manners of the people, but in this part of St. Ann's the people have always been courteous and polite." He said that he was certainly disposed to attribute this to the fact that the children of the neighbourhood had been well cared for in the schools and had been under religious influences. (1897.) Mr. E. H. Lindo (builder, Bath) said that he thought the manners of the children were much better than they were years ago. (2342.) Mr. W. J. Calder (Inspector of Constabulary for the parish of St. Elizabeth) said that the younger children were not as respectful as their parents. That he accounted for by the parents' lack of authority. He spoke of the parents, having seen that their children were more educated than themselves and so having lost control over their children, looking up to them and regarding them as very much smarter people than themselves. (1277–81.) Mr. T. F. Forbes (master of a private secondary school in Falmouth) said that he had been teaching for sixteen years, and could not say from his observation during that period that the morals of the people had deteriorated. " The morals are more the result of home influence than school influence. Children with moral parents are usually moral and well-behaved." (1762.)

Mr. S. Dell Smith (storekeeper, of Port Antonio) said that the present system is as good as can be desired, subject of course to improvement (2241), and Mr. C. A. Gale (Inspector of the Poor) testified that the system had worked fairly well to his knowledge. " I have had acquaintance with it because I have had boys at elementary schools for a number of years. I have felt great satisfaction at the education they get from the elementary schools." (2250.)

The following judicious observations, made by Mr. J. R. Williams (Inspector of Schools), will suitably close this summary of extracts. " The difficulties attending the education of the lower classes are not fully realised: we have had to evolve our own system, and it may well be that we do not know what is most suitable for the race that we have to do with. We have had to make teachers, and that cannot be done in a generation; irregularity of attendance cripples the efforts of such teachers as we have; and their efforts are still further thwarted by the influence of the children's lives at home and the examples of their parents. A system can hardly be said to be fairly and thoroughly at work till those who have passed through the schools fill the parents' class — and it will be many years before that is true here. Finally, we are apt to forget that Elementary Education is only one of the means of civilisation. While the present percentage of illegitimacy gauges, partially at least, current morality, and while the home life of most of the peasantry continues to be as uncivilised and demoralising as it is, the expenditure on elementary education must be partially wasted and disappointing: we need concurrent effort to improve house and home life and to elevate sexual morality." (1464.)

III.—EDUCATION IN JAMAICA, 1898–9.

The Annual Reports of the Education Department, and of the Board of Education of Jamaica for the years ending March 31st, 1898, and March 31st, 1899, published in 1899 and 1900 respectively, contain much important information, parts of which are summarised or quoted below.

(i.) *Educational Statistics,* 1897–9.

Year.	Schools on Annual Grant List.	Schools Inspected.	Scholars on Books.	Scholars in average attendance at Inspection.	Average Attendance from monthly return.	Percentage in average attendance of numbers on books.	First Class Schools.	Second Class Schools.	Third Class Schools.	Total Payments to Elementary Schools and Teachers.
1897–8	913	869	98,205	57,983	50,627	59·04	160	389	330	£ 53,554
1898–9	893	876	97,091	57,508	54,041	59·23	176	397	267	51,561

The Hon. T. Capper points out in his report for 1898–9, that "the number of schools on the Annual Grant List continues to decrease owing to the closing of small inefficient schools, the scholars from which could in nearly every instance easily attend neighbouring schools. The closing of these unnecessary schools has been accompanied by a remarkable rise in the number of first-class and second-class schools, showing that the large amount spent by the country on training teachers has not been wasted."

(ii.) *Memorandum on educational matters addressed by the Board of Education to the Legislative Council, April,* 1897.

In the report of the Board of Education for the year 1897–8, there is given the text of an important memorandum addressed by the Board of Education to the Legislative Council, in which the following paragraphs occur with reference to contemplated proposals for the reduction of the estimates for education :—

"The present public expenditure on Elementary Education in Jamaica is on an economical scale as compared with other British countries and colonies, including West Indian ones, such as Barbados and Trinidad and also Demerara. This is true both as regards the cost per head of the general population and the cost per head of the number of children on the books.

"The character of the education given no doubt admits of improvement; but in its methods and results it is on the same general lines as education given elsewhere, and deemed by most of the leaders of public opinion everywhere to be necessary in the interests of progress. It has not yet reached effectively half the juvenile population; and some of the defective results attributed to the present educational system are attributable to the fact that a large portion of the population has not been brought under its influence.

"The Board of Education, recognising the importance, to all classes, of the Agricultural interests of this country, has taken steps to introduce into the elementary schools theoretical and practical teaching bearing on agriculture and handicrafts, and though to their full extent these plans cannot be carried out, nor can their value be realised, all at once, they will in the very beginning include more than is done in this direction in other British countries and colonies or in the United States of America. This branch of our educational efforts could in several respects be more rapidly and effectively extended if more public funds were available. What needs to be shown when criticisms and suggestions are made on this subject is, not only that certain changes (which should be specified) are desirable, but how they can be made with the resources available, and in keeping with those general principles of education which are declared by experienced men in all countries to be vital.

". . . There is a considerable body of statesmen and philanthropists in the Mother Country who are watching with deep and very special interest the educational, social, and general development of Jamaica for many reasons; but chiefly because here, more fully than elsewhere, is being tested the possibility of progressively developing such mixed races as inhabit this island, into a civilised, united, and advancing community. And any action of the Jamaica Legislature of a retrograde character, educationally and socially, will produce a most profound and unfavourable impression in the Mother Country. This remark does not affect any well thought out and coherent plans for reforming and improving our educational methods; but it does apply clearly and strongly to the hasty adoption of measures likely to have permanent detrimental results for the purpose of meeting temporary financial difficulties."

(iii.) *Educational Finance,* 1897–9.

The following table shows the total amounts spent on education in its various branches, in the years 1897–8 and 1898–9.

Year.	Grants to Elementary Schools and Teachers.	Building Grants.	Administration and Inspection.	Government Training College for Women.	Aid to Training Colleges not under Government.	Board of Education.	Jamaica High School.	Scholarships.	Secondary School, Montego Bay.	Total.
	£	£	£	£	£	£	£	£	£	£
1897–8	53,554	510	5,684	1,574	4,380	172	1,800	1,161	300	68,585
1898–9	51,561	—	5,377	1,558	4,513	102	1,800	1,212	300	66,123

The annual payments from the Treasury for Elementary Schools have thus decreased by nearly £2,500, of which £500 is accounted for by the discontinuance of Building grants, and £1,500 by the discontinuance of the Appliances grant. There was also an actual decrease in the amount actually paid to the Training Colleges for the work during the year 1898-9, but this decrease is converted into an apparent increase in the figures given above by reason of the payment in 1898-9 of £800, which should have been paid in 1897-8. From January 1, 1899, there has been a reduction in the number of students maintained at the Training Colleges.

In his report for 1897-8, the Superintending Inspector of Schools wrote as follows with regard to the retrenchments then made :—

" On a representation being made to it by the Government that the expenditure of the colony must be cut down in every possible way, the Board of Education reluctantly agreed to recommend the discontinuance for one year only of the appliances grant of 6d. per unit of average, amounting to some £1,500 in all. This recommendation received the assent of His Excellency the Governor in Privy Council, and Article 106 of the Code was accordingly suspended for the year.

" Early in 1898 the Board of Education drew up and submitted to the Governor in Privy Council two articles of the Code supplementary to Article 30, laying down the mode in which it proposed to deal with the amalgamation or closing of a list of schools laid before it by the Department as being superfluous, and causing unnecessary and useless public expenditure. Recognising the urgency of the case, and the necessity for stopping all such useless expenditure, the Governor in Privy Council approved the Articles, understanding that on their becoming law the Board would proceed to deal with the various schools in the list on their merits."

In the report for 1898-9 it is explained that " in view of the serious financial position of the colony no amount for building grants was placed on the Estimates for 1899-900, and Article 106 of the Code of Regulations, providing for grants for appliances, has not been revived."

Mr. Capper added in his report for 1897-8 : " In my last report I gave some figures showing that Jamaica spent less on elementary education, and less on administration and inspection, than five other colonies that could fairly be compared with it as regards general conditions" (viz., Barbados, Mauritius, Demerara, Trinidad, and the Cape of Good Hope). " The comparison would, of course, have been far more striking if the Mother Country and other European countries, the United States, Canada, and the Australian Colonies had been taken into account. The United Kingdom spends three times as much as Jamaica per unit of average, and a larger proportion of its revenue ; and the self-governing Colonies spend more even than the Mother Country for each child educated."

(iv.) Monthly Average Attendance at School and Classification
of Scholars.

Mr. Capper remarks, in his report for 1898–9, that "the monthly averages show a steady increase in attendance throughout the Island, an increase which I believe to be a sign, amongst other things, of returning prosperity, as well as of a growing appreciation of the constantly improving quality of the education placed within the reach of the people."

In 1897–8 the majority of children in the schools had not reached the second standard. Mr. Capper records his opinion that this is a fact of "most serious import. It is hard to see how any great change can be effected without compulsion. Irregularity of attendance is responsible for this as for many other evils." Writing in 1899, he said that there was no material change in the position of affairs above described, and that the remarks quoted were still applicable. The following tables (from the report for 1897–8) shows the statistics of age and distribution into standards.

TABLE I.

Standard.	A.	B.	I.	II.	III.	IV.	V.	VI.	VII.
Average Age of Scholars -	7½	9	10	10	10	11	11	11½	12½

TABLE II.

Standard.	A.	B.	I.	II.	III.	IV.	V.	VI.	VII.
Number of Scholars -	32,917	14,308	13,101	10,278	8,917	7,04	5,064	2,580	141

Writing in the report for 1897–8, Mr. J. R. Williams (Inspector of Schools) remarks as follows: "Considering our system and difficulties, it does not seem to me that the proportion of children who go to school at some time or other is so very discreditably small. It is the irregularity of the attendance that wastes the teachers' efforts and so much of our expenditure on elementary education. I see no cure for this except compulsory education, and perhaps this might be tried gradually in towns, beginning with the youngest children. But while the illegitimacy rate is what it is, and so many of the illegitimate children are the main support of their families, I cannot bring myself to the opinion that compulsion is as yet practicable in the country parts, where children's services are of most value, and where also absence from school does not to anything like the same extent mean idleness or vagrancy."

(v.) *Teachers.*

The following table shows the number of teachers in the years 1897-8 and 1898-9 :—

	1897-8.	1898-9.
Number of Principal Teachers	913	893
„ Assistant Teachers	19	19
„ Additional Women Teachers ...	89	100
„ Pupil Teachers	590	533
Certificated Teachers, and Teachers who have passed the Certificate Examination...	315	411

(vi.) *Manual Training, Kindergarten Class, and Teaching of Elementary Science in its bearing on Agriculture.*

The report of the Board of Education for 1898-9 records that at the Board School in Kingston there has been carried on during the year—

(*a*) Hand and eye training class for teachers.
(*b*) Woodwork classes for teachers and students.
(*c*) A class for the instruction of teachers in drawing.
(*d*) Three woodwork classes for boys from the Board school.
(*e*) A Kindergarten class for teachers.

The Board " expresses its satisfaction that so much progress has been made in the organisation of such an important branch of education as manual training is now allowed on all hands to be."

During the year 1898-9 eight schools earned a grant for agricultural teaching. Mr. Hicks (Inspector of Schools) wrote : " More attention has been paid than heretofore to that portion of elementary science which deals with tillage, and my impression is that the instruction given has been brought home to the intelligent comprehension of the children to a more satisfactory degree than has been usual. So far, however, this instruction has not been so effectually transferred from school to home as to make any appreciable difference in the actual tillage of the people, who (with some exceptions here and there) follow the custom of their forefathers." In the report on the industrial school at Hope, the Inspector states that the lessons given in the gardens were decidedly good, and followed with great interest and intelligence by some of the boys. The long contemplated plan of encouraging the admission of other classes of boys into the school has been fully dealt with by the Education Commissioners in their report, in which they recommend the development of the school as an Agricultural Industrial School.

(vii.) *Training Colleges.*

In the report of the Education Department for 1899 the announcement is made that "after a good deal of negotiation, an agreement was arrived at, towards the close of the financial year, between the Government and a number of persons interested in the Shortwood Training College (for women students) and anxious to avert the closing which seemed imminent, whereby the latter undertook to carry on the Institution with 30 students, on their own responsibility, on receipt of a subsidy of £1,200 a year." Mr. Capper states in the same report that he has made "searching enquiry into the after history of all the students of the college," and that in this enquiry he included even those who had only been inmates of the College for a few months on probation, and had then left for various reasons. It transpired that of 103 students received into the College from its opening in September, 1885, to the end of 1895, there were only six as to whom no information could be obtained. Of 69 who had completed their course in the College, 50 were still teachers; 13, after completing their stipulated term of service, married and left the profession, several being married to managers of schools; 3 had died; and only 3 had failed to render the due term of service, in one case only from misconduct. All were now reported to be of good character. Of 20 who withdrew, from various reasons, after from one to two years' training, 8 were still teachers, 8 others had taught for various periods and then had left the profession, and 4 were not teaching at all. Information was got about all these except two, and all were reported as being of good character. Of the 14 who had left Shortwood after less than a year's residence, 4 had become teachers and were still teachers. Of only one Shortwood ex-student had other than a favourable report been received. Mr. Capper adds: "I trust that these results show clearly that Shortwood has not been a failure, especially when we consider the high character of very many of the Shortwood students and the unquestioned influence for good exercised by these in remote parts of the country." In the report for 1898, Mr. Capper, referring to the services of Miss Johnson, who had retired from the Principalship on account of ill health, after many years of zealous and able service, wrote as follows: "In every corner of the island are now to be found women teachers trained by Miss Johnson, who have carried there and are disseminating, not only book education, but the lessons of thrift, industry, self-respect, and right thinking which they received from her during their college career."

An interesting point is thus referred to in the report of the Board of Education for 1898: "The Board submitted to the Secretary of State for the Colonies, through the Government, a statement as to the sum of over £70 which it appeared that Mr. Peet, the headmaster of the Board School, was liable to refund to the Imperial Government on account of the expenses of his training in an English Training College for teachers. Such a refund is, when possible, collected from teachers who leave the profession; but the Board pointed out that it would be unfair to Mr. Peet to exact it in his case, as he had in no sense left the profession, and was carrying on, in a British Colony, the work for which he had been trained. The Board further pointed out that the inevitable tendency of the exaction of such a forfeit in similar cases would be to seriously increase the difficulty of obtaining teachers from Great Britain, and force upon the colonies the necessity of seeking them in the United States of America, where no such rule exists. The Board is glad to record that it was decided not only not to exact the refund in Mr. Peet's case, but also that in the future it should not be demanded in similar cases."

(viii.) *Scholarships and Secondary Education.*

In their report for 1899 the Board of Education state that the average number of boys on the books of the Montego Bay Secondary School for the three terms of the year was 20, an increase of two over the number for the previous year. The Local Board of Management had urged the Board of Education to consent to a reduction in the amount of the fee charged, and in view of the special knowledge of the circumstances possessed by the Local Board, the Board of Education had consented to the change, which, in the belief of the Local Board, would increase the number of scholars and enlarge the revenue of the school.

Assistance to Secondary Education continues to be given in Jamaica in two forms, viz., in an annual subsidy granted by the Legislative Council to the school for boys at Montego Bay, which is the only such school established under the provisions of Law 32 of 1892, and by means of scholarships. Under a new scheme decided upon by the Government before the end of the financial year 1898-9, the number of smaller one-year scholar-ships provided under Law 32 of 1892 has been reduced from 15 to 6, and the Jamaica Scholarship of £200 a year, tenable for three years, which does not depend on that law, has been given in place of one of the £60 scholarships awarded under that law. Mr. Capper, in his report for 1899, expresses the hope that "this change will not retard the rapid advance that has been, and is still, taking place in secondary education in the colony." The report of the Board of Education refers to " the great importance of the Jamaica Scholarship not merely to the holders but on account of the impetus given by it to the education of the middle class in the Island."

The University College and Jamaica High School are main-tained from public funds. Over the several endowed schools the Jamaica Schools Commission exercises general control. And, in addition to these, there are the high schools or grammar schools supported by religious bodies, such as the York Castle

High School (Wesleyan), the Church of England High School (Kingston), etc. (See Jamaica Report for 1898–9, Colonial Reports—Annual, No. 283.)

(ix.) *Remarks of the Superintending Inspector on the Report of the Education Commission.*

In his report for 1898–9, the Superintending Inspector writes as follows with reference to the above report after giving a brief summary of some of its recommendations: "It appears to have been the opinion of some persons that this report would be 'adopted' by the Government and the Legislative Council, and its recommendations put into practice immediately. Such an opinion could not have been entertained if the history and nature of Commissions generally had been better known and understood. Of the recommendations of the very strong Commission of 1886, some have been simply passed over without notice, some were carried into effect six years later, in 1892, and only one or two were dealt with at the time. Such is and must be the fate of the reports of all Commissions. The suggestions and recommendations which such reports contain must stand the test of free and public discussion before it can be shown which of them are practicable and valuable and which are not. Of the former, in nearly every case some only can be dealt with at once, and others have to stand over until the time is ripe for carrying them into effect. Of the recommendations of the present Commission a much larger proportion have been considered and adopted by the Government than was done in the case of the . . . Commission of 1886. The presence on the Board of Education of several members of the Commission is sufficient guarantee that the other recommendations will not be overlooked."

SELECTION OF THE ARTICLES

CONTAINED IN THE

NEW CODE OF REGULATIONS

OF THE

EDUCATION DEPARTMENT

IN FORCE FROM MAY 10, 1900.

PRELIMINARY.

The object of the grant is to maintain, or aid in maintaining—
(a) Elementary Schools, including Trade and Farm Schools ;
(b) Training Colleges for Teachers.

Object of Grant for Public Elementary Education in Jamaica.

PART I.

PUBLIC ELEMENTARY SCHOOLS.

CHAPTER I.—INTRODUCTORY.

DEFINITIONS.

The term "Government School" shall mean a Public Elementary School Government held in a building which is either the property of the Government or placed School. during ordinary school hours at the disposal of the Government, and which is managed by persons appointed by the Department, who constitute the Board of Management and have equal power in the management of the School.

The term "Voluntary School" shall mean a school at present on the list Voluntary of schools in receipt of annual grants managed according to the system School. heretofore existing, the corresponding manager being usually a minister of the religious denomination to which the buildings belong.

The term "Manager" shall include all persons who have the management Manager. of any public elementary school, whether the legal interest in the school is or is not vested in them.

"The Manager" shall mean in a Voluntary School, the Corresponding The Manager. In a Government School it shall mean the Board of Management. Manager.

MANAGEMENT.

5. Every public elementary school shall have, in general, not less than Three three managers, of whom one shall be accepted by the Department as Managers Correspondent and two at least shall if possible be resident in the vicinity. generally The Department may refuse to accept or may require the withdrawal of required. any person as manager whom it considers for any reason unsuitable ; and no teacher of any public elementary school can, under any circumstances, be accepted as a manager of his own or any other such school. In the case of voluntary schools if the Department is satisfied that suitable managers, willing to act and acceptable to the Corresponding Manager, cannot be found in the vicinity of the school, a public elementary school may be recognised though it has less than three managers.

Visitors. 6. When the co-managers are not resident in the vicinity, or where co-managers acceptable to the Corresponding Manager cannot be found, the Corresponding Manager may appoint Visitors, who shall have all the duties of supervision specified under Art. 7. The appointment of any person as Visitor must be at once entered by the Corresponding Manager in the log-book of the school and a notification of the appointment, accompanied by a letter, written by the Visitor, expressing his willingness to act, must be at the same time forwarded to the Department. The Department may require the withdrawal of any person from the position of Visitor whom it may consider for any reason unsuitable.

Duties of Managers. 7. The managers are held responsible by the Department for the conduct and supervision of their schools and their maintenance in efficiency : for the provision of needful furniture, books and apparatus ; for the arrangement of school terms, so that the number of sessions required by this Code may be held ; for fixing the dates on which or between which holidays may be given ; and for the making of all returns required from them by the Department. Supervision includes the payment of a visit to the school during ordinary school hours, sometimes without previous notice, by one at least of the managers or a Visitor at least once in each month, and once in three months, at least, by the Corresponding Manager. At each such monthly visit an entry must be made in the log-book by the Manager or Visitor, as the case may be, giving the date and hour of the visit, number of children present at the time of the visit, the number of children last entered in the attendance register and the date of such entry, and any other particulars that may seem advisable. All such entries should be confined to the statement of facts observed, without any reflections or opinions ; provided that the Corresponding Manager may also add such directions to the teacher as shall seem to be needful. Any serious irregularity must at once be reported to the Department by the Corresponding Manager or the Correspondent.

ATTENDANCE.

Attendance. 17. An "attendance" means attendance at secular instruction during at least two hours after the roll-call is completed [with specified exceptions].

General Age Limits. 18. Except as provided in the two following Articles, no child that has not attained his sixth or that has attained his fourteenth birthday shall be admitted into or retained in any public elementary school.

Older Scholars for whom no grant will be paid. 19. Up to 31st December, 1900, any pupil that has attained his fourteenth but has not attained his sixteenth birthday may, if of the same sex as the principal teacher, be admitted into or retained in any public elementary school, provided that the attendance of such pupil shall not be recorded in the attendance register nor allowed in any way to affect Government grants to the school.

Infant Schools or Departments 20. In schools specially sanctioned by the Governor with a trained Kindergarten mistress or other teacher approved in writing by the Department, children may be received and retained who have attained their fourth but not their eighth birthday ; and grants may be made to such schools on account of the attendance of such children as provided by this Code.

Special Register. 21. In every school in which children are received who have attained their fourteenth birthday, a special register shall be kept for recording the attendance of all such children and the fees collected from them.

Average Attendance. 25. For the average attendance return on the examination class list, as calculated on the schedule, every session need not be taken into account, but only the best sessions at the rate of 24 for each month from the beginning of the month in which the last inspection took place to the end of the month next before the date of the present inspection. When not otherwise implied, "average attendance" in this Code shall mean the average attendance thus calculated. Provided that when the Inspector of a district certifies that it was desirable that the older children of a country school should be absent temporarily to meet special demands for agricultural labour in that school district, and that upon application made to him he had given assent to such absence, the Department may direct that the attendances for a specified continuous period equal to one month may be omitted altogether in calculating average attendance, which will then be calculated upon sessions selected from the remaining part of the year, the number required being for one month less than the school year ; but this will be allowed only where the Department shall be satisfied that the school had been duly kept in operation for the number of sessions required by the Code for the school year, and that during the exempted period the work of teaching the scholars who attended during that period had been faithfully done.

The average attendance at the sewing class, to be entered on the examination class list, must be calculated upon as many sessions of the sewing class as will include a number of hours equal to one-fourth the number of sessions selected as directed in the first part of this Article.

26. The average attendance required for the monthly returns is the number found by dividing the total aggregate number of attendances (exclusive of those on Friday mornings) of all the scholars during the month, by the number of times the school has met during the month (exclusive of Friday sessions). ˙ *Average Attendance for Monthly Returns.*

CHAPTER II.—SCHOOLS ON ANNUAL GRANT LIST.—INSPECTION.

28. Public elementary schools are inspected, and the scholars are examined in the prescribed subjects (Schedule A), and marks are given upon the following scale :— *Scale of Marks.*

I.—STATE OF THE SCHOOL.		
Organization - - - - -	5	10
Discipline - - - - - -	5	
II.—WORK OF THE SCHOOL.		
CHIEF SUBJECTS { Reading and Recitation - - - -	16	48
Writing and English (including Orthography, Composition, Elements of Grammar) - - - - - -	16	
Arithmetic—Mental, and on Slates and Paper - - - - - -	16	
OBLIGATORY SUBJECT { Elementary Science (through Object Lessons, practical illustrations, and simple experiments), having special reference to Agriculture. (See Note 1)		10
SECONDARY SUBJECTS { Scripture and Morals. (See Note 3) - -	5	16
Drawing and Manual Occupations. (See Note 2) - - - - - - -	5	
Geography (with incidental History) - -	3	
Singing - - - - - - - -	3	
		84

SPECIAL SUBJECTS.

(A) Needlework (for all schools as a rule).

(B) { Practical Agriculture and Horticulture.
     Manual Training.

IN INFANT SCHOOLS.

I. - STATE OF THE SCHOOL.

{	Organization - - - - - -	10 }	
	Discipline - - - - - - -	10 }	20

II. WORK OF THE SCHOOL.

{	(A) - *Work of a Kindergarten nature;*		
	Manual work (including Drawing) -	8 }	
	Songs and Kindergarten Games -	8 }	24
	Nature Study and Home Geography	}	
	(taught through conversational		
	lessons and Object Lessons) -	8 }	

(B)—Scripture and Morals - - - -	—	6

{	(C)—*Chief Elementary Subjects :*		
	Reading and Recitation - - -	12 }	
	Writing and English (oral and written)	12 }	34
	Arithmetic—Mental and on Slate -	10 }	

                                           84

NOTES.

1. *Obligatory Subject.*—Until teachers have had opportunity to more fully qualify themselves to teach this subject, a faithful, intelligent use of the Tropical Readers will enable teachers to meet the requirements as regards the subject to a degree that will be deemed satisfactory. As soon as such opportunity shall have been afforded to any teacher a thorough teaching of the subject will be required from him.

2. *Drawing and Manual Occupations.*—Until schools can be prepared for the work in "Manual Occupations," full marks can be earned by excellence in Drawing alone; but where Drawing falls below the highest excellence, any degree of success that may be attained in Manual Occupations will receive due credit in awarding marks for this subject.

3. The marks for discipline having been increased, a larger degree of credit can be given for the practical result of efficient instruction in Morals, as shown in the conduct of the children.

4. In Infant Schools it will not be required that children under six years of age be examined in the chief elementary subjects, but upon the express request of the teacher, children not under five and a half years may be so examined. The efficiency of the instruction given to children under six years will be estimated by the exhibit of work done and such exercises in the presence of the Inspector as shall be selected by the teacher and conducted by her or under her direction. These exercises, and the specimens of work shown, and the work done at inspection under the direction of the teacher, will indicate to the Inspector the merit and success of the methods used to make the little children acquainted with Language, Number, Colour and Form, and to develop in them a degree of self-activity, and to impress upon them fundamental principles of right conduct.

5. First class schools which have obtained 65 marks or upward in three successive years, shall be fully examined only in alternate years, if the staff remains substantially the same; provided that the Department shall order the inspection if it considers it necessary. Notice of the intention to omit the annual inspection will be given by the Department with the report for the previous year.

29a. If the Department shall consider that any school on the Annual Cessation of Grant List is, on account of proximity to other schools, shifting of the Grants-in-population, improvement of means of communication, or for any other aid. reason unnecessary, or that the cost of such school to the Government is, under existing circumstances, out of proportion to its usefulness, a report from the Department to that effect shall be laid before the Board of Education ; and the Board of Education shall, at the next meeting after that at which the report is received, forward it to the Governor with its recommendations and advice. The Governor may then, in his discretion, remove the said school from the annual grant list, provided that, except in the case of schools to which a provisional notice of cessation of grants has been issued at a time when they (a) were not in operation, (b) had been for three months of the current school year and were still in charge of an unregistered teacher, or (c) were not, after due notice, ready for inspection, three months' notice shall be given of the cessation of grants to any school.

29b. i. When any school is removed from the annual grant list under the How provisions of Art. 29a, the Department may make such requirements of the neighbouring managers of neighbouring voluntary schools as shall secure either (i.) the Managers are appointment of the manager of the said school to be a manager of a affected. neighbouring school, or (ii.) the amalgamation of two or more voluntary schools into one Government school ; and any voluntary school whose manager fails to comply with such requirements may be removed from the annual grant list.

ii. When a Government school is held in a building not the property of Government, the Government, the building shall be placed at the disposal of the Schools. Government during the ordinary school hours. In such case there shall be Grant to keep paid, by way of nominal rent, to be used in keeping the building and premises in premises in fit condition for school purposes, a sum of money at the rate of fit condition. one shilling per annum per unit of average attendance. Beyond this the Limit of re-Government assumes no financial responsibility in connection with a sponsibility. Government school, other than what is provided in the Code for public elementary schools.

29c. So long as Roman Catholic Schools at present on the Annual Grant Roman List meet such requirements as are laid down in the Code for exceptional Catholic schools in districts sparsely populated and difficult of access, and in Schools. Kingston and Spanish Town have further not less than 80 in average attendance, they shall be retained on the said annual grant list, and aided as at present ; provided that if any such school has less than fifty scholars in average attendance the grant to such school per unit of average attendance shall not exceed the grant per unit that would have been earned had the said school had an average attendance of fifty : and provided also that nothing in this Article shall prevent the amalgamation of Roman Catholic schools with one another.

29d. No denominational school which meets the requirements of the Code Consent to as regards ordinary or exceptional schools shall be amalgamated with another Amalgama-denominational school without the consent of the manager or managers tion. concerned.

30. No new voluntary school shall be placed on the annual grant list ; and Application no new Government School shall be placed on the said list until it has been for Grants-in-declared necessary by the Governor, after the matter has been submitted to aid for new the Board of Education for its consideration and advice. The question Schools. whether a proposed new school is necessary may either be brought before the Board by the Department, or by an application made, in the form pre-scribed, to the Secretary of the Board, signed by all ministers of religion having a place of worship within four miles, by ordinary roads, of the proposed site, and stating that they are willing to act as managers of the proposed school, and jointly and severally to fulfil all the requirements of Arts. 5 to 9 of the Code. If the Board of Education decide that, having regard to the population of the district and the free school accommodation already provided, the proposed school is necessary, the Department may, if the Governor so direct, take steps to establish a Government school, and make such advance to it as the circumstances may justify.

Trust Schools.   30c. All public elementary schools in connection with Trusts, under the supervision of the Schools Commission, shall be considered Government Schools, and the managers appointed according to the regulations governing the Trust shall be recognised as the Managers of the Schools as if appointed by the Department.   Provided that such Trust Schools shall not be entitled to the grant to Government Schools on account of rent under Article 29b.

CHAPTER III.--TEACHERS.

Classes of Teachers.   37. No teacher is recognised by the Department whose name is not on one of the registers of teachers kept by the Department, under one of the following heads :—A. Teachers not qualified to take charge of a school, viz.—(i.) Pupil-teachers (ii.) Additional teachers ; B. Teachers qualified to take charge of a school, viz.—(i.) Uncertificated teachers (ii.) Certificated teachers.

Employment of Teachers.   38. Teachers are employed by the managers and not by the Department. Managers and teachers shall make their own agreements as to salary and other details, subject to the provisions of the Code, and it is desirable that such agreements should in all cases be in writing. In accordance with Section 25 of the Elementary Education Law, 1892, the terms of the agreement with the teacher or teachers of the school under this or the succeeding Article must be stated in the returns required by Article 122.

Condition of engagement.   39. It shall not be required as a condition of the engagement of any teacher, unless in a separate agreement, that he shall perform any duties unconnected with his work as an elementary school teacher.

Termination of engagement.   40. Unless for grave misconduct, no engagement between manager and teacher shall be terminable, except by mutual consent, at less than three calendar months' notice on either side given at any time. Such notice must in every case be in writing.

PUPIL-TEACHERS.

Definition.   41. A pupil-teacher is a boy or girl engaged by the manager of a public elementary school on condition of teaching in the school under the superintendence of the principal teacher and receiving suitable instruction. Such pupil-teachers shall not be considered to be scholars in such schools, nor be subject to the limitations of Article 18.

Where they may be employed.   42. In every public elementary school having an average attendance of not less than 60, in charge of a qualified teacher, one or more pupil-teachers may be employed, and grants will be made on their behalf, subject to the following requirements.

Qualification for training them.   43. A qualified teacher for the purpose of Articles 41-60 is one who (i.) has completed the required course at a recognised training college and has passed the Government examination at the end of such course ; or (ii.) holds a Jamaica or British Government certificate or other certificate approved by the Superintending Inspector of Schools ; or (iii.) has passed a school first class at least at the preceding Government inspection, having been in charge of it for not less than six months ; or (iv.) has twice passed a school second class at least in the last two years.

Number recognised.   44. The number of pupil-teachers shall not exceed two for a registered principal teacher, and one for each registered assistant. In a school with an average attendance of 60 there may be one pupil-teacher, and in a school having an average attendance of 90, where there is not an Additional Teacher, there may be a second pupil-teacher.

Age and Attainments.   45. No pupil-teacher can be engaged under these rules :—

(i.) who at the time of entering upon engagement as a first year pupil-teacher is less than thirteen or more than seventeen years of age ;

(ii.) who has not been for six months, previous to engagement, in at least the fifth standard in reading and writing and in arithmetic ;

(iii.) who does not possess good health (including freedom from any infirmity likely to interfere with the profession of teaching), good moral character, and aptitude to teach.

46. Every pupil-teacher on engagement must, in conjunction with his **Engagement** parent or guardian, enter into an agreement with the manager of the school in which he is to be employed, in the form prescribed (in duplicate), as issued by the Department, and the duplicate copy of such agreement must be forwarded to the Superintending Inspector of Schools. The engagement of a pupil-teacher must begin on January 1st, and the memorandum of agreement must be signed before that date. Provided that in the case of a vacancy occurring in the number of pupil-teachers, or for any other special reason, engagements may, with the permission of the Department, begin on a date other than January 1st. In such case the year of service shall be considered to begin on the first of the month next after the signing of the agreement.

During the year 1900 engagements may also begin on April 1st, July 1st or October 1st.

47. The length of the engagement is ordinarily four years, but may be **Length of** three, two, or one, provided that (*a*) the candidate passes before engage- **Engagement.** ment the examination fixed for the first, second, or third year, respectively ; and (*b*) the end of the reduced term of service falls beyond the completion of the candidate's seventeenth year, and before the completion of his twenty-first year.

48. From the date of engagement every pupil-teacher, besides constant **Instruction** supervision and training during school hours, must receive not less than **and Super-** four hours' special, separate and personal instruction from the teacher, out **vision.** of the ordinary school hours, in every week that the school has been open, of which four hours not more than two shall be part of the same day. This shall not, however, prevent the formation of combination classes in towns, and other districts where such arrangements are practicable and are sanctioned by the Department.

49. Pupil-teachers should, as a rule, be of the same sex as the principal **Conditions** teacher of the school in which they are engaged. In cases where the **when they** teacher and pupil-teacher are of different sexes some other person or **are not of the** persons, approved of by the manager, must on every occasion be present for **same sex as** the whole time during which this special instruction is being given. **the teacher.**

50. The Department is not a party to the engagement, and will confine **Department** itself to ascertaining whether the prescribed conditions are fulfilled. **not a party to Engagement.**

51. A pupil-teacher who has been employed in any school agreeably to **Completion** these regulations may be allowed, at the discretion of the Superintending **of Engage-** Inspector of Schools, to complete the period of his engagement in that **ment.** school and to receive the usual grants, even though it should subsequently have become ineligible from loss of class or from falling off in average attendance.

52. A pupil-teacher may be transferred from one school to another, pro- **Change of** vided that the circumstance be reported to the Department, and the condi- **School.** tions laid down in the Code as to the attendance and staff of the school complied with. If the teacher of a school in which a pupil-teacher is employed agreeably to these regulations leaves the school during the currency of the said pupil-teacher's engagement, such engagement can only be continued at the same school if the new teacher is qualified in accordance with the requirements of Article 43, or under written permission from the Superintending Inspector of Schools.

53. At the termination of their engagements pupil-teachers are free to **At termina** choose their employment. **tion of Engagement.**

Examination   54. An examination of pupil-teachers in public elementary schools, and others, will be held annually on the third Friday in July in each year, or on such other day or days as may be fixed by previous notice in the "Jamaica Gazette." The examination will extend to the subjects specified in Schedule D. A pupil-teacher who fails to pass his examination may be presented once more only, at the next subsequent pupil-teachers' examination, in the same standard. If he then passes, the actual year of service in which the examination takes place will be considered the year for which he shall receive the grant provided in Article 59, but if he fails a second time he will cease to be recognised by the Department as a member of the school staff. No pupil-teacher under engagement shall be admitted to the second, third, or fourth year examination respectively until he has passed the previous examination.

Time and place of Examination   55. Application to be admitted to the examination must be made, in the form prescribed, on behalf of each pupil-teacher, by the teacher of the school in which the pupil-teacher is employed. Application for forms of entry must be addressed to the Superintending Inspector of Schools not later than May 21st, and the forms of entry must be returned not later than May 31st. Late applications may be received by the Department, provided that the arrangements for conducting the examination are not so far advanced as to make this impracticable. In the case of every such application a sum not exceeding £1, to be fixed by the Department, at its discretion, will be deducted from the next advance to the school from which the pupil-teacher is presented, and charged against the Merit Grant.

Conditions for a Pass.   56. Pupil-teachers will be considered to have passed the examination who are fairly proficient in reading and teaching; and who obtain one-half of the total number of marks attainable in Writing and English, Arithmetic, Elementary Science and Agriculture, and, in the case of fourth year pupil-teachers, in the written examination in Teaching; and one-third of the total marks attainable in Scripture, Geography including History, Drawing, and Manual Occupations, and in the written examination in Teaching, respectively.

Conditions for a Grant.   57. Every pupil-teacher engaged under these regulations shall, during the currency of his engagement, attend for the whole of every session of the school in which he is engaged, unless certified to be unable to do so from illness or other urgent cause. If this is certified in the case of every absence from school, a deduction proportionate to the number of sessions he has been absent shall be made from the grants awarded under Articles 59 and 60. If this cannot be certified in the case of every absence, the whole or any portion of the grants under the said Articles may be withheld at the discretion of the Department. He shall not be required to teach during the last hour of any afternoon session, and shall have that hour for joining in the Reading, Science, or other lessons given to the highest standard, or for private study.

Record of Instruction.   58. A clear and distinct record must be kept by the teacher of the attendance of the pupil-teacher at the school, and the hours and subjects of special instruction. This record must also show the reasons for the pupil-teacher's absence from any school session.

Payment for Instruction of Pupil-teachers.   59. i. For every pupil-teacher who passes the first, second, third, or fourth year annual examination, the following payment will be made to the manager of the school on the completion of the corresponding year of service, provided that the conditions laid down in these regulations are complied with. Such payment will be made on the receipt by the Superintending Inspector of Schools of an application for the same, in the form prescribed, as issued by the Department, signed by the manager and teacher. This certificate must be dated as on the last day of the year of service, and all the particulars must have reference to that year, and that year only.

		£	s.	d.
Payment for the First Year - - - -	-	2	0	0
,, ,, Second Year - - -	-	3	0	0
,, ,, Third Year - - -	-	4	0	0
,, ,, Fourth Year - - -	-	5	0	0

ii. For every pupil-teacher who, having first passed the first year Pupil Teachers' Examination, has completed his year of service with credit, and who has during the year sat for the corresponding examination but has failed to pass it, not having failed in more than two subjects, a grant not exceeding half the above may, at the discretion of the Department, be made on the receipt of a certificate of good character and service from the manager of the school at the close of the calendar year in which the examination has taken place.

60. A payment shall be made to the teacher for the instruction of every Payment for pupil-teacher who passes his examination (whether the first, second, third, Instruction or fourth year) provided such instruction has been duly given and recorded of Pupil-daily in accordance with Art. 58, at the rate of £3 for one pupil-teacher and teachers. £1 10s. for each additional pupil-teacher taught in the same school. If the number of hours of instruction given has been less than is required by Art. 48, this payment may be withheld or reduced, at the discretion of the Department. In the case of combination classes (Art. 48) the expense of any such arrangement must be met from this grant.

61. Of the candidates who pass the fourth year examination, the four Government who stand highest on the list and who enter a recognised training college Exhibi-the following January, will be styled Government exhibitioners. For each tioners. of the four on their entering such a training college and at the termination of each year of their residence in such training college, on the production of a certificate of good conduct from the principal, the sum of five pounds will be paid to such principal. The first sum of five pounds is to be applied to defraying the entrance fee to the college, and the subsequent payments are for the exhibitioner's personal expenses.

62. Volunteer candidates, whether or not they are scholars in any public Volunteer elementary school, on whose behalf a fee of 5s. has been lodged in the Candidates. Treasury and a receipt for the same sent to the Superintending Inspector of Schools on or before the date fixed by the Department in each year, accom-panied by a statement in each case of the name, age, and school, if any, of the candidate, the year, whether first, second, third, or fourth, for which he desires to take papers, and the centre at which he will attend, in the form prescribed, will be examined in the same way as the pupil-teachers, but first, second, and third year candidates shall not be examined in teaching. Candidates presented from public elementary schools for the first or second year examination are required to present a certificate showing that they have been for six months in at least the fifth standard in reading and writing and in arithmetic.

ADDITIONAL TEACHERS.

63. In mixed, girls', and infant schools, a woman over eighteen years of Additional age, whose character and attainments satisfy the Department and who is Teachers. employed during the whole of the school hours in the general instruction of the scholars and in teaching needlework, will, if her engagement be expressly sanctioned in writing by the Department, be recognised as an additional woman teacher. In schools for boys only an additional male teacher may be employed on like terms and conditions, except as to teaching needlework.

REGISTRATION OF TEACHERS.

64. All persons of at least 18 years of age who produce satisfactory Registration. certificates of good character and (a) have spent at least one year at a recognised training college, or (b) have passed the Cambridge Senior, or

London Matriculation, or other examination recognised by the Department will on application be provisionally registered as teachers and recognised by the Department. Such provisional registration and recognition will continue for three years from the date of such recognition, after which period they will, on application, be permanently placed on the register if they are recommended by an Inspector as showing practical ability in teaching, and on passing an examination in the subjects specified in Schedule C, unless they have already passed the same or an equivalent or higher examination. If they are not so recommended the term of provisional recognition may be extended, at the discretion of the Department, beyond the period of three years for a further period not exceeding two years if it seems probable that they will, during the further period of probation, acquire such practical ability. In special cases, upon application made to the Department and leave granted, the examination qualifying for permanent registration may be taken after two years of teaching instead of three. Students on leaving a training college at the close of their course are registered permanently, if they have passed the second year examination,—provisionally, if they have not passed that examination.

> Until further notice the passing of the Fourth Year Pupil-Teachers' Examination will be recognised by the Department as entitling a teacher to provisional registration under (b).

Qualifications for Teachers of Infant Schools or departments.
65. No person is allowed to take charge of an Infant school or department except (a) a trained and certificated Kindergarten mistress, or (b) a Teacher eligible for the position of Principal or Assistant Teacher of a Public Elementary School, who, under arrangements to be made by the Department, shall sit for and shall pass the First Year Training College Examination in Infant Teaching, and who shall produce a certificate satisfactory to the Superintending Inspector of Schools from the Kindergarten Mistress of the Board School in Kingston, or from some other person authorised by the Department to give such certificate, that such teacher has practical ability in the use of gifts III. and IV. and four at least of the occupations specified in the Training College curriculum, and has shown aptitude in gaining the attention of little children and instructing them. Persons qualified under (a) and, for the present and until further provisions are made for training Kindergarten Mistresses, those qualified under (b) shall be deemed to meet the requirements of the Department under Art. 20 ; provided that in exceptional cases a teacher who fails to fully meet the requirements above specified may at the discretion of the Department be permitted to take charge of an Infant School or department for a limited period not exceeding twelve months.

CERTIFICATED TEACHERS.

Certificates after full College Course.
66. Every teacher who has passed the third year training college examination (Art. 156) as a student, and who has subsequently served for two years in public elementary schools or in a training college, whose character is good, and who has been favourably reported on by an Inspector in each such year of service, will receive, on application, a certificate. If he has passed in honours, that fact will be stated on the certificate.

Certificates otherwise obtained.
66a. Every teacher who in December, 1900, or at any subsequent date, shall have passed the second year's training college examination and subsequently for three years served as described in Art. 66, and with a like favourable report, and who shall pass the third year's examination having spent not less than three months immediately preceding the examination in a training college, will receive on [application a certificate. If a teacher fulfils the above conditions, except the three months' additional course in a training college and passing the third year's examination, he may then, after four years of further service in one of which his school shall pass first class, he having been in charge of it for at least six months, upon application receive a certificate ; provided that, in exceptional cases, the Department may grant a certificate although the condition as to passing his school first class has not been fulfilled.

67. Registered uncertificated teachers (whether permanently or pro- Examination visionally registered) whose schools have taken at least a second class, of Teachers whether under their charge or in which they were teaching as members of for Certifi- the school staff at the previous inspection, may be examined with the third cates. year students at the training college examination in December, if the Superintending Inspector of Schools is satisfied of their good character and competency.

68. The conditions for a pass will be the same as for third year training Conditions college students (Articles 163 and 164), with for the present the following for a Pass. modifications : only a first year's course in Geometry will be required, and a pass will not be insisted on in Algebra, Manual Training, and Drawing.

69. Application for the admission of teachers to the third year training Application college examination must be made to the Superintending Inspector of for admission Schools not later than October 1st in each year, stating the centre at which for examina- the applicant wishes to attend. tion.

70. As soon after the examination as possible a list of the successful Pass List. candidates will be published in the "Jamaica Gazette."

71. Teachers who pass the examination will receive a certificate, so soon Certificates, as they have been continuously engaged in teaching in public elementary without full schools for four years (whether before, or after, or partly before and partly College after the examination) if their schools have passed at least in the second course. class at the last two inspections. If a candidate passes in honours that fact will be stated on his certificate.

CHARGES OF MISCONDUCT AGAINST TEACHERS.

72. If a manager or visitor of a public elementary school hears that a Investigation teacher employed in such school is charged with serious professional mis- by Manager. conduct of any kind, or with any grave moral offence, it shall be his duty, if not himself the corresponding manager, to at once inform the correspond- ing manager. It shall be the duty of the corresponding manager in any such case, if he considers that the circumstances justify it, or if such a charge be brought to his notice by the Department, to hold such investiga- tion as he deems under the circumstances to be necessary (giving full opportunity to the teacher to defend himself), and to report the details and result without unnecessary delay to the Department. If the Department is satisfied, whether from such report, with or without further information, or after inviting and considering any answer to such charge that may be made by the accused teacher, that any such charge against a teacher is clearly proved, or if the accused has admitted his guilt in writing, or in the presence of witnesses, the accused's name shall be struck off the register and his certificate, if he has one, shall be suspended. On this decision being communicated to the manager of the school the teacher shall, unless the manager in the exercise of his discretion have already dismissed him, be summarily dismissed. In any case both he and the manager shall be informed without delay of the decision of the Department in the case.

73. i. When a teacher in a public elementary school is charged by the Official In- manager or other responsible person with the commission of any such vestigation. offences as are referred to in the preceding article, the Superintending Inspector of Schools will, if he considers that a prima facie case has been made out, but that the accused's guilt is not clearly proved, send to the accused a registered letter stating the nature of the charge and asking whether he admits that he is guilty, or demands an official enquiry. If an enquiry is demanded, the Inspector for the district will appoint a day and place for holding such enquiry (for which it shall be the duty of the manager to afford every facility) and will give ten days' notice by registered letter (the notice counting from the date of registration) both to accuser and accused, who will be expected to appear at the enquiry and produce their witnesses. When possible the Inspector will secure that two managers of schools, not interested in the case under investigation, shall sit with him at the enquiry. At its conclusion he will make a report to the Department giving the evidence and stating his views and those of the managers, if any, who sat

with him ; upon which, if in the opinion of the Department the charge is substantiated, the teacher's name will be struck off the register, and in the case of a certificated teacher his certificate will be suspended. The decision arrived at will be communicated to the teacher and the manager without delay.

ii. If the letter stating the charge remains unanswered for two weeks from the date of its registration, the accused's name will be provisionally struck off the register. If at any subsequent time the accused satisfies the Department that through no fault of his own he did not receive the letter, an enquiry may be then held as above at the discretion of the Superintending Inspector of Schools.

iii. The Department may, at its discretion, appoint some other officer to take the place of the Inspector for the district, or may hold the investigation in Kingston.

Reinstatement.

74. When a teacher is informed by the Department that his name has been struck off the register, he shall be at the same time informed after what interval, if at all, he may apply for reinstatement. Such an application must be supported by at least two certificates from responsible persons as to the teacher's life and character (one, at least, if possible, being from a minister of religion), between them covering the whole period during which his name has been off the register, and showing how his time has been occupied. On receipt of such an application, so supported, the Superintending Inspector of Schools may, in his discretion, replace the teacher's name on the register, with such restrictions, if any, as to the locality in which the teacher may again take charge of a school, or on any other point, as he may deem necessary, and may at the same time, or after any such further period of probation as he may deem necessary, reissue the teacher's certificate, if he have possessed one. The decision arrived at will be communicated to the teacher, and a statement of the facts entered in the register.

Temporary exclusion from the Register.

75. A teacher who leaves any school without due notice to, or the consent of, the manager, or who fails to take charge of any school, in violation of his written agreement so to do, and without the consent of the manager to whom he has engaged himself, or who fails to leave a school when summarily dismissed by the manager or at the expiration of due notice, or who on leaving a school, or at any other time upon demand made by the manager, fails to hand over to the manager, in good order, the school records entered up to date, maps, and other school appliances, will, when reported by the manager, have his name taken off the register for a period not exceeding six months, or, at the discretion of the Department, until such records, maps or appliances are returned or replaced. The Department may, as above, make such restrictions as appear desirable as to the locality in which the teacher may again take charge of a school.

Information as to Status of Teachers.

76. Managers can ascertain the status of any teacher, as affected by this Code, so far as the facts are known to the Department, upon application to the Superintending Inspector of Schools, but they will in all cases be presumed to be in possession of all information which could have been obtained from the manager of the school in which such teacher has been employed, and if they engage him without reference to such manager, do so at their own risk.

School Staff.

77. The recognised teachers in any school form the school staff.

Minimum Staff.

79. In estimating the minimum school staff required the Department considers a principal teacher to be sufficient for an average attendance of 80, each assistant teacher for an additional average of 70, each additional teacher approved under Article 63 for an additional average of 50, and each pupil-teacher for an additional average of 30 ; except that where there is an additional teacher or an assistant teacher, the first pupil-teacher shall be considered sufficient for an additional average of 10. Before an engagement of an assistant or additional teacher is entered into the sanction of the Department must first be obtained.

CHAPTER IV.—ANNUAL GRANT.

81. The conditions required to be fulfilled by a public elementary school General
in order to obtain an annual grant are those set forth in this Code. Conditions.

82. The school must submit to inspection when required, comply with all Inspection
the regulations of the Department and make all the returns called for by and returns.
the Department.

83. Except in vacation time, or during special interruptions of school School days.
work morning and afternoon school shall be held on the first four
working days of every week in every public elementary school, and on
Friday morning school shall be held in every public elementary school
in the city of Kingston and in the towns of Annotto Bay, Black River,
Brown's Town, Buff Bay, Falmouth, Half-way Tree, Linstead, Lucea,
Manchioneal, Mandeville, Montego Bay, Morant Bay, Old Harbour,
Oracabessa, Port Antonio, Port Maria, Porus, St. Ann's Bay, Savanna-
la-Mar and Spanish Town ; but no pressure shall be put upon any children
residing outside the limits of the places named to make them attend school
on Friday if it appears that their parents require their services. School
may, however, be held in any public elementary school in the morning or
afternoon of any working day.

84. The usual hours of school shall be not less than three in the morning School hours.
and two in the afternoon. School shall in every case be held for two full
hours after each roll-call, but the time-table must provide that infants and
scholars of 1st and 2nd Standards shall have recess during each session of
not more than twenty minutes, and the other scholars recess of not more
than ten minutes ; provided that the scholars dismissed from school at the
expiration of one hour after the afternoon roll-call, need not have recess in
the afternoon session.

85. The annual grant-in-aid to the school must be applied only for the Application
purposes of public elementary schools. This must not include any outlay of Grant.
on the premises beyond the cost of ordinary repairs, nor for any other
purpose not recognised by the Department as educational.

86. No child suffering from yaws, or other contagious or infectious Infectious
disease, shall be admitted into or retained in any public elementary school. Diseases.

87. No person unauthorised by the Department is allowed to be present Persons
in a schoolroom during school time ; provided that visitors occasional or allowed to be
regular, besides those specified in Art. 6, interested in educational questions, present in
may be admitted by the teacher or introduced by a manager ; provided also School.
that assistants (unrecognised by the Department) of the same sex as the
teacher and not less than 14 years of age may be regularly engaged with the
sanction of the Inspector for the district, but may not receive instruction
during school time ; except that such assistants, under 16 years of age, may
join in the work of the highest Standard during the last hour of the afternoon session ; and except also that the limitation as to sex shall not
prevent a teacher from employing his own wife or daughter as an unrecognised assistant, provided that the other requirements of the Article
are met.

88. No child otherwise eligible may be refused admission as a scholar to Refusal of
any public elementary school in which there is available accommodation, Admission.
or may be excluded from such school on other than reasonable grounds,
such as persistent misconduct, insubordination, or the like. The final
decision as to whether the grounds of refusal in any particular case are
reasonable shall rest with the Superintending Inspector of Schools.

89. All public elementary schools must be classified in accordance with Wall Sheets
the Standards and Divisions of Schedule A. A copy of the time-table must to be put up
be presented to the Inspector at the annual inspection, together with a in the School.
detailed statement showing the number of hours per week (or month) given
to each subject in each Standard ; and the work of the school must
regularly be conducted according to the time-table. A copy of the time-
table and the conscience clause must be kept posted in a conspicuous place
in the school.

Superfluous Schools.

90. No school shall receive a grant-in-aid, the establishment of which is considered superfluous by reason of the existence of another available school in the vicinity or of any other valid objection.

"The vicinity" in this regulation shall mean, in general, except in towns and large village centres, within a distance of three miles by any practicable road.

Minimum Average.

·91· No school shall receive any grant-in-aid unless the average attendance is not less than thirty or in the towns named in Article 83 not less sixty ; provided that in the case of schools on the annual grant list which are inspected for the first time, and schools which are situated in districts sparsely populated and difficult of access, schools may be recognised if the average attendance is not less than twenty.

Managers responsible for expenses.

94. The managers shall be responsible for the payment of teachers and all other expenses of the school.

Temporary employment of un-registered Teachers.

96. No school shall, except as herein provided, receive a grant-in-aid for any month in any part of which it is not in charge of a registered teacher. Nevertheless, a school previously in receipt of annual grants may continue to receive them for an interval or intervals not exceeding three months in all in any school year, during the temporary absence of the teacher in consequence of illness or other unavoidable cause, or between the leaving of one and the coming of another teacher qualified under this Code to have charge of it, provided the school is kept open under a temporary teacher approved by the Department and the other regulations of the Code are observed during the interval or intervals.

Number of sessions required.

97. No school shall receive a grant-in-aid unless it shall have met for a number of sessions during the school year not less in the aggregate than twenty-eight, or thirty where Friday sessions are required, for every month therein. Allowance may be made for any unavoidable circumstances occurring to prevent this, when such are satisfactorily explained to the Superintending Inspector of Schools ; but the plea of rainy weather, unless such weather has been altogether exceptional in the district, will not be accepted. The explanation of any deficiency must be made in writing, and handed to the Inspector at the inspection. A deduction may be made from the grant-in-aid, at the discretion of the Superintending Inspector of Schools, for any deficiency in the number of sessions.

Report of Inspector.

98. No school shall receive a grant-in-aid which has not been visited and reported on by an Inspector during the school year unless a continued epidemic or other cause accepted as sufficient by the Department prevent such visit and report.

Conditions.

99. The Department must be satisfied—

Premises.

(i.) that the school buildings are properly constructed, are supplied with suitable offices and contain sufficient accommodation (in general not less than 8 square feet per unit of average attendance) for the scholars attending the school. (This sub-section is not intended to prohibit managers from fixing with the approval of the Department a higher minimum of accommodation than 8 square feet per unit of average attendance in any school.)

Staff, furniture and Apparatus.

(ii.) that the school has a sufficient staff (see Art. 79) and is properly provided with furniture, books, maps and other apparatus of elementary instruction ;

Registers and Accounts.

(iii.) that the admission and daily attendance of the scholars are carefully registered by the principal teacher or under his supervision by some member of the recognised staff, not being a pupil-teacher, and periodically verified by the manager ;

(iv.) that the book of school accounts contains an accurate record of income and expenditure, and that all returns may be accepted as trustworthy ;

(v.) that the teachers are not allowed to undertake duties not con- Employment nected with the school which occupy any part of the school hours, of Teachers. or of the time appointed for the special instruction of pupil-teachers.

99a. In the case of an Infant School or Infant Department the Super- In case of intending Inspector of Schools must be further satisfied that the school- Infant room and premises, the furniture and appliances are sufficient and suitable Schools. for an Infant School in which a portion of the work done will be of a Kindergarten nature.

100. The Inspector will bear in mind in recommending the grant the Visits with-result of any visits without any notice made in the course of the school out notice. year.

101. In cases where any of the conditions of annual grants set forth in Power to this Code (except such conditions as are specially imposed by the warn instead Education Law) are found not to have been fulfilled, the Department shall of withhold-have power, after considering all the circumstances, to pay the whole or a ing grant. portion of the grant, either at once or when such conditions are complied with, and give a warning to the managers that the grant may be withheld next year.

102. Schools deserving of a grant-in-aid will be marked by the Inspector Classification and ranked as schools of the first, second or third class. The classification of Schools. will be decided not by the size but by the quality of the school, that is to say, by the amount and character of the work done, and this will be measured by a set of standards applied to each branch of instruction and school management by the Inspectors at their annual inspection of the school (see Schedule A).

103. To have a place in the third class a school must obtain 30 marks or Classes of more, including at least a third of the aggregate marks in the chief Schools. subjects and at least five marks in each of them, and also three marks in the obligatory subject and three marks in the aggregate for Organization and Discipline. To have a place in the second class a school must obtain at least 42 marks, at least eight marks being obtained for each of the chief subjects, and at least four marks in the obligatory subject, and at least five marks in the aggregate for Organization and Discipline, and at least two marks in each of them ; to have a place in the first class a school must obtain at least 56 marks, including at least two-thirds of the maximum aggregate marks in the chief subjects and at least ten marks in each of them and at least five marks in the obligatory subjects and at least seven marks of the maximum aggregate for Organization and Discipline and at least three marks in each of them ; provided that after Jan. 1st, 1903, the marks in the obligatory subject required for a pass will be 4, 5, and 6 respectively in 3rd, 2nd and 1st class schools.

104. If any school at its annual inspection fails to obtain the minimum Failure at number of marks or average qualifying it for a grant-in-aid under this Inspection. Code, no further payment of any kind shall be made for the school year then concluded, and after three months' notice, during which the school shall receive such reduced advances as the Department may determine, it may either be struck off the annual grant list in accordance with the provisions of Art. 29a, or, if the Department considers the school a necessary one, may be retained on the list, and reduced advances may be paid of such amount and on such conditions as the Department may think proper, until the school can be again inspected. Provided that the Superintending Inspector of Schools shall make a quarterly return to the Governor of the particulars of all cases in which this discretion has been exercised, indicating the reason in each case.

106. A grant of not more than sixpence for each pupil in average Appliances attendance will be available for keeping up the supply of school materials Grant. and appliances. In order to take advantage of this grant, a form supplied by the Department, showing what is required for the new school year, must be presented to the Inspector on the day of inspection, to be forwarded to the Department. When approved, the necessary arrangements for the

execution of the order will be made by the Department. Until announce-ment is duly made in the *Gazette* that the Government will grant the larger sum, the grant under this Article will be threepence for each pupil in average attendance.

School Library Grant. 106a. A grant will be available to a limited extent to aid, at the discretion of the Department, in the purchase of books for the beginning of a School Library, where the manager has already in hand not less than twenty shillings available for this purpose ; provided that the Department must be satisfied that the books selected are suitable, and provided also that, ordinarily, the grant to a school under this Article will not exceed twenty shillings and in no case shall exceed 50 per cent. of the cost of the books.

Aid to Infant schools when first established. 106b. A grant not exceeding £4 may be given at the discretion of the Department, instead of the appliances grant above provided for, and according to the special needs in each case, to assist the Manager of an Infant School during its first year in providing it with suitable Kindergarten appliances as shall be approved by the Department.

Merit Grant. 107. In schools in which the average attendance is not less than 80, the merit grant will be at the rate of one pound for each mark obtained on inspection ; or if the average attendance is less than 80, at the rate of fifteen shillings, together with one penny for every unit of such average attendance over 20, for each mark obtained on inspection ; provided that in third class schools 10s. a mark only will be paid for each mark over 41, and in second-class schools 10s. only for each mark over 55. This grant is to be paid by the manager to the teacher without deductions unless in accordance with a written agreement previously approved by the Department.

Sewing Grant. 109. In all schools where a woman teacher is on the ordinary staff needle-work must regularly be taught ; and if in such case this be neglected the Department may discontinue advances for the woman teacher so long as such neglect continues. To schools in which there is no woman teacher on the ordinary staff and in which girls are satisfactorily taught sewing in accordance with Schedule A, an allowance will be given of one shilling or one shilling and sixpence according to the quality of the work, for each girl so taught, calculated on the average number of girls attending the sewing class. To every school in which the instruction is in strict accordance with the Code, and the work done is of exceptional excellence, a bonus at the rate of £1, £2, or £3 per annum may be recommended by the Inspectress of Needlework according to the excellence of the work and the size of the school.

Grant for Sewing Materials. 109a. When the Corresponding Manager of a school shall certify that the sewing class has been taught regularly for the three preceding months, and that such teaching is to be continued, and that aid is needed to keep the class supplied with necessary sewing materials, the Department may grant to such manager a sum of money equal to threepence per unit of average attendance of the sewing class, to be used in the course of the school year by the sewing mistress as an aid towards providing such materials. If, in any such case, the school shall be entitled at the end of the school year to receive a sewing grant (either ordinary or bonus), the amount sent as aid as aforesaid shall be deducted from the amount of such sewing grant.

Sessions of Sewing Class. 110. The sewing class must have been held during the school year for a number of hours equal in the aggregate to at least six times the number of calendar months therein, provided that it be not held in any case for less than one and a half or for more than two hours in any one day, nor for less than six in any month during which the school has been in continuous operation. A deduction will in any case be made from the grant for any deficiency in the aggregate number of hours, and may be made at the discretion of the Department for any month or months in which the number of hours sewing has been less than six.

Practical Agriculture and Horti-culture. 112. i. A grant not exceeding £10 may be made to any public elementary school in which the Inspector certifies that evidence has been put before him at inspection to show that satisfactory teaching in Agriculture or Horticulture has been given in a plot of land approved for this purpose, out of school hours, for at least four hours a week on an average during the whole of the school year ; but no grant will be made under this Article unless an application has been made to the Inspector at the previous inspection in the form prescribed, and the manager has certified that suitable and efficient arrangements have been made for the giving of such teaching, and unless one of the teachers in the school is competent to give it. The amount of the grant will depend upon the efficiency and completeness of the teaching, according to the report of the Inspector, and the number of children taught.

ii. A further grant may be made of one half the cost of the tools purchased during the year so long as the number of tools purchased does not exceed, for the first year the number of children in the class, and for any subsequent year one-third of that number.

113. A grant not exceeding £10 per annum may be made to a teacher Grant for who having been duly qualified to the satisfaction of the Department, by a Advanced special course in manual instruction, shall give satisfactory teaching in Manual advanced manual training for an average of at least six hours per week Training. during the school year, of which four at least shall be out of ordinary school hours, the instruction to be given in a place suitably fitted and supplied with necessary tools, and where the average number of boys so instructed is not less than 20. Where the average is greater, the grant may be increased to a sum not exceeding £12. An initial grant of a sum not exceeding £30 may be made by the Department at its discretion, and upon conditions to be prescribed to aid in fitting a suitable room for the purpose of manual instruction, and to procure necessary tools.

114. A payment at the rate of £20 per annum for an additional teacher Payment for (see Article 63) may be made, at the discretion of the Department, to Additional schools in which the staff would otherwise be below the minimum required Teacher. by Art. 79.

115. In schools with an average attendance of over 150 a payment in Payment for addition to the grants above specified may be made at the rate of £30 per Assistant annum for a registered uncertificated assistant and £36 for a certificated Teacher. assistant, and another such payment may be similarly made for each additional 70 in average attendance ; provided that no grant shall be given for any member of the staff whose withdrawal would not bring the staff below the minimum required by Art. 79. A further grant may be made for any recognised assistant teacher who has taught as such in any school for the whole of the school year of £1 per annum for every completed year within ten years previous to such school year during which he has taught either as principal teacher or assistant in a school that has taken at least a second class at inspection ; provided that such further grant shall not exceed £6.

116. All first class and second class schools with an average attendance of Additional over 80 shall be treated as special schools, and shall receive in addition to Grant. the payments otherwise provided in this Code a grant of 3s. per head on each scholar above the number of 80 in average attendance. Schools which had in the year 1898 an average attendance of over 250 may continue to receive a grant of 4s. per unit of average attendance above 80, so long as the principal teachers who were in charge in 1898 remain in charge of these schools. Where a department of a school is kept in a separate building under an assistant or additional teacher, such teacher shall receive as much of the grant under this Article as does not exceed 3s. per unit of average attendance in the department. This grant shall not, however, be paid for any children in excess of the number for which the school has staff and accommodation. [Articles 79 and 99 (i).]

117. If the monthly average attendance at any school (Art. 26) falls to Reduction of such an extent as to make it clear that the staff is greater than the average Advances. attendance at the next inspection will justify, the Department may require that the services of any additiona or assistant teacher shall be discontinued after due notice not exceeding 3 months, and the advances will after the expiration of such notice be reduced accordingly.

Superfluous Schools.

90. No school shall receive a grant-in-aid, the establishment of which is considered superfluous by reason of the existence of another available school in the vicinity or of any other valid objection.

"The vicinity" in this regulation shall mean, in general, except in towns and large village centres, within a distance of three miles by any practicable road.

Minimum Average.

·91. No school shall receive any grant-in-aid unless the average attendance is not less than thirty or in the towns named in Article 83 not less sixty; provided that in the case of schools on the annual grant list which are inspected for the first time, and schools which are situated in districts sparsely populated and difficult of access, schools may be recognised if the average attendance is not less than twenty.

Managers responsible for expenses.

94. The managers shall be responsible for the payment of teachers and all other expenses of the school.

Temporary employment of un- registered Teachers.

96. No school shall, except as herein provided, receive a grant-in-aid for any month in any part of which it is not in charge of a registered teacher. Nevertheless, a school previously in receipt of annual grants may continue to receive them for an interval or intervals not exceeding three months in all in any school year, during the temporary absence of the teacher in consequence of illness or other unavoidable cause, or between the leaving of one and the coming of another teacher qualified under this Code to have charge of it, provided the school is kept open under a temporary teacher approved by the Department and the other regulations of the Code are observed during the interval or intervals.

Number of sessions required.

97. No school shall receive a grant-in-aid unless it shall have met for a number of sessions during the school year not less in the aggregate than twenty-eight, or thirty where Friday sessions are required, for every month therein. Allowance may be made for any unavoidable circumstances occurring to prevent this, when such are satisfactorily explained to the Superintending Inspector of Schools; but the plea of rainy weather, unless such weather has been altogether exceptional in the district, will not be accepted. The explanation of any deficiency must be made in writing, and handed to the Inspector at the inspection. A deduction may be made from the grant-in-aid, at the discretion of the Superintending Inspector of Schools, for any deficiency in the number of sessions.

Report of Inspector.

98. No school shall receive a grant-in-aid which has not been visited and reported on by an Inspector during the school year unless a continued epidemic or other cause accepted as sufficient by the Department prevent such visit and report.

Conditions.

99. The Department must be satisfied—

Premises.

(i.) that the school buildings are properly constructed, are supplied with suitable offices and contain sufficient accommodation (in general not less than 8 square feet per unit of average attendance) for the scholars attending the school. (This sub-section is not intended to prohibit managers from fixing with the approval of the Department a higher minimum of accommodation than 8 square feet per unit of average attendance in any school.)

Staff, furni- ture and Apparatus.

(ii.) that the school has a sufficient staff (see Art. 79) and is properly provided with furniture, books, maps and other apparatus of elementary instruction;

Registers and Accounts.

(iii.) that the admission and daily attendance of the scholars are carefully registered by the principal teacher or under his supervision by some member of the recognised staff, not being a pupil-teacher, and periodically verified by the manager;

(iv.) that the book of school accounts contains an accurate record of income and expenditure, and that all returns may be accepted as trustworthy;

made proper provision for the preparation of pupils to pass the Cambridge Local Examination.

125. Candidates for the scholarships must be not more than thirteen years of age on the day of examination and must produce certificates of age and good character from a magistrate or minister of religion. Age of Candidates.

126. The examination for the scholarship will be the same as that for first year pupil-teachers, omitting the subject of teaching, and candidates will be required to pay the fee of 5s. paid by volunteer candidates at that examination (see Art. 62). The fourteen scholarships will be awarded to the fourteen who pass highest out of all those who comply with the conditions of these Articles. Examination.

127. These scholarships will be paid by the Superintending Inspector of Schools in quarterly instalments to the treasurer or principal of any school, approved by the Board, at which the scholar is being educated, to be by him applied in reduction of the payments required to be made for such scholar, on receipt of a certificate from the principal that (*a*) the scholar has attended at not less than nine-tenths of the number of sessions during which the school has been open during the quarter, or giving reasons, satisfactory to the Superintending Inspector of Schools, for any further deficiency not exceeding one-half of the whole number of sessions : and (*b*) that the scholar has been well behaved and diligent and has made satisfactory progress in his studies. If the requirements of good behaviour, diligence, and progress be not met, all further payment on behalf of such scholar shall cease. No quarterly payment will be made if the scholar has been absent for more than one-half the number of sessions during which the school has been open during the quarter. Certificates required for Payments.

127a. i. Five Scholarships, each of the value of £25 per annum and lasting for a maximum period of five years, shall be annually granted to five boys selected by examination as provided below, who shall be willing to enter into articles of apprenticeship with tradesmen to be selected from the following list :— Trade Scholarships to Pupils in Elementary Schools.

Tradesmen.	Period of Training.
5 Carpenter	
3 Fitter	
3 Shipwright	
3 Boiler-maker	5 years
3 Blacksmith	
2 Plumber and Coppersmith	
2 Cooper	
2 Wheelwright	2 years
2 Bricklayer and Mason	

When a scholarship falls vacant before the maximum period of five years has been completed, each such vacancy may be filled up by granting an extra scholarship in addition to the five mentioned above, provided that when all the scholarships allowed by the scheme are filled up there shall not be at any time more than 25 scholarships of the total aggregate value of £625.

·ii. A candidate for these scholarships must not be less than thirteen years of age on the day of examination nor of such an age as will cause him to reach the age of 21 years before the termination of his articles of apprenticeship, and must produce certificates of age and good character from a magistrate or minister of religion.

iii. The examination for these scholarships will be the same as that for second year pupil-teachers with an examination in drawing substituted for the pupil-teachers' examination in teaching, and candidates will be required to pay the fee of five shillings paid by volunteer candidates at that examination (see Art. 62).

iv. The priority in choice of scholarships shall be offered in order of merit to the competitors who stand· highest on the list, and if any competitor refuse to make a selection from the scholarships offered to him, the choice shall be offered to the next competitor on the list ; provided that no scholarship can be awarded until the candidate has passed a medical examination prescribed by the Superintending Inspector of Schools.

v. The sum of £1 17s. 6d. shall be paid monthly by the Superintending Inspector of Schools to such person as he may approve on behalf of each scholar, for his board, clothing, and other expenses, on the receipt from the employer of such scholar of a certificate that he has been during the month for which payment is claimed industrious and well-behaved, and that he is making progress in learning his trade. The remainder of the scholarship, or the sum of £2 10s. for each year of apprenticeship, shall be retained by the Government, and that sum shall be applied at the end of such apprenticeship to the purpose of providing an outfit for the apprentice.

vi. In case the engagement shall be terminated before the term of apprenticeship has expired, and it shall be shown by the decision of a justice of the peace that such termination was due to the fault of the apprentice, the said apprentice shall forfeit both the aforesaid £2 10s. per annum reserved from the scholarship, and also any unaccrued portion of the scholarship. If, however, the engagement be terminated before its expiry, and it shall be shown by the decision of a justice of the peace, or otherwise, that such expiry is not due to the fault of the apprentice, he shall be allowed to retain his scholarship, provided that at any time within three months from the date of such expiry he enter into fresh articles of apprenticeship with another master for the completion of the term of his apprenticeship. In case an apprentice, whose engagement has expired otherwise than by his own fault, shall fail to enter into such fresh articles of apprenticeship within three months from the date of such expiry he shall be entitled to receive the £2 10s. per annum reserved under the provisions of section 5, but shall forfeit all claim to any unaccrued portion of the scholarship.

vii. Every master applying for an apprentice must be approved of by the Superintending Inspector of Schools, and will be required to produce evidence satisfactory to the Director of Public Works that he is competent to teach his trade and take charge of apprentices.

viii. Articles of apprenticeship to country tradesmen can in general only be sanctioned if each such tradesman and his apprentice agree in writing, on signing the articles of apprenticeship, that after two years they shall be transferred to a tradesman of the same trade in Kingston who shall be approved by the Superintending Inspector of Schools and the Director of Public Works.

CHAPTER VI.—BUILDING GRANTS.

Objects of Grants.

128. Application for grants-in-aid towards the erection of schoolhouses in places where no school operations have been previously conducted, or where further school provision is needed, or towards the improvement or repairs of schoolhouses already in use, or for the erection of teachers' houses where none exist, or for the improvement of teachers' houses for which no building grant has been made, will be considered by the Department ; and a limited amount of aid may be afforded according to the amount available for such purposes and in accordance with the conditions laid down in the following Articles.

Application.

129. No application for a building grant will be entertained for any school not on the annual grant list. An application for a building grant may, however, be made to the Superintending Inspector of Schools at the same time as the application for the recognition of the school.

131. The site selected for the school must be approved by the Depart- Site. ment as healthy. central and suitable.

132. Except when enlargement is necessary in consequence of the closing Grant must or amalgamation of any school or schools in the vicinity, in which case a be supple-larger proportion of the total cost may be borne by the Government, the meated, manager applying for such aid must be prepared to raise by local effort or by the assistance of any society with which the school may be connected, at least one half the amount needed to complete the building, or the proposed enlargement or repairs, and meet all claims. The total amount which may be given by the Government to any one school for such purpose shall not in any case exceed one hundred pounds nor shall any grant given towards the erection or improvement of a teacher's house in any case exceed fifty pounds.

133. No grant can be recommended until the Superintending Inspector Plans and of Schools shall have approved the plans and estimates submitted and shall Estimates. have satisfied himself by personal investigation, or by a full and special report from one of the Inspectors, that there is a necessity for the erection of a new school or teacher's house, or the enlargement or repair of an established school, or for the improvement of a teacher's house, and that the estimate of the entire cost of the work to be performed, sent in with the application, is reasonable and fairly accurate. The grant will not, except under the circumstances referred to in the preceding Article, exceed one half of this estimate which must be sufficient for the completion of the work. No application for supplementary grants will be entertained.

134. No building or repairing grant will be given unless the land on Guarantees. which the building or proposed building is erected or to be erected is, at least (unless with the express consent and approval of the Department) one quarter of an acre in area, and is vested in a trustee or body of trustees approved by the Department, nor unless such trustee or trustees guarantee (a) that the building or repairs will be completed according to specifications within two years from the date of receiving the grant or first instalment of the grant, under the penalty of forfeiting any unpaid balance of the grant or of refunding one-twelfth of the aggregate amount already paid for every calendar month over the said period of two years during which the building or repairs shall remain uncompleted, and (b) that if the building is diverted from public elementary school purposes within twelve years of the date of completion of such building or repairs they shall refund one-twelfth of the grant for every year and part of a year remaining unexpired of the said period of twelve years.

136. As only a limited amount of funds can be devoted to this class of Principle of special grant, the Department does not pledge itself to recommend grants distribution-for all applications that may be received. The number of grants and the amount that may be given will wholly depend upon the funds available for the purpose ; and in the distribution of whatever may be given, the cases which may be considered by the Superintending Inspector of Schools the most necessitous and deserving will always receive the first consideration. The rejection of unsuccessful applications will not, therefore, necessarily be final, and they may be repeated.

CHAPTER VII.—TRADE AND FARM SCHOOLS.

137. Any schemes for the establishment of special Trade and Farm Schools Schemes to combining manual labour with school instruction, in which skilled labour be con-and improved systems of cultivation are introduced on really useful and sidered. successful methods, will have the consideration of the Department : and pecuniary aid may be afforded to such schools according to their respective merits and the funds that may be available for extra grants of this description,

PART II.—TRAINING COLLEGES.

For Resident or Day Students.

148. A Training College is an institution for boarding, lodging, and instructing, or for instructing only, students who are preparing to become certificated teachers in public elementary schools. It is required to include, either on its premises or within a convenient distance, a practising school in which the students may learn the practical exercise of their profession.

Admission of Students.

151. No resident student on whose behalf the Government aid is sought can be admitted into a training college who has not previously at some time or other passed the final Pupil Teachers' examination, except by permission of the Department. Non-resident students may be admitted and grants may be made for them, though they have not passed the final Pupil Teachers' examination, provided they have passed such other examination as shall be satisfactory to the Department.

Age Limit.

152. Every student admitted into a training college must be at least 17 years of age, and, on being enrolled, a certificate of age and good character, in the form prescribed, must be sent to the Superintending Inspector of Schools by the Principal.

Two Years' and Three Years' Course.

153. The period of training for students will ordinarily be two years before leaving college. Students who pass not below First Class in first and second years, and in Honours in one of the two years, shall, with the approval of the Department, be permitted to remain in College for a third year's course of training ; and others, who pass in the First Class in the second year examination, may, with the like approval, upon the special recommendation of the Principal of the College, also be permitted to remain for the third year's course.

Supplementary Third Year's Course.

153a. Students who shall have taken the two years' course in college and passed the second year examination, and subsequently have had three years of actual work as teacher in public elementary schools, may take the third year's course in part as home study, and complete it as prescribed in Schedule B.

Provision for Teachers who take the third year's course.

153b. A teacher, upon leaving a school which is in his charge, in order to attend a Training College to complete the third year's course, may make arrangements, with the sanction of the Department, for the continuance of the work of the school during his temporary absence, on such terms as will secure to him a portion of the grant paid to the school for such period of absence.

One Year's Course.

154. Teachers who have taught in public elementary schools for two years and have been favourably reported on by the Inspector at the inspection in each year may be admitted to a training college for the second year's course, at the discretion of the authorities, on passing the first year training college examination. They will be considered as second year students to all intents and purposes.

Number of Students allowed.

155. The authorities of a training college may, subject to the power reserved to the Department, select and admit on their own terms as many students as they think fit, provided that they satisfy the conditions laid down in Article 168.

EXAMINATION OF STUDENTS IN TRAINING COLLEGES.

Date and place of Examination.

156. An examination of students in training colleges will be held in their respective colleges every year, commencing on the Monday next before December 18th ; but the Oral Examination of Students will be held at each College within six weeks previous to this date.

Subjects.

157. The annual examination will extend to the subjects specified in the annexed Schedule B. Except as herein before provided or by special permission of the Department, no student will be admitted to the second or third year examination, unless he has passed the examination for the previous year, nor unless he has spent the number of hours required by Schedule B during the year in the practising school under proper superintendence.

158. In training colleges for men special arrangements will be made for Manual the examination in Manual Training. The students in training colleges Training for women will be examined in needlework, in accordance with Schedule B, and Needle- in November of each year. work.

160. Subject to the foregoing requirements the examination will be Residence or open to— Attendance

(*a*) Students who have resided in training colleges for at least 250 required. days during the year preceding the examination.

(*b*) Students who have attended training colleges for at least 210 days in the preceding year.

The Superintending Inspector of Schools may at his discretion, in special cases, waive the requirement of the full number of days.

163. Candidates will be considered to have passed the examination who Conditions have obtained one-half the total aggregate marks as well as one-half of the for a pass. total marks in each of the primary subjects and one-third of the total marks in each of the secondary subjects.

164. A candidate will be said to have passed with honours if he obtain Pass with two-thirds or more of the total aggregate marks, provided he has obtained Honours. the marks in each subject required in Article 163.

164a. The scale of marks for the different subjects is as follows :— Scale of Marks.

PRIMARY SUBJECTS.

Reading and Recitation	180
English	180
Writing - 60 } Drawing - 120 }	180
Arithmetic	180
School Management, Theory and Practice	180
Science, General and Agricultural	180

SECONDARY SUBJECTS.

Scripture and Morals	120
Geography	120
Geometry	120
Vocal Music	120
Manual Training for Men } Domestic Economy for Women }	120
Algebra for Men (third year)	120

165. A classified list of the successful candidates will be published in the Publication "Jamaica Gazette" as early as practicable. Unsuccessful candidates may of Pass List. be presented for examination in the same standard in a subsequent year, but must again take up every subject and pass in all.

166. All students in training colleges, unless prevented by ill health, are All Students expected to be qualified and presented for each December examination to be during the term of their residence or attendance. presented.

GRANTS TO TRAINING COLLEGES.

167. All grants made by the Department to training colleges will be Object of exclusively for the training of those who are to follow teaching as a pro- Grants. fession. Any one for whom such a grant shall have been paid who, through his own choice or fault or without justifying cause, shall fail to serve as teacher for the minimum period of six years in a public elementary school in Jamaica or other School approved by the Department, shall, if and when called upon by the Department, refund to the Department for each year of the six years in which he shall so fail an amount equal to one-sixth part of the amount so paid for his training ; provided that if such grant to a training college shall in any case be for one year's training only, the minimum term of service in such case shall be three years, and the

amount liable to be refunded because of failure to serve as teacher shall be one-third of such grant for every year of the three years in which there shall be such failure.

Declaration and Certificates.

168. Before any grant is made on behalf of any student in a training college (a) he must sign a declaration that he intends *bona fide* to adopt and follow the profession of a teacher in a public elementary school or training college, or with the express consent of the Department in such other school as it may approve, and must enter into bond with a surety that he will serve as such teacher for the minimum period specified in Article 167 ; (b) the principal of the college must certify that the authorities of the college are satisfied that such student has shown inclination, aptitude and general suitability of character for the said profession; and (c) a qualified medical officer must certify that the student is in good health and free from any bodily infirmity likely to interfere with the practice of the said profession. Students who comply with the requirements of this Article are hereinafter called normal students. These declarations and certificates in the form prescribed must be repeated for all normal students at the commencement of each year.

Maintenance Grant.

169. The managers of every training college will be informed in October of each year for what number of students the Government will give them a maintenance grant. Within this limit, for every resident normal student admitted into a training college in accordance with these regulations, a payment at the rate of £25 per annum shall be paid as maintenance grant, in monthly instalments, so long as he continues to reside and be taught in the college, passes the annual Government examination, and otherwise satisfies the conditions laid down in this Code, and until he shall have completed his residence in the college. For students admitted in January this annual payment will be calculated as from January 1st.

Grant for a Pass.

170. Grants will be made to training colleges at the rate of £10 for every normal student who passes the examination, whether of the first, second, or third year, provided that for students who have been under training for less than six months of the year the grant shall be £5.

Bonus for a Pass with Honours.

172. Every third year student who passes with honours will receive a bonus of five pounds in addition to the amount paid on his account to his college.

SCHEDULE A.

Course of Study and Standards of Classification.

All Schools on the Annual Grant List will be examined according to these Standards. The maximum marks attainable will only be given at Inspection when the whole of the subjects mentioned in the Syllabus are taken, and when the school as a whole has attained to the highest degree of proficiency that would be possible under any teaching. Every lower degree of proficiency will receive a proportionately smaller number of marks, which may be fractional.

Children in higher Standards (Chief Subjects) or Divisions (Obligatory Subject and Secondary Subjects) may be examined in any of the subjects for Lower Standards or Divisions as well as in their own.

All Scholars are required to be placed in the same Standards in Reading and Writing ; and it is expected that, as a general rule, the Scholars will also be in the same Standard in Arithmetic.

First Class Schools, of at least 60 marks, will be examined upon the full course of study for each Standard and Division in the school. Other First Class Schools will not be examined in " Elements of Grammar " beyond 5th Standard requirements.

Second Class Schools as a rule will not be examined beyond the 5th Standard in chief subjects, and in " Elements of Grammar " not beyond 4th Standard requirements ; and in other subjects not beyond Middle Division requirements. By the special approval, first obtained, of the Inspector for the District, such school may undertake full 5th Standard work, and 6th Standard work in Reading, and the obligatory subject for the Upper Division.

Third Class Schools will not be examined beyond 4th Standard work in chief subjects and the Middle Division in other subjects except that with the special approval, first obtained, of the Inspector for the District, such school may undertake 5th Standard work in Reading.

It will not be expected that the full work of the several Divisions will be accomplished, except by the highest standard in each Division--that is, as a rule, by Scholars who have been in that Division for more than one year.

In the case of any school where, in the opinion of the Teacher, a different distribution of Standards into Divisions is desirable, the desired change may be made with the approval of the Inspector for the District.

The first inspection of a school after the date of the coming into operation of this Code, will be under the requirements of the former Code ; except that schools which at that date had already been inspected in 1900 may, upon request of the teacher, be next examined under the new Code. At the first inspection under this Code, and until teachers have had opportunity to bring their schools into full harmony with the new requirements, all reasonable allowances will be made for disadvantages incidental to a change of curriculum.

CHIEF SUBJECTS.

READING AND RECITATION.

JUNIOR STANDARD.

READING.

To read from blackboard, chart and book, short sentences ·in script and print, expressing simple thoughts in easy and familiar words of one and two syllables.

Spelling. Division of words into syllables. Word-building. ...

RECITATION.

To recite a single poem of 8 to 12 lines ; also two to four bright gems of thought, each of 4 lines or less.

NOTES AND SUGGESTIONS.

Beginners should be taught by a judicious combination of the sentence or word method, phonic method, and letter or spelling method. As a rule the child should read individually ; sometimes two or three together ; and sometimes, but more rarely, the whole class may be permitted to read simultaneously. To prevent rote reading, the sentences, put on the blackboard, should be varied from day to day, using new words and known words in new combinations. The Object Lessons, lessons in Scripture and Morals, lessons in Geography and Number, will often yield material for a reading lesson—some useful fact or striking thought being expressed in a short sentence, in simple words, to be read from the blackboard. The repeated reading from day to day of the same lessons from a chart should be avoided. The lessons should be chiefly from blackboard to ensure variety, to compel attention, and to maintain fresh interest. It will be well to transcribe each new sentence from the blackboard on a narrow slip of cardboard. These slips, distributed among the children once a week, will admirably serve the purpose of review.

Words and Sentences.—Children should be taught to recognize at sight the written and printed forms of the words, and to pronounce them readily as wholes. They should be taught to read by phrase rather than by single words, "a" and "the" to be pronounced as if a syllable of the following word ; to observe, carefully, the three chief marks of punctuation —period, note of interrogation, and comma ; to read to express a thought ; to read in an easy natural tone of voice as one would talk, but with special distinctness.

Phonics and Letters.—The children should be taught to enunciate clearly the vowel sounds. Also the consonant sounds at the beginning and ending of a word, the consonant sound to be enunciated, usually, in combination with a vowel, forming a syllable. The children should know the names of the letters representing these several sounds.

Word-building. Spelling.—The children should be taught to separate words into syllables, and words and syllables into their component sounds and letters ; to build up these components into new words and syllables, by addition to or change of initial or terminal consonant, or by adding or changing a vowel ; to know the change of sound usually produced by having two vowels instead of one in a monosyllable, as pin, pine ; got, goat ; fed, feed ; ran, rain ; pond, pound ; to spell by letter easy words of regular formation and those other words of irregular formation which most frequently recur in the reading lessons. In word-building much use should be made of the more common combinations of two or three letters, forming part of a word or a distinct syllable, to be known at sight. When these combinations are well known at sight, the form of many familiar words can be acquired with great rapidity. For example : With an, ed, er, it, ain, ack, ing, many words can be built by prefixing one or more consonants, as can, fan, pan, plan, bed, fed, bred, fled, her, lit, split, rain, stain, strain, lack, sack, slack, sing, sting, &c. ; or by prefixing a syllable, as, reader, singer, playing, walking, &c. The aim to be kept constantly in view in this drill on the components of words is that the child may acquire without much delay, and gradually more and more, the power to pronounce new word forms without the aid of the teacher.

A careful following (not slavishly but with intelligent adaptation) of the method described in detail in Miss Fundenburg's "First Lessons in Reading—Teacher's Edition," will ensure a fair amount of progress every month, and will enable a teacher, ordinarily, to accomplish the work of the Standard in less than twelve months. The *method* of teaching is commended ; the *sentences to be read* should be such as are above indicated.

A sufficient supply of blackboards is indispensable. It is also indispensable that the teaching of this Standard be not entrusted to a pupil teacher or monitor who has not first been specially instructed how to conduct the teaching.

Recitation.--The children should be taught to recite their little poem individually, in small groups, and simultaneously. Other choice selections —gems of thought or "memory gems"—usually of two to four lines, should be known by heart. One such gem, learned every three or four months, would give three or four for the year. In every case the meaning of what is memorized is to be clearly understood by the pupils.

It is believed that the child who enters school at six years of age, and attends with a fair degree of regularity, may be expected to master the work of the Standard in one year. When the attendance is quite irregular two years may be required. For purposes of instruction the teacher may sometimes find it desirable to divide the Standard into two sections.

STANDARD I.

READING.

To read a passage of one to three paragraphs, or one or two verses of poetry, from a First Reader (or other reading book used in this Standard) with intelligence, correct pronunciation, and distinct articulation. To read lessons in dialogue form with animation and natural expression.

Pronunciation of special lists of words in the reading book.

Spelling ; phonics ; word-building.

RECITATION.

To recite a simple poem of 16 to 24 lines. Also, three or more gems of thought learned during the school year.

NOTES AND SUGGESTIONS.

The pupils in this Standard should be taught to find, readily, any selected lesson in the reading book, the number of the page being given ; to read simple poetry without a sing-song tone or uniformly recurring cadence ; to observe, carefully and intelligently, all marks of pronunciation ; to pronounce correctly the words in the lists given in the First Reader ; to know the marks of pronunciation used in their reading book and to be able to use them as a guide in pronouncing the words in the lists and similar new words.

STANDARD II.

READING.

To read a passage selected from a Second Reader, or the First Tropical Reader, or other reading book used in the Standard.

Pronunciation of special lists of words in the reading book.

Spelling ; phonics ; word-building.

RECITATION.

To recite a poem of 20 to 30 lines ; also four or more gems of thought learned during the school year.

STANDARD III.

READING.

To read a passage from a Third Reader, or 1st or 2nd Tropical Reader or other reading book used in the Standard.

RECITATION.

To recite a poem of 30 lines or more ; also four or more gems of thought learned during the school year.

[It is suggested that pupils of the 3rd Standard be taught how to use the dictionary, to find the meaning of words and their pronunciation.]

STANDARD IV.

READING.

To read a passage from a Fourth Reader, or 2nd Tropical Reader, or other reading book used in the Standard.
Use of the Dictionary.

RECITATION.

To recite a poem of 40 lines or more ; also four or more gems of thought learned during the school year.

STANDARD V.

READING.

To read a passage selected from a Fifth Reader, or other approved reading book.

To read a news paragraph from a local newspaper.

Habitual use of the Dictionary.

RECITATION.

To recite 50 or more lines of verse—either a complete poem or (if part of a longer poem) a portion having unity in itself. Gems of thought, as in Standard IV.

STANDARD VI.

READING.

To read from a Sixth Reader, or other approved reading book, containing choice selections from Shakespeare, Tennyson, Longfellow, and other standard authors, or from a book in the school library.

To read selections from the "Journal of Agriculture" or "Bulletin"; also, selections from a current newspaper, including telegrams, market reports, and shipping news.

Habitual use of the Dictionary.

RECITATION.

To recite with expression about 60 lines of verse from a standard author Gems of thought, as in previous Standards.

GENERAL NOTES AND SUGGESTIONS.

Reading with intelligence, and with due regard to marks of punctuation, italics, etc., will be required in all the Standards, and increased fluency and expression in successive years. In all Standards above Junior, at least two sets of reading books must be provided, one of which, in the Second Standard, will be the 1st Tropical Reader, and in higher standards the 2nd Tropical Reader.

The Inspector may examine from any of the books in use in the Standard, and from Standard III. and upwards from any book or passage suitable for the purpose which he may select. The intelligence of the reading will be tested partly by questions on the meaning of what is read, .

Correct and intelligent reading includes complete mastery of the words, distinct articulation, just emphasis and right inflection, the mind taking in the thought and the reading expressing the thought. While pupils should read loud enough to be heard distinctly by the teacher and every member of the class, undue loudness should be checked. Not special loudness of tone but distinctness of pronunciation is required. In all the Standards the pupils should be trained to open the mouth well, and not to read with closed teeth. The power to use the dictionary readily and intelligently in Standard III. is highly desirable; and in the higher Standards, with full knowledge of all the marks of pronunciation, will be regarded by the Inspector as very important, and will usually be tested.

Intelligence and expression, with due attention to articulation, inflection and emphasis, will be required in the recitation of all Standards. The "intelligence" will include not only a knowledge of the meaning of the individual words but a full understanding of the meaning of the poem, and of all its phrases, and the force and pertinency of its allusions. The teacher should select with care the "gems of thought" to be committed to memory during the course of the year. They will be but a light tax upon the time of teacher and pupils; they will add variety to the recitation that is required; they will, if wisely chosen, store the mind with what will be valuable as a life-long possession, and will greatly aid the teacher in his effort to impress upon children a high sense of duty, and a deep appreciation of what is right and good, what is unselfish, noble and patriotic. Suitable verses can be found in the reading books and can be used until the teacher has gathered others which he may prefer from standard authors.

Reading, like talking, is so much a matter of imitation, that it is important the children should hear much good reading. This is best secured when all other exercises in the school are suspended and the teacher reads to the whole school. Three minutes a day given to this exercise, reading interesting selections from books in the school library, or the most interesting of the penny reading books, and reading with care in the best manner, will, in the course of a year, exert a controlling influence in determining the manner of reading in all the Standards. This might be the last exercise before dismissing the school for the noon recess, or the first exercise after reassembling the school, or at any other convenient time when all the scholars are present and can give attention.

WRITING AND ENGLISH.

JUNIOR STANDARD.

WRITING AND ORTHOGRAPHY.

To form letters in script and write simple words on slate, slowly and carefully, in a bold hand, from script copy on slate or blackboard.

To form with sticks capital letters composed of straight lines; to draw them on the slate; to draw like letters from copy on chart or blackboard, or from dictation.

To copy on slate short sentences written on blackboard, with correct use of capitals, period, note of interrogation, and apostrophe followed by s.

COMPOSITION.

To answer questions in the form of simple sentences. To tell in complete sentences simple facts about actual objects shown or represented in pictures. To ask questions respecting such objects.

STANDARD I.

WRITING AND ORTHOGRAPHY.

To copy sentences written on blackboard.

To transcribe a paragraph of two or three sentences from First Reader with correct use of capitals and marks of punctuation.

To copy from blackboard a very short letter to a relative or friend. The pupil to write his own name and the name of the school.

To write an easy sentence from dictation.

Copybooks to be shown.

COMPOSITION.

As in previous Standard. Also, to answer easy questions on slate in very simple sentences.

[The pupils in this Standard should have much practice in the correct use in sentences of--is, are ; I, me, ; it, they, them. The pupils should distinguish between one and more than one thing :—as book, books, etc.]

STANDARD II.

WRITING AND ORTHOGRAPHY.

To write a passage of two or three short sentences from a Second Reader, or equivalent sentences,—each sentence to be slowly read once, and then dictated by single words, or phrases of two or three words ; the period, note of interrogation and apostrophe to be put in by the pupil correctly, without aid.

Copybooks and exercise books to be shown.

COMPOSITION.

To answer in writing, in whole sentences, questions about familiar events and objects.

To write a very simple letter.

Note.—The pupils in the Second Standard should be carefully taught to begin and end their simple letters in proper form.

[While in every lesson in every subject some attention should be given to the use of correct English, the pupils in this Standard should have sufficient practice in the use, in short sentences, of the forms previously mentioned, and also such as—he, his, him ; she, her ; their ; has, have, had ; was, were ; come, comes, came ; walk, walks, walked ; receive, receives, received ; etc.]

STANDARD III.

WRITING AND ORTHOGRAPHY.

To write a passage of four to eight lines of prose from a reading book used in the Standard, slowly read once and then dictated—the period, note of interrogation, comma and quotation marks to be correctly put in by the pupil without aid.

To write four lines selected from the poem memorized for recitation.

Copybooks and exercise books to be shown.

COMPOSITION.

Writing simple sentences containing specified nouns, verbs, adjectives, adverbs.

To use correctly in sentences the more common words in the reading books pronounced alike but spelt differently.

To write a simple letter ; a receipt for money ; also a very simple bill, showing amount due for an article sold or for services rendered.

Note.—The exercise books of this Standard should contain, among other matters, forms of letters with suitable beginning and ending, varied according to the person addressed ; forms of receipts for money and simple bills ; a simple form of household accounts, one page containing entries of money received and the opposite page of money expended.

Special attention should be given in this and the higher Standards to the right use of words, and the use of simple rather than pretentious words

ELEMENTS OF GRAMMAR.

Simple analysis of easy sentences. Different parts of speech. Number —nouns and pronouns. Different forms of verbs as determined by singular or plural form of the subject. Gender of nouns. Different forms of pronouns as modified by the gender of nouns for which they stand. Cases of nouns and pronouns. Modification of nouns to show the possessive case. Personal pronouns. Inflection of personal pronouns, showing case, number and gender. Modification of the form of verbs determined by the 3rd personal pronoun in the singular number. Different forms of verbs, to indicate present, past, and future.

[Only ordinary forms and variations are required to be known. When, however, a child encounters an unusual form in his reading lesson, the teacher should give such explanation as is needful for the intelligent understanding of what is read.]

STANDARD IV.

WRITING AND ORTHOGRAPHY.

To write with correct punctuation eight lines of prose or poetry, slowly read once, and then dictated.
Copybooks and exercise books to be shown.
The simpler rules of spelling, and the common affixes, to be known.

COMPOSITION.

Business letters and other letters ; receipts for money ; promissory notes ; bills ; simple household accounts.

ELEMENTS OF GRAMMAR.

Modification of subject, predicate and object by words and phrases. Parsing an easy sentence, to show the relation of each word to other words in the sentence.

Note.—Pupils in this Standard should have a knowledge of the plainest rules of spelling and word-building, including rules governing such cases as step, stepping ; sleep, sleeping ; hat, hatter ; heat, heater.

STANDARD V.

WRITING AND ORTHOGRAPHY.

Dictation.
Further rules of spelling.
Copy books and exercise books to be shown.

COMPOSITION.

Paraphrase of a simple and short poetical passage, being chiefly a transposition of the words into the order of prose.
Writing from memory the substance of a short story read out twice.
Letter writing. Business forms and correspondence.

ELEMENTS OF GRAMMAR.

Modification of subject, predicate and object by words, phrases and sentences. Analysis of easy complex sentences.

Note.—The rules of spelling and word-building known by pupils in this Standard should include rules governing such cases as : pin, pinning ; pine, pining ; print, printing ; happy, happier ; play, player.

STANDARD VI.

WRITING AND ORTHOGRAPHY.

As in Standard V.

COMPOSITION.

As in Standard V.

To write an abstract or synopsis of a letter or other simple document

ELEMENTS OF GRAMMAR.

Parsing and Analysis of complex sentences. Word-building. Knowledge of English prefixes. Making sentences illustrative of the right use of given words and phrases.

GENERAL NOTES AND SUGGESTIONS.

Writing.—The slates of the Junior Standard and 1st and 2nd Standard should be ruled on one side permanently, with lines to indicate height of loop and small letters. On the slates of the Junior and 1st Standard there should be permanently marked three linear inches and one square inch.

At the inspection, the writing of Standard I. and II. may be on slates or paper, at the discretion of the teacher; in Standard III. and upwards it should be on paper.

Exercise Books.—It is important that the letters and business forms, after all errors have been carefully marked, be re-written in correct form to serve as models for future use. The memory gems, learned from time to time, should also be preserved in the exercise books.

Every exercise in the exercise books and every page in the copy books should be dated.

ARITHMETIC.

JUNIOR STANDARD.

To count objects up to 12, forwards and backwards. The same, by intervals of 2, beginning at 1 and 2; intervals of 3, beginning at 1, 2, and 3; intervals of 4, beginning at 1, 2, 3, and 4.

To make calculations by the actual handling of objects, in addition, subtraction, multiplication and division, to involve no number beyond 12. To represent these processes by figures and symbols.

The meaning of $\frac{1}{2}$ and $\frac{1}{4}$ by concrete examples;—also, 1 dozen; $\frac{1}{2}$ dozen.

Easy problems on common objects and in tables as follows: Money, up to 1 shilling; capacity, to 1 quart; length, to 1 yard.

Besides the above,—counting forwards to 100, and addition and subtraction to 20.

Note.—The signs $+$, $-$, $\times$, $\div$, $=$, to be known.

TABLES.

Money.—4 farthings = 1*d*.; 2 half-pennies = 1*d*.; 2 penny-half-pennies = 3*d*.; 2 threepences = 6*d*.; 2 sixpences = 1*s*.

Capacity.—4 gills = 1 pint; 2 pints = 1 quart.

Length.—12 inches = 1 foot; 3 feet = 1 yard.

[A half-penny coin may be used as an inch measure.]

STANDARD I.

To count to 100 forwards and backwards :—by intervals of 5 ; by intervals of 2, the odd and even numbers ; by intervals of 10, beginning with each of the numbers from 1 to 10 and from 100 to 91. To count forwards to 30 by intervals of 3 and 4, beginning with 1, 2, 3 and 4, and backwards in reverse order,—*i.e.*, beginning with 30, 29, 28, 27.

The multiplication table to 6 times 12.

Mental addition of any two digits, and subtraction of any digit from a number not exceeding 18. Adding by decades, thus : 7 + 4 ; 17 + 4 ; 27 + 4 ; 37 + 4, etc.

The four rules up to 100 ; addition not to exceed 5 lines ; neither multiplier nor divisor to exceed 6.

Easy problems on common objects and on the tables in Money, Capacity, Length, Weight and Time to the extent specified in the Notes.

The meaning, by concrete examples, up to 40, of $\frac{1}{2}$, $\frac{1}{4}$, $\frac{1}{3}$, $\frac{1}{6}$, 1-10, 1-12.

Roman numbers to XXX.

Note.—" Concrete examples :" $\frac{1}{2}$, $\frac{1}{4}$, $\frac{1}{3}$, 1-12 of a shilling, or of a foot ; 1-10 of £1 ; etc.

TABLES.

Money.—20*s.* = £1 ; 2*s.* = 1 florin ; 10 florins = £1.

Time.—24 hours = 1 day ; 7 days = 1 week—(names of the days in order) ; 12 months = 1 year—(names of the months in order).

Capacity.—4 quarts = 1 gallon.

Length.—22 yards = 1 chain ; 66 feet = 1 chain. (Actual measurement in school yard or on roadside marked by stakes.)

Weight.—16 oz. = 1 lb. [Practical use of $\frac{1}{2}$ lb. and $\frac{1}{4}$ lb. weights and $\frac{1}{2}$ oz. and $\frac{1}{4}$ oz. weights is recommended.]

STANDARD II.

To count forwards to 60, by intervals of 2, 3, 4, etc., up to 9, beginning with each of the digits, and backwards in reverse order.

The multiplication table to 12 times 12.

Mental addition of two or three numbers, and subtraction of any number from another, the total or minuend not to exceed 100. The same in money, the total or minuend not to exceed 10*s.* Mental calculation of the cost of dozens of articles, up to 4 dozen, at a given number of pence or farthings each.

The pence table to 10*s.*

The four simple rules ; no number or amount to exceed 1,000 ; no multiplier to exceed 24 ; no divisor to exceed 12.

Addition and subtraction of money. (See Note.) Easy sums in the tables.

To know, practically, the meaning of a square inch, foot and yard. To make simple calculations of area, not to exceed 144 square inches.

To know the meaning of any proper fraction with denominator 3, 4, 5, 6, 8, 10, or 12. To add and subtract halves and fourths ; thirds and sixths ; fourths and eighths.

Roman numbers to C.

Time by the clock. The meaning of 1.35, 3.20, etc., as applied to the clock.

Note.—In mental calculations, in money, only two denominations to be used,—shillings and pence, or pence and farthings. In written sums in addition of money, the lines not to exceed five nor any number used to exceed 20. In subtraction, farthings to be used in minuend or subtrahend, not in both.

4226.

3 D

TABLES.

Money.—5 shillings = 1 crown ; 2 shillings and sixpence = 1 half-crown ; 4 crowns = £1 ; 8 half crowns = £1.

Time.—60 seconds = 1 minute ; 60 minutes = 1 hour ; 365 days = 1 year [52 weeks in a year].

Length.—1760 yards = 1 mile ; 80 chains = 1 mile.

Weight.—28 lbs. = 1 qr. ; 4 qrs. = 1 cwt. ; 112 lbs. = 1 cwt.

Surface.—144 square inches = 1 square foot. [To show, by ruling on slate or paper, that—for instance—an area of 6 in. by 4 in. contains 24 square inches.]

STANDARD III.

Mental.—Simple exercises in addition and subtraction of money up to £2. Reduction from one denomination to the next with numbers not exceeding 100. Calculation of the cost of articles by the dozen, score and gross. To calculate prices by the easier aliquot parts of a sovereign and a shilling.

Written.—The four simple rules, with numbers to 100,000. Reduction. The compound rules, with multiplication by factors up to 144 only, and divisor not exceeding 12. Money table in full : other tables as specified in the Notes, but calculations usually confined to two denominations,—*e.g.*, days and hours, feet and inches.

To know the meaning of a cubic inch, foot and yard, and to work very simple easy sums in measuring contents.

The meaning of any proper fraction with denominator not exceeding 24. Easy operations in addition and subtraction of halves, fourths, eighths ; halves, thirds, sixths ; halves, fifths, tenths.

To know the meaning of 5 and 2½ per cent., and to work easy sums mentally with exact hundreds.

Roman numbers to CC.

Notes.—The shorter process of division, with terminal noughts in divisor and dividend, should be known.

There should be actual measurement in cubic measure to find the contents of a box, the schoolroom, &c.,—using only one denomination—feet or inches.

TABLES.

Length.—5½ yards = 1 pole ; 4 poles = 1 chain ; 80 chains = 1 mile.

Weight.—20 cwt. = 1 ton ; 2240 lbs. = 1 ton.

Capacity.—8 gallons = 1 bushel ; 32 qts. = 1 bushel.

Surface.—9 sqr. feet = 1 sqr. yard ; 30½ sqr. yds. = 1 sqr. pole ; 40 sqr. poles = 1 rood ; 4 roods = 1 acre ; 10 sqr. chains = 1 acre.

Solidity.—1728 cubic inches = 1 cubic foot ; 27 cubic feet = 1 cubic yard.

[Inasmuch as some of the pupils in this Standard will not remain in school beyond this year, the teacher should endeavour to fit them for the simple business calculations that will enter into their life. It is therefore desirable that they know the tables in full ; also American money : 1 cent = 1 British half-penny ; 100 cents = 1 dollar ($) ; also, $7\frac{92}{100}$ inches (very nearly 8 inches) = 1 link ; 100 links = 1 chain. (These are to be taught to Standard IV., if not to Standard III.) It is also desirable that Standard III. should have some practice in simple household accounts, thus anticipating the next Standard.]

STANDARD IV.

Full knowledge of the four rules in simple and compound numbers, including weights and measures.

To measure rectangular areas and the cubic contents of rectangular tanks.

Household accounts. Ordinary bills and invoices.

To find the interest on a sum of money for years and even months, at 4, 5, 6, 10 per cent.

Easy sums in addition and subtraction of simple fractions, with denominators not exceeding 12.

To know the meaning of .5, .25, .75 ; to learn these decimals as tenths and hundredths, and as corresponding to ½, ¼, ¾.

Easy percentages, and ordinary trade discount.

To solve, mentally, by the method of first principles, (unitary method) easy problems occurring in actual life.

STANDARD V.

More familiar knowledge of compound numbers, household accounts, and bills and invoices.

Easy vulgar and decimal fractions.

Percentages. Interest,—principal, rate per cent. and time being given. Simple Practice. Simple proportion. Averages. The measurement of a triangle, or a four-sided figure with two sides parallel.

STANDARD VI.

Fraction. Percentages. Interest. Compound Proportion.

The work of previous standards, with increased rapidity and accuracy.

Notes and Suggestions.

Teachers are recommended to form a plan for the year's work in Arithmetic, so as to take up in each Standard the several portions of the prescribed work, progressively, month by month,—taking all, in a simple way, with frequent reviews, during the first six months of the school year, and the same afterwards more fully and with thorough reviews. With such definite plan, and a wise distribution of the work, success can be achieved which otherwise could not be expected. The following are suggestions as to teaching this subject :—

(a) All numbers should be learned and all processes explained by actual observation and handling of suitable objects by the pupils, or (if this is not practicable) by diagrams. Compound numbers and fractions so explained will be easily comprehended to the extent required in the several Standards. For the first lessons the objects might be small sticks, nuts, pebbles, and the like ; objects in the schoolroom (books, etc.) ; lines, dots, O's, X's, squares, triangles, etc., on blackboard and on slates ; and also balls on the numeral frame, which, however, should not be used exclusively nor chiefly. Coins, weights and measures, to a limited extent, should be introduced from the beginning, and learned, so far as possible, by actual observation and handling on the part of the pupils. The objects are to be gradually discarded as the facts are learned.

(b) For teaching addition and subtraction, small sticks (single and combined into bundles of tens and tens into hundreds) could be used (or some equivalent device) and the same principles illustrated by the use of farthings pence and shillings.

(c) The sum of any two digits added together should be as well known as the multiplication table. In addition and subtraction sums at the Examination, counting by fingers or by strokes on slate will very greatly detract from the credit due for a correct answer.

(*d*) To ensure correct notation, there should be frequent special exercises in writing numbers from dictation.

(*e*) Mental exercises, with small numbers, but of the same nature as the written exercises, should precede the written in all the Standards.

(*f*) All problems of applied arithmetic should bear principally on current coins, weight and measures, and be suitable to the life and experience of the children.

(*g*) Accuracy should be the especial aim in the Lower Standards. To secure rapidity with accuracy the scholars of the 3rd Standard and upwards should be required to add columns of pounds, shillings and pence within a specfied time.

(*h*) The tables to be learned include those weights and measures only which are in ordinary use, viz. :—

Length.—The mile, furlong, chain, rod or pole, yard, foot and inch.

Weight.—The ton, hundredweight, quarter, stone, pound, ounce and drachm.

Capacity.—Bushel, peck, gallon, quart, pint and gill.

Area.—The square mile, acre, rood, square pole or perch, the square yard, foot and inch.

Time.—Year, month, week, day hour, minute and second.

At inspection liberal allowances will be made in marking the work of any Standard with respect to that portion of the work not prescribed in the former Code, until there has been opportunity to take up in the lower Standards, from which the pupils have been advanced, the preliminary work of a like nature.

OBLIGATORY SUBJECT.

ELEMENTARY SCIENCE, GENERAL AND AGRICULTURAL.

LOWER DIVISION.—*Junior Standard and Standard I.*

A course of 36 lessons dealing with the simple phenomena of animal and plant life ; e.g. :—

I. *Animal Life.*

(*a*) *Domestic Animals.*—Their uses. How they repay kindness and care. The Cat (compare with Dog) ; Cow (compare with Sheep and Goat) ; Horse (compare with Mule and Donkey.)

(*b*) *Domestic Birds.*—Fowl (compare with Duck), Turkey, Pigeon, etc.

(*c*) *Wild Animals, Birds, Reptiles, etc.*—Their usefulness ; their harm-fulness. Lessons upon some of the following :—Bat, Rat, and Mouse ; Lizards and Crocodiles ; Tadpoles and Frogs ; Bees and Humming Birds ; etc.

II. *Plant Life.*

(*a*) Study of Plants as growing things. Very simple lessons upon the structure and purpose of roots, stems, leaves, flowers, fruit and seeds.

(*b*) Simple lessons to be given upon some of the more useful plants in Jamaica—such as sugar cane, coffee, bananas, oranges, yams, cocoes, etc.

MIDDLE DIVISION - *Standards II. and III.*

A course of at least 25 lessons embracing the following subjects :

I. *General Science.*

Matter.—The three states of matter. Simple experiments to show their properties, especially those of water. Effect of heat and cold, boiling and freezing.

Movements of the air.—Land and sea breezes—winds—hurricanes.

Moisture in the air.—Water turns to vapour. (Wet cloth dried in the wind.) Vapour turns to water. (Breathing on slate. Clouds on hills. Evening mists.)

Clouds in the sky. Rain (size of drops—effect of heavy rain in tearing up roads, etc. Disposition of sand and pebbles washed to a distance.)

II. Agricultural Science.

Plant Life.—Water necessary for plants. Seeds.—Germination of seeds (examples to be shown). Functions of water, soil and air in supplying plant food.

UPPER DIVISION—*Standards above Middle Division.*

A course of at least 25 lessons embracing the following subjects :

I. General Science.

As in Middle Division.

The Atmosphere.—Composition of the air. Properties of Oxygen and Carbon-dioxide.

Use of Barometer and Thermometer.

General ideas of the structure of the human body and functions of its chief organs, given in simple language. A few main laws of health. Necessity for wholesome food, pure water, airy dwelling, bodily cleanliness.

II. Agricultural Science.

Action of water, air, etc., on rocks and soil.

Soils—how formed—different kinds — condition — how improved by tillage, drainage, watering and manuring, etc.

Agricultural work at different periods of the year.

Tools. Uses of the different sorts. How to keep in order.

Common objects of cultivation in Jamaica. Condition of soil and situation best suited to their growth.

Plant food required by chief Jamaica crops—how obtained and utilised.

Preparation of fruit and other products for market

NOTES AND SUGGESTIONS.

1. The lessons generally, and very specially in the Lower Division, should be conversational, as far removed as possible from a formal lecture.

2. The lessons must, whenever possible, be illustrated by actual objects, specimens, pictures, diagrams, blackboard drawings or clay models.

3. Children should be encouraged to bring with them to the lesson illustrative specimens, which they have collected or obtained from friends.

4. Children should be encouraged to make simple drawings illustrative of their observations. Those in the upper division should be required to write brief weekly compositions in which they may express in a written form the ideas which they have acquired through observation and oral instruction and also through reading.

5. Plants, in pots, boxes or glasses, should be grown in the school room for illustrative purposes. As far as possible, knowledge respecting plants should be gained through practical illustrations and simple experiments.

6 When the teacher of a country school finds it needful to give only selected portions of the course in this subject, the lessons most closely connected with agriculture should be chosen.

SECONDARY SUBJECTS.

SCRIPTURE, INCLUDING THE TEACHING OF MORALS.

LOWER DIVISION.—*(Junior Standard and Standard I.)*

Scripture Knowledge.

To answer intelligently questions on 30 lessons given during the year, consisting chiefly of simple stories from the life of Christ ; also from the lives of prominent Bible characters, to illustrate moral lessons and the greatness, goodness and providence of God.

To learn by heart : Lord's Prayer ; Psalm xxiii. Standard I. to learn, also, Prov. xii. 17, 18, 19, 22.

Morals.

Instruction and training throughout the year in reverence for God, truthfulness, honesty, purity, gentleness, obedience to parents, to teachers, and to persons in authority, politeness, kindness towards playmates and animals

MIDDLE DIVISION.—*(Standards II. and III.)*

Scripture Knowledge.

Leading facts in Life of our Lord. A few of the chief parables. History of Creation and Flood. Simple Stories as in Lower Division, including most prominent facts in life of Moses.

To learn by heart : Ten Commandments ; Matt. v. 1-12, and xxii. 35-40. Standard III. to learn, also, Deut. xxviii. 1-14.

Morals.

Reverence, love of country, respect for authority, obedience to law, honour, industry, temperance, purity, politeness, good behaviour at home, in school, in places of worship, in company, avoiding evil speaking and profanity.

UPPER DIVISION.—*(Standard IV. and upwards.)*

Scripture Knowledge.

Our Lord's Life and Teaching. The main facts in Old Testament history, and in lives of the Apostles.

To learn by heart : John xiv. 15-31. Standards V. and VI. also to learn Proverbs xiv. 25 ; xvi. 24 ; xix. 22 ; xx. 1 ; xxiii. 31 and 32 ; xxvi. 28 ; xxviii. 13 ; Ephesians vi. 1-8. Standard VI. also to learn : 1 Cor. xii. 31, and xiii.

Morals.

Reverence, self-respect, patriotism, courage, self-control, self-denial, confession of wrong, forgiveness, duties of the citizen, fidelity to official trust.

Note.—There can profitably be some stated lessons in Morals, teaching the rules of politeness and good behaviour and the principles of right conduct underlying the rules ; the duties of a citizen ; etc. As a rule, however, Morals will be taught incidentally, in connection with Scripture lessons and the school life of the children. The most effectual teaching will be the daily life of the teacher. Much use should be made of stories and brief biographies, as illustrative examples. Besides appropriate Scripture texts, children should learn by heart suitable and striking verses and proverbs and the like, and it will be well to have these written on slate or paper and (in the higher Standards) carefully copied into exercise books.

DRAWING AND MANUAL OCCUPATIONS.

LOWER DIVISION—*Junior Standard, Standards I. and II.*

DRAWING.

(a) *Drawing*—On chequered slates, or paper, of lines (Vertical, Horizontal, Oblique and Curved) and combinations of these to form simple figures and patterns and to represent common objects of simple form.

(b) To know the use of the ruler and to be able to measure short distances in inches and half inches.

(c) To draw with the ruler (using inches or inches and half-inches) straight lines in the different positions, and also to combine these to form angles and simple geometrical figures.

MANUAL OCCUPATIONS.

(a) *Stick-laying.*—On a plane surface to illustrate direction of lines and formation of simple geometrical figures. To combine sticks so as to illustrate simple arithmetical processes.

(b) *Colour-work.*—To colour (with crayons) squares, oblongs, triangles, etc., so as to gain an accurate conception of their form, as distinguished from outline ; *or*

(c) *Clay-modelling.*—Modelling with fingers or very simple tools to illustrate lessons in Geography, Science, Drawing, etc. ; e.g., Island, Lake, Cape, Bay, Orange, Banana, Square, Sphere, etc.

MIDDLE DIVISION—*Standards III. and IV.*

DRAWING.

(a) *Freehand Drawing* of regular forms and of simple curved and right lined figures from the flat.

(b) Very simple drawing from objects ; also memory drawing—to reproduce impressions of the size and shape of objects under observation in the Science, Geography or other lessons.

(c) *Simple Geometrical Figures* with the ruler or with the ruler and set square ; e.g., square, oblong, triangle, pentagon, hexagon, octagon, etc.

MANUAL OCCUPATIONS.

(a) *Paper and Cardboard Modelling.*—To cut out and mount simple geometrical forms and right lined figures.

To make a few simple models ; e.g., an Envelope, Box, Tray, etc.

(b) *Clay Modelling.*—To illustrate lessons in Science, Geography, Drawing, etc.

To model some of the Solid Geometrical Forms; e.g., Cube, Cylinder, Cone, Prism, etc. ; *or*

(c) *Colour Work.*—To colour with crayons some of the items of the Drawing Course for the year—more particularly the object   awn.

DIVISION III.—*Standards V. and VI.*

DRAWING.

(a) *Freehand Drawing* and drawing from objects more advanced than in Division II.

(b) *Simple Scales and Drawing to Scale :*

1. Scales ; e.g. : 1 inch, 1½ inch, or 3 inches to a foot to show feet, or 1 or 2 inches to 10 feet to show feet.

2. To draw and take dimensions from a scale of feet and inches.

3. To draw a plan or other figure on squared paper from a sketch having dimensions marked on it.

4. To enlarge or reduce plane figures to scale.

(c) *The use of Compasses.*—To construct a square, triangle, circle, polygon, etc., and to bisect a line or angle.

MANUAL OCCUPATIONS.

(a) *Clay Modelling.*—As in previous Divisions ; also Modelling of solid geometrical forms from dimensioned drawing.

(b) *Paper or Cardboard Modelling.*—A few simple models executed accurately from a dimensioned drawing.

(c) *Modelling in Wood.*—A few easy exercises such as can be accomplished by the use of simple tools, such as a knife and saw ; e.g.: Flower stick, Setting stick, String winder, Plant label, etc.

GEOGRAPHY—(WITH INCIDENTAL HISTORY).

LOWER DIVISION—*Junior Standard and Standard I.*

Land and water. Simple notions of natural features—hills, mountains, valleys, plains ; bodies of water and water courses ; these notions to be gained from observation of natural features in the locality of the school, and from illustrations by diagrams, pictures, and clay models.

Simple notions of a district ; a parish ; a country ; a town or city.

Cardinal points. Localities surrounding school and district.

The simplest plans. Plan of schoolroom ; of school and school yard. Simple notions of a map. To point out on a map of Jamaica the parish ; capital of the parish ; Kingston ; Spanish Town ; Montego Bay ; Port Antonio.

MIDDLE DIVISION—*Standards II. and III.*

A. Very general broad outlines of the geography of the world. General ideas of the physical, political and commercial geography of Jamaica. Ports of Jamaica. British and American ports commercially connected with Jamaica. Interchange of products.

B. General knowledge of the Geography of the British Empire ; of the West Indies, North America, and Europe. The five Zones. The most prominent events of Jamaica History.

UPPER DIVISION—*Standards above the Middle Division.*

Physical, political and commercial geography of Great Britain and the United States—the general and more prominent features. The British Empire—very prominent features. General geography of the world. Latitude and Longitude. To find on the map any place, its latitude and longitude being known, and *vice versa.*

Climate. Interchange of productions, especially as between countries in different Zones.

Biographies of six leading persons prominently connected with the history of England or Jamaica, as Alfred, Henry V., Columbus, Queen Elizabeth, Cromwell, Rodney, Nelson, Wilberforce, Wellington, General Gordon, etc.

Leading events in the reign of Queen Victoria.

[Third Class Schools will not be examined in Geography beyond Section A, Middle Division, except with the sanction of the Inspector for the District first obtained.]

SINGING.

LOWER DIVISION—*Junior Standard and Standard I.*

To sing the Scale of C. Major (the ordinary scale) from staff or modulator, and the notes (tones) of the key-chord of C (or a Do-chord) in any easy order.

To sing sweetly an appropriate hymn, and three simple songs, two of them to be action songs.

The words of hymn and songs should be such as children can understand and such as will excite their interest.

The compass of the songs as a rule should not exceed the limit of an octave.

MIDDLE DIVISION—*Standards II. and III.*

NOTE TEST.

Staff Notation.—To sing slowly as pointed out by the examiner and using the sol-fa syllables, the ascending and descending notes of the scale of C, (Do) the notes of the key-chord of C (Do Mi Sol Do), in any order, and also small groups of consecutive notes of the scale of C as written by the examiner.

Tonic Sol-fa Notation.—To Sol-fa slowly from the examiner's pointing on the modulator in any key—the key tone and chord being given ; the tones of the Do chord in any order, and the other tones of the scale in stepwise succession.

TIME TEST.

Staff Notation.—To sing on one sound to the syllable "laa" an exercise in 2-2 or 4-4 time, which shall include minims and crotchets.

Tonic Sol-fa Notation :—To sing on one ·tone to the syllable "laa" an exercise including one pulse and two pulse tones, in two pulse or four pulse measure.

SONG TEST.

To sing in unison in good time and tune, and sweetly, any one of at least five school songs previously prepared.

UPPER DIVISION—*Standards IV. and upwards.*

NOTE TEST.

Staff Notation.—To sing slowly as pointed out by the examiner, using the Sol-fa syllables, a series of notes in the key of C containing an F sharp contradicted by an F natural, and a B flat contradicted by a B natural. The F sharp should be approached by the note G and return to G, and the B flat should be approached by C and followed by A.

Tonic Sol-fa Notation.—(Modulator) (*a*) To Sol-fa from the examiner's pointing on the Modulator, or from dictation in any key, simple passages in the major diatonic scale, including fe and ta, in stepwise progression used thus : s fe s—d' ta l.

(*Written or printed*) (*b*).—To Sol-fa at sight a written or printed exercise including the notes of do-chord in any order, and any other notes of the major diatonic scale in stepwise succession. The exercise not to contain any difficulties of time.

TIME TEST.

Staff Notation.—To sing on one sound to the syllable "laa" an exercise in 4-4 or 3-4 time containing semibreves, minims, crotchets, and quavers, with dotted minims, and rests on non-accented portions of the bar.

Tonic Sol-fa Notation.—To sing on one sound to the syllable "laa" an exercise in three pulse or four pulse measure, containing one pulse notes, half pulse notes and whole pulse rests on the non-accented pulses of the measure.

Song Test.

To sing in unison or parts, in good time and tune and with due expression, any one of at least five school songs previously prepared.

Notes and Suggestions.

1. The singing should not be too loud.

2. The songs should be varied in character and include the National Anthem.

3. Some new songs should be learned every year.

SPECIAL SUBJECTS.

Needlework.

Lower Division.—*(Junior Standard and Standard I.)*

1.—Needle Drill.   Position Drill.

2.—A strip of calico or other cotton material in simple hemming with coloured cotton in two colours in order.   Not less than 4 inches should be shown in each colour.

3.—Hemming, seaming, felling.   Any useful articles showing these three stitches.

Middle Division.—*(Standards II. and III.)*

1.—The work of the previous division.   Stitching on coarse material, pleating, putting on a band, sewing on strings.   A simple untrimmed garment ; *e.g.*, an apron, pinafore, or petticoat.

2.—Simple darning on stocking web or on single thread canvas or cheese cloth.

Upper Division.—*(Standards IV. and upwards.)*

1.—The work of the previous division.   Gathering and setting in. Making a button-hole.   A simple untrimmed garment ; *e.g.*, a child's overall or chemise.

2.—Patching a calico or print garment.

3.- Herring-bone stitch.

4.—Darning a thin place, a hole, a tear.

Practical Teaching in Agriculture and Horticulture.

[All schools are required to illustrate the teaching in Elementary Science, General and Agricultural, by experiments—including simple experiments on plant germination, life and growth, the different kinds of soil and their improvement and use of manures —carried on by means of plants grown in pots or boxes.]

To obtain the extra grant under Article 112 the following conditions must be met :—

1. A plot of land at least a quarter of an acre in extent must be provided.

2. The plot must be surrounded by a good and sufficient fence, and the possession of it legally defined.

3. The plot must be used as an experiment ground to illustrate the lessons on Agriculture given in the school : *i.e.*, to illustrate plant life and

growth, to show the effect of different methods of preparing the soil, the necessity of the presence of moisture and plant food, the results of the use of different manures ; to produce practical skill in agricultural operations such as preparing and tending the ground for crops, planting, pruning, grafting, &c., treatment of pests, culture of the ordinary products of Jamaica (not necessarily *only* those generally found in the district) and rotation of crops.

4. Every boy in the school above 11 years of age must attend the practical teaching in the experiment plot for at least two of the four hours required to be given to it, and the teaching shall be open to girls ; all who take part in it must undertake such work as their strength and state of progress enables them to do ; *e.g.*, the younger children can water, weed, and tidy the ground, the less advanced among the older boys dig, mix and carry manure, &c., and the more advanced prune, graft, &c. : all must be taught to observe the condition and growth of the plants as affected by the different methods of cultivation, the different effects of surface digging and deep trenching, &c., what to do with leaves, weeds and other refuse, &c.

5. The list of tools provided must be approved by the Inspector ; as a rule the following will be required for each dozen children :

       3 Light Machettes.
       2 Rakes.
       2 Garden Spades : small size.
       2 Demerara Forks—3 or 4 prongs.
       3 Hoes, small size only, for friable soil (loam or marl). Pruning Knives ; &c.

6. Everything grown should if possible be sold, and after the payment of necessary expenses one-third of the net proceeds must go to the Teacher, and the other two-thirds must be used for the purchase of tools or other necessaries of cultivation, text-books, and other books dealing with country life.

7. No credit will be given to any school for ordinary cultivation conducted on unscientific methods : but only for cultivation in the methods of experiment and teaching laid down by the Agricultural Experiment Station, and taught to the Teachers and Students by the officers of the Station or others in the Training College and elsewhere.

Note.—For the present and until further notice grants will continue to be given for intelligent and careful teaching and cultivation on the lines of the last revision of the Code of 1899 to teachers who have not had the opportunity of instruction in proper methods of teaching Practical Agriculture.

ADVANCED COURSE OF MANUAL TRAINING.

The following advanced course is prepared for boys of Standard V. and VI. in town schools, where a central place is fitted with appliances for manual training. A special grant for fairly efficient teaching of this subject will be given.

DRAWING.

Mechanical Drawing.—To understand and be able to execute a full working drawing (plan, elevation, section and isometric or oblique projection) of an exercise or model to be afterwards executed in wood.

To make rapid freehand sketches of exercises or models that have been executed in wood.

To construct all the ordinary plane figures by geometry.

MANUAL OCCUPATIONS.

Woodwork—1st Year.

Combined exercises in drawing and modelling. Acquaintance with principal tools used ; their construction, proper use, method of sharpening, &c.

Graduated practical exercises in planing and sawing ; also simple joints and simple models.

Woodwork—2nd Year.

More advanced practical exercises involving the use of additional tools. Ability to sharpen a plane-iron, chisel, gouge, &c.
Knowledge of timber—its growth, felling, seasoning, market forms, value, &c., &c.
Knowledge of nails, screws, glue and other material used in the workshop.

ORGANIZATION AND DISCIPLINE.

Marks are awarded to schools for Organization and Discipline.

Organization.—In awarding marks for Organization, the Inspector will have regard (a) to [the neatness and order of the school premises and furniture and their suitability ; (b) the proper classification of the scholars both for teaching and examination ; (c) the suitableness of the programme of work for the several Standards and for the members of the staff, as shown in the time-table ; and (d) the Inspector will take into account the condition of the school records, and the thoroughness with which the requirements of the Department with regard to them have been met. The marking of Organization will be affected by the results of any special visits the Inspector may have been able to pay during the year.

In Infant Schools much importance will be attached to the adequate supply of suitable furniture and appliances and the sufficiency of material for work (especially of the younger scholars) along Kindergarten lines.

Discipline.—The ordinary discipline of the school, to be satisfactory, must be prompt and exact, yet maintained without harshness and without noisy demonstration of authority. In Infant Schools the quiet tone, the gentle, pleasing manner of the teacher with the little children, will be specially noted.

Managers and Teachers will be expected to satisfy the Inspector that all reasonable care is taken, in the ordinary conduct of the school, to bring up the children in the habits of punctuality, of good manners and language of cleanliness and tidiness, and also to impress upon the children the importance of cheerful obedience to duty, of consideration and respect for others, and of honour and truthfulness in word and act. In particular, the honesty of the scholars under examination, and the degree of interest they show in their work, will be taken into account ; and high marks will not be given unless the Inspector is satisfied that the school is a place for the formation of right habits as well as a place of instruction.

INFANT SCHOOLS.

The scholars in an Infant School will comprise two Divisions :

Division I.—Preparatory Standard (A)— 4 to 6 years.

Division II.—Junior Standard (B) and Standard I.—6 to 8 years. [It will often be advisable, for the benefit of all, that children prepared to enter Standard I. be transferred to an ordinary school, leaving only the Preparatory Standard and the Junior Standard.]

The course of instruction for the Junior Standard and Standard I. will be that prescribed for those Standards in Schedule A, together with such portions of the Special Course of Infant Instruction as are appropriate to those Standards, including the "Manual Occupations" prescribed for them in Schedule A.

The course of instruction for the Preparatory Standard will be chiefly of a Kindergarten nature, but will include, at the discretion of the teacher and to the extent that shall be determined by her, some of the simpler work of the Junior Standard. [See Art. 28, Notes.]

SPECIAL COURSE OF INFANT INSTRUCTION.

I.—LANGUAGE.—Through conversation and in connection with all lessons.

II.—NUMBER; COLOUR; FORM—(*direction, position, dimension, surface, outline*). To be learned through observation, and chiefly in the use of Kindergarten Gifts and by Kindergarten Occupations. In the Occupations the child is to be so taught that his own powers of construction and arrangement will be developed, and also his power of expression through the work of the hand.

Gifts.—The chief gifts are: 1, 2, 3, 4, 7, 8.

Occupations.—The chief occupations are: Building; stick-laying; drawing; paper-folding, cutting, and pasting; modelling in clay simple and familiar objects of household use, or of plant and animal life. [Other Occupations, serving in a like purpose, are sewing (outlines of figures), and peas-work.]

III.—MORALS.—To be taught (in part) through (a) Action Songs; (b) Kindergarten Games.

[The action song and the organized play lead the child to self-activity and to reproduce in a simple way some of the doings he observes in the social world about him. He is thus to learn his moral relations to others; to respect their rights while maintaining his own.]

SCHEDULE B.

CURRICULUM FOR TRAINING COLLEGES.

PREPARATORY STATEMENT.

The revision of the Curriculum for Training Colleges has become necessary, in order to provide a two years' course of training to be taken by the majority of Students, and to be supplemented at a later stage ; to provide for fuller instruction, through observation and experiment and practical demonstration, in agriculture, and elementary science chiefly connected therewith ; and to introduce a practicable amount of manual training, along Kindergarten lines for women, and more extended manual training for men.

A prominent aim in arranging the Curriculum has been to ensure that the Students who become Teachers shall have a thorough and familiar knowledge of what they will teach to school children, together with an intelligent grasp of the true principles and best methods of teaching, and, as far as practicable, actual experience in the use of such methods in the elementary (practising) school. It is expected that in all the subjects the lessons as given to the Students by the College Tutors will to a very considerable extent exemplify the best method of giving lessons to children upon the same or similar subjects.

Another prominent aim has been to secure general intelligence and alertness of mind ; also, a taste for reading with some knowledge of the books most desirable to be read, fitting students to guide and assist their future pupils in the reading of books which it is to be hoped will ere long be found in school libraries in many schools. The fact is recognised in the Curriculum that a Teacher's range of knowledge should extend beyond what he will be required to teach.

The Curriculum has been framed so as to exclude, as far as may be, the mere memorizing of such details as are not necessary for the equipment of an efficient teacher ; but for purposes of illustrating general truths and principles, Tutors will frequently find it profitable to go further into details than is prescribed. The Curriculum is to be regarded not as indicating the maximum of instruction that may profitably be given, but as prescribing the minimum of instruction that is required. The examination tests are to be based upon what is prescribed.

After completing their two years' course in College many Students will enter upon their work as teachers, while a smaller number of Students will continue in College for a third year. Teachers who, after taking a two years' course in College, have had three years of actual work as teachers, may take the third year's course, in part as home study, to be completed as a rule in a Training College for a period not exceeding six months. The Department may accept a shorter term than six months in a Training College, but not less than three months, in cases where a course of additional reading, to be prescribed, is pursued with intelligent comprehension to the satisfaction of the Department as ascertained by an examination to be arranged for.

READING AND RECITATION.

FIRST YEAR :—

To read with fluency, ease and expression, with full understanding and ability to explain to a class, lessons from the ordinary books used in the elementary schools of the Island. Special weight will be attached to distinct articulation and clear enunciation. [See Note 1.]

Ability to use a dictionary intelligently, with knowledge of marks of pronunciation and the several uses of italics.

To recite, with appropriate expression, three or four simple poems of varied character, of an aggregate of not less than 120 lines.

In the case of each Student a certificate will be required from the Principal that the Student has read during the year, under supervision, at least one prose work by a standard author. [See Notes 2 and 3.]

SECOND YEAR :—

Reading, as in first year, and of a more advanced character. One-third of the reading lessons should be historical, including current history. To read newspapers, and current periodicals, including educational periodicals. [See Note 4.]

Full knowledge of abbreviations ordinarily occurring in current literature.

To recite with appropriate expression two poems, differing in character, of an aggregate of not less than 120 lines.

A certificate from the Principal, as above,--the book to be of a different character from that of the first year ; also, a certificate that the student has read a short history of the reign of Queen Victoria.

THIRD YEAR :—

Advanced Reading. Reading from newspapers and periodicals.

To recite with appropriate expression one or two poems of not less than 120 lines in the aggregate.

A certificate from the Principal as above, that the Student has read two standard works, prose or poetry ; also, a certificate that the Student has read a book of general history.

NOTES AND SUGGESTIONS.

1.—To secure distinct articulation and clear enunciation there will need to be systematic exercises in vocal drill throughout the course.

2.--The book to be read by the Student should be selected by the Principal and the selection approved by the Department. The contents of the work should form the subject of conversational discussion between the Tutors and Students, and the volume might be the same for a group of four to eight Students in cases where there would be several such groups.

3.—The book read by the Student may be one of the books from which an extract is selected by the Examiner to be read at the Oral Examination. An intelligent understanding of the extract read will be expected.

4.—A list of the educational periodicals to be provided for the reading of Students should be given to the Education Department at the beginning of each year.

5.—In their reading the Students should be trained to the habitual use of the dictionary and atlas, and should be accustomed to make use of other books of reference.

6.—It is not expected that in any year the reading will be limited to the Syllabus.

WRITING.

FIRST SECOND, AND THIRD YEAR :—

Specimens of penmanship shown in setting copies in text hand and small hand.

Writing on blackboard.

NOTES AND SUGGESTIONS.

The penmanship shown in the examination papers, generally, will be taken into consideration.

Blackboard writing will be tested at the same time with practice teaching. It will include the writing of sentences to serve as a reading lesson, and the setting of sums for any Standard.

It is important that Students acquire a large, bold, clear style of blackboard writing.

ENGLISH.

FIRST YEAR :—

To write from dictation passages (prose and poetry) of moderate difficulty, involving the use of the common punctuation marks.

Spelling ; word-building ; common prefixes and affixes.

Business forms ; letter-writing, to include business letters.

To write from memory the substance of a short simple story, read with ordinary quickness—(120 to 150 words).

Paraphrasing of simple modern poetry.

Simple analysis and parsing.

SECOND YEAR :—

Dictation as in first year, with full knowledge of marks of punctuation.

More extended exercises in word-building.

Fuller knowledge of letter-writing and business forms.

Writing in simple language short essays on given subjects.

To give a concise report of a public lecture or a discussion.

Paraphrasing as in first year.

Full analysis and parsing of modern prose and poetry.

THIRD YEAR :—

As in previous years, with more difficult essay writing and more extended reports of lectures and discussions.

Paraphrasing of modern poetry.

Analysis and parsing as above.

Structure of words ; roots ; prefixes and affixes.

ARITHMETIC.

FIRST YEAR :—

Elementary Rules ; Money ; Weights and Measures : Fractions, Vulgar and Decimal ; Metric System ; Practice ; Bills of Parcels ; Simple household Accounts ; Proportion, Unitary Method.

Exercises in Mental Arithmetic.

SECOND YEAR :—

Proportion ; Percentages ; Interest ; Profit and Loss ; Simp Problems, occurring in every-day life, in Linear, Square, and Cub Measure ; Square Root.

Exercises in Mental Arithmetic.

THIRD YEAR :—

Review of the work of previous years, with more advanced question and more extensive applications of percentages, including Stocks.

NOTES AND SUGGESTIONS.

1.—In addition to special exercises in Mental Arithmetic, a portion of the time given to each lesson in Arithmetic—ten to twenty-five per cent.— should, as a rule, be devoted to simple mental exercises introductory to the lesson.

2.—Students may be required to do addition and multiplication sums in money, within a specified time, as a test of accuracy and speed.

3.—It is expected that all written work will be done with such regard to neatness and method as would make it a satisfactory model for scholars in elementary schools.

4.—To the Arithmetic paper for the Second Year there will be appended a certain proportion of questions in Algebra, which may be taken, optionally, as alternative to certain questions in Arithmetic, by those Students who passed in first class in Arithmetic in the 1st Year Examination ; also, by others, in exceptional cases, who receive special permission from the Department to take the alternative questions in Algebra.

These questions in Algebra will not extend beyond the four simple rules, and simple equations of one unknown quantity, with easy problems leading to such equations.

SCHOOL MANAGEMENT

FIRST YEAR :—

Characteristics of Children. Leading Principles of Teaching, as founded upon fundamental laws of the mind affecting the acquisition of knowlege, and as applied in methods of teaching Reading, Arithmetic, and Object Lessons.

Notes of Lessons. A lesson in Reading or Arithmetic to be given in presence of the Examiner. Three lessons to be prepared.--[See Note 2a.]

Also—in Women's Colleges,—

INFANT TEACHING.

Characteristics of Infants—4 to 6 and 6 to 8 years of age.
Characteristics of a successful Infant School Teacher.
Principles of Kindergarten Teaching. Adaptation of same to teaching the following to children in Infant Schools, and the lower Standards in elementary schools ; Language and Reading ; Number ; Object Lessons chiefly on common natural objects.

SECOND YEAR :—

Principles of Teaching : (i.) as founded upon fundamental laws of the mind affecting the acquisition of knowledge, the attainment of intellectual power and manual skill, and the formation of character ; (ii.) as applied in methods of teaching the several subjects in the Code.

The adaptation of Kindergarten methods and manual training to ordinary elementary schools ; the practicable extent and necessary limitations.

Best methods of organization ; time table ; school appliances ; school records and forms.

Discipline.

A lesson, which may be on any subject in the Code, to be given in presence of the Examiner. Four lessons to be prepared.—[See Note 2b.]
In addition to the above, the Examiner may require a Student to conduct a class in Swedish Drill.

Also—in Women's Colleges—

INFANT TEACHING.

Aim of an Infant School ; best method of organization ; essential elements of good discipline.

How to teach Language and Reading ; Number ; Writing ; Object Lessons, to include Lessons on Form and Colour ; Singing ; Drill ; Games ; Story-telling ; Drawing on blackboard.

How most effectively to give direct and indirect instruction in Scripture and Morals.

Practice in the following occupations : building (Gifts iii. and iv.) ; drawing—on chequers, and free hand ; stick-laying ; paper-folding ; clay-moulding.

The best methods of teaching these to scholars in Infant Schools and the lower Standards of ordinary elementary schools ; limitations of their profitable use.

THIRD YEAR :—

For Men : Review of the work of previous years.
Educational Reformers : Comenius ; Pestalozzi ; Frœbel ; Spencer. Their educational principles, and their life, so far as directly connected with their educational work.

For Women : Review of the work of previous years.
Frœbel's life and educational work. The essential harmony of his educational principles with those of Comenius and Pestalozzi. The

3 E

adaptation of his methods to Infant Schools in Jamaica, and the lower Standards of ordinary elementary schools.

NOTES AND SUGGESTIONS.

1. (a) First Year Students will be required to spend, during the latter half of the year, fifty hours in the practising school. Part of this time, at the discretion of the Tutor, may be spent in observation.

(b) Second Year Students will be required to spend in the practising school during the year 100 hours, of which at least seventy-five are to be spent in actual teaching; provided that the hours spent during the latter half of the year in visiting neighbouring schools under guidance will be accepted, to the extent of fifteen hours, as equivalent to that number of hours in the practising school.

(c) Third Year Students will be required to spend at least sixty hours during the year in teaching in the practising school. Two periods of not more than a week each, at the discretion of the Principal, should be granted to Third Year Students to visit the best neighbouring schools. The Students should be required to furnish to the Principal notes of the visit to each school.

2. (a) The three lessons prepared by First Year Students shall consist of one in the Arithmetic and two in Reading, or *vice versa*, one lesson of the two to be for a lower Standard and the other for a higher Standard.

(b) The lessons to be given by Second and Third Year Students at the Examination should include in the aggregate (if possible) all subjects of instruction in the Code, (except Sewing and Manual Training) and should be distributed among all Standards or Divisions of the school.

3. Third Year Students will be present at the practice teaching of some First or Second Year Students, at the Examination, and shall then prepare for the Examiner a written criticism of the teaching and the Notes of Lesson. One hour will be allowed for this exercise.

4. Besides special questions set on the subject of School Management, it is intended that the Examination tests in each subject shall include questions as to methods of teaching the subject, and reasons for processes.

5. The Students should be proficient in such exercises in Swedish Drill as can be introduced advantageously into elementary schools.

6. In addition to any other instruction given in lectures by College Tutors, it will be expected of Students that they show an intelligent knowledge of the text-books, as follows :—

First Year.—The text-books prescribed for Pupil Teachers, and the following portions of Roark's "Method in Education"; pp. 12–39; 63–70; 103–134; 260–280. *Also—(in Women's Colleges)* [Text-book prescribed by the Department].

Second Year.—As above; Roark complete, excepting chapters XIII. and XIV. *Also—(in Women's Colleges)* [Text-book prescribed by the Department].

Third Year.—As above. Quick's Essays on Comenius, Pestalozzi, Frœbel, Spencer. Spencer's Essay on Education, Chapters II. and III. *In Women's Colleges*, [Text-book prescribed by the Department].

It is recommended that College Tutors themselves make free use of, and train the Students to use, for reference, the text-books used heretofore and any others of high repute in which principles and methods of teaching are set forth.

SCRIPTURE AND MORALS.
SCRIPTURE KNOWLEDGE.

(A) Chief facts recorded in Genesis to Judges, inclusive. Matthew.

(B) Chief facts recorded in the Books of Samuel and Kings. Luke, Leading facts in Life of the Apostle Paul.

(C) The chief Prophets. Outlines of History of Israel from the Captivity to the Christian Era   John. Acts.

In 1901, and every alternate year thereafter, First and Second Year Students will be examined in A, and in 1902, and every alternate year thereafter, they will be examined in B.

In 1901, Third Year Students will be examined in A ; and every year thereafter they will be examined in C.

[In 1900, all Students will be examined in Scripture under the former Code.]

Students to commit to memory the passages required to be learnt by the pupils in the elementary schools :—

First Year—Passages for Lower and Middle Division.
Second Year—Passages for Upper Division.
Third Year—As above.

MORALS.

Lessons in Morals, distributed as above, covering the subjects prescribed Elementary Schools.

GEOGRAPHY.

FIRST YEAR :—
       Meaning and uses of maps, exemplified by drawing maps of school premises and district surrounding school. General notions of latitude and longitude.

The world. Distribution of land and water. Geographical definitions with prominent illustrations.

The continents ; island groups ; chief islands ; relative size compared with Jamaica ; chief mountain ranges and plains ; chief peninsulas, isthmuses and capes.

The oceans ; chief seas, lakes, rivers, river systems, bays, gulfs, straits.

The chief countries, with their capitals ; relative size compared with Great Britain.

The chief productions of these countries ; the interchange direct or indirect, of these products with those of Jamaica.

An outline map of one of the continents to be supplied. Students will be expected to fill in the chief physical features and most important towns.

SECOND YEAR :
       Outlines of the Geography of the British Empire and the United States of America, also of the West Indies and the Isthmus of Panama. [Minute details not required.]   Geography of Jamaica, more in detail. A general knowledge of localities made prominent through current political events.

Races and Religions of Mankind. Types of Government. Students will be expected to know the different types of government, and to what type the government of every important country of the world belongs.

Mathematical Geography : General Notions of the Earth as a planet in the solar system. Form and size, and motions of the Earth. Day and Night, and the Seasons. The Zones. Fuller knowledge of latitude and longtitude.

Physical Geography. Formation of land by the action of water and other agencies. Mountains, rivers, and river valleys. Climate, winds, rain, dew, etc. [See Note.]

Students will be required to fill in chief physical features and important towns in an outline map to be supplied to them of the British Isles, or any considerable dependency of the British Empire, or the United States, or (with fuller details) Jamaica.

THIRD YEAR :—
       Fuller knowledge of the work of first and second years.   More detailed knowledge of the Government of Great Britain and the Colonies. Geography of Europe (Minute details not required).
Maps as in Second Year. Also, to show proficiency in drawing maps on blackboard.

Note.—Second Year Students in Women's Colleges will be exempted from examination in Physical Geography. The teaching of Physical Geography should, as far as possible, be exemplified and illustrated by the physical features of Jamaica.

ELEMENTARY SCIENCE [GENERAL AND AGRICULTURAL]

FIRST YEAR :—

1. A course of elementary physics and chemistry preparatory to the study of the life and food of plants and to a knowledge of the composition of soils and manures. The course to consist of :—

The properties of solids, liquids, and gases.

Chemical and physical changes.

Elements and compounds, atoms and molecules.

Use of symbols and chemical formulæ.

The occurrence, preparation, and properties of Oxygen, Hydrogen, Chlorine, Hydrochloric Acid, Nitrogen, and Carbon.

The composition of the Atmosphere and of substances found in it such as water, carbon-dioxide, ammonia.

Chemical combination—Examples of its various forms being given that the following terms may be understood :—*Oxidation, acids, salts (e.g., nitrates, chlorides, sulphates, &c.).*

2. An intelligent knowledge of the Tropical Readers : Book i. Part ii. ; Book ii., Parts i and iv.

3. One lesson each week to be given by the Tutors of the College, dealing with the ordinary phenomena of common life and with objects familiar to school children. The lesson to be of such a nature and given in such a manner as to indicate the kind of lessons suited for elementary schools, and the best methods of giving such lessons to school children.

The illustrations and the apparatus used for experiments should be chiefly of such a nature and so inexpensive that they may be provided for and made use of, in the elementary schools in the Island.

SECOND YEAR :—

1. AGRICULTURE. General ideas of Scope of Subject :

Atmosphere. Composition and action of.

Soils. Origin and formation ; constituents and properties.

Plant Structure. Root, stem, leaf, flower, fruit, and seed.

Plant Life. Germination, nutrition, storing of food, chemica composition of plants.

Cultivation. Tillage, drainage, irrigation, manuring.

Crops.

Box-Gardening.—In addition to out-door cultivation, experiments and illustrations such as are recommended in the French Scheme of Agriculture for Elementary Schools, with plants grown in boxes, &c., should receive much attention. Disused soap boxes, kerosine oil tins, &c., might be utilized for this purpose.

2. Object lessons as in first year, during the first term of the second. For the latter part of the year the general laws of health in connection with a general knowledge of the human body.

3. Students to have opportunities of obtaining useful knowledge by visits to museums, public gardens, manufacturing establishments, etc.

Note.—The object lessons given to students during the first two years of their training must include all subjects in Schedule A, not otherwise covered by the work prescribed in the Training College Syllabus,

DOMESTIC ECONOMY.

FOR WOMEN'S COLLEGES.

FIRST YEAR :—

A. Care of the body.

B. Needlework.

1. To cut out on sectional and plain paper the undermentioned garments and to make one of them: *a.* Child's pinafore and overall ; *b.* Cotton petticoat ; *c.* Chemise or woollen vest.

2. Darning on materials of different kinds : *a.* A thin place ; *b.* A hole ; *c.* Tears of different kinds.

3. To give after careful preparation, and under supervision, the following lessons to a class : 1. Drills of different kinds ; 2. Fixing a hem and hemming ; 3. Seaming ; 4. Sewing and felling ; 5. Herring-boning ; 6. Running and felling.

SECOND YEAR :—

A. Care of Children from birth with special reference to cleanliness, food and clothing.

B. 1. Treatment of simple accidents.

2. Nursing hints : a. Care of a sick person ; b. The sick room.

C. Needlework.

1. To cut out the undermentioned garments on sectional and plain paper, and to make one of them : a. A combination ; b. A simple working dress ; c. A pair of drawers.

2. To put a patch on—a. Calico or linen ; b. Print ; c. Flannel.

3. To give after careful preparation and under supervision, the following lessons to a class : 1. Darning—a thin place, a hole, a tear ; 2. Making a band ; 3. Making a button hole ; 4. Fixing a tape on a band ; 5. Fixing a button on a band ; 6. Cutting out a simple pinafore.

THIRD YEAR :—

A. Cookery.

1. Principles of boiling, stewing, roasting, baking, frying, broiling.

2. Practice in the cooking of meat, fish, vegetables, soup, porridge, cakes and puddings.

3. Invalid food (practice in preparation).

B. Laundry work.

1. Hints as to the best methods to be used in washing different materials and in starching and ironing.

2. Practice in washing, starching and ironing, including the getting up of skirts, blouses, collars, and cuffs.

C. Needlework.

1. To cut out on sectional and on plain paper the undermentioned garments, and to make any two of them : *a.* A blouse ; *b.* A skirt ; *c.* A boy's shirt ; *d.* A night dress.

2. To revise darning and patching.

3. To give after careful preparation and under supervision, the following lesson to a class : *a.* Stitching ; *b.* Plaiting ; *c.* Setting in gathers ; *d.* Cutting out an apron, chemise or any other simple garment ; *e.* Marking ; *f.* Making and fixing a gusset ; *g.* Putting on a strengthening tape ; *h.* Patching a woollen, calico or print garment.

MANUAL TRAINING.

FOR MEN'S COLLEGES.

FIRST YEAR :—

1. Paper folding and designing.
2. Colour work.
3. Paper modelling and cardboard modelling.
4. Clay modelling.
5. Simplified woodwork.

A short course in making three or four simple models, with knife and saw as cutting tools, such as may be done on a simple desk or table.

SECOND YEAR :—

A. Woodwork.

1. *Exercises in Joint Work.*—Simple joints, e.g., Housing, Halving, Half-lap, Mortise and Tenon, Bridle, etc.

2. *Models.*— Simple geometrical figures. Plant label, Square prism, Flat ruler, Octagonal prism, Round ruler, Flower-pot cross, etc.

3. *Tools.*— Rip and tenon saws, Jack and Smoothing planes, Firmer chisels, Gouges, Marking Gauge, Mortise Gauge, Rule, Brace and bits, etc.

B. Drawing.

1. *Orthographic Projection.*—Simple plans and elevations, etc., drawn accurately to scale.

2. Isometric Projection drawn to scale.

THIRD YEAR :—

A. Woodwork.

1. *Exercises in Joint Work.*—More advanced than in 2nd Year, and with simple combinations, e.g., Tongue and groove, Notched Halving Oblique Halving, Scarfing, etc.

2. *Models.*—Bench Hook, Pen Tray, Flower Pot Stand, Hat Rack, Nailed Box, Bracket, Tee and Set Squares, etc.

3. *New Tools.*—Rebate Plane, Trying Plane, Mitre Block, Bevel Spoke-shave, Bow Saw, etc.

B. Drawing.

1. *Orthographic Projection.*-- Plan (Elevation Section) of simple solids and Joints and also simple combinations of Joints drawn accurately to scale.

2. *Isometric and Oblique Projection.* –More advanced than in the 2nd year.

Note.--Two hours per week are to be given to this work.

In 1900 the Students of all years will take the First Year's course. In 1901 the 2nd and 3rd year Students will take the Second Year's course.

Besides the examination in the work for their own year, Second and Third Year Students will be tested in the work prescribed for the first year, of which they will be expected to show such mastery as will enable them to teach the same to scholars in elementary schools.

GEOMETRY.

FIRST YEAR—FOR MEN AND WOMEN :—

Practical Geometry

Geometrical figures with instruments and to scale.

1. To divide a straight line into any number of equal parts.

2. To draw a straight line parallel to a given straight line with ruler and set square and also by construction.

3. To draw perpendicular lines with ruler and set square and also by construction.

4. To construct a square, oblong, triangle, and any regular polygon, the length of side or sides being given.

5. To bisect an angle. To construct an angle equal to a given angle.

Also the following :

1. To find the centre of a circle.

2. To draw a tangent to a circle at a point in its circumference.

3. To draw a tangent to a circle from a point outside its circumference.

4. To describe two circles of given radii touching each other.

5. To describe a circle to pass through three given points.

6. To describe a circle to touch three given straight lines.

7. To find the centre of a triangle.

8. To inscribe a circle within or describe a circle about a given triangle.

9. To construct, by a general method, any regular polygon, one of its sides being given.

10. To construct, by a general method, any regular polygon, its circumscribing circle being given.

SECOND YEAR.—FOR MEN.
Euclid—Book I. 1-26, and Easy Riders.

THIRD YEAR.—FOR MEN.
Book I. 27–48, and Easy Riders.

ALGEBRA.

FOR MEN OF THE THIRD YEAR :—

To Least Common Multiple ; Fractions : Simple Equations involving one or two unknowns ; Simple problems involving the same.

VOCAL MUSIC.

FIRST YEAR :—

THEORY.—STAFF NOTATION.

Notes.—Position on treble and bass staves. The major scales C, G, and F. Diatonic intervals. Relations as noted by the terms tonic, dominant, and sub-dominant.

Time.—Value of notes, dotted notes, tied notes, rests. Signatures of simple time. Accent. Contents of measures (bars).

TONIC SOL-FA NOTATION.

Notes.—Common major scale ; its chordal structure. Diatonic intervals. Relations as noted by the terms tonic, dominant, and sub-dominant. The standard scale of pitch, and the relations (in pitch) of various keys.

Time.—The accent of pulses. Two, three, and four pulse measure. Contents of measures. Continuations, rests, and simple division of pulses.

PRACTICE.

Singing from Modulator.

SECOND YEAR :—

THEORY.

Musical terms in common use.
Compass of children's voices. General rules relating to voice-traning.

STAFF-NOTATION.

Notes.—As in first year. Major and minor scales, not beyond four sharps and four flats. Diatonic and chromatic intervals.
Time.—As in first year. Compound time.
Accent and syncopation.

TONIC SOL-FA NOTATION.

Notes.—As in first year. Major and minor scales. Diatonic and chromatic intervals. Names of chromatic tones. Removes of key ; bridge, notes and distinguishing tones.
Time.—The measures in common use. Division of pulses into thirds and quarters. Transcription of values by halving, doubling, etc. Accent and syncopation.

PRACTICE.

To sing an easy passage in a major scale.

THIRD YEAR :—

As in previous years. Singing at sight a passage or tune of only moderate difficulty, in a major or minor key, in either notation.
To repeat and afterwards name the notes of a simple diatonic phrase, comprising not more than four notes of the scale of C, which the Examiner may twice sing to laa, (or play), the common chord having first been given.

NOTES AND SUGGESTIONS.

1. Singing of simple part songs and glees by the Students should be practised.

2. It is desirable that Tutors allot a certain portion of time in which Second and Third Year Students may practise Harmonium playing.

DRAWING.

FIRST YEAR : –

(a) A course of Kindergarten Drawing to cover the Code requirements for Standards I. and II.

(b) Free hand, and with the ruler and set square, of lines, angles, parallels and the simplest right lined forms.

(c) Free hand Drawing of regular forms and of curved and right lined figures from the flat.

SECOND YEAR :—

(a) Free hand Drawing more advanced than in the First Year.

(b) *Drawing to Scale.*

1. Simple scales, e.g., ¾ inch, 1 inch, 1½ inches, 3 inches to the foot to show inches ; or 1, 2, or 3 inches to 10, 20 feet, etc., to show feet.

2. To draw and take dimensions from a scale of feet and inches.

3. To draw a plan or other figure on squared paper from a sketch having dimensions marked on it.

4. To enlarge or reduce plane figures to scale.

(c) Drawing from models of regular form and from easy common objects.

THIRD YEAR :—

Thorough revision of work of previous years, with abundant practice in blackboard drawing, and more extended drawing from models and common objects.

NOTES AND SUGGESTIONS.

1. Drawing should be taught regularly throughout the year for at least 1½ hours per week to enable Students to gain the facility necessary for teaching Drawing.

2. Great attention should be paid to the principles and practice of teaching the subject, and very much attention should be given to drawing on the blackboard to ensure facility in illustrating ordinary school lessons.

3. Care should be taken to overcome the general tendency to make the copies in " Free hand " and " Model " too small. The work of the Students should conveniently fill a sheet of paper 11 inches by 7 inches.

4. The Examination in Drawing will consist of paper work, blackboard work (to which much importance will be attached) and a short paper on the Theory and Practice of teaching Drawing.

SCHEDULE C.

REGISTRATION EXAMINATION FOR TEACHERS.

The Examination will include the following selected portions of the First Year and Second Year Training College Examination :—

First Year Subjects :

Scripture and Morals ;
Manual Training
or
Domestic Economy ;
Geography ;
Singing ;
Drawing, including blackboard work.

Second Year Subjects :

Reading and Recitation ;
English ;
Writing ;
Arithmetic ;
School Management—Theory and Practice
Elementary Science.

SCHEDULE. D.

READING AND RECITATION.

FIRST YEAR :—

Reading. To read from a school reading book with fluency, ease and expression.

Recitation. To recite one or two simple poems of an aggregate of not more than 50 lines from any standard author.

SECOND YEAR :—

Reading. As above.

Recitation. To recite one or two poems of an aggregate of not less than 60 lines.

THIRD YEAR :—

Reading. As above.

Recitation. To recite a poem of not less than 80 lines, or two poems of varied character of an aggregate of not less than 80 lines, from some standard author.

FOURTH YEAR :—

Reading. As above : also from newspapers or magazines.

Recitation. To recite a passage from Shakespeare or Milton not exceeding 100 lines.

Note.—In each year the pupil teachers are expected to have a full knowledge of meanings and allusions.

WRITING AND ENGLISH.

FIRST YEAR :—

Specimens of penmanship in text-hand and small ; to set simple copies on blackboard.

SECOND YEAR :—

As above, with greater proficiency.

THIRD YEAR :—

As above with increased proficiency.

FOURTH YEAR :—

As above, with increased proficiency,

NOTES :—

I. A bold, neat style of writing is expected.

II. Blackboard work should be neat and very clear.

III. Good figures, both on paper and blackboard, will be required. The blackboard work of the pupil teachers will be tested at the inspection of the school.

DICTATION.

A passage of moderate difficulty to be written from Dictation in a fair legible hand.

COMPOSITION.

FIRST YEAR :—

To

SECOND YEAR :—

To write from memory the substance of a short story read by the Examiner.

THIRD YEAR :—

As above. Also business forms, such as bills and receipts

FOURTH YEAR :—

As above ; also a short essay on a subject prescribed by the Examiner.

GRAMMAR.

FIRST YEAR :—

1. Analysis of very simple sentences. 2. Parsing of same. 3. Word-building. 4. Knowledge of prefixes.

SECOND YEAR :—

1. Analysis of simple sentences. 2. Parsing of same. 3. Word-building. 4. Fuller knowledge of prefixes. 5. Paraphrasing of very simple poetry.

THIRD YEAR :—

1. Analysis of complex and compound sentences. 2. Full parsing of sentences of ordinary difficulty. 3. Word-building. 4. Prefixes and affixes. 5. Paraphrasing of simple modern poetry.

FOURTH YEAR :—

1. Analysis and parsing as above. 2. Paraphrasing of modern poetry. 3. Word-building.

ARITHMETIC.

FIRST YEAR :—

To be fairly proficient in the practical application of all the Compound Rules, *i.e.*, of Money, and the Weights and Measures in general use.

SECOND YEAR :—

Elementary Vulgar Fractions ; Practice ; Tradesmen's and household accounts.

THIRD YEAR :—

Simple interest ; Simple proportion ; Vulgar Fractions ; Unitary Method ; Decimals.

FOURTH YEAR :—

Compound Proportion ; Percentage ; Averages.

ELEMENTARY SCIENCE AND AGRICULTURE.

FIRST YEAR :—

1st Tropical Readers—Part I. Colour. Form.

SECOND YEAR :—

1st Tropical Reader—Part II.

THIRD YEAR :—

2nd Tropical Reader—Parts I. and II.

FOURTH YEAR :—

2nd Tropical Reader—Parts III. and IV.

GEOGRAPHY, WITH INCIDENTAL HISTORY.

FIRST YEAR :—

As required in Schedule A for Lower Division and Section A of Middle Division. Map of Jamaica (on paper or blackboard).

SECOND YEAR :—

As required in Schedule A for the Middle Division, Sections A and B. Map of North America (on paper or blackboard).

THIRD YEAR :

As required in Schedule A for Upper Division. Map of British Isles on paper or blackboard.

FOURTH YEAR :—

As in third year in fuller detail. Map of the West Indies on paper or blackboard.

DRAWING AND MANUAL OCCUPATIONS.

FIRST YEAR :—

As required in Schedule A for Lower Division.

SECOND YEAR :—

As required in Schedule A for Middle Division.

THIRD YEAR :—

Drawing as required in Schedule A for Upper Division ; and Manual Occupations as required for Middle Division.

FOURTH YEAR :—

Drawing and Manual Occupations as required in Schedule A for Upper Division.

SCRIPTURE.

FIRST YEAR :—

Leading facts of Bible History as connected with—The Creation ; Fall ; Deluge ; Lives of the Patriarchs. The Life of Christ. To repeat the Scripture required in Schedule A of Standards below III.

SECOND YEAR :—

The Bondage in Egypt ; the Exodus ; Journeying to and Conquest of Canaan. The Life of Christ in fuller detail. To repeat the Scripture required of Standards III. and IV.

THIRD YEAR :—

Leading facts connected with the most prominent Judges, and the Kings of Israel, before the division of the Kingdom. The chief parables of the New Testament. To repeat the Scripture required of Standard V.

FOURTH YEAR :—

Leading facts connected with the most prominent Kings of Judah and Israel after the division, and the most prominent prophets of the Old Testament. Lives of the Apostles. To repeat the Scripture required of Standard VI.

TEACHING.

FIRST YEAR :—

To teach a class in Reading or Writing in 2nd or 3rd Standard. To answer simple questions on how to secure attention. .

SECOND YEAR :—

As above, Standards 1 to 4, with improved skill in instruction and discipline.

To answer simple questions on how to secure attention, and how to question.

THIRD YEAR :—

To teach the lowest class (Junior Standard) in Reading, also a class in Arithmetic, to the satisfaction of the Inspector.

To answer questions on how to teach Reading and Arithmetic to beginners.

FOURTH YEAR :—

As above ; also to give a lesson to pupils in any secondary subject taught in the school.

To prepare notes of lesson.

TEXT-BOOKS ON TEACHING FOR PUPIL TEACHERS.

First Year :—" How to Secure and Retain Attention."—(Hughes.)

Second Year :—" How to Question."—(Fitch.)

Third Year :—" First Lessons in Reading—Teacher's Edition."—(Miss Fundenburg.)

Fourth Year :—" Mistakes in Teaching."—Chapter IV.—(Hughes.)

NOTES AND SUGGESTIONS.

1. (*a*) Pupil Teachers should make themselves familiar with the suggestions in Schedule A and follow them faithfully. (*b*) They should be guided by the principles of teaching set forth in the prescribed text-books. (*c*) Specific directions for teaching different classes will be found in Cowham's School Method, which, in the main, and subject to (*a*) and (*b*), may be safely followed.

2. Pupil teachers of the Fourth Year will be expected to have a thorough knowledge of the text-books prescribed for each year.

3. At the end of the Fourth Year Students will be expected to have an intelligent grasp of all the subjects required to be taught in Elementary Schools on the lines laid down in Schedule A.

THE
SYSTEM OF EDUCATION
IN
BRITISH GUIANA

I. PRIMARY EDUCATION.

Introductory - - - . - - . . 7ι3
Early History - - - - - - - - ιϋ3
Mr. Canning's Resolutions - - - - - 754
First Grants for Educational Purposes - - 754
Lady Mico's Legacy, etc. - - - - - - 755
Establishment of the Grammar School - - - 755
Education Commission - - - - - - 756
Ordinance of 1855 - - - - - - - 756
School Commission of 1874 - - - - - 757
Ordinance of 1882 - - - - - - - 758
Reduction of State Grants to Education - - - 760
The New Code of 1890 - - - - - - 761
Schools for Aboriginal Indians - - - - - 762
Statistics - - - - - - - - 762

II. SECONDARY EDUCATION.

Queen's College - - - - - - - - 763
The Catholic Grammar School - - - - - 765
Ursuline Convent High Schools - - - - 766
Wesleyan High Schools - - - - - - 766

III. REFORMATORIES. - - - - - - - 766

IV. EDUCATIONAL ENDOWMENTS - - - - - - 768

SUPPLEMENTARY NOTE - - - - - - - 770

APPENDICES.

A. Report of the Commissioners on Primary Education,
    1897 - - - - - - - - - 771
B. Code of Regulations for Grant-in-Aid Schools, 1900 - 774
C. An Ordinance (1900) to amend the Elementary Educa-
    tion Ordinance, 1876 - - - - - - - 793

THE SYSTEM OF EDUCATION IN BRITISH GUIANA.*

I. Primary Education.

BRITISH GUIANA, which includes the counties of Demerara, Introductory. Essequebo and Berbice, extends from Point Playa, east of the mouth of the Orinoco, to the River Corentyne, by which it is separated from Dutch Guiana. It has a seaboard of over 300 miles and its area is calculated at 92,296 square miles, of which only 130 square miles are under cultivation.

It was discovered by Columbus in 1498, and in the course of about a century the whole of its coast line had been traced by Dutch sailors and adventurers, while during the same period the Spaniards occupied themselves along the Orinoco and in vain efforts to penetrate into the interior, behind the Dutch coast lands, in search of the mythical golden city. It may be easily imagined how the early visitors from Europe to the South American coast, finding rivers beyond all others in size and volume, which poured down with many tributaries through rich tropical lands, drew for themselves a picture of vastness and riches, and gave it definite form and shape as a city or land of gold.

The cultivated portions of the colony are for the most part alluvial flats, just above the level of the sea, and are liable to inundations during the spring tides. The sugar estates are protected against these inundations by a front dam or sea-wall, and inside this front dam is a public road, kept up partly at the expense of the estate through which it passes, and partly by the Government. But during the rainy season the estates and provision grounds are also liable to inundations from behind. Against these they are protected by a back dam. The interior of the country is diversified by ranges of mountains, the most notable of which is Mount Roraima, 8,400 feet high, and the dense forests furnish timber of the most valuable, durable and beautiful kinds. The chief exports are about 105,000 tons of sugar and 125,000 ounces of gold. The revenue of the colony for the last financial year amounted to $2,667,719.12 and the expenditure to $2,834,957.54, of which $161,101 or 6·03 per cent. was voted for education.

The first European attempts at settlement within the limits of Early British Guiana were by the Dutch about 1620. A century later, History. during the war with France, a squadron under Du Casse entered

---

* This report, which in its original form was prepared by Mr. Blair in January, 1898, was revised by him in September, 1900.

4226.

3 F

the Berbice River and laid waste some of its plantations. In 1781, during the American War, in which France and Holland united against Britain, Lord Rodney's fleet captured Demerara and Essequebo; but those provinces were afterwards recaptured by France, and at the Peace of Paris in 1784 they were restored to the Dutch. They were recaptured by the British in 1796 and again restored to the Dutch at the Treaty of Amiens in 1802, but during the following year they surrendered again to the British, and were formally ceded by the Netherlands to Great Britain in 1814.

The London Missionary Society in 1808 sent out a missionary who was a teacher as well as a preacher. There were at the time only one church in Berbice, the Lutheran, and one in Essequebo, the Dutch Reformed, and two years later (1810) the first Episcopal church (St. George's) was opened in Georgetown, Demerara. At this period the population was estimated at,—slaves, 101,710, and freemen, 8,000; and as the education of slaves was discouraged, it will readily be understood that teaching was at a very low ebb.

Mr. Canning's Resolutions.

On the 23rd March 1824 the Right Honourable G. Canning's resolutions, " to ameliorate the condition of the slave population and to prepare them for freedom," passed the House of Commons, and the " Royal Gazette," August 1824, contained an advertisement to the effect that a large number of children whose parents were unable to pay high school fees were acquiring habits of indolence and vice, and it was proposed to establish free schools for boys and girls. His Excellency the Governor and Lady D'Urban approved of the scheme, and having such patronage it was liberally supported. In

First grants for educational purposes.

1830 the sum of £150 was placed on the estimate of the colony as a grant to schools. In 1838 His Excellency Sir James Carmichael Smyth, Bart., in a message to the legislature, laid particular stress on the desire of apprenticed labourers for religious and secular instruction, and the sum of 28,000 guilders (£1,866 13s. 4d.) was voted for churches and schools in the county of Berbice, and 1,500 guilders (£100) for Georgetown.

The keen interest evinced by the British Parliament in the education of the negro was shared by the London Missionary Society and the British and Foreign School Society, whose school at New Amsterdam, Berbice, at this time under two trained teachers, was the most efficient in the colony, and Mr. Latrobe, reporting to Lord Glenelg in August 1838, said, " Notwithstanding the indifference still evinced by the bulk of the residents of the superior classes; the inertness and indecision with reference to the subject which still reigns in the majority of colonial legislatures; the slight value which the negro may yet place upon instruction; the various difficulties interposed in the way of rapid diffusion from the character of the climate and the weakness of the agency employed, and above all the want of sufficient funds, it is undeniable that, compared with the past, the present furnishes abundant cause for thankfulness and satisfactory anticipation."

Educational progress during the next two years was preeminently satisfactory, and a Blue-book for 1840 reported that a strong desire prevailed among the working classes to have their children taught to read and write, of which it was politic to take advantage. The Church of England had 42 schools, the Church of Scotland and the London Missionary Society each 27, and the Wesleyan Missionary Society 5; and the Combined Court for the year 1841 voted the sum of £3,159 for the establishment and maintenance of schools. This was a little less than 2 per cent. of the colony's revenue.

In 1834 the funds of the Lady Mico's legacy for the suppression of Algerian piracy and the release of Christian slaves had increased to £120,000. At the instance of Sir Thomas Fowell Buxton, these funds, together with large parliamentary grants, were set aside for the promotion of education of the black and coloured population in British Guiana and the West Indies. Six undenominational schools were established, and they were said by the Governor to be the most efficient in the colony; and after doing excellent work for some years, a letter was written by their superintendent in Georgetown to the Government, intimating that the trustees of the charity were prepared to increase their grants on certain conditions. Nearly every section of the Christian Church opposed these proposals, and the fears of the clergy were hardly allayed by the assurance of the Governor that it was not intended to interfere with existing schools, but to establish others in remote and sparsely populated localities where none existed. One memorial was sent to the Court praying that no part of the educational vote should be alienated from the churches. It was decided however that the offer of the trustees of the Mico Charity should be accepted, inasmuch as it enabled the Government to extend the means of instruction to the rural population, particularly to districts where no schools were established. But about this period the withdrawal of the Imperial Parliamentary grant crippled the finances of the Charity, and the trustees decided to leave their schools to the clergy. We are, however, to this day, still indebted to the charity for some efficiently trained schoolmasters.

Lady Mico's legacy and Imperial grants devoted to the support of schools for the coloured population.

On the 7th December, 1842, Bishop Austin addressed the Governor and the Court of Policy, urging the importance of establishing a grammar school in Georgetown. His Lordship had at his disposal the sum of £1,500, and he asked the legislature to subscribe an equal amount, and to make a small vote in payment of salaries. Government grants were first made in 1844, and in 1848 an ordinance incorporating the college passed the court. It is however proposed to deal with Queen's College and other similar institutions in separate chapters.

Establishment of the Grammar School.

Early in 1849 it was pointed out by the Secretary of State, the Right Hon. Earl Grey, that a good school ought, as soon as possible, to be provided within easy reach of every place where more than a certain number of inhabitants were to be found: but the expense of these schools ought not to be provided for out of the general revenue. It should fall (in the shape of a rate) upon the districts for whose benefit the schools were intended. Earl Grey's suggestions were not adopted.

Education Commission.

About this time an Education Commission, having the functions of a board of education, was appointed. Its secretary was Mr., afterwards Sir John, Lucie Smith, and a sum of £550 was devoted to pay the salary of an inspector of schools. Mr. George Dennis, the first inspector, after receiving a short training in England, returned to the colony and presented a report, which showed that better results should have been obtained from the large sums of money which from time to time had been voted. The only books used were the Bible and " Fenning's Spelling-book "; the teacher for the most part was grievously deficient in attainments and in educational training, and corporal punishment was inflicted by leathern straps, frequently cut at the end into thongs, according to the disposition and temper of the schoolmaster, or even more wantonly and freely by a monitor, on boys and girls alike. Mr. Dennis also urged the importance of compulsory attendance at school, and the establishment of a normal or training school for teachers, and of industrial schools, and he had the satisfaction of seeing a seminary for teachers established by Bishop Austin, known as Bishop's College, where teachers of all denominations were trained. This institution was purchased by the Government in 1877 and closed in 1882 by Sir Henry T. Irving. The ordinance abolishing the Bishop's College also abolished the Board of Education and conferred its powers on the chief inspector of schools.

Reverting again to 1852, resolutions were passed in the Court of Policy requesting the commissioners to submit a Bill for making better provision for education. The Bill was drafted by Lieutenant-Governor William Walker, who was also the chairman of the commissioners, and the Secretary of State expressed his approval of its purport and provisions. It was brought up for a second reading 6th February, 1854, was postponed several times, and finally withdrawn, the education commissioners observing that they deeply "lamented that prejudice and indifference " that prevailed among the upper classes.

Ordinance of 1855.

In 1855 a short ordinance was passed, the main features of which were :—

(a.) That assistance should only be given to schools in which religious instruction, founded on the precepts of the Holy Scriptures, was imparted daily.

(b.) That school fees should be paid.

(c.) That the teachers should receive fixed salaries according to their classes after examination.

To carry out this ordinance, His Excellency P. E. Woodhouse asked the Court "to sanction under the head of schools the amount of 37,600 dollars, being 5,000 dollars less than was voted for the past year. In this sum are comprised 6,000 dollars for the orphan asylum, a charitable perhaps more than an educational establishment, and 5,500 dollars for special training institutions. The remaining 26,100 dollars will with your approval be expended under the provisions of the ordinance just passed. . . . . I am not without hope that if you should be pleased to vote the funds necessary for carrying it out, it may effect a gradual improvement in the moral condition of the people, and prepare them for the introduction at some future day of that more perfect plan which at present we do not seem to possess the means of developing."

The total expenditure on education in 1854 was 37,720 dollars, compared with 201,252 dollars for prisons and police, and Inspector Dennis asked for an increased vote, remarking that "money laid out for the encouragement of virtue and the removal of ignorance is a far more profitable investment than that expended on the repression and punishment of crime." In 1856 the vote was 44,040 dollars, distributed as follows:—

	Dollars.
Orphan Asylum	6,000
Queen's College Grammar School	3,000
Salary of Inspector	3,600
Salaries of Teachers	22,000
Rents and Repairs of School Houses	4,000
Support of Pupils at Training College	1,500
Support of Training Masters	1,000
School Books, Maps and Furniture	1,500
(English Church) Indian Mission Schools	720
(Scotch Church) Indian Missions	720
Total	44,040

Mr. George Dennis, after 10 years efficient service as inspector of schools, was succeeded by the Rev. W. G. G. Austin, M.A., in 1862, and from that date the amount voted for primary education was gradually increased from 56,809 dollars in 1862 to 93,724 dollars in 1874,* during which year Sir James R. Longden, K.C.M.G., appointed a commission of 17 members to enquire into and report on the education of the colony.

The schools were divided into five classes according to their efficiency (A, B, C, D, E,), receiving respectively 8 dollars, 7 dollars,

The School Commission of 1874.

* The amount spent on Education in 1862 was $56,809; in 1863, $56,756.79; in 1864, $59,413.16; in 1865, $63,008.05; in 1866, $70,210.19; in 1867, $72,912.16; in 1868, $82,902.96; in 1869, $86,875.30; in 1870, $84,875.64; in 1871, $83,264.90; in 1872, $93,102.99; in 1873, $91,449.49; in 1874, 93,724.34; in 1875, $91,422.63.

6 dollars, 5 dollars, and 4 dollars for each scholar in average attendance, on the condition that the fees of the scholars and the local contributions amounted to at least one-third of the Government grant. In addition to these sums, the Board of Education, on the recommendation of the inspector, made special gratuities to efficient teachers, assisted the managers in erecting schoolhouses, keeping them in repair, and supplying them with books and apparatus.

The Education Commission above alluded to sent in an exhaustive and a most valuable report and made a large number of recommendations for placing education (primary, secondary, and industrial) on a more satisfactory basis. These were adopted by the legislature, and three ordinances—(a) to enforce elementary education, (b) to vest in the colony Queen's College Grammar School and the property known as Bishop's College, (c) to establish a more representative Board of Education—came into force on February 3rd, 1877. Seven months later an ordinance was passed to establish and regulate an institution for the training of teachers.

Ordinance of 1882.

In 1882 a short ordinance was passed abolishing the Board of Education and conferring its powers on the inspector of schools, and the following are the chief provisions of the Act now in force :—

1. Her Majesty may appoint an inspector of schools and the Governor one or more assistant inspectors, receiving such salaries as may be voted by the Combined Court.

2. The inspector is required to submit an annual report in such form, and giving such information, as the Government may direct.

3. Inspectors and assistant inspectors may visit an assisted school with or without notice and at any time.

4. The Governor and Court of Policy are empowered to make rules and regulations for :—

(*a.*) The government and discipline of the schools and teachers.

(*b.*) The distribution of the funds voted.

(*c.*) Maintaining an efficient system of elementary education throughout the colony.

5. The inspector of schools may refer any charge of cruelty or immorality made against a schoolmaster to a district stipendiary magistrate. The magistrate will submit the evidence and his report thereon to the inspector, who may cancel or suspend the teacher's certificate.

6. For enforcing attendance at school the colony may be

divided into districts by proclamation, and the governor may appoint district educational officers, whose duties are briefly:—

(*a*) To keep a register of all children under 12 years of age, (*b*) to report to the inspector any parents neglecting to send their children to school, (*c*) to sue for and recover fees.

7. District educational officers are empowered to enter any house or yard and make enquiry, and persons obstructing them or giving false information are liable to fines or imprisonment.

8. The parents or guardians of children not attending school may be summoned before a magistrate, who for the first offence may make an order. If that order is not carried out, the punishment is fine or imprisonment.

9. Children under nine years of age may not be employed as domestic servants or as agricultural labourers. If over nine they may be so employed if they have obtained a certificate of proficiency in reading, writing and elementary arithmetic. Persons giving false information or disregarding this rule are liable to a penalty of 24 dollars.

10. The proprietors of estates are bound to provide schools for the children of immigrants, provided none exist. They can claim grants for such schools on the same terms as the clergy.

11. Schools receiving a grant are to be opened by repeating the Lord's Prayer and reading a portion of the Scriptures without comment. Further religious instruction may be given during the first or last hour, but parents are allowed to withdraw their children from such instruction without being placed at a disadvantage in secular subjects.

12. The parents are bound to pay a fee of not less than a penny a week per scholar. In cases of poverty the fee may be paid by the inspector on behalf of the Government.

After the passing of this ordinance the Board of Education passed rules and regulations providing liberal salaries and grants for teachers and managers as follows:—

Certificate Salaries.	Per Annum.
	Dollars.
Class I. - - - - - - - - - - -	480
Class II. - - - - - - - - - - -	300
Class III. - - - - - - - - .- - -	120
Provisional - - - - - - - - - - -	96

For every pass in one of the subjects, reading, writing or arithmetic, 1 dollar; in two 4 dollars; and in three 7 dollars. With 1 dollar additional for grammar, geography, needlework, and any other subject approved by the Board.

Pupil teachers were also employed, receiving salaries ranging from 3 dollars to 6 dollars per month, and grants were made paying one-half of the cost of the new school houses erected, a sum for rent and repairs, and a vote to cover part of the cost of books and apparatus. At the end of 1881 there were 181 schools, said to have had an average attendance of 11,398 scholars, presenting 10,900 for examination, earning a grant of 101,947.02 dollars, or 9.35 dollars per scholar, equal to £1 18s. 11½d. In addition to this, large sums were spent in maintaining a Government training college (8,380 dollars), the payment of the salaries of inspectors and educational officers, &c. (15,140 dollars). During the following year, with a revenue of a little over 2,000,000 dollars, the expenditure on education was over 150,000 dollars.

Reduction of State Grants to Education. On the 10th June, 1881, the following resolution passed the Combined Court :—

> "Whereas a very large amount has been spent by the
> "Government for elementary education, and whereas such
> "expenditure has been excessive without any adequate
> "results; Be it resolved, that the vote for elementary
> "education be reduced on and after the first day of October
> "next, and that His Excellency the Governor and the
> "Honourable Court of Policy give effect to this resolution
> "by amendment of the law."

Sir Henry Irving, addressing the Combined Court on May 30th, 1882, stated that he concurred in the opinion of the Court that the amount spent on primary education had been excessive and without commensurable results. Comparing our expenditure with that of Jamaica he showed that the same number of scholars in this colony would cost 65,000 dollars more than in Jamaica. He further insisted on the payment of school fees and local contributions. The fees amounted to about 1s. 6d. per scholar and the local contributions were practically nil. He was of opinion that this was demoralising in its effects and injurious to the cause of education. He was convinced that a large reduction might be made in the grants with positive advantage. The expenditure of the colony had for some time been in excess of its income, and the Combined Court lost no time in giving effect to His Excellency's suggestions, making changes of a sweeping character. A law was passed abolishing the Board of Education and conferring its powers on the Inspector of Schools; the ordinance to establish and regulate an institution for the training of schoolmasters was allowed to remain on the Statute-book, but no money being voted for its maintenance it was abandoned.

Teachers' certificate salaries, the salaries of pupil teachers and grants for building and furnishing schools were swept away. In lieu of the grants and salaries the only sum now paid was a capitation grant of 4, 5 or 6 dollars, on the estimated average attendance, to be adjusted at the end of the school year, and a further sum, varying from 1 to 4 dollars for each child in average attendance, according to the percentage of full passes in reading, writing and arithmetic. Schools obtaining less than 50 per cent. of full passes received no grant, and schools obtaining 80 per cent. or over received the maximum grant of 8 dollars for each child. There was also a grant for each pass in needlework. Frequently the amount advanced was more than the amount earned, but in no cases were the managers called upon to make a refund, while in other cases the balance due to a school which had increased in numbers and efficiency sometimes amounted to 1,000 dollars. The immediate result of this scheme was a reduction in the amount of the grants to schools from 101,000 to 69,000 dollars, or from 9.35 to 7.96 dollars for each scholar examined.

The number of scholars however soon began to increase, and at the close of 1889 the grants amounted to 119,968.94, or 8.41 dollars for each scholar presented for examination.

The Lieutenant-Governor, Sir Charles Bruce, K.C.M.G., who had formerly held the appointment of rector of the Royal College, Mauritius, and Director of Public Instruction in Ceylon, being of opinion that the system of education was capable of improvement, introduced into the Court a new code of rules and regulations, which came into force on the 1st April, 1890. The chief features of this code are:— *The New Code of 1890.*

> 1. Granting salaries to certificated teachers at the rate of 240 dollars, 180 dollars, and 96 dollars for first, second, and third-class respectively.
>
> 2. Paying the salaries of pupil-teachers at rates varying from 4 dollars to 8 dollars per month, with a bonus of 25 dollars to the schoolmaster.
>
> 3. An allowance of 1.50 dollars for each pass in reading, writing, and arithmetic, but no payment is made on account of any scholar who failed to pass in more than one subject.
>
> 4. Scholars obtaining a full pass may be examined in two of the three subjects, grammar, geography, and history, receiving for each pass 1.50 dollars.
>
> 5. A grant of 1 dollar to each girl who passed in one of the three R's and in needlework.
>
> 6. A capitation grant of 1 dollar for each child over four and under seven years of age who had made over 200 attendances.

These grants are withheld (a) if the school fails to obtain 35 per cent. of full passes at the annual examination, (b) if the teacher neglects to collect 50 per cent. of the fees chargeable, (c) unless provision is made for teaching the girls needlework, and (d) unless the school is supplied with suitable books and apparatus, and contains 8 square feet and 60 cubic feet for each child, and unless there are separate latrines for the children of each sex.

The grant is paid in 12 monthly instalments, and nine-tenths of it must be disbursed in paying the salaries of teacher and assistants. The remaining tenth may be retained by the manager for the purpose of providing a suitable school and the necessary furniture, on the condition that the amount of the school fees and the local contributions exceed the sum retained by the manager.

Before the code came fully into force the Rev. W. G. G. Austin retired on pension, and the writer of this article, who had been associated with Sir Charles Bruce in Ceylon, and who had been appointed by Sir James Longden to act for him as Director of Public Instruction, was transferred by the Secretary of State to British Guiana.

Shortly after arrival he was instructed by the Right Honourable Viscount Gormanston to prepare rules for making more liberal grants to schools for aboriginal Indians, to mission schools, and to schools in remote and sparsely populated localities. Advantage was taken of this to mitigate the penal clauses in the code which had become law the year before, to make grants to industrial schools in which technical instruction was given, to grant certificates to teachers trained in England or the Colonies, and to permit the managers to give the teachers and assistants the whole of the Government grant.

Schools for Aboriginal Indians. The regulations for the encouragement of schools for aboriginal Indians have been an unqualified success, while those with regard to industrial schools have been a hopeless failure. Schools for teaching carpentry, printing and tailoring have been opened and closed, accomplishing little or no good, but the agriculture schools failed altogether. One of the most promising of these was established by Canon Sloman in the county of Berbice, in which some 50 boys received two hours instruction in carpentry on Mondays, Wednesdays and Fridays, and in agriculture on Tuesdays and Thursdays. Mr. Sloman had some trouble at the outset in inducing the children to work, but he made their attendance at the industrial school compulsory, and it was hoped they would soon become self-supporting. But, on resuming work after the Midsummer holidays, the boys, encouraged by their parents, remained away from school altogether. Mr. Sloman called a meeting of the parents and endeavoured to conciliate them, but they obstinately refused to allow their children " to work cutlass and shovel." The cause of the failure in this and every other case is the unwillingness of the parents to allow their children to be engaged in agricultural pursui s.

Statistics. The total amount spent on primary education for thet year ended 31st March 1897 was 110,727.05 dollars, of which 99,779.49 dollars was paid to the schools as certificate salaries, salaries to pupil-teachers or grants in aid. The total amount spent on primary education in 1898–9 was $115,223.90, of which $102,958.59 was paid in Grants-in-Aid. The following table shows the distribution of the grant for 1891-7 :—

Year.	Certificate Salaries.	P. T. Salaries.	Grants in Aid.
	$	$	$
1891-2	15,756.19	5,288.01	65,913.45
1892-3	17,883.96	6,417.73	61,350.83
1893-4	18,658.18	6,647.72	64,444.18
1894-5	19,002.19	5,948.96	67,309.77
1895-6	20,319.50	7,083.64	71,491.22
1896-7	20,527.92	7,524.09	71,178.03

The following table shows the progress from 1880–1899 :—

Year.	No. of Schools on the Government List.	No. on the Books.	Average Attendance.	Number present at Inspection.	Examined.	Grants in Aid.	Average Cost per Scholar examined.
						$	$
1880 . .	181	20,809	10,889	16,155	10,104	93,174.19	9.22
1881 . .	183	21,486	11,398	16,806	10,900	101,974.02	9.35
1882 . .	183	22,378	11,710	17,208	11,475	101,498.64	8.84
1883 . .	173	18,747	10,671	14,190	8,754	69,706.55	7.96
1884 . .	176	17,941	10,084	14,175	9,190	76,139.08	8.28
1885 . .	166	17,793	10,628	14,386	9,799	77,075.53	7.86
1886 . .	160	18,919	11,323	16,109	10,707	83,375.53	7.78
1887 . .	162	21,225	12,820	18,097	12,355	99,095.68	8.02
1888 . .	159	21,384	13,191	17,819	12,489	101,396.26	8.11
1889 . .	163	23,664	14,717	19,850	14,053	119,968.94	8.51
1890 . .	177	26,734	16,706	22,648	16,622	122,907.22	7.85
1891-92 . .	181	25,841	14,387	20,467	16,013	86,958.25	5.43
1892-93 . .	187	25,734	13,831	20,553	16,458	85,893.02	5.21
1893-94 . .	197	26,872	14,721	22,143	17,756	90,248.09	5.08
1894-95 . .	205	28,002	15,445	23,514	19,094	92,677.70	4.85
1895-96 . .	208	28,339	16,806	24,230	20,375	99,311.10	4.87
1896-97 . .	207	28,452	16,627	24,419	20,647	99,779.49	4.83
1897-98 . .	210	28,691	—	—	—	—	—
1898-99 . .	210	28,689	15,969	—	—	102,958 59	—

In December 1896, His Excellency Sir Augustus Hemming, K.C.M.G., appointed a commission " to enquire into the advisability or otherwise of retaining the present system of grants based on the results of examination, and into the advisability or otherwise of establishing a Board of Education as the central authority."

The report of the commission is given as Appendix A, and a code of regulations, prepared at the commissioners' request by the writer, as Appendix B.

II. SECONDARY EDUCATION.

The oldest and most important institution for secondary educa- Queen's
tion is Queen's College, established in 1844 by the Bishop of College.
Guiana, as a Church of England Grammar School " for the instruction of boys of all classes in classical literature, mathematics and other branches of education, on the principles of King's College, London."

It was incorporated by ordinance in 1848, and annual grants towards maintenance, varying from 1,200 dollars to 4,000 dollars, were made by the Government until 1876. For many years this grant was made on the condition that the Bishop should contribute not less than 960 dollars a year, and his lordship accordingly contributed from 200*l.* to 500*l.* a year, in augmentation of the salaries of the masters.   After 1861, however, the grant was unconditional.

The governing body, in consideration of this vote, placed ten free exhibitions at the disposal of the Governor and the Court of Policy.

From 1844, to the appointment of Sir James Longden's Education Commission in 1874, 500 boys received instruction, the average yearly attendance being 35.   And for rather more than twenty years the institution was under the direction of the Rev. George Fox, whose name and work are still gratefully remembered.

The commissioners reported on the work of the school as follows :—

" Many of the pupils educated solely, or principally, at Queen's College are occupying good positions in the public service, and in other employments. . . . It has filled an important place in the colony in supplying the means of education to the higher and middle classes.   Until 1866, when the Roman Catholic Grammar School was opened, Queen's College stood alone in the gap.   It owes its existence to the zealous exertions of the Bishop of Guiana, and to the liberality of his lordship and of those on whom he could bring his influence to bear, generously aided by the legislature of the colony, who have shewn their appreciation of the institution, and their confidence in the promoters and in the governing body, by liberal grants."

The commissioners at the same time recommended that the school should be taken over by the Government, and that changes should be made in the staff, and their report being adopted by the Court of Policy, the Combined Court was asked, and agreed to vote the necessary funds.

Sir James Longden, in addressing the Court on the subject, made the following remarks on the aims and object of the school :—

" With regard to the Queen's College, I must express my great satisfaction at learning that this Court is favourable to the proposition.   My own opinion is that higher education is most necessary.   We have not here in this colony any of the liberal foundations which our ancestors have left in England, and which are growing in America, and we have therefore to provide for education from the public funds.   I believe that it would be better that there should be one establishment, and that that establishment should be a colonial institution of an undenominational character, in which all the youths of the colony might obtain such an education as is required in the circumstances of the present day.   I hope, with the aid of this Court and under such arrangements as may be sanctioned by the Court of Policy, to see it recognised on a systematic plan, so that it will be a credit to the colony, and afford to everybody here an opportunity of obtaining at a moderate expense as good an education as can be obtained in any grammar school in England.   I do not hope to go beyond the Local Examinations of Oxford and Cambridge.

If we educate our children up to such a point that they will enter into competition with those at schools and colleges in England on fair terms, if we educate them up to that point at which University education begins, we shall have done all that our duty to the colony demands. I do not propose to•go so far as to establish University teaching, but simply the standard of the Oxford and Cambridge Local Examinations."

"The Queen's College of British Guiana" was reopened as a Government institution on January 22nd, 1877. Mr. Exley Percival, B.A., Oxon., the first principal, assumed his duties on March 5th, 1877, and held the office with conspicuous ability until his death on March 5th, 1893.

During his tenure of the principalship considerable success was attained, and the number of students largely increased. The number of entries from 1877 to 1897 was 661, giving an average attendance of 83. Mr. Percival was succeeded by Mr. J. A. Potbury, M.A., St. John's, Cambridge.

These examinations were first held in the colony in December Cambridge 1881. Since then 104 pupils from the college have gained Local Ex- honours, 122 have gained pass certificates, and 85 marks of special aminations. distinction have been gained, including one "first," and three "bracketed first" among all candidates, English and Colonial.

Students are also prepared for the examination of the University of London, for which British Guiana has been constituted a centre.

The standard therefore, as laid down by Sir James Longden, has been fully attained, and the college very well fulfils the objects for which it was founded. Those parents who are able to do so send their sons to be educated in England, where climatic and general conditions are far superior to those prevailing in a tropical country. But Queen's College boys have proved that they can hold their own in competition with others from any part of the Empire, and to quote the words of one of Mr. Percival's annual reports—"The old boys of Queen's College are to be found everywhere and in every capacity in the ranks of workers, acquitting themselves as loyal and useful citizens of the land."

The Catholic Grammar school was opened in 1866, closed shortly The Catholic after the Queen's College was taken over as a Government insti- Grammar tution, and reopened by order of the Catholic Bishop in School. 1879. It is intended for boys of Catholic parentage who are precluded on conscientious grounds from availing themselves of the advantages of Queen's College.

Its average daily attendance is about 70, of whom more than one-half are Portuguese, who are prepared for the examination of the College of Preceptors and the Cambridge Locals. It is located in the ground floor of the Catholic presbytery, is under the able direction of the Rev. Father Barraud, S.J., and is supported mainly by generous donations from Bishop Butler and fees from the scholars.

An effort was made in 1894 to provide a more suitable building, and a petition was presented to the Combined Court asking for a vote of 5,000 dollars, on the condition that an equal amount should be raised by private contributions, and Father Barraud has informed the writer that they could only collect 1,200 dollars, and that the Government was not in a position to render the assistance asked for.

Ursuline Convent High Schools.

The following information has been furnished by the Rev. Father Barraud :—

"The Convent High Schools were opened in 1847. The teaching sisters were then six in number. Now 17 nuns are engaged in teaching 200 pupils.

"In 1887 the Kensington Examinations were first applied as a means of raising the standard of teaching, and they have served their purpose by exciting emulation among the scholars, and have proved a very excellent preparation for the more difficult examinations of Edinburgh and Cambridge.

"Over 360 girls have entered for these London examinations, a large number gaining senior, junior and preliminary certificates. The convent pupils have latterly been very successful at Edinburgh and Cambridge also.

"Two new schools have been founded by the Demerara Sisters, one at New Amsterdam, the second city of the colony, and the other at Barbados. Both are succeeding beyond all expectation.

"It ought to be mentioned that the colour prejudice, as well as more important considerations, has necessitated the establishment of two distinct high schools at the Georgetown Convent. For admission to the select school legitimate birth is an indispensable qualification."

Wesleyan High Schools.

A high school for boys and one for girls were established about five years ago by the Rev. D. J. Reynolds. Both have been successful in carrying off the Mitchell Scholarships.

There is also a private high school for girls at Minto House, taught by Mrs. Vyfhuis, and a staff of able assistants. The pupils of Mrs. Vyfhuis have been very successful at the Cambridge senior and junior local examinations.

III. REFORMATORIES.

Onderneeming Reformatory for Boys.

Early in 1879 the Combined Court voted a sum of money to make provision for the establishment and regulation of a school for the instruction and training of vagrant boys and youthful male offenders, who should as far as possible be employed in agricultural pursuits.

It was established in July of that year, under the supervision of Mr F. A. Gall, and the direction of the Inspector-General of Prisons. It had accommodation for 54 boys, but the number gradually increased to 204 in 1893, and the number now varies from about 150 to 200.

Boys under 16 years of age who are found—

(a) Begging or receiving alms in any public street or place;

(*b*) Wandering in the streets, having no guardians or settled place of abode and no visible means of support;

(*c*) Frequenting the company of reputed thieves or whose surviving parent is undergoing penal servitude;

(*d*) Committing an offence punishable by a magistrate, may be sent to this reformatory.

The teaching staff consists of a superintendent, a chief officer, a first-class certified schoolmaster, an assistant, and a number of officers and wardens, and the main objects of the school may be briefly summarised as follows :—

(*a*) "To instil into the minds of the boys sound moral principles, and to induce in them practical habits of industry, regularity and good conduct." Rule 10.

(*b*) To enforce habits of cleanliness. Rule 17.

(*c*) That the officers in charge are to be kind and persuasive, not harsh and irritating, Rule 32, but at the same time firm in their dealings and report at once insubordination and dereliction of duty.

(*d*) And, finally, every boy on his admission shall be taught to consider the school as a place of improvement, and not of punishment, unless by breaches of its rules he makes it such, and while by every means the well disposed will be furnished with manifold encouragements to continue in their course of amendment, the ill-conducted will be sure of prompt punishment.

The estimated expenditure for the current year is 14,414 dollars, and the value of the farm crops is about 3,000 dollars.

In 1852 an ordinance was passed to establish an orphan Orphan asylum and school of industry in Georgetown. The institution Asylum. was supported by a vote of the Combined Court, and to a small degree by private subscriptions, bequests and donations. In addition to the three R's, the boys were instructed in certain trades and branches of agriculture, and the girls in sewing, cooking and domestic economy. At the age of 14 years the children were apprenticed out for any period not exceeding five years.

The first annual report of the "Industrial and Reformatory School" (the legal title of the institution) was written in May 1880 by Mr. J. Brummell, the managing director. At that time there were on the books of the institution 124 children, classified as Creoles, Coolies, Chinese, Portuguese and "other countries." The chief industry was the cultivation of Para grass, and the revenue derived from this source was over 900 dollars. When not thus employed, the boys were turned into the field with hoes, or sent as messengers, etc.

From 1880 to the present time the numbers have fluctuated slightly (average about 120), while the work of the institution has been carried on with little change from the passing of the ordinance in 1852.

The amount for its upkeep for the current year is 6,479 dollars.

Reformatory for Girls.   There is also a reformatory for girls conducted on similar lines, held in the building which was formerly used as a training school for teachers.   Under the efficient management of Mr. J. R. Wilcocks, formerly the head master of the training school, it is doing a good and useful work.

Its estimated cost to the Government is, for the current year, 4,092 dollars.

IV. Educational Endowments.

De Saffon Endowments.   (1.) Pierre Louis de Saffon, a native of France and a land surveyor by profession, died in 1784, leaving a considerable sum of money and property for the education and maintenance of ten orphans or half-orphans, natives of the colony, without distinction of sex, but born in lawful marriage, preferring always the most poor and indigent and those born of white parents.   The net annual revenue of the estate is divided into ten parts, each legatee being entitled to receive one-tenth until he attains the age of 16 years or dies.   Should this amount be more than sufficient for his education and maintenance, the surplus may be allowed to accumulate for his benefit any time after he may have attained the age of 16.   Five boys are being educated at Queen's College and five girls at a private school.   The accumulated funds amount to 102,330·23 dollars, of which 75,375 dollars are invested in mortgages and the remainder in bonds .

Mitchell Scholarships.   2. Walter Mitchell died in 1862, directing that 15 years after his death his residuary estate should be placed at the disposal of the legislature for the endowment of a church college or charitable institution similar to the De Saffon, though not with the same exclusion, but under the same rules.   In July 1895 the Court of Policy resolved that two scholarships (one for boys and one for girls) tenable for four years, should be awarded on the result of the Cambridge Preliminary Local Examination, having an annual value of 72 dollars.   The competitors at this examination must be under 14 years of age, and if no girls attain the qualifying standard, two scholarships may be awarded to the first two boys who have so qualified, and *vice versâ*.   Kingston High School (Wesleyan) and Minto House School (Mrs. Vyfhuis) won the scholarships in 1895, and Queen's College and Trinity High School (Wesleyan) in 1896.

The accumulated funds amount to 21,114.85 dollars and are invested in Government Securities.

The Guiana Scholarships.   3. The Guiana scholarship was instituted in 1882, and is either of the annual value of 200*l.* for three years, or of 150*l.* for five years if the scholar elects to study medicine.   The first scholar was elected in May 1882 on the result of an examination conducted by the Inspector of Schools.   But since then the Cambridge Local Senior Examination has been constituted the test, the standard to be obtained being, 1st or 2nd Class Honours, or 3rd Class Honours with distinction in some special subject.   In 1884 and 1885 the scholarship lapsed, no candidate obtaining the required qualification.   Since then, however, the scholarship has been won each year by a Queen's College boy, and the standard attained has never been below First Class Honours.   The vote for the current year amounts to 3,360 dollars.

4. The Percival exhibition was instituted by past and present The Percival Queen's College boys as a memorial to Mr. Percival. It is of the value Exhibition. of about 40 dollars, and is awarded annually to the first Junior in the Cambridge Local Examinations, provided he attains a certain standard in Honours.   It is open for competition to the whole colony, but is only tenable at the college.   It has been won for three years in succession by a Queen's College boy.

5. In 1895 the Combined Court voted the sum of 1,000 dollars Primary to be continued annually and to be competed for by boys and Scholarships. girls attending the Government aided and private schools.   Six scholarships are awarded every year, four for boys and two for girls, the value of each being 30 dollars per annum and free tuition at any High School approved by the Governor.   Thirteen of the most promising boys are now attending Queen's College. The girls select the Convent and the Wesleyan High School in about equal numbers.   The total cost of these Primary Scholarships for the year ended December 1897 was 1,119 dollars.

The amounts voted for educational purposes by the Combined Court may be thus briefly recapitulated :—

	Dollars.		£.	*s.*	*d.*
1. Primary Schools, Inspecting Staff, and Miscellaneous Expenses . . .	117,870	=	24,556	5	–
2. Secondary Education, Queen's College .	13,266	=	2,763	15	–
3. Miscellaneous, including Scholarships and Prizes	4,980	=	1,037	10	–
4. Onderneeming Reformatory . . .	14,414	=	3,002	18	4
5. Girls' Reformatory	4,092	=	852	10	–
6. Orphan Asylum	6,479	=	1,349	15	10
Total . . .	161,101	=	33,562	14	2

These sums are exclusive of large amounts for the repairs and upkeep of the Government Buildings in which schools and colleges are held.

W. BLAIR.

Education Office,
   Georgetown, British Guiana.

Maps of British Guiana and photographs of schools can be seen at the Board of Education Library, St. Stephen's House, Cannon Row, Whitehall, London, S.W.

SUPPLEMENTARY NOTE.

The following is extracted from the Annual Report for British Guiana 1898-9, published June, 1900. It will be observed that on an earlier page of the above Report some later statistics have been embodied from the same source :—

There are at present 210 schools having 28,689 scholars on the books, with an average daily attendance of 15,959, and maintained at a cost of $115,223.90, distributed as follows :—

	Dollars.		Per cent.
Administration and Inspection - - - -	8,789.18	or	7·62
Stationery, Office, and Miscellaneous Expenses	2,167.13	„	1·88
Scholarships and Prizes - - - -	1,309.00	„	1·13
Grants-in-Aid - - - - - -	102,958.59	„	89·35
Total - - -	115,223.90		

It is required that not less than nine-tenths of the grant shall be paid to the teachers and assistant teachers. The remaining tenth may be retained by the manager for providing a school-house, and furnishing it with books and school apparatus. All the schools. with the exception of thirteen estate schools, are denominational as follows :—Church of England, 72; Church of Scotland, 36; Congregational, 30; Wesleyan, 29: Roman Catholic, 27; Estate, 13; Moravian, 2; Lutheran, 1.

APPENDIX A.

REPORT OF THE COMMISSIONERS ON PRIMARY EDUCATION, 1897.

To His Excellency Sir Augustus William Lawson Hemming, Knight Commander of the Most Distinguished Order of Saint Michael and Saint George, Governor and Commander-in-Chief in and over the Colony of British Guiana, Vice-Admiral and Ordinary of the same, &c.

WE, the Commissioners appointed by Your Excellency to enquire into certain matters in connection with Primary Education in this Colony, to wit :—The advisability or otherwise of retaining the present system of Grants based on the results of Examinations, and the desirability or otherwise of establishing a Board of Education as the Central Authority, have the honour to report as follows :—

We have held thirteen meetings, viz. : On the following days—31st December, 1896 ; 4th, 12th, 22nd January ; 12th, 15th, 22nd February ; 1st, 8th, 15th, 22nd March ; 27th April, and 9th July, 1897. The following Witnesses were examined :—

Mr. William Blair, Inspector of Schools,
Mr. J. F. Rose, Assistant Inspector of Schools,
Mr. E. J. R. Wilcocks, Secretary, Poor Law Commissioners, and Superintendent, Girls' Reformatory, and Secretary to the Old Education Board,
Mr. C. T. Cox, Assistant Government Secretary,
Mr. W. H. Hinds, Proprietor and Editor of the " Echo,"
The Lord Bishop of Guiana,
The Reverend D. J. Reynolds, Superintendent Wesleyan Missions,
The Reverend W. B. Ritchie, Moderator of the Presbytery,
The Reverend F. C. Glasgow,
The Ven. Archdeacon Gwyther,
The Reverend Father Rigby,
The Reverend J. B. Cropper,
The Reverend Father Barraud,
The Reverend J. Highwood.

Messrs. C. T. Holder, Ivry Hart, D. V. Jacobs, E. D. Sharples H. E. Smith, W. A. Osborne, T. Y. Carrington, T. N. Durant, S. Robertson, E. Joseph, E. Linton, D. N. Mitchell, P. Saunders.

We have confined ourselves as strictly as possible to the objects named in our Commission, but we have found it impossible to exclude some cognate subjects from our consideration.

1. With regard to the payment of grants, we are of opinion that the present system based on the results of examinations should be retained, with such modifications as will admit of the grant being to some extent dependent on the general proficiency of the whole school, and not as at present solely on the individual excellence of the pupils.

2. As regards the establishment of a Board of Education as the central authority, we consider that this is neither necessary nor desirable ; but we are of opinion that, in all important matters relating to primary education, there should be an appeal to the Governor in Council.

3. The question of payment of teachers is one which has demanded and which has received careful consideration. On the one hand, there is the almost unanimous opinion on the part of the teachers, supported in some considerable measure by the managers of schools, that there should be a greater degree of fixity given to the emoluments of the teachers than is possible under the present code. On the other hand, there is the danger

4226.   3 G 2 that if the teacher's income be made altogether independent of the results of his teaching in his school, one of the greatest inducements to the attainment of a high standard of efficiency will be removed. We have, therefore, come to the conclusion that the fixed salaries of the different classes of certificates should be increased, the per caput grant-in-aid being proportionately reduced so as to avoid any necessity for a larger appropriation than at present from public funds for the purposes of primary education.

4. The present standards, we consider, may be retained. They certainly should not be lowered ; if any alteration be made, it should be in the other direction.

5. With regard to the number of attendances to qualify for examination, we are of opinion that the requirement should, as regards the town schools, remain as at present, *i.e.*, at 200. As regards the country schools, we think that the minimum number might be fixed at 150.

6. Under the present code the maximum age at which a pupil teacher may receive Government aid is 20 years, and no teacher under the age of 21 is allowed the sole charge of a school. The certificate salary is paid only to a teacher in charge. We recommend that while there should be no reduction in the minimum age at which a teacher can have sole charge of a school, there should be no hiatus between that minimum age and the maximum age at which a pupil teacher may receive Government aid as such. We attach much importance to this recommendation.

7. With reference to the payment of bonuses to teachers for training pupil teachers, we are of opinion that the teachers should be required to furnish to the inspector of schools a monthly return, showing the hours of instruction given by them to the pupil teachers. The return to be countersigned by the manager, and payment of the bonus to be withheld if the return be not furnished as required.

8. We have given careful consideration to the question of the tenure of office by teachers, and we have arrived at the conclusion that the present system under which a teacher can be arbitrarily dismissed by his manager should be modified. We accordingly recommend that the manager should be given the power to suspend a teacher, reporting at once such suspension, together with the reasons thereof, to the Inspector of Schools, who should have power to confirm or disallow the same. Both the manager and teacher to be given the right of appeal to the Governor-in-Council.

9. With regard to the supervision of the schools by the managers, there is before us abundant evidence to show that, in some cases at least, very little, if any, exists. It must be remembered that the managers of schools, as such, are the recipients of public money for disbursements in connection with their schools, and we are strongly of opinion that they, should be required to pay more frequent visits of inspection to and generally to exercise greater supervision over, their schools than at present. In short, they should be managers in fact and not in name only.

10. As has already been said, managers of schools are the recipients for disbursement of public money, and we consider that they should be required like all other persons to furnish vouchers of such expenditure.

11. With regard to the question of fees, the evidence before us shows very clearly that the present system, under which the collection of fees is made compulsory, leads to falsification of returns and other underhand proceedings. We strongly recommend the repeal of the penal clauses in connection with the collection of fees.

12. We understand that in some of the popular schools the parents of the scholars readily pay fees at a higher rate than is required by the regulations. There does not appear to be any objection to this, but we think that in order that the financial returns may be as complete as possible the fees should be fixed at not less than two cents per caput per week ; all fees, of whatever amount, to be accounted for.

13. The question of the support given to their schools by the different denominations has been considered by us, and we are of opinion that the denominations should be called upon to contribute (apart from school buildings) directly to the maintenance of their schools, and that the Government Grant in Aid should be paid only on the production of a certificate to the effect that the denominational contribution (which should bear some fixed proportion to the fees chargeable) had been duly collected. Mission schools, and schools in remote and sparsely populated localities, to be exempted from payment of the denominational contribution.

14. We would also recommend the continuance in the educational law of the principle of compulsory attendance at schools ; but in doing so we are not unmindful of the present difficulties which underlie the carrying out of the law in its entirety.

15. Although not strictly within the terms of our commission, we strongly advise that as soon as the state of the public exchequer will allow, a training school for teachers should be provided as the law now directs.

In the meantime, and as a tentative measure, we would suggest that a certain number of schools, to be approved of by the Governor-in-Council, be selected at which pupil teachers may, after passing their examination as such, be trained in the art of teaching and receive practical lessons under the supervision of the principal teacher.

16. We understand that there are at present certain teachers who, though uncertificated, have for years successfully conducted their schools. To meet cases of this kind we would suggest that the Inspector of Schools should be given power to issue, with the approval of the Governor-in-Council, a certificate of competency to any uncertificated teacher who has to the knowledge of the Educational Department successfully conducted a school for a period of not less than ten years.

17. With regard to the question referred to us in the letter from the Government Secretary of the 15th March 1897, we would recommend that the Inspector of Schools be given power to issue certificates of the 1st, 2nd, or 3rd class, as the case may be, to any person who has been trained in any recognised normal or training school, or who has taken a degree at any recognised university in any part of Her Majesty's dominions, and holds a certificate thereof.

18. Our attention has been called to a scheme for providing pensions for deserving teachers propounded in the draft regulations of the Inspector of Schools, and we would recommend its adoption ; the funds for the purpose could be obtained by the diversion of the Capitation Grant to that purpose.

All of which is respectfully submitted.

Henry Kirke,
C. B. Hamilton,
B. Howell Jones,
D. M. Hutson,
E. C. Luard,
J. Thomson.

J. Hampden King, Secretary.
29 July 1897.

I dissent from Paragraph 12. I am of opinion that all the law can stipulate for is a minimum fee. Anything paid voluntarily over that amount is a tribute to the teacher of a purely ultra-official nature. No evidence as to the payment of a higher rate of fee was given before the Commission.

J. Thomson.

APPENDIX B.

CODE OF REGULATIONS FOR GRANT-IN-AID SCHOOLS 1900.

PRELIMINARY CHAPTER.

Short title.
 1. These Regulations may be cited for all purposes as the Education Code, 1900.

Condition of grants-in-aid
 2. The grants-in-aid to primary schools are dependent on the amount voted annually for that purpose by the Combined Court, and nothing in this code shall be regarded as constituting any vested right or interest to or in such grants.

Administration of grants.
 3. The grants are administered by the Inspector of Schools, hereinafter called "the Inspector" subject to the control and direction of the Governor-in-Council.

Mode and conditions of making grants.
 4. Aid to maintain a school on the list of aided schools is given by annual grants, payable by equal monthly instalments, conditional upon the attendance and proficiency of the scholars and the state of the school at the time of the annual examination and during the twelve months immediately following. The payment of any instalment or instalments may, with the previous sanction of the Governor-in-Council be wholly or in part withheld if any breach of these Regulations is committed.

Inspectors and Assistant Inspectors.
 5. Officers are appointed and employed by the Government to verify the fulfilment of the conditions on which grants are made. These officers are called Inspectors and Assistant Inspectors.

Power to visit School.
 6. The Inspector or an Assistant Inspector may visit any school at any time with or without notice.

Placing School on, &c., list of Aided Schools.
 7. No school shall be placed on the list of aided schools or be removed herefrom without the consent of the Governor-in-Council.

Making of application for grant.
 8. Every application for a grant-in-aid must be made on a printed form which can be obtained at the office of the Education Department. The application must be sent to the inspector, who will submit the same, together with his report thereon, to the Governor-in-Council.

General rules as to grants.
 9. No steps should be taken to establish a school with the expectation of obtaining aid from the Government. Grants cannot be claimed irrespective of the circumstances of the case and the limits of the sum placed at the disposal of the department. If a grant is refused, the reason for its refusal will be communicated to the applicant.

Restriction on making of grants to new Schools.
 10. As a general rule, no application will be entertained for a grant to any new school if there already exists an efficient school of the same class having available accommodation within two miles.

Notification of application for grant to new School.
 11.—(1.) Every application for a grant to a new school shall be notified in the Gazette, so as to enable managers of existing aided schools within two miles to state any objections which they may have to its being placed on the list of aided schools.

 (2.) A copy of the Gazette will be sent to all the managers interested in the application.

Management of Schools.
 12. Every school shall be under the control of one or more managers, who shall be responsible that the regulations subject to which aid is granted are conformed and enforced. If there are two or more managers, one of

their number must be appointed in writing to communicate with the department on all matters relating to the school, and he will receive the Government grant and be responsible to the department for its proper distribution.

13. No schoolmaster can be recognised as the manager of an aided school, nor can any person be recognised as the manager of an aided school if he derives any profit or emolument therefrom. *Restrictions as to Managers.*

14.—(1.) No school shall be conducted for private profit or shall be farmed out by the manager to the teachers. *Responsibility of Managers.*

(2.) The manager shall be responsible for the payment of the teachers' salaries and all other expenses of the school.

15.—(1.) Schools shall be classified as "A schools," "B schools," "C schools," and "D schools." *Classifications of Schools.*

(2.) Schools which fulfil all the conditions of Regulation 17 (2) to (8) inclusive of this code and whose daily average attendance for the six months before any examination is not less than 25 are called "A schools."

(3.) Schools which do not fulfil all these conditions are called "B schools."

(4.) Mission schools for Aboriginal Indians and schools in remote and sparsely populated localities are called "C schools."

(5.) Industrial schools in which theoretical and practical instruction in agriculture, or in a trade or trades, or both, is given are called "D schools."

16. The schedules annexed to this Code shall form part of and have the same effect as the regulations of the Code. *Effect of Schedules to the Code.*

CHAPTER I.

ANNUAL GRANTS.

A and B Schools.

17. Before any school is placed on the list of Aided Schools the Governor-in-Council shall be satisfied— *Requirements to be satisfied before School is placed on list of Aided Schools as A School.*

(1.) That the average daily attendance for the six months before the date of the application was not less than 40 ;

(2.) That the principal teacher is over 20 years of age, and is certificated ;

(3.) That the registers of admission and attendance, of the form and in the manner hereinafter described, are accurately kept ; that the returns required by the Government or the Department are trustworthy ; and that the school is conducted in accordance with an approved time-table (a copy of which signed by the Inspector shall be hung up in the schoolroom), and in an orderly and efficient manner ;

(4.) That adequate provision is made for the instruction of the girls in needlework ;

(5.) That the school buildings, including covered galleries, are in good repair ; that they are well ventilated, and contain not less than 80 cubic feet (space) and 8 square feet (area) for each child in average attendance ;

(6.) That the school is provided with a sufficient number of benches of suitable heights to seat all the children without overcrowding ; a sufficient number of desks of suitable heights to permit at least one-half of the children to be engaged in writing at the same time ; reading books for each standard, copy books, slates, maps, blackboards, clock, log-book, account-book &c. ;

(7.) That the school is provided with separate latrines for the children of each sex ; and

(8.) That all reasonable care is taken in the ordinary management of the school to bring up the children in habits of punctuality, of good manners and language, of cleanliness and neatness, and also to impress upon the children the importance of cheerful obedience to duty, of consideration and respect for others and of honour and truthfulness in work and act.

B Schools. 18.—(1.) Any aided school, hereinafter called "school," the daily average attendance at which for the six months before any examination is less than 25, or which ceases to fulfil any of the conditions 2 to 8 (inclusive) of Regulation 17, shall be classed as a B school.

(2.) No school will be allowed to remain a B school for more than two consecutive years.

Subjects of examination. First Schedule. 19. Scholars will be examined in the subjects prescribed in Part II. of the schedule to this code.

Computation of grant to A Schools. Second Schedule. 20. The annual grant payable to A and B schools shall be computed according to Part III. of the schedule to this code.

Qualification of instruction and attendance for individual grants. 21. Subject to the proviso hereinafter contained, no grant will be allowed for any scholar who has been a pupil for less than six months during the 12 months immediately preceding the examination in the school in which he is examined, and who has made less than 150 attendances.

Provided always (1) that if the parents of any pupil remove from the locality in which his school is to another residence more than two miles distant from such school, and necessitating the attendance of the child at another school, the periods for which he has been a pupil and the attendances at both schools shall be taken into account ; (2) a grant may be allowed for any child not previously on the register of any school, or for any child who has been removed from any school for any reason approved at the time by the Inspector, and in respect of whom no grant is payable to any other school, provided in either case such child has made the requisite number of attendances.

Qualification of age for individual grants. 22.—(1.) No grant will be allowed for any scholar over 15 years of age on the day of examination.

(2.) No grant will be allowed for any scholar in Standard I. who is over 12 years of age on the day of examination.

Proof of age of scholar. 23. If in the opinion of the Inspector the ages of any scholars are incorrectly entered on the examination schedules he may call upon the manager to furnish him with the names of the parents of such scholars, the districts in which they were born, and refer the cases to the Registrar General, whose decision shall be final.

Examination in standards. 24.—(1.) At the first examination scholars may be grouped in any standard fixed by the manager, but scholars may not afterwards be presented for examination in the same standard as, or a lower standard than, that in which they have previously passed.

(2.) If scholars fail to pass in two of the subjects, reading, writing, and arithmetic, they will be considered to have failed altogether, and no grants will be allowed for them.

C Schools.

Definition of sparsely populated locality. 25. No school shall be considered to be in a sparsely populated locality if the population within a radius of two miles exceeds 200.

Number of C Schools. 26. The number of C schools shall not at any time exceed 25.

Qualification of average attendance for C Schools. 27. No school shall be accepted or retained on the list as a C school, unless the average daily attendance for the year is at least 12.

28. Subject to the proviso hereinafter contained, no grant will be allowed for any scholar who has been a pupil for less than six months in a C school during the 12 months immediately preceding the examination, and who has made less than 100 attendances ; provided always that if the parents of any pupil remove from the locality in which his school is to another residence more than two miles distant from such school and necessitating the attendance of the child at another school, the periods for which he has been a pupil and the attendance at both schools shall be taken into account. Qualifications of instruction and attendance for individual grants.

29. The annual grants to C schools shall be 50 per cent. more than the amounts prescribed in Part III. of the schedule to this Code in respect of reading, writing, and arithmetic, and needlework, and the same amounts in respect of all other subjects. Grants to C Schools.

30. Regulations 17 (2) to (8) inclusive, 19, 22, 23, and 24 shall apply to C schools as well as to A and B schools.

D Schools.

31. The number of D schools shall not at any time exceed twelve. Number of D Schools.

32.—(1) Before any school is placed on the list of aided schools as a D school Regulation 17 must be complied with, and in addition the Governor-in-Council be satisfied :— Conditions of grant to D Schools.

   (a.) That the school teaches a trade or trades approved by the Inspector ; or gives more advanced theoretic and practical instruction in agriculture than is given in the ordinary Elementary Schools, or provides both such teaching and such instruction.

   (b.) That the school shall be sufficiently provided with appliances for elementary instruction in agriculture or in the trade or trades to which the school is devoted ; and

   (c.) That the master or mistress appointed to teach agriculture or the trade or trades is duly qualified for that purpose, and has obtained such certificate (if any) as may be required by the Education Department.

(2.) Any D school which for two consecutive years fails to fulfil any of these conditions—(a), (b), and (c)—or of those prescribed for A schools, shall be removed from the list of aided schools.

33. The manager of a D school shall receive, in addition to the grants payable according to Part III. of the schedule to this Code, the sum of 7.50 dols. for each scholar, being over 12 and under 17 years of age, who may be certified to have been in attendance for not less than 100 days and to have received daily not less than two hours' instruction in agriculture or in the workshop, and who is able to work at his trade to the satisfaction of the Inspector : Provided that the grant to any one D school shall not exceed the sum of 250 dols. for one year. Special grant to D Schools.

34. Regulations 19 to 24 (both inclusive) shall apply to D schools, 17 years being substituted for 15 in Regulation 22 (1).

CHAPTER II.

MANAGERS.

35. The manager shall be responsible to the Inspector of Schools for the conduct of the school, for the maintenance of its efficiency, and for the provision of suitable buildings, books, and apparatus. General responsibility of Manager.

School fees.

36. The manager may require every scholar attending the school who is over 12 years of age, or who has passed the Fourth Standard to pay a school fee not exceeding two cents per week, payable in advance.

Appropriation of one-tenth of grant for school buildings, &c.

37. The manager may retain not more than one-tenth of the grant made to his school for the purpose of providing and maintaining suitable buildings, books, and apparatus for the school. He may also retain for this purpose any fees paid by the scholars and any local contributions entrusted to him.

Appropriation of nine-tenths of grant for Teachers.

38. Not less than nine-tenths of the grant shall be divided between the principal teacher and the assistant teacher or teachers or sewing mistress (but not pupil teachers), in such proportions as may, after considering the recommendation of the manager on the subject, be decided by the Inspector. The decision of the Inspector shall be subject to an appeal to the Governor-in-Council.

Furnishing of quarterly accounts of income and expenditure.

39. The manager shall furnish quarterly to the inspector a detailed account certified by him to be correct of the income and expenditure of the school, attaching thereto vouchers for the expenditure of the Government Grant, including certificate salaries and salaries of pupil teachers. The manager shall personally, if practicable, pay the salaries of all assistant teachers and of the sewing mistress and of pupil teachers, but in any event a receipt for each salary paid must be entered in the school account book and dated and signed by the recipient.

Furnishing of returns.

40. The manager shall furnish all returns that may be required by the Government or the Inspector.

Duty of Manager at annual examination.

41. (a) Due notice, not being less than 14 days, will be given of the annual examination, and the manager will be furnished with the examination forms given in Part V. of the schedule to the Code in duplicate, which, together with the declarations thereon, he must have ready for inspection, and duly signed by himself and the principal teacher on the morning of the day of the examination. He will also inform the Inspector at least five clear days before the examination of the probable number of children that will be examined in each standard and of the number to be examined in the extra subjects.

(b) The manager will also be required to produce the School Registers, Log Book, and School Account Book at the annual examination.

(c) The Account Book shall state the names of the principal teacher and all the assistant teachers, including sewing teachers and pupil teachers and the respective amounts of their salaries.

Duty of Manager. Fourth Schedule.

42. Before the examination the manager shall sign the declaration set forth in Form (1) in Part V. of the schedule to this Code. If he is unable to do so, he shall state his reasons in writing for such inability, and the case will be dealt with in such manner as the Governor-in-Council may decide.

Duty of Manager as to visiting Schools.

43. The manager shall personally visit the school at least once a month, examine and sign the registers, record the results of his visit in the log book, and forward a copy to the Inspector with his monthly school accounts ; provided that it shall be sufficient if schools in remote districts, more than 10 miles from the manager's residence, are visited not less than once a quarter.

Powers of Manager as to Teachers.

44. (1) The manager shall have the exclusive right of appointing and dismissing teachers and assistant teachers, and subject as in hereinafter provided, pupil teachers, but all changes in the teaching staff shall be notified by the manager to the Inspector. Any change, permanent or temporary, will be recognised only from the date on which the same is notified to the Inspector.

(2.) Every teacher who is dismissed by the manager of any school may within ten days thereafter appeal from the decision to any body of the denomination to which such school belongs, appointed by the authorities of such denomination to hear such appeal and approved of by the Governor, and any such body shall hear and decide any such appeal within fourteen days after it is received, and either party may appeal from such decision to the Governor-in-Council. If there is no such body, or such body does not decide the appeal within the said fourteen days, the manager shall obtain the papers and forward them to the Governor-in-Council, who shall decide the appeal.

(3.) If the manager fails to comply with such final decision public aid may be withdrawn from the school.

CHAPTER III.

TEACHERS.

46. Every teacher hereafter appointed to the charge of an Aided school shall be required to hold a certificate of competency, hereinafter called " a certificate," granted after due examination. *Require-ment as to Certificate of Competency.*

47. (1) The Inspector shall have the power to issue a certificate of the second or third class to any person who— *Power to issue Second or Third Class Certificates to certain persons.*

(a.) Holds a certificate from any recognised normal or training school ; or

(b.) Having been trained in any recognised normal or training school, holds a certificate from the Government of the country or colony in which such school is situated ; or

(c.) Has taken a degree at any recognised university in any part of Her Majesty's dominions or in the United States of America, or has obtained an honour certificate at the Oxford or Cambridge Local Examination for seniors or a certificate in the First Division of the First Class at the College of Preceptors ; provided that in any of the three preceding cases the Inspector may in any particular instance if there is, in his opinion, sufficient cause for so doing, refuse to issue such certificate, but in such case the applicant shall have a right of appeal against such refusal to the Governor-in-Council, whose decision shall be final.

(2.) The Inspector may, with approval of the Governor-in-Council, issue a certificate of competency without an examination to any provisionally-certificated teacher who for ten consecutive years has successfully conducted a school to the knowledge of the Inspector of Schools. The holder of such certificate shall be entitled to the same salary as if he held a third-class certificate.

(3.) The Inspector may issue a second-class certificate to any teacher who at the commencement of these Regulations is and has been for ten years previously rendering efficient service as a teacher, and who in 1877 held a second-class certificate which was subsequently cancelled by the then existing Board of Education, because the holder had not in 1877 completed ten years' service.

48. Any certificate of the second class issued under this code or under the Education Regulations, 1890, may, subject to the like power of refusal of appeal as is contained in sub-section (1) of the preceding regulation, be raised to a certificate of the first class after three consecutive years efficient service as a teacher in any aided school of the colony. Provided always that no teacher whose certificate is so raised in any year shall be entitled to claim any increase of certificate salary in that year, unless such increase has been provided for in the sum granted by the combined courts on the Annual Estimates in respect of Grants to Primary Schools. *Power to raise Second Class Certificates.*

Power to issue Provisional Certificate, and effect thereof.

49. The inspector shall have the power to issue a provisional certificate to any person who, in his judgment, may be properly employed in a school. The holder of any such provisional certificate shall nevertheless be under obligation to present himself for examination at the first certificate examination subsequently held in the colony, provided that the date of such examination does not fall within six months of the issue of the certificate. If the date of the examination falls within those six months, the teacher must present himself at the next succeeding examination. The provisional certificate may be suspended if the holder fails to pass or for any other reason which is, in the opinion of the inspector, sufficient.

Effect of Provisional Certificate.

50. A provisional certificate shall not entitle its owner to a certificate salary, nor shall the holder of one be entitled to be entrusted with the training of pupil teachers.

Recognition of existing Certificates.

51. Teachers holding certificates recognised under the regulations which came into force on the 1st day of January, 1883, or under the Education Regulations, 1890, shall be considered as holding certificates of the same class under this code.

Salaries attached to Certificates.

52. The following salaries shall, subject to the proviso hereinafter contained, be attached to certificates held by males or females who are principal teachers of schools—

> For a First Class Certificate - - - 240 dols. per annum.
> For a Second Class Certificate - - 180 „ „
> For a Third Class Certificate - - 96 „ „

Provided always that the salary to be received by a certificated teacher in respect of his certificate shall be reduced by one-fifth if, at the annual examination, the school of which he is the principal teacher fails to obtain 50 per cent. of full passes calculated on the number presented for examination ; and by one-third should his school fail to obtain 40 per cent. of full passes.

Employment of Assistant Teachers in large Schools.

53. In a school having had an average daily attendance for the preceding six months of 120 or more, a certificated teacher may be employed as an assistant at a salary of 8 dols. a month, and such portion of the grant as may be determined by the manager and approved by the Inspector, in lieu of two pupil teachers ; and in a school having an average daily attendance of 200 or more, two certificated teachers may be employed as assistants, in lieu of four pupil teachers, on similar conditions.

Holding of examinations for Certificates.

54.—(1.) Examinations for certificates of the second and third classes will be held annually in the month of January, at the Queen's College, Georgetown, and at such other times and places as may be necessary. There shall not be any examination for certificates of the first class.

(2.) A syllabus of the subjects of examination is set out in Part VI. of the schedule of this Code, and will be sent to school managers in the month of February.

(3.) Candidates desiring to sit at any such examination shall apply for a card of admission, and each application shall be accompanied by unused postage or revenue stamps to the value of one dollar or such other sum as may be fixed by the Governor-in-Council.

Position of successful Candidates at examination.

55. A successful candidate at his examination, if employed as the principal teacher of a school, will be entitled to draw a certificate salary from the first day of the month immediately following that in which the examination is held.

Suspension or cancellation of Certificate.

56.--(1.) A certificate may at any time be suspended or cancelled by the Inspector for misconduct, whether the holder thereof is employed as a teacher or not. The Inspector may impose on a teacher guilty of negligence or carelessness without any intention of fraud a fine according to the following scale, namely, for the first offence a fine not exceeding 5 per cent. of the teacher's salary (including his certificate salary, if any) for one month, and for a second or any subsequent offence a fine not exceeding 10 per cent. thereof

(2.) The Inspector shall not suspend or cancel a certificate or impose a fine until the teacher has been informed of the charge against him and has been allowed an opportunity of making his defence.

(3.) If a certificate is suspended or cancelled, or a fine imposed the holder may appeal to the Governor-in-Council, whose decision shall be final.

57. All communications from a teacher relating to the discipline or management of his school must be forwarded through the manager. Statistical information, letters with reference to certificate examinations, &c., may be sent direct. No reply will be sent to letters when this regulation is disregarded. *Conduct of correspondence.*

58. Teachers will be required to furnish any statistical information, or any information with reference to the attendance of any scholar or scholars, which may be required by the Inspector, or assistant inspectors, or an educational district officer. *Furnishing of information by Teachers.*

CHAPTER IV.

PUPIL TEACHERS.

59. Pupil teachers are boys and girls selected by the manager to assist in maintaining discipline and in instructing the lower classes. A pupil teacher must not be employed for more than five hours in any one day or more than twenty hours in any one week. *Status, &c., of Pupil Teachers.*

60. The manager is bound to see—

(1.) That the pupil teacher receives, without cost, special instruction from the principal teacher for not less than five hours during every week, out of the regular school hours, not more than two hours being on the same day ; and

(2.) That he, during his last year, attends such classes of instruction in Agricultural Science (including Botany and Chemistry) as may be held for the instruction of teachers. *Right of Pupil Teacher to special instruction.*

61.—(1.) Any school having an average daily attendance of 80, for six months, shall be entitled to one pupil teacher, and to one additional pupil teacher for every 40 above the first 80 ; but the number of pupil teachers shall in no case exceed four. One or two certificated assistant teacher or teachers may be employed in lieu of two or four pupil teachers. *Proportion of Pupil Teachers to scholars.*

(2.) If the daily average attendance for any three consecutive months falls below the above numbers respectively, a pupil teacher's services shall be dispensed with at the end of that period without previous notice.

62.—(1.) An application for the appointment of a pupil teacher shall be made in the form of Part VII. of the schedule to this Code or such form as may for the time being be approved by the Inspector. *Making of application for appointment of Pupil Teachers.*

(2.) A copy of such form may be obtained on application to the department.

63. Before a candidate can be employed as a pupil teacher he will be required to produce a certificate of birth or baptism, showing he is eligible for the examination, a certificate of good character from a minister of religion, and a medical certificate showing that he is not suffering from any infirmity likely to impair his usefulness as a teacher, and to pass an examination in the subjects specified in Part VIII. of the schedule to this Code. *Qualifications for employment of Pupil Teachers.*

Examination of Pupil Teachers.

64.—(1.) No candidate under 14 or over 16 years of age shall be eligible for the first examination as a pupil teacher.

(2.) A pupil teacher's engagement shall cease when he or she attains the age of 21 years.

(3.) Pupil teachers shall attend such annual examinations as may be appointed by the Inspector, and be examined in the subjects prescribed in Part VIII. of the schedule to this Code. Candidates desiring to sit at any such examination shall apply for a card of admission.

Restrictions on employment of Pupil Teacher.

(4.) At the examination every pupil teacher shall produce his note books and a certificate of good character from his manager.

65.—(1.) No pupil teacher shall be employed as such for more than five years.

(2.) A pupil teacher voluntarily leaving or being dismissed from one school shall not as a rule be eligible for employment in another.

(3.) After two consecutive failures to pass the annual examination, except such failure is due to illness or other sufficient cause, a pupil teacher will no longer be recognized by the Inspector of schools.

Salaries of Pupil Teachers.

66. Pupil teachers, whilst actually employed in teaching, shall be paid the following salaries :—$3 monthly during the first year, $4 monthly during the second, $5 monthly during the third, $6 monthly during the fourth, and $7 monthly during the fifth : provided always that these increments shall be conditional on their passing at the commencement of the second and subsequent years the annual examination.

Bonus to successful Pupil Teacher.

67. Every pupil teacher who passes with credit the five consecutive examinations, and is able to produce a certificate of good character from his manager, shall be entitled to a bonus of $20.

Bonus to Principal Teacher for passing of Pupil Teacher.

68. A bonus of $20 shall be paid to the principal teacher of a school for every pupil teacher employed therein who passes the annual examination, if such teacher produces a certificate from the manager showing that such principal teacher has complied with the requirements of Regulation No. 60 in respect of such pupil teacher. Such bonus, if more than one principal teacher of the same school has taken part in the tuition of a pupil teacher, shall be apportioned between such persons in proportion to the periods during which such persons respectively have filled the office of principal teacher of such school.

Pupil Teachers' Time-Table.

69. A pupil teachers' time table shall be hung up in a conspicuous place in the schoolroom.

CHAPTER V. [omitted].

REGISTERS.

CHAPTER VI.

GENERAL RULES.

General right of admission to School.

79. No child over five years of age may be refused admission as a scholar into any school on other than reasonable grounds.

Restrictions on right of admission.

80. No child under four years of age, and no child suffering from any contagious, cutaneous, or infectious disease, or coming from a house in which such disease is known to exist, shall be admitted into any school, and the attendance of any child whose name is on the register but who comes from such house, or is so diseased, shall be prevented by the teacher.

81. It shall not be required, as a condition of being admitted into or con- *Prohibition* tinuing in a school, that a scholar shall attend or abstain from attending *of condition* any Sunday school or any place of religious worship, or that he shall, or *as to attend-* shall not, attend any religious observance whatever. *ance at Sunday School, &c.*

82. —(1.) The time or times during which any religious observance is *Rules as to* practised, or instruction in religious subjects is given, shall be specified in *religious* the school time table, which shall be approved by the Inspector and kept *instruction.* permanently and conspicuously affixed in the school-room.

(2.) Any scholar may be withdrawn from any such religious instruction without forfeiting any of the other benefits of the school.

83 Members of the Executive Council and of the Combined Court, the *Persons* Judges of the Supreme Court, Justices of the Peace, and any other persons *having right* authorised by the Governor may visit any school, and they shall have full *to visit* liberty to examine the registers and to record the result of their visit in the *Schools.* school log-book. Visitors are requested to report the results of their visits to the Inspector of Schools.

84. Every school shall be kept open for at least five days in each week, *Working* except on the fixed holidays and any special holidays granted by the *days.* inspector.

85.—(1) In addition to all public holidays, a school may be closed for two *Holidays.* weeks at Christmas, commencing on the Friday before Christmas Day, one week at Easter, and four weeks in August, commencing with the first Monday in August. The Easter and August vacations may be changed to other periods, but all such changes must be notified to the inspector before-hand.

86. The school hours shall be from 9 a.m. to 12 noon, and from 1 p.m. to *School hours.* 3 p.m., or such hours as may be appointed by the inspector.

87. Any child over five years of age whose name is on the register of *Examination* any school, and who has not passed the fourth standard, but who has made *of children* fewer attendances or has been a pupil for a shorter time than is prescribed *whose names* by Regulations 21, 28, and 34 (as the case may be) shall be presented for *are on the* examination when the annual examination of such school is being held, and *register, but* shall be examined in the standard in which children of his age are usually *in respect of* examined, but no grant shall be made in respect of any pass obtained by *whom no* any such child. *grant is to be made.*

88. As soon as possible after the annual examination the Inspector of *Return of* Schools shall prepare a return of all such scholars, and this return shall be *children so* forwarded to the manager. *examined.*

89. The Education Regulations, 1880, and the Education Regulations, 1891, are hereby revoked. Provided always that—

(1.) Any school receiving a grant under the said Regulations shall continue to receive the same up to 1st November, 1900, but no longer.

(2.) Any school examined on or before the 1st March, 1901, shall be examined in the standards prescribed by Regulation 32 of the Education Regulations, 1890 ; and

(3.) The salary of any pupil teacher employed at the commencement of these regulations shall, until the 1st day of November, 1900, but no longer, be that prescribed by Regulation 30 of the Education Regulations, 1890, but in all other respects he shall be subject to these Regulations.

Pensions to Teachers.*

Appropria-
tion of sum
for pensions.

*88. A sum not exceeding $1,000 per annum, or such other amount as may be voted by the Combined Court, shall be appropriated for paying pensions to deserving teachers.

Number of
pensioners,
&c.

*89. The number of pensioners at any time shall not exceed 15, namely, five at 100 dollars per annum, and ten at 50 dollars per annum, or such other less amount as may be allowed by the Governor-in-Council.

Selections of
pensioners.

*90. The pensioners will be selected by the Governor-in-Council.

Qualifica-
tions of ap-
plicant for
pension.

*91. An applicant for a pension shall—

(1.) Be a certificated teacher in charge of an aided school at the time when the pension is applied for ;

(2.) Have become incapable, from age or infirmity, of continuing to teach a school efficiently ;

(3.) Have, as a rule, been employed as a teacher in an elementary school for 20 years or more ; and

(4.) Be 55 years of age or more, unless the pension is applied for on the ground of infirmity.

Sending in
of applica-
tions for
pensions.

*92. Applications for pensions shall be sent to the inspector, who will submit them quarterly (in January April, July, and October), with a complete record of the applicants' services, to the Governor-in-Council.

Preferential
claims of
certain
Teachers.

*93. Teachers holding certificates for the first class and of upwards of 30 years' service will be regarded, *cæteris paribus*, as having the first claim.

Payment of
pensions.

*94. The pensions will be paid quarterly on certificates forwarded to the inspector proving identity and good behaviour.

---

* Regulations of 1897 revoked by the Regulations of 1900.

SCHEDULE.

PART II. Reg. 19.

INFANTS' SCHOOLS AND CLASSES. —*Age from 5 to 7 years.

Reading.—To read from a Reading Sheet or from an easy Primer containing words of three or four letters.

Writing.—To copy on Slate from the Blackboard words of two or three letters.

Arithmetic.—To point out, and write on slate, figures from 1 to 10, and count up to 20.

No child shall be entered for this examination who is under the age of 5 or over the age of 7 years.

STANDARD I.—*Age from 7 to 9 years.

Reading.—To read a few sentences from an Infant School Primer containing not less than 40 pages.

Writing.—Short words on paper. Small letters on slates from Dictation.

Arithmetic.—Notation to 100. To add and subtract mentally numbers up to 20.

STANDARD II.—*Age from 9 to 10 years.

Reading.—Nelson's Royal Reader for Standard I. or any similar book. Slowly and distinctly.

Writing.—Text or round hand on paper, and words or sentences from the Reading Book from Dictation on Slates.

Arithmetic.—Notation to tens of thousands. Easy sums in Simple Addition and Subtraction. The Multiplication Table up to 6 times 12.

STANDARD III.—*Age from 10 to 11 years.

Reading.—Nelson's Royal Reader for Standard II., or any similarly graduated book. Clearly and intelligibly.

Writing.—Transcription on paper. To write a paragraph from the Reading Book from Dictation on Slates.

Arithmetic.—Notation to hundreds of thousands. The multiplication table. Sums in the simple Rules up to Short Division (inclusive.)

STANDARD IV.— *Age from 11 to 12 years.

Reading.—Nelson's Royal Reader for Standard III., or any similarly graduated book. Clearly and intelligibly.

Writing.—To write on paper a paragraph from the Reading Book from Dictation.

Arithmetic.—Notation to millions. Sums in the simple Rules. Miscellaneous Questions.

---

* Approximate, but no grant will be made for any child passing the 1st Standard who is over 12 years of age on the day of examination.

STANDARD V.—*Age from 12 to 13 years.

Reading.—Nelson's Royal Reader for Standard IV., or any similarly graduated book. Fluently and with expression.

Writing.—To write neatly on paper, a paragraph from the Reading Book from Dictation.

Arithmetic.—Any sums (including Miscellaneous Questions) in the Compound Rules and Reduction of money, English and Colonial.

Grammar.—The parts of speech.

Geography.—Definitions and British Guiana in detail.

STANDARD VI.—*Age from 13 to 14 years.

Reading.—Nelson's Royal Reader for Standard V., or any similarly graduated book. Fluently and intelligibly to the Inspector without the book.

Writing.—Dictation on paper from any book or newspaper.

Arithmetic.—Miscellaneous Questions and Reduction of common Weights and Measures.

Grammar.—The inflections of words.

Geography.—British Guiana and the West Indies.

Agriculture.—Blackie's Tropical Reader, Part I.

STANDARD VII.—*Age from 14 to 15 years.

Reading.—To read from any book or newspaper. Good reading at sight.

Writing.—To write from dictation with increased proficiency.

Arithmetic.—Vulgar and Decimal Fractions, Practice and Simple Proportion, and the work of the preceding standards.

Grammar.—Similar to that required of Standard VI., but with increased proficiency. Parsing.

Geography.—The British Colonies.

Agriculture.—Blackie's Tropical reader, Part II.

STANDARD VIII.

Reading.—The same as Standard VII., with increased proficiency.

Writing.—To write a short essay or letter, or to reproduce a story.

Arithmetic.—All the above rules. Practice, Proportion, Interest and Discount.

Grammar.—Parsing and analysis of sentences.

Geography.—America, and all the above with increased proficiency.

Agriculture.—Blackie's Tropical Reader, Part II., with greater proficiency.

N.B.—Reading may be tested in the ordinary class book if approved by the Inspector, but the books must be of reasonable length and difficulty. If only one set of Reading Books is provided for the lower standards, or if the lessons appear to have been learned by rote, the reading may be tested from a book for the same standard brought by the Inspector. Scholars in the fifth and higher standards will be required to understand what they read, and to answer questions on the subject matter of the reading lesson.

---

* Approximate, but no grant will be made for any child passing the 1st Standard who is over 12 years of age on the day of examination.

NEEDLEWORK.

I. STANDARD.	II. STANDARD.	III. STANDARD.	IV. STANDARD.	V. STANDARD.	VI. STANDARD.	VII. STANDARD.	VIII. STANDARD.
Threading Needles. Hemming.	Seaming or Sewing. Felling.	Stitching. Sewing on strings. Patching calico garments.	Sewing on linen, buttons. Stroking. Gathering.	Pleating. Plain darning. Button holing. Fixing the work in a plain cotton shirt.	Whipping. Running tucks. Sewing on frills. Setting in gathers. Darning stockings.	Herring-boning. Fine darning. Marking with cotton or silk.	Darning and patching fine linen, diaper, and calico. Feather stitch. Grafting. Cutting out and fixing a plain garment.
e.g. A plain pocket handkerchief.	e.g. A child's pinafore.	e.g. A pillow case or a plain chemise without bands or gathers.	e.g. A plain night shirt.	e.g. A plain day shirt.	e.g. A night dress with frills.	e.g. A cambric handkerchief.	e.g. A plain shirt.

PART III.

Regulations 20, 29, 33.

GRANTS.

I. The sum of two dollars ($2.00) shall be paid for every scholar over 5 and under 7 years of age, who, having been a scholar for over six months, shall pass in the standard for infants' schools and classes in two subjects.

II. A grant of $1.25 shall be made for each pass in reading, writing or arithmetic, according to the standard in which the child is examined : provided such child passes in at least two out of the said three subjects. No grant will be made to any school which for two consecutive years fails to obtain 35 per cent. of full passes at the annual examination in Reading, Writing and Arithmetic calculated on the number of children presented for examination in accordance with regulation 21.

III. No grant will be paid for any scholar who fails in more than one subject.

IV. Scholars who pass fully in reading, writing and arithmetic shall be eligible for examination in two of the subjects grammar, geography, agriculture and such other subjects as may be approved by the Governor-in-Council and shall be paid for at the rate of one dollar ($1.00) for a pass in any one of those subjects. The additional sum of one dollar ($1.00) will be paid for every girl who, having passed in two of the three subjects first mentioned, passes also in needlework.

MERIT GRANTS.

V. If at the expiration of any Financial Year the sum voted on the Annual Estimates for that Year in respect of "Grants to Primary Schools" has been only in part expended, the remainder may be divided as a Merit Grant among those Schools which are efficient in Discipline and Instruction, well supplied with Books, Slates, and School Apparatus and conducted in commodious and well-ventilated buildings, and which contain more than 50 per cent. of full Passes in such proportions as shall, from time to time, be determined by the Governor-in-Council, and published in the Gazette.

VI. Twenty-five prizes of $20 each shall be awarded annually in the month of March to the most efficient assistant teachers, sewing mistresses, and pupil teachers whose classes shall obtain not less than 90 per cent. of full passes, preference being given to the largest classes and work in the highest standards. Not more than two prizes shall be awarded to the teachers in any one school.

PART VI.

SYLLABUS OF SUBJECTS IN WHICH CANDIDATES FOR CERTIFICATES OF COMPETENCY WILL BE EXAMINED.

THIRD CLASS CERTIFICATES.

READING –To read with fluency, ease and expression.

WRITING—To write a Paragraph from Dictation, neatly and correctly Copy Setting.

ARITHMETIC--To work sums mentally. Fractions, Decimals, Practice, Proportion, and Interest.

GRAMMAR—The Elements of Grammar, including Parsing, Analysis of Sentences, and Shakespeare's "Merchant of Venice," with paraphrasing and questions on the subject matter.

SCHOOL MANAGEMENT--To answer questions on the Expedients of Instruction in the elementary subjects— (Gladman's School Method).
To answer questions on the Government Education Regulations.
The method of keeping School Registers.

GEOGRAPHY AND HISTORY—Lucas' Historical Geography of British Guiana, Trinidad, Barbados, and Jamaica.

EUCLID AND ALGEBRA--(For Males only).

AGRICULTURAL-- (For Males only).—The elements of Tropical Agriculture.

NEEDLEWORK- (For Females only).-- Plain Needlework, including Cutting Out.

DOMESTIC ECONOMY—(For Females only).—Mann's Domestic Economy, pp. 38 to 175. Special importance will be attached to the nature and action of food, and to the preparation of it

EUCLID, BOOKS I. AND II.— Two hours will be allowed for the paper, which will consist of two parts. The first part will contain book work questions only, and will be collected at the expiration of an hour and a quarter; the second part will contain Easy Geometrical Exercises.

ALGEBRA.—The Multiplication and Division of Algebraic quantities; Theory of Indices ; Greatest Common Measure and Least Common Multiple ; the Extraction of Square Root ; Easy Equations.

SECOND CLASS CERTIFICATES.

READING—Candidates will be expected to show proficiency in the higher qualities of good reading and to read with ease, fluency and accuracy long and involved sentences.

WRITING—To write a more difficult paragraph from Dictation neatly and correctly.

ARITHMETIC—The whole subject, including Mental Arithmetic, and Elementary Mensuration.

HISTORY AND GEOGRAPHY—The Historical Geography of British Guiana and the British West Indies. To draw Maps from Memory of the more important Colonies. (LUCAS.)

GRAMMAR—Parsing, Paraphrasing, Analysis of Sentences, Syntax, and to write plain prose on a given subject. One of Shakespeare's Plays of which notice will be given at least one year before the examination. Questions on language, and subject matter.

SCHOOL MANAGEMENT—To answer questions on the expedients of Instruction in Elementary subjects.
To draw time tables for use in a school, under given conditions.
To answer questions on the Government Education Regulations, and on the keeping of School Registers.

EUCLID AND ALGEBRA—(For Males only).

EUCLID—BOOKS I., II., III.—See requirements for Class III. More difficult Geometrical Exercises.

ALGEBRA.—Same as for Class III., and the Solution of Quadratic Equations, and problems producing such equations, Ratio and Proportion, Progressions, Permutations and Combinations.

AGRICULTURE—(Males).—Tropical Agriculture. The questions will at present be confined to the subjects treated in the Book on this subject published by the Government of Jamaica, and Blackie's Tropical Readers or other Books, of which due Notice will be given.

DOMESTIC ECONOMY—(Females).—The whole subject as treated by Dr. MANN. Questions will be asked on the making of poultices, nourishing Puddings, and teas for Invalids; the treatment of scalds and burns, &c., &c.

NEEDLEWORK—(Female).—Candidates will be required to show excellence in plain Needlework.

N.B.—Candidates must bring lead pencil, thimble and scissors

OPTIONAL SUBJECTS.

ALL CLASSES.

MUSIC—(1) Notation in the Treble and Bass Clefs, Time, Accent, and the Major and Minor Scales.
(2) To write down in correct time, short and simple passages played in the presence of the Candidate.

DRAWING—Any of the following exercises in any order, no candidate
taking up more than three :—
      (1.) Free hand from flat examples.
      (2.) Linear Geometry, with Instruments.
      (3.) Linear Perspective.
      (4.) Model Drawing.
      (5.) Drawing on the Blackboard.

SCIENCE—Elementary Botany and Chemistry—Sanitary.

SCALE OF MARKS.

	Full marks.
READING * - - - - -	100
WRITING * - - - -	100
ARITHMETIC * - - - -	150
GRAMMAR * - - - -	120
SCHOOL MANAGEMENT * - - -	100
HISTORY and GEOGRAPHY - - -	100
EUCLID and ALGEBRA - - -	120
AGRICULTURE - - - -	60
MUSIC - - - - -	60
DRAWING (20 for each subject) - -	60
DOMESTIC ECONOMY - - -	100
NEEDLEWORK * - - -	100
Total Males - - -	970
Total Females - - -	990

Minimum Marks for a Pass—
| III. Class - - - - | 450 |
| II. Class - - - - | 500 |

Failure to obtain 30 per cent. in the Subjects marked * excludes a
candidate from a Certificate.

No value will be given to Papers for Second and Third Classes marked
below 40 and 35 per cent. respectively.

Reg. 62

PART VII.

EDUCATION DEPARTMENT, BRITISH GUIANA.

GRANT-IN-AID SCHOOLS.

PUPIL TEACHER'S CERTIFICATE.

Date :   19

SIR,— I have the honour to inform you that I have this day nominated
as Pupil Teacher in the
School, believing   to be well qualified for the office in respect of
health, character, habits, and parentage.

I further certify that   passed the VI. Standard in
Reading, Writing, Arithmetic, Grammar, and Geography, and at an Examination held at   School on the   day of   , 19

        I am, Sir,
        Your obedient Servant,

                Manager.

Registered this   day of   , 19   No.
                              Inspector of Schools.

PART VIII.

PUPIL TEACHERS' EXAMINATION.

READING.

For Admission.	To read fluently and correctly a passage of prose from a fifth reading book.
End of First Year.	As above, from any book or newspaper.
End of Second Year.	As above, and to repeat 40 consecutive lines of poetry.
End of Third Year.	As above, and to repeat 60 consecutive lines of poetry or prose.
End of Fourth Year.	Vide Requirements for Teachers' Certificates, Class III.

WRITING.

For Admission.	To write from Dictation a passage from a fifth reading book.
End of First Year.	A more difficult piece from a newspaper.
End of Second Year.	A still more difficult paragraph —Narrative Composition.
End of Third Year.	A short Essay.
End of Fourth Year.	Vide requirements for Teachers' Certificates, Class III.

ARITHMETIC, &c.

For Admission.	To work sums in the Compound Rules, Money, Colonial and English, and Weights and Measures.
End of First Year.	Vide requirements for Standard VII.
End of Second Year.	Vide requirements for Standard VIII.
End of Third Year.	The same with increased proficiency.
	(Males—Euclid, Book 1, Propositions 1 to 15. Algebra to Division.)
End of Fourth Year.	Vide requirements for Teachers' Certificates, Class III.

ENGLISH GRAMMAR.

For Admission.	Definitions, and to tell the parts of speech in a simple sentence.
End of First Year.	The inflections of words. Simple parsing.
End of Second Year.	More difficult parsing. The analysis of Sentences.
End of Third Year.	More difficult Analysis and easy paraphrasing.
End of Fourth Year.	Vide requirements for Teachers' Certificates, Class III.

GEOGRAPHY.

For Admission.	Geographical Definitions. British Guiana.
End of First Year.	British Guiana in detail. The West Indies—(British).
End of Second Year.	The British Empire.
End of Third Year.	The same, with increased proficiency. Maps.
End of Fourth Year.	Vide requirements for Teachers' Certificates, Class III.

TEACHING.

At the end of the Second Year, Pupil Teachers will be required to teach a class to the satisfaction of the Inspector. Each subsequent year he will be required to show increased proficiency, and to satisfy the Inspector of his power to conduct a school.

NEEDLEWORK.

V. STANDARD.	VI. STANDARD.	VII STANDARD.	VIII. STANDARD.
Pleating. Plain darning. Button holing. Fixing the work in a plain cotton shirt.	Whipping. Running tucks. Sewing on frills. Setting in gathers. Darning stockings.	Herringboning. Fine darning. Marking with cotton or silk.	Darning and patching fine linen, diaper, and calico. Feather stitch. Grafting. Cutting out and fixing a plain garment.
e.g. A plain day shirt.	e.g. A night dress, with frills.	e.g. A cambric handkerchief.	e.g. A plain shirt.

AGRICULTURE, &c.

End of Second Year.   Blackie's Tropical Reader, part I.
End of Third Year.   Blackie's Tropical Reader, part II.
End of Fourth Year.   Vide requirements for III. Class Certificates.

During the Fifth Year Pupil Teachers will be required to attend a course of Lectures on Chemistry and Botany, and to pass the examination held in connection therewith.

APPENDIX C.

AN ORDINANCE (1900) TO AMEND THE ELEMENTARY EDUCATION ORDINANCE, 1876.

Be it enacted by the Governor of British Guiana, with the advice and consent of the Court of Policy thereof, as follows :—

1. This Ordinance may be cited as the Elementary Education Ordinance, 1876, Amendment Ordinance, 1900. *Short title.*

2. The Elementary Education Ordinance, 1876, (hereinafter referred to as the Principal Ordinance), and this Ordinance shall be construed together as one Ordinance. *Construction.*

3. In Section 2 of the principal Ordinance the following provisions shall be inserted, namely :— *Interpretation of terms*

"Authorised person" means any person who, under this Ordinance has, and is entrusted with the same rights, powers, privileges, and functions as an educational district officer ;

"Prescribed" means prescribed by any Regulations made under this Ordinance :

And the following definitions, namely, —

"Aided School" means an elementary school, the managers of which receive any grant-in-aid from the colonial revenues ;

"Colonial School" means an elementary school established by the Inspector of Schools and maintained from the colonial revenues ;

"Industrial School" means any elementary school in which theoretic and practical instruction in agriculture or in any trade or trades, or in both is given and which is recognised under the regulations as an Industrial School,

are hereby substituted for the definitions of "Public Elementary School," "Colonial School," "Industrial School" and "Day Industrial School," in that section given.

4. In Section 7 (1) and Section 8 of the principal Ordinance the words "or pupils" are hereby inserted after the words "the children," and the words "as Teacher or otherwise," after the words "immoral conduct" whereever appearing in those sections. *Amendment of Sec. 7 (1) and Sec. 8 of Ord. 3 of 1876.*

5. The following sub-section shall be added to Section 10 of the principal Ordinance :— *Amendment of Sec. 10 of Ord. 3. of 1876.*

(3.) Every member of the Combined Court, Minister of Religion, Justice of the Peace, Inspector of Schools, Assistant Inspector of Schools, School Manager, Certificated principal Teacher of a school authorised in writing by the manager of his school, Member of any Town or Village Council, Commissary of Taxation, Government Officer appointed under the Crown Lands Ordinance, 1887, or the Mining Ordinance, 1887, member of the Police Force, or person authorised by the Governor shall have and may exercise all the rights, powers, privileges and functions vested in an Educational District Officer by the Principal Ordinance : . provided always that no Police Constable shall have and exercise the powers given to an Educational District Officer by Section 15 or Section 52 of the Principal Ordinance unless authorised or empowered as therein mentioned and provided also that nothing herein contained shall impose on any person hereinbefore specified the duties imposed on Educational District Officers by Section 11 of the principal Ordinance.

6. In Section 14 (1) of the Principal Ordinance, the words "if such parent has previously been warned without effect to provide such instruction" are hereby inserted after the words "district officer may." *Amendment of Sec. 14 (1) of Ord. 3 of 1876.*

7. In Section 15 of the principal Ordinance, in sub-section (1) the words 'elementary school other than an Industrial School" are hereby substituted for the words "Public Elementary School"; and in sub-section (3) the *Amendment of Sec. 15 (3) of Ord. 3 of 1876.*

words "the person taking the child into custody" are hereby substituted for the words "Educational District Officer."

Amendment of Sec. 24 (3) of Ord. 3 of 1876.

8. In Section 24 (3) of the Principal Ordinance the words "the person enquiring into the matter" are hereby substituted for the words "Educational District Officer."

Industrial Schools.

Teacher's power of detention over children.

9. Every child required to attend or sent by his parent to an industrial school may be detained by the teacher during such hours as may be prescribed.

Employment of children.

10.—(1.) Every child attending an industrial school may be employed in the vicinity of such school during prescribed hours in agricultural pursuits on any plantation or lands or in any workshop: Provided always that the full value of any labour performed by a child after deducting the cost of the instruction and of the food (if any) supplied at the cost of the school to such child shall be paid to the parent of or secured for such child.

(2.) The amount that may be deducted for such cost shall be fixed by the Inspector of Schools.

Provision for children required to attend School for part only of a day.

11. Provision shall be made at every industrial school for allowing children who are only required to attend an elementary school for two and a half hours in the day to receive instruction in elementary education in such school without becoming subject to the industrial training at such school.

Execution of order requiring child to be sent to school.

12. Every child ordered by a Stipendiary Magistrate to be sent to an industrial school may at any time, while the order continues in force, be taken to the industrial school named in the order by an Educational District Officer or authorised person, or by any person authorised in writing by an Educational District Officer or authorised person.

Powers of Stipendiary Magistrate under Ord. 1 of 1852.

13. Nothing in this or the principal Ordinance shall affect the power and jurisdiction of any Stipendiary Magistrate under the Industrial and Reformatory Schools Ordinance, 1852, and in any case coming before a Stipendiary Magistrate under Section 15 or 16 of this Ordinance, such Magistrate may, in lieu of dealing with the case thereunder, order the child to be sent to the industrial school mentioned in the said Ordinance as if the case had arisen under and was expressly provided for by that Ordinance, and its provisions shall apply to every such order and to any child and the parent and father (as in this Ordinance defined) of any child sent to such school under such order.

Amendment of sections 35 and 41 (3) of Ord. 3 of 1876.

14. In Sections 35 and 41 (3.) of the Principal Ordinance, the words "aided school" are hereby substituted for the words "Public Elementary School."

15. Section 37 of the Principal Ordinance is hereby repealed and the following substituted therefor :—

Payment and application of school fees.

37.—(1.) Every parent of a pupil who attends an aided school or a colonial school, after he has ceased to be a child or has passed the prescribed fourth standard, shall be bound to pay to the teacher of such school for every week in which such pupil attends the school, a school fee not exceeding such sum as may be prescibed.

(2.) All school fees must be paid not later than during the week next following the week in respect of which the same may have become payable.

(3.) All school fees shall be applied for the maintenance of the school.

Amendment of Sec. 41 (1) of Ord. 3 of 1876.

16. In Section 41 (1.) of the Principal Ordinance, the words "or if in any district the Governor-in-Council on economical or other grounds direct him to do so" are hereby inserted before the words "the Inspector of Schools."

Amendment of Sec. 42 (2) of Ord. 3 of 1876.

17. In Section 42 (2.) of the Principal Ordinance, the words "or entitled" are hereby inserted after the words "proprietor shall be compelled."

18. In Section 46 of the Principal Ordinance, the words "the Inspector of Schools, every person authorised in writing by him and " are hereby inserted before the words "every Educational District Officer." — Amendment of Sec. 46 of Ord. 3 of 1876

19. Any school fee or any sum payable under Section 21 of this Ordinance which is due and unpaid may be sued for and recovered in any Court of competent jurisdiction by the manager of the school or any teacher authorised in writing by such manager to recover it, or in the case of a colonial school by the Inspector of Schools or any one authorised in writing by him, and shall in all Courts be deemed a debt due to the person suing, by the parent. — Recovery of school fees, &c.

20. In Section 51 of the Principal Ordinance, the words " in proceedings other than those taken for the recovery of school fees " are hereby inserted after the words " Plaintiff or." — Amendment of Sec. 51 of Ord. 3 of 1876.

21.—(1.) If a child whose name is on the register of any school and who has not passed the prescribed fourth Standard (a) is absent from the prescribed annual examination, or (b) is not a pupil of such school for the prescribed period, before such examination, or (c) does not make the prescribed number of attendances before it, and also fails in any of such cases to pass such examination in the standard in which children of his age are usually examined, the parent of such child shall in the absence of any reasonable excuse, be liable to pay to the manager of such school within two months after the date of the examination, a sum equal to the grant which would have been made to such school in respect of such child if such child had passed the examination. Provided always that no liability shall be incurred under this sub-section unless the parent of such child has a reasonable time before such examination been warned of the liability he is incurring hereunder. — Liability of parent whose child does not attend examination, &c.

(2.) Any return or certificate purporting to be signed by the Inspector of Schools and to state the absence of any such child from or the failure of any such child to pass the prescribed examination shall be *prima facie* evidence thereof.

22. The words "or authorised person " are hereby inserted after the words "educational district officer," wherever such words occur in Sections 12, 14, 15, 16, 22, 24, and 52, and in Forms No. 2, No. 3, No. 4, No. 6, and No. 7 of the Principal Ordinance. — Insertion of words " authorised person " in specified parts of Ord. 3 of 1896.

23. The words "aided school or colonial school" are hereby substituted for the words "Public Elementary School or any Day Industrial School" in Section 14 (2) a) and Section 23 (1) of the Principal Ordinance. — Amendment of Sects. 14 and 23 of Ord. 3 of 1876.

24. The words " to sue for and recover the school fees herein required to be paid and " in Section 11 (4): the words " or to a Day Industrial School " in Section 15 (2) (b) and in Section 16 (1) (a) and (b): Sections 27 to 33 (both inclusive), 38, 39, 40, 48, 50, of the Principal Ordinance and Form No. 11 : the words " or be sent to the Day Industrial School at " in Form No. 5, and the words " or to the Day Industrial School at " in the note to Form No. 7, in the schedule to the same Ordinance, are hereby repealed. — Repeal.

25. If the principal Ordinance is at any time reprinted under the authority of the Government, it shall be reprinted as amended by this Ordinance, and it shall be lawful to insert therein the additional sections hereby enacted in such places as may be deemed by the Government most suitable and to renumber, if necessary, all or any of the sections of the Principal Ordinance. — Reprinting of Principal Ordinance.

26. Any regulations in force at the commencement of this Ordinance shall have effect as if enacted immediately after such commencement. — Application to Regulations.

THE

TEACHING OF AGRICULTURE IN ELEMENTARY AND HIGHER SCHOOLS IN THE WEST INDIES.

———

Recommendations of the West India Royal Commission   799
    Extracts from Report: A system of Peasant Pro-
      prietors - - - - - - - - 799
      Establishment of a Department of Economic
        Botany in the West Indies - - - - 801
    Education: Elementary, Agricultural and Industrial   802
    Extracts from Subsidiary Report: - - - - 802
      Scheme for the Establishment of a Department
        of Economic Botany and for Agricultural
        Instruction in the West Indies - - - 802
      Administration; Head Office - - - - 803
      Tobago, Botanic Station - - - - - 804
      Grenada, Botanic Station - - - - - 804
      St. Vincent, Botanic Station and Industrial
        School - - - - - - - - 805
      St. Lucia, Botanic Station and Industrial
        School - - - - - - - - 805
      Barbados, Botanic Station and Experimental
        Cane Cultivation - - - - - - 806
      Dominica, Botanic Station and Industrial
        School - - - - - - - - 806
      Montserrat, Botanic Station - - - - 806
      Antigua, Botanic Station and Sugar Cane
        Experiments - - - - - - - 807
      St. Kitts-Nevis - - - - - - - 807
      Summary: Botanic Stations and Industrial
        Schools - - - - - - - - 807
      British Guiana - - - - - - - 808
      Horticultural Shows - - - - - 808
      Grants to Elementary Schools - - - 808
      Bulletins, Leaflets, etc. - - - - 808
      Grants to Colleges and Schools - - - 808
      Summary: Botanic Department - - - 809
Debate in the House of Commons, 2nd August, 1898 - 809
Letter from the Secretary of State - - - - 810

First Agricultural Conference : President's Address - 811

    The Sugar Industry - - - - 812

    Other Industries - - - - - 815

    Botanical Institutions - - - - 817

    Agricultural Instructors - - - - 817

    Agricultural Exhibitions - - - - - 818

    Bulletins, Handbooks and Leaflets - - - 819

    Agricultural Teaching in Primary Schools - 819

    Agricultural Schools - - - - - 820

    Teaching Scientific Agriculture in the Higher Schools and Colleges - - - - - 820

    Fungoid and Insect Pests - - - 821

    New Steamship Services - - - - 821

Second Agricultural Conference - - - - 821

    Extracts from President's Address : Agricultural Education - - - - - 821

    Teaching Agriculture in High Schools and Colleges : Discussion - - - - 824

    Teaching Agriculture in Elementary Schools : Discussion - - - - - 828

Postscript on Agricultural Education in the West Indies in 1900 - - - - - - 833

THE TEACHING OF AGRICULTURE IN ELEMENTARY AND HIGHER SCHOOLS IN THE WEST INDIES.

In an interesting paper on *Agricultural Education in Greater Britain*, read before the Society of Arts on February 27, 1900,* Mr. Hedger Wallace arrives at the conclusion that "throughout Greater Britain, irrespective of climatic, racial, and political divergencies, there is a universal movement to give all interested in the culture of land every opportunity, facility, and assistance possible to improve themselves, their art and craft, and the land and its produce."

In the developments which have taken place in this direction during recent years few, if any, are more important and interesting than that which has resulted from the Report of the West India Royal Commission (Sir H. W. Norman, Sir E. Grey, and Sir D. Barbour), published in 1897.†

The Commissioners observed that while it was possible that no industry or series of industries could be introduced into the West Indies which would ever completely take the place of sugar, and certainly that no such results would be attained within the space of a few years, they regarded it as being of the utmost importance that no time should be lost in making a beginning of substituting other industries for the cultivation of the sugar-cane. They unanimously recommended *inter alia* :—

(1) The settlement of the labouring population on small plots of land as peasant proprietors.

(2) The establishment of minor agricultural industries and the improvement of the system of cultivation, especially in the case of small proprietors.

(3) The improvement of the means of communication between the different islands, and

(4) The encouragement of a trade in fruit with New York and, possibly, at a future time, with London.

Recommendations of the West India Royal Commission.

On the subject of a system of peasant proprietors, the Commissioners remarked as follows :—

" If the sugar estates are thrown out of cultivation, it is extremely improbable, and, in fact, it may be stated to be impossible, that any industry to be conducted on large estates can ever completely take its place, we have therefore no choice but to consider how means can be found

Extracts from Report —A System of Peasant Proprietors.

---

* Printed in the *Journal of the Society of Arts*, March 9, 1900 ; for a "Supplementary Note" see the same Journal for July 13, 1900.

† Cd. 8655, 2s. 8d.

to enable the mass of the population to support themselves in other ways than as labourers on estates. If work cannot be found for the labouring population on estates, they must either emigrate or support themselves by cultivating small plots of land on their own account. No large industry, other than agriculture, offers any prospect of success, except possibly the gold industry in British Guiana, and when large estates cannot be profitably worked the adoption of the system of cultivation by petty proprietors is inevitable.

"The labouring population in the West Indies is mainly of negro blood, but there is also, in some of the Colonies, a strong body of East Indian immigrants, and the descendants of such immigrants. The negro is an efficient labourer, especially when he receives good wages. He is disinclined to continuous labour, extending over a long period of time, and he is often unwilling to work if the wages offered are low, though there may be no prospect of his getting higher wages from any other employer. He is fond of display, open-handed, careless as to the future, ordinarily good humoured, but excitable and difficult to manage, especially in large numbers, when his temper is aroused.

"The East Indian immigrant, ordinarily known as the coolie, is not so strong a workman, but he is a steadier and more reliable labourer. He is economical in his habits, is fond of saving money, and will turn his hand to anything by which he can improve his position.

" The cultivation of the sugar-cane has been almost entirely carried on in the past on large estates, but both the negro and the coolie like to own small patches of land by which they may make their livelihood, and take a pride in their position as landholders, though in some cases they also labour at times on the larger estates, and are generally glad to have the opportunity of earning money occasionally by working on such estates, and on the construction and maintenance of roads and other public works. The existence of a class of small proprietors among the population is a source of both economic and political strength.

"The settlement of the labourer on the land has not, as a rule, been viewed with favour in the past by the persons interested in sugar estates. What suited them best was a large supply of labourers, entirely dependent on being able to find work on the estates, and, consequently, subject to their control and willing to work at low rates of wages. But it seems to us that no reform affords so good a prospect for the permanent welfare in the future of the West Indies as the settlement of the labouring population on the land as small peasant proprietors ; and in many places this is the only means by which the population can in future be supported. The drawbacks to the system of peasant proprietors have hitherto been their want of knowledge and care in cultivation, and the habit of what is called prædial larceny. The latter term is applied to the theft of growing crops, which is said to be very prevalent. We do not believe it will disappear until such practices are universally condemned by native public opinion, which, unfortunately, does not appear to be the case at present, and in the meantime each Colony must deal with the question as may seem best. The small proprietors show some desire to improve their modes of cultivation, and we shall have some suggestions to make on this subject.

"But whilst we think that the Governments of the different Colonies should exert themselves in the direction of facilitating the settlement of the labouring population on the land, we see no objection to the system of large estates when they can be maintained under natural economic conditions. On the contrary, we are convinced that in many places they afford the best, and, sometimes, the only profitable means of cultivating certain products, and that it is not impossible for the two systems, of large estates and peasant holdings, to exist side by side with mutual advantage."

*   *   *   *   *   *

The Commissioners then proceed to make the following proposal for the establishment of a Department of Economic Botany in the West Indies, at the expense of the Imperial Exchequer, and in connexion with that proposal to suggest certain changes in the course of education in the public schools of the Islands.

" Establishment of a Department of Economic Botany in the West Indies.

" The practical work of cultivating new products must be left in the hands of private persons, whether owners of large estates or peasant proprietors, but there are certain directions in which assistance can be given by the State.

" Your Majesty's West Indian possessions are, as a rule, not of large extent, and some of them, though possessing separate administrative and financial systems, are of very limited area. Communication between them is difficult, and with the outside world it is both tedious and expensive. The persons engaged in cultivation suffer from this state of isolation, and are often without any information as to what is being done elsewhere. The cultivator of one product is often quite ignorant of the best means of cultivating any other, and does not know whether his soil and climate might be better adapted for something else. These remarks have special reference to the small cultivators, but they are not wholly inapplicable to persons interested in the larger estates.

" The botanical establishments in the larger Colonies, such as Jamaica, Trinidad, and British Guiana, have already rendered considerable assistance in improving agricultural industries, and they are capable of being made increasingly useful in this respect. In the Windward and Leeward Islands and Barbados, small establishments called botanic stations were established a few years ago on the advice of the director of Kew Gardens, and the results, though not yet extensive, have been of a distinctly promising character. It is evident that to grapple with the present circumstances, there is required for the smaller islands a special public department capable of dealing with all questions connected with economic plants suitable for growth in tropical countries, and we recommend the establishment of such a department, under which should be placed the various botanic stations already in existence. These stations should be enlarged in their scope and character, and be organised on the lines found so successful in Jamaica. In the latter Colony it is admitted that intelligent and progressive action in the direction of encouraging a diversity of industries has produced most satisfactory results. To achieve this result has, however, taken more than 20 years of persistent effort, and the Government has spent more than £100,000 during that period on its botanical establishments. The department has distributed seeds and plants at nominal prices by means of the post office, Government railways, and coastal steam service; it has supplied information orally or by means of bulletins, regarding the cultivation of economic plants, and has encouraged the careful preparation of the produce by sending agricultural instructors on tour through the island to give lectures, demonstrations, and advice.

" The special department recommended for carrying on similar work in the Windward and Leeward Islands should be under the charge of a competent Imperial officer, whose duty it would be to advise the Governors in regard to all matters affecting the agricultural development of the islands. He would take part in consultations with the object of improving agricultural teaching in colleges and schools, and of training students in agricultural pursuits, and would attend to the preparation of suitable literature on agricultural subjects. The existing botanic stations should be placed under his supervision, and the charge of maintaining them transferred to Imperial funds. Each botanic station would be actively engaged in the introduction and improvement of economic plants, and in propagating and distributing them throughout the island. It would carry out the experimental cultivation of new plants to serve as an object lesson to cultivators, and it would be prepared to give the latest information to inquirers regarding economic products, and to provide suitable men as agricultural instructors. To effect all this will require funds entirely beyond the present resources of the smaller islands. We are, therefore, of opinion that as the necessity for such a department is urgent, the cost should be borne by the Imperial Exchequer.

"The promising experimental work connected with raising new varieties of canes, and increasing the production of sugar by the use of manures and other means, should receive special attention. The cost of some of this work would be a legitimate portion of the charge above stated. The chief experiments might be carried on as hitherto by the officers in charge of them in British Guiana, Barbados, and Antigua, but continued and extended, if found desirable, in Trinidad and Jamaica. In addition, the botanic stations in the Leeward and Windward Islands would maintain nurseries for the introduction of all new and promising canes, and would undertake the distributing them within their respective spheres of action. [The Commissioners then refer to Dr. Morris' Memorandum, as printed below.]

"In dealing with the question of introducing new industries into the West Indian Colonies, or of extending existing industries, it must be borne in mind that for many of the special products of the West Indies there is only a limited demand. There is, for example, a comparatively large market for coffee, but not for such products as arrowroot or nutmegs, and if they were extensively grown in a number of the Islands they would soon cease to command a remunerative price. This has actually happened in the case of arrowroot.

" *Education :—Elementary, Agricultural, and Industrial.*

"In the course of our stay in the West Indies our attention was frequently called to the question of the progress of general education, and we obtained a considerable amount of information on this subject. There has been a marked increase of expenditure on this account in recent years, and, no doubt, the efforts made for the extension of education have been largely successful. The total expenditure on education amounted to about £95,000 in 1882, and to nearly £180,000 in 1896, showing an increase of about 90 per cent. It may be hoped that in Jamaica and Grenada, and probably in Trinidad also, it will not be found necessary, on financial grounds, to curtail this expenditure, but if the sugar industry fails in British Guiana and in the islands not mentioned above, the revenue may be quite unequal to the maintenance of the whole of the existing schools.

"At the present time a system of training in agricultural occupation is much needed We think that some, at least, of the botanic stations should have agricultural schools attached to them, where the best means of cultivating tropical plants would be taught, and if elementary training in agriculture were made a part of the course of education in the public schools generally, the Botanic Department would be in a position to render valuable assistance.

"Agriculture, in one form or another, must always be the chief and the only great industry in the West Indies, but a system of training in other industial occupations, on a limited scale, is desirable, and would be beneficial to the community."

Extracts from Subsidiary Report. Appended to the Commissioners' Report was a subsidiary report by Dr. Morris, C.M.G. (at that time Assistant-Director of the Royal Gardens, Kew, and now Imperial Commissioner of Agriculture for the West Indies). Dr. Morris's report comprised the following

Scheme for the Establishment of a Department of Economic Botany and for Agricultural Instruction in the West Indies.

At the request of the Chairman the following scheme has been prepared for the special public department suggested by the Commission for developing the resources of the Leeward and Windward Islands and Tobago, and for affording assistance to the experimental cane cultivation to be carried on, in continuance of present efforts, in British Guiana, Barbados, and Antigua.

It is understood that concurrently with the working of this scheme steps will be taken by the Government in each island to open roads, to settle the people on the land, and provide facilities for delivering produce at the nearest shipping ports.

It is further understood that a subsidy will be granted by the Imperial Government—(1) to establish direct steam communication (weekly or fortnightly as required) between Dominica and St. Vincent and New York, and (2) for cheap and regular steam communication by means of two or more small steamers between the several members of the Leeward and Windward groups, connecting with each other, and with the New York steamers, at a central point such as Barbados or St. Lucia.

It would be desirable to arrange for such tariffs by these steamers as would afford facilities for the conveyance of produce at specially low rates of payment, and supply a ready and convenient means of moving from one island to another to all classes of the community.*

The probable amount of the subsidies required would be £5,000 for the service to New York, and £1,800 to £2,500 each for the local steamers; £10,000 should be sufficient for both services.

It may be pointed out that the islands under consideration form an extended chain, the component parts of which are divided by intervals of sea varying from 20 to 100 miles across. They extend, in fact, north and south over seven degrees of latitude and form the eastern boundary of the Caribbean Sea. The extreme points are distant seven days by the route taken at present by the Royal Mail Company's steamers, which require a detention of two days and nights at Barbados.

The duties to be entrusted to the proposed department have been described in the report as follows :—(1) to supervise and extend the work of the present botanic stations ; (2) to start industrial schools for training boys in agricultural pursuits ; (3) to encourage the theoretical (and to some slight extent the practical) teaching of agriculture in elementary schools ; (4) to promote the teaching of scientific agriculture in colleges and schools ; (5) to organise horticultural shows and exhibitions of implements and machinery suitable for cultivating and curing tropical products ; and (6) to prepare bulletins, leaflets, and other literature on subjects suitable for cultivation in the West Indies.

The duties devolving on the botanic stations may be more fully described. They are to devote themselves in a systematic manner to the work of introducing, propagating, and distributing all the promising economic plants of the tropics ; they are to initiate the experimental cultivation of new or little known plants, and assist in the efforts made in the larger colonies to secure improved varieties of the sugar cane. They are to act as centres for diffusing accurate information, and as training institutions for the practical teaching of tropical agriculture ; also as the headquarters from which agricultural instructors would be sent to give lectures and demonstrations bearing upon the selection of land for tropical economic plants, their suitable cultivation, and the best methods for curing and packing the produce.

No provision is made in this scheme for the purchase of land or for buildings required, as these might be provided by the local governments in lieu of continuing the present payments to the botanic stations. It is desirable that the funds contributed by the Imperial Government should be wholly devoted to the efficient working of the department, and not to establishing gardens or erecting permanent structures.

ADMINISTRATION.

It is recommended by the Commission that "a competent Imperial officer" be appointed to take charge of the department, whose duty, briefly

---

* The Royal Mail Company might also be asked to afford special facilities for the conveyance of bulletins, seeds, and economic plants between all parts of the West Indies. In fact such articles should be carried free of charge when exchanged between the several botanic gardens for the purpose of improving the general welfare of these Colonies.

stated, would be to develop the agricultural resources of the Windward and Leeward Islands and Barbados.

It has been suggested that this officer should act under the direct authority of the Secretary of State, and should locally administer and be responsible for all the funds contributed by the Imperial Government. The most convenient headquarters in every way would be Barbados.

This scheme might be submitted beforehand, and receive the careful consideration of the several governments concerned, but when the general policy has been settled it should be understood that all administrative details, and the charge of all the existing and any further botanic stations established in the Windward and Leeward Islands, are left entirely in the hands of the Imperial officer, who might also act, as occasion required, as consulting authority to the other Colonies.

It is an essential part of the scheme now set forth that it should be consistently carried out for a period of ten years at least.

Head Office.

		£
*Chief officer - - - - - - -	-	1,000
†Travelling superintendent - - -	-	400
Clerk - - - - - - -	-	200
Travelling and office expenses - - -	-	600
Total - - -	-	2,200

TOBAGO.

The Commissioners state that "it is desirable that a botanic station be established at Tobago subordinate to the Botanic Department at Trinidad, and having for its object the attainment of the same end." The island is too poor to support such a station itself, and it is very improbable that Trinidad, at present at least, will be prepared to assist it. The only alternative is to include it under the present scheme. The supervision might very well be left to the Superintendent of the Trinidad Department. The grant proposed might be expended as follows :—

Botanic Station, Tobago.

		£
Curator, £150-£200 - - - -	-	200
Agricultural Instructor, £70-£100 -	-	100
Foreman - - - - - -	-	50
‡8 labourers, £15 - - - -	-	120
Tools, manure, &c. - - - -	-	30
		500
‡or 6 labourers, £15 - - - -	·	90
3 students, £10 - - - -	-	30

GRENADA.

The present Botanic Garden, with the limited means at its command, does useful work, but, in accordance with the recommendation of the Commission, "this work should be extended and the station held respon-

---

* The Director of the Botanical Department in Jamaica receives salary and emoluments of £800 a year; the Government analytical chemist at British Guiana receives £1,000 a year.

† To complete one visit of inspection through all the islands, staying a fortnight in each one, would occupy about four months. It is, therefore, essential to have the services of a superintendent to assist in organising the various agencies, and to be in charge of the head office when the chief officer is on tour.

sible for agricultural instruction, for the introduction and experimental cultivation of tropical plants of economic importance." Provision is suggested for additional land to be placed under experimental cultivation, for the employment of an agricultural instructor, and for the training of students. The latter are to be boys selected from the elementary schools and given a small weekly sum (in fact, a scholarship) to support them while being trained at the Garden. The full course should be for five years. Some assistance might be given from Grenada to the Island of Carriacou as indicated in the report on that island.

The details of the vote are as follows :

Botanic Station, Grenada.

						£
Curator - - - - - - -						200
Agricultural Instructor, £130–£150	-	-	-	150
Travelling and house allowance	-	-	-	-	70
Foreman - - - - - -					-	70
10 labourers, £15 - - - - - -						150
4 students, £10 - - - - - -						40
Tools, plants, &c. - - - - - -						50
						730

St. Vincent.

This island and Dominica require not only immediate assistance to prevent the people from becoming absolutely destitute, but they promise to be more readily rescued from this condition by establishing a trade in bananas and other fruit with New York. This subject has been already dealt with in the preceding report. It is proposed to employ two agricultural instructors, to increase the number of students to six, and start in each island an industrial school to train 25 boys in agricultural pursuits. These boys are not to be criminals, but those placed under training by the consent of their parents, or orphans, and destitute children. The estimated cost of the industrial schools proposed in this scheme is based on the working of the successful reformatory schools now existing in Barbados and Antigua. No provision is made for buildings. These may be loaned from the local governments. The total grant of £1,500 is proposed to be expended as follows :

Botanic Station and Industrial School, St. Vincent.

						£
Curator - - - - - - -						200
2 agricultural instructors, £150	-	-	-	-	300
Travelling allowances - - - - -					-	80
1 foreman - - - - - -					-	70
1 foreman - - - - - -					-	60
12 labourers, £15 - - - - - -						180
6 students, £10 - - - - - -						60
Tools, manure, &c. - - - - - -						50
						1,000
Industrial School - - - - -						500
						1,500

St. Lucia.

It is stated in the Commissioners' report that "more suitable land for the purpose of experimental cultivation in connexion with the botanic station is very much required." The Local Government might assist in providing the land and the necessary buildings. St. Lucia offers an excellent field for the development of minor industries. Everything hitherto has been stopped by want of means. The grant proposed may be applied as follows :—

Botanic Station and Industrial School, St. Lucia.

		£
Curator - - - - - - -	-	200
Agricultural instructor, £130–£150 -	-	150
Travelling and house allowance	- - -	70
Foreman - - - - -	- -	70
10 labourers, £15 - - -	- -	150
4 students - - - -	- -	40
Tools, plants, &c. - - -	- -	50
		730
Industrial School	- - - -	500
		1,230

BARBADOS.

Provision is suggested for maintaining two experimental stations for sugar-cane cultivation at Barbados, one at Dodds, and the other on the highlands in the ratooning districts of the island. The complete dependence of this colony on sugar renders it necessary to devote special attention to the raising of new canes and in improving their saccharine contents. The officers in charge of the present experiments, or others selected for the purpose, should give their whole time to the work, regularly visit the estates, and publish information at frequent intervals. The detailed working of these stations might be arranged after consultation with the Government of Barbados. The contribution of £20 per annum hitherto made by the botanic station at Barbados to the Jamaica Gardens would cease under the working of this scheme.

Botanic Station and Experimental Cane Cultivation at Barbados, £1,500.

DOMINICA.

Remarks on this vote have already been given under St. Vincent. The details are here repeated.

Botanic Station and Industrial School at Dominica.

		£
Curator - - - - -	- -	200
2 agricultural instructors, £150	- -	300
Travelling allowance	- - -	80
1 foreman - - -	- -	70
1 foreman - - - -	- -	60
12 labourers, £15 - -	- -	180
6 students, £10 - -	- -	60
Tools, manure, &c. - -	- -	50
		1,000
Industrial School - -	- -	500
		1,500

MONTSERRAT.

The station established in this island in 1890 was abandoned for want of funds to carry it on. An agricultural instructor is much needed to visit and encourage the peasants (in case shipping facilities are provided) in the cultivation of fruit and other products for export. For training boys in agriculture, arrangements might be made with Antigua. This vote is arranged on the same lines as that for Tobago, where the circumstances are very similar.

Botanic Station at Montserrat.

	£
Curator, £150–£200 - - - - - -	200
Agricultural instructor, £70–£100 - - - -	100
Foreman - - - - - - - -	50
*8 labourers, £15 - - - - - -	120
Tools, manure, &c. - - - - - -	30
	500
* or 6 labourers - - - - - -	90
3 students - - - - - - -	30

ANTIGUA.

The chief and practically only interest in this island is sugar. Hence it is proposed to provide for systematic experiments in raising new varieties of cane, and in improving the cultivation by the use of manures and other means, as in Barbados and British Guiana. The Botanic Station should co-operate in this work and also endeavour to improve the pine-apple and any other minor industry that offers hope of success. There is already a good industrial school at Antigua which should be maintained on its present lines.

Botanic Station and Sugar Cane Experiments at Antigua.

	£
Botanic station - - - - - -	450
Sugar cane experiments - - - - - -	550
	1,000

ST. KITTS-NEVIS.

The same organisation is suggested in St. Kitts-Nevis as in Antigua with the addition of an industrial school and an agricultural instructor. The latter should devote special attention to the peasant proprietors at Nevis.

St. Kitts-Nevis.

	£
Curator, £150–£200 - - - - -	200
Agricultural instructor - - - - -	70
6 labourers, £15 - - - - - -	90
3 students, £10 - - - - - -	30
Manure, tools, &c. - - - - - -	50
	440
Sugar cane experiments - - - - -	300
Industrial school - - - - - -	500
	1,240

SUMMARY.

Botanic Stations and Industrial Schools.

	£
Tobago - - - - - - - -	500
Grenada - - - - - - -	730
St. Vincent - - - - - - -	1,500
St. Lucia - - - - - - -	1,230
Barbados - - - - - - -	1,500
Dominica - - - - - - -	1,500
Montserrat - - - - - - -	500
Antigua - - - - - - -	1,000
St. Kitts-Nevis - - - - - -	1,240
	9,700

BRITISH GUIANA.

The important character of the investigations carried on by Messrs. Harrison and Jenman in raising and testing new varieties of canes has already been noticed.   There is such good promise of success that it would be a calamity if these experiments are not continued on the present lines. It is suggested to make a special provision for these investigations and to leave the detailed arrangements to be settled after consultation with the Government of British Guiana.

Sugar cane experiments in British Guiana   -   - £1,000

HORTICULTURAL SHOWS.

These shows are suggested as effective means of bringing into prominence the resources of the islands and of creating an intelligent interest in improving the cultivation of the soil and in prosecuting new industries. The funds set apart for this purpose would be chiefly spent in bringing together implements of field and garden husbandry, in explaining the construction and mode of working of suitable machinery for cleaning and curing produce, and in exhibiting samples of produce skilfully selected and packed for export purposes.   One or two shows might be held annually in each island co-operating with any local efforts made in the same direction.

Grant   -   -   -   -   -   -   -   £500

GRANTS TO ELEMENTARY SCHOOLS.

Following the example set by the Education Department in Jamaica, it is proposed to make small grants in aid in two classes, (A) to schools in which the theory of agriculture is satisfactorily taught, and (B) a slightly increased grant in cases where in addition to the teaching of the theory of agriculture school gardens or experimental plots are maintained by the efforts of the teachers and scholars.   The amount of the grant proposed for each school in Class A would be from £1 to £3 ; in Class B from £2 to £5, depending in each case on the number of children who reach a satisfactory standard of attainments.   For the first year or two the total amount of these grants would necessarily be very small, as the chief outlay would consist of expenses incurred in giving instruction to and in training the teachers.

Grants   -   -   -   -   -   -   .   -   £500

BULLETINS, LEAFLETS, &c.

Bulletins, such as are now issued by the Botanical Institutions in the West Indies, are regarded as indispensable means for reaching the more intelligent members of the community and of diffusing amongst them accurate information in regard to tropical products.   The leaflets proposed in addition would be distributed amongst the labouring classes after lectures and demonstrations by the agricultural instructors, and copies would be supplied free to magistrates, medical and government officers, clergy, police officers, and all persons having influence with or coming into contact with the peasantry.   The leaflets would contain hints, expressed in simple and clear language, on the treatment of the soil and plants, and worded so as to be used for dictation lessons in the higher classes in elementary schools.   Readers would be prepared for use in elementary and industrial schools dealing with the familiar plants of the tropics.

Grant   -   -   -   -   -   -   -   £500

GRANTS TO COLLEGES AND SCHOOLS.

There are no institutions existing at present in any part of the West Indies where the scientific teaching of Agriculture is carried on.   All the better class of students attending the higher schools turn their attention either to the learned professions or to Government clerkships, while the better paid appointments connected with agriculture are filled from outside or by a small number of local men who by hard plodding and the slow teaching of practical experience have qualified themselves to undertake charge of plantations. These local men are useful but they have had no scientific training, and necessarily, from their position, are restricted not only in their capability of realising the progress made in other countries, but of adapting such progress to their own circumstances. Unless brought up on family estates, agriculture is seldom regarded as a suitable career by young men in the West Indies ; in fact they avoid it as much as possible, and their example is unfortunately followed by the better class of peasant proprietors, who prefer to educate their children for positions as clerks or as assistants in stores to any work connected with agriculture. A long period must elapse before there is a considerable change in this respect, but in certain colonies such as Barbados, Jamaica, Trinidad, and British Guiana, where there exist colleges and schools of high standing, it is very desirable to make provision for the higher agricultural education necessary to instruct those who may afterwards become managers and proprietors of estates, and fit them for availing themselves of the results of modern advances in improving local agriculture. The teaching and training given in temperate countries are of little service to men who are destined for tropical planting. Such men must be trained amidst the special circumstances of the tropics.

Grants might be offered for sound agricultural teaching to the Codrington College at Barbados, the Queen's Colleges at Trinidad and British Guiana, and to the Jamaica High School. The amount of the grant paid in each case would depend on the number of pupils who show ability to pass a written and oral examination, and on the character of the provision made for laboratory teaching and field work. Some assistance in this direction might be rendered by the officers and establishments connected with the Department, but special teachers, one at each college, would be necessary, at salaries from £250 to £500 per annum.

Grants   -   -   -   -   -   -   -   -   £2,600

SUMMARY.

Botanic Department.

	£
Head office - - - - - - - -	2,200
Nine botanic stations and four industrial schools	9,700
Sugar cane experiments at British Guiana - -	1,000
Horticultural shows, exhibition of implements, &c.	500
Printing bulletins, leaflets, and distribution - -	500
Grants to elementary schools for teaching the theory of agriculture and care of school gardens	500
Grants to colleges and schools for teaching scientific agriculture - - - - - - -	2,600
	17,000

To this might be added the subsidies estimated at £10,000 for steamer services, making a total of £27,000.

In the course of the debate in the House of Commons on August 2, 1898, the Secretary of State for the Colonies (Mr. Chamberlain) spoke as follows, when introducing the supplementary estimate providing for the erection of an Imperial Department of Agriculture for the West Indies:— Debate in the House of Commons, Aug. 2, 1898.

"The recommendations of the West Indian Royal Commission in this regard were twofold. In the first instance they suggested that a special Department [of Agriculture] should be established dealing with all questions of economic plants and botanic stations in all the islands—we propose to adopt that suggestion and that this establishment should be placed under the direction of Dr. Morris, Assistant Director at Kew, who is marked out, as I think any one who knows anything of Kew will admit, by special qualifications for an important position of this kind. Not only has he all the scientific and other knowledge in the possession of the authorities at Kew, but also special acquaintance with the West Indies, and, if those other industries are to be successful, there is no one more capable of doing it than Dr. Morris. In order to carry out this scheme, which we owe entirely to the Royal Commission—because, except in detail, I know no way of improving on their recommendation—we ask for a grant of £4,500, all the money we can spend during the present financial year. But we estimate that the annual charge will be £17,500. . . . . As regards the grants which we ask from the Imperial exchequer, I have to point out that it is absolutely impossible for the colonies to bear the cost under the present circumstances. We hope they may be in the future self-supporting, but at present it is absolutely impossible for them to do anything for themselves. If these grants were thrown on the revenue of the Colonies, the only result would be that their deficit would be increased, and we should have to ask for an increased grant in aid instead of a grant in aid for communication, agriculture, and technical instruction. The advantage of taking the whole matter into our hands is that we shall have it under our control, and we shall not be hampered by local jealousies, and shall be able to introduce something like a general scheme, which would be impossible if local Legislatures in each case had to be consulted, and local jealousies were brought into play. I regard the whole of this cost as being an expenditure intended to relieve the British Government of future charges. The object is to assist the West Indian Colonies in every possible way."

Sir Edward Grey, M.P. (one of the West India Royal Commissioners), said :—

"Part of the vote is a grant in aid of an Agricultural Department, and I am exceedingly glad to hear that Dr. Morris is to be in charge of this department. He will bring to the discharge of his duties a knowledge of tropical produce, the possibilities and conditions of the cultivation of that produce, which I do not think can be surpassed by any one. He will bring to the administration of the department the greatest ability, energy, enterprise and devotion to work. His knowledge and assistance in reference to the prospects of the islands we visited, were of the greatest value to the Commission, and I am sure his work at the head of the department will be of the highest value to the islands, and will be of increasing value year by year."

Letter from the Secretary of State. The following are extracts from an Official letter addressed by the Secretary of State to the Governors of all the West Indian Colonies (including the Bahamas and British Honduras) respecting the organization and working of the Imperial Department of Agriculture : —

Downing Street,
6th September, 1898.

Sir,—You will have learnt from public sources of information that Her Majesty's Government have decided that, in accordance with certain of the recommendations of the West India Royal Commission, a Department of Agriculture shall be established in the West Indies. The cost of this Department for a period of ten years will be provided from Imperial funds, and grants will also be made in aid of the Public Revenues of Trinidad and Tobago (for the benefit of the latter Island), British Guiana, Barbados, the Windward Islands, and the Leeward Islands, to provide for or to assist in the maintenance of Agricultural and Botanical Establishments, Industrial Schools, or other kindred purposes, as has been done for the last half of the current financial year under Sub-Head S 3 of the Supplementary Estimate aid before Parliament last Session, of which a copy is enclosed.

2. The headquarters of the Imperial Department of Agriculture in the West Indies will be at Barbados and the staff will consist of a Commissioner of Agriculture, a Travelling Superintendent and a Clerk. Dr. D. Morris, C.M.G., Assistant Director of the Royal Gardens, Kew, has been appointed Commissioner of Agriculture and will take up his duties in Barbados early in October next. He will correspond directly with the Colonial Office upon all matters concerning the general work of the Department; on matters affecting Colonial Establishments and expenditure he will correspond with the several Colonial Governments through the Colonial Secretaries.

3. He should be consulted on all Botanic and Agricultural questions, and on all matters affecting the organization, duties and expenditure of the Botanic Departments or other kindred institutions wherever their cost is to be reimbursed out of the Imperial Grant in Aid; and his services and those of his assistants should be made use of in every way possible with a view to the development of the resources of the Colonies.

Mr. Chamberlain specially called attention, in a later part of this letter, to the proposal for arranging a Conference of the chief chemical and botanical officers in the West Indies at an early date, with a view to the prosecution of a policy of co-operative effort.

The first Agricultural Conference held in the West Indies met First in the Chamber of the House of Assembly, Barbados, on Agricultural January 7, 1899. The President was Dr. Morris, C.M.G., M.A., Conference. D.Sc., F.L.S., Imperial Commissioner of Agriculture for the West Indies. Representatives were present from Jamaica (3), British Guiana (4), Trinidad (5), the Windward Islands (3), the Leeward Islands (3), and Barbados (6).

The President then delivered the following address* :—

This is the first Conference assembled in the West Indies to discuss the practical details of agricultural work. I re-echo the welcome just offered to you by Her Majesty's Representative in this Colony, and I trust that your visit and the important subjects that will be brought before you will be conducive to the welfare and prosperity of the communities among whom we live.

There is no doubt that at the present time the circumstances of the West Indies generally are not in a satisfactory condition. In December, 1896, a Royal Commission was appointed to examine into the present condition and future prosperity of the West Indies. This Commission made an exhaustive inquiry extending over several months, and in August, 1897, it presented a Report containing valuable suggestions calculated to restore and maintain the prosperity of these colonies and their inhabitants It is generally admitted that the Royal Commissioners were men of excep tional ability and experience, and that their conclusions were entitled to be received as conveying a true and adequate account of the circumstances of the West Indies.

The recommendations of the Commission have since been adopted by Parliament, and a beginning has been made in giving effect to them by the establishment of a Department of Agriculture for the West Indies. The duties of the Department are twofold: (1) to endeavour to restore the sugar industry to a condition in which it could be profitably carried on;

---

* Reprinted from the *West Indian Bulletin, the Journal of the Imperial Agricultural Department of the West Indies*, vol. i., No. 1. (Barbados: Messrs. Bowen and Sons. London agents: Messrs. Dulau and Co., 37, Soho Square, W.)

(2) to encourage the establishment of other industries in such colonies as afford suitable conditions to supplement the staple industry.

The funds at the disposal of the Department up to the 31st March next amount to £6,500. It is estimated that the annual provision afterward will be £17,500. As stated in the speech of the Secretary of State in the House of Commons in August last, this "must continue, if the experiment shows a prospect of success, until the colonies are once again placed in a self-supporting condition."

As you are aware, the duty of organising the Department of Agriculture n the West Indies has been entrusted by Her Majesty's Government to me, and I look forward with great interest to the work, and am prepared to devote all my time and energies to the important concerns committed to my charge. I ask, and I know I shall not ask in vain, for your cordial co-operation in the task of improving the agricultural interests of the West Indies.

There has been a disposition in some quarters to represent the scheme of the Agricultural Department as a weak alternative to the demands of the sugar planters. As a friendly critic has pointed out : "It is nothing of the kind. On the contrary, it is founded on a close and keen study of the needs of the Colonies, and is devised not only to improve the methods of sugar cultivation, but to promote that variety of industries, that independent cultivation of the soil, which is necessary if these communities are ever to become stable, well-ordered, and flourishing."

The Sugar Industry.

The Agricultural Department is specially charged to assist the sugar industry wherever the conditions are favourable for its continuance. It is a cardinal point in the policy of the Department to prevent, if possible, a single acre of land now under canes from being thrown out of cultivation. Whether this will be practicable in every case will depend on circumstances, many of them beyond the control of the Department. Nevertheless, as far as the Department is concerned, it will discharge the important duties intrusted to it with fidelity and care. If its efforts are well supported and its recommendations fully carried out, there can be no doubt the sugar industry will eventually reach a more prosperous condition than at present. There are in the West Indies certain colonies in which the cultivation of the sugar cane has continued for a long period to be the staple industry. These may be termed sugar colonies. They are British Guiana, Trinidad in part, Barbados, Antigua, and St. Kitts-Nevis. The others, namely Jamaica, Grenada, St. Vincent, St. Lucia, Dominica, Montserrat, and the Virgin Islands, although at one time, and still to some extent, dependent on the sugar industry, have found themselves quite unable to withstand the keen competition of recent years. If they are to exist at all, they will have to depend on other industries than sugar.

The operations of the Department must, therefore, be so distributed as to give adequate assistance to each of these groups. The population to be supported is almost equally divided between them. In the interest of the people themselves, it is, therefore, as important to give attention to the non-sugar Colonies as to the sugar Colonies.

Referring to the sugar industry, apart from the operations of certain political and fiscal changes which cannot be discussed here, there is a very considerable amount of work to be done to assist the sugar planters ; for instance, in enabling them to improve their methods and in reducing the cost of production. We must, I think, assume that if the production of sugar goes on steadily increasing everywhere, prices cannot increase to any appreciable extent.

With the wider areas placed under cultivation, and the energy displayed by many European nations, the tendency is for the price of all tropical produce to fall rather than to rise. In order, therefore, to meet this, there must be cheaper production ; and cheaper production in the case of sugar demands the highest skill and knowledge in cultivation with the latest and best appliances in manufacture.

In every sugar-producing country great importance is attached to improving the quality of the particular plant yielding sugar. In European countries the amount of sugar yielded by the beet has been nearly doubled within a comparatively short period. Until within the last ten years nothing had been done on similar lines to improve the quality of the sugar cane. This work was only possible when by a fortunate circumstance the power of the sugar cane to produce fertile seed was fully realised. This occurred almost simultaneously in the East and West Indies—in Java and Barbados. This island is, therefore, to be congratulated, no less than those personally connected with it, in having been among the first to grasp the practical bearing of this fact.

The point now is to utilise to the utmost the capabilities of the cane in this direction, and endeavour to place it in an equally favourable position as the beet. The experiments so far carried on, though on a limited scale, have been most encouraging. We have results from Java, the Hawaiian Islands, and Louisiana, all confirming those obtained in the West Indies. I have recently cited those obtained in British Guiana. I would now draw attention to a seedling cane obtained in Barbados of a most promising character. [Dr. Morris here exhibited a bunch of fine canes that had previously been brought in and placed in the upper part of the hall.] It was raised at Dodd's Botanical Station, and is known as Barbados, (or shortly) B. 147. I quote from a letter written by Mr. Bovell (who raised this cane) as follows : "This cane has been under cultivation here for the past five years, and it has during that time given an average yield of nearly half a ton of available sugar per acre over the 'Caledonian Queen,' which comes next, and more than three-quarters of a ton more than the 'Bourbon.' All the planters who have tried it speak favourably of it, and I have no hesitation in recommending planters in the black soil districts to plant this year about a third of their estate with it."

Mr. Bovell adds the following comparative statement of the average results for five years obtained at Dodd's with the Seedling Cane B. No. 147, and certain other canes usually cultivated in Barbados :—

Name of Cane.	Sucrose per Imperial Gallon. lbs.	Glucose per Imperial Gallon. lbs.	Average available Sugar per acre. lbs.	REMARKS.
Seedling No. 147 - -	1·794	·114	7,190	
Caledonian Queen - -	1·980	·041	6,137	
Rappoe - - - -	1·922	·041	5,920	
Naga B. - - -	1·937	·051	5,894	
Bourbon - - -	1·775	·086	5,210	
White Transparent -	1·804	·086	5,275	3 yrs. only.

The best proof of the value attached to this cane is the keen demand which has arisen for it amongst the planters themselves.

Several fields of it exist in different parts of the island, and it is reported as having actually yielded as high as three tons per acre. This year about 200 acres will be established on one group of estates. Further, in an island where new canes have hitherto been regarded with a certain amount of suspicion, it is a promising sign that those in possession of B. 147 find it advantageous to sell canes in large quantities to their neighbours. One planter alone has disposed of over one million plants this season. The demand for this cane from the neighbouring colonies is also considerable.

There are numerous other directions in which the sugar industry might be improved. It is proposed to undertake a series of experiments with various kinds of manures to find out the sorts best adapted to certain soils, and the period in regard to the age and condition of the canes at which they should be applied. Further, there is the treatment of the various insect and fungoid pests to which the sugar cane is subject. In previous years the loss arising from these causes has been very considerable. This loss is largely preventable, and it will be the business of the Department to study the circumstances and advise the planters to the best of its ability.

At Barbados, the experiments in these directions have already been started. Mr. Bovell has been placed in charge of the field work with the title of " Agricultural Superintendent of Sugar Cane Experiments," while Professor d'Albuquerque will be in charge of the chemical work. With the hearty co-operation of the proprietors of estates, I have pleasure in stating that there will be established four Principal or Central experimental Stations, and eight Local Stations for the improvement of the sugar cane in this island. The Central Stations will be devoted to raising seedlings and to carrying out their treatment in the early stages until they are accepted as distinctly improved varieties. They will also afford opportunity for carrying on several series of manurial experiments. The Local Stations will be entirely concerned in the practical and final testing under normal conditions of the best varieties and their adaptability as sugar producers in different soils and climates of the island. At the Local Stations the planters in each parish will have opportunities of observing the growth and habits of the selected canes treated like all the other canes on the estate, and of afterwards obtaining plants or tops for establishing their own plantations. The total area covered by these experimental stations will be about 130 acres. It is arranged that experiments on similar lines will be started at once at Antigua and St. Kitts. In regard to Trinidad, the experiments started by Mr. Hart will, it is hoped, be largely extended, while the chemical work will be undertaken by a competent officer. At Jamaica, where the experimental cultivation of canes introduced from other countries was started more than 20 years ago, and whence many varieties have been distributed to the neighbouring Colonies, it is anticipated that Messrs. Fawcett and Watts will be able to take up experiments of a thoroughly useful character. I am unable to give information at present in regard to what is likely to be done in British Guiana. There is, however, before the Government of that Colony a proposal to provide funds, as advised by the Royal Commission, for continuing, on a large scale, the experiments which have already produced such good results.

The total amount so far proposed to be expended on the special sugar cane experiments in Barbados, British Guiana, Antigua, and St. Kitts–Nevis is £3,350. As all previous efforts in these islands have not cost more than about £350 annually, which, which provide for the entire service of several competent officers, the ultimate results of the experiments cannot fail to be of great assistance to the sugar industry.

I do not, however, disguise the fact that outside British Guiana and Trinidad, and to some extent St. Lucia, whatever improvement may take place in regard to new·varieties of the sugar cane, the application of manures, the treatment of disease and the reduction of expenses in cultivation, the sugar industry in the smaller islands will never be in a satisfactory condition so long as the processes of crushing the canes and manufacturing the sugar remain as at present.

We have in the report of the Royal Commission the most painful demonstration of the inadequacy of the methods now in use. For instance, owing to defective treatment it is recorded (based on experiments extending over seven years) that there " is an average of over 2,000 pounds of sugar per acre left in the canes after crushing which is burnt in the megass." A large part of this could have been recovered by better machinery. At present in these islands it is said to require about 13 tons of cane to produce one ton of sugar. With the best machinery about 9 tons should be sufficient to produce a ton of sugar. There is, according to reliable authority, a further heavy loss in boiling the juice and in converting it into sugar. I quote the exact words:—"For every 100 pounds of crystallisable sugar contained in the juice, not more than an average of 75 pounds of ordinary muscovado sugar is now recovered."

Apart, therefore, from the loss incurred by imperfect crushing, the loss in actually manufacturing the sugar amounts to one-fourth of the total quantity produced. These statements appear to apply generally to the sugar industry as carried on in the smaller islands. As already stated, they do not apply to British Guiana and Trinidad, and to some localities in the island of St. Lucia. There, very efficient machinery and appliances are used, and any improvements in other directions should add to the advantages already existing. As you are aware, the remedy recommended by the Royal Commission to prevent such a loss in the smaller islands was the establishment of Central Factories. This subject, as you will notice, is down for discussion by the Conference this afternoon. I trust that the information which will be placed before us by those competent to speak on the subject will lead to one or two experimental factories being established during the present year.

The time has evidently arrived when it is absolutely necessary for the planters to decide what the future of the sugar industry in these islands is to be. In commercial, as in natural life, the perpetual struggle for existence necessitates continual adjustment to new and fresh conditions. When this adjustment is wanting or imperfect, the industry, or being, is pushed aside and disappears. It is now imperative for the sugar planters to adapt themselves to the conditions of their environment, or they become "unfit." In other words, they will be unable to hold their own and they and their industry must disappear.

With your permission I would touch upon one or two other points. Rule of thumb methods, wherever existing, must be abandoned, and with them must be abandoned the crude and empirical notions in regard to agricultural subjects that have long since been discarded by our rivals amongst the intelligent communities of Europe and America. A simplification of methods for working sugar estates as well as for disposing of the produce (already adopted in some instances) is also necessary. This should tend to reduce the costs of management and, further, should enable the planters to obtain all estate supplies at reasonable prices.

Formerly, when the price of sugar was high, it was possible for the industry to bear charges that are now quite impossible. Times have changed, and simple and more direct methods, all culminating in reducing expenses, must now be adopted, otherwise West Indian sugar will have no chance of competing successfully in the markets of the world.

OTHER INDUSTRIES.

In discussing the steps necessary to place the West Indies generally in a more satisfactory condition, the Royal Commissioners drew special attention to the need for expanding the number and extent of other industries. Their words, which I quote in full, are as follows :--

"The recommendations involving expenditure by the mother country which we have considered it our duty to make, are based primarily on the present and prospective depression of the sugar industry in the West Indies, but they are of such a nature that they should, in our opinion, be carried out even if the sugar industry were restored temporarily to a condition of prosperity. It is never satisfactory for any country to be entirely dependent upon one industry. Such a position is, from the very nature of the case, more or less precarious, and must, in the case of the West Indies, result in a preponderating influence in one direction tending to restrict development in other ways.

"The general statement regarding the danger of depending on a single industry applies with very special force to the dependence of the West Indian Colonies upon the sugar industry, for the cultivation of sugar collects together a larger number of people upon the land than can be employed or supported in the same area by any other form of cultivation.

In addition to this, it also unfits the people, or at any rate gives them no training, for the management or cultivation of the soil for any other purpose than that of growing sugar cane. The failure, therefore, of a sugar estate not only leaves destitute a larger number of labourers than can be supported upon the land in other ways, but leaves them also without either the knowledge, skill, or habits requisite for making a good use of the land.

"Whilst, therefore, the vital importance of the sugar industry to the present prosperity of nearly all the Colonies is beyond dispute, we wish to observe that, so long as they remain dependent upon sugar, their position can never be sound or secure. It has become a commonplace criticism to remark upon the perpetual recurrence of crises in the West Indian Colonies, and we submit that the repeated recurrence of such crises, as well as the fact that the present crisis is more ominous than any of the previous ones, illustrates the danger to which we have referred, and adds much force to our recommendations for the adoption of special measures to facilitate the introduction of other industries."

The coast lands in the West Indies have been under cultivation in many instances for more than a hundred years. In several districts large tracts have been abandoned as useless, and the casual visitor seeing these only is under the impression that the West Indies "are played out." A reference to the Report of the Royal Commission will show, what few realise, that so far from being exhausted, the total area of cultivable land not beneficially occupied at present, amounts to more than 22 million acres. Leaving out British Guiana, which is only partially explored, and confining our attention only to the Islands, viz., Trinidad, the Windward Islands, Barbados, the Leeward Islands and Jamaica, we find even within this smaller area, that leaving out swamps, rocky and other useless land, and allowing for land to be reserved in forest, there are still over 2 million acres suitable for bearing crops. The actual area under cultivation is only about a million acres. Practically, therefore, only one-third of the cultivable land in the West Indian Islands is at present utilised. These facts appear in the following table compiled from the official returns supplied to the Royal Commission:—

Place.	Area in Acres.	Area now Cultivated.	Area of cultivable land not beneficially occupied.
		Acres.	Acres.
British Guiana - - - -	65,836,000	325,000	20,000,000
Trinidad and Tobago - - -	1,193,313	310,000	550,000
Windward Islands - - -	328,122	95,000	135,000
Barbados - - -	106,470	90,000	10,000
Leeward Islands - - -	390,840	100,000	150,000
Jamaica - - - -	2,692,480	693,674	1,500,000
Total - - -	70,547,225	1,613,674	22,345,000

Taking the colonies as a whole, we find the area now under cultivation is only a little over 2 per cent. of the total area, and only a little over 7 per cent. of the estimated cultivable area.

From the consideration of the land, we now pass to the circumstances of the population. It is admitted that even in Sugar Colonies like British Guiana, only one-third of the total population is directly engaged in the industry. If we allow another third for those indirectly engaged and for Indians, we shall still have a third of the population contributing little or nothing to the exports of the Colony. In St. Vincent, St. Lucia, Dominica, Montserrat, Antigua, and St. Kitts-Nevis and Jamaica, there are thousands of people whose labour at present is devoted to raising casual food crops. They thus destroy land that with suitable treatment should yield valuable crops for export.

The object of starting other industries is first of all to realise to the best advantage the extensive tracts of unused lands in these islands; and, secondly, to find remunerative employment for people who are now almost without the means of subsistence. Other industries are, therefore, essential.

In taking up this work I fully realise the difficulties of the situation. I am also sensible of the enormous amount of labour involved, and the slow and tedious character of the operations necessary to produce results at all commensurate with the cost of the undertaking. I have, however, a close acquaintance with the circumstances of these Colonies. I have carefully studied their resources and I am not unused to deal with what is termed the "labour difficulty." In spite of these I retain, after an experience of twenty years, a strong faith in the future of these Colonies, and I believe that, rightly guided and assisted in these days of their adversity, they will realise the destiny designed for them by nature, and they will yet become happy and prosperous communities.

It is needless to enter into details. The work immediately at hand is to give attention to the sugar industry. When efforts are fully started in that direction, then I hope within a short time to devote the energies of the Department and the funds at my command in building up those other industries which the exceptionally able men on the Royal Commission regarded as essential to the permanent well-being of the West Indies.

Botanical Institutions.

The Royal Commissioners stated that the botanical institutions in the West Indies have rendered considerable assistance in improving agricultural industries, and "they are capable of being made increasingly useful in this respect." Twenty years ago there were only three such institutions in existence. Now, owing to the organisation of the small establishments known as Botanic Stations, there are thirteen of these institutions. The results at the latter, "though not yet extensive, have been of a distinctly promising character." As the Colonies of Jamaica, Trinidad and British Guiana were regarded by the Royal Commission as in a position to maintain their own Botanical Establishments, no grants-in-aid in their case have been voted by Parliament. As regards the Botanic Stations, it is proposed to place them under the direct control of this Department, and the charge of maintaining them is transferred to Imperial Funds. The Botanic Stations so transferred are those at Tobago, Grenada, St. Vincent, Barbados, St. Lucia, Dominica, Montserrat, Antigua, and St. Kitts-Nevis. Amongst the duties to be discharged by the Botanic Stations, the Royal Commissioners indicated the following:—"They are to devote themselves in a systematic manner to the work of introducing, propagating and distributing all the promising economic plants of the tropics. They are to initiate the experimental cultivation of new or little known plants, and assist in the efforts made in the larger colonies to secure improved varieties of the sugar cane. They are to act as centres for diffusing accurate information, and as training institutions for the practical teaching of tropical agriculture, also as the headquarters from which agricultural instructors would be sent to give lectures and demonstrations bearing upon the selection of land for tropical economic plants, their suitable cultivation, and the best methods for curing and packing the produce."

Agricultural Instructors.

A considerable experience has shown that it is not sufficient to provide Botanic Gardens and Experimental Stations to influence the large body of

cultivators in the West Indies. They must be reached in a more direct
and effective manner. The first attempt to employ travelling instructors
was made on my recommendation in Jamaica in 1891. Two Cacao instructors were appointed by Sir Henry Blake, and the results since that
time have fully justified the use of this method of assisting in the development of rural industries. Great care is necessary in selecting men possessing the necessary qualifications. In Dominica, St. Lucia, and Grenada it
would be an advantage for them also to be able to speak the local *patois*.
It is important to arrange beforehand with the leading personages in each
district, so that the people are prepared to receive the Instructor and made
thoroughly acquainted with the objects of his visit. A public meeting is
useful as a first step, to be followed by visits to gardens and cultivated
areas in the neighbourhood where the Instructor is able to give practical
demonstration in the right methods of preparing the soil, in draining and
manuring, and in putting out the plants in a neat and suitable manner.
Later, he would show how the plants are to be cared for and pruned, and
ultimately he would give a regular course of instruction in curing and
preparing produce for export. These details carefully instilled into the
minds of the people would be part of the general training necessary to
direct the raw labour material of these islands into the right channels. I
am absolutely convinced of the efficiency of the system, and it would not
be difficult to mention several striking instances of the success that has
attended it when the right men are employed and they are placed under
favourable circumstances for carrying out the duties entrusted to them.
It is proposed to attach an Agricultural Instructor to each of the Botanic
Stations, and an officer with a similar training will have charge of the
cultural work at the Agricultural Schools. Where it is not possible to
attach an Instructor to the Botanic Station, arrangements will be made to
allow the Instructor's duty, in part at least, to be undertaken by the
Curator, leaving the garden meanwhile in charge of a competent foreman.
In addition, Instructors, or experts, with special experience in budding
and pruning fruit trees, curing tobacco, bee-keeping, selecting and packing
fruit for export, will be employed to spend a month or two in each island
and thus distribute practical knowledge over a wider area. For some
years to come, the peripatetic instructors must be relied upon to carry out
a large share of the training necessary amongst the adult portion of the
community. In spite of the disadvantages incidental to their isolated
position, these people are not slow to follow the advice given them once
they are convinced of its practical utility and of its direct bearing upon
their future welfare.

AGRICULTURAL EXHIBITIONS.

Agricultural Shows or Exhibitions are not new in the West Indies.
They have been held for some years in the larger Colonies. They are
practically unknown in the smaller Colonies. The purely educational
side of these Exhibitions, especially in regard to small cultivators,
has not been so fully recognised as it should be. The prizes are in
many cases given for produce possessing intrinsically little or no merit.
It is often badly prepared and presented in a slovenly and uninviting
condition. Such prizes are calculated to do more harm than good, as
they encourage the people in unskilful and careless habits which destroy
any chance of their obtaining remunerative prices for their produce. The
work of substituting careful and intelligent methods for those already
so prevalent in the West Indies, will be a long and tedious task. It is,
however, of so important a character that it must be dealt with. Possibly,
the best way to start a better system in handling and marketing produce,
is to offer several prizes at Agricultural Shows, but award them only in
cases where the articles are presented in a thoroughly satisfactory condition. The Department might exhibit similar articles, especially those
intended for export, as object lessons, and arrange for some of its officers to
be present to explain exactly what is necessary in order to reach a high
standard of merit

It is understood that the prizes offered by the Department are in aid of local efforts and not to supersede them. Further, the Department will bring together implements of field and garden husbandry and explain the construction and mode of working of suitable machinery for cleaning and curing produce. It will also exhibit cases skilfully packed with fruit and other produce ready for shipment.

It has been arranged that preliminary exhibitions will be held shortly at St. Lucia, Dominica, and Montserrat.

BULLETINS, HANDBOOKS AND LEAFLETS.

The Royal Commissioners stated that "in the West Indies persons engaged in cultivation suffer from isolation and are often without any information as to what is being done elsewhere." In addition to the employment of travelling instructors it is proposed to meet the difficulties of isolation by preparing and distributing bulletins, handbooks and leaflets affording information on subjects of general interest. The principal publication of the Department will be the "West Indian Bulletin." This will probably be issued at the end of this month, and will contain amongst other matter the proceedings of this Conference. The handbooks will contain hints and directions in simple language on the cultivation of certain crops such as Coffee, Cacao, Oranges, Pineapples, Bananas, Ginger, Vanilla, etc. The handbooks will be stitched in canvas covers and form a series similar to those issued in England and the United States. The leaflets will be of a more modest character and will contain information expressed in simple and clear language suitable for distribution after addresses and demonstrations given to small cultivators by the Agricultural instructors. These leaflets will also be supplied free to magistrates, medical and revenue officers, the clergy, police officers, and all having influence, or coming into contact, with the peasantry. Both the handbooks and leaflets will be regularly supplied to schools, and the teachers will be encouraged to use them in dictation lessons and take an interest in diffusing the information contained in them amongst the people of the district.

AGRICULTURAL TEACHING IN PRIMARY SCHOOLS.

In all agricultural communities the need of the hour is the education of the rising generation in the knowledge how to obtain from the soil those products for which there is a good demand in the markets of the world. Ignorance and ineptitude can never produce successful results. The prevailing practice in the West Indies is to take everything out of the land and abandon it immediately afterwards. This is a vicious and destructive system ; but to suddenly change the habits of centuries is impossible. We must take the children and gradually teach them other ways. At least, the principles of sound agricultural methods must be taught in the elementary schools. Large sums are being spent in these Colonies on general education. The total quoted in the Report of the Royal Commission for the year 1896 was £180,000. It is admitted that "efforts made on general education have been largely successful." In some colonies steps have already been taken to teach agriculture as a part of elementary education. The chief difficulty is the want of knowledge on the part of the teachers. It is hoped that the Agricultural Department, as suggested by the Royal Commissioners, "will be in a position to render valuable assistance" in this direction. With the co-operation of the central educational authorities in each colony, the teachers will be given a course of instruction in the principles of Agriculture. They will also be taught how to impart the knowledge thus obtained to their pupils in a series of object lessons. They will further be supplied with a school reader containing agricultural information in simple and plain language. This will form the basis of all the theoretical and practical teaching required for the first few years in elementary schools. Great hopes are based on the educational value of school gardens where the teachers and children will carry out practically operations suggested by the lessons taught in school. In England, the Education Department recently referred to school gardens as follows :—"We fully recognise the improvement which a thorough knowledge of cottage gardening may effect in the condition of the working classes in agricultural districts; but as a school subject its teaching also serves a general educational purpose." Following the example set by the Education Department in Jamaica, it is proposed to make small grants in aid in two classes : (A) to schools in which the theory of Agriculture is satisfactorily taught; and (B) a slightly increased grant in cases where, in addition to the teaching of the theory of Agriculture school gardens or experimental plots are maintained by the efforts of the teachers and scholars.

The amount of the grant proposed for each school in class A would be from £1 to £3 ; in class B from £2 to £5 ; depending in each case on the number of children who reach a satisfactory standard of attainments. For the first year or two the total amount of these grants would necessarily be very small, as the chief outlay would consist of expenses incurred in giving instruction to and in training the teachers.

AGRICULTURAL SCHOOLS.

The Royal Commissioners recommended that "a system of training in agricultural occupation was much needed" in the West Indies. It was suggested that "some at least of the Botanic Stations should have agricultural schools attached to them where the best means of cultivating tropical plants would be taught." It is proposed to carry out this valuable suggestion. Provision has been made to establish an agricultural school immediately at Dominica, and as soon as the necessary land has been obtained, similar schools will be started at St. Vincent, St. Lucia, and St. Kitts-Nevis. These schools are not to be reformatories, and will not deal with criminals. This would defeat the object in view. The more suitable plan for obtaining pupils would be to admit, preferably from the country districts, orphans and destitute children over nine years of age, or those voluntarily placed at the schools by their parents or guardians. The order for their admission will require to be signed before a magistrate, and provide that the child remain at the school without molestation of any kind for a period of not less than five years. It is hoped by means of these agricultural schools to train a certain number of the children of respectable black people in sound agricultural methods. They will, first of all, be employed in raising their own food and will be accustomed to neat, intelligent and active methods of carrying on various operations of garden and field husbandry. Further, they will be carefully taught to handle tools, how to raise and prune fruit trees, the best means for getting rid of fungoid and insect pests, and how to bud and graft. The boys thus trained should be most useful afterwards in diffusing practical knowledge of this kind amongst their own people.

TEACHING SCIENTIFIC AGRICULTURE IN THE HIGHER SCHOOLS AND COLLEGES.

On this important subject a paper is to be read before the Conference by the Rev. William Simms, who has given considerable attention to it. He has also visited the United States and Canada with the view of studying the methods there adopted. It is hoped from the paper itself and from the discussion that will follow, it may be possible to suggest a plan for at least starting the teaching of scientific agriculture in the colleges in the West Indies.

So far, little or nothing has been attempted in that direction. In consequence the students attending the higher educational institutions turn their attention to the learned professions or to Government clerkships. Both these are now overcrowded, while the better paid appointments connected with scientific agriculture are filled from outside. We must endeavour to make agriculture a popular and remunerative career for young men in the West Indies. To do this would be an effective means of generally increasing the resources of the colonies. It is understood that the training in agriculture given in European countries is not suited to men who are destined for tropical planting. Such men are always better taught amid the special circumstances of the tropics.

The Department is prepared to offer grants to enable certain institutions to employ teachers in agricultural science, and possibly provide a number of scholarships for the most promising pupils. The heads of these institutions with whom I have conferred are thoroughly sympathetic in this direction. I therefore anticipate as one of the results of this Conference, that it will be possible to prepare a scheme for the teaching of agricultural science that will meet with the approval of the Imperial Government.

FUNGOID AND INSECT PESTS.

The injury done to food crops and fruit trees by fungoid and insect pests is very considerable. The discouragement thus met with by those anxious to follow a better system of cultivation is no doubt responsible for the little progress that has hitherto been made in this direction. Usually the small cultivators regard a disease in their crop as a fatalism, and make little or no effort to deal with it. They also leave the diseased crops on the land, which, in the case of fungoid disease, becomes infected with spores, and so the crops of succeeding seasons are also injured or destroyed. I estimate that the total loss to crops from preventable diseases in the West Indies amounts to several thousand pounds yearly. Mr. Fawcett will bring forward some suggestions on this subject before the Conference on Monday afternoon.

NEW STEAMSHIP SERVICES.

As directly associated with the work of the Imperial Department of Agriculture, I may mention that tenders were invited in London, in September last, for four new steamer services for the West Indies. Service A. is intended to provide a fortnightly service between all the islands from St. Kitts southward as far as Trinidad. The object of this service, in accordance with the recommendations of the Royal Commission, is to afford with the existing Royal Mail Service a regular weekly service between the islands. Service B. is intended to be a fortnightly service between Trinidad, British Guiana, Barbados and Canada. This, it is hoped, will encourage trade in sugar and other products between the West India Colonies specified above and the Dominion of Canada. Service C. provides for a fortnightly fruit-steamer service between St. Vincent, Dominica, and the United States or Canada. The steamers are to be specially fitted for the carriage of fruit, and the contractors are to undertake to purchase fruit at fixed rates. If circumstances require it, it has been suggested that this service be modified so as to provide fruit steamers between St. Vincent, Dominica, and the United Kingdom. Service D. is intended to supply a direct tri-weekly fruit service between a port or ports in Jamaica and a port in the United Kingdom.

The second West Indian Agricultural Conference was opened in the Hall of the House of Assembly, Barbados, on January 6, 1900. Dr. Morris presided, and there were present forty representatives, including the heads of all the botanical, chemical and educational departments, as well as representatives of the principal agricultural societies in the West Indies.

In the President's Address* the following passages occurred :—

Second Agricultural Conference.

I regard it as a great privilege to meet you, as the chosen representatives of the West Indies, in Conference to-day. I appreciate deeply the action of the several Governments in sparing the services of their officers to attend this Conference, and no less the Government of Barbados for its continued hospitality in lending us the use of this hall as a meeting place.

Extracts from President's Address.

---

* *West Indian Bulletin,* vol. i., No. 2.

Not only is every colony prominently represented by those engaged in botanical, chemical, and educational efforts in the West Indies, but we have also amongst us gentlemen deputed to attend in behalf of the principal agricultural societies in these colonies. We have, therefore, not only official but non-official representation. This should tend to give our deliberations a wider scope, and bring them into closer sympathy with those actually engaged in agricultural pursuits.

I regard your presence here as a proof that you share with me in realising the grave character of the present circumstances of these colonies. Also of your earnest desire to do all in your power to improve them by the special knowledge with which each of you, in his own particular branch, is equipped. Many now present were here last year, and since that time they have, I know, been busily engaged in carrying out some of the recommendations then adopted. I doubt not that by such efforts we shall, before long, do much to increase the material prosperity of these colonies.

In reviewing the work of the past year, there is much to encourage us ; but, on the other hand, I frankly admit we are more and more sensible of the enormity of the task before us, and the need for active and united action to overcome the difficulties which confront us.

I believe no single agency is likely to prove so useful in this direction as these Conferences. It is recognised that isolated and individual efforts, however earnest and judicious, are bound to flag and, sooner or later, to be abandoned. The *vis inertia* in the West Indies is too great to be overcome by merely spasmodic efforts. Hence the suggestion of these Conferences. We have here an opportunity of renewing and strengthening our forces, and, after careful consideration, of utilising them to the best advantage. There are also the indirect benefits likely to arise from these Conferences —the result of friendly intercourse and a mutual exchange of ideas amongst those engaged in a common work. It would, I admit, add to the interest and value of these Conferences if we could change our meeting place and visit each colony in turn. At present, at least, I regret to find this is not practicable. It would not only extend the period during which representatives would require to be absent from their duties, but it would increase their expenses nearly three-fold.

Under existing arrangements attendance at the Conference involves an absence, in the majority of cases, of scarcely a week. If the Conference were to meet, as suggested, at Trinidad, British Guiana, or Jamaica, it would require an absence of nearly three weeks. An annual Conference under these circumstances would be impossible.

*   *   *   *

Dr. Morris discussed the subject of Agricultural Instruction in the following paragraphs :—

AGRICULTURAL EDUCATION.

A careful study of the subject of Agricultural Education appears to show that the tendency of the existing educational system in most, if not all, of the West Indian Colonies, has been to give the peasant a dislike for manual labour and to disassociate him from the cultivation of the soil. This has no doubt been, primarily, due to the absence of suitable training on the part of the teachers and to the educational methods in these Colonies following too closely those of the British Isles. It is inconceivable in communities so closely interested in the cultivation of the soil that Agriculture should not only have been entirely neglected, but that the encompassment of school life should have discouraged attention to it. Owing to the early period at which many of the children are removed from school and the irregularity of their attendance, it is not possible that much, if any, direct teaching in agriculture or what has been called "farming" can be given in elementary schools. What is first required is that a series of object lessons be given by intelligent and sympathetic teachers in all classes of schools, so that, to adopt the words of the Archbishop of the West Indies, "the entire youth of these purely agricultural communities should be trained in an atmosphere favourable to agriculture, that they should grow up interested in it, and that they should learn that tilling the soil and caring for crops is a work worthy of being studied by intelligent minds and likely to lead to greater health as well as greater profit than the purely clerical work which is now so keenly sought for by the more capable peasant boys in the West Indies."

The scheme of agricultural instruction suggested to meet the immediate requirements of elementary schools aims first of all at rendering the existing teachers competent to give simple object lessons bearing on Agriculture and illustrate them by experiments and actual specimens. Examples of growing plants should be grown in pots and boxes under the eyes of the children, and every stage of their growth as well as the conditions favourable for rapid and successful development should be clearly explained. This much is within the reach of the poorest school in the West Indies. All, however, depends on the amount of knowledge and the interest thrown into the subject on the part of the teachers. It is proposed to assist the teachers at present in charge of schools by affording them the means of attending courses of lectures during their holidays. While attending these lectures all out-of-pocket expenses (except in British Guiana, Trinidad and Jamaica) are paid by the Imperial Department of Agriculture. Lectures to elementary teachers were started last year at Trinidad, St. Lucia and Barbados, in each case with singular success. They will be continued next week at Tobago, Grenada, St. Vincent and Dominica. The teachers so far have shown themselves most anxious to acquire knowledge of the principles of Agriculture, and it is anticipated that during the next two years most of the existing teachers throughout the West Indies will have passed through the initial course of training. The teachers now at the training colleges and all future students passing through such colleges should be fully instructed and be competent to teach Agriculture before they are placed in charge of schools. For the present, Blackie's "Tropical Readers," Books I. and II., are recommended for use in schools, but great care is required to prevent mere book knowledge, which is worthless, taking the place of the intellectual education and the hand and eye training necessary for agricultural pursuits. To explain clearly what should be aimed at in this connection, I cannot do better than quote from a publication recently issued by the French Government on the "Teaching of Elementary Ideas of Agriculture in Rural Schools":—

"Instruction in the elementary principles of agriculture such as can be properly included in the programme of primary schools, ought to be addressed less to the memory than to the intelligence of the children. It should be based on observation of the everyday facts of rural life, and on a system of simple experiments appropriate to the resources of the school, and calculated to bring out clearly the fundamental scientific principles underlying the most important agricultural operations. Above all, the pupils of a rural school should be taught the reasons for these operations, and the explanations of the phenomena which accompany them, but not the details of methods of execution, still less a resumé of maxims, definitions or agricultural precepts. To know the essential conditions of the growth of cultivated plants, to understand the reasons for the work of ordinary cultivations, and for the rules of health for man and domestic animals—such are matters which should first be taught to everyone who is to live by tilling the soil; and this can be done only by the experimental method."

As a higher stage in Agricultural education it is proposed to maintain agricultural schools—the first at St. Vincent, St. Lucia, Dominica and St. Kitts. The boys will be fed, clothed, and trained free. Admission to these schools will be offered as an exhibition to boys in elementary schools of about 14 years of age who have passed the IV. Standard and who show moral and intellectual aptitude for such instruction.

We have next the scheme of instruction in Agriculture to boys in Secondary and High Schools assisted by the special lecturers in Agriculture provided by the Imperial Department. At the same schools scholarships are offered to boys from the country districts, the sons of planters in moderate circumstances, who intend to devote themselves to agricultural pursuits.

Lastly, there are lectures to the younger generation of planters and others engaged in Agricultural pursuits to afford information and assistance in elucidating the scientific problems which underlie the practical work in which they are daily engaged.

This is a brief sketch only of the scheme of Agricultural Education now being actively carried on in these Colonies. The details have been carefully and gradually evolved in conjunction with thoughtful and leading men with great educational experience, and it may be confidently anticipated that if efforts are consistently sustained for a generation at least, we shall lay the foundations of a larger measure of prosperity for all classes of people in these Colonies, both white and black, than has been possible in any previous portion of their history.

During the Conference several papers were read on educational subjects, and two of these (Mr. Deighton's paper on *Teaching Agriculture in High Schools and Colleges*, and the Rev. J. E. Reece's paper on *Teaching Agriculture in Elementary Schools*) are printed below, together with the official report of the discussion which followed each paper.* It will be seen that there took part in the discussions several eminent authorities on education in the West Indies—the Rev. Canon Simms (Principal of University College, Jamaica), Mr. Potbury (Principal of Queen's College, British Guiana), the Rev. W. Caroll (St. Mary's College, Trinidad), Mr. G. B. R. Burton (Headmaster of Combermere School, Barbados), Mr. G. Hicks (Acting Superintending Inspector of Schools for Jamaica), Mr. W. Blair (Inspector of Schools, British Guiana), and Mr. J. H. Collens (Acting Inspector of Schools, Trinidad).

TEACHING AGRICULTURE IN HIGH SCHOOLS AND COLLEGES.

By HORACE DEIGHTON, M.A., F.R.A.S.,
Headmaster of Harrison College, Barbados.

Agricultural Science has been taught at Harrison College for some time, but the resources of the college did not admit of this being done in a perfectly satisfactory way, the time at the disposal of the masters who conducted the science department being inadequate for the purpose. When it was proposed to me that additional aid might be given by the Imperial Department of Agriculture, I had to consider what change could be made in the curriculum of the college, which, whilst giving full scope to the teaching of agriculture to those boys for whom such a course was desired, would not injuriously affect the general education given at the college. As I had always been of opinion that it would be an advantage to education to have elementary science systematically taught in our lower forms, I gladly welcomed the proposal. I mention this because had I thought for one moment that the change in the curriculum which would be necessitated would interfere with the general education given at the college, I should have considered it my bounden duty to decline the offered help. My firm opinion, on the contrary, is that educationally we shall be great gainers.

This is not the place to discuss the question of the position which science should occupy in a school curriculum. But to justify my position that the

---

* *West Indian Bulletin,* vol. i., No. 3.

systematic teaching of science in the lower forms is a gain to education I may add that "educate" means to "draw out" and not "stuff in": in other words education (and I am necessarily limiting the term to intellectual education) is the discipline of the intellect, the training of the mind, and not an attempt to cram the memory with facts. Now as a mental discipline, science possesses this special value, that it not only appeals to the reasoning faculties, but also—through the experiments which necessarily form an important part of every science course cultivates the powers of observation.

At the beginning of the third term of last year, with the aid of an Imperial Grant recommended by Dr. Morris, Mr. Albert Howard, B.A., F.C.S., was appointed Lecturer in Agricultural Science at Harrison College, and the teaching of chemistry was begun in earnest in the first, second, third, and lower fourth forms; two hours a week in each of these forms being allotted to the subject. It is early yet to gauge the results accurately; but I can say this, that in every form there are boys who show themselves interested in the work, and Professor d'Albuquerque tells me that he was more than satisfied with the general results of the examination, which he himself conducted at the end of the term. No doubt there are boys in each form who take little or no interest in the work, but the same may be said of every subject: *e.g.*, has not every one who has had to teach Euclid to beginners found immense difficulty at first in getting the majority of the boys to take any interest in the work? Have they not, on the contrary, shown a marked distaste for it? But nobody would venture to say that therefore Geometry ought not to be taught. "It is a very laudable effort," says John Stuart Mill, "to render as much as possible of what the young are required to learn easy and interesting to them. But when this principle is pushed to the length of not requiring them to learn anything but what has been made easy and nteresting, one of the chief objects of education is sacrificed."

This elementary course affects two classes of boys: (1) Those who do not intend to continue the study of science, and (2) those who do intend to do so. In the case of a boy of the first class the course will prove a valuable intellectual training, and it will be his own fault if he is not able to take an intelligent interest in many scientific subjects which otherwise would be quite incomprehensible to him. Considering how largely and increasingly the practical applications of science enter into everyday life ought not some knowledge of science to be now considered a necessary part of a liberal education? The advantages to a boy of the second class are sufficiently evident: he will be able to attack his new work well equipped for the struggle.

The study of science as a separate branch of school work begins in the upper fourth form. When a boy, who intends to take up science, reaches this form, he drops Greek and Latin, and devotes the time thus liberated to the study of science. The particular form at which this divergence should occur has been carefully considered by me. All authorities are unanimous in insisting that a sound general education must be acquired before any special work is attacked. It may therefore appear too early to allow a boy to specialise when in the upper fourth form; and I should myself prefer putting it off till he reaches the fifth form; but I believe that local conditions, for the present at least, require the earlier period to be adopted.

Dr. Morris has supplemented the appointment of a Lecturer in Agricultural Science by instituting Exhibitions to be held by boys from the country districts who are thereby pledged to become Agriculturists. At present there are five such exhibitioners at Harrison College. I believe this step to be as wise as it is liberal: probably, especially valuable as a sort of pioneer movement leading the way in which it is hoped that many will follow.

I am aware that there are many who regard this educational movement as likely to prove of little value. I think this is principally because the benefits to be derived from it cannot be immediate and must be very gradual. The problem before us is this—granting that there is room for improvement in the cultivation of the sugar-cane, on which the life of this island depends, how is this improvement to be brought about except by gradually placing the charge of the estates in the hands of men who have been scientifically trained for that very purpose? All experts tell us that Practice must not be divorced from Theory, but that all practical work ought to to be based on theoretic knowledge. The wise man is he who learns by the experience of others. If we in Barbados are willing to learn by the experience of others, we shall certainly avail ourselves to the utmost of the great advantages which the foresight of Dr. Morris and the liberality of the Home Government have placed so easily within our reach.

I have explained shortly the arrangements made at Harrison College for the teaching of Science. I am confident that with the additional help which has been afforded us we shall be able to turn out scientific agriculturists just as we have turned out successful classical and mathematical scholars ; and that the slight change which has been made in our curriculum, so far from interfering with the advance of those boys who do not eventually take up the study of science, will educationally be a distinct advantage to them. But if we are to be as successful in Agriculture as in classics and mathematics, we must work under similar conditions—the boys must come to us when quite young.

DISCUSSION.

Rev. CANON SIMMS (University College, Jamaica): There can be no doubt that Mr. Deighton's paper describes the only way in which it is possible for our High Schools and Colleges to take part in this work : namely, the teaching of elementary science in the lower forms, and then gradually extending it as boys reach the higher forms. I would, however, suggest that boys should specialise in the fifth form instead of the upper fourth. The paper requires little or no criticism. Every one must agree with Mr. Deighton that, apart from any value it may have on the educational side, the teaching of elementary science in these days is an absolute necessity. The boys who are going to take up agricultural work must specialise in the science of agriculture. Technical agriculture I should regard as the work of post-school days and not a work of school days. In the last two or three years of his school life the boy should lay the scientific foundation on which technical agriculture could be built. That is the way in which good work could be done. We must first of all overcome many difficulties—difficulties arising from our slender staff, difficulties arising from the overcrowded condition of our time table, and difficulties arising from the fact that our more intelligent boys at present chiefly turn their attention to University requirements and conditions. I find few of the sons of planters and overseers in Jamaica make up their minds to go in for agriculture. The fact is, the planter tells his son that sugar does not pay, and the son naturally wants to take up something else that does pay. The only way of meeting difficulties of this kind is that so clearly indicated by Mr. Deighton.

Mr. J. A. POTBURY (Queen's College, British Guiana): All the West Indies naturally look to Harrison College for a lead in educational matters. We in British Guiana have done so for a long time. But Mr. Deighton during the past twelve months has enjoyed the advantage which the Colleges in other colonies so far have not had, that is, a supplemented staff. I should be very glad if the Imperial Department would similarly aid us in the matter. Given a staff, we are quite prepared to take up the teaching of scientific agriculture.

Rev. W. CAROLL (St. Mary's College, Trinidad): I regret to learn that my criticism last year on this subject was considered to some extent a destructive one. However, I believe it is well to see both sides of a question. It is not by ignoring our difficulties that we can surmount them. And that there are difficulties in the way of introducing the teaching of agriculture into our secondary schools I think will be pretty generally admitted. I agree with Canon Simms and the other gentlemen who have spoken as to the nature of these difficulties. First, it must be borne in mind that in our secondary schools the system of education that has existed and does exist, is and has been classical and literary rather than scientific; and so far at least, every attempt that has been made to introduce anything else has failed. Mr. Deighton and the leading educational authorities in these colonies have given us to understand that the boys should not be allowed to specialise too early. Now I think the best thing is to fix the age at which a boy should branch off to special studies, say at seventeen or eighteen years, and then, only when he has passed through a regular course in the ordinary subjects taught in our secondary schools. Then it becomes a question how far agricultural instruction is likely to succeed by grafting it on to our present system. It would be very unwise to overcrowd our time table. As far as my experience goes our boys are not very favourably disposed to agricultural studies. It is true that hitherto they have not had a favourable opportunity of manifesting their appreciation, but where they have had such opportunity they have not availed themselves of it to the extent one would expect. My experience of the College of which I have charge is this: that within the last three years as many as thirty young men left us to continue or complete their studies in Europe, many of them the sons of planters and agriculturists—sons of men whose whole life was associated with agricultural pursuits; some of them went to England, some to France, some to Germany. Not a single one has so far offered to take up a course of agricultural instruction. There is a reason for it, and it is this: the impossibility of a young man making a living out of agricultural pursuits. That is at the root of our difficulty. Given that a young man could reach the same success in life as an agriculturist that he could in other professions, I am of opinion that trained agriculturists would be forthcoming. These are the points that suggest themselves to me, but in stating them I wish it to be understood that I do not oppose the teaching of agriculture in our secondary schools. Furthermore, I am of opinion that the Imperial Department of Agriculture is endeavouring to overcome the difficulties I have indicated, and it is right that it should have the sympathy, co-operation, and active support of everyone in the West Indies. We came last year looking for light. We saw a glimmer then. Having heard Mr. Deighton's very explicit paper to-day, I begin to think we have streaks of dawn. I hope that when next we meet we shall be in full light, and in a position to make agricultural teaching in secondary schools the success which it deserves to be.

The PRESIDENT: Mr. Burton, the Headmaster of Combermere School, Barbados, has asked to be allowed to address a few words on the subject now before the Conference.

Mr. G. B. R. BURTON: I am of opinion we should start to teach agricultural science in the second grade schools in the West Indies for the following reasons: The majority of boys attending these schools will in time be engaged in agricultural pursuits as managers and book-keepers, and through them we would gradually reach the lower classes—that is, the labourers on the estates. I do not speak specially of the Combermere School because most of the pupils there will probably enter commercial life. Arrangements might, however, be made for the small number of our pupils intended for agricultural pursuits to attend the agricultural classes at the Government Laboratory, which happens to be quite near to our school. In extending agricultural education to second grade schools it is necessary to avoid two mistakes: (1) The teaching must not be given at so-called centres—classes will have to be formed at each school; (2) it is necessary that more than one lecture be given per week at each school, otherwise little good will be done. I may add that we shall never get agricultural science earnestly taken up until we place it on an equal footing with other subjects and give the boys equal attention and encouragement.

TEACHING AGRICULTURE IN ELEMENTARY SCHOOLS.

BY THE REV. J. E. REECE, M.A.,
Inspector of Schools, Barbados.

I have been asked to give a short account of the recent effort made in this Island by the Imperial Department of Agriculture to give instruction and a measure of practical training to some of the teachers of our elementary schools. Also to suggest how the work may be continued in future years.

About the middle of August last year a circular was sent by the Education Board to each supervising minister stating that a course of lectures on agricultural science would be given during the September vacation, and asking that the names of those teachers who were willing to attend should be sent in. About seventy teachers volunteered, but as it was impossible to accommodate so large a number at once it was decided to select forty-six of the teachers who were in charge of Primary and Combined Schools to attend. In consequence of the absence of Dr. Morris from the Island the Very Rev. the Dean of St. Michael, a member of the Education Board, gave the opening address. Mr. R. Radclyffe Hall, the Assistant Professor of Chemistry, delivered eight lectures. The course comprised life and the elementary chemistry of it; plants, their nature and work; the nature, structure, and functions of roots; stems, leaves, and flowers, and the cultivation and care of plants.

Mr. J. R. Bovell, the Superintendent of the Botanic Station, gave demonstrations on practical horticulture on four afternoons, and on two other afternoons conducted the teachers over the gardens at Government House and Queen's House. The teachers were most regular in their attendance, although many of them daily made a journey of over twenty miles. Several teachers have informed me that they considered Mr. Hall's lectures most interesting and instructive, and that they learned many things from Mr. Bovell's demonstrations which would be of great value to them in giving instruction to their pupils. An examination was held by each lecturer on the subject matter of the lectures. Thirty teachers attended this examination. The papers of nine of these were considered of sufficient merit to entitle the writers of them to be placed in the first rank. I have every reason to believe that the teachers who attended these lectures derived much good from them, and they will doubtless get more good from a similar course in the future. What has been done can only be regarded as a beginning, and I would venture to suggest that those teachers (whether teachers of primary schools or infant schools) who are interested in agricultural pursuits should be invited to attend a course of lectures to be delivered, say on the third Saturday in each month, with three or four extra lectures given during the Whitsuntide or September vacation (or both, if deemed necessary) and followed by an examination at the end of the year. Another course of lectures of a more elementary character might be arranged for on the fourth Saturday in each month, which assistant teachers and pupil teachers might be required to attend, and at their annual examination questions might be set on the subjects in which they had thus received instruction.

Then arises the question: What can be done to give regular and intelligent instruction in this subject to the children in our Elementary Schools? I have proposed to the Education Board that they should allow the teachers who gained a certain number of marks in the examination held by Messrs. Hall and Bovell to prepare at once their pupils for examination in Blackie's Tropical Readers, and to grant a premium for each scholar who passes this examination successfully. The smaller book would be used by children in the fourth standard and the larger book by those in the higher standards. In the lower standards much useful information could be given by means of object lessons carefully selected, and intelligently taught. These in good hands would brighten school life and interest the children, but too often they are nothing but bare recitals of facts, and little is done to train the faculty of observation. It may also be possible to do something in the way of growing plants in pots or boxes; and in this connection it has been suggested to me by one of our teachers that prizes might be offered at one of our annual Exhibitions for plants grown in pots or boxes by our school children. As time goes on it may be possible to start a school garden here and there where a spot of land near the school house can be obtained; and these plots may be inspected by officers of the Agricultural Department, and prizes awarded. This no doubt will be a work of time, and it is right that it should be so. No greater mistake could be made than to force this matter on those who are unwilling to enter heartily into the scheme. Our motto in this case must be " *festina lente.*" By the last issued report of the Committee of Council on Education (England and Wales), I find that in 1895 only one school out of the 19,739 inspected by Her Majesty's Inspectors of Schools obtained a grant for the practical teaching of cottage gardening; in the following year 42 schools received the grant, in 1897, 72 schools, and last year 84. In the same publication I find in the general report of one of Her Majesty's Chief Inspectors on the Schools in the Welsh Division the following remarks :— " A great part of Wales is agricultural, and the people gain their livelihood by farming. It might naturally have been thought that in many rural schools the elder boys would have received instruction in cottage gardening, just as in many country villages, especially in Carnarvonshire, their sisters have lessons in cookery. Yet this subject practically receives no attention, and only 31 boys throughout the length and breadth of Wales received last year the cottage gardening grant. To anybody who has seen the zest with which boys enter into such a congenial occupation as outdoor work, and the stimulus which it gives to other studies, it seems strange that this should be the case."

The time has arrived when it is absolutely necessary that elementary education should be made more practical; and I feel sure that these West Indian Colonies will do their utmost, with the limited means at their disposal, to make it so. There has been very little attempt made in the past to draw out and train the faculties of children. Our system must be remodelled so as to draw out these faculties. "In too many cases" (to quote from a paper by Mr. F. J. Lloyd) "the sole object of education has been to cram a certain number of useless and disconnected facts, or pseudo-facts, into what is termed the brain. Teachers recognise one faculty and one only, viz., memory; and to train this one faculty to the neglect of every other has been the sole object of education for ages past, and remains so mainly to the present day. It has entirely neglected to develop manual skill, it has neglected to draw out or cultivate any mental faculty save memory, and even for this purpose has utilised subjects, the recollection of which would in no wise benefit the future farmer. But far worse than this, it has neglected the most valuable of nature's gifts to all of us, the strongest natural faculty we possess, observation. What is the most striking faculty possessed by a child from three to six years of age? The power of observation. Watch that same child between the ages of thirteen and sixteen, and the power, though at times manifesting itself, is gradually becoming dormant, partly because it has not been cultivated, partly from its constant suppression by the ignorance and heedlessness of those who surround the child. Ten years later the faculty is practically non-existent, lost from neglect of use, as a singer may lose the power of song or a musician the power of execution. The difficulty now found in improving Agricultural Education depends greatly upon this failure of the past." Be ours the task, as far as lies in our power, to try and remedy this defect in our Educational systems in the West Indies.

DISCUSSION.

The PRESIDENT : The Lectures so successfully given at Barbados and St. Lucia will shortly be extended to Grenada, St Vincent and Dominica. Great interest has been taken in these lectures in every part of the West Indies. It is evident that we are working on right lines. We have among us to-day leading educational authorities whose counsel based on long experience we would gladly welcome. In Jamaica, for instance, the vote for Elementary Education amounts to about £60,000 yearly. There are in all about 900 teachers. Strenuous efforts are being made to adapt the educational system in that island to the requirements of the people and on lines very similar to those advocated by the Imperial Department of Agriculture. As Representative of Jamaica we have here the Acting Superintending Inspector of Schools, Mr. George Hicks, who is one of the most earnest educationists in the West Indies. I would ask Mr. Hicks to be kind enough to open the discussion following Mr. Reece's paper.

Mr. HICKS : The interesting and useful paper just read is full of encouragement to those about to undertake similar work. The systematic instruction of the teachers is of course essential before they can embark on the instruction of their pupils. Provision was made for agricultural instruction in the Jamaica elementary shools and special grants offered, but without accomplishing very much. We now propose to make such instruction an integral part of the curriculum. We are liable to fall into a mistake in introducing agricultural education into the elementary schools in the West Indies. Statements have been made that country boys prefer a town life and clerical work to a country life and tilling the soil. But this is not peculiar to the West Indies. It appears to be universal. In France what we know as the "French scheme" of agricultural instruction has been introduced for the express purpose of preventing the French country boys from yielding to the tendency of drifting into the towns and neglecting the cultivation of the soil. As in France, so in America ; leading educationists there also are seeking to counteract the same tendency.

Dr. MORRIS : In European countries and in America there are factories and other means of employment in towns to attract the people. Here we have none.

Mr. HICKS : Because that is so, our problem is not so difficult. The boys here, forsaking the soil, drift into towns, and if they find no employment there they drift back again to engage unwillingly in agricultural work. Our aim should be to equip them for such work and enable them to live comfortably by it. It is now believed, and I am satisfied the belief is well founded, that education can be given on wiser and more extended lines than formerly, and that the country boy so educated will find country life both remunerative and attractive. It is currently believed that there is on the part of the people of the West Indies an aversion to manual labour. We are liable, I think, to give this too large an interpretation. "Little labour, little gains" is quoted by our President. I would add "The greatest gain with the least labour" as the universal rule. The aversion to manual labour is, after all, only a desire for greater gain with less labour. When increase of gain is offered the manual labour is forthcoming. This has been fully proved everywhere in the West Indies. I believe if we base our educational efforts upon the general truth that the people in these colonies are like other people, that they have essentially the same desires and are actuated by the same motives, we shall be on safe ground. It is fortunate that the proposed agricultural instruction which seems to be urgently needed in the West indies, is also that which is best from the educational standpoint. The Imperial Department of Agriculture is therefore promoting educational methods in the best interests of all. The new lines of education, the hand and eye training, the training of the powers of observation, the learning to see things and to do things, are I believe truer lines, upon which, generally speaking, a more valuable education will be gained. Our attitude should be not that of standing aloof and offering the tillers of the soil that which is for them and not for us, but as offering what we share with them—that which is best for them and best for all. The eyes of the country child should be unsealed. He should be made to see the beauties and wonders that lie about his feet, and are to be found in profusion all around him. A sympathetic, skilful teacher will invest rural life with an interest that will attract and fascinate. The life that was monotonous, dull, insipid, and purely mechanical will be changed into one full of interest ; and with this there will be gained a discipline of the mind, a development of intellectual power, which are prominent aims of all true education. The new knowledge and skill will be to the country boy as a new tool, the possession of a new power, and he will be eager to make use of it. What is done on a small scale in a corner of the school plot, or in the box-garden, will be reproduced at home on a larger scale and with added interest. It will be his delight to show what he can do, and the useful results of his doing. He will find use for his knowledge of reading, writing, and arithmetic in connection with his observations and experiments in the study and mastery of some of the secrets of nature. He will have a desire to read ; and, if we are wise, we shall see that he has opportunity by providing the school with a suitable library, and some of the books specially applicable to country life.*

The educationists of France and America are zealously endeavouring to make rural life more attractive, and I feel sure that they will find this possible, and also that we, moving upon like lines, will find it to be possible in the West indies. The Imperial Department of Agriculture will certainly accomplish much in the efforts now put forth to make rural life more interesting and more profitable, and therefore more attractive. I am sure that we who are engaged in educational work will most heartily co-operate with the Imperial Department of Agriculture in its present effort to introduce a wise and feasible degree of agricultural instruction into the elementary schools of the West Indies.

Mr. W. BLAIR (Inspector of Schools, British Guiana) : A few days after my arrival in British Guiana I received a letter from the Government Secretary asking me to submit a Code of Rules and Regulations awarding special grants to Mission Schools for Aboriginal Indians, and to schools in remote and sparsely populated localities. I will not take up your time in giving you the details of these rules, but it appeared to me that having had some experience of Agricultural and Technical Schools in the Island of Ceylon I could at the same time prepare a Code for Agricultural and Industrial Schools for British Guiana, and I had the satisfaction of seeing my proposals adopted by the Governor and the Court of Policy, and the Combined Court passed a vote of $1,500.

I divided the Schools into 4 classes, A, B, C, D.

The following regulations were adopted :—

(1) Industrial Schools in which technical instruction is given shall be classed as " D " Schools.

(2) An application for a grant-in-aid to an Industrial School will be entertained on the following conditions :—(a) that the school shall teach agriculture or a trade or trades approved by the Inspector of Schools ; (b) that the school shall be sufficiently provided with appliances for elementary instruction in agriculture or in the trade or trades to which the school is devoted ; and (c) that the master or mistress appointed to teach agriculture or the trade or trades is duly qualified.

(3) The Manager of a " D " School shall receive in addition to the general grants payable under No. 12 (a), (b), and (c) of the Education Regulations, 1890, the sum of $7.50 for each pupil, being over twelve and under seventeen years of age, who may be certified to have been in attendance for not less than 100 days, and to have received daily not less than two hours' instruction in agriculture or in the workshop, and who is able to work at his trade to the satisfaction of the Inspector of Schools ; provided that the grant to any single " D " School shall not exceed the sum of $200 (£41 13s. 4d.).

(4) The number of " D " Schools shall not exceed ten.

---

* Note added :—Some Schools in Jamaica now have Libraries, mainly through the personal efforts of Mr. Hicks. There is a proposal before the Government to assist the formation of School Libraries by the offer of a grant to defray one-half the total cost. [Ed. W.I.B.]

The first to ask for a grant were the Nuns of the Ursuline Convent for the establishment of a school laundry, which has been an unqualified success, and it is impossible to visit that institution without admiring the skill and dexterity with which young girls between the ages of twelve and seventeen years wash, starch, and iron ladies' underclothes of every sort and description, and under the direction of the Nuns the finest altar linen. Without the Government grant it more than pays its way, and if the Government grant were withdrawn to-morrow, which it will not be, the School would be carried on just the same. Lady Sendall visited the laundry a fortnight ago and saw the girls at work, and spoke of their performance in terms of the highest commendation.

A tailors' shop was started in Georgetown by Canon Josa in connection with Christ Church School, which for the last five years has been fairly successful. A carpenters' shop at Plaisance School was opened with a flourish of trumpets, but it was never a success, and in three years had to be abandoned. Two Agricultural Schools, one in Demerara, East Coast, and one in Berbice, at Rose Hall, were opened, but both these schools were close to sugar estates, on which the boys who were inclined to work could readily find employment and earn from 6d. to 8d. a day. The more ambitious of them considered working in the fields was degrading, and they were anxious to attain what Mr. Gladstone described as the "supposed paradise of pen and ink." The parents supported their children, and the schools were hopeless failures. We have been more successful at the Roman Catholic Mission Station at Santa Rosa. I have not had an opportunity of visiting the school, but my assistant reports that it is doing a good and useful work. I am afraid that one of the causes of failures was my want of respect for the prejudices of the parents. If I had required less I should have probably achieved more.

Simultaneously with the establishment of Industrial Schools I made important changes in the Syllabus of Subjects for Teachers' Certificates, introducing Agriculture for males and Domestic Economy for females. Dr. Nicholls' work is our text book, and the Hon. B. Howell Jones, a planter of wide and varied experience, is the Examiner. I have already handed to Dr. Morris copies of the Examination Questions set at the examination held last week, and I shall be glad if he will give you his opinion on them. Arrangements are also being made for giving a few of our most intelligent schoolmasters a course of lectures in Chemistry and Botany. Professor Harrison has submitted the course to the Government, and we are now only waiting on the Combined Court for a vote. I am hopeful for the future, and if I am privileged to attend the Conference next year I trust that I shall be able to give you an interesting account of what we have done.

Mr. J. H. COLLENS (Acting-Inspector of Schools, Trinidad): I have listened with considerable attention to the valuable paper read by Mr. Reece, and I fully endorse all that he has said. We have embarked in Trinidad on pretty well the same lines as in Barbados, and in Jamaica. I cannot, however, say for Trinidad what Mr. Hicks said with regard to Jamaica—that our people have no antipathy to manual labour. I am sorry to say they have : consequently, the colony finds it necessary to import a large number of East Indian labourers, or it would be impossible to get all our agricultural work done. If there is an attempt to make a child in the schools do manual labour, the parents state their objections very forcibly. I agree with Mr. Hicks that if our attempts to teach agriculture in elementary schools are to be successful, the greatest possible tact must be shown by the officers concerned. We must not drive or coerce the people ; above all, we must try and instil into the children's minds a love of nature, and the necessity of learning nature's methods. If we succeed in doing that, we may hope in time to turn their attention to field pursuits and to agriculture generally as a means of earning a livelihood. We must, however, proceed very cautiously. In Trinidad it has been decided that the teachers should, first of all, have a course of lectures, and in the event of their showing aptitude in teaching agriculture and passing an examination in the syllabus laid out, they are to be rewarded by receiving a bonus on the results of the examination of their schools at the end of each year. That is one encouragement; but we have another. We have made the examination the means for promotion from the third class to the second. That is an important means of influencing the teacher, because it directly touches his pocket. Then with regard to teaching in the schools, we make considerable use of Blackie's Tropical Readers. These are used as alternate reading books. I feel a deep personal interest in this subject of teaching agriculture in elementary schools. I have given considerable thought to it, and I am convinced if we are to do any real good we must exercise great caution and always place the pleasantest side before the parents and the teachers. Otherwise, we shall fail.

POSTSCRIPT OF AGRICULTURAL EDUCATION IN THE WEST INDIES IN 1900.

The report of the proceedings of the third West Indian Agricultural Conference, held in the Hall of the House of Assembly, Barbados, on 5th January, 1901, has arrived just as this volume is going to press. The President (Dr. Morris) devoted part of his address to an account of the progress made in Agricultural Education in the West Indies during the year 1900. He reported that lectures to teachers in charge of elementary schools had been successfully carried on in every part of the West Indies, and proceeded to remark as follows:—"Within another year or two, in the smaller islands at all events, every teacher in charge of a school should be qualified not only to give a certain amount of instruction in the principles of agriculture, but to interest his children by simple experiments, followed by practical demonstrations, in the cultivation of plants suited to each district. The plants may be grown in pots or boxes, or on small plots attached to the schools. This work must necessarily progress slowly and be carried on with the hearty co-operation of all concerned. I fully realise the difficulties to be overcome, but provided we proceed with due deliberation and keep clearly in view the fact that we cannot attempt to teach practical farming to children in elementary schools, we shall be on the right lines."

Seven scholarships in agriculture, tenable at Harrison College (Barbados) have now been awarded by the Imperial Department of Agriculture. Two scholarships, each of the annual value of £75, have just been awarded in the Windward and Leeward Islands.

The first Agricultural School in the West Indies, affording secondary education to selected boys who may afterwards become managers of estates or cultivate their own lands, was opened at St. Vincent in September, 1900. A similar Agricultural School was opened in December, 1900, at Dominica. Dr. Morris hopes that two more agricultural schools will be opened in 1901, one at St. Lucia, and the other, which is to combine the characters of an Agricultural School and a Grammar School, at St. Kitts.

It will be seen that the scheme of agricultural education is intended to reach every section of the community. Special stress was laid by Dr Morris on the necessity for united effort on the part of three sections of the community, namely, (1) the scientific experts, (2) the practical leaders of industry and agriculture, and (3) the representatives of educational agencies, and of all grades of schools from the highest to the lowest.   The following passage in his presidential address (1901) gives an admirable statement of the aim in view. " Our conjoined aim should be so to educate, according to his station, the peasant and the planter as to give to each the particular training and knowledge necessary to equip him for the battle of life.   We start with the fundamental idea that those who have to depend on the cultivation of the soil as the sole means of existence should, at least, be taught to observe and study intelligently the every-day facts of rural life, and to clearly comprehend the cardinal principles underlying the most important agricultural operations.   By adding a reasonable amount of teaching in Science and Agriculture to the curriculum of their schools, our educational colleagues will, I believe, widen the scope and add to the interest of their own work."

The following appear periodically, and can be subscribed for :—

TRADE OF THE UNITED KINGDOM WITH BRITISH POSSESSIONS AND FOREIGN COUNTRIES, showing the Quantities and the Declared Value of the Articles.

The Proceedings of Parliament in Public and Private Business are published daily— House of Lords, price 1d. per 4 pp.; House of Commons, 1d. per 8 pp.

TRADE REPORTS of the several British Colonies, with information relative to their population and general condition.

TRADE REPORTS by His Majesty's Representatives in Foreign Countries, and Reports on Commercial and General Interests.

Special Reports on Educational Subjects. Issued by Board of Education:—
PUBLIC LIBRARY AND PUBLIC ELEMENTARY SCHOOL. The connection between.
<table>
<tr><td></td><td>Price 2½d.</td></tr>
<tr><td>HEURISTIC METHOD OF TEACHING.</td><td>Price 3d.</td></tr>
<tr><td>MODERN LANGUAGE TEACHING IN BELGIUM, HOLLAND, AND GERMANY.</td><td>Price 6½d.</td></tr>
<tr><td>SECONDARY SCHOOLS IN BADEN.</td><td>Price 5½d.</td></tr>
<tr><td>SECONDARY SCHOOLS IN PRUSSIA.</td><td>Price 1s.</td></tr>
<tr><td>UNIVERSITY AND SECONDARY EDUCATION IN FRANCE.</td><td>Price 4d.</td></tr>
<tr><td>INTERMEDIATE EDUCATION IN WALES, AND THE ORGANISATION OF EDUCATION IN SWITZERLAND.</td><td>Price 1s.</td></tr>
</table>

Military :—
ARMY. PAY, APPOINTMENT, PROMOTION AND NON-EFFECTIVE PAY. Royal Warrant. 1900. Price 1s.
BALKAN STATES. ARMIES OF. Hand-book. By Capt. M. C. P. Ward, R.A. Price 6d.
DRESS REGULATIONS, 1900. Price 4s. 6d., or interleaved 5s. 6d.
ENGINEERING. MILITARY. Instruction in. Part IV. Mining and Demolition. Price 1s. 6d.
GOLD COAST. NORTHERN TERRITORIES OF. Report on. Compiled by the late Lt.-Col. H. P. Northcott, C.B. Price 6s.
TURKISH ARMY. Hand-book. By Capt. M. C. P. Ward, R.N. Price 4d.
VOLUNTEER FORCE. Regns. 1901. Price 1s.

Hydrographical :—
PACIFIC CABLE ROUTE. PROPOSED. Report on Soundings of H.M.S. "Egeria." Price 9d.
RED SEA AND GULF OF ADEN PILOT, 1900. Price 3s. 6d.

Geological :—
FIFE, CENTRAL AND WESTERN, AND KINROSS. Sheet 40 and parts of Sheets 32 & 48. By Sir Archibald Geikie. Price 5s. 6d.

Local Government Board :—
SANITARY CIRCUMSTANCES OF THE FARNWORTH REGISTRATION SUB-DISTRICT OF THE BOLTON (LANCS.) REGISTRATION DISTRICT. Report on. Price 4d
EPIDEMIC ENTERIC FEVER IN NUNEATON AND CHILVERS COTON URBAN DISTRICT Report on. Price 4d

Emigrants' Information Office, 31, Broadway, Westminster, viz. :—
COLONIES, HANDBOOKS FOR. April 1900. 8vo. Wrapper.
No. 1. Canada. 2. New South Wales. 3. Victoria. 4. South Australia. 5. Queensland. 6. Western Australia. 7. Tasmania. 8. New Zealand. 9. Cape Colony. 10. Natal
Price 1d. each.
No. 11. Professional Handbook dealing with Professions in the Colonies. 12. Emigration Statutes and General Handbook. Price 3d. each.
No. 13 (viz., Nos. 1 to 12 in cloth). Price 2s.
CONSULAR REPORTS, 1899. SUMMARY OF. America, North and South. July 1900.
Price 2d.
INTENDING EMIGRANTS, INFORMATION FOR :—Argentine Republic, price 2d. California, price 1d. Ceylon, Oct. 1900, price 1d. Federated Malay States, Jan. 1900, Price 6d. Maryland, price 1d. Newfoundland, price 1d. South African Republic, price 3d. West Indies, price 6d.

Excise Laws. PRACTICAL ARRANGEMENT OF THE LAWS RELATIVE TO THE EXCISE, &c., &c. By Nath. J. Highmore, Assist. Solicitor of Inland Revenue. 2nd Edition. 2 Vols. Price 30s.

Foreign Office :—
AFRICA BY TREATY. The Map of. By Sir E. Hertslet, K.C.B. 3 Vols. Price 31s. 6d.
COMMERCIAL TREATIES. (Hertslet's.) A complete collection of Treaties, &c., between Great Britain and Foreign Powers so far as they relate to Commerce and Navigation, &c. By Sir E. Hertslet, K.C.B., &c., Vols. I. to XX. Price 15s. each.
STATE PAPERS. British and Foreign. Vol. 80. General Index (chronologically and alphabetically arranged) to Vols. 65 to 79. (1873 to 1888.) Vols. :—81. 1888–1889. 82. 1889–1890. 83. 1890-1. 84. 1891-2. 85. 1892-3. 86. 1893-4. 87. 1894-5. 88. 1895-6. Price 10s. each.

Board of Trade Journal, of Tariff and Trade Notices and Miscellaneous Commercial Information. Published weekly. Price 1d.
Index to Vols. 1 to 14. Price 2s. And to Vols XV. to XX., July, 1893, to June, 1896.
Price 1s. 6d.

Kew : Royal Botanic Gardens. Bulletins of Miscellaneous Information. Volume for 1898, price 3s.; and Monthly parts, 1899, price 4d.

PORT OF LONDON COMMISSION. Minutes of Evidence. Price per day 4d.

BOARD OF EDUCATION.

SPECIAL REPORTS

ON

EDUCATIONAL SUBJECTS.

VOLUME 4.

EDUCATIONAL SYSTEMS OF THE CHIEF COLONIES OF THE BRITISH EMPIRE.

(DOMINION OF CANADA : NEWFOUNDLAND: WEST INDIES).

Presented to both houses of parliament by command of her Majesty.

LONDON :
PRINTED FOR HIS MAJESTY'S STATIONERY OFFICE,
BY WYMAN AND SONS, LIMITED, FETTER LANE, LONDON, E.C.

And to be purchased, either directly or through any Bookseller, from
EYRE & SPOTTISWOODE, EAST HARDING STREET, FLEET STREET, E.C.; and
32, ABINGDON STREET, WESTMINSTER, S.W.; or
JOHN MENZIES & Co., ROSE STREET, EDINBURGH, and
90, WEST NILE STREET, GLASGOW; or
HODGES, FIGGIS & Co., LIMITED, 104, GRAFTON STREET, DUBLIN.

1901

[Cd. 416.]   Price 4s. 8d.

Lightning Source UK Ltd.
Milton Keynes UK
UKHW020840110119
335238UK00009B/1021/P

9 780260 178923